# Commands Guide Tutorial for SolidWorks® 2010

A comprehensive reference guide with over 230 tutorials

David C. Planchard & Marie P. Planchard CSWP



ISBN: 978-1-58503-548-9

SDC PUBLICATIONS

Schroff Development Corporation

www.schroff.com

**Schroff Development Corporation**
P.O. Box 1334
Mission KS 66222
(913) 262-2664
www.schroff.com

Publisher: Stephen Schroff

## Trademarks and Disclaimer



## Copyright© 2010 by David C. Planchard and Marie P. Planchard



## Examination Copies



## Electronic Files

# INTRODUCTION

The **Commands Guide Tutorial for SolidWorks® 2010** is a comprehensive reference book written to assist beginner to intermediate users of SolidWorks. SolidWorks is an immense software package, and no one book can cover all topics for all users. The book provides a centralize reference location to address many of the System and Document properties, FeatureManagers, PropertyManagers, ConfigurationManagers and RenderManagers along with 2D and 3D Sketch tools, Sketch entities, 3D Feature tools, Motion Study, SustainabilityXpress, DFMXpress, SimulationXpress, Sheet Metal, PhotoView 360 and more.

Chapter 1 provides a basic overview of the concepts and terminology used throughout this book using SolidWorks® 2010 software. If you are completely new to SolidWorks, you should read Chapter 1 in detail and complete Lesson 1, Lesson 2 and Lesson 3 in the SolidWorks Tutorials.

If you are familiar with an earlier release of SolidWorks, you still might want to skim Chapter 1 to be acquainted with some of the commands, menus and features that you have not used; or you can simply jump to any section in any chapter.

Each chapter (17 total) provides detail PropertyManager information on key topics with individual stand alone short tutorials to reinforce and demonstrate the functionality and ease of the SolidWorks tool or feature. All models for the 230 plus tutorials are located on the enclosed book CD with their solution (initial and final). Learn by doing, not just by reading!

Formulate the skills to create, modify and edit sketches and solid features. Learn the techniques to reuse features, parts and assemblies through symmetry, patterns, copied components, design tables, configurations and more.

The book is design to compliment the Online Tutorials and Online Help contained in SolidWorks 2010. The goal is to illustrate how multiple design situations and systematic steps combine to produce successful designs.

The authors developed the tutorials by combining their own industry experience with the knowledge of engineers, department managers, vendors and manufacturers. These professionals are directly involved with SolidWorks everyday. Their responsibilities go far beyond the creation of just a 3D model.

# About the Book

You will find a wealth of information in this book. Short stand-alone step-by step tutorials are written for each topic with the new and intermediate user in mind.

The following conventions are use throughout this book:

1. The term document is used to refer a SolidWorks part, drawing or assembly file.

2. The list of items across the top of the SolidWorks interface is the Main menu. Each item in the Main menu has a pull-down menu. When you need to select a series of commands from these menus, the following format is used; Click **Insert ➢ Reference Geometry ➢ Plane** from the Main bar. The Plane PropertyManager is displayed.

3. The book is organized into 17 chapters. You can read any chapter without reading the entire book. Each chapter has short stand-alone step-by-step tutorials to practice and reinforce the chapter subject matter and objectives. Learn by doing, not just by reading!
4. This book is written to provide defaults for the ANSI drafting standard and Third Angle projection. IPS (inch, pound, second) and MMGS (millimeter, gram, second) unit systems are used.
5. Copy the SolidWorks files and folders from the enclosed CD to create the tutorials and to check your results.
6. Compare your results with the tutorial documents in the Summary folder. All summary models for the stand-alone tutorials are included.

---

# About the Authors

David Planchard is the Founder of D&M Education LLC. Before starting D&M Education, he spent over 27 years in industry and academia holding various engineering, marketing, and teaching positions and degrees. He holds five U.S. patents and one International patent. He has published and authored numerous papers on Machine Design, Product Design, Mechanics of Materials, and Solid Modeling. He is a member of the New England Pro/Users Group, New England SolidWorks Users Group, and the Cisco Regional Academy Users Group. David holds a BSME, MSM and a Certified SolidWorks Associate (CSWA) Certification. David is a SolidWorks Solution Partner and an Adjunct at Worcester Polytechnic Institute.

Marie Planchard is the Director of World Education Markets at SolidWorks Corporation. Before she joined SolidWorks, Marie spent over 10 years as an engineering professor at Mass Bay College in Wellesley Hills, MA. She has 14 plus years of industry software experience and held a variety of management and engineering positions. Marie holds a BSME, MSME and a Certified SolidWorks Professional (CSWP) Certification. She is an active member of the American Society of Mechanical Engineers (ASME) and the American Society for Engineering Education (ASEE).

David and Marie Planchard are co-authors of the following books:

- **A Commands Guide for SolidWorks® 2010**, 2009 and 2008
- **A Commands Guide Reference Tutorial for SolidWorks® 2007**

- **Assembly Modeling with SolidWorks® 2008**, 2006, 2005-2004, 2003 and 2001Plus
- **Drawing and Detailing with SolidWorks® 2010,** 2009, 2008, 2007, 2006, 2005, 2004, 2003, 2002 and 2001/2001Plus
- **Engineering Design with SolidWorks® with Multimedia CD 2010**, 2009, 2008, 2007, 2006, 2005, 2004, 2003, 2001Plus, 2001 and 1999
- **SolidWorks® The Basics with Multimedia CD 2010**, 2009, 2008, 2007, 2006, 2005, 2004 and 2003
- **SolidWorks® Tutorial with Multimedia CD 2010**, 2009, 2008, 2007, 2006, 2005, 2004, 2003 and 2001/2001Plus
- **The Fundamentals of SolidWorks®: Featuring the VEXplorer robot**, **2008** and 2007
- **Official Certified SolidWorks® Associate Examination Guide, Version 2**, Version 1
- **Applications in Sheet Metal Using Pro/SHEETMETAL & Pro/ENGINEER**

## Acknowledgements

Writing this book was a substantial effort that would not have been possible without the help and support of my loving family and of my professional colleagues. I would like to thank Professor Holly Keyes Ault and the community of scholars at Worcester Polytechnic Institute who have enhanced my life, my knowledge, and helped to shape the approach and content to this book.

A special acknowledgment goes to my wife for her support and encouragement and to our loving daughter Stephanie who supported us during this intense and lengthy project.

## Contact the Authors

This is the 3rd edition of this book. We realize that keeping software application books current is imperative to our customers. We value the hundreds of professors, students, designers, and engineers that have provided us input to enhance our book. We value your suggestions and comments. Please visit our website at **www.dmeducation.net** or contact us directly with any comments, questions or suggestions on this book or any of our other SolidWorks books at dplanchard@msn.com.

## Trademarks, Disclaimer and Copyrighted Material



## Note to Instructors

Please contact the publisher **www.schroff.com** for additional presentation and classroom materials and the Instructor's Guide with model solutions, and tips that support the usage of this text in a classroom environment.

## References


- SolidWorks Users Guide, SolidWorks Corporation, 2010
- ASME Y14 Engineering Drawing and Related Documentation Practices
- Beers & Johnson, Vector Mechanics for Engineers, 6th ed. McGraw Hill, Boston, MA
- Betoline, Wiebe, Miller, Fundamentals of Graphics Communication, Irwin, 1995
- Hibbler, R.C, Engineering Mechanics Statics and Dynamics, 8th ed, Prentice Hall, Saddle River, NJ
- Hoelscher, Springer, Dobrovolny, Graphics for Engineers, John Wiley, 1968
- Jensen, Cecil, Interpreting Engineering Drawings, Glencoe, 2002
- Jensen & Helsel, Engineering Drawing and Design, Glencoe, 1990
- Lockhart & Johnson, Engineering Design Communications, Addison Wesley, 1999
- Olivo C., Payne, Olivo, T, Basic Blueprint Reading and Sketching, Delmar, 1988

- Planchard & Planchard, Drawing and Detailing with SolidWorks, SDC Pub., Mission, KS 2009
- Walker, James, Machining Fundamentals, Goodheart Wilcox, 1999
- 80/20 Product Manual, 80/20, Inc., Columbia City, IN, 2009
- Reid Tool Supply Product Manual, Reid Tool Supply Co., Muskegon, MI, 2007
- Simpson Strong Tie Product Manual, Simpson Strong Tie, CA, 2008
- Ticona Designing with Plastics – The Fundamentals, Summit, NJ, 2008
- SMC Corporation of America, Product Manuals, Indiana, 2009
- Gears Educational Design Systems, Product Manual, Hanover, MA, 2009
- Emhart – A Black and Decker Company, On-line catalog, Hartford, CT, 2009

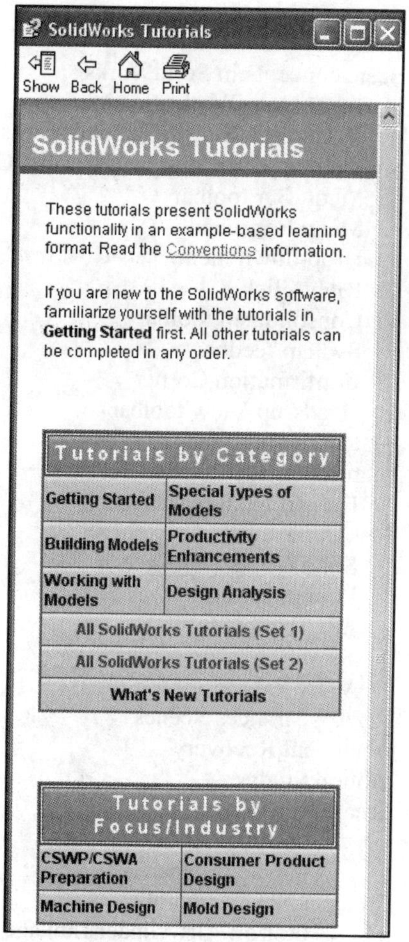


There are over 200 enhancements in SolidWorks 2010. Over 90% of these enhancements were requested directly by customers.

New in SolidWorks 2010 is the What's New Tutorials.

Every license of SolidWorks 2010, obtains a copy of SolidWorks SustainabilityXpress. SustainabilityXpress calculates environmental impact on a model in four key areas: *Carbon Footprint, Energy Consumption, Air Acidification and Water Eutrophication*. Material and Manufacturing process region and Transportation Usage region are used as input variables.

During the initial SolidWorks installation, you are requested to select either the ISO or ANSI drafting standard. ISO is typically an European drafting standard and uses First Angle Projection. The book is written using the ANSI (US) overall drafting standard and Third Angle Projection for drawings.

# TABLE OF CONTENTS

## Command Syntax

The following command syntax is used throughout the text. Commands that require you to perform an action are displayed in **Bold** text.

| Format: | Convention: | Example: |
|---|---|---|
| Bold | • All commands actions.<br>• Selected icon button.<br>• Selected geometry: line, circle.<br>• Value entries. | • Click **Options** from the Menu bar toolbar.<br>• Click the **Extruded Boss/Base** feature.<br>• Click **Corner Rectangle** from the Consolidated Sketch toolbar.<br>• Click the **centerpoint**.<br>• Enter **3.0** for Radius. |
| Capitalized | • Filenames.<br>• First letter in a feature name. | • Save the **Flashlight** assembly.<br>• Click the **Fillet** feature. |

## Windows Terminology in SolidWorks

The mouse buttons provide an integral role in executing SolidWorks commands. The mouse buttons execute commands, select geometry, display Shortcut menus and provide information feedback. A summary of mouse button terminology is displayed below:

| Item: | Description: |
|---|---|
| Click | Press and release the left mouse button. |
| Double-click | Double press and release the left mouse button. |
| Click inside | Press the left mouse button. Wait a second, and then press the left mouse button inside the text box.<br>Use this technique to modify Feature names in the FeatureManager design tree. |
| Drag / Drop | Point to an object, press and hold the left mouse button down.<br>Move the mouse pointer to a new location.<br>Release the left mouse button. |
| Right-click | Press and release the right mouse button.<br>A Shortcut menu is displayed. Use the left mouse button to select a menu command. |
| ToolTip | Position the mouse pointer over an Icon (button). The tool name is displayed below the mouse pointer. |

# CHAPTER 1: QUICK START

## Chapter Objective

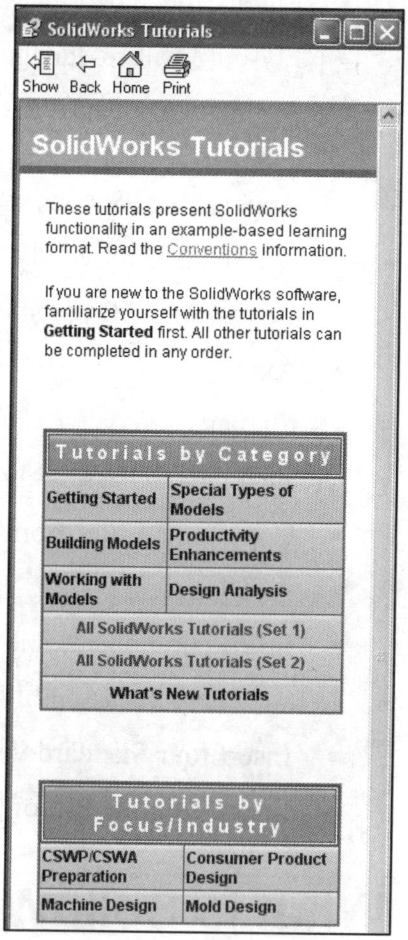


Chapter 1 provides a basic overview of the concepts and terminology used throughout this book using SolidWorks® 2010 software. If you are completely new to SolidWorks, you should read Chapter 1 in detail and complete Lesson 1, Lesson 2 and Lesson 3 in the SolidWorks Tutorials under the Getting Started category.

New in 2010 is the What's New Tutorials.

If you are familiar with an earlier release of SolidWorks, you still might want to skim Chapter 1 to be acquainted with the feature and interface enhancements that are incorporated into 2010.

Chapter 1 introduces you to many of the basic operations of SolidWorks such as; definitions, starting a SolidWorks session, using the User Interface along with opening and closing files, creating a part, assembly and a multi-view drawing with a Bill of Materials.

Every license of SolidWorks 2010, obtains a copy of SolidWorks SustainabilityXpress. SustainabilityXpress calculates environmental impact on a model in four key areas: *Carbon Footprint, Energy Consumption, Air Acidification and Water Eutrophication*. Material and Manufacturing process region and Transportation Usage region are used as input variables.

On the completion of this chapter, you will be able to:

- Comprehend what is SolidWorks
- Understand basic concepts in SolidWorks:
  - Associativity, Base sketch, document, geometric constraint, dimensions, 2D drawing, 3D feature, SolidWorks model and refining the design
- Start a SolidWorks session
- Use the SolidWorks User Interface (UI) and CommandManager:
  - Menu Bar toolbar, Menu Bar menu, Drop-down menu, Right-Click Pop-up menus, Consolidated flyout tool buttons, System feedback, Confirmation Corner, Heads-up View toolbar and more

- Know the FeatureManager Design Tree:
  - Show or Hide
  - Filter
  - Fly-out FeatureManager
- Comprehend the Task Pane:
  - SolidWorks Resources, Design Library, File Explorer, Search, View Palette, Appearances/Scenes, Custom Properties and Document Recovery
- Understand Motion Study
- Create two new 3D parts:
  - Axle
  - Flatbar
- Create a new 3D assembly:
  - Copy model files from the CD in the book
  - AirCylinder
  - Insert components and Standard mates
- Create a new 2D assembly drawing:
  - Insert four Standard views: Front, Top, Right, and Isometric
  - Insert a simple Bill of Materials

# What is SolidWorks?

SolidWorks® is a mechanical design automation software package used to build parts, assemblies and drawings that takes advantage of the familiar Microsoft® Windows graphical user interface.

SolidWorks is an easy to learn design and analysis tool, (SolidWorks SimulationXpress, SolidWorks Motion, SolidWorks Flow Simulation, Sustainability, etc.) which makes it possible for designers to quickly sketch 2D and 3D concepts, create 3D parts and assemblies and detail 2D drawings.

Model dimensions in SolidWorks are associative between parts, assemblies and drawings. Reference dimensions are one-way associative from the part to the drawing or from the part to the assembly.

The book is written for the beginner user with six or more months of experience to the intermediate user and assumes that you have some working knowledge of an earlier release of SolidWorks.

# Basic concepts in SolidWorks

Below is a list of basic concepts in SolidWorks to review and to comprehend. These concepts are applicable to all versions of SolidWorks. All of these concepts are addressed in this book.

- *Associativity*. Model dimensions between parts, assemblies and drawings assure that changes made to one document are automatically made to all other documents.

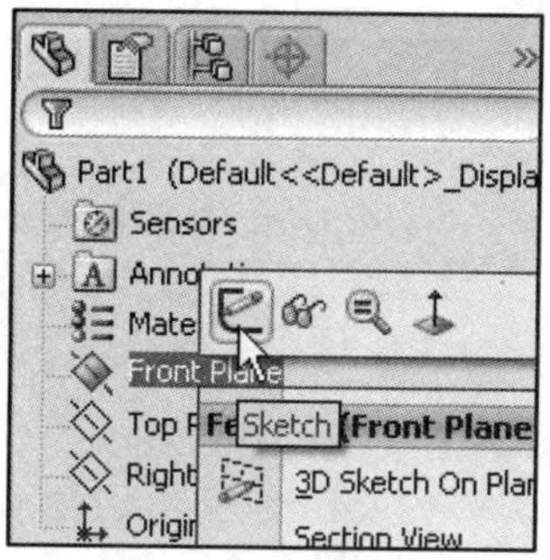


- *Base Sketch*. The first sketch in the part is called the Base sketch. The Base sketch is the foundation for the 3D model. Create a 2D sketch on a default plane: *Front*, *Top* or *Right* or on a created plane or face. You can also import a surface or solid geometry. In a 3D sketch, the Sketch Entities exist in 3D space.
- *Document*. A SolidWorks file containing a part, assembly or drawing.
- *Features*. The individual shapes that, when combined, make up the part. You can also add some types of features to assemblies.

DimXpert creates Reference dimensions not model dimensions.

- *SolidWorks model*. Consist of 3D solid geometry in a part or assembly document. Typically, you begin with a sketch, create a Base feature, and then add additional features to your model. Note: You can also begin with an imported surface or solid geometry.
- *Refining the design*. Perform the following types of editing feature operations:
  - Rollback the part to the state it was in before a selected feature was added either with the:
  - Rollback bar in the FeatureManager.

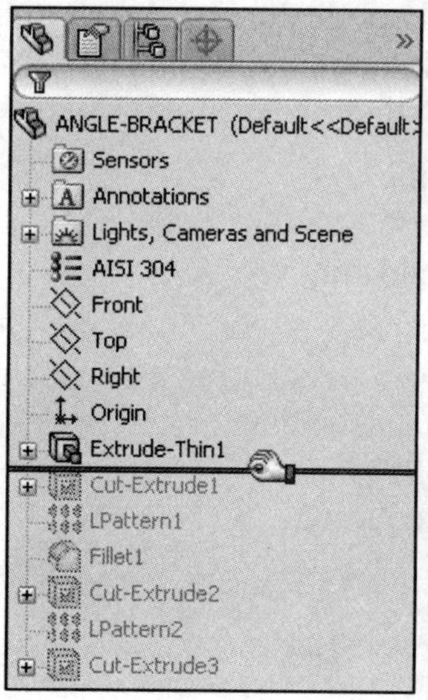


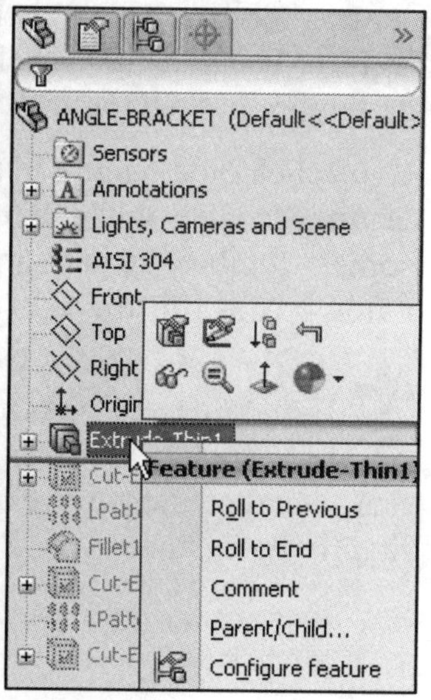

- Roll to Previous command from the Feature dialog box.
- Rollback command from the Pop-up Context toolbar.

Edit the definition, the sketch, or the properties of a feature by:

- Selecting the feature or sketch in the FeatureManager. The Pop-up Context toolbar is displayed. Select the Edit command.
- Selecting the feature or sketch in the FeatureManager, right-click in the Graphics window. The Feature dialog box is displayed. Select the Edit command.
- Control the access to selected dimensions. Click on either a feature or sketch in the FeatureManager or Graphics window. View the illustrated dimensions.
- View the Parent and Child relationships of a feature.
- Use the feature handles to move and resize features.
- Modify the order in which features are reconstructed when the part is rebuilt.

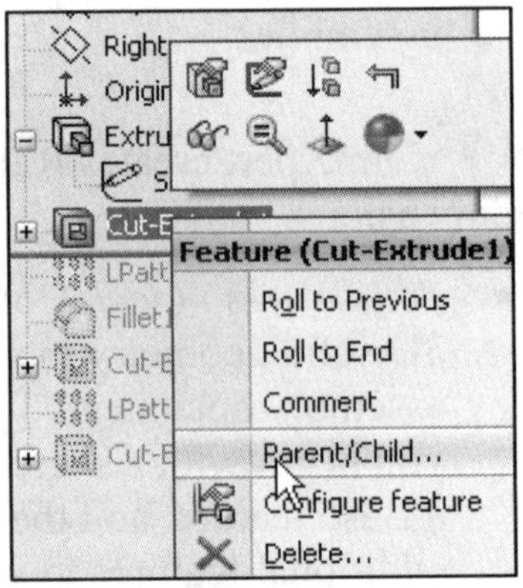


To activate the Pop-up toolbar, (also know as the Context toolbar) either click the feature or sketch in the FeatureManager, right-click, or click the feature in the Graphics window.

Right-click on a feature in the FeatureManager will active the Context toolbar, Feature and Body dialog box as illustrated.

There are over 200 enhancements in SolidWorks 2010. Over 90% of these enhancements were requested directly by customers.

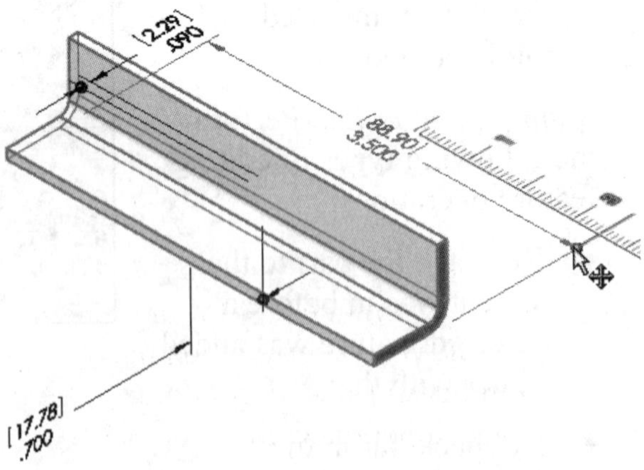

- *Geometric Constraint*. SolidWorks supports numerous constraints. Constraints are geometric relations such as: *Perpendicular, Horizontal, Parallel, Vertical, Coincident, Concentric, etc.* Apply equations to establish mathematical relationships between parameters. Insert equations and constraints to your model to capture and maintain design intent.
- *2D Drawing*. Create 2D drawings of any 2D or 3D part or assembly. Parts, assemblies, and drawings are linked documents. This means that any change incorporated into the part or assembly changes the drawing document. A drawing generally consists of several views generated from the model. Views can also be created from existing views. Example: A Section view is created from an existing drawing view.

# Starting a SolidWorks session

Start a SolidWorks session and familiarize yourself with the SolidWorks User Interface. As you read and perform the tasks in this chapter, you will obtain a sense on how to use this book and the structure. To help you learn the material, short quick tutorials are provided throughout the chapters. Actual input commands or required actions in the tutorial are displayed in bold.

At the time of publication, SolidWorks (http://www.solidworks.com/sw/support/SystemRequirements.html) did not have their 2010 system requirements available. Displayed are the system requirements up to SW 2009 SP4. SolidWorks will not support XP Professional next year and will start supporting Windows 7.

**Requirements for Data Management products** (PDMWorks Workgroup and Enterprise).

**Microsoft® Windows® Supported Operating Systems** (9)

| | SolidWorks 2006 | SolidWorks 2007 | SolidWorks 2008 | SolidWorks 2009 |
|---|---|---|---|---|
| Vista (64-bit) (12)(11) | ✘ | ✘ | ✔ | ✔ |
| Vista (32-bit) (11) | ✘ | ✘ | ✔ | ✔ |
| XP Professional (32-bit) (1) | ✔ | ✔ | ✔ | ✔ |
| XP Professional (64-bit) | ✔ (4) | ✔ | ✔ | ✔ |
| 2000 Professional (2) | ✔ | ✘ | ✘ | ✘ |

**Computer and Software Requirements:**

| | |
|---|---|
| RAM | • **Minimum**: 512MB RAM (SolidWorks 2009 1GB RAM)<br>Parts (< 200 features) and assemblies (< 1000 components)<br>• **Recommended**: 1GB or more (SolidWorks 2009 and higher 2GB or higher RAM)<br>Parts (> 200 features) and assemblies (> 1000 components)<br>• **Very Large Models:** X64 processor with 6GB or more, Parts > 1000 features, assemblies > 10000 components or models that exceed the limit of 32 bit architecture.<br>• Virtual memory recommended to 2X the amount of RAM. |
| Video | • A certified OpenGL workstation graphics card and driver.<br>For a listing of tested and certified graphics cards and driver combinations visit the **Graphics Cards and Systems web site**. |
| CPU | • Intel® and AMD® processors.<br>**Note**: SolidWorks is not supported on Apple Mac® based machines.<br>• eDrawings® is supported on Apple Mac®-based machines. |
| Other | • Mouse or other pointing device<br>• DVD drive<br>• Microsoft Excel 2002, 2003, or 2007<br>• Internet Explorer version 6.x or 7.x<br>• Adobe Acrobat version 7.0.7 or higher |
| Network | • SolidWorks is tested only with Microsoft's Windows Networking and Active Directory network environments.<br>• Novell networks and non-Windows based network storage devices are not tested or recommended. |

The book is written using SolidWorks Professional 2010 with Windows XP Professional SP2 on a Windows Classic desktop theme.

All models were created using SolidWorks 2010 SP0.

The book does not cover starting a SolidWorks session in detail for the first time.
A default SolidWorks installation presents you with several options. For additional information for an Education Edition, visit the following site:
http://www.solidworks.com/sw/docs/EDU_2009_Installation_Instructions.pdf

In the next section, start a SolidWorks session. The SolidWorks application is located in the Programs folder.

***Tutorial: Starting a SolidWorks Session 1-1***

1. Click **Start ➢ All Programs ➢ SolidWorks 2010 ➢ SolidWorks 2010** from the Windows taskbar. The SolidWorks program window opens as illustrated. *Do not open a document at this time.* If you do not see this screen, click the **SolidWorks Resources** icon in the Task Pane on the right side of the SolidWorks Graphics window.

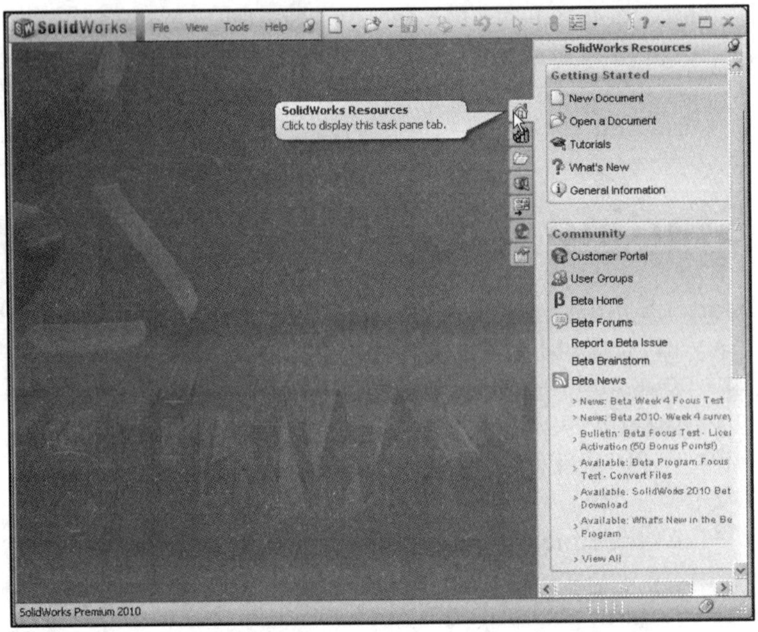


2. **Read** the Tip of the Day.

Double-click the **SolidWorks 2010 icon** on the Windows Desktop to start a SolidWorks session.

# SolidWorks User Interface (UI)

## Menu Bar toolbar

The SolidWorks 2010 (UI) is design to make maximum use of the Graphics window. The Menu Bar toolbar contains a set of the most frequently used tool buttons from the Standard toolbar.

The available default tools are:

- **New** – Creates a new document
- **Open** – Opens an existing document
- **Save** – Saves an active document
- **Print** – Prints an active document
- **Undo** – Reverses the last action
- **Select** – Selects Sketch entities, components and more

- **Rebuild** – Rebuilds the active part, assembly or drawing
- **Options** – Changes system options, document properties, and Add-Ins for SolidWorks

Expand the drop-down menu to display additional options and tools.

Until a file is converted to the current version of SolidWorks and saved, a warning icon is displayed on the Save tool as illustrated.

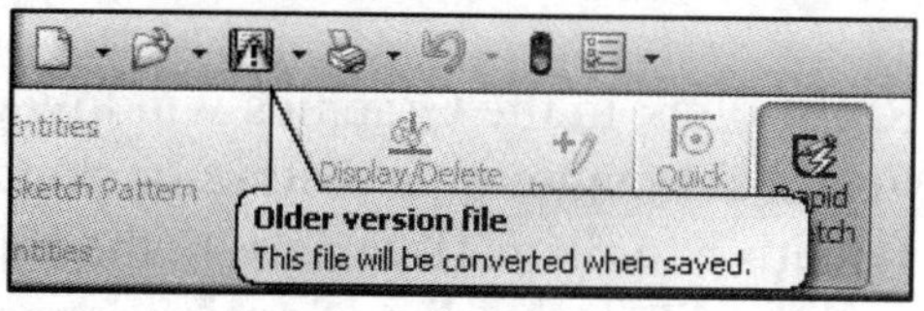


## Menu Bar menu

Click SolidWorks to display the default Menu Bar menu as illustrated. SolidWorks provides a Context-sensitive menu structure. The menu titles remain the same for all three types of documents, but the menu items change depending on which type of document is active. The display of the menu is also dependent on the work flow customization that you have selected. The default menu items for an active document are: *File*, *Edit*, *View*, *Insert*, *Tools*, *Window*, *Help* and *Pin*.

The Pin option displays the Menu Bar toolbar and the Menu Bar menu as illustrated. In future chapters, the Menu Bar menu and the Menu Bar toolbar remains pinned and are refer to as the Menu bar.

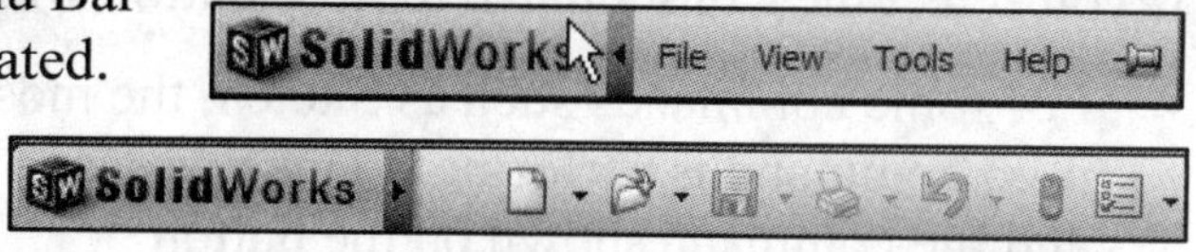


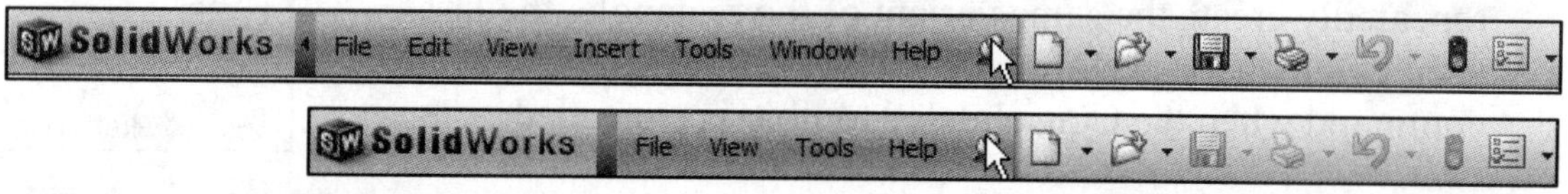


## Drop-down menu

SolidWorks takes advantage of the familiar Microsoft® Windows user interface. Communicate with SolidWorks through drop-down menus, Context sensitive toolbars, Consolidated toolbars or the CommandManager tabs.

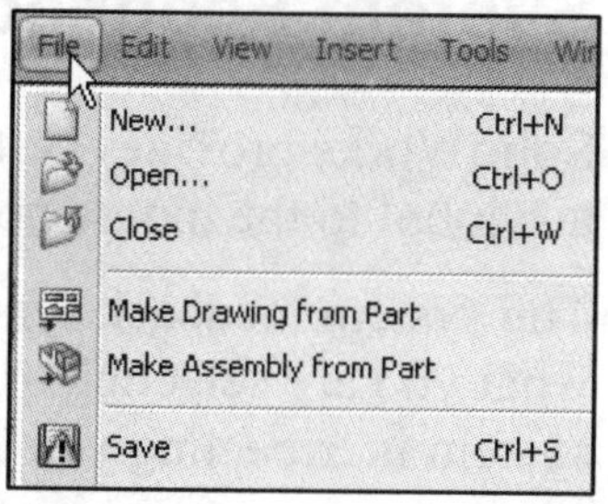

A command is an instruction that informs SolidWorks to perform a task.

Press the **Esc** key to close a SolidWorks drop-down menu. You can also click any other part of the SolidWorks Graphics window, or click another drop-down menu.

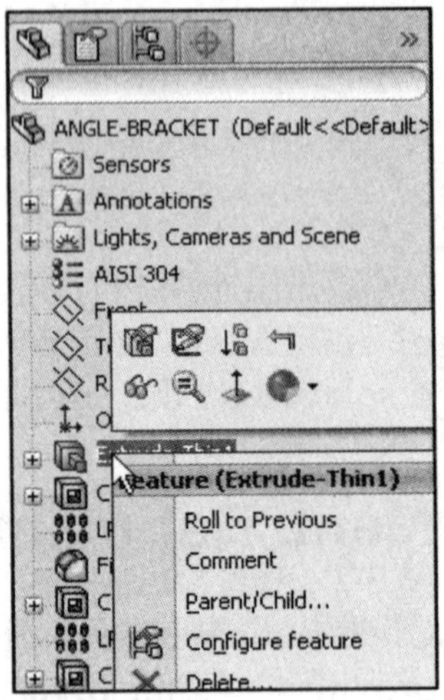


## Right-Click

Right-click in the Graphics window on a model, or in the FeatureManager on a feature or sketch to display a Context-sensitive toolbar. If you are in the middle of a command, this toolbar displays a list of options specifically related to that command.

The most commonly used tools are located in the Pop-up Context toolbar and CommandManager.

## Consolidated toolbar

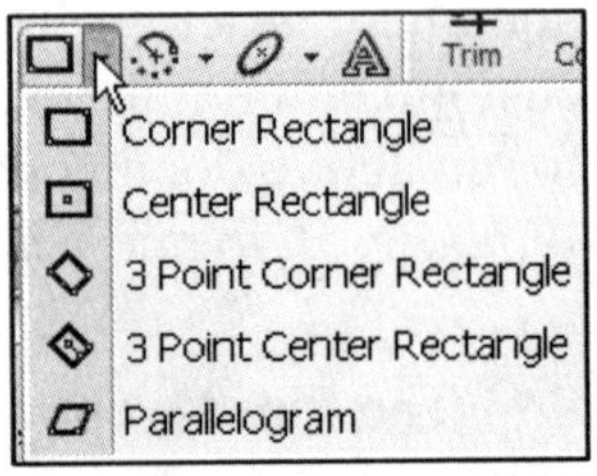


Similar commands are grouped together in the CommandManager. Example: Variations of the Rectangle sketch tool are grouped in a single fly-out button as illustrated.

If you select the Consolidated toolbar button without expanding:

- For some commands such as Sketch, the most commonly used command is performed. This command is the first listed and the command shown on the button.
- For commands such as rectangle, where you may want to repeatedly create the same variant of the rectangle, the last used command is performed. This is the highlighted command when the Consolidated toolbar is expanded.

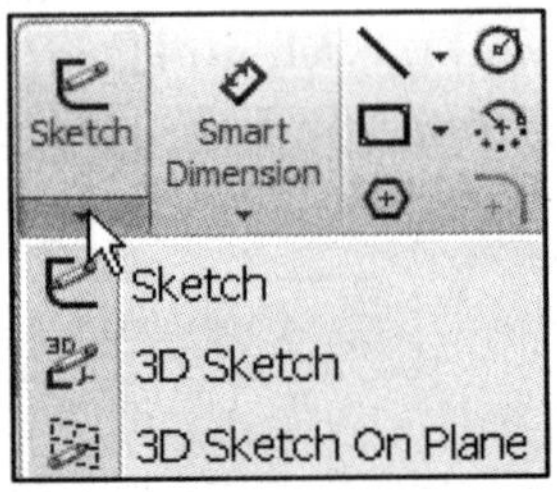


## System Feedback

SolidWorks provides system feedback by attaching a symbol to the mouse pointer cursor.

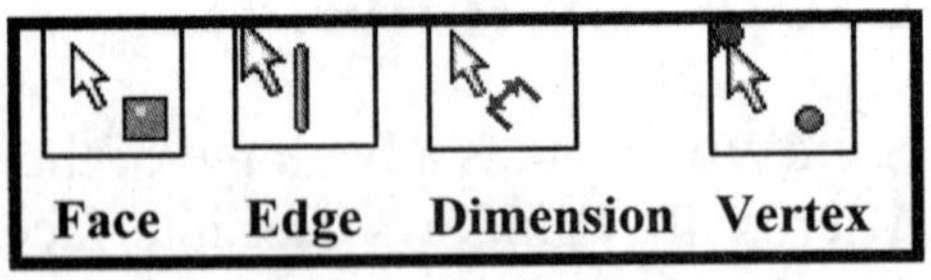


The system feedback symbol indicates what you are selecting or what the system is expecting you to select.

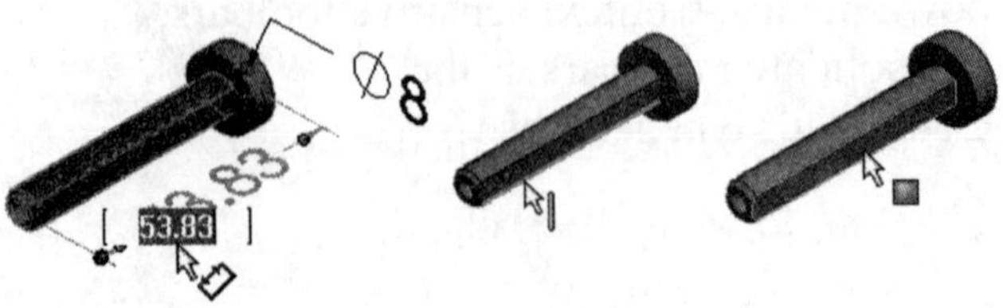

As you move the mouse pointer across your model, system feedback is displayed in the form of symbols, riding next to the cursor.

## Confirmation Corner

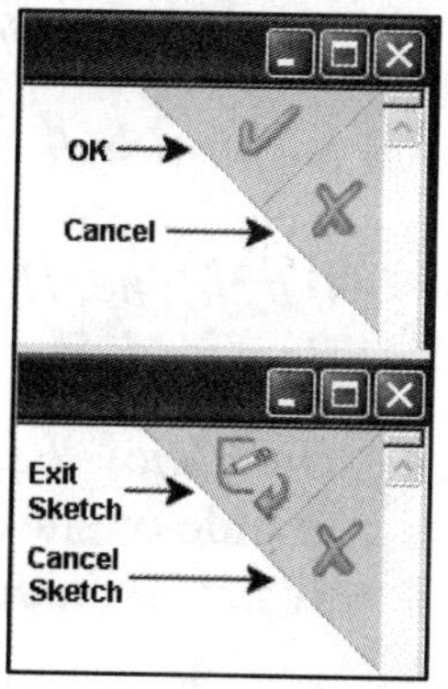


When numerous SolidWorks commands are active, a symbol or a set of symbols are displayed in the upper right hand corner of the Graphics window. This area is called the Confirmation Corner.

When a sketch is active, the confirmation corner box displays two symbols. The first symbol is the sketch tool icon. The second symbol is a large red X. These two symbols supply a visual reminder that you are in an active sketch. Click the sketch symbol icon to exit the sketch and to saves any changes that you made.

When other commands are active, the confirmation corner box provides a green check mark and a large red X. Use the green check mark to execute the current command. Use the large red X to cancel the command.

## Heads-up View toolbar

SolidWorks provides the user with numerous view options from the Standard Views, View and Heads-up View toolbar.

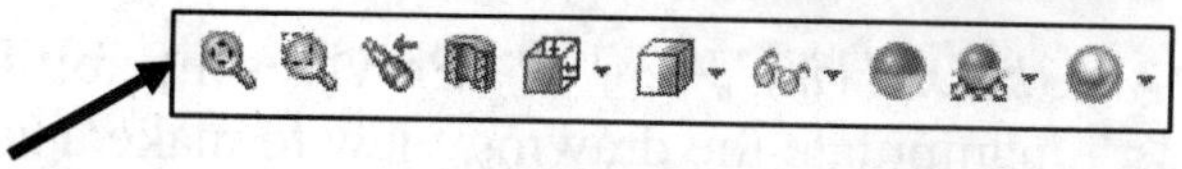

For an active part or assembly document

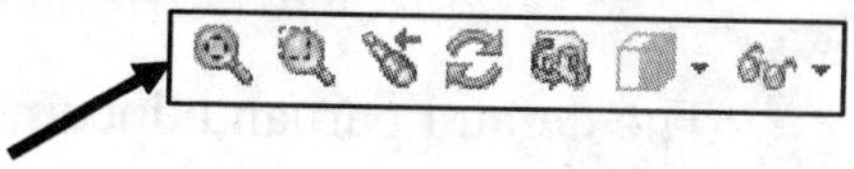

For an active drawing document

The Heads-up View toolbar is a transparent toolbar that is displayed in the Graphics window when a document is active.

You can't hide nor move the Heads-up View toolbar. You can modify it. To modify the Heads-up View toolbar, right-click on a tool, and select or deselect the tools that you want to display.

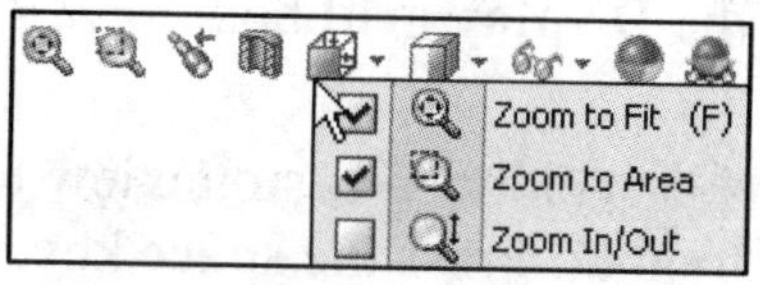


The following views are available: Note: <u>*The available views are document dependent*</u>.

- *Zoom to Fit* : Zooms the model to fit the Graphics window.
- *Zoom to Area* : Zooms to the areas you select with a bounding box.
- *Previous View* : Displays the previous view.
- Section View : Displays a cutaway of a part or assembly, using one or more cross section planes.

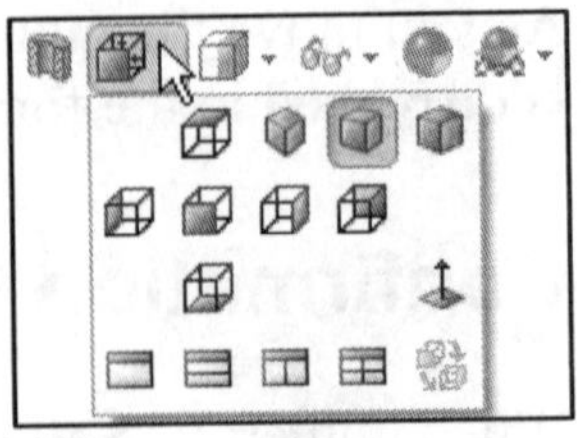

- *View Orientation* : Provides the ability to select a view orientation or the number of viewports. The available options are: *Top, Isometric, Trimetric, Dimetric, Left, Front, Right, Back, Bottom, Single view, Two view - Horizontal, Two view - Vertical Four view.*

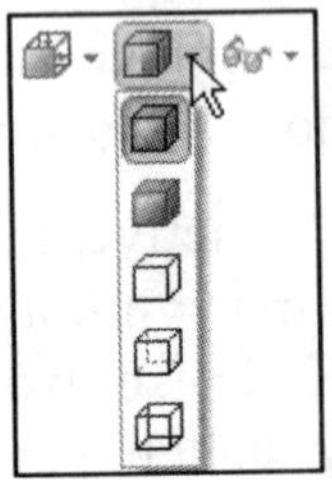

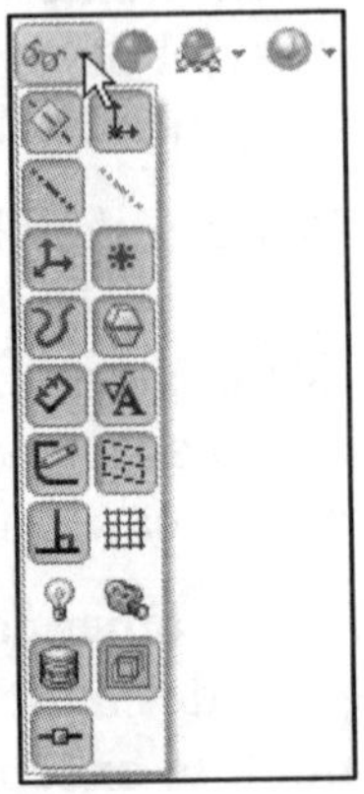

- *Display Style* : Provides the ability to display the style for the active view: The available options are: *Wireframe, Hidden Lines Visible, Hidden Lines Removed, Shaded, Shaded With Edges.*
- *Hide/Show Items* : Provides the ability to select items to hide or show in the Graphics window. Note: *The available items are document dependent.*
- *Edit Appearance* : Provides the ability to edit the appearance of entities of the model.
- *Apply Scene* : Provides the ability to apply a scene to an active part or assembly document. View the available options.

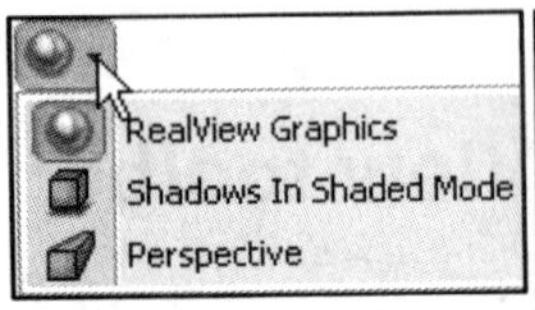


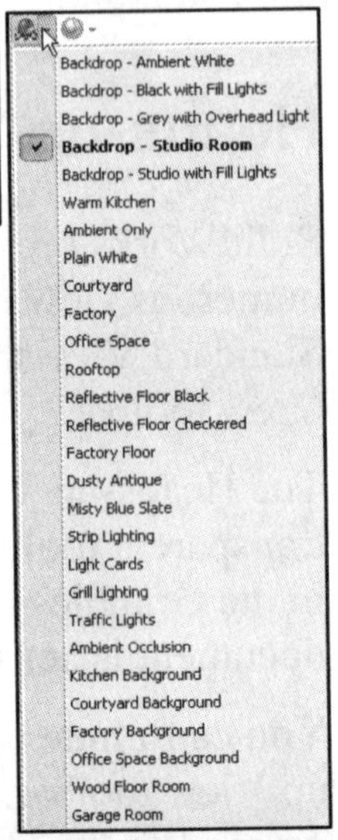


- *View Setting* : Provides the ability to select the following settings: *RealView Graphics, Shadows in Shaded Mode* and *Perspective.*
- *Rotate view* : Provides the ability to rotate a drawing view.
- *3D Drawing View* : Provides the ability to dynamically manipulate the drawing view to make a selection.

The default part and document setting displays the grid. To deactivate the grid, click **Options**, **Document Properties** tab. Click **Grid/Snaps**, uncheck the **Display grid** box.

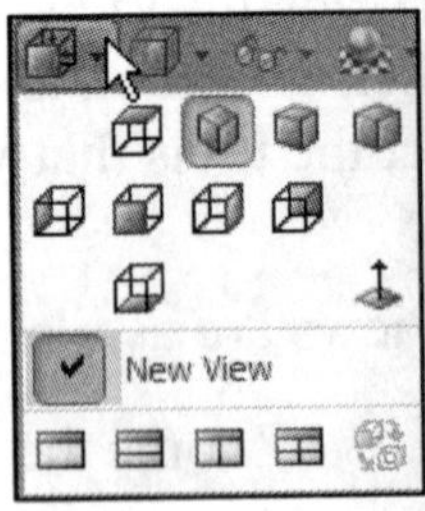


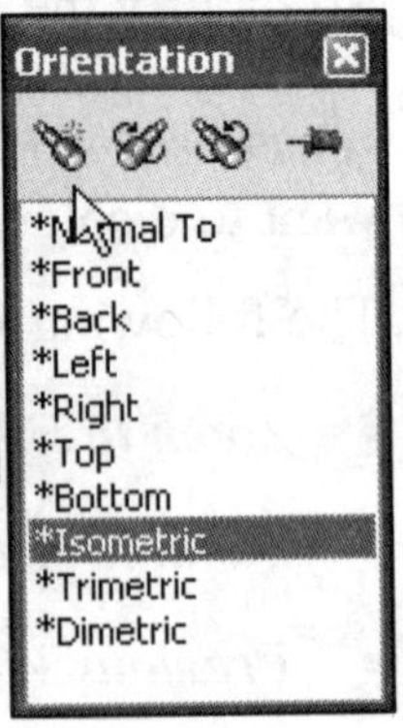


Adding a custom view to the Heads-up View toolbar. Press the **space** key. The Orientation dialog box is display. Click the **New View** tool. The Name View dialog box is displayed. Enter a new **named** view. Click **OK**.

Press the **g** key to activate the Magnifying glass tool. Use the Magnifying glass tool to inspect a model and make selections without changing the overall view.

## SolidWorks CommandManager

The SolidWorks CommandManager is a *context-sensitive toolbar* that automatically updates based on the toolbar you want to access. By default, it has toolbars embedded in it based on your active document type. When you click a tab below the CommandManager, it updates to display that toolbar. Example, if you click the Sketch tab, the Sketch toolbar is displayed. The default Part tabs are: *Features, Sketch, Evaluate, DimXpert* and Office *Products*.

Below is an illustrated CommandManager for a default Part document.

If you have SolidWorks, SolidWorks Professional, or SolidWorks Premium, the Office Products tab appears on the CommandManager.

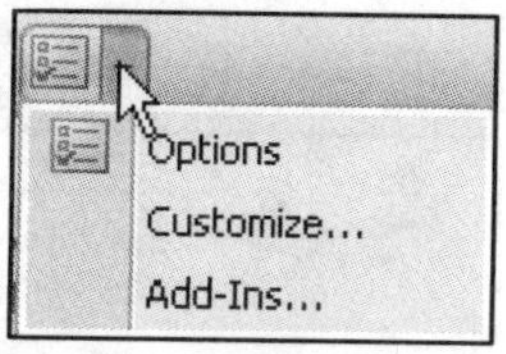


The Office Products toolbar display is dependent on the activated Add-Ins during a SolidWorks session.

Instant3D and Rapid Sketch are on by default.

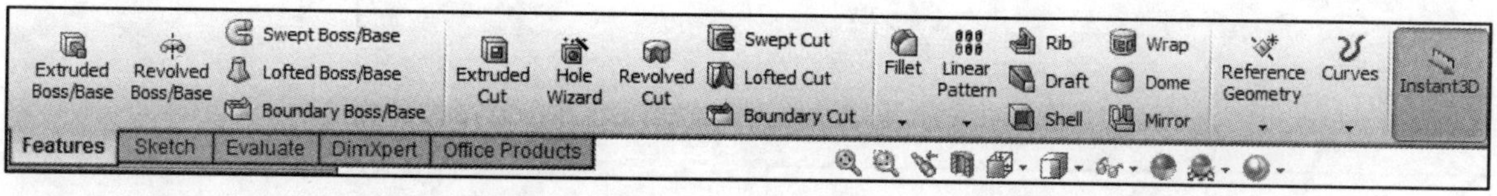


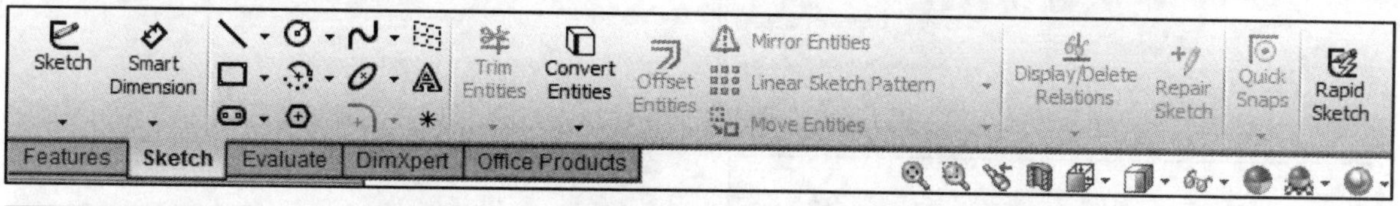


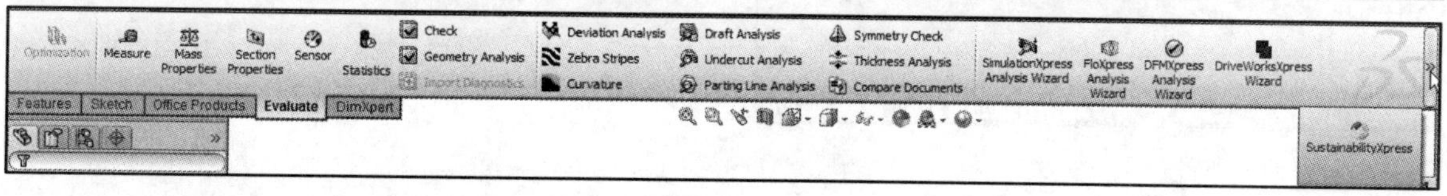


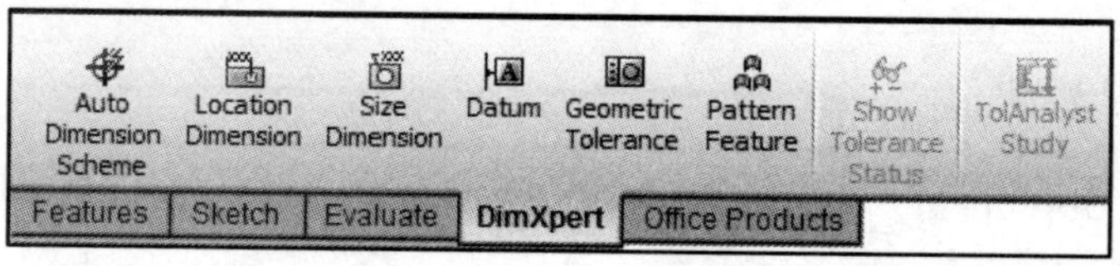


To customize the CommandManager, right-click on a tab and select Customize CommandManager.

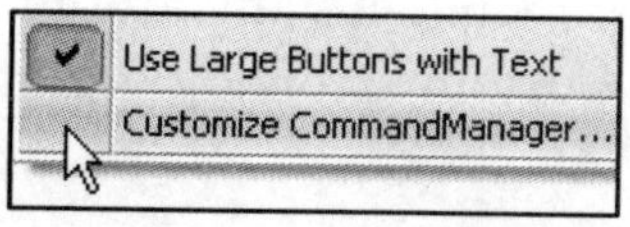

Below is an illustrated CommandManager for the default Drawing document. The default Drawing tabs are: *View Layout*, *Annotation*, *Sketch*, *Evaluate* and *Office Products*.

If you have SolidWorks, SolidWorks Professional, or SolidWorks Premium, the Office Products tab appears on the CommandManager.

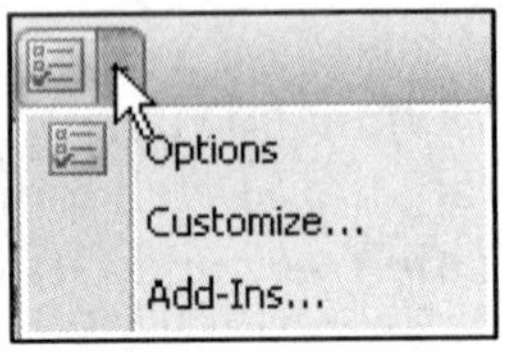


The Office Products toolbar display is dependent on the activated Add-Ins during a SolidWorks session.

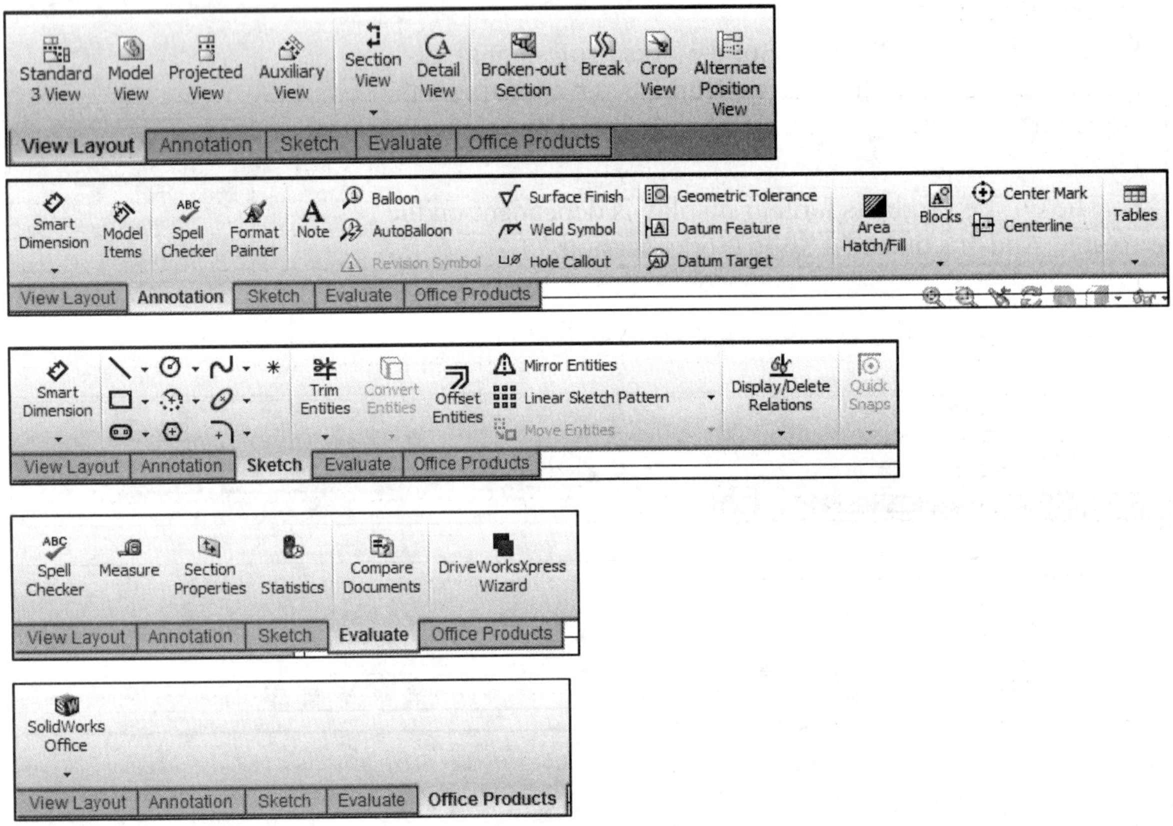


If you want to add a custom tab to your CommandManager, right-click on a tab and select the toolbar you want to insert. You can also select to add a blank tab as illustrated and populate it with custom tools from the Customize dialog box.

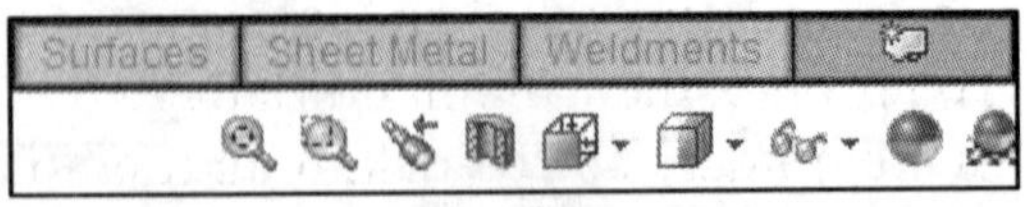

Below is an illustrated CommandManager for the default Assembly document. The default Assembly tabs are: *Assembly*, *Layout*, *Sketch*, *Evaluate* and *Office Products*.

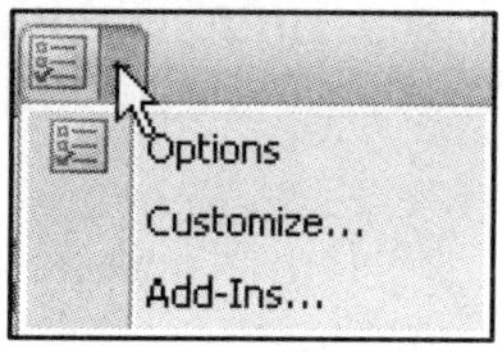


The Office Products toolbar display is dependent on the activated Add-Ins during a SolidWorks session.

*Rapid Sketch* and *Instant3D* are active by default.

If you have SolidWorks, SolidWorks Professional, or SolidWorks Premium, the Office Products tab appears on the CommandManager.

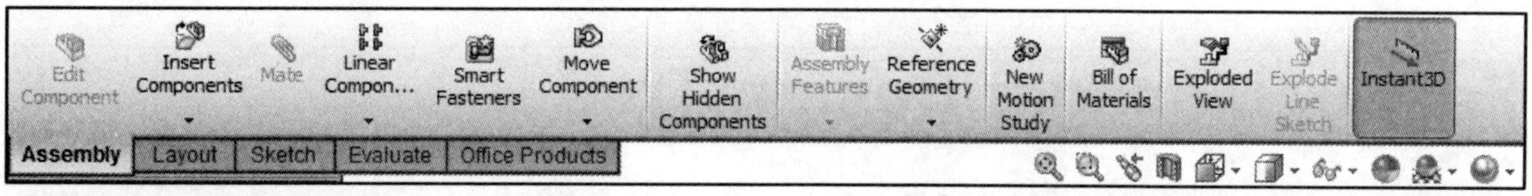

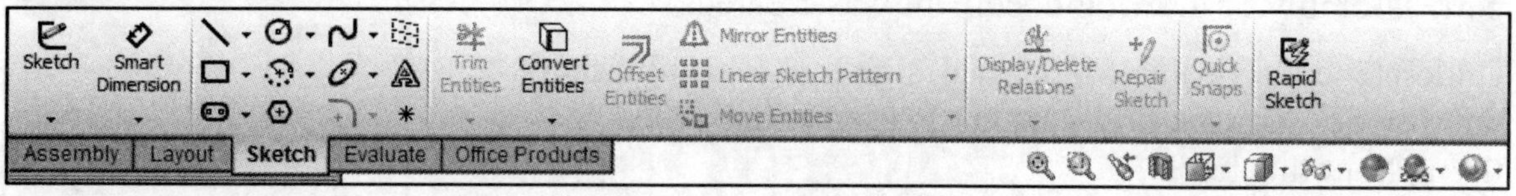


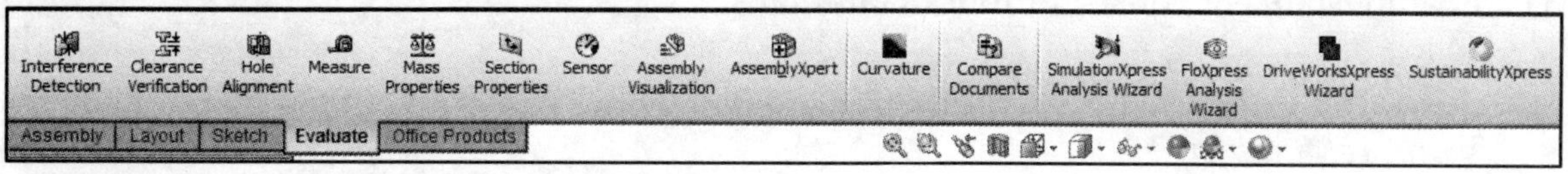


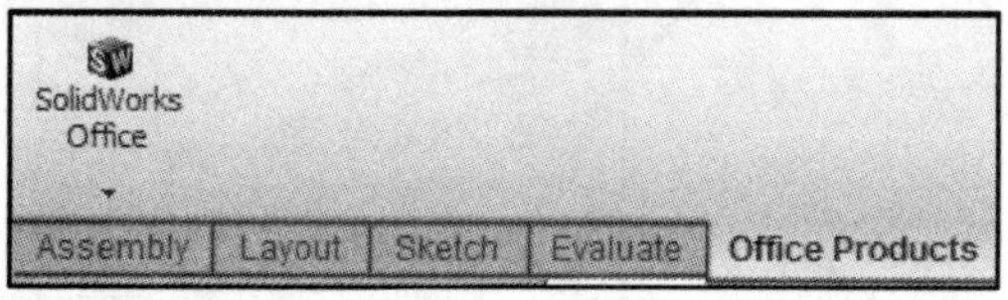


You can dock your CommandManager to the left or right in your Graphics window. To un-dock the CommandManager, click and drag on any non-toolbar button area, such as the border. To re-dock, drag it onto one of the docking stations around the Graphics window.

SustainabilityXpress, Assembly Visualization and Compare Documents are a few of the new 2010 tools under the Evaluate tab in SolidWorks Premium.

To save space in the CommandManager, right-click in the CommandManager and un-check the Use Large Buttons with Text box. This will eliminate the text associated with the tool.

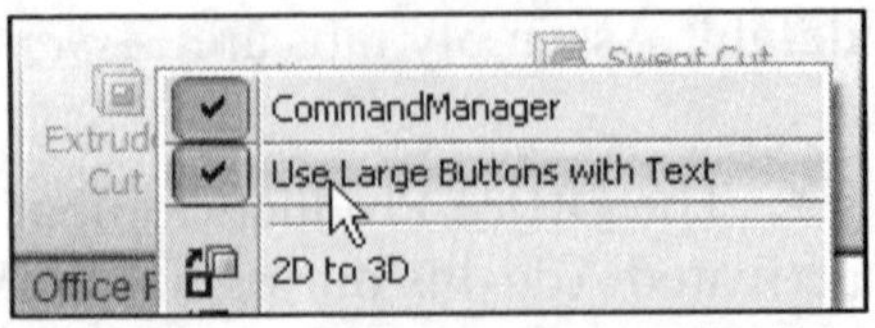


DimXpert provides the ability to graphically check if the model is fully dimensioned and toleranced. DimXpert automatically recognize manufacturing features. Manufacturing features are *not SolidWorks features*. Manufacturing features are defined in 1.1.12 of the ASME Y14.5M-1994 Dimensioning and Tolerancing standard. See SolidWorks Help for additional information.

---

# FeatureManager Design Tree

The FeatureManager design tree is located on the left side of the SolidWorks Graphics window. The FeatureManager provides a summarize view of the active part, assembly, or drawing document. The tree displays the details on how the part, assembly or drawing document was created.

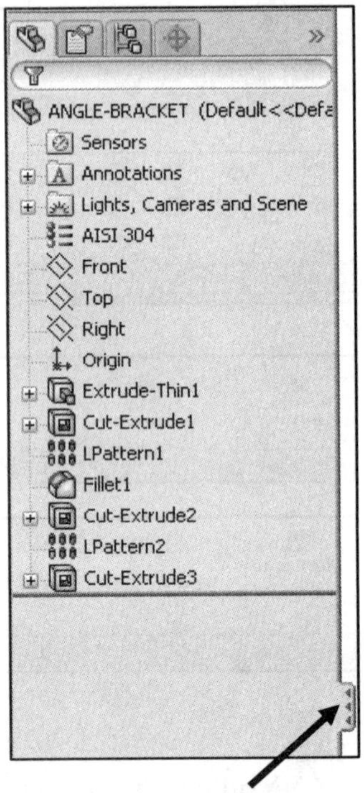


Understand the FeatureManager design tree to troubleshoot your model. The FeatureManager is used extensively throughout this book.

The FeatureManager consist of four default tabs:

- *FeatureManager design tree*
- *PropertyManager*
- *ConfigurationManager*
- *DimXpertManager*

Select the Hide FeatureManager Tree Area arrows  as illustrated to enlarge the Graphics window for modeling.

The Sensors tool 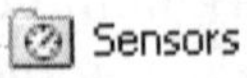

located in the FeatureManager monitors selected properties in a part or assembly and alerts you when values deviate from the specified limits. There are four sensor types: *Mass properties*, *Measurement*, *Interference Detection* and *Simulation data*.

Various commands provide the ability to control what is displayed in the FeatureManager design tree. They are:

1. Show or Hide FeatureManager items.

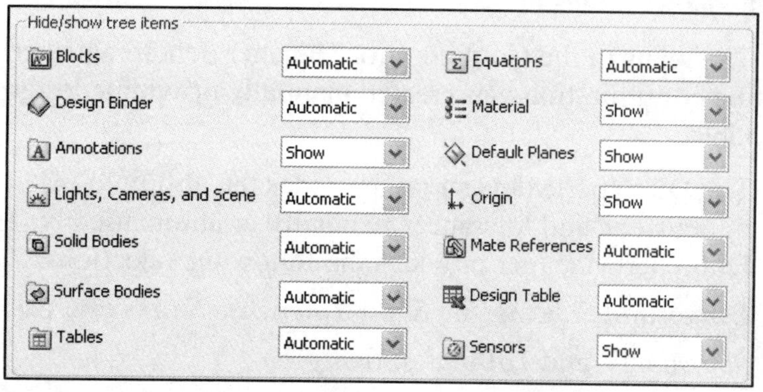


Click **Options** from the Menu bar. Click **FeatureManager** from the System Options tab. **Customize** your FeatureManager from the Hide/Show Tree Items dialog box.

2. Filter the FeatureManager design tree. Enter information in the filter field. You can filter by: *Type of features, Feature names, Sketches, Folders, Mates, User-defined tags and Custom properties*.

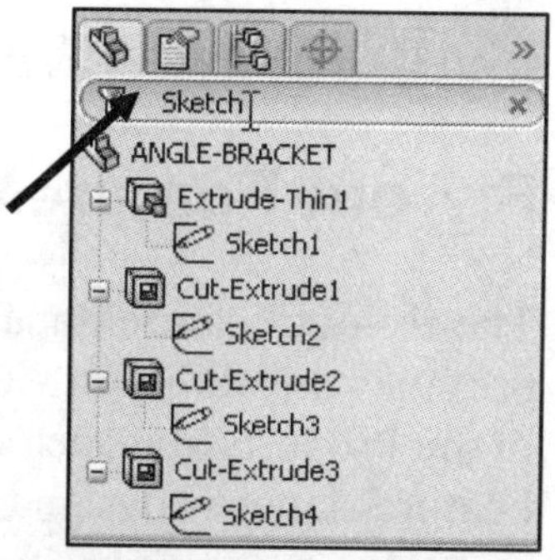


Tags are keywords you can add to a SolidWorks document to make them easier to filter and to search. The Tags icon is located in the bottom right corner of the Graphics window.

To collapse all items in the FeatureManager, **right-click** and select **Collapse items**, or press the **Shift** +**C** keys.

The FeatureManager design tree and the Graphics window are dynamically linked. Select sketches, features, drawing views, and construction geometry in either pane.

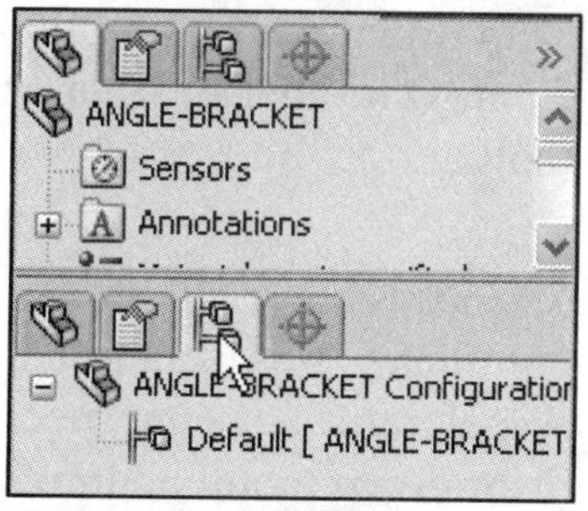


Split the FeatureManager design tree and either display two FeatureManager instances, or combine the FeatureManager design tree with the ConfigurationManager or PropertyManager.

Move between the FeatureManager design tree, PropertyManager, ConfigurationManager, and DimXpertManager by selecting the tabs at the top of the menu.

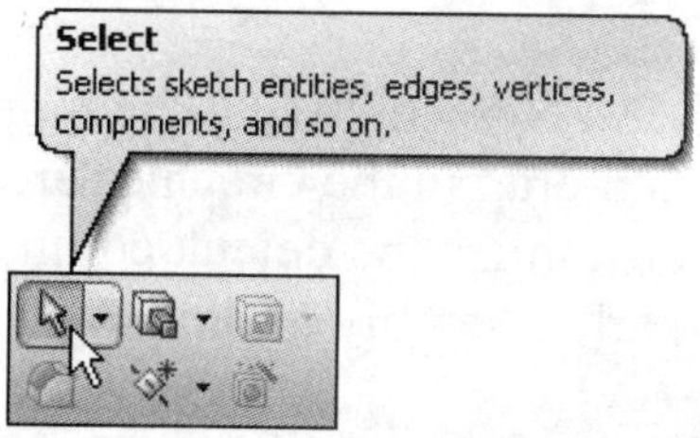


Press the **s** key to view the Shortcut toolbar. Shortcut menus provide convenient access to previous applied tools and commands.

Illustrations may vary depending on your SolidWorks release version.

The ConfigurationManager is located to the right of the FeatureManager. Use the ConfigurationManager to create, select, and view multiple configurations of parts and assemblies.

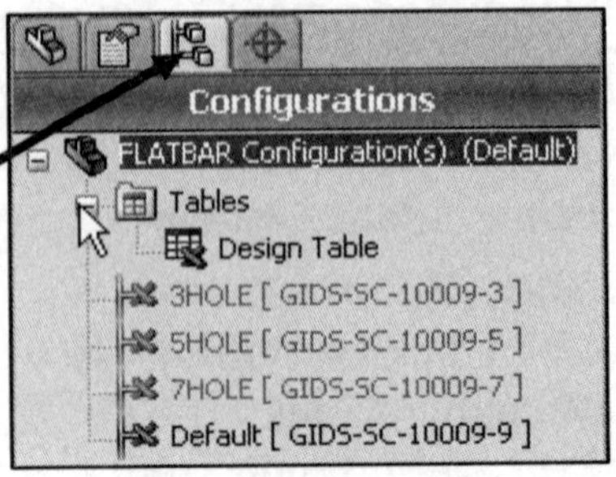


The icons in the ConfigurationManager denote whether the configuration was created manually or with a design table.

The DimXpertManager tab provides the ability to insert dimensions and tolerances manually or automatically. The DimXpertManager provides the following selections: *Auto Dimension Scheme*, *Show Tolerance Status*, *Copy Scheme* and *TolAnalyst Study*.

TolAnalyst is available in SolidWorks Premium.

## Fly-out FeatureManager

The fly-out FeatureManager design tree provides the ability to view and select items in the PropertyManager and the FeatureManager design tree at the same time.

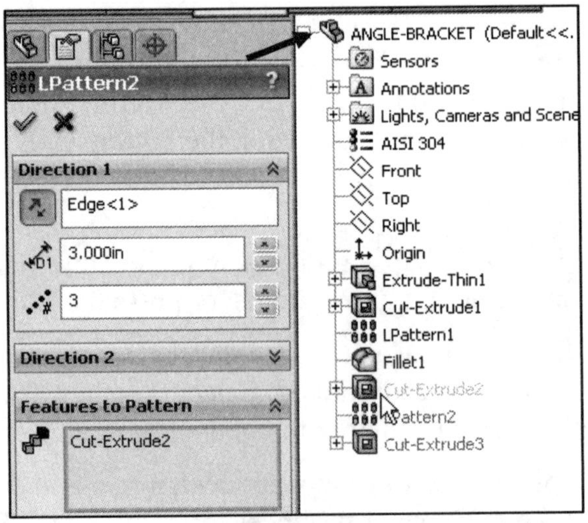


Throughout the book, you will select commands and command options from the drop-down menu, fly-out FeatureManager, Context toolbar or from a SolidWorks toolbar.

Another method for accessing a command is to use the accelerator key. Accelerator keys are special keystrokes which activates the drop-down menu options. Some commands in the menu bar and items in the drop-down menus have an underlined character.

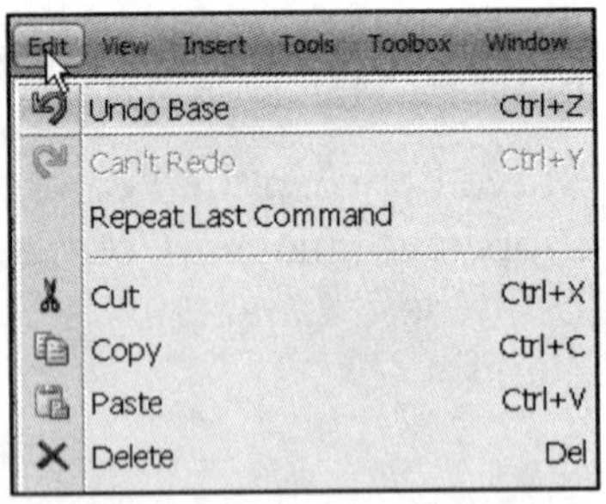


New in 2010 is the mouse gesture wheel. Right-click and drag in the Graphics area to display the wheel. You can customize the default commands for a sketch, part, assembly or drawing.

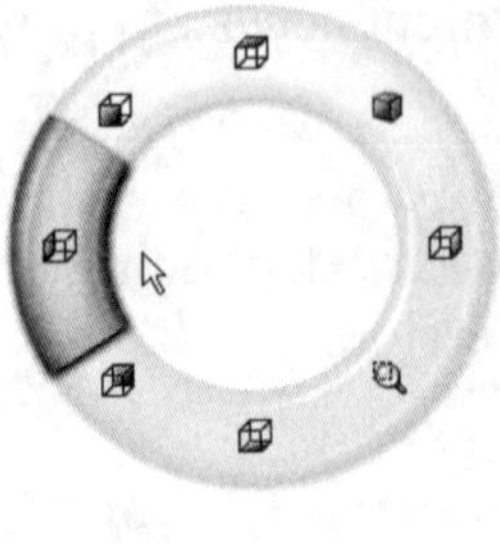

# Task Pane

The Task Pane is displayed when a SolidWorks session starts. The Task Pane can be displayed in the following states: *visible or hidden, expanded or collapsed, pinned or unpinned, docked or floating*. The Task Pane contains the following default tabs: *SolidWorks Resources*, *Design Library*, *File Explorer*, *SolidWorks Search*, *View Palette*, *Appearances/Scenes* and *Custom Properties*.

The Document Recovery tab is displayed in the Task Pane if your system terminates unexpectedly with an active document and if auto-recovery is enabled in System Options.

## SolidWorks Resources

The basic SolidWorks Resources menu displays the following default selections: *Getting Started*, *Community*, *Online Resources*, and *Tip of the Day*.

Other user interfaces are available: *Machine Design*, *Mold Design* or *Consumer Products Design* during the initial software installation selection.

## Design Library

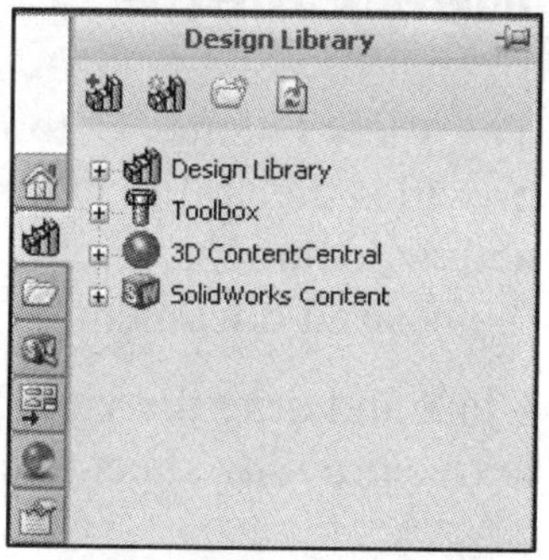


The Design Library contains reusable parts, assemblies, and other elements including library features.

The Design Library tab contains four default selections. Each default selection contains additional sub categories. The default selections are: *Design Library*, *Toolbox*, *3D ContentCentral* and *SolidWorks Content*.

Click **Tools**, **Add-Ins..**, check the **SolidWorks Toolbox** and **SolidWorks Toolbox Browser** box to activate the SolidWorks Toolbox.

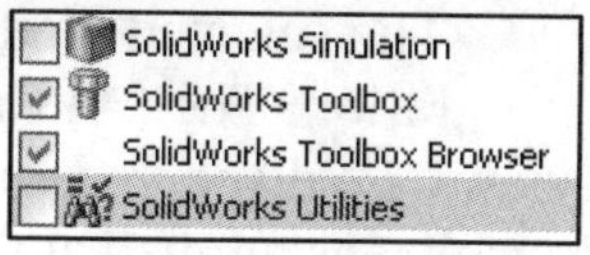


To access the Design Library folders in a non-network environment, click **Add File Location**, enter: **C:\Documents and Settings\All Users\Application Data\SolidWorks\SolidWorks 2010\design library**. Click **OK**. In a network environment, contact your IT department for system details.

# File Explorer

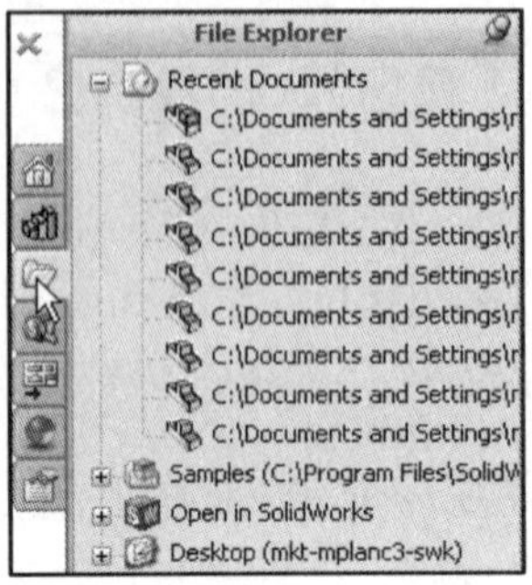


File Explorer duplicates Windows Explorer from your local computer and displays *Resent Documents*, *directories* and the *Open in SolidWorks and Desktop* folders.

# Search

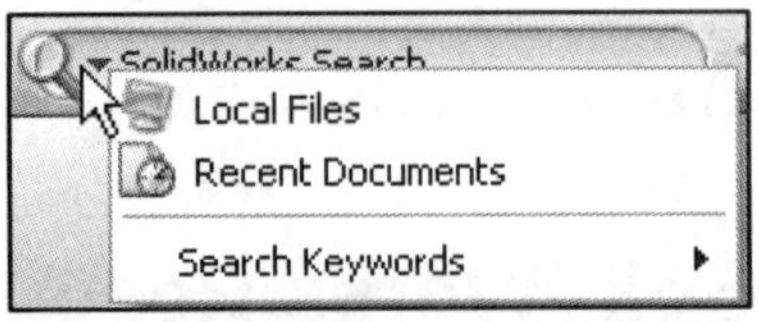


SolidWorks Search is installed with Microsoft Windows Search and indexes the resources once before searching begins, either after installation, or when you initiate the first search.

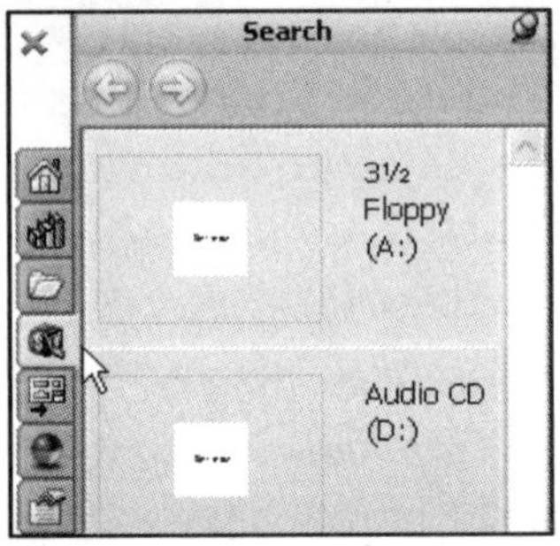


The SolidWorks Search box is displayed in the upper right corner of the SolidWorks Graphics window. Enter the text or key words to search. Click the drop-down arrow to view the last 10 recent searches.

The Search tool in the Task Pane searches the following default locations: *All Locations*, *Local Files*, *Design Library*, *SolidWorks Toolbox and 3D ContentCentral*.

Select any or all of the above locations. If you do not select a file location, all locations are searched.

# View Palette

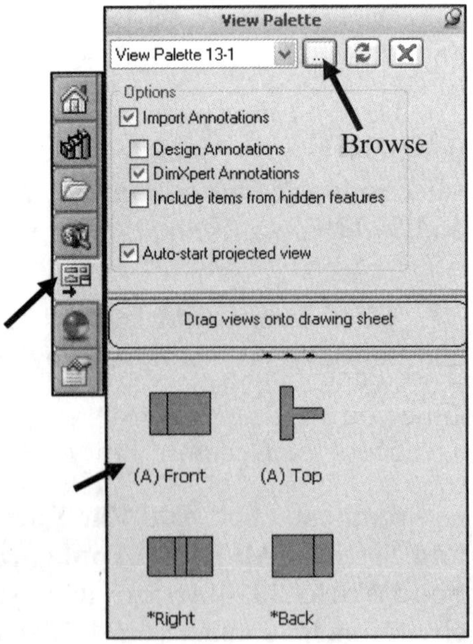


The View Palette tool located in the Task Pane provides the ability to insert drawing views of an active document, or click the Browse button to locate the desired document.

Click and drag the view from the View Palette into an active drawing sheet to create a drawing view.

The selected model is View Palette 13-1 in the illustration. The **(A) Front** and **(A) Top** drawing views are displayed with DimXpert Annotations which was applied at the part level.

## Appearances/Scenes

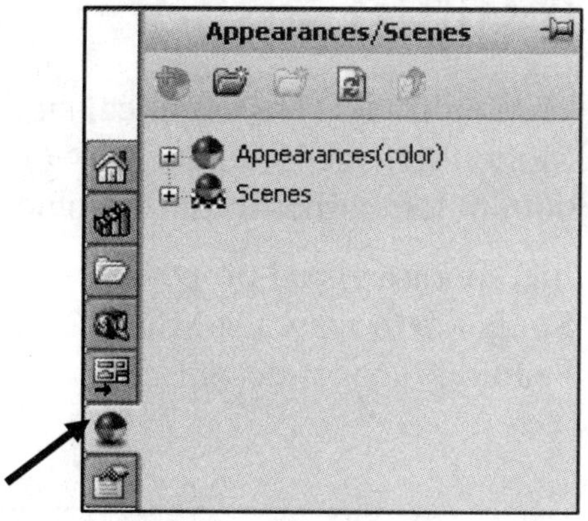


Appearances/Scenes provide a simplified way to display models in a photo-realistic setting using a library of Appearances and Scenes. Note: Appearances/Scenes require graphics card support.

On Appearances/Scenes compatible systems, you can select Appearances and Scenes to display your model in the Graphics window. Drag and drop a selected appearance onto the model or FeatureManager. View the results in the Graphics window. Note: PhotoWorks needs to be active to apply the scenes tool.

Appearances/Scenes graphics is only available with supported graphics cards. For the latest information on graphics cards that support Appearances/Scenes Graphics display, visit: www.solidworks.com\pages\services\videocardtesting.html.

## Custom Properties

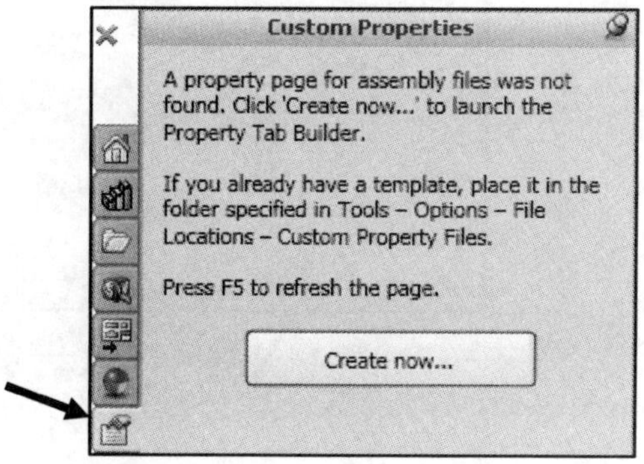


The Custom Properties tool provides the ability to enter custom and configuration specific properties directly into SolidWorks files.

## Document Recovery

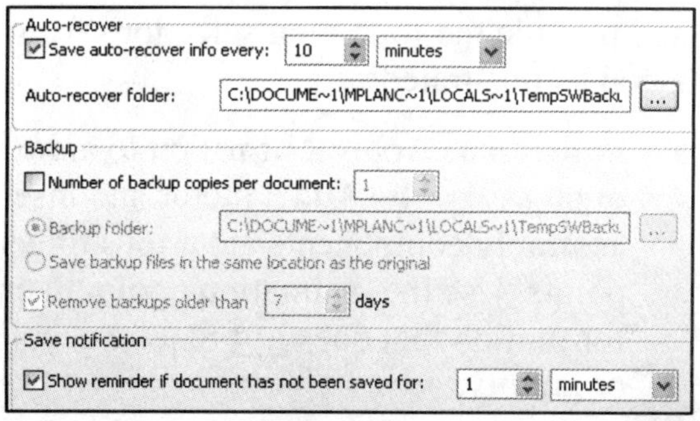


If auto recovery is initiated in the System Options section and the system terminates unexpectedly with an active document, the saved information files are available on the Task Pane Document Recovery tab the next time you start a SolidWorks session.

Run DFMXpress from the Evaluate tab or from Tools, DFMXpress in the Menu bar menu. The DFMXpress icon is displayed in the Task Pane.

# Motion Study

Motion Studies are graphical simulations of motion for an assembly. Access MotionManager from the Motion Study tab. The Motion Study tab is located in the bottom left corner of the Graphics window.

Incorporate visual properties such as lighting and camera perspective. Click the Motion Study tab to view the MotionManager. Click the Model tab to return to the FeatureManager design tree.

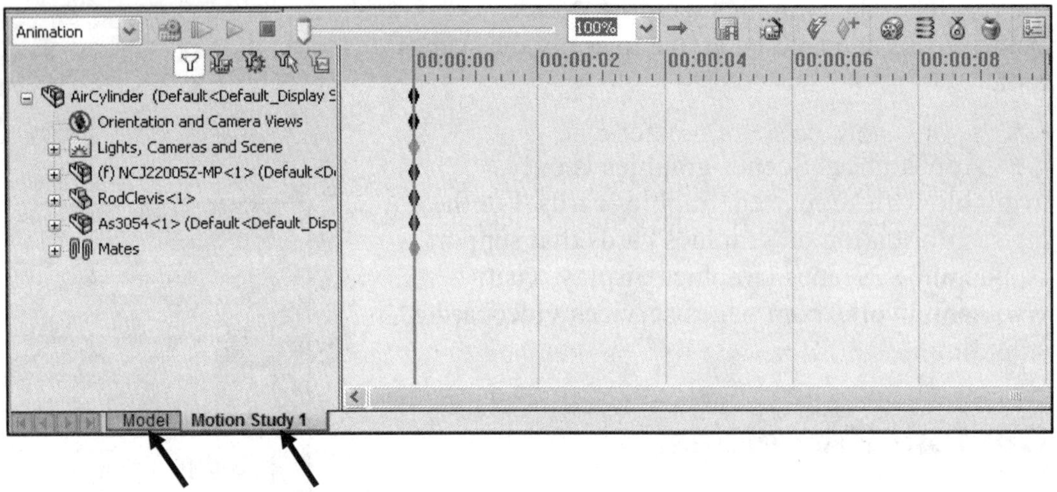


The MotionManager display a timeline-based interface, and provide the following selections from the drop-down menu as illustrated:

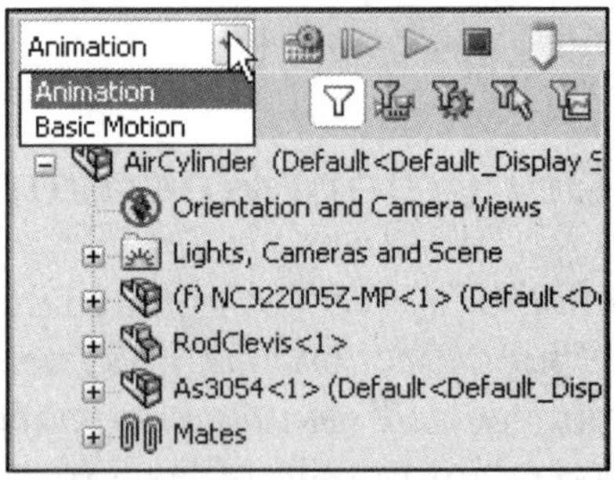


- *Animation:* Apply Animation to animate the motion of an assembly. Add a motor and insert positions of assembly components at various times using set key points. Use the Animation option to create animations for motion that does **not** require accounting for mass or gravity.
- *Basic Motion:* Apply Basic Motion for approximating the effects of motors, springs, collisions and gravity on assemblies. Basic Motion takes mass into account in calculating motion. Basic Motion computation is relatively fast, so you can use this for creating presentation animations using physics-based simulations. Use the Basic Motion option to create simulations of motion that account for mass, collisions or gravity.

If the Motion Study tab is not displayed in the Graphics window, click **View ➢ MotionManager** from the Menu bar.

Older assemblies created before 2008, the Animation1 tab may be displayed. View the Assembly Chapter for additional information.

# Create a New Part

A part is a 3D model which consists of features. What are features?

- Features are geometry building blocks.
- Features add or remove material.
- Features are created from 2D or 3D sketched profiles or from edges and faces of existing geometry.
- Features are an individual shape that combined with other features, makes up a part or assembly. Some features, such as bosses and cuts, originate as sketches. Other features, such as shells and fillets, modify a feature's geometry.
- Features are displayed in the FeatureManager as illustrated.

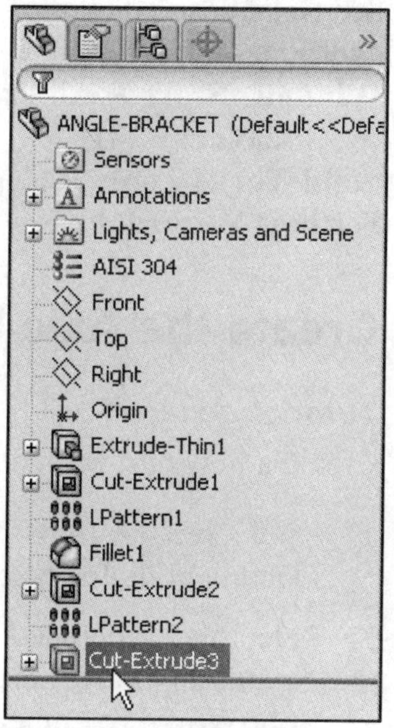


You can suppress a feature such as Cut-Extrude3 in the ANGLE-BRACKET FeatureManager. A suppressed feature is display in light gray in the FeatureManager.

The first sketch of a part is called the Base Sketch. The Base sketch is the foundation for the 3D model.

SolidWorks provides two modes in the New SolidWorks Document dialog box: ***Novice*** and ***Advanced***.

The ***Novice*** mode is the default mode with three default templates (Part, Assembly and drawing).

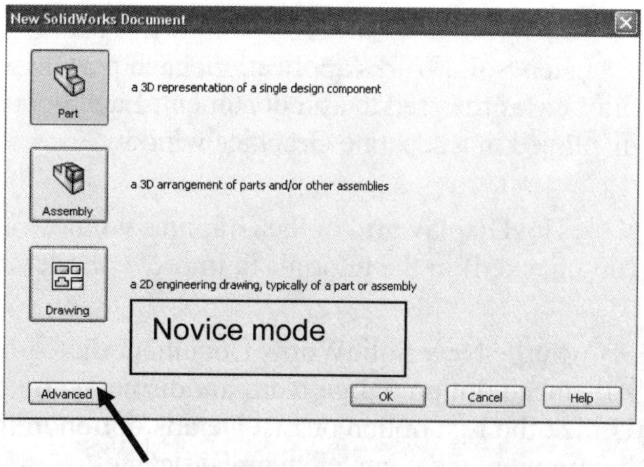

The ***Advanced*** mode contains access to create additional templates. In this book, use the ***Advanced*** mode.

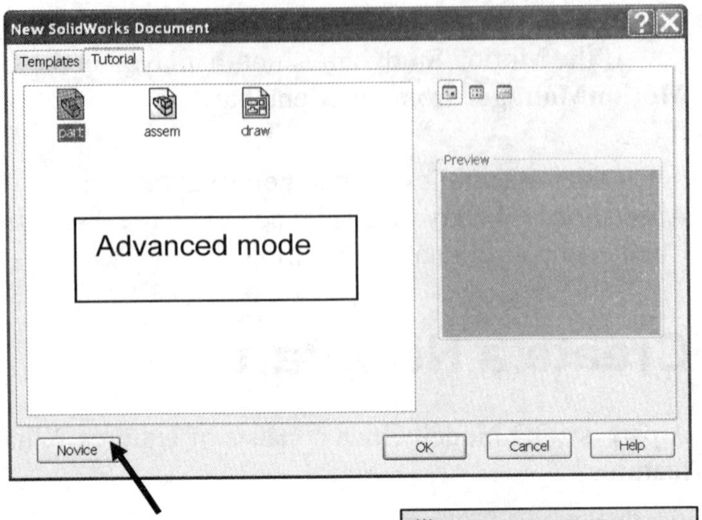


The SolidWorks Copy Settings Wizard provides the ability to save or restore customization settings for SolidWorks toolbar, shortcuts, menus and system preferences. See SolidWorks Help for additional information. Click **Windows Start ➤ All Programs ➤ SolidWorks 2010 ➤ SolidWorks Tools ➤ Copy Settings Wizard**. Follow the instructions.

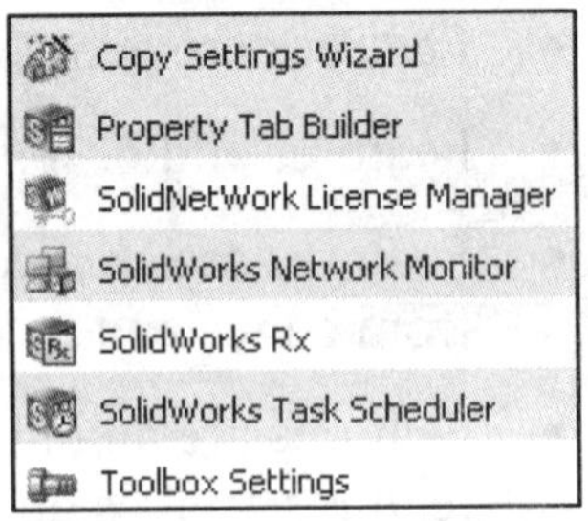


## Create the Axle Part

### *Tutorial: Axle 1-1*

Create a new part named Axle.

1. Click **New** from the Menu bar. The New SolidWorks Document dialog box is displayed.
2. Select the **Advanced mode**. The Templates tab is the default tab. Part is the default template from the New SolidWorks Document dialog box.
3. Click **OK** from the New SolidWorks Document dialog box.

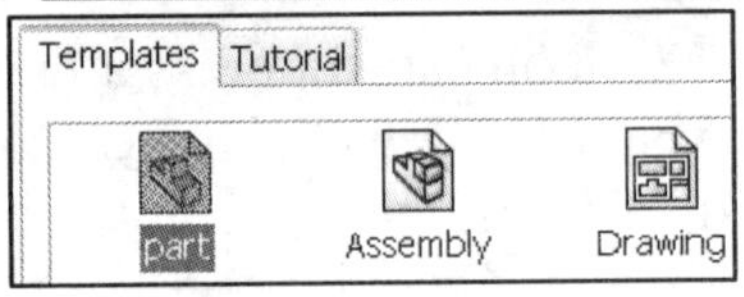


In a SolidWorks application, each part, assembly and drawing is referred to as a document. Each document is displayed in a separate Graphics window.

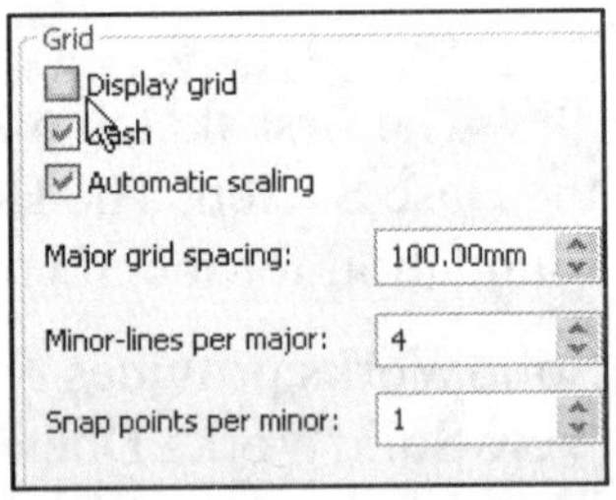


The Display grid in the Graphics window is deactivated (un-checked) in the tutorials to improve model visibility.

In the New SolidWorks Document dialog box, Advanced option, Large icons are displayed by default. Utilize the List option or List Details option in the dialog box to view the complete template name.

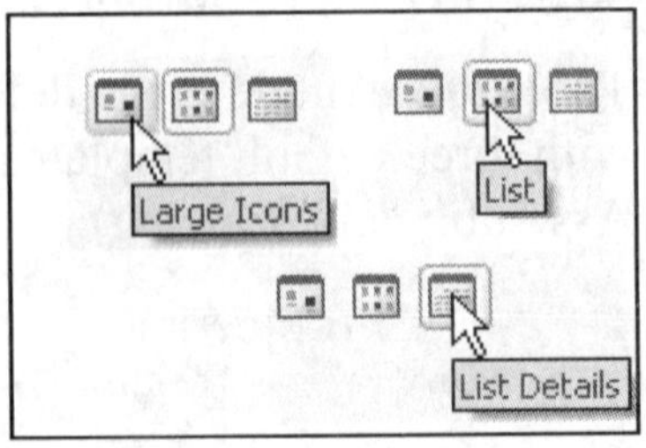

The ***Advanced*** mode remains selected for all new documents in the current SolidWorks session. The ***Advanced*** mode setting is saved when you exit SolidWorks. The default SolidWorks installation contains two tabs in the New SolidWorks Document dialog box: *Templates*, and *Tutorial*. The Templates tab corresponds to the default SolidWorks templates. The Tutorial tab corresponds to the templates utilized in the Online SolidWorks Tutorials.

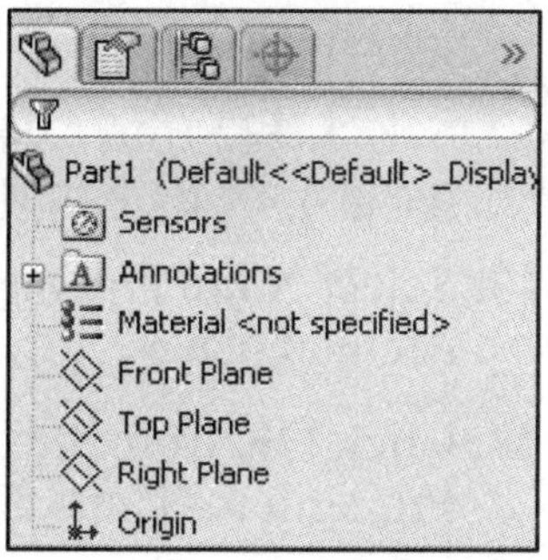


In SolidWorks, the first default part filename is named: Part1. SolidWorks attaches the .sldprt suffix to the created part. Part1 is displayed in the FeatureManager.

4. Click **Save** from the Menu bar.
5. Create a new folder named **SolidWorks 2010**.
6. Enter **Axle** for the File name in the SolidWorks 2010 folder.
7. Click **Save** from the Save As dialog box.

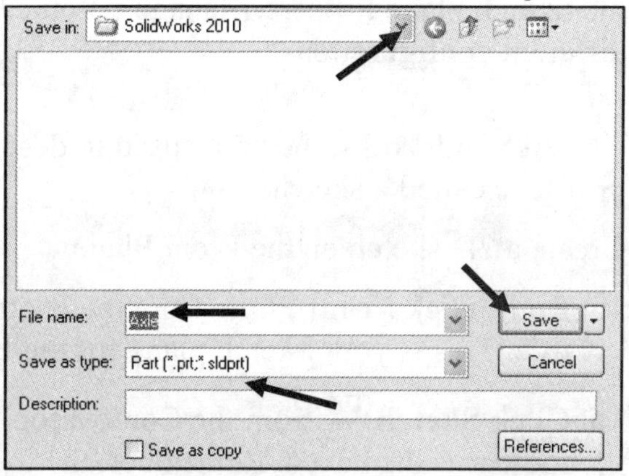


Organize parts into file folders. Use the SolidWorks 2010 folder as the main file folder for this book.

Set the Overall drafting standard, Unit system and precision for the Axle part.

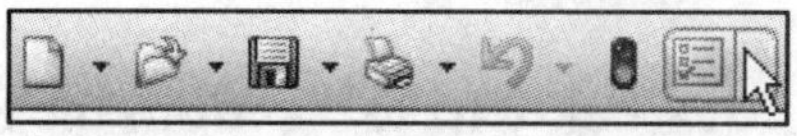

8. Click **Options** ➤ **Document Properties** tab. The Document Properties – Drafting Standard dialog box is displayed.

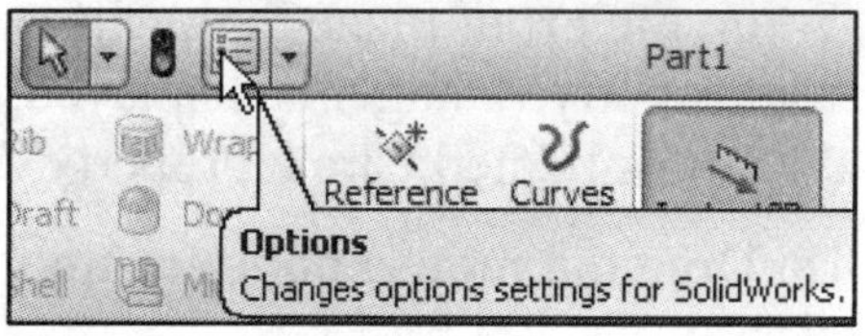


9. Select **ANSI (American National Standards Institute)** from the Overall drafting standard drop-down menu. ANSI is an American drafting standard and uses Third Angle Projection.

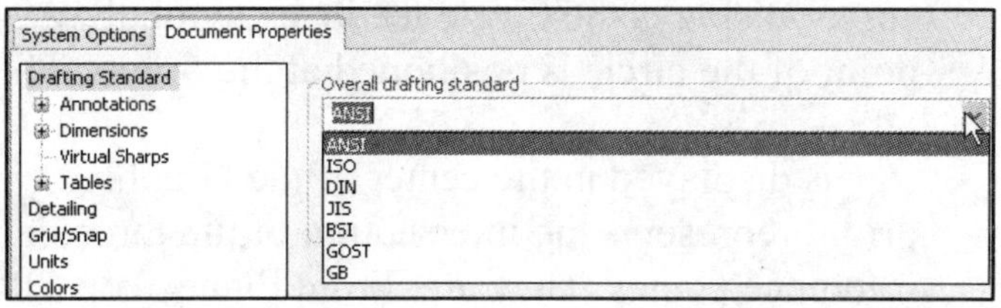


During the initial SolidWorks installation, you were requested to select either the ISO or ANSI drafting standard. ISO is typically a European drafting standard and uses First Angle Projection. The book is written using the ANSI (US) overall drafting standard and Third Angle Projection for drawings.

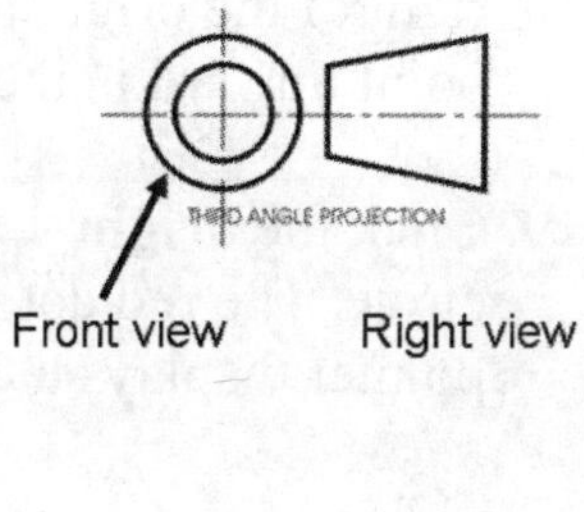

10. Click **Units**.

11. Select **IPS** (inch, pound, second) for Unit system.

12. Select **.123** (three decimal places) for Length Basic Units.

13. Select **None** for Angular unit decimal places.

14. Click **OK** from the Document Properties – Units dialog box.

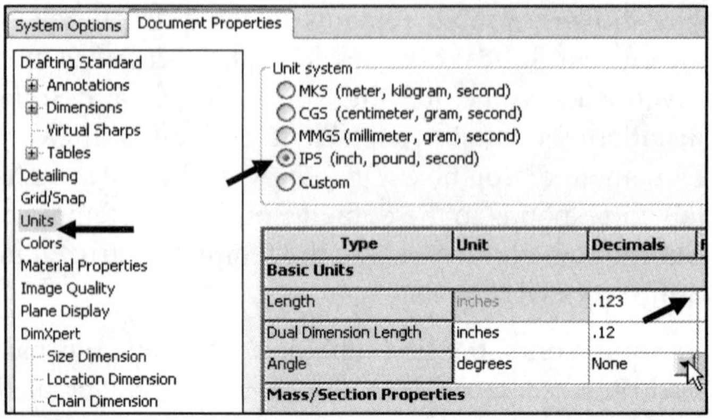


Identify the Sketch plane. The Sketch plane is the plane on which a sketch (2D or 3D) lies and is configurable through the Sketch plane PropertyManager. You can place a single sketch on various planes in different configurations.

In SolidWorks, the name used to describe a 2D or 3D profile is called a sketch.

Create a 2D sketch on the Front Plane.

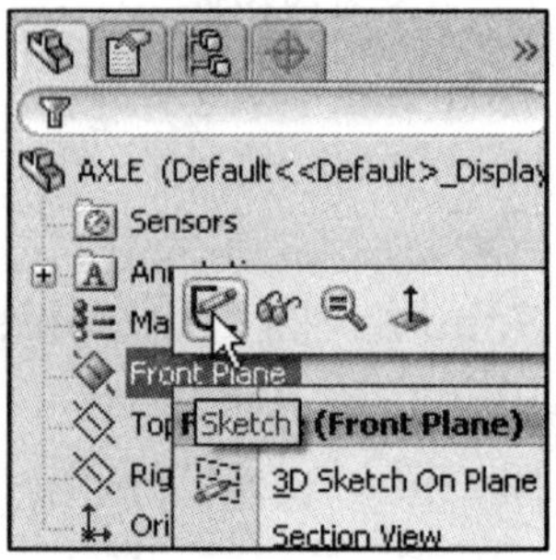


15. Right-click **Front Plane** from the FeatureManager design tree. This is your Sketch plane for the first feature.

16. Click **Sketch** from the Context toolbar. The Sketch toolbar is displayed. Remember, the toolbar is document dependent.

17. Click **Circle** from the Sketch toolbar. The Sketch opens on the Front Plane in the Front view by default. The Circle PropertyManager is displayed. Note: The Circle tools use a Consolidated Circle PropertyManager.

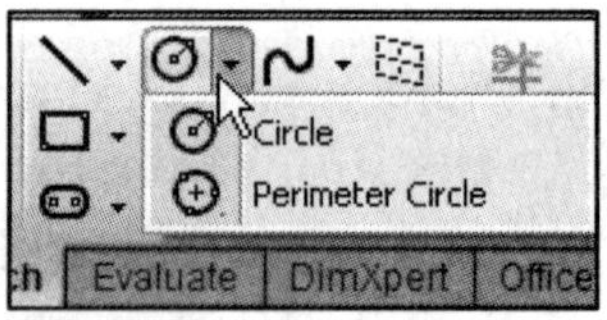


18. Drag the **mouse pointer** into the Graphics window. The cursor displays the Circle feedback symbol. The center point of the circle is positioned at the origin. The part origin is displayed in the center of the Graphics window. The origin represents the intersection of the three default reference planes. They are: Front Plane, Top Plane and Right Plane. The positive X-axis is horizontal and points to the right of the origin in the Front view. The positive Y-axis is vertical and point upward in the Front view.

19. Click the **origin** from the Graphics window. This is the first point of the circle. The red dot feedback indicates the origin point location. The mouse pointer displays the Coincident to point feedback symbol.

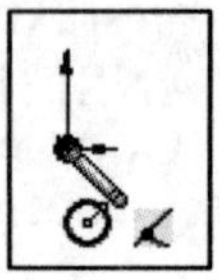

Sketch the circle.

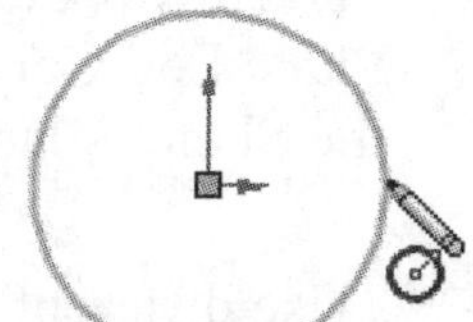

20. Drag the **mouse pointer** to the right of the origin.
21. Click a **position** to create the circle.

To control the Sketch relation display, click **View ➢ Sketch Relations** from the Menu bar.

Insert a dimension. Apply the Smart Dimension tool.

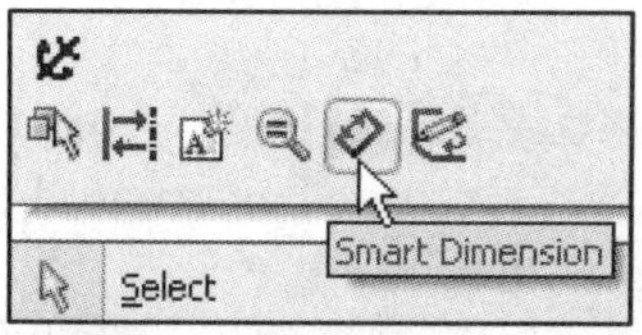


22. Right-click the **Smart Dimension** tool from the Context toolbar. The mouse cursor displays the dimension icon.
23. Click the **circumference** of the circle.

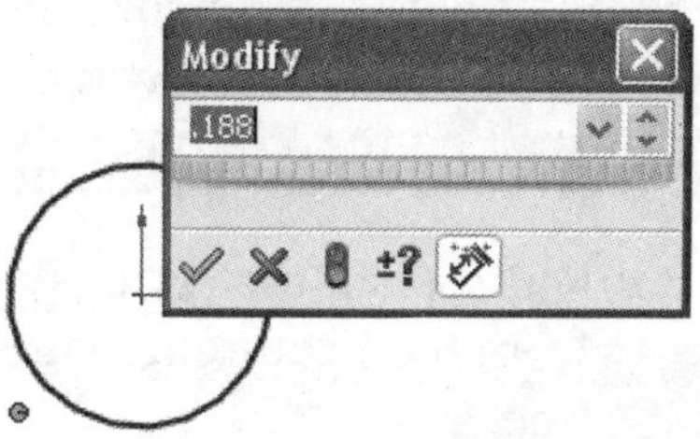


24. Click a **position** to locate the dimension in the Graphics window. The Dimension PropertyManager is displayed.
25. Enter **.188**in the Modify dialog box. The circular sketch is centered at the origin.

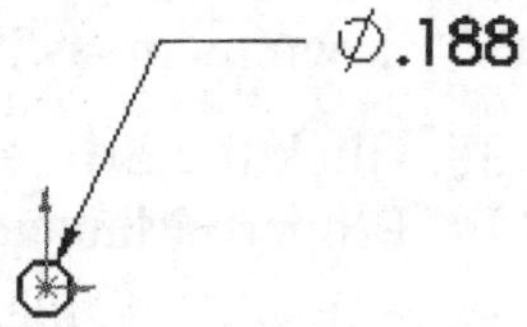


If your sketch is not correct, select **UNDO** from the Menu bar.

To fit your sketch to the Graphics window, press the **f** key or the **Zoom to Fit** tool from the Heads-up View toolbar.

Create your first feature. Create an Extruded Boss/Base feature. The Extruded Boss/Base feature adds material to a part. The Extruded Boss/Base feature is the first feature of the AXLE part. An extrusion extends a profile along a path normal to the profile plane for some distance. The movement along that path becomes the solid model. The 2D circle is sketched on the Front Plane.

An Extruded Boss/Base feature is a feature in SolidWorks that utilizes a sketched profile and extends the profile perpendicular (⊥) to the Sketch plane. The Base feature is the first feature that is created. Keep the Base feature simple.

26. Click the **Features** tab from the CommandManager. The Features toolbar is displayed. Remember, the toolbar is document dependent.

27. Click **Extruded Boss/Base** from the Features toolbar. The Boss-Extrude PropertyManager is displayed. The Boss-Extrude PropertyManager displays the parameters utilized to define the feature.

28. Select **Mid Plane** for End Condition in Direction 1. The Mid Plane End Condition extrudes the sketch equally on both sides of the Sketch plane.

Use different End Condition options to affect the Design Intent of your model and design symmetry.

29. Enter **1.375**in for Depth. The Depth defines the distance.
30. Click **OK** from the Boss-Extrude PropertyManager. Boss-Extrude1 is created and is displayed in the FeatureManager design tree.
31. Fit the Model to the Graphics window. Press the **f** key.
32. **Save** the part. View the created FeatureManager.

Modify the color (appearance) of the Axle part.

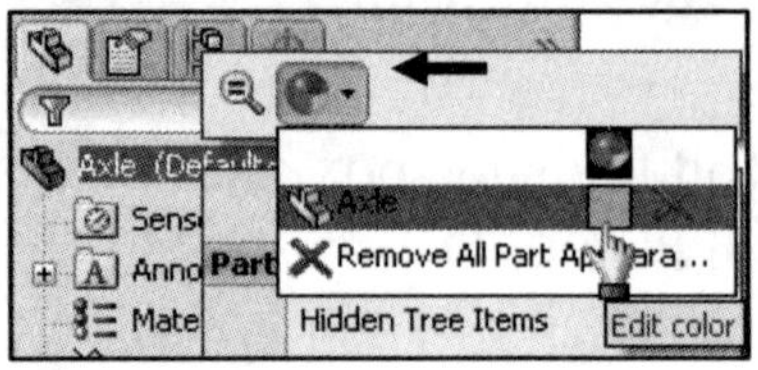


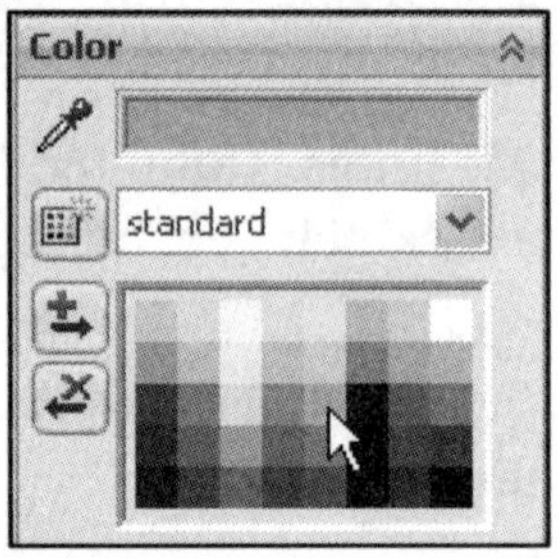


33. Right-click the **Axle** AXLE icon from the FeatureManager design tree.
34. Click the **Appearances** drop-down menu as illustrated.
35. Click the **Edit color** box as illustrated. The Color PropertyManager is displayed.
36. Select a **color** from the Color box as illustrated.

    Note: The Appearances/Scenes tab in the Task Pane to add additional patterns and textures.

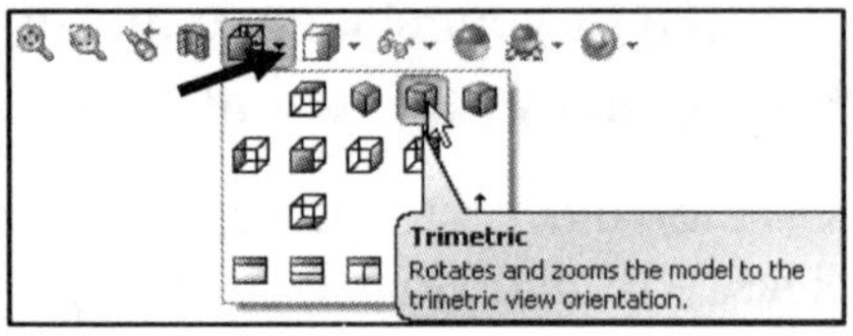


37. Click **OK** from the Color PropertyManager. The Axle is displayed with the selected color.
38. Click **Isometric view** from the Heads-up View toolbar.
39. **Save** the part. You completed the AXLE part using the Extruded Boss/Base feature with the Mid Plane End Condition option. You also applied a color to the part.

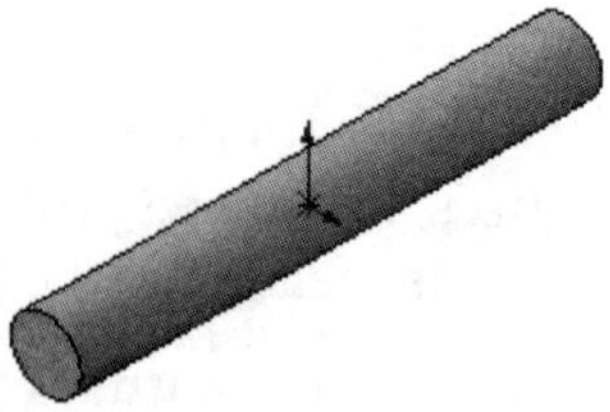

SolidWorks utilizes default colors to indicate status of sketches and features. Example: Default colors indicate the status of a sketch.

Sketches are generally defined in one of the following states. Color indicates the state of individual sketch entities. The states of individual sketch entities are:

1. *Under Defined.* There is inadequate definition of the sketch, (Blue). The FeatureManager displays a minus (-) symbol before the Sketch name.

2. *Fully Defined.* Has complete information, (Black). The FeatureManager displays no symbol before the Sketch name.

3. *Over Defined.* Has duplicate dimensions, (Red). The FeatureManager displays a (+) symbol before the Sketch name. The What's Wrong dialog box is displayed.

It is possible to create geometry that is unsolvable or invalid. The items that prevent the solution are displayed in pink (unsolvable) or yellow (invalid). Sketches with these types of geometry are labeled **No Solution Found** or **Invalid Solution Found**.

## Create the Flatbar Part

***Tutorial: Flatbar 1-2***

Create a new part named Flatbar.

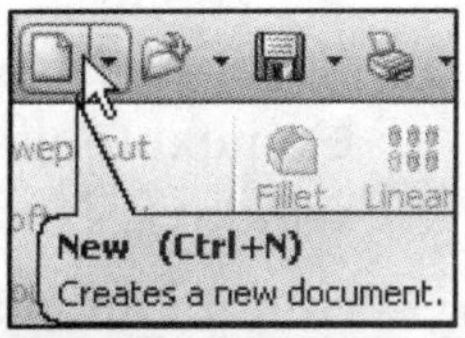


1. Click **New** from the Menu bar. The New SolidWorks Document dialog box is displayed. Part is the default template.
2. Double-click the **Part** icon. Note: The ***Advanced*** mode is selected.

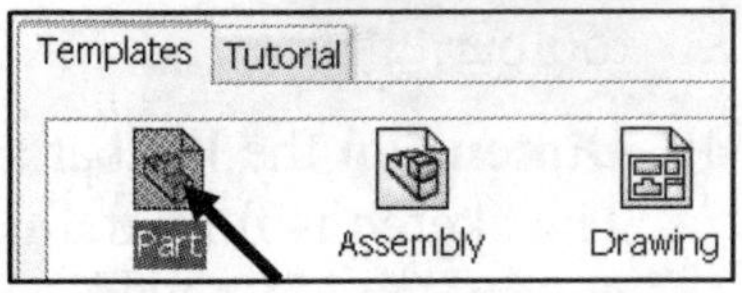


3. Click **Save** from the Menu bar.
4. Enter **Flatbar** in the SolidWorks 2010 folder.
5. Click **Save**. Flatbar is displayed in the FeatureManager design tree.

Set the Overall drafting standard, Unit system and precision for the Flatbar part.

6. Click **Options** ➤ **Document Properties** tab. The Document Properties – Drafting Standard dialog box is displayed.

7. Select **ANSI** from the Overall drafting standard drop-down menu.
8. Click **Units**. Click **IPS** for Unit system.
9. Select **.123** (three decimal places) for Length Basic Units.
10. Select **None** for Angular units decimal places.
11. Click **OK** from the Document Properties - Unit dialog box.
12. Right-click **Front Plane** from the FeatureManager design tree. This is your Sketch plane.
13. Click **Sketch** from the Context toolbar. The Sketch toolbar is displayed.

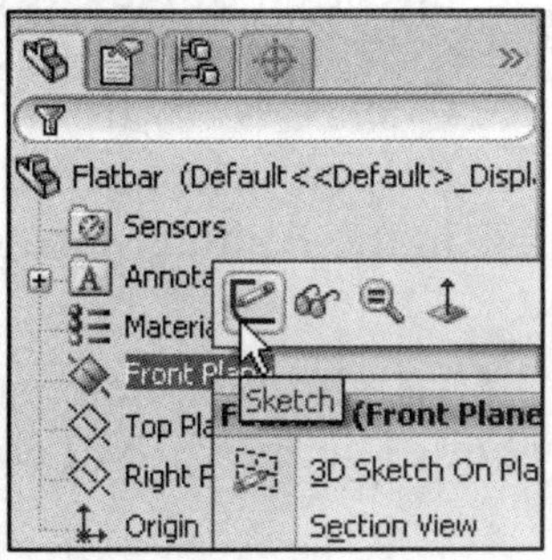

The Consolidated Slot Sketch toolbar is great to create a slot in three easy steps.

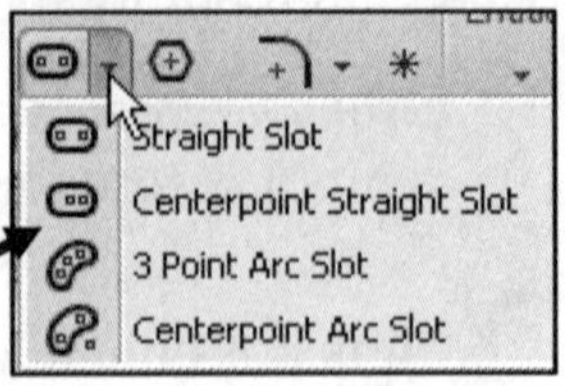


14. Click **Centerpoint Straight Slot** from the Consolidated Slot Sketch toolbar as illustrated. The Slot PropertyManager is displayed.

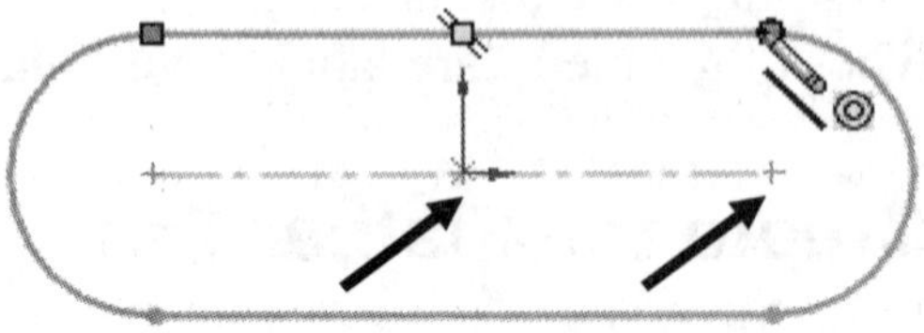

15. Click the **Origin**. This is your first point.

16. Click a **position** directly to the right of the Origin. This is your second point.

17. Click a **position** directly above the second point as illustrated. This is your third point.

Dimension the sketch.

18. Right-click **Smart Dimension** from the Context toolbar in the Graphics window. Note: You can also click the Smart Dimension icon in the Sketch toolbar.

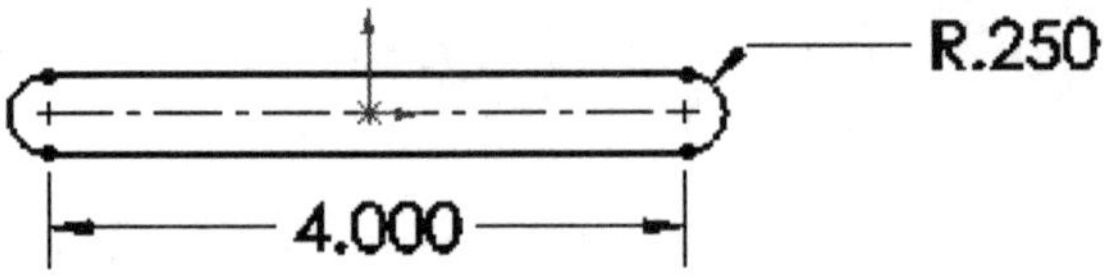


19. **Dimension** the Flatbar as illustrated. The sketch is fully defined. The sketch is displayed in black.

Create the first feature for the Flatbar. Create an Extruded Boss/Base feature. The Extruded Boss/Base feature adds material to a part. Extrude the sketch to create the first feature.

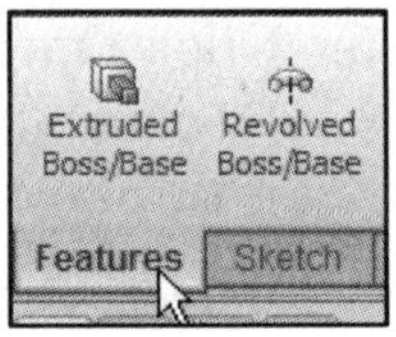


20. Click the **Features** tab from the CommandManager. The Features toolbar is displayed.

21. Click **Extruded Boss/Base** from the Features toolbar. Blind is the default End Condition in Direction 1.

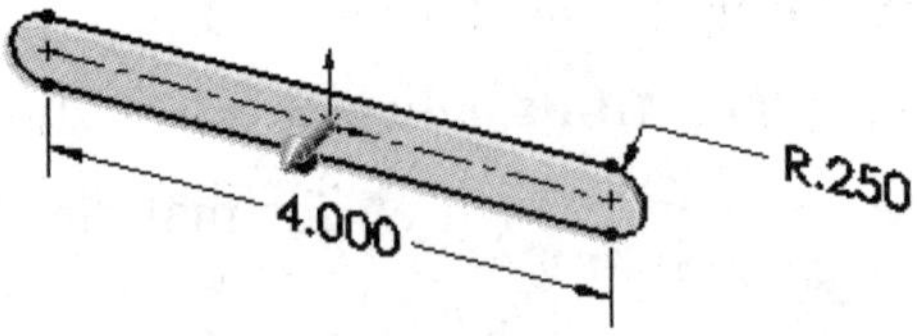


22. Enter **.060**in for Depth in Direction 1. Note the direction of the extrude feature.

23. Click **OK** from the Boss-Extrude PropertyManager. Boss-Extrude1 is displayed in the FeatureManager design tree.

Right-click Select to deselect a tool and to choose geometry and entities.

24. **Expand** Boss-Extrude1 from the FeatureManager design tree. Sketch1 is fully defined.

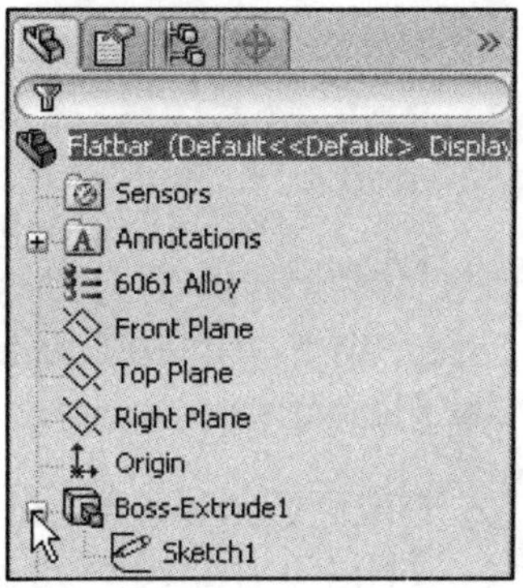


25. **Fit** the model to the Graphics window.

26. **Save** the model.

Instant3D provides the ability to drag geometry and dimension manipulator points to resize and create features directly in the Graphics window. Click the face. Select a manipulator point. Click and drag. Click a location along the ruler for the required dimension. The rule increments are set in System Options.

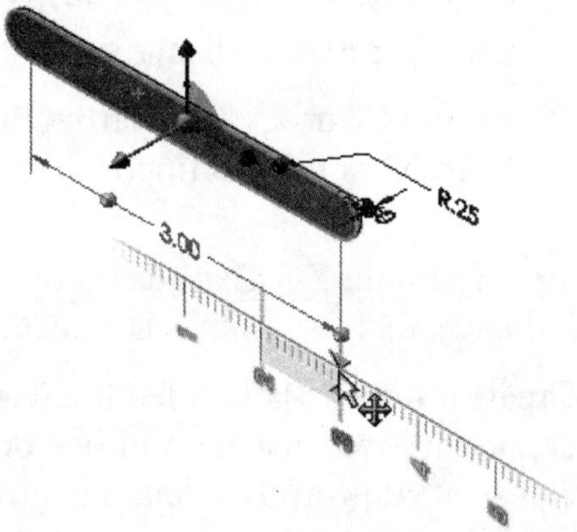


RapidSketch provides the ability to select planar faces or planes, and with any sketch tool active, start to sketch. As you move to each planar face, a plane is created and a sketch is opened.

Utilize the Extruded Cut feature to create the first hole. Insert a new sketch for the Cut-Extrude1 feature.

27. Right-click the **front face** of Boss-Extrude1 for the Sketch plane. This is your Sketch plane.

28. Click Sketch from the Context toolbar. The Sketch toolbar is displayed.

29. Display a **Front view** from the Heads-up View toolbar.

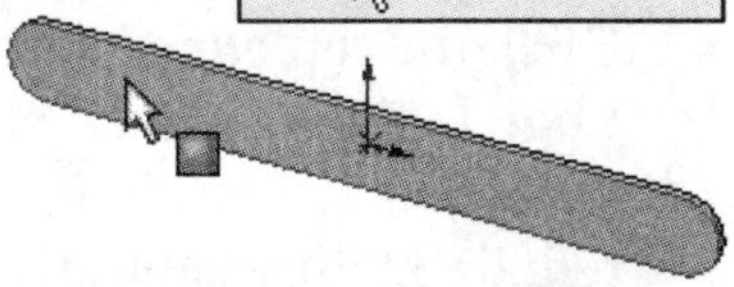

30. Click the **Circle** Sketch tool. The Circle PropertyManager is displayed.

Wake-up the centerpoint.

31. Place the **mouse pointer** on the left arc. Do not click! Wake-up the centerpoint of the Flatbar. The centerpoint of the slot arc is displayed.

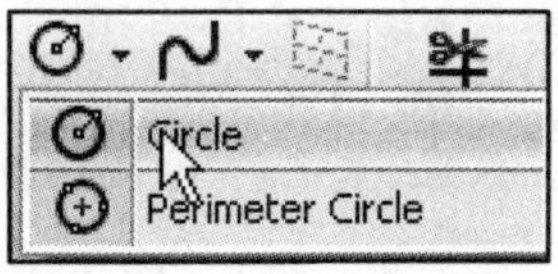


The process of placing the mouse pointer over an existing arc to locate its center point is call "wake up".

32. Click the **centerpoint** of the arc.

33. Click a **position** to the right of the centerpoint to create the circle.

Add a dimension.

34. Right-click **Smart Dimension** from the Context toolbar.

35. **Dimension** the circle as illustrated.

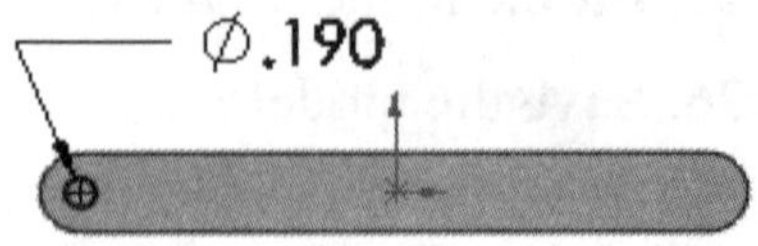


Insert an Extruded Cut feature to create the first hole in the Flatbar part.

36. Click **Extruded Cut** from the Features toolbar. The Cut-Extrude PropertyManager is displayed.

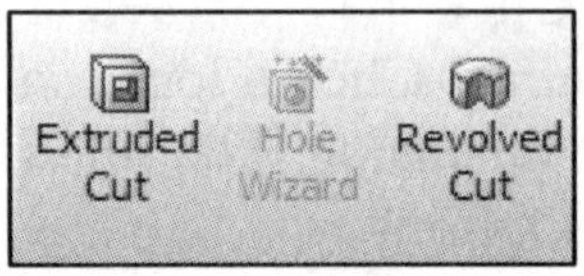


37. Select **Through All** for End Condition in Direction 1.

38. Click **OK** from the Cut-Extrude PropertyManager. Cut-Extrude1 is displayed in the FeatureManager.

39. **Expand** Cut-Extrude1 from the FeatureManager. Sketch2 is fully defined.

The blue Cut-Extrude1 icon in the FeatureManager indicates that the feature is selected.

Create a Linear Pattern feature. Use a linear pattern to create multiple instances of one or more features that you can space uniformly along one or two linear paths. Utilize the Linear Pattern feature to create additional holes in the Flatbar part.

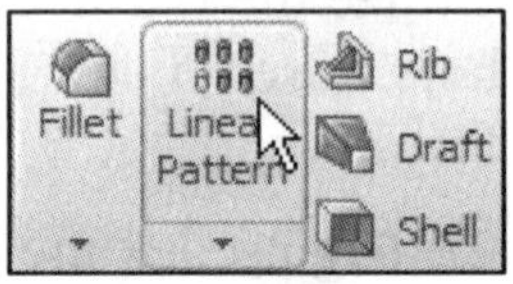


40. Click **Linear Pattern** from the Features toolbar. The Linear Pattern PropertyManager is displayed.

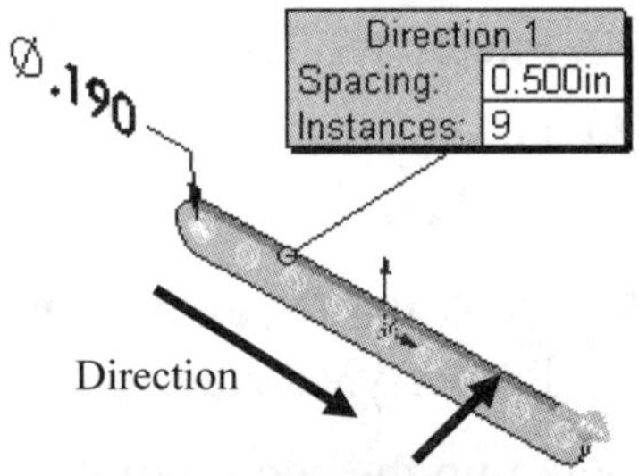


41. Click **Isometric view** from the Heads-up View toolbar.

42. Click the **top edge** of Boss-Extrude1 for Direction 1. Edge<1> is displayed in the Pattern Direction box for Direction 1. The direction arrow points to the right. If required, click the Reverse Direction button.

43. Enter **0.5**in for Spacing.

44. Enter **9** for Number of Instances. Instances are the number of occurrences of a feature. Note: Cut-Extrude1 is displayed in the Features to Pattern box.

45. Click **OK** from the Linear Pattern PropertyManager. LPattern1 is displayed in the FeatureManager.

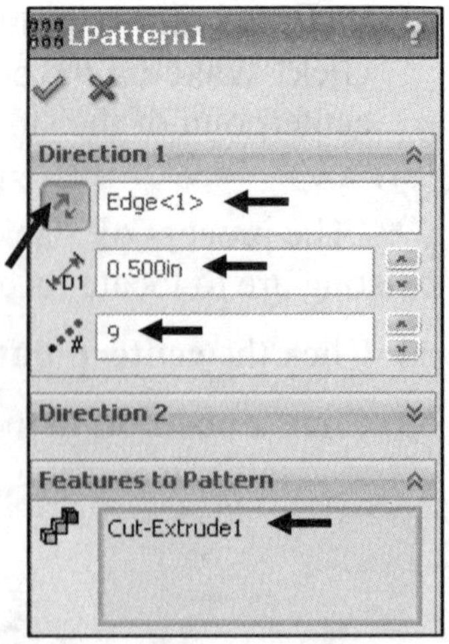

Apply material properties to the Flatbar part.

46. Right-click **Material** from the Flatbar FeatureManager design tree.

47. Click **Edit Material**.

48. Select **6061 Aluminum Alloy** for material. View the Physical Properties of the material. The Material dialog box provides the ability to apply *Appearance*, *CrossHatch*, *Custom*, *Application Data and Favorites* options.

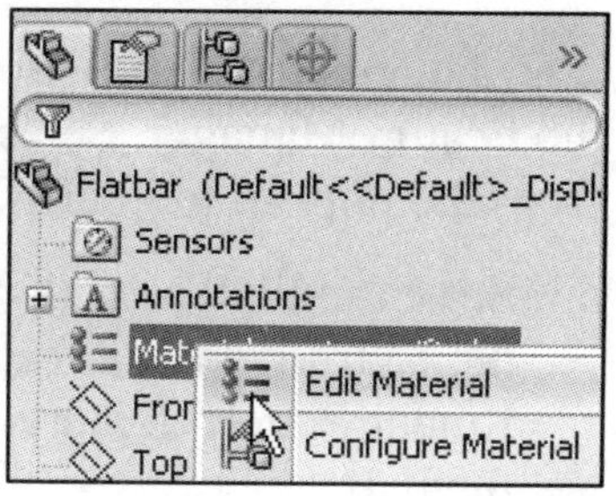


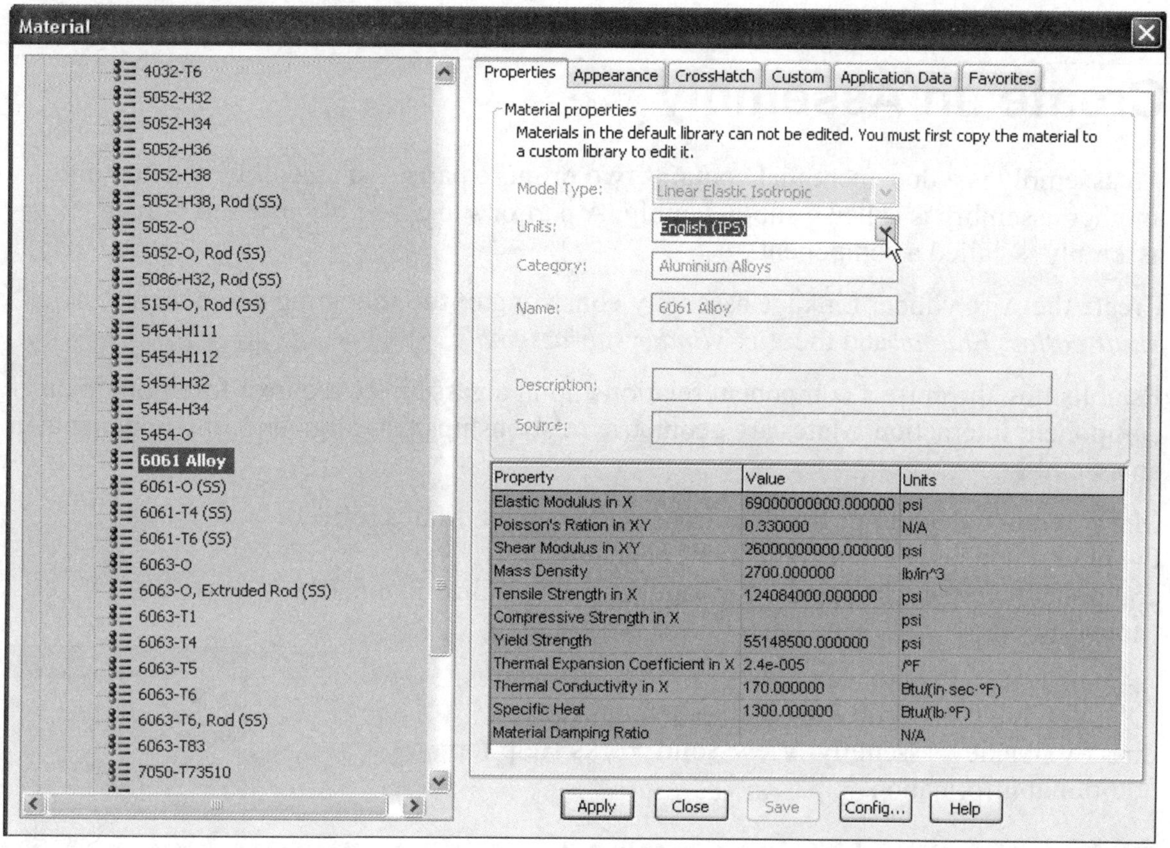


If needed, select the English (IPS) Units category. Note additional material information from SW 2010.

49. Click each **tab** and explore the options.

50. Click **Apply** from the Materials dialog box.

51. Click **Close** from the Materials dialog box. 6061 Alloy is displayed in the FeatureManager design tree.

52. Click **Isometric view** from the Heads-up View toolbar.

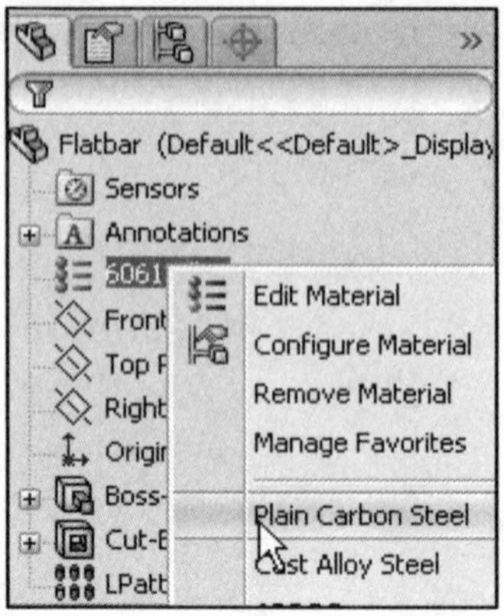


To apply material properties, right-click **Material** from the FeatureManager. Select the needed material if available from the pop-up toolbar. The material is applied to the model.

53. **Save** the Flatbar part. You completed the Flatbar part using the Extruded Base feature, Extruded Cut feature, and the Linear Pattern feature. You applied 6061 Alloy material to the part.

# Create an Assembly

An assembly is a document that contains two or more parts. An assembly inserted into another assembly is called a sub-assembly. A part or sub-assembly inserted into an assembly is called a component.

Create the AirCylinder Linkage assembly consisting of the following components: *Axle*, *Shaft-collar*, *Flatbar* and the *AirCylinder sub-assembly*.

Establishing the correct component relationship in an assembly requires forethought on component interaction. Mates are geometric relationships that align and fit components in an assembly.

Mates remove degrees of freedom from a component. Mates reflect the physical behavior of a component in an assembly. The components in the AirCylinder Linkage assembly utilize Standard Mate types only.

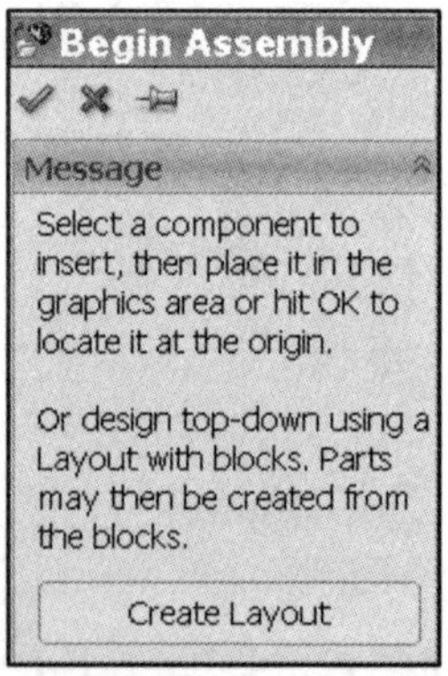


You have the ability to create a layout sketch directly in a new assembly. View SolidWorks Help for additional information.

### *Tutorial: AirCylinder Linkage assembly 1-3*

Create the AirCylinder Linkage assembly.

1. **Copy** the content of the provided CD (SolidWorks 2010 folder) to the SolidWorks 2010 folder on your computer. The CD in the book provides access to over 230 models and their solutions.

2. Click **New** from the Menu bar.

3. Double-click the **Assembly** icon from the New SolidWorks Document dialog box. The Begin Assembly PropertyManager is displayed.

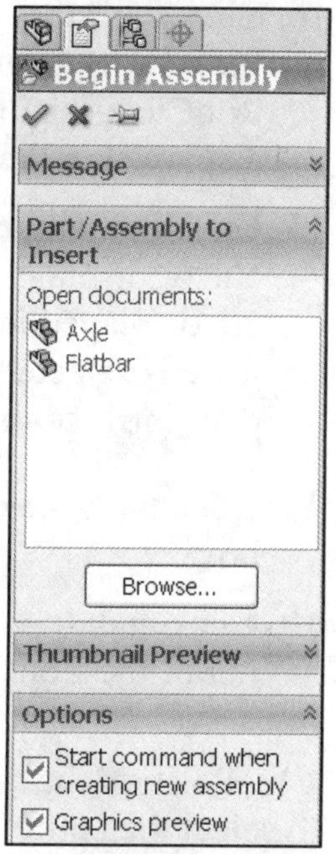


The Begin Assembly PropertyManager is displayed when the Start command when creating new assembly option box is checked.

4. Activate the origins. Click **View** ➤ check the **Origins** box from the Menu bar.
5. Click **Browse** from the Part/Assembly to Insert box.
6. Double-click the **AirCylinder** assembly from the SolidWorks 2010 folder on your computer.
7. Accept the default. If needed, check the **Don't ask me again** box. Click **OK**. The AirCylinder assembly is displayed in the Graphics window.

Fix the AirCylinder assembly to the origin.

8. Click **OK** from the Begin Assembly PropertyManager. Assem1 is displayed in the FeatureManager design tree and the AirCylinder sub-assembly is fixed to the origin.
9. Click **Save As** from the Menu bar.

10. Enter **AirCylinder Linkage** for File name.
11. Click **Save**. The AirCylinder Linkage FeatureManager design tree is displayed. The AirCylinder is the first sub-assembly in the AirCylinder Linkage assembly and is fixed (f). The (f) symbol is placed in front of the AirCylinder name in the FeatureManager.

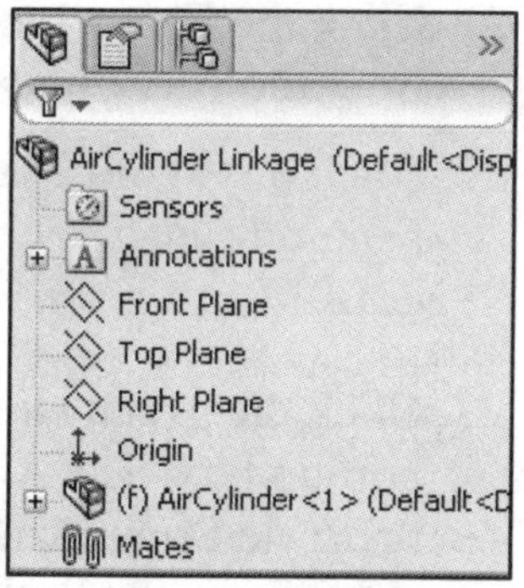


12. Click the **Insert Components** tool from the Assembly toolbar. The Insert Component PropertyManager is displayed.
13. Click **Axle** from the Open documents box in the Insert Component PropertyManager.
14. Click a **position** to the front of the AirCylinder assembly as illustrated.
15. **Deactivate** the Origins.

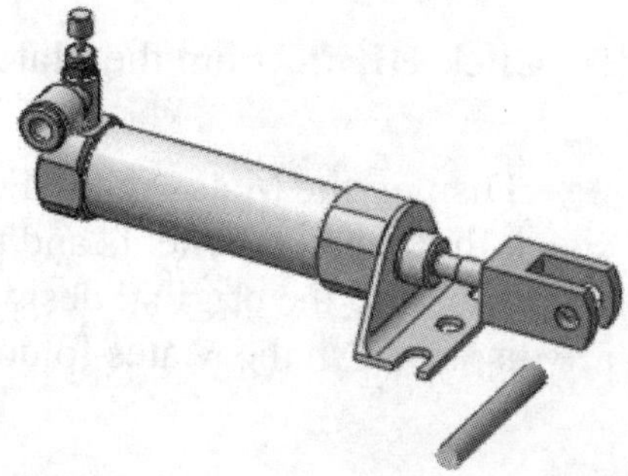

Insert a Concentric mate between the RodClevis and the Axle. A Concentric mate forces two cylindrical faces to become concentric. The faces can move along the common axis, but cannot be moved away from this axis.

16. Click the **Mate** tool from the Assembly toolbar. The Mate PropertyManager is displayed. Click the **inside hole face** of the RodClevis as illustrated. Face<1>@Air Cylinder is displayed in the Mate Selections box.

17. Click the **long cylindrical face** of the Axle. The cursor displays the Face feedback symbol. The faces are displayed in the Mate Selections box. Concentric mate is selected by default. The Axle is positioned concentric to the RodClevis hole.

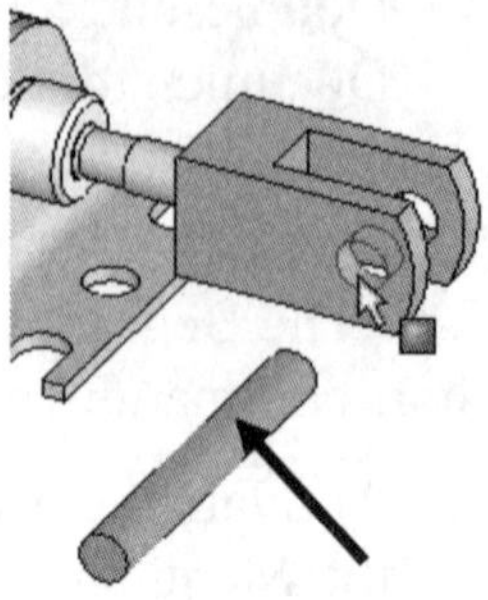

18. Click the **green check mark** in the Mate pop-up box.

19. Click and drag the **Axle**. The Axle translates in and out of the RodClevis holes.

Position the mouse pointer in the middle of the face to select the entire face. Do not position the mouse pointer near the edge of the face.

Insert a Coincident mate. A Coincident mate forces two planar faces to become coplanar. The faces can move along one another, but cannot be pulled apart.

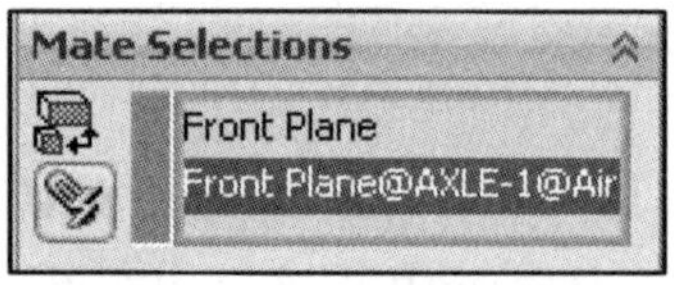


20. **Expand** the fly-out AirCylinder Linkage FeatureManager.

21. Click the **Front Plane** of the AirCylinder assembly from the AirCylinder Linkage fly-out FeatureManager.

22. Click the **Front Plane** of the Axle part from the fly-out FeatureManager. Coincident mate is selected by default.

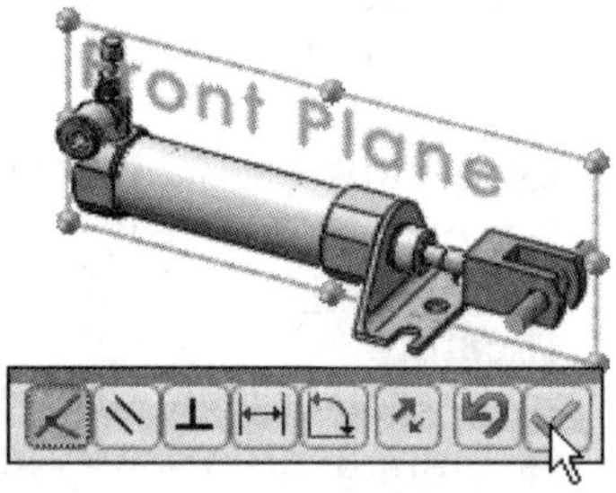


23. Click the **green check mark** in the Mate pop-up box. The AirCylinder Front Plane and the Axle Front Plane are Coincident. The Axle is centered in the RodClevis.

24. Click **OK** from the Mate PropertyManager.

Display the Mates in the FeatureManager to check that the components and the mate types correspond to the original design intent. Mate icons are displayed in the Mates folder.

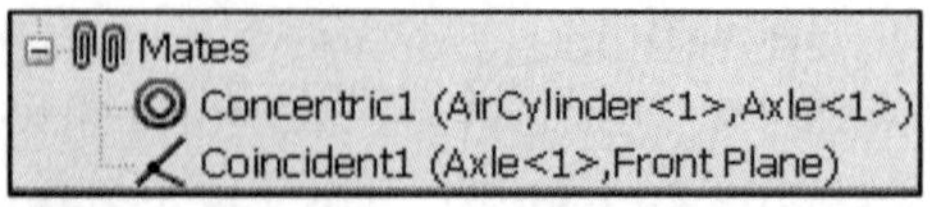

If you delete a mate and then recreate it, the mate numbers will be in a different order.

25. Click the **Insert Components** tool from the Assembly toolbar.
26. Click **Flatbar** from the Open documents box in the Insert Component PropertyManager.
27. Click a **position** to the front of the AirCylinder assembly.

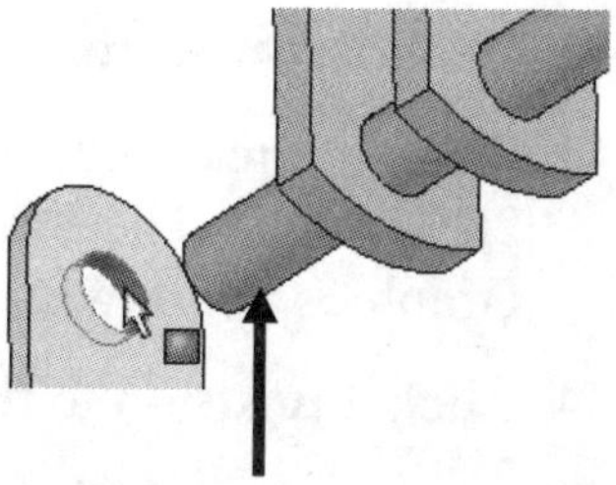

28. Click the **Mate** tool from the Assembly toolbar.
29. Click the **inside left hole face** of the Flatbar.
30. Click the **long cylindrical face** of the Axle. The faces are displayed in the Mate Selections box. Concentric mate is selected by default.

31. Click the **green check mark** in the Mate pop-up box.
32. Click and drag the **Flatbar** in the Graphics window. The Flatbar translates and rotates along the Axle.
33. Insert a Coincident mate between the **back face** of the Flatbar and the **front face** of the RodClevis. Coincident mate is selected by default.

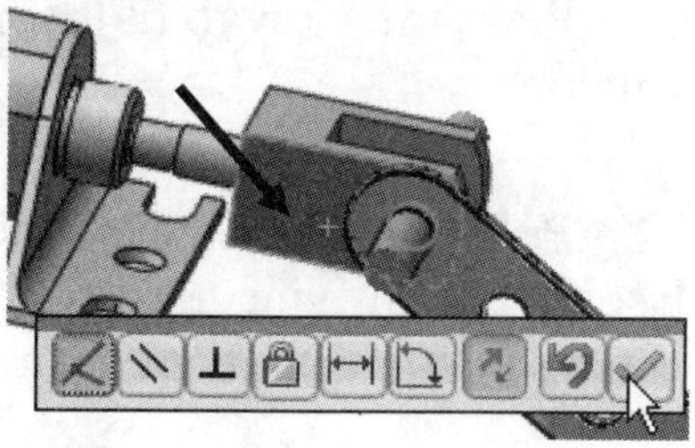

34. Click the **green check mark** in the Mate pop-up box.
35. Click **OK** from the Mate PropertyManager.
36. **Expand** the Mates folder from the FeatureManager design tree. View the inserted mates.

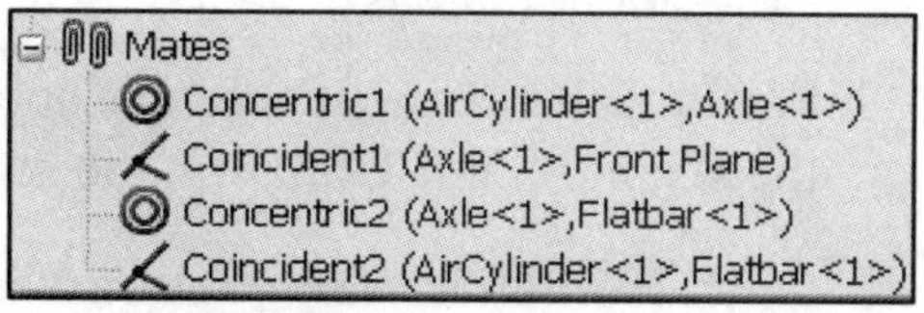


37. Perform the **same procedure** above to insert the second Flatbar component on the back side of the RodClevis.
38. Insert a Parallel mate between the **top narrow face** of the first Flatbar and the **top narrow face** of the second Flatbar. A Parallel mate places the selected items so they lie in the same direction and remain a constant distance apart from each other.

39. Click **OK** from the Mate PropertyManager. View the created Mates.

40. Click and drag the **second Flatbar**. Both parts move together.

41. Click the **Insert Components** tool from the Assembly toolbar.

42. Click **Browse** from the Part/Assembly to Insert box.

43. Double-click the **Shaft-collar** part from the SolidWorks 2010 folder. The Shaft-collar is displayed in the Graphics window.

44. Click a **position** to the front of the Axle as illustrated.

45. Insert a Concentric mate between the inside **hole face** of the Shaft-Collar and the **long cylindrical face** of the Axle. Concentric mate is selected by default.

Press the **Shift-z** keys to Zoom in on the model.

Press the **z** key to Zoom out on the model.

Press the **f** key to fit the model to the Graphics window.

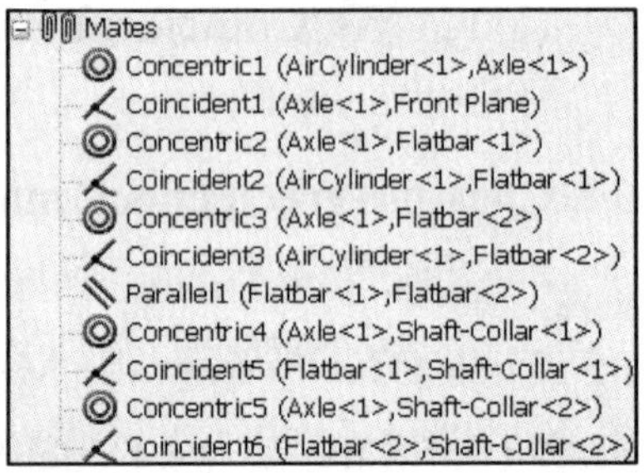


Press the **g** key to activate the Magnifying glass tool. Use the Magnifying glass tool to inspect a model and make selections without changing the overall view.

46. Insert a Coincident mate between the **back face** of the Shaft-collar and the **front face** of the first Flatbar. Coincident mate is selected by default.

47. Perform the **same procedure** above to insert the second Shaft-Collar on the second Flatbar.

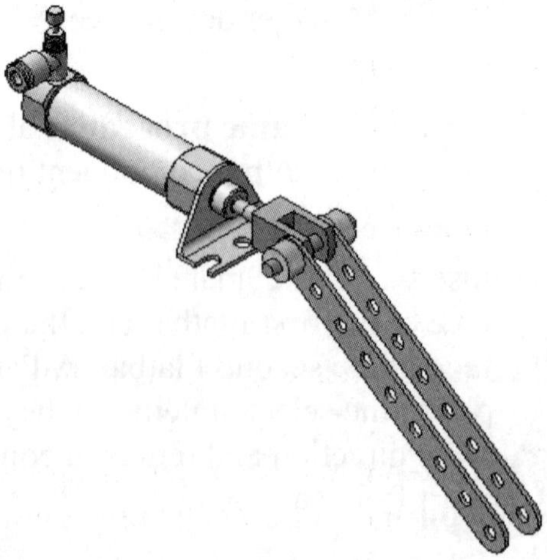

48. Click **Isometric view** from the Heads-up View toolbar.

49. **Save** the model. You completed the AirCylinder Linkage assembly. View the inserted mates from the FeatureManager. Note: This model is located in the Solutions folder on the CD in the book.

# Create a New Assembly Drawing

A SolidWorks drawing displays 2D and 3D views of a part or assembly. The foundation of a SolidWorks drawing is the drawing template. Drawing size, drawing standards, company information, manufacturing, and or assembly requirements, units and other properties are defined in the drawing template. In this section, use the default drawing template.

The sheet format is incorporated into the drawing template. The sheet format contains the border, title block information, revision block information, company name and or logo information, Custom Properties and SolidWorks Properties. Because this section of the book is a Quick Start section, you will not address these items at this time.

Custom Properties and SolidWorks Properties are shared values between documents. Utilize an A (ANSI) Landscape size Drawing Template with a custom Sheet Format for the Air Cylinder Linkage assembly drawing.

A drawing contains views, geometric dimensioning and tolerances, notes and other related design information. When a part or assembly is modified, the drawing automatically updates. When a dimension in the drawing is modified, the part or the assembly is automatically updated.

***Tutorial: AirCylinder Linkage Drawing 1-4***

Create the ANSI AirCylinder Linkage assembly (Third Angle Projection) drawing. Display the Front, Top, Right and Isometric views. Utilize the Model View tool from the View Layout tab in the CommandManager.

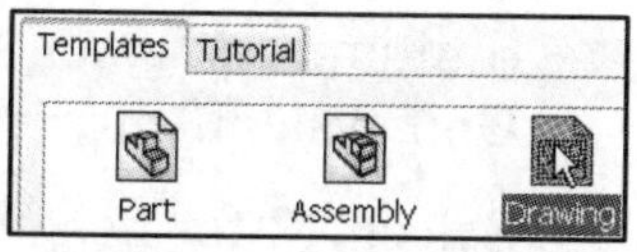


1. Click **New** from the Menu bar.
2. Double-click **Drawing** from the Templates tab.
3. Select **A (ANSI) Landscape** from the Sheet Format/Size dialog box.
4. Click **OK**. The Model View PropertyManager is displayed.
5. Click **Cancel** from the Model View PropertyManager. Draw1 is displayed.

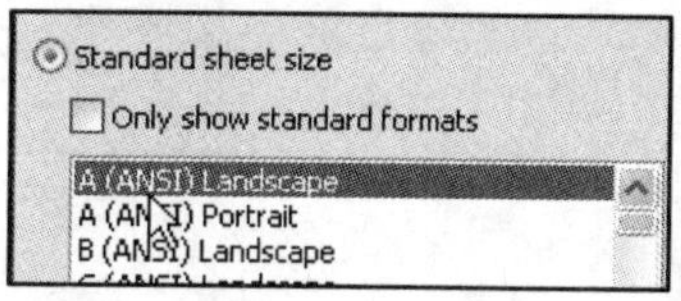


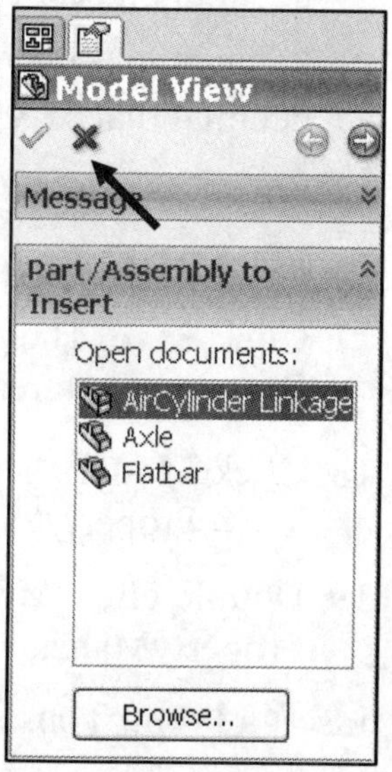


The Model View PropertyManager is displayed if the Start command when creating new drawing option is checked.

The book was written using the ANSI default drafting standard and Third Angle projection.

6. Set the Sheet1 Properties in the drawing. Right-click **Properties** in Sheet1. The Sheet Properties is displayed. Draw1 is the default drawing name. Sheet1 is the default first sheet name. The CommandManager area alternates between the *View Layout, Annotation, Sketch, Evaluate and Office Products* tabs.

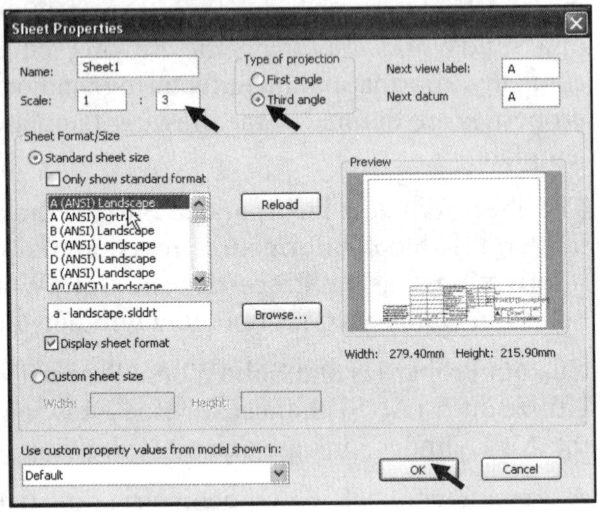


7. Enter Sheet Scale **1:3**.
8. Check **Third angle** for Type of projection.
9. Click **OK** from the Sheet Properties box. The A-Landscape paper is displayed in a new Graphics window. The sheet border defines the drawing size, 11″ × 8.5″ or (279.4mm × 215.9mm). The View Layout toolbar is displayed in the CommandManager.

Set the Document Properties for your drawing.

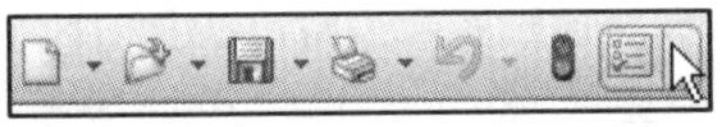

10. Click **Options** ➢ **Document Properties** tab.
11. Select **ANSI** for Overall drafting standard.

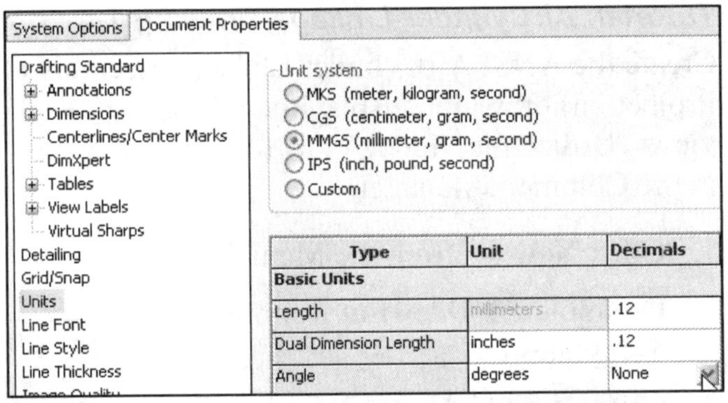


12. Click **Units**. Select **MMGS** (millimeters, gram, second) for Unit system.
13. Select **.12** for Length units decimal places.
14. Select **None** for Angular units decimal places. Click **OK**.
15. **Save** the drawing.

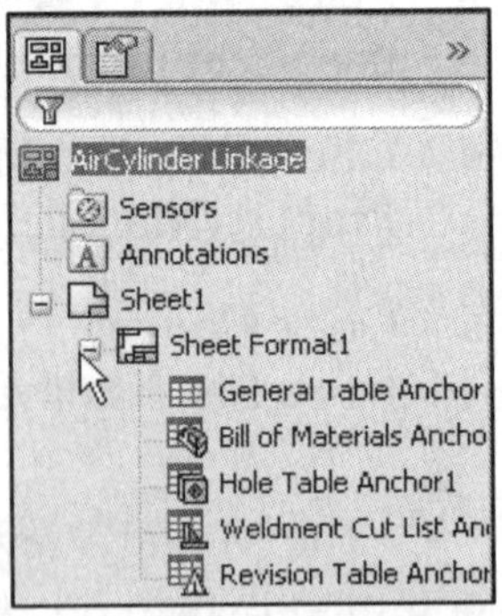


16. Enter **AirCylinder Linkage** for file name.
17. Click **Save**. The AirCylinder Linkage is displayed in the Drawing FeatureManager design tree.
18. Click **Model View** from the View Layout tab. The Model View PropertyManager is displayed.
19. Double-click **AirCylinder Linkage** from the Model View PropertyManager.

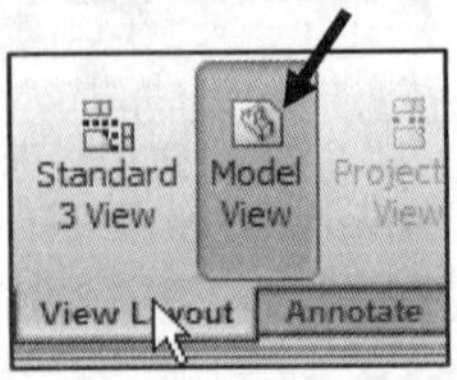


Insert a Front, Top, Right and Isometric view.

20. Check the **Create multiple views** box.

21. Select ***Front, *Top**, and ***Right** from the Orientation box. *Isometric view is activated by default.

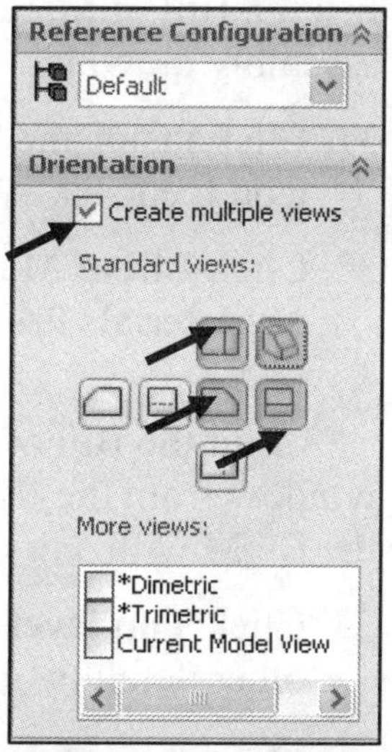


22. Click **OK** from the Model View PropertyManager.
23. Click **Yes** to use Isometric true dimensions. The four views are displayed in Sheet1.

The Title block is located in the lower right hand corner of Sheet1. A drawing contains two modes: *Edit Sheet* and *Edit Sheet Format*.

Insert views and dimensions in the Edit Sheet mode. Modify the Sheet Format text, lines or title block information in the Edit Sheet Format mode. The CompanyName Custom Property is located in the title block above the TITLE box. There is no value defined for CompanyName. A small text box indicates an empty field.

Activate the Edit Sheet Format Mode.

24. Right-click in **Sheet1**. Do not select a view boundary.

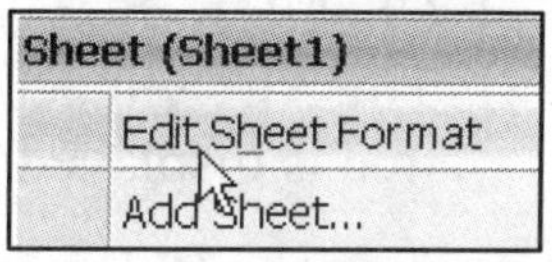


25. Click **Edit Sheet Format**. The Title block lines turn blue. View the right side of the Title block.
26. Double-click the **AirCylinder Linkage** text in the DWG NO. box.

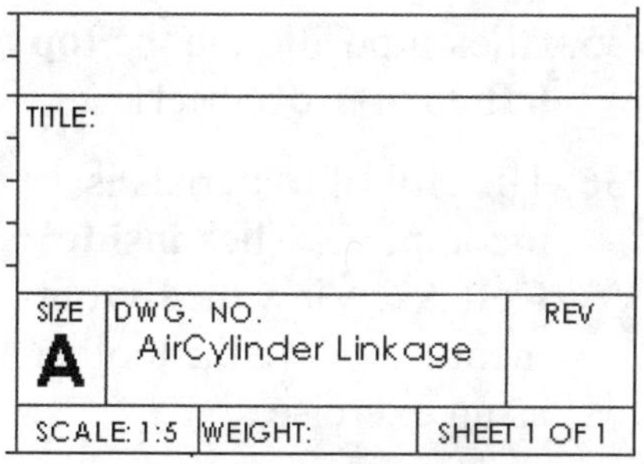


27. Click the **drop-down arrows** to set the Text Font to **12** from the Formatting dialog box.
28. Click **OK** from the Note PropertyManager.
29. Right-click **Edit Sheet** in Sheet1.
30. **Save** the drawing.

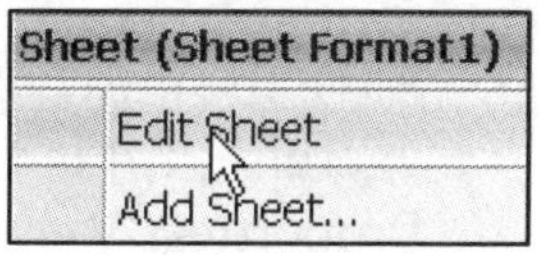


Fit and scale drawing text into the title box, Bill of Materials or any tight area on the drawing. Select **Fit text** from the Formatting dialog box. **Size** the selected text.

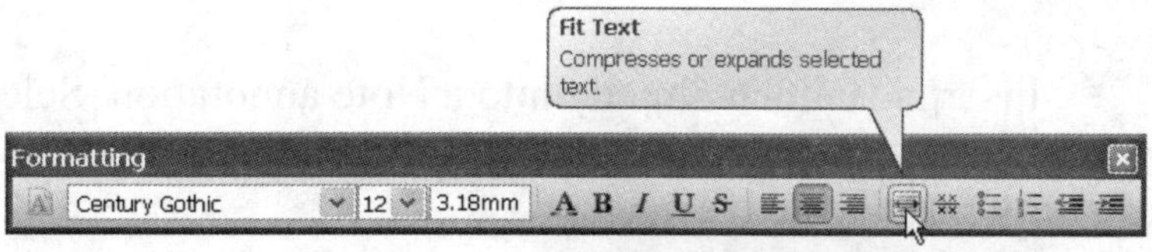


Check **use specified color for drawings paper color** in the System Options, Color section to display a difference drawing sheet color.

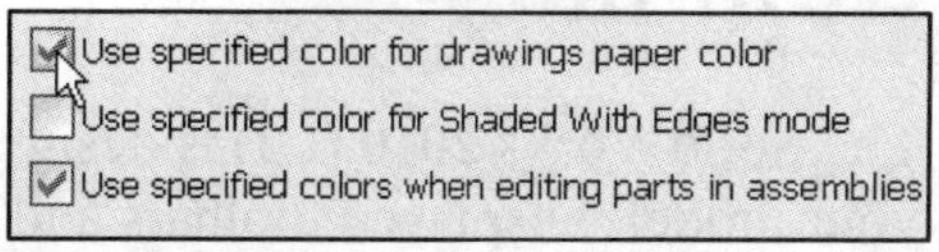

Insert a Bill of Material into the AirCylinder Linkage assembly drawing.

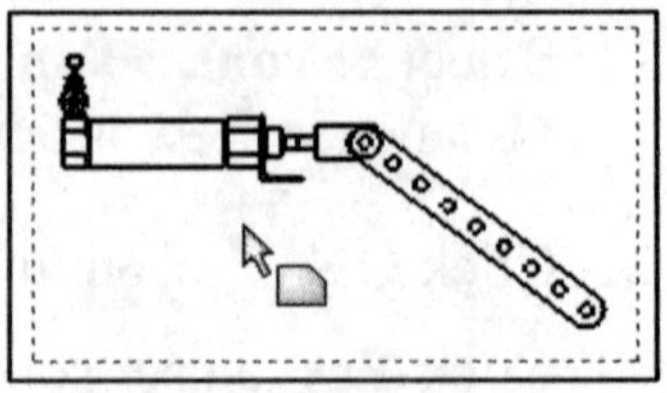

31. Click inside the **Front view**, Drawing View1. Note the icon feedback symbol.

32. Click **Bill of Materials** from the Annotation tab. The Bill of Materials PropertyManager is displayed.

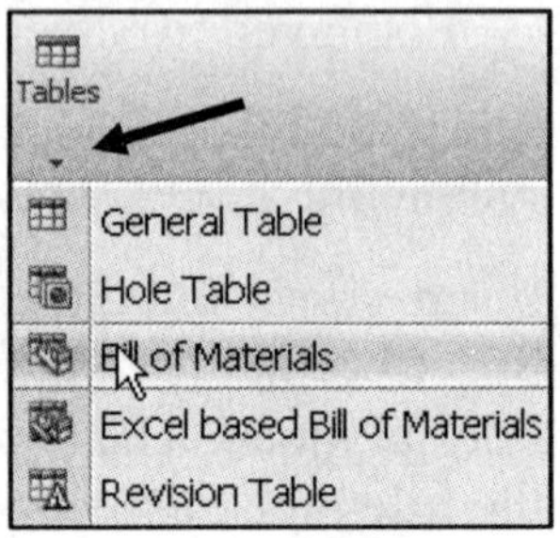


Edit the Bill of Materials table items in the Graphics window from the fly-out toolbar. Reorder rolls and columns in the BOM with a drag and drop interfaces.

33. Click **Top level only** from the BOM Type box. Accept all other defaults.

34. Click **OK** from the Bill of Materials PropertyManager. The AirCylinder Linkage assembly FeatureManager design tree is displayed.

Position the BOM.

35. Click a position in the **top left corner** of Sheet1.

36. The Bill of Materials is incomplete. Click **inside Cell A2**. View the fly-out menu. Explore the toolbar as an exercise.

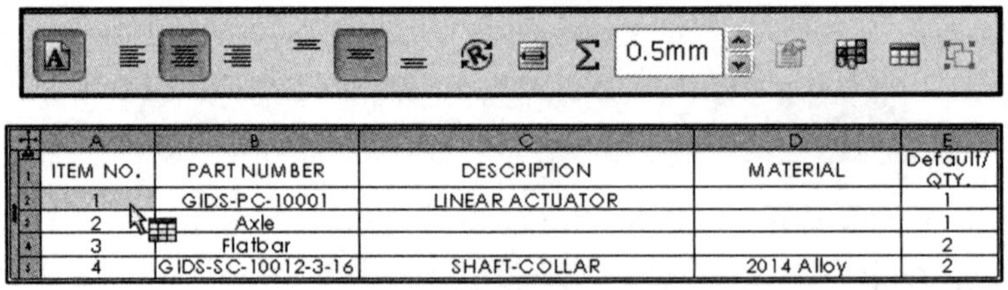


| ITEM NO. | PART NUMBER | DESCRIPTION | MATERIAL | Default/ QTY. |
|---|---|---|---|---|
| 1 | GIDS-PC-10001 | LINEAR ACTUATOR | | 1 |
| 2 | Axle | | | 1 |
| 3 | Flatbar | | | 2 |
| 4 | GIDS-SC-10012-3-16 | SHAFT-COLLAR | 2014 Alloy | 2 |

37. Click inside **Sheet1**.

38. **Save** the drawing. As an exercise, fill in the rest of the BOM cells with Custom Properties. View SolidWorks Help on Custom Properties.

39. **Close** the model.

Insert a Balloon directly into a Note annotation. Select the target Note annotation. Select the Balloon, the Balloon is inserted directly into the active note.

# Summary

The SolidWorks 2010 (UI) is design to make maximum use of the Graphics window for your model. Displayed toolbars and commands are kept to a minimum.

In this chapter, you started a SolidWorks session and applied the SolidWorks User Interface and CommandManager. You learned about the basic concepts in SolidWorks: *Terminology, 2D Base sketch, Sketch tools, 3D Feature tools, Assemblies, Standard Mates, refining the design, associativity, 2D drawings, dimensions and geometric constraints*.

You created a simple Axle part. You selected the correct Sketch plane and applied the Circle sketch tool. You then applied the Extruded Boss/Base 3D feature with the Mid Plane End Condition option. You applied color (appearance) and material to the part.

You created the Flatbar part. You selected the correct Sketch plane and applied various (Slot, and Circle) Sketch tools. You then applied the Extruded Boss/Base 3D feature with the Blind End Condition option, Extruded Cut feature with the Through All option, and the Linear Pattern feature. You applied material to the Flatbar using the Material dialog box.

You copied key components and models from the CD in the book. You created the AirCylinder Linkage assembly by inserting six components and three Standard mates: Concentric, Coincident and Parallel.

You created an ANSI, Third Angle Projection AirCylinder Linkage drawing with a Front, Top, Right and Isometric view. In the drawing, you edited the Title block and inserted a simple Bill of Materials.

In Chapter 2, explore the System Options in SolidWorks. System Options provides the ability to customize SolidWorks functionality for your needs.

A key goal of this book is to expose various SolidWorks design tools and features.

During the initial SolidWorks installation, you are requested to select either the ISO or ANSI drafting standard. ISO is typically an European drafting standard and uses First Angle Projection. The book is written using the ANSI (US) overall drafting standard and Third Angle Projection for drawings.

# Key Terms

**Assembly:** A document in which parts, features, and other assemblies (sub-assemblies) are put together. A part in an assembly is called a component. Adding a component to an assembly creates a link between the assembly and the component. When SolidWorks opens the assembly, it finds the component file to show it in the assembly. Changes in the component are automatically reflected in the assembly. The filename extension for a SolidWorks assembly file name is .SLDASM.

**CommandManager:** A Context-sensitive toolbar that dynamically updates based on the toolbar you want to access. By default, it has toolbars embedded in it based on the document type. When you click a tab below the Command Manager, it updates to display that toolbar. For example, if you click the **Sketches** tab, the Sketch toolbar is displayed.

**ConfigurationManager:** Located on the left side of the SolidWorks window and provides the means to create, select, and view multiple configurations of parts and assemblies in an active document. You can split the ConfigurationManager and either display two ConfigurationManager instances, or combine the ConfigurationManager with the FeatureManager design tree, PropertyManager, or third party applications that use the panel.

**Coordinate System:** SolidWorks uses a coordinate system with origins. A part document contains an original Origin. Whenever you select a plane or face and open a sketch, an Origin is created in alignment with the plane or face. An Origin can be used as an anchor for the sketch entities, and it helps orient perspective of the axes. A three-dimensional reference triad orients you to the X, Y, and Z directions in part and assembly documents.

**Cursor Feedback:** System feedback symbol indicates what you are selecting or what the system is expecting you to select. As you move the mouse pointer across your model, system feedback is provided.

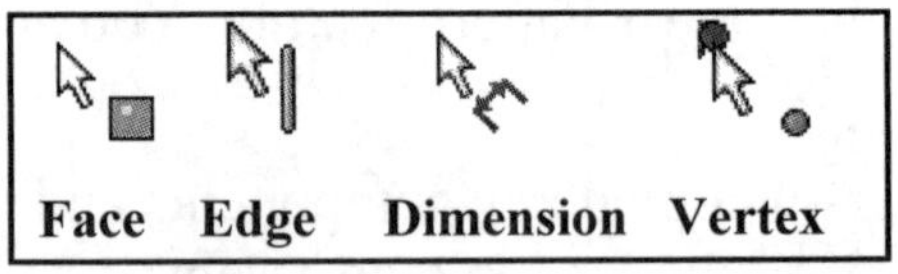


**Dimension:** A value indicating the size of the 2D sketch entity or 3D feature. Dimensions in a SolidWorks drawing are associated with the model, and changes in the model are reflected in the drawing, if you DO NOT USE DimXpert.

**DimXpertManager:** Lists the tolerance features defined by DimXpert for a part. Displays DimXpert tools that you use to insert dimensions and tolerances into a part.

**Document:** In SolidWorks, each part, assembly, and drawing is referred to as a document, and each document is displayed in a separate window.

**Drawing:** A 2D representation of a 3D part or assembly. The extension for a SolidWorks drawing file name is *.slddrw. Drawing refers to the SolidWorks module used to insert, add, and modify views in an engineering drawing.

**Feature:** Features are geometry building blocks. Features add or remove material. Features are created from 2D or 3D sketched profiles or from edges and faces of existing geometry.

**FeatureManager:** Located on the left side of the SolidWorks window provides an outline view of the active part, assembly, or drawing. This makes it easy to see how the model or assembly was constructed or to examine the various sheets and views in a drawing. The FeatureManager and the Graphics window are dynamically linked. You can select features, sketches, drawing views, and construction geometry in either pane.

**Graphics window**: The area in the SolidWorks window where the part, assembly, or drawing are displayed.

**Heads-up View toolbar:** A transparent toolbar located at the top of the Graphic window.

**Model:** 3D solid geometry in a part or assembly document. If a part or assembly document contains multiple configurations, each configuration is a separate model.

**Motion Studies:** Graphical simulations of motion and visual properties with assembly models. Analogous to a configuration, they do not actually change the original assembly model or its properties. They display the model as it changes based on simulation elements you add.

**Origin:** The model origin is displayed in blue and represents the (0,0,0) coordinate of the model. When a sketch is active, a sketch origin is displayed in red and represents the (0,0,0) coordinate of the sketch. Dimensions and relations can be added to the model origin, but not to a sketch origin.

**Part:** A 3D object that consist of one or more features. A part inserted into an assembly is called a component. Insert part views, feature dimensions and annotations into 2D drawing. The extension for a SolidWorks part filename is *.sldprt.

**Plane:** Planes are flat and infinite. Planes are represented on the screen with visible edges.

**PropertyManager:** Most sketch, feature, and drawing tools in SolidWorks open a PropertyManager located on the left side of the SolidWorks window. The PropertyManager displays the properties of the entity or feature so you specify the properties without a dialog box covering the Graphics window.

**Rebuild:** A tool that updates (or regenerates) the document with any changes made since the last time the model was rebuilt. Rebuild is typically used after changing a model dimension.

**Relation:** A relation is a geometric constraint between sketch entities or between a sketch entity and a plane, axis, edge or vertex.

**Rollback**: Suppresses all items below the rollback bar.

**Sketch:** The name to describe a 2D profile is called a sketch. 2D sketches are created on flat faces and planes within the model. Typical geometry types are lines, arcs, corner rectangles, circles, polygons, and ellipses.

**Task Pane:** Displayed when you open the SolidWorks software. It contains the following default tabs: SolidWorks Resources, Design Library, File Explorer, Search, View Palette, Appearances/Scenes and Custom Properties.

**Toolbars:** Provide shortcuts enabling you to access the most frequently used commands. When you enable add-in applications in SolidWorks, you can also display their associated toolbars.

**Units:** Used in the measurement of physical quantities. Decimal inch dimensioning and Millimeter dimensioning are the two types of common units specified for engineering parts and drawings.

# Notes:

# CHAPTER 2: SYSTEM OPTIONS

## Chapter Objective

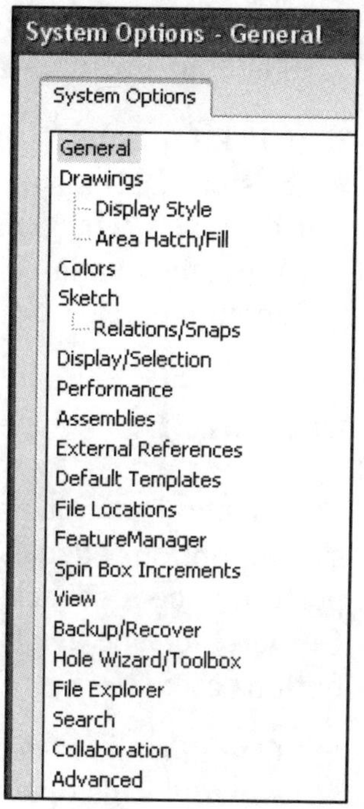


Chapter 2 provides a comprehensive understanding and the ability to use and modify the System Options in SolidWorks.

On the completion of this chapter, you will be able to:

- Setup and modify the available tools from the System Options section: *General, Drawings, Colors, Sketch, Display/Section, Performance, Assemblies, External References, Default Templates, File Locations, FeatureManager, Spin Box Increments, View, Backup/Recover, Hole Wizard/Toolbox, File Explorer, Search, Collaboration and Advanced*

## Systems Options

System Options are stored in the registry of your computer. System Options are not part of your document. Changes to the System Options affect all current and future documents. In Chapter 3, explore and address the Document Properties Options.

In a SolidWorks application, each part, assembly and drawing is referred to as a document.

The selections grouped under the System Options tab are displayed in a tree format on the left side of the System Options – General dialog box. Click an item in the tree, the options for the selected item is displayed on the right side of the dialog box. The title bar displays the title of the tab and the title of the options page.

System Options provides the ability to customize SolidWorks functionality for your needs. Review the System Options – General dialog box structure.

***Tutorial: Close all open models in SolidWorks 2-1***

Close all parts, assemblies, and drawings. Access the System Options dialog box.

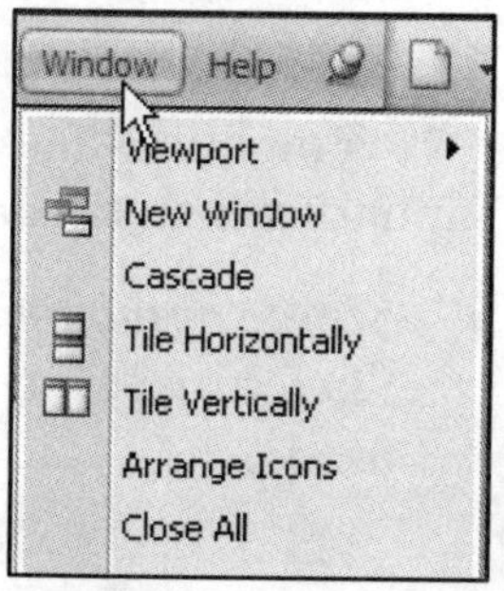


1. Click **Window ➢ Close All** from the Menu bar.

Access the System Options dialog box.

1. Click **New** from the Menu bar. The Templates tab is the default tab. Part is the default template from the New SolidWorks Document dialog box.
2. Click **OK** from the New SolidWorks Document dialog box. The Part FeatureManager is displayed.

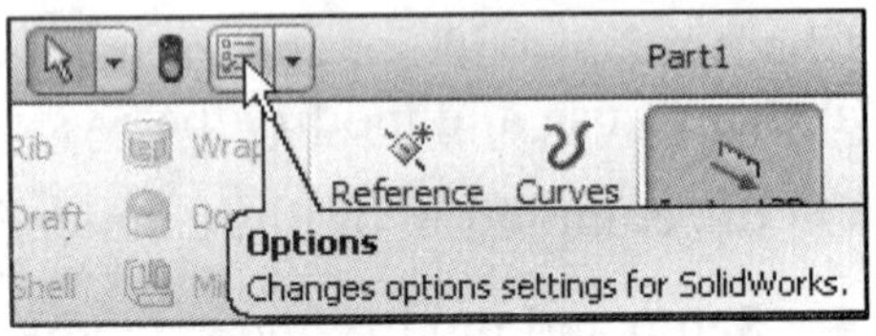


3. Click **Options** from the Menu bar. The System Options – General dialog box is displayed. The General tab is selected by default. View the available selections for a Part document.

## General

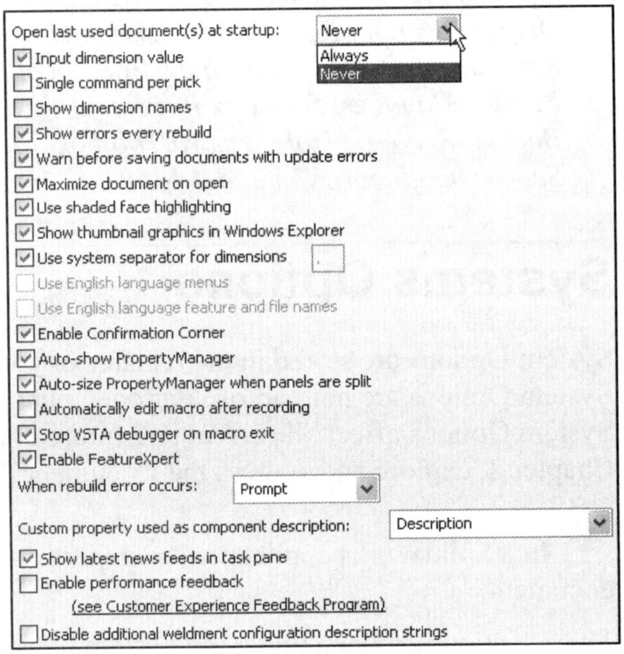


The General section provides specify system options such as enabling the performance feedback, the Confirmation Corner, etc. The available default options are:

- ***Open last used documents(s) at startup***. This option provides two selections:
  - **Always**. Provides the ability to open your last document automatically when a SolidWorks session starts.
  - **Never**. Default setting. Provides the ability for SolidWorks not to open any documents automatically.
- ***Input dimension values***. Default setting. Provides the ability to specify that the Dimension Modify dialog box is displayed automatically for the input of a new dimension value.

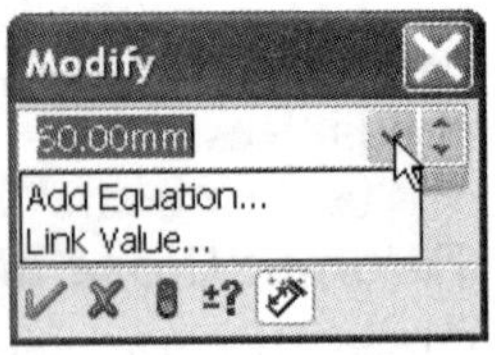


You must double-click the dimension to modify the value, if the Input dimension values option is not checked.

- ***Single command per pick***. Provides the ability to specify that Sketch and Dimension tools are cleared after each time they are used.

Double-clicking a tool will cause the tool to remain selected for additional use.

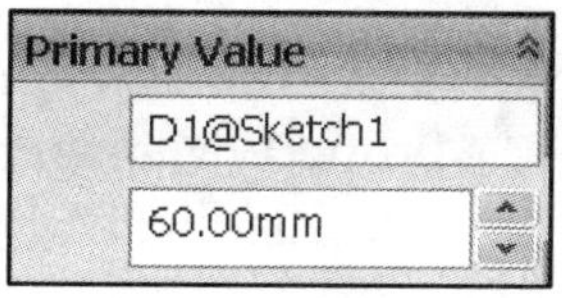


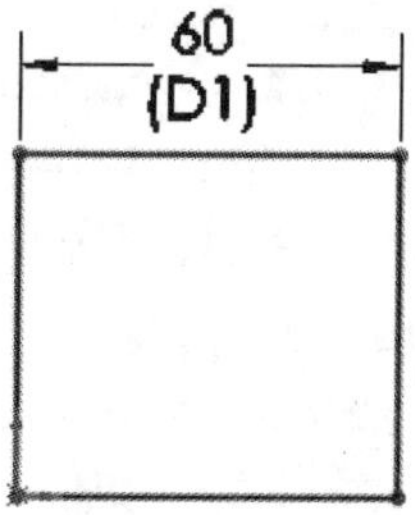


- ***Show dimension names***. Provides the ability to display the dimension name in parentheses below the actual value. Note: Dimension name is displayed in the Primary Value box of the Dimension PropertyManager.
- ***Show errors every rebuild***. Default setting. Provides the ability to display an error message each time you rebuild the model, if an error is present.
- ***Warn before saving documents with update errors***. Default setting. Provides the opportunity to fix errors before saving the document.
- ***Maximize document on open***. Default setting. Provides the ability to open each document to its largest size in the SolidWorks Graphics window for viewing.
- ***Use shaded face highlighting***. Default setting. Provides the ability to display the selected faces in a solid color. Modify the default color, solid green by using the following commands: **Options ➢ Systems Options ➢ Colors** from the Menu bar.
- ***Show thumbnail graphics in Windows Explorer***. Default setting. Provides the ability to display a thumbnail graphic instead of an icon in Windows Explorer for each SolidWorks part or assembly document. The displayed thumbnail graphic is based on the view orientation of the model when you saved the document.
- ***Use system separator for dimensions***. Default setting. Provides the ability to specify that the default system decimal separator is used when displaying decimal numbers. Use the Windows Control Panel to set your system default. To set a decimal separator different from the system default, **clear** this option, type a **symbol**, usually a period or comma.
- ***Use English language menu***. Not active by default if you installed SolidWorks 2010 with English as your installed language.
- ***Use English language feature and file names***. Not active by default if you installed SolidWorks 2010 with English as your language. Provides the ability to display feature names in the FeatureManager design tree and to automatically create files names in English.

Existing feature and file names in a foreign language do not update when you select this option.

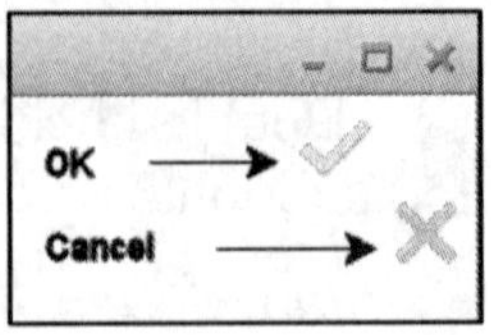


- ***Enable Confirmation Corner***. Default setting. Display the Confirmation Corner controls in the upper right corner of the Graphics window.
- ***Auto-show PropertyManager***. Default setting. Display the PropertyManager when you select an existing sketch entities, dimensions, and or annotations from the SolidWorks Graphics window.

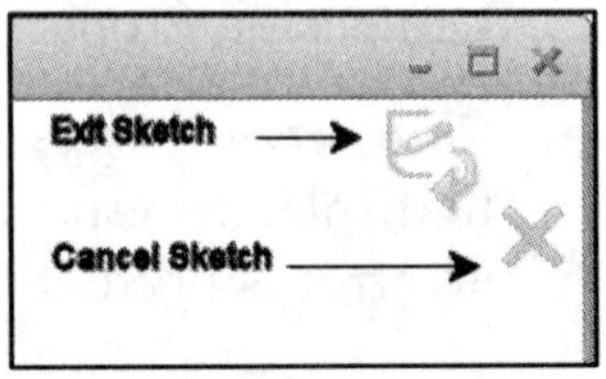


- ***Automatically edit macro after recording***. Opens the macro editor after you recorded and saved your macro in SolidWorks.
- ***Enable FeatureXpert***. Default setting. FeatureXpert is based on the SolidWorks Intelligent Feature Technology SWIFT™. This option provides the ability to automatically fix parts, so you can issue a successful rebuild. The Enable FeatureXpert option enables: MateXpert, FilletXpert, DraftXpert, etc.
- ***When rebuild error occurs***. Prompt is the default option. There are three options from the drop-down menu. They are: **Stop, Continue** and **Prompt**.

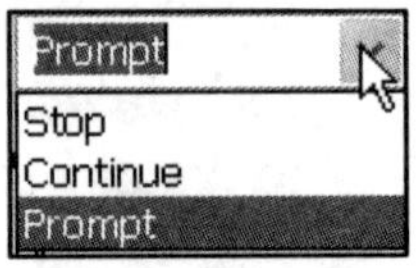


- ***Custom property used as component description***. Description is the default custom property. There are 39 custom property options from the drop-down menu. Provides the ability to set or type a name to define a custom description label. Example: Open dialog box has a Description label which displays the model description.

If you change the **Custom property used as component description** in a document that has already been saved, you must manually add the new description to the Summary Information dialog box.

- ***Enable performance feedback***. Default setting. Provides performance feedback directly to SolidWorks. The process is transparent and reports only system and command usage information for quality and usage evaluation. All information is confidential.
- ***Disable additional weldment configuration dialog***. Default setting. Removes the As Welded and As Machined configuration descriptions when you insert a weldment feature into a new part.

## Drawings

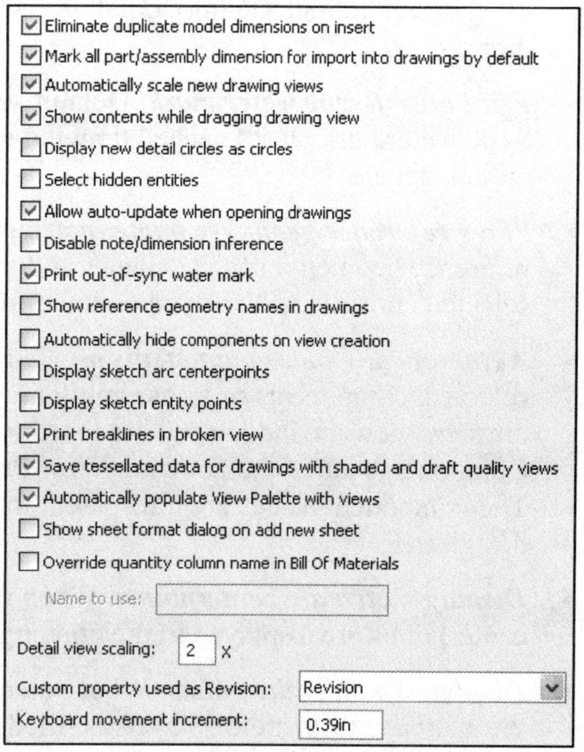


Customize setting for your drawings in this section. The Drawings section provides the following default options:

- ***Eliminate duplicate model dimensions on insert***. Default setting. Provides the ability to duplicate dimensions which are not inserted into a drawing when you use the Model dimensions tool. Note: This option is overridden by Eliminate duplicates in the Model Items PropertyManager.
- ***Mark all part/assembly dimension for import into drawings by default***. Default setting. Provides the ability to set any dimension inserted in a model as Mark For Drawing.
- ***Automatically scale new drawing views***. Default setting. Provides the ability to automatically scale new drawing views to fit the drawing sheet, regardless of the selected paper size.
- ***Show contents while dragging drawing view***. Default setting. Provides the ability to display the contents as you drag a view in the drawing. If this option is deselected, you will only see the view boundary as you drag the model in the drawing.
- ***Display new detail circles as circle***. By default, the sketched profiles are displayed. When activated, new profiles, "loops" for detail views are displayed as circles. Note: A detail circle refers to any closed loop that is applied to create a Detail view. This option displays the loop as a circle, regardless of whether you drew it as a rectangle, hexagon, ellipse or any other closed sketch profile.
- ***Select hidden entities***. When selected, you can select hidden tangent edges and edges that you have hidden manually. Move the mouse pointer over the hidden edge, the edge is displayed in phantom line font.
- ***Allow auto-update when opening drawings***. Default setting. Provides the ability for your drawing views to be updated automatically as the drawing is opened.

- ***Disable not/dimension inference***. If cleared, when you place a note or dimension, a line appears to indicate horizontal or vertical alignment with other notes or dimensions.
- ***Print out-of-sync water mark***. Default setting. Provides the ability to print an Out-of-Sync watermark on a detached drawing sheet that has not been updated since the last model change.
- ***Show reference geometry name in drawings***. Provides the ability to assign names to reference geometry, such as planes and axes and to controls whether or not the selected entities are displayed on the drawing.
- ***Automatically hide components on view creation***. When selected, components of an assembly not visible in a new drawing view are hidden and are listed on the Hide/Show Components tab of the Drawing View Properties dialog box. The component names are transparent in the FeatureManager design tree.
- ***Display sketch arc centerpoints***. When selected, sketch arc centerpoints are displayed in the drawing.
- ***Display sketch entity points***. When selected, the endpoints of the sketch entities are displayed as filled circles in drawing sheets and drawing sheet formats. They are not displayed in the drawing views.
- ***Print breaklines in broken view***. Default setting. Prints the break lines in the Broken view.
- ***Save tessellated data for drawings with shaded and draft quality views***. Default setting. When not selected, your file size is reduced by not saving the tessellated data in drawing documents with Shaded and draft quality views.

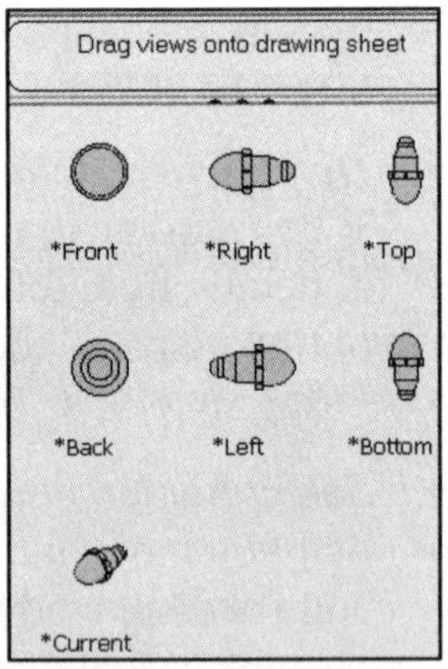


- ***Automatically populate View Palette with views***. Default setting. Provides the ability to display the available drawings views of an active document in the View Palette.
- ***Show sheet format dialog on add new sheet***. Displays the Sheet Format dialog when you add a new drawing sheet.
- ***Override quantity column name in Bill Of Materials***. When selected, uses the name you enter in Name to use for the quantity in a BOM.

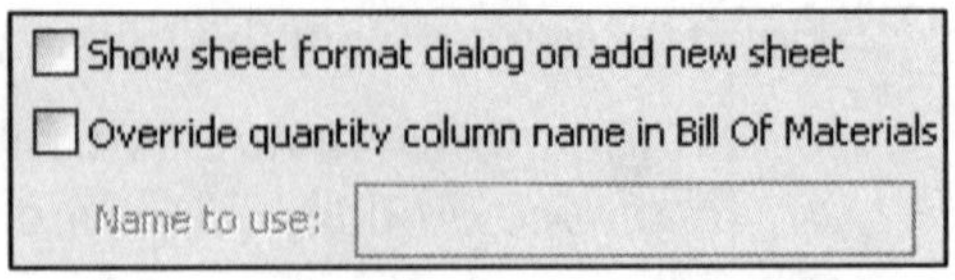

- ***Detail view scaling***. 2X, is the default setting. Specifies the scaling for your detail views. The scale is relative to the scale of the drawing views from where the detail view is generated from.

- ***Custom property used as Revision***. Revision, is the default setting from the drop-down menu. This option provides the ability to specify the document custom property to be regarded as the revision data when checking a document into PDMWorks. There are 33 selections from the drop-down menu.

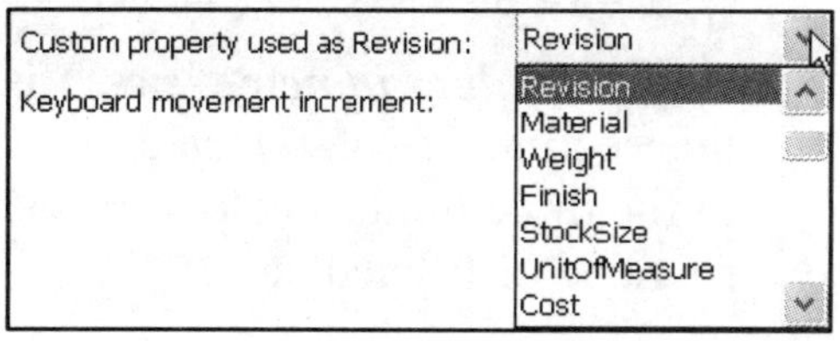


- ***Keyboard movement increment***. 0.39in, (10mm) default setting. Provides the ability to specify the unit value of movement when you utilize the arrow keys to move or nudge drawing views, annotations or dimensions in small increments.

## Drawings – Display Style

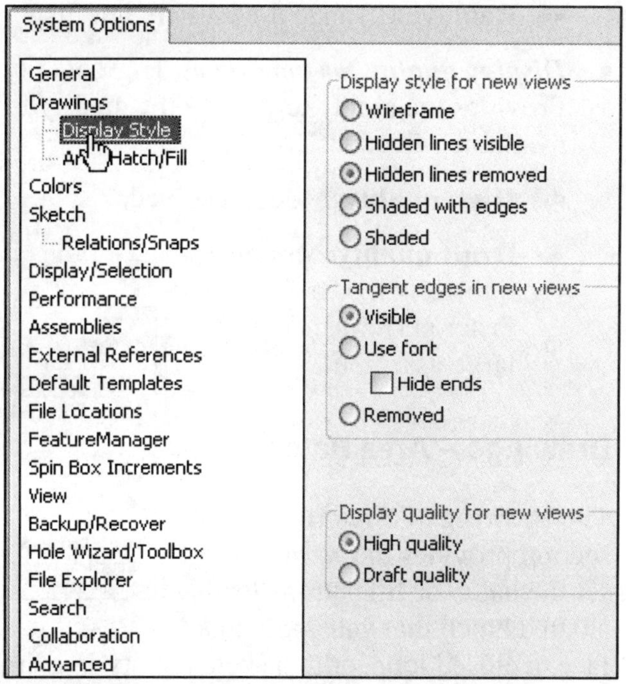


The Drawings – Display Style section provides the ability to set options for the default display of edges in all drawing documents.

The specified display types apply to new drawing views, except for new views created from existing views. If you create a new drawing view from an existing view, the new view uses the display settings of the source view. Example: Projected view.

The Drawings – Display Style section provides the following default options:

- ***Default style for new***. Hidden lines removed selected by default. There are five display view modes. Each view mode specifies the way a part or assembly is displayed in a drawing. The display options are:
  - **Wireframe**: All edges are displayed in a drawing view.
  - **Hidden lines visible**: All visible edges as specified in the Line Font Options are displayed. Hidden edges are displayed in black.
  - **Hidden lines removed**: Default setting. Only edges that are visible at the chosen angle are displayed. Obscured lines are removed from all views.

- **Shaded with edges**: Views in Shaded mode with Hidden lines Removed are displayed. Click **Options** ➤ **Colors** from the Menu bar to specify a color for the edges, or use the specified color or a color slightly darker than the model color.
- **Shaded**: Parts are displayed shaded.

- ***Tangent edges in new views***. Visible selected by default. There are three options in this section. If you selected Hidden lines visible or Hidden lines removed, select one of the three options below for viewing the tangent edges, transition edges between rounded or filleted faces.
  - **Visible**: A solid line is displayed.
  - **Use font**: A line using the default font for tangent edges is displayed. A drawing document is required to active this option.
    - **Hide ends**: Hides the start and end segments of tangent edges. You can also set the color for this type of tangent edge.
  - **Removed**: Tangent edges are not displayed.
- ***Display quality for new views***. High quality selected by default. Provides the ability to display the quality for a new view. The available selections are:
  - **High quality**: Model resolved.
  - **Draft quality**: Model lightweight. Use for faster performance with large assemblies.

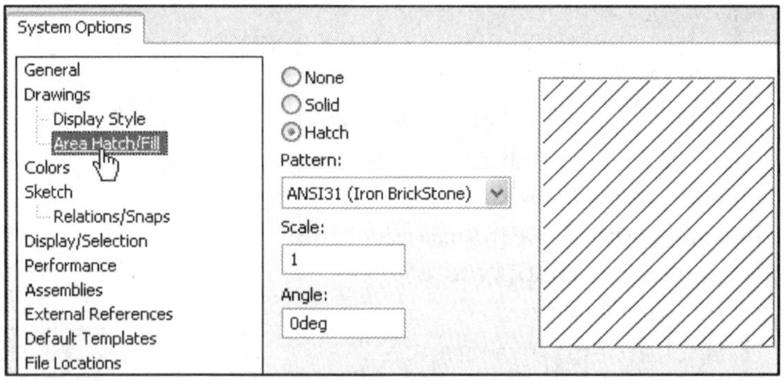


## Drawings – Area Hatch/Fill

The Drawings – Area Hatch/Fill section provides the ability to set the hatch or fill options for an area hatch that you apply to a face, a closed loop, or to a sketch entity in a drawing.

The Drawings – Areas Hatch/Fill section provides the following options:

- ***Type of hatch or fill***. Hatch selected by default. The default color of the solid fill is black. There are three pattern modes available. Modify the color of the fill by selecting the **area hatch** in the Graphics window, click **Line Color** from the Line Format toolbar. This procedure does not work for a Section view. The three pattern modes are: **None**, **Solid** and **Hatch**.

- ***Pattern***: Available only for the Hatch option. ANSI31 Iron BrickStone selected by default. Select a crosshatch pattern from the drop-down menu.

- ***Scale***: Available only for the Hatch option. The default Scale value is 1.
- ***Angle***: Available only for the Hatch option. The default Angle value is 0.

Material Hatch Pattern selected in a part propagates to a Section view in a drawing.

The default color of the solid fill is black.

## Colors

The Colors section provides the ability to set colors in the user interface: backgrounds, FeatureManager design tree, drawing paper, sketch status, etc.

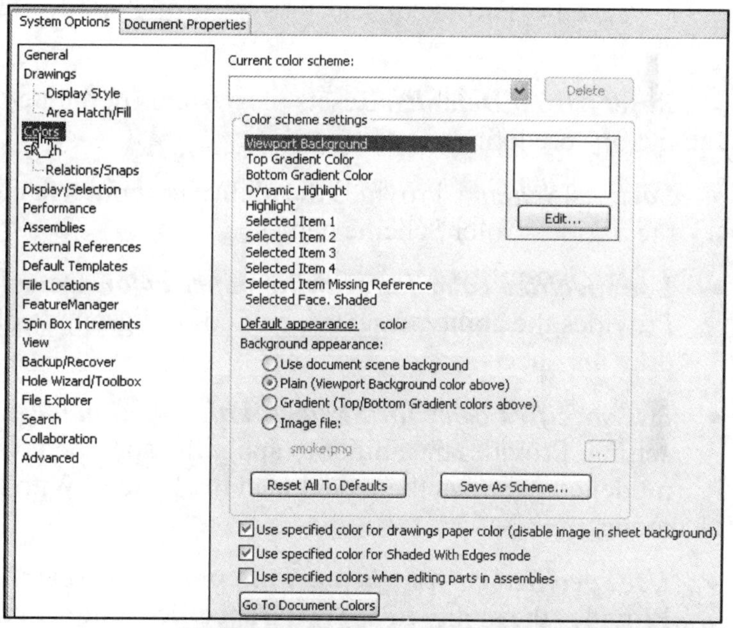


The Colors section provides the following default options:

- ***Current color scheme***. Provides the ability to choose from various background color schemes. Corresponding image file names are displayed in the Image file under Background appearance. Note: Specifying an Image file takes precedence over schemes in the list. Schemes created with Save As Scheme are displayed in the list.

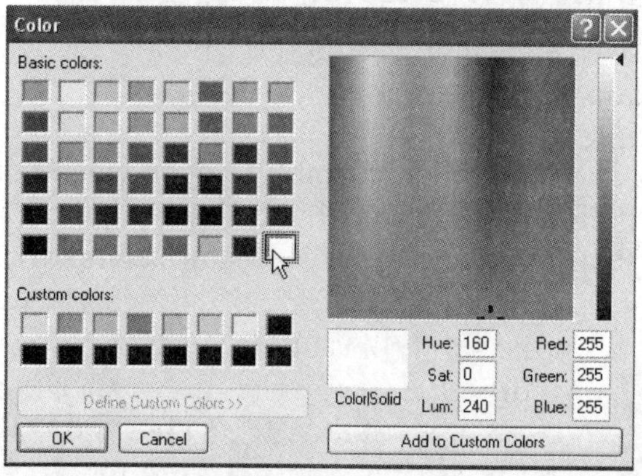


A plain white Graphics window background is displayed in this book.

- ***Color scheme settings***. Provides the ability to select an item in the list to display its color. Click **Edit** to modify the color of the selected item. Review the Color scheme settings by clicking on each item.
- ***Background appearance***. Plain selected by default. There are four appearance options:
    - **Use document scene background**. The scene background that is saved with the document is used when it is opened in SolidWorks.
    - **Plain**. The color scheme selected for the Viewport Background is used as the background color.
    - **Gradient**. The color scheme selected for the Top and Bottom Gradient is used as the background color.
    - **Image file**. Various files are provided with the application, corresponding to the color schemes listed in Current color scheme. Browse to select a system file or any other image file.

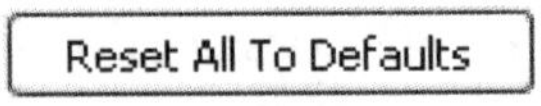


- ***Reset All To Defaults***. Resets the systems default colors to factory predefined conditions.
- ***Save As Scheme***. Provides the ability to input a name to Save the various Color Scheme names.
- ***Use specified color for drawing paper color***. Default setting. Provides the ability to set a specified background color on all drawing sheets.
- ***Use specified color for Shaded With Edges mode***. Default setting. Provides the ability to apply the specified color to model edges when the model is in the Shaded With Edges mode.
- ***Use specified colors when editing parts in assemblies***. Provides the ability to apply the specified colors to the faces, features, and bodies of a part while it is being edited in any assembly.

If a part or assembly is open when you set system color options, you can go to the **Colors** options on the **Document Properties** tab to set the feature colors for models.

## Sketch

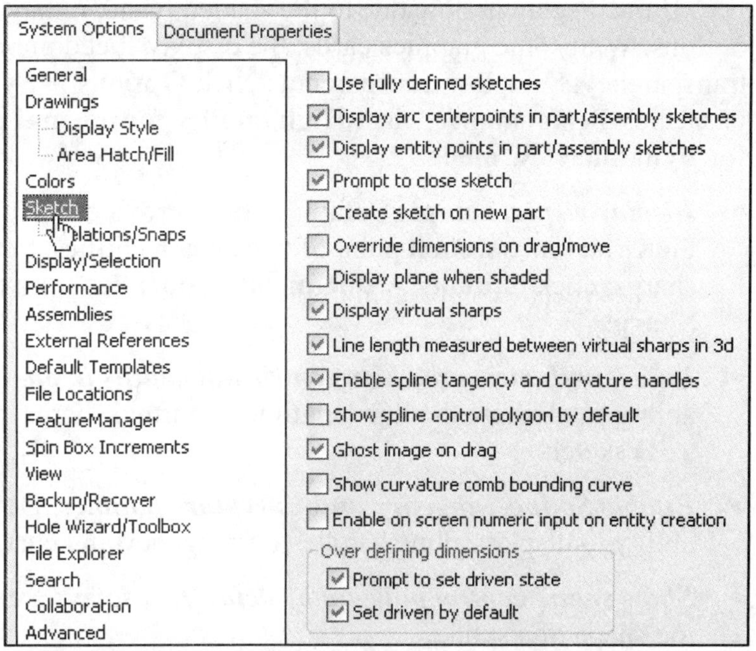


The Sketch section provides the ability to set the default system options for a sketch. When you open a new part document, first you create a sketch. The sketch is the base for a 3D model.

The Sketch section provides the following default options:

- ***Use fully defined sketches***. Requires sketches to be fully defined before they are used to create a feature in your model.
- ***Display arc centerpoints in part/assembly sketches***. Default setting. Displays arc centerpoints in the sketch. Note: Arc centerpoints can be useful to select for relations or dimensions.
- ***Display entity points in part/assembly sketches***. Default setting. Displays endpoints of sketch entities as filled circles. The color of the filled circles indicates the status of your sketch entity.

Black – Fully defined, Blue – Under defined, Red / Yellow – Over defined and Green – Selected.

- ***Prompt to close sketch***. Default setting. Provides the ability to display a dialog box with the question, Close Sketch With Model Edges? Use the model edges to close the sketch profile and to select the direction in which to close your sketch.
- ***Create sketch on new part***. Provides the ability to open a new part with an active sketch located on the Front plane. The Front plane is your active Sketch plane.
- ***Override dimensions on Drag/Move***. Provides the ability to override a dimension when you select and drag sketch entities or move your sketch entity in the Move or Copy PropertyManager. The dimension updates after the drag is finished.
- ***Display plane when shaded***. Provides the ability to display the Sketch plane when you edit your sketch in the Shaded With Edges or the Shaded mode.

If the display is slow due to the shaded plane, it may be because of the Transparency options. With some graphics cards, the display speed improves if you use low transparency. Set a low transparency; click **Options ➤ System Options** from the Menu bar. Click **Performance**, clear **High quality for normal view mode** and **High quality for dynamic view mode**.

- ***Display virtual sharps***. Default setting. Provides the ability to create a sketch point at the virtual intersection point of two sketch entities. Set the display options for virtual sharps; click **Options ➤ Document Properties** from the Main bar. Click **Virtual Sharps**.
- ***Line length measured between virtual sharps in 3d***. Default setting. Provides the ability to measure the line length from virtual sharps, as opposed to the end points in a 3D sketch.
- ***Enable Spline Tangency and Curvature handles***. Default setting. Provides the ability to display spline handles for tangency and curvature.
- ***Show spline control polygon by default***. Displays a control polygon to manipulate the shape of a spline.

A control polygon is a sequence of nodes (manipulators) in space used to manipulate an object's shape. The control polygon displays when you sketch and edit a 2D or 3D Spline sketch.

- ***Ghost image on drag.*** Default setting. Provides the ability display a ghost image of a sketch entities' original position while you drag a sketch.
- ***Show Curvature Comb Bounding Curve***. Provides the ability to display or hide the bounding curve used with curvature combs.
- ***Enable on screen numeric input on entity creation.*** Provides the ability to view dimensions during a sketch.

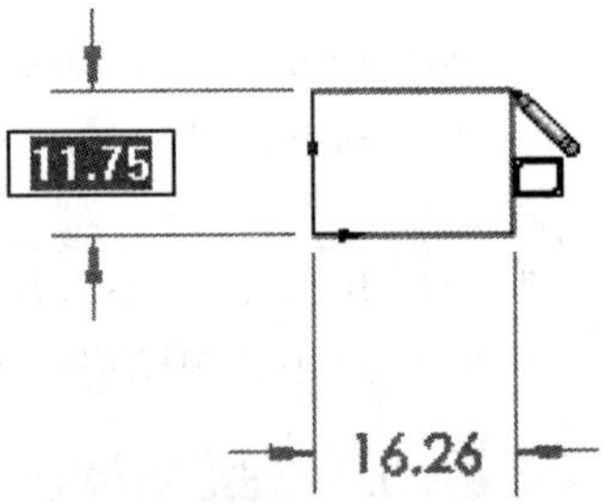


- ***Over defining dimensions***. There are two options. They are:
  - **Prompt to set driven state**. Default setting. Provides the ability to display a dialog box with the question, Make Dimension Driven? This question is displayed when you add an over defining dimension to your sketch.

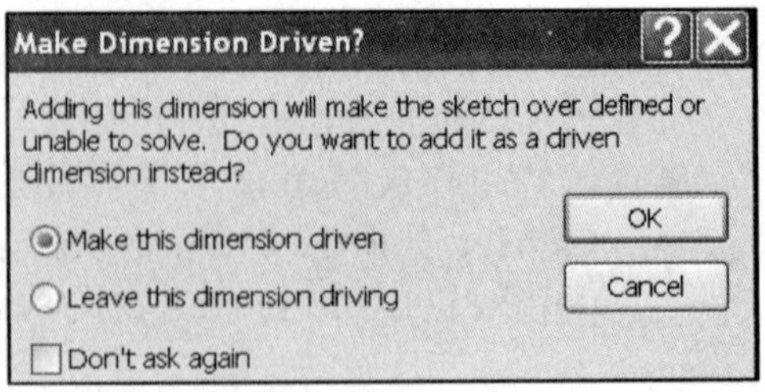

- **Set driven by default**. Default setting. Provides the ability to set the dimension to be driven by default when you add an over defining dimension to a sketch.

## Sketch – Relations/Snaps

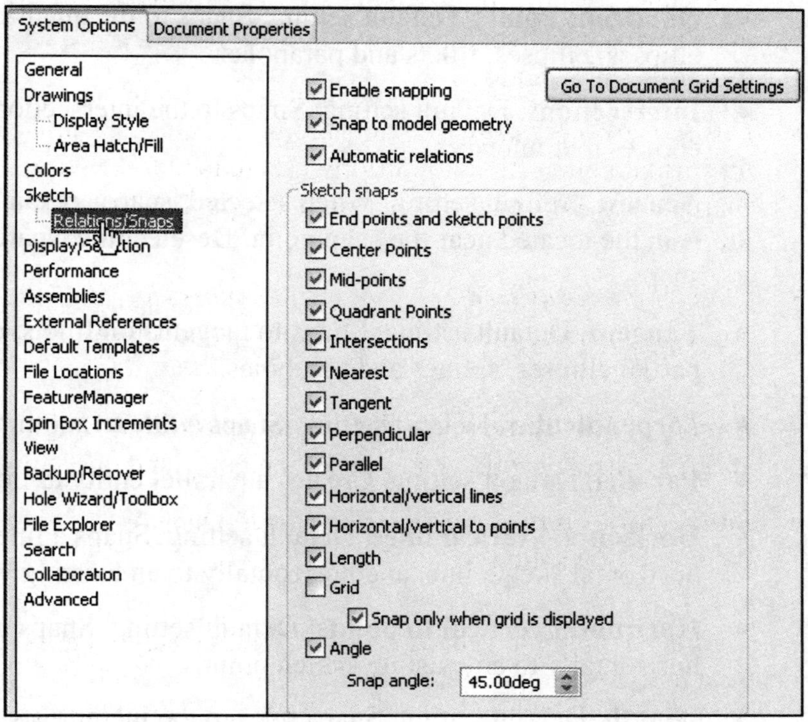


The Sketch – Relations/Snaps section provides the ability to set the default system options for various Sketch Snaps when you are sketching.

Most of the Sketch Snaps functions can be accessed through the Quick Snaps toolbar.

The Sketch – Relations/Snaps section provides the following default options:

- ***Enable snapping***.
  Default setting.
  Provides the ability to toggle all automatic relations, snapping and inferencing.
- ***Snap to model geometry***. Default setting. Allows sketch entities to snap to model geometry.
- ***Automatic relations***. Default setting. Provides the ability to create geometric relations as you add sketch elements.

Relations to the global axes are called: AlongX, AlongY and AlongZ. Relations that are local to a plane are called: Horizontal, Vertical, and Normal.

- ***Sketch Snaps***. There are sixteen selections under Sketch Snaps. They are:
  - **End points and sketch points**. Default setting. Snaps to the center of arcs. The End points and sketch points option Snaps to the end of the following sketch entities: centerlines, chamfers, polygons, parabolas, rectangles, parallelograms, fillets, partial ellipses, splines, points and lines.
  - **Center Points**. Default setting. Snaps to the center of arcs, filets, circles, parabolas, and partial ellipses sketch entities.

- **Mid-points**. Default setting. Snaps to the midpoints of rectangles, chamfers, fillets, lines, polygons, parallelograms, splines, points, centerlines, arcs, parabolas and partial ellipses.
- **Quadrant Points**. Default setting. Snaps to the quadrants of circles, arcs, partial ellipses, ellipses, fillets and parabolas.
- **Intersections**. Default setting. Snaps to the intersections of entities that meet or entities that intersect.
- **Nearest**. Default setting. When selected, snaps are enabled only when the pointer is in the located near the snap point. Deselect the Nearest option to enable all snaps.
- **Tangent**. Default setting. Snaps to tangents on fillets, circles, arcs, ellipses, partial ellipses, splines and parabolas.
- **Perpendicular**. Default setting. Snaps a line to another line.
- **Parallel**. Default setting. Creates a parallel entity to lines.
- **Horizontal/vertical lines**. Default setting. Snaps a line vertically to an existing horizontal sketch line, and horizontally to an existing vertical sketch line.
- **Horizontal/vertical to points**. Default setting. Snaps a line vertically or horizontally to an existing sketch point.
- **Length**. Default setting. Snaps lines to the increments that are set by the grid option.
- **Grid**. Snaps sketch entities snap to the grid's vertical and horizontal divisions.
  - **Snap only when grid is displayed**. Default setting.
- **Angle**. Default setting. Snaps to a selected angle.
- **Snap angle**. 45deg selected by default. Provides the ability to select your required angle from the spin box.

## Display/Selection

The Display/Selection section provides the ability to set the default options for the display and selection of edges, planes, etc. in your sketch. The following options are available:

- ***Hidden edges displayed as***. Dashed selected by default. Specifies how hidden edges are displayed in the Hidden Lines Visible (HLV) mode for a part and assembly document. There are two display modes:
  - **Solid**. Displays Hidden edges in solid lines.

- **Dashed**. Default setting. Displays Hidden edges in dashed lines.

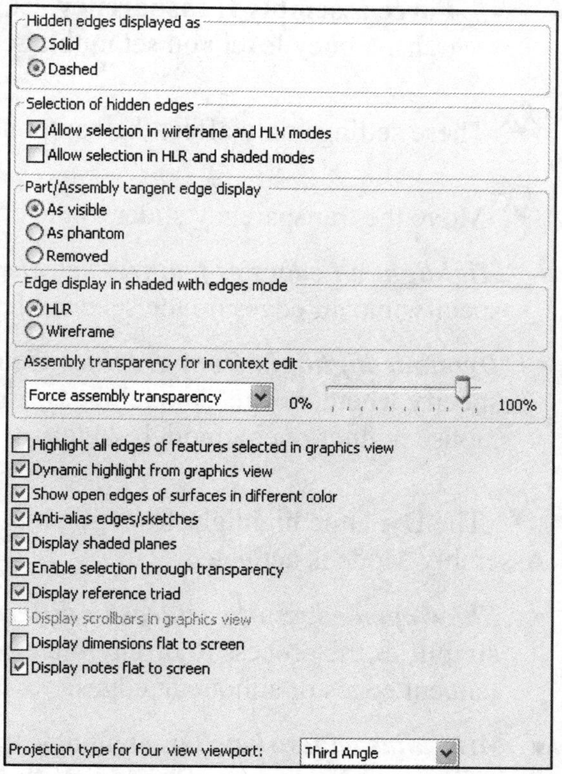


- ***Selection of hidden edges***. Allow selection in wireframe and HLV modes is selected by default. There are two display options. They are:
  - **Allow selection in wireframe and HLV modes**. Default setting. Allows you to select hidden edges or vertices in Wireframe and Hidden Lines Visible modes.
  - **Allow selection in HLR and shaded modes**. Allows you to select hidden edges or vertices in Hidden Lines Removed (HLR), Shaded With Edges, and Shaded modes.
- ***Part/Assembly tangent edge display***. As visible selected by default. Controls how tangent edges are displayed in various view modes. There are three display options:
  - **As visible**. Default setting. Displays Tangent edges.
  - **As phantom**. Provides Tangent edges to be displayed using the Phantom style line font.
  - **Removed**. Does not display the Tangent edges.
- ***Edge display in shaded with edges mode***. HLR is selected by default. There are two display options:
  - **HLR**. Default setting. Displays edges in the Hidden Lines Removed mode and in the Shaded With Edges mode.
  - **Wireframe**. Displays edges in the Shaded With Edges mode and in the Wireframe mode.
- ***Assembly transparency for in context edit***. Force assembly transparency with a 90% transparency setting is selected by default. Provides the ability to control the transparency display when you edit your assembly components. There are three display options. They are:
  - **Opaque assembly**. Default setting. Components not being edited are opaque.
  - **Maintain assembly transparency**. Components not being edited retain their individual transparency settings.

- **Force assembly transparency**. Components not being edited use the transparency level you set in this section.

These settings only affect the components that are not being edited.

Move the transparency slider to the desired level, to the right increases transparency.

- ***Highlight all edges of features selected in graphics view***. Provides the ability to specify that all edges on the selected feature are highlighted when selected.
- ***Dynamic highlight from graphics view***. Default setting. Provides the ability to specify whether edges, model faces, and vertices are highlighted when you drag your mouse pointer over a model, sketch, or drawing.

The Dynamic highlight from graphics view option is not available when the Large Assembly Mode is activated.

- ***Show open edges of surfaces in different color***. Default setting. This option simplifies the process to differentiate between the open edges of a surface and any tangent edges or silhouette edges.
- ***Anti-alias edges/sketches***. Default setting. Flattens out the jagged edges in the following view modes: **Shaded With Edges**, **Wireframe**, **Hidden Lines Removed** and **Hidden Lines Visible**.

The Anti-alias edges/sketches option is not available when the Large Assembly Mode is activated.

- ***Display shaded planes***. Default setting. Provides the ability to display transparent shaded planes with a Wireframe edge that have different front and back colors.
- ***Enable selection through transparency***. Default setting. Provides the ability to select opaque objects behind transparent objects in the Graphics window. This includes opaque components through transparent components in an assembly as well as edges, interior faces, and vertices through transparent faces in a part. Move the pointer over opaque geometry which is behind transparent geometry, the opaque edges, faces, and vertices are highlight.

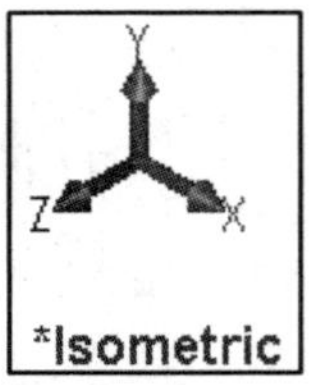


- ***Display reference triad***. Default setting. Provides the ability to display a reference triad. The triad is for reference only. You can not select it or use it as an inference point.

Specify the triad colors, click **Options ➢ Systems Options ➢ Colors** from the Menu bar. Select any of the three axes to apply a color.

- ***Display scrollbars in graphics view***. This option is unavailable when a document is open. To change this setting, you must close all documents.
- ***Display dimensions flat to screen***. Select to display dimension text in the plane of your computer screen. Clear to display dimension text in the plane of the dimension's 3D annotation view. Note: SolidWorks part and assembly documents support 3D annotations according to the ASME Y14.41-2003 standard.
- ***Display notes flat to screen***. Select to display notes in the plane of your computer screen. Clear to display notes in the plane of the dimension' s 3D annotation view. Note: SolidWorks part and assembly documents support 3D annotations according to the ASME Y14.41-2003 standard.

3D annotations in parts are not dynamically linked to their corresponding drawings. If you change a 3D annotation in a part, the drawing is not updated. You need to re-insert the drawing view for the change to take effect.

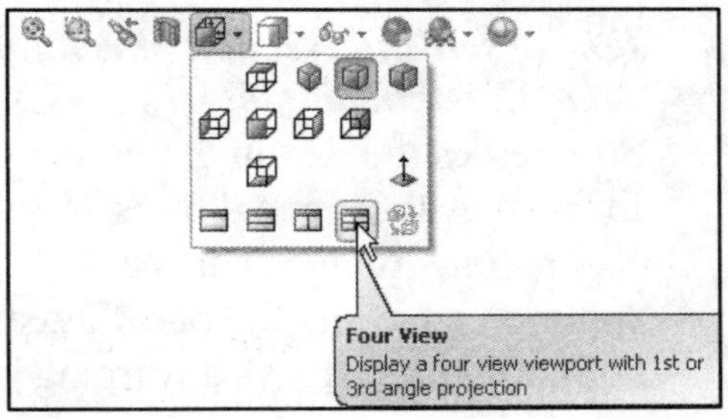


- ***Projection type for four view viewport***. Default is dependent on your initial system install. This options controls which views are displayed in the viewports when you click the Four View command from the Heads-up View toolbar. There are two view options from the drop-down menu:
  - **First Angle**. Displays the Front, Left, Top and Trimetric views. Note: ISO is typically a European drafting standard and uses First Angle Projection.
  - **Third Angle**. Displays the Front, Right, Top and Trimetric views. Note: ASNI is an American drafting standard and uses Third Angle Projection.

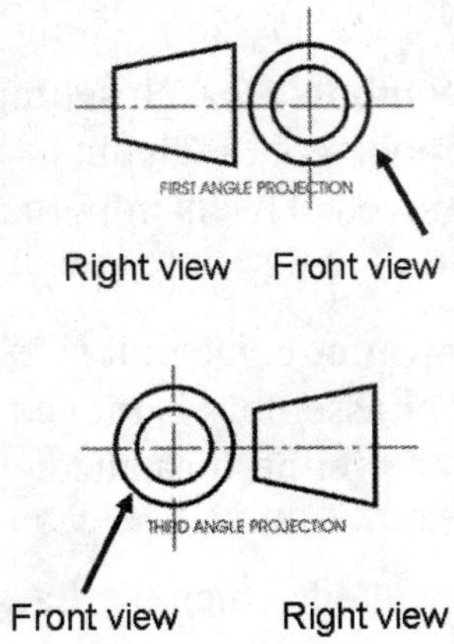


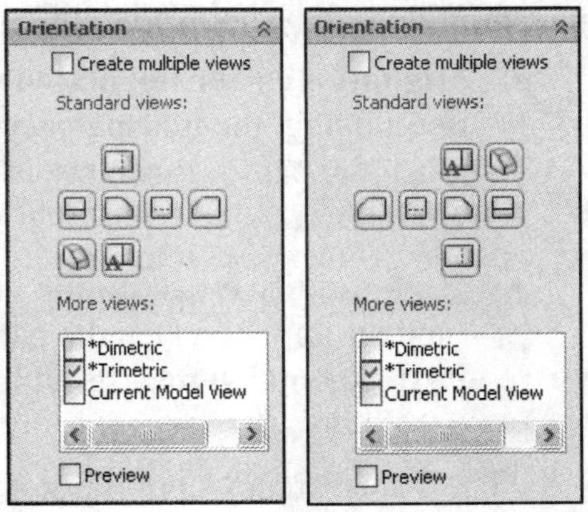


First Angle Third Angle

# Performance

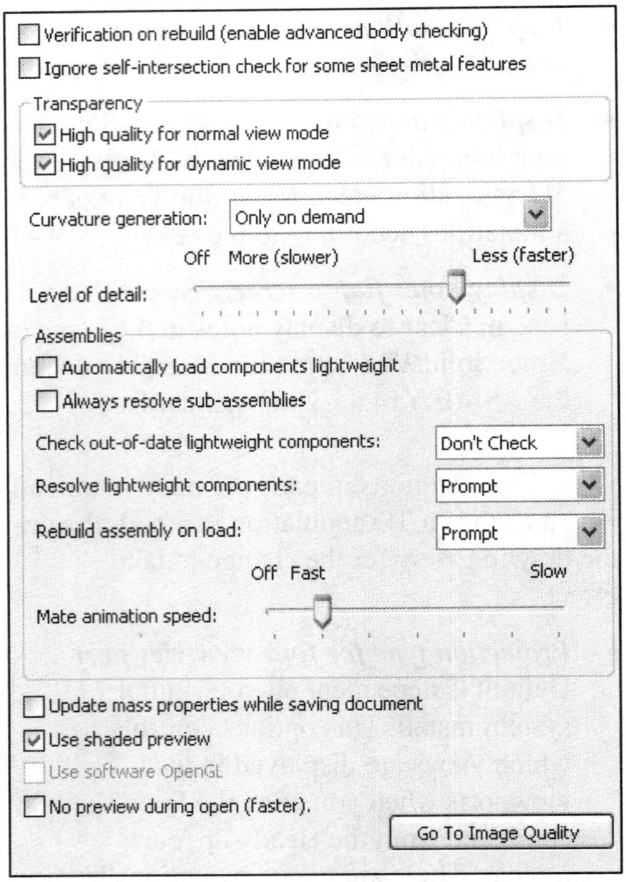


The Performance section provides the ability to set system options as it relates to the performance of the software on your system.

Changes to the performance settings will not affect documents which are open.

The Performance section provides the following default options:

- ***Verification on rebuild***. Provides the ability to control the level or error checking when you create or modify features. In most applications, the default setting is adequate, and will result in a faster model rebuild time.
- ***Ignore self-intersection check for some sheet metal features***. Suppresses the warning messages for certain sheet metal parts. Example: A flange shares a common edge and the part flattens correctly but displays a warning message.
- ***Transparency***. High quality for normal view mode and High quality for dynamic view mode selected by default. There are two display options:
  - **High quality for normal view mode**. Default setting. If the part or assembly is not moving, the transparency mode is of high quality. Low quality is applied when the part or assembly is moved. This is important if the part or assembly is complex.
  - **High quality for dynamic view mode**. Default setting. High quality transparency mode is applied when the part or assembly is moved. Depending on your graphics card, this option may result in slower performance.

The Transparency option is not available when the Large Assembly Mode is activated.

- ***Curvature generation***. Only on demand selected by default. There are two options. They are:
  - **Only on demand**. Uses less system memory, but will provide a slower initial curvature display on your system.
  - **Always (for every shaded model)**. Uses more system memory, but will provide a faster initial curvature display on your system.

The Curvature generation option is not available when the Large Assembly Mode is activated.

- ***Level of detail***. Provides the ability to move the slider from More (slower) or Less (faster) to specify the level of detail during dynamic viewing operations.

The Level of detail option is not available when the Large Assembly Mode is activated.

- ***Automatically load components lightweight***. Loads the individual components into assemblies which are opened as lightweight. Sub-assemblies are not lightweight, but the parts that they contain are.
- ***Always resolve sub-assemblies***. Sub-assemblies are resolved when an assembly opens in a lightweight mode. The components in the sub-assemblies are lightweight.
- ***Check out-of-date lightweight components***. Don't check selected by default. Provides the ability to specify how you want the system to load lightweight components which are out-of-date. There are three options:
  - **Don't check**. Loads the assemblies without checking for out-of-date components.
  - **Indicate**. Loads the assemblies and marks them with a lightweight icon, only if the assemblies contain an out-of-date component.
  - **Always Resolve**. Resolves the out-of-date assemblies during the loading process.

Right-click an out-of-date top down level assembly and select Set Lightweight to Resolved.

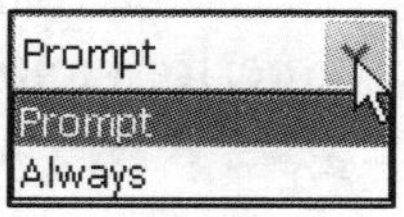


- ***Resolve lightweight components***. Prompt selected by default. Some operations require certain model data that is not loaded in lightweight components. This option controls what happens when you request one of these operations in an assembly which has lightweight components. There are two selections:
  - **Prompt**. Resolves lightweight components each time one of these operations is requested. In the dialog box that appears, click **Yes** to resolve the components and continue, or click **Cancel** to cancel the operation.

- **Always**. Automatically resolves lightweight components.

- ***Rebuild assembly on load***. Prompt selected by default. Provides the ability to specify whether or not you want your assemblies to be rebuilt so the components are updated the next time you open them. There are three options. They are:

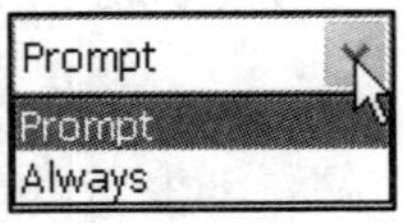


  - **Prompt**. Asks if you want to rebuild each time an assembly is opened. Click **Yes** or **No** in the dialog box. If you check the Don't ask me again box, the option is updated to reflect your choice. Yes changes the option to Always. No will change the option to Never.
  - **Always**. Rebuilds an assembly when it is open.
  - **Never**. Opens your assembly without performing a rebuild.

- ***Mate animation speed***. Fast selected by default. Enables animation of mates and controls the speed of your animation. When you add a mate, Click **Preview** or **OK** in the PropertyManager to view an animation of the mate.

- ***Update mass properties while saving document***. Updates the Mass properties information when you save a document. If the document did not change, the next time you access the Mass properties, the system does not need to recalculate them.

The Update Mass properties while saving document option is not available when the Large Assembly Mode is activated.

- ***Use shaded preview***. Default setting. Displays shaded previews to help you visualize features that you create. Rotate, pan, zoom, and set standard views while maintaining the shaded preview.

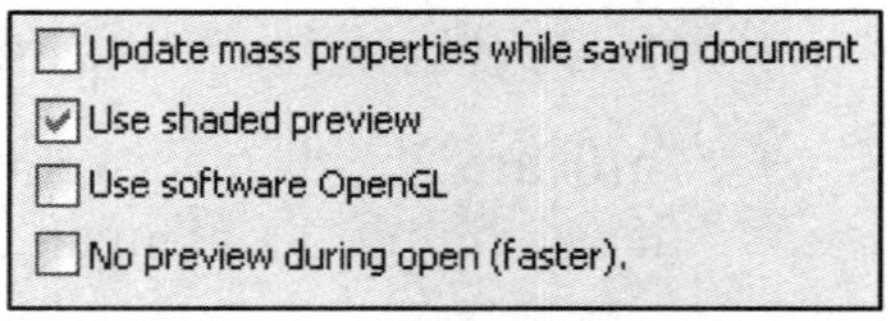


- ***Use Software OpenGL***. Disables the graphics adapter hardware acceleration and enables graphics rendering using only software. For many graphics cards, this will results in slower system performance.

Only active the Use Software OpenGL option when instructed by SW technical support.

- ***No preview during open (faster)***. Select this option to disable the interactive preview. This will reduce the time to load your models. Clear to display the interactive preview while the model is loading.

## Assemblies

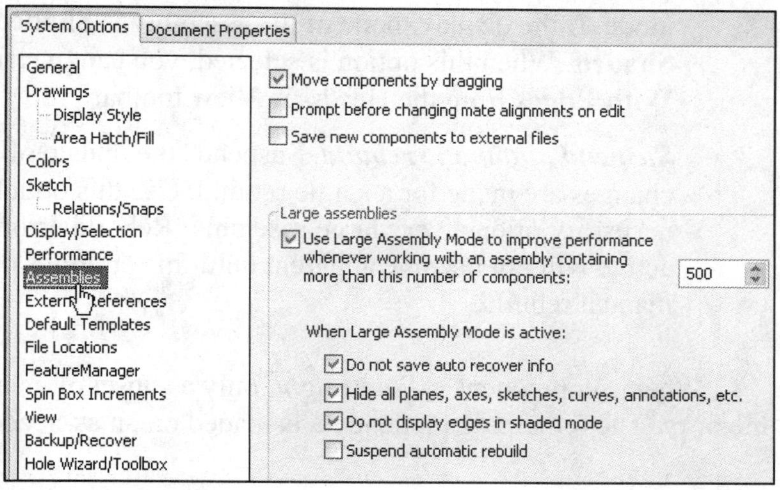


The Assemblies section provides the ability to set the behavior options for dragging components in an assembly.

The Assemblies section provides the following default options:

- ***Move components by dragging***. Default setting. Provides the ability to move or rotate components within their degrees of freedom. When you deselect, you can still move or rotate a component with the Move with Triad function or the Move Component tool and Rotate Component tool located in the Assembly toolbar.
- ***Prompt before changing mate alignments on edit.*** When changes that you make to mates result in errors that the software can fix by flipping mate alignments, the software asks if you want it to make the changes. Otherwise, the software makes the changes automatically (without asking).
- ***Save new component to external file.*** If selected, prompts you to name and save new in-context components to external files. If cleared, saves new in-context components in the assembly file as *virtual components***.**
- ***Use Large Assembly Mode to improve performance whenever working with an assembly containing more than this number of components***. Default setting. Set the number of resolved components above which Large Assembly Mode automatically activates when opening or working in an assembly. When the Large Assembly Model is active, select the following options to improve performance:
  - ***Do not save auto recover info***. Default setting. Disables automatic save of your model. (Set in Backup Options for normal use.)
  - ***Hide all planes, axes, sketches, curves, annotations, etc***. Default setting. Selects Hide All Types on the View menu. When this option is selected, you can override it by clearing Hide All Types on the View menu, then selecting to show or hide individual types.

- ***Do not display edges in shaded mode***. Default setting. Turns off edges in shaded mode. If the display mode of the assembly is **Shaded With Edges**, it changes to **Shaded**. When this option is selected, you can override it by clicking **Shaded With Edges** from the Heads-up View toolbar.
- ***Suspend automatic rebuild***. Suspends the update of an assembly until all of the changes are made for a single rebuild. Use this option only when absolutely necessary or on a very large assembly. Rebuild errors created while this option is active will not become apparent until this option is deactivated, or you perform a manual rebuild.

When a component is *lightweight*, only a subset of its model data is loaded in memory. The remaining model data is loaded on an as-needed basis.

You can improve performance of large assemblies significantly by using lightweight components. Loading an assembly with lightweight components is faster than loading the same assembly with fully resolved components. Assemblies with lightweight components rebuild faster because less data is evaluated.

## External References

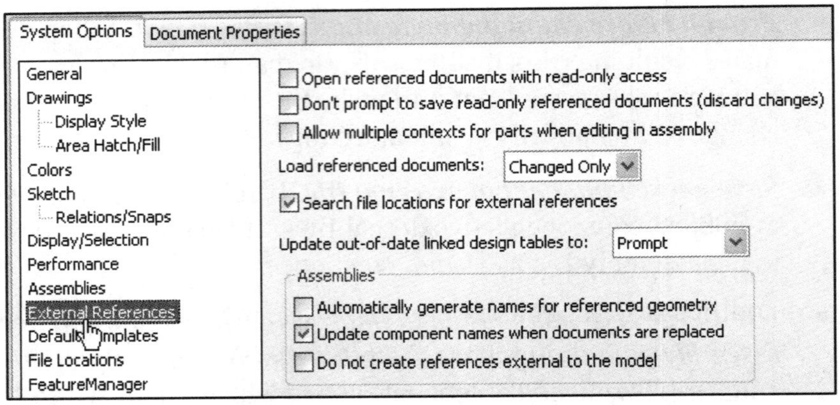


The External References section provides the ability to specify how a part, assembly or a drawing with external references is opened and managed.

An external reference is created when a document depends on another document for a solution. In an assembly (Top-down) when a component references geometry from another component, an in-context feature and an external reference are created.

The External References section provides the following default options:

- ***Open referenced documents with read-only access***. Specifies that all referenced documents will be opened with read-only access.

- ***Don't prompt to save read-only referenced documents (discard changes)***. Specifies that when a parent document is saved or closed, no attempt will be made to save its read-only, referenced documents.
- ***Allow multiple contexts for parts when editing in assembly***. You can create external references to a single part from more than one assembly context. However, any individual feature or sketch within the assembly may only have one external reference.

Any individual feature or sketch within an assembly can only have one External reference.

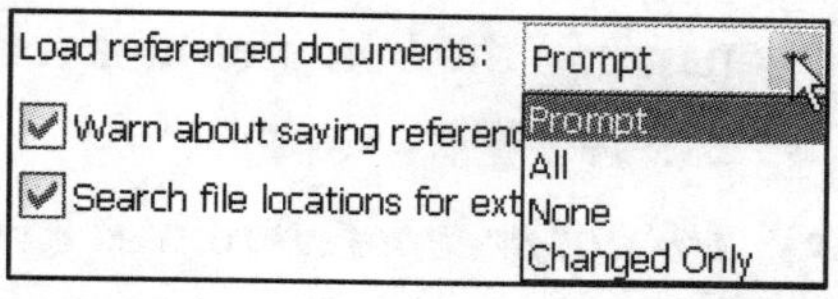


- ***Load referenced documents***. Prompt selected by default. Specifies whether to load the referenced documents when you open a part that is derived from another document. There are four options. They are:
  - **Prompt**. Prompts you about loading externally referenced documents each time you open a document with External references.
  - **All**. Opens all of the externally referenced documents.
  - **None**. Does not open any External referenced documents. External references can be shown as out of context until you open the External referenced documents.
  - **Changed Only**. Opens the Externally referenced documents which changed since the last time you opened the original document.
- ***Search file locations for external references***. Default setting. Displays a message for modified external reference models. The message will asks it you want to save the referenced model. If the option is deselected, no message is displayed and the reference model is saved automatically.

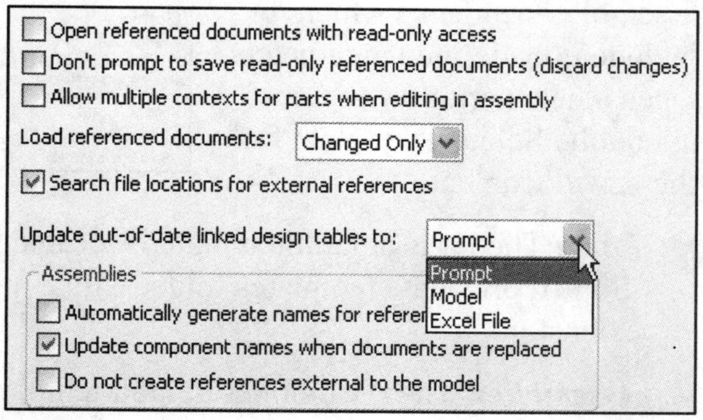


- ***Update out-of-date linked design tables to***. Prompt selected by default. The Update out-of-date linked design tables to option determines what happens to linked values and parameters if the model and the design table are out-of-sync. There are three options:
  - **Prompt**. Default setting. Prompts you when you open a document with a design table that is out-of-sync with the model.
  - **Model**. The design table updates with the model's values.

- **Excel File**. The model updates with the design table's values.

- ***Automatically generate names for referenced geometry***. When this option is not selected, you can mate to parts for which you have read-only access because you are only using the internal face IDs of the parts.

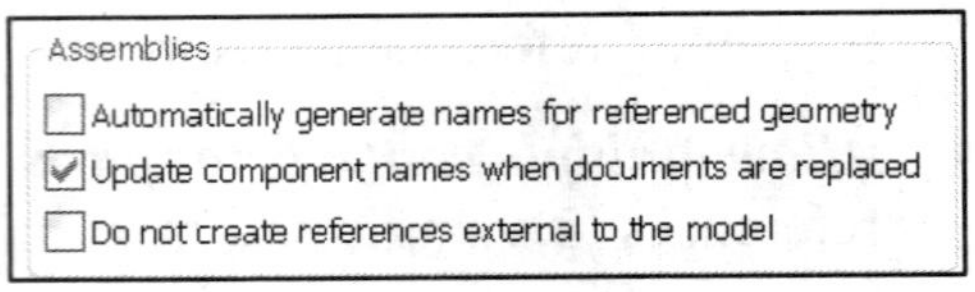


In a multi-user environment, leave this option deactivated.

- ***Update component names when documents are replaced***. Default setting. Clear this option only if you use the Component Properties dialog box to assign a component name in the FeatureManager design tree that is different from the filename of the component.

- ***Do not create references external to the model***. Select this option to NOT create External references when designing In-Context of an assembly. No In-Place mates are created when you create a new component in a Top-down assembly.

## Default Templates

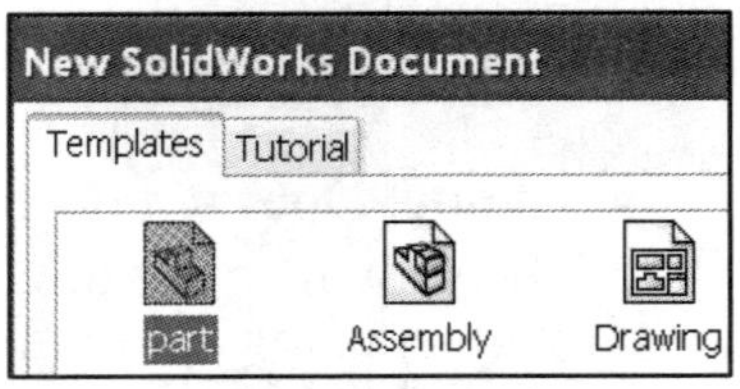


The Default Templates section specifies the folder and template file for parts, assemblies and drawings which are created automatically. Example: When you import a file from another application or create a derived part, the default template is used as the new document if your do not want to apply a template that you created.

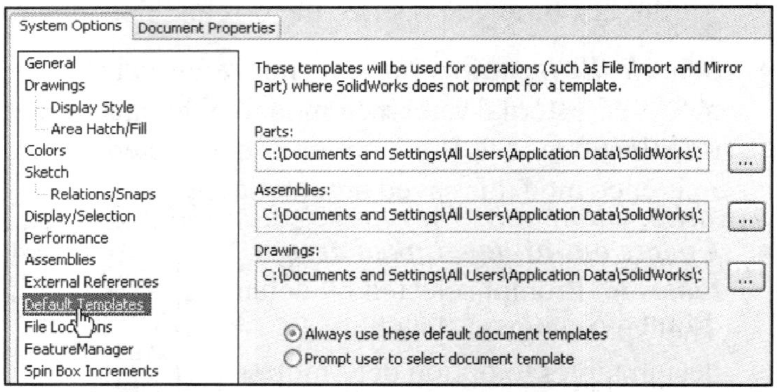


Templates are part, drawing and assembly documents which include user-defined parameters. Open a new part, drawing or assembly. Select a template for the new document.

- ***Parts***. The Parts default template is located in the \SolidWorks\data\templates folder with a .prtdot file extension.

- ***Assemblies***. The Assemblies default template is located in the \SolidWorks\data\templates folder with an .asmodot file extension.

- ***Drawings***. The Drawings default template is located in the \SolidWorks\data\templates folder with a .drwdot file extension.

## File Locations

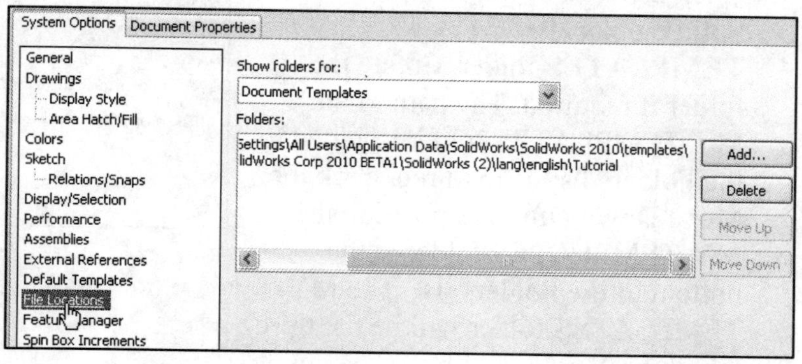


The File locations section provides the ability to specify the location of the folders to be searched for using the specified document type. Folders are searched in the order in which they are listed. Each folder is listed under **Options ➢ System Options ➢ File Locations**. The tab is visible when the folder contains one or more SolidWorks Part, Assembly or Drawing Templates.

SolidWorks utilizes a compound file structure that creates file references between documents. When you open an assembly drawing, SolidWorks searches for the referenced assembly document. If the assembly document cannot be located, SolidWorks performs a search to locate the missing document. In the file open process, the search order is as follows:

- Documents loaded in memory.
- Optional user-defined search lists.
- Show folders for*:* The Show folders for option displays the various available search paths in SolidWorks.

### *Tutorial: Document Templates Location 2-2*

Add a new Document Templates tab.

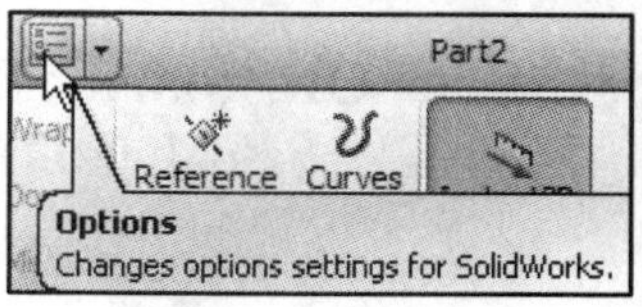


1. **Start** a SolidWorks session.
2. Click **New** from the Menu bar. The Templates tab is the default tab. Part is the default template from the New SolidWorks Document dialog box.
2. Click **OK** from the New SolidWorks Document dialog box. The Part FeatureManager is displayed.
3. Click **Options** ➢ **System Options** tab ➢ **File Locations**.
4. Select **Document Templates** from the show folders for box as illustrated.

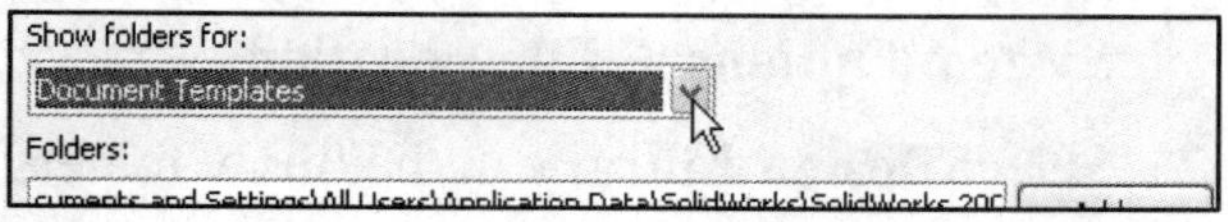

5. Click the **Add** button. Browse to the **SolidWorks 2010\MY-TEMPLATES** folder. Create the folder if required. The path to the MY-TEMPLATES folder is added to the Folders list. If required, click the Move Down button to position the MY-TEMPLATES folder at the bottom of the Folders list. The MY-TEMPLATES folder will be the third tab in the New dialog box. The new tab is only displayed if there is a document in the folder. Note: Part and Drawing templates are provided in the MY-TEMPLATES folder on the CD in the book.

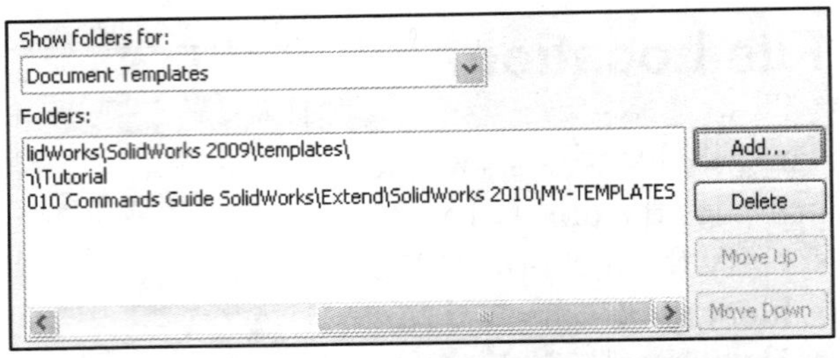


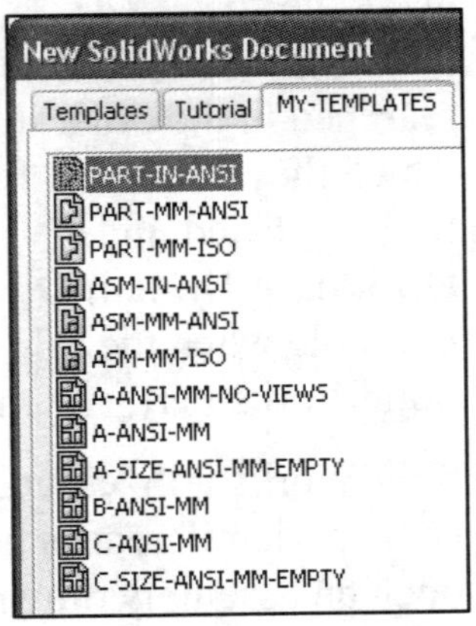


6. Click **OK** from the Browse For Folder dialog box. Click **OK** from the System Options – File Locations dialog box. Click **OK** to change search paths.

7. **Close** all models.

### *Tutorial: Referenced Document Location 2-3*

Add a folder for the Referenced Documents.

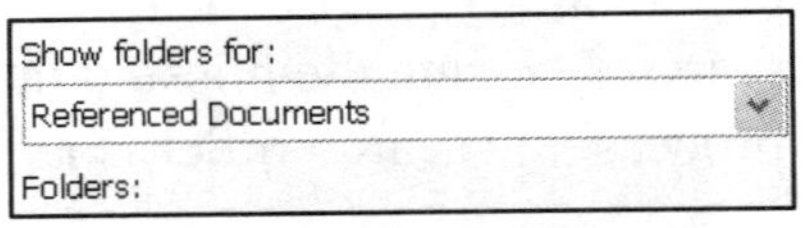


1. **Start** a SolidWorks session. Click **Options** ➢ **System Options** ➢ **File Locations**.
2. Select **Referenced Documents** in the Show folders for box. Click the **Add** button.
3. Select the **SolidWorks 2010\Delivery** folder. Create the folder if required.
4. Click **OK** from the Browse For Folder dialog box.
5. Click **OK** from the System Options – File Locations dialog box. Click **OK** to change search paths.
6. **Close** all models.

### *Tutorial: Design Library Location 2-4*

Add two folders to the Design Library.

1. **Start** a SolidWorks session. Click **Options** ➢ **System Options** ➢ **File Locations**.

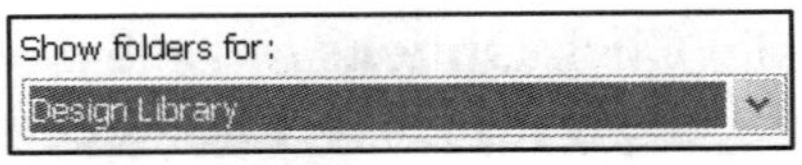


2. Select **Design Library** in the Show folders for box.
3. Click the **Add** button. Select the **SolidWorks 2010\MY-TOOLBOX** folder. Create the folder if required. Click **OK** from the Browse For Folder dialog box.
4. Select the **SolidWorks 2010\SMC** folder. Create the folder if required.

5. Click **OK** from the Browse For Folder dialog box. Click **OK** from the System Options – File Locations dialog box. Click **OK** to change search paths.
6. **Close** all models. **View** the two new folders in your Design Library.

## FeatureManager

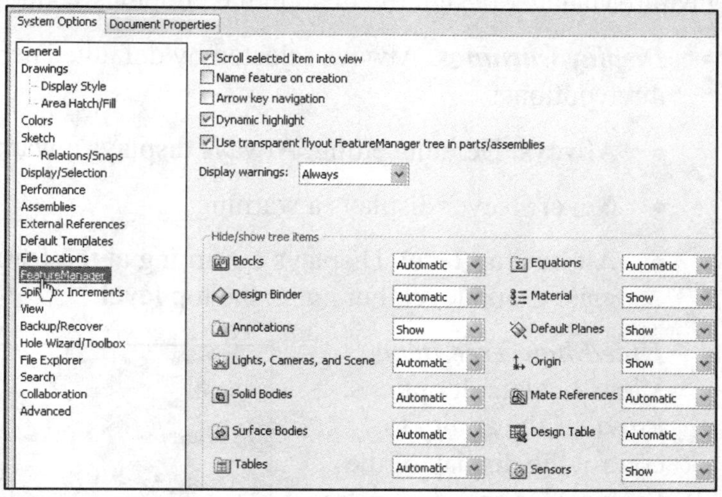


The FeatureManager section provides the ability to configure the FeatureManager design tree.

The FeatureManager design tree is located on the left side of the SolidWorks Graphics window. The FeatureManager provides an outline view of the active part, assembly, or drawing. This provides insight on how the document was constructed and aids you to examine and edit the document.

The FeatureManager design tree and the Graphics window are dynamically linked. Select sketches, features, drawing views, and construction geometry in either pane. The FeatureManager section provides the following default options:

- ***Scroll selected item into view***. Default setting. Provides the ability for the FeatureManager design tree to scroll automatically to display features corresponding to items selected in the Graphics window.
- ***Name feature on creation***. Provides the ability to name features and sketches for design intent.
- ***Arrow key navigation***. When you create a new feature, the feature name in the FeatureManager design tree is automatically selected and is ready to enter a name.
- ***Dynamic highlight***. Default setting. This option provides the ability for the geometry in the graphics area; edges, faces, planes, axes, etc. is highlighted when the pointer passes over the item in the FeatureManager design tree.
- ***Use transparent flyout FeatureManager in parts/assemblies***. Default setting. The flyout design tree is transparent. When cleared, the flyout design tree is not transparent.

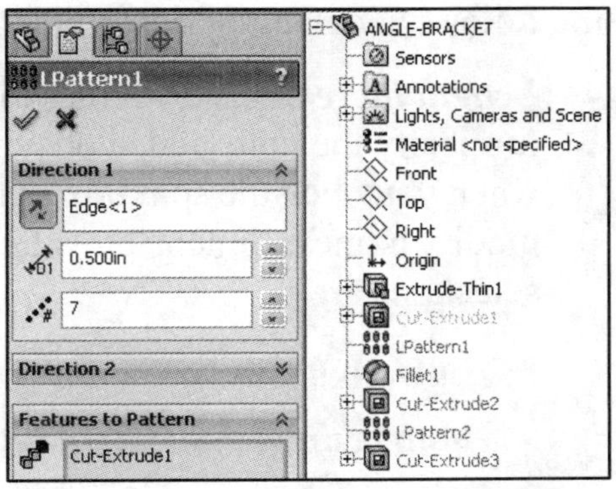

The fly-out FeatureManager design tree allows you to view both the FeatureManager design tree and the PropertyManager at same time. Sometimes it is easier to select items in the flyout FeatureManager design tree than in the Graphics window.

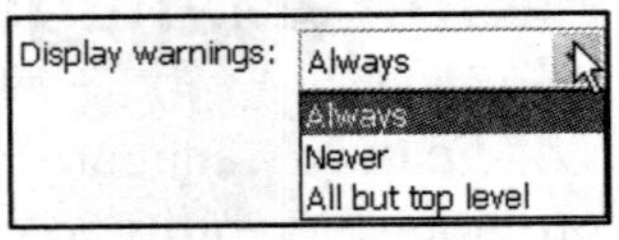


- ***Display warnings***. Always selected by default. There are three options:
  - **Always**. Default setting. Always displays a warning.
  - **Never**. Never displays a warning.
  - **All but top level**. Displays a warning at the feature and mate group level, but not at the top level.

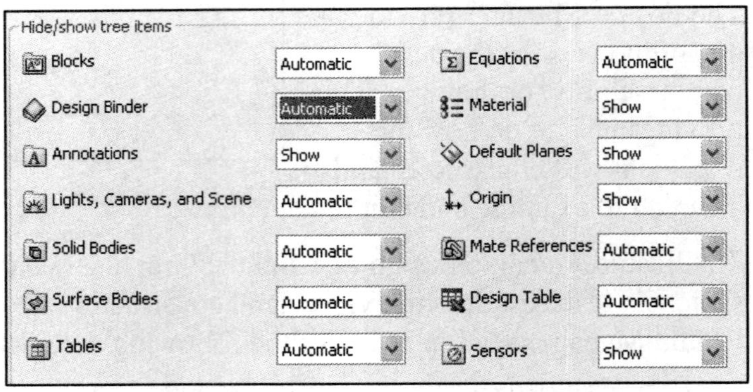


- ***Hide/Show Tree Items***. View the default options. Provides the ability to control the display of the FeatureManager design tree folders and tools. The three options are:
  - **Automatic**. Displays the item if present. Otherwise, it is hidden.
  - **Hidden**. Always hides the item.
  - **Show**. Always shows the item.

## Spin Box Increments

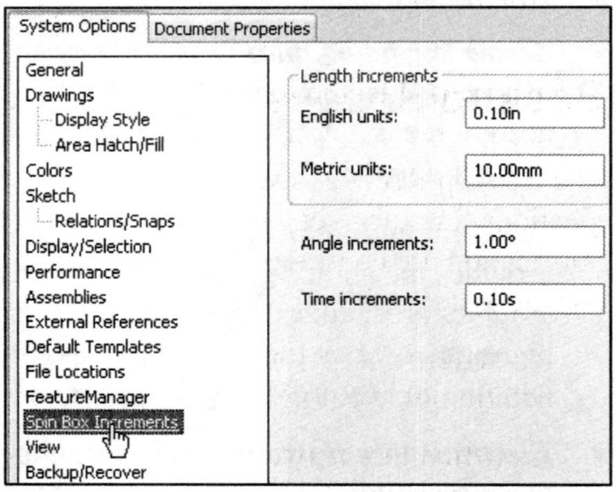


The Spin Box Increments section provides the ability to set the spin box increment value for both English and Metric units.

The Spin Box Increments section provides the following default options:

- ***Length increments***. Provides the ability to specify the units added or subtracted when you click the spin box arrow to modify a linear dimension value. The selections are:
  - **English units**. Specifies English units in inches.
  - **Metric units**. Specifies Metric units in mm.
  - **Angle increments**. Specifies the angle increments, 1 degree added or subtracted when you click a spin box arrow to change an angular dimension value.

## View

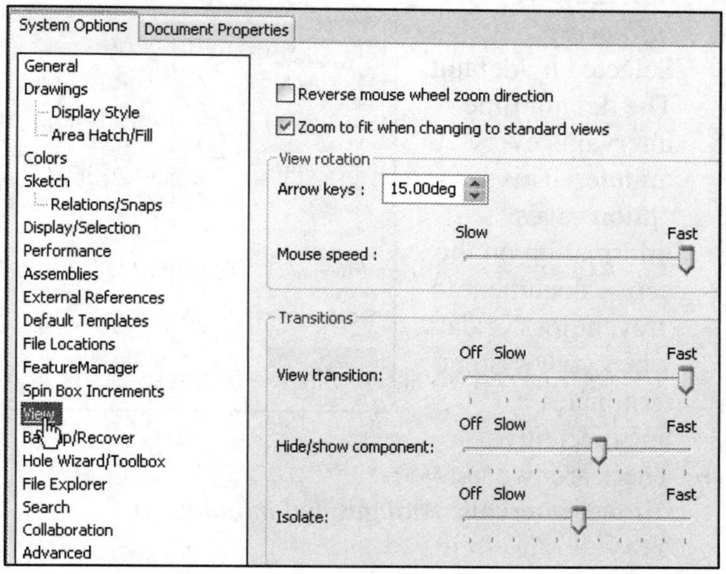


The View section provides the ability to set the default view rotation and transitions.

- ***Reverse mouse wheel zoom direction***. Changes the direction of the mouse wheel for Zooming in and out.
- ***Zoom to fit when changing to standard views***. Default setting.
- ***Arrow keys***. 15deg selected by default. Specifies the angle increment for view rotation when you use the arrow keys to rotate the model.
- ***Mouse speed***. Mouse speed by default is set to Fast. Provides the ability to specify the speed of rotation when you use the mouse to rotate the model or assembly component. Move the slider to the left to obtain finer control and slower rotation.
- ***View Transitions***. Changes from one view orientation to another. For example, from a front view to an isometric view.
- ***Hide/Show Component***. In assemblies, when you turn the visibility of selected components off or on.
- ***Isolate***. In assemblies and multi-body parts, when you isolate selected components.

## Backup/Recover

The Backup/Recover section provides the ability to set time frequency and folder locations for auto-recovery, backup, and save notification. Auto-recovery and save notification are controlled by a specified number of minutes or the number of changes. A change is defined by the following:

1. An action in a part or assembly document which requires a rebuild. Example: An addition of a feature.
2. An action in a drawing document which requires a rebuild. Example: A modification to a dimension.

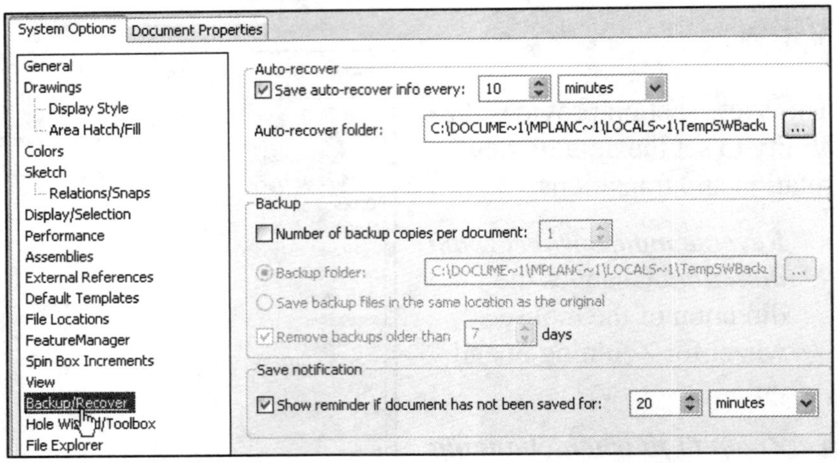


- ***Save auto-recover info every***. Selected by default. The default time interval is every 10 minutes. This option saves information on the active document to prevent loss of data when your system terminates unexpectedly. There are two auto-recover intervals: *changes* and *minutes*.

Auto-recover does not save over the original file. You can save the recovered document over the original file. The status bar displays the number of minutes since the last save and to the next scheduled save, if the save interval is specified in minutes.

- ***Auto recover folder***. Provides the ability to specify the folder to store auto recovered files or browse to select a new location. The default location: \TempSW\BackupDirectory\swauto.

- ***Backup***. Stores a backup of the original document before any changes are saved to the file. It is a version before the last saved version of the document. Backup files are named Backup of <*document_name*>. Multiple backups of a document, are named with the most recent version in Backup (1), the next most recent in Backup (2), etc.

If changes to an active document are saved in error, opening the backup file brings the document back to the point before the changes were made.

If you save a document without making any changes, the backup file is the same as the original.

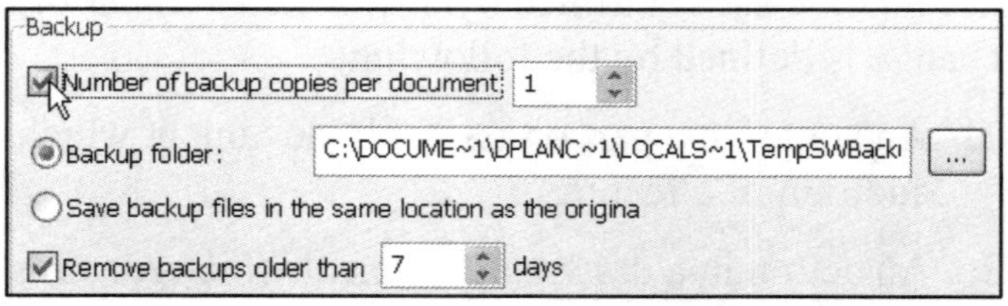


- ***Number of backup copies per document***. Not selected by default. When this option is selected, you can specify from 1 to 10 copies to be saved for each document.

- ***Save notification***. Provides a transparent message, Un-Saved Document Notification, is displayed in the lower right corner of the Graphics window if the active document has not been saved within the specified interval; time or number of changes.

Click the commands in the message to save the active document or save all open documents. The message fades after a few seconds.

- ***Show reminder if document has not been saved for***. Default setting is 20 minutes. When notification is enabled, you can specify the interval in minutes or number of changes.

## Hole Wizard\Toolbox

The Hole Wizard\Toolbox section provides the ability to create new standards or to edit existing standards used by the Hole Wizard holes and SolidWorks Toolbox components. You can add administrative access to these standards and the options of the SolidWorks Toolbox Add-in.

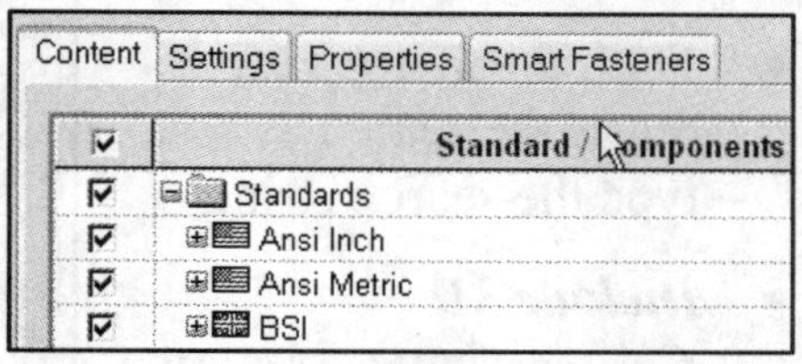


The Hole Wizard\Toolbox section provides the following default options:

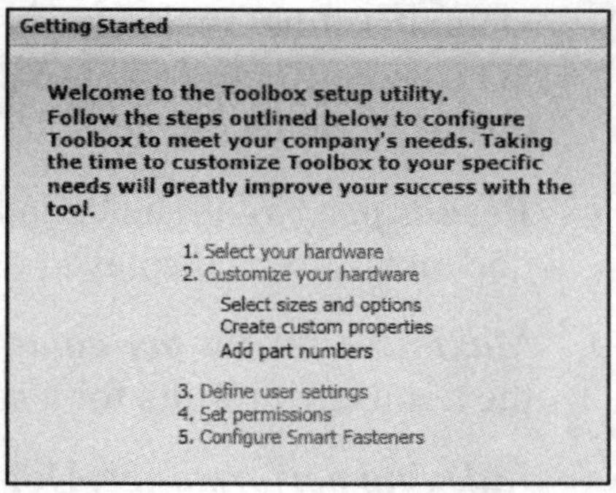


- ***HoleWizard\ToolBox folder***. The default HoleWizard\ToolBox folder location is C:\program files\common files\solidworks data.
- ***Configure***. Provides the ability to access the Getting Started\Configure Data dialog box to configure contents, settings, properties, etc. for the SolidWorks toolbox.

## File Explorer

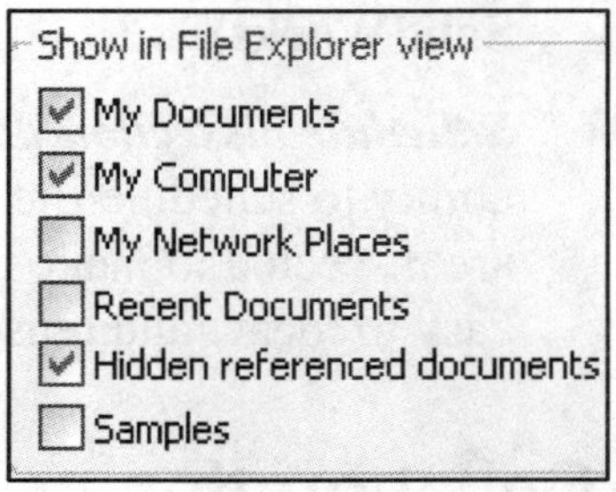


The File Explore section duplicates Windows Explorer from your local computer and displays the following directories: Recent Documents and Open in SolidWorks. The File Explorer section provides the following default options:

- ***Show in File Explorer View***. Provides the ability to show or hide the following folders and files on the File Explorer tab of the Task Pane. The following options are:
  - **My Documents**. Default setting.

- **My Computer**. Default setting.
- **My Network Places.**
- **Recent Documents**.
- **Hidden referenced documents**. Default setting.
- **Samples**. The Samples option is for the Online Tutorial and *What's New* examples.

## Search

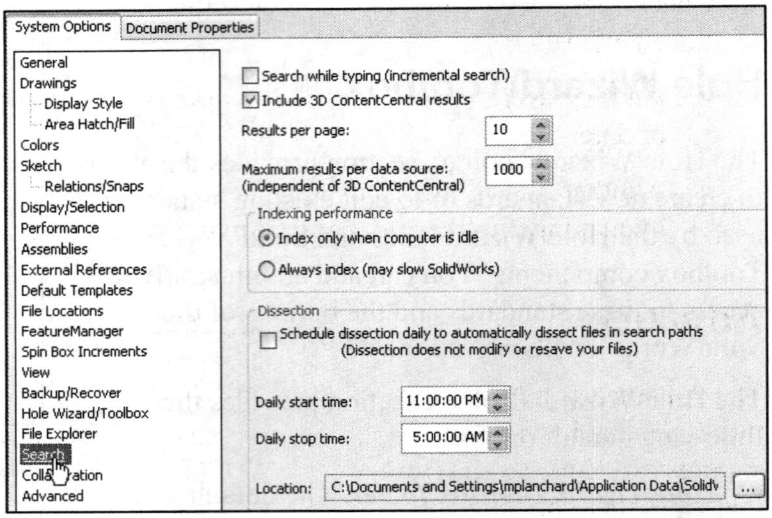


The Search section locates key items. The Search section provides the following default options:

- ***Search while typing***. Starts the search as you type the search string.
- ***Include 3D ContentCentral results***. Default setting. Includes 3D ContentCentral results from the search.
- ***Results per page***. The default Results per page = 10. Specifies the number of documents to be displayed on each page of the Task Pane Search Results tab.
- ***Maximum results per data***. The default Maximum results per data = 1000. Specifies the number of results for a search attempt.
- ***Indexing performance***. Default setting. Updates the index to improve performance. All locations in the list on the Task Pane Search Results tab are indexed. There are two selections: **Index only when computer is idle** and **Always index (may slow SolidWorks)**.
- ***Schedule dissection daily to automatically dissect files in search paths***. Provides the ability to schedule file dissection for Design Clipart. The SolidWorks files you search are dissected to make their components easy to locate and reuse.

## Collaboration

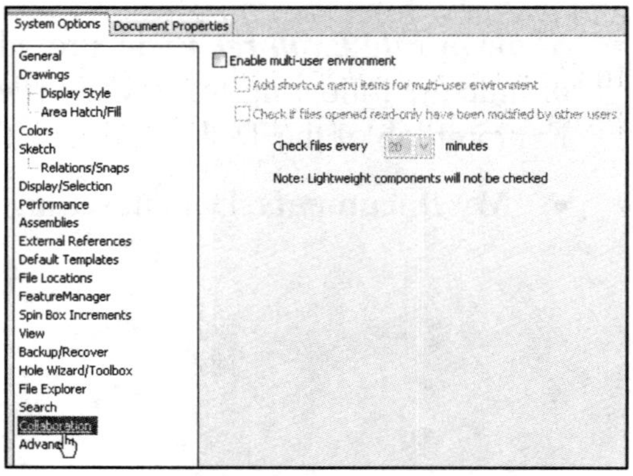


The Collaboration section provides the ability to specify options for a multi-user environment. The Collaboration section provides the following options:

- ***Enable multi-user environment***. Enables the other options below. Note: The Enable multi-user environment option is activated in the illustration to improve visibility of the screen shot.
- ***Add shortcut menu items for multi-user environment***. Provides menu items; Make Read-Only and Get Write Access are available on the File menu part documents and for assemblies.
- ***Check if files opened read-only have been modified by other users***. Default time is 20 minutes. Checks files you have opened as read-only at the interval specified in Check files every X minutes to view if the files have been modified in one of the following ways:
  - Another user saves a file that you have open in SolidWorks, making your file out of date.
  - Another user relinquishes write access to a file that you have open in SolidWorks by making the file read-only, allowing you to take write access.

## Advance

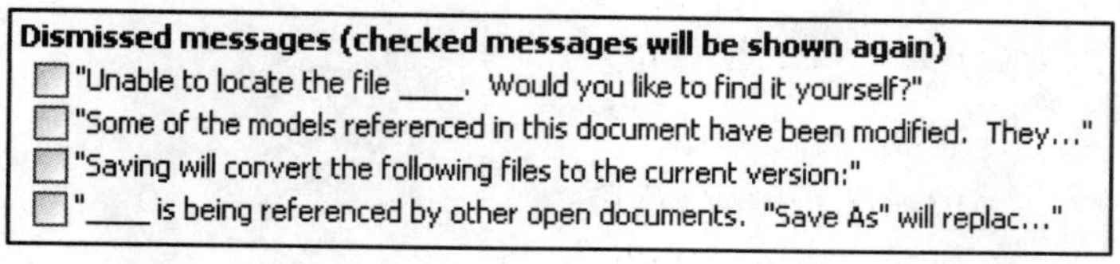


The Advance section restores messages that have been suppressed. You can suppress messages that you view frequently if you know that you will always choose the default response. The dismissed messages are illustrated.

# Summary

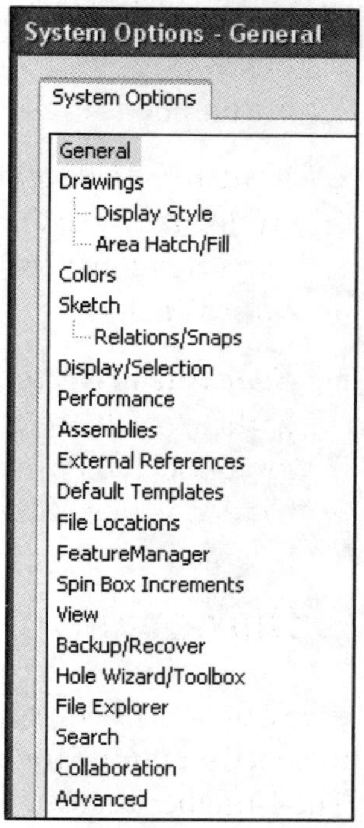


In this chapter, you learned about using and modifying the System Options in SolidWorks. System Options are stored in the registry of your computer. System Options are not part of your document. Changes to the System Options affect all current and future documents.

You added a new Document Template in the File Locations section. You added a new folder to the Referenced Documents and two new folders to the Design Library.

In Chapter 3, explore and address Templates and Document Properties for a Part, Assembly and Drawing document.

**Notes:**

# CHAPTER 3: DOCUMENT PROPERTIES

## Chapter Objective

Chapter 3 provides a comprehensive understanding of the Document Properties section.

The available options under the Document Properties tab are document dependent as illustrated from left to right: *Part*, *Drawing* and *Assembly*.

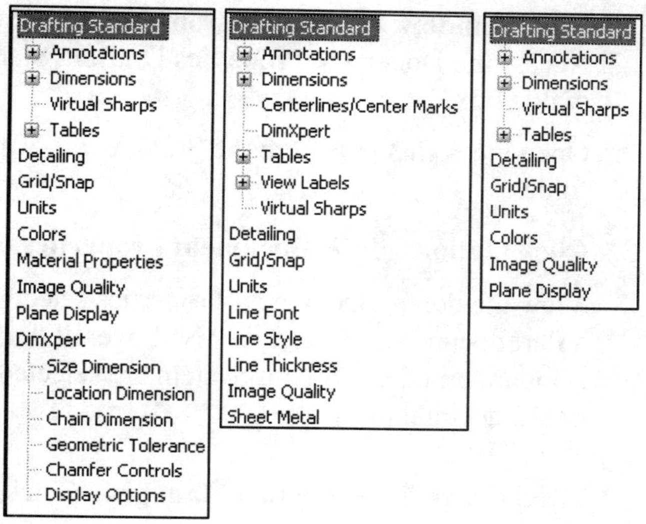


On the completion of this chapter, you will be able to:

- Understand a document template.
- Setup and modify the available tools from the Document Properties section.

The ANSI drafting standard using the IPS unit system is the default standard in the book.

The first half of the chapter addresses the Document Properties for a Part or Assembly document. The second half of the chapter addresses the Drawing document, specific Document Properties.

## Document Properties / Templates

Templates are documents, (part, drawing and assembly documents) which forms the basis of a new document. It can include user-defined parameters, annotations, predefined views, geometry, etc. You can maintain numerous different document templates. Example:

- **Part Templates (*.prtdot)**
- **Assembly Templates (*.asmdot)**
- **Drawing Templates (*.drwdot)**

- A document template using an *ANSI* drafting standard.
- A document template using an *ISO* drafting standard.

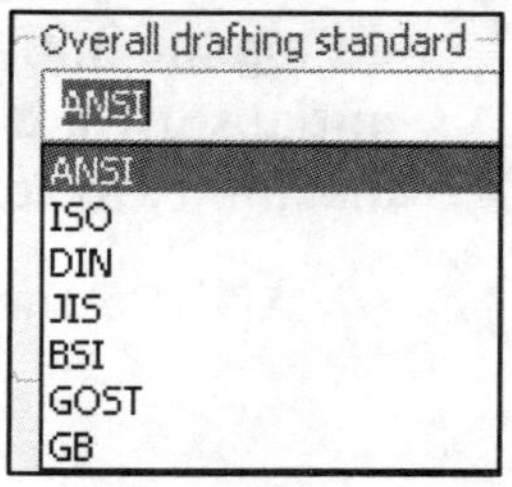

- A document template using inches and another document template using millimeters with predefined views and notes.

Organize your document templates by placing them on different tabs in the New SolidWorks Document dialog box. Create custom tabs to organize your templates.

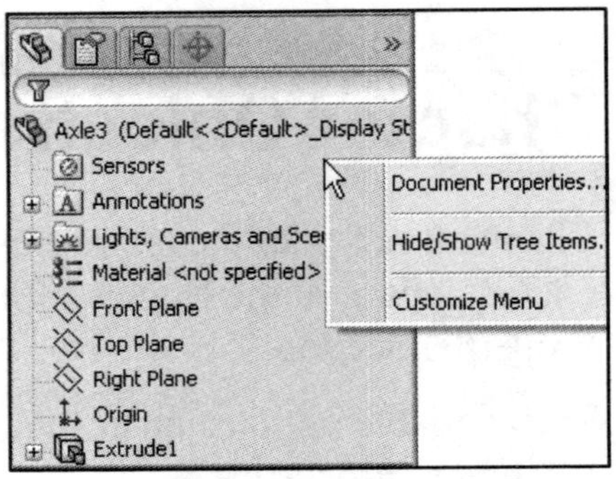


***Tutorial: Close all open models in SolidWorks 3-1***

Close all parts, assemblies, and drawings. Access the Document Properties dialog box.

1. Click **Window** ➢ **Close All** from the Menu bar. Access the Document Properties Drafting Standard dialog box.
2. Open the **Axle3** part from the SolidWorks 2010 folder.
3. Click **Options** ➢ **Document Properties** tab.
4. **View** the default Document Properties selection for a Part document. Note: The ANSI overall drafting standard and the IPS Unit System are selected for this part document with a precision of .12 decimal places.

Right-click in the **FeatureManager** ➢ click **Document Properties** to access the Document Properties dialog box.

The available options under the Document Properties tab are document dependent: *Part, Assembly* and *Drawing*.

# Drafting Standard

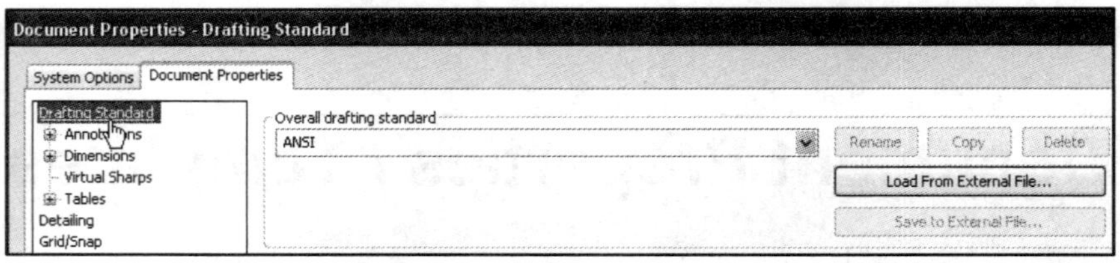


The Drafting Standard feature provides the ability to select default standards for an active Part, Assembly or Drawing document from the drop-down menu or to create a custom drafting standard.

- ***Overall drafting standard***. The default setting was chosen and set during the initial software installation. The default standard during this initial software installation was ANSI. The drop-down menu provides the ability to select the following default drafting standards:
    - **ANSI**. American National Standards Institute

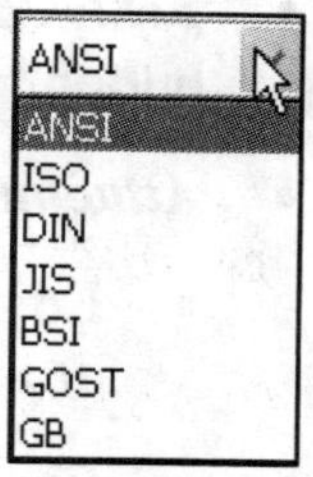


- **ISO**. International Standards Organization
- **DIN**. Deutsche Institute fur Normumg
- **JIS**. Japanese Industry Standard
- **BSI**. British Standards Institution
- **GOST**. Gosndarstuennye State standard
- **GB**. Guo Biao

The Overall drafting standard provides the ability to create or modify a default standard. Modification to a standard drafting standard creates a modified standard.

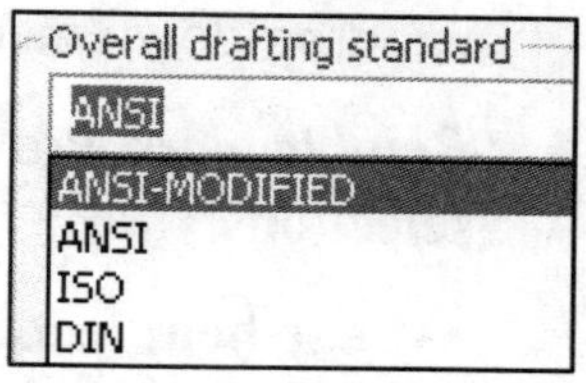


- ***Rename***. Only available for a modified drafting standard. Provides the ability to rename the default modified drafting standard.
- ***Copy***. Only available for a modified drafting standard. Provides the ability to copy the modified drafting standard.
- ***Delete***. Only available for a modified drafting standard. Provides the ability to delete the modified drafting standard from the drop-down menu.
- ***Load From External File***. Load a drafting standard from an external file.
- ***Save to External File***. Only available for a modified drafting standard. Saves a modified drafting standard to an external file.

## Annotations

The Annotations section provides six sub-sections: *Balloons, Datums, Geometric Tolerances, Notes, Surface Finishes* and *Weld Symbols*.

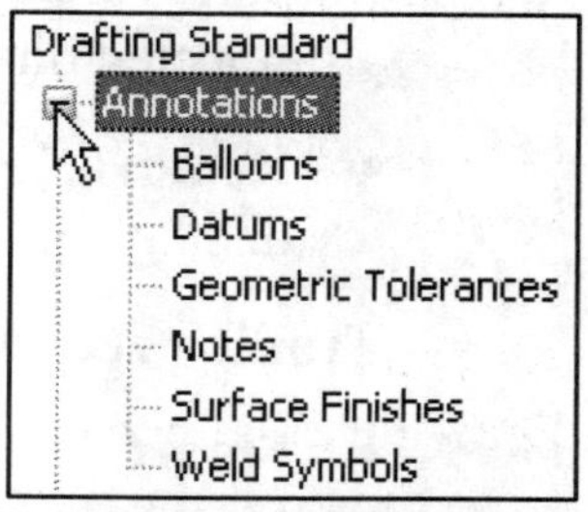


The Annotations section provides the ability to select the following:

- ***Overall drafting standard***. Displays the selected drafting standard.

- ***Text***. Century Gothic selected by default. Click the Font button to select a custom font style and size.
- ***Attachments***. Provides the following arrow style options:
  - **Edge/vetex**. Select from 11 arrow styles from the drop-down menu.
  - **Face/surface**. Select from 11 arrow styles from the drop-down menu.
  - **Unattached**. Select from 11 arrow styles from the drop-down menu.

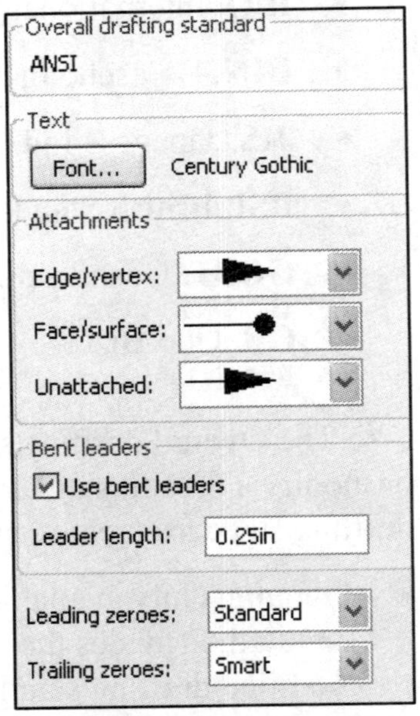


- ***Bend leaders***. Provides the following selections:
  - **Use bent leaders**. Selected by default. Deselect to enter leader length. Note: Modify from a default standard creates a modfied standard as illustrated.
  - **Leader length**. Default leader length is 0.25in for the IPS system and 6.35mm for the MMGS system.

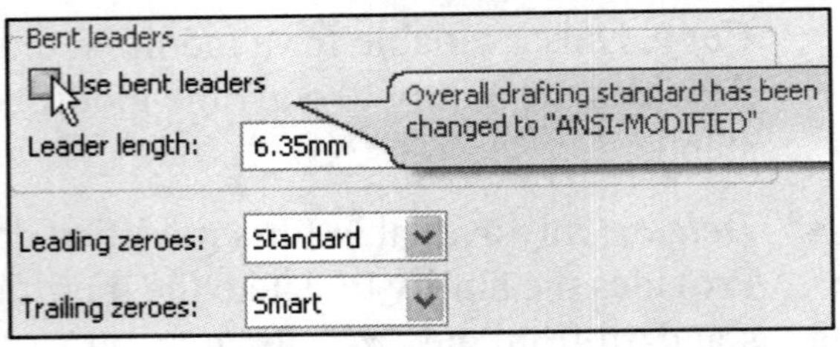


  - **Leading zeroes**. Standard selected by default. Select one of three options from the drop-down menu:
    - **Standard**. Zeros are displayed based on the selected dimensioning standard.
    - **Show**. Zeros before the decimal points are displayed on the selected dimensioning standard.
    - **Remove**. Zeros are not displayed.

  - **Trailing zeroes**. Provides the following selections:
    - **Smart**. Default setting. Trailing zeros are trimmed for whole metric values. Conforms to ANSI and ISO standards.
    - **Show**. Dimensions have trailing zeros up to the number of decimal places specified in **Options**, **Document Properties** and **Units**.

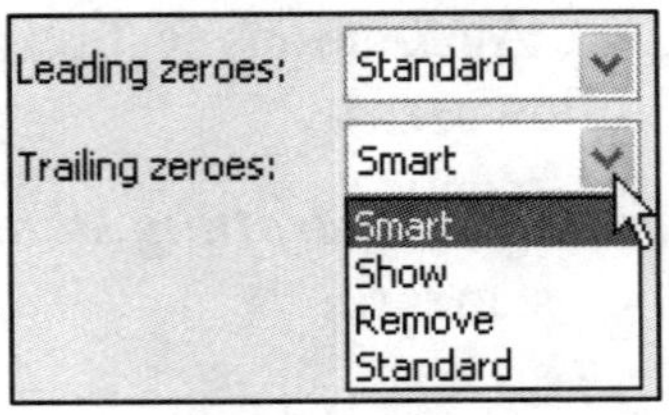

- **Remove**. All trailing zeros are removed.
- **Standard**. Trims trailing zeros to the ASME Y14.5M-1994 standard.

## Annotations – Balloons

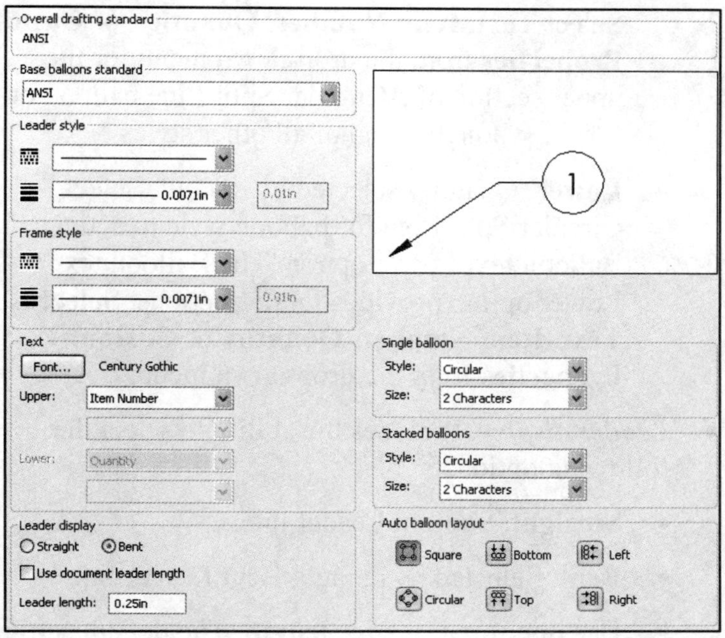


The Annotations – Balloons section provides the ability to set the default properties of balloons in a drawing document or in a note.

Create balloons in a drawing document or in a note. The balloons label the parts in the assembly and relate them to item numbers on the bill of materials (BOM).

You do not have to insert a BOM in order to add balloons. If the drawing has no BOM, the item numbers are the default values that the software would use if you did insert a BOM. If there is no BOM on the active sheet, but there is a BOM on another sheet, the numbers from that BOM are applied.

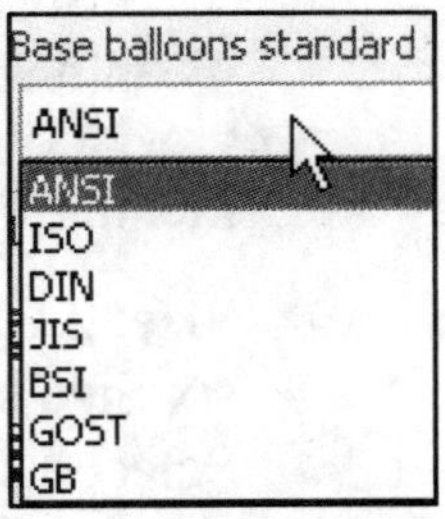


- ***Overall drafting standard***. Displays the selected drafting standard.
- ***Base balloons standard***. Provides the ability to select a default standard for an active Part, Assembly, or Drawing document from the drop-down menu or to create a custom Base balloons standard.
- ***Leader Style***. Provides the ability to use the default Leader style or to select a custom Leader style and thickness from the drop-down menus.
- ***Frame Style***. Provides the ability to use the default Frame style or to select a custom Frame style and thickness from the drop-down menus.

- ***Text***. Century Gothic selected by default. Click the Font button to select a custom font style and size. There are two options for Balloon text. They are:

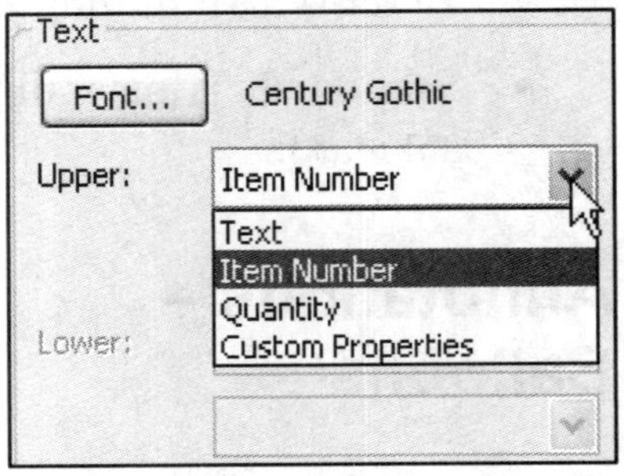


  - **Upper**. Item Number selected by default. There are four selections from the Upper Balloon text. Select **Text**, **Item Number**, **Quantity**, or **Custom Properties** from the drop-down menu for the upper section of a Circular Split Line balloon or for the whole balloon of all other styles.

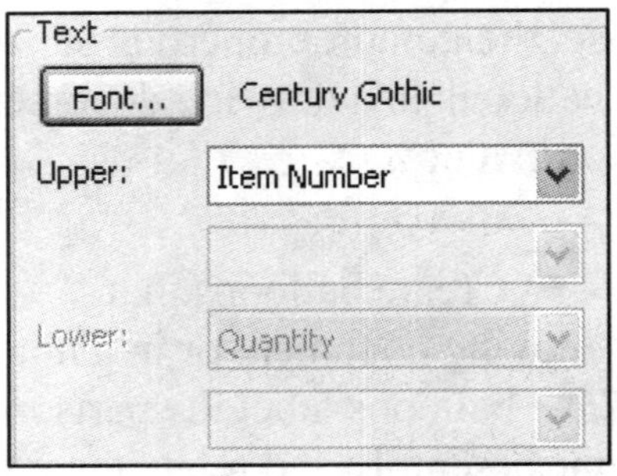


  - **Lower**. Quantity selected by default. Select Circular Split Line for balloon style to activate the Balloon text Lower option. The Balloon text Lower option provides four selections. **Select Text**, **Item Number**, **Quantity** or **Custom Properties** from the drop-down menu.

- ***Leader display***. Provides the ability to select the following options:

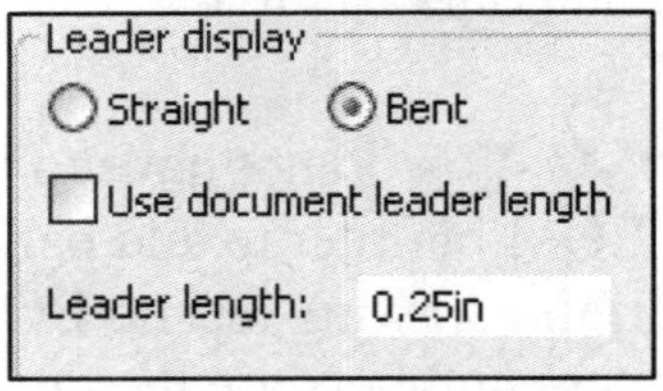


  - **Straight**. Straight Leader line.
  - **Bent**. Selected by default. Bent Leader line.
  - **Use document leader length**. The default setting is 0.25in for the IPS system and 6.35mm for the MMGS system. Provides the ability to enter a default value for the length of the leader nearest to the balloon.

- ***Single balloon***. Circular and 2 Characters selected by default. There are two selections for the Single balloon option:

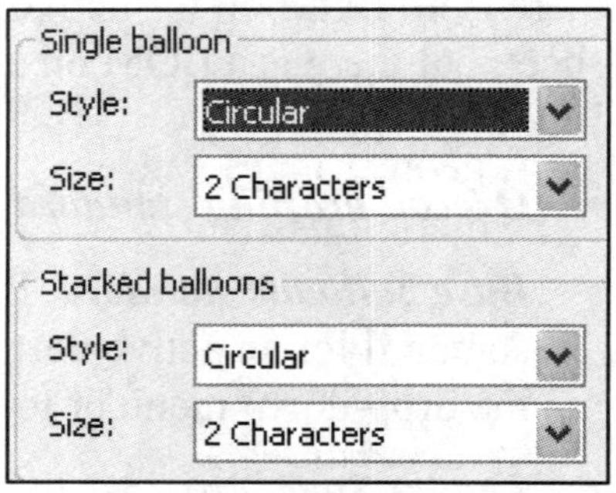


  - **Style**: Circular selected by default. There are eleven Style selections from the drop-down menu. Select a balloon style option.
  - **Size**: 2 Characters selected by default. There are six Size selections from the drop-down menu. Select a size to accommodate your requirements. Note: Select Tight Fit to adjust balloon size to the text or select the number of characters.

- ***Stacked balloons***. Circular and 2 Characters selected by default. There are two selections for the Stacked balloons option:
  - **Style**: There are ten Style selections from the drop-down menu. Select a balloon style.
  - **Size**: There are six Size options from the drop-down menu. Select a balloon size. Note: Select Tight Fit to adjust balloon size to the text or select the number of characters.

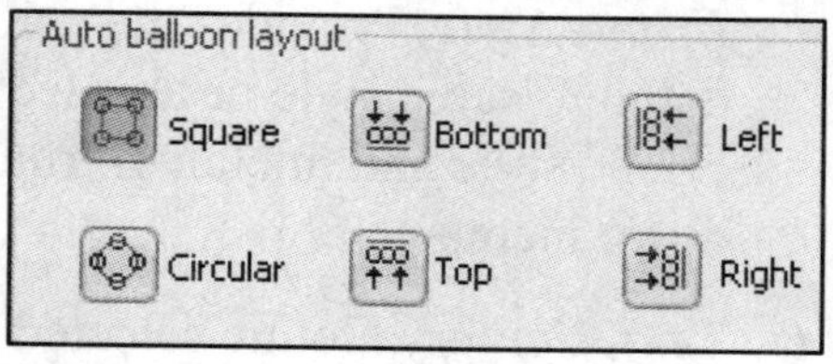


- ***Auto Balloon Layout***. Square layout selected by default. There are six selections for the Auto Balloon Layout option. The option provides the ability to select a layout as the default for inserting Auto Balloons. The six selections are: **Square**, **Bottom**, **Circular**, **Left**, **Top** and **Right**.

## Annotations – Datums

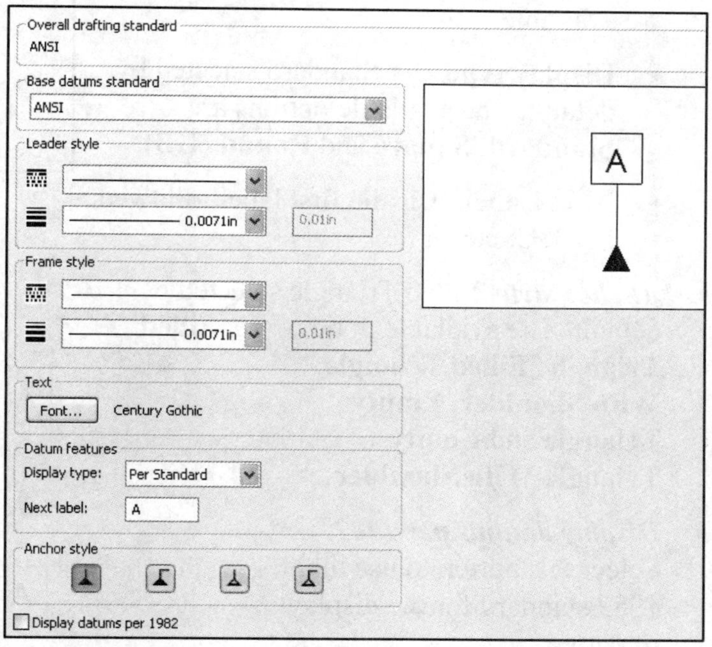


You can attach a datum feature symbol to the following items:

- A part or assembly
- On a planar model surface or on a reference plane
- In a drawing view
- On a surface that appears as an edge (not a silhouette) or on a section view surface
- A geometric tolerance symbol frame
- A note
- On a dimension, except for: Ordinate dimensions, Chamfer dimensions, Angular dimensions and Arc dimensions

The Annotations – Datums section provides the following selections:

- ***Overall drafting standard***. Displays the selected drafting standard.

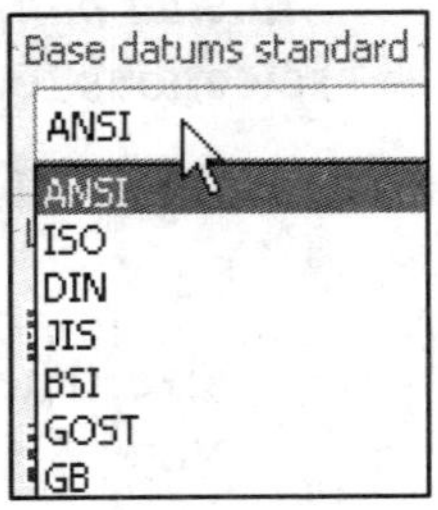


- ***Base datums standard***. Provides the ability to select a default standard for an active Part, Assembly or Drawing document from the drop-down menu or to create a custom Base datums standard.
- ***Leader Style***. Provides the ability to use the default Leader style or to select a custom Leader style and thickness from the drop-down menus.
- ***Frame Style***. Provides the ability to use the default Frame style or to select a custom Frame style and thickness from the drop-down menus.

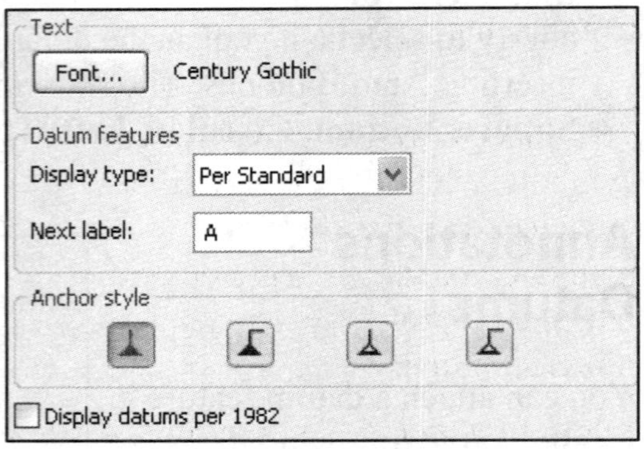


- ***Text***. Century Gothic selected by default. Click the Font button to select a custom font style and size.
- ***Datum features***. The following selections are available:
  - **Display type**. Per Standard selected by default. The available options are: **Standard, Square** and **Round (GB)**.
  - **Next Label**. A is the first label followed by B, C, etc.
- ***Anchor style***. Filled Triangle selected by default. The available options are: **Filled Triangle**, **Filled Triangle With Shoulder**, **Empty Triangle** and **Empty Triangle With Shoulder**.
- ***Display datums per 1982***. Select this option to use the 1982 standard for the display of datums.

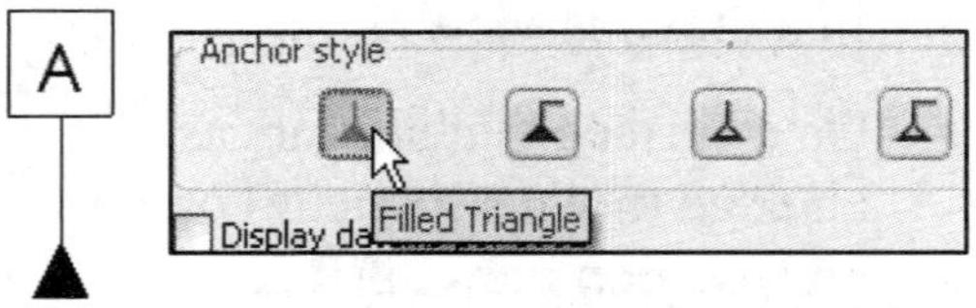

The Display datums per 1982 option only available if you select the American National Standards Institute, ANSI dimensioning standard.

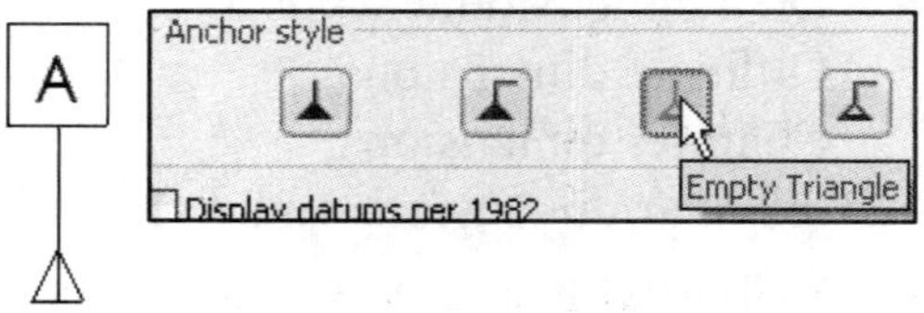

## Annotations – Geometric Tolerance

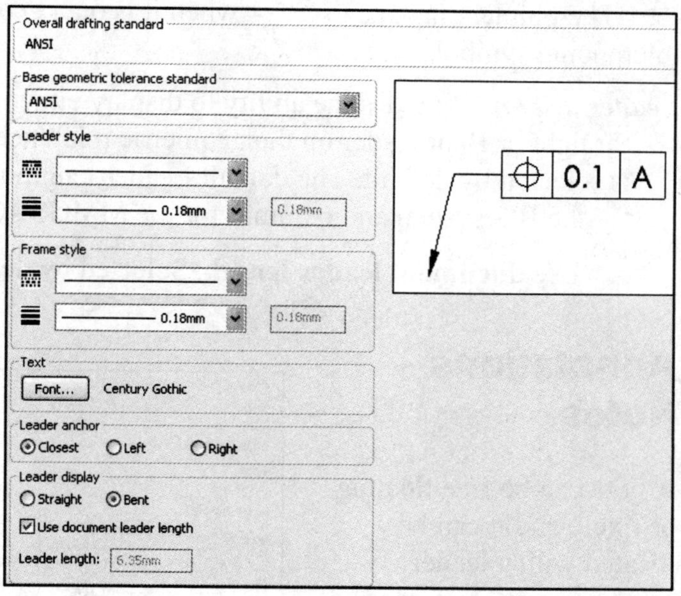


The Annotations – Geometric Tolerance section provides the ability to specify the properties when you create a geometric tolerance symbol. The SolidWorks software supports the ANSI Y14.5 Geometric and True Position Tolerancing guidelines.

Place Geometric tolerancing symbols, with or without leaders, anywhere in a drawing, part, assembly, or sketch, and you can attach a symbol anywhere on a dimension line.

The Annotations – Geometric Tolerance section provides the following selections:

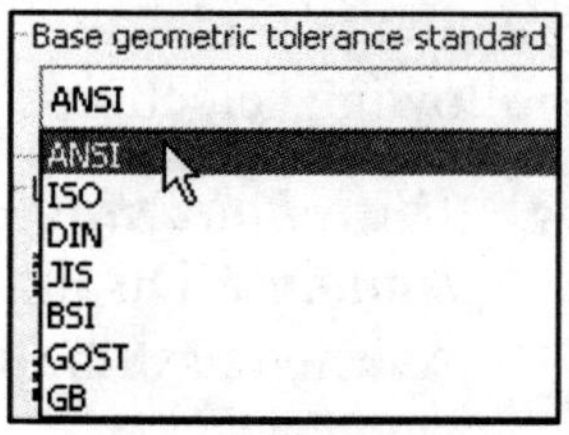


- ***Overall drafting standard***. Displays the selected drafting standard.
- ***Base geometric tolerance standard***. Provides the ability to select a default standard for an active Part, Assembly or Drawing document from the drop-down menu or to create a custom Base geometric tolerance standard.
- ***Leader Style***. Provides the ability to use the default Leader style or to select a custom Leader style and thickness from the drop-down menu.
- ***Frame Style***. Provides the ability to use the default Frame style or to select a custom Frame style and thickness from the drop-down menu.
- ***Text***. Century Gothic selected by default. Click the Font button to select a custom font style and size.
- ***Leader anchor***. Anchor the leader to the specified location on the geometric tolerance. Closest this selected by default. The three options are: **Closest**, **Left** and **Right**.

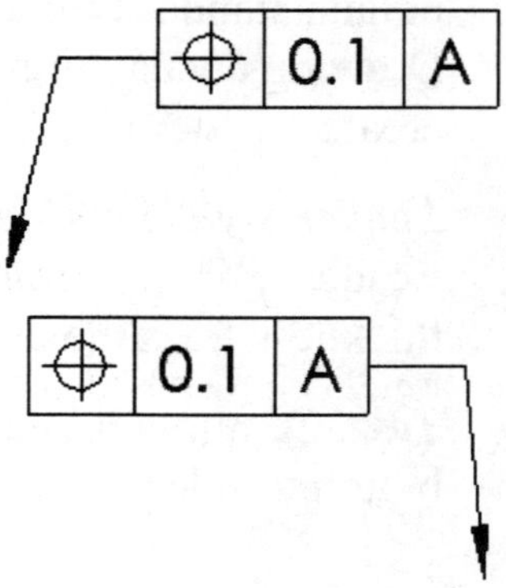

The pointer changes to when it is on a geometric tolerancing symbol.

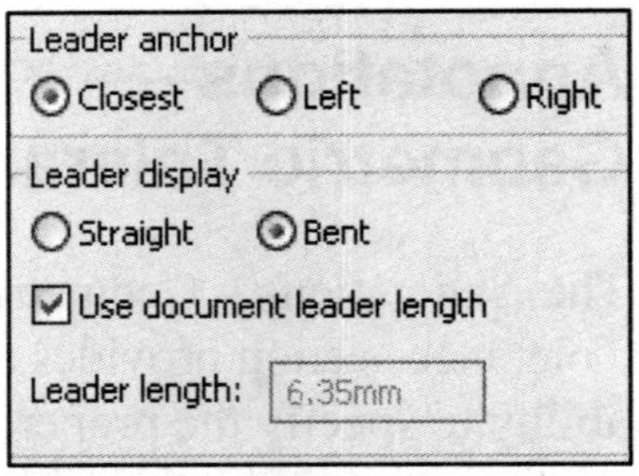


***Leader display***. Provides the ability to display either a Straight or Bent leader on the geometric tolerance. Bent is selected by default. The default Leader length is .25in for the IPS system and 6.35mm for the MMGS system.

- **Use document leader length**. Selected by default.

## Annotations – Notes

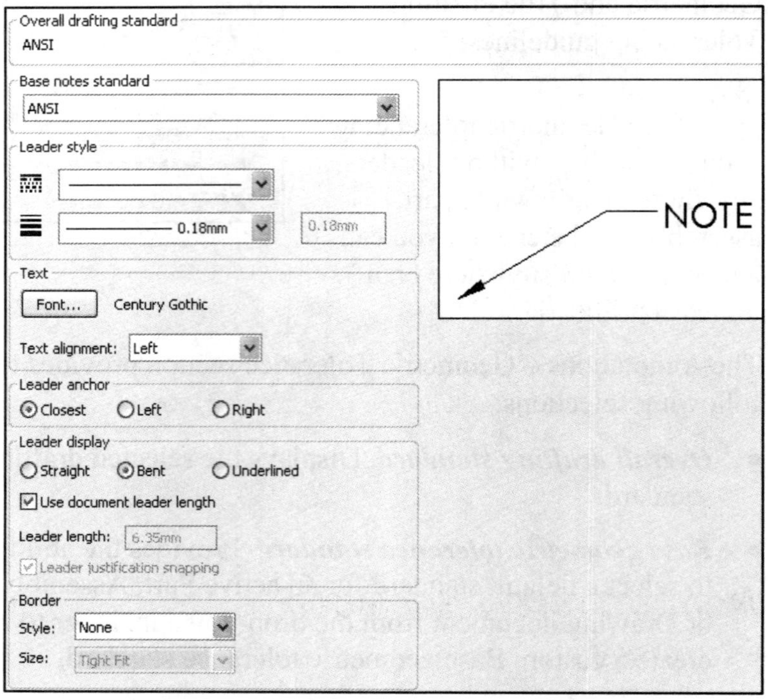


A note can be free floating or fixed, and it can be located with a leader pointing to an item, face, edge, or vertex in the document. It can also contain simple text, symbols, parametric text, and hyperlinks.

The Annotations - Notes section provides the following selections:

- ***Overall drafting standard***. Displays the selected drafting standard.
- ***Base notes standard***. Provides the ability to select a default standard for an active Part, Assembly or Drawing document from the drop-down menu or to create a custom Base notes standard.

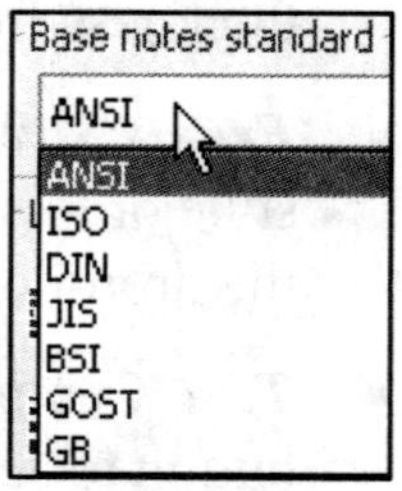


- ***Leader Style***. Provides the ability to use the default Leader style or to select a custom Leader style and thickness from the drop-down menus.
- ***Text***. Century Gothic selected by default. Click the Font button to select a custom font style and size.

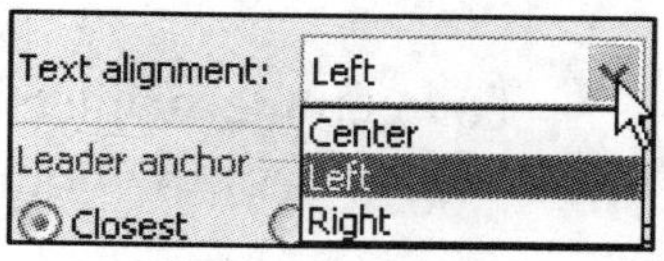


- **Text alignment**. Left is selected by default. The three options are: **Center**, **Left** and **Right**.

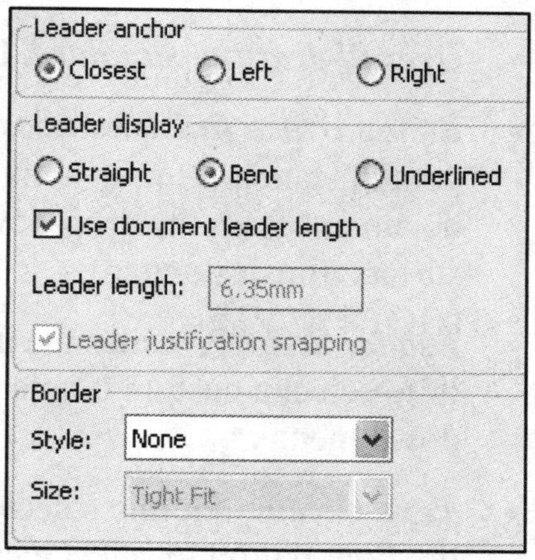


- ***Leader anchor***. Anchor the leader to the specified location on the note. Closest this selected by default. The three options are: **Closest**, **Left** and **Right**.
- ***Leader display***. Provides the ability to display either a Straight, Bent, or Underlined leader on the note. Bent is selected by default. The default Leader length is .25in for the IPS system and 6.35mm for the MMGS system.
  - **Use document leader length**. Selected by default.
- ***Border***. Provides the ability to insert a border around the note.
  - **Style**. None selected Style by default. Select a border style from the drop-down menu as illustrated.
  - **Size**. Select a border size from the drop-down menu as illustrated.

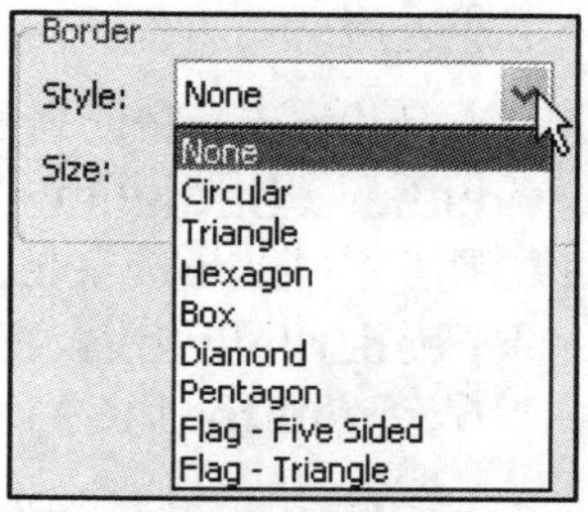


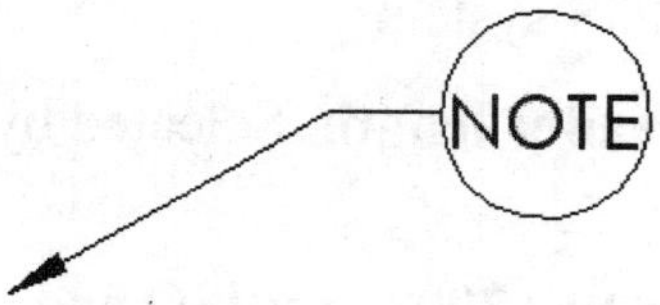


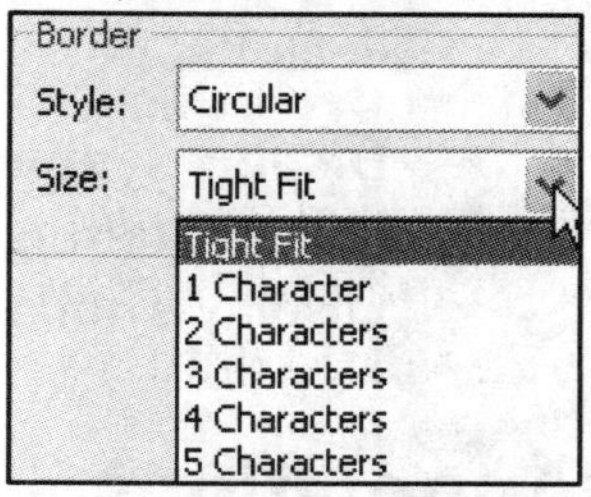


## Annotations – Surfaces Finishes

Specify the surface texture of a part face by using a surface finish symbol. Select the face in a part, assembly or drawing document.

Drag a surface finish symbol with a leader to any location. If you attach a leaderless symbol to an edge, then drag it off the model edge, an extension line is created.

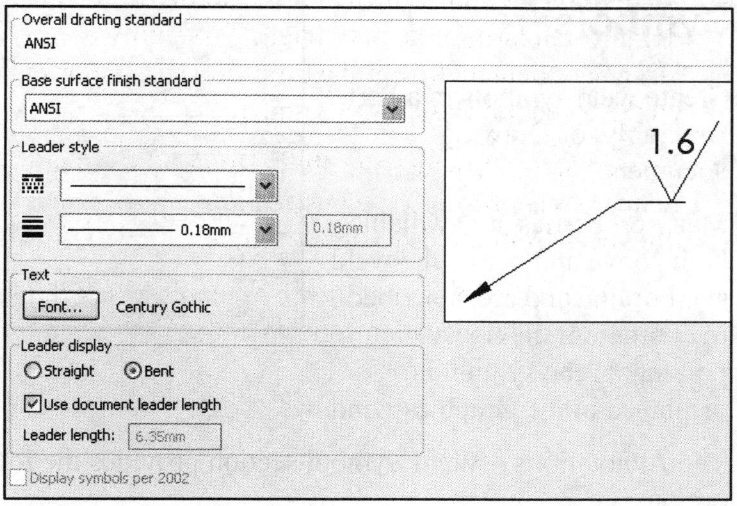

To keep the surface finish symbol locked on an edge, drag the symbol from anywhere except the bottommost handle.

The Annotations – Surface Finishes section provides the following options:

- ***Overall drafting standard***. Displays the selected drafting standard.
- ***Base surface finish standard***. Provides the ability to select a default standard for an active Part, Assembly or Drawing document from the drop-down menu or to create a custom Base surface finish standard.

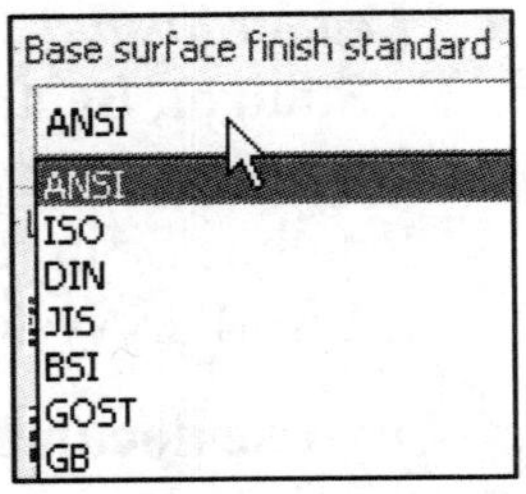


- ***Leader Style***. Provides the ability to use the default Leader style or to select a custom Leader style and thickness from the drop-down menus.
- ***Text***. Century Gothic selected by default. Click the Font button to select a custom font style and size.

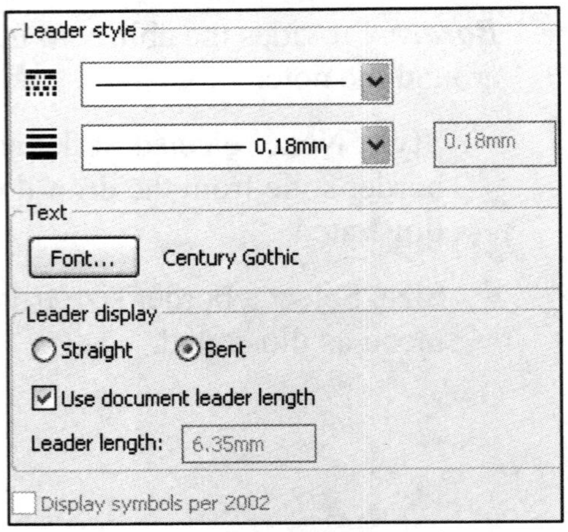


- ***Leader display***. Provides the ability to display either a Straight or Bent leader on the surface finish. Bent is selected by default. The default Leader length is .25in for the IPS system and 6.35mm for the MMGS system.
  - **Use document leader length**. Selected by default.
  - **Display symbols per 2002**. For ISO and related drafting standards, you can specify Display symbols per 2002.

## Annotations – Weld Symbols

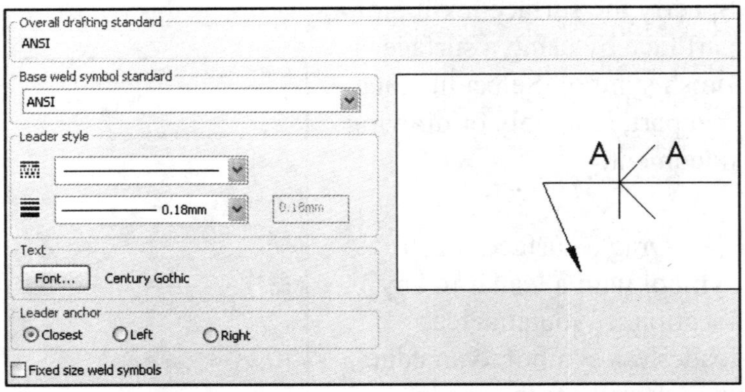


Create weld symbols in a Part, Assembly, or Drawing document.

Many properties are available both above and below the weld symbol line and are described in order from the line. A preview of the symbol is displayed in the Graphics window.

The Annotations – Weld Symbol section provides the following options:

- ***Overall drafting standard***. Displays the selected drafting standard.
- ***Base weld symbol standard***. Provides the ability to select a default standard for an active Part, Assembly or Drawing document from the drop-down menu or to create a custom Base weld symbol standard.
- ***Leader Style***. Provides the ability to use the default Leader style or to select a custom Leader style and thickness from the drop-down menu.

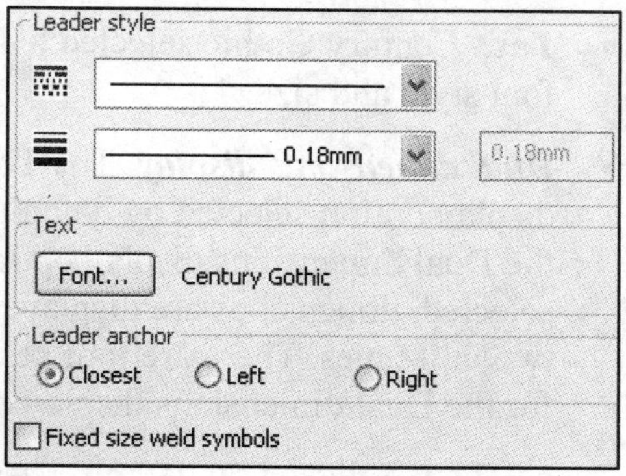


- ***Text***. Century Gothic selected by default. Click the Font button to select a custom font style and size.
- ***Leader anchor***. Anchor the leader to the specified location on the note. Closest selected by default. The three options are: **Closest**, **Left** and **Right**.

# Dimensions

The Dimensions section has eight sub-sections: *Angle, Arc Length, Chamfer, Diameter, Hole Callout, Linear, Ordinate and Radius.* Note: See the Drawing document section for additional information.

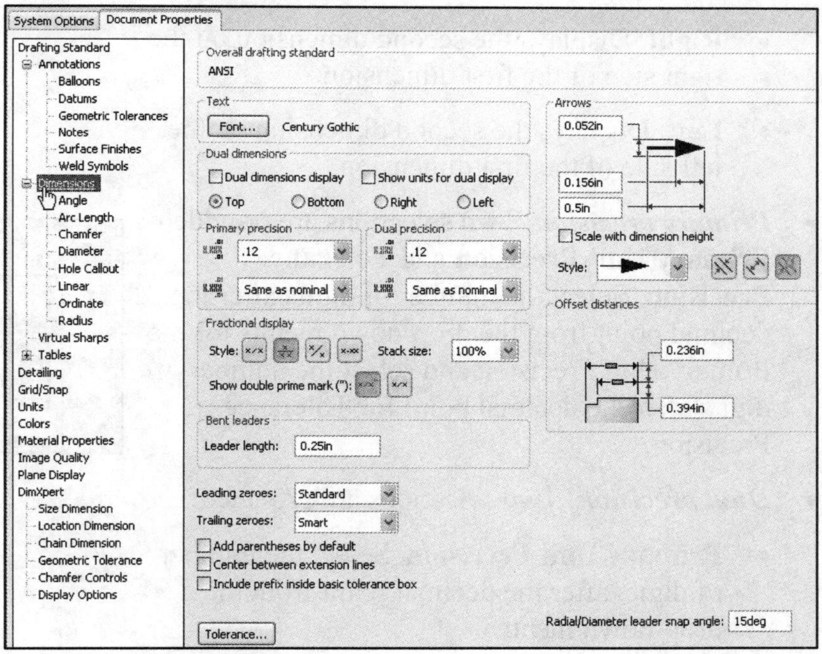


The Dimensions section provides the ability to set various options for dimensioning in an active document. The Dimensions/Relations toolbar and the Tools, Dimensions and Tools, Relations menus provide tools to dimension and to add and delete Geometric relations.

The type of dimension is determined by the items you select. For some types of dimensions, point-to-point, angular, and circular, where you place the dimension also affects the type of dimension that is applied.

- ***Overall drafting standard***. Displays the selected drafting standard.
- ***Text***. Century Gothic selected by default. Click the Font button to select a custom font style and size.
- ***Dual dimensions display***. The Top display option selected by default. When the Dual dimensions display option is selected, dimensions are displayed in two unit types. There are four selections for the Dual dimensions display option:

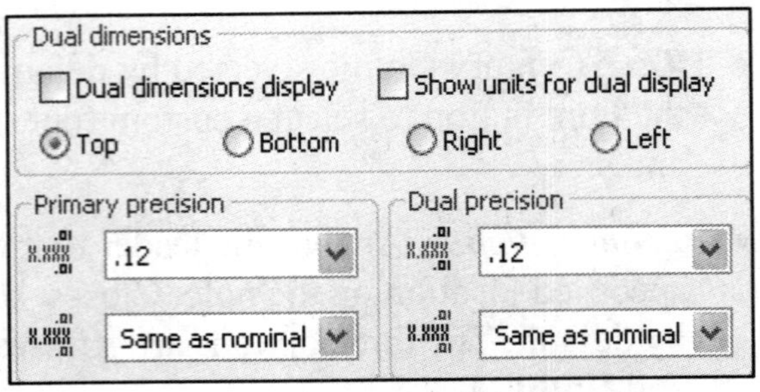


  - **Top**. Selected by default. Displays the second dimension on the top of the first dimension.
  - **Bottom**. Displays the second dimension on the bottom of the first dimension.
  - **Right**. Displays the second dimension on the right side of the first dimension.
  - **Left**. Displays the second dimension on the left side of the first dimension.
- ***Primary precision***. Two selections are provided: **Primary Unit Precision** and **Tolerance Precision**. Select the number of digits after the decimal point from the drop-down menus for the Primary Unit Precision and select the number of digits after the decimal point for Tolerance Precision.

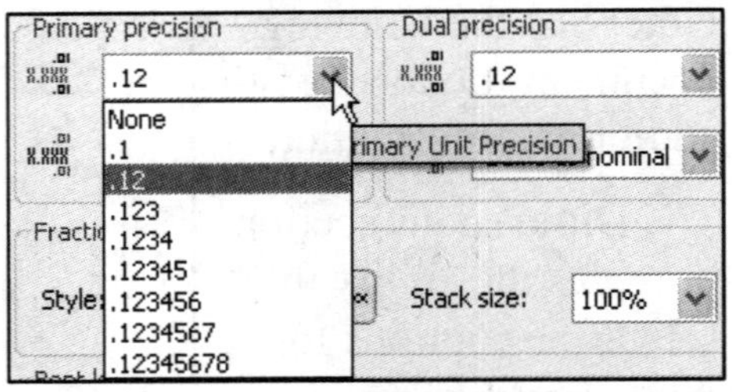


- ***Dual precision***. Two selections are provided:
  - **Primary Unit Precision**. Select the number of digits after the decimal point from the drop-down menu.
  - **Tolerance Precision**. Select the number of digits after the decimal point from the drop-down menu.

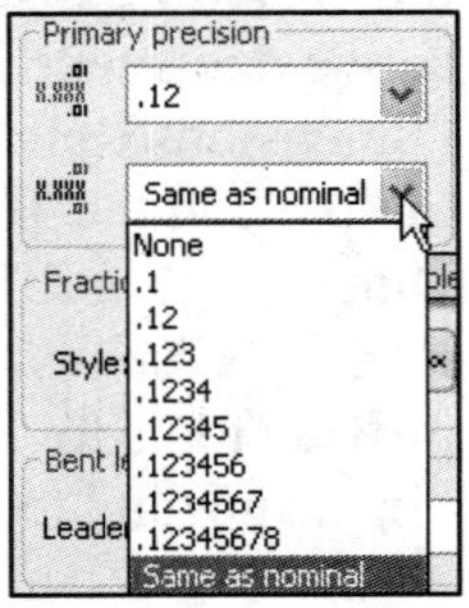

- ***Fractional display***. Fractional dimensions are available only for lengths in IPS (inch-pound-second) units. View the illustration for Style and Stack size.

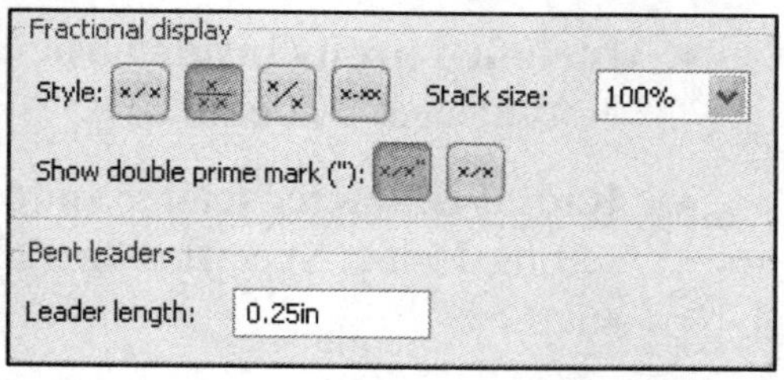


- ***Bent leaders***. Enter the length of the unbent portion of the leader. The default leader length is 0.25in for the IPS system and 6.35mm for the MMGS system.

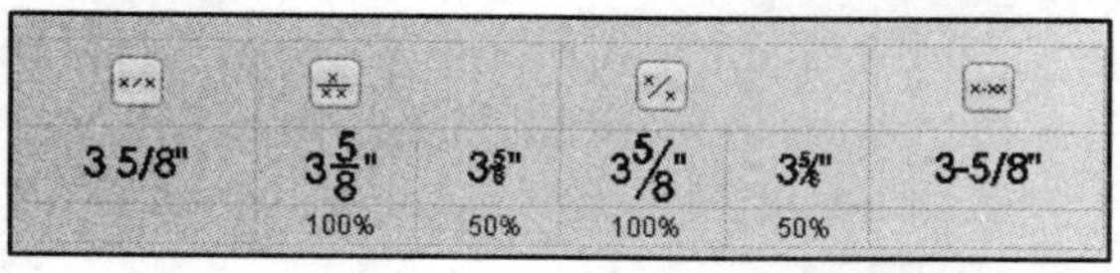


  - **Leading zeroes**. Standard selected by default. Select one of three options from the drop-down menu:

    - **Standard**. Zeros are displayed based on the selected dimensioning standard.
    - **Show**. Zeros before the decimal points are displayed on the selected dimensioning standard.
    - **Remove**. Zeros are not displayed.
  - **Trailing zeroes**. Provides the following selections:

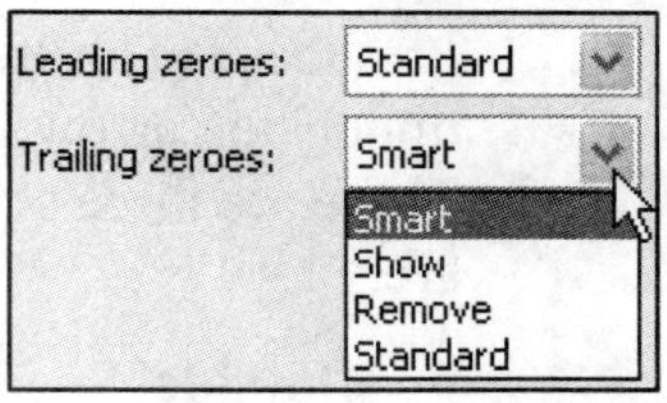


    - **Smart**. Selected by default. Trailing zeros are trimmed for whole metric values. Conforms to ANSI and ISO standards.
    - **Show**. Dimensions have trailing zeros up to the number of decimal places specified in **Options, Document Properties, Units**.
    - **Remove**. Trailing zeros are removed
    - **Standard**. Trims trailing zeros to the ASME Y14.5M-1994 standard.
  - **Add parentheses by default**. Provides the ability to display reference dimensions in a drawing with parentheses.

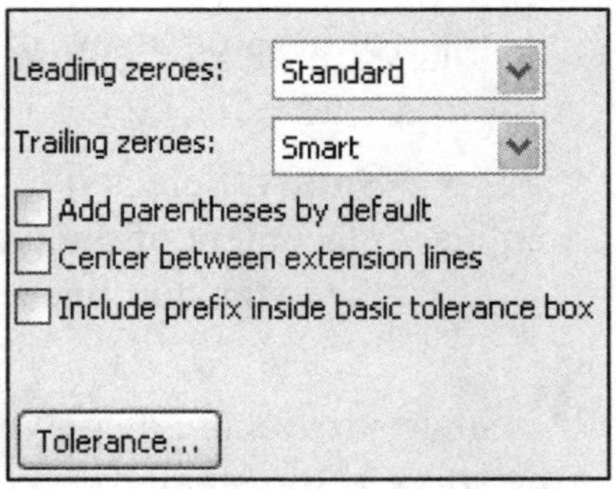


  - **Center between extension lines**. Provides the ability to center dimensions between the extension lines.

- **Included prefix inside basic tolerance box**. Not selected by default.
- **Radial/Diameter leader snap angle**. Default setting 15deg. Specifies the radial angle of the snap.

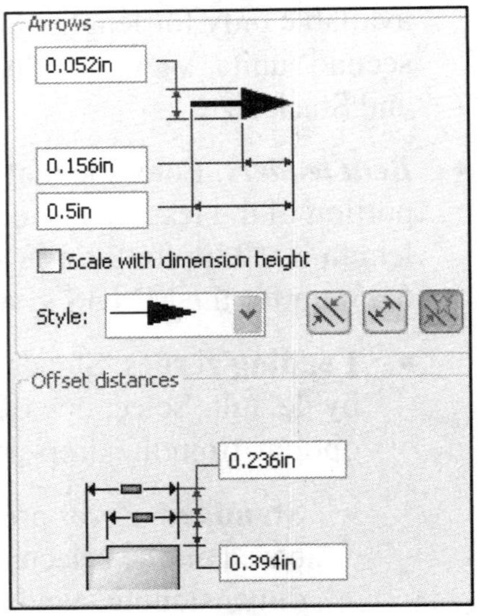


- ***Arrows***. The Arrows selection provides the ability to set the display options for arrows which are used in drawings. The default option is drafting standard dependent.
  - **Size**. The default height of the arrowhead is 0.04in, (1.02mm). The default width of the arrowhead is 0.13in, (3.3mm). The default complete arrow is .25in, (6.35mm). The size boxes provides the ability to specify the height and width of the arrowhead, and the length of the complete arrow, for leaders on notes, dimensions, and other drawing annotations.
  - **Scale with dimension height**.

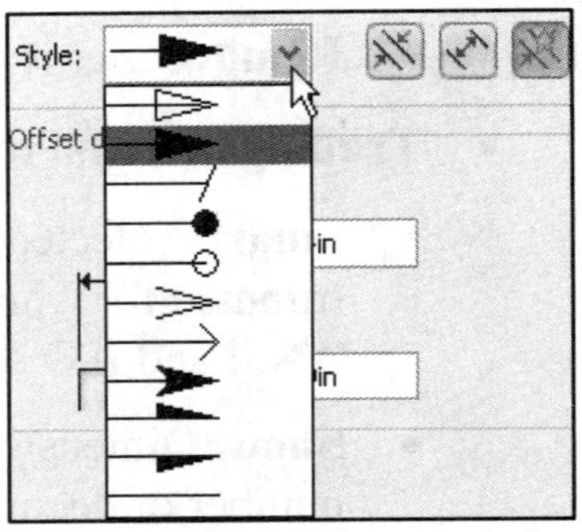


  - ***Style***. The default style is solid filled with Smart. Provides the ability to specify the placement of the dimension arrow in relation to the extension lines. There are three selections for the Style option. They are:
    - **Outside**. Specifies the outside placement of the dimension arrow in relation to the extension lines.
    - **Inside**. Specifies the inside placement of the dimension arrow in relation to the extension lines.
    - **Smart**. Selected by default. Specifies the placement of the dimension arrow in relation to the extension lines.

Smart arrows are displayed outside of extension lines, if the space is too small to accommodate the dimension and the arrowheads.

  - ***Offset distances***. The default Offset distances is 0.24in, (6mm) and 0.39in, (10mm) respectively using the ANSI standard. Provides the ability to specify values for the distances between baseline dimensions. Baseline dimensions are reference dimensions used in a drawing. You cannot change their values or use the values to drive the model.

## Dimensions – Angle

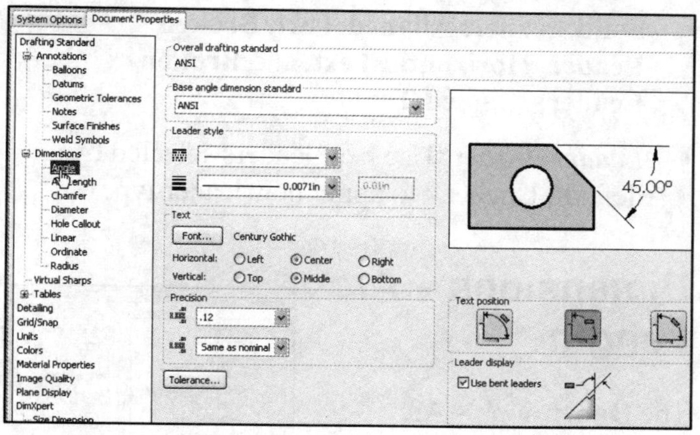


The Dimensions – Angle section provides the ability to place an angular dimension between two lines or a line and a model edge. Select the two entities, then move the pointer to observe the dimension preview.

The angle to be dimensioned changes based on the pointer position.

The Dimensions – Angle section provides the following options:

- ***Overall drafting standard***. Displays the selected drafting standard.
- ***Base angle dimension standard***. Provides the ability to select a default standard for an active Part, Assembly, or Drawing document from the drop-down menu or to create a custom Base angle dimension standard.
- ***Leader Style***. Provides the ability to use the default Leader style or to select a custom Leader style and thickness from the drop-down menu.
- ***Text***. Century Gothic selected by default. Click the Font button to select a custom font style and size. The Text options provides the following locations relative to the angle:

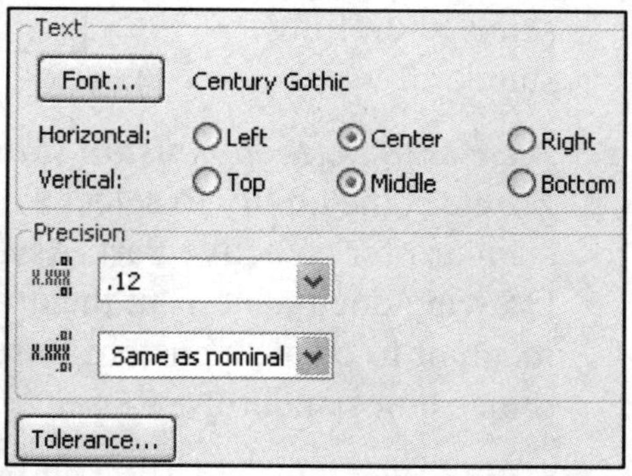


  - **Horizontal. Left, Center, Right**
  - **Vertical. Top, Middle, Bottom**
- ***Precision***. Two selections are provided: **Unit Precision** and **Tolerance Precision**. Select the number of digits after the decimal point from the drop-down menu for the Primary Unit Precision and select the number of digits after the decimal point for Tolerance Precision.

- ***Tolerance***. Select the Tolerance button to access the Tolerance dialog box.

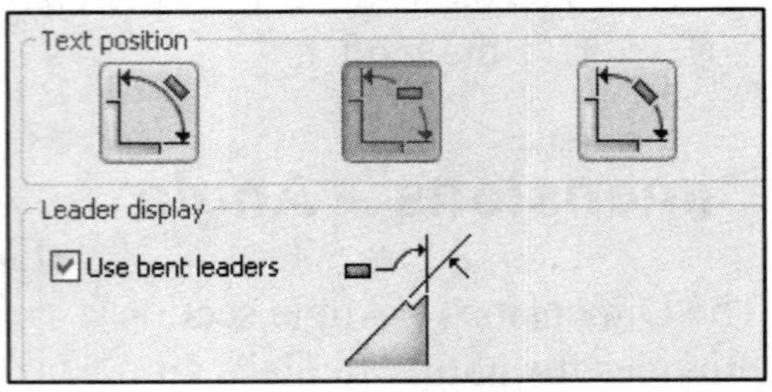


- ***Text position***. Broken Leader, Horizontal Text selected by default. The options are: **Solid Leader**, **Aligned Text**, **Broken Leader**, **Horizontal Text**, and **Broken Leader**, **Aligned Text**.
- ***Leader display***. Use bent leaders selected by default. Uncheck to apply new leader type.

## Dimensions – Arc Length

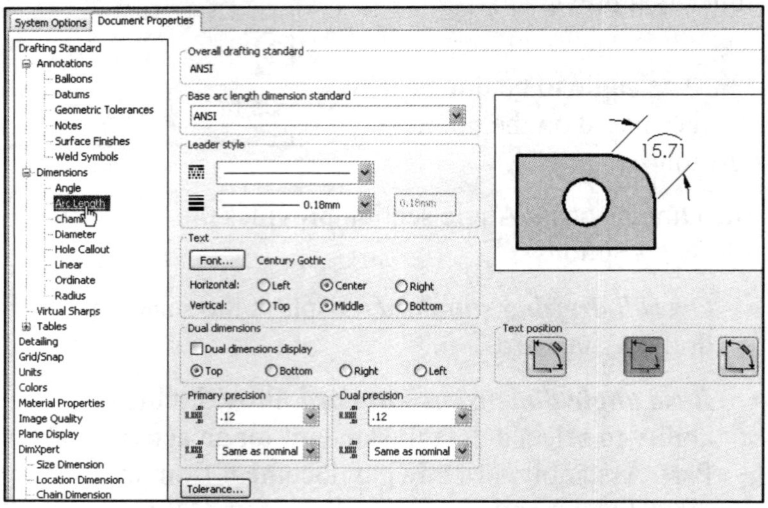


The Dimensions – Arc Length section provides the ability to dimension the true length of an arc. The Dimensions – Angle section provides the following options:

- ***Overall drafting standard***. Displays the selected drafting standard.
- ***Base arc length dimension standard***. Provides the ability to select a default standard for an active Part, Assembly, or Drawing document from the drop-down menu or to create a custom Base arc length dimension standard.

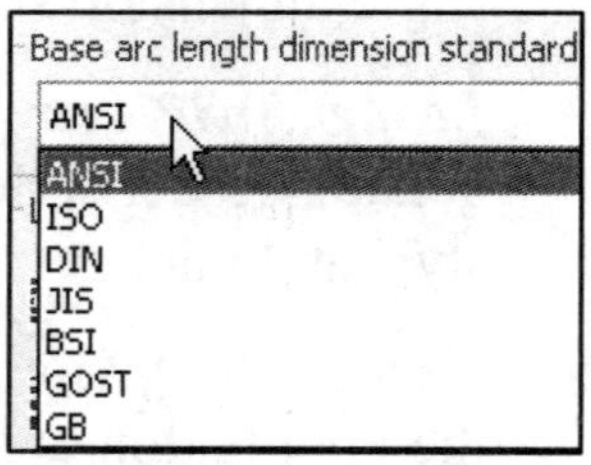


- ***Leader Style***. Provides the ability to use the default Leader style or to select a custom Leader style and thickness from the drop-down menus.
- ***Text***. Century Gothic selected by default. Click the Font button to select a custom font style and size. The Text options provides the following locations relative to the angle length:
  - **Horizontal**. **Left**, **Center**, **Right**

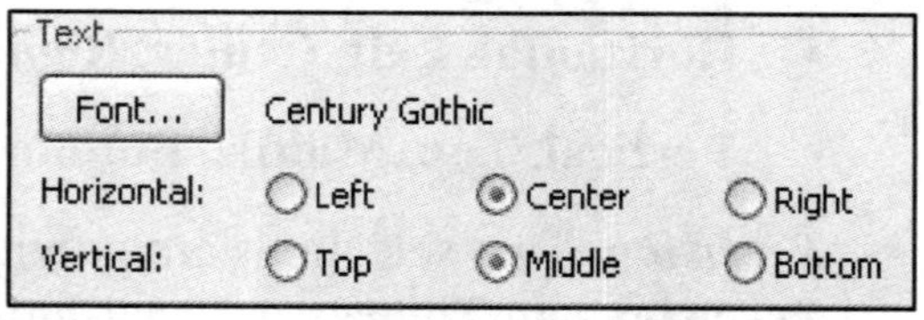

- **Vertical**. **Top, Middle, Bottom**

- ***Dual dimensions display***. The Top display option selected by default. When the Dual dimensions display option is selected, dimensions are displayed in two unit types. There are four selections for the Dual dimensions display option:

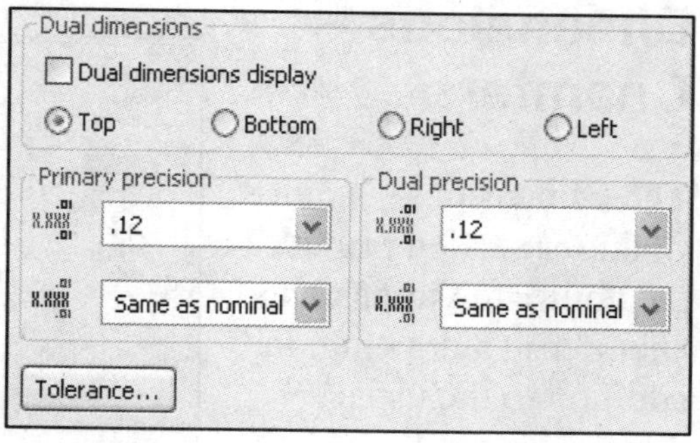


  - **Top**. Selected by default. Displays the second dimension on the top of the first dimension.
  - **Bottom**. Displays the second dimension on the bottom of the first dimension.
  - **Right**. Displays the second dimension on the right side of the first dimension.
  - **Left**. Displays the second dimension on the left side of the first dimension.

- ***Primary precision***. Two selections are provided: **Primary Unit Precision** and **Tolerance Precision**. Select the number of digits after the decimal point from the drop-down menus for the Primary Unit Precision and select the number of digits after the decimal point for Tolerance Precision.

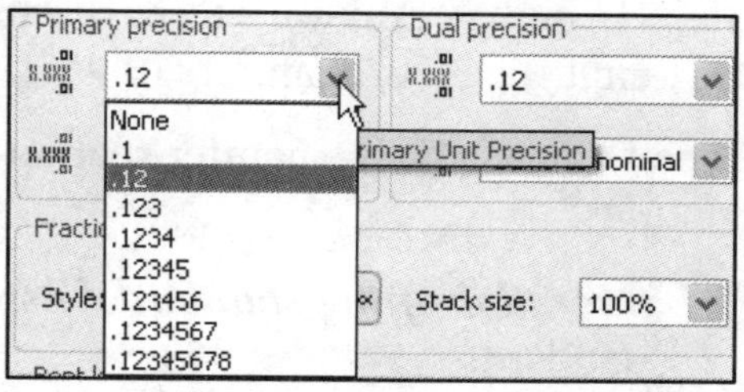


- ***Dual precision***. Two selections are provided:

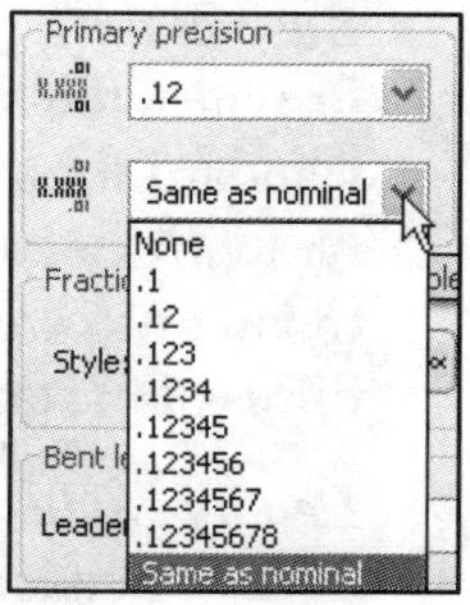


  - **Primary Unit Precision**. Select the number of digits after the decimal point from the drop-down menu.
  - **Tolerance Precision**. Select the number of digits after the decimal point from the drop-down menu.
  - ***Tolerance***. Select the Tolerance button to access the Tolerance dialog box.
  - ***Text position***. Broken Leader, Horizontal Text selected by default. The options are: **Solid Leader, Aligned Text, Broken Leader, Horizontal Text**, and **Broken Leader, Aligned Text**.

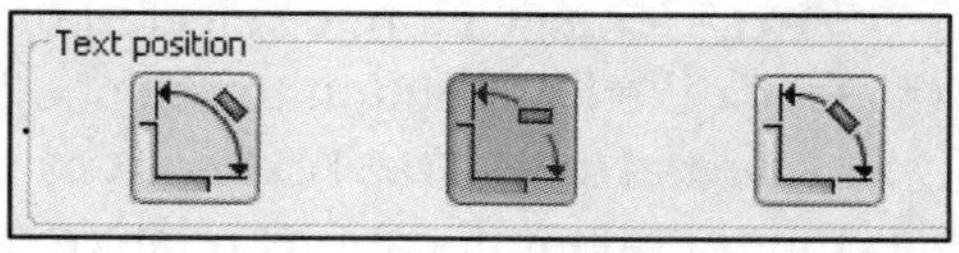

## Dimensions – Chamfer

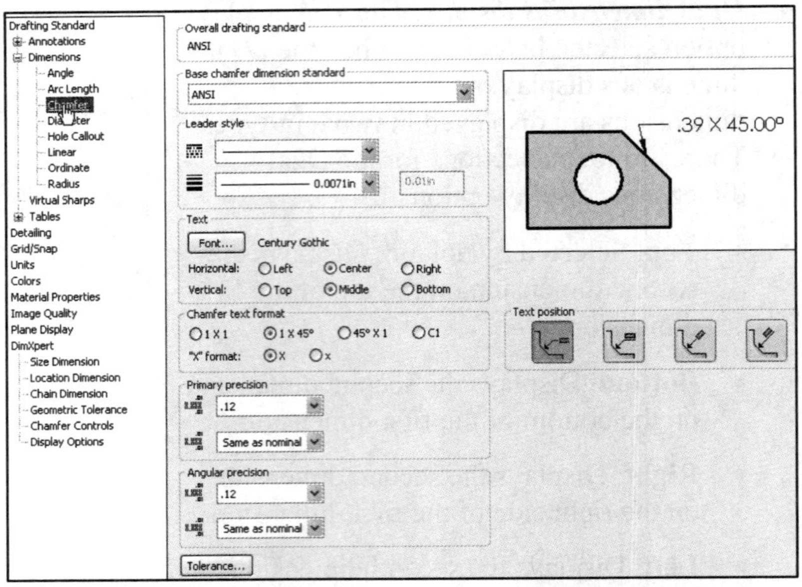


The Dimensions – Chamfer section provides the ability to dimension a chamfer in a drawing. In addition to the usual dimension display properties, chamfer dimensions have their own options for leader display, text display, and X display. X display is the size of the X in a chamfer dimension with two numbers, such as 1 X 45° (Length X Angle), 45° X 1 (Angle X Length), 1 X 1 (Length X Length) or C1 (chamfers of 45°).

The Dimensions – Chamfer section provides the following options:

- ***Overall drafting standard***. Displays the selected drafting standard.

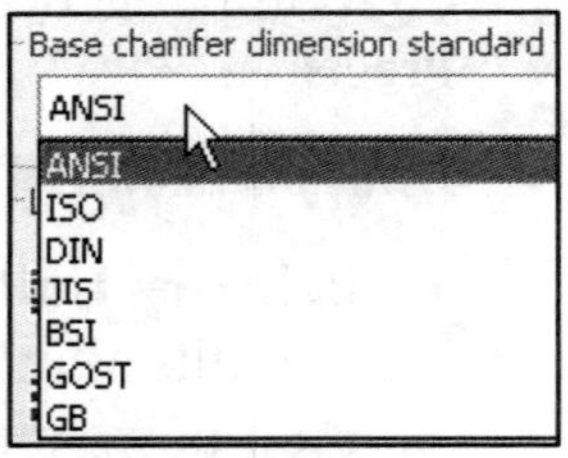


- ***Base chamfer dimension standard***. Provides the ability to select a default standard for an active Part, Assembly, or Drawing document from the drop-down menu or to create a custom Base chamfer dimension standard.

- ***Leader Style***. Provides the ability to use the default Leader style or to select a custom Leader style and thickness from the drop-down menus.

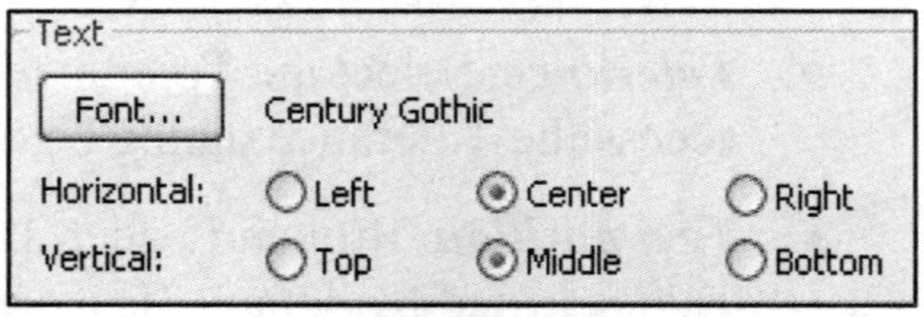


- ***Text***. Century Gothic selected by default. Click the Font button to select a custom font style and size. The Text options provides the following locations relative to the chamfer:
  - **Horizontal**. **Left**, **Center**, **Right**
  - **Vertical**. **Top**, **Middle**, **Bottom**

- ***Chamfer text format***. Provides the ability to dimension the chamfer with a leader display, text display, and X display. X display is the size of the X in a chamfer dimension with two numbers, such as 1 X 45° (Length X Angle), 45° X 1 (Angle X Length), 1 X 1 (Length X Length) or C1 (chamfers of 45°).

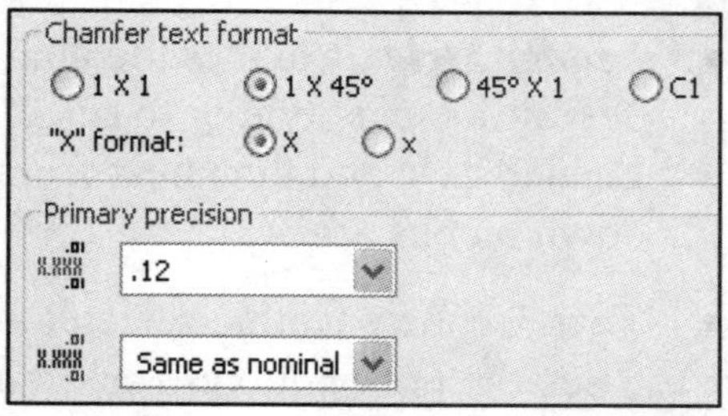


- ***Primary precision***. Two selections provided: **Primary Unit Precision** and **Tolerance Precision**. Select the number of digits after the decimal point from the drop-down menu for the Primary Unit Precision and select the number of digits after the decimal point for Tolerance Precision.

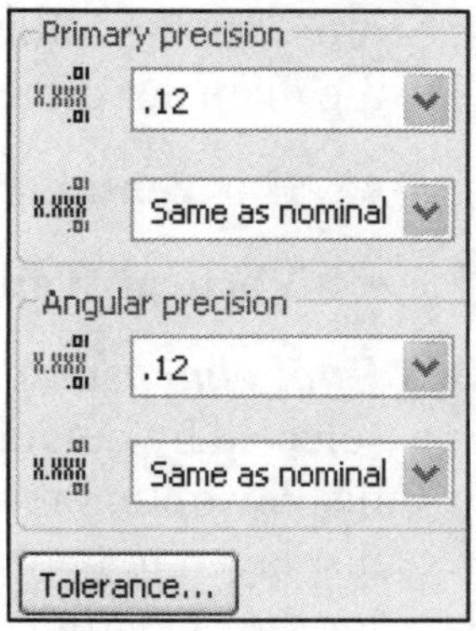


- ***Angular precision***. Two selections provided: **Primary Unit Precision** and **Tolerance Precision**. Select the number of digits after the decimal point from the drop-down menus for the Primary Unit Precision and select the number of digits after the decimal point for Tolerance Precision

- ***Tolerance***. Select the Tolerance button to access the Tolerance dialog box.

- ***Text position***. Provides the following text position for the chamfer dimension. Horizontal Text, Underlined Text selected by default. The available selections are: **Horizontal Text, Horizontal, Underlined Text, Angled Text, Angled, Underlined Text.**

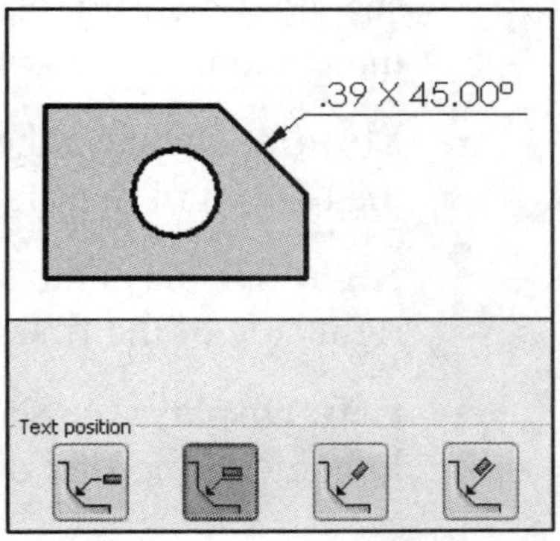


Tolerance types for chamfer dimensions are limited to **None**, **Bilateral**, and **Symmetric**.

## Dimensions – Diameter

The Dimensions – Diameter section provides the following options:

- ***Overall drafting standard***. Displays the selected drafting standard.

- ***Base diameter dimension standard***. Provides the ability to select a default standard for an active Part, Assembly, or Drawing document from the drop-down menu or to create a custom Base diameter dimension standard.

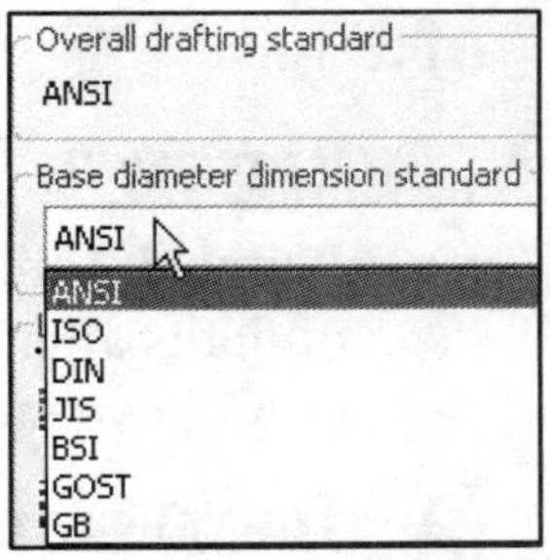

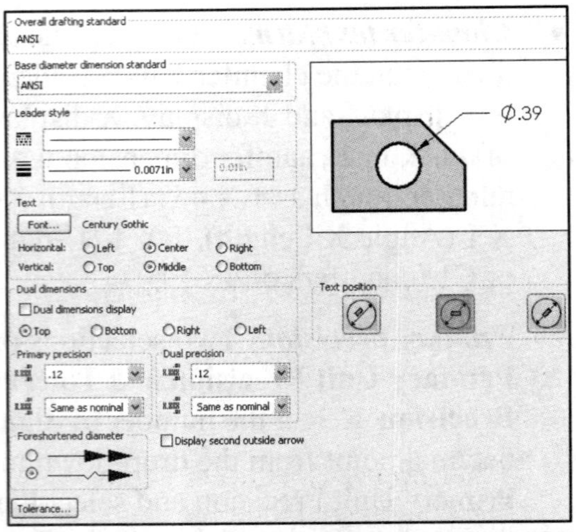


- ***Leader Style***. Provides the ability to use the default Leader style or to select a custom Leader style and thickness from the drop-down menus.
- ***Text***. Century Gothic selected by default. Click the Font button to select a custom font style and size. The Text options provides the following locations relative to the diameter dimension:
  - **Horizontal. Left, Center, Right**
  - **Vertical. Top, Middle, Bottom**

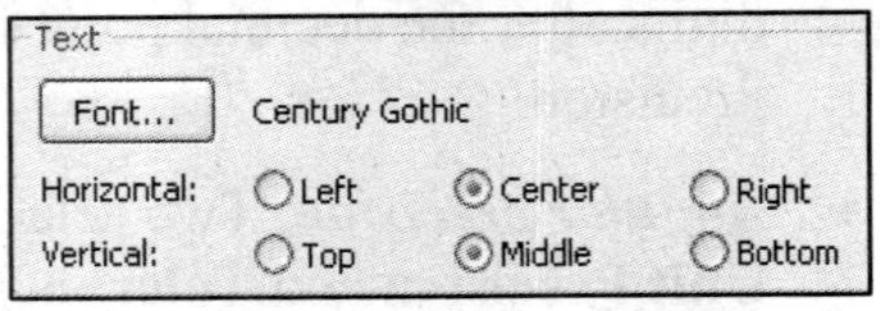


- ***Dual dimensions display***. Top display option selected by default. When the Dual dimensions display option is selected, dimensions are displayed in two unit types. The four selections for the Dual dimensions display option are:
  - **Top**. Selected by default. Displays the second dimension on the top of the first dimension.
  - **Bottom**. Displays the second dimension on the bottom of the first dimension.
  - **Right**. Displays the second dimension on the right side of the first dimension.
  - **Left**. Displays the second dimension on the left side of the first dimension.

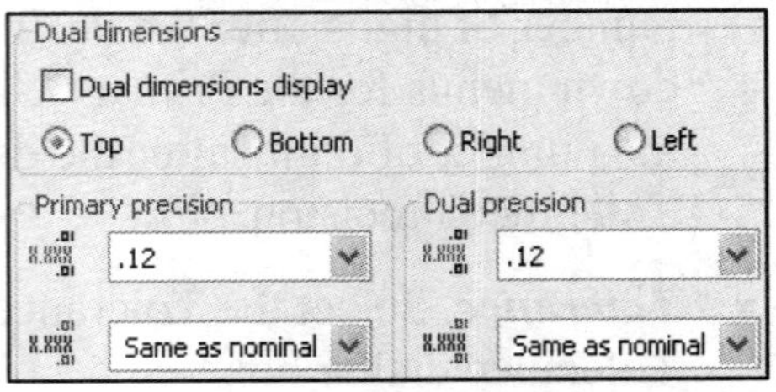


- ***Primary precision***. Two selections are provided: **Primary Unit Precision** and **Tolerance Precision**. Select the number of digits after the decimal point from the drop-down menu for the Primary Unit Precision and select the number of digits after the decimal point for Tolerance Precision.

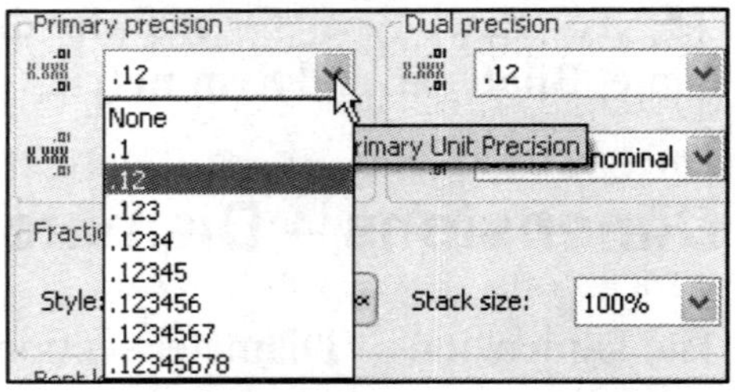


- ***Dual precision***. Two selections are provided:
  - **Primary Unit Precision**. Select the number of digits after the decimal point from the drop-down menus.
  - **Tolerance Precision**. Select the number of digits after the decimal point from the drop-down menu.

- ***Foreshortended diameter***. The default option is Zigzag selected by the ANSI standard. The Foreshortened diameter option provides two selections. The selections are: **Double arrow** and **Zigzag arrow**.

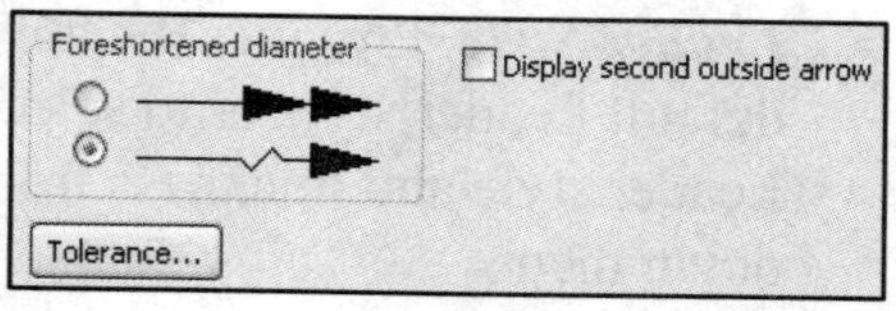


Create foreshortened diameters in drawing documents. When SolidWorks detects that the diameter is too large for the drawing view, the dimension is automatically foreshortened.

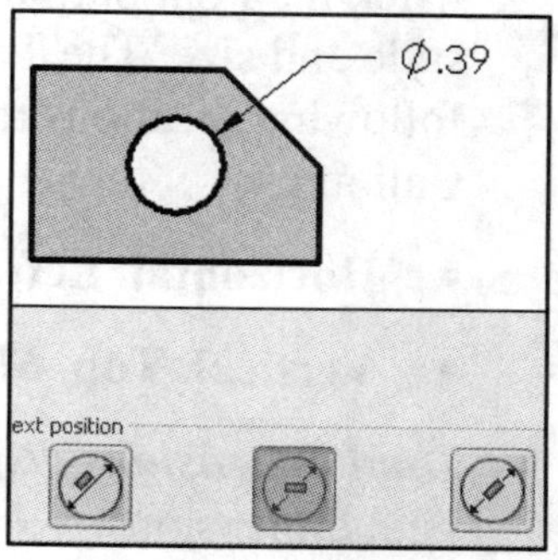


- ***Tolerance***. Select the Tolerance button to access the Tolerance dialog box.
- ***Text position***. Provides the following text position for the diameter dimension. Broken Leader, Horizontal Text selected by default. The available selections are: **Solid Leader**, **Aligned Text**, **Broken Leader**, **Horizontal Text**, **Broken Leader** and **Aligned Text**.

## Dimensions – Hole Callout

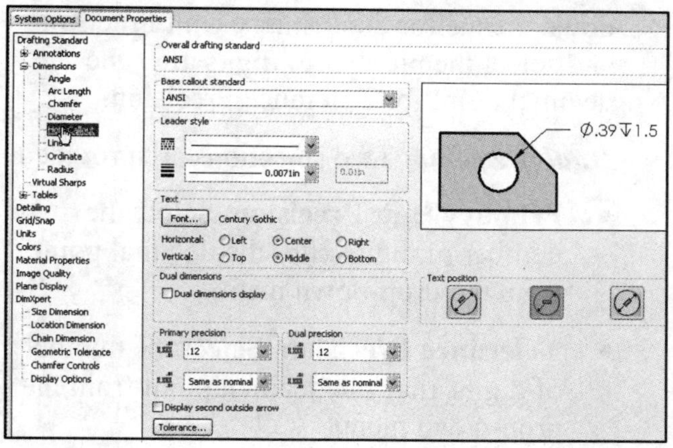

If you change a hole dimension in the model, the callout updates automatically.

The callout contains a diameter symbol and the dimension of the hole diameter. If the depth of the hole is known, the callout also contains a depth symbol and the dimension of the depth. If the hole is created in the **Hole Wizard**, the callout contains additional information (the dimensions of a countersink or number of hole instances, for example).

The Dimensions – Hole Callout section provides the following options:

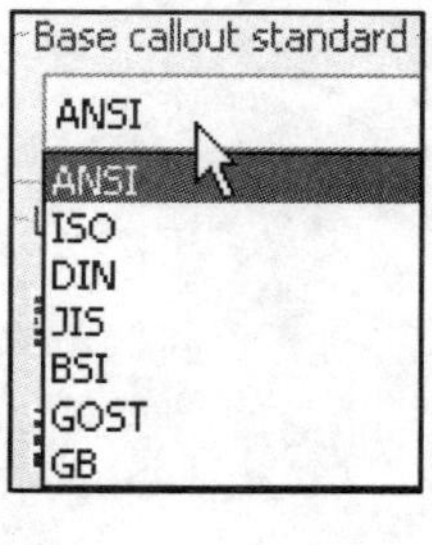


- ***Overall drafting standard***. Displays the selected drafting standard.
- ***Base callout standard***. Provides the ability to select a default standard for an active Part, Assembly, or Drawing document from the drop-down menu or to create a custom Base callout standard.

- ***Leader Style***. Provides the ability to use the default Leader style or to select a custom Leader style and thickness from the drop-down menu.

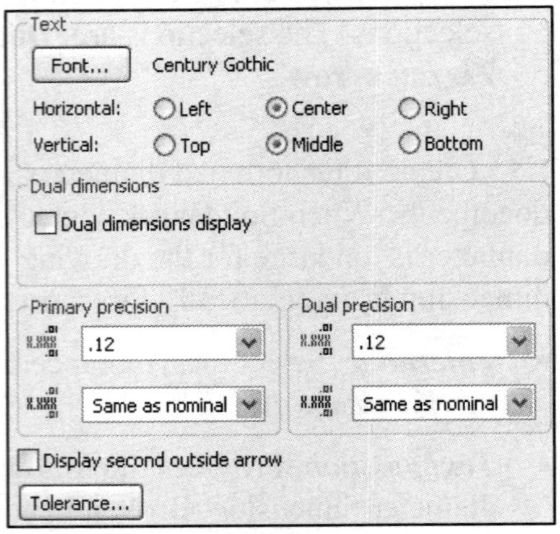


- ***Text***. Century Gothic selected by default. Click the Font button to select a custom font style and size. The Text options provides the following locations relative to the Hole Callout:
  - **Horizontal. Left, Center, Right**
  - **Vertical. Top, Middle, Bottom**
- ***Dual dimensions display***. Check to display dual dimensions.
- ***Primary precision***. Two selections are provided: **Primary Unit Precision** and **Tolerance Precision**. Select the number of digits after the decimal point from the drop-down menus for the Primary Unit Precision and select the number of digits after the decimal point for Tolerance Precision.

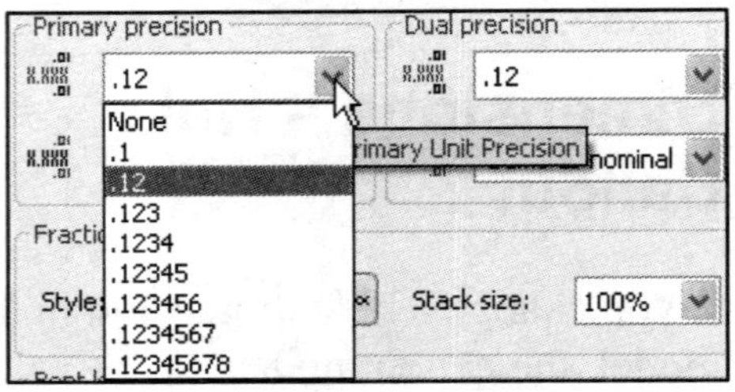


- ***Dual precision***. Two selections are provided:
  - **Primary Unit Precision**. Select the number of digits after the decimal point from the drop-down menu.
  - **Tolerance Precision**. Select the number of digits after the decimal point from the drop-down menu.

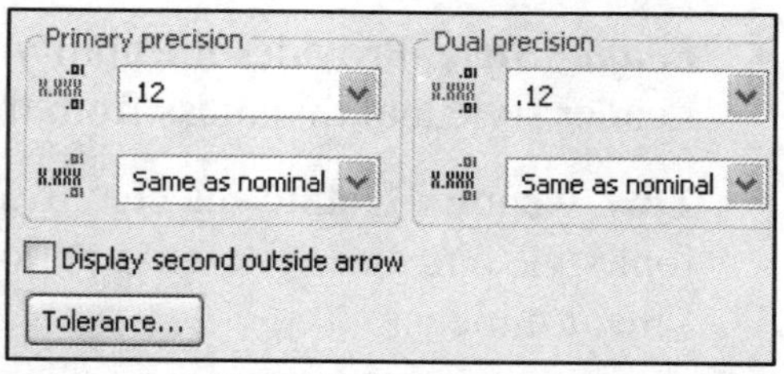


- ***Display second outside arrow***.
- ***Tolerance***. Select the Tolerance button to access the Tolerance dialog box.
- ***Text position***. Provides the following text position for the diameter dimension. Broken Leader, Horizontal Text selected by default. The available selections are: **Solid Leader, Aligned Text**, **Broken Leader**, **Horizontal Text**, **Broken Leader** and **Aligned Text**.

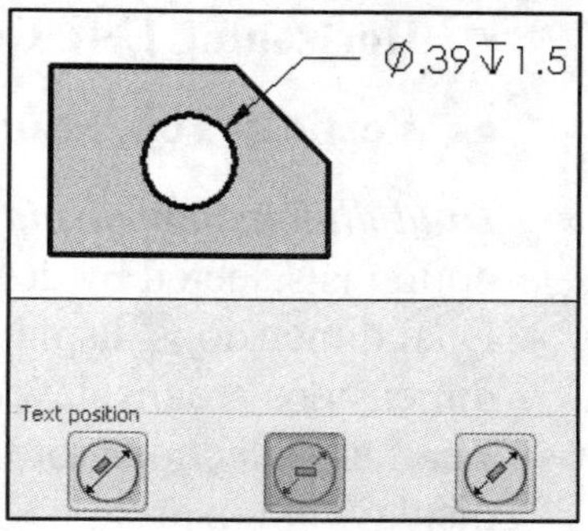


If you attach a hole callout to a tapped hole in ANSI inch standard and the current drawing units are millimeters, the drill diameter and hole depths are reported in mm but the thread description retains the ANSI inch size designation. You might want to replace the thread description with other variables from the **Callout Variables** dialog box.

## Dimensions – Linear

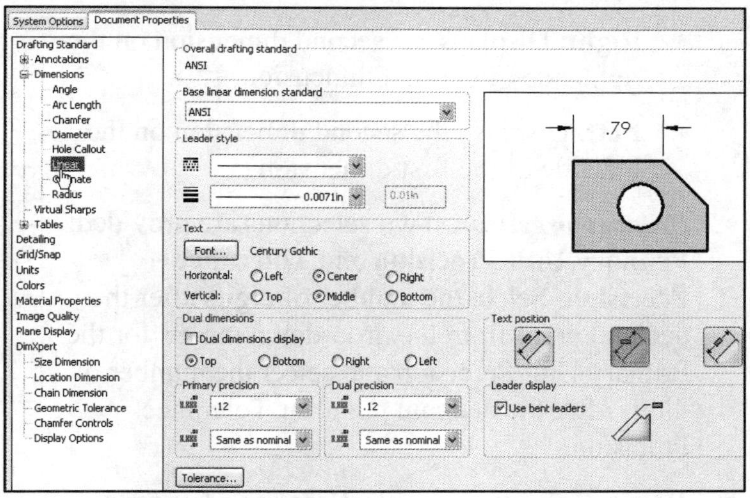


The Dimensions – Linear section provides the ability to measure the distance between two points. Since two points define a line, the units of distance are sometimes called "linear" units or dimensions.

The Dimensions – Linear section provides the following options:

- ***Overall drafting standard***. Displays the selected drafting standard.

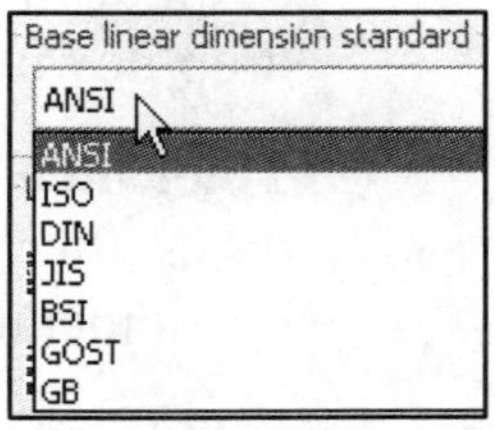


- ***Base linear dimension standard***. Provides the ability to select a default standard for an active Part, Assembly or Drawing document from the drop-down menu or to create a custom Base linear dimension standard.

- ***Leader Style***. Provides the ability to use the default Leader style or to select a custom Leader style and thickness from the drop-down menu.
- ***Text***. Century Gothic selected by default. Click the Font button to select a custom font style and size. The Text options provides the following locations relative to the Linear dimension:
  - **Horizontal. Left, Center, Right**
  - **Vertical. Top, Middle, Bottom**
- ***Dual dimensions display***. Top display option is selected by default. When the Dual dimensions display option is selected, dimensions are displayed in two unit types. The four selections for the Dual dimensions display option are:

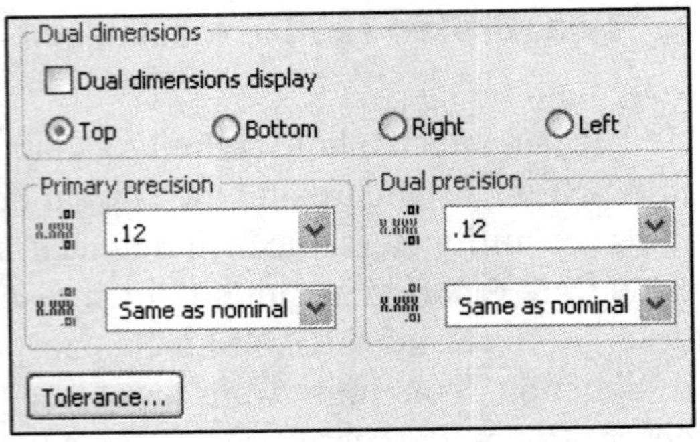


  - **Top**. Selected by default. Displays the second dimension on the top of the first dimension.
  - **Bottom**. Displays the second dimension on the bottom of the first dimension.
  - **Right**. Displays the second dimension on the right side of the first dimension.
  - **Left**. Displays the second dimension on the left side of the first dimension.

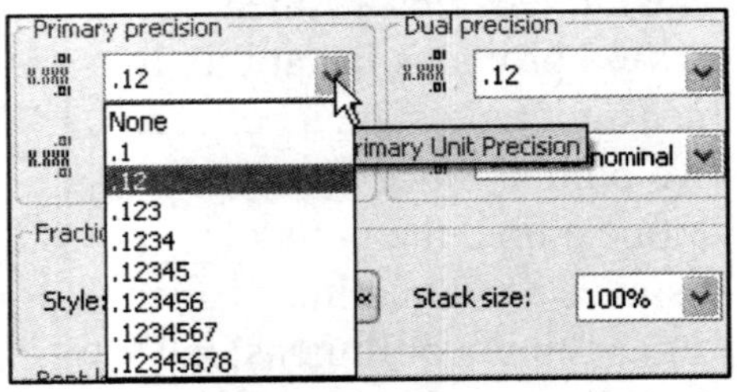


- ***Primary precision***. Two selections are provided: **Primary Unit Precision** and **Tolerance Precision**. Select the number of digits after the decimal point from the drop-down menus for the Primary Unit Precision and select the number of digits after the decimal point for Tolerance Precision.
- ***Dual precision***. Two selections are provided:
  - **Primary Unit Precision**. Select the number of digits after the decimal point from the drop-down menu.
  - **Tolerance Precision**. Select the number of digits after the decimal point from the drop-down menu.
- ***Tolerance***. Select the Tolerance button to access the Tolerance dialog box.

- ***Text position***. Provides the following text position for the Linear dimension placement. Broken Leader, Horizontal Text selected by default. The available selections are: **Solid Leader**, **Aligned Text**, **Broken Leader**, **Horizontal Text**, **Broken Leader** and **Aligned Text**.

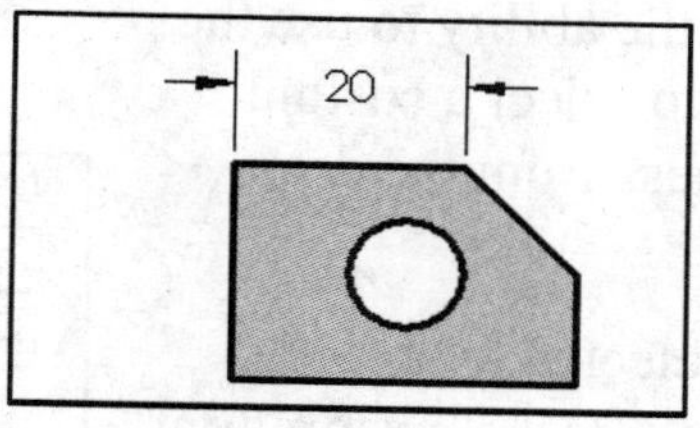


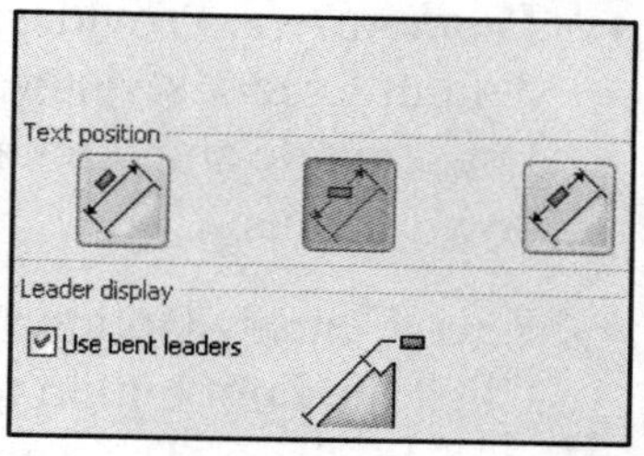


- ***Use bent leaders***. Selected by default.

## Dimensions – Ordinate

Ordinate dimensions are a set of dimensions measured from a zero ordinate in a drawing or sketch. In drawings, they are reference dimensions and you cannot change their values or use the values to drive the model.

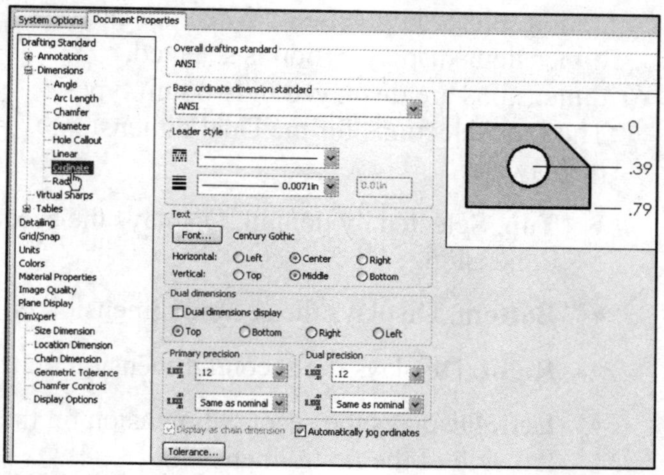


Ordinate dimensions are measured from the axis you select first. The type of ordinate dimension (horizontal or vertical) is defined by the orientation of the points you select.

Ordinate dimensions are automatically grouped to maintain alignment. When you drag any member of the group, all the members move together. To disconnect a dimension from the alignment group, right-click the dimension, and select Break Alignment.

The Dimensions – Ordinate section provides the following options:

- ***Overall drafting standard***. Displays the selected drafting standard.

- ***Base ordinate dimension standard***. Provides the ability to select a default standard for an active Part, Assembly, or Drawing document from the drop-down menu or to create a custom Base ordinate dimension standard.

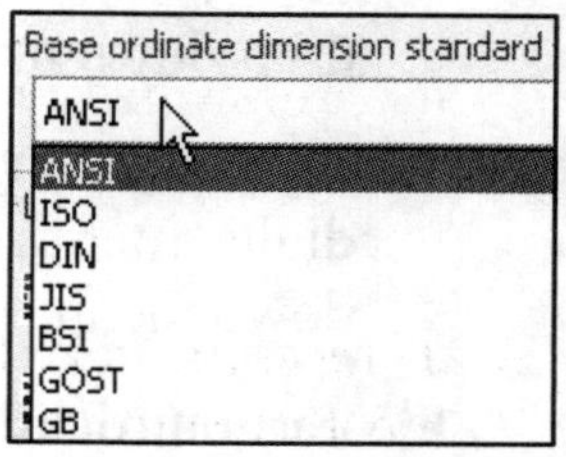

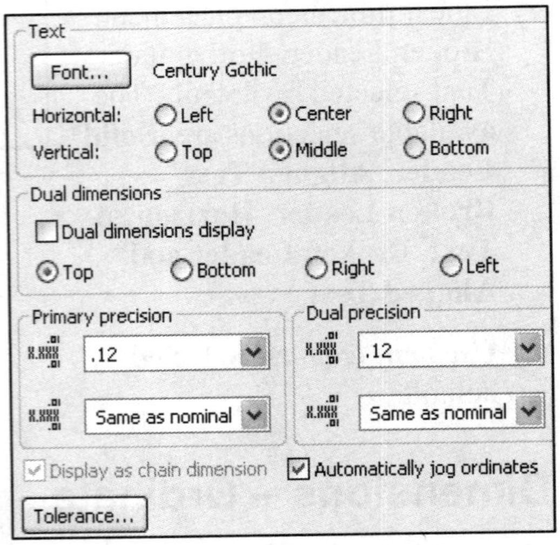


- ***Leader Style***. Provides the ability to use the default Leader style or to select a custom Leader style and thickness from the drop-down menus.
- ***Text***. Century Gothic selected by default. Click the Font button to select a custom font style and size. The Text options provides the following locations relative to the Ordinate dimension:
  - **Horizontal**. **Left**, **Center**, **Right**
  - **Vertical**. **Top**, **Middle**, **Bottom**
- ***Dual dimensions display***. Top display option selected by default. When the Dual dimensions display option is selected, dimensions are displayed in two unit types. The four selections for the Dual dimensions display are:
  - **Top**. Selected by default. Displays the second dimension on the top of the first dimension.
  - **Bottom**. Displays the second dimension on the bottom of the first dimension.
  - **Right**. Displays the second dimension on the right side of the first dimension.
  - **Left**. Displays the second dimension on the left side of the first dimension.

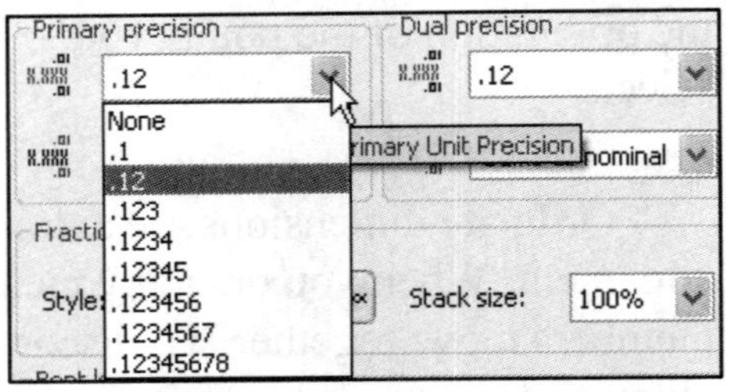


- ***Primary precision***. Two selections are provided: **Primary Unit Precision** and **Tolerance Precision**. Select the number of digits after the decimal point from the drop-down menu for the Primary Unit Precision and select the number of digits after the decimal point for Tolerance Precision.
- ***Dual precision***. Two selections are provided:
  - **Primary Unit Precision**. Select the number of digits after the decimal point from the drop-down menu.
  - **Tolerance Precision**. Select the number of digits after the decimal point from the drop-down menu.
  - **Automatically jog ordinates**. Automatically bends the leader line of the ordinates.

- ***Tolerance***. Select the Tolerance button to access the Tolerance dialog box.

You can drag the zero dimension to a new position, and all the ordinate dimensions update to match the new zero position.

## Dimensions – Radius

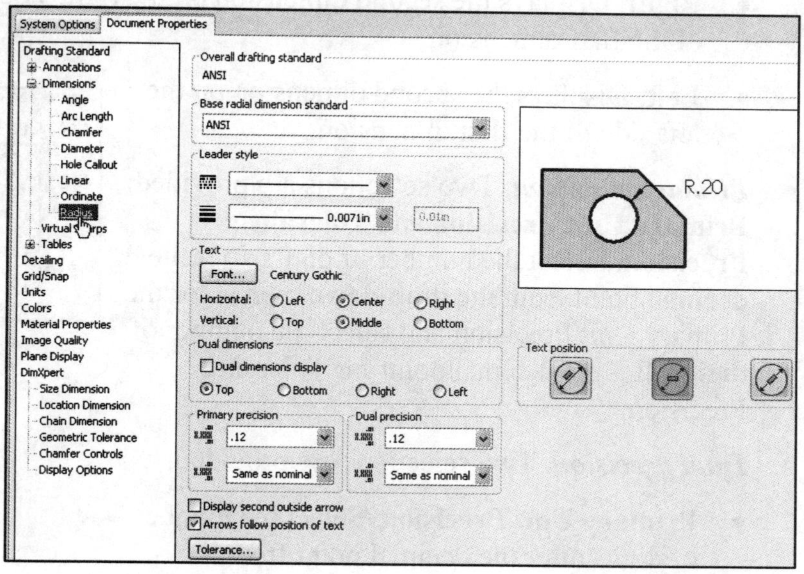


The Dimensions – Radius section provides the following options:

- ***Overall drafting standard***. Displays the selected drafting standard.
- ***Base radial dimension standard***. Provides the ability to select a default standard for an active Part, Assembly, or Drawing document from the drop-down menu or to create a custom Base radial dimension standard.

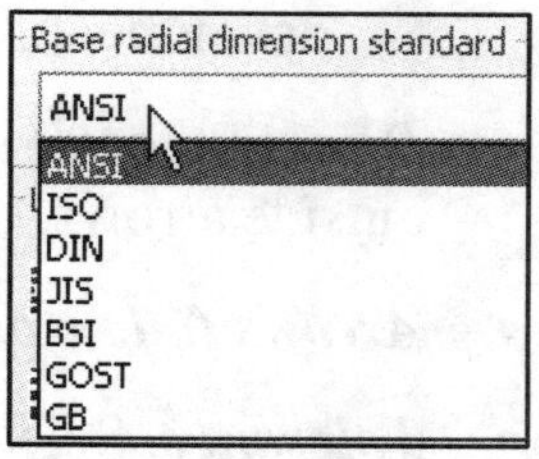


- ***Leader Style***. Provides the ability to use the default Leader style or to select a custom Leader style and thickness from the drop-down menus.
- ***Text***. Century Gothic selected by default. Click the Font button to select a custom font style and size. The Text options provides the following locations relative to the radius dimension:
  - **Horizontal**. **Left, Center, Right**
  - **Vertical**. **Top, Middle, Bottom**
- ***Dual dimensions display***. Top display option selected by default. When the Dual dimensions display option is selected, dimensions are displayed in two unit types. The four selections for the Dual dimensions display are:

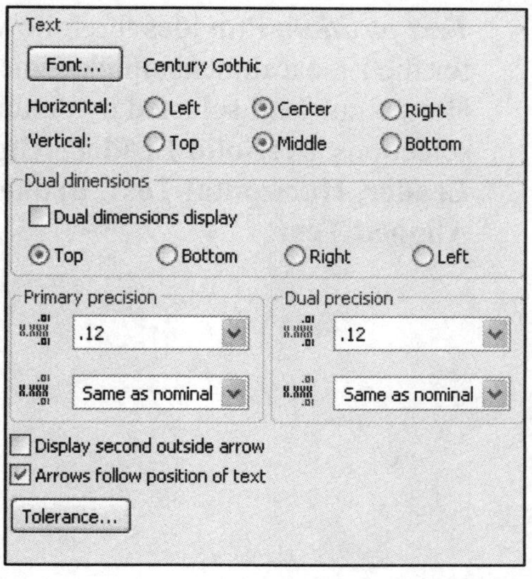

- **Top**. Selected by default. Displays the second dimension on the top of the first dimension.
- **Bottom**. Displays the second dimension on the bottom of the first dimension.
- **Right**. Displays the second dimension on the right side of the first dimension.
- **Left**. Displays the second dimension on the left side of the first dimension.

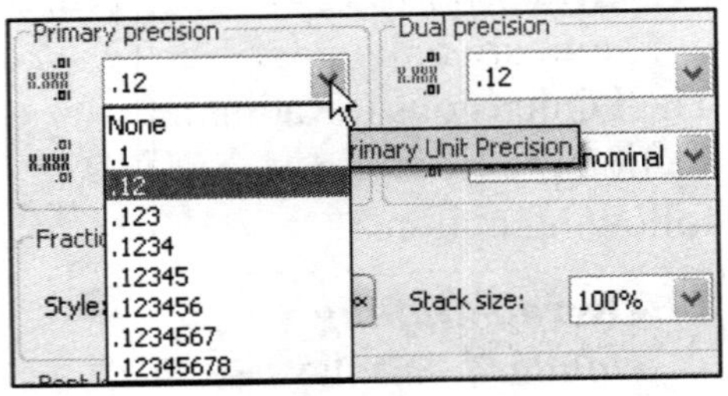


- ***Primary precision***. Two selections are provided: **Primary Unit Precision** and **Tolerance Precision**. Select the number of digits after the decimal point from the drop-down menus for the Primary Unit Precision and select the number of digits after the decimal point for Tolerance Precision.
- ***Dual precision***. Two selections are provided:
  - **Primary Unit Precision**. Select the number of digits after the decimal point from the drop-down menu.
  - **Tolerance Precision**. Select the number of digits after the decimal point from the drop-down menu.

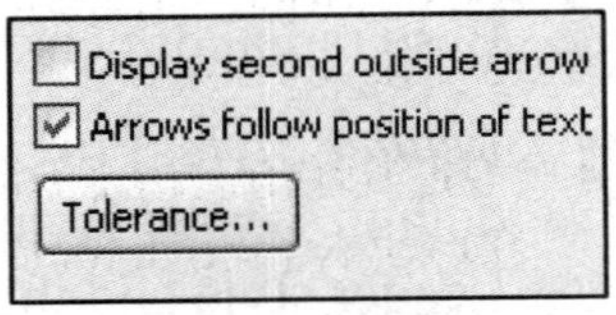


- ***Display second outside arrow***. Select to display two outside arrows.
- ***Arrows follow position of text.*** Select to display.
- ***Tolerance***. Select the Tolerance button to access the Tolerance dialog box.
- ***Text position***. Provides the following text position for the Linear dimension placement. Broken Leader, Horizontal Text selected by default. The available selections are: **Solid Leader, Aligned Text, Broken Leader, Horizontal Text, Broken Leader** and **Aligned Text**.

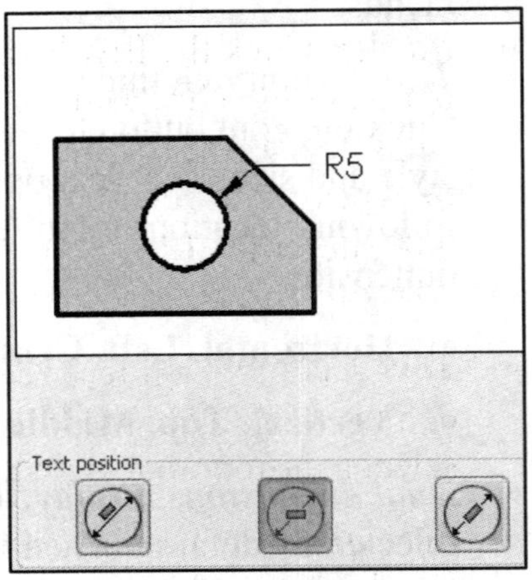

## Virtual Sharps

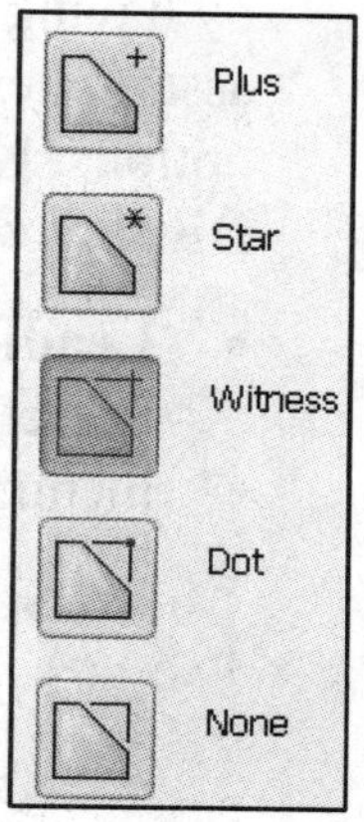


- ***Virtual Sharps***. Witness style selected by default. There are five style selections: **Plus, Star, Witness, Dot** and **None**. This option provides the ability to set the display options for the virtual sharps. A virtual sharp creates a sketch point at the virtual intersection point of two sketch entities. Dimensions and relations to the virtual intersection point are retained, even if the actual intersection no longer exists. Example: When a corner is removed by a using a Fillet or a Chamfer feature.

# Tables

The Tables section for a Part or Assembly document provides the ability to select text fonts and options for a Bill of Materials. Note: The second half of this chapter addresses Drawing document specific Document Properties.

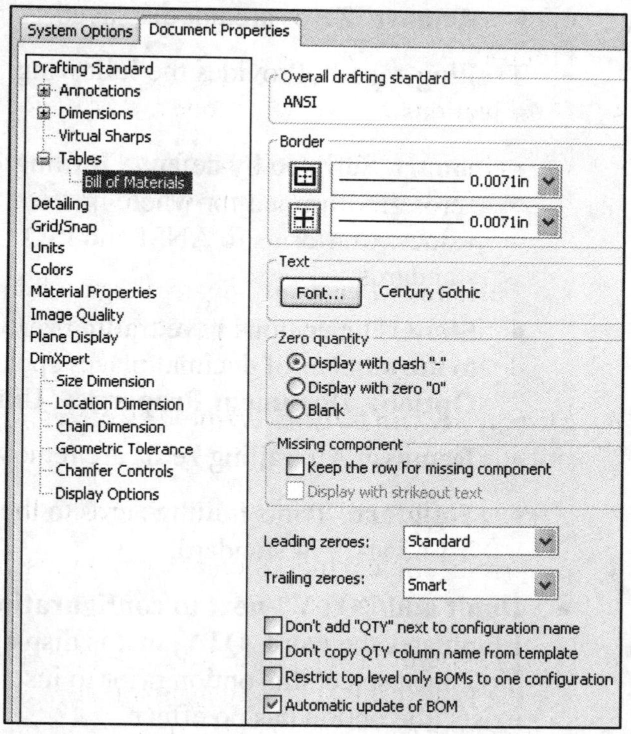


The Bill of Materials section for a Part or Assembly document provides the following options:

- ***Overall drafting standard***. Displays the selected drafting standard.
- ***Border***. Click the **Box Border** option or the **Grid Border** option and select a corresponding thickness. The default thickness is 0.007in for the IPS system and .18mm's for the MMGS system.
- ***Text***. Century Gothic selected by default. Click the Font button to select a custom font style and size.
- ***Zero quantity***. Display with dash '-' is selected by default. Provides the ability to select whether to display zero quantities with a dash (-) or a zero (0), or to leave the cell blank.

- ***Missing component***. A Missing component created by having deleted or suppressed parts or sub-assemblies in the top-level assembly. There are two options: **Keep the row for missing component** and **Display with strikeout text**.

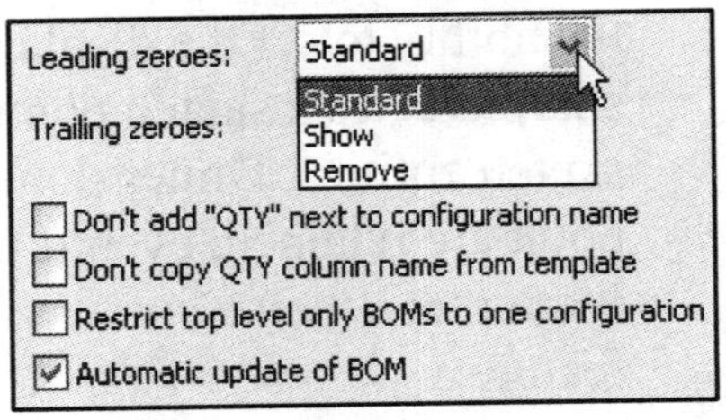


- **Leading zeroes**. Standard selected by default. Select one of three options from the drop-down menu:
  - **Standard**. Zeros are displayed based on the selected dimensioning standard.
  - **Show**. Zeros before the decimal points are displayed on the selected dimensioning standard.
  - **Remove**. Zeros are not displayed.

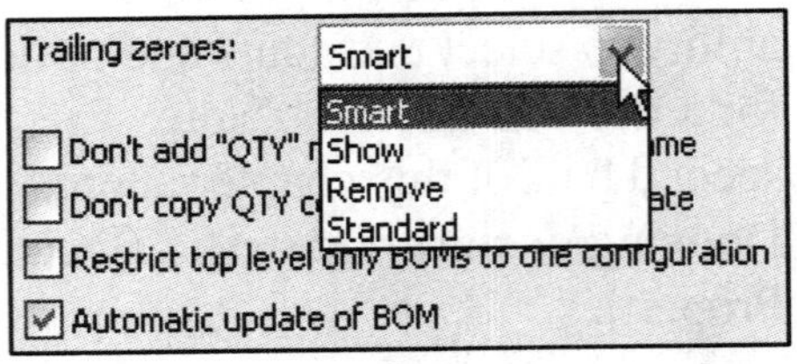


- **Trailing zeroes**. Provides the following selections:
  - **Smart**. Selected by default. Trailing zeros are trimmed for whole metric values. Conforms to ANSI and ISO standards.
  - **Show**. Dimensions have trailing zeros up to the number of decimal places specified in **Options, Document Properties, Units.**
  - **Remove**. All trailing zeros are removed.
  - **Standard**. Trims trailing zeros to the ASME Y14.5M-1994 standard.
- **Don't add "QTY" next to configuration name**. Eliminates the word, **QTY**, that is displayed in the configuration column. Note: You must select this option prior to inserting a BOM. If you select it after a BOM exists, the option has no effect.
- **Don’t copy QTY column name from template**. Select to use the configuration name appended by the string /QTY for the quantity column header.
- **Restrict top level only BOMs to one configuration**. Select to limit Top-level only BOMs to one configuration. When you change the configuration in the BOM, the quantity column label does not change.

- **Automatic update of BOM**. Select to update the BOM when you add or delete components in the associated assembly.

# Detailing

Set options for detailing in the active document. You can also set the detailing options in Document Templates.

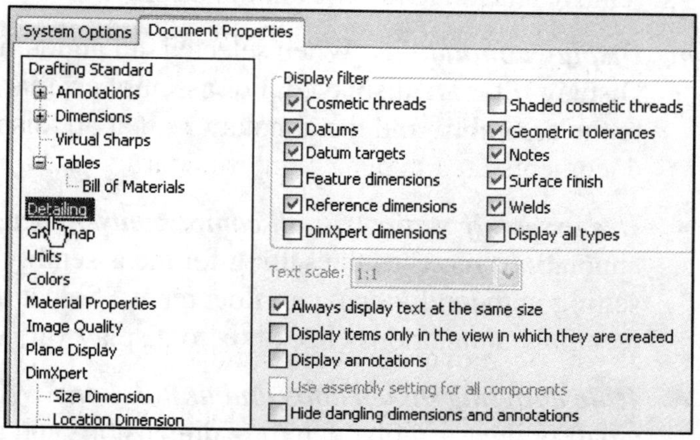


- ***Display filter***. The Display filter option provides the ability to specify the detailing display filters. The Display filter option provides twelve selections. To apply a filter, select **Display all types**, or clear **Display all types** and select one of the following filters:
  - **Cosmetic threads**. Selected by default.
  - **Datums**. Selected by default.
  - **Datum targets**. Selected by default.
  - **Feature dimensions**. Not selected by default.
  - **References dimensions**. Selected by default.
  - **DimXpert dimensions**. Not selected by default.
  - **Shaded cosmetic threads**. Not selected by default.
  - **Geometric tolerances**. Selected by default.
  - **Notes**. Selected by default.
  - **Surface finish**. Selected by default.
  - **Welds**. Selected by default.
  - **Display all types**. Not selected by default.
- ***Text scale***. Text scale 1:1 is selected by default. Use the text scale option only for part and assembly documents. Deselect the Always display text at the same size option to active the Text scale and to specify a scale for the default size of the annotation text.

- ***Always display text at the same size***. Selected by default. When selected, all annotations and dimensions are displayed at the same size regardless of zoom.
- ***Display items only in the view in which they are created***. When selected, annotation is displayed only when the model is viewed in the same orientation as when the annotation was added. Rotating the part or selecting a different view orientation removes the annotation from the display.
- ***Display annotations***. When selected, all annotation types which are selected in the Display filter are displayed. For assemblies, this includes the annotations that belong to the assembly, and the annotations that are displayed in the individual part documents.
- ***Use assembly setting for all components***. When selected, the display of all annotations matches the setting for the assembly document. This is regardless of any setting in the individual part documents. Select this option along with the Display assembly annotations check box to display various combinations of annotations.
- ***Hide dangling dimensions and annotations***. When selected, if you delete features in a part or an assembly, dangling dimensions and annotations are automatically hide in the drawing. If a feature is suppressed, this option will automatically hide any dangling reference dimensions in the drawing.

## Grid/Snap

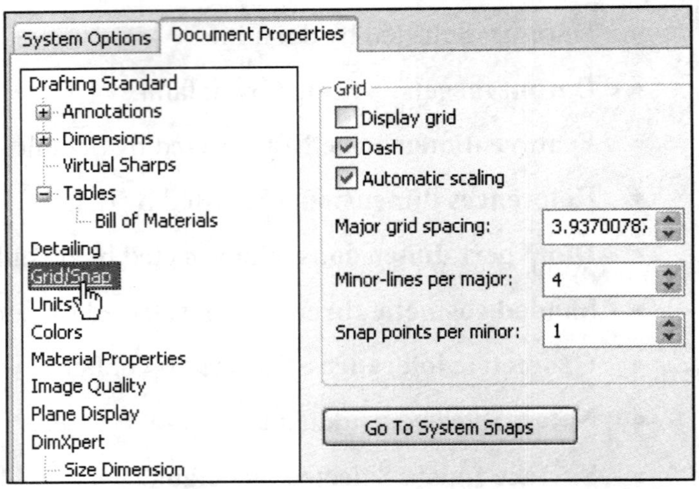


The Grid/Snap selection provides the ability to display a sketch grid in an active sketch or drawing and to set the options for the snap functionality and grid display.

The options for grid spacing and minor grid lines per major lines apply to the rulers in drawings, drawing grid lines, and sketching.

A drawing window displays rulers at the top and left side of the Graphics window. The rulers and the status bar display the position of your mouse pointer on the active sheet.

- ***Grid***. The Grid option provides the following selections:
  - ***Display grid***. Activates the sketch grid on or off.
  - ***Dash***. Selected by default. Toggles between solid and dashed grid lines.
  - ***Automatic scaling***. Selected by default. Automatically adjusts the display of the grid when you zoom in and out on a view.
  - ***Major grid spacing***. Provides the user the ability to specify the space between major grid lines.
  - ***Minor-lines per major***. The Minor-lines per major option default is 4. Provides the user the ability to specify the number of minor grid lines between major grid lines.
  - ***Snap points per minor***. The Snap point per minor option default is 1. Provides the ability to set the number of snap points between the minor grid lines.
  - ***Go To System Snaps***. This option locates you to the System Options, Relations/Snap section. See Chapter 2 for detail information on System Options.

## Units

The Units option provides the ability to specify units and precision for an active part, assembly, or drawing document.

If you use small units such as angstroms, nanometers, microns, mils, or microinches; it is helpful to create a custom template as the basis for your document.

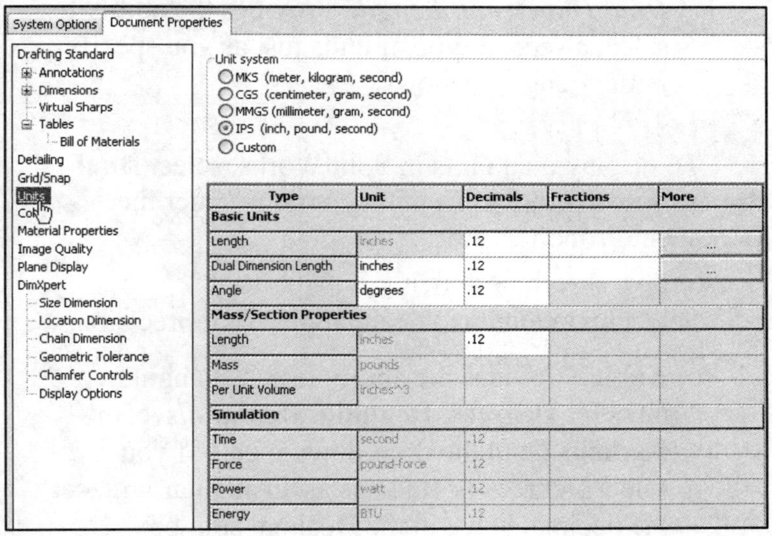

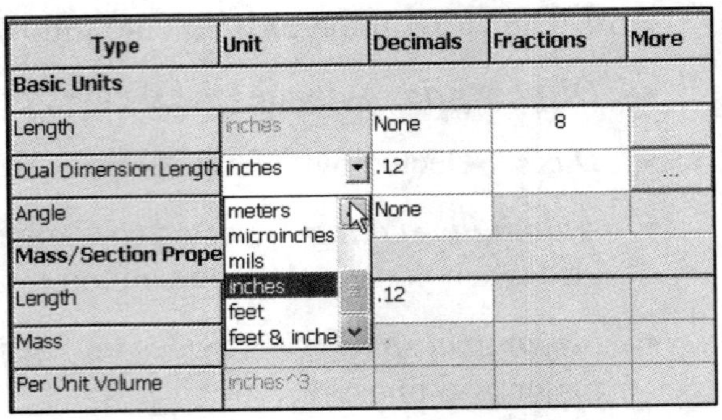


- ***Units System***. The Unit system option provides the ability to select from four unit systems and a Custom system. The selections are: **MKS (meter, kilogram, second), CGS (centimeter, gram, second), MMGS (millimeter, gram, second), IPS (inch, pound, second)** and **Custom**. The Custom unit system provides the ability to set the Length units, such as feet and inches, Density units, and Force.
- ***Basic Units***. Provides the ability to select **Length, Dual Dimension Length**, and **Angle** from the drop-down menu.
  - **Length**. Provides the ability to select length precision from the drop-down menu as illustrated.
  - ***Dual Dimension Length***. Provides the ability to select a second type of units just as you specify in the Length section.

To display dual units in SolidWorks, select **Dual dimensions display** in Detailing options under the Document Properties tab.

Select up to eight (8) decimal places of precision.

  - **Angle**. Provides the ability to select angular units in: **Degrees, Deg/min, Deg/min/sec**, or **Radians** from the drop-down menu. If you select Degrees or Radians as an angular unit, set the decimal place in the Decimal spin box.
- ***Mass/Section Property***. Provides the ability to select **Length, Mass**, and **Per Unit Volume** from the drop-down menu.
- ***Simulation***. For Assemblies only. Provides the ability to perform simulations (Motion Study). Available options: **Time, Force, Power** and **Energy** from the drop-down menu.

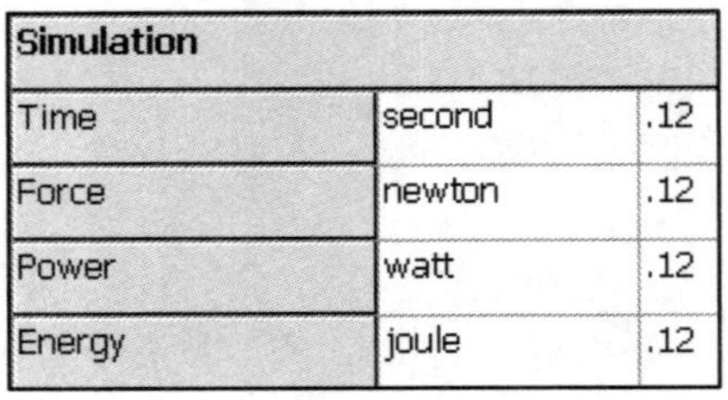

# Color

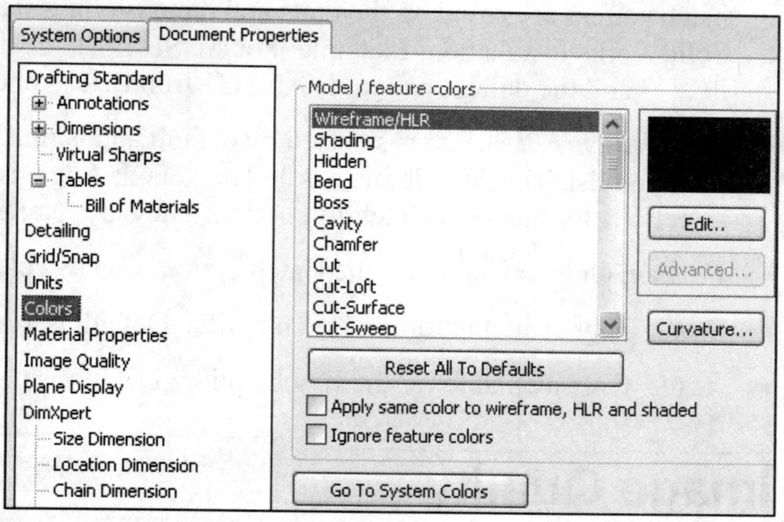


The Colors selection provides the ability to modify the color default options in an active part or assembly document. This selection also provides the ability to modify the default color in a part or assembly document to be used as a template.

- ***Mode/Feature colors***. Provides the ability to select a feature type or view mode. In an assembly document, the Shading, for Shaded view mode and the Hidden, Hidden Lines Visible view modes are available.

If you edit the color for Shading, the Advanced button is active. Set values for Shininess, Transparency, etc.

- ***Apply same color to wireframe, HLR and shaded***. Applies the same color.
- ***Ignore feature colors***. Only available in a part document. Part colors take precedence over feature colors.
- ***Go To System Colors***. Brings you directly to the System Options, Color box to set the colors for the system. See Chapter 2 for additional information.

# Material Properties

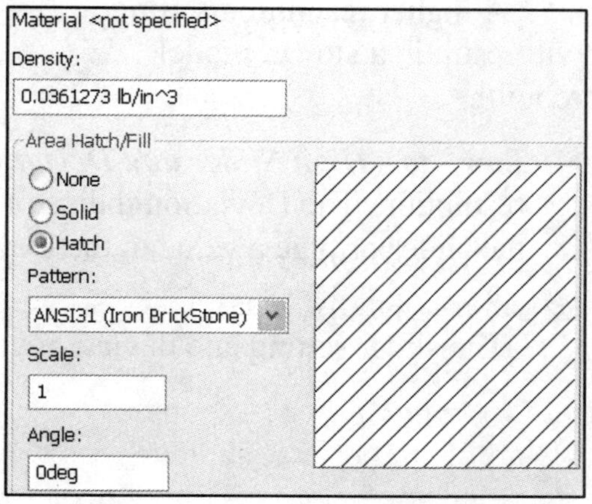


The Material Properties selection provides the ability to set crosshatch options and material density in an active part. These options are not available for drawing or assembly documents. The applied crosshatch pattern in the part document is displayed in the Section view of the part in the associative drawing.

If you applied material to the part document, you must remove it before you set the Material Properties.

- ***Density***. Provides the ability to set density of a material. The default density and hatch pattern are based on the units and dimensioning standard selected during the SolidWorks installation. Example: For ANSI (IPS), the default density is 0.03612 lb/in^3 and the default pattern is ANSI31 Iron Brickstone.
- ***Area Hatch/Fill***. Hatch is selected by default and is illustrated to the right of the selection list. The default Scale is 1. The default Angle is 0deg. There are three selections for the Area Hatch/Fill option. They are: **None**, **Solid** and **Hatch**.
- ***Pattern***. Only available for the Hatch option. ISO (Steel) selected by default.
- ***Scale.*** Only available for the Hatch option. Default is 1.
- ***Angle***. Only available for the Hatch option. Default is 0.

# Image Quality

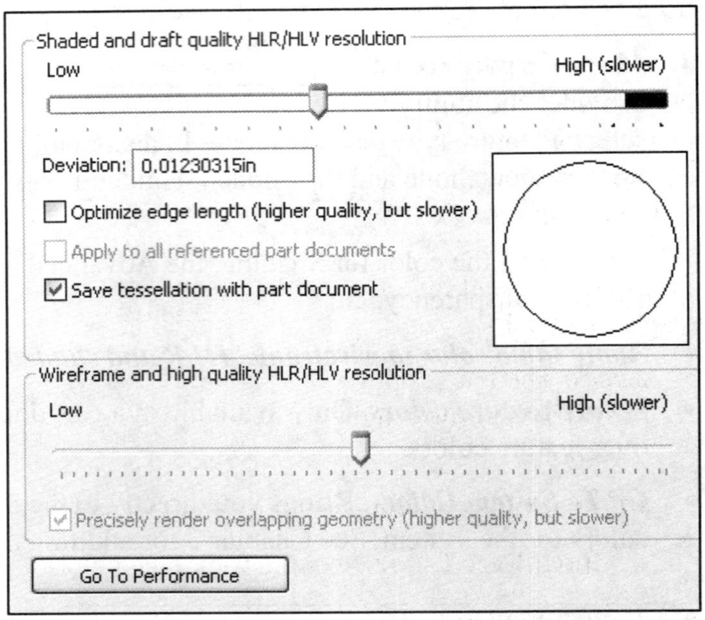


The Image Quality selection provides the ability to set the image display quality in the SolidWorks Graphics window on your system.

- ***Shaded and draft quality HLR/HLV resolution***. Provides the ability to control the tessellation of curved surfaces for shaded rendering output.

A higher resolution setting will result in a slower model rebuild.

- ***Low - to - High Slider and Deviation indicator***. Controls the image quality resolution. The Deviation indicator is the maximum chordal deviation in effect. Drag the slider or type a value in the Deviation indicator to modify the screen resolution.

The slider setting and deviation value are coupled and are inversely proportional.

- ***Optimize edge length (higher quality, but slower)***. Increases image quality if, after you move the slider to the highest setting, you still require a higher image quality.
- ***Apply to all referenced part documents (assemblies only)***. Provides the ability to apply the settings to all of the part documents referenced by the active document.
- ***Save tessellation with part document (parts only)***. Selected by default. Provides the ability to save the display information. When cleared, file size is reduced significantly. The model is not displayed when the file is opened in the view-only mode, in the SolidWorks Viewer, or in SolidWorks eDrawings. The display data is regenerated when the file is opened again in SolidWorks.

# Plane Display

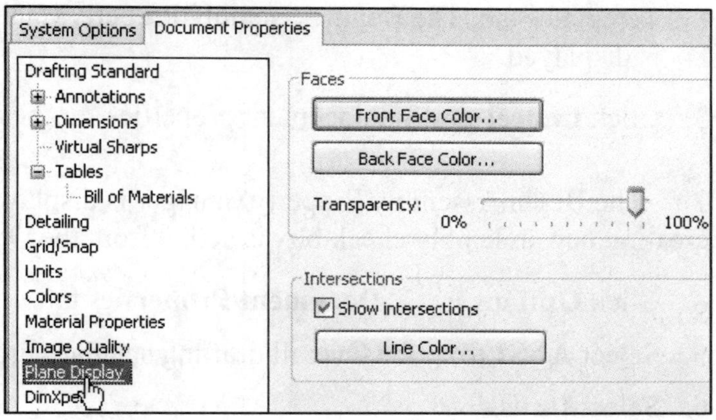


The Plane Display selection provides the ability to set the plane display options for a part or assembly document. The following options can be addressed: Face color, Transparency, and Intersection display and color.

- ***Faces***. The Faces option provides the following selections:
  - **Front Face Color**. Sets the front face color of planes using the Color dialog box.
  - **Back Face Color**. Sets the back face color of planes using the Color dialog box.
- ***Transparency***. The default setting is approximately 95%. Controls the planes transparency. 0% displays a solid face color. 100% displays no face color.
- ***Intersections***. Provides the following selections:
  - **Show intersections**. Selected by default. Displays the intersecting planes.
  - **Line Color**. Sets the plane intersection line color using the Color dialog box.

## *Tutorial: Assembly Template 3-2*

Create a custom Assembly template. The custom Assembly template begins with the default assembly template. Templates require System Options, File Locations. System Options are addressed in Chapter 2. Note: The Assembly Template is located in the MY-TEMPLATES folder on the CD with many other templates!

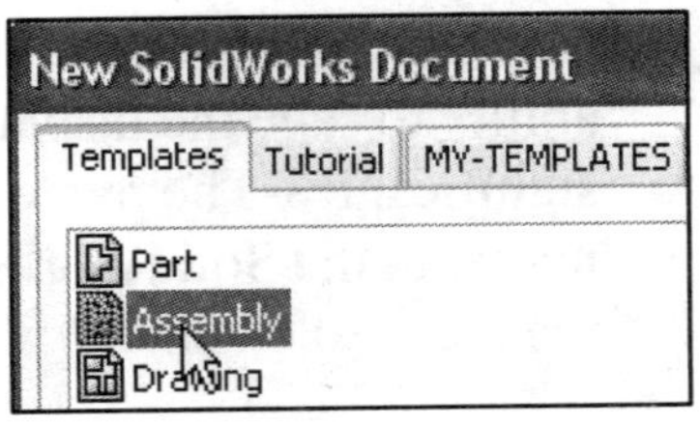


Create a custom Assembly Template.

1. Click **New** from the Menu bar.
2. Double-click the **Assembly** icon from the default Templates tab. The Begin Assembly PropertyManager is displayed.
3. Click **Cancel**. Set document properties for the assembly template.

The Begin Assembly PropertyManager is displayed if the Start command when creating new assembly check box is active from the Options dialog box.

4. Click **Options** ➤ **Document Properties** tab.
5. Select **ANSI** from the Overall drafting standard drop-down menu.
6. Select **Units**.
7. Select **MMGS (millimeter, gram, second)** for Unit system.
8. Select **.12** for Length Decimal places.
9. Click **OK**.
10. Save the Assembly template. Select **Assembly Templates (*.asmdot)** for Save as type.
11. Select the **SolidWorks 2010\MY-TEMPLATES** folder.

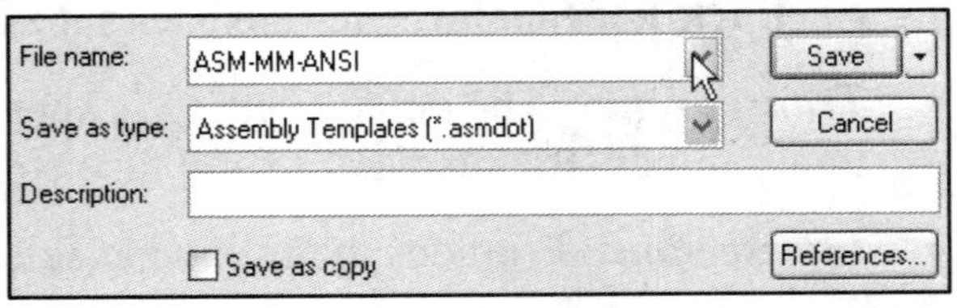


Create the SolidWorks 2010\MY-TEMPLATES folder to save all custom templates for this book.

12. Enter **ASM-MM-ANSI** for File name.
13. Click **Save**.
14. **Close** all files.
15. Click **New** from the Menu bar. The MY-TEMPLATES tab is displayed. The MY-TEMPLATES folder was created in Chapter 2. The MY-TEMPLATES folder is only displayed when there is a document in the folder.

16. Click the **MY-TEMPLATE** tab. The ASM-MM-ANSI Assembly template is displayed. **Close** all models.

***Tutorial: Part Template 3-3***

Create a custom Part template. The custom Part template begins with the default part template.

1. Click **New** from the Menu bar.
2. Double-click **Part** from the default Templates tab.

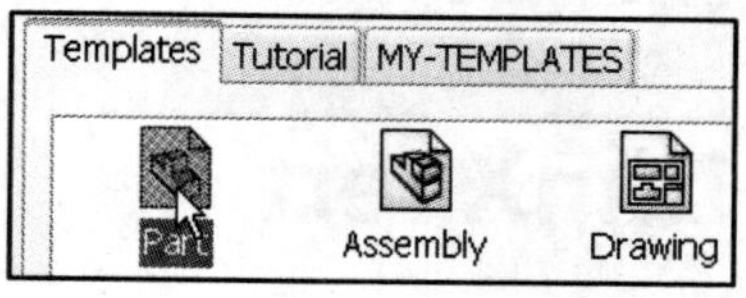


Set the document properties.

3. Click **Options** ➢ **Document Properties** tab.
4. Select **ANSI** for Overall drafting standard.
5. Click **Units** from the left text box. Click **MMGS (millimeter, gram, second)** for Unit system.
6. Select **.12** for Length Decimal places.
7. Click **OK**.

Apply material to the Part template.

9. Right-click **Material** from the FeatureManager design tree.
10. Click **Edit Material**.
11. Select **6061** from the Aluminum Alloys folder.
12. Click **Apply**.
13. Click **Close** from the Materials dialog box. 6061 Alloy is displayed in the Part FeatureManager design tree.

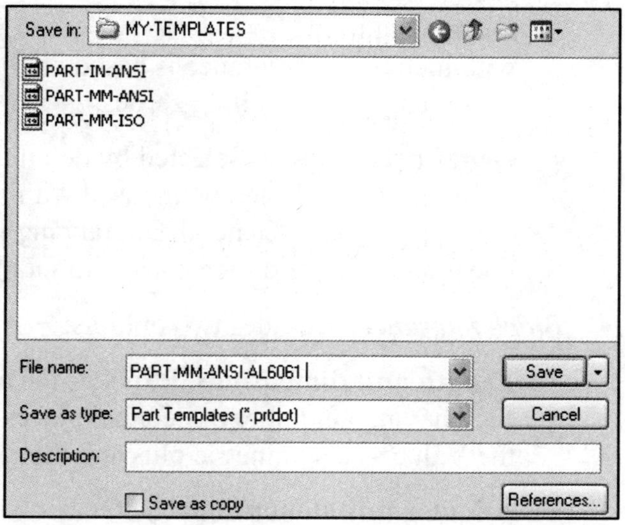


Save the Part template.

14. Click **Save**. Select **Part Templates (*.prtdot)** from the Save As type list box.
15. Select the **SolidWorks 2010\MY-TEMPLATES** folder from the Save in list box.
16. Enter **PART-MM-ANSI-AL6061** in the File name text box.
17. Click **Save**.
18. **Close** all files.

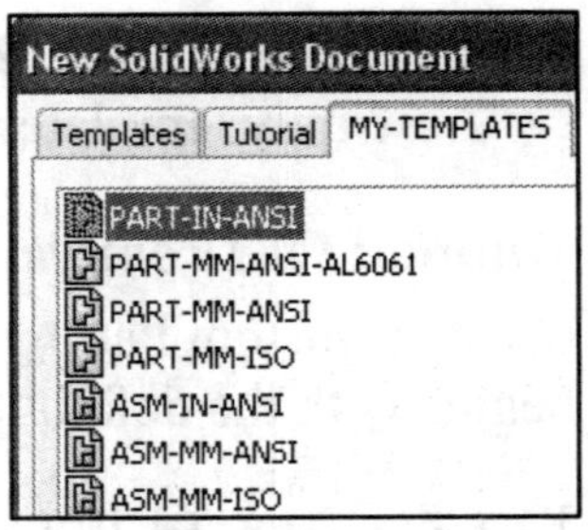


19. Click **New** from the Menu bar. The MY-TEMPLATES tab is displayed. The MY-TEMPLATES folder was created in Chapter 2. The MY-TEMPLATES folder is only displayed when there is a document in the folder.
20. Click the **MY-TEMPLATE** tab. The PART-MM-ANSI-AL6061 Part template is displayed.
21. **Close** all models.

# DimXpert

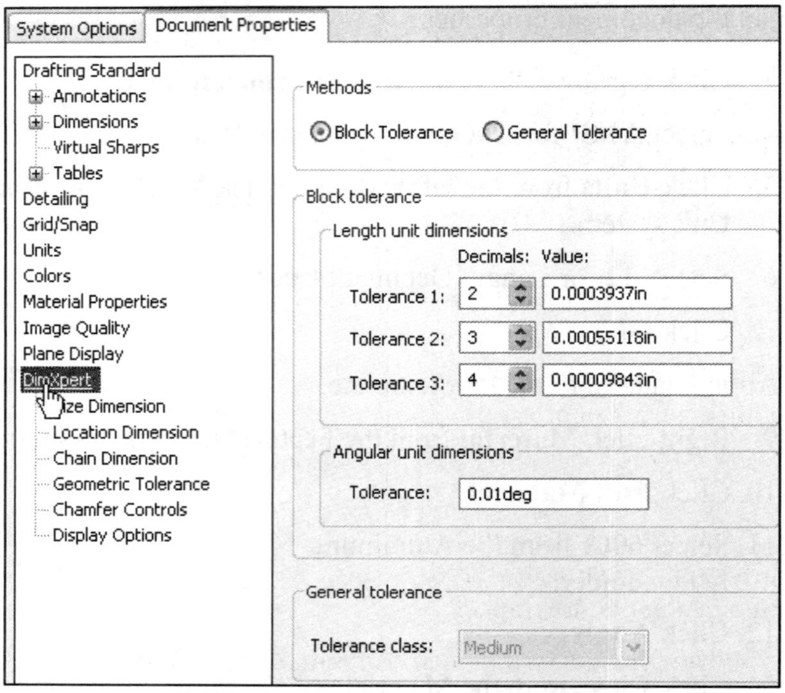


The DimXpert section provides the ability to define whether DimXpert uses Block Tolerances or General Tolerances on dimensions that do not contain tolerances.

- ***Methods***. The Methods section provides two options:
  - **Block Tolerance**. Selected by default when you set system units to IPS. A common form of tolerancing used with inch units. Tolerance is based on the provided precision of each dimension. You must specify trailing zeroes.
  - **General Tolerance**. Selected by default when you set system units to MMGS. A common form of tolerancing used with metric units in conjunction with the ISO drawing standard. General Tolerancing is based on ISO 2768-1 Tolerances for linear and angular dimensions without individual tolerance indications.
- ***Block tolerance***. Provides two options:
  - **Length unit dimensions**. Provides the ability to set up three block tolerances, each having a number of decimal places and tolerance value. DimXpert applies the Value as a symmetric plus and minus tolerance.
  - **Angular unit dimensions**. Default is 0.01deg. Provides the ability to set the tolerance value to use for all angular dimensions, including those applied cones and countersinks, and angle dimensions created between two features. DimXpert applies the Tolerance value as a symmetric plus and minus tolerance.

- **General tolerance**. Default is Medium. Provides the ability to set the part tolerance for the following: **Fine (f)**, **Medium (m)**, **Coarse (c)**, and **Very Coarse (v)**.

## DimXpert – Size Dimension

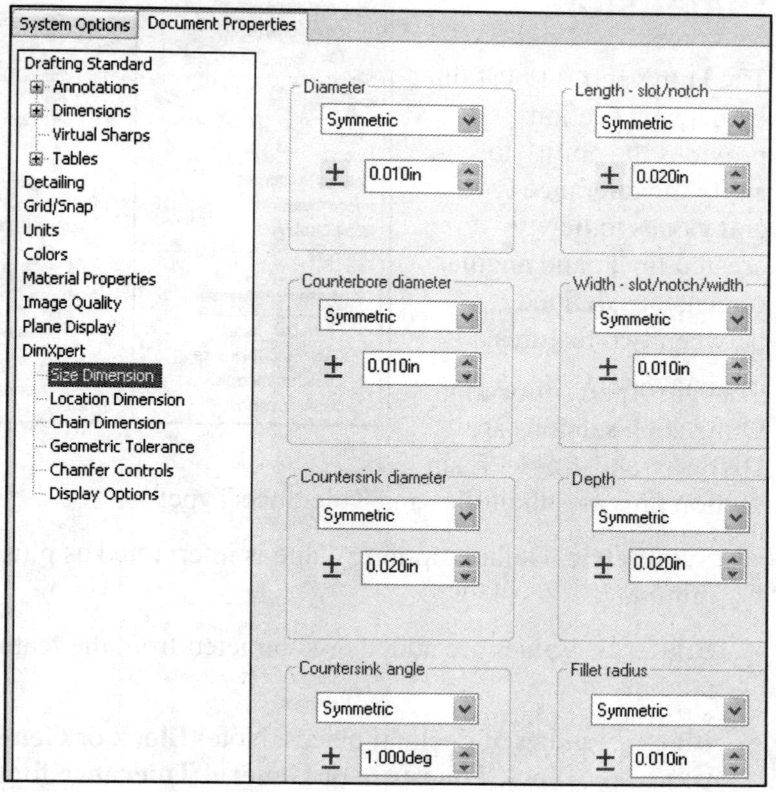


The DimXpert – Size Dimension section defines the tolerance type and value to apply to newly created size dimensions, including dimensions created with the *Size Dimension* tool and the *AutoDimenson Scheme* tool.

Click Location Dimension from the DimXpert toolbar or **Tools**, **DimXpert**, **Location Dimension**.

These options do not affect pre-existing features, dimensions, or tolerances.

The DimXpert - Size Dimension options are: **Diameter** (Symmetric, Bilateral, and Block), **Counterbore diameter** (Symmetric, Bilateral, and Block), **Countersink diameter**, **Countersink angle**, **Length - slot/notch**, **Width - slot/notch/width**, **Depth** (Symmetric, Bilateral, and Block), and **Fillet radius** (Symmetric, Bilateral, and Block).

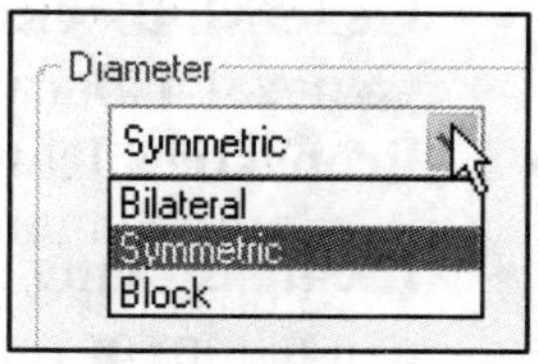


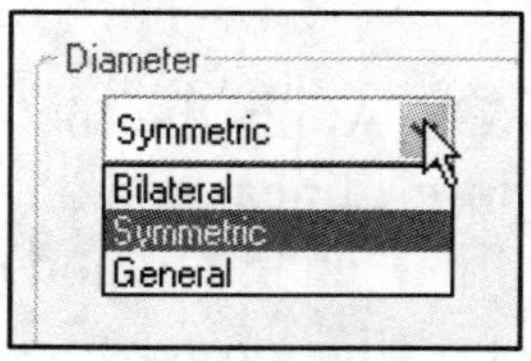


**Block** or **General** appears based on whether you select **Block Tolerance** or **General Tolerance** for the **DimXpert** method.

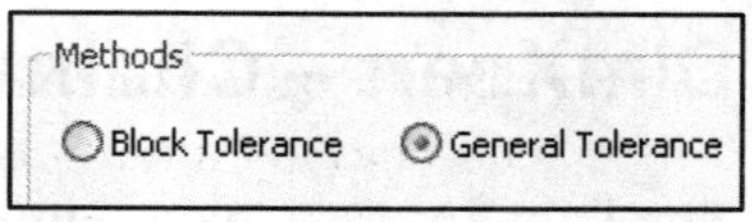

## DimXpert – Location Dimension

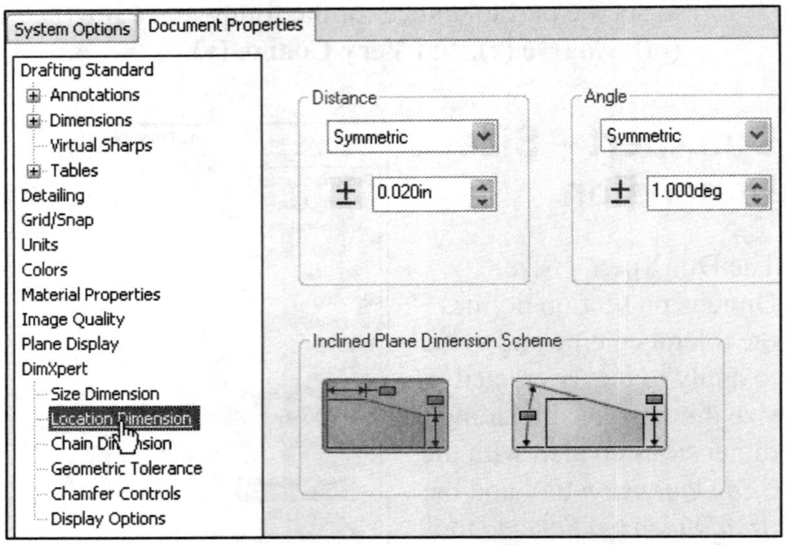


The DimXpert – Location Dimension section provides the ability to apply the tolerance type and values to newly created linear and angular dimensions defined between two features.

The DimXpert – Location Dimension sections are: **Distance** and **Angle**. Each section provides the following Tolerance Type:

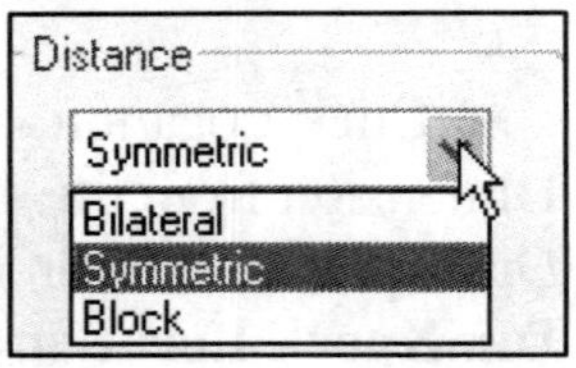


- **Symmetric**. Default option. Value is interpreted as plus and minus.
- **Bilateral**. Values are added or subtracted from the feature's nominal size.
- **Block**. Number of decimal places. Note: **Block** or **General** appears based on whether you select **Block Tolerance** or **General Tolerance** for the **DimXpert** method.
- **General**. **Block** or **General** appears based on whether you select **Block Tolerance** or **General Tolerance** for the DimXpert **Method**. See **Tools**, **Options**, **Document Properties**, **DimXpert**.
- **Inclined Plane Dimension Scheme**. Applies angle dimensions to planes at an angle to a datum or reference plane.

Apply the Inclined Plane Dimension Scheme tool from the DimXpert toolbar to insert linear and angular dimensions between two DimXpert features, excluding surface, fillet, chamfer, and pocket features.

## DimXpert – Chain Dimension

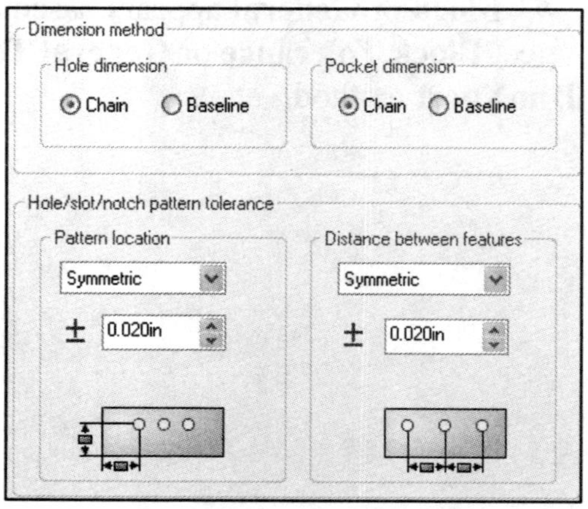


The DimXpert – Chain Dimension section provides the ability to define the type of dimension scheme to apply to pattern and pocket features and the tolerance type and values applied to chain dimension schemes.

The options in this section only apply to dimensions that were created with the Auto Dimension Scheme tool when you set the Tolerance Type to Plus and Minus.

- ***Dimension Method***. Provides the ability to define the dimension scheme used for pattern and pocket features.
  - **Hole dimension**. Chain selected by default. Provides the ability to define the type of dimension used for patterns of counterbores, countersinks, cylinders, holes, slots, and notches. The available options are: **Chain** and **Baseline**.
  - **Pocket dimension**. Chain selected by default. Provides the ability to define the type of dimension used for patterns of counterbores, countersinks, cylinders, holes, slots, and notches. The available options are: **Chain** and **Baseline**.
  - **Hole/slot/notch pattern tolerance**. Provides the ability to set the tolerance type and values used when creating chain dimension schemes. This options offers three tolerance types: **Symmetric**, **Bilateral** and **Block**. Symmetric is selected by default.
    - **Pattern location**. Provides the ability to set the tolerance type and value used for the features locating the pattern from the origin features. Note: For two features, the feature nearest the origin is used to locate the pattern.
    - **Distance between features**. Provides the ability to set the tolerance type and value used for the dimensions applied between the features in the pattern.

## DimXpert – Geometric Tolerance

The DimXpert – Geometric Tolerance section provides the ability to set the tolerance values and criteria for generating geometric tolerance schemes created by the Auto Dimension Scheme tool.

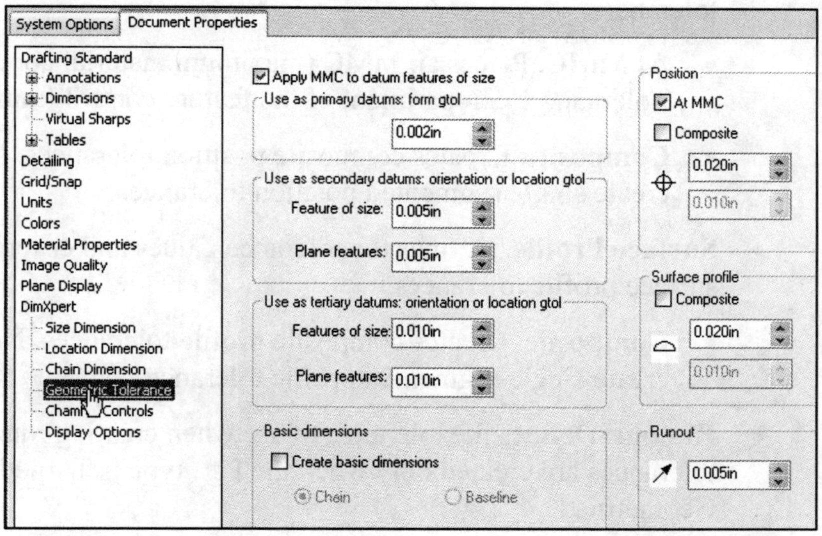

- ***Apply MMC to datum features of size***. Selected by default. Defines whether an MMC symbol is placed in the datum fields when the datum feature is a feature of size.
  - **Use as primary datums: form gtol**. Sets the tolerance value for the tolerances that are applied to primary datum features. DimXpert uses this option when the primary datum feature is a plane, in which case a flatness tolerance is applied.
  - **Use as secondary datums: orientation or location gtol**. Sets the tolerance value for the orientation and location tolerances that are applied to secondary datum features.
  - **Use as tertiary datums: orientation or location gtol**. Sets the tolerance value for the orientation and location tolerances that are applied to tertiary datum features.
  - **Basic dimensions**. Provides the ability to enable or disable the creation of basic dimensions, and to select whether to use Chain or Baseline dimension schemes. This option only applies to position tolerances created by the **Auto Dimension Scheme, Geometric Tolerance** and **Recreate basic dim** commands.
    - **Chain**. Creates chain dimensions between parallel pattern features. When the features are not parallel, baseline dimensions are used.
    - **Baseline**. Creates baseline dimensions that can be applied to any pattern regardless of their orientation to one another. In the example, the features within the pattern are not all parallel.
  - **Position**. Defines the tolerance values and criteria to use when creating position tolerances.
    - **At MMC**. Places an MMC (maximum material condition) symbol in the Tolerance 1 compartment of the feature control frame when applicable.
    - **Composite**. Creates composite position tolerances. Note: Clear Composite to create single segmented position tolerances.
  - **Surface Profile**. Defines the tolerance values and criteria to use when creating surface profile tolerances.
    - **Composite**. Creates composite profile tolerances. Note: Clear Composite to create single segmented profile tolerances.
  - **Runout**. Defines the tolerance to use when creating runout tolerances. Runout tolerances are created only when the Part type is Turned and the Tolerance type is Geometric.

## DimXpert – Chamfer Controls

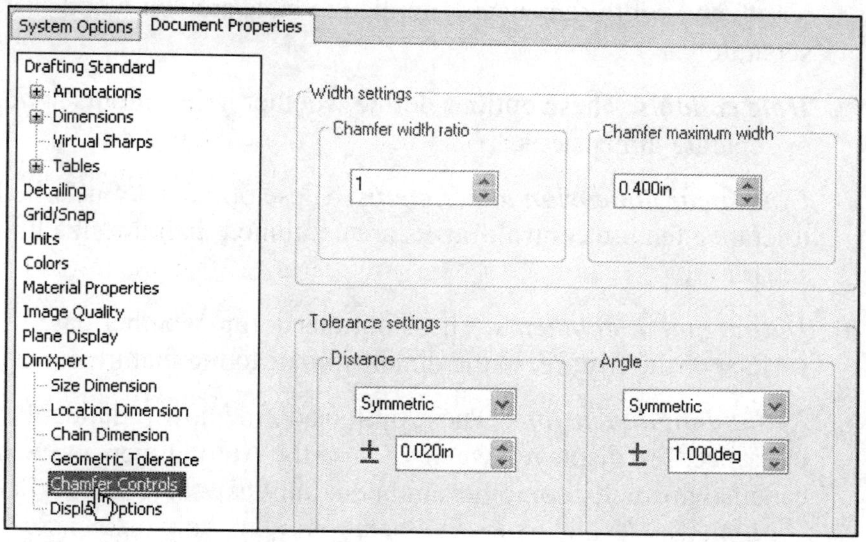


The DimXpert – Chamfer Controls section provides the ability to influence how Chamfer features are recognized by DimXpert, and define the tolerance values used when size tolerances are created by the Auto Dimension Scheme tool or the Size Dimension tool.

- ***Width settings***. Controls when faces can be considered as candidates for chamfer features.
  - **Chamfer width ratio**. Sets the chamfer width ratio, which is computed by dividing the width of a face adjacent to a candidate chamfer by the width of the candidate chamfer.
  - **Chamfer maximum width**. Sets the maximum chamfer width.
- ***Tolerance settings***. Provides two options: **Distance** and **Angle**. Offers three tolerance types: *Symmetric*, *Bilateral* and *Block*. Symmetric is selected by default.

## DimXpert – Display Options

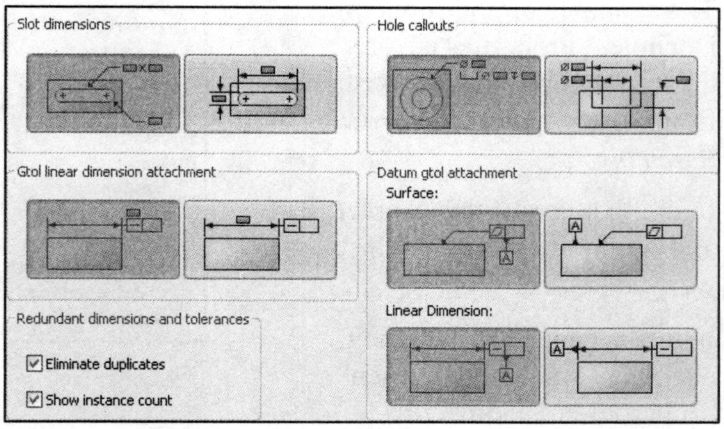


The DimXpert – Display Options section provides the ability to define the dimensioning style used for slot dimensions, hole dimensions, Gtol linear dimension attachments and Datum gtol attachments and how duplicate dimensions and instance counts are managed.

- ***Slot dimensions***. Combined selected by default. These options define whether the length and width dimensions applied to slots are combined as a callout or are placed separately.
- ***Hole callouts***. These options define whether hole callouts are displayed as combined or separate dimensions.
- ***Gtol linear dimension attachments***. These options define whether the geometric tolerance feature control frames are combined with the size limits or placed separately.
- ***Datum gtol attachments***. These options define whether datums are attached to the surface of the feature, to the dimension, or to the feature control frame.
- ***Redundant dimensions***. These options define how redundant dimensions and tolerances are displayed when you use the Auto Dimension Scheme tool. Note: You can also manually combine and break duplicates.
    - **Eliminate duplicates**. Selected by default. Specifies if dimensions are individually stated or combined into a group.
    - **Show instance count**. Selected by default. Defines whether instance counts are displayed with grouped dimensions.

The available options under the Document Properties tab is document dependent: part, assembly, drawing. In the next section, address the six additional options that are only available for a drawing document under the Document Properties tab: **DimXpert**, **Tables**, **View Labels**, **Line Font**, **Line Style** and **Sheet Metal**.

# Drawing Document Properties Section

The available options under the Document Properties tab are document dependent as illustrated from left to right: *Part*, *Drawing* and *Assembly*.

In the first part of this chapter, Part and Assembly Document Properties were addressed.

In this next section, Drawing document specific Document Properties are addressed.

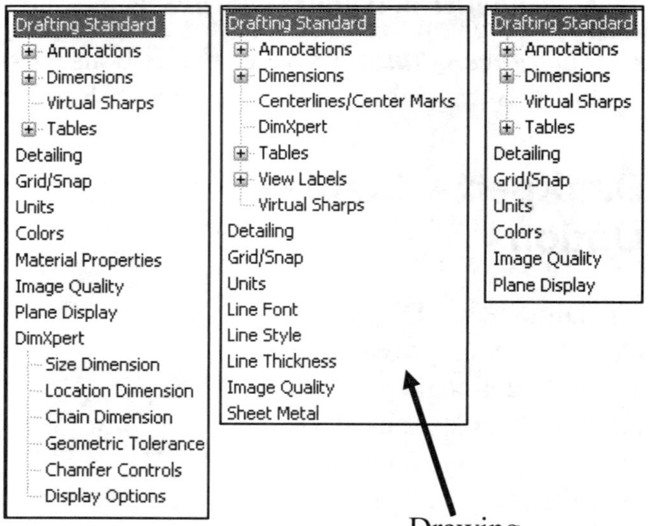

Drawing

# Dimensions – Centerlines/Center Marks

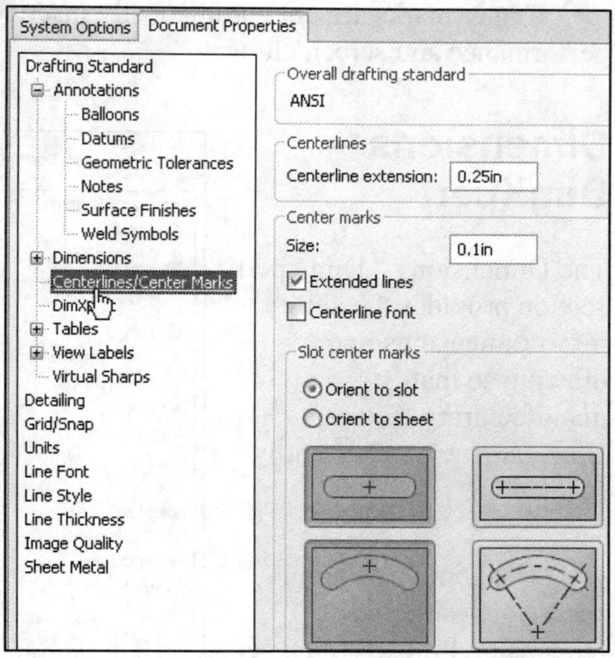


The Dimensions – Centerlines/Center Marks section for a Drawing document provides the following options:

- ***Overall drafting standard***. Displays the selected drafting standard.
- ***Centerlines extension.*** The default is 0.25in for the IPS system and 6.35mm's for the MMGS system. The default value is set according to the ANSI standards. The extension value controls the centerline's extension length beyond the section geometry in a drawing view.
- ***Center marks***. Provides the ability place center marks on circles or arcs in a drawing. The center mark lines can be used as references for dimensioning. Two options are provided:
  - **Extended lines.** Select to display center mark extension lines.
  - **Centerline font**. Select to make the center mark extension lines follow the font selected for centerlines.

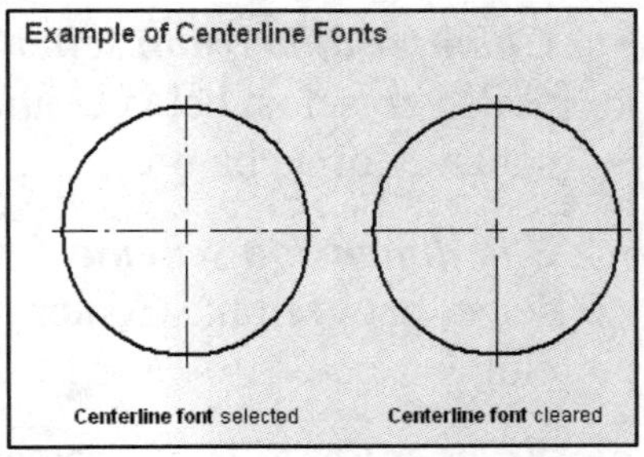


Center marks are available as single marks, in linear patterns, or in circular patterns. Linear patterns can include connection lines. Circular patterns can include circular lines, radial lines, and base center marks. Display attributes include mark size, extended lines and specifying the centerline font for the center mark lines.

- ***Slot center marks***. Two options are provided:
  - **Orient to slot**.
  - **Orient to sheet**.

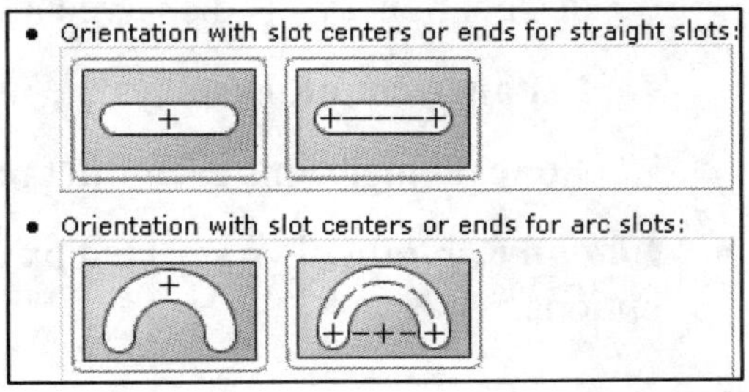

Center marks are not automatically inserted into assembly drawings because of performance and screen clutter.

## Dimensions – DimXpert

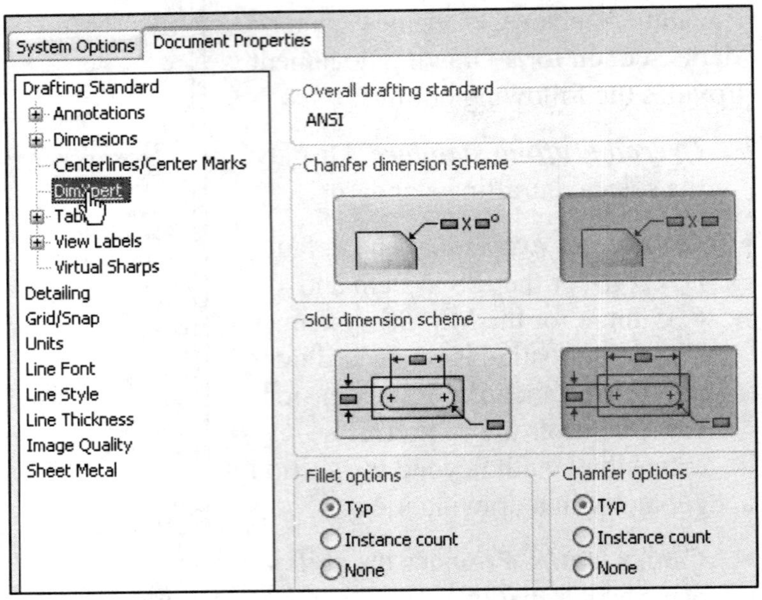


The Dimensions – DimXpert section provides the ability to insert dimensions in a drawing so that manufacturing features; *slots*, *patterns*, *etc*. are fully-defined.

The DimXpert tool is accessible using the Dimension PropertyManager or from the DimXpert tab in the CommandManager.

The Dimensions – DimXpert section provides the following options:

- ***Overall drafting standard***. Displays the selected drafting standard.
- ***Chamfer dimension scheme***. Distance X Distance is selected by default. Provides the ability to select between the Distance X Angle or the Distance X Distance dimension scheme for a chamfer.
- ***Slot dimension scheme***. Overall Length is selected by default. Provides the ability to select between the Center to Center or the Overall Length dimension scheme for a slot.
- ***Fillet options***. Typ is selected by default. Provides the ability to select three fillet options:
  - **Typ**. Inserts single or multiple dimensions to fillets of the same size. The designation Typ is displayed after the dimension.
  - **Instance count**. Displays the number of instances of fillets of the same size.
  - **None**. Dimensions each fillet regardless if they are the same size.
- ***Chamfer options***. Typ selected by default. Provides the ability to select three chamfer options:

- **Typ**. Inserts single or multiple dimensions to chamfers of the same size. The designation Typ is displayed after the dimension.
- **Instance count**. Displays the number of instances of chamfers of the same size.
- **None**. Dimensions each chamfer regardless if they are the same size.

## Tables – General

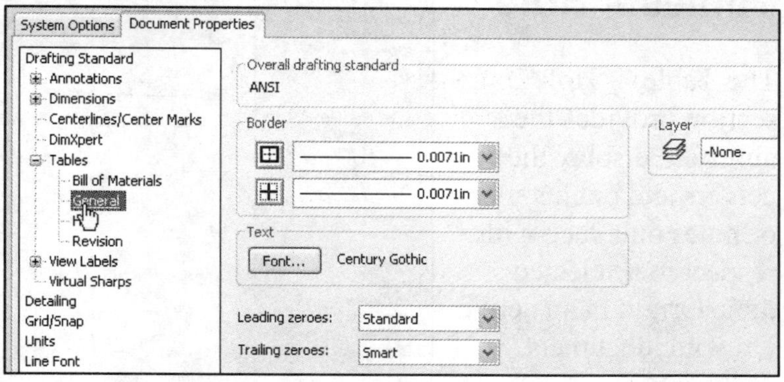


The Tables – General section provides the following options for an active Drawing document:

- ***Overall drafting standard***. Displays the selected drafting standard.
- ***Border***. Click the **Box Border** option or the **Grid Border** option and select a corresponding thickness. The default thickness is 0.007in for IPS and .18mm's for MMGS unit system.
- ***Text***. Century Gothic selected by default. Click the Font button to select a custom font style and size.

  - **Leading zeroes**. Standard selected by default. Select one of three options from the drop-down menu:
    - **Standard**. Zeros are displayed based on the selected dimensioning standard.
    - **Show**. Zeros before the decimal points are displayed on the selected dimensioning standard.
    - **Remove**. Zeros are not displayed.

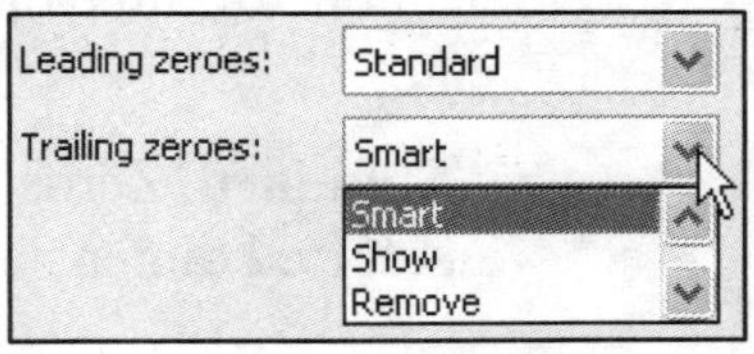


  - **Trailing zeroes**. Provides the following selections:
    - **Smart**. Selected by default. Trailing zeros are trimmed for whole metric values. Conforms to ANSI and ISO standards.
    - **Show**. Dimensions have trailing zeros up to the number of decimal places specified in **Options**, **Document Properties**, and **Units**.

- **Remove**. All trailing zeros are removed.
- **Standard**. Trims trailing zeros to the ASME Y14.5M-1994 standard.

- ***Layer***. Select a Layer property to evaluate a drawing view.

## Tables – Hole

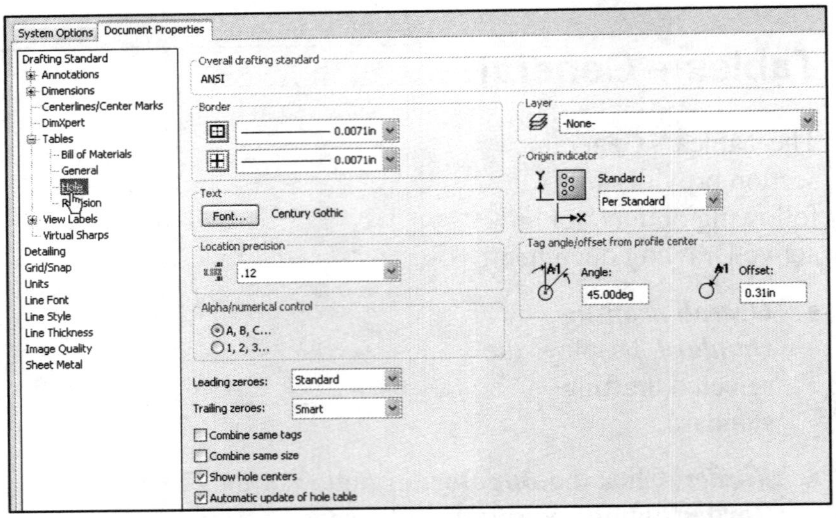


The Tables – Hole section provides the ability to display the centers and diameters of holes on a face with respect to a selected table Origin in an active Drawing document.

Hole Tables use a separate template.

The Tables – Hole section provides the following options:

- ***Overall drafting standard***. Displays the selected drafting standard.
- ***Border***. Click the **Box Border** option or the **Grid Border** option and select a corresponding thickness. The default thickness is 0.007in for the IPS system and .18mm's for the MMGS system.
- ***Text***. Century Gothic selected by default. Click the Font button to select a custom font style and size.
- ***Location precision***. Specifies the number of significant digits for the hole location value.
- ***Alpha/numerical control***. Specifies the tags identifying the holes to be letters or numbers.
  - **Leading zeroes**. Standard selected by default. Select one of three options from the drop-down menu:

    - **Standard**. Zeros are displayed based on the selected dimensioning standard.
    - **Show**. Zeros before the decimal points are displayed on the selected dimensioning standard.
    - **Remove**. Zeros are not displayed.

- **Trailing zeroes**. Provides the following selections:

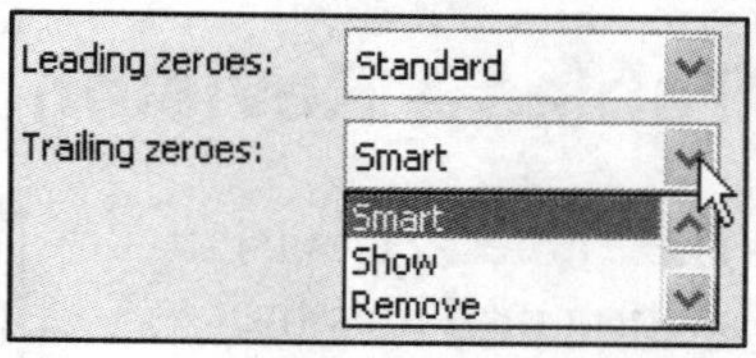


  - **Smart**. Selected by default. Trailing zeros are trimmed for whole metric values. Conforms to ANSI and ISO standards.
  - **Show**. Dimensions have trailing zeros up to the number of decimal places specified in **Options**, **Document Properties**, and **Units**.
  - **Remove**. All trailing zeros are removed.
  - **Standard**. Trims trailing zeros to the ASME Y14.5M-1994 standard.

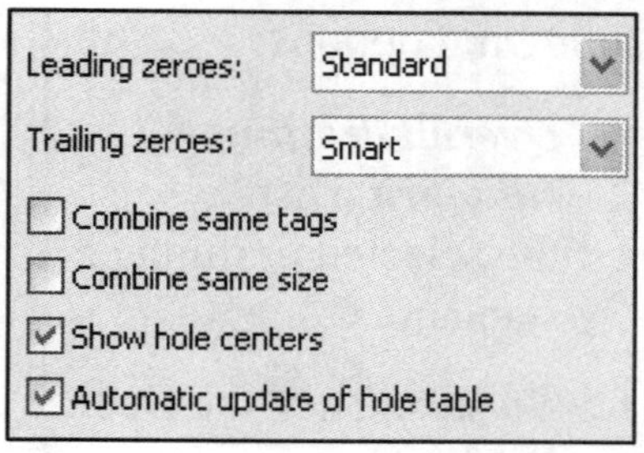


  - **Combine same tags**. Combines rows with holes in the same pattern, which also combines holes with the same sizes. The columns of location values are removed.
  - **Combine same size**. Available only if Combine same tags is cleared. Merges cells for holes of the same size. The columns of location values remain.
  - **Show hole centers.** Selected by default.
  - **Automatic update of hole table**. Selected by default.

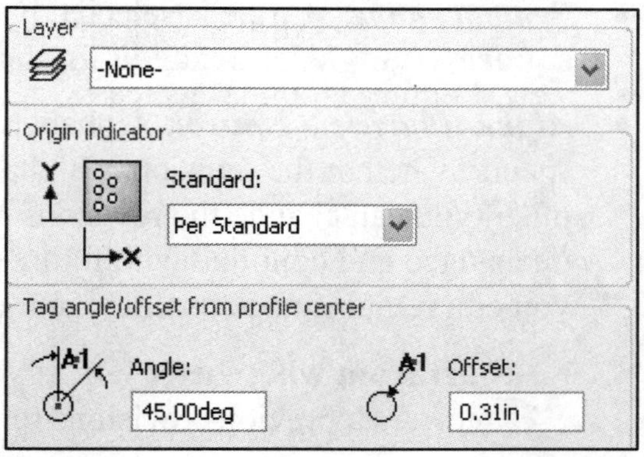


- ***Layer***. Select a Layer property to evaluate a drawing view.
- ***Origin indicator***. Per Standard is selected by default. Provides the ability to specify the appearance of the indicator of the Origin from which the software calculates the hole position by selecting a standard. There are eight options. They are: **Per Standard, ANSI, ISO, DIN, JIS, BSI, GOST** and **GB**.
- ***Tag angle/offset from profile center***. Provides the ability to position the text at an angle and distance from the center of the hole. There are two available options:
  - **Angle**. Angle from a vertical line through the center of the hole.
  - **Offset**. Distance from the hole profile.

# Tables – Revision

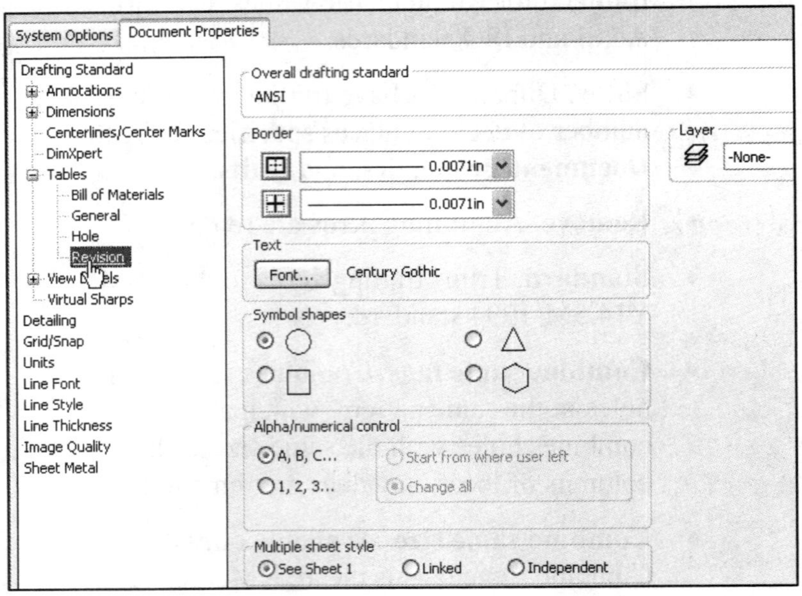


The Tables – Revision section provides the ability to track drawing revisions. The revision level is stored in a custom property in the file.

The Tables – Revision section provides the following options:

- ***Overall drafting standard***. Displays the selected drafting standard.
- ***Border***. Click the **Box Border** option or the **Grid Border** option and select a corresponding thickness. The default thickness is 0.007in for IPS and .18mm's for MMGS unit system.
- ***Text***. Century Gothic selected by default. Click the Font button to select a custom font style and size.
- ***Symbol shapes***. Circle is selected by default. Provided the ability to select a **circle**, **square**, **triangle**, or **hexagon** for the revision symbol in a drawing.
- ***Alpha/numerical control***. Alphabetic is selected by default. Provides the ability to specify whether the revision is alphabetic or numeric. If you switch from one to the other, you can change the revisions already in the table, or you can leave them unchanged and continue with future revisions in the new format. Any revision text you edit remains unchanged by automatic operations. The options are:
  - **Start from where user left**. If you change control from alphabetic to numeric or vice versa, previous revisions remain as they are.
  - **Change all**. If you change control from alphabetic to numeric or vice versa, previous revisions, except any you have edited change to the new format.
- ***Multiple sheet style***. Provides the ability to control revision tables in drawings with multiple sheets. The three options are:
  - **See Sheet1**. Selected by default. The revision table on the first sheet is the active table. On all other drawing sheets, the revision table is labeled See Sheet 1.

- **Linked**. A copy of the revision table from Sheet 1 is created on all sheets, and all revision tables update as one.
- **Independent**. The revision table on each sheet is independent of any other revision table in the drawing. Updates to a revision table are not reflected in tables on other sheets.

- ***Layer***. Select a Layer property to evaluate a drawing view.

## View Labels

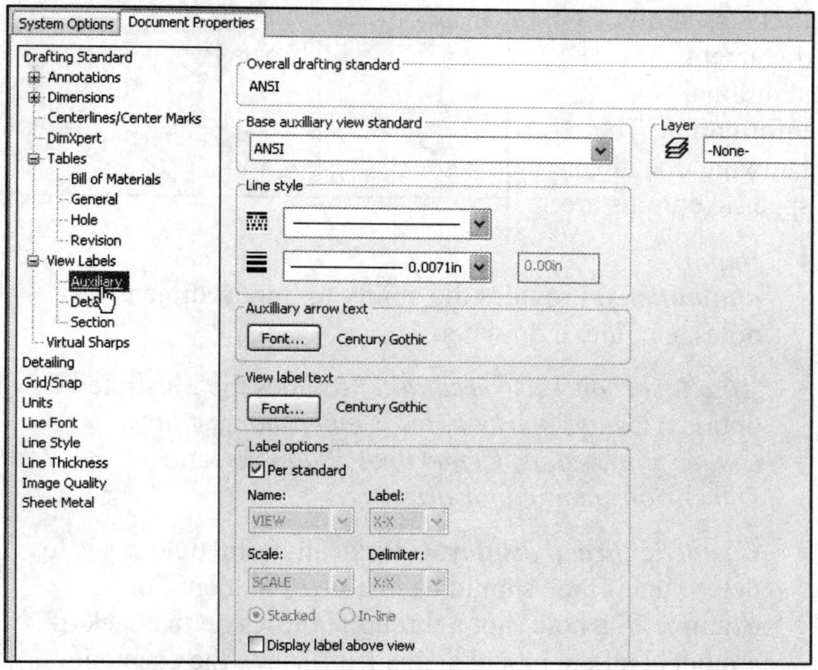


The View Labels section provides the ability to set options for *Auxiliary*, *Detail* and *Section* view labels in an active drawing document. The default option is Per standard.

The Per standard follows the standard specified in the **Options, Document Properties, Detailing, etc** command procedure from the Menu bar toolbar. See SolidWorks Help for additional detail information.

The available Label options are:

- **Name**. Select a title to be displayed in the view label.
- **Label**. Select whether the label letter corresponding to the label on the parent view is displayed in the view label.
- **Scale**. Select whether the word SCALE is displayed next to the scale.
- **Delimiter**. Select the delimiter between the two scale numbers and whether the scale is displayed in parentheses. If you select **#X**, the number in (#) can be an integer or a real number.
- **Preview**. Display the view label with name and label stacked on top of the scale (Stacked), or all data on the same line (In-line).
- **Display label above view**. Places view labels above the drawing view. This applies to new drawing views only.

## Detailing

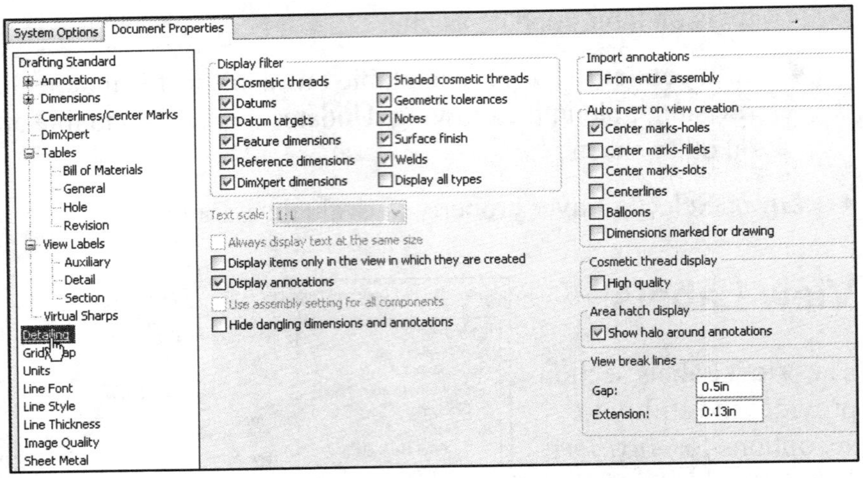


Additional tools are available for a Drawing document. See the Detailing section on Part/Assembly documents for additional information. The Drawing document specific options are:

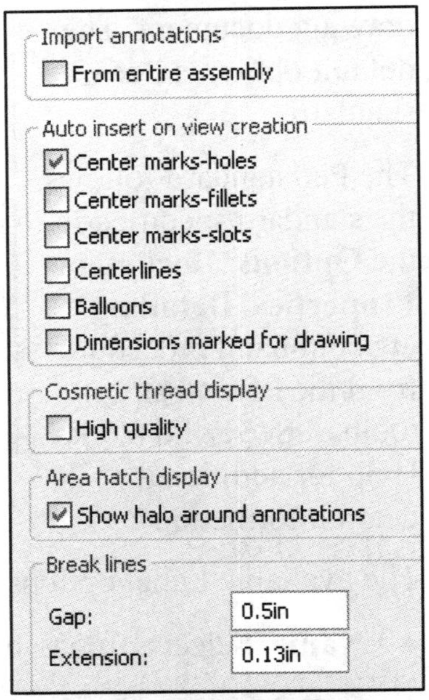


- ***Import annotations***. Provides the ability to import dimensions, notes, etc. into a drawing.
- ***Auto insert on View creation***. Provides the illustrated options: *Center marks-holes, Center marks-fillets, Center marks-slots, Centerlines, Balloons*, and *Dimensions marked for drawing*.
- ***Cosmetic thread display***. Checks all cosmetic threads to determine if they should be visible or hidden. For example, if a hole (not a through hole) is on the back of a model and the model is in a front view, the cosmetic thread is hidden. You can set the display for each drawing view individually in the drawing view PropertyManager under **Cosmetic Thread Display**.
- ***Area hatch display***. Displays space around dimensions and annotations that belong to the drawing view or a sketch and are on top of an area hatch.

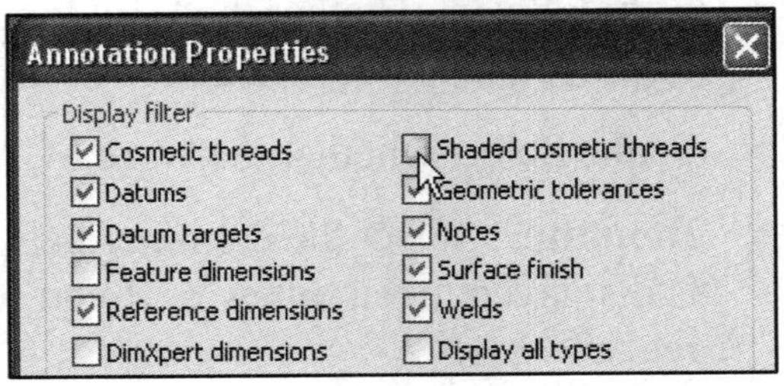


- ***Break lines***. Set a value for the distance between the model and dimension extension lines. This also controls the gap between dimensions and center marks.

## Line Font

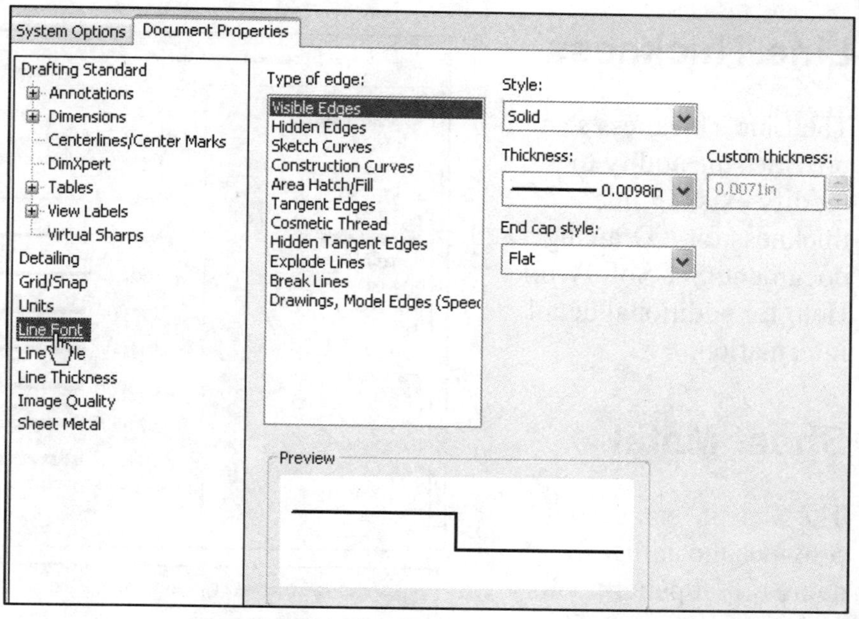


The Line Font section provides the ability to set the style and weight of a line for various edge types in a Drawing document. The available options are:

- ***Type of edge***. Visible Edges selected by default. Select an edge type from the drop-down menu.

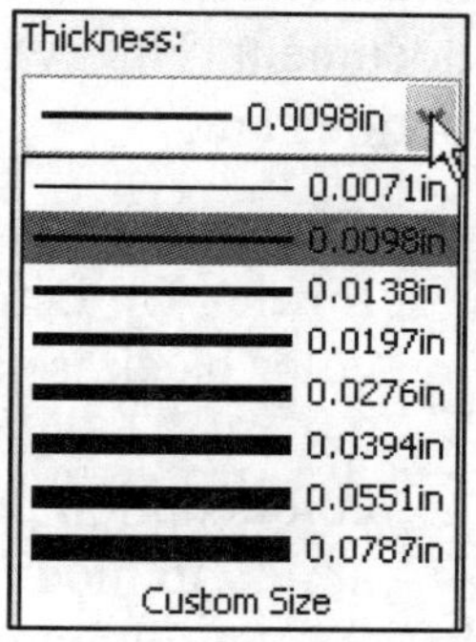


- ***Style***. Solid selected by default. Select a style from the drop-down menu. There are seven options: **Solid**, **Dashed**, **Phantom**, **Chain**, **Center**, **Stitch**, and **Thin/Thick Chain**.
- ***Thickness***. Select a thickness from the drop-down menu or select custom size in input a dimension.
- ***End Cap Style***. Flat selected by default. Select a style that defines the ends of edges: **Flat**, **Round** or **Square**.

## Line Style

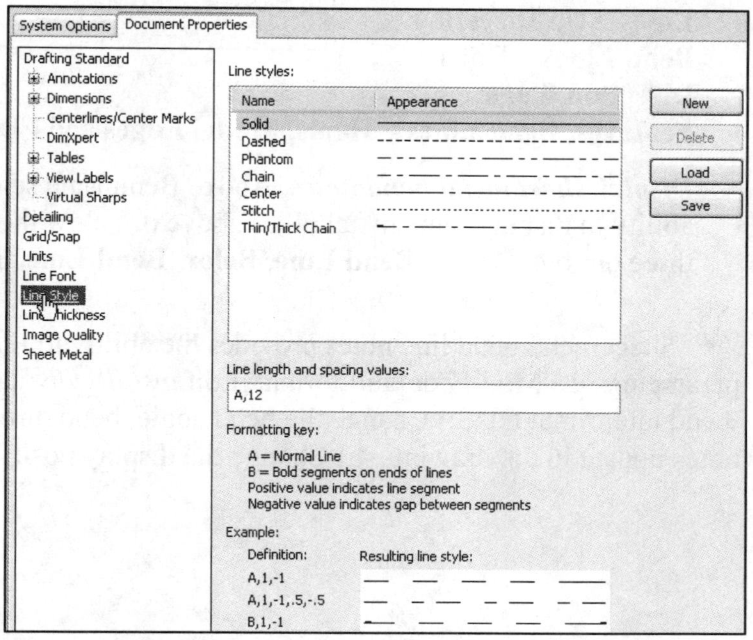


The Line Style section provides the ability to create or modify existing line styles for a Drawing document.

Apply a simple code which is illustrated to create a special line style. See SolidWorks Help for additional detail information.

## Line Thickness

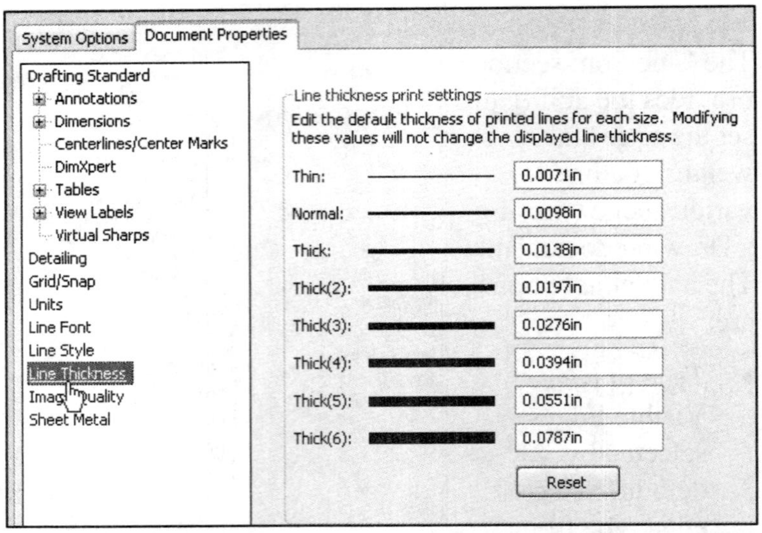


The Line Thickness section provides the ability to modify existing line thickness for a Drawing document. See SolidWorks Help for additional detail information.

## Sheet Metal

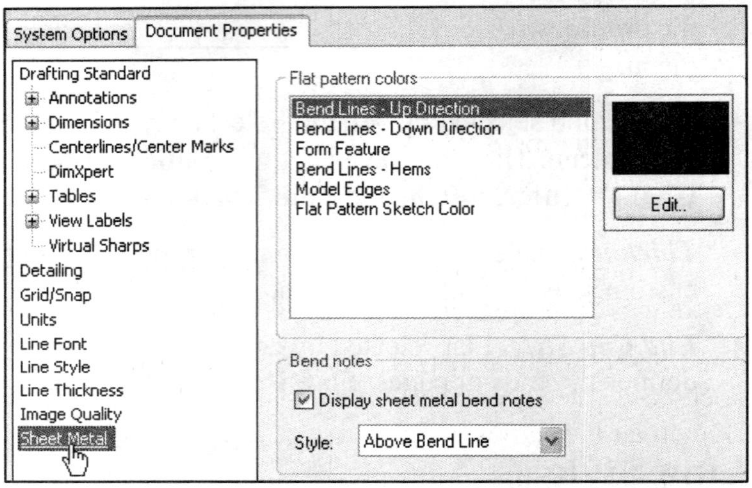


The Sheet Metal section provides the ability to address Flat pattern colors and Bend notes to a Drawing document. The available options are:

- ***Flat pattern colors***. Bend Lines – Up Direction, color black is selected by default. The Flat pattern colors option provides the ability to modify colors for the following: **Bend Lines – Up Direction**, **Bend Lines – Down Direction**, **Form Features**, **Bend Lines – Hems**, **Model Edges** and **Flat Pattern Sketch Color**.
- ***Display sheet metal bend notes***. Above Bend Line selected by default. Provides the ability to display sheet metal notes above of below the bend line. Select one of the three options: **Above Bend Line**, **Below Bend Line** and **With Leader**.

Sheet metal bend line notes provides the ability to: 1.) Edit text outside the note parameters. 2.) Modify default format. Edit *install_dir*>\lang\<*language*> \bendnoteformat.txt. 3.) Change the bend angle, bend direction, or bend radius, and the notes update in the drawing. 4.) Change the display position of the bend notes.

# Summary

This chapter was intended to provide a general overview of the available Document Properties for a Part, Assembly and Drawing document.

The available options under the Document Properties tab are document dependent as illustrated from left to right: *Part*, *Drawing* and *Assembly.*

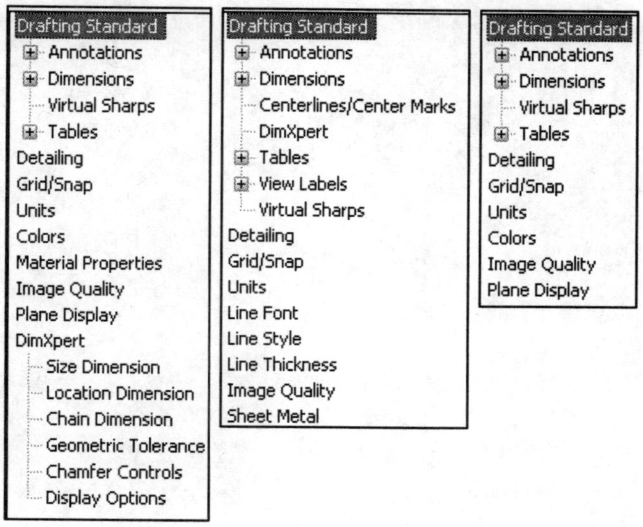


Templates are documents, (part, drawing, assembly) which include user-defined parameters and are the basis for a new document.

You created a custom Assembly template using the ANSI, MMGS Unit system and a Part template with an applied material.

The Document Properties applied to a template allows you to work efficiently. However, Document Properties in the current document can be modified at any time.

The first half of this chapter addressed the Document Properties for a Part or Assembly document. The second half of the chapter addressed Drawing document specific Document Properties.

In Chapter 4, explore and address Design Intent, 2D and 3D Sketching, Sketch states, Parent/Child relationships, Sketch Entities tools, and the Block and Spline toolbar.

**Document Properties**

## Notes:

# CHAPTER 4: DESIGN INTENT, SKETCHING AND SKETCH ENTITIES

## Chapter Objective

Chapter 4 provides a comprehensive understanding of Design Intent, Sketching and the available Sketch Entities in SolidWorks. On the completion of this chapter, you will be able to:

- Define and incorporate Design Intent in a:
  - Sketch, Feature, Part, Assembly and Drawing
- Utilize the available SolidWorks Design Intent tools:
  - Comments, Design Binder, ConfigurationManager, dimensions, equations, design tables and features
- Identify the correct Reference planes:
  - 2D Sketching
  - 3D Sketching
- Insert sketch Reference planes
- Comprehend the Parent/Child relationship
- Recognize and address Sketch states:
  - Fully Defined, Over Defined, Under Defined, No Solution Found and Invalid Solution Found
- Identify and utilize the following Sketch Entities tools:
  - Line, Corner Rectangle, Center Rectangle, 3 Point Corner Rectangle, 3 Point Center Rectangle, Parallelogram, Straight Slot, Centerpoint Straight Slot, 3 Point Arc Slot, Centerpoint Arc Slot, Instant3D, Polygon, Circle, Perimeter Circle, Centerpoint Arc, Tangent Arc, 3 Point Arc, Ellipse, Partial Ellipse, Parabola, Spline, Spline on Surface, Equation Driven Curve, Point, Centerline, Text, Plane, Route line and Belt/Chain
- Classify and utilize the following Block tools:
  - Make Block, Edit Block, Insert Block, Add/Remove, Rebuild, Saves Block, Explode Block and Belt/Chain
- Recognize and utilize the following Spline tools:

- Add Tangency Control, Add Curvature Control, Insert Spline Point, Simplify Spline, Fit Spline, Show Spline Handle, Show Inflection points, Show Minimum Radius and Show Curvature Combs

# Design Intent

What is design intent? All designs are created for a purpose. Design intent is the intellectual arrangements of features and dimensions of a design. Design intent governs the relationship between sketches in a feature, features in a part and parts in an assembly.

The SolidWorks definition of design intent is the process in which the model is developed to accept future modifications. Models behave differently when design changes occur.

Design for change! Utilize geometry for symmetry, reuse common features, and reuse common parts. Build change into the following areas that you create: sketch, feature, part, assembly & drawing.

When editing or repairing geometric relations, it is considered best practice to edit the relation vs. deleting it.

## Design Intent in a sketch

Build design intent in a sketch as the profile is created. A profile is determined from the Sketch Entities. Example: Rectangle, Circle, Arc, Point, Slot etc. Apply symmetry into a profile through a sketch centerline, mirror entity and position about the reference planes and Origin.

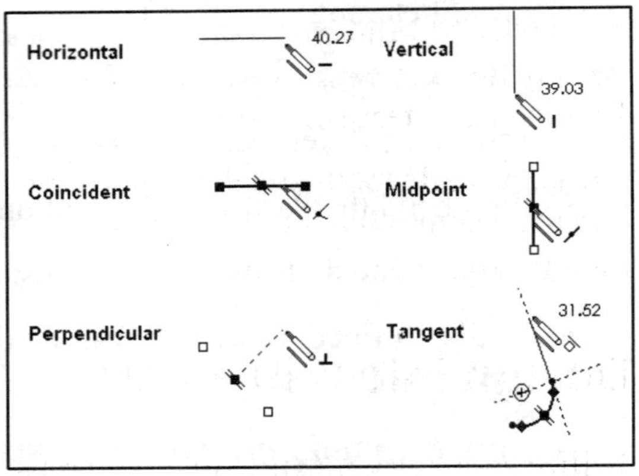


Build design intent as you sketch with automatic Geometric relations. Document the decisions made during the up-front design process. This is very valuable when you modify the design later.

A rectangle (Center Rectangle Sketch tool) contains Horizontal, Vertical and Perpendicular automatic Geometric relations.

Apply design intent using added Geometric relations if needed. Example: Horizontal, Vertical, Collinear, Perpendicular, Parallel, Equal etc.

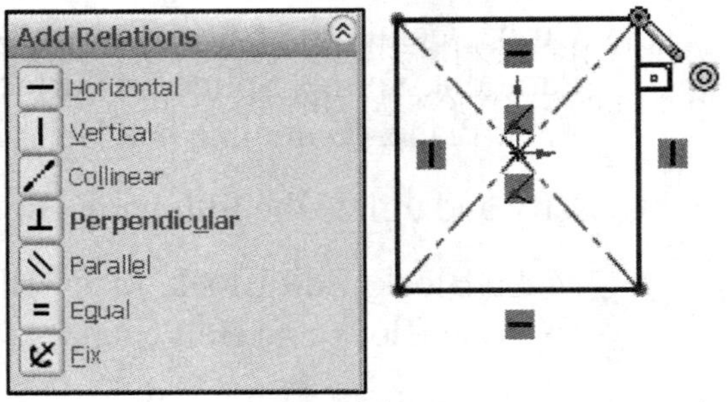

Example A: Apply design intent to create a square profile. Sketch a rectangle. Apply the Center Rectangle Sketch tool. Note: No construction reference centerline or Midpoint relation is required with the Center Rectangle tool. Insert dimensions to fully define the sketch.

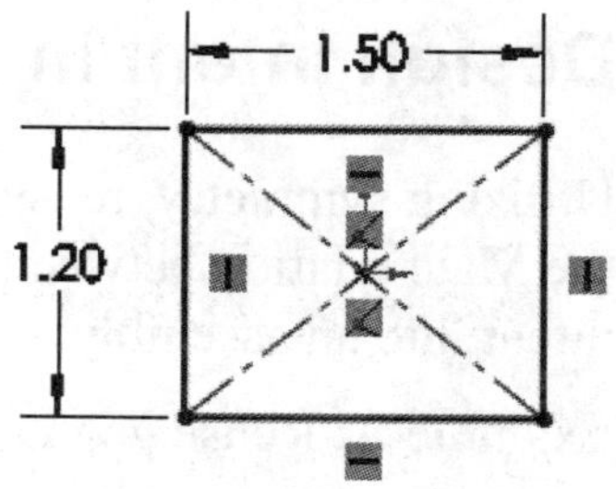


Example B: Develop a rectangular profile. Apply the Corner Rectangle Sketch tool. The bottom horizontal midpoint of the rectangular profile is located at the Origin. Add a Midpoint relation between the horizontal edge of the rectangle and the Origin. Insert two dimensions to fully define the rectangle as illustrated.

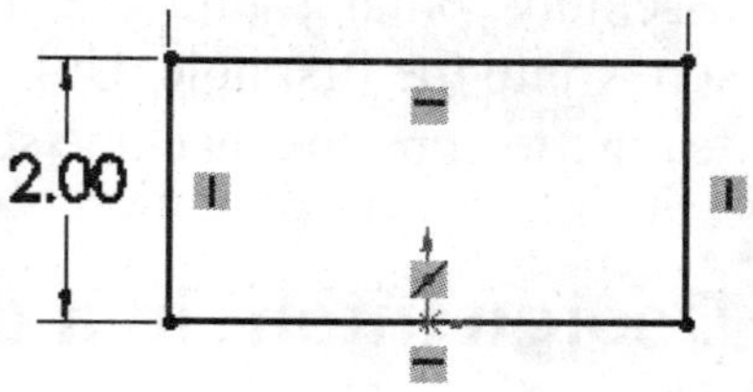


## Design intent in a feature

Build design intent into a feature by addressing symmetry, feature selection, and the order of feature creation.

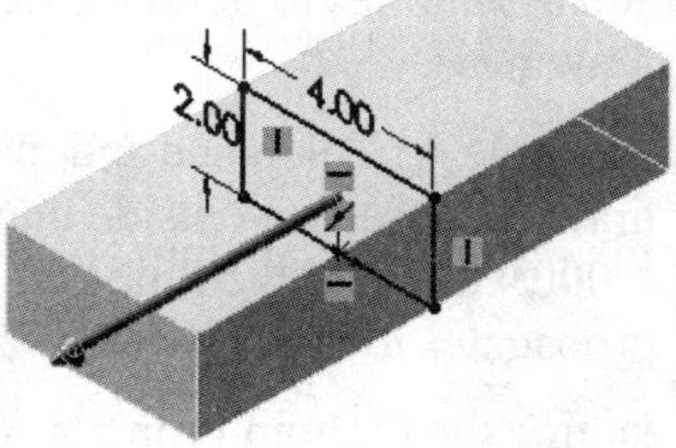


Example A: The Extruded Base feature remains symmetric about the Front Plane. Utilize the Mid Plane End Condition option in Direction 1. Modify the depth, and the feature remains symmetric about the Front Plane.

Example B: Create 34 teeth in the model. Do you create each tooth separate using the Extruded Cut feature? No.

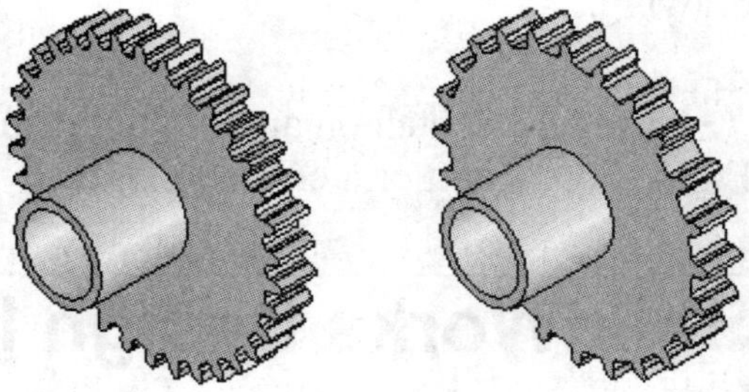

Create a single tooth and then apply the Circular Pattern feature. Modify the Circular Pattern from 32 to 24 teeth.

## Design intent in a part

Utilize symmetry, feature order and reusing common features to build design intent into a part. Example A: Feature order. Is the entire part symmetric? Feature order affects the part.

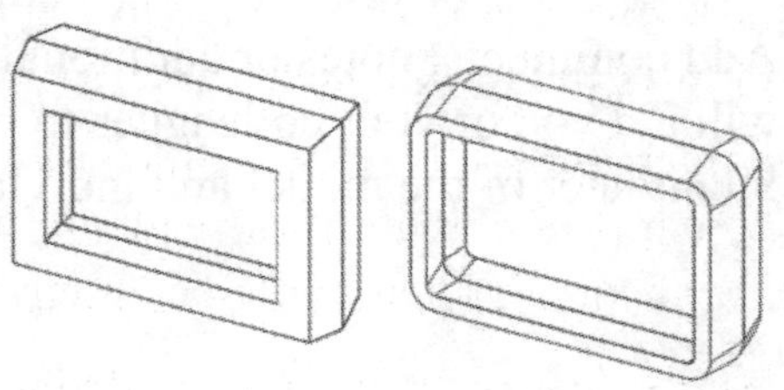

Apply the Shell feature before the Fillet feature and the inside corners remain perpendicular.

## Design intent in an assembly

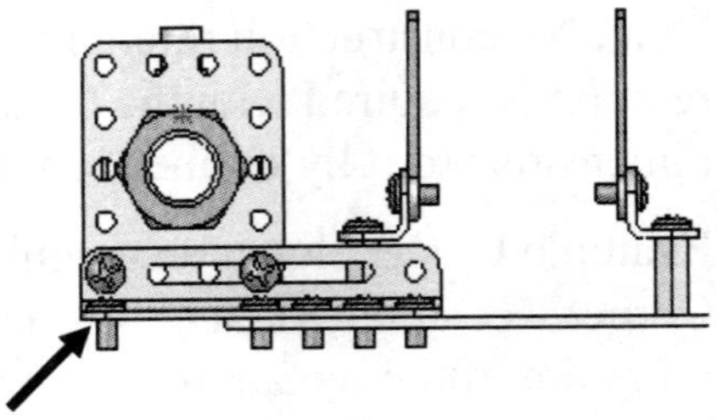

Utilizing symmetry, reusing common parts and using the Mate relation between parts builds the design intent into an assembly.

Example A: Reuse geometry in an assembly. The assembly contains a linear pattern of holes. Insert one screw into the first hole. Utilize the Component Pattern feature to copy the machine screw to the other holes.

## Design intent in a drawing

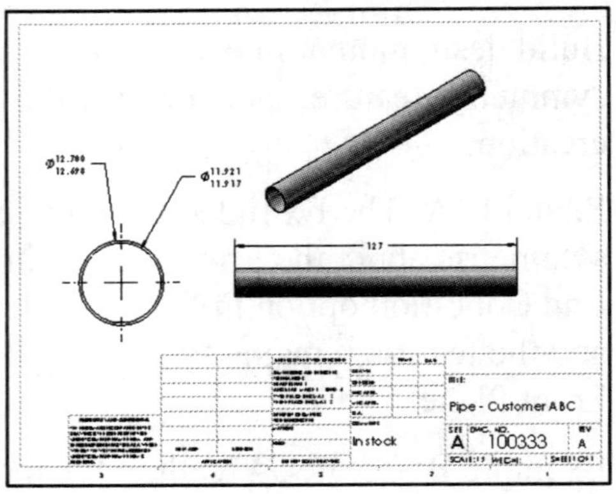


Utilize dimensions, tolerance and notes in parts and assemblies to build the design intent into a drawing.

Example A: Tolerance and material in the drawing. Insert an outside diameter tolerance +.000/-.002 into the Pipe part. The tolerance propagates to the drawing.

Define the Custom Property Material in the Part. The Material Custom Property propagates to your drawing.

Create a sketch on any of the default planes: Front, Top, Right or a created plane.

# SolidWorks Design Intent tools

## Comments

Add comments, notes or additional information to features during the design period. This will aid you or your colleagues to recall and to better understand the fundamental design intent later of the model and individual features.

Right-click on the **FeatureManager name**. Click **Comment ➤ Add Comment** from the FeatureManager design tree. The Comment dialog box is displayed. Enter the information. Move your mouse pointer over the feature. The created comment is shown in a balloon format.

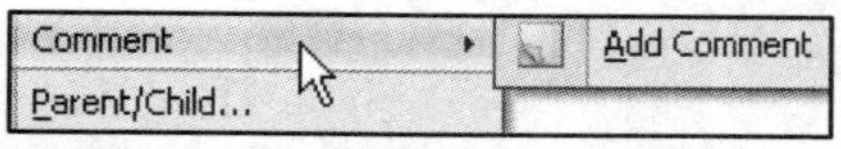

You can also add a Date/Time stamp to your comment.

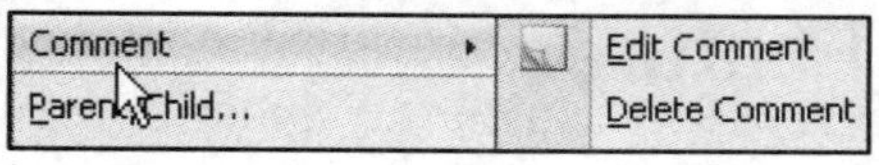


## Design Binder

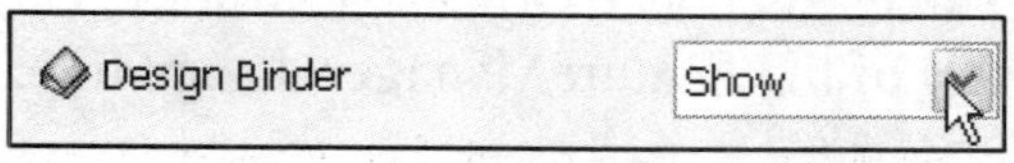


Activate the Design binder. Click **Options** ➤ **System Options** tab ➤ **FeatureManager**. Select **Show** from the drop-down menu. The Design Binder is an embedded Microsoft Word document that provides the ability for the user to capture a screen image and to incorporate text into a document.

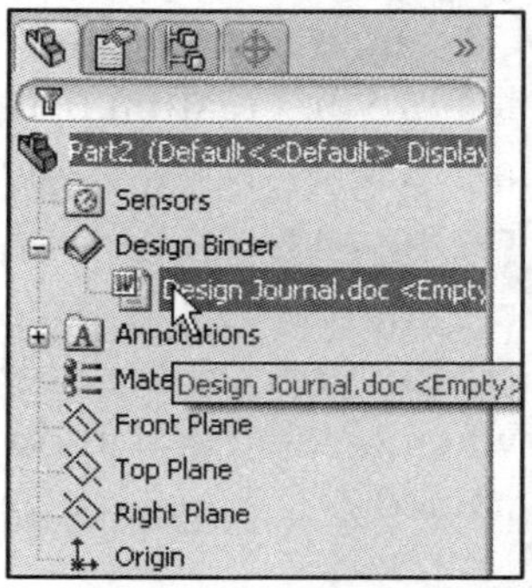


## ConfigurationManager

When you create various configurations for assemblies, design tables, etc., use the comment area to incorporate a comment for these configurations.

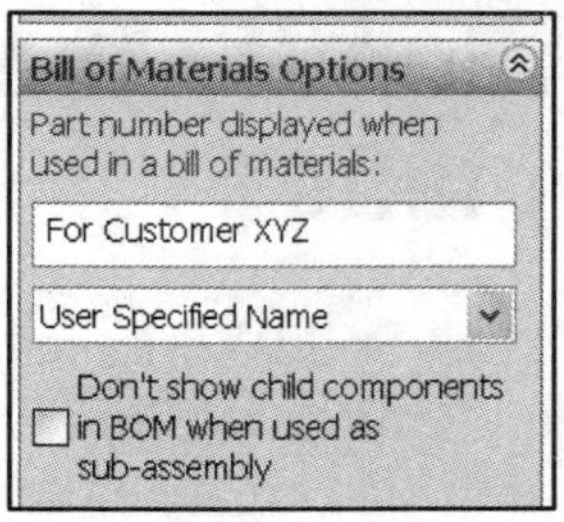


## Dimensions

To be efficient, reuse existing geometry. Provide dimensions with descriptive names.

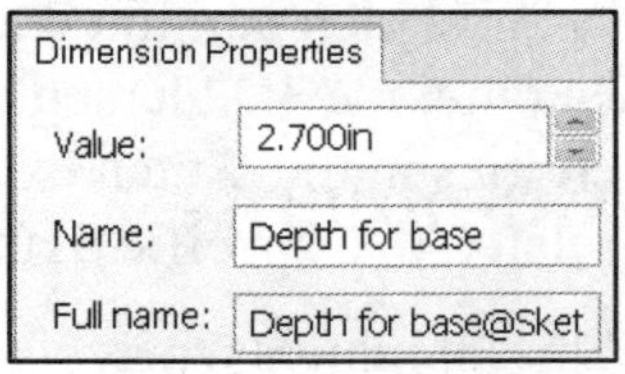


## Equations

Add a comment to the end of an equation to provide clarity for the future. Use descriptive names and organize your equations for improve clarity. SolidWorks equations ignore everything from the right of the apostrophe.

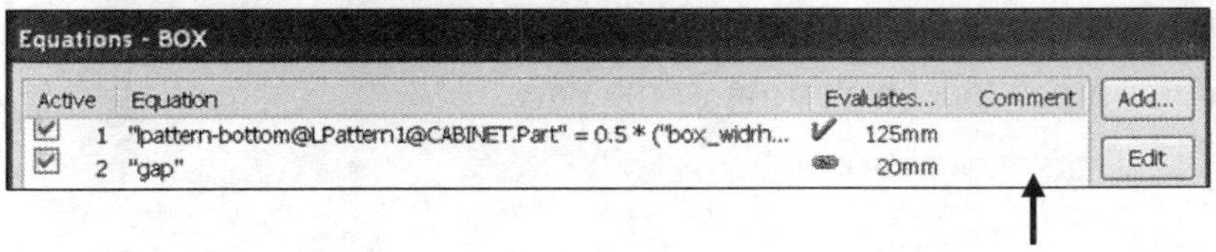

## Design Tables

There are a number of ways to incorporate a comment into a design table. One way is to add "$COMMENT" to the heading of a column. This provides the ability to add a comment in a design table.

## Features

Always use descriptive names in the FeatureManager design tree, not the default feature names such as Extrude1, Extrude1, LPattern1, etc. Group important features toward the top of the FeatureManager design tree.

Enable the FeatureManager Name feature on creation option, click **Options** ➤ **System Options** ➤ **FeatureManager** ➤ **Name feature on creation** box. The Name feature on creation option highlights the feature name when created and allows the feature to be named.

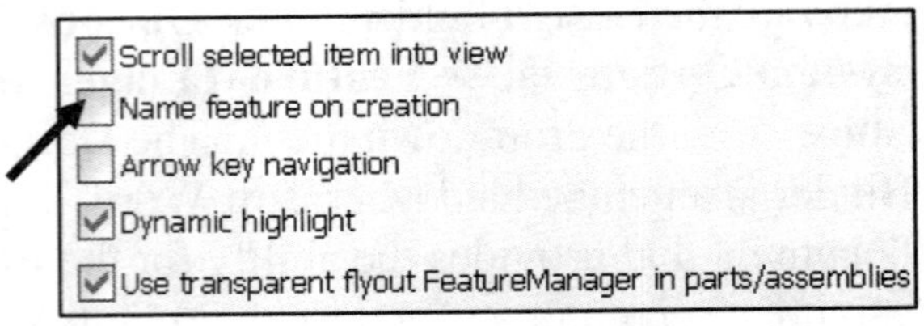


# Identify the Correct Reference planes

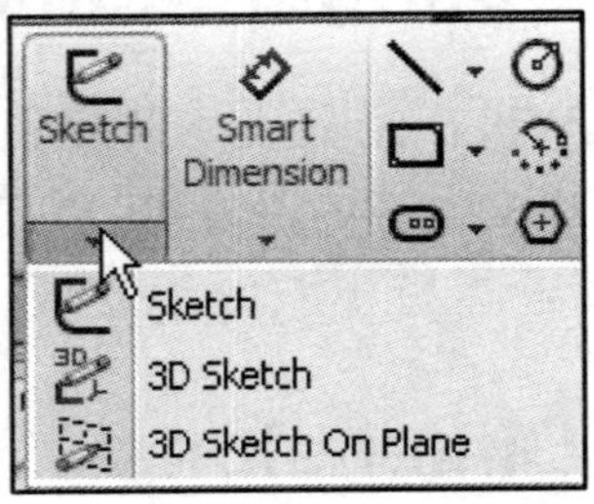


Most SolidWorks features start with a 2D sketch. Sketches are the foundation for creating features. SolidWorks provides the ability to create either 2D or 3D sketches.

A 2D sketch is limited to a flat 2D Sketch plane. A 3D sketch can include 3D elements. As you create a 3D sketch, the entities in the sketch exist in 3D space. These entities are not related to a specific Sketch plane as they are in a 2D sketch.

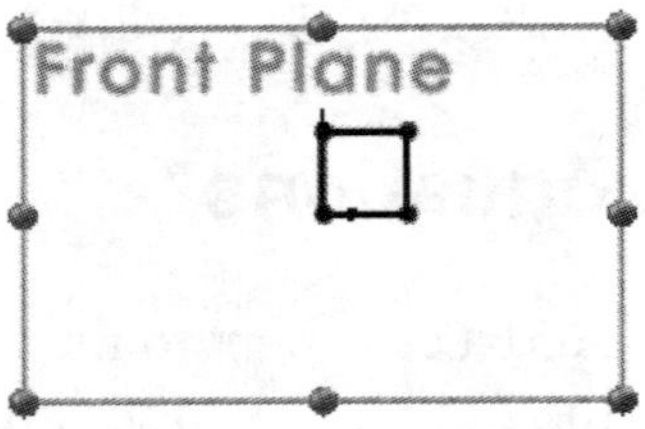


Does it matter where you start sketching? Yes! When you create a new part or assembly, the three default planes are aligned with specific views. The plane you select for your first sketch determines the orientation of the part. Selecting the correct plane is very important.

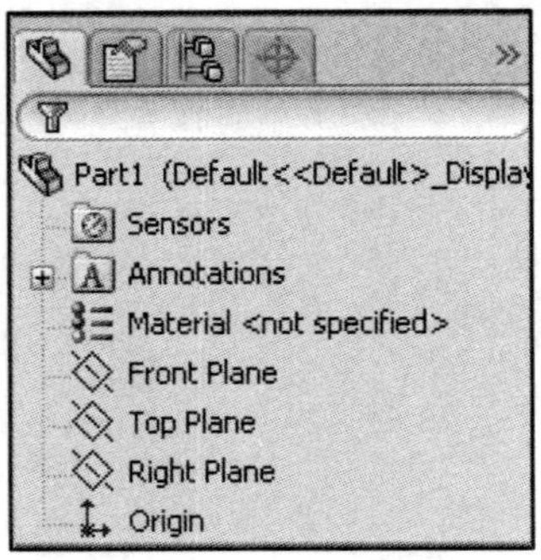


The plane or face you select for the Base sketch determines the orientation of the part.

## 2D Sketching / Reference planes

The three default ⊥ reference planes, displayed in the FeatureManager design tree represent infinite 2D planes in 3D space. They are:

- Front
- Top
- Right

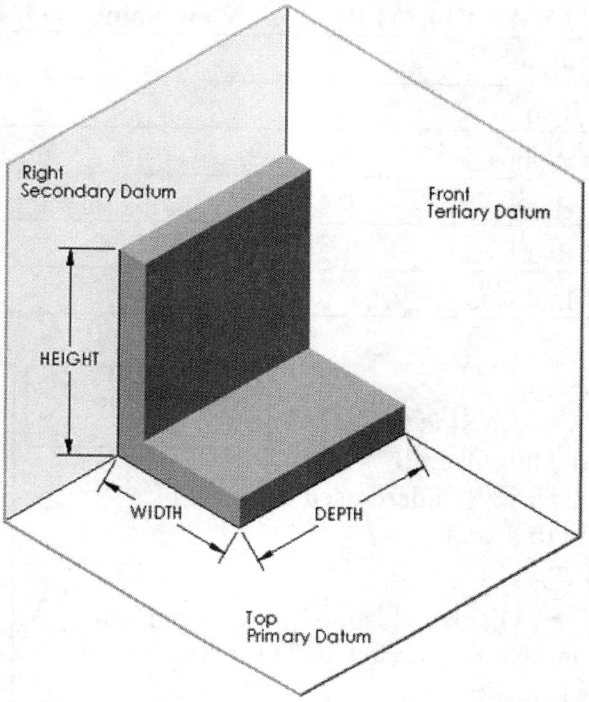


Planes have no thickness or mass. Orthographic projection is the process of projecting views onto parallel planes with ⊥ projectors. The default ⊥ datum planes are:

- Primary
- Secondary
- Tertiary

Use the following planes in a manufacturing environment:

- Primary datum plane: Contacts the part at a minimum of three points
- Secondary datum plane: Contacts the part at a minimum of two points
- Tertiary datum plane: Contacts the part at a minimum of one point

The part view orientation depends on the sketch plane. Compare the Front, Top and Right Sketch planes for an L-shaped profile in the following illustration.

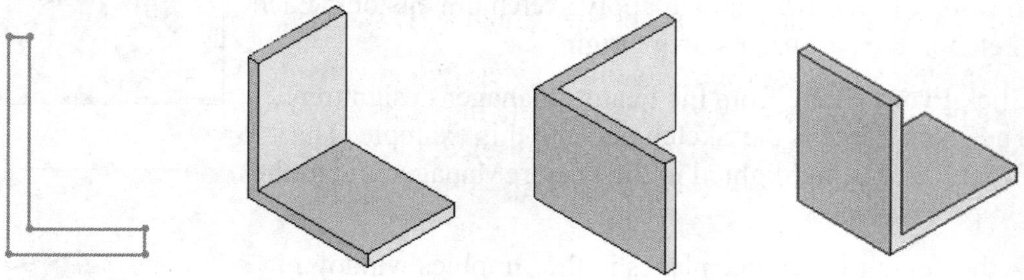

2D Profile    Front Plane    Top Plane    Right Plane

The six principle views of Orthographic projection listed in the ASME Y14.3M standard are: *Front, Top, Right, Bottom, Rear and Left*. SolidWorks Standard view names correspond to these Orthographic projection view names.

| ASME Y14.3M Principle View Name: | SolidWorks Standard View: |
|---|---|
| Front | Front |
| Top | Top |
| Right side | Right |
| Bottom | Bottom |
| Rear | Back |
| Left side | Left |

ANSI is the default Overall drafting standard used in this book.

Displayed is the Front, Top, Right and Isometric view in Third Angle Projection.

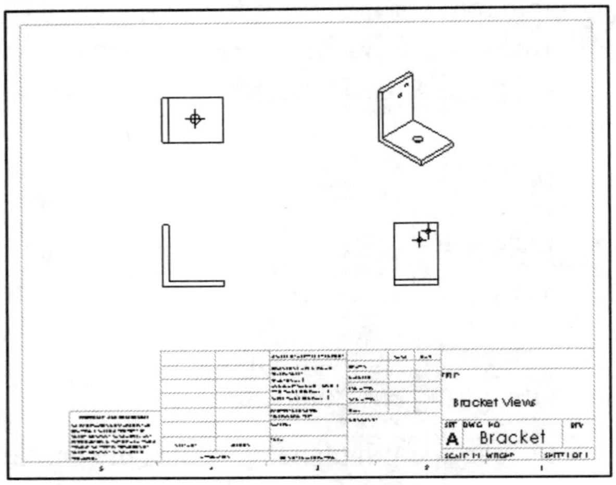


### *Tutorial: Default Reference Planes 4-1*

Create a new part. Show the default Reference planes in the Graphics window.

1. Click **New** from the Menu bar. The Templates tab is the default tab. Part is the default template from the New SolidWorks Document dialog box.

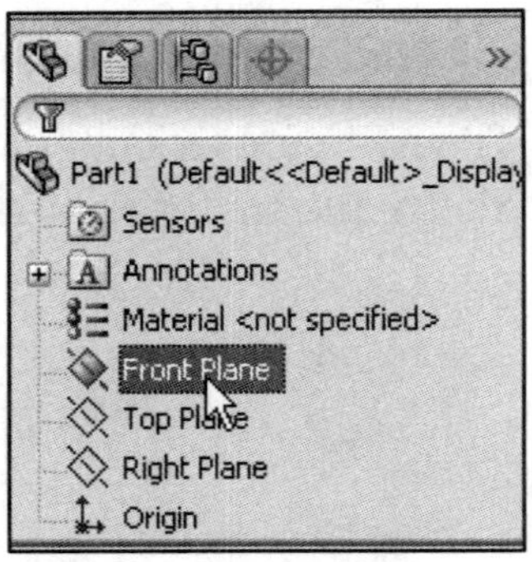


2. Click **OK**. The Part FeatureManager is displayed. Use the sketch Origin to help understand the (X,Y) coordinate location of the sketch and to apply sketch dimensions. Each sketch in the part has its own Origin.
3. Click **Front Plane** from the FeatureManager design tree. The Front Plane is the Sketch plane in this example. The Front Plane is highlighted in the FeatureManager and in the Graphics window.

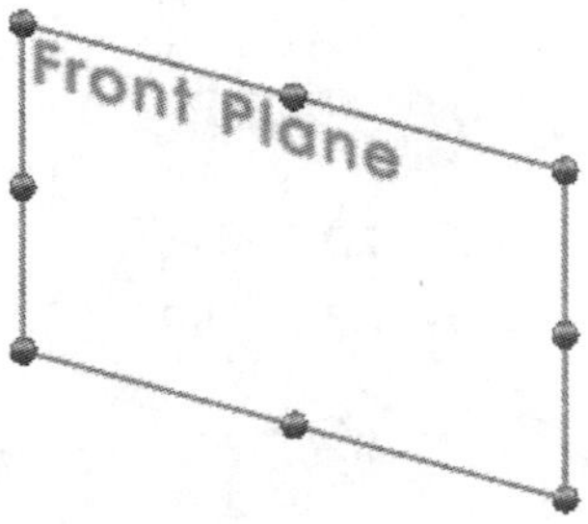


Show the default Reference planes in the Graphics window.

4. Hold the **Ctrl** key down.

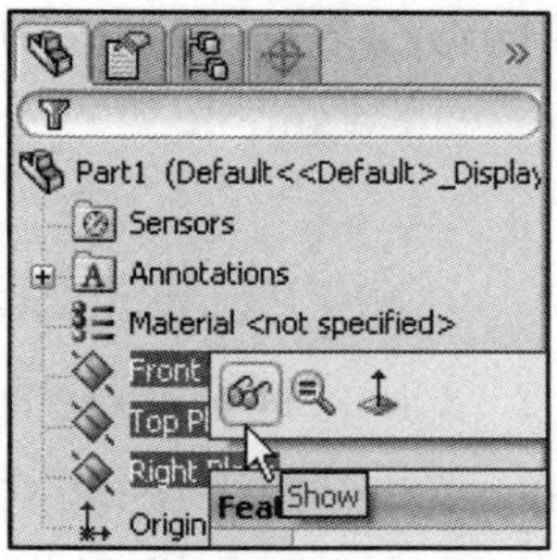


5. Click **Top Plane** and **Right Plane** from the FeatureManager design tree.
6. Release the **Ctrl** key.
7. Right-click **Show** from the Context toolbar. If needed click **View**, check **Planes** from the Menu bar.
8. Click **inside** the Graphics window. The three planes are displayed in the Graphics window. Note the Plane icon in the FeatureManager.

Rename the default Reference planes.

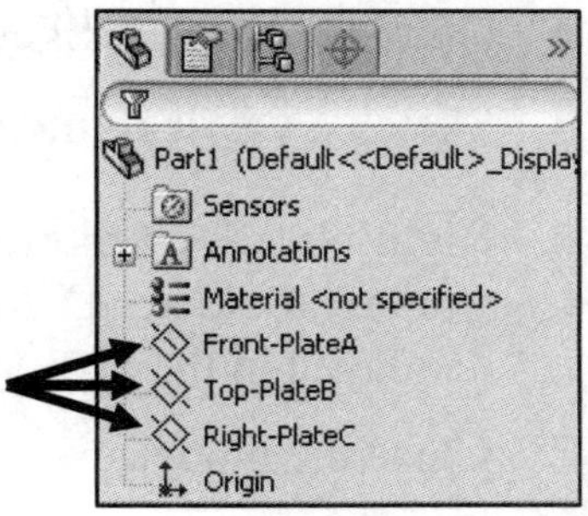


9. Rename the **Front Plane** to **Front-PlateA**.
10. Rename the **Top Plane** to **Top-PlateB**.
11. Rename the **Right Plane** to **Right-PlateC**.
12. **Rebuild** the model.
13. **Close** the model.

## 3D Sketching / Reference planes

Create a 3D sketch in SolidWorks. A 3D sketch is typically used for advanced features such as Sweeps and Lofts. Most basic features are created from a 2D sketch.

See the Hole Wizard section for additional 3D sketch information.

There are two approaches to 3D sketching. The first approach is called 2D sketching with 3D Sketch planes. In this approach, you:

1. Activate a planar face by adding a 3D Sketch plane.
2. Sketch in 2D along the plane.
3. Add 3D Sketch planes each time you require to move sketch entities to create a 3D sketch.

Using the 2D sketching with 3D Sketch planes approach provides the ability to:

- Add relations:
  - Between planes
  - Between sketch entities on different planes
  - To planes
  - Define planes
  - Move and resize planes

***Tutorial: 3D Sketching 4-1***

Create a simple 2D sketch with 3D Sketch planes.

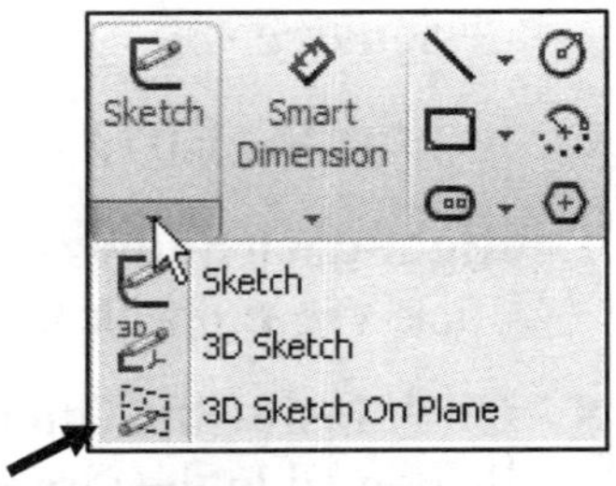


1. Create a **New** part in SolidWorks. Use the default ANSI Part template.
2. Click **Top Plane** from the FeatureManager.
3. Click **3D Sketch On Plane** from the Sketch Consolidated toolbar as illustrated. 3DSketch1 is active.
4. Click the **Line** Sketch tool.
5. Sketch a **vertical line** through the origin.
6. Right-click **Exit Sketch** from the Context toolbar. 3DSketch1 is displayed in the FeatureManager.
7. **Close** the model.

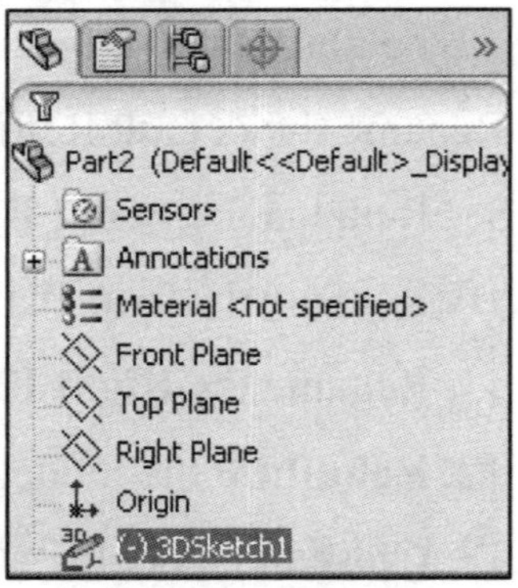


***Tutorial: 3D Sketching 4-2***

Create the illustrated model. Insert two features: Boss-Extrude1 and Cut-Extrude1. Apply the 3D Sketch tool to create the Cut-Extrude1 feature. System units = MMGS.

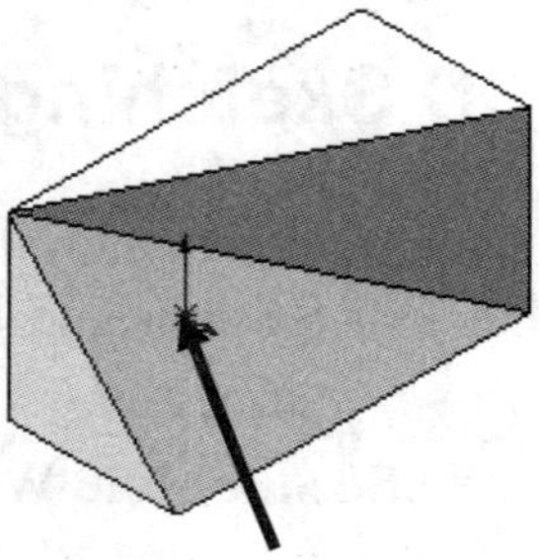

Origin

1. Create a **New** part in SolidWorks. Use the default ANSI, MMGS Part template.
2. Right-click **Front Plane** from the FeatureManager. This is your Sketch plane.
3. Click **Sketch** from the Context toolbar. The Sketch toolbar is displayed.
4. Click the **Corner Rectangle** tool from the Consolidated Rectangle Sketch toolbar. The PropertyManager is displayed.
5. Sketch a **rectangle** as illustrated. The part Origin is located in the bottom left corner of the sketch.

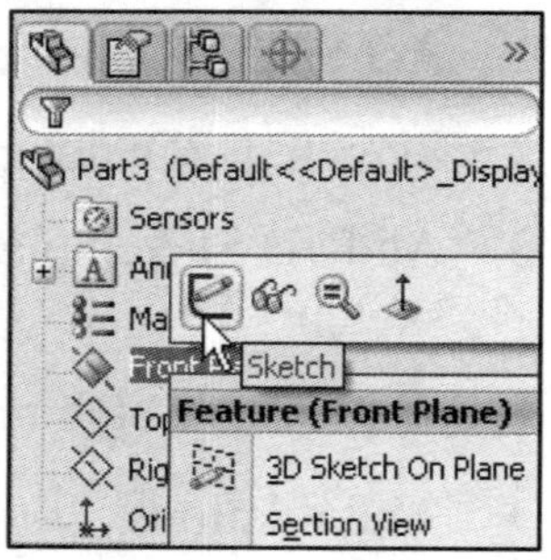


Insert Dimensions.

6. Right-click **Smart Dimension** from the Context toolbar.
7. **Dimension** the sketch as illustrated. The sketch is fully defined. The sketch is displayed in black.

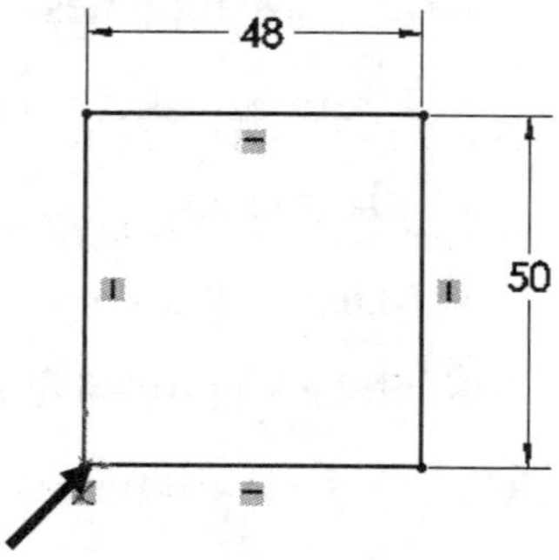


Origin

Create the first feature for the model. The Extruded Boss/Base feature adds material to a part. Extrude the sketch to create the first feature.

8. Click **Extruded Boss/Base** from the Features toolbar. Apply symmetry.
9. Select the **Mid Plane** End Condition in Direction 1. Enter **100.00**mm for Depth in Direction 1. Accept the default conditions. Click **OK** from the Boss-Extrude PropertyManager.

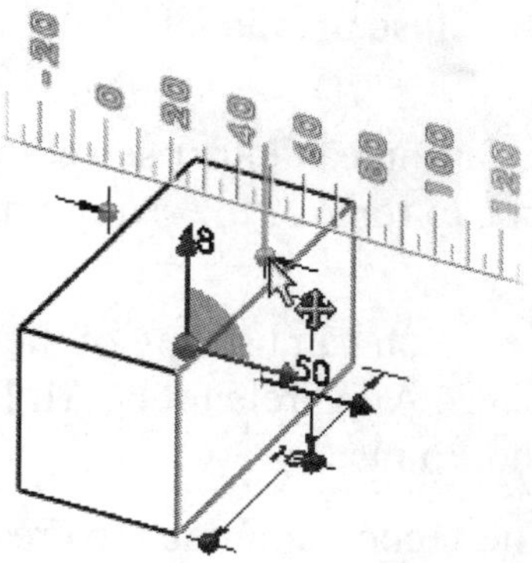


Instant3D provides the ability to drag geometry and dimension manipulator points to resize features or to create new features directly in the Graphics window. Click the face. Select a manipulator point. Click and drag. Click a location along the ruler for the required dimension. The rule increments are set in System Options.

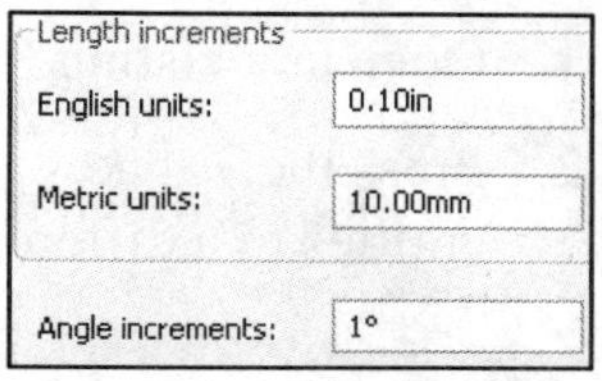


10. Create 3DSketch1. 3DSketch1 is a four point sketch. Click **3D Sketch On Plane** from the Consolidated Sketch toolbar as illustrated.
11. Click the **Line** Sketch tool. 3DSketch1 is a four point sketch as illustrated. 3DSketch1 is the profile for Cut-Extrude1.
12. Locate the first point of the sketch. Click the **back right bottom point** as illustrated. Locate the second point of the sketch. Click the **top left front point** as illustrated. Locate the third point of the sketch.
13. Click the **bottom right front point** as illustrated.

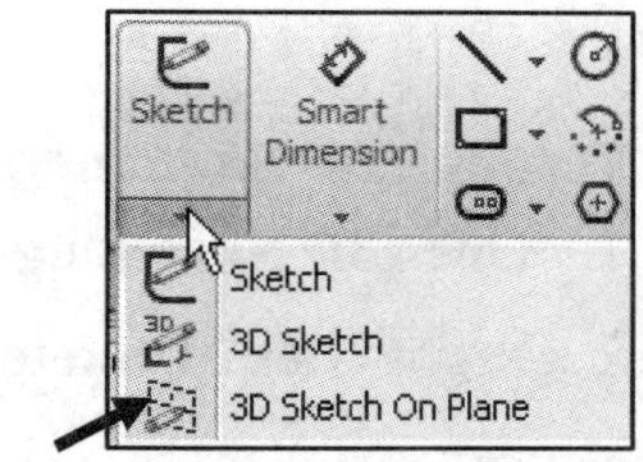


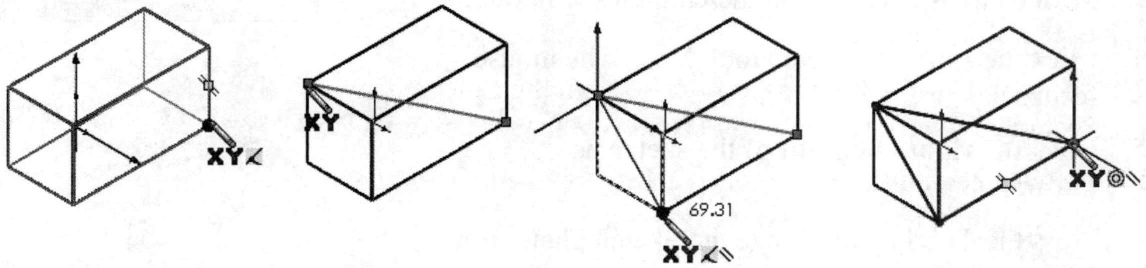


Locate the fourth point of the sketch.

14. Click the **back right bottom** point as illustrated to close the sketch.

Create the Cut-Extrude1 feature.

15. Click **Extruded Cut** from the Features toolbar.

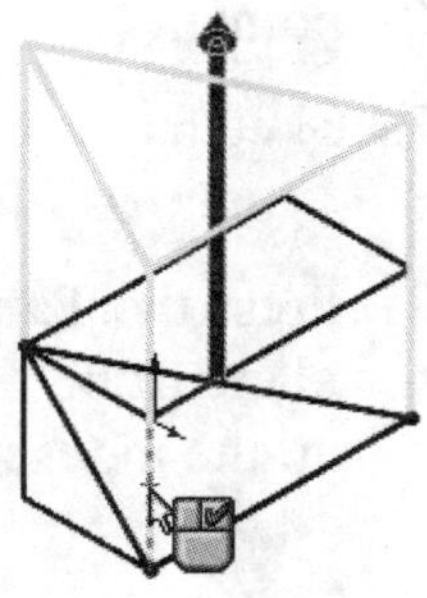

16. Click the **front right vertical edge** as illustrated to remove the material. Edge<1> is displayed in the Direction of Extrusions box.

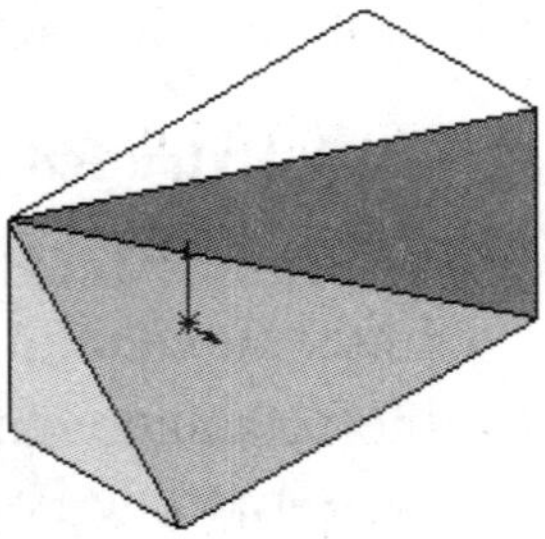

17. Click **OK** from the Cut-Extrude PropertyManager. Cut-Extrude1 is displayed in the FeatureManager.

18. **Close** the model.

You can either select the front right vertical edge or the Top face to remove the require material in this tutorial.

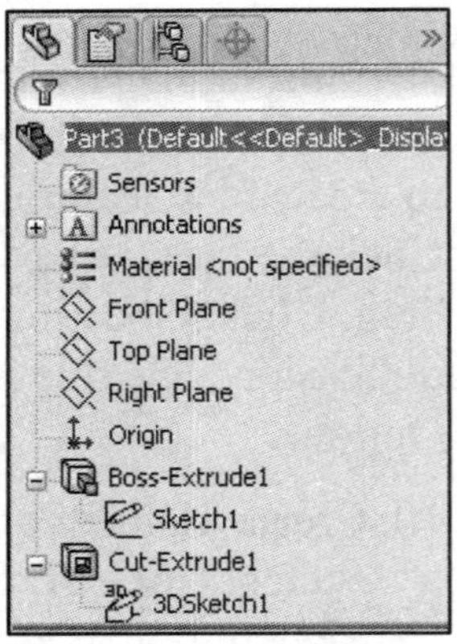


You can use any of the following tools to create 3D sketches: Lines, All Circle tools, All Rectangle tools, All Arcs tools, Splines and Points.

The second approach to create a 3D sketch with SolidWorks is 3D sketching. In this approach:

1. Open an existing 3D sketch.
2. Press the Tab key each time you need to move your sketch entities to a different axis.

The sketch origin is placed wherever you start your sketch.

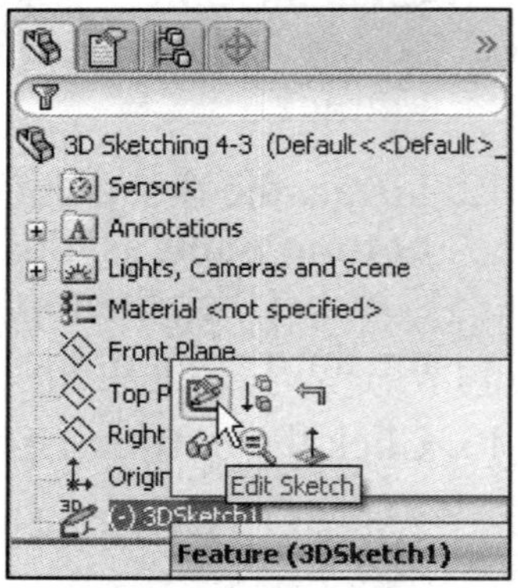


### *Tutorial: 3D Sketching 4-3*

1. Open **3D Sketching 4-3** from the SolidWorks 2010 folder.
2. Right-click **3DSketch**.
3. Click **Edit Sketch** from the Context toolbar. 3DSketch1 is displayed in the Graphics window.
4. Click the **Line** Sketch tool. Note: The mouse feedback icon
5. Click the **right endpoint** of the sketch as illustrated.

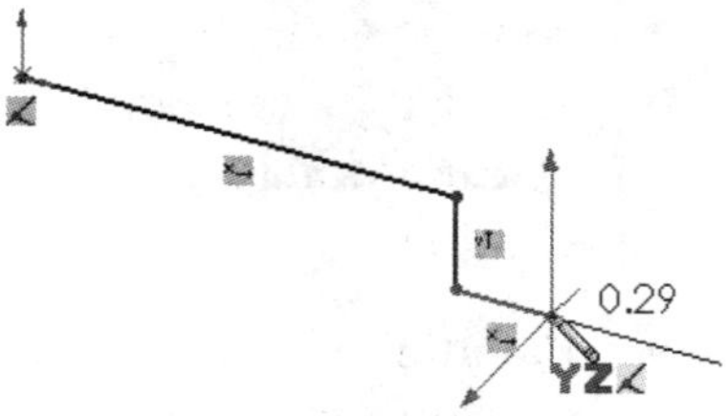


6. Press the **Tab** key to change the Sketch plane from XY to YZ. The YZ icon is displayed on the mouse pointer.
7. Sketch a **line** along the Z axis approximately 130mm as illustrated.

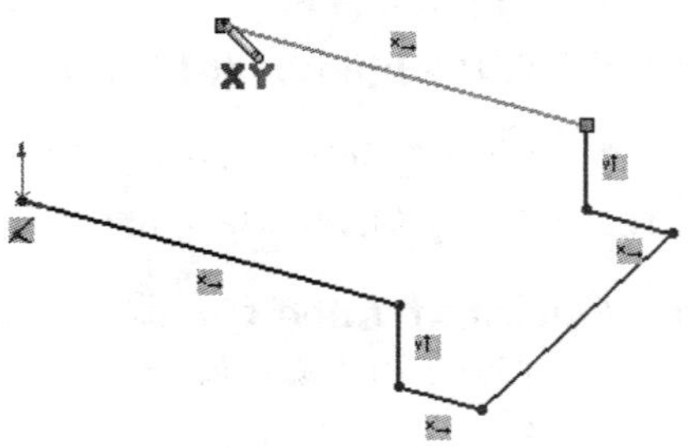


8. Press the **Tab** key twice to change the sketch plane from YZ to XY. The XY icon is displayed on the mouse pointer.

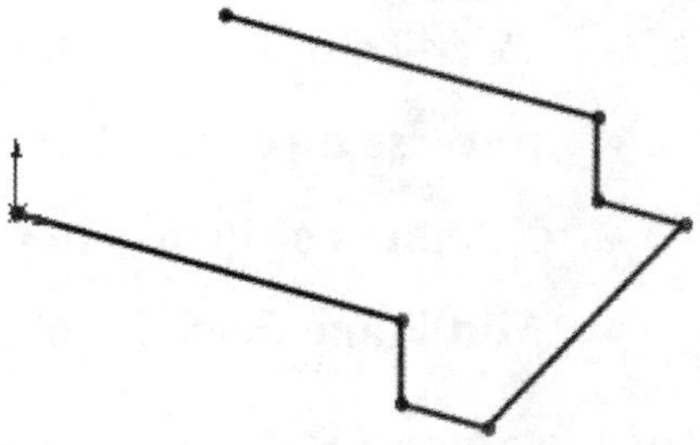

9. Sketch a **line** back along the X axis approximately 30mm.
10. Sketch a **line** on the Y axis approximately 30mm.
11. Sketch a **line** along the X axis of approximately 130mm.

Deselect the Line Sketch tool.

12. Right-click **Select**. View the 3D Sketch.
13. **Rebuild** the model.
14. **Close** the model.

## 2D Sketching / Inserting Reference planes

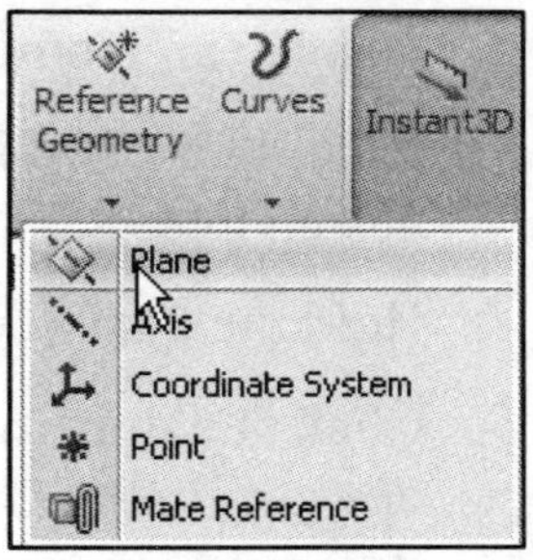


Reference Planes are geometry created from existing planes, faces, vertices, surfaces, axes, and or sketch geometry. To access the Plane PropertyManager, click **Insert ➤ Reference Geometry ➤ Plane** from the Menu bar or click the **Plane** tool from the Consolidated Reference Geometry Features toolbar.

### Plane Tool

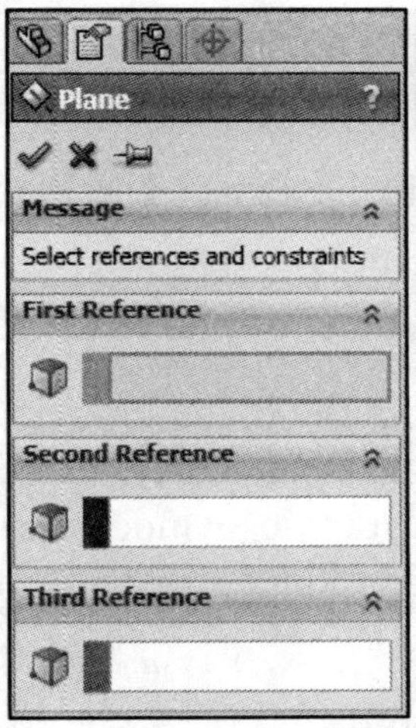


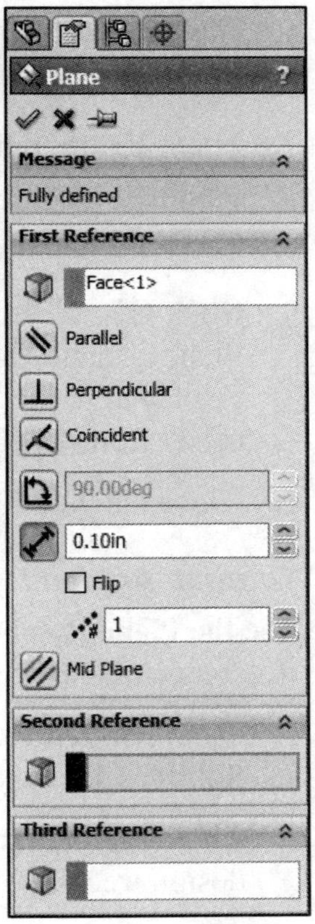


The Plane tool uses the Plane PropertyManager. The Plane PropertyManager (new in 2010) provides the following selections:

- ***First Reference***. Select a face, plane or edge to create a reference plane. The options are available:
  - **Reference Entities**. Displays the selected planes either from the FeatureManager or from the Graphics window.
  - **Parallel**. Creates a plane through a point parallel to a plane or a face.
  - **Perpendicular**. Creates a plane through a point perpendicular to a plane or a face.
  - **Coincident.** Creates a plane through a point coincident to a plane or a face.
  - **Angle**. Creates a plane through an edge, axis, or sketch line at an angle to your plane or face. Enter the angle value in the angle box.

- **Distance**. Creates a plane parallel to a face or plane, which is offset by your specified distance. Enter the Offset distance value in the distance box.
- **Reverse direction**. Reverses the direction of the angle if required.
- **Numbers of Planes to Create**. Displays the selected number of planes.
- **Mid Plane**. Equally spaced on both sides.

### *Tutorial: Insert Reference Planes 4-2*

Create three Reference planes using the Offset Distance option from the Plane PropertyManager.

1. Create a **New** part in SolidWorks. Use the default ANSI Part template. Set system units to MMGS.
2. Display an **Isometric view**.
3. Right-click **Top Plane** from the FeatureManager design tree.
4. Hold the **Ctrl** key down.
5. Click and drag the **boundary** of the Top Plane upwards in the Graphics window. The Plane PropertyManager is displayed. Top Plane is displayed in the First Reference box.
6. Release the **Ctrl** key and **mouse** pointer.
7. Enter **25**mm in the Distance. The Plane is offset by 25mms.
8. Enter **3** in the Number of planes to create box.
9. Click **OK** from the Plane PropertyManager. Plane1, Plane2 and Plane3 are created and are displayed in the Graphics window. Each Plane is offset from the Top Plane a distance of 25mm.
10. **Close** the part.

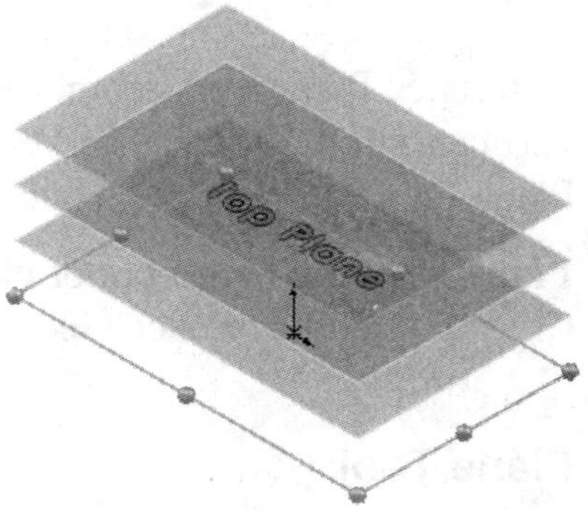


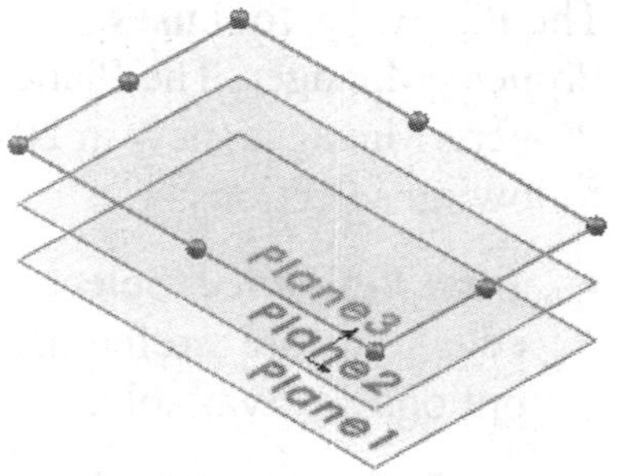


### *Tutorial: Angled Reference Plane 4-3*

Use the Plane PropertyManager to create two angled Reference planes from an edge at a 45 degree angle.

1. Open **Angled Reference Plane 4-3** from the SolidWorks 2010 folder.
2. Click **Right Plane** from the FeatureManager design tree.

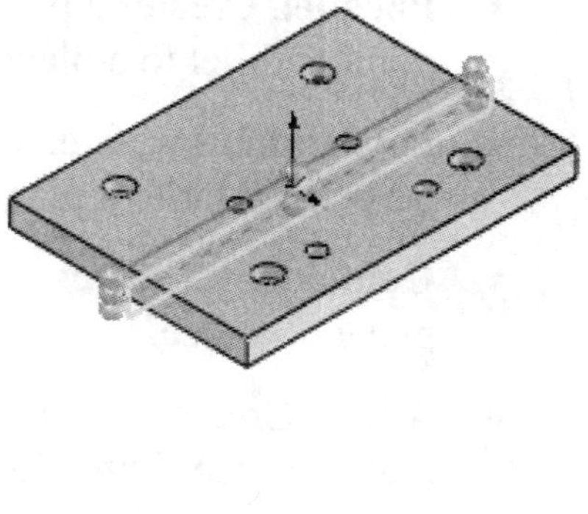

3. Click **Insert ➢ Reference Geometry ➢ Plane** from the Menu bar. The Plane PropertyManager is displayed. Right Plane is displayed in the First Reference box.
4. Click the **At angle** button.
5. Enter **45**deg for Angle.
6. Click the **front vertical edge** of Extrude1 as illustrated. Do not select the midpoint. Edge<1> is displayed in the Selections box. The model is fully defined.

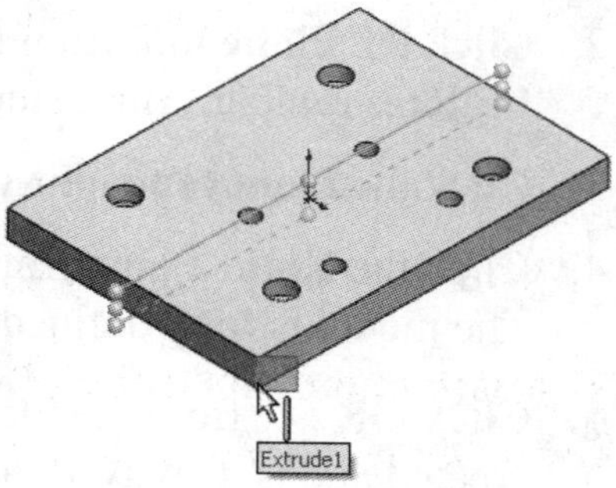


7. Enter **2** in the Number of planes to create box.
8. Click **OK** ✔ from the Plane PropertyManager. Plane1 and Plane2 are displayed in the FeatureManager and in the Graphics window.
9. **Close** the model.

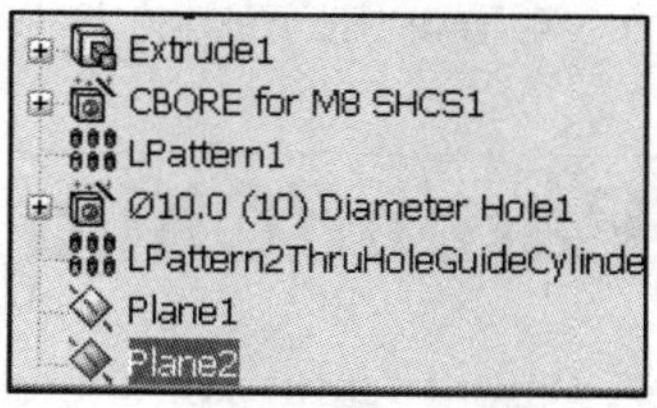


### *Tutorial: Reference Plane 4-4*

Use the Plane PropertyManager to create a Reference plane using three vertices of Extrude1.

1. Open **Reference Plane 4-4** from the SolidWorks 2010 folder.
2. Click **Insert ➢ Reference Geometry ➢ Plane**. The Plane PropertyManager is displayed.
3. Click **three Vertices** as illustrated. Vertex<1>, Vertex<2> and Vertex<3> are displayed in the Reference Entities boxes. The model is fully defined.
4. Click **OK** ✔ from the Plane PropertyManager. The angled Plane1 is created and is displayed in the FeatureManager and the Graphics window.
5. **Close** the model.

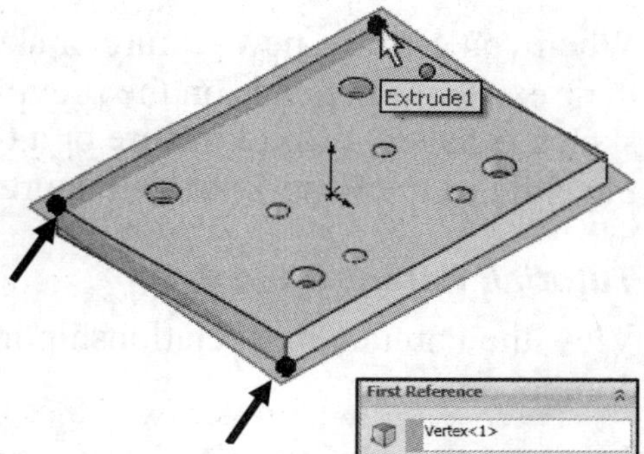


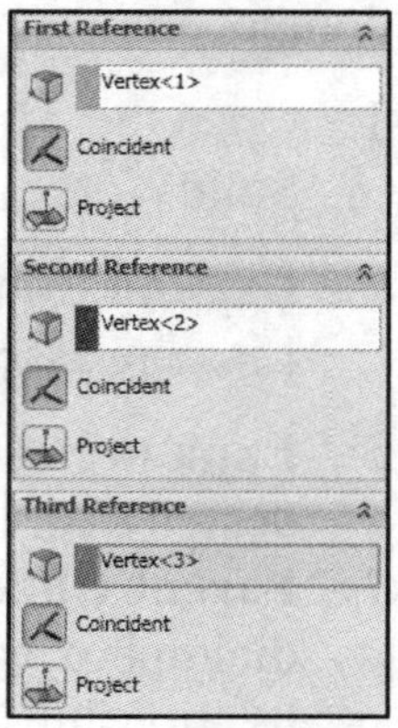


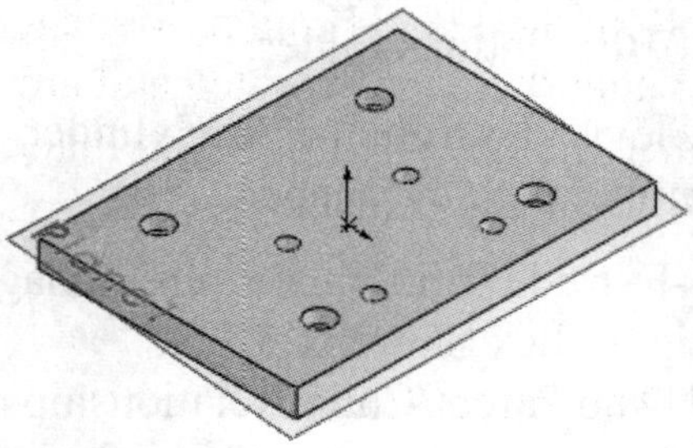

### *Tutorial: Reference Plane 4-5*

Use the Plane PropertyManager to create a Reference plane parallel to an existing plane, through a selected point.

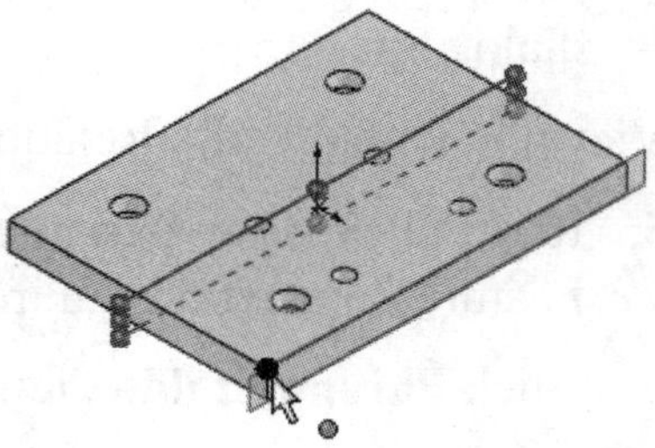

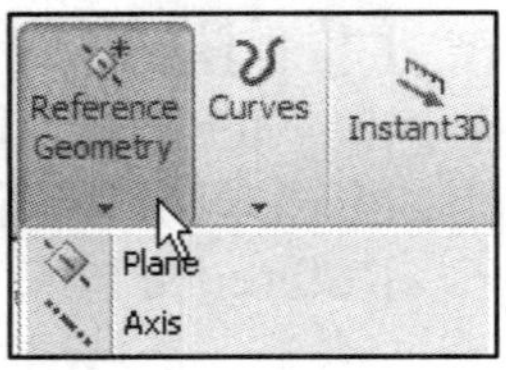


1. Open **Reference Planes 4-5** from the SolidWorks 2010 folder.
2. Click the **Plane** tool from the Consolidated Reference Geometry Features toolbar. The Plane PropertyManager is displayed.
3. Click the **front top right vertex**.
4. Click the **Right Plane** from the fly-out FeatureManager. The model is fully defined.
5. Click **OK** ✔ from the Plane PropertyManager. Plane1 is created and is displayed in the FeatureManager and Graphics window.
6. **Close** the model.

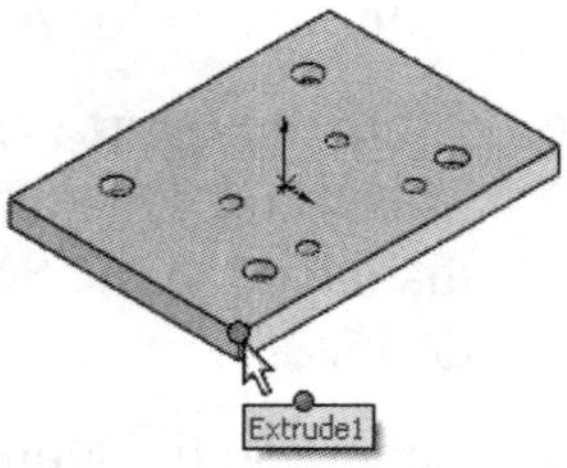


# Parent/Child Relationship

A Parent feature or sketch is an existing feature or sketch on which others depend on. Example of a Parent feature: An Extruded feature is the Parent feature to a fillet which rounds the edges.

When you create a new feature or sketch which is based on other features or sketches, their existence depends on the previously built feature or sketch. The new feature or sketch is called a Child feature or a Child sketch. Example of a Child feature: A hole is the child of the Base-Extrude feature in which it is cut.

***Tutorial: Parent-Child 4-1***

View the Parent/Child relationship in an assembly for a sketch and a feature from a component.

1. Open the **AirCylinder Linkage** assembly from the SolidWorks 2010\Solutions folder.
2. **Expand** RodClevis<1> from the AirCylinder Linkage assembly FeatureManager.
3. **Expand** Base-Extrude from the FeatureManager design tree. Right-click **Sketch2**. Click **Parent/Child**. The Parent/Child Relationships dialog box is displayed. View the Sketch2 relationships.
4. Click **Close** from the Parent/Child Relationships dialog box.

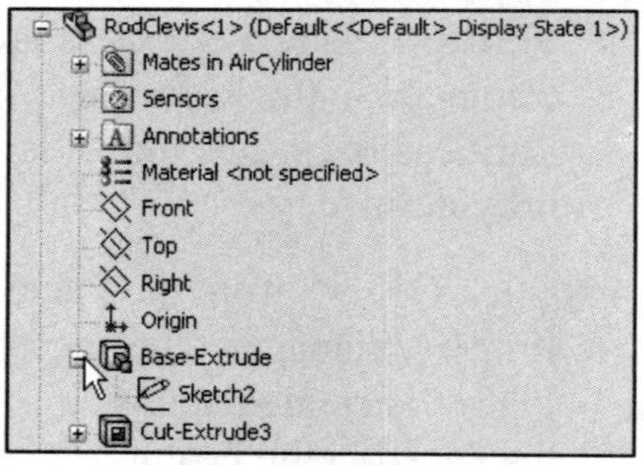


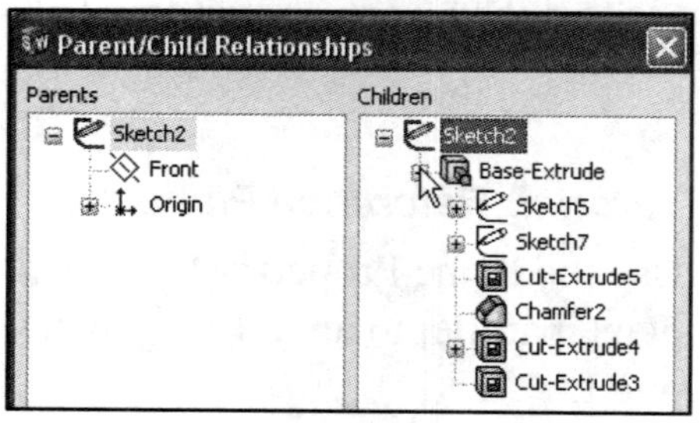


View the Parent/Child Relationships for a feature.

5. Right-click **Base-Extrude** from the FeatureManager design tree.
6. Click **Parent/Child**. View the Base-Extrude feature relationships.

7. Click **Close** from the Parent/Child Relationships dialog box.
8. **Close** the model.

# Sketch States

Sketches can exist in any of five states. The state of the sketch is displayed in the status bar at the bottom of the SolidWorks window. The five sketch states in SolidWorks are:

Color indicates the state of the individual Sketch entities.

1. *Under Defined.* Inadequate definition of the sketch, (blue). The FeatureManager displays a minus (-) symbol before the Sketch name.
2. *Fully Defined.* Complete information, (black). The FeatureManager displays no symbol before the Sketch name.
3. *Over Defined.* Duplicate dimensions and or relations, (red). The FeatureManager displays a (+) symbol before the Sketch name. The What's Wrong dialog box is displayed.
4. *Invalid Solution Found.* Your sketch is solved but results in invalid geometry. Example: such as a zero length line, zero radius arc or a self-intersecting spline (yellow).
5. *No Solution Found.* Indicates sketch geometry that cannot be resolved, (Brown).

The SolidWorks SketchXpert is designed to assist in an over defined state of a sketch. The SketchXpert generates a list of causes for over defined sketches. The list is organized into Solution Sets. This tool enables you to delete a solution set of over defined dimensions or redundant relations without compromising your design intent.

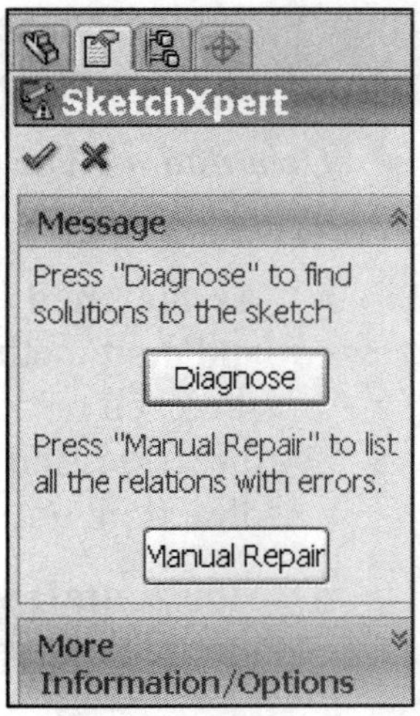


With the SolidWorks software, it is not necessary to fully dimension or define sketches before you use them to create features. You should fully define sketches before you consider the part finished for manufacturing.

Click **Options** ➤ **System Options** ➤ **Sketch**, and click the **Use fully defined sketches** option to use fully defined sketches for created features.

The plane or face you select for the Base sketch determines the orientation of the part.

# Sketch Entities

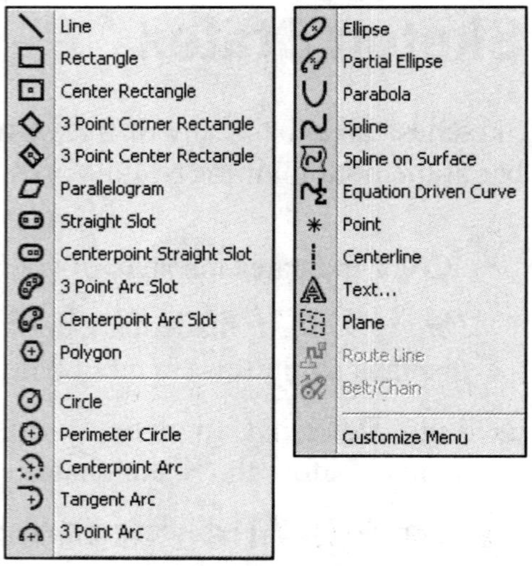


Sketch entities provide the ability to create lines, rectangles, parallelograms, circles, etc. during the sketching process. To access the available sketch entities for SolidWorks, click **Tools ➢ Sketch Entities** from the Menu bar menu and select the required entity. This book is targeted towards a person with a working knowledge of SolidWorks. The book will not go over each individual Sketch entity in full detail but will address the more advance entities.

To obtain additional information of each sketch entity, active the sketch entity and click the question mark icon located at the top of the entity PropertyManager or click **Help ➢ SolidWorks Help Topics** from the Menu bar and search by using one of the three available tabs: **Contents**, **Index**, or **Search**.

## Line Sketch entity

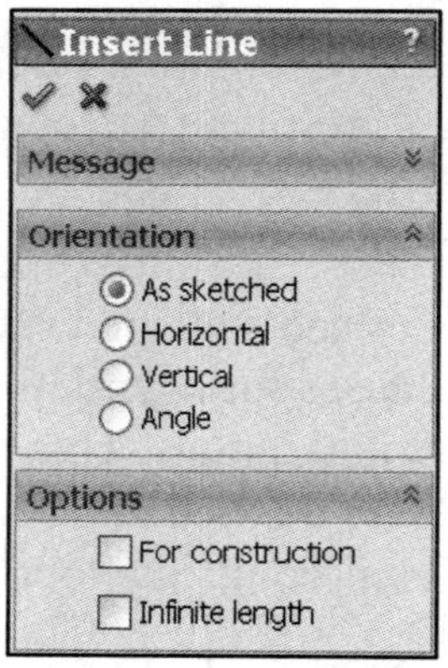


The Line Sketch entity tool provides the ability to sketch multiple 2D lines in a sketch. The Line Sketch entity uses the Insert Line PropertyManager. The Insert Line PropertyManager provides the following selections:

- ***Orientation***. The Orientation box provides the following options:
  - **As sketched**. Sketch a line in any direction using the click and drag method. Using the click-click method, the As sketched option provides the ability to sketch a line in any direction, and to continue sketching other lines in any direction, until you double-click to end your process.
  - **Horizontal**. Sketch a horizontal line until you release your mouse pointer.
  - **Vertical**. Sketch a vertical line until you release your mouse pointer.
  - **Angle**. Sketch a line at an angle until you release your mouse pointer.

The angle is created relative to the horizontal.

- ***Options***. The Options box provides two line types. They are:

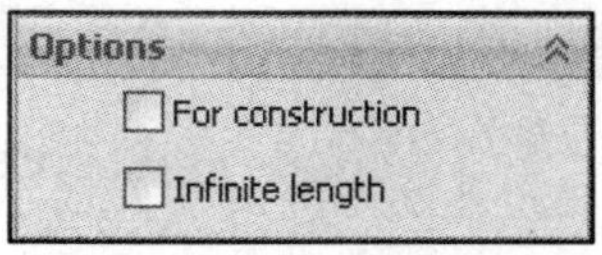


  - **For construction**. Converts the selected sketch entity to construction geometry.
  - **Infinite length**. Creates a line of infinite length which you can later trim in the design process.

Use Construction geometry to assist in creating your sketch entities and geometry that are ultimately incorporated into the part. Construction geometry is ignored when the sketch is used to create a feature. Construction geometry uses the same line style as a centerline.

## Rectangle and Parallelogram Sketch Entity

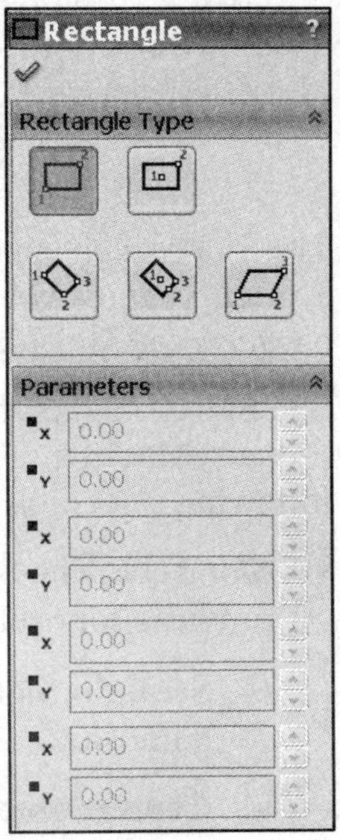


The Rectangle Sketch entity tool provides the ability to sketch a *Corner Rectangle*, *Center Rectangle*, *3 Point Corner Rectangle* and a *3 Point Center Rectangle*. The Parallelogram Sketch entity provides the ability to sketch a *Parallelogram*.

The Rectangle and Parallelogram Sketch entity uses the Consolidated Rectangle PropertyManager. The Rectangle PropertyManager provides the following selections:

- ***Rectangle Type***. The Rectangle Type box provides five selections. They are:
  - **Corner Rectangle**. Sketch a standard rectangle at a corner point. Click to place the first corner of the rectangle, drag, and release when the rectangle is the correct size and shape.
  - **Center Rectangle**. Sketch a rectangle at a center point. Click to define the center. Drag to sketch the rectangle with centerlines. Release to set the four edges.
  - **3 Point Corner Rectangle**. Sketch a rectangle at a selected angle. Click to define the first corner. Drag, rotate, and then release to set the length and angle of the first edge. Click and drag to sketch the other three edges. Release to set the four edges.

   - **3 Point Center Rectangle**. Sketch a rectangle with a center point at a selected angle. Click to define the first corner. Drag and rotate to set one half the length of the centerlines. Click and drag to sketch the other three edges and centerlines. Release to set the four edges.
   - **Parallelogram**. Sketch a standard parallelogram. A Parallelogram is a rectangle whose sides are not horizontal or vertical with respect to the sketch grid. Click to define the first corner. Drag, rotate, and then release to set the length and angle of the first edge. Click, rotate, and drag to set the angle and length of the other three edges. Release to set the four edges.

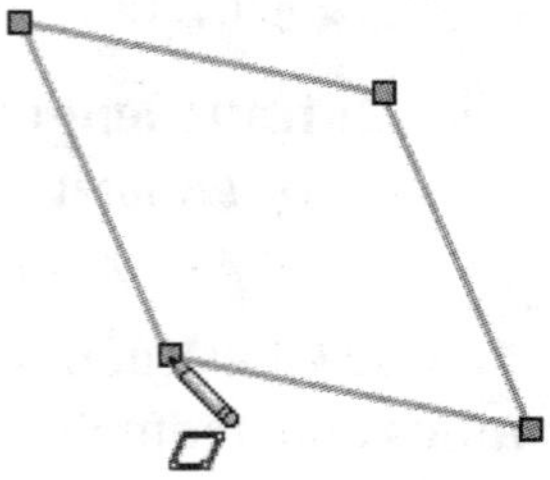

- ***Parameters***. Specify the appropriate combination of parameters to define the rectangle or parallelogram if they are not constrained by relations.

## Slot Sketch entity

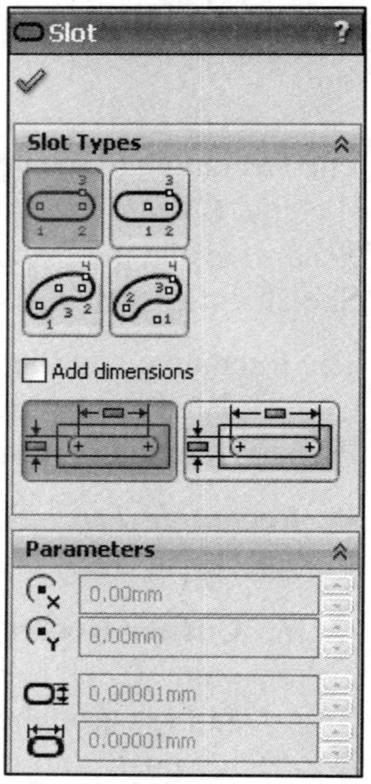


The Slot Sketch entity  tool provides the ability to sketch a *Straight Slot*, *Centerpoint Straight Slot*, *3 Point Arc Slot* and a *Centerpoint Arc Slot* from the Consolidated Slot toolbar.

The Slot Sketch entity uses the Consolidated Slot PropertyManager. The Slot PropertyManager provides the following selections:

- ***Slot Type***. The Slot Type box provides four selections. They are:

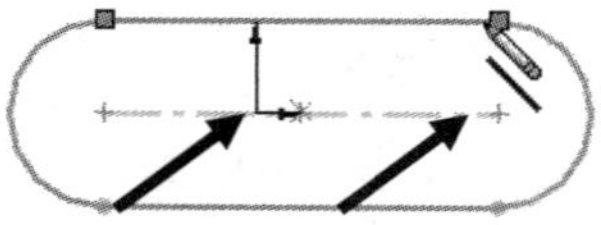

   - **Straight Slot**. Sketch a three point slot.

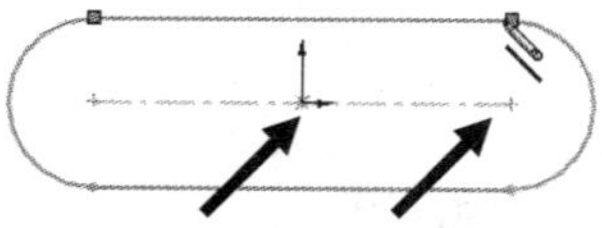

   - **Centerpoint Straight Slot**. Sketch a three point slot located at an Origin or centerpoint.

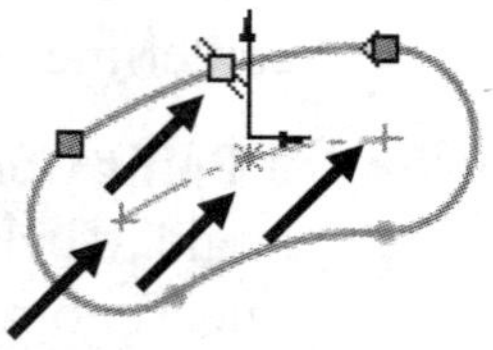

   - **3 Point Arc Slot**. Sketch a four point arc slot.
   - **Centerpoint Arc Slot**. Sketch a four point arc slot located at an Origin or reference point.

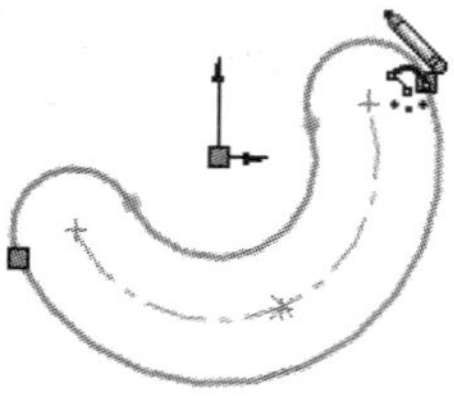

- **Add dimensions**. Insert dimensions as you sketch the slot.
- **Center to Center**. Insert center to center dimension if the Add dimensions box is checked.
- **Overall Length**. Insert overall length if the Add dimensions box is checked.

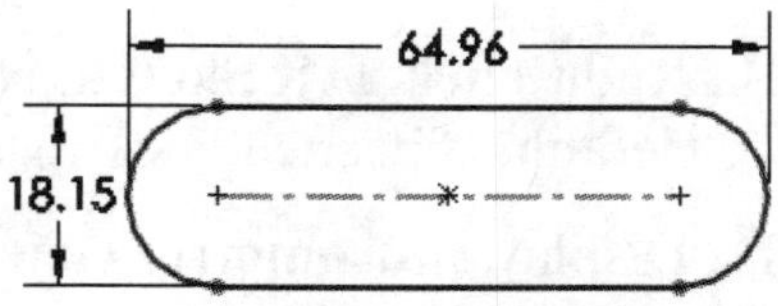


- **Parameters**. Provides the ability to specify the appropriate combination of parameters to define slot if they are not constrained by relations. The parameters box provides the following options: **Center X Coordinate**, **Center Y Coordinate**, **Radius of Arc**, **Angle of Arc**, **Slot Width** and **Slot Length**.

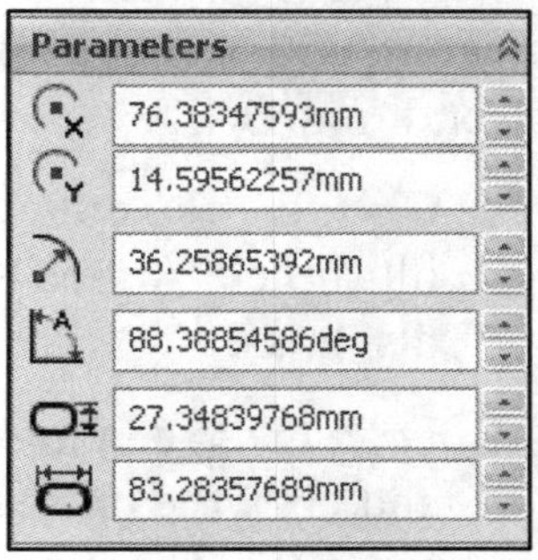


### *Tutorial: Slot Sketch - Instant3D 4-1*

Utilize the Slot Sketch tool. Create an Extruded Boss/Base and Extruded Cut feature using the Instant3D tool.

1. Create a **New** part in SolidWorks. Use the default ANSI, IPS Part template.
2. Right-click **Front Plane** from the FeatureManager. This is your Sketch plane.
3. Click **Sketch** from the Context toolbar. The Sketch toolbar is displayed.
4. Click **Centerpoint Straight Slot** from the Consolidated Slot toolbar as illustrated. The Slot PropertyManager is displayed. If needed, uncheck the Add dimension box.
5. Click the **Origin**.
6. Click a **position** directly to the right of the Origin.
7. Click a **position** directly above the second point as illustrated.

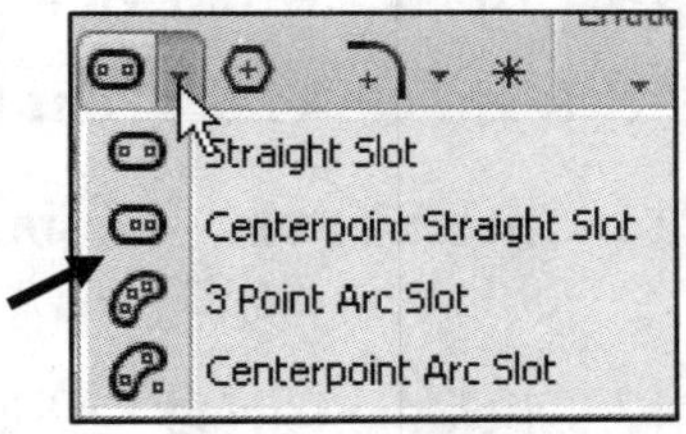


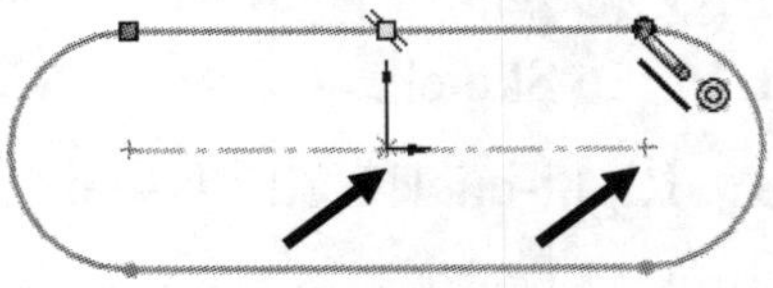

Dimension the slot sketch.

8. Right-click **Smart Dimension** from the Context toolbar in the Graphics window.
9. **Dimension** the model as illustrated. The sketch is fully defined.

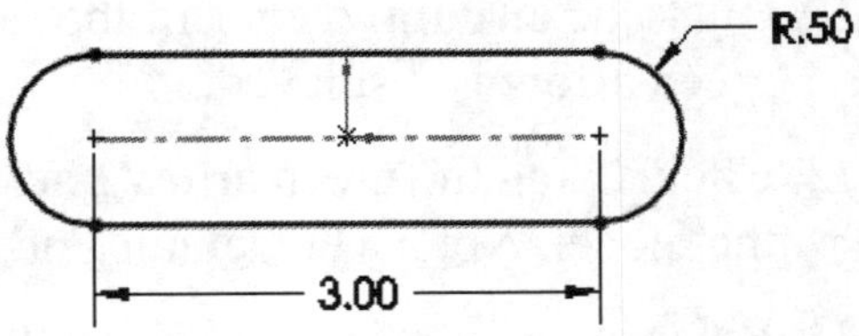

Apply the Instant3D tool. Create an Extruded Boss/Base feature. The Extruded Boss/Base feature adds material to a part. Note: Edit the feature, view the PropertyManager to confirm that you picked the correct dimension with the on-screen ruler.

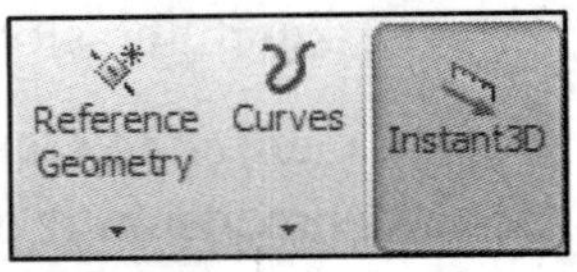


Exit Sketch1.

10. Right-click **Exit Sketch**. Note: Instant3D is active by default. If needed click Instant3D from the Features tab.

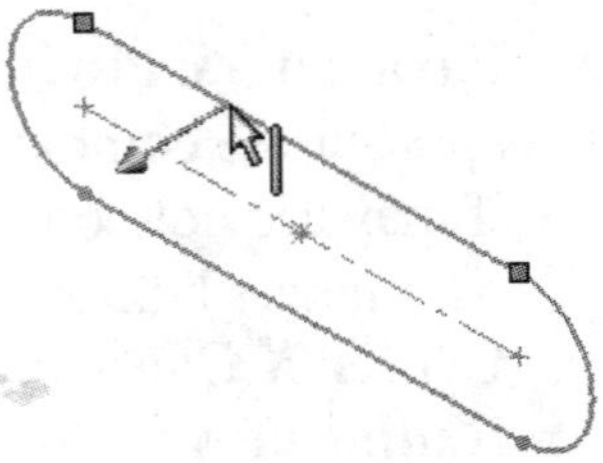

11. Display an **Isometric view**.

Create an Extruded Boss/Base feature with a default Blind End Condition.

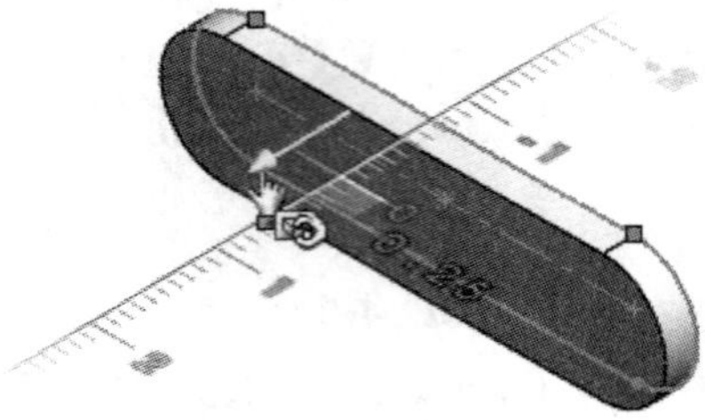

12. Click the **top edge** as illustrated. A green arrow is displayed.

13. Drag the **green arrow** forward and click the on-screen ruler at the **0.25** dimension. View Boss-Extrude1 in the FeatureManager. Depth = .25in.

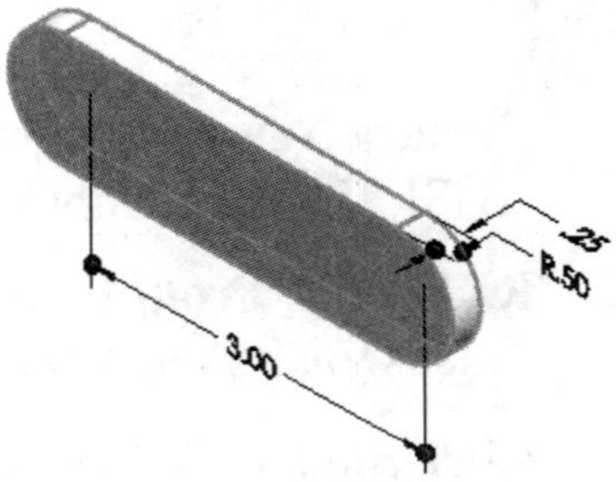


Create an Extruded Cut feature using Instant3D.

14. Display a **Front view**.

15. Right-click the **Front face**. This is you Sketch plane.

16. Click **Sketch** from the Context toolbar. The Sketch toolbar is displayed.

17. Click the **Circle** Sketch tool.

18. Sketch a **circle** centered at the Origin as illustrated.

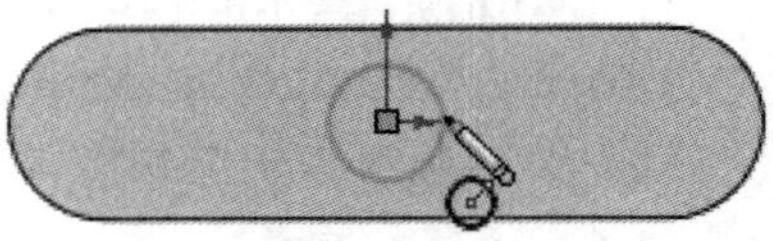

Exit the Sketch.

19. Right-click **Exit Sketch**.

20. Display an **Isometric view**.

Create an Extruded Cut feature.

21. Click the **circumference** of the sketch as illustrated. A green arrow is displayed.

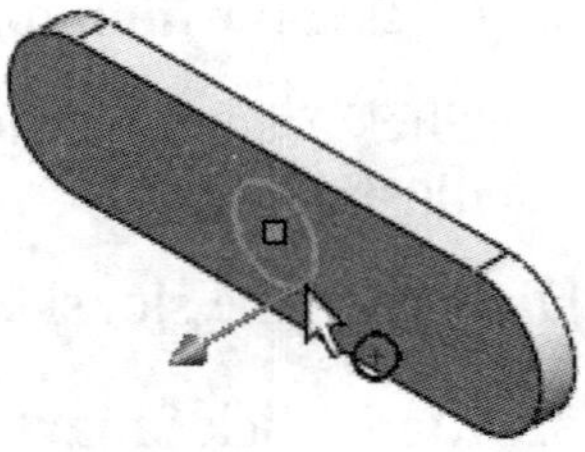

22. Click a drag the green arrow **backwards** to create a hole in the model. Note: The default End Condition is Blind.

23. **Release** the mouse icon behind the model. The Cut-Extrude1 feature is displayed. View the model.

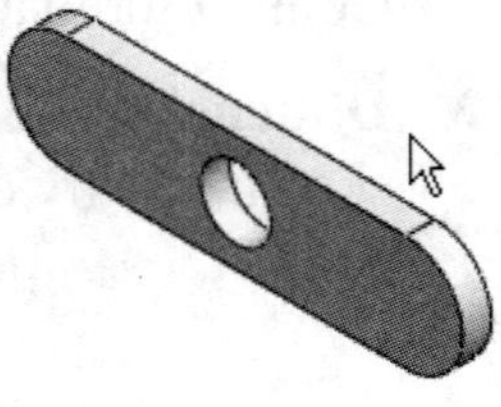

24. **Close** the model.

## Polygon Sketch Entity

The Polygon Sketch entity tool provides the ability to create equilateral polygons with any number of sides between 3 and 40. The Polygon Sketch entity uses the Polygon PropertyManager. The Polygon PropertyManager provides the following selections:

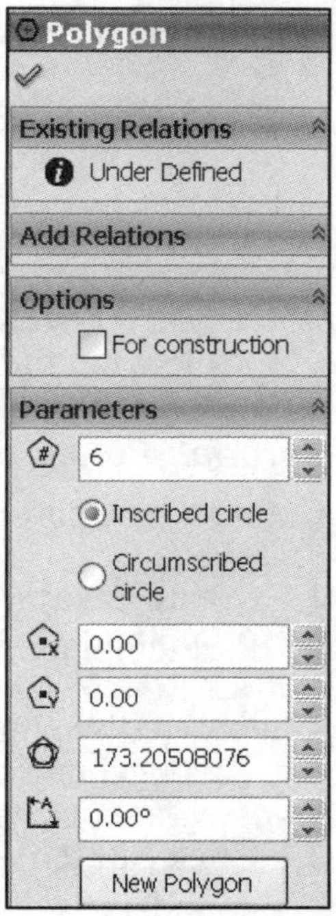


- ***Existing Relations***. The Existing Relations box displays information on existing relations of the polygon sketch.
- ***Add Relation***. The Add Relation box displays the selected relations to the points and lines of your polygon sketch.

You can not add a relation to a complete polygon. You can only add a relation to the points and lines of the polygon.

- ***Options***. The Options box provides the following selection:
  - **For construction**. Not selected by default. Converts the selected sketch entity to construction geometry.
- ***Parameters***. The Parameters box provides the ability to specify the appropriate combination of parameters to define the polygon. When you modify or change one or more parameters, the other parameters update automatically. The available selections are:
  - **Number of Sides**. Sets the number of sides in your polygon.
  - **Inscribed circle**. Selected by default. Displays an inscribed circle inside the polygon. This option defines the size of the polygon. The circle is construction geometry.

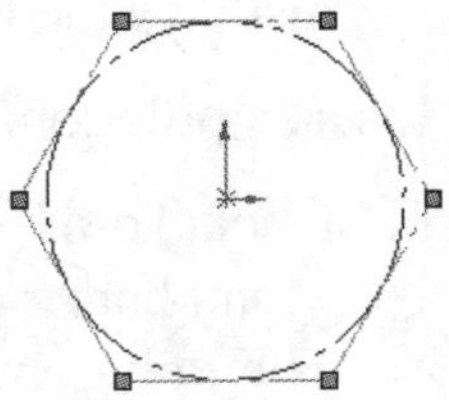

  - **Circumscribed circle**. Displays a circumscribed circle outside of the polygon. This option defines the size of the polygon. The circle is construction geometry.

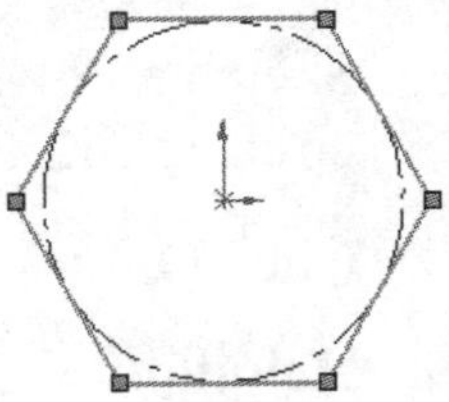

  - **Center X Coordinate**. Displays the X coordinate for the center of your polygon.

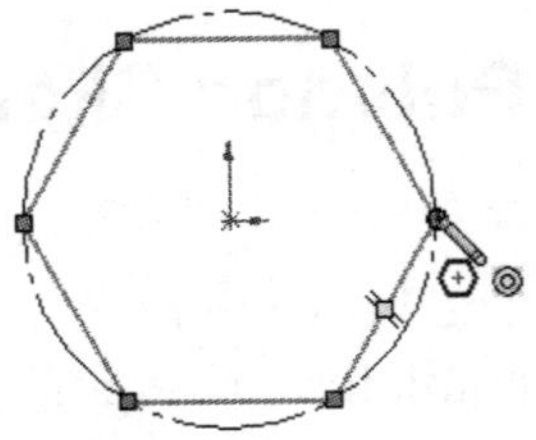

- **Center Y Coordinate**. Displays the Y coordinate for the center of your polygon.
- **Circle Diameter**. Displays the diameter of the inscribed or circumscribed circle.
- **Angle**. Displays the angle of rotation.
- **New Polygon**. Creates more than a single polygon without leaving the PropertyManager.

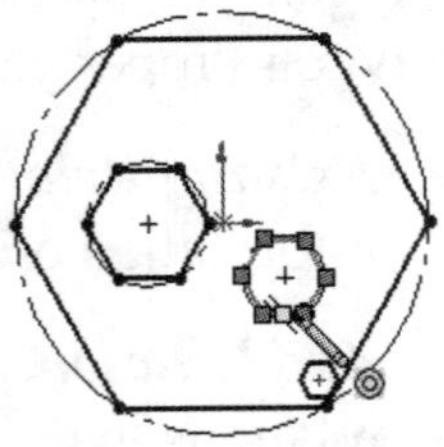

### *Tutorial: Polygon 4-1*

Create a new part using the Polygon Sketch entity.

1. Create a **New** part in SolidWorks. Use the default ANSI Part template.
2. Right-click **Top Plane** from the FeatureManager design tree. This is your Sketch plane.

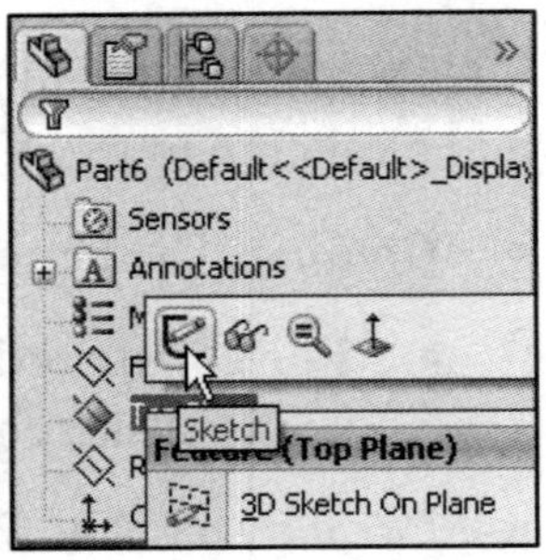


3. Click **Sketch** from the Context toolbar. The Top Plane boundary is displayed in the Top view in the Graphics window.
4. Click the **Circle** Sketch tool. The Circle PropertyManager is displayed.
5. Sketch a **circle** centered at the origin. The mouse cursor displays the Circle icon symbol.

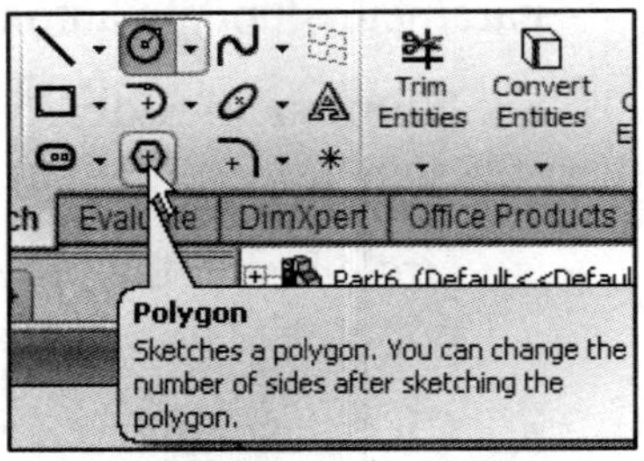


Insert a polygon.

6. Click **Tools ➢ Sketch Entities ➢ Polygon** from the Menu bar or click **Polygon** from the Sketch toolbar. The Polygon PropertyManager is displayed. The mouse cursor displays the Polygon icon symbol.
7. Sketch a **Polygon** centered at the Origin larger than the circle as illustrated.

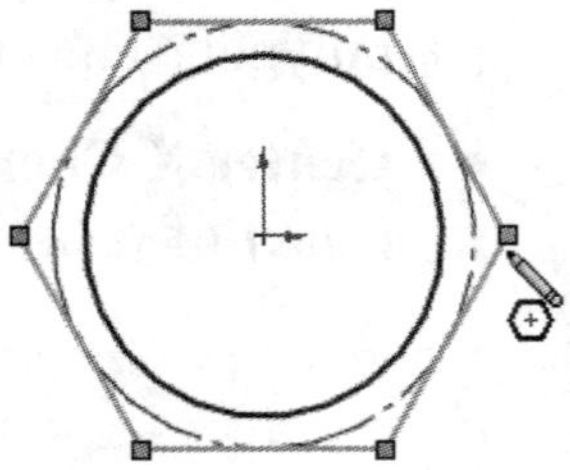

8. Click **OK** from the Polygon PropertyManager.
9. **Rebuild** the model. View the created Polygon in the Graphics window.
10. **Close** the model.

For illustration purposes, the Reference planes and grid are hidden.

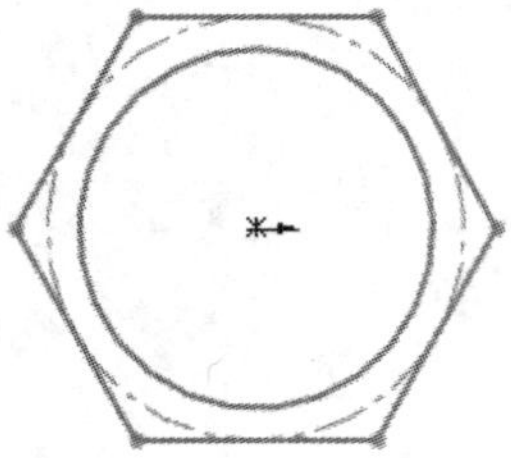

## Circle Sketch and Perimeter Circle Sketch Entity

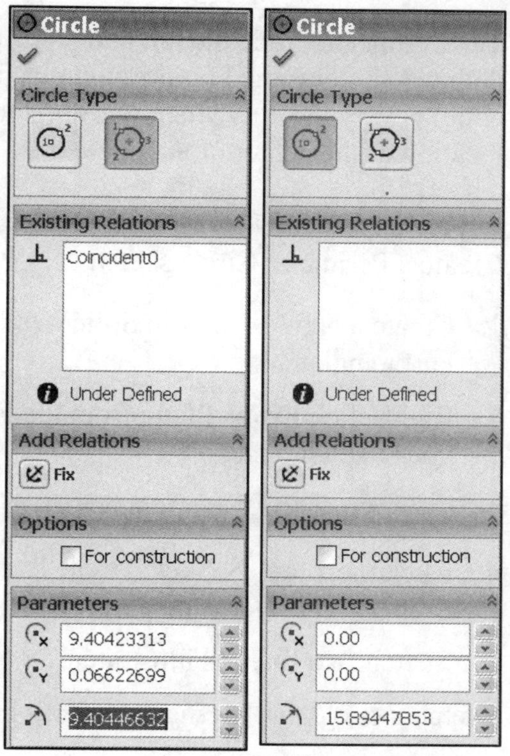


The Circle Sketch and Perimeter Circle Sketch entity tool provides the ability to control the various properties of a circle.

The Circle Sketch and Perimeter Circle Sketch entity uses the consolidated Circle PropertyManager. The consolidated Circle PropertyManager provides the following selections:

- ***Circle Type***. Provides the ability to select either a center based circle or a perimeter-based circle sketch entity.
- ***Existing Relations***. The Existing Relations box provides the following options:
  - **Relations**. Displays the automatic relations inferenced during sketching or created manually with the Add Relations tool. The callout in the Graphics window is highlighted when you select a relation in the dialog box. The Information icon in the Existing Relations box displays the sketch status of the selected sketch entity. Example: Under Defined, Fully Defined, etc.
- ***Add Relations***. Provides the ability to add relations to the selected entity. Displays the relations which are possible for the selected entity.
- ***Options***. The Options box provides the following selection:
  - **For construction**. Not selected by default. Converts the selected entity to construction geometry.
- ***Parameters***. Specifies the appropriate combination of parameters to define the circle if the circle is not constrained by relations. The available selections are:
  - **Center X Coordinate**. Sets the Center X Coordinate value.
  - **Center Y Coordinate**. Sets the Center Y Coordinate value.
  - **Radius**. Sets the Radius value.

The Perimeter Circle Sketch entity provides the ability to define a circle using 3 points along its perimeter. This sketch entity is very usefully when you are not concern about the location of the center of the circle.

### *Tutorial: Perimeter Circle 4-1*

Create a Perimeter Circle sketch.

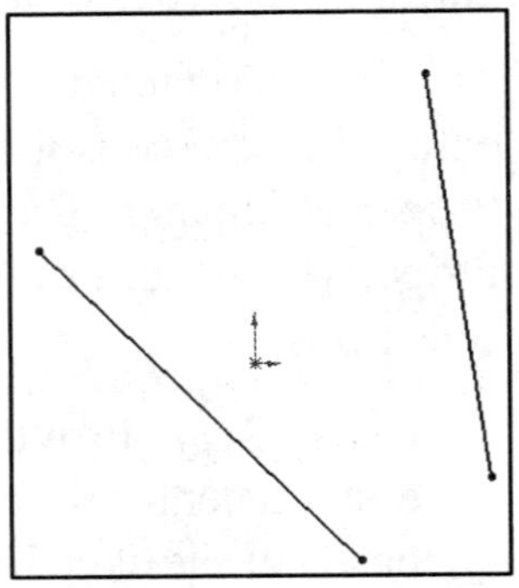

1. Create a **New** part in SolidWorks. Use the default ANSI Part template.
2. Right-click **Front Plane** from the FeatureManager. This is your Sketch plane.
3. Click **Sketch** from the Context toolbar.
4. Click the **Line** Sketch tool. The Insert Line PropertyManager is displayed.
5. Sketch **two lines** as illustrated.

Sketch a circle that is tangent to both lines.

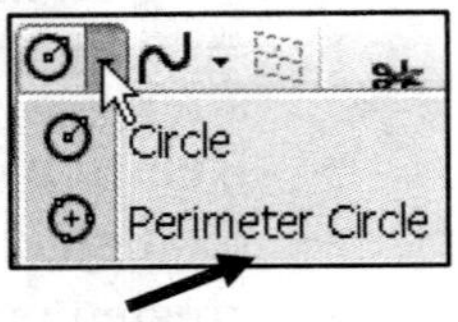


6. Click **Perimeter Circle** from the Consolidated Circle Sketch toolbar. The Circle PropertyManager is displayed.
7. Click **each line** once.
8. Click a **position** as illustrated to determine the size of the circle. The X coordinate, Y coordinate, and Radius is displayed in the Parameters box. The two lines are tangent to the circle. You created a simple circle using the Perimeter Circle sketch entity.

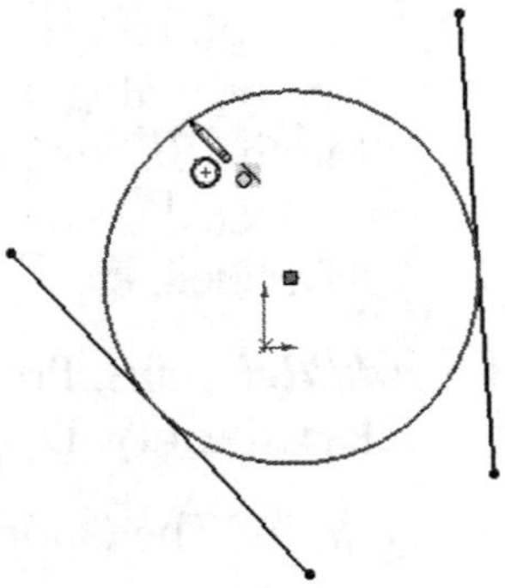

9. Click **OK** from the Circle PropertyManager. View the model.
10. **Rebuild** the model.
11. **Close** the model.

If the two lines change, the circle remains tangent to the lines.

In System Options, apply the Ghost image on drag option. The option displays a ghost image of a sketch entities' original position while you drag the sketch in the Graphics window.

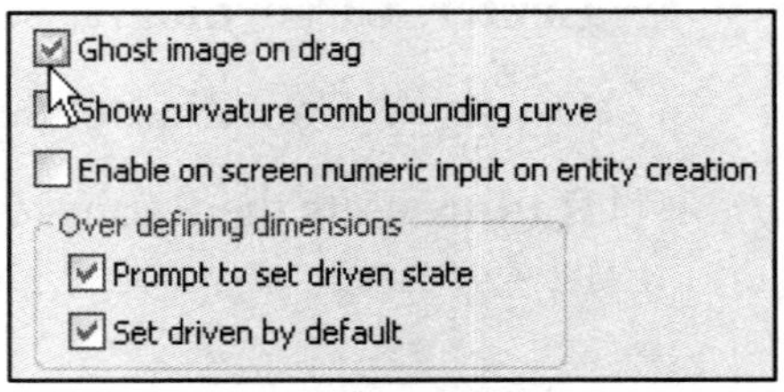

## Centerpoint Arc Sketch Entity

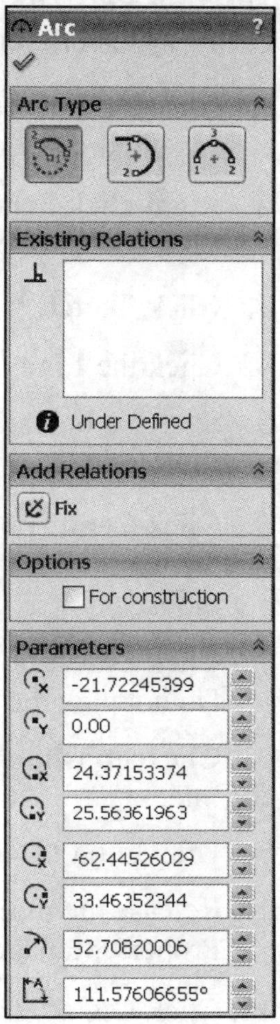


The Centerpoint Arc Sketch entity  tool provides the ability to create an arc from a centerpoint, a start point, and an end point. The Centerpoint Arc Sketch entity uses the consolidated Arc PropertyManager.

The Arc PropertyManager controls the properties of a sketched *Centerpoint Arc, Tangent Arc and 3 Point Arc*.

The consolidated Arc PropertyManager provides the following selections:

- ***Arc Type***: Provides the ability to select a Centerpoint Arc, Tangent Arc or 3 Point Arc sketch entity.
- ***Existing Relations***. The Existing Relations box provides the following options:
  - **Relations**. Displays the automatic relations inferenced during sketching or created manually with the Add Relations tool. The callout in the Graphics window is highlighted when you select a relation in the dialog box. The Information icon in the Existing Relations box displays the sketch status of the selected sketch entity. Example: Under Defined, Fully Defined, etc.
- ***Add Relations***. Provides the ability to add relations to the selected entity. Displays the relations which are possible for the selected entity.
- ***Options***. The Options box provides the following selection:
  - **For construction**. Converts the selected entity to construction geometry.
- ***Parameters***. Provides the ability to specify any appropriate combination of parameters to define your arc if the arc is not constrained by relations. The available selections are: **Center X Coordinate, Center Y Coordinate, Start X Coordinate, Start Y Coordinate, End X Coordinate, End Y Coordinate, Radius** and **Angle**.

Press the **g** key to activate the Magnifying glass tool. Use the Magnifying glass tool to inspect a model and make selections without changing the overall view.

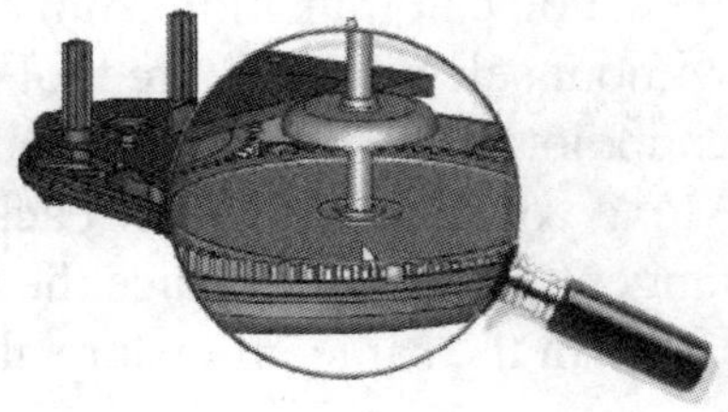

***Tutorial: Certerpoint Arc 4-1***

Create a Centerpoint Arc sketch.

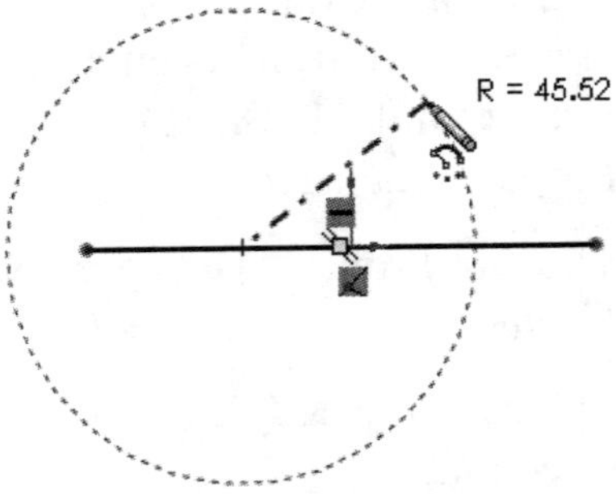


1. Create a **New** part in SolidWorks. Use the default ANSI Part template.
2. Right-click **Front Plane** from the FeatureManager. This is your Sketch plane.
3. Click **Sketch** from the Context toolbar.
4. Click the **Line** Sketch tool.
5. Sketch a **horizontal line** through the origin as illustrated.
6. Click **Centerpoint Arc** from the Consolidated Arc Sketch toolbar. The Arc icon is displayed on your mouse pointer.

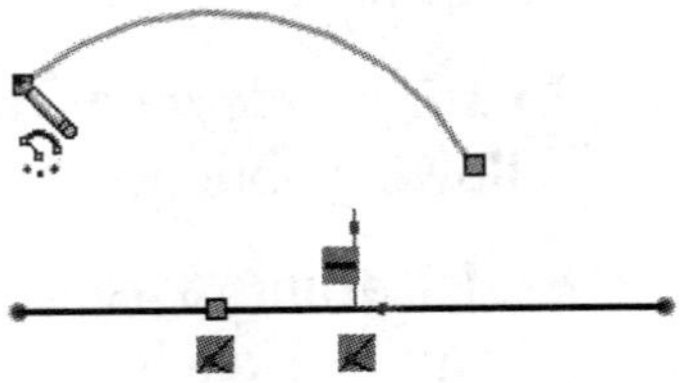

7. Click a location on the **horizontal line** left of the origin. Do not pick the origin or the endpoint.
8. Click a **position** to the right and up on the horizontal line.
9. Drag to set the **angle** and the radius of the arc.
10. Release the **mouse** button to place the arc. View the Arc PropertyManager and the coordinates.
11. Click **OK** from the Arc PropertyManager.
12. **Rebuild** the model.
13. **Close** the model.

## Tangent Arc Sketch Entity

The Tangent Arc Sketch entity tool provides the ability to create an arc, which is tangent to a sketch entity. The Tangent Arc Sketch entity uses the Arc PropertyManager. View the Centerpoint Arc Sketch entity section above for additional information on the Arc PropertyManager.

You can transition from sketching a line to sketching a Tangent Arc, and vice versa without selecting the Arc tool from the Sketch toolbar. Example: Create a line. Click the endpoint of the line. Move your mouse pointer away. The Preview displays another line. Move your mouse pointer back to the selected line endpoint. The Preview displays a tangent arc. Click to place the arc. Move the mouse pointer away from the arc endpoint. Perform the same procedure above to continue.

***Tutorial: Tangent Arc 4-1***

Create a Tangent Arc sketch.

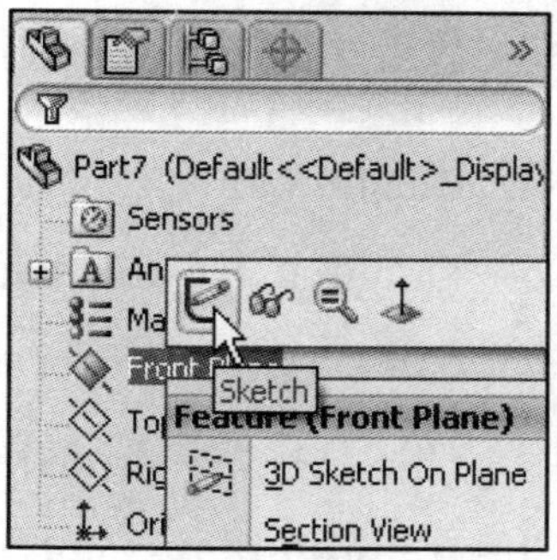


1. Create a **New** part in SolidWorks. Use the default ANSI Part template.
2. Right-click **Front Plane** from the FeatureManager.
3. Click **Sketch** from the Context toolbar.
4. Click the **Line** Sketch tool.
5. Sketch a **horizontal line** through the Origin.

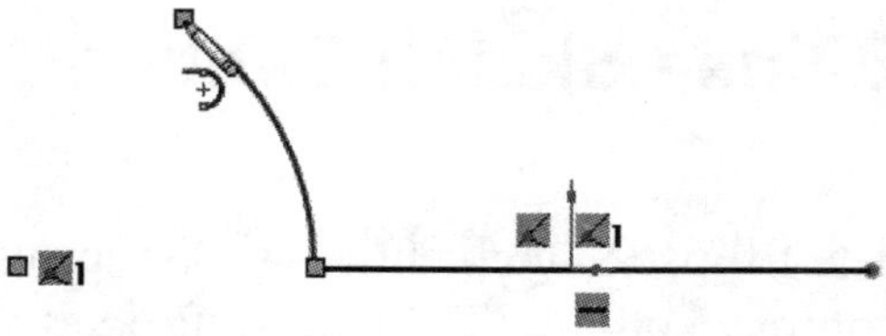

6. Click **Tangent Arc** from the Consolidated Arc Sketch toolbar. The Arc icon is displayed on the mouse pointer. Click the **left end point** of the horizontal line.
7. Drag the **mouse pointer** upward and to the left for the desired shape.
8. Click an **end point**. You created a Tangent Arc. The Arc PropertyManager is displayed.
9. Right-click **Select** in the Graphics window to deselect the Sketch tool.
10. Click **OK** from the Arc PropertyManager.
11. **Exit** the sketch. **Close** the model.

You can select an end point of a line, ellipse, arc or a spline. The Tangent Arc tool creates both Normal and Tangent Arcs.

# 3 Point Arc Sketch Entity

The 3 Point Arc Sketch entity tool provides the ability create an arc by specifying three points; a starting point, an endpoint, and a midpoint. View the Centerpoint Arc Sketch entity section for additional information on the Arc PropertyManager.

***Tutorial: 3Point Arc 4-1***

Create a 3Point Arc sketch.

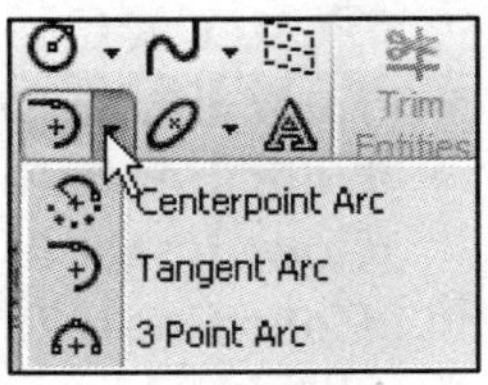


1. Open **3Point Arc 4-1** from the SolidWorks 2010 folder.
2. **Edit** Sketch1.
3. Click **3Point Arc** from the Consolidated Arc Sketch toolbar.

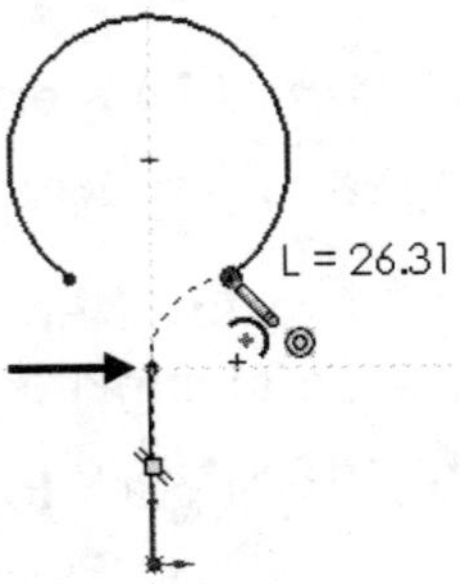


4. Click the **top point** of the vertical line for the start point as illustrated.
5. Click the **right point** of the open circle for the end point as illustrated.
6. Drag the **arc** downward to set the radius.
7. Click a **position** for the midpoint of the 3Point Arc.
8. Click **OK** from the Arc PropertyManager.
9. **Rebuild** the model. **Close** the model.

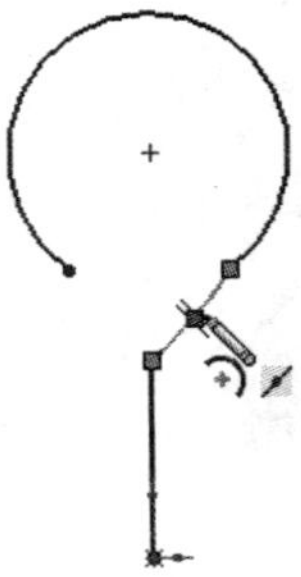

## Ellipse Sketch Entity

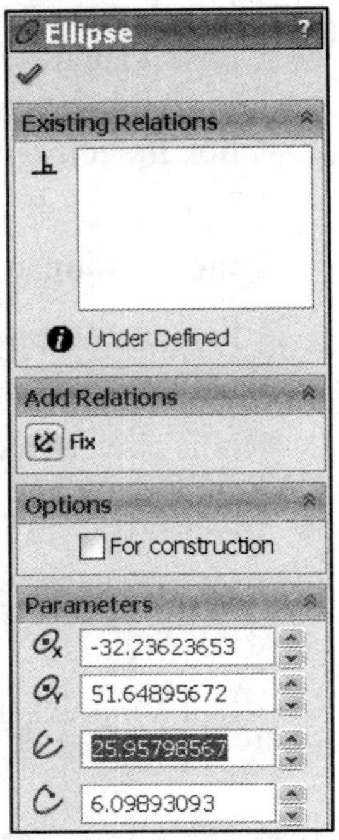


The Ellipse Sketch entity tool provides the ability to create a complete ellipse. The Ellipse PropertyManager controls the properties of a sketched Ellipse or a Partial Ellipse. The Ellipse PropertyManager provides the following selections:

- ***Existing Relations***. The Existing Relations box provides the following options:
  - **Relations**. Displays the automatic relations inferenced during sketching or created manually with the Add Relations tool. The callout in the Graphics window is highlighted when you select a relation in the dialog box. The Information icon in the Existing Relations box displays the sketch status of the selected sketch entity. Example: Under Defined, Fully Defined, etc.
- ***Add Relations***. Provides the ability to add relations to the selected entity. Displays the relations which are possible for the selected entity.
- ***Options***. The Options box provides the following selection:
  - **For construction**. Converts the selected entity to construction geometry.
- ***Parameters***. Provides the ability to specify any appropriate combination of parameters to define the ellipse if the ellipse is not constrained by relations. The available selections are: **Center X Coordinate**, **Center Y Coordinate**, **Start X Coordinate** (only available for a Partial Ellipse), **Start Y Coordinate** (only available for a Partial Ellipse), **End X Coordinate** (only available for a Partial Ellipse), **End Y Coordinate** (only available for a Partial Ellipse), **Radius 1**, **Radius 2** and **Angle** (only available for a Partial Ellipse).

***Tutorial: Ellipse 4-1***

Create an Ellipse sketch.

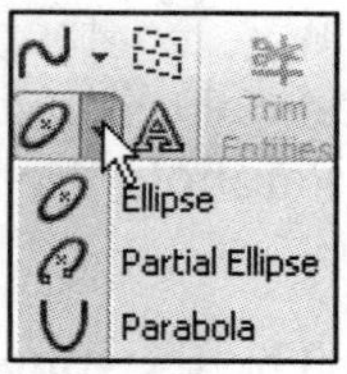


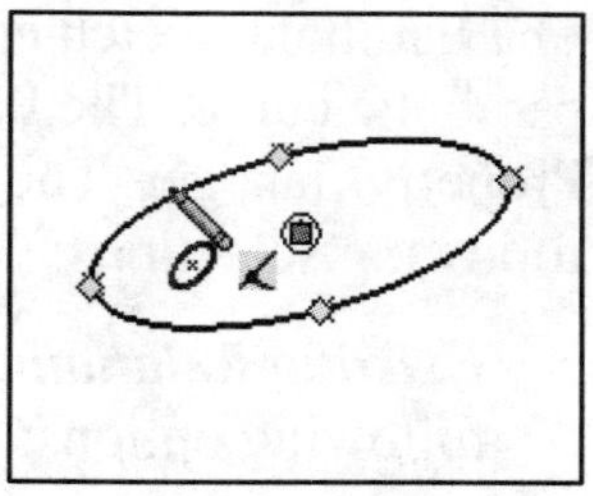

1. Create a **New** part in SolidWorks. Use the default ANSI Part template.
2. Right-click **Front Plane** from the FeatureManager. This is your Sketch plane.
3. Click **Sketch** from the Context toolbar.
4. Click the **Ellipse** Sketch tool. The Ellipse icon is displayed on the mouse pointer.
5. Click a **location** in the Graphics window. This is the start location.

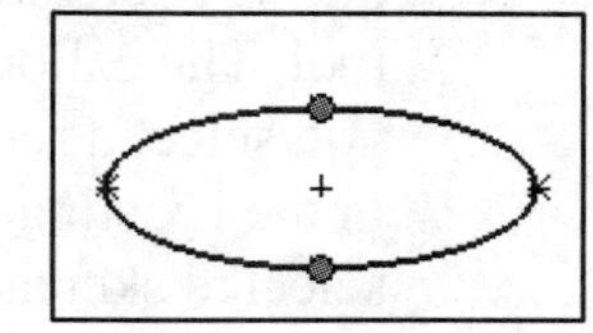

6. Drag and click to set the **major axis** of the ellipse. The ellipse PropertyManager is displayed.
7. Drag and click again to set the **minor axis** of the ellipse.
8. Right-click **Select** in the Graphics window.

Add a Vertical relation.

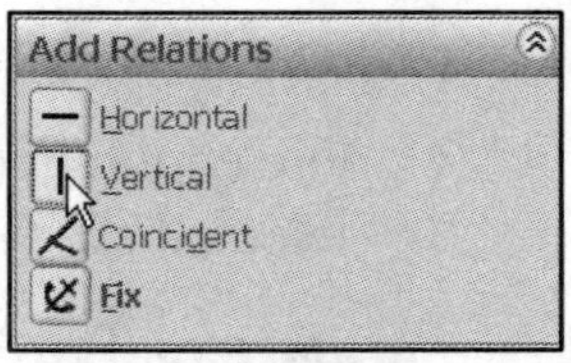


9. Hold the **Ctrl** key down.
10. Click the **top vertical** point and the **bottom vertical** point of the Ellipse.
11. Release the **Ctrl** key. The Properties PropertyManager is displayed.

12. Click **Vertical** from the Add Relations box. Note: You can also use the pop-up Context toolbar and click Make Vertical.
13. Click **OK** from the Properties PropertyManager.
14. **Rebuild** the model. View the sketch.
15. **Close** the model.

# Partial Ellipse Sketch Entity

The Partial Ellipse Sketch entity tool provides the ability to create a partial ellipse or an elliptical arc from a centerpoint, a start point, and an end point. You use a similar procedure when you created a Centerpoint Arc. The Ellipse PropertyManager controls the properties of a sketched Ellipse or a Partial Ellipse. View the Ellipse section for additional information on the Ellipse PropertyManager.

## Parabola Sketch Entity

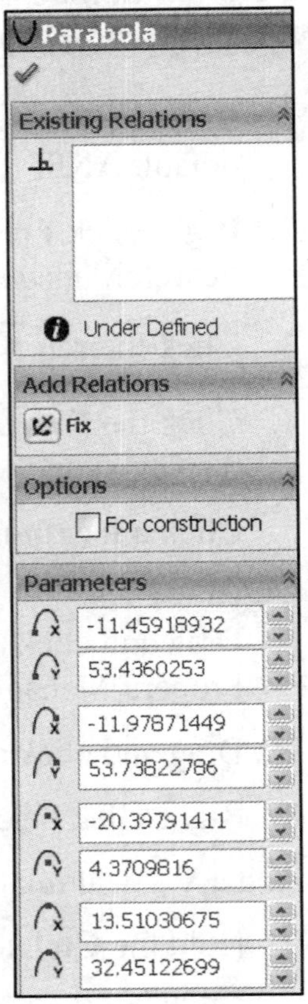


The Parabola Sketch entity tool provides the ability to create a parabolic curve. The Parabola Sketch entity uses the Parabola PropertyManager. The Parabola PropertyManager provides the following selections:

- ***Existing Relations***. The Existing Relations box provides the following options:
  - **Relations**. Displays the automatic relations inferenced during sketching or created manually with the Add Relations tool. The callout in the Graphics window is highlighted when you select a relation in the dialog box. The Information icon in the Existing Relations box displays the sketch status of the selected sketch entity. Example: Under Defined, Fully Defined, etc.
- ***Add Relations***. Provides the ability to add relations to the selected entity. Displays the relations which are possible for the selected entity.
- ***Options***. The Options box provides the following selection:
  - **For construction**. Not selected by default. Converts the selected entity to construction geometry.
- ***Parameters***. Provides the ability to specify the appropriate combination of parameters to define the parabola if the parabola is not constrained by relations. The available selections are: **Start X Coordinate, Start Y Coordinate, End X Coordinate, End Y Coordinate, Center X Coordinate, Center Y Coordinate, Apex X Coordinate** and **Apex Y Coordinate**.

### *Tutorial: Parabola 4-1*

Create a Parabola sketch.

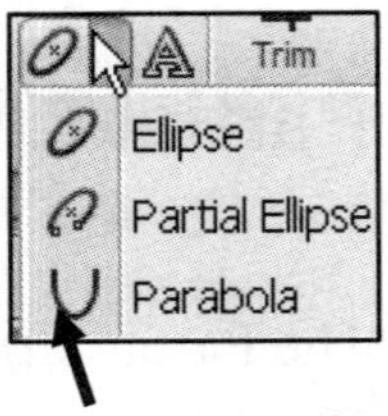


1. Create a **New** part in SolidWorks. Use the default ANSI, IPS Part template.
2. Right-click **Front Plane** from the FeatureManager. This is your Sketch plane.
3. Click **Sketch** from the Context toolbar.
4. Click the **Parabola** Sketch tool from the Consolidated Sketch toolbar. The Parabola icon is displayed on the mouse pointer.

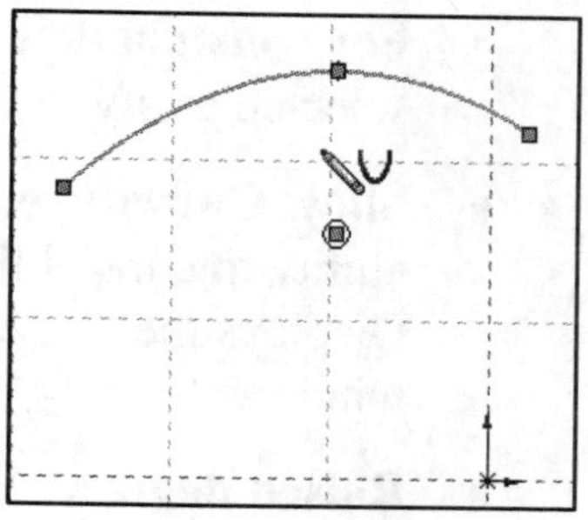

5. Click a **position** in the Graphics window to locate the focus of your parabola.
6. Drag to **enlarge** the parabola. The parabola is outlined.
7. Click on the **parabola** and drag to define the extent of the curve. The Parabola PropertyManager is displayed.
8. Click **OK** from the Parabola PropertyManager.
9. **Rebuild** the model.
10. **Close** the model.

## Spline Sketch Entity

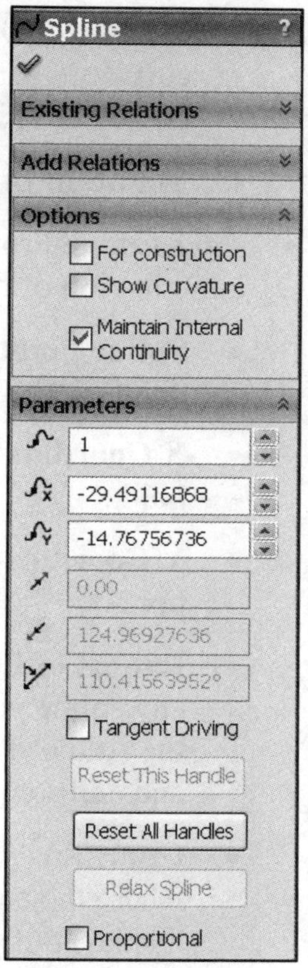


The Spline Sketch entity tool provides the ability to create a profile that utilizes a complex curve. This complex curve is called a Spline, (Non-uniform Rational B-Spline or NURB). Create a spline with control points. With spline control points, you can:

- Use spline points as handles to pull the spline into the shape you want.
- Add dimensions between spline points or between spline points and other entities.
- Add relations to spline points.

The 2D Spline PropertyManager provides the following selections:

- ***Existing Relations***. The Existing Relations box provides the following options:
  - **Relations**. Displays the automatic relations inferenced during sketching or created manually with the Add Relations tool. The callout in the Graphics window is highlighted when you select a relation in the dialog box. The Information icon in the Existing Relations box displays the sketch status of the selected sketch entity. Example: Under Defined, Fully Defined, etc.
- ***Add Relations***. Provides the ability to add relations to the selected entity. Displays the relations which are possible for the selected entity.
- ***Options***. The Options box provides the following selection:

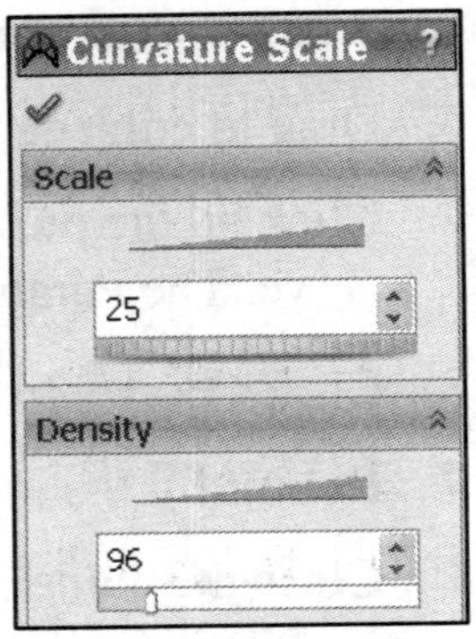


- **For construction**. Not selected by default. Converts the selected entity to construction geometry.
- **Show Curvature**. Not selected by default. Provides the ability to control the Scale and Density of the curvature. Displays the Curvature of the spline in the Graphics window.
- **Raised degree**. Only available with splines that include curvature handles at each end. Raises or lowers the degree of the spline. You can also adjust the degrees by dragging the handles.
- **Standard**. Only available with splines that include curvature handles at each end. Displays when you first create the spline or if Raised degree is cleared.
- **Maintain Internal Continuity**. Selected by default.

- ***Parameters***. Provides the ability to specify the appropriate combination of parameters. The available parameters are:
  - **Spline Point Number**. Highlights your selected spline point in the Graphics window.
  - **X Coordinate**. Specifies the x coordinate of your spline point.
  - **Y Coordinate**. Specifies the y coordinate of your spline point.
  - **Radius of Curvature**. Controls the radius of curvature at any spline point. This option is only displayed if you select the Add Curvature Control option from the Spline toolbar, and add a curvature pointer to the spline.
  - **Curvature**. Displays the degree of curvature at the point where the curvature control was added. This option is only displayed if you add a curvature pointer to the spline.
  - **Tangent Weighting1**. Controls the left tangency vector by modifying the spline's curvature at the spline point.
  - **Tangent Weighting 2**. Controls the right tangency vector by modifying the spline's curvature at the spline point.
  - **Tangent Radial Direction**. Controls the tangency direction by modifying the spline's angle of inclination relative to the X, Y or Z axis.

- **Tangent Polar Direction**. Controls the elevation angle of the tangent vector with respect to a plane placed at a point perpendicular to a spline point. This is only for the 3D Spline PropertyManager.
- **Tangent Driving**. Enables spline control by using the Tangent Magnitude option and the Tangent Radial Direction option.
- **Reset This Handle**. Returns the selected spline handle to the initial state.
- **Reset All Handles**. Returns the spline handles to their initial state.
- **Relax Spline**. Sketch your spline and display the control polygon. You can drag any node on the control polygon to change shape. If your dragging results in a spline which is not smooth, re-select the spline to display the PropertyManager. Click the Relax Spline selection under the Parameters option. This will re-parameterize or smooth the shape of your spline.
- **Proportional**. Retains the spline shape when you drag the spline.

# Spline toolbar

Use the tools located on the Spline toolbar to control properties of a sketched spline. The Spline toolbar provides the following tools:

- ***Add Tangency Control***. The Add Tangency Control tool adds a tangency control handle. Drag the control handle along the spline and position it to control the tangency at the selected point.

- ***Add Curvature Control***. The Add Curvature Control tool adds a curvature control handle. Drag the control handle along the spline and position the control handle to control the spline shape at the selected point.

- ***Insert Spline Point***. The Insert Spline Point tool adds a point to the spline. Drag spline points to reshape the spline.

You can insert dimensions between the spline points.

- ***Simplify Spline***. The Simplify Spline tool reduces the number of points in the spline. This function improves the performance in the model for complex spline curves.

- ***Fit Spline***. The Fit Spline tool adds a spline based on the selected sketch entities and edges.

- ***Show Spline Handles***. The Show Spline Handles tool displays all handles of the selected spline in the Graphic window. Use the spline handles to reshape the spline.
- ***Show Inflection Points***. The Show Inflection Points tool displays all points where the concavity of a selected spline changes.
- ***Show Minimum Radius***. The Show Minimum Radius tool displays the measurement of the smallest radius in the selected spline.
- ***Show Curvature Combs***. The Show Curvature Combs tool displays the scalable curvature combs which visually enhances the curves of your selected spline.

***Tutorial: Spline 4-1***

Create a 2D Spline sketch.

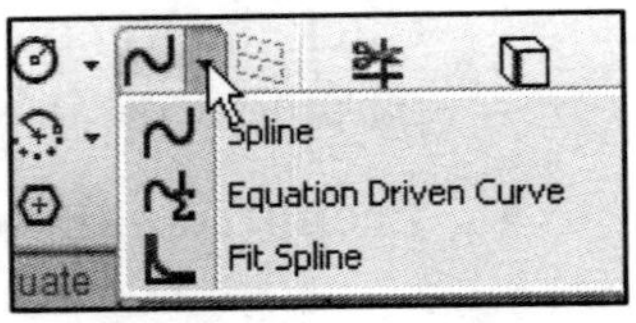


1. Create a **New** part. Use the default ANSI, IPS Part template.
2. Right-click **Right Plane** from the FeatureManager. This is your Sketch plane.
3. Click **Sketch** from the Context toolbar.
4. Click the **Spline** Sketch tool. The spline icon is displayed on the mouse pointer.
5. Create a **seven point control** spline as illustrated. Do not select the origin. The Spline PropertyManager is displayed.
6. Right-click **End spline** on the last control point.
7. **Exit** the Spline tool.
8. Click and drag the **spline** from left to right. Do not select a control or handle. The spline moves without changing its shape.
9. Click **OK** from the Spline PropertyManager.
10. **Rebuild** the model. View the results.
11. **Close** the model.

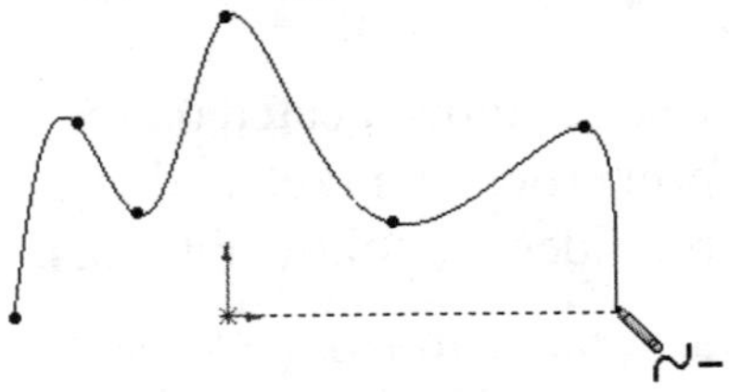

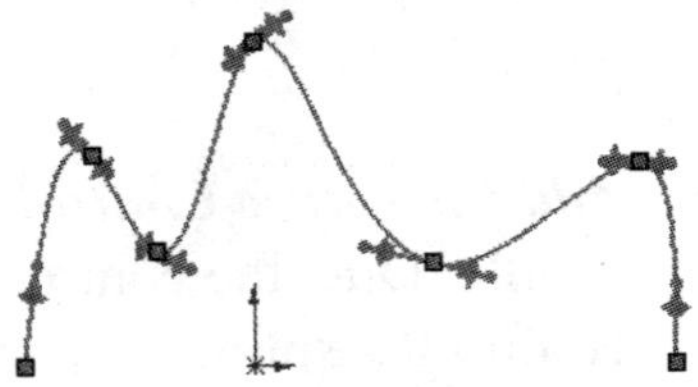

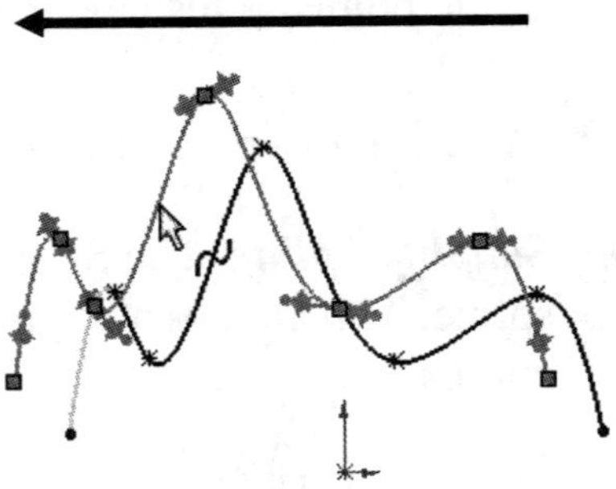

Spline handles are displayed by default. To hide or display spline handles, click the **Show Spline Handles** tool from the Spline toolbar or click **Tools ➤ Spline Tools ➤ Show Spline Handles**.

***Tutorial: 2D Spline 4-2***

Dimension a 2D Spline handle.

1. Open **2D Spline 4-2** from the SolidWorks 2010 folder.
2. **Edit** Sketch1.

Use the Smart Dimension tool to dimension the spline handles. Display the handles.

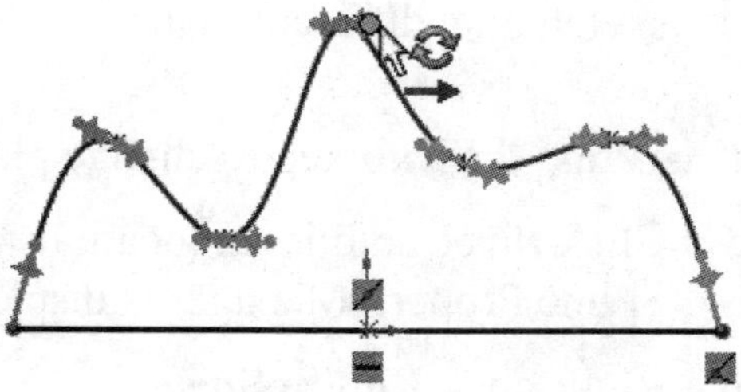

3. Click the **Spline** in the Graphics window. The Spline PropertyManager is displayed. Locate the pointer on the top handle. The rotate icon is displayed.
4. Click the **top handle tip**.
5. **Rotate** the handle upwards as illustrated to create a Tangent Driving.

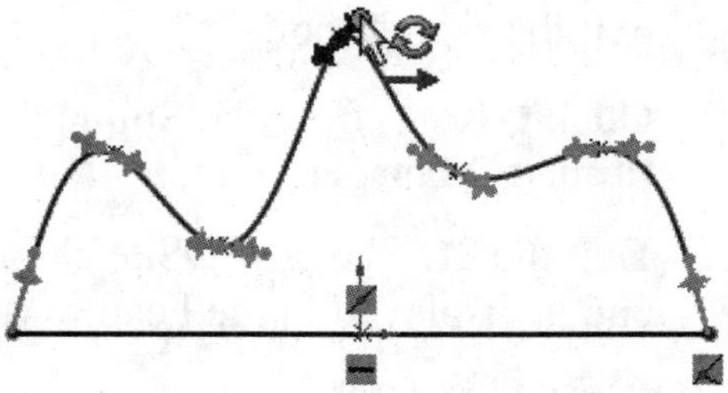

6. Right-click **Smart Dimension** from the Context toolbar.

Create a Tangent Radial dimension.

7. Click the **handle arrow tip**.
8. Click the **horizontal** line.
9. Enter **40**deg.
10. Set **precision** to none.
11. Click **OK** from the Dimension PropertyManager.
12. **Rebuild** the model. View the results.
13. **Close** the model.

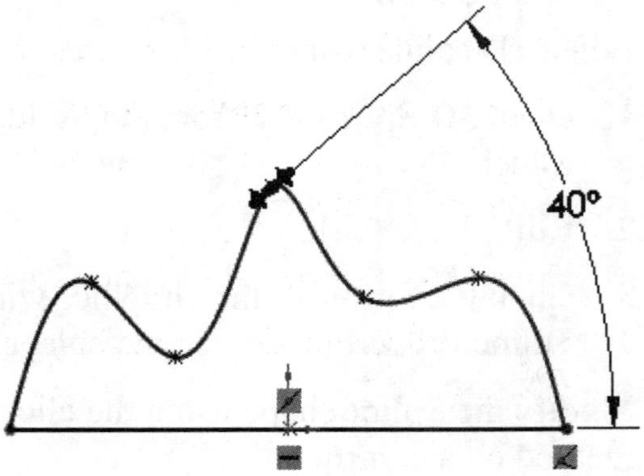


For a Tangent Magnitude select the arrow tip on the handle to add the dimension.

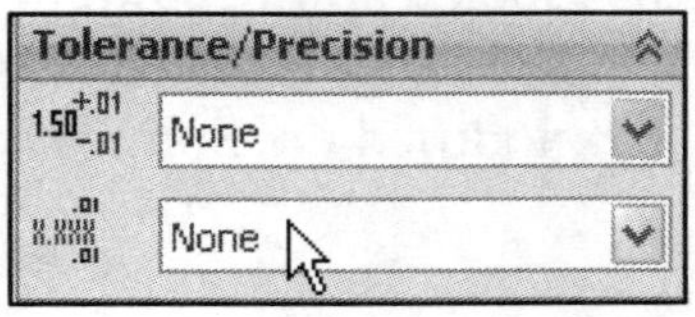

### *Tutorial: 3D Spline 4-1*

Create a 3D Spline part.

1. Create a **New** part. Use the default ANSI Part template.
2. Click **Insert ➢ 3D Sketch** from the Menu bar menu.
3. Click the **Spline** Sketch tool.

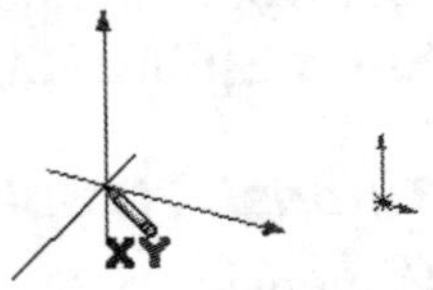

4. Click a **location** in the Graphics window to place the first spline point. Each time you click a different location, the space handle is displayed to help you sketch on a different plane.

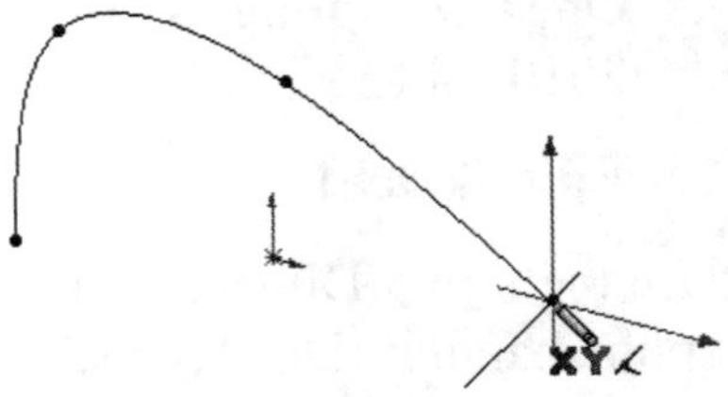

Press the **Tab** key to change planes.

5. Click **three** additional locations as illustrated. The Spline PropertyManager is displayed.
6. Right-click **End Spline**.
7. Click **Spline** from the Sketch toolbar to exit the sketch tool.
8. Click **OK** from the Spline PropertyManager.
9. **Exit** the 3D Sketch. 3DSketch1 is created and is displayed in the FeatureManager.
10. **Close** the sketch.

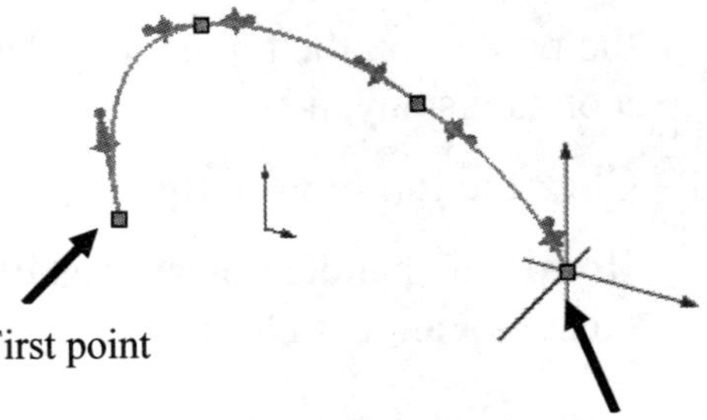

First point

Last point

### *Tutorial: 3D Spline 4-2*

Edit a 3D spline using the current elements.

1. Open **3D Spline 4-2** from the SolidWorks 2010 folder.
2. **Edit** 3DSketch1.
3. Click the **Spline** in the Graphics window. The Spline PropertyManager is displayed.

Modify the Spline shape using the click and drag method on a control point.

4. Click a **spline control point** and drag it upward. The Point PropertyManager is displayed. You modified the Spline shape.

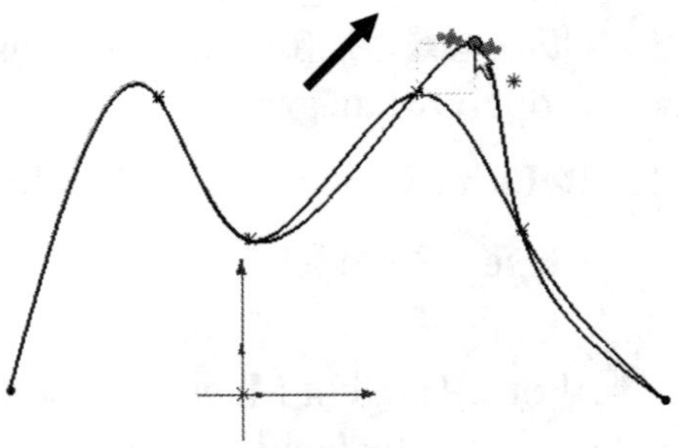

Modify the Spline shape using the X, Y and Z coordinates method on a control point.

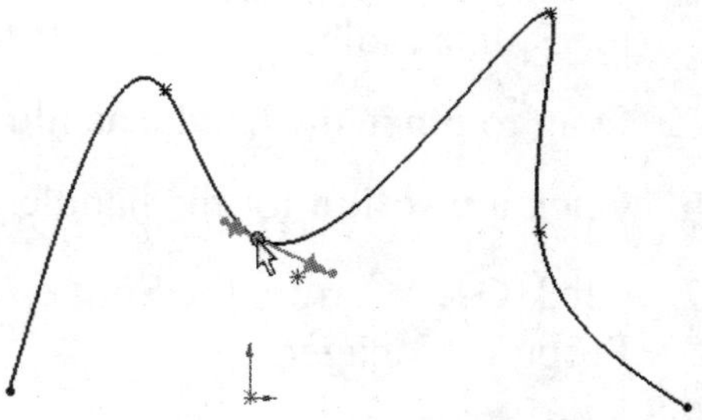

5. Click a **spline point** as illustrated. The Point PropertyManager is displayed.
6. Set values for **X, Y**, and **Z** coordinates from the Point PropertyManager. You modified the Spline shape.

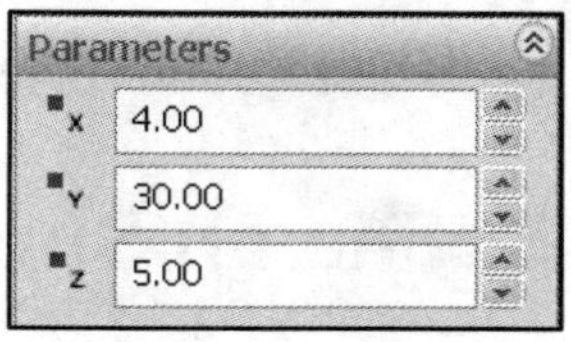


Modify the Spline shape using the click and drag method on a handle.

7. Click a **spline handle** as illustrated.
8. Drag the selected **spline handle** to control the tangency vector by modifying the spline's degree of curvature at the spline point. The Spline PropertyManager is displayed.

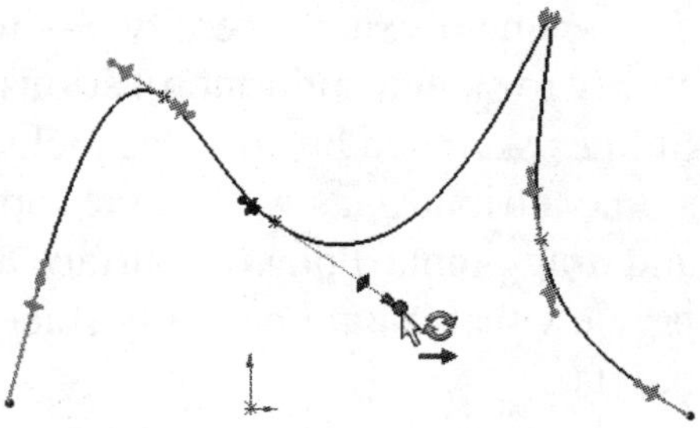

Reset the handle to the original location.

9. Click the **Reset This Handle** option. All values relative to the selected handle return to their original value.

Move the spline.

10. Check the **Proportional** box.
11. Click and drag the **spline** from left to right. Do not select a control point. As the spline is moved, it retains its shape.
12. Click **OK** from the Spline PropertyManager.
13. **Exit** the 3D Sketch. View the results.
14. **Close** the model.

### *Tutorial: 3D Spline 4-3*

Add new elements to a 3D Spline.

1. Open **3D Spline 4-3** from the SolidWorks 2010 folder.
2. **Edit** 3DSketch1.
3. Click the **spline** from the Graphics window. The Spline PropertyManager is displayed.

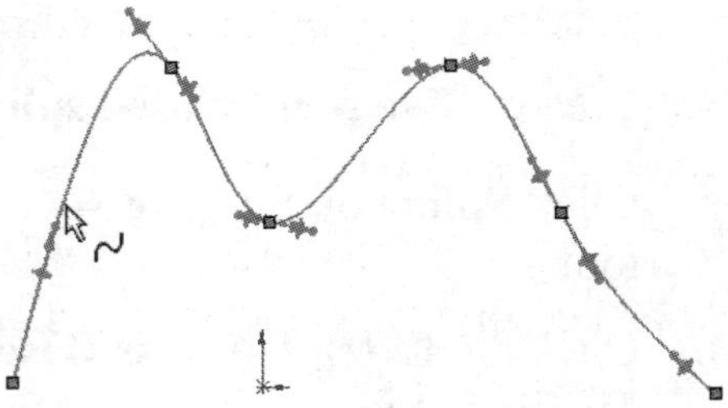

4. Click the **Add Tangency Control** tool from the Spline toolbar.
5. Drag to **place** the handle as illustrated.
6. Click a **position** for the handle.
7. Click **OK** from the Spline PropertyManager.
8. **Exit** the 3D Sketch. View the results.
9. **Close** the model.

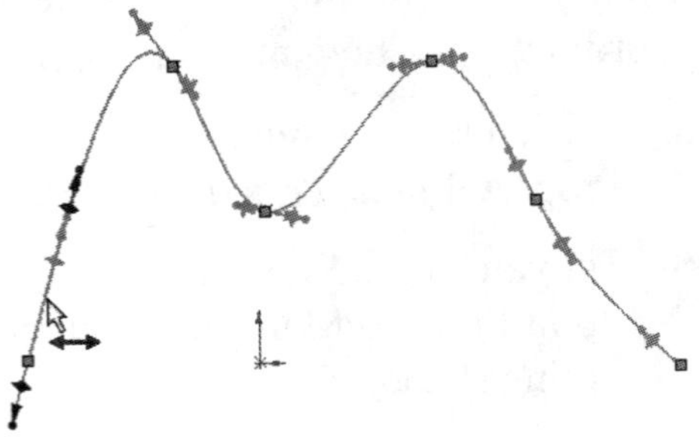

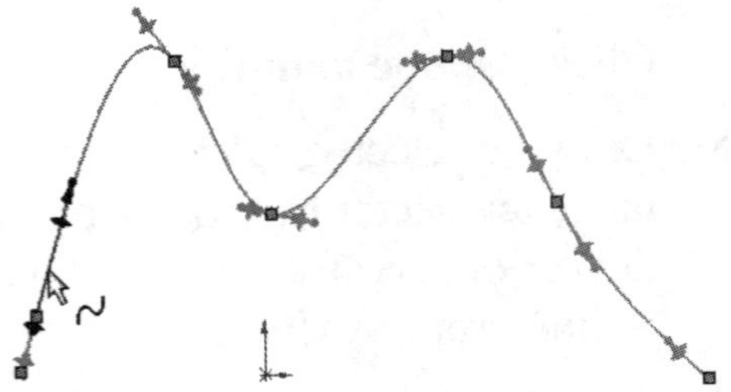

## Spline on Surface Entity

The Spline on Surface entity tool provides the ability to sketch splines on various surfaces. Splines sketched on surfaces include standard spline attributes, as well as the capabilities to add and drag points along the surface and to generate a preview that is automatically smoothed through the points.

All spline points are bounded to the surface on which they are sketched.

***Tutorial: Spline on Surface 4-1***

Create a Closed Spline on Surface feature.

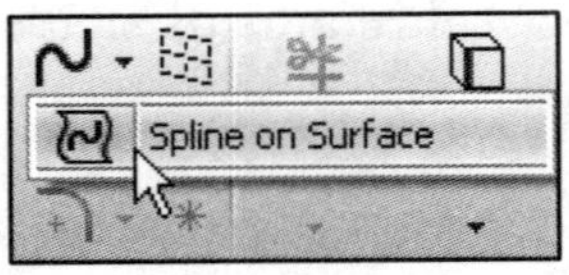


1. Open **Spline on Surface 4-1** from the SolidWorks 2010 folder.
2. Click the **top left face** as illustrated.
3. Click the **Spline on Surface** Sketch tool.

   The spline icon is displayed on the mouse pointer.
4. Create a **five point closed spline** as illustrated.
5. Click **Spline on Surface** to close the sketch tool.
6. Click the **Extruded Boss/Base** Features tool. The Boss-Extrude PropertyManager is displayed.

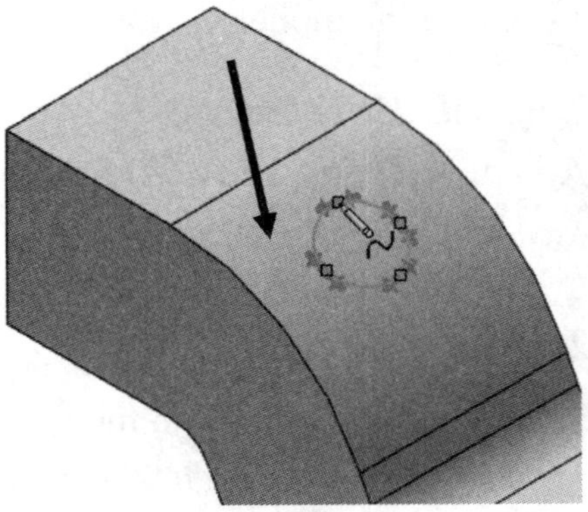

7. Click the **left vertical line** as illustrated for Direction 1.
8. Enter **10**mm for Depth.
9. Click **OK** from the Boss-Extrude PropertyManager. Boss-Extrude1 is displayed. View the results in the Graphics window.
10. **Close** the model.

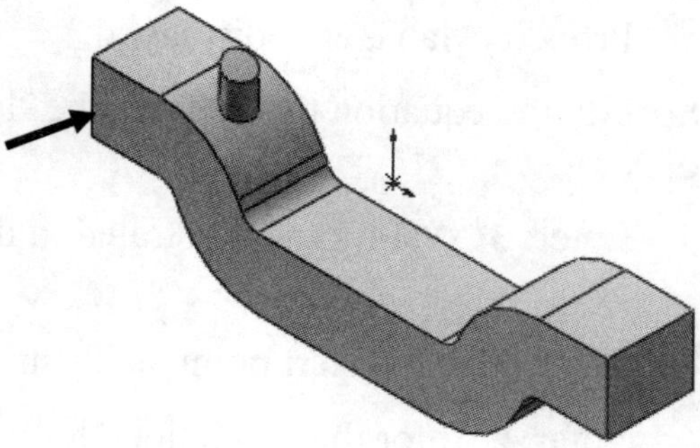

## Equation Driven Curve

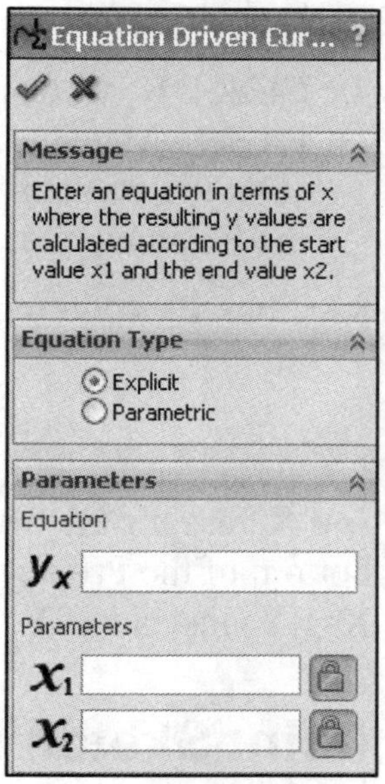


The Equation Driven Curve tool is a 2D sketch spline driven by an equation. This Sketch entity provides the ability to create a curve by specifying the equations that defines the curve. Equations defining a curve specify Y as a function of X. You can use any function that is supported in the Equations dialog box.

The Equation Driven Curve entity uses the Equation Driven Curve PropertyManager. The PropertyManager provides the following selections:

- ***Equation Type***. There are equation types available: *Explicit* and *Parametric*.
- ***Parameters***. The Parameters box provides the following options:
  - **Equation**. Provides the ability to enter an equation as a function of X. If you enter an equation that can't be resolved, the text color is displayed in red.
  - **Parameters**. Provides the ability to enter the start and end X value of the equation.
  - **Transform**. Provides the ability to enter the translation of X, Y and angle for the curve.

### *Tutorial: Equation Driven Curve 4-1*

Create an Equation Driven Curve.

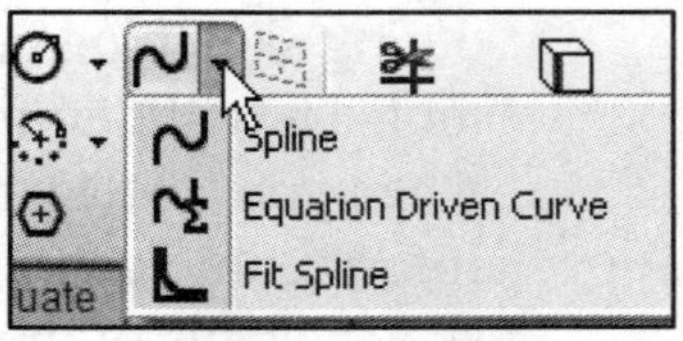


1. Create a **New** part. Use the default ANSI, IPS Part template. Right-click **Front Plane** from the FeatureManager.
2. Click **Sketch** from the Context toolbar. The Sketch toolbar is displayed.

3. Click the **Equation Driven Curve** Sketch tool. The Equation Driven Curve PropertyManager is displayed.

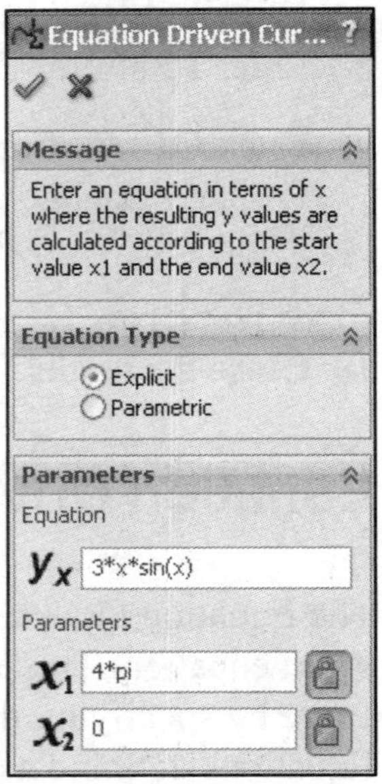


Specify the equation that defines the sketch. Note: Y is a function of X.

4. Enter: **3*x*sin(x)** as illustrated in the Equation box.
5. Enter **0** for the start point as illustrated.
6. Enter **4*pi** for the end point. Note: You can fix the end points of the curve by applying the Fix tool.
7. Click **OK** from Equation Driven Curve PropertyManager. View the created curve. Note click the curve in the Graphics window to edit the Parameters of the curve.
8. Click **Exit Sketch**. View the results. **Close** the model.

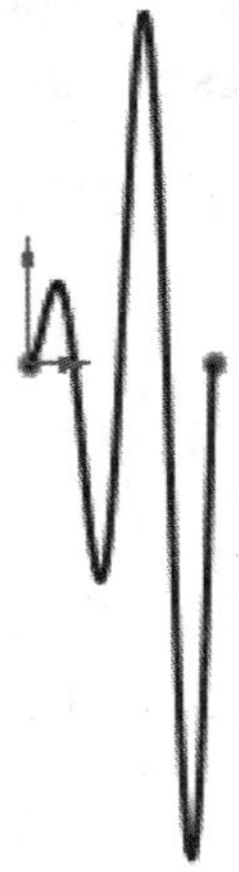

Use regular mathematical notation and order of operations to write an equation. X1 and X2 are for the beginning and end of the curve. Use the transform options at the bottom of the PropertyManager to move the entire curve in X, Y or rotation. To specify X=f(Y) instead of Y = f(x), use a 90 degree transform.

## Point Sketch Entity

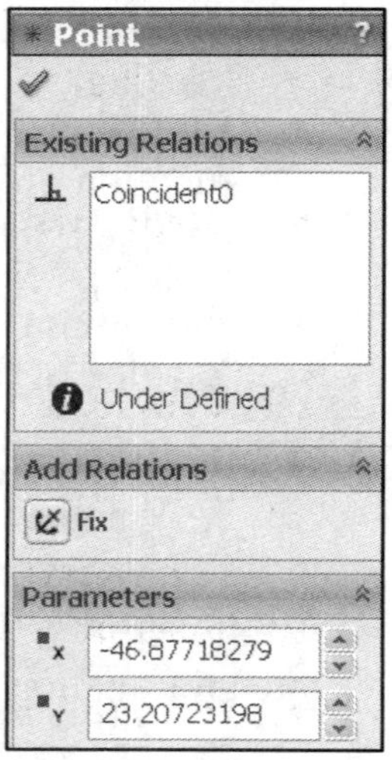


The Point Sketch entity tool provides the ability to insert points in your sketches and drawings. To modify the properties of a point, select the point in an active sketch, and edit the properties in the Point PropertyManager. The Point PropertyManager provides the following selections:

- ***Existing Relations***. The Existing Relations box provides the following options:
  - **Relations**. Displays the automatic relations inferenced during sketching or created manually with the Add Relations tool. The callout in the Graphics window is highlighted when you select a relation in the dialog box. The Information icon in the Existing Relations box displays the sketch status of the selected sketch entity.
- ***Add Relations***. Provides the ability to add relations to the selected entity. Displays the relations which are possible for the selected entity.

- ***Parameters***. Provides the ability to specify the appropriate combination of parameters for your point only is the point is not constrained by relations. The available parameters are:
  - **X Coordinate**. Specifies the x coordinate of your point.
  - **Y Coordinate**. Specifies the y coordinate of your point.

## Centerline Sketch Entity

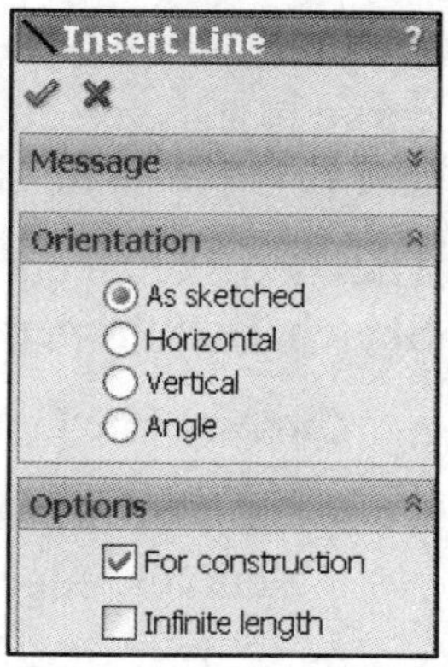


The Centerline Sketch entity tool provides the ability to use centerlines to create symmetrical sketch elements and revolved features, or as construction geometry. The Centerline sketch entity uses the Insert Line PropertyManager. The Insert Line PropertyManager provides the following selections:

- ***Orientation***. The Orientation box provides the following options:
  - **As sketched**. Sketch a line in any direction using the click and drag method. Using the click-click method, the As sketched option provides the ability to sketch a line in any direction, and to continue sketching other lines in any direction, until you double-click to end your process.
  - **Horizontal**. Sketch a horizontal line until you release your mouse pointer.
  - **Vertical**. Sketch a vertical line until you release your mouse pointer.
  - **Angle**. Sketch a line at an angle until you release your mouse pointer.

The angle is created relative to the horizontal.

- ***Options***. The Options box provides two line types. They are:
  - **For construction**. Selected by default. Converts the selected sketch entity to construction geometry.
  - **Infinite length**. Not selected by default. Creates a line of infinite length which you can later trim in the design process.

Use Construction geometry to assist in creating your sketch entities and geometry that are ultimately incorporated into the part. Construction geometry is ignored when the sketch is used to create a feature. Construction geometry uses the same line style as a centerline.

# Text Sketch Entity

The Text Sketch entity tool provides the ability to sketch text on the face of a part and extrude or cut the text. Text can be inserted on any set of continuous curves or edges. This includes circles or profiles which consist of lines, arcs or splines.

Convert the sketch entities to construction geometry if the curve is a sketch entity, or a set of sketch entities, and your sketch text is in the same sketch as the curve.

The Text sketch entity uses the Sketch Text PropertyManager. The Sketch Text PropertyManager provides the following selections:

- ***Curves***. The Curves box provides the following options:
  - **Select Edges, Curves Segment**. Displays the selected curves, edges, sketches, or sketch segments.
- ***Text***. The Text box provides the following options:
  - **Text**. Displays the entered text along the selected entity in the Graphics window. If you do not select an entity, the text is displayed horizontally starting at the origin.
  - **Bold Style**. Bold the selected text.
  - **Italic Style**. Italic the selected text.
  - **Rotate Style**. Rotate the selected text.
  - **Left Alignment**. Justify text to the left. Only available for text along an edge, curve or sketch segment.
  - **Center Alignment**. Justify text to the center. Only available for text along an edge, curve or sketch segment.
  - **Right Alignment**. Justify text to the right. Only available for text along an edge, curve or sketch segment.
  - **Full Justify Alignment**. Justify text. Only available for text along an edge, curve or sketch segment.
  - **Flip**. Provides the ability to flip the text.

- **Flip Vertical direction and back**. The Flip Vertical option is only available for text along an edge, curve or sketch segment.
- **Flip Horizontal direction and back**. The Flip Horizontal option is only available for text along an edge, curve or sketch segment.
- **Width Factor**. Provides the ability to widen each of your characters evenly by a specified percentage. Not available when you select the Use document's font option.
- **Spacing**. Provides the ability to modify the spacing between each character by a specified percentage. Not available when your text is fully justified or when you select the Use document's font option.
- **Use document's font**. Selected by default. Provides the ability to clear the initial font and to choose another font by using the Font option button.
- **Font**. Provides the ability to choose a font size and style from the Font dialog box.

***Tutorial: Text 4-1***

Apply text on a curved part. Use the Sketch Text PropertyManager.

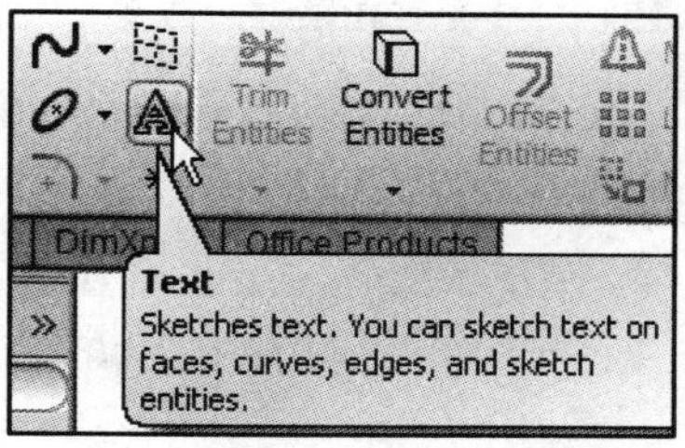


1. Open **Text 4-1** from the SolidWorks 2010 folder. The Lens Cap is displayed in the Graphics window.
2. Click **Front Plane** from the FeatureManager.
3. Click the **Text** Sketch tool. The Sketch Text PropertyManager is displayed.
4. Click **inside** the Text box.
5. Type **SolidWorks**. SolidWorks is displayed horizontally in the Graphics window starting at the origin, because you do not select an entity.

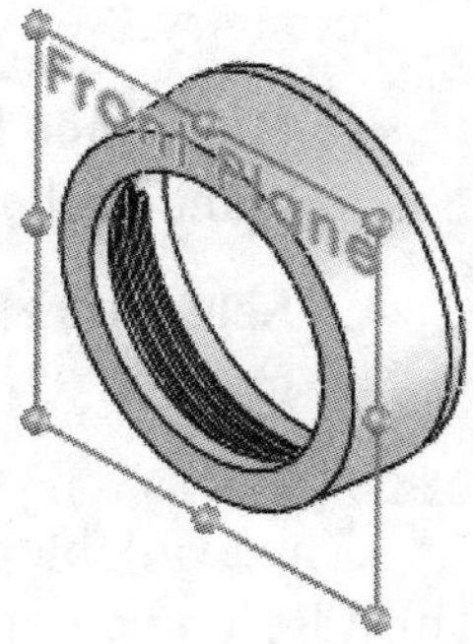


6. Click the **front edge** of Base Extrude. Edge<1> is displayed in the Curves option box. The SolidWorks text is displayed on the selected edge.
7. Uncheck the **Use document font** box.
8. Enter **250%** in the Spacing box.
9. Click the **Font** Button. The Choose Font dialog box is displayed.
10. Select **Arial Black, Regular, Point 14**.

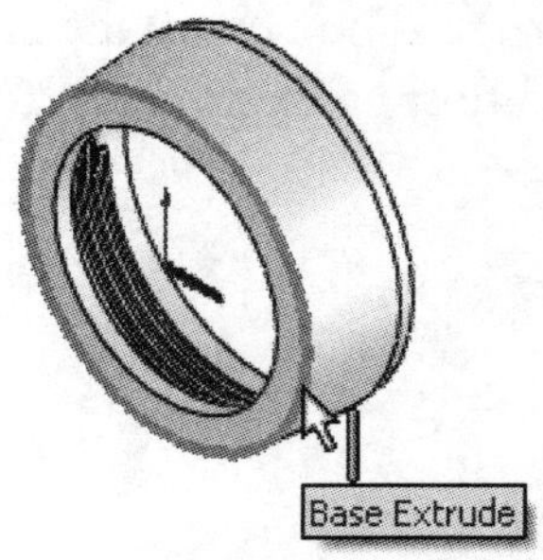

11. Click **OK** from the Choose Font dialog box.

12. Click **OK** from the Sketch Text PropertyManager. Sketch7 is created and is displayed in the FeatureManager. Zoom in on the created text.

13. **Close** the model.

If the curve is a sketch entity, or a set of sketch entities, and the sketch text is in the same sketch as the curve, convert the sketch entities to construction geometry.

## Plane Sketch Entity

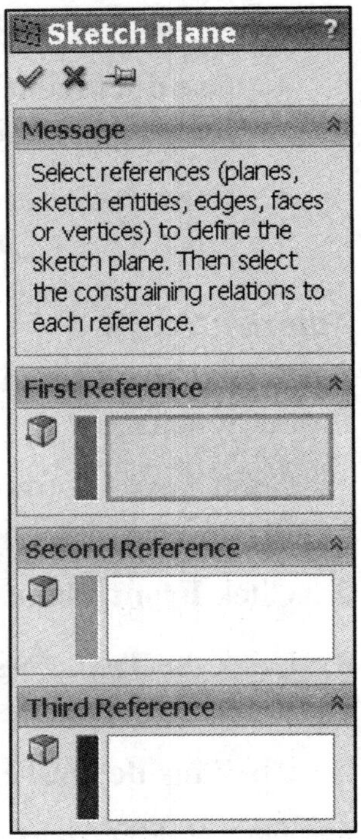


The Plane Sketch entity tool provides the ability for the user to add Reference entities to a 3D sketch. Why? To facilitate sketching and to add relations between sketch entities. Once you add the plane, you need to activate it to display its properties and to create a sketch. The Plane sketch entity uses the Sketch Plane PropertyManager.

The Sketch Plane PropertyManager provides the following selections:

- ***First Reference***. Provides the ability to select Reference entities from the FeatureManager or from the Graphics window. Select the constraining relations to each reference. The available relations selection is based on the selected geometry.
  - **Reference Entities**. Displays the selected sketch entity or plane as the reference to position the 3D Sketch plane.
  - **Select a relation**. Select a relation based on the selected geometry.

The available relations displayed under First, Second, and Third References are based on existing geometry.

The new planes in a 3D Sketch are sketch entities, just like lines, arcs, splines, etc.

- ***Second Reference***. Provides the ability to select Reference entities from the FeatureManager or from the Graphics window. Select the constraining relations to each reference. The available relations selection is based on the selected geometry.
  - **Reference Entities**. Displays the selected sketch entity or plane as the reference to position the 3D Sketch plane.
  - **Select a relation**. Selects a relation based on the selected geometry.
- ***Third Reference***. Provides the ability to select Reference entities from the FeatureManager or from the Graphics window. Select the constraining relations to each reference. The available relations selection is based on the selected geometry.
  - **Reference Entities**. Displays the selected sketch entity or plane as the reference to position the 3D Sketch plane.
  - **Select a relation**. Selects a relation based on the selected geometry.

With existing geometry, add a plane by referencing the entities that are present. You can use any number of references required to achieve the desired results.

***Tutorial: Sketch Plane 4-1***

Add a 3D Sketch plane. Add a plane using references. Select two corner points of a 3D sketch. The corner points of the rectangle reference the position of the 3D sketch plane.

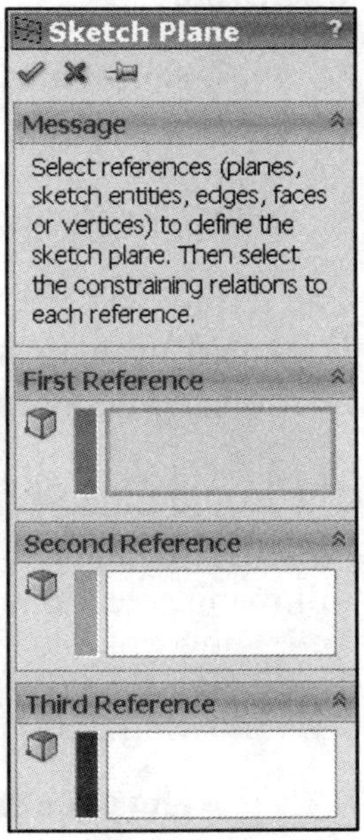


1. Open **Sketch Plane 4-1** from the SolidWorks 2010 folder.
2. **Edit** 3DSketch1 from the FeatureManager.
3. Click **Tools ➢ Sketch Entities ➢ Plane**. The Sketch Plane PropertyManager is displayed.

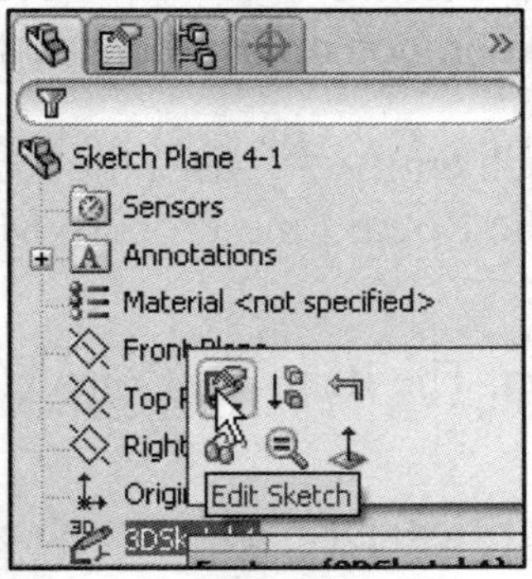


The available relations are displayed in the Sketch Plane PropertyManager under the First, Second and Third Reference. The relations are based on existing geometry.

4. Click the **top front corner point** of the rectangle as illustrated. Point3 is displayed in the First Reference box.
5. Click the **bottom back corner point** of the rectangle. Point4 is displayed in the Second Reference box.
6. Click **OK** from the Sketch Plane PropertyManager.
7. **Rebuild** the model. Plane2@3DSketch1 is created and is displayed in the Graphics window.
8. **Close** the model.

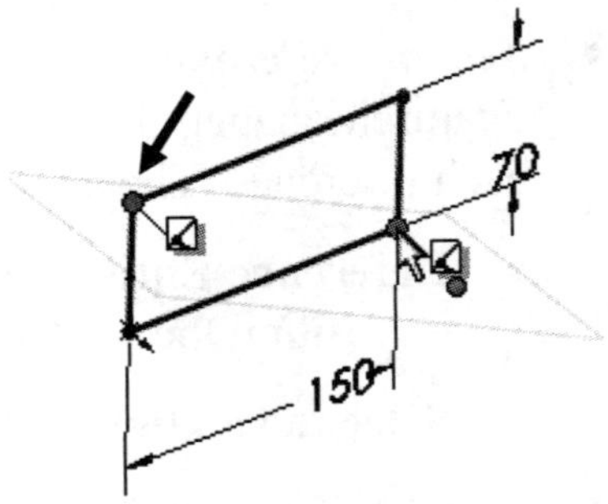


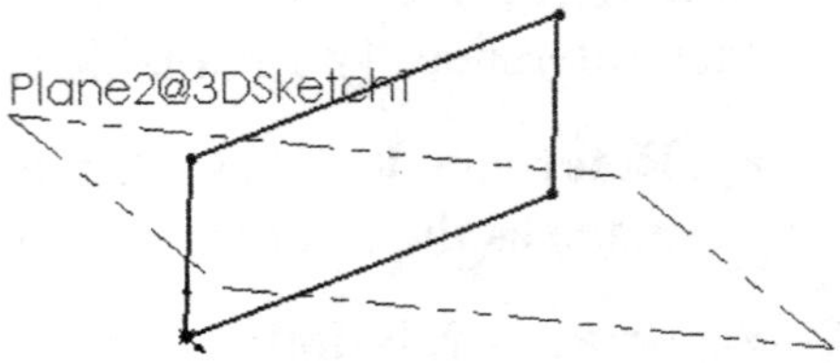


## Route Line Sketch Entity

The Route Line Sketch entity tool provides the ability to insert a Route line between faces, circular edges, straight edges, or planar faces. The Route Line Sketch entity is active when you:

- Create an Explode Line Sketch.
- Edit an Explode Line Sketch.
- Select the Route Line tool in a 3D sketch.

The Exploded Line Sketch tool is a 3D sketch added to an Exploded View in an assembly. The explode lines indicate the relationship between components in the assembly.

The Route Line Sketch entity uses the Route Line PropertyManager. The Route Line PropertyManager provides the following selections:

- ***Items To Connect***. The Items To Connect box provides the following option:
  - **Reference entities**. Displays the selected circular edges, faces, straight edges or planar faces to connect with your created route line.
- ***Options***. The Options box provides the following selections:
  - **Reverse**. Reverses the direction of your route line. A preview arrow is displayed in the direction of the route line.
  - **Alternate Path**. Displays an alternate possible path for the route line.
  - **Along XYZ**. Creates a path parallel to the X, Y and Z axis directions.

Clear the Along XYZ option to use the shortest route.

### *Tutorial: Route Line 4-1*

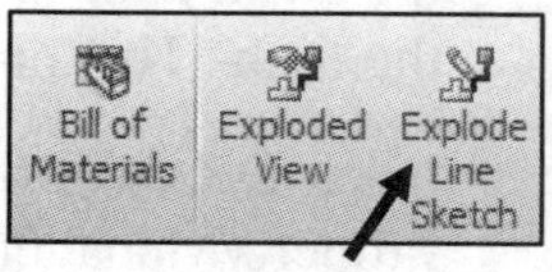


Create an Explode Line sketch using the Route Line Sketch entity.

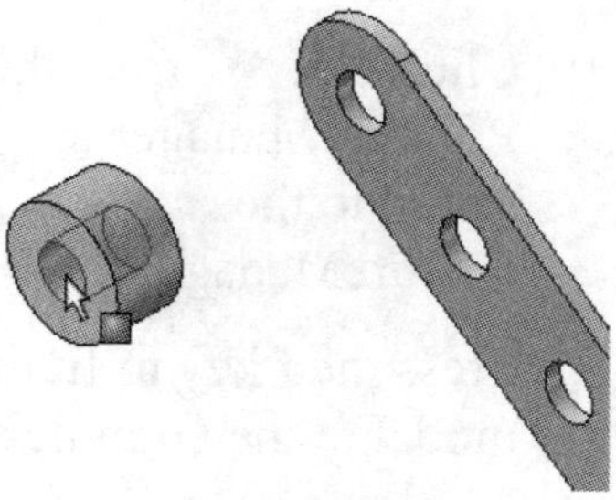

1. Open the **Route Line 4-1** assembly from the SolidWorks 2010 folder. The assembly is displayed in an Exploded view.
2. Click the **Explode Line Sketch** tool from the Assembly toolbar. The Route Line PropertyManager is displayed.
3. Click the **inside face** of Cut-Extrude1 of Shaft-Collar<1>. The direction arrow points towards the back. If required, check the Reverse direction box. Face<1> @Shaft-Collar-1 is displayed in the Items To Connect box.

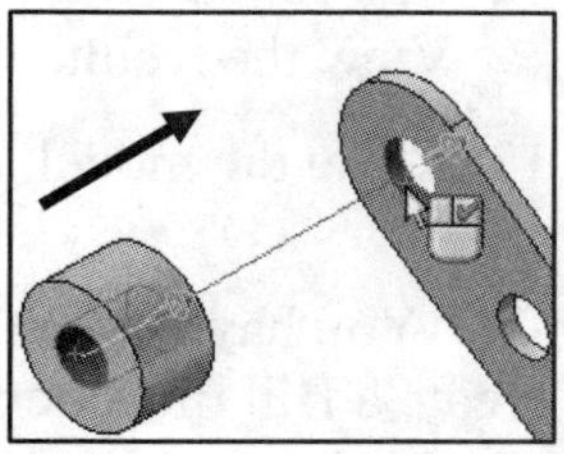

4. Click the **inside face** of the top hole of Cut-Extrude1 of the Flatbar<1> component. Face<2>@Flatbar-1 is displayed in the Items To Connect box. The arrow points towards the right.

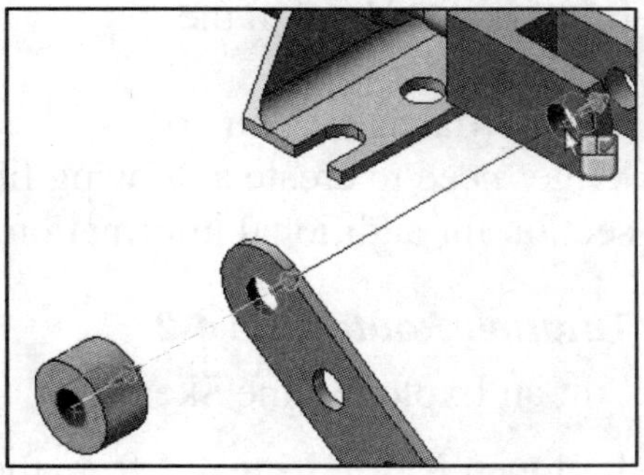

5. Click the **inside face** of Cut-Extrude5 of RodClevis<1>. Face<3>@AirCylinder-1is displayed in the Items To Connect box. The Arrow points towards the back.
6. Click the **inside face** of the second Cut-Extrude5 feature of RodClevis<1>. Face<4>@ AirCylinder-1 is displayed in the Items To Connect box.
7. Click the **inside face** of the top hole of Cut-Extrude1 of the Flatbar<2> component. Face<2>@Flatbar-2 is displayed in the Items To Connect box. The arrow points towards the back.

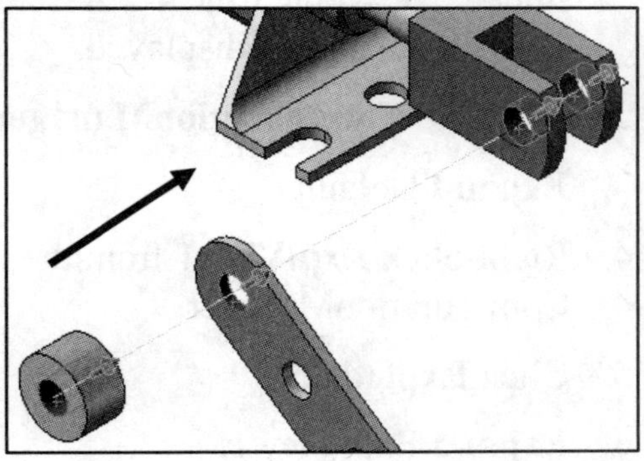

8. Click the **inside face** of Cut-Extrude1 of SHAFT-COLLAR<2>. The direction arrow points towards the back. Face<1> @Shaft-Collar<2> is displayed in the Items To Connect box.

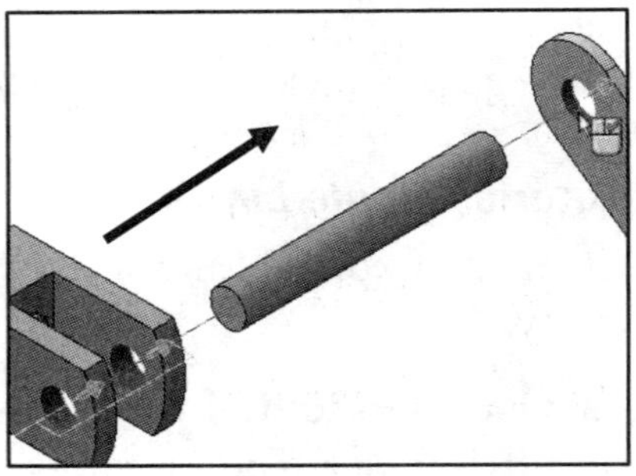

9. Click **OK** ✔ from the Route Line PropertyManager. View the created Route Line.

10. Click **OK** ✔ from the PropertyManager to return to the FeatureManager.

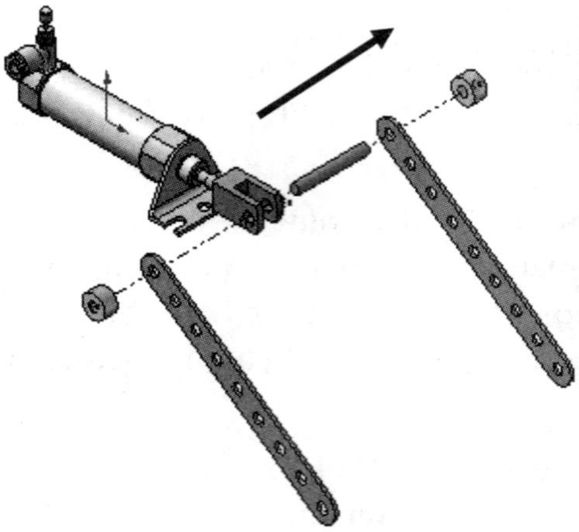

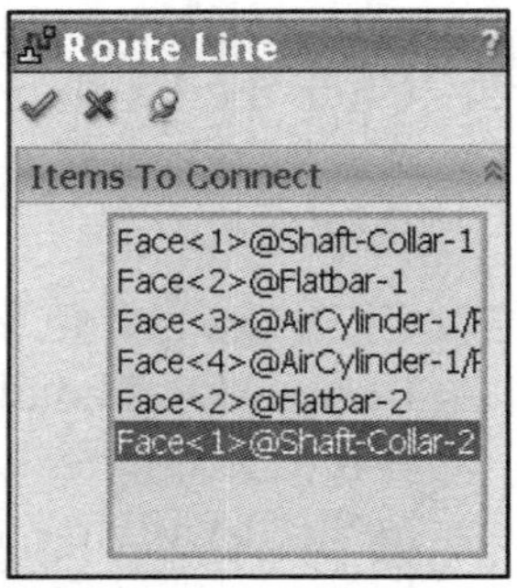


11. Press the **f** key to fit the model to the Graphics window.

12. Click **Isometric view**. View the results.

13. **Close** the model.

You have the ability to create a Bill of Materials (BOM) in an assembly. The BOM is displayed in the Tables folder of the FeatureManager. You no longer need to create a drawing first. See the Assembly section for additional information.

***Tutorial: Route Line 4-2***

Edit an Explode Line Sketch.

1. Open **Route Line 4-2** from the SolidWorks 2010 folder. The Route Line 4-2 Assembly FeatureManager is displayed.

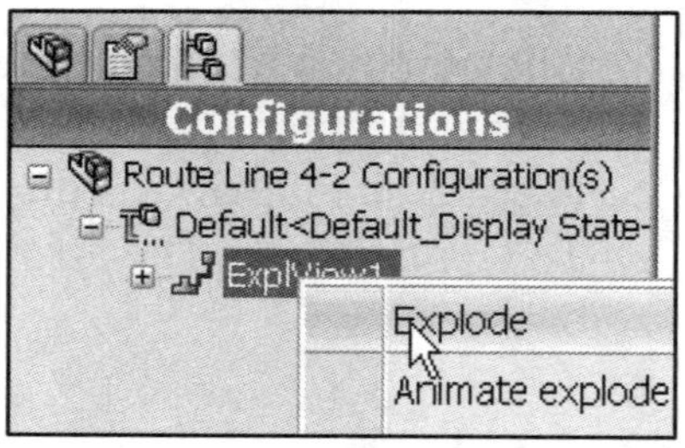


2. Click the **ConfigurationManager** tab.

3. **Expand** Default.

4. Right-click **ExplView1** from the ConfigurationManager.

5. Click **Explode**.

6. **Expand** ExplView1.

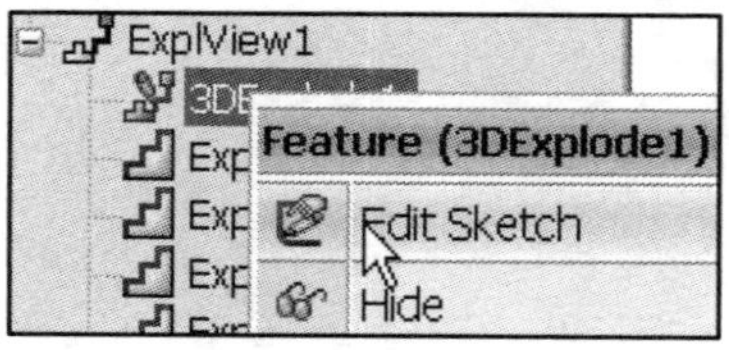

Edit the Explode Line Sketch.

7. Right-click **3DExplode1** from the ConfigurationManager.
8. Click **Edit Sketch**.
9. Display a **Top** view.
10. Click **Centerline** from the Sketch toolbar. The Insert Line PropertyManager is displayed.
11. Click the **endpoints** of the Route Line as illustrated.

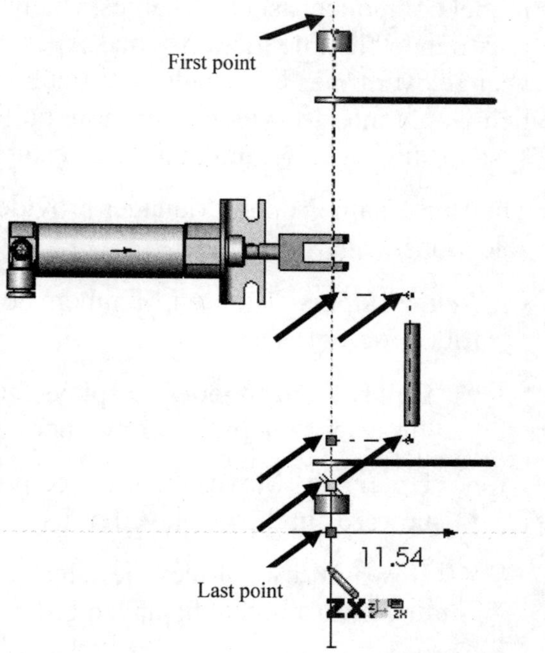


Create a new path.

12. Click a **point** to the right of the Route Line endpoint and over the top of the axle.
13. Click a **point** below the axle as illustrated.
14. Click a **point** to the left of the axle over the Flatbar.
15. Click a **point** below the Flatbar and a **point** above the SHAFT-COLLAR.
16. Click a **point** below the Shaft-Collar.

Deselect the Sketch tool.

17. Right-click **Select** in the Graphics window.
18. **Rebuild** the model. View the results.
19. **Close** the model.

## Belt/Chain Sketch Entity

This option provides the ability to create layout sketches for pulleys or sprocket mechanisms. The Belt/Chain feature simulates a cable-pulley mechanism. The Belt/Chain entity uses the Belt/Chain PropertyManager.

In the past, it was difficult using SolidWorks to effectively model components such as cables, chains, and timing belts due to their flexible motion. The shapes of these items could change over time. This made it difficult to examine the way a belt would interact with two or more pulleys, or a cable system shifts a lever, or crank with a solid assembly model.

The Belt/Chain PropertyManager provides the following selections:

- ***Belt Members***. The Belt Members box provides the following options:
  - **Pulley Components**. Displays the selected arcs or circles for the pulley components.
  - **Up arrow**. Moves the selected pulley component upwards in the displayed order.
  - **Down arrow**. Moves the selected pulley component downward in the displayed order.
  - **Flip belt side**. Changes the side on which the belt is located in the pulley system.

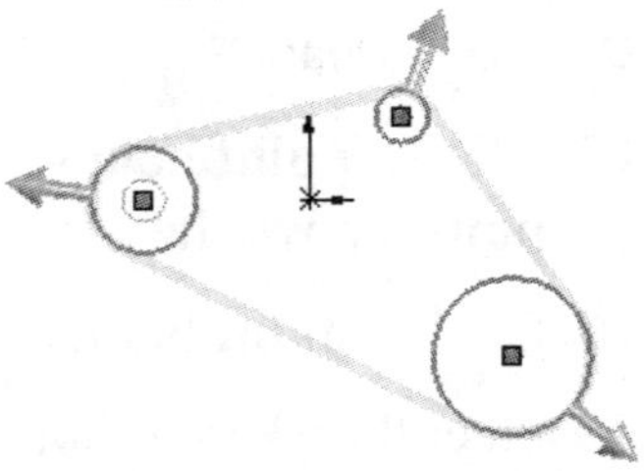

- ***Properties***. The Properties box provides the ability to define the following belt conditions. They are:
  - **Driving**. Cleared by default. Provides the ability to calculate the length of your belt. When checked, enter a value if you do not want the system to calculate your belt length. Based on the constraints, one or more of the components may move to adjust for the length of the belt.
  - **Use belt thickness**. Specifies the thickness value of the belt.

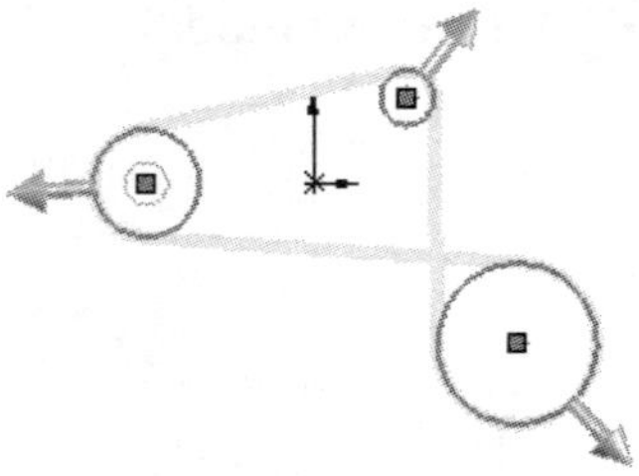

- **Engage belt**. Selected by default. Disengages the belt mechanism.

Only circle entities in a block can be selected for a belt member.

Before you use the Belt/Chain sketch entity in an example, review Blocks in general and the Block toolbar.

# Blocks

Blocks are a grouping of single or multiple sketch entities. In SolidWorks, the origin of the block is aligned to the orientation of the sketch entity. Previously, blocks inherited their origin location from the Parent sketch. Additional enhancements to Blocks are:

- Modeling pulleys and chain sprockets.
- Modeling cam mechanisms.

Blocks are used in the Belt/Chain sketch entity. You can create blocks from a single or multiple sketch entities.

Why should you use Blocks? Blocks enable you to:

- Create layout sketches using the minimum of dimensions and sketch relations.
- Freeze a subset of sketch entities in a sketch to control as a single entity.
- Manage complicated sketches.
- Edit all instances of a block simultaneously.

You can also use blocks in drawings to conserve drawing items such as standard label positions, notes, etc.

# Blocks toolbar

The Blocks toolbar controls blocks in sketching. The Blocks toolbar provides the following tools:

- ***Make Block***. The Make Block tool provides the ability to create a new block.
- ***Edit Block***. The Edit Block tool provides the ability to add or remove sketch entities and to modify dimensions and relations in your sketch.

- ***Insert Block***. The Insert Block tool provides the ability to add a new block to your sketch or drawing. This option provides the ability to either create multiple instances of existing blocks or to browse for existing blocks.
- ***Add/Remove***. The Add/Remove tool provides the ability to add or remove sketch entities to or from your block.
- ***Rebuild***. The Rebuild tool provides the ability to update the parent sketches affected by your block changes.
- ***Saves Block***. The Saves Block tool provides the ability to save the block to a file. Adds an .sldblk extension.
- ***Explode Block***. The Explode Block tool provides the ability to explode the selected block.
- ***Belt/Chain***. The Belt/Chain tool provides the ability to insert a belt.

Exploding a single instance of your block will only affect that instance of the block.

***Tutorial: Block 4-1***

Create a Block using the Blocks toolbar.

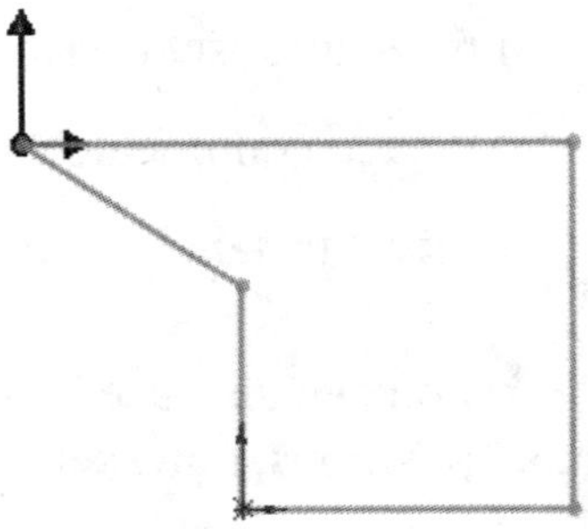

1. Create a **New** part in SolidWorks. Use the default ANSI Part template.
2. Click **Top Plane** from the FeatureManager. This is your Sketch plane.
3. Sketch a **closed sketch** using sketch entities as illustrated. The sketch consists of five lines.

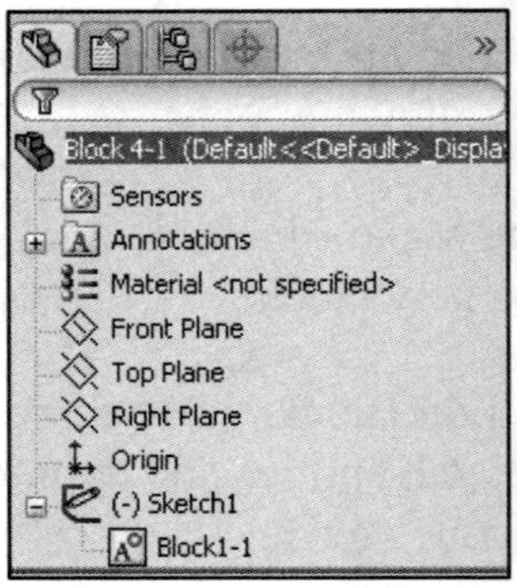

4. Click **Make Block** from the Block toolbar or click **Tools ➢ Blocks ➢ Make**. The Make Block Property Manager is displayed.
5. Box-select the **sketch entities** from the Graphics window. The selected sketch entities are is displayed in the Block Entities box.
6. Click **OK** from the Make Block PropertyManager. Note the location of the insertion point. Block1-1 is displayed in the FeatureManager.
7. **Rebuild** the model. **Close** the model.

Create a block for a single or combination of multiple sketch entities. Saving each block individually provides you with extensive design flexibility.

***Tutorial: Belt-chain 4-1***

Use the Belt/Chain Sketch entity function. Create a pulley sketch.

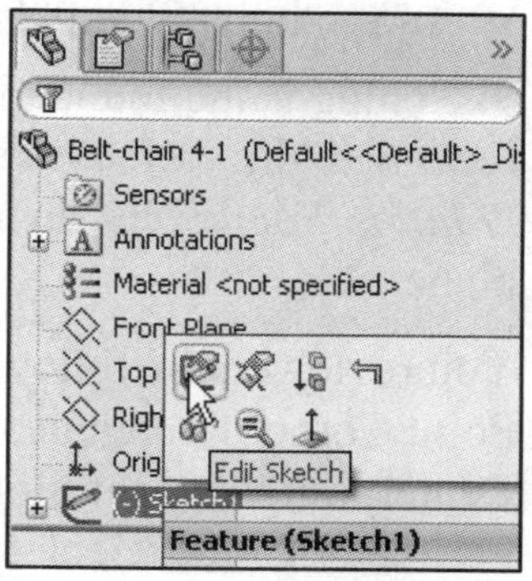


1. Open **Belt-chain 4-1** from the SolidWorks 2010 folder. View the three created blocks in the Belt-chain FeatureManager.
2. Edit **Sketch1** from the FeatureManager.
3. Click **Tools ➤ Sketch Entities ➤ Belt/Chain**. The Belt/Chain PropertyManager is displayed.
4. Select the **three circles** from left to right. The select circles are displayed in the Belt Members dialog box.
5. Check the **Driving** box.
6. Enter **460**mm for Belt Length.
7. Check the **Use belt thickness** box.
8. Enter **20**mm for belt thickness.
9. Click **OK** from the Belt/Chain PropertyManager.
10. **Expand** Sketch1. Belt1 is created and is displayed in the FeatureManager. The calculated belt length was larger than the belt length entered in the PropertyManager. The system moved the entities to correct for the entered 460mm belt length.
11. **Rebuild** the model. View the results.
12. **Close** the model.

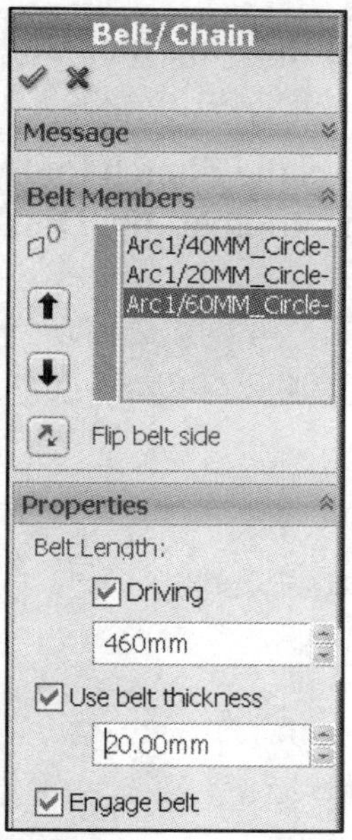


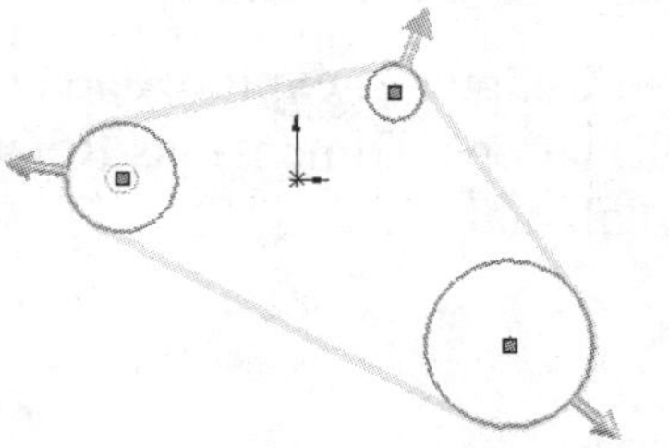

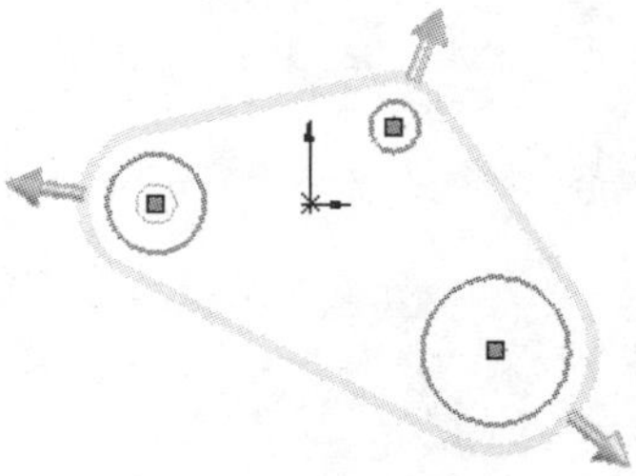

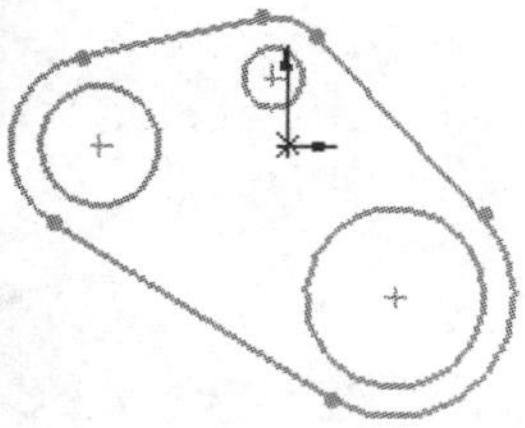

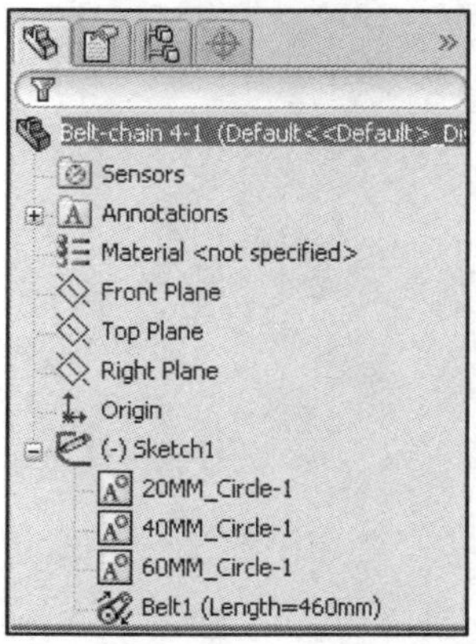

# Summary

In this chapter, you learned about the available tools to incorporate Design Intent into your sketch, feature, part, assembly and drawing.

Sketching is the foundation of a model. You addressed 2D and 3D sketching and how to recognize the various sketch states: *Fully Defined, Over Defined, Under Defined, No Solution Found and Invalid Solution Found* along with identifying the correct reference plane.

You reviewed the following Sketch Entities; Line, Corner Rectangle, Center Rectangle, 3 Point Corner Rectangle, 3 Point Center Rectangle, Parallelogram, Straight Slot, Centerpoint Straight Slot, 3 Point Arc Slot, Centerpoint Arc Slot, Polygon, Circle, Perimeter Circle, Centerpoint Arc, Tangent Arc, 3 Point Arc, Ellipse, Partial Ellipse, Parabola, Spline, Spline on Surface, Equation Driven Curve, Point, Centerline, Text, Plane, Route line and Belt/Chain.

You utilized and addressed the following toolbars; Block toolbar and Spline toolbar and applied the Instant3D tool.

In Chapter 5, explore and address the Sketch tools, 2D to 2D toolbar, Geometric Relations, Dimensions/Relations toolbar, the DimXpertManager and learn about TolAnalyst.

# CHAPTER 5: SKETCH TOOLS, GEOMETRIC RELATIONS AND DIMENSIONS/RELATIONS TOOLS

## Chapter Objective

Chapter 5 provides a comprehensive understanding of the available Sketch tools, Geometric relations, Dimensions/Relations tools and the DimXpertManager in SolidWorks.

On the completion of this chapter, you will be able to:

- Understand and use the following Sketch tools:
  - Fillet, Chamfer, Offset Entities, Convert Entities, Intersection Curve, Face Curves, Trim, Extend, Split Entities, Jog Line, Construction Geometry, Make Path, Mirror Entities, Dynamic Mirror, Stretch Entities, Move Entities, Rotate Entities, Scale Entities, Copy Entities, Linear Pattern, Circular Pattern, Create Sketch From Selections, Repair Sketch, SketchXpert, Align, Modify, Close Sketch to Model, Check Sketch for Feature, 2D to 3D and Sketch Picture
- Comprehend the 2D to 3D toolbar:
  - Front, Top, Left, Bottom, Back, Auxiliary, Sketch from Selections, Repair Sketch, Align Sketch, Extrude and Cut
- Recognize and apply Geometric relations in 2D sketches:
  - Automatic relations
  - Manual relations
- Know and apply Geometric relations in 3D sketches
- Understand and utilize the following Dimensions/Relations tools:
  - Smart Dimension, Horizontal Dimension, Vertical Dimension, Baseline Dimension, Ordinate Dimension, Horizontal Ordinate Dimension, Vertical Ordinate Dimension, Chamfer Dimension, Baseline Dimension, Add Relations, Display/Delete Relations and Fully Defined Sketch
- Understand DimXpertManager and the following tools:
  - Auto Dimension Scheme, Show Tolerance Status, Copy Scheme and TolAnalyst

# Sketch tools

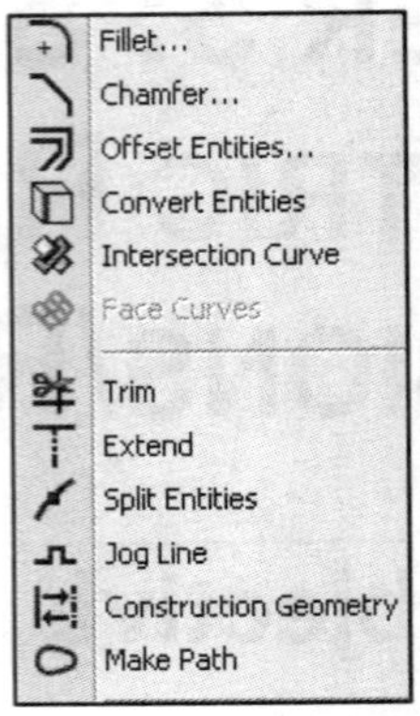

Sketch tools control the various aspects of creating and modifying a sketch. To access the available sketch tools for SolidWorks, click **Tools ➢ Sketch Tools** from the Menu bar and select the required tool.

To obtain additional information of each sketch tool, active the sketch tool and click the question mark icon located at the top of the tool PropertyManager or click **Help ➢ SolidWorks Help Topics** from the Menu bar and search by using one of the three available tabs: **Contents**, **Index** or **Search**. Note: To view the three tabs, the Use SolidWorks Web Help option is de-activated.

## Sketch Fillet Sketch tool

The Sketch Fillet tool provides the ability to trim the corner at the intersection of two sketch entities to create a tangent arc. This tool is available for both 2D and 3D sketches.

The Sketch Fillet tool uses the Sketch Fillet PropertyManager. The Sketch Fillet PropertyManager provides the following selections:

- ***Fillet Parameters***. The Fillet Parameters box provides the following options:
  - **Radius**. Displays the selected fillet sketch radius. Enter a radius value.
  - **Keep constrained corners**. Selected by default. Maintains the virtual intersection point, if the vertex has dimensions or relations.
  - **Undo**. Deletes your last action.

The Fillet tool from the Consolidated Features toolbar fillets entities such as edges in a part, not in a sketch. The Sketch Fillet tool is applied to a sketch, not a feature.

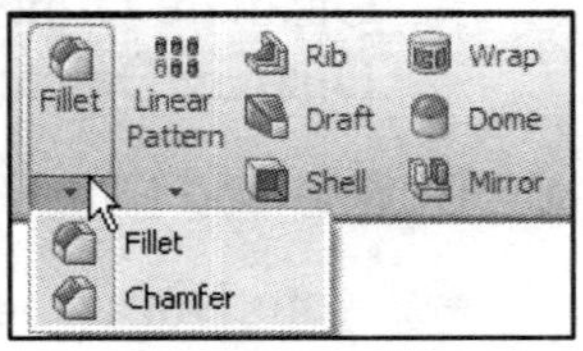

***Tutorial: 2D Sketch Fillet 5-1***

Create a Sketch Fillet 2D sketch. Fillet the four corners of the rectangle with a 15mm Radius. Edit the Sketch Fillet and modify the corners.

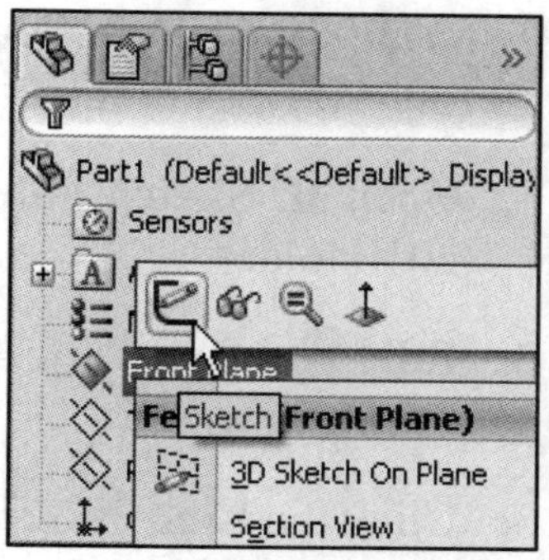


1. Create a **New** part. Use the default ANSI, MMGS Part template.
2. Right-click **Front Plane** from the FeatureManager.
3. Click **Sketch** from the Context toolbar.
4. Click **Center Rectangle** from the Consolidated Rectangle Sketch toolbar.

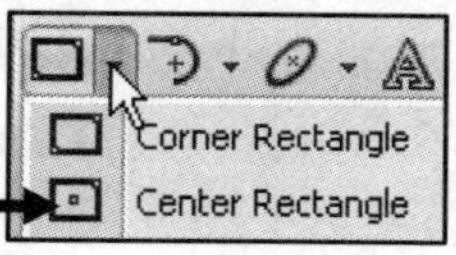


5. Click the **Origin**.
6. Sketch a **rectangle** as illustrated.

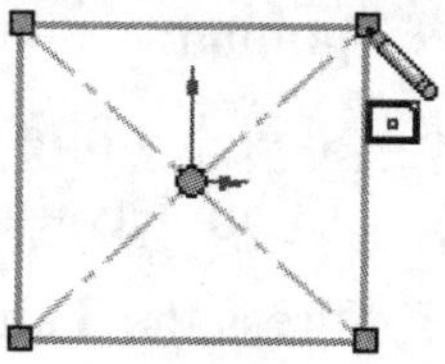

7. Right-click **Smart Dimension** from the Context toolbar.
8. **Dimension** the sketch as illustrated.

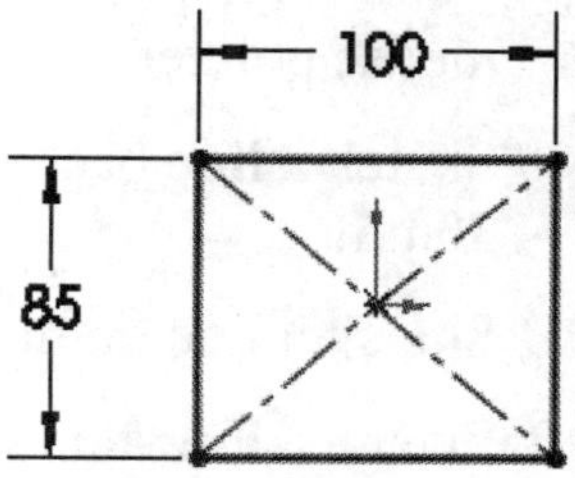


9. Click **Sketch Fillet** the Consolidated Sketch toolbar. The Sketch Fillet PropertyManager is displayed.
10. Enter **15**mm in the Radius box.
11. Click the **first** corner of the rectangle. The 15mm radius is applied to the first corner.
12. Click the other **three corners** of the rectangle. The four corners are displayed with a Sketch Fillet.

13. Click **OK** from the Sketch Fillet PropertyManager.

Modify the sketch fillet radius.

14. Double-click the **R15** dimension from the Graphics window. The modify dialog box is displayed.

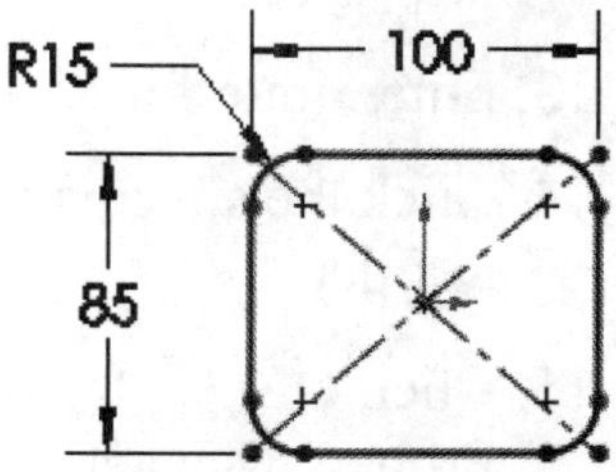


15. Enter **10**mm.
16. Click **OK** from the Dimension PropertyManager.
17. **Rebuild** the model. View the results.
18. **Close** the model.

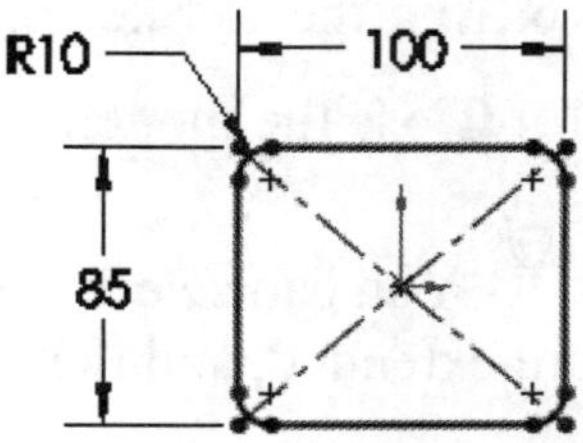

### *Tutorial: 3D Sketch Fillet 5-2*

Create a 3D sketch fillet.

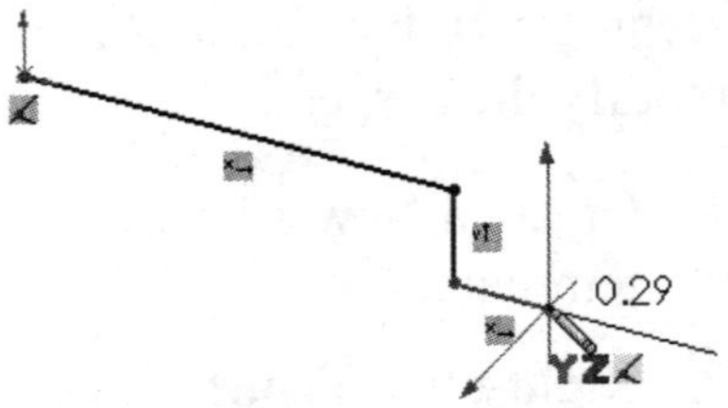


1. Open **3D Sketch Fillet 5-2** from the SolidWorks 2010 folder.
2. **Edit** 3DSketch1. 3DSketch1 is displayed in the Graphics window.
3. Click the **Line** Sketch tool.
4. Click the **right endpoint** of the sketch as illustrated.
5. Press the **Tab** key to change the Sketch plane from XY to YZ. The YZ icon is displayed on the mouse pointer.

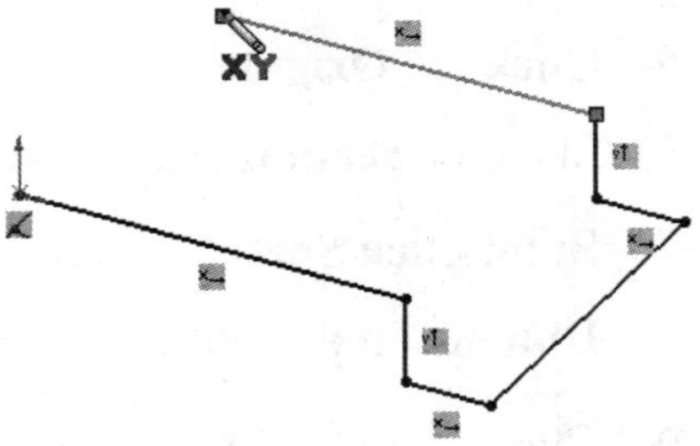


6. Sketch a **line** along the Z axis approximately 130mm as illustrated.
7. Press the **Tab** key twice to change the sketch plane from YZ to XY. The XY icon is displayed on the mouse pointer.
8. Sketch a **line** back along the X axis approximately 30mm.
9. Sketch a **line** on the Y axis approximately 30mm.
10. Sketch a **line** along the X axis of approximately 130mm.
11. Right-click **Select** in the Graphics window.

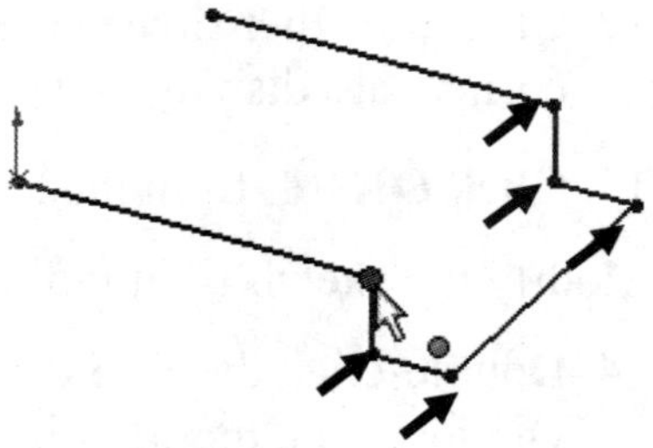

12. Click **Sketch Fillet** from the Consolidated Sketch toolbar. The Sketch Fillet PropertyManager is displayed.
13. Enter **4**mm for Radius.
14. Click the **six corner points** of the sketch as illustrated to fillet.
15. Click **OK** from the Sketch Fillet PropertyManager.

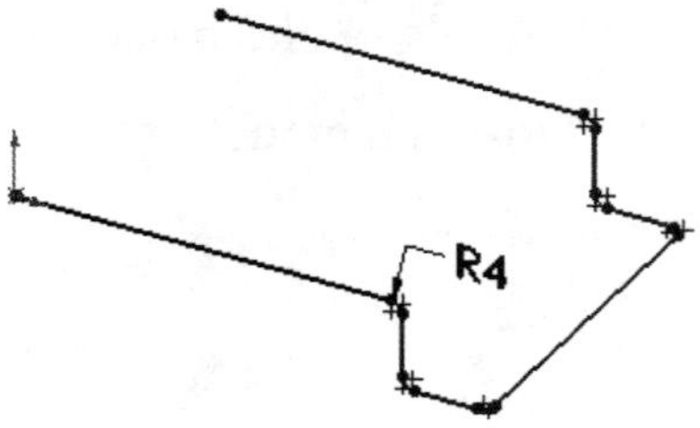


16. **Exit** the 3DSketch. View the results.
17. **Close** the model.

You can select non-intersecting entities. The entities are extended, and the corner is filleted.

## Sketch Chamfer Sketch tool

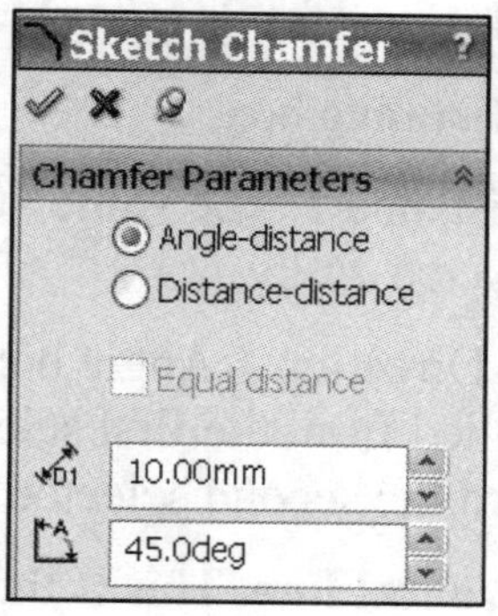


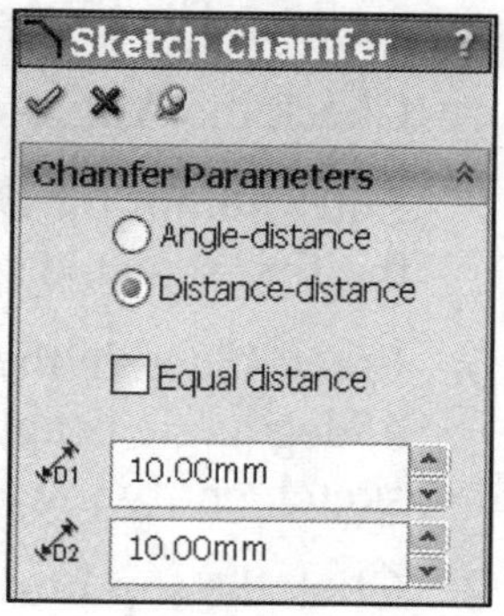


The Sketch Chamfer Sketch tool provides the ability to apply a chamfer to an adjacent sketch entity either in a 2D and 3D sketch. The Sketch Chamfer tool uses the Sketch Chamfer PropertyManager. The Sketch Chamfer PropertyManager provides the following selections:

- ***Chamfer Parameters***. Provides the ability to control the following options:
  - **Angle-distance**. The Angle-distance option provides two selections:
    - **Distance 1**. The Distance 1 box displays the selected value to apply to the first selected sketch entity.
    - **Direction 1 Angle**. The Direction 1 Angle box displays the selected value to apply from the first sketch entity toward the second sketch entity.
  - **Distance-distance**. Selected by default. Provides the following selections. They are:
    - **Equal distance**. Selected by default. When selected, the Distance 1 value is applied to both sketch entities. When cleared, the Distance 1 value is applied to the first selected sketch entity. The Distance 2 value is applied to the second selected sketch entity.
    - **Distance 1**. Displays the selected value to apply to the first selected sketch entity.

The Chamfer tool from the Features toolbar chamfers entities such as edges in a part, not in a sketch.

### *Tutorial: Sketch Chamfer 5-1*

Create an Angle-distance Sketch chamfer for a 2D sketch.

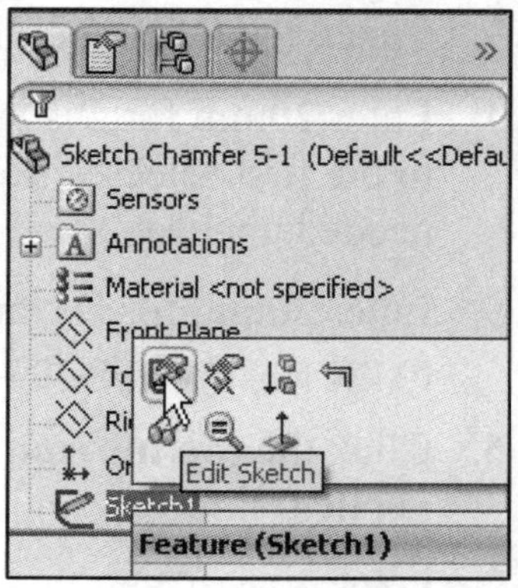


1. Open **Sketch Chamfer 5-1** from the SolidWorks 2010 folder. A rectangle is displayed in the Graphics window.
2. **Edit** Sketch1.

3. Click the **Sketch Chamfer** tool from the Consolidated Sketch toolbar. The Sketch Chamfer PropertyManager is displayed.

4. Check the **Angle-distance** box.
5. Enter **40**mm for Distance 1. The value 40mm is applied to the first selected sketch entity.

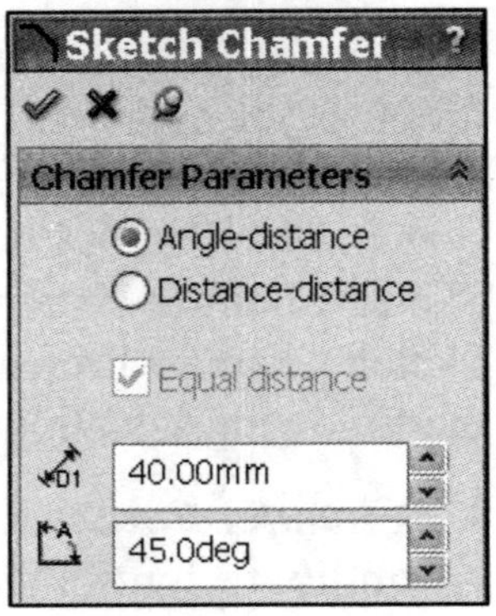


6. Enter **45**deg in the Direction 1 Angle box. The 45deg angle is applied from the first selected sketch entity toward the second selected entity.
7. Click the **top horizontal line**. This is the first selected entity.
8. Click the **left vertical line**.
9. Click **Yes** to confirm. This is the second selected entity. View the created chamfer.
10. Click **OK** from the Sketch Chamfer PropertyManager.

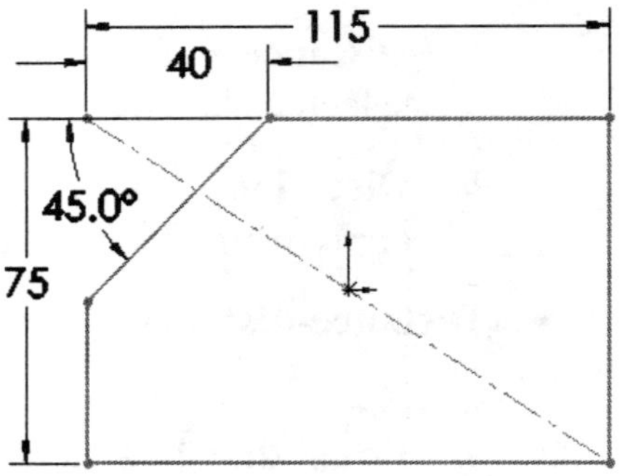


11. **Rebuild** the model. View the results.
12. **Close** the model.

***Tutorial: Sketch Chamfer 5-2***

Create a Distance-distance Sketch chamfer for a 2D sketch.

1. Open **Sketch Chamfer 5-2** from the SolidWorks 2010 folder. The sketch is displayed in the Graphics window.

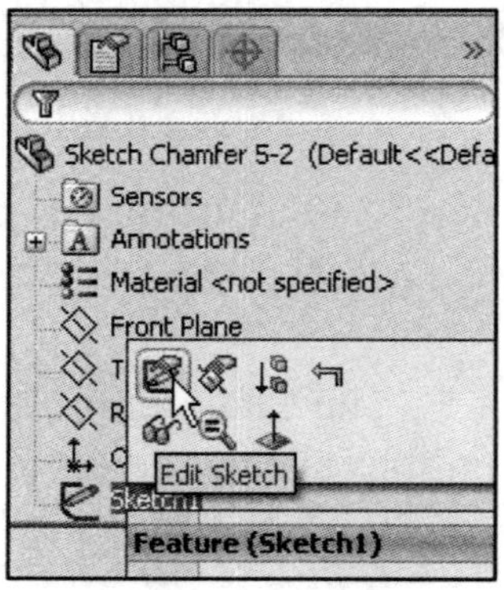


2. **Edit** Sketch1. Click the **Sketch Chamfer** tool from the Sketch toolbar. The Sketch Chamfer PropertyManager is displayed.
3. Check the **Distance-distance** box.
4. Enter **20**mm for Distance 1. 20mm is applied to the first selected sketch entity. Note: if needed uncheck the Equal distance box.
5. Enter **30**mm for Distance 2. 30mm is applied to the second selected sketch entity.

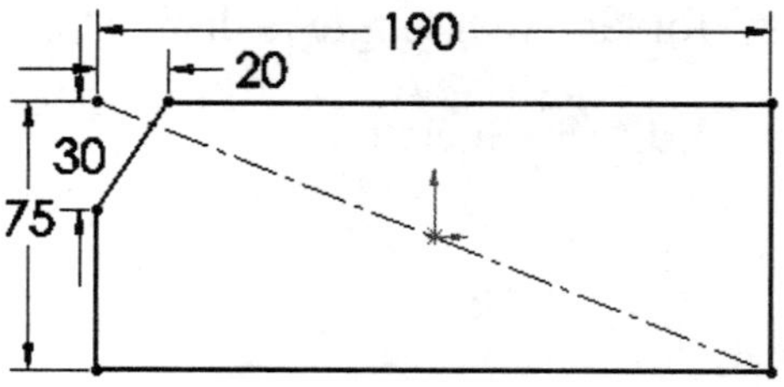


6. Click the **top horizontal line**. Click the **left vertical line**.
7. Click **Yes** to continue. View the created chamfer.

8. Click **OK** from the Sketch Chamfer PropertyManager.
9. **Rebuild** the model. View the results.
10. **Close** the model.

***Tutorial: Sketch Chamfer 5-3***

Create an Angle-distance Sketch chamfer for a 3D sketch.

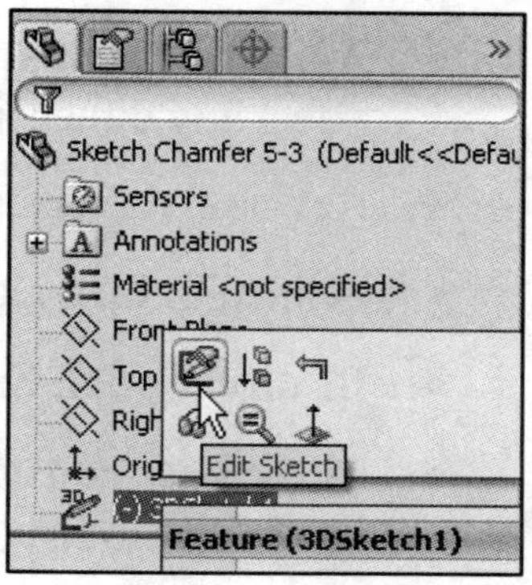


1. Open **Sketch Chamfer 5-3** from the SolidWorks 2010 folder. The rectangle is displayed in the Graphics window.
2. **Edit** 3DSketch1.
3. Click the **Sketch Chamfer** tool from the Sketch toolbar. The Sketch Chamfer PropertyManager is displayed.
4. Check the **Angle-distance** box.
5. Enter **10**mm for Distance 1. The value 10mm is applied to the first selected sketch entity.
6. Enter **25**deg in the Direction 1 Angle box. The 25deg angle is applied from the first selected sketch entity toward the second selected entity.
7. Click the **top horizontal line**. This is the first selected entity.
8. Click the **left vertical line**. View the created chamfer.
9. Click **OK** from the Sketch Chamfer PropertyManager. View the model.
10. **Rebuild** the model. View the results.
11. **Close** the model.

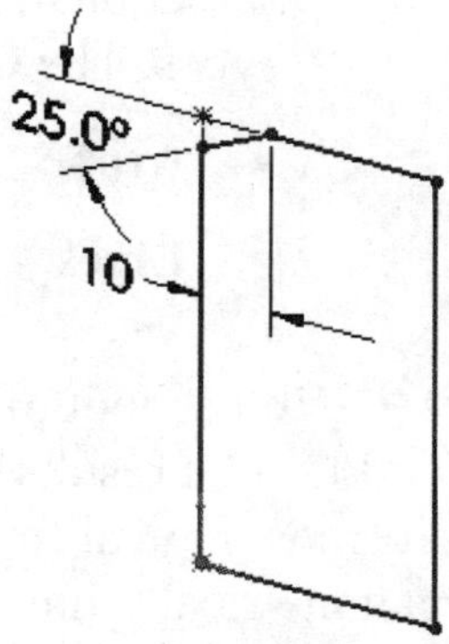


## Offset Entities Sketch tool

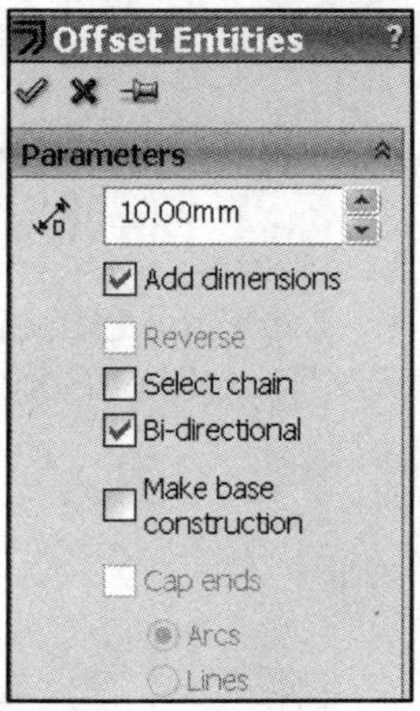


The Offset Entities Sketch tool provides the ability to offset one or more sketch entities, selected model edges, or model faces by a specified distance. Example: You can offset sketch entities such as arcs, splines, loops, or sets of model edges etc.

The Offset Entities PropertyManager controls the following selections:

- *Parameters*. Provides the ability to control the following options:
  - **Offset Distance**. Displays the selected distance value to offset the sketch entity. To view a dynamic preview, hold the mouse button down and drag the pointer in the Graphics window. When you release the mouse button, the Offset Entity is complete.
  - **Add dimensions**. Includes the Offset Distance tool in the sketch. This does not affect any dimensions included with the original sketch entity.
  - **Reverse**. Reverses the direction of the offset if required.
  - **Select chain**. Creates an offset of all contiguous sketch entities.
  - **Bi-directional**. Creates offset entities in two directions.
  - **Make base construction**. Converts the original sketch entity to a construction line.
  - **Cap ends**. Extends the original non-intersecting sketch entities by selecting Bi-directional, and adding a cap. You can create Arcs or Lines as extension cap types. The Cap ends check box provides two option types:
    - **Arcs**
    - **Lines**

You cannot offset Fit splines, previously offset splines, or entities that results in self-intersecting geometry. A Fit spline chooses the most logical fit to the geometry you select. A Fit spline is parametrically linked to underlying geometry. If the geometry changes, the spline is updated automatically.

***Tutorial: Offset Entity 5-1***

Create an Offset Entity using the Offset Distance option.

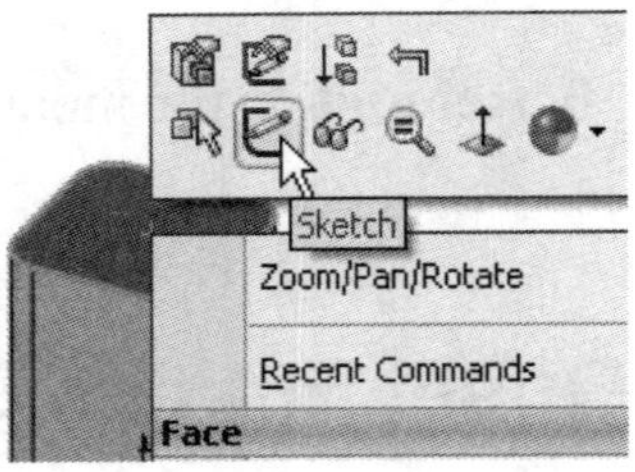


1. Open **Offset Entity 5-1** from the SolidWorks 2010 folder.
2. Right-click the **Top face** of the model. Base Extrude is highlighted in the FeatureManager.
3. Click **Sketch** from the Context toolbar.
4. Click **Top view** from the Heads-up View toolbar.
5. Click the **Offset Entities** tool from the Sketch toolbar. The Offset Entities PropertyManager is displayed.
6. Enter **.150**in for the Offset Distance.

7. The new Offset orange/yellow profile is displayed inside the original profile. Check the **Reverse** check box if needed.
8. Click **OK** from the Offset Entities PropertyManager.
9. Drag the **dimension** off the model.
10. **Rebuild** the model. Sketch2 is created in the FeatureManager. View the results.
11. **Close** the model.

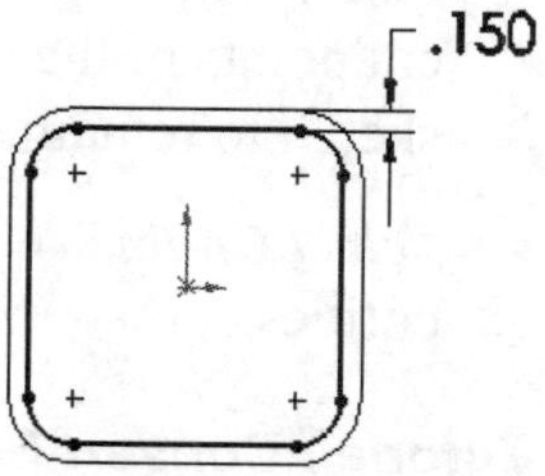


***Tutorial: Offset Entity 5-2***

Create an Offset Entity using the Cap ends option.

1. Open **Offset Entity 5-2** from the SolidWorks 2010 folder.
2. **Edit** Sketch1.
3. Click the **spline construction** line. The Spline PropertyManager is displayed.

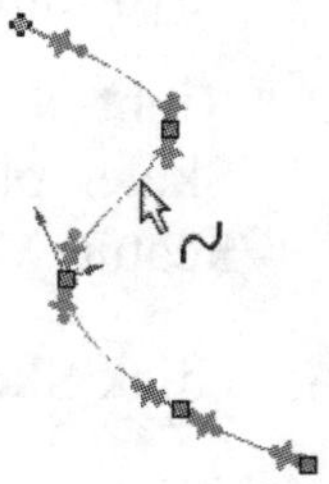

4. Click the **Offset Entities** tool from the Sketch toolbar. The Offset Entities PropertyManager is displayed.
5. Enter **5mm** for the Offset Distance value.
6. Check the **Bi-directional** box.
7. Check the **CAP ends** box.
8. Check the **Arcs** box.
9. Click **OK** from the Offset Entities PropertyManager. View the results.

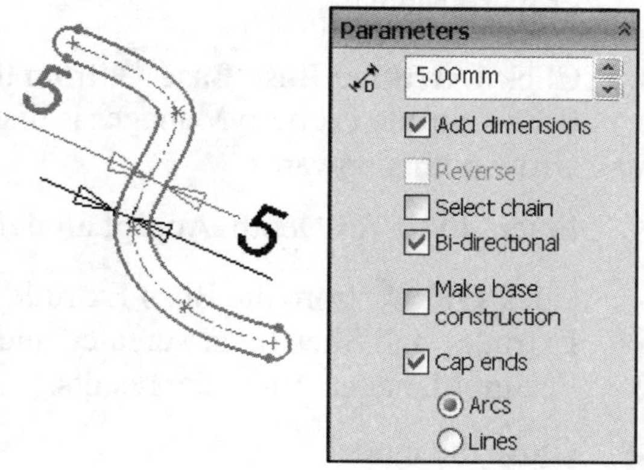


10. **Rebuild** the model. View the results.
11. **Close** the model.

## Convert Entities Sketch tool

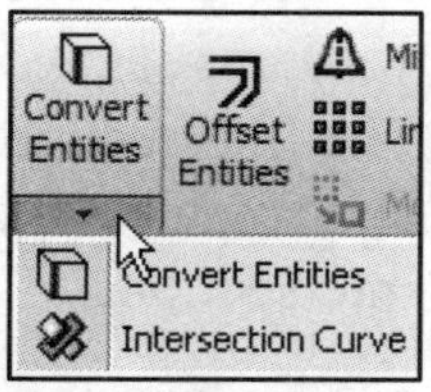


The Convert Entities Sketch tool provides the ability to create one or more curves in a sketch by projecting an edge, loop, face, curve, or external sketch contour, set of edges, or set of sketch curves onto a selected Sketch plane. New in 2010, is the Convert Entities PropertyManager. The following relations are created when the Convert Entities tool is used:

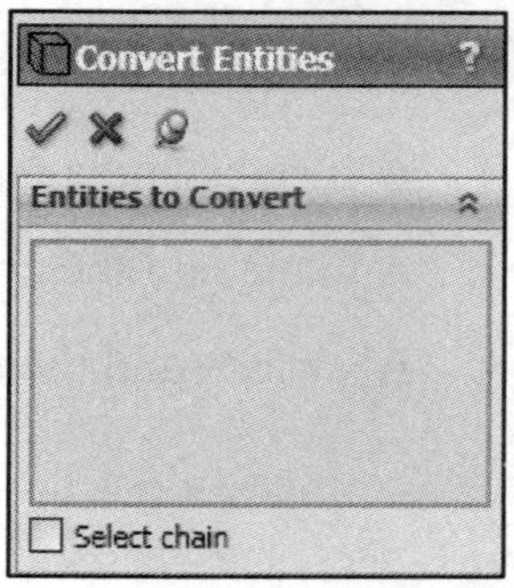


- *On Edge*. The On Edge relation is created between the new sketch curve and the entity. The On Edge relation causes the curve to update if the entity changes.

- *Fixed.* The Fixed relation is created internally on the endpoints of the sketch entity. The Fixed relation causes the sketch to remain in a fully defined state.
- *Select Chain.* To convert all contiguous sketch entities.

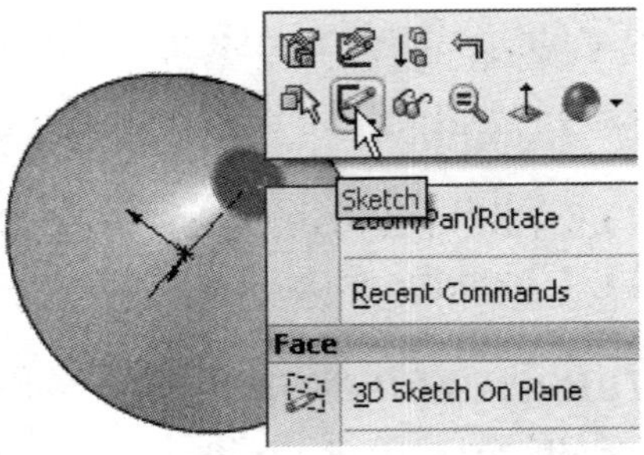


***Tutorial: Convert Entity 5-1***

Create a Convert Entities feature on a Flashlight lens.

1. Open **Convert Entities 5-1** from the SolidWorks 2010 folder.
2. Right-click the **back face** of the model. This is the Sketch plane. The BaseRevolve feature is highlighted in the FeatureManager.

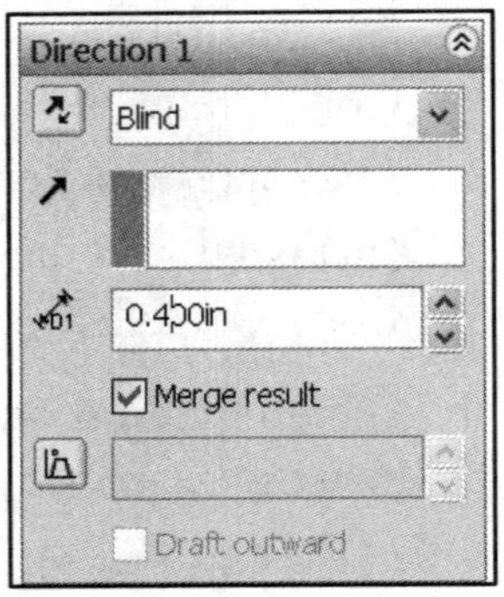


3. Click **Sketch** from the Context toolbar.
4. Click the **Convert Entities** tool from the Consolidated Sketch toolbar. Click **OK** from the Convert Entities PropertyManager
5. Click **Extruded Boss/Base** from the Features toolbar. The Boss-Extrude PropertyManager is displayed. The direction arrow points upwards.
6. Enter **.400**in for Depth. Accept all defaults.
7. Click **OK** from the Boss-Extrude PropertyManager. Boss-Extrude1 and Sketch2 are created and are displayed in the FeatureManager. View the results.

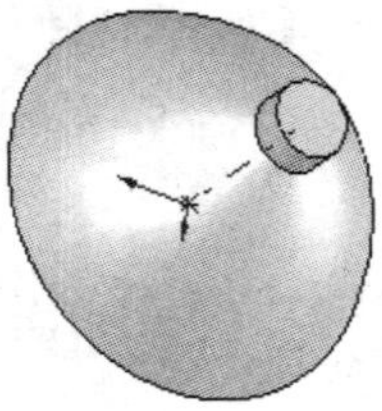

8. **Close** the model.

## Intersection Curve Sketch tool

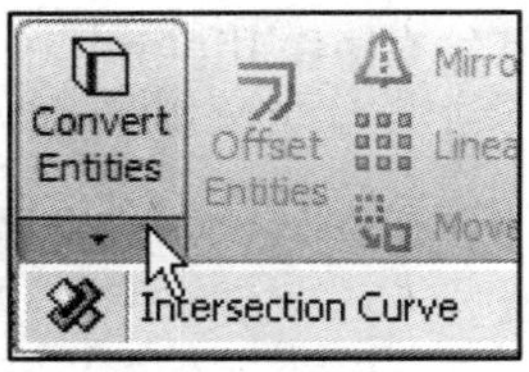


The Intersection tool provides the ability to activate a sketch and creates a sketched curve at the following types of intersections:

- A plane and a surface or a model face
- Two surfaces
- A surface and a model face
- A plane and the entire part
- A surface and the entire part

In a 2D sketch use the Intersection Curve tool to extrude a feature. Select the **plane**, click the **Intersection Curve** tool.

In a 3D sketch, use the Intersection Curve tool to extrude a feature. Click the **Intersection Curve** tool, select the **plane**.

***Tutorial: Intersection Curve 5-1***

Measure the thickness of a cross section of a part for a 2D sketch.

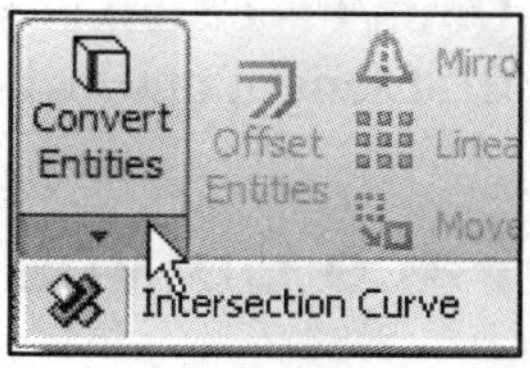


1. Open **Intersection Curve 5-1** from the SolidWorks 2010 folder.
2. Click **Right Plane** from the FeatureManager.

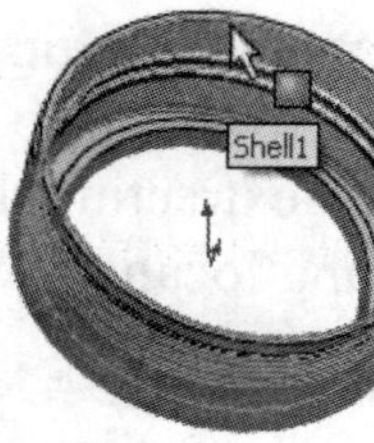

3. Click **Tools ➢ Sketch Tools ➢ Intersection Curve** or click the **Intersection Curve** tool from the Consolidated Sketch toolbar.
4. Click the **front outside face** of the part as illustrated.
5. Rotate the **part** to view the top inside face.
6. Click the **top inside** face of the part.
7. Click **OK** from the PropertyManager. Sketched splines are displayed on the top inside face and the outside face.

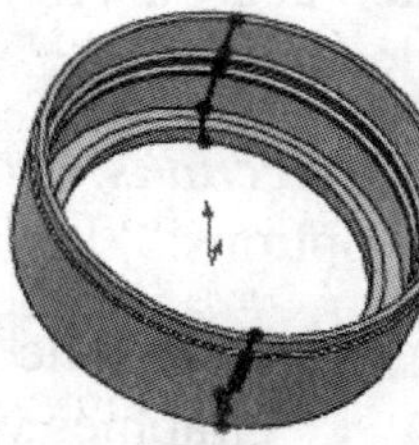

Measure the thickness of the part.

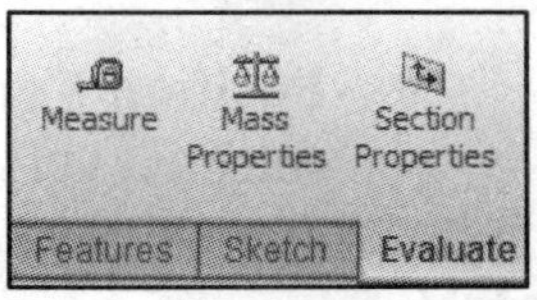


8. Click the **Evaluate** tab from the CommandManager.
9. Click the **Measure** tool from the Evaluate toolbar. The Measure dialog box is displayed.
10. Click the **inside** and **outside** faces of the model to obtain the measured value. View the results.
11. **Close** the Measure dialog box.

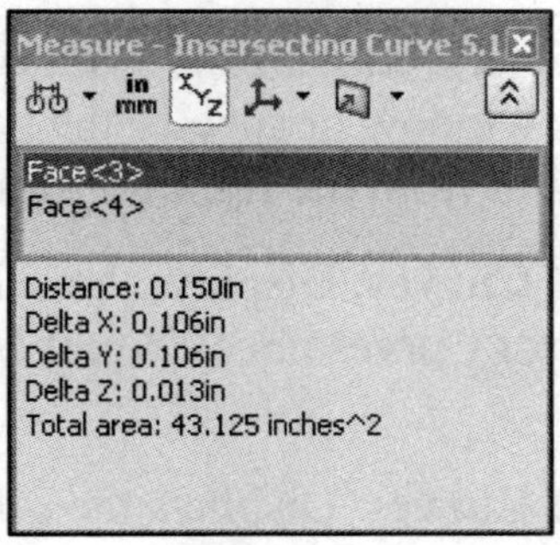


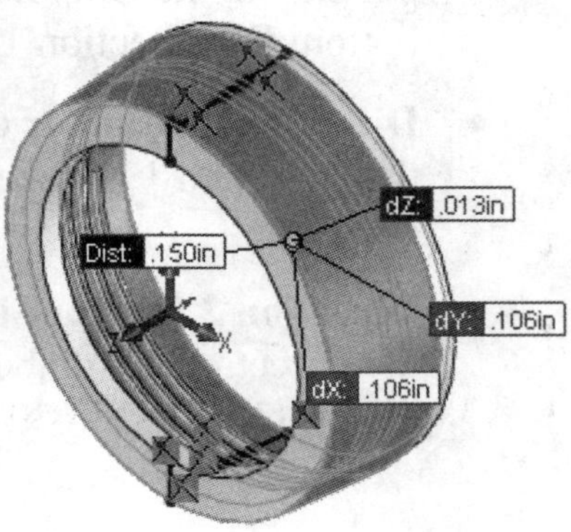

12. **Rebuild** the model. Sketch7 is created and is displayed in the FeatureManager.

13. Click **Isometric view** from the Heads-up View toolbar. View the results.

14. **Close** the model.

Configure the Measure tool to display two different units of measurement. Click the **Units/Precision** box in the Measure dialog box. Select **Use custom settings**. Select the **first** length unit. Click **Use Dual Units**. Select the **second** length unit. Click **OK**.

## Face Curves Sketch tool

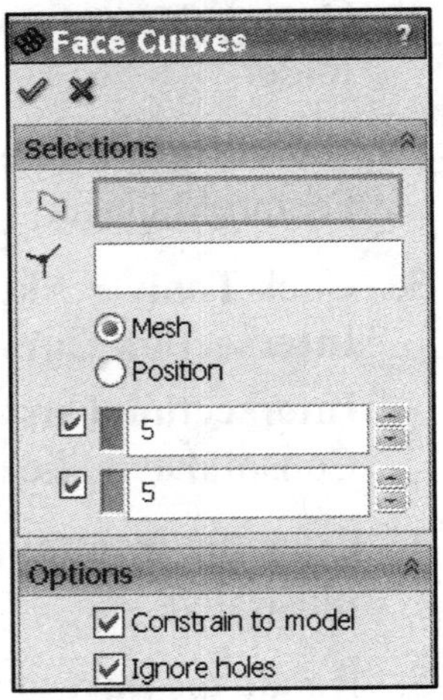


The Face Curves Sketch tool provides the ability to extract iso-parametric (UV) curves from a face or surface. Applications of this functionality include extracting the curves for imported surfaces and then performing localized cleaning using the face curves.

The Face Curves Sketch tool specifies a mesh of evenly spaced curves or a position which creates two orthogonal curves. The Face Curves Sketch tool uses the Face Curves PropertyManager. The Face Curves PropertyManager provides the following selections:

- ***Selections***. Provides the ability to control the following options:
  - **Face**. The Face box displays the selected faces from the Graphics window.
  - **Position Vertex**. The Position Vertex box displays the selected vertex or point for the intersection of the two curves. You can not drag the vertex.
  - **Mesh**. Selected by default. Evenly spaces the curves. Specify the number of curves for Direction 1 and Direction 2.
  - **Position**. Positions the intersection of the two orthogonal curves. Drag the position in the Graphics window or specify the percentage distance from the bottom for Direction 1 and from the right for Direction 2.
  - **Direction 1 Number of Curves**. Displays the selected number of curves. Clear the Direction 1 Number of Curves check box if a curve is not required in the first direction.
  - **Direction 2 Number of Curves**. Displays the selected number of curves. Clear the Direction 2 Number of Curves check box a curve is not required in the second direction.

- ***Options***. The Options box controls the following selections:
  - **Constrain to model**. Selected by default. Updates the curves if the model is modified.
  - **Ignore holes**. Selected by default. Generates curves across holes as though the surface was intact. When cleared, this option stops the curves at the edges of holes.

Each curve created by this process becomes a separate 3D sketch. However, if you are editing a 3D sketch when you invoke the Face Curves tool, all extracted curves are added to your active 3D sketch.

***Tutorial: Face Curve 5-1***

Extract iso-parametric curves using the Face Curve Sketch tool.

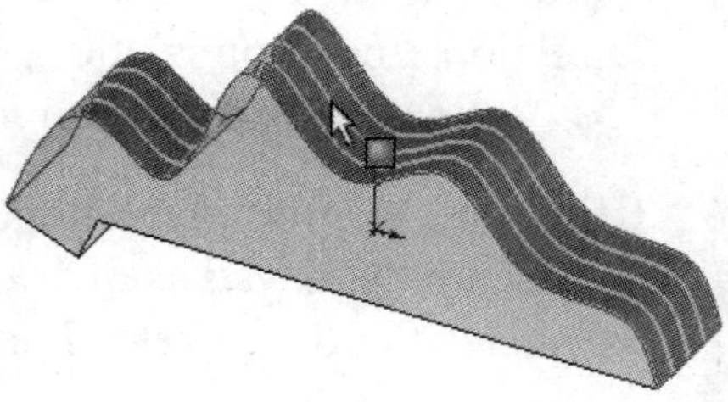

1. Open **Face Curve 5-1** from the SolidWorks 2010 folder.
2. Click **Tools ➢ Sketch Tools ➢ Face Curves**. The Face Curves PropertyManager is displayed.
3. Click the **top face** of the model. Face<1> is displayed in the Face box. A preview of the curves is displayed on the face in the Graphics window. The curves displayed, are one color in one direction and another color in the other direction.

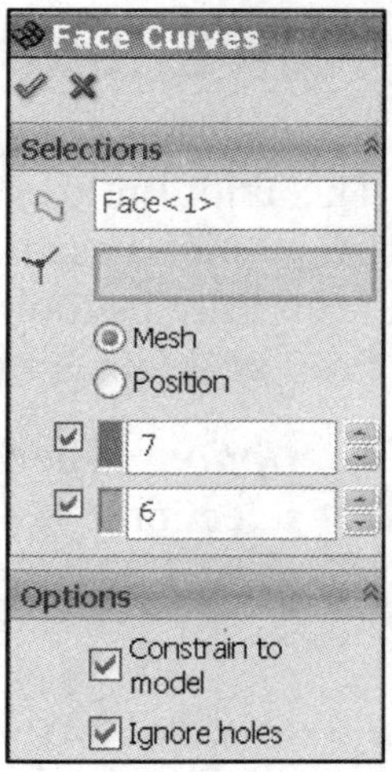


4. Check the **Mesh** box.
5. Enter **7** for Direction 1 Number of Curves.
6. Enter **6** for Direction 2 Number of Curves.
7. Click **OK** ✔ from the Face Curves PropertyManager. The curves are displayed as 3D sketches in the FeatureManager. 3DSketch1 - 3DSketch13 are displayed.

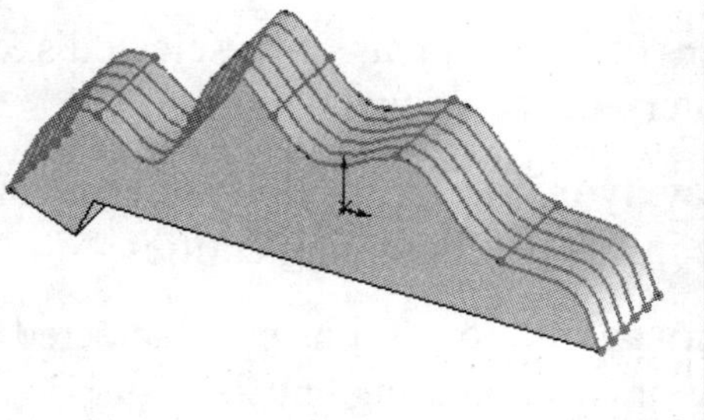

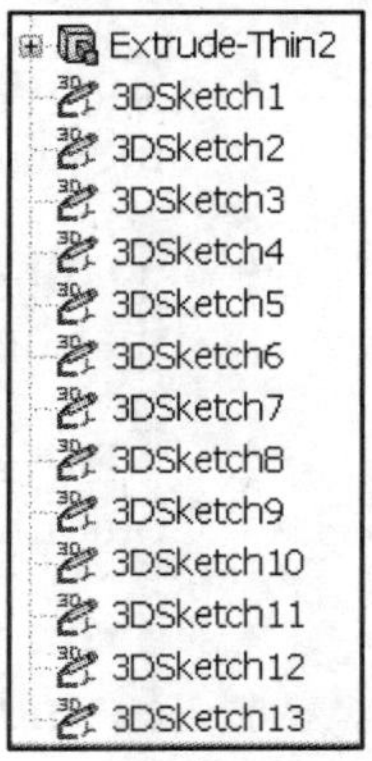

***Tutorial: Face Curve 5-2***

Extract iso-parametric curves using the Face Curve Sketch tool.

1. Open **Face Curve 5-2** from the SolidWorks 2010 folder.
2. Click **Tools** ➢ **Sketch Tools** ➢ **Face Curves**. The Face Curves PropertyManager is displayed.
3. Click the **top face** of the model. Face<1> is displayed in the Face box. A preview of the curves is displayed on the face in the Graphics window. The curves displayed, are one color in one direction and another color in the other direction.

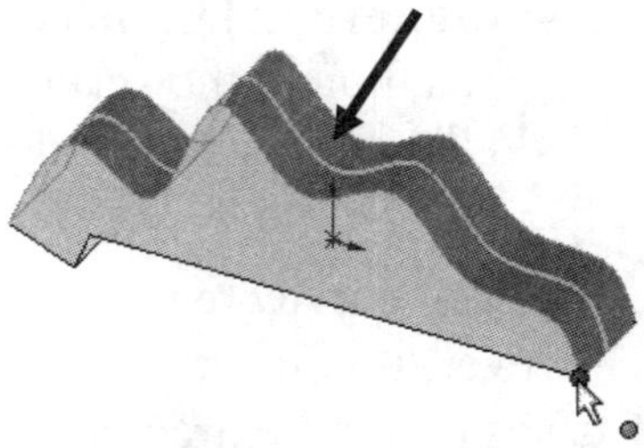

4. Check the **Position** box.
5. Click the **front right vertex** point of the model. The Direction 1 position is 100%. The Direction 2 position is 0%. Vertex<1> is displayed in the Position Vertex box.
6. Click **OK** from the Face Curve PropertyManager. The curves are displayed as 3D sketches in the FeatureManager. 3DSketch1 and 3DSketch2 are created and are displayed.

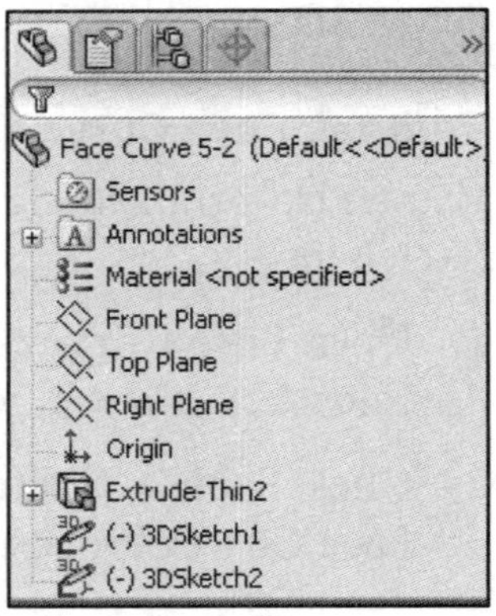


## Trim Entities Sketch tool

The Trim Entities Sketch tool provides the ability to select the trim option based on the entities you want to trim or extend. The Trim Entities tool uses the Trim PropertyManager. The Trim PropertyManager provides the following selections:

- ***Options***. The Options box controls the following trim selections:
  - **Power trim**. Trims multiple, adjacent sketch entities by clicking and dragging the pointer across each sketch entity and to extend your sketch entities along their natural paths. Power trim is the default option.
  - **Corner**. Extends or trims two selected sketch entities until they intersect at a virtual corner.
  - **Trim away inside**. Trims open selected sketch entities that lie inside two bounding entities.
  - **Trim away outside**. Trims open selected sketch entities outside of two bounding entities.
  - **Trim to closest**. Trims each selected sketch entity or extended to the closest intersection.

### *Tutorial: Trim Entity 5-1*

Use the Trim Entities Sketch tool with the Trim to closest option.

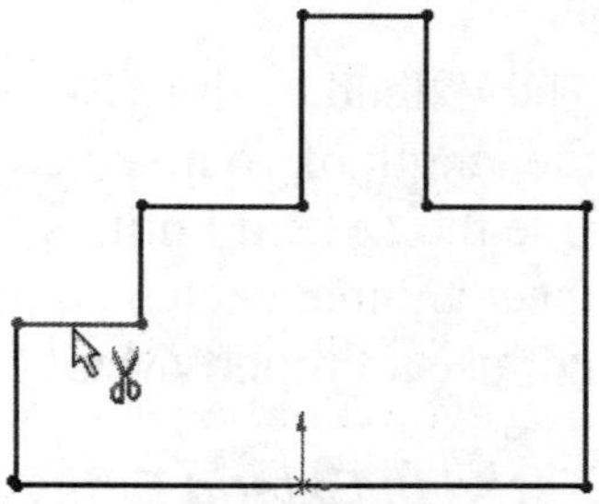

1. Open **Trim Entities 5-1** from the SolidWorks 2010 folder.
2. **Edit** Sketch1.
3. Click the **Trim Entities** Sketch tool. The Trim Entities PropertyManager is displayed. The Trim icon is located on the mouse pointer.
4. Click the **Trim to closest** box.
5. Click the **first left horizontal line.**
6. Click the **second left horizontal line.**
7. Click **Yes**. Both horizontal lines are removed.
8. Click **OK** from the Trim PropertyManager.
9. **Rebuild** the model.
10. **Close** the model.

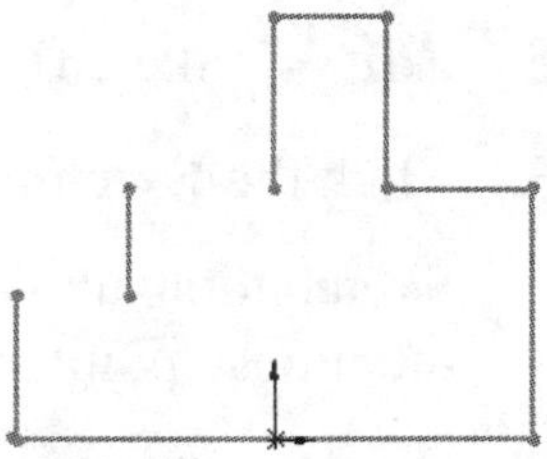

### *Tutorial: Trim Entity 5-2*

Use the Trim Entities Sketch tool with the Power Trim option.

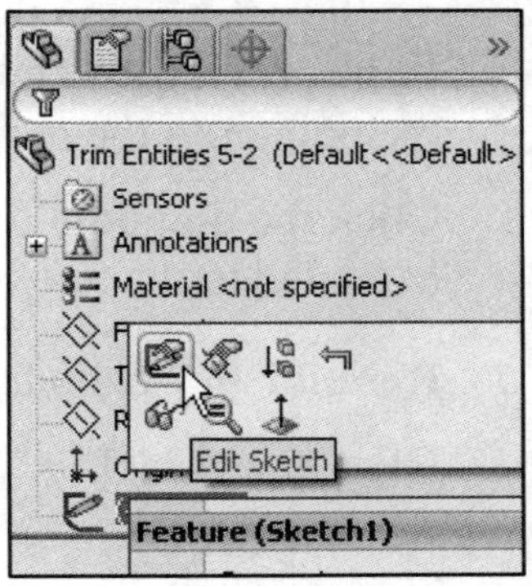


1. Open **Trim Entities 5-2** from the SolidWorks 2010 folder.
2. **Edit** Sketch1.
3. Click the **Trim Entities** Sketch tool. The Trim PropertyManager is displayed.
4. Click the **Power Trim** option box.
5. Click a **location** above the spline as illustrated.
6. Drag the **mouse point** to any location on the spline. The spline is removed.
7. Click **OK** from the Trim PropertyManager.
8. **Rebuild** the model. View the results.
9. **Close** the model.

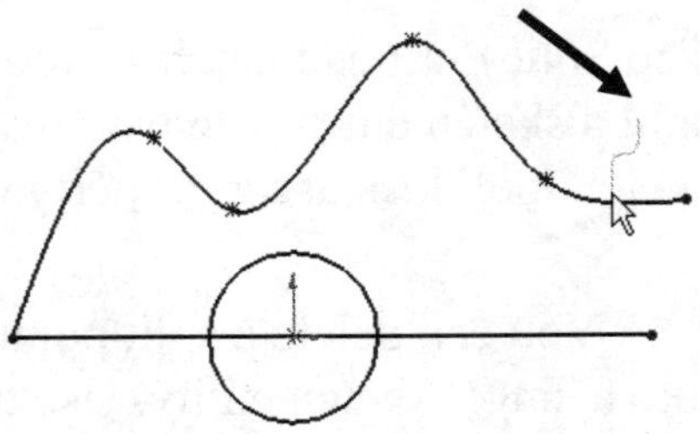

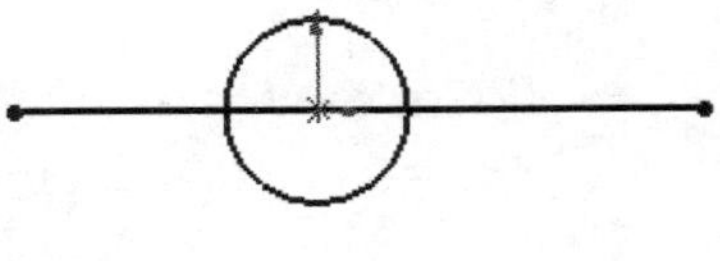

# Extend Entities Sketch tool

The Extend Entities Sketch tool provides the ability to add to the length of your sketch entity. Example: line, centerline or arc. Use the Extend Entities sketch tool to extend a sketch entity to meet another sketch entity. The Extend Entities sketch tool does not use a PropertyManager.

***Tutorial: Extend Entity 5-1***

Create an Extend Entity sketch.

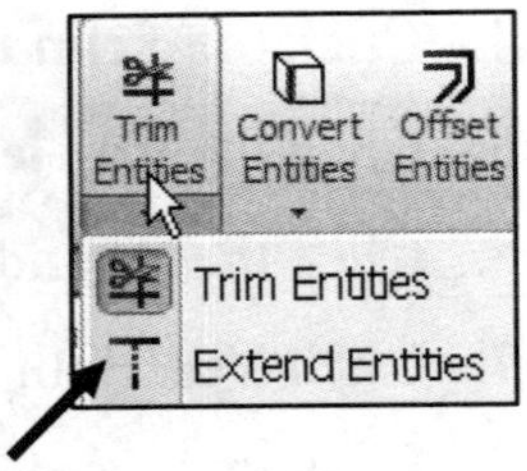


1. Open **Extend Entities 5-1** from the SolidWorks 2010 folder.
2. **Edit** Sketch1.
3. Click the **Extend Entities** tool from the Consolidated Sketch toolbar. The Extend icon is displayed on the mouse pointer.
4. Drag the **mouse pointer** over the diagonal line. The selected entity is displayed in red. A preview is displayed in red in the direction to extend the entity. If the preview extends in the wrong direction, move the pointer to the other half of the line.
5. Click the **diagonal** line. The First selected entity is extended to the top horizontal line.
6. **Rebuild** the model. View the results.
7. **Close** the model.

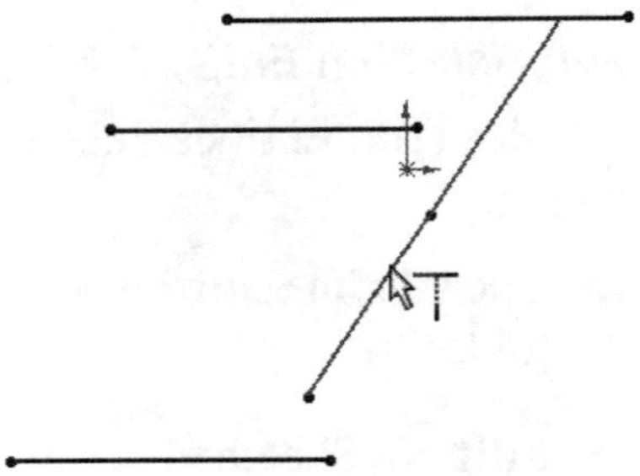

# Split Entities Sketch tool

The Split Entities Sketch tool provides the ability to split a sketch entity to create two sketch entities. The Split Entities sketch tool does use a PropertyManager.

You can delete a split point to combine two sketch entities into a single sketch entity. Use two split points to split a circle, full ellipse or a closed spline.

***Tutorial: Split Entity 5-1***

Apply the Split Entities Sketch tool.

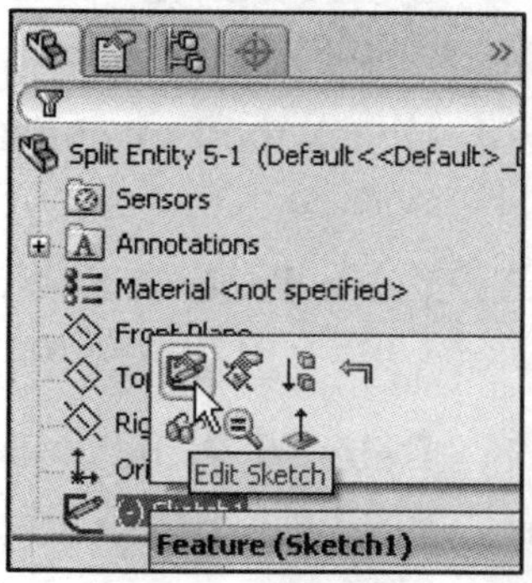


1. Open **Split Entity 5-1** from the SolidWorks 2010 folder.
2. **Edit** Sketch1.
3. Click **Tools ➤ Sketch Tools ➤ Split Entities**. The Split Entities icon is displayed in the mouse pointer.
4. Click the **right bottom horizontal line**.
5. Right-click **OK**. The sketch entity splits into two entities at the selected location sketch. A split point is added between the two sketch entities.
6. **Rebuild** the model. View the results.
7. **Close** the model.

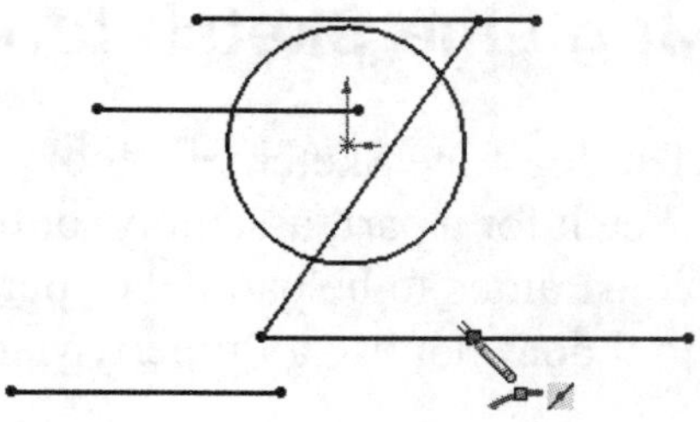

# Construction Geometry Sketch tool

The Construction Geometry Sketch tool provides the ability to convert sketch entities in a sketch or drawing to construction geometry. Construction geometry is used to assist in creating the sketch entities and geometry that are ultimately incorporated into the part. Construction geometry is ignored when the sketch is used to create a feature. Construction geometry uses the same line style as centerlines. Construction Geometry tool does not use a PropertyManager.

Any sketch entity can be specified for construction. Points and centerlines are always construction entities.

***Tutorial: Construction Geometry 5-2***

Convert existing geometry to Construction geometry.

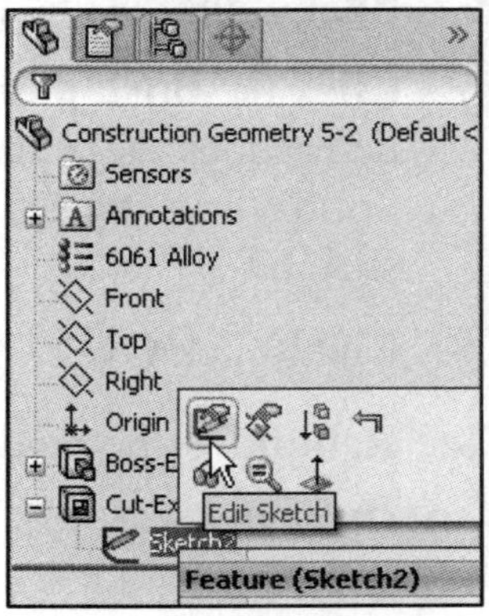


1. Open **Construction Geometry 5-2** from the SolidWorks 2010 folder.
2. **Expand** Cut-Extrude1 from the FeatureManager.
3. Right-click **Sketch 2** from the FeatureManager as illustrated.
4. Click **Edit Sketch** from the Context toolbar.

5. Click the **circular edge** of the circle as illustrated. The Circle PropertyManager is displayed.
6. Check the **For construction** box in the Options section.
7. Click **Tools ➢ Sketch Tools ➢ Construction Geometry**.
8. **Rebuild** the model. View the results.
9. **Close** the model.

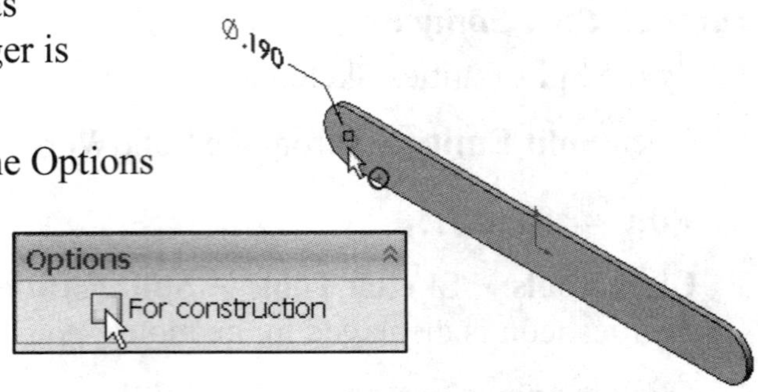


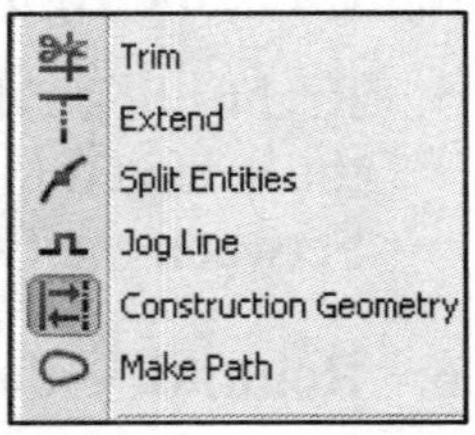


## Jog Line Sketch tool

The Jog Line Sketch tool provides the ability to jog sketch lines in either a 2D or 3D sketch for a part, assembly, or drawing documents. Jog lines are automatically constrained to be parallel or perpendicular to the original sketch line. The Jog Line sketch tool does not use a PropertyManager.

You can drag and dimension Jog lines.

***Tutorial: Jog line 5-1***

Create a Jog line in a 2D sketch.

1. Open **Jog line 5-1** from the SolidWorks 2010 folder.
2. **Edit** Sketch1.
3. Click **Tools ➢ Sketch Tools ➢ Jog Line**.
4. Click a starting **point** midway on the top horizontal line.
5. **Drag** the **mouse pointer** directly above the starting point. This point determines the height of the Jog.
6. **Drag** the **mouse pointer** directly to the right of the second point.
7. Click the **third point** location. This point determines the width of the Jog. SolidWorks created a Jog in the rectangle sketch.
8. Right-click **OK**.
9. **Rebuild** the model. View the results.
10. **Close** the model.

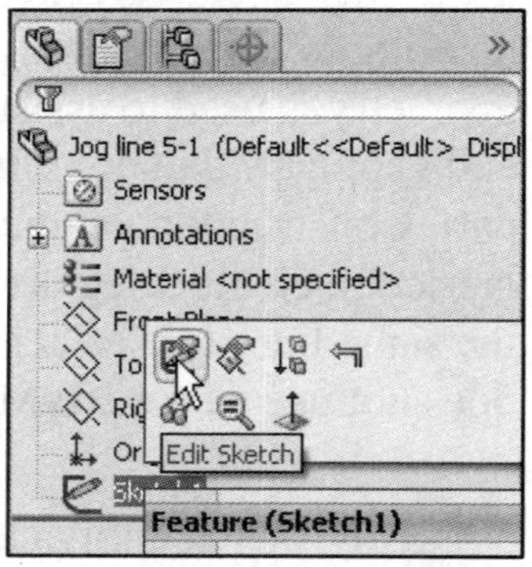


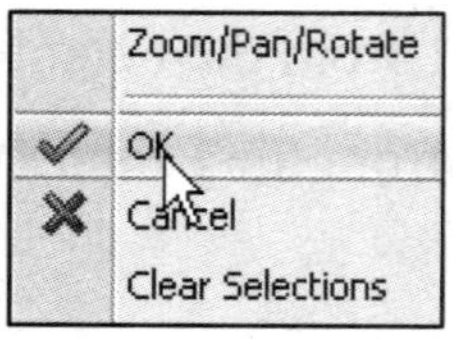


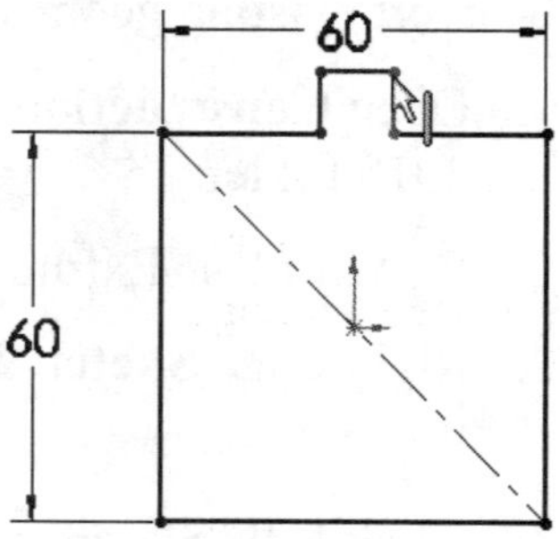

The Jog Line tool stays active so you can insert multiple jogs.

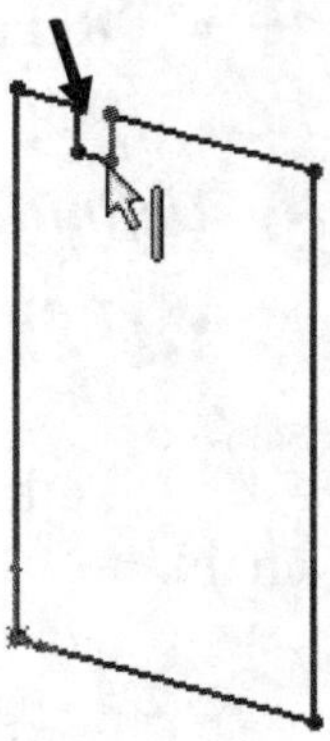


***Tutorial: Jog line 5-2***

Create a Jog line in a 3D sketch.

1. Open **Jog line 5-2** from the SolidWorks 2010 folder.
2. **Edit** 3DSketch1.
3. Click **Tools ➢ Sketch Tools ➢ Jog Line**.
4. Click a starting **point** on the top horizontal, X line as illustrated. Drag the **mouse pointer** down and to the right to create the first Jog.
5. Click a **position** as illustrated.

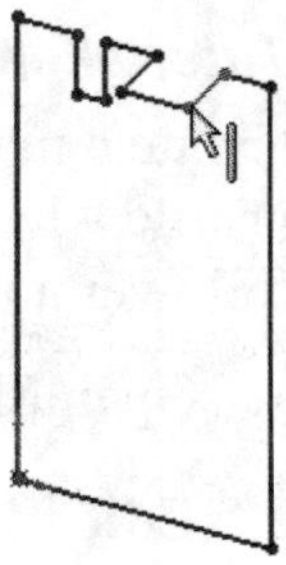

Create a second Jog.

6. Click a starting **point** on the top horizontal, X line as illustrated.
7. Drag the **mouse pointer** down and to the right to create the second Jog.
8. Press the **Tab** key to change the plane of the Jog. The Jog is in the Z plane.
9. Click a **position**.
10. Create the **third** and **fourth** Jog as illustrated.
11. Right-click **OK**.
12. **Rebuild** the model. View the results.
13. **Close** the model.

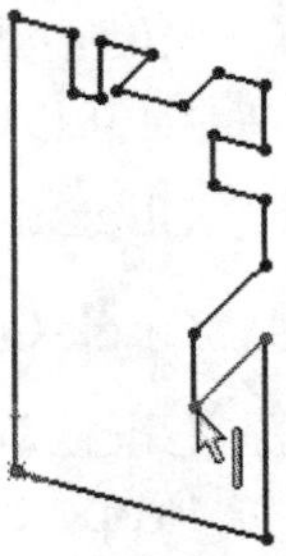

Jog lines are automatically constrained to be perpendicular or parallel to your original sketch line.

# Make Path Sketch tool

The Make Path Sketch tool provides the ability to create a path with end-to-end coincident sketch entities. A path consists of sketch entities which are coincident end to end to form a single chain. The selected sketch entities are highlighted in the Graphics window. The Make Path Sketch tool uses the Path Properties PropertyManager. The Path Properties Manager provides the following selections:

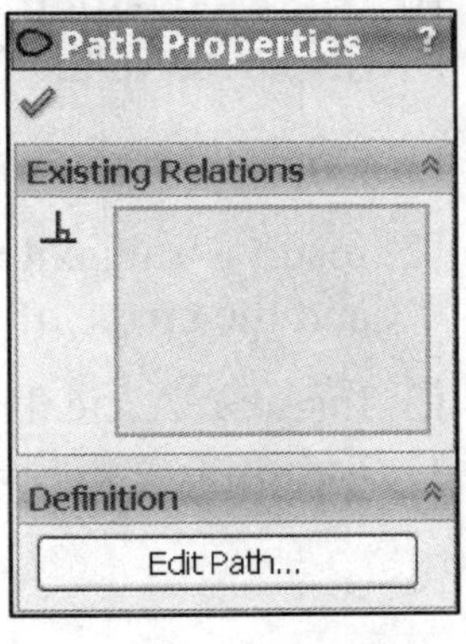


It is recommend to create the sketch entities into a block. A chain of sketch entities can belong only to a single path.

- ***Existing Relations***. Provides the following option:
  - **Relations**. Displays the relations between the sketch entities that consist of the path and the sketch entities with which the path interacts.
- ***Definition***. Provides the following option:
  - **Edit Path**. Adds sketch entities to create a path.

A Path consists of sketch entities that are coincident end to end, forming a single chain.

Edit paths in the Path Properties PropertyManager.

### *Tutorial: Make Path 5-1*

Create a machine design 2D layout sketch. Model a cam profile where the tangent relation between the cam and a follower automatically transitions as the cam rotates.

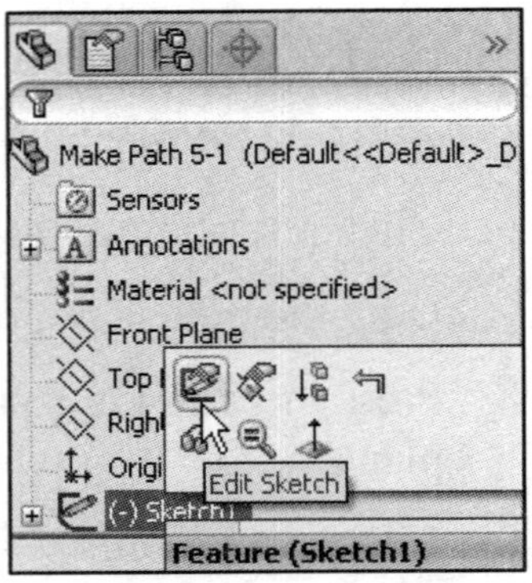


1. Open **Make Path 5-1** from the SolidWorks 2010 folder.
2. **Edit** Sketch1.
3. Click the **spline boundary** of the CAM block. The Block PropertyManager is display

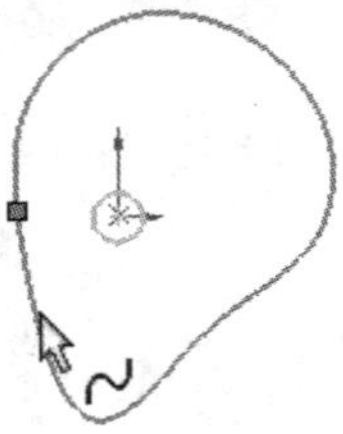

4. Right-click **Make Path** from the Context toolbar. The Path Properties PropertyManager is displayed.
5. Click the **Edit Path** button to view the Selected entities.
6. Click **OK** from the Path Properties PropertyManager.
7. Click **Tools ➤ Blocks ➤ Insert**. The Insert Block PropertyManager is displayed.

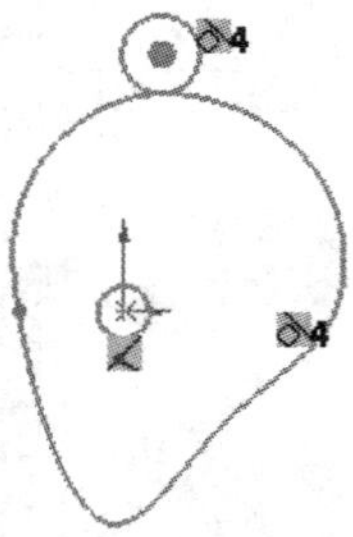

8. Click the **Browse** button from the Blocks to Insert box.
9. Double-click **Follower.sldblk** from the SolidWorks 2010 folder.
10. Click a **position** above the CAM. Follower and Block2 are displayed in the Open Blocks box.
11. Click **OK** from the Insert Block PropertyManager.

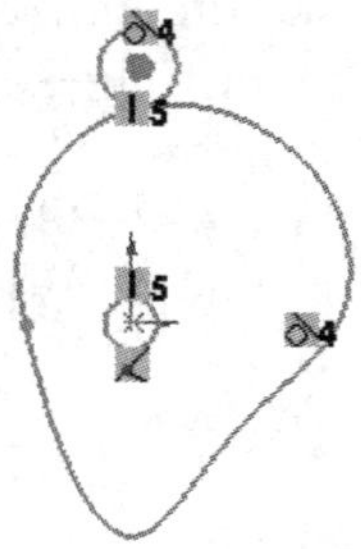

12. Insert a Tangent relation between the **spline of the CAM** and the **circle of the Follower**.
13. Insert a Vertical relation between the **center point of the Follower** and the center point of the **CAM**.

14. Slowly **rotate** the CAM block. View the model in the Graphics window.
15. **Rebuild** the model. View Block 2-3 and Block Follower-1 in the FeatureManager and in the Graphics window.
16. **Close** the model.

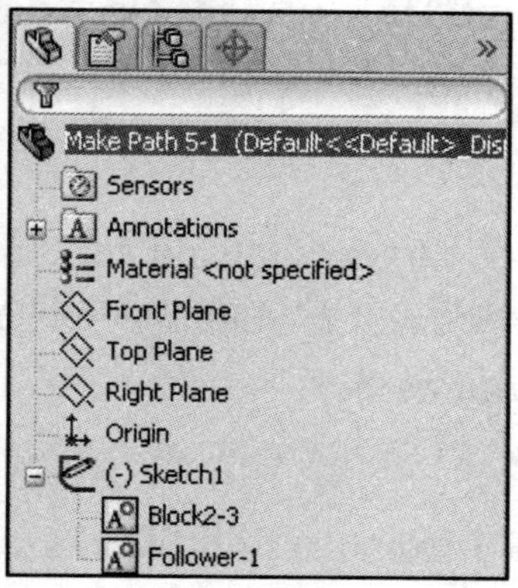


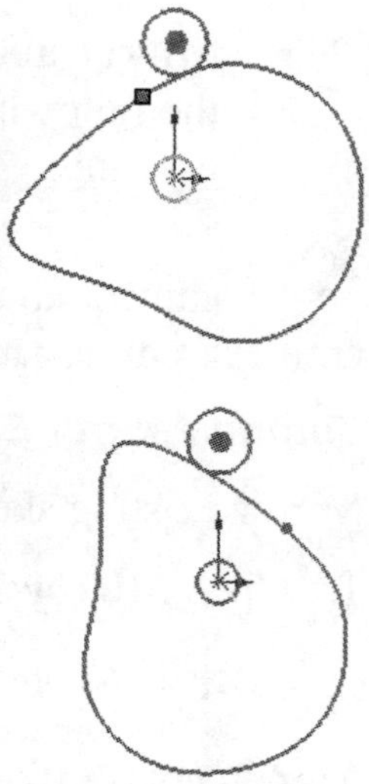

The Make Path tool enables you to create a tangent relation between a chain of sketch entities and another sketch entity.

## Mirror Entities Sketch tool

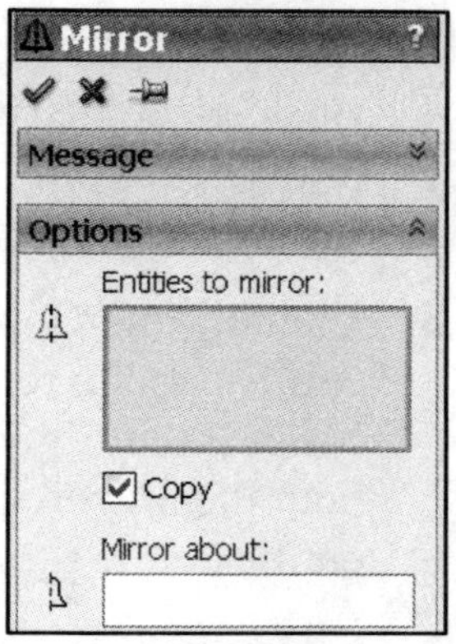


The Mirror Entities Sketch tool provides the ability to mirror existing sketch entities. This tool is not available for 3D sketches. The tool provides the following capabilities which are the same as the Dynamic Mirror sketch tool. They are:

- Mirror to only include the new entity, or both the original and the mirrored entity.
- Mirror some or all of the sketch entities.
- Mirror about any type of line, not just a construction line.
- Mirror about edges in a drawing, part, or assembly.

When you create mirrored entities, SolidWorks applies a symmetric relation between each corresponding pair of sketch points (the ends of mirrored lines, the centers of arcs, etc). If you change a mirrored entity, its mirror image also changes.

The Mirror Entities Sketch tool uses the Mirror PropertyManager. The Mirror PropertyManager provides the following options:

- ***Options***. Controls the following selections:
  - **Entities to mirror**. Displays the selected sketch entities to mirror.
  - **Copy**. Selected by default. Includes both the original and mirrored entities. Clear the Copy check box if you only want the mirrored entities and not the original entity.

- **Mirror about**. Displays the selected item to mirror about. You can Mirror about the following items: Centerlines, Lines, Linear model edges, and Linear edges on drawings.

To mirror about a linear drawing edge, your sketch entities to mirror must lie within the boundary of the drawing.

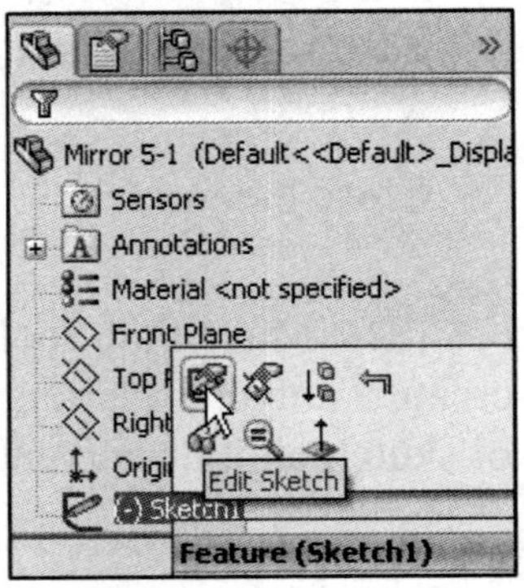


***Tutorial: Mirror Entities 5-1***

Mirror existing sketch entities with the Mirror Sketch tool.

1. Open **Mirror 5-1** from the SolidWorks 2010 folder.
2. **Edit** Sketch1.
3. Click the **Mirror Entities** Sketch tool. The Mirror PropertyManager is displayed.
4. Box-Select the **two rectangles** and the **circle** on the left side of the centerline. The selected entities are displayed in the Entities to mirror box.
5. Uncheck the **Copy** box to add a mirror copy of the selected entities and to remove the original sketch entities. Note: if the Copy box is checked, you will include both the mirrored copy and the original sketch entities.
6. Click inside the **Mirror about** box.
7. Click the **centerline** to Mirror about. Line1 is displayed in the Mirror about box.
8. Click **OK** from the Mirror PropertyManager. The selected entities are mirrored about the centerline. No original entities are displayed due to the unchecked Copy box.
9. **Rebuild** the model. View the results.
10. **Close** the model.

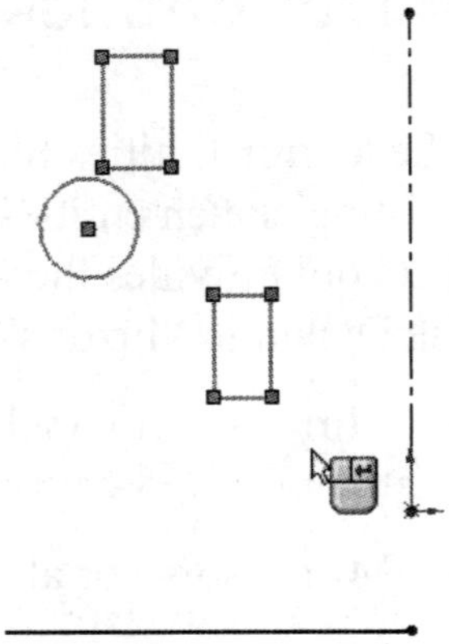

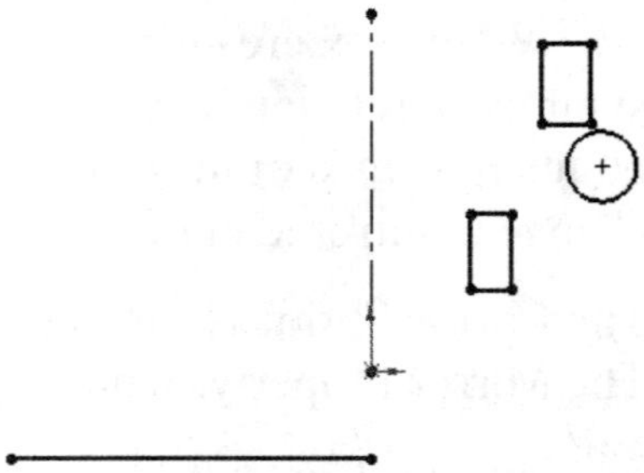

## Dynamic Mirror Sketch tool

The Dynamic Mirror Sketch tool provides the ability to mirror sketch entities as you sketch them. Dynamics Mirror is not available for 3D sketches. The Dynamic Mirror sketch tool does not use a PropertyManager.

The Dynamic Mirror sketch tool provides the following capabilities which are the same as the Mirror sketch tool. They are:

- Mirror to only include the new entity, or both the original and the mirrored entity.
- Mirror some or all of the sketch entities.
- Mirror about any type of line, not just a construction line.
- Mirror about edges in a drawing, part, or assembly.

***Tutorial: Dynamic Mirror 5-1***

Mirror sketch entities as you sketch them. Use the Dynamic Mirror Sketch tool.

1. Open **Dynamic Mirror 5-1** from the SolidWorks 2010 folder.
2. **Edit** Sketch1.
3. Click the **vertical line**. The Line Properties PropertyManager is displayed.
4. Click **Tools ➤ Sketch Tools ➤ Dynamic Mirror**. The Mirror PropertyManager is displayed. A Symmetry symbol is displayed at both ends of the vertical line in the Graphics window.
5. Create **two circles** on the left side of the vertical line. The circle entities are mirrored as you sketch them.

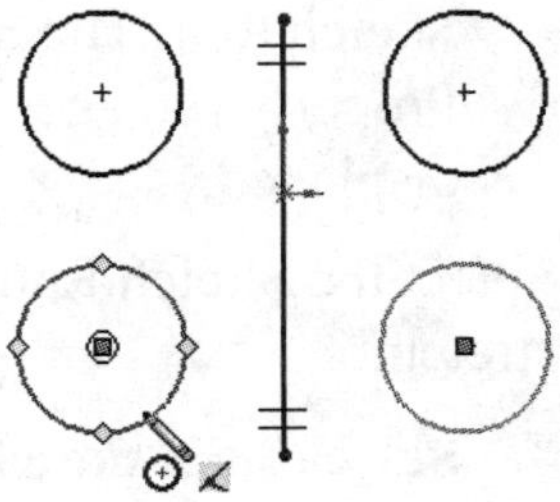

Deactivate the Dynamic Mirror tool.

6. Click **Tools ➤ Sketch Tools ➤ Dynamic Mirror.**
7. **Rebuild** the model. View the results.
8. **Close** the model.

## Stretch Entities

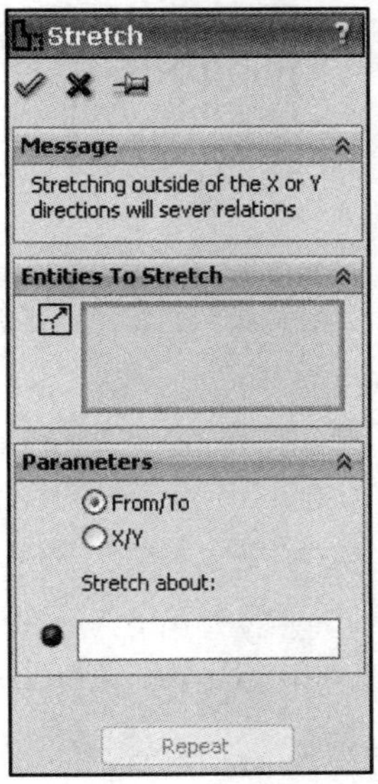


The Stretch Entities tool provides the ability to stretch multiple sketch entities as a single group in a 2D sketch. The Stretch Entities tool uses the Stretch PropertyManager.

The Stretch PropertyManager provides the following options:

- ***Entities To Stretch***. Displayed the selected sketch entities.
- ***Parameters***. Provides the following options:

- **From/To**. Selected by default. Adds a Base point to set the Start point. Drag the mouse pointer and click a location in the Graphics window to set the destination point.
- **X/Y**. Sets the value for the Delta X and Delta Y coordinate.
- **Base Point**. Displays the selected vertex to Stretch the sketch in the Graphics window.
- **Repeat**. Moves your sketch entities again by the same distance when using the X/Y option.

### *Tutorial: Stretch Entities 5-1*

Apply the Stretch Entities tool.

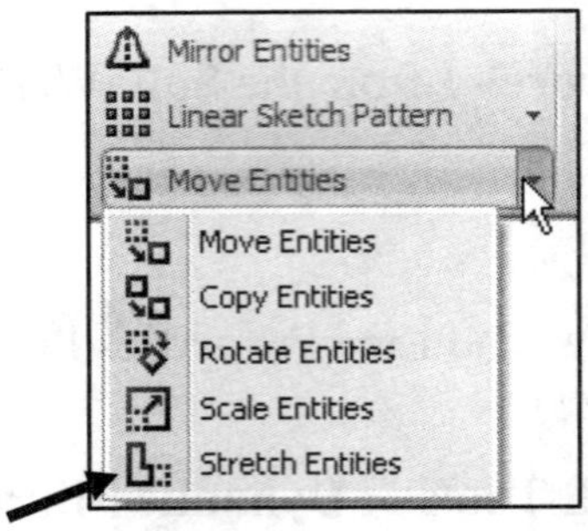


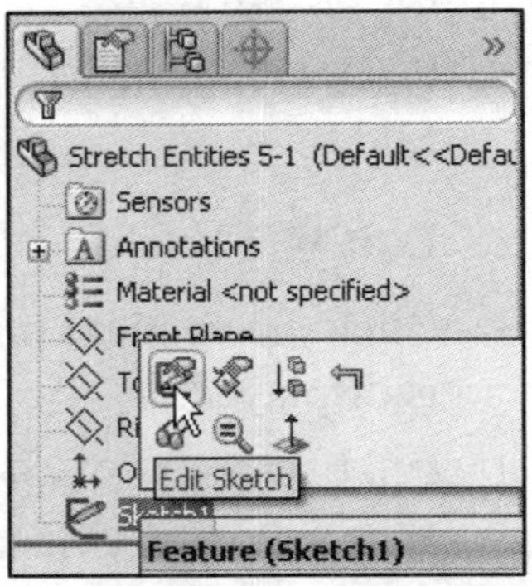


1. Open **Stretch Entities 5-1** from the SolidWorks 2010 folder.
2. **Edit** Sketch1.
3. Click the **Stretch Entities** Sketch tool. The Stretch PropertyManager is displayed.

Select the Sketch Entities to stretch.

4. Select the **5 sketch entities** as illustrated. The selected entities are displayed in the Entities to Stretch box
5. Click the **From/To** box.
6. Click inside the **Base point** box.

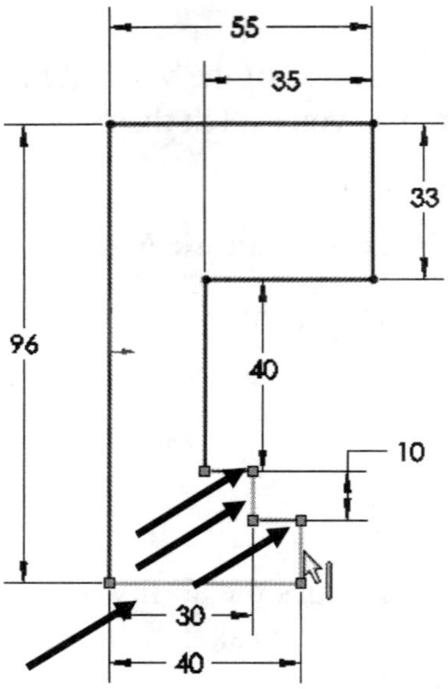


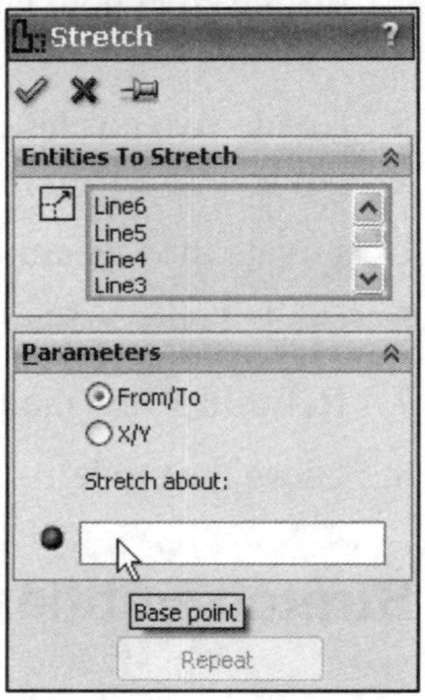

Select a Stretch about point.

7. Click the **left bottom vertex** in the Graphics window as illustrated. Base defined is displayed in the Base point box.

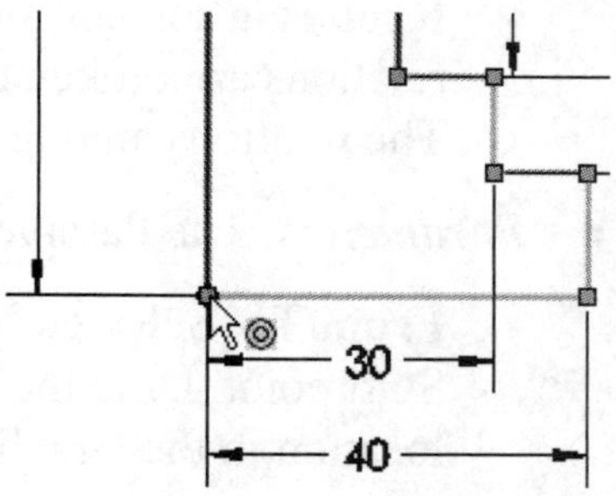


8. Drag the mouse pointer directly to the **right** for the stretch.
9. Click the stretch **end point**. View the results. The dimensions are updated.
10. **Close** the model.

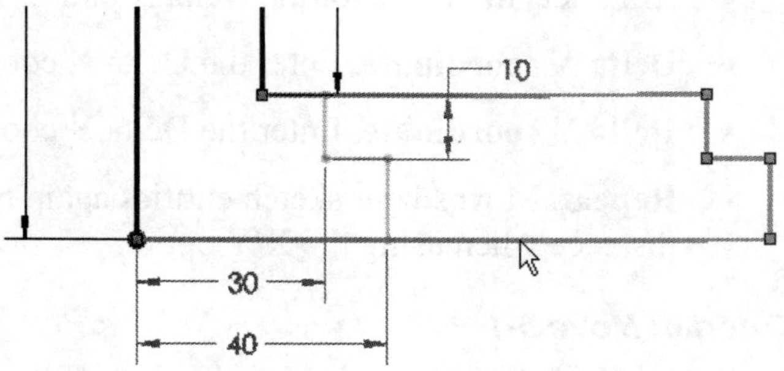


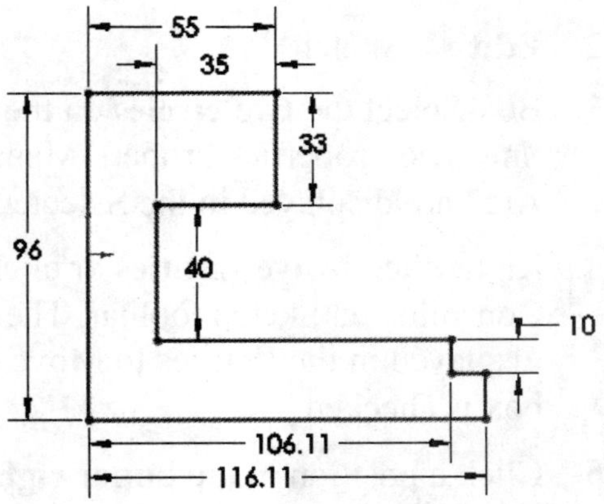


## Move Entities Sketch tool

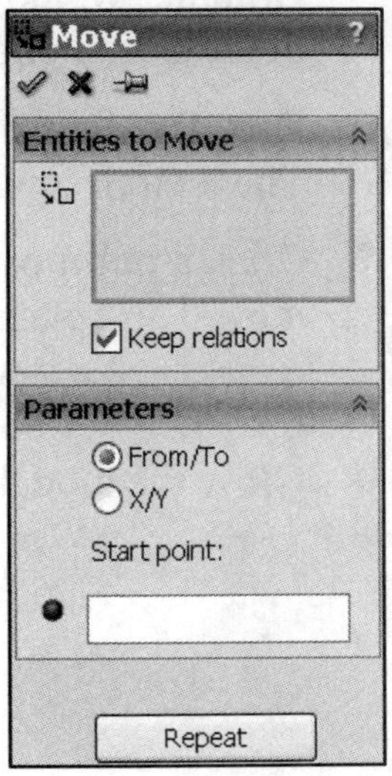


The Move Entities sketch tool provides the ability to move entities by selecting from and to points or by using the X and Y destination coordinates. Using the Move sketch tool does not create relations.

The Move Entities sketch tool uses the Move PropertyManager. The Move PropertyManager provides the following selections:

- ***Entities to Move***. Provides the following options:
  - **Sketch Items or annotations**. Displays the selected sketch entities to move.

- **Keep relations**. Maintains relations between sketch entities. If un-checked, sketch relations are broken only between selected entities and those that are not selected. The relations among the selected entities are still maintained.

- ***Parameters***. The Parameters box controls the following options:
  - **From/To**. Selected by default. Adds a Base point to set the Start point. Drag the mouse pointer and double-click a location in the Graphics window to set the destination point.
  - **X/Y**. Sets the value for the Delta X and Delta Y coordinate.
  - **Delta X coordinate**. Enter the Delta X coordinate value.
  - **Delta Y coordinate**. Enter the Delta Y coordinate value.
  - **Repeat**. Moves your sketch entities again by the same distance when using the X/Y option.

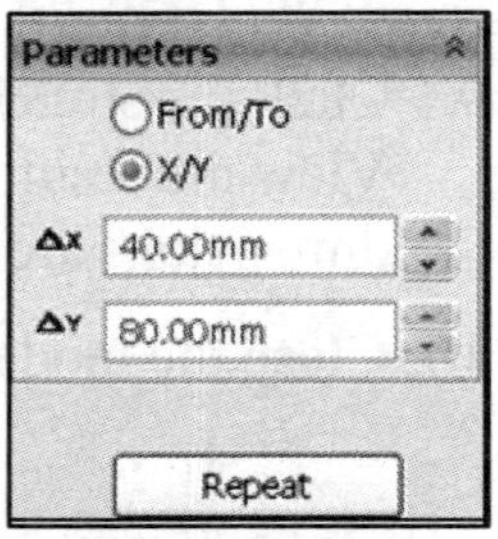


### *Tutorial: Move 5-1*

Apply the Move Entities tool using the From/To option.

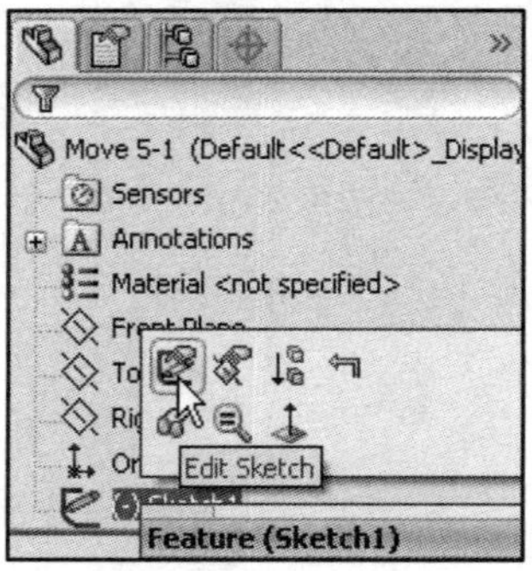


1. Open **Move 5-1** from the SolidWorks 2010 folder.
2. **Edit** Sketch1.
3. Box-Select the **two circles** on the left side of the vertical line. The Properties PropertyManager is displayed. Arc1 and Arc3 are displayed in the Selected Entities box.
4. Right-click **Move Entities** or click Move Entities from the Consolidated Sketch toolbar. The two selected circles are displayed in the Entities to Move box. Note: The **From/To** box is checked.

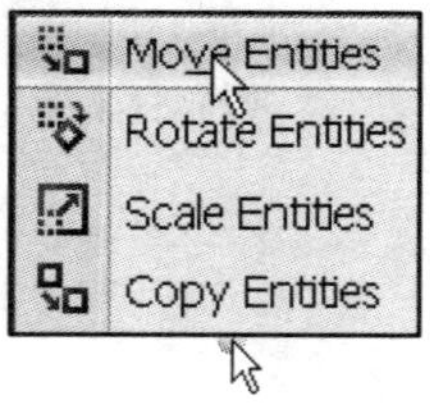


5. Click a position in the **upper right** section of the Graphics window. A base point is displayed in the Graphics window. From Point Defined is displayed in the Base point box.
6. Drag the **mouse pointer** in the Graphics window. The 4 circles move keeping their relations.
7. Click a **point** over the vertical line. The circles are moved and placed.
8. **Rebuild** the model. View the results.
9. **Close** the model.

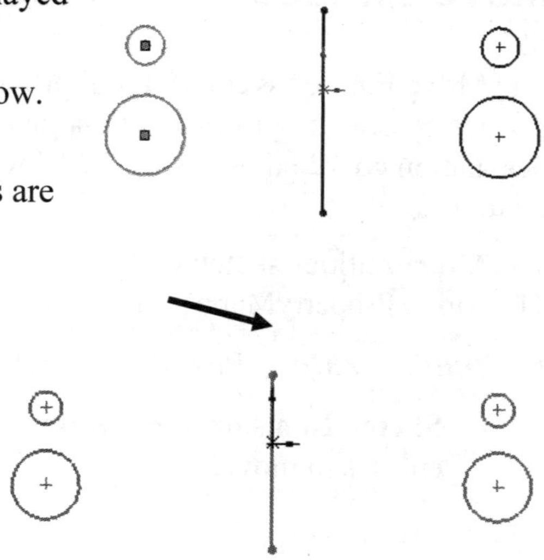

## Copy Entities Sketch tool

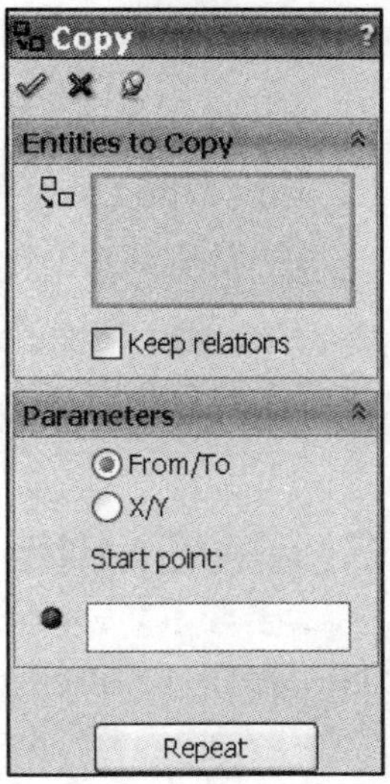


The Copy Entities sketch tool provides the ability to copy entities by selecting from and to points or by using the X and Y destination coordinates. This tool does not create relations. The Copy Entities tool uses the Copy PropertyManager. The Copy PropertyManager provides the following selections:

- ***Entities to Copy***. The Entities to Copy box provides the following options:
  - **Sketch Items or annotations**. Displays the selected sketch entities to copy.
  - **Keep relations**. Maintains relations between sketch entities. If un-checked, sketch relations are broken only between selected entities and those that are not selected. The relations among the selected entities are still maintained.
- ***Parameters***. The Parameters box controls the following options:
  - **From/To**. Adds a Base point to set the Start point. Move the mouse pointer and double-click to set the destination point in the Graphics window.
  - **X/Y**. Sets the value for the Delta X and Delta Y coordinate.
  - **Delta X coordinate**. Enter the Delta X coordinate value.
  - **Delta Y coordinate**. Enter the Delta Y coordinate value.
  - **Repeat**. Moves your sketch entities again by the same distance when using the X/Y option.

### *Tutorial: Copy sketch 5-1*

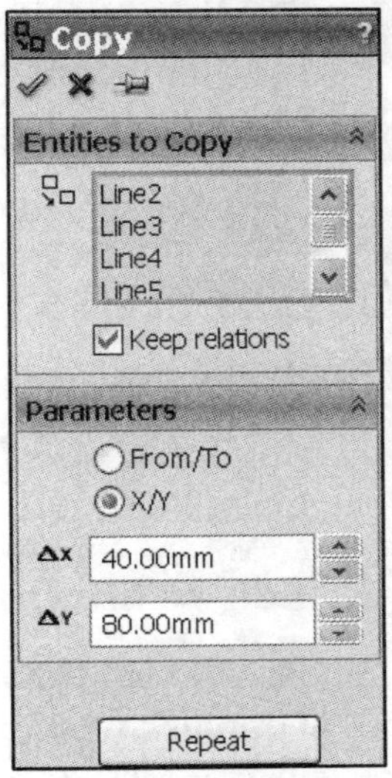


Apply the Copy Entities tool using the X/Y option.

1. Open **Copy 5-1** from the SolidWorks 2010 folder.
2. **Edit** Sketch1. Box-Select the **rectangle** in your Graphics window. The Properties PropertyManager is displayed with the selected sketch entities.
3. Right-click **Copy Entities** from the Context toolbar. The lines of the rectangle are displayed in the Entities to Copy box.
4. Check the **X/Y** box.
5. Enter **40**mm for Delta X. Enter **80**mm for Delta Y. View the copied rectangle displayed in yellow above and to the right of the original entity.

6. Click the **Repeat** button. The copied rectangle moves again by the same X and Y coordinate value. The new values are displayed in the Parameters box.
7. Click **OK** from the Copy PropertyManager.
8. Press the **f** key to fit the model to the Graphics window. View the copy sketch entity.
9. **Rebuild** the model. View the results.
10. **Close** the model.

## Scale Entities Sketch tool

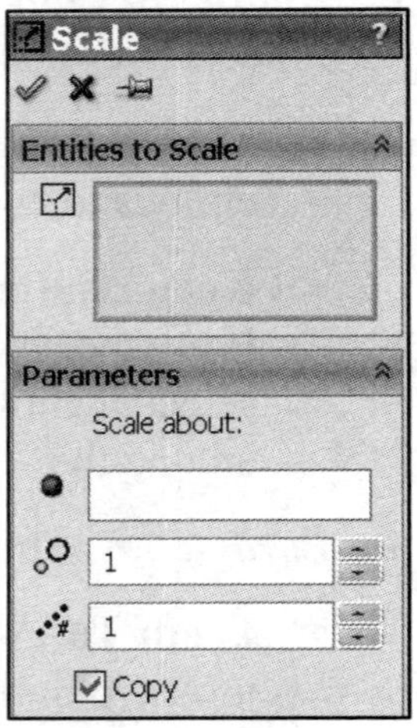


The Scale Entities sketch tool provides the ability to scale and create copies of sketch entities by selecting a Base point, a Scale Factor, and the number of copies required. The Scale Entities tool uses the Scale PropertyManager. The Scale PropertyManager provides the following selections:

- ***Entities to Scale***. The Entities to Scale box provides the following option:
  - **Sketch Items or Annotations**. Displays the selected sketch entities to scale from the Graphics window.
- ***Parameters***. The Parameters box controls the following options:
  - **Scale about**. Display the selected Base point as the point to scale about.
  - **Scale Factor**. Display the selected scale required. Enter the Scale Factor.
  - **Number of Copies**. Display the selected value of the Number of Copies required. Enter the Number of Copies.
  - **Copy**. Selected by default. Creates one or more copies of your scaled entities.

### *Tutorial: Scale 5-1*

Apply the Scale Entities sketch tool using a 1.5 Scale Factor and multiple copies.

1. Open **Scale 5-1** from the SolidWorks 2010 folder.
2. **Edit** Sketch1.
3. Box-Select the **small rectangle** in the top left corner of the Graphics window. The Properties PropertyManager is displayed with the selected sketch entities.

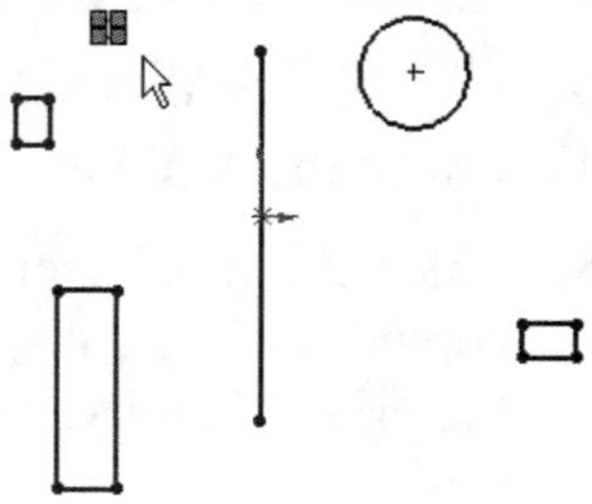

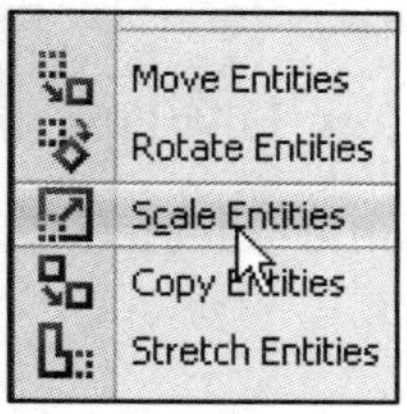


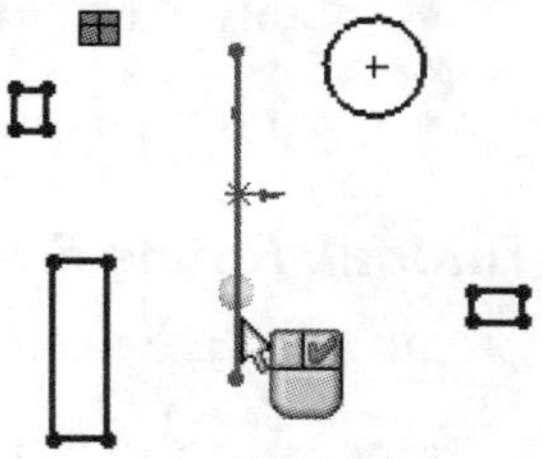

4. Right-click **Scale Entities** from the Context toolbar. The selected sketch entities are displayed in the Entities to Scale box.
5. Click inside the **Base point** box.
6. Click the **vertical** line as illustrated. Scale Point Defined is displayed in the Base point box. A base point is displayed in the Graphics window on the vertical line.
7. Enter **1.5** in the Scale Factor box.
8. Check the **Copy** box.

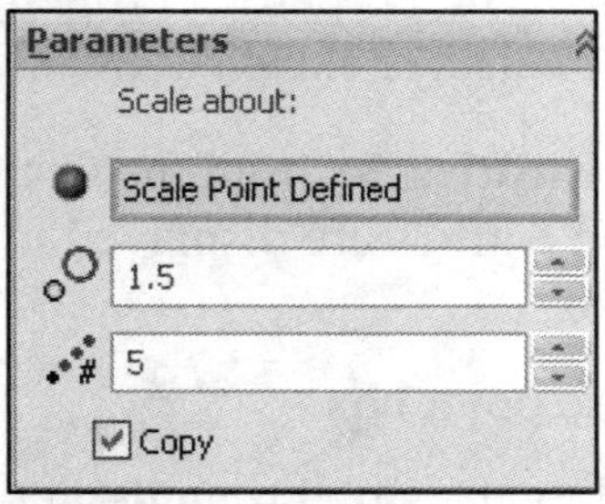


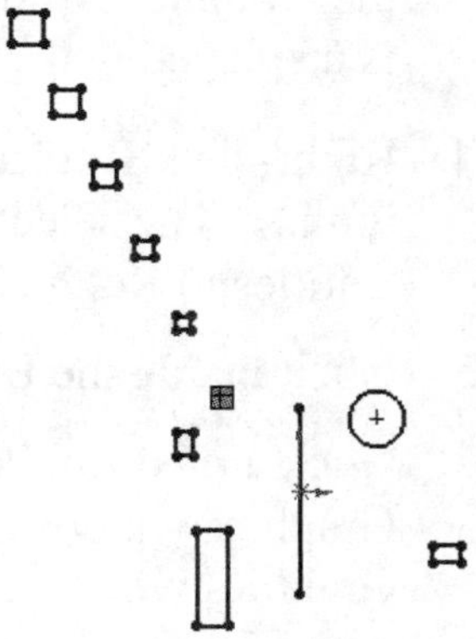

9. Select **5** for the Number of Copies using the increment arrow box. The scale of each copy is increased by 1.5. The 5 copies of the small rectangle are displayed in yellow in the Graphics window.
10. Click **OK** from the Scale PropertyManager.
11. **Zoom out** to view the created copies of the rectangle in the Graphics window.
12. **Rebuild** the model. View the results.
13. **Close** the model.

## Rotate Entities Sketch tool

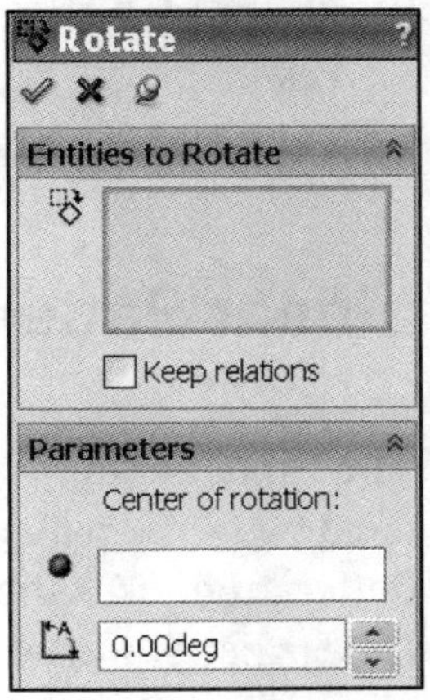


The Rotate Entities sketch tool provides the ability to rotate entities by selecting a center of rotation and the number of degrees to rotate. The Rotate Entities tool uses the Rotate PropertyManager. The Rotate PropertyManager provides the following selections:

- ***Entities to Rotate***. The Entities to Rotate box provides the following options:
  - **Sketch Items or Annotations**. Displays the selected sketch entities from the Graphics window.
  - **Keep relations**. Maintains relations between sketch entities. If un-checked, the sketch relations are broken only between the selected entities and those that are not selected. The relations among the selected sketch entities are still maintained.

- ***Parameters***. The Parameters box controls the following option:
  - **Center of rotation**. Displays the selected Base point as the Center of rotation.
  - **Angle**. Displays the selected value for the Angle.

***Tutorial: Rotate 5-1***

Create a Rotate sketch.

1. Open **Rotate 5-1** from the SolidWorks 2010 folder.
2. **Edit** Sketch1.
3. Box-Select the **small triangle** in the top left corner of the Graphics window. The Properties PropertyManager is displayed with the selected sketch entities.
4. Right-click **Rotate Entities** from the Context toolbar. The selected entities are displayed in the Entities to Rotate box.

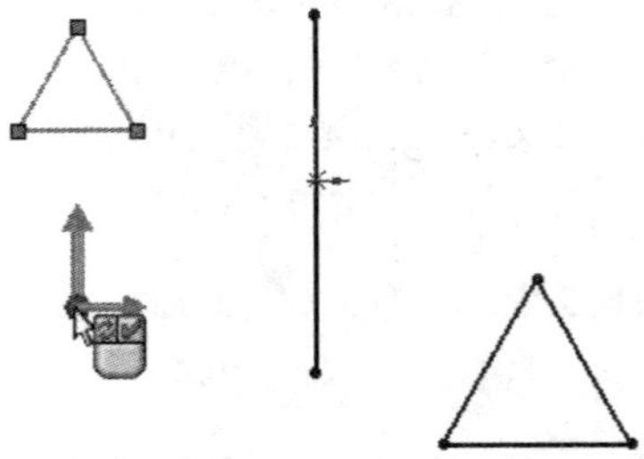

5. Click **inside** the Base point box.
6. Click a **position** below the small triangle in the Graphics window. A point triad is displayed in the Graphics window.
7. Enter **135**deg for Angle. View the triangle rotated 135 degrees in the Graphics window.
8. Click **OK** from the Rotate PropertyManager.
9. **Rebuild** the model. View the results.
10. **Close** the model.

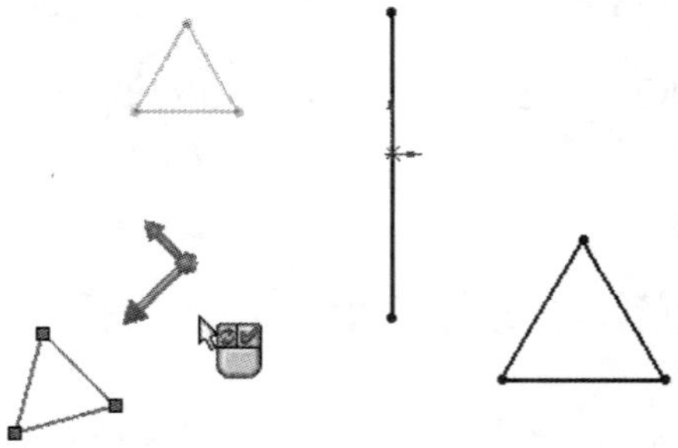

## Linear Pattern Sketch tool

The Linear Pattern Sketch tool provides the ability to create a linear pattern along one or both axes. The Linear Pattern tool uses the Linear Pattern PropertyManager. The Linear Pattern PropertyManager provides the following selections:

- ***Direction 1***. The Direction 1 box provides the following options:

- **Pattern Direction**. Displays the selected edge from a part or an assembly to create a linear pattern in the X direction.
- **Reverse direction**. Reverses the pattern direction in the X direction if required.
- **Number**. Displays the selected number of pattern instances in the X direction. The number includes the original feature.
- **Spacing**. Displays the selected spacing value between the pattern instances for Direction 1.
- **Add dimension**. Dimensions between the pattern instances.
- **Angle**. Displays the selected angular value direction other than horizontal for the pattern instances.

Set a value for the Number option to activate the Direction 2 box settings.

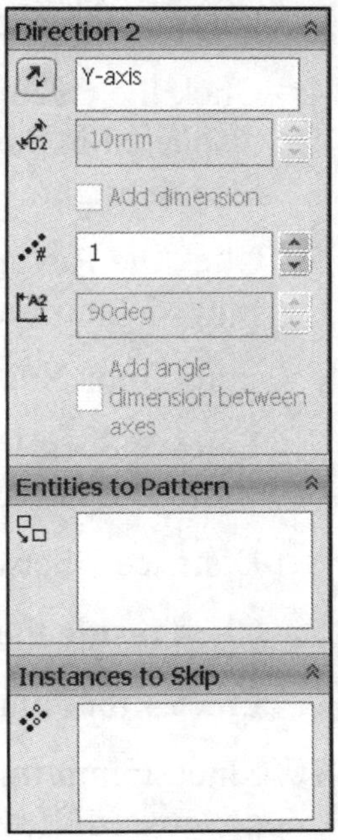


- ***Direction 2***. The Direction 2 box provides the following options:
  - **Pattern Direction**. Displays the selected edge from a part or an assembly to create a linear pattern in the Y direction.
  - **Reverse direction**. Reverses the pattern direction in the Y direction if required.
  - **Spacing**. Displays the selected spacing value between the pattern instances for Direction 2.
  - **Add dimension**. Dimensions between the pattern instances.
  - **Number**. Displays the selected number of pattern instances in the Y direction. The number includes the original feature.
  - **Angle**. Displays the selected angular value direction other than vertical for the pattern instances.
  - **Add angle dimension between axes**. Selected by default. Displays the angle dimension between the patterns along the X and Y axis.
- ***Entities to Pattern***. The Entities to Pattern box provides the following option:
  - **Entities to Pattern**. Displays the selected sketch entities from the Graphics window.

- ***Instances to Skip***. The Instances to Skip box provides the following option:
  - **Instances to Skip**. Displays the selected instances from the Graphics window which you want to skip. Click to select a pattern instance. The coordinates of the pattern instance are displayed in the Graphics window.

### *Tutorial: Linear Pattern sketch 5-1*

Create a Linear Pattern sketch using the Instances to Skip option.

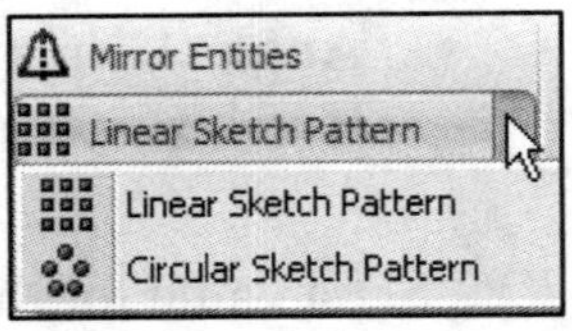


1. Open **Linear Pattern 5-1** from the SolidWorks 2010 folder.
2. **Edit** Sketch2.
3. Click the **Linear Sketch Pattern** Sketch tool. The Linear Pattern PropertyManager is displayed. The Linear Sketch Pattern icon is displayed on the mouse pointer.
4. Click the **circumference** of the small circle. Arc 1 is displayed in the Entities to Pattern box. The pattern direction is to the right.
5. Click the **Reverse** direction check box option if required. Enter **50**mm for Spacing in Direction 1.
6. Enter **3** for Number of sketch entities in Direction 1.
7. Enter **355**deg for Angle at which to pattern the sketch entities in Direction 1.

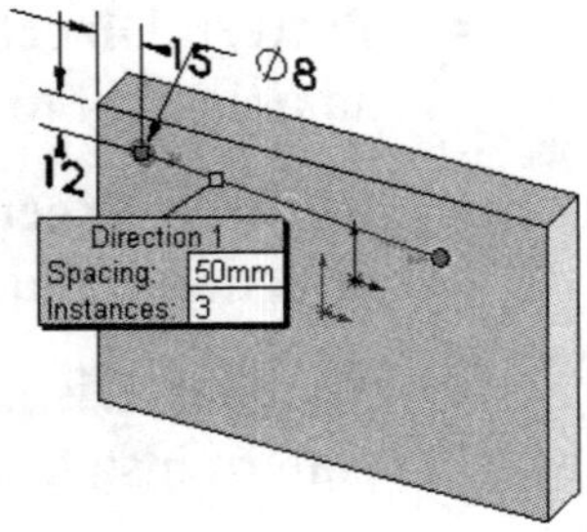


Set Distance 2 between sketch entities along the Y-axis.

8. Click **inside** the Y-axis box.
9. Enter **4** for Number of sketch entities.
10. Enter **25**mm for Spacing. The pattern direction arrow points downward. If required, click the **Reverse** direction check box.

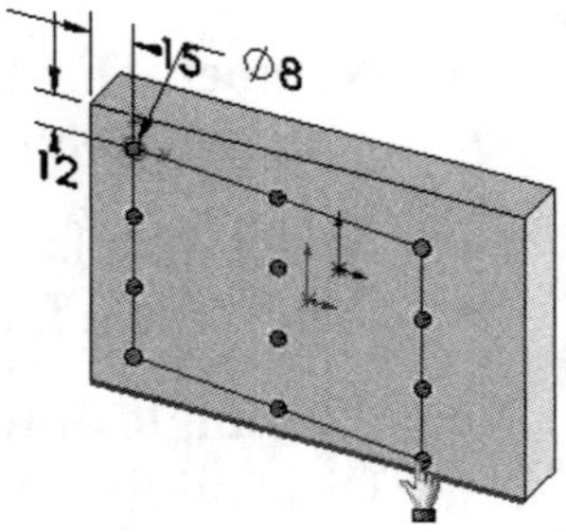


11. **Expand** the Instances to Skip option box.
12. Click **inside** the Instances to Skip box.
13. Click the two bottom right corner pattern points, **(2,4)**, **(3,4)**. The selected sketch entities, (2,4) and (3,4) are displayed in the Instances to Skip option box.
14. Click **OK** from the Linear Pattern PropertyManager.
15. **Rebuild** the model. View the results.
16. **Close** the model.

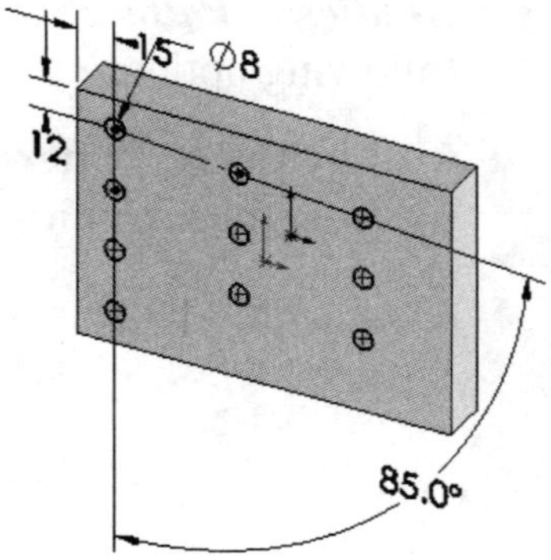

## Circular Pattern Sketch tool

The Circular Pattern Sketch tool provides the ability to create a circular sketch pattern along one or both axes. The Circular Pattern tool uses the Circular Pattern PropertyManager. The Circular Pattern PropertyManager provides the following selections:

When you active the Circular Pattern sketch tool, the Entities to Pattern option is selected. The circular pattern defaults to 4 equally spaced pattern instances.

- ***Parameters***. The Parameters box controls the following options:
  - **Entities to Pattern**. Displays the selected entity to pattern from the Graphics window.
  - **Reverse direction**. Reverses the circular pattern direction if required.
  - **Center X**. Patterns the center along the X axis.
  - **Center Y**. Patterns the center along the Y axis.
  - **Number**. Displays the selected number of pattern instances along the circular pattern.
  - **Spacing**. Displays the selected number of total degrees in the circular pattern.
  - **Radius**. Displays the selected radius value of the circular pattern.
  - **Arc Angle**. Displays the selected angle measured from the center of the selected entities to the center point or vertex of the circular pattern.
  - **Equal Spacing**. Selected by default. Patterns the circular instances equidistant from each other.
  - **Add dimensions.** Displays a dimension between the circular pattern instances.
- ***Entities to Pattern***. The Entities to Pattern box provides the following option:
  - **Entities to Pattern**. Displays the selected sketch entities from the Graphics window.

- ***Instances to Skip***. The Instances to Skip box provides the following option:
  - **Instances to Skip**. Displays the selected instances from the Graphics window which you want to skip. Click to select a pattern instance. The coordinates of the pattern instance are displayed in the Graphics window.

***Tutorial: Circular Pattern sketch 5-1***

Create a Circular Pattern sketch.

1. Open **Circular Pattern 5-1** from the SolidWorks 2010 folder.
2. **Edit** Sketch1.
3. Click **Circular Sketch Pattern** from the Consolidated Sketch toolbar. The Sketch Circular Pattern PropertyManager is displayed.

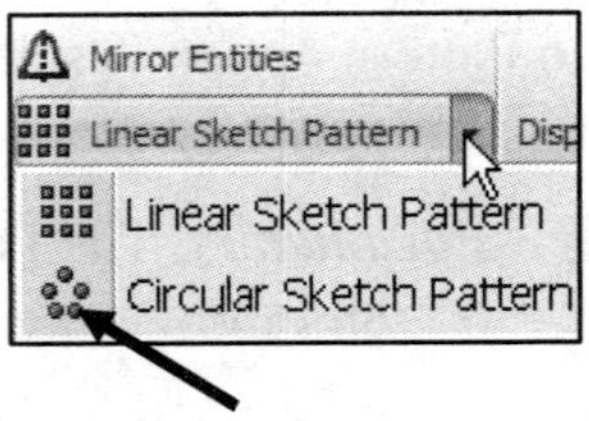


4. Click the **circumference** of the small circle in the Graphics window. Point-1 is displayed in the Parameters box. The direction arrow points downward. If required, click the Reverse direction box. Arc 2 is displayed in the Entities to Pattern box.
5. Enter **8** for spacing.
6. Check the **Equal spacing** box.

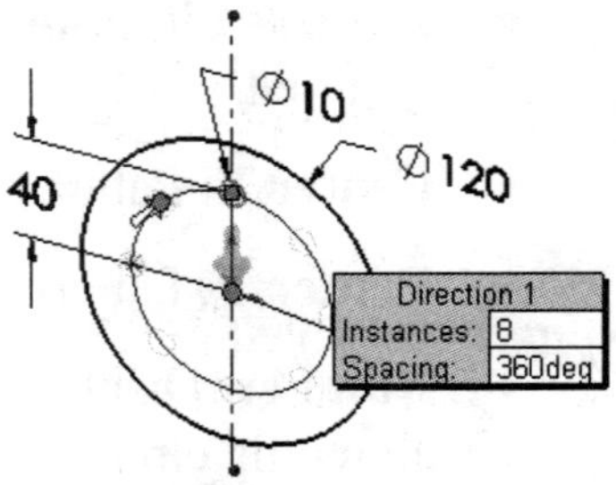


Center X, Center Y, and Arc Angle are values generated by the location of your circular pattern's center. You can edit each of these values independently.

7. **Expand** the Instances to Skip box.
8. Click **inside** the Instances to Skip box.
9. Click **Point 8** and **Point 4** from the Graphics window. Point (8) and Point (4) are displayed in the Instances to Skip box.

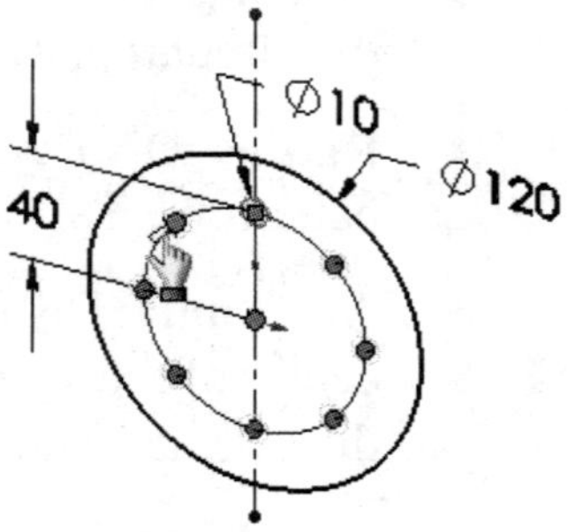


10. Click **OK** from the Circular Pattern PropertyManager. The sketched Circular Pattern is displayed in the Graphics window.
11. **Rebuild** the model. View the results.
12. **Close** the model.

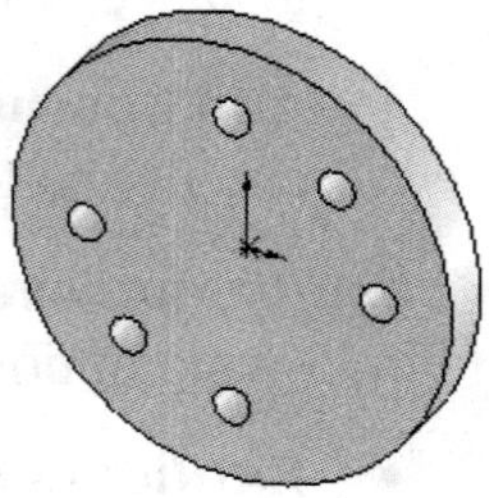

## SketchXpert Sketch tool

The SketchXpert Sketch tool provides the ability to resolve over-defined sketches. Color codes are displayed in the SolidWorks Graphics window to represent the sketch states. The SketchXpert tool uses the SketchXpert PropertyManager. The SketchXpert PropertyManager provides the following selections:

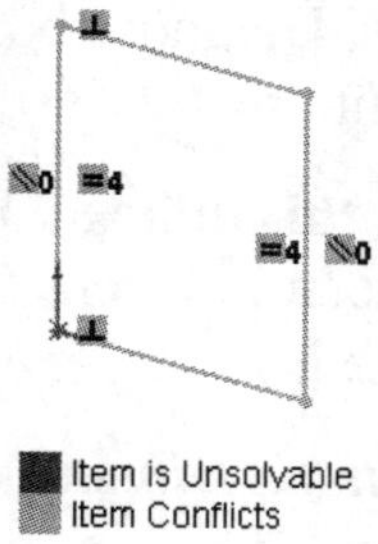


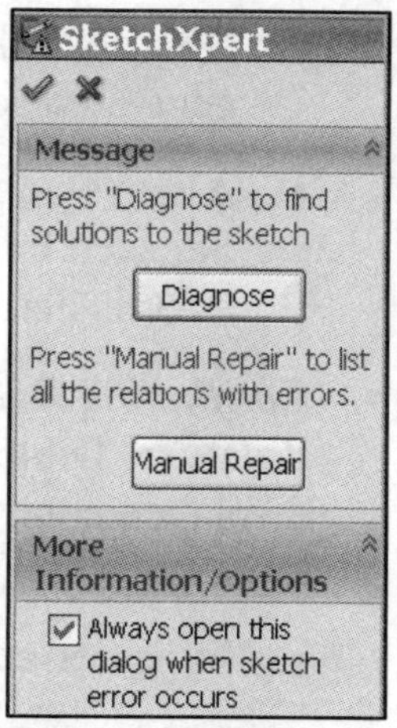


- ***Message***. The Message box provides access to the following selections:
  - **Diagnose**. The Diagnose button generates a list of solutions for the sketch. The generated solutions are displayed in the Results section of the SketchXpert PropertyManager.
  - **Manual Repair**. The Manual Repair button generates a list of all relations and dimensions in the sketch. The Manual Repair information is displayed in the Conflicting Relations/Dimensions section of the SketchXpert PropertyManager.

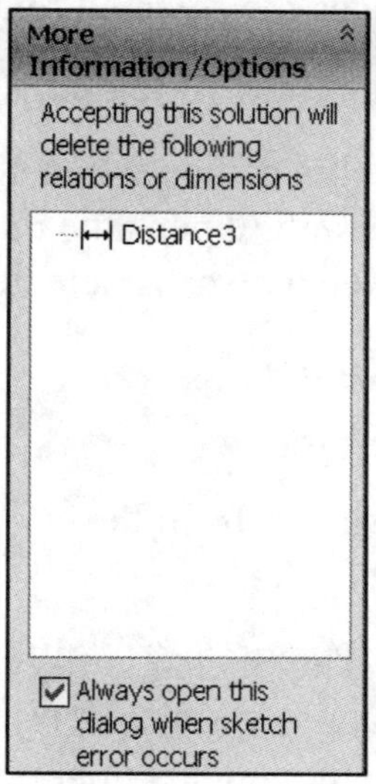


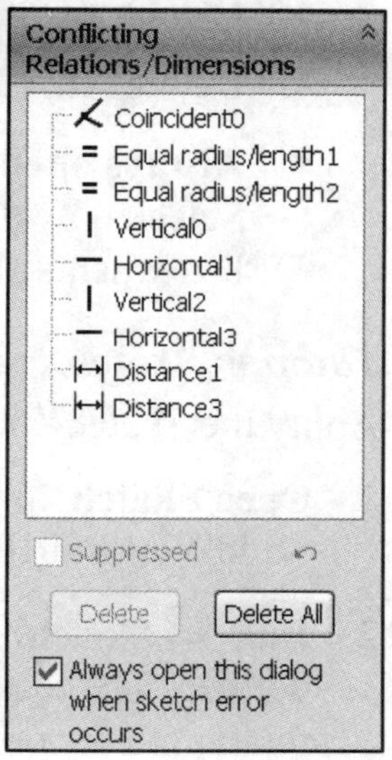


- ***More Information/Options***. Provides information on the relations or dimensions that would be deleted to solve the sketch.
  - **Always open this dialog when sketch error occurs**. Selected by default. Opens the dialog box when a sketch error is detected.
- ***Results***. The Results box provides the following selections:
  - **Left or Right arrows**. Provides the ability to cycle through the solutions. As you select a solution, the solution is highlighted in the Graphics window.
  - **Accept**. Applies the selected solution. Your sketch is no longer over-defined.

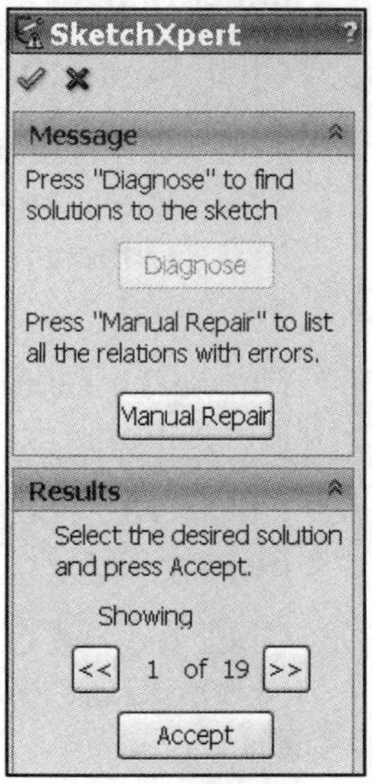

- ***More Information/Options***. The More Information/Options box provides the following selections:
  - **Diagnose**. The Diagnose box displays a list of the valid generated solutions.
  - **Always open this dialog when sketch error occurs**. Selected by default. Opens the dialog box when a sketch error is detected.

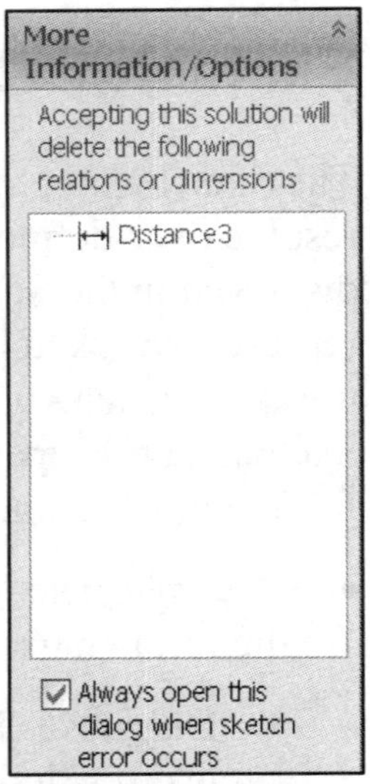


- ***Conflicting Relations/Dimensions***. The Conflicting Relations/Dimensions box provides the ability to select a displayed conflicting relation or dimension. The select item is highlight in the Graphics window. The options include:
  - **Suppressed**. Suppresses the relation or dimension.
  - **Delete**. Removes the selected relation or dimension.
  - **Delete All**. Removes all relations and dimensions.
  - **Always open this dialog when sketch error occurs**. Selected by default. Opens the dialog box when a sketch error is detected.

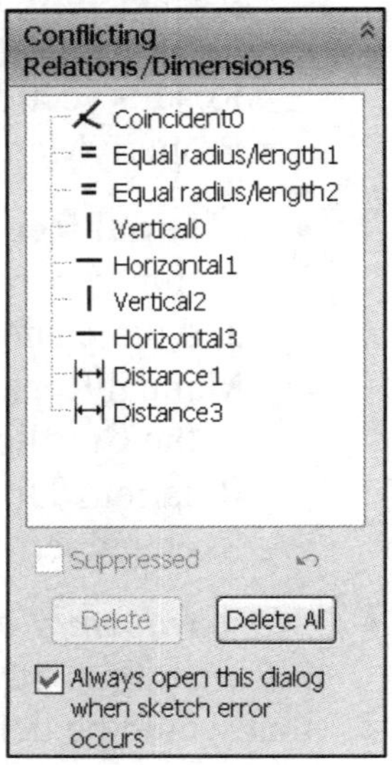


### *Tutorial: SketchXpert 5-1*

Apply the SketchXpert tool.

1. Open **SketchXpert 5-1** from the SolidWorks 2010 folder.
2. **Edit** Sketch1. The Sketch is fully defined. The rectangle has a midpoint relation to the origin, and an equal relation with all for sides. The top horizontal line is dimensioned.
3. Click **Smart Dimension**.
4. Add a dimension to the **left vertical line**. This makes the sketch over-defined. The Make Dimension Driven dialog box is displayed.

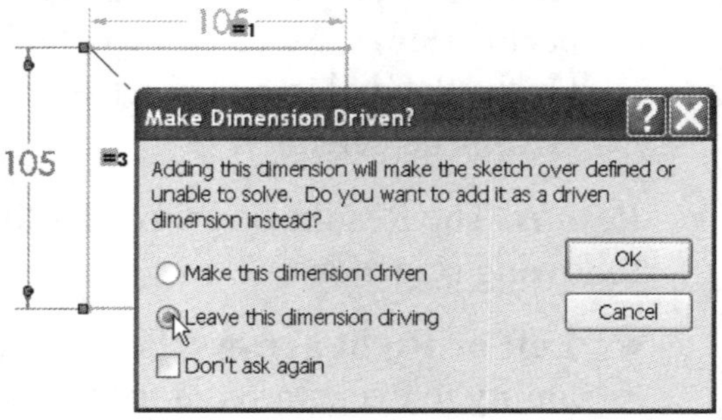


5. Check the **Leave this dimension driving** box option.
6. Click **OK**. The Over Defined warning is displayed.

7. Click the **red Over Defined** message. The SketchXpert PropertyManager is displayed.

Color codes are displayed in the Graphics window to represent the sketch states.

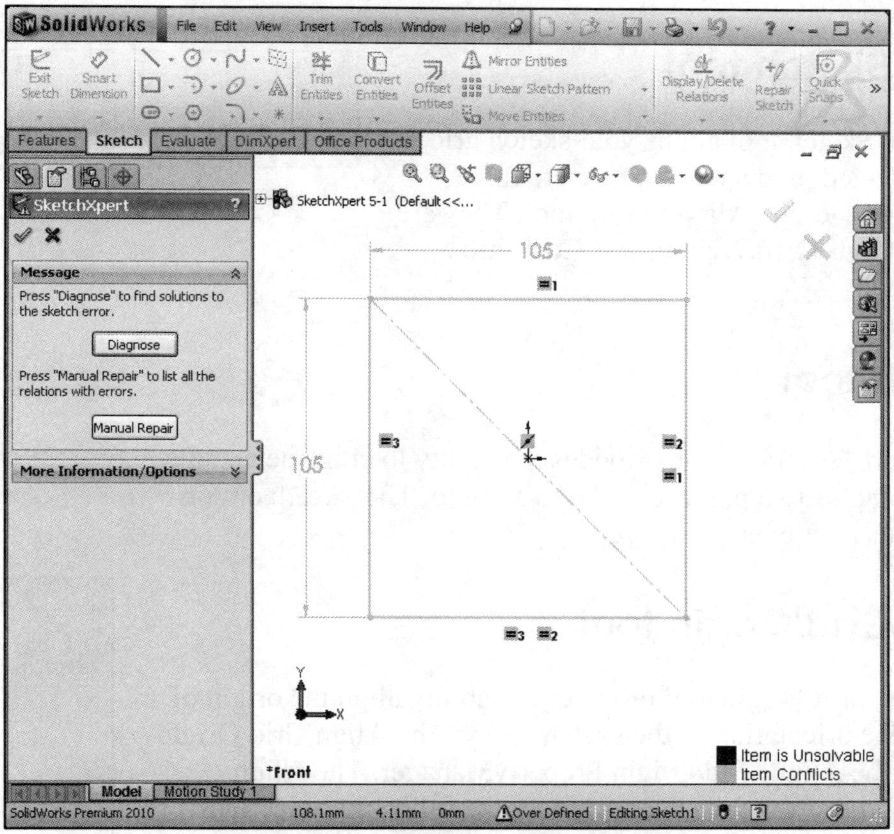


8. Click the **Diagnose** button. The Diagnose button generates a list of solutions for your sketch. You can either accept the first solution or click the Right arrow key in the Results box to view the section solution. The first solution is to delete the vertical dimension of 105mm.

9. View the second solution. Click the **Right arrow** key in the Results box. The second solution is displayed. The second solution is to delete the horizontal dimension of 105mm.

10. View the third solution. Click the **Right arrow** key in the Results box. The third solution is displayed. The third solution is to delete the Equal relation between the vertical and horizontal lines.

11. Accept the second solution. Click the **Left arrow** key to obtain the second solution.

12. Click the **Accept** button. The SketchXpert tool resolves the over-defined issue. A message is displayed.

13. Click **OK** from the SketchXpert PropertyManager.

14. **Rebuild** the model. View the results. **Close** the model.

## Align Sketch tool

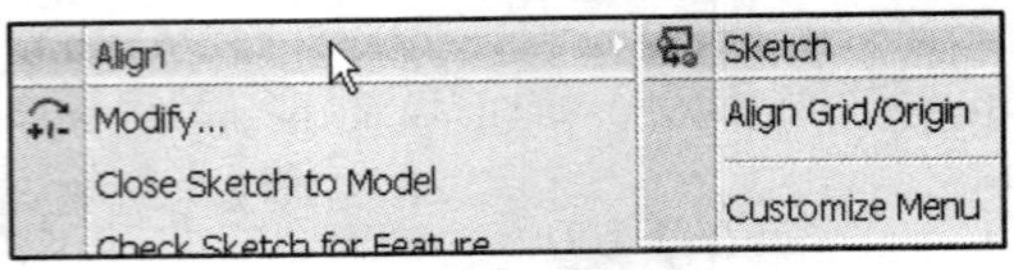


The Align Sketch tool aligns your sketch grid with a selected model edge. There are three selections under the Align Sketch tool. They are: **Sketch**, **Align Grid/Origin**, and **Customize Menu**.

## Sketch tool

The Sketch tool option provides the ability to either select one sketch point, or two points or lines to align to. The Sketch option does not use a PropertyManager.

## Align Grid/Origin tool

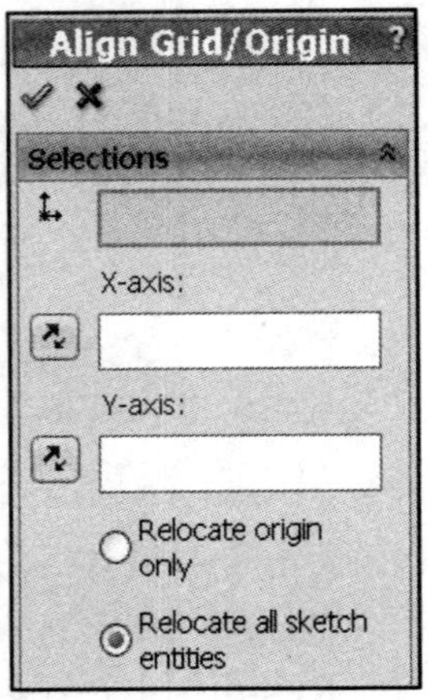


The Align Grid/Origin tool provides the ability align the origin of a block to the orientation of the sketch entity. The Align Grid/Origin tool uses the Align Grid/Origin PropertyManager. The Align Grid/Origin PropertyManager provides the following selections:

- ***Selections***: The Selections box provides the following options:
  - **Selections**. Displays the selected point or vertex from the Graphics window for the Sketch origin location.
  - **X-axis**. Displays the selected X-axis.
  - **Flip X-axis**. Flips the orientation of the origin by 180deg.
  - **Y-axis**. Displays the selected Y-axis.
  - **Flip Y-axis**. Flips the orientation of the origin by 180deg.
  - **Relocate origin only**. Moves the location of the origin.
  - **Relocate all sketch entities**. Selected by default. Moves the sketch's location based on relocating:

## Custom Menu tool

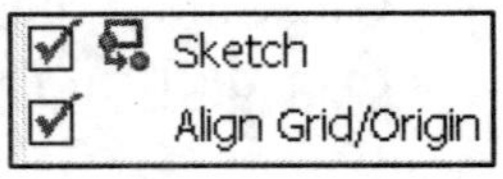


The Custom Menu tool provides the ability to create a custom menu for the Align Sketch tool. The Custom Menu tool does not use a PropertyManager.

***Tutorial: Align 5-1***

Create a block. Display the origin orientation location for a block.

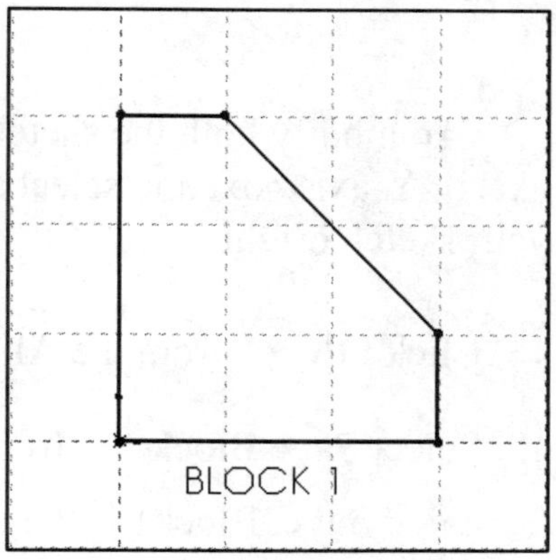


1. Create a **New** part in SolidWorks. Accept the default Part template.
2. Right-click **Front Plane** from the FeatureManager.
3. Click **Sketch** from the Context toolbar.
4. Sketch several **sketch entities** as illustrated with the Line Sketch tool.
5. Click **Insert ➢ Annotations ➢ Note**. The Note PropertyManager is displayed.
6. Click a **position** below the sketch entities.
7. Enter **BLOCK 1** for name. The Formatting toolbar is displayed to change font type and size.
8. Select **None** for Border style.

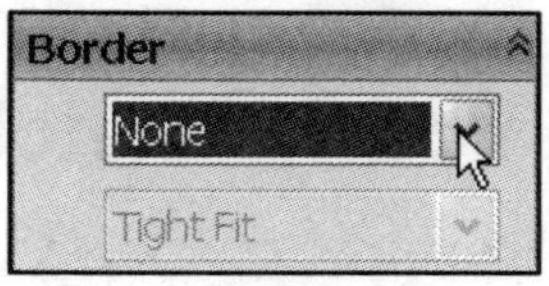


9. Click **OK** from the Note PropertyManager.
10. Box-Select the **sketch entities**. Line1 - Line5 are displayed in the Selected Entities box. Create a Block.
11. Click **Tools ➢ Blocks ➢ Make**. The Make Block PropertyManager is displayed.
12. Click **OK** from the Make Block PropertyManager. Block 1-1 is displayed in the FeatureManager.

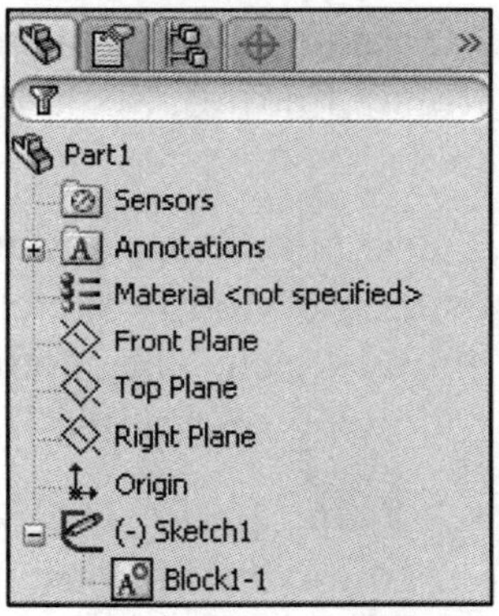


13. **Rebuild** the model.
14. Right-click **Block1-1** from the FeatureManager.
15. Click **Edit Block**. You are in Edit mode. The Blocks toolbar is displayed.

16. Click **Tools ➢ Sketch Tools ➢ Align ➢ Align Grid/Origin**. The Align Grid/Origin PropertyManager is displayed.

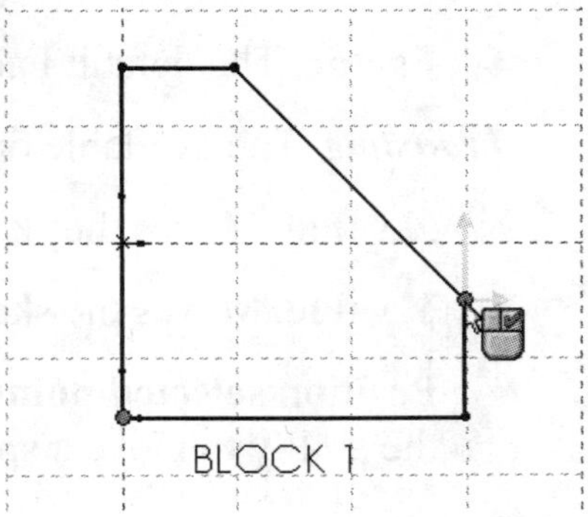


To modify the sketch origin, select a vertex or point.

17. Click the **right middle vertex** as illustrated for the sketch origin location. The point is displayed in the Selections box of the Align Grid/Origin PropertyManager.

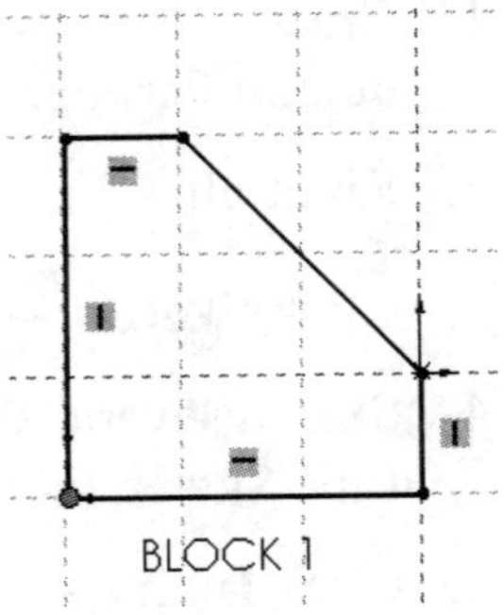


To modify both the sketch and orientation, click inside the X-axis or Y-axis box, and select a line to modify the orientation of your sketch origin

18. Click **OK** from the Align Grid/Origin PropertyManager.

19. Select **Save Block** from the Block toolbar.

20. Click **Save**. Block1 is the default name.

21. **Rebuild** the model. View the results.

22. **Close** the model.

## Modify Sketch tool

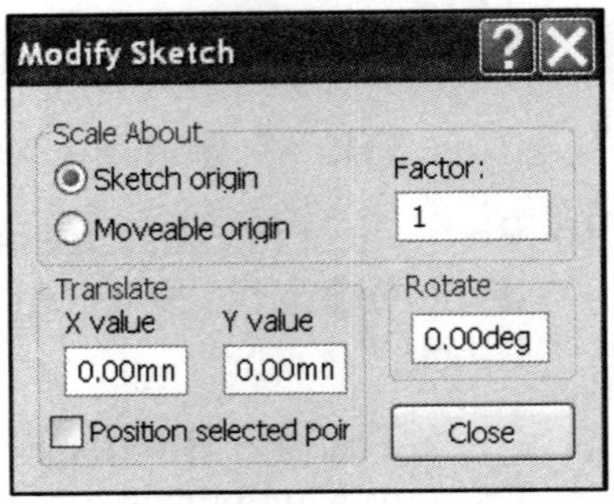


The Modify Sketch tool provides the ability to move, rotate, or scale the entire sketch. To move, rotate, scale or copy an individual sketch entity, use the Move Entities, Rotate Entities, Scale Entities or Copy Entities sketch tools.

The available options are dependent on whether you are using the Modify sketch tool to move, rotate or scale an entire sketch. The Modify Sketch dialog box provides the following selections:

- ***Scale About***. The Scale About section provides the following options:
  - **Sketch origin**. Selected by default. Applies a uniform scale about the origin of your sketch.
  - **Moveable origin**. Scales the sketch about the moveable origin.
  - **Factor**. The default Factor is 1. Enter the required factor scale.
- ***Translate***. The available options are:
  - **X value**. Moves the sketch geometry incrementally in the X direction.
  - **Y value**. Moves the sketch geometry incrementally in the Y direction.
  - **Position selected point**. The Position selected point option check box provides the ability to move a specified point of the sketch to a specific location.

- ***Rotate***. The available options are:
  - **Rotate**. Sets the value of the rotation.
- ***Close***. Closes the dialog box.

***Tutorial: Modify 5-1***

Move and scale a sketch using the Modify Sketch tool.

1. Open **Modify 5-1** from the SolidWorks 2010 folder.
2. **Edit** Sketch1. Click **Tools ➢ Sketch Tools ➢ Modify**. The Modify Sketch dialog box is displayed. Note: The sketch can't contain a relation.

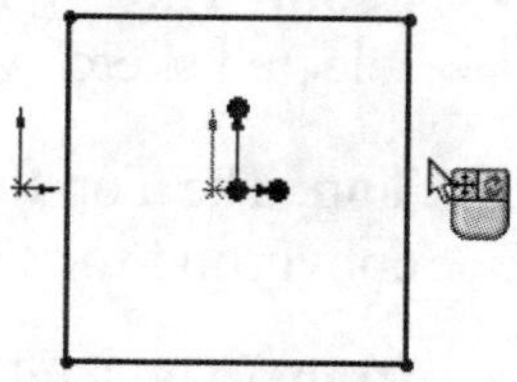

3. Click **outside** of the sketch in the Graphics window.
4. Drag the **mouse pointer** to the desired location. The Sketch moves with the mouse pointer.
5. Click **Close** from the Modify Sketch dialog box.
6. Click **Tools ➢ Sketch Tools ➢ Modify**. The Modify Sketch dialog box is displayed.
7. Right-click **outside** of the sketch. Rotate the **mouse pointer** to the desired location. The Sketch rotates with the mouse pointer.
8. Click **Close** from the Modify Sketch box. Scale the sketch using the Modify Sketch tool.
9. Click **Tools ➢ Sketch Tools ➢ Modify**. The Modify Sketch dialog box is displayed. Scale the sketch geometry.

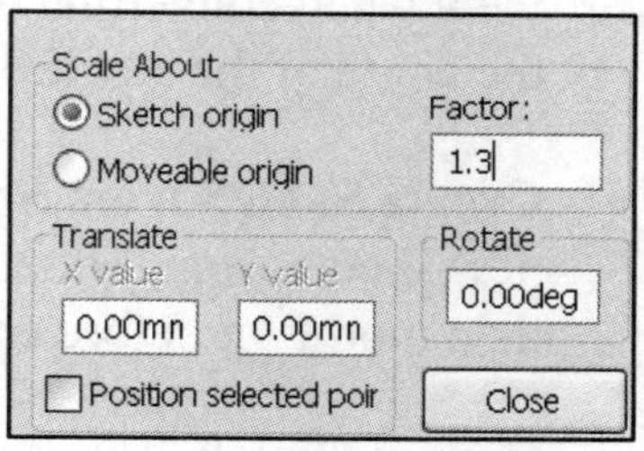


10. Check the **Sketch origin** box.
11. Enter **1.3** for Factor. The model increases in size.
12. Click **Close** from the Modify Sketch box.
13. **Rebuild** the model. **Close** the model.

The Modify Sketch tool translates your entire sketch geometry in relation to the model. This includes the sketch origin. The sketch geometry does not move relative to the origin of the sketch.

# 2D to 3D Sketch tool

The 2D to 3D Sketch tool provides the ability to convert your 2D sketches into 3D models. Your 2D sketch can be an imported drawing, or it can be a simple 2D sketch.

You can copy and paste the drawing from a drawing document, or you can import the drawing directly into a 2D sketch in a part document.

The 2D to 3D Sketch tool does not use a PropertyManager. The 2D to 3D toolbar provides the following selections:

- **Front**. The Front tool displays the selected sketch entities in a front view when converting to a 3D part.
- **Top**. The Top tool displays the selected sketch entities in a top view when converting to a 3D part.
- **Right**. The Right tool displays the selected sketch entities in a right view when converting to a 3D part.
- **Left**. The Left tool displays the selected sketch entities in a left view when converting to a 3D part.
- **Bottom**. The bottom tool displays the selected sketch entities in a bottom view when converting to a 3D part.
- **Back**. The Back tool displays the selected sketch entities in a back view when converting to a 3D part.
- **Auxiliary**. The Auxiliary tool displays the selected sketch entities in auxiliary view when converting to a 3D part. A line in another view must be selected to specify the angle of the auxiliary view.
- **Create Sketch from Selections**. The Create Sketch from Selections tool creates a new sketch from the selected sketch entities. Example: You can extract a sketch and then modify it before creating a feature.
- **Repair Sketch**. The Repair Sketch tool repairs the errors in your sketch. Example: Typical errors can be overlapping geometry, small segments which are collected into a single entity, or small gaps.
- **Align Sketch**. The Align Sketch tool provides the ability to select an edge in one view and to align to the edge selected in a second view. The order of selection is very important.
- **Extrude**. The Extrude tool extrudes a feature from the selected sketch entities. You do not have to select a complete sketch.
- **Cut**. The Cut tool cuts a feature from the selected sketch entities. You do not have to select a complete sketch.

***Tutorial: 2D to 3D Sketch tool 5-1***

Import a part and use the 2D to 3D tool.

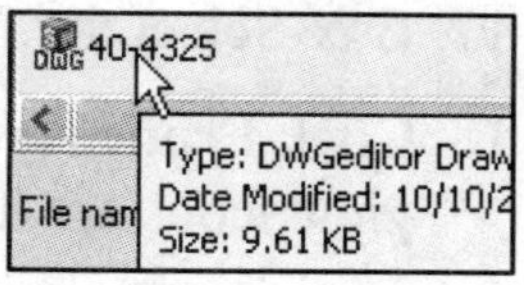


1. Open the **40-4325.DWG** drawing from the SolidWorks 2010 folder.
2. Check the **Import to a new part** check box from the DXF/DWG Import dialog box.
3. Click **Next>**.
4. Check the **White background** check box.
5. Click **Next>**.
6. Select **Millimeters** for Units for the Imported data.
7. Check the **to a 2D sketch** check box.
8. Click **Finish**.
9. Click **OK**.

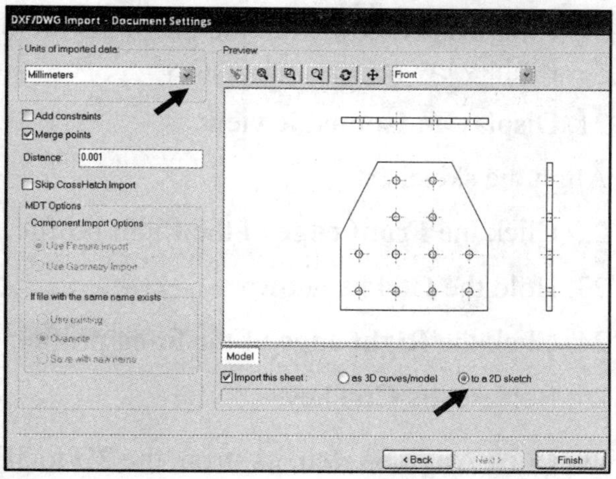


The current sketch displays the Top, Front and Right views. SolidWorks displays the part and the 2D to 3D toolbar in the Graphics window.

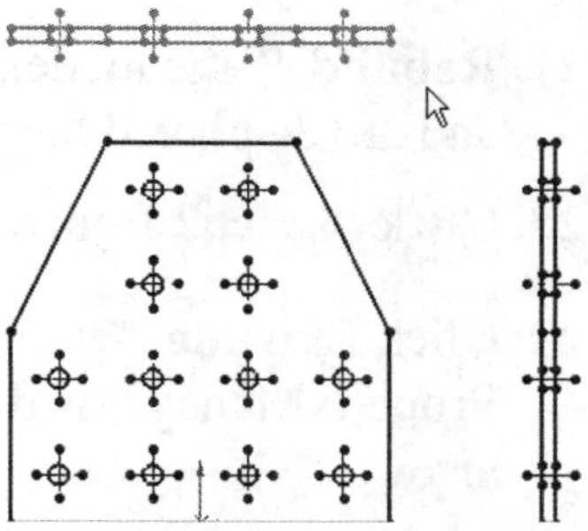

The Front view and Right view are required to extrude the sketch.

Delete the top view.

10. Box-Select the **Top view** of Sketch1. The Properties PropertyManager is displayed.
11. Press the **Delete** key.

Set the Front view.

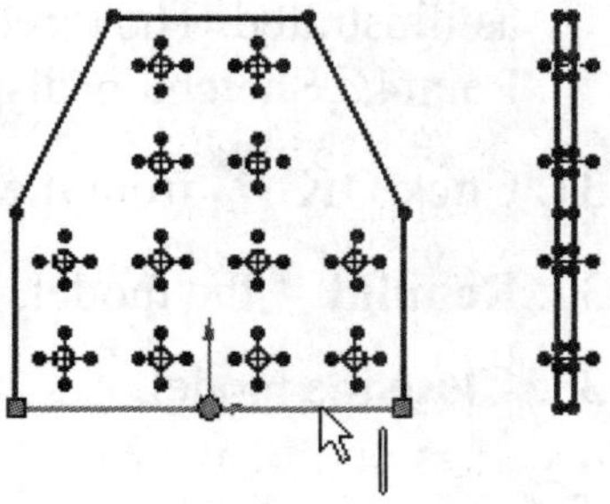

12. Insert a Midpoint relation between the **origin** and the **bottom horizontal line**.
13. Click **OK** from the Properties PropertyManager.
14. Box-Select the **Front profile**.
15. Click **Fix** from the Add Relations box.

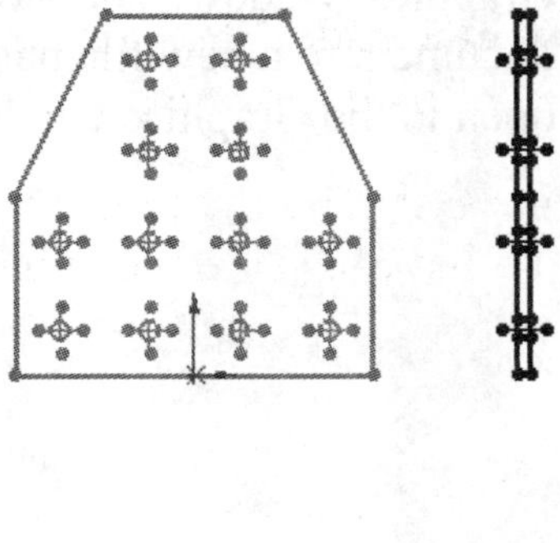

16. Click **OK** ✔ from the Properties PropertyManager.

17. Box-Select the **Front profile**.

18. Click **Front** view from the 2D to 3D toolbar. The view icons are highlight in the 2D to 3D toolbar.

19. Box-Select the **Right profile**.

20. Click **Right** view from the 2D to 3D toolbar. The Right view moves and rotates.

21. Display an **Isometric** view.

Align the sketches.

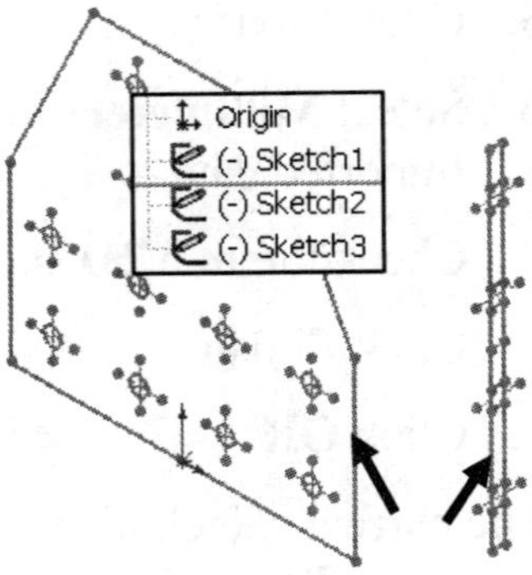


22. Click the **Front edge** of the Right profile.

23. Hold the **Ctrl** key down.

24. Click the **Right edge** of the Front profile.

25. Release the **Ctrl** key.

26. Click **Align Sketch** from the 2D to 3D toolbar. The two profiles are aligned.

27. **Rebuild** the model. Sketch2 and Sketch3 are created and are displayed in the FeatureManager.

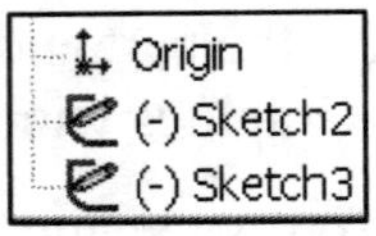


28. Click **Sketch2** from the FeatureManager.

29. Click **Extrude** from the 2D to 3D toolbar. The PropertyManager is displayed. View the extrude direction arrow.

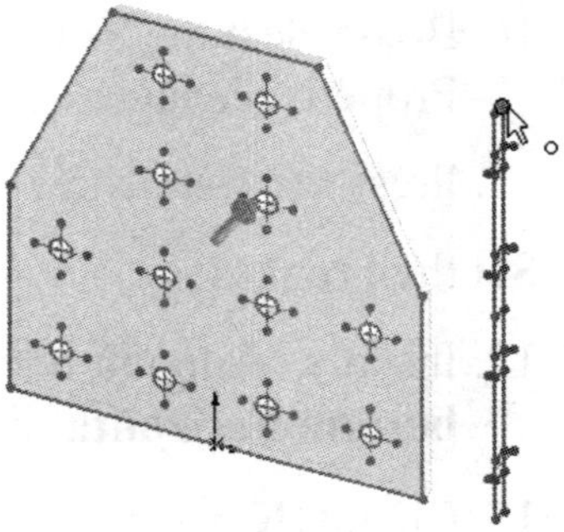

30. Click the **top back point** on the Right profile of Sketch3 as illustrated. The direction arrow points into the screen. Point4@Shetch3 is displayed in the Vertex box.

31. Click **OK** ✔ from the Extrude PropertyManager.

32. **Rebuild** the model. View the results.

33. **Close** the model.

The Save As option displays the new part name in the Graphics window. The Save as copy option copies the current document to a new file name. The current document remains open in the Graphics window.

## Creates Sketch from Selections Sketch tool

The Create Sketch from Selections tool provides the ability to only extract the elements of your sketch, usually in an imported drawing that you need to create a feature. Example: Extract a sketch, and then modify it before creating a feature. The Create Sketch from Selections is a tool on the 2D to 3D toolbar. The Create Sketch from Selections does not use a PropertyManager.

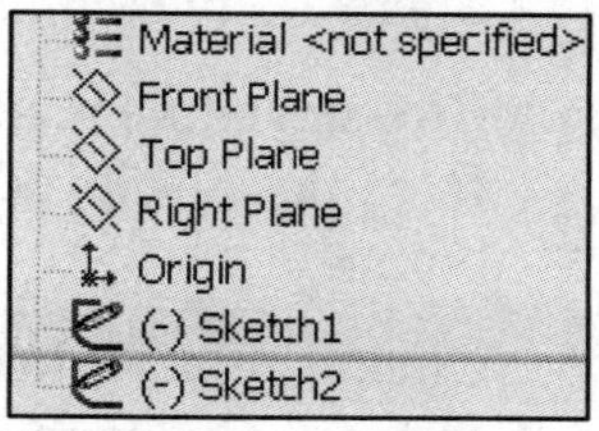


### *Tutorial: Create Sketch from Selections 5-1*

1. Open **Create Sketch from Selections 5-1** from the SolidWorks 2010 folder.
2. **Edit** Sketch1. Box-Select the **top view**. The Properties PropertyManager is displayed with the selected sketch entities. Click **Tools ➢ Sketch Tools ➢ Create Sketch from Selections**.
3. Click **OK** from the Properties PropertyManager. A new sketch is displayed in the FeatureManager design tree, Sketch2.
4. **Exit** the Sketch. **Close** the model.

## Repair Sketch tool

The Repair Sketch tool provides the ability to repair errors in your sketch. Example: Some tools; Extrude and Cut repair sketches automatically when the tool detects an error which it can fix. You can also repair sketches manually. The Repair Sketch tool is useful for sketches created by importing DXF/DWG files. The Repair Sketch is a tool located on the 2D to 3D toolbar. The Repair Sketch tool does not use a PropertyManager. The Repair Sketch proceeds automatically as follows:

- Delete zero line length and arc segments. A zero line length is a segment that is less than ±1.0e-8 meters.
- Merges Coincident lines which are separated by less than ±1.0e-8 meters into a single line.
- Merges co-linear lines which overlap.
- Collect small segments in co-linear lines with no gaps that are greater than ±1.0e-8 meters.
- Eliminates gaps of less than ±1.0e-8 meters in co-linear lines.

***Tutorial: Repair Sketch 5-1***

Repair a sketch automatically with the Repair Sketch tool.

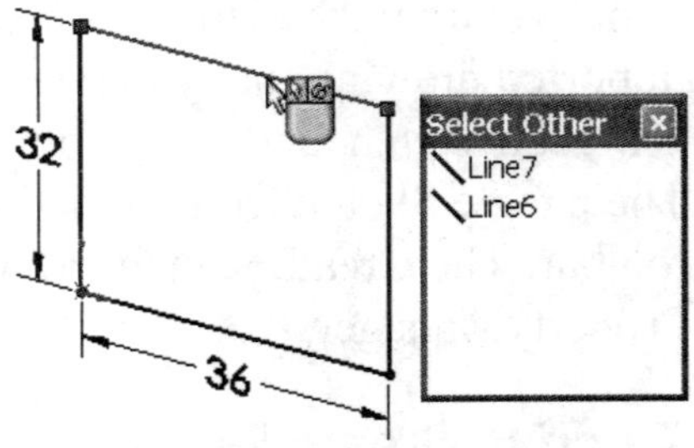


1. Open **Repair Sketch 5-1** from the SolidWorks 2010 folder.
2. **Edit** Sketch1 from the FeatureManager.
3. Click the **top horizontal line**. The Line Properties PropertyManager is displayed.
4. Click **Select Other** from the shortcut toolbar. There are two coincident lines selected.
5. **Box-select** the rectangular sketch. There are five lines displayed in the Selected Entities box.

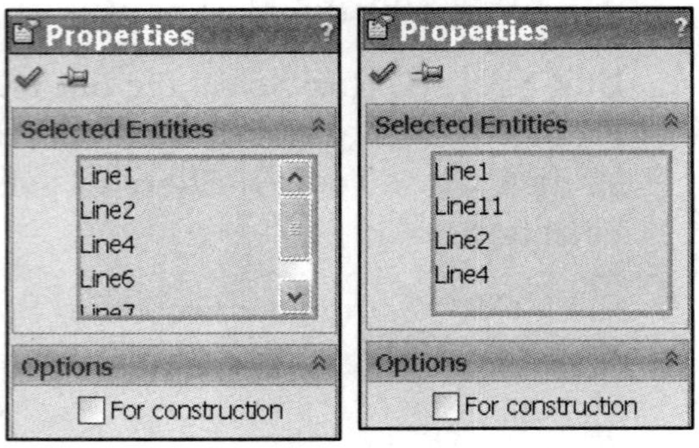


6. Click **Tools ➤ Sketch Tools ➤ Repair Sketch**. The two Coincident lines merge and the sketch can be extruded.
7. **Box-select** the rectangular sketch. Four lines displayed in the Selected Entities box.
8. Click **OK** from the Properties PropertyManager. Sketch1 does not have an open contour.
9. **Rebuild** the model. View the results.
10. **Close** the model.

## Sketch Picture Sketch tool

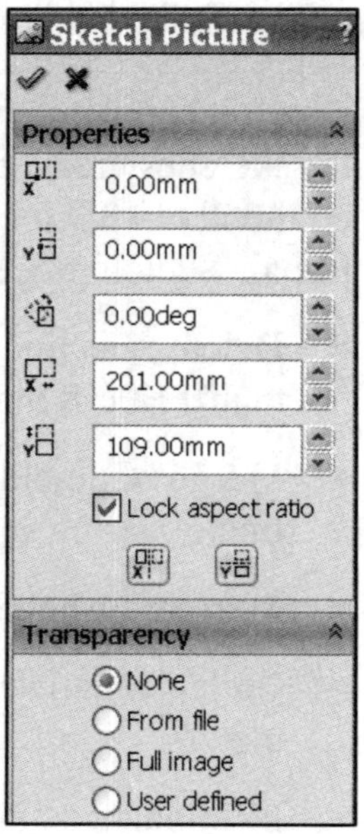


The Sketch Picture Sketch tool provides the ability to insert a picture in the following formats: (.bmp, .gif, .jpg, .jpeg, .tif and .wmf) on your Sketch plane. Use picture as an underlay for creating 2D sketches. The Sketch Picture tool uses the Sketch Picture PropertyManager. The Sketch Picture PropertyManager provides the following selections:

- ***Properties***. The Properties box provides the following options:
  - **Origin X Position**. Displays the selected X coordinate value for the origin of your picture.
  - **Origin Y Position**. Displays the selected Y coordinate value for the origin of your picture.

  - **Angle**. Displays the selected angle value in degrees. A positive angle rotates your picture counterclockwise.
  - **Width**. Displays the selected width value for the picture. If the Lock aspect ratio option check box is selected, the height adjusts automatically.
  - **Height**. Displays the selected height value for the picture height. If the Lock Aspect Ratio option is selected, the width adjusts automatically.
  - **Lock aspect ratio**. Selected by default. Keeps a fixed width and height aspect ratio.
  - **Flip Horizontally**. Flips your picture horizontally within its borders.
  - **Flip Vertically**. Flips your picture vertically within its borders.
- ***Transparency***. The Transparency box provides the following options:
  - **None**. Selected by default. Does not use any transparency attributes.
  - **From file**. Keeps the transparency attributes which exist presently in the file.
  - **Full image**. Sets the whole image transparent.

Slide the slider to adjust the degree of transparency when you select the Full image option.

  - **User defined**. Provides the ability to select a color from the image, define a tolerance level for that color, and to apply a transparency level to the image.

The picture is inserted with its (0, 0) coordinate at the sketch origin, an initial size of 1 pixel per 1 mm, and locked aspect ratio.

The picture is embedded in the document (not linked). If you change the original image, the sketch picture does not update. If you sketch on top of your picture, there is no snap to picture, inferencing, or autotracing capability. The sketch does not update if the image is moved, or deleted and replaced.

The picture is hidden if you hide your sketch. Pictures can be inserted into assemblies when editing a part In-Context. Pictures cannot be inserted into assembly sketches.

***Tutorial: Sketch Picture 5-1***

Insert a picture into an existing sketch.

1. Open **Sketch Picture 5-1** from the SolidWorks 2010 folder.
2. **Edit** Sketch2 from the FeatureManager.

3. Click **Tools** ➢ **Sketch Tools** ➢ **Sketch Picture**.
4. **Browse** to locate a picture file in the SolidWorks 2010 folder. Double-click the **logo** picture file. The SolidWorks logo is displayed in the Graphics window.

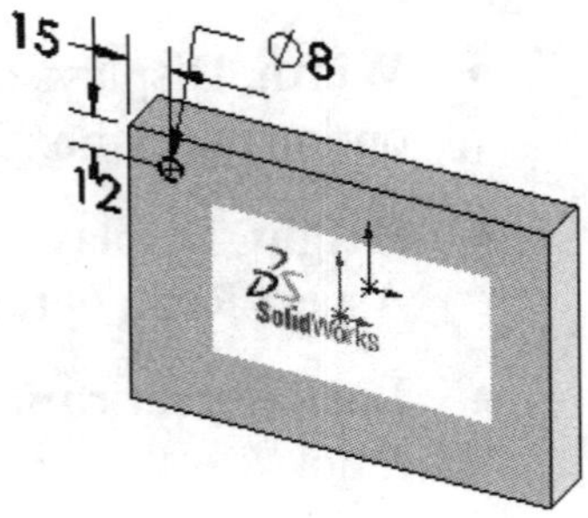


5. Set the **properties** from the Sketch Picture PropertyManager or use the picture handles in the Graphics window to move and size the logo on the model. Click **OK** from the Sketch Picture PropertyManager.
6. **Rebuild** the model.
7. Right-click **Sketch2** from the FeatureManager.
8. Click **Show**. View the results.
9. **Close** the model.

# Geometric Relations 2D Sketches

Relations between sketch entities and model geometry, in either 2D or 3D sketches, are an important means of building in design intent. Sketch relations are geometric constraints between sketch entities or between a sketch entity and a plane, axis, edge, or vertex. Relations can be added automatically or manually.

To select or clear the Automatic relations option; click **Tools** ➢ **Sketch Settings** ➢ **Automatic Relations** or click **Options** ➢ **System Option** ➢ **Relations/Snaps**, and click **Automatic relations**.

## Automatic Relations

As you sketch, allow the SolidWorks application to automatically add relations. Automatic relations rely on: Inferencing, Point display, and Sketch Snaps and Quick Snaps. When the Automatic relations tool is activated, the following relations can be added:

- *Horizontal*
  - Entities to select: One or more lines or two or more points.
  - Resulting Relations: The lines become horizontal as defined by the current sketch. Points are aligned horizontally.
- *Coincident*
  - Entities to select: A point and a line, arc or ellipse.
  - Resulting Relations: The point lies on the line, arc or ellipse.

- *Perpendicular*
    - Entities to select: Two lines.
    - Resulting Relations: The two items are perpendicular to each other.
- *Vertical*
    - Entities to select: One or more lines or two or more points.
    - Resulting Relations: The lines become vertical as defined by the current sketch. Points are aligned vertically.
- *Midpoint*
    - Entities to select: Two lines or a point and a line.
    - Resulting Relation: The point remains at the midpoint of the line.
- *Tangent*
    - Entities to select: An arc, ellipse, or spline and a line or arc.
    - Resulting Relations: The two items remain tangent.

## Manual Relations

After you sketch, manually add any required relations to fully define the sketch, or edit existing relations using the Display/Delete Relations tool.

The Properties PropertyManager is displayed when you select multiple sketch entities in the Graphics window. You can manually create geometric relations between sketch entities, or between sketch entities and planes, axes, edges or vertices.

The following are a few of the common 2D Sketch relations and how to create them:

- *Coincident*
    - Entities to select: A point and a line, arc or ellipse.
    - Resulting Relations: The point lies on the line, arc or ellipse.

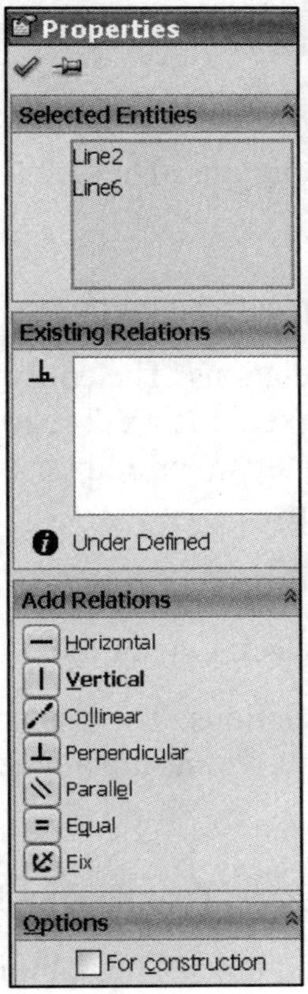


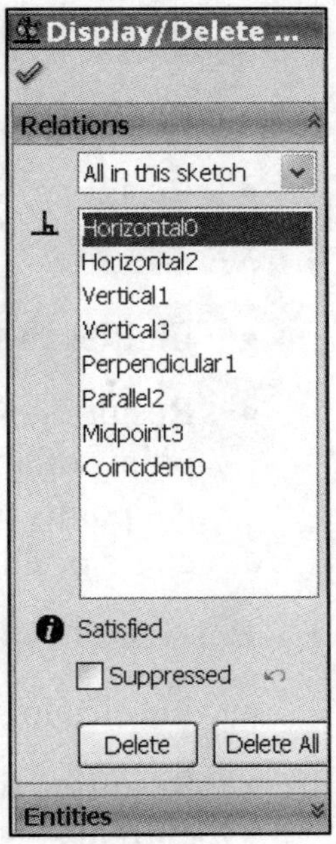

- *Collinear*
  - Entities to select: Two or more lines.
  - Resulting Relations: The items lie on the same infinite line.

When you create a relation to a line, the relation is to the infinite line, not just the sketched line segment or the physical edge. As a result, some items may not touch when you expect them to.

- *Concentric*
  - Entities to select: Two or more arcs, or a point and an arc.
  - Resulting Relations: The arcs share the same centerpoint.
- *Coradial*
  - Entities to select: Two or more arcs.
  - Resulting Relations: The items share the same centerpoint and radius.

When you create a relation to an arc segment or elliptical segment, the relation is actually to the full circle or ellipse.

- *Equal.*
  - Entities to select: Two or more lines or two or more arcs.
  - Resulting Relations: The line lengths or radii remain equal.
- *Fix*
  - Entities to select: An entity.
  - Resulting Relations: The entity's size and location are fixed. However, the end points of a fixed line are free to move along the infinite line the underlies it. The endpoints of an arc or elliptical segment are free to move along the underlying full circle or ellipse.
- *Horizontal or Vertical*
  - Entities to select: One or more lines or two or more points.
  - Resulting Relations: The lines become horizontal or vertical as defined by the current sketch. Points are aligned horizontally or vertically.
- *Intersection*
  - Entities to select: Two lines and one point.
  - Resulting Relations: The point remains at the intersection of the lines.

- *Merge Points*
  - Entities to select: Two sketch points or endpoints.
  - Resulting Relations: The two points are merged into a single point.
- *Midpoint*
  - Entities to select: Two lines or a point and a line.
  - Resulting Relations: The point remains at the midpoint of the line.
- *Parallel*
  - Entities to select: Two or more lines in a 2D sketch. A line and a plane in a 3D sketch. A line and a planar face in a 3D sketch.
  - Resulting relations: The items are parallel to each other in the 2D sketch. The line is parallel to the selected plane in the 3D sketch.

If you create a relation to an item that does not lie on the sketch plane, the resulting relation applies to the projection of that item as it is displayed on the Sketch plane.

- *Perpendicular*
  - Entities to select: Two lines.
  - Resulting Relations: The two items are perpendicular to each other.
- *Pierce*
  - Entities to select: A sketch point and an axis, edge, line or spline.
  - Resulting Relations: The sketch point is coincident to where the axis, edge, or curve pierces the sketch plane. The pierce relation is used in Sweeps with Guide Curves.
- *Symmetric*
  - Entities to select: A centerline and two points, lines, arcs or ellipses.
  - Resulting Relations: The items remain equidistant from the centerline, on a line perpendicular to the centerline.
- *Tangent*
  - Entities to select: An arc, ellipse, or spline, and a line or arc.
  - Resulting Relations: The two items remain tangent.

# Geometric Relations in 3D Sketches

Many relations available in 2D sketches are available in 3D sketches. Additional sketch relations are supported with 3D sketching include:

- Perpendicular relations between a line through a point on a surface.
- Symmetric relations about a line between 3D sketches created on the same plane.
- Midpoint relations.
- Equal relations.
- Relations between arcs such as concentric, tangent, or equal.
- Normal to applied between a line and a plane, or between two points and a plane.
- Relations between 3D sketch entities created on one sketch plane, and 3D entities created on other sketch planes.

## 3D Sketch Relations

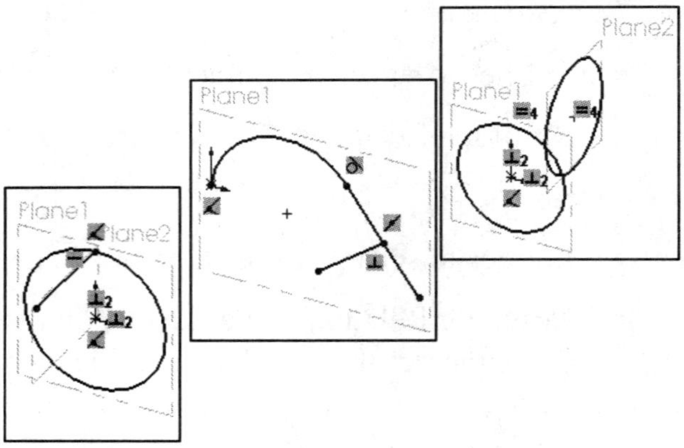


- Example 1: Equal arcs created on perpendicular planes.
- Example 2: An Arc with a tangent line and perpendicular line to the midpoint between the sketch entities.
- Example 3: An Arc with a perpendicular line created on the perpendicular planes.

The following are a few of the common 3D Sketch relations and how to create them:

- *AlongZ*
  - Entities to select: A line and a plane in a 3D sketch. A line and a planar face in a 3D sketch.
  - Resulting Relations: The line is normal to the face of the selected plane.

Relations to the global axes are called AlongX, AlongY and AlongZ. Relations that are local to a plane are called Horizontal, Vertical and Normal.

- *ParallelYZ*
  - Entities to select: A line and a plane in a 3D sketch. A line and a planar face in a 3D sketch.
  - Resulting relations: The line is parallel to the YZ plane with respect to the selected plane.
- *ParallelZX*
  - Entities to select: A line and a plane in a 3D Sketch. A line and a planar face in a 3D sketch.
  - Resulting relations: The line is parallel to the ZX plane with respect to the selected plane.
- *Parallel*
  - Entities to select: A line and a plane in a 3D sketch. A line and a planar face in a 3D sketch.
  - Resulting relations: The line is parallel to the selected plane in the 3D sketch.

# Dimension/Relations toolbar

The Dimensions/Relations toolbar, **Tools ➢ Dimensions** menu, **Tools ➢ Relations** menu, and the Consolidated Sketch toolbar provide the required tools to dimension and to add and delete Geometric relations.

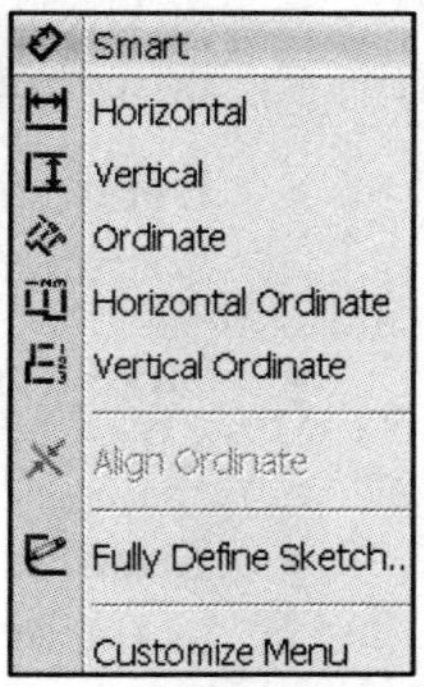


Not all toolbar buttons have corresponding menu items; conversely, not all menu items have corresponding toolbar buttons.

The book focuses on providing the most common tools and menu options. Not all dimension/relations tools are addressed.

To modify the dimension font size, click **Options, Document Properties, Detailing,** and check the **Always display text at the same size** box.

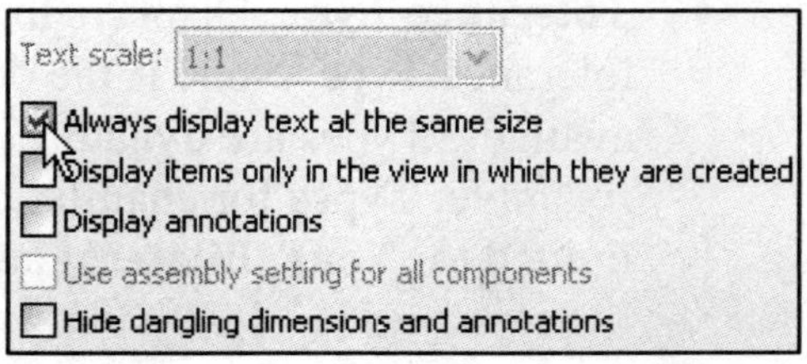

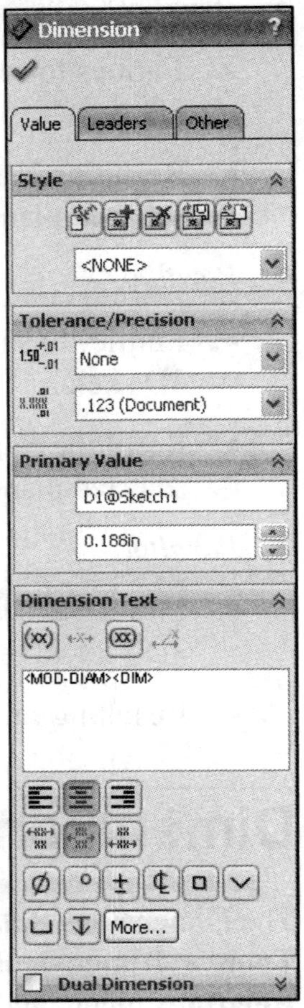


# Smart Dimension tool

The Smart Dimension tool uses the Dimension PropertyManager. The Dimension PropertyManager provides the ability to either select the **Value**, **Leaders** or **Other** tab. Each tab provides a separate menu. Note: The Value tab is selected by default.

## Smart Dimension tool: Value tab

The Value tab provides the following selections:

- ***Style***. The Style box provides the ability to define your favorite styles and various annotations, (Notes, Geometric Tolerance Symbols, Surface Finish Symbols, and Weld Symbols). The available options are:
  - **Apply the default attributes to selected dimensions**. Resets the selected dimension or dimensions to the document defaults.
  - **Add or Update a Style**. None is the default. Opens the Add or Updates dialog box. Review your styles using the drop-down menu.
  - **Delete a Style**. Delete the selected style from your document.
  - **Save a Style**. Opens the Save As dialog box with Style (.sldfvt) as the default file type. Save the existing style.
  - **Load Style**. Opens the Open dialog box with style (.sldfvt) as the active file type. Note: Use the Ctrl key or the Shift key to select multiple files.
  - **Set a current Style**. NONE is the default. Set a current style from the drop-down menu.
- ***Tolerance/Precision***. The Tolerance/Precision box provides the following selections:
  - **Tolerance Type**. Displays the selected tolerance Type. None is the default type. The available Types are dynamic in the list. Example: Types for chamfer dimensions are limited to: **None**, **Bilateral** and **Symmetric**.

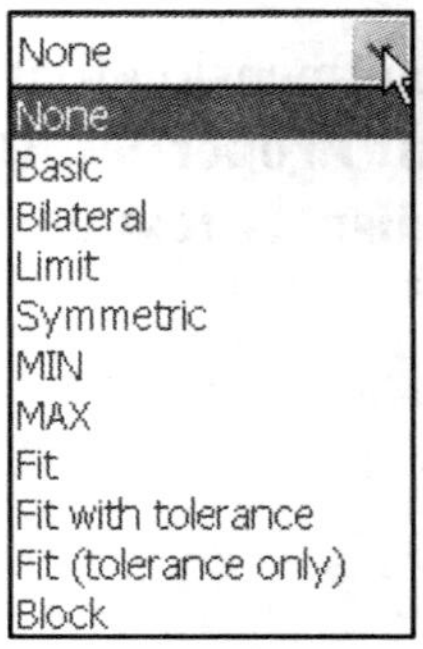


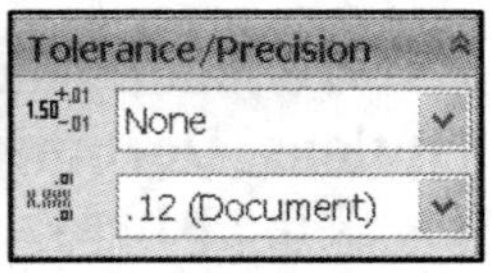

- **Maximum Variation**. Set the maximum variation value.
- **Minimum Variation**. Set the minimum variation value.
- **Show Parentheses**. Only available for Bilateral, Symmetric, and Fit with tolerance types. Displays parentheses when values are set for the Max and Min Variation.
- **Primary Unit Precision**. .12(Document) is the default. Displays the selected number of digits after the decimal point for primary unit precision.

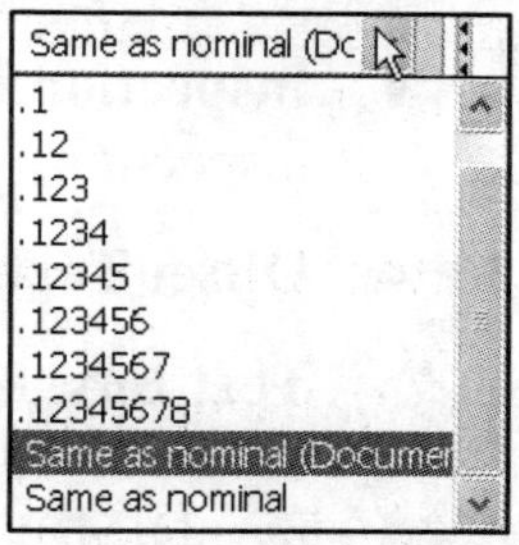


- **Tolerance Precision**. Same as nominal (Document) is the default. Displays the selected the number of digits after the decimal point for tolerance precision.
- **Classification**. Only available if you select Fit, Fit with tolerance, or Fit (tolerance only) types. This option provides the following selections: **User Defined**, **Clearance**, **Transitional** and **Press**. User Defined is selected by default.

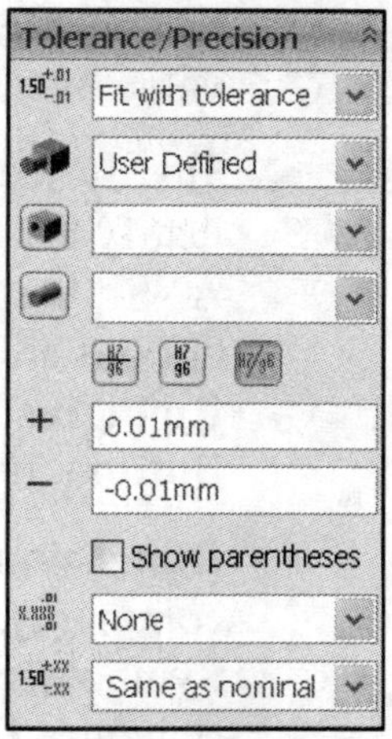


- **Hole Fit**. Only available if you select Fit, or Fit with tolerance, or Fit (tolerance only) types. Displays the selected Hole fit type from the drop-down menu.
- **Shaft Fit**. Only available if you select Fit, or Fit with tolerance or Fit (tolerance only) types. Displays the selected Shaft Fit type from the drop-down menu.
- **Stacked with line display**. Only available if you select Fit, or Fit with tolerance or Fit (tolerance only) types.
- **Stacked without line display**. Only available if you select Fit, or Fit with tolerance or Fit (tolerance only) types.
- **Linear display**. Only available if you select Fit, or Fit with tolerance or Fit (tolerance only) types.

A second Tolerance/Precision section is available for Chamfer Dimensions.

- ***Primary Value***. The Primary Value box provides the following two selections:
  - **Sketch name**. Displays the dimension name of the sketch.
  - **Sketch entity dimension**. Displays the dimension of the selected entity in the Graphics window.

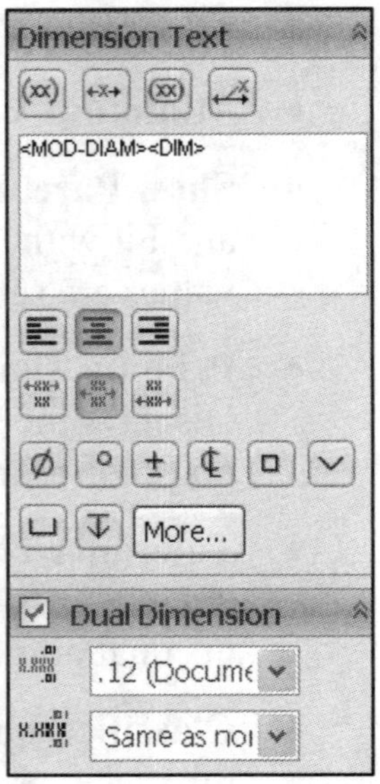


- ***Dimension Text***. The Dimension Text box provides the following selections:
  - **Add Parenthesis**. Displays the dimension with parentheses.
  - **Center Dimension**. Centers the displayed dimension.
  - **Inspection Dimension**. Displays the dimension for inspection.
  - **Offset Text**. Displays an offset text from the dimension.
  - **Text Box**. Provides the ability for the dimension text to be automatically displayed in the center text box, represented by <DIM>. Place the mouse pointer anywhere in the text box to insert text. If you delete <DIM>, you can reinsert the value by clicking **Add Value**.
  - **Justify section**. The Justify section provides the ability to justify the text horizontally and for some standards, such as ANSI, you can justify the leader vertically. The available options are: **Horizontal – Left Justify**, **Center Justify**, **Right Justify**, **Vertical – Top Justify**, **Middle Justify** and **Bottom Justify**.
  - **Dimension text symbols**. SolidWorks displays eight commonly used symbols and a More button to access the Symbol Library. The eight displayed symbols from left to right are: **Diameter**, **Degree**, **Plus/Minus**, **Centerline**, **Square**, **Countersink**, **Counterbore** and **Depth/Deep**.
  - ***Dual Dimension***. The Dual Dimension box provides the ability to display dual dimensions for the present model.

## Smart Dimension tool: Leaders tab

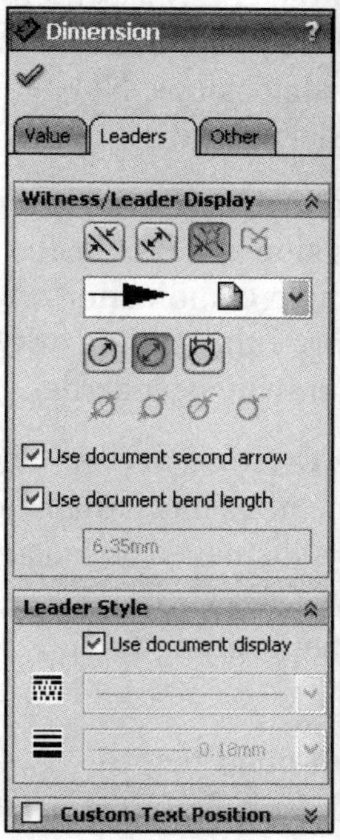

The Leaders tab provides the following selections: Note: Geometry type dependent (diameter, length, arc, etc.).

- ***Witness/Leader Display***. The Witness/Leader Display box provides the ability to display the selected type of arrows and leaders available, which depends on the type of dimension selected. There are three selections available for Witness/Leader placement. They are: **Outside**, **Inside** and **Smart**. Smart is selected by default.

Smart specifies that arrows are displayed automatically outside of extension lines if the space is too small to accommodate the dimension text and the arrowheads.

- **Style**. Geometry type dependent. The Style drop-down menu provides the ability to select separate styles for each arrow when there are two arrows for a dimension. This feature supports the JIS dimensioning standard.

  Two lists are displayed in the Dimension PropertyManager only when separate styles are specified by the dimensioning standard.

  - **Radius**. Specifies that the dimension on an arc or circle displays the radius.
  - **Diameter**. Specifies that the dimension on an arc or circle displays the diameter.
  - **Linear**. Specifies the display of a diameter dimension as a linear dimension (not radial).
  - **Foreshortened**. Specifies that the radius dimension line is foreshortened, broken. This is helpful when the centerpoint of a radius is outside of the drawing or interferes with another drawing view.

- **Solid Leader** . Specifies the display of a solid line across the circle for radial dimensions. Not available with ANSI standard.
- **Dimension to inside of arc**. Specifies that the dimension arrow is inside the arc. Use this option in combination with the **Arrows** setting, either **Inside** or **Outside** to meet your drawing standards.

- **Use document second arrow**. Checked by default. Specifies that a diameter dimension, not displayed as linear with outside arrows follows the document default setting for a second arrow.
- **Use document bend length**. Checked by default. Uses the value for Bent leader length in the Options, Document Properties, Dimensions section.

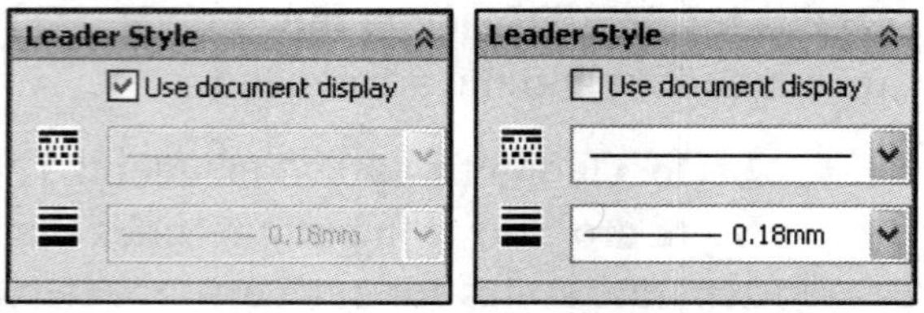


- ***Leader Style***. Provides the ability use the default document style set in Options or to select a custom style for the drop-down menus.
- ***Custom Text Position***. Provides the ability to locate and select leader type. The available selections are: **Solid leader**, **aligned text**, **Broken leader**, **horizontal text**, **Broken leader** and **aligned text**.

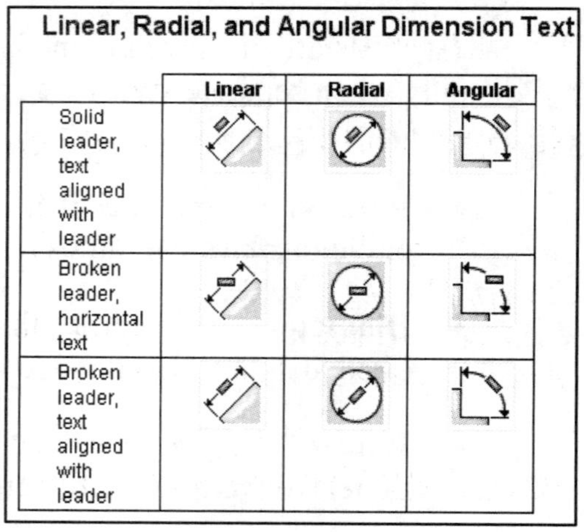


- ***Arc Condition***. Provides the ability to set the dimension between an arc or circle. Set First and Second arc condition. In the illustration, the First arc condition is Center, and the Second arc condition is set as noted.

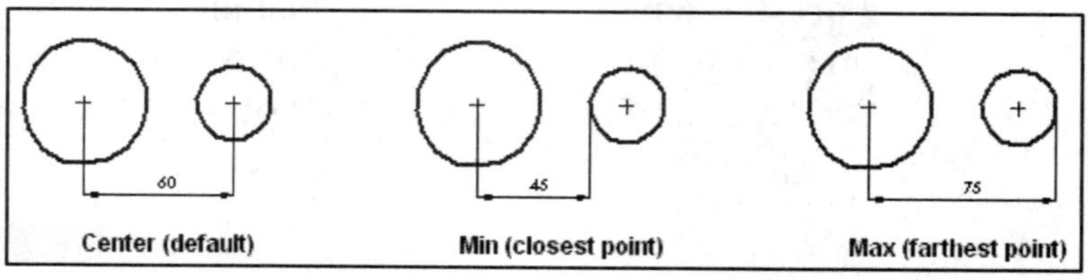

### Smart Dimension tool: Other tab

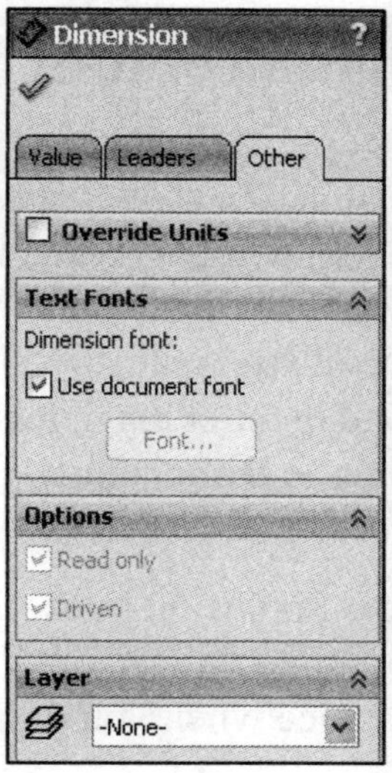


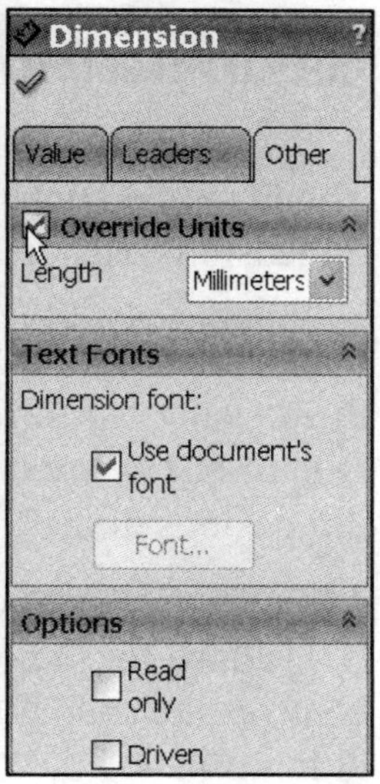


The Other tab provides the ability to specify the display of dimensions. If you select multiple dimensions, only the properties that apply to all the selected dimensions are available: The followings options are available:

- ***Override Units***. Provides the ability to override the units that were set in the Document Properties section of the active document. The available options depend on the type of dimensions that you select.
- ***Text Fonts***. Provides the following options:
  - **Dimension font**. Specifies the font used for the dimension.
    - **Use document's font**. Selected by default. Provides the ability to use the current document's font.
    - **Font** button. Provides the ability to select a new font type, style and size for the selected items.
- ***Options***. The Options box provides the following dimension selections: **Read only** and **Driven**. Driven specifies that the dimension is driven by other dimensions and conditions, and cannot be changed.

## Horizontal Dimension tool

The Horizontal dimension tool creates a horizontal dimension between two selected entities. The horizontal direction is defined by the orientation of the current sketch. The Horizontal dimension tool uses the Dimension PropertyManager. View the Smart Dimension tool section for detail Dimension PropertyManager information.

## Vertical Dimension tool

The Vertical dimension tool creates a vertical dimension between two points. The vertical direction is defined by the orientation of the current sketch. The Vertical dimension tool uses the Dimension PropertyManager. View the Smart Dimension tool section for detail Dimension PropertyManager information.

# Baseline Dimension tool

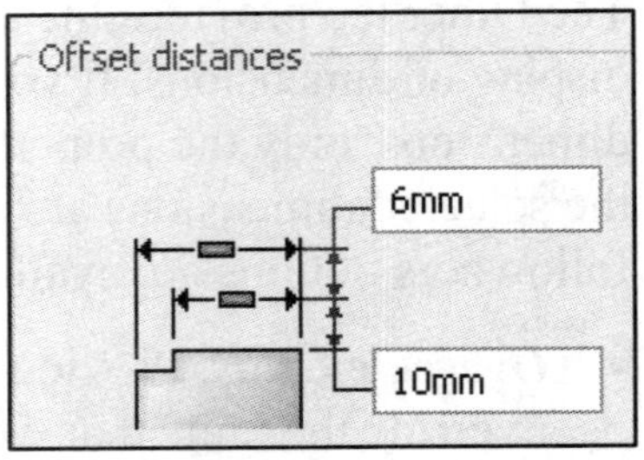


The Baseline Dimension tool creates reference dimensions used in a drawing. You cannot modify their values or use their values to drive the model. Baseline dimensions are grouped automatically. They are spaced at the distances specified by clicking **Tools ➢ Options ➢ Document Properties ➢ Dimensions**. Enter the Baseline dimensions under the Offset distances option.

The distance between dimension lines, From last dimension (B) is used for the baseline dimension. This value also controls the snap distance when you drag a linear dimension.

The distance between the model and the first dimension, From model (A) is used for the baseline dimension.

You can dimension to midpoints when you add baseline dimensions.

### *Tutorial: Baseline Dimension Drawing 5-1*

Insert a Baseline Dimension into a drawing.

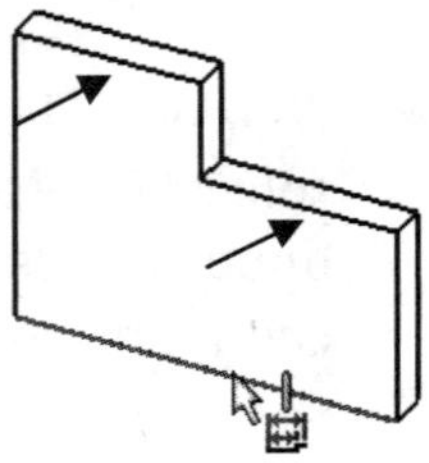

1. Open **Baseline 5-1.slddrw** from the SolidWorks 2010 folder.

Activate the Dimensions/Relations toolbar.

2. Click **View ➢ Toolbars ➢ Dimensions/Relations**.
3. Click **Baseline Dimension** from the Dimensions/Relations toolbar.
4. Click the **bottom horizontal edge** as illustrated for the baseline reference.

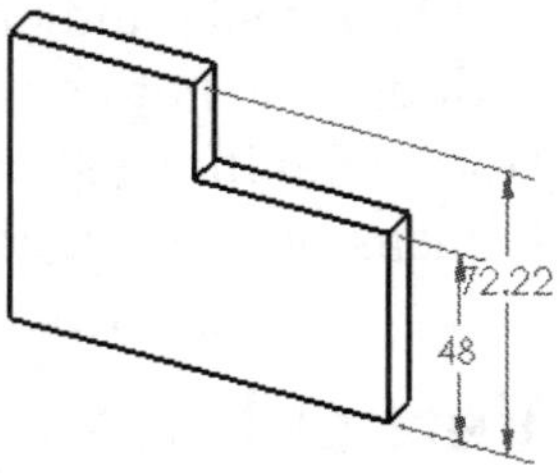


5. Click the other two **horizontal edges** to dimension.
6. Select **Baseline Dimension** from the Dimensions/Relations toolbar to deactivate the tool.
7. Click a **position** in Sheet1. View the drawing.
8. **Close** the drawing.

If you select a vertex, dimensions are measured point-to-point from the selected vertex. If you select an edge, dimensions are measured parallel to the selected edge.

# Ordinate Dimension tool

The Ordinate Dimension tool provides the ability to create a set of dimensions measured from a zero ordinate in a drawing or sketch. You can dimension to edges, vertices, and arcs, centers and minimum and maximum points.

In drawings, the Ordinate dimension tool provides reference dimensions and you cannot change their values or use the values to drive your model. Ordinate dimensions are measured from the first selected axis. The type of ordinate dimension, vertical or horizontal is defined by the orientation of the points you select. Ordinate dimensions are automatically grouped to maintain alignment. When you drag any member of the group, all the members move together. To disconnect a dimension from the alignment group, right-click the dimension, and select Break Alignment.

New in 2010, when you insert ordinate dimensions in parent views, the dimensions continue in the detail view. The detail view uses the existing 0 point in the parent view. Conversely, when you insert ordinate dimensions in detail views and apply ordinate dimensions in parent views, the parent view uses the 0 point from the detail view.

***Tutorial: Ordinate Dimension Drawing 5-1***

Insert Ordinate dimensions into a drawing.

1. Open **Ordinate 5-1.slddrw** from the SolidWorks 2010 folder.
2. Click **Ordinate Dimension** from the Dimensions/Relations toolbar.

You can also select the Horizontal Ordinate Dimension tool or the Vertical Ordinate Dimension tool to specify the direction of the dimensions.

3. Click the **centerline** from which all other sketch entities are measured from, (the 0.0 dimension).
4. Click a **position** above the large circle to locate the 0.0 dimension.
5. Click the circumference of the **three small circles** as illustrated from left to right. As you click each circumference, the dimension is placed in the view, aligned to the zero ordinate.
6. Click **Ordinate Dimension** from the Dimensions/Relations toolbar to deactivate the tool.

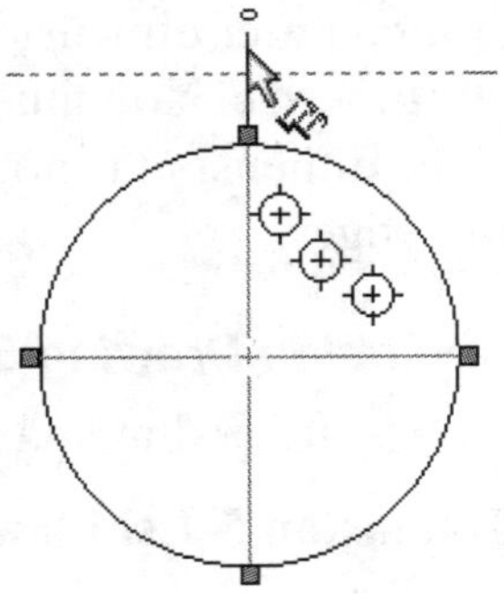


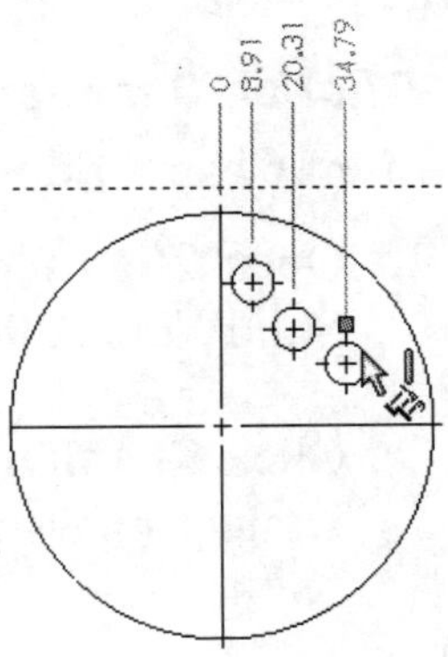

7. Click a **position** in Sheet1. View the dimensions. **Close** the drawing.

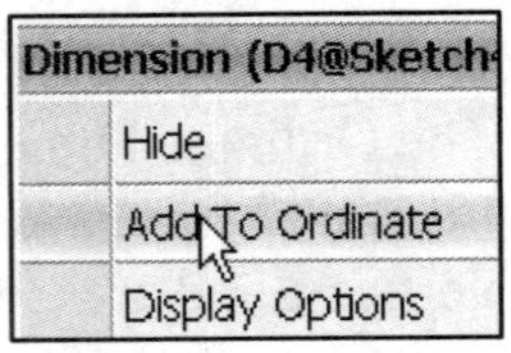


To add additional dimensions along the same ordinate, Right-click an **ordinate dimension** and select **Add To Ordinate**. Click the edges, or vertices, or arcs you want to dimension using the same ordinate.

## Horizontal Ordinate Dimension tool

The Horizontal Ordinate dimension tool provides the ability to create a horizontal dimension between two entities. The horizontal direction is defined by the orientation of the current sketch. View the above section on Ordinate Dimension tool for additional information.

## Vertical Ordinate Dimension tool

The Vertical Ordinate dimension tool provides the ability to create a vertical dimension between two points. The vertical direction is defined by the orientation of the current sketch. View the above section on Ordinate Dimension tool for additional information.

## Chamfer Dimension tool

The Chamfer Dimension tool provides the ability to create chamfer dimensions in drawings. The Chamfer Dimension tool uses the Dimension PropertyManager.

Tolerance types for chamfer dimensions are limited to **None**, **Bilateral** and **Symmetric**. You must select the chamfered edge first. The dimension is not displayed until you select one of the lead-in edges.

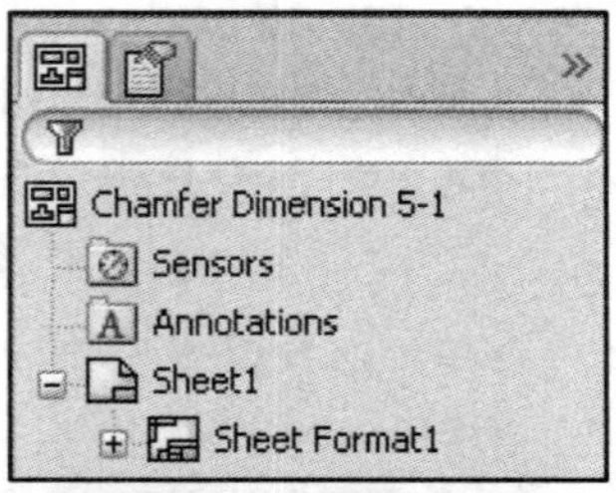


### *Tutorial: Chamfer Dimension Drawing 5-1*

Insert Chamfer dimensions into a drawing.

1. Open **Chamfer Dimension 5-1.slddrw** from the SolidWorks 2010 folder.

2. Click **Chamfer Dimension** from the Dimensions/Relations toolbar.

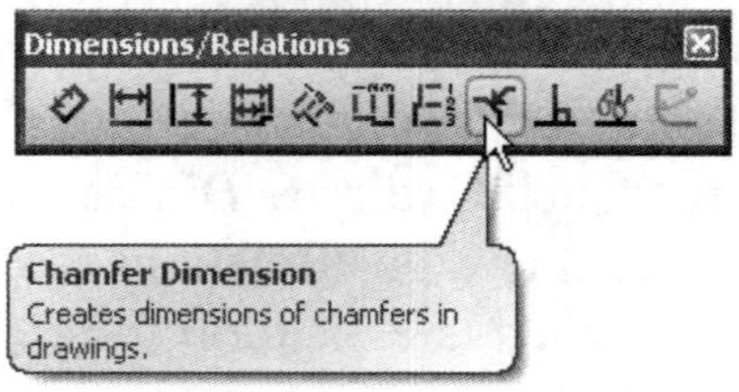

3. Click the **chamfered edge** as illustrated.
4. Click the **top horizontal edge**. The dimension is displayed.
5. Click a **position** in the Graphics window to place the dimension. The Dimension PropertyManager is displayed.
6. Click **OK** from the Dimension PropertyManager. View the drawing.
7. **Close** the drawing.

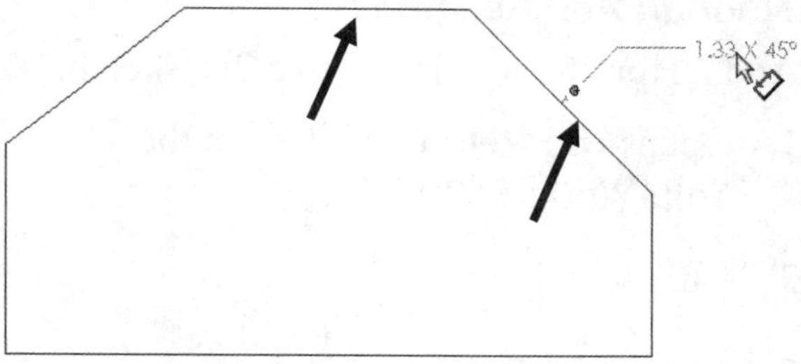


## Add Relation tool

The Add Relation tool provides the ability to create geometric relations between sketch entities, or between sketch entities and axes, planes, edges, or vertices. The Add Relation tool uses the Add Relations PropertyManager.

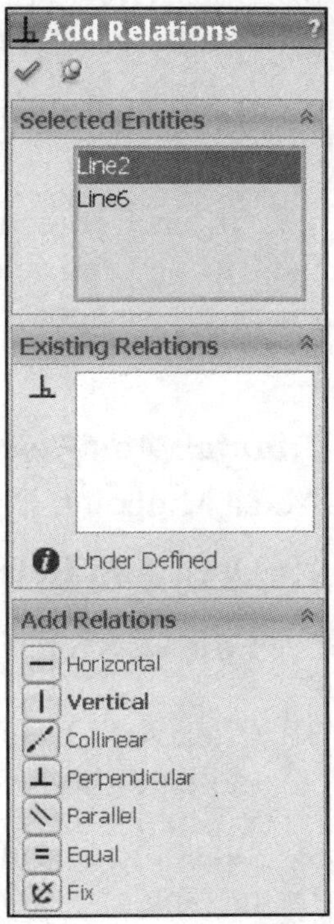


The Add Relations PropertyManager provides the following selections:

- ***Selected Entities***. The Selected Entities box provides the following option.
  - **Selected Entities**. Displays the names of selected sketch entities from the Graphics window.
- ***Existing Relations***. The Existing Relations box provides the following options:
  - **Relations**. Displays the existing relations for the selected sketch entity.
  - **Information**. Displays the status of the selected sketch entity.
- ***Add Relations***. The Add Relations box provides the following option.
  - **Relations**. Provides the ability to add a relation to the selected entities from the list. The list includes only relations that are possible for the selected entities.

***Tutorial: Add Relation 5-1***

Add a Horizontal relation to a 2D Sketch.

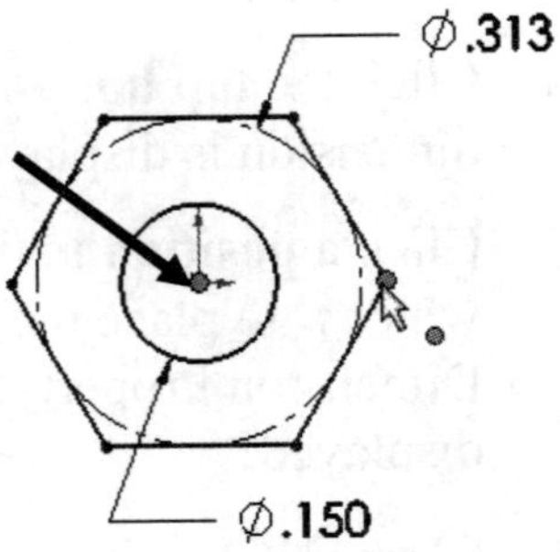


1. Open **Add Relation 5-1** from the SolidWorks 2010 folder.
2. **Edit** Sketch1.
3. Click **Add Relation** from the Consolidated Sketch toolbar. The Add Relations PropertyManager is displayed.

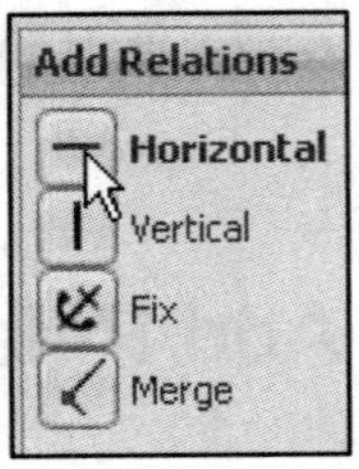


4. Click the **origin**. Click the **right most point** of the hexagon.
5. Click **Horizontal** from the Add Relations box.
6. Click **OK** from the Add Relations PropertyManager. A Horizontal relation is applied.
7. **Rebuild** the model. View the results. **Close** the model.

Insert Geometric relations without the Add Relations tool by using the Ctrl key and selecting two or more sketch entities. The Properties PropertyManager is displayed. The Add Relation tool is not required with this process.

***Tutorial: Add Relation 5-2***

Add a Midpoint, Equal, and Tangent relation to a 2D Sketch.

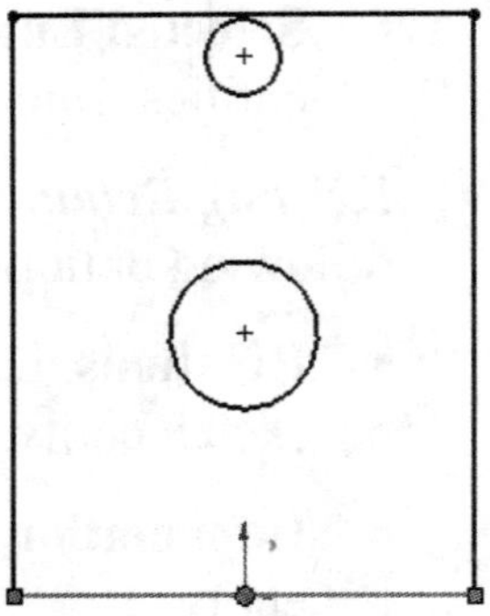

1. Open **Add Relation 5-2** from the SolidWorks 2010 folder.
2. **Edit** Sketch1.
3. Click **Add Relation** from the Consolidated Sketch toolbar. The Add Relations PropertyManager is displayed.
4. Click the **origin**. Click the **bottom horizontal** line of the rectangle.
5. Click **Midpoint** from the Add Relations box. A Midpoint relation is added.

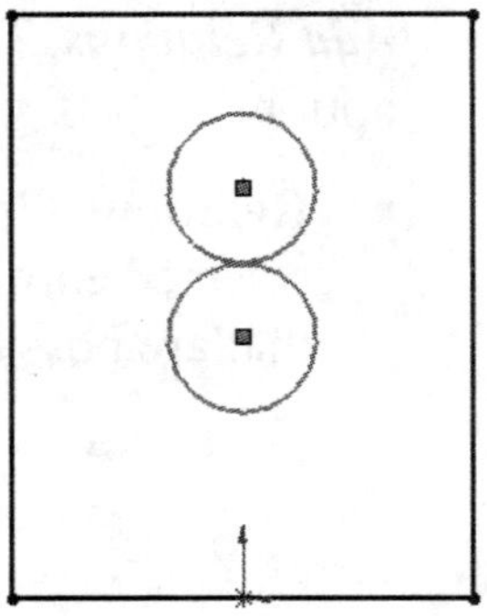

6. Click the **circumference** of the two circles.
7. Click **Equal** from the Add Relations box.
8. Click **Tangent** from the Add Relations box. An Equal and Tangent relation is applied to the circles.
9. Click **OK** from the Add Relations PropertyManager.
10. **Rebuild** the model. View the results. **Close** the model.

***Tutorial: Add Relation 5-3***

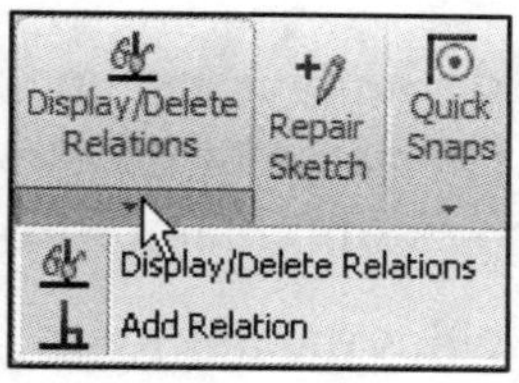


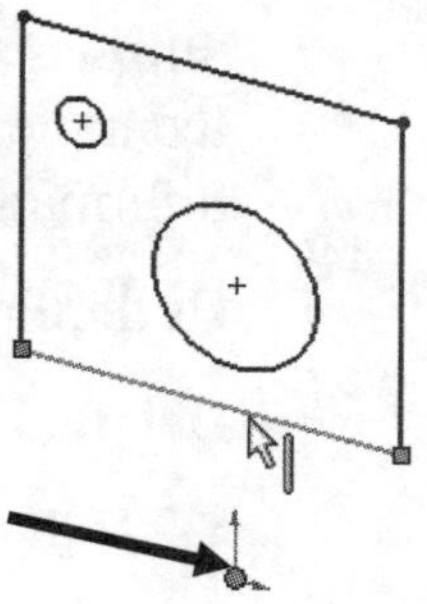

Add a Coincident, Midpoint, and Equal relation in a 3DSketch.

1. Open **Add Relation 5-3** from the SolidWorks 2010 folder.
2. **Edit** 3DSketch1.
3. Click **Add Relation** from the Consolidated Sketch toolbar. The Add Relations PropertyManager is displayed.
4. Click the **origin**.
5. Click the **bottom horizontal** X axis line.
6. Select **Midpoint** from the Add Relations box.
7. Click the circumference of the **small circle**.
8. Click the circumference of the **large circle**.
9. Click **Equal** from the Add Relations box.
10. Click **OK** from the Add Relations PropertyManager.
11. **Rebuild** the model. View the results.
12. **Close** the model.

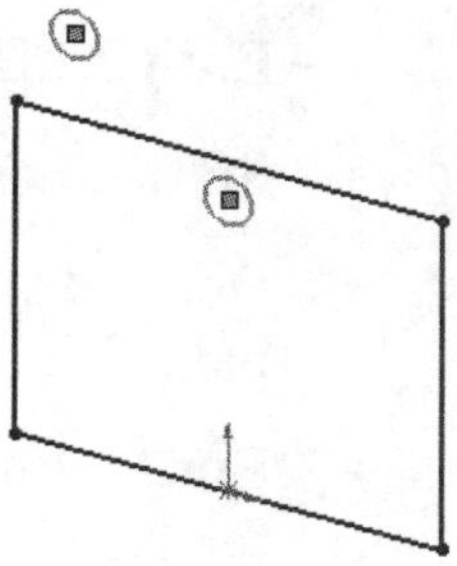

## Display/Delete Relations tool

The Display/Delete Relations tool provides the ability to edit existing relations after you added the relations to your sketch. The Display/Delete Relations dimension tool uses the Display/Delete Relations PropertyManager. The Display/Delete Relations PropertyManager provides the following selections:

- ***Relations***. The Relations box displays the selected relation based on the option selected from the filter box. The appropriate sketch entities are highlighted in your Graphics window. The Relations box provides the following options:
  - **Filter**. The Filter box provides the ability to specify which relation to display. The selections are: **All in this sketch**, **Dangling**, **Over Defined/Not Solved**, **External**, **Defined In Context, Locked**, **Broken** and **Selected Entities**.

If the relation was created In Context of an assembly, the status can be Broken or Locked.

- **Information icon**. Displays the status of the selected sketch entity.
- **Suppressed**. Suppresses the selected relation for the current configuration. Example: The name of the suppressed relation is displayed in gray and the Information status changes from Satisfied to Driven.
- **Undo**. Provides the ability to change the last relation.
- **Delete**. Deletes or replace your last action.
  - **Delete All**. Deletes your selected relations or to delete all of your relations.

- ***Entities***. The Entities box provides the ability to view the selected relation on each selected entity. The Entities box provides the following information:
  - **Entity**. Lists each selected sketch entity.
  - **Status**. Displays the status of your selected sketch entity.
  - **Defined In**. Displays the location where the sketch entity is defined. Example: Same Model, Current Sketch, or External Model.
  - **Entity**. Information for external entities in an assembly. Displays the entity name for sketch entities in the Same Model or External Model.
  - **Owner**. Information for external entities in an assembly. Displays the part to which the sketch entity belongs to.
  - **Assembly**. Information for external entities in an assembly. Displays the name of the top-level assembly where the relation was created for sketch entities in an External Model.
  - **Replace**. Replaces your selected entity with a different entity.

***Tutorial: Display/Delete Relations 5-1***

Delete and view the relations in a 3D Sketch.

1. Open **Display-Delete Relations 5-1** from the SolidWorks 2010 folder.
2. Click **Close** to the Error message.
3. **Edit** 3DSketch1 from the FeatureManager.
4. Click **Display/Delete Relations** from Sketch toolbar. The Add Relations PropertyManager is displayed. View the relation in the Relations box.
5. **Delete** the Coincident6 relation.
6. Select **All in this sketch** from the Relations box. View the relations in the Relations box.

7. Click **OK** from the Display-Delete Relations PropertyManager.
8. **Rebuild** the model. View the results.
9. **Close** the model.

## Fully Defined Sketch tool

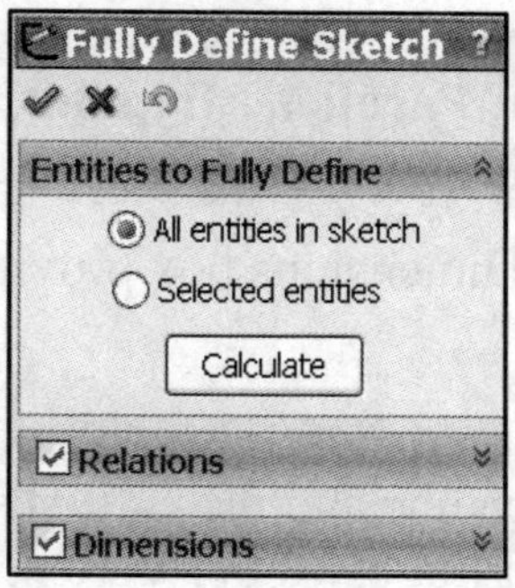


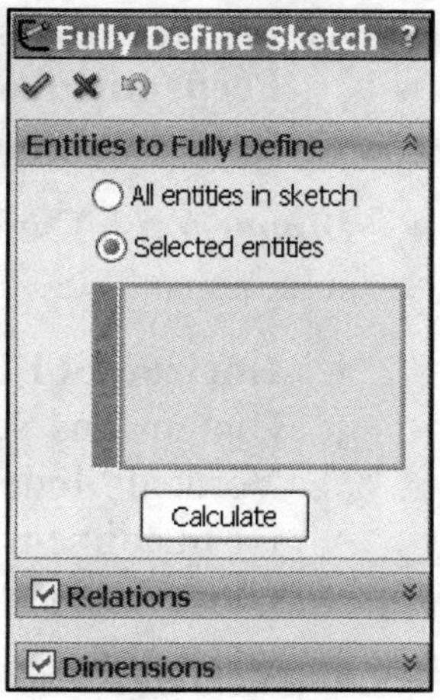


The Fully Defined Sketch tool provides the ability to calculate which dimensions and relations are required to fully define under defined sketches or selected sketch entities. You can access the Fully Define Sketch tool at any point and with any combination of dimensions and relations already added.

Your sketch should include some dimensions and relations before you use the Fully Define Sketch tool.

The Fully Defined Sketch tool uses the Fully Define Sketch PropertyManager. The Fully Define Sketch PropertyManager provides the following selections:

- ***Entities to Fully Define***. The Entities to Filly Define box provides the following options:
  - **All entities in sketch**. Fully defines the sketch by applying combinations of relations and dimensions.
  - **Selected entities**. Provides the ability to select sketch entities.
    - **Entities to Fully Define**. Only available when the Selected entities box is checked. Applies relations and dimensions to the specified sketch entities.
  - **Calculate**. Analyzes the sketch and generates the appropriate relations and dimensions.

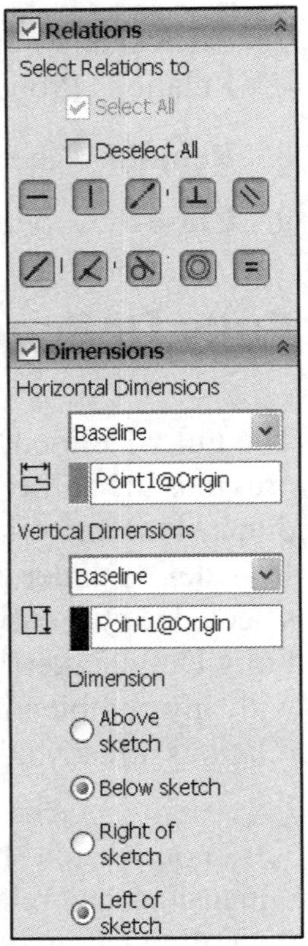


- ***Relations***. The Relations box provide the following selections:
  - **Select All**. Includes all relations in the results.
  - **Deselect All**. Omits all relations in the results.
  - **Individual relations**. Include or exclude needed relations. The available relations are: **Horizontal, Vertical, Collinear, Perpendicular**, **Parallel, Midpoint**, **Coincident**, **Tangent**, **Concentric** and **Equal radius/Length**.
- ***Dimensions***. The Dimensions box provides the following selections:
  - **Horizontal Dimensions**. Displays the selected Horizontal Dimensions Scheme and the entity used as the Datum - Vertical Model Edge, Model Vertex, Vertical Line or Point for the dimensions. The available options are: **Baseline**, **Chain** and **Ordinate**.
  - **Vertical Dimensions.** Displays the selected Vertical Dimensions Scheme and the entity used as the Datum - Horizontal Model Edge, Model Vertex, Horizontal Line or Point for the dimensions. The available options are: **Baseline**, **Chain** and **Ordinate**.
  - **Dimension**. Below sketch and Left of sketch is selected by default. Locates the dimension. There are four selections: **Above sketch**, **Below the sketch**, **Right of sketch** and **Left of sketch**.

### *Tutorial: Fully Defined Sketch 5-1*

Create a fully defined sketch.

1. Open **Fully Defined Sketch 5-1** from the SolidWorks 2010 folder.
2. **Edit** Sketch1.
3. Click **Fully Defined Sketch** from the Consolidated Sketch toolbar. The Fully Defined Sketch PropertyManager is displayed.
4. Check the **All entities in sketch** box.
5. Click **Calculate** from the Entities to Fully Define box. The dimensions are displayed in the Graphics window.

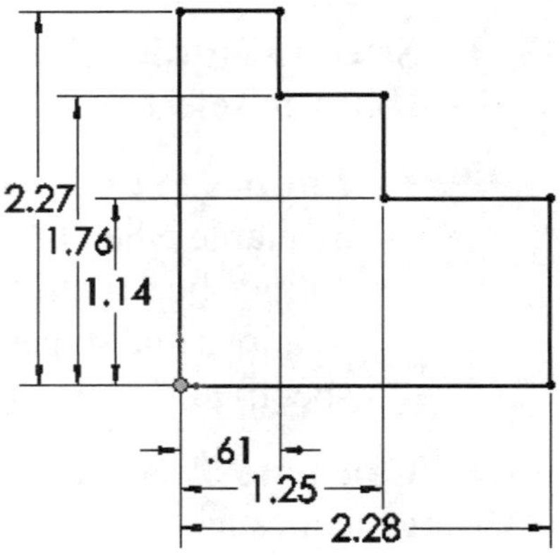

6. Click **Undo** from the PropertyManager.
7. Check the **Selected entities** box.
8. Click the **bottom horizontal** line.
9. Click the **top horizontal** line.
10. Click **Calculate**. The dimensions are displayed in the Graphics window.
11. Click **Undo** from the PropertyManager.
12. Check the **Above sketch** box and the **Right of sketch** box from the Dimension section.
13. Click **Calculate**. The dimensions are displayed in the Graphics window.
14. Click **OK** from the Fully Define Sketch PropertyManager.
15. **Rebuild** the model. View the results.
16. **Close** the model.

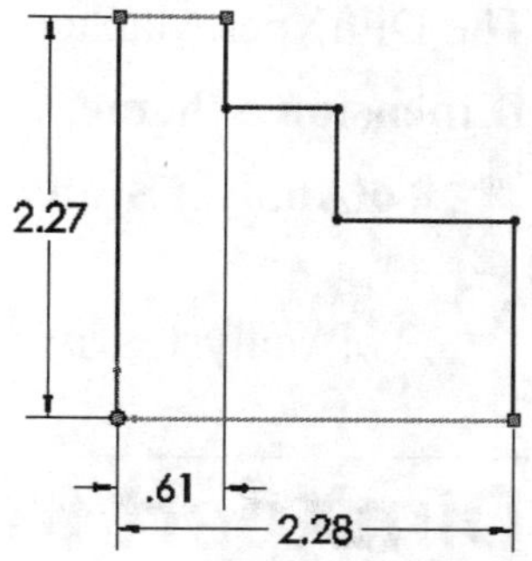


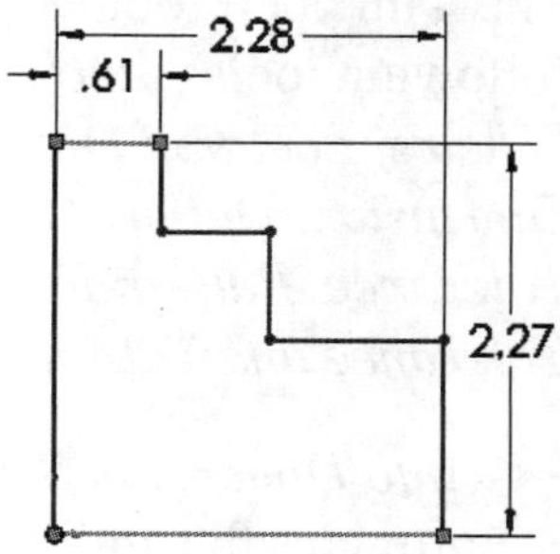


# DimXpertManager

The DimXpertManager provides access to the DimXpert. DimXpert for parts is a set of tools you use to apply dimensions and tolerances to parts according to the requirements of the ASME Y14.41-2003 standard.

You can then use the tolerances with TolAnalyst to perform stack analysis on assemblies, or with downstream CAM, other tolerance analyses, or metrology applications.

Model dimensions are associative between parts, assemblies, and drawings. Reference dimensions and DimXpert dimensions are one-way associative from the part to the drawing or from the part to the assembly. DimXpert dimensions show up in a different color to help identify them from model dims and reference dims. DimXpert dims are the dimensions that are used when calculating tolerance stack-up using TolAnalyst.

DimXpert applies dimensions in drawings so that manufacturing features (patterns, slots, pockets, etc.) are fully-defined.

DimXpert for parts and drawings automatically recognize manufacturing features. What are manufacturing features? Manufacturing features are *not SolidWorks features*. Manufacturing features are defined in 1.1.12 of the ASME Y14.5M-1994 Dimensioning and Tolerancing standard as: "The general term applied to a physical portion of a part, such as a surface, hole or slot.

The DimXpertManager provides the following selections: **Auto Dimension Scheme**, **Show Tolerance Status**, **Copy Scheme**, **TolAnalyst Study**.

TolAnalyst is available in SolidWorks Premium.

# DimXpert toolbar

The DimXpert toolbar provides the following tools: *Auto Dimension Scheme, Location Dimension, Size Dimension, Datum, Geometric Tolerance, Pattern Feature, Show Tolerance and TolAnalyst Study.*

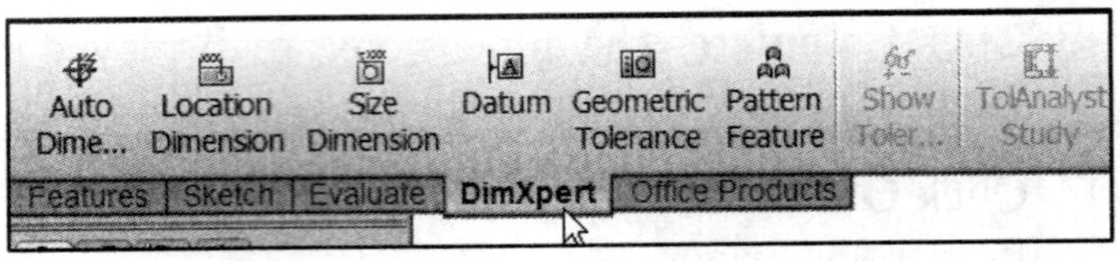


- *Auto Dimension Scheme* provides the ability to automatically apply dimensions and tolerances to the manufacturing features of a part.
- *Location Dimension* provides the ability to apply linear and angular dimensions between two DimXpert features, (excluding surface, fillet, chamfer, and pocket features).
- *Size Dimension* provides the ability to place tolerance size dimensions on DimXpert features.
- *Pattern Feature* provides the ability to create or edit pattern features and collection features.
- *Datum* provides the ability to define datum features. The tool supports these feature types: Boss, Cylinder, Notch, Plane, Simple Hole, Slot, Width.
- *Geometric Tolerance* provides the ability to apply geometric tolerances to DimXpert features. Note: When you apply geometric tolerances to features defined as datums or to features with pre-existing size tolerances, DimXpert automatically places the feature control frame and pre-existing annotation in an annotation group.

- *Show Tolerance Status* provides the ability to identify the manufacturing features and faces that are fully constrained, under constrained, and over constrained from a dimensioning and tolerancing perspective. Note: The DimXpert identification process is unlike that used in sketches, which utilizes dimensional and geometrical relationships to determine the constraint status of the sketch entities. DimXpert is based solely on dimension and tolerance constraints. Geometrical relationships, such as Concentric relationships, are not considered.

- *Copy Tolerance Scheme* provides the ability to copy a DimXpert tolerance scheme from one configuration of a part to another configuration. Note: Copied schemes are not synchronized with the Source configuration. Making changes to one scheme has no affect on the other.

- *Delete All Tolerances* provides the ability to delete the entire DimXpert database. Note: To reinstate the DimXpert database, click **Undo** from the Menu bar toolbar.

DimXpert tools provide the ability to place dimensions and tolerances on parts. Access DimXpert from the DimXpertManager tab or from the DimXpert tab in the CommandManager. The DimXpertManager provides the ability to list the tolerance features defined by DimXpert in chronological order and to display the available tools.

Care is required to apply DimXpert correctly on complex surfaces or with some existing models. See SolidWorks help for detail information on DimXpert with complex surfaces.

## Auto Dimension Scheme tool

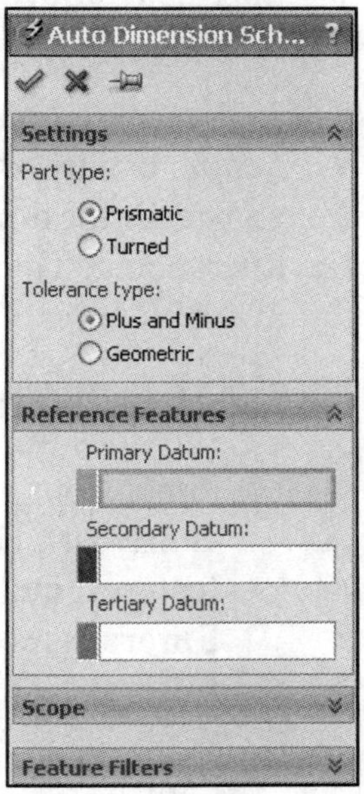


The Auto Dimension Scheme tool / DimXpert automatically insert dimensions and tolerances to the manufacturing features of a part. View SolidWorks Help for additional detail information on "manufacturing features".

The Auto Dimension Scheme tool / DimXpert use the Auto Dimensional PropertyManager. The Auto Dimensional PropertyManager provides the following selections:

- ***Settings***. Set the PropertyManager options described below:
  - **Part type**. Defines the part based on how it is manufactured.

- **Prismatic**. Selected by default. Used with Geometric Tolerance type. DimXpert applies position tolerances to locate holes and bosses. For annotation views, size dimensions are displayed as callouts with open leaders.
- **Turned**. Used with Geometric Tolerance type. Applies circular run-out tolerances to locate holes and bosses. For annotation views, size dimensions are displayed as linear dimensions, parallel to the axis.

- **Tolerance type**. Provides the ability to control how features of size (hole types, slots, notches, widths, and cones), pockets, and surfaces are located relative to the datum or reference features.
  - **Plus and Minus**. Selected by default. Locates the features with linear plus and minus dimensions. Does not apply dimensions to surface features in plus and minus mode.
  - **Geometric**. DimXpert locates axial features with position and circular runout tolerances. Pockets and surfaces are located with surface profiles.

- ***Reference Features /Datum Selection***. Defines the *Primary, Secondary and Tertiary* reference features for **Plus and Minus** schemes or datums for **Geometric** schemes. The selection provides the ability to select one to three reference features to use to generate linear plus and minus location dimensions. DimXpert validates reference features according to the rules defined for establishing datum reference frames, per ASME Y14.5.1M-1994.

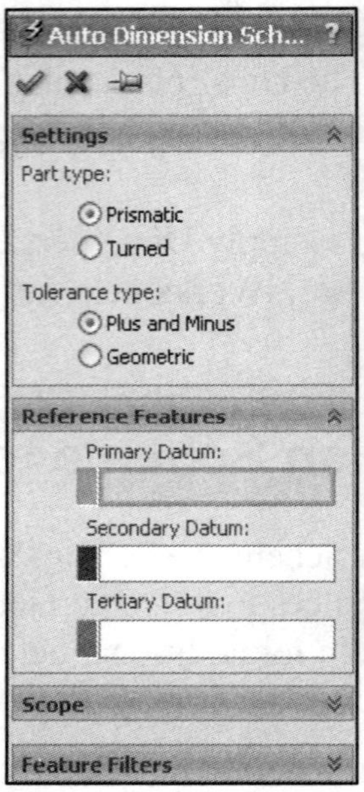


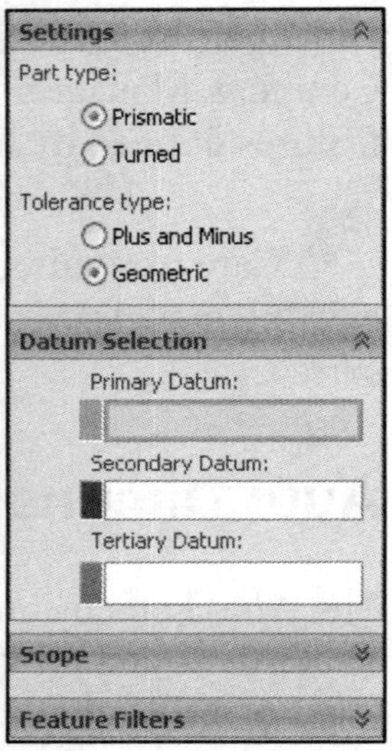


- ***Scope***. Controls which features DimXpert considers for dimensioning and tolerancing. The following selections are available:
  - **All features**. Selected by default. Provides the ability to apply dimensions and tolerances to the entire part. DimXpert considers all previously defined features, including those not listed under **Feature Filters**, as well as those features listed under **Feature Filters**.

The All features option is best suited for simple parts or parts for which all dimensions and tolerances are relative to a single datum reference frame or origin.

- **Selected features**. The objective is to dimension and tolerance the selected features.

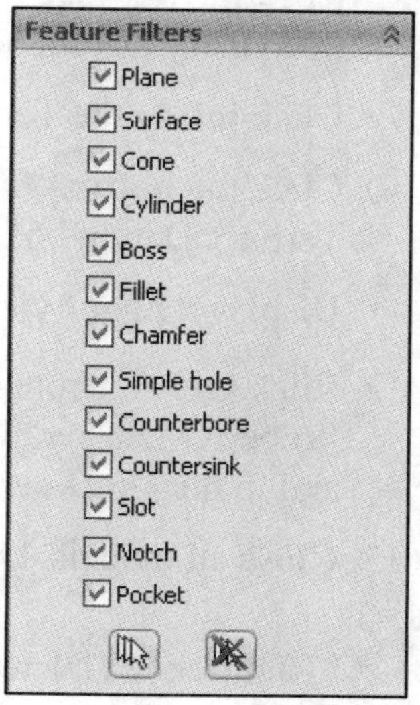


The Selected features option is useful for more complex parts that have multiple datum schemes or require features to be dimensioned from different origins.

- ***Feature Filters***. Provides the ability to control which features DimXpert recognizes and considers for dimensioning and tolerance when you select the All Features option in the Scope dialog box.

Clearing features omits further recognition of those types. For example, if the part has no DimXpert dimensions or tolerances, and you clear **Plane**, DimXpert does not dimension or tolerance plane features, nor does DimXpert use the planar faces to derive a complex feature type such as a slot or notch.

### *Tutorial: DimXpert 5-1*

Apply the DimXpert tool. Apply Prismatic and Geometric options.

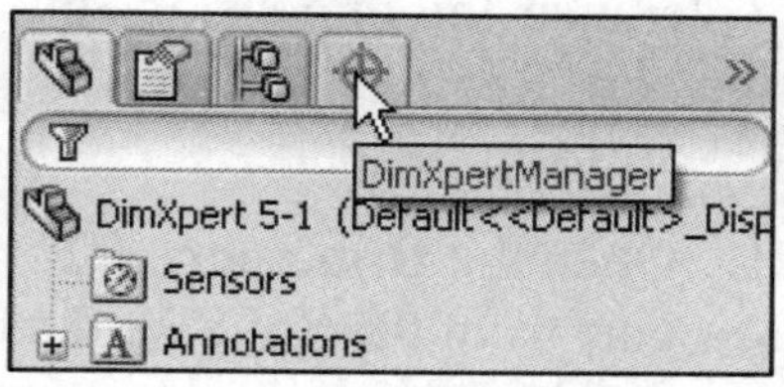


1. Open the **DimXpert 5-1** part from the SolidWorks 2010 folder.
2. Click the **DimXpertManager** tab as illustrated.
3. Click the **Auto Dimension Scheme** tab from the DimXpertManager. The Auto Dimension Scheme PropertyManager is displayed.
4. Click the **Prismatic** box.
5. Click the **Geometric** box.
6. Click the **front face** of the model. Plane1 is displayed in the Primary Datum box.
7. Click **inside** the Secondary Datum box.

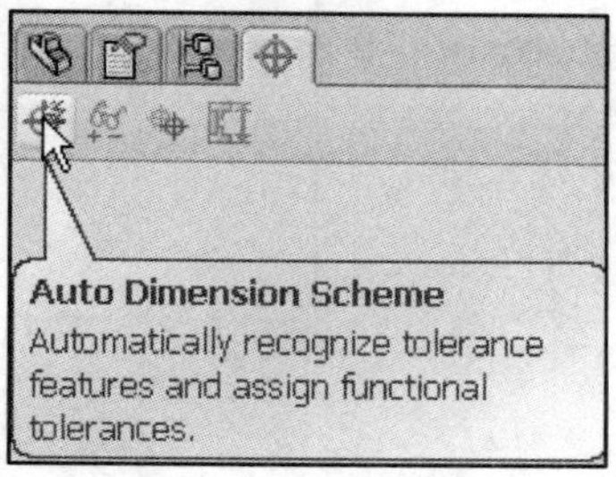


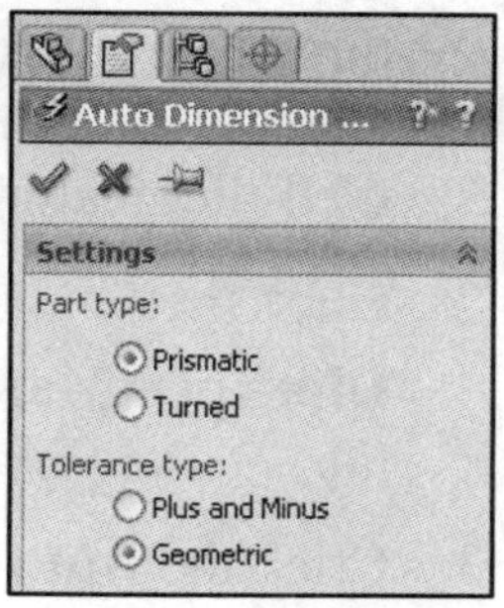

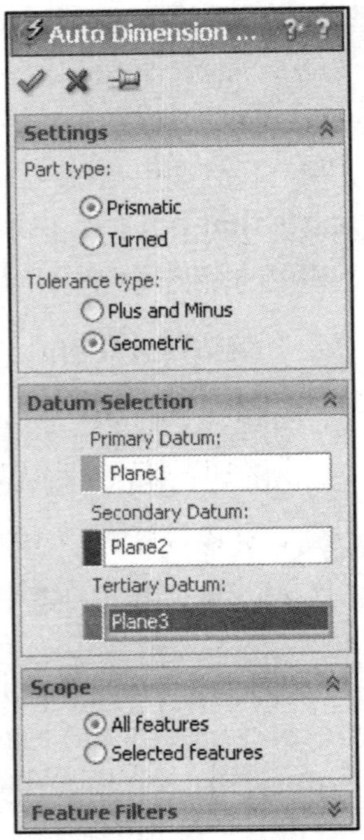


8. Click the **left face** of the model. Plane2 is displayed in the Secondary Datum box.
9. Click **inside** the Tertiary Datum box.
10. Click the **bottom face** of the model. Plane3 is displayed in the Tertiary Datum box. Accept the default options.
11. Display a **Front view**.
12. Click **OK** from the Auto Dimension Scheme PropertyManager. View the results in the Graphics window and in the DimXpertManager.
13. **Close** all models. Do not save the updates.

Right-click Delete to delete the Auto Dimension Scheme in the DimXpert PropertyManager.

### *Tutorial: DimXpert 5-2*

Apply DimXpert: Plus and Minus option. Modify Tolerance and dimensions in the part. Remove Instance Count from the part.

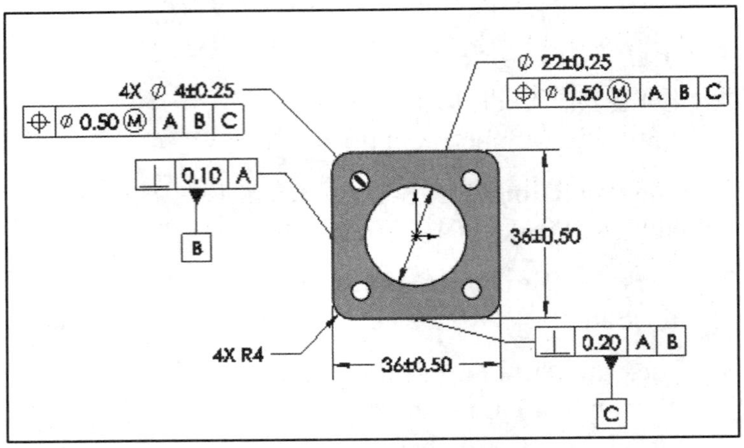


1. Open the **DimXpert 5-2** part from the SolidWorks 2010 folder. View the three Extrude features, Linear Pattern feature, and the Fillet feature.
2. Click the **DimXpertManager** tab.
3. Click the **Auto Dimension Scheme** tool from the DimXpertManager. The Auto Dimension PropertyManager is displayed.

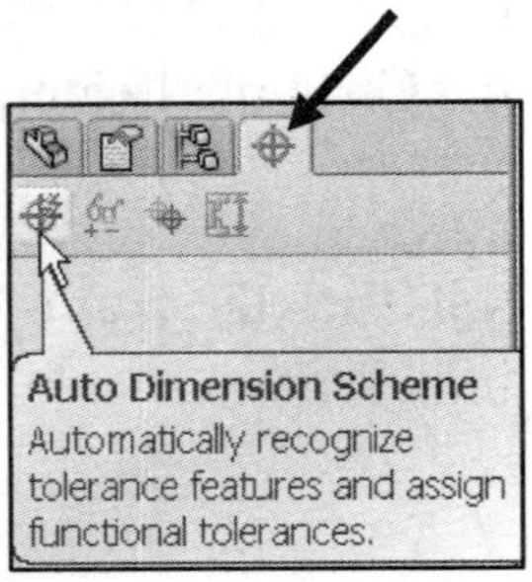


4. Click the **Prismatic** box.
5. Click the **Plus and Minus** box.

A key difference between the *Plus and Minus* option versus the *Geometric* option is how DimXpert controls the four-hole pattern, and how it applies tolerances to interrelate the datum features when in *Geometric* mode.

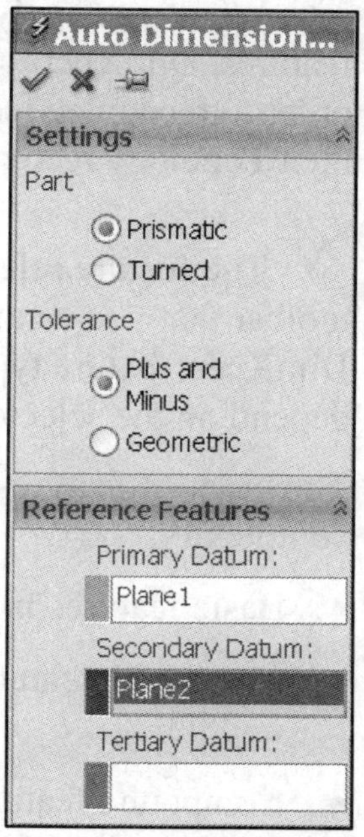


6. Click the **back face** of the model. Plane1 is displayed in the Primary Datum box.
7. Click **inside** the Secondary Datum box.
8. Click the **left face** of the model. Plane2 is displayed in the Secondary Datum box.
9. Click **OK** from the Auto Dimension PropertyManager.
10. Click **Isometric view**. View the dimensions. View the features displayed in green and yellow. Note: Additional dimensions are required for manufacturing. View the DimXpertManager.

The DimXpertManager displays either *no mark*, *(+)*, or a *(-)* sign next to the Plane or Feature.

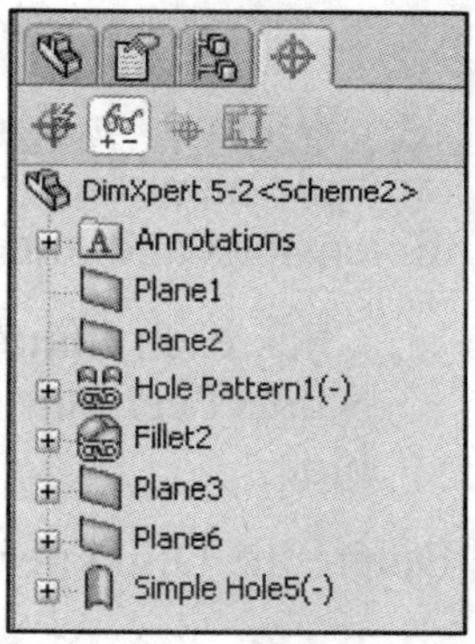


- Features with *no mark* after the name are fully constrained, as illustrated in the DimXpertManager and are displayed in green.
- Features with the *(+)* sign following the name are over constrained and are displayed in red in the Graphics window.
- Features with the *(-)* sign following the name are under constrained and are displayed in yellow in the Graphics window.

DimXpert dimensions and tolerances are magenta in color by default.

For DimXpert, features mean manufacturing features. For example, in the CAD world, you create a "shell" feature, which is a type of "pocket" feature in the manufacturing world. See SolidWorks Help for additional information.

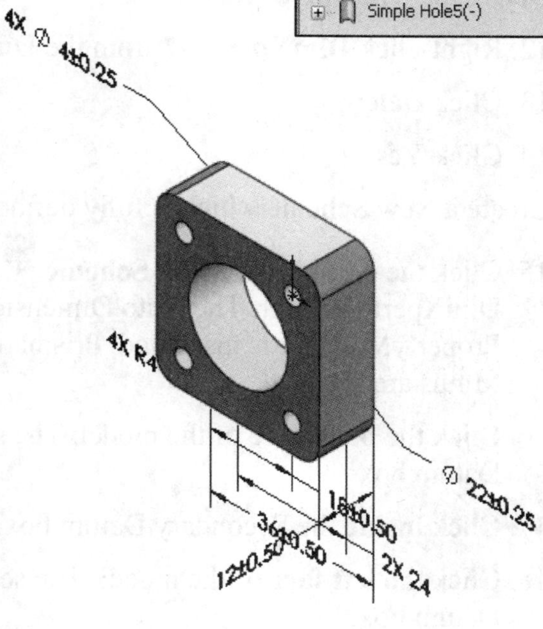

When you apply DimXpert dimensions to manufacturing features, DimXpert uses the following two methods in this order to recognize features: Model feature recognition and then Topology recognition.

The feature selector is a floating, context sensitive toolbar that you can use to distinguish between different DimXpert feature types. The available feature selector choices depend on the selected face and the active command.

The order of features in the feature selector is based on their complexity:

- Basic features like planes, cylinders, and cones are on the left.
- Composite features like counterbore holes, notches, slots, and patterns are in the middle.
- Compound features like compound holes and intersect points are on the right. Compound features require additional selections.

Within DimXpert, a single face can typically define multiple manufacturing feature types that require different dimensions and tolerances.

11. Click each **Plane** and **feature** in the Show Tolerance Status FeatureManager. The selected item is displayed in blue.

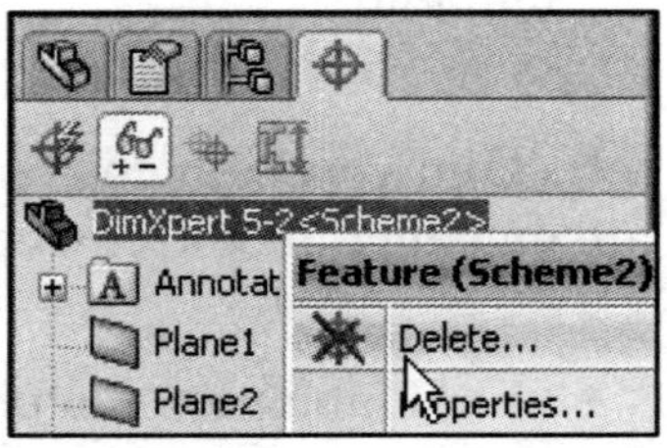


Delete the DimXpert Scheme.

12. Right-click **DimXpert 5-2** from the DimXpertManager.
13. Click **Delete**.
14. Click **Yes**.

Create a New Scheme which is fully defined.

15. Click the **Auto Dimension Scheme** tool from the DimXpertManager. The Auto Dimension PropertyManager is displayed. Prismatic and Plus and Minus are selected.
16. Click the **back face** of the model. The selected plane is displayed in the Primary Datum box.
17. Click **inside** the Secondary Datum box.
18. Click the **left face** of the model. The selected plane is displayed in the Secondary Datum box.

19. Click **inside** the Tertiary Datum box.
20. Click the **top face** of the model. The selected plane is displayed in the Tertiary Datum box.
21. Click **OK** ✔ from the Auto Dimension PropertyManager.
22. Click **Isometric view**. View the dimensions. All features are displayed in green.

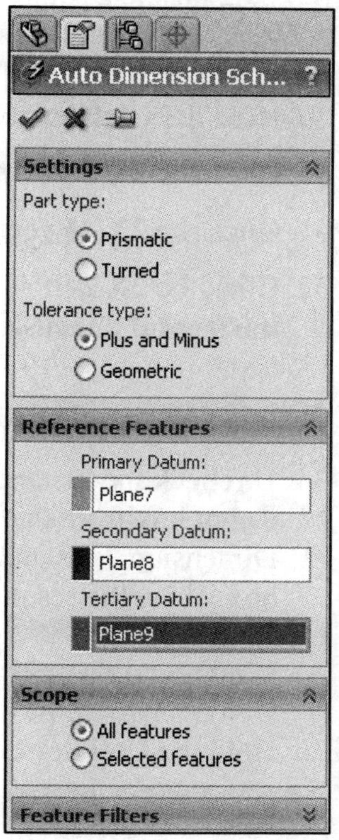


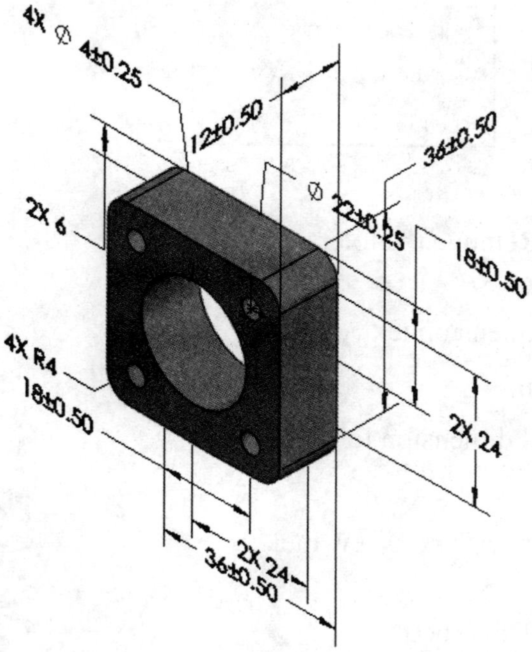


Modify Tolerance and dimensions in the part.

23. Click the **36 horizontal** dimension text

Create a Bilateral Tolerance.

24. Select **Bilateral** from the Tolerance Type drop-down menu.
25. Enter **0** for Maximum Variation.
26. Repeat the above procedure for the **36 vertical** dimension text.
27. Click **OK** ✔ from the DimXpert PropertyManager. View the results.

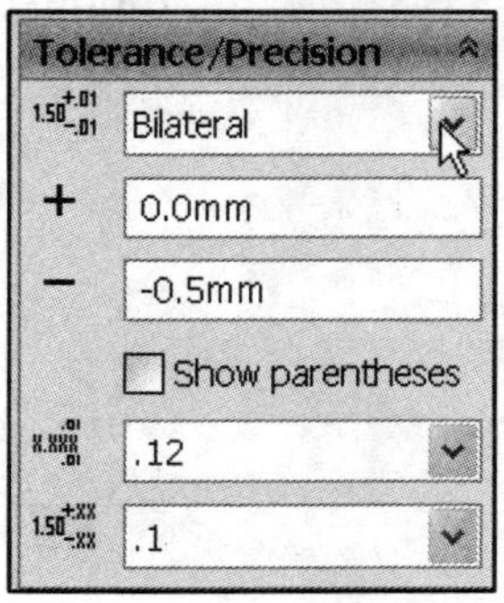

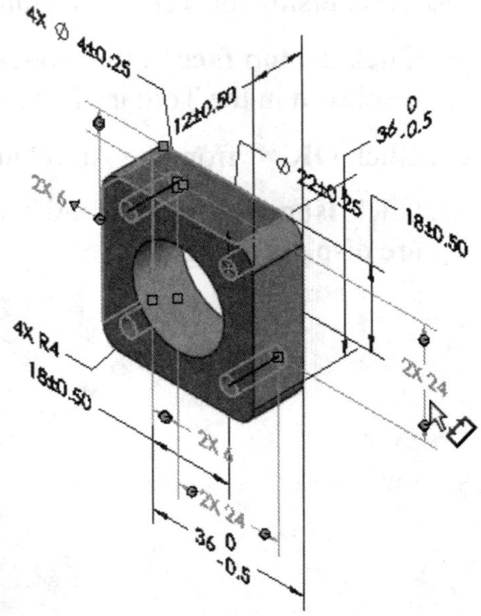


Remove Instance Count from the part.

28. Click the **2X 6 vertical** dimension text.
29. Hold the **Ctrl** key down.
30. Click the **2X 6 horizontal** dimension text.
31. Click the **2X 24 vertical** dimension text.
32. Click the **2X 24 horizontal** dimension text.

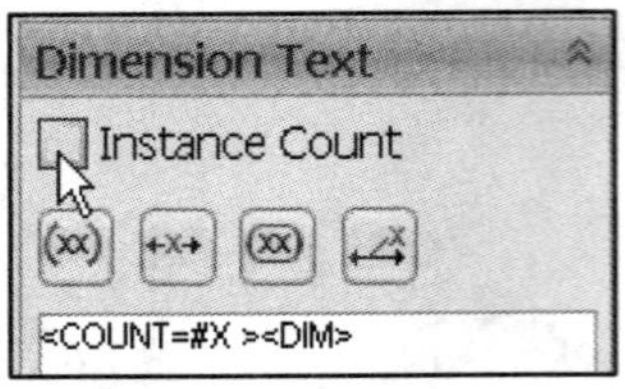


33. Release the **Ctrl** key.
34. **Uncheck** the Instance Count box from the Dimension Text dialog box. View the results. Remove the tolerance from the part.
35. Click the **18 vertical** dimension text.
36. Hold the **Ctrl** key down.
37. Click the **18 horizontal** dimension text.
38. Release the **Ctrl** key.
39. Select **None** for Tolerance Type. View the results.
40. Click **OK** ✔ from the DimXpert PropertyManager.
41. **Close** the model. Do not save the model.

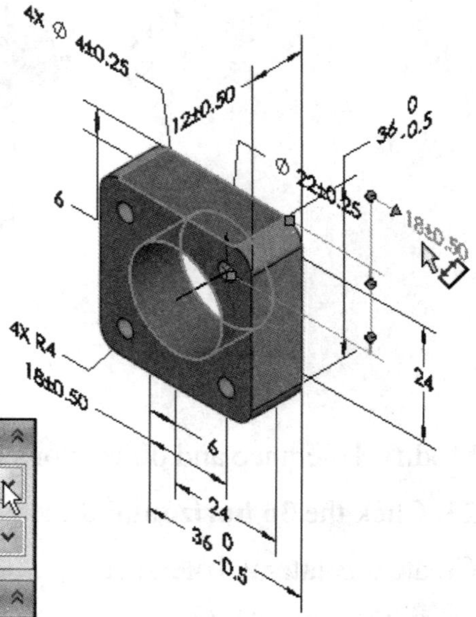


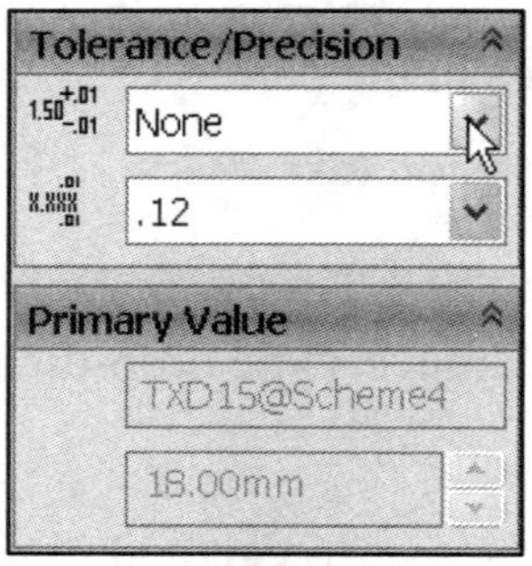

### *Tutorial: DimXpert 5-3*

Apply DimXpert: Geometric option.
Edit a Feature Control Frame.

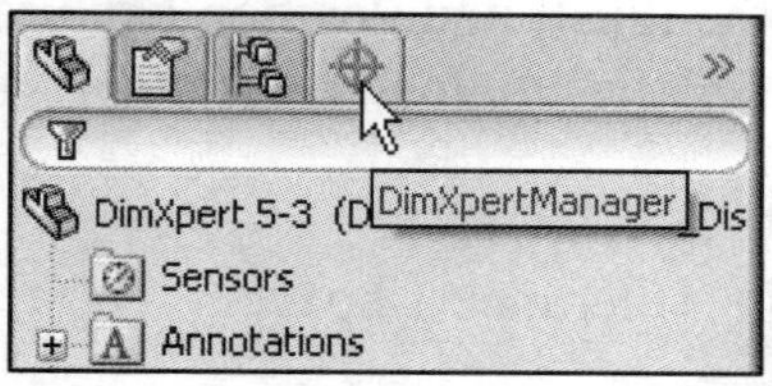


1. Open the **DimXpert 5-3** part from the from the SolidWorks 2010 folder.

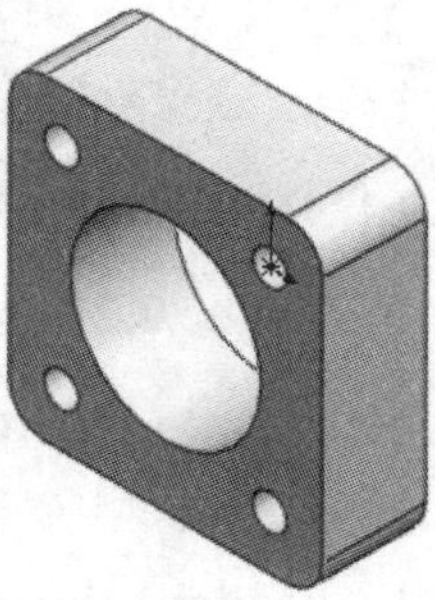

2. Click the **DimXpertManager** tab.
3. Click the **Auto Dimension Scheme** tool from the DimXpertManager. The Auto Dimension PropertyManager is displayed. Prismatic and Plus and Minus is selected by default. In this section, you will select the Geometric option.

DimXpert: Geometric option provides the ability to locate axial features with position and circular runout tolerances. Pockets and surfaces are located with surface profiles.

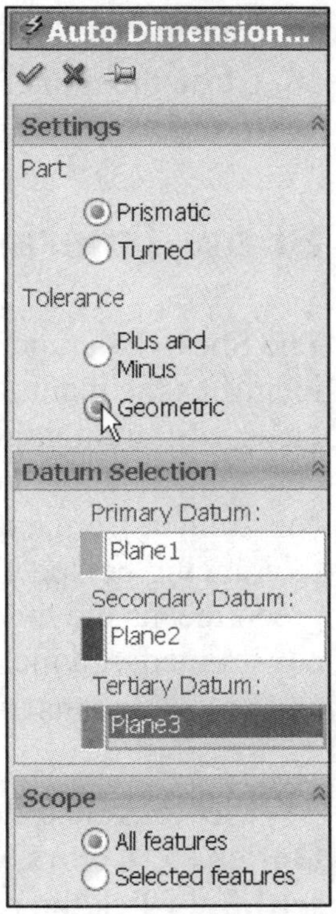


4. Click the **Geometric** box as illustrated. Note: the Prismatic box is checked.
5. Click the **back face** of the model. Plane1 is displayed in the Primary Datum box.
6. Click **inside** the Secondary Datum box.
7. Click the **left face** of the model. Plane2 is displayed in the Secondary Datum box.
8. Click **inside** the Tertiary Datum box.
9. Click the **top face** of the model. Plane3 is displayed in the Tertiary Datum box.
10. Click **OK** from the Auto Dimension PropertyManager.
11. Click **Isometric view** from the Heads-up View toolbar. View the Datum's, Feature Control Frames, and Geometric tolerances. All features are displayed in green.

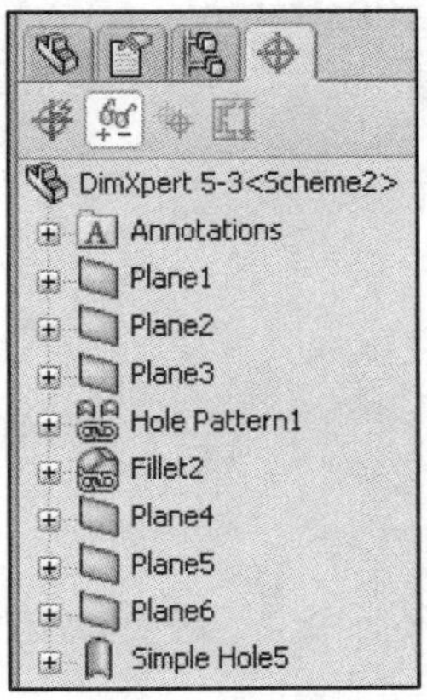

Edit a Feature Control Frame.

12. **Double-click** the illustrated Position Feature Control Frame. The Properties dialog box is displayed.

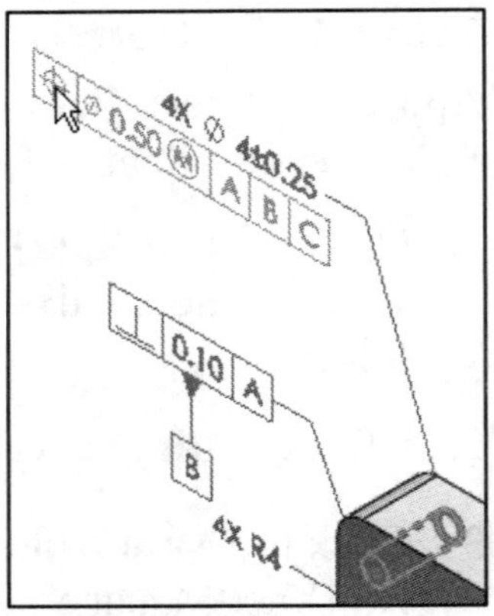


Modify the 0.50 tolerance.

13. Click **inside** the Tolerance 1 box.
14. **Delete** the existing text.
15. Enter **0.25**.
16. Click **OK** from the Properties dialog box.
17. **Repeat** the above procedure for the second Position Feature Control Frame. View the results.
18. **Close** the model. Do not save the model.

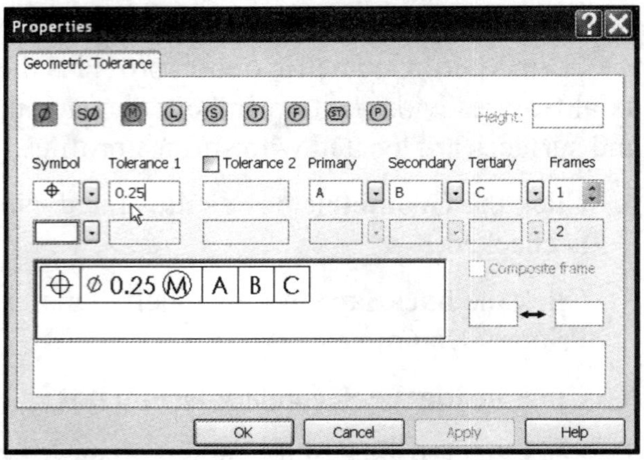


## Show Tolerance Status

The Show Tolerance Status option identifies the manufacturing features and faces, (different colors) which are fully constrained, under constrained, and over constrained from a dimensioning and tolerancing perspective. Example: All green means the model is fully constrained, red means over constrained, and yellow means under constrained.

Set tolerance status color, click **Options ➢ Colors, Color Scheme settings**. Click the required **setting** as illustrated.

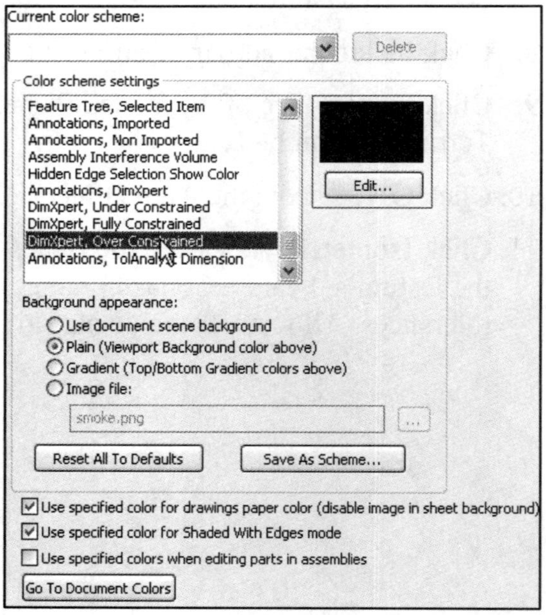

To exit tolerance status mode, click **Show Tolerance Status** or another SolidWorks command.

In the DimXpertManager:

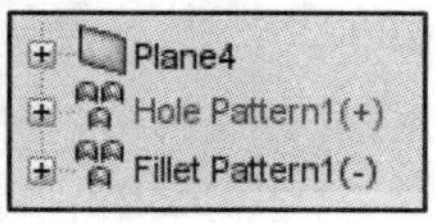


- Features with no mark after the name are fully constrained.
- Features with **(+)** following the name are over constrained.
- Features with **(-)** following the name are under constrained.

## Copy Scheme

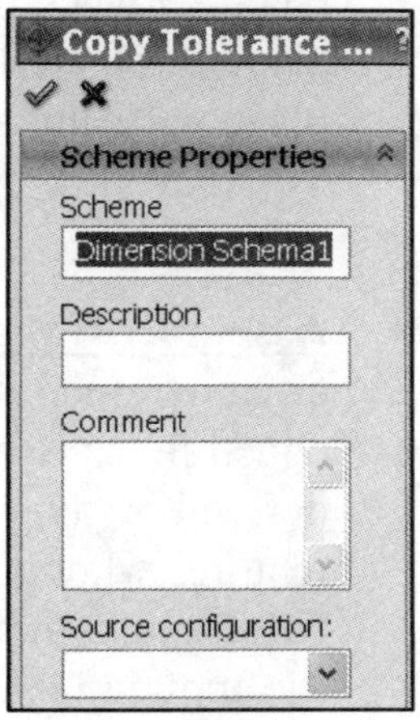


The Copy Scheme option provides the ability to copy a DimXpert tolerance scheme from one configuration of a part to another configuration. The Copy Scheme uses the Copy Tolerance PropertyManager. The Copy Tolerance PropertyManager provides the following selections:

- ***Scheme Properties***.
  - **Scheme**. DimXpert automatically enters a name (**Copy of** <*source configuration name*>), which you can modify.
  - **Description**. Add a description.
  - **Comment**. Add a comment.
  - **Source configuration**. Provides the ability to select the configuration with the tolerance scheme to copy.

## TolAnalyst Study

TolAnalyst is available in SolidWorks Premium. TolAnalyst is a tolerance analysis application that determines the effects that dimensions and tolerances have on parts and assemblies.

Use the DimXpert tools to apply dimensions and tolerances to a part or component in an assembly, then you use the TolAnalyst tools to leverage that data for stack-up analysis.

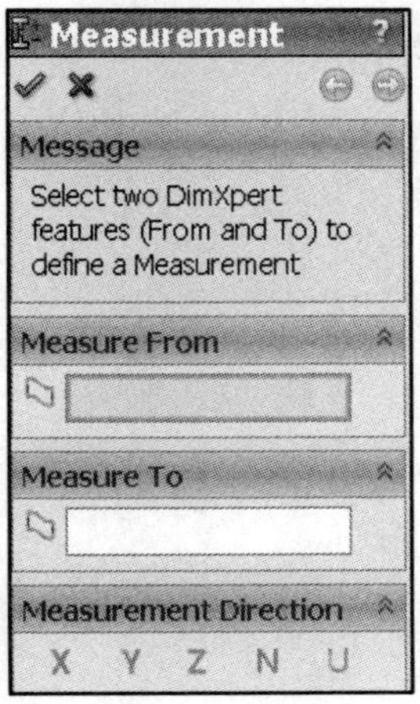


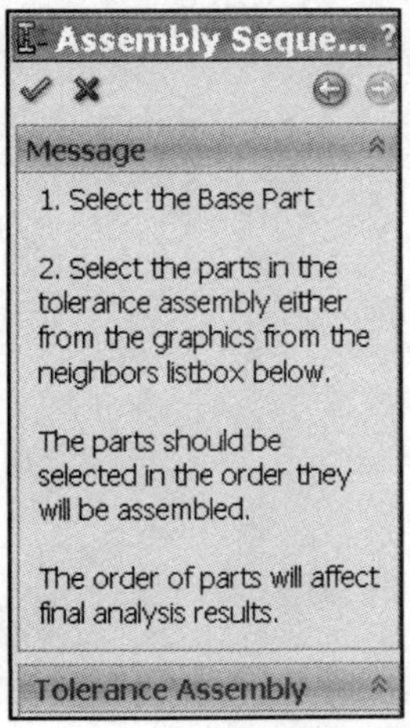

TolAnalyst performs a tolerance analysis called a study, which you create using a four-step procedure:

- **Measurement**. Establish the measurement, which is a linear distance between two DimXpert features. The first step in creating a TolAnalyst study is to specify the measurement as a linear dimension between two DimXpert features.
- **Assembly Sequence**. Select the ordered set of parts to establish a tolerance chain between the two measurement features. The selected parts form the "simplified assembly." A simplified assembly includes, at a minimum, the parts necessary to establish a tolerance chain between the two measurement features. This step also establishes the sequence or order in which you place parts into the simplified assembly, which TolAnalyst replicates when computing the worst case conditions.

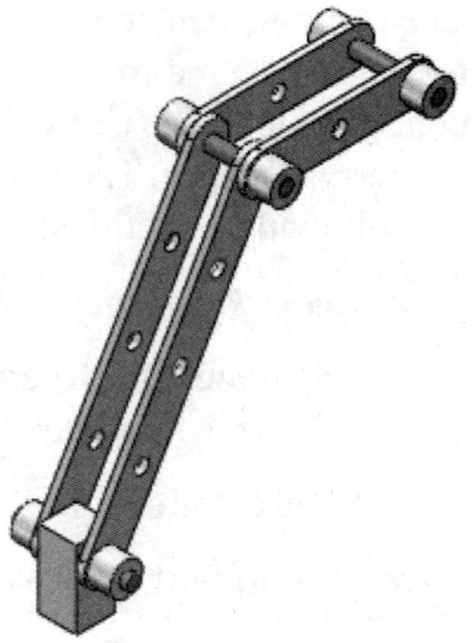

- **Assembly Constrains**. Define how each part is placed or constrained into the simplified assembly. Assembly constraints are analogous to mates. Constraints are derived by the relationships between DimXpert features whereas mates are derived by the relationships between geometric entities. Additionally, constraints are applied in sequence, which can play an important role and have significant impact on the results.
- **Analysis Results**. Evaluate and review the minimum and maximum worst case tolerance stacks. When the Results PropertyManager is activated, the results are automatically computed with the default or saved settings.

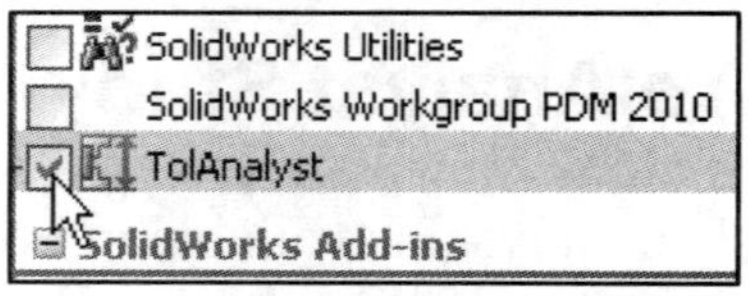


TolAnalyst is an Add-In in SolidWorks Premium.

## Summary

In this chapter, you learned about the available Sketch tools, Geometric Relations and Dimensions/Relations tools in SolidWorks. Sketch tools control the various aspects of creating and modifying a sketch. You reviewed and addressed the following tools from the Sketch toolbar: Fillet, Chamfer, Offset Entities, Convert Entities, Intersection Curve, Face Curves, Trim, Extend, Split Entities, Jog Line, Construction Geometry, Make Path, Mirror, Dynamic Mirror, Move, Rotate, Scale, Copy, Linear Pattern, Circular Pattern, Create Sketch From Selections, Repair Sketch, SketchXpert, Align, Modify, Close Sketch to Model, Check Sketch for Feature, 2D to 3D and Sketch Picture.

You utilized the 2D to 3D toolbar and reviewed the following tools: Front, Top, Left, Bottom, Back, Auxiliary, Sketch from Selections, Repair Sketch, Align Sketch, Extrude and Cut.

You addressed and applied Geometric Relations for 2D sketches using both Automatic and Manual Relations. You reviewed and applied Geometric Relations to 3D sketches.

You reviewed and used the tools from the Dimensions/Relations toolbar: Smart Dimension, Horizontal Dimension, Vertical Dimension, Baseline Dimension, Ordinate Dimension, Chamfer Dimension, Autodimension, Baseline Dimension, Add Relations and Display/Delete Relations.

You also addressed the DimXpertManager tools and learned about TolAnalyst.

In Chapter 6 explore and address the Extruded Boss/Base feature, Extruded Cut feature, Extruded Solid/Thin feature and the Extruded Surface feature. Also, address the Fillet feature using the Fillet and FilletXpert PropertyManager and Cosmetic threads.

**Notes:**

# CHAPTER 6: EXTRUDED BOSS/BASE, EXTRUDED CUT, FILLET AND COSMETIC FEATURES

## Chapter Objective

Chapter 6 provides a comprehensive understanding of Extruded and Fillet features in SolidWorks. On the completion of this chapter, you will be able to:

- Understand and utilize the following Extruded features:
  - Extruded Boss/Base
  - Extruded Cut
  - Extruded Solid/Thin
  - Extruded Surface:
    - Cut With Surface
- Comprehend and utilize the following information on Fillets:
  - Fillets in General
  - Fillet PropertyManager:
    - Manual tab
      - Constant Radius fillet
      - Variable Radius fillet
      - Face fillet
      - Full Round fillet
    - Control Points
    - FilletXpert PropertyManager:
      - Add tab
      - Change tab
      - Corner tab
- Apply the Cosmetic Thread feature

# Extruded Boss/Base Features

Once a sketch is complete, you can extrude the sketch to create a feature. An Extruded Boss/Base feature is created by projecting a 2D sketch perpendicular to the Sketch plane to create a 3D shape. An Extrude Base feature (Boss-Extrude1) is the first feature that adds material in a part.

A Boss feature (Boss-Extrude2) adds material onto an existing feature. An Extruded Cut feature removes material from the part. The Extrude-Thin feature parameter option provides the ability to specific thickness of the extrusion. Extrude features can be solids or surfaces. Solids are utilized primary for machined parts and contain mass properties. Surfaces are utilized surfaces for organic shapes which contain no mass properties.

For an Extruded Boss/Base feature, you need to identify a Start Condition from the Sketch plane and an End Condition. The Boss-Extrude PropertyManager provides the ability to select four Start Conditions options. Sheet metal features are addressed later in the Sheet metal chapter of the book.

# Extruded Boss/Base Feature

The Extruded Boss/Base feature uses the Boss-Extrude PropertyManager. The Boss-Extrude PropertyManager provides the following selections:

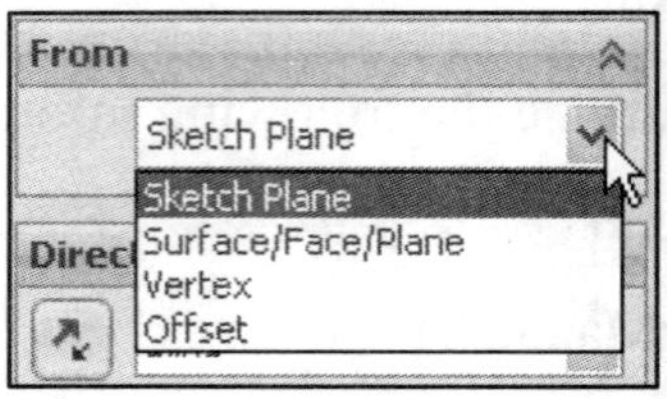


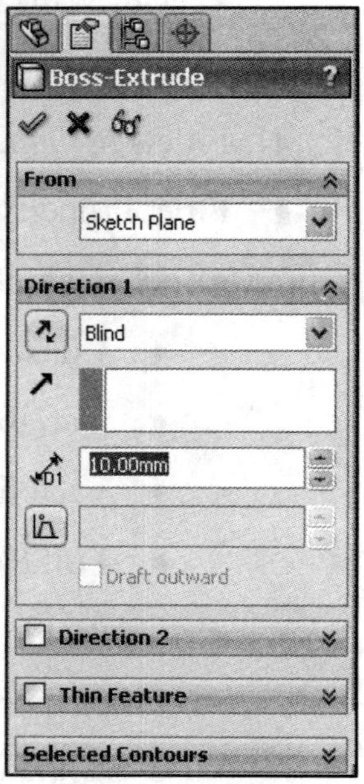


- ***From***. Displays the location of the initial extrude feature or the Start condition. The available options are:
  - **Sketch Plane**. Selected by default. Initiates that the extrude feature is from the selected Sketch plane.
  - **Surface/Face/Plane**. Initiates that the extrude feature is from a valid selected entity. A valid entity is a surface, face or plane.

The entity can be planar or non-planar. Planar entities do not require to be parallel to the Sketch plane. The sketch must be entirely contained within the boundaries of the non-planar surface or face. The sketch follows the shape of the non-planar entity at the starting surface or face.

  - **Vertex**. Initiates that the extrude feature is from the selected vertex.

- **Offset**. Initiates that the extrude feature is from a plane that is offset from the current Sketch plane. Set the Offset distance in the Enter Offset Value box from the Offset option.

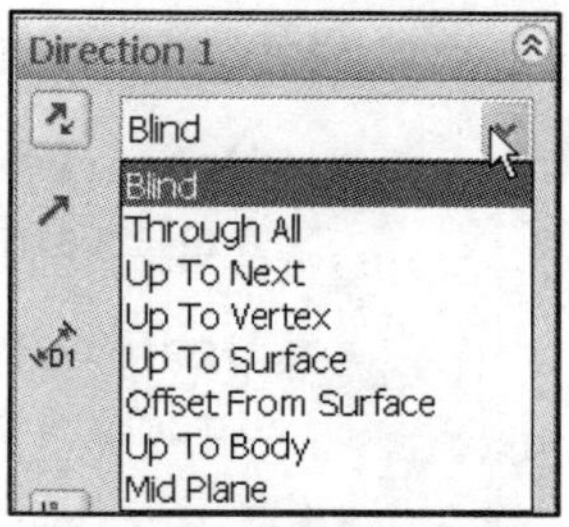


- ***Direction 1***. Provides the ability to select an End Condition Type. Extrudes in a single direction from the selected option. The available End Condition Types for Direction 1 are feature dependent:
  - **Blind**. Selected by default. Extends the feature for a specified depth.
  - **Through All**. Extends the feature from the sketch plane through all existing geometry.
  - **Up To Next**. Only available for a Boss feature. Extrudes the feature from the Sketch plane to the next surface that intercepts the entire profile. The intercepting surface must be on the same part to use the Up To Next option.
  - **Up To Vertex**. Extends the feature from the Sketch plane to a plane which is parallel to the Sketch plane, and passes through the specified vertex. Sketch vertices are valid selections for the Up To Vertex option extrusions.
  - **Up To Surface**. Extends the feature from the Sketch plane to a selected surface. The extrusion is shaped by the selected surface. Only one surface selection is allowed.
  - **Offset From Surface**. Extends the feature from the Sketch plane to the specified distance from the selected surface. An Offset From Surface value in required with this option as illustrated.

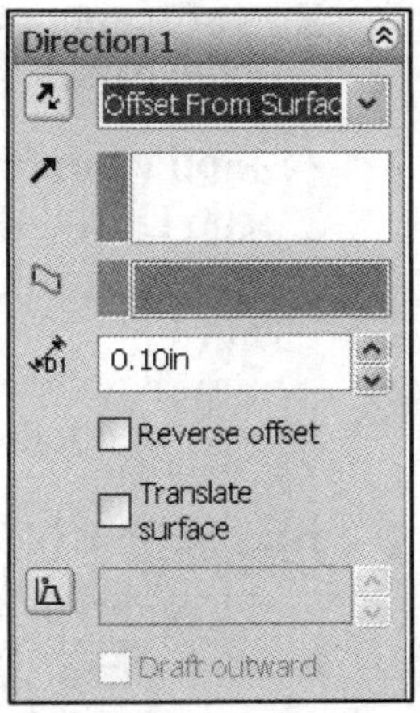


  - **Up To Body**. Extends the feature from the Sketch plane to a specified body. Use the Up To Body type option with assemblies, mold parts, or multi-body parts.
  - **Mid Plane**. Extends the feature from the Sketch plane equally in both directions. Direction 2 is not available with this option.
  - **Reverse Direction**. Only available for the following options: Blind, Up To Surface, Offset From Surface, and Up To Body. Reverses the direction of the extrude feature if required.

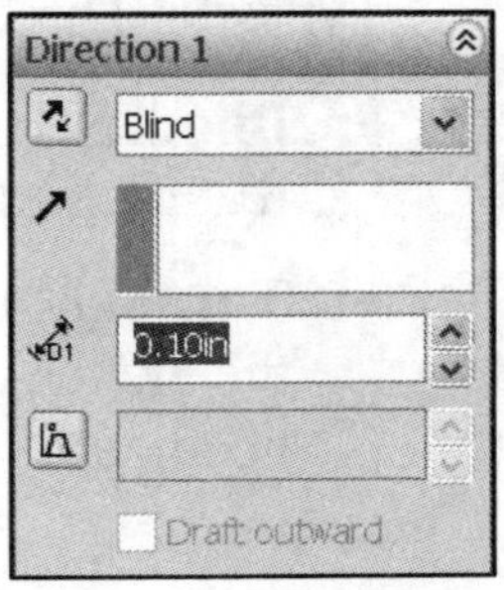


  - **Direction of Extrusion**. The Direction of Extrusion box provides the ability to display the selected direction vector from the Graphics Window to extrude the sketch in a direction other than normal to the sketch profile.

- **Depth**. Displays the selected depth of the extruded feature.
- **Draft On/Off**. Adds a draft to the extruded feature. The Draft On/Off option provides two selections:

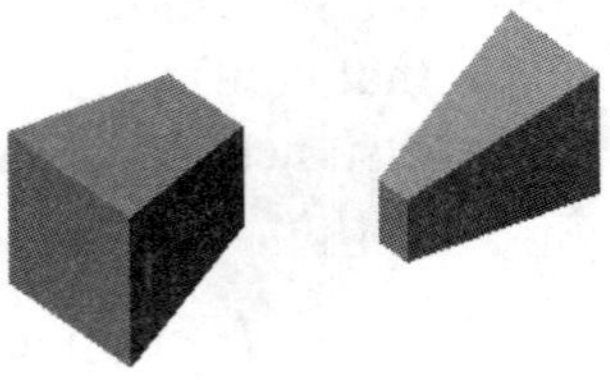

10° draft angle outward    10° draft angle inward

  - **Required draft angle**. Input the required draft angle value.
  - **Draft outward**. Modifies the direction of the draft if required.

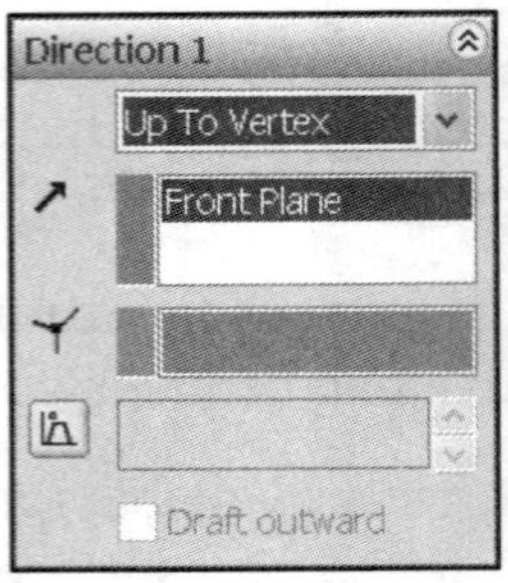

- **Vertex**. Only available for the Up To Vertex option. Displays the selected vertex for the extruded feature.
- **Face/Plane**. Only available for the Up To Surface and Offset From Surface option. Displays the selected face or plane and provides the ability to select either a face or plane from the Graphics window or FeatureManager.
- **Reverse offset**. Only available for the Offset From Surface option. Reverses the offset direction if required.
- **Translate surface**. Only available for the Offset From Surface option. Provides the ability to make the end of the extrusion a translation of the reference surface, rather than a true offset.
- **Solid/Surface Body**. Only available for the Up To Body option. Displays the selected solid or surface body and provides the ability to select either a solid or surface from the Graphics window or FeatureManager.

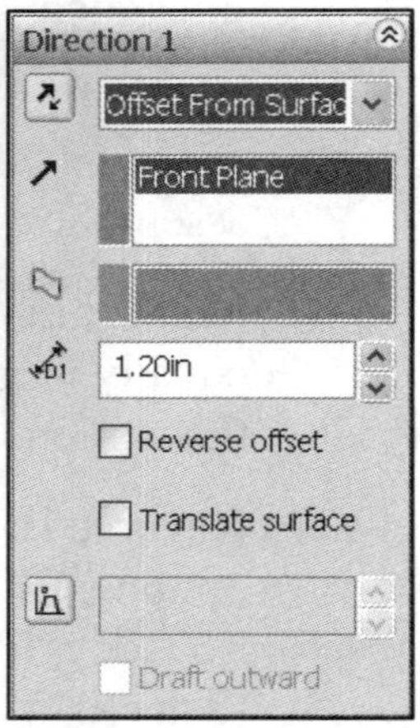


- ***Direction 2***. Provides the ability to select an End Condition Type for Direction 2. Extrudes in a single direction from the selected option. The available End Condition Types for Direction 2 are feature dependent:
  - **Blind**. Selected by default. Extends the feature for a specified depth.
  - **Through All**. Extends the feature from the Sketch plane through all existing geometry.

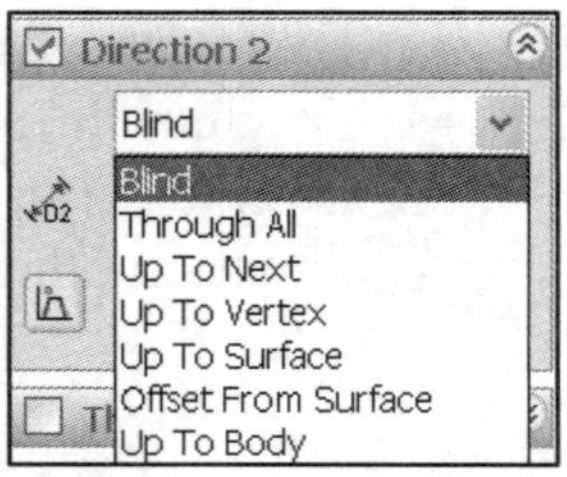

- **Up To Next**. Only available for a Boss feature. Extrudes the feature from the Sketch plane to the next surface that intercepts the entire profile. The intercepting surface must be on the same part to use the Up To Next option.
- **Up To Vertex**. Extends the feature from the Sketch plane to a plane which is parallel to the Sketch plane, and passes through the specified vertex. Sketch vertices are valid selections for the Up To Vertex option extrusions.
- **Up To Surface**. Extends the feature from the Sketch plane to a selected surface. The extrusion is shaped by the selected surface. Only one surface selection is allowed.
- **Offset From Surface**. Extends the feature from the Sketch plane to the specified distance from the selected surface. An Offset From Surface value in required with this option.

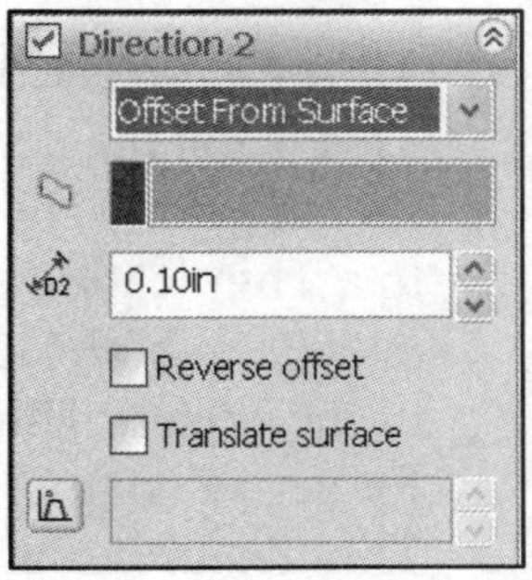


- **Up To Body**. Extends the feature from the Sketch plane to a specified body. Use the Up To Body type option with assemblies, mold parts, or multi-body parts.
- **Reverse Direction**. Only available for the following options: Blind, Up To Surface, Offset From Surface, and Up To Body. Reverses the direction of the extrude feature if required.
- **Depth**. Displays the selected depth of the extruded feature.
- **Draft On/Off**. Adds a draft to the extruded feature. The Draft On/Off option provides two selections:
  - **Required draft angle**. Input the required draft angle value.
  - **Draft outward**. Modifies the direction of the draft if required.

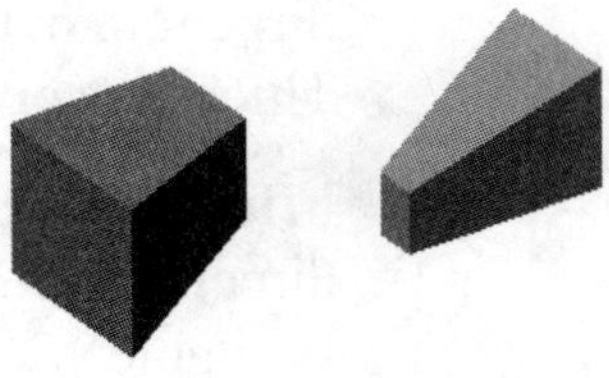

10° draft angle outward 10° draft angle inward

- **Vertex**. Only available for the Up To Vertex option. Displays the selected vertex for the extruded feature.
- **Face/Plane**. Only available for the Up To Surface and Offset From Surface option. Displays the selected face or plane and provides the ability to select either a face or plane from the Graphics window or FeatureManager.

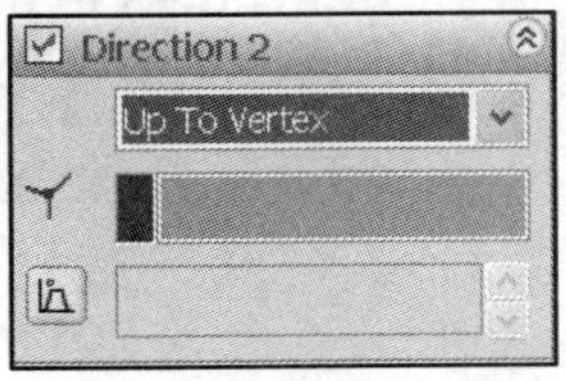


- **Reverse offset**. Only available for the Offset From Surface option. Reverses the offset direction if required.
- **Translate surface**. Only available for the Offset From Surface option. Provides the ability to make the end of the extrusion a translation of the reference surface, rather than a true offset.

- **Solid/Surface Body**. Only available for the Up To Body option. Displays the selected solid or surface body and provides the ability to select either a solid or surface from the Graphics window or FeatureManager.

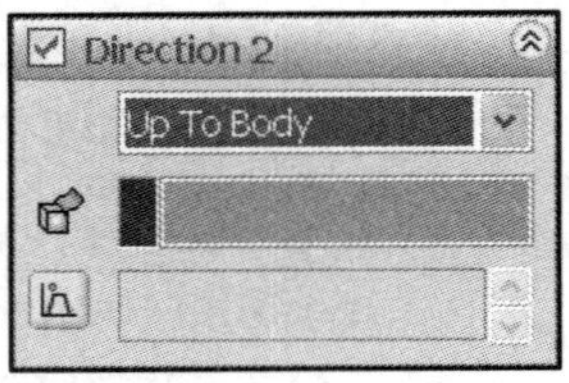


Set an End Condition Type for Direction 1 and Direction 2 to extrude in two directions with unequal depths. Direction 1 and Direction 2 are always separated by 180 degrees. Direction 2 becomes inactive if you select the Mid Plane End Condition in Direction 1.

- ***Thin Feature***. Controls the extrude thickness of the profile. This is not the depth. Create a Thin feature by using an active sketch profile and applying a wall thickness. Apply thickness to a Thin feature either to the inside or outside of the sketch, evenly on both sides of the sketch, or unevenly on either side of the sketch. Thin feature creation is automatically invoked for active contours that are extruded or revolved. Create a Thin feature from a closed contour. There are three conditions to select from:

  - **Type**. Displays the selected type of a thin extrude feature extrude. There are three options. They are:

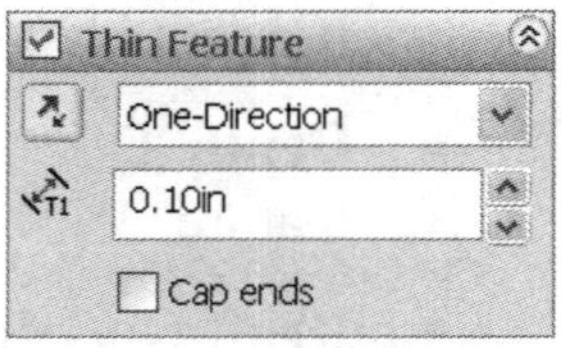


    - **One-Direction**. Sets the extrude thickness in one direction, outwards from the sketch. The Direction 1 Thickness option is available.
    - **Mid-Plane**. Sets the extrude thickness equally in both directions from the sketch. The Thickness option is available.

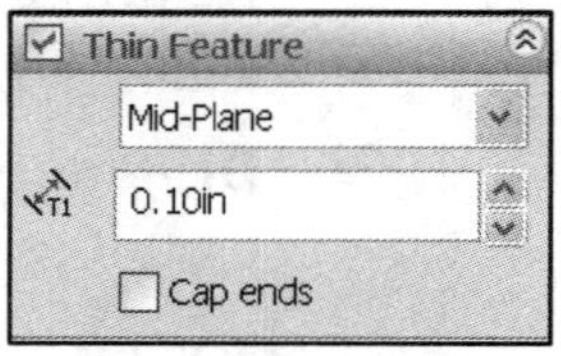


    - **Two-Direction**. Sets the extrude thickness in two directions, outward from the sketch. The Direction 1 and Direction 2 Thickness option is available.
  - **Direction 1 Thickness**. Displays the selected extrude thickness in one direction, outward from the sketch.
  - **Direction 2 Thickness**. Displays the selected extrude thickness in a second direction, outward from the sketch.

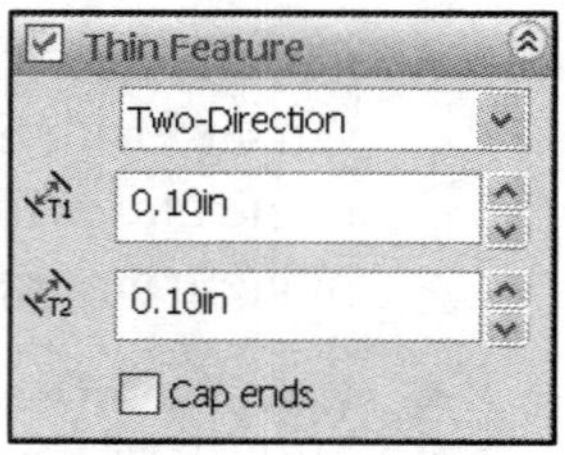

- **Cap ends**. Covers the end of the thin feature extrude, creating a hollow part. Provides the ability to set the Cap Thickness option. This option is available only for the first extruded body in a model.
- **Cap Thickness**. Displays the selected extrude thickness of the cap.

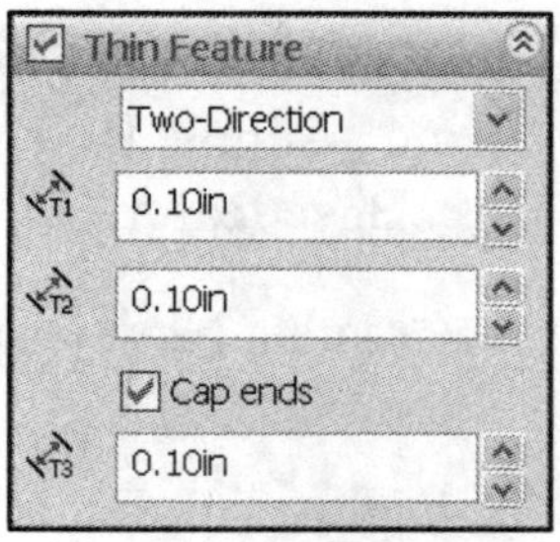


The Cap ends option is only available for the first extruded body in your model. This option specifies the end of the Thin feature extrude, which creates a hollow part. A thickness of the Cap is required.

- **Auto-fillet corners**. Selected by default. Only available for an open sketch. Rounds each edge where the lines meet at an angle.
- **Fillet Radius**. Only available if the Auto-fillet corners option is selected. Sets the inside radius of the round.

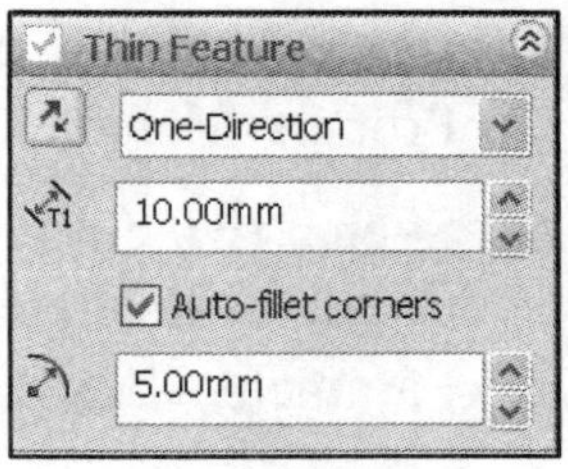


- ***Selected Contours***. Displays the selected contours and provides the ability to use a partial sketch to create the extrude feature. Select sketch contours and model edges from the Graphics window or FeatureManager.

- ***Feature Scope***. Apply features to one or more multi-body parts. The Feature Scope box provides the following selections:
  - **All bodies**. Applies the feature to all bodies every time the feature regenerates. If you add new bodies to the model that are intersected by the feature, these new bodies are also regenerated to include the feature.

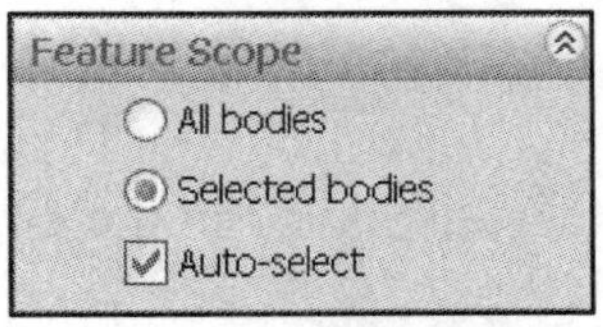


  - **Selected bodies**. Selected by default. Applies the feature to the selected bodies.
  - **Auto-select**. Only available if you select the Selected bodies option. When you first create a model with multi-body parts, the feature automatically processes all the relevant intersecting parts. Auto-select is faster than All bodies because it processes only the bodies on the initial list and does not regenerate the entire model.

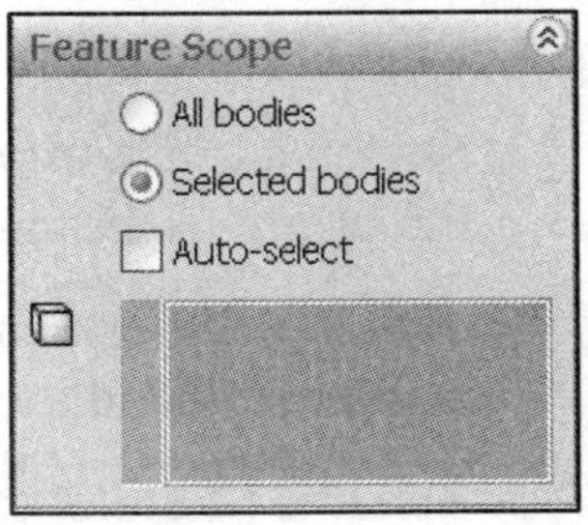


  - **Solid Bodies to Affect**. Only available if Auto-select is not active. Displays the selected bodies to affect from the Graphics window.

### *Tutorial: Extrude 6-1*

Create a simple Rod part on the Front Plane using the Extruded Boss/Base feature.

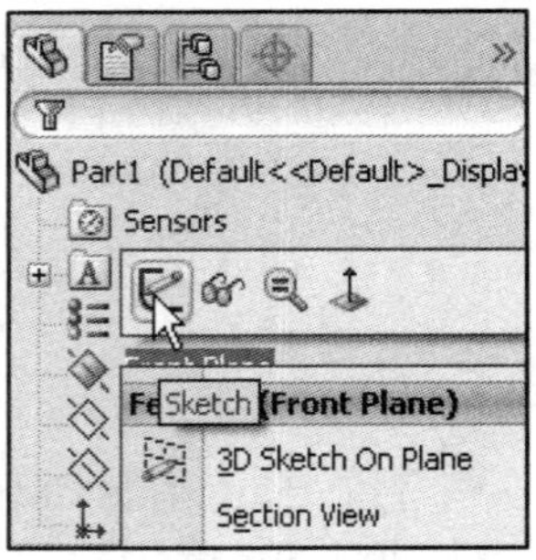


1. Create a **New** part. Use the default ANSI, MMGS Part template.
2. Right-click **Front Plane** from the FeatureManager. This is your Sketch plane.
3. Click **Sketch** from the Context toolbar.
4. Click **Circle** from the Sketch toolbar. The Circle PropertyManager is displayed.

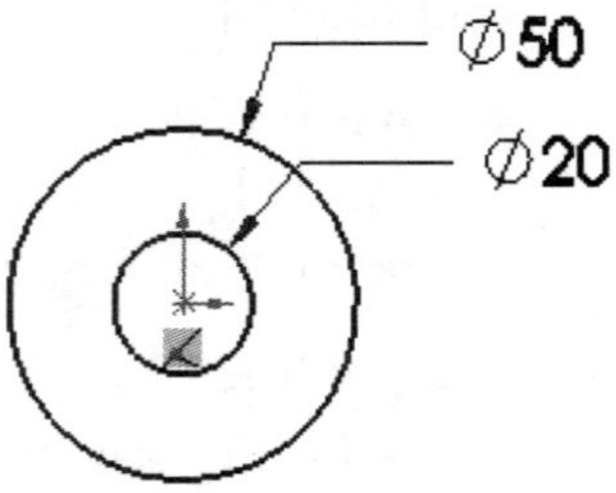


5. Sketch **two circles**, one inside the other centered at the origin as illustrated. Center creation is check in the Parameters box. Click **Smart Dimension**.
6. Enter a **20**mm dimension for the small circle. Enter a **50**mm dimension for the large circle.
7. Click **OK** from the Dimension PropertyManager.
8. **Rebuild** the model.
9. Rename **Sketch1** to **Sketch1-Profile**.
10. Right-click **Right Plane** from the FeatureManager.

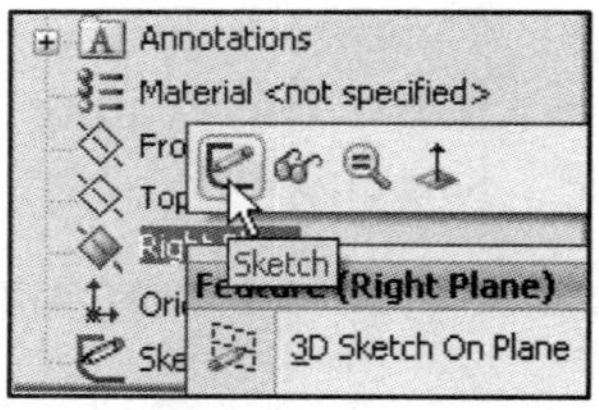


11. Click **Sketch** from the Context toolbar. Click **Right view** from the Heads-up View toolbar. Right Plane is displayed in the Graphics window.
12. Click **Centerline** from the Consolidated Line Sketch tool bar.
13. Sketch a **horizontal centerline** 50mm from the origin to the right.
14. Sketch a **30deg centerline** horizontal from the origin. **Rebuild** the model.

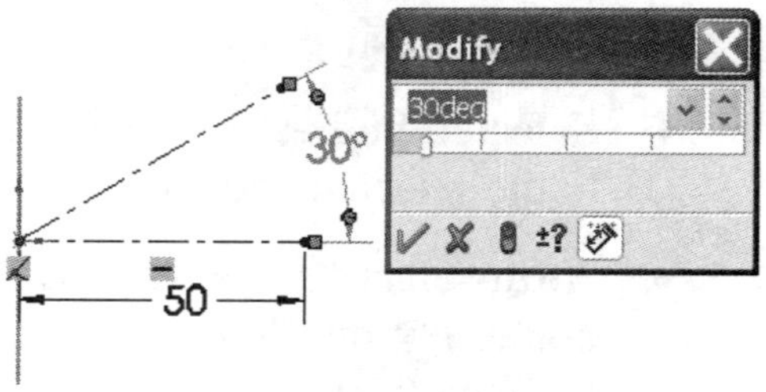


15. Rename **Sketch2** to **Sketch2-Vectors**.
16. Click **Sketch1-Profile** from the FeatureManager.
17. Click **Isometric view** from the Heads-up View toolbar.
18. Click the **circular edge** of the 20mm circle. Note: The Instant3D green arrow.

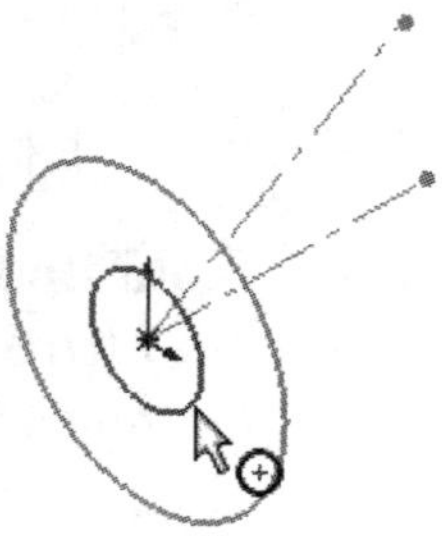

19. Click **Extruded Boss/Base** from the Features toolbar. The Boss-Extrude PropertyManager is displayed.

20. Select **Offset** for the Start Condition in the From dialog box.
21. Enter **20**mm for Offset value.
22. Select **Up To Vertex** for the End Condition Type in Direction 1.

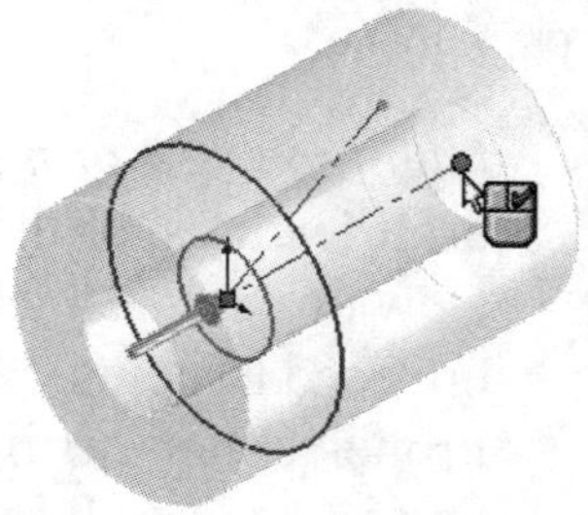

23. Click the **horizontal centerline** endpoint as illustrated. Point2@Sketch2-Vector is displayed in the vertex box. The extrude arrow points to the right.
24. Click inside the **Direction of Extrusion** box for Direction 1.
25. Click the **30deg centerline** from the Graphics window. Line2@Sketch2-Vector is displayed in the Direction of Extrusion box. The Extrusion is angled 30 degrees from horizontal.

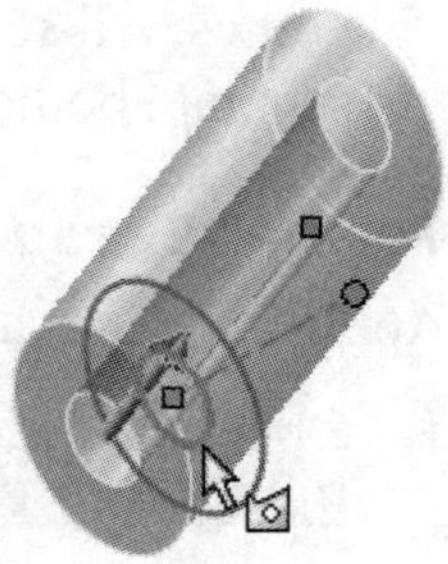

26. **Expand** the Selected Contours box.
27. Click the **circular edge** of the 20mm circle. The Sketch1-Profile Contour is displayed in the Selected Contours box.

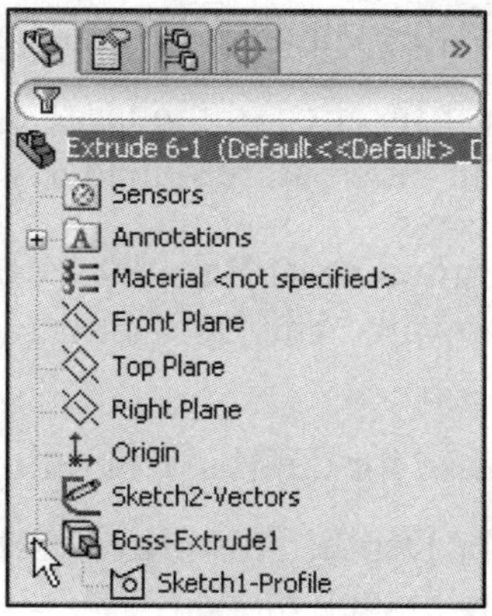


28. Click **OK** from the Boss-Extrude PropertyManager. Boss-Extrude1 is displayed in the FeatureManager. The Extrusion is perpendicular to the Sketch plane. Sketch1-Profile is displayed under the Boss-Extrude1 feature in the FeatureManager design tree.

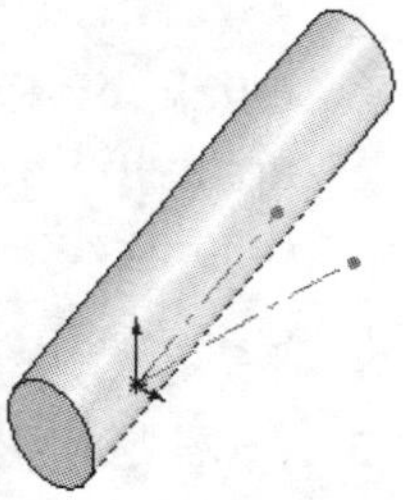

29. **Save** the part.
30. Enter the name **Extrude 6-1**.
31. **Close** the model.

By default, the direction of Extrusion is normal to the Sketch plane, but you can also select a linear entity such as an edge or axis as the direction.

## Detailed Preview PropertyManager

The Detailed Preview PropertyManager provides the ability to display detailed previews and control what is displayed in the Graphics window for the following features: Extrudes, Ribs and Drafts.

There are two selections in the Detailed Preview PropertyManager. They are:

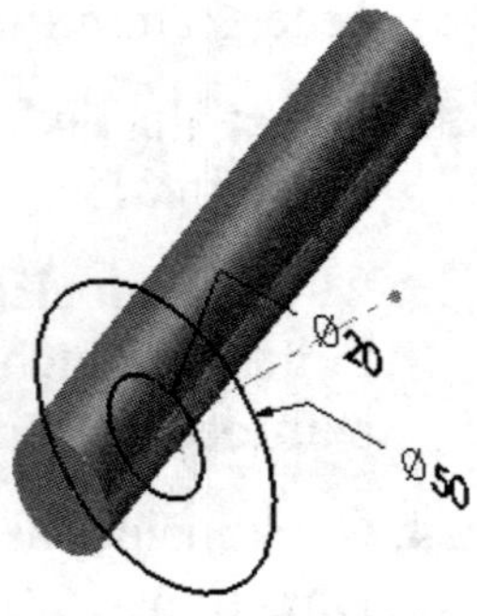


- *Highlight new or modified faces.* Displays new extrude, rib, or draft features, or the faces that were changed by your last edit. New or modified faces are highlighted in a different color, as opposed to being displayed shaded as they do in the standard PropertyManager if the Highlight new or modified faces check box is active. All individual bodies are displayed in the preview.
- *Show only new or modified bodies*. Displays new or modified bodies. All separate bodies are hidden in the preview. Only separate bodies are affected by this option.

***Tutorial: Extrude 6-2***

Apply a few advanced Extruded Boss/Base feature options.

1. Open **Extrude 6-2** from the SolidWorks 2010 folder. The Extrude 6-2 FeatureManager is displayed.
2. Click the **circumference** of the large circle. Sketch1-Profiles is highlighted in the FeatureManager.
3. Click the **Extruded Boss/Base** Features tool. The direction arrow points upward. The Boss-Extrude PropertyManager is displayed.

4. Select **Mid Plane** for the End Condition in Direction 1.
5. Enter **20**mm for Depth. This provides 10mm's of extrusion on each side of the Sketch plane.
6. Click **OK** from the Boss-Extrude PropertyManager. Boss-Extrude1 is created and is displayed in the FeatureManager.
7. Click the **circumference** of the small circle. Sketch1-Profiles is highlighted in the FeatureManager under Extrude1.

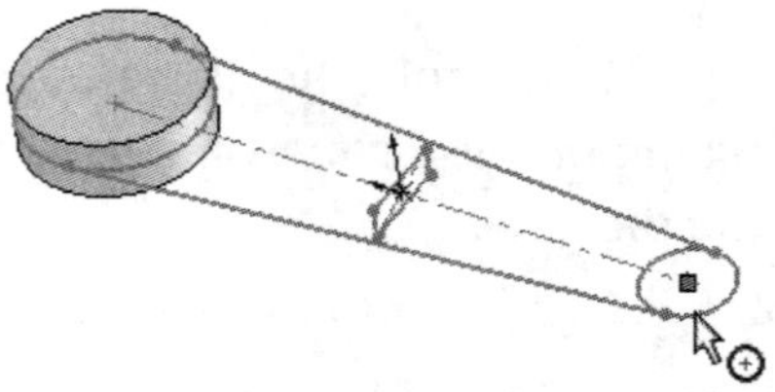

8. Click the **Extruded Boss/Base** Features tool. The Boss-Extrude PropertyManager is displayed.
9. Select **Mid Plane** for the End Condition in Direction 1. The extrude arrow points in an upward direction as illustrated.

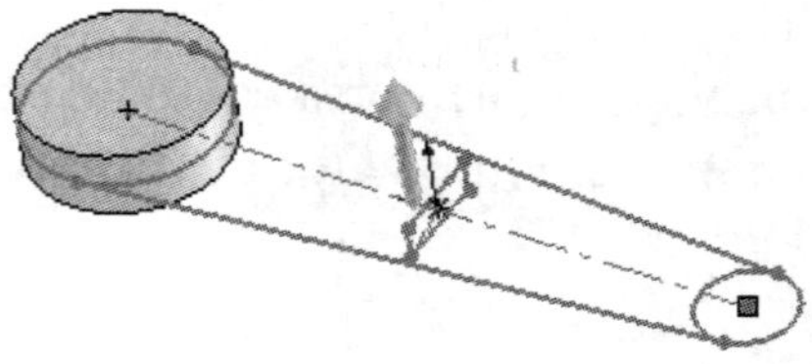

10. Enter **40**mm for Depth.
11. Click inside the **Selected Contours** box.
12. Click the **circumference** of the small circle. Sketch1-Profies-Contours<1> is displayed in the Selected Contours box.

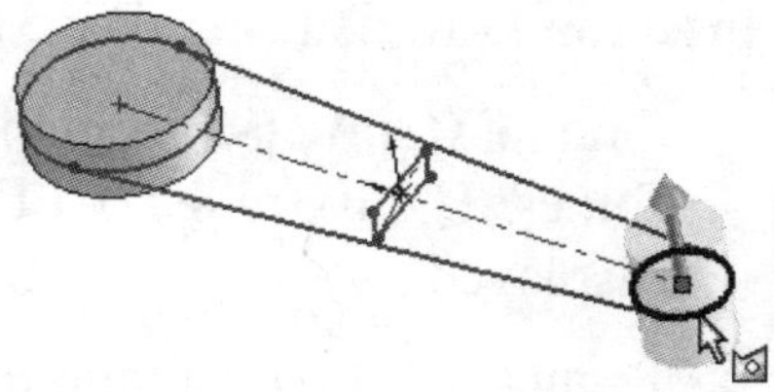

13. Click **OK** from the Boss-Extrude PropertyManager. Boss-Extrude2 is created and is displayed from the FeatureManager.

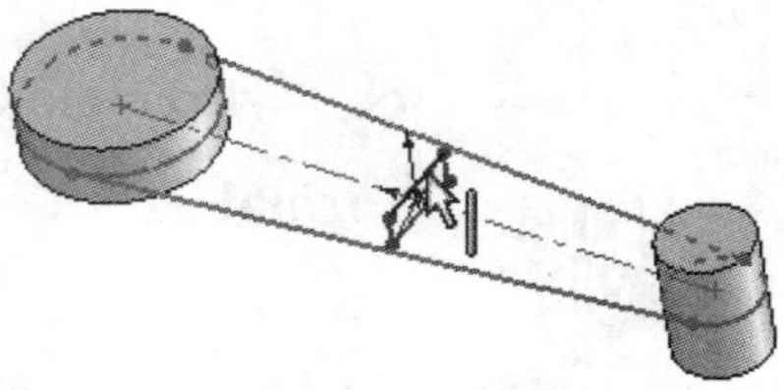

Extrude the sketch handle.

14. Click the **Top profile line** on the rectangular handle. Sketch2-Handle is highlighted in the FeatureManager.
15. Right-click **Select Chain**. You selected all sketch entities of the handle.
16. Click **Extruded Boss/Base** from the Features toolbar. The direction arrow point to the left. The Boss-Extrude PropertyManager is displayed.
17. Select **Up To Surface** for the End Condition in Direction 1.

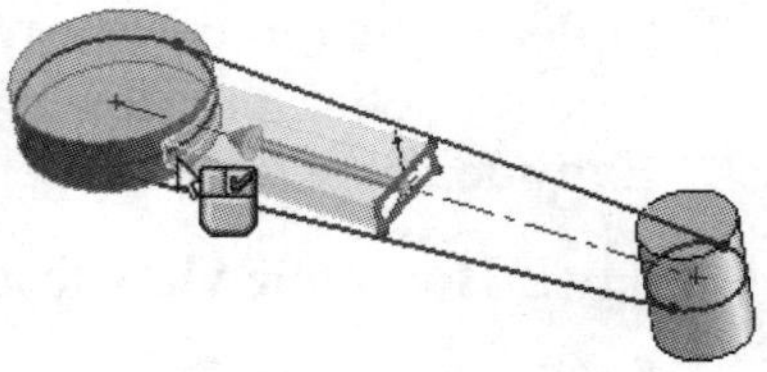

18. Click the **cylindrical face** of the large cylinder. Face<1> is displayed in the Face/Plane box.
19. **Expand** the Direction 2 box from the Extrude PropertyManager.
20. Select **Up To Surface** for the End Condition in Direction 2.

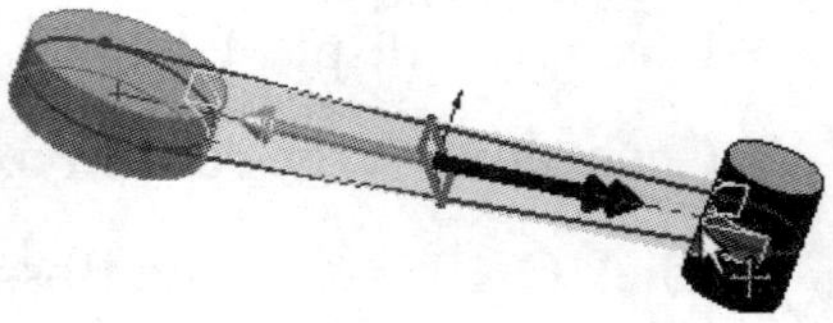

21. Click the **inside cylindrical face** of the small cylinder. Face<2> is displayed in the Solid/Surface Body box.
22. Click **OK** from the Boss-Extrude PropertyManager. Boss-Extrude3 is created.
23. Display an **Isometric view**. You created three extrusions using advance features of the Boss-Extrude PropertyManager.

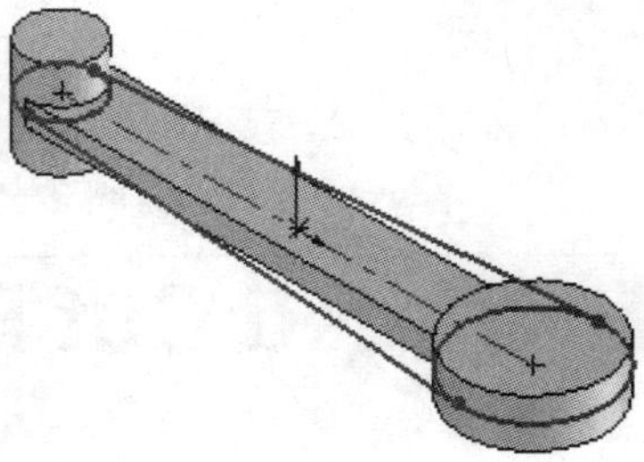

24. **Close** the model.

***Tutorial: Extruded 6-3***

Insert an Extruded Boss/Base feature in a 3D model.

1. Open **Extrude 6-3** from the SolidWorks 2010 folder. The Extruded 6-3 FeatureManager is displayed.
2. Right-click **Front Plane** from the FeatureManager.
3. Click **Sketch** from the Context toolbar.
4. Display a **Normal To view** from the Heads-up View toolbar.

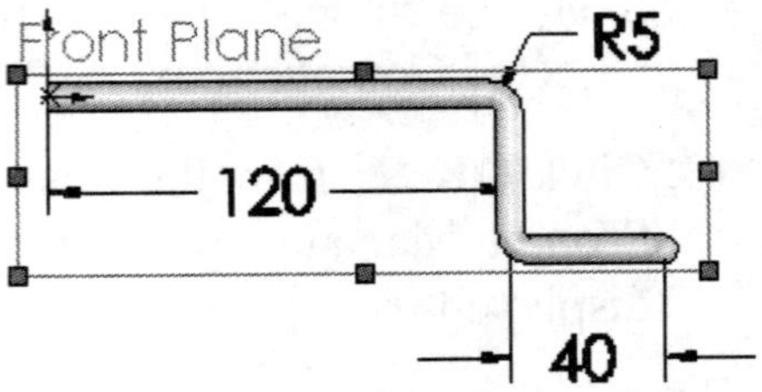


5. Click the **Circle** Sketch tool. The Circle PropertyManager is displayed.
6. Sketch a **circle** on the face of the tube as illustrated.
7. **Dimension** the circle with a 3mm diameter.

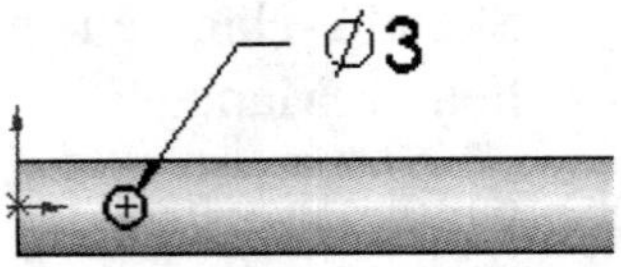


8. Click **Extruded Boss/Base** from the Features toolbar. The direction arrow points towards the back. If required, click the Reverse Direction box The Boss-Extrude PropertyManager is displayed.
9. Click **Isometric view** from the Heads-up View toolbar.
10. Select the **Up to Surface** End Condition for Direction1.
11. Click the **opposite side** of the frame as illustrated. Face<1> is displayed in the Face/Plane box.
12. Check the **Merge result** box.
13. Click **OK** from the Boss-Extrude PropertyManager. Boss-Extrude1 is created and is displayed in the FeatureManager.
14. **Close** the model.

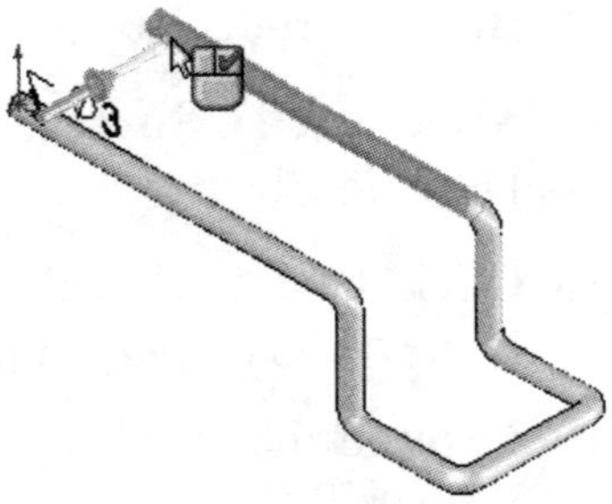

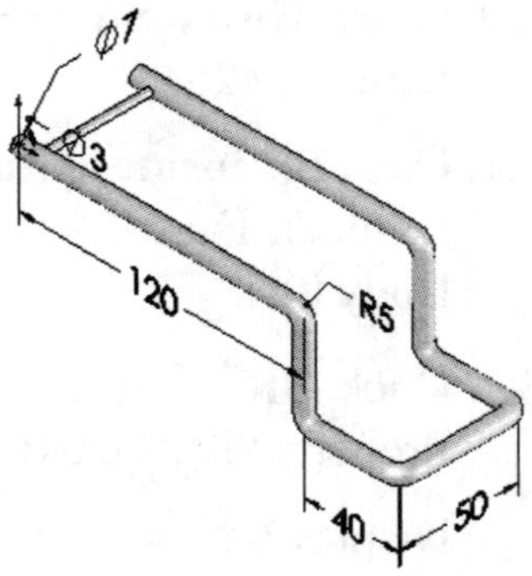


# Extruded Cut Feature

The Extruded Cut feature procedure is very similar to the Extruded Boss/Base feature. First create a sketch, second select the required options from the Extrude PropertyManager. You need a Start Condition from the Sketch plane and an End Condition.

The Cut-Extrude PropertyManager provides four Start Condition options from the drop-down menu. Note: The four Start Condition options are the same as for the Extruded Boss/Base feature.

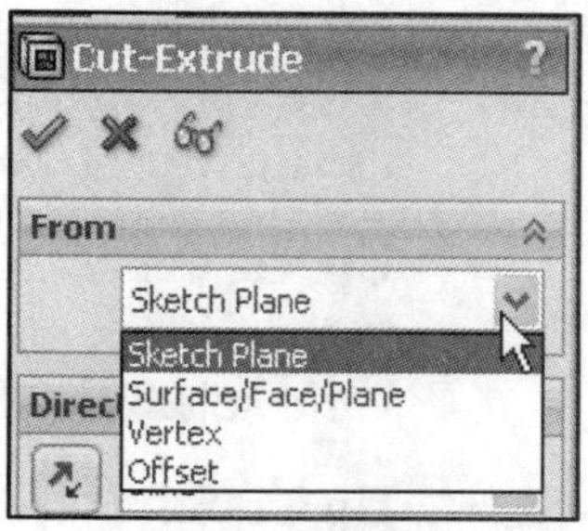


In multi-body parts, use the Extruded Cut feature to create disjoint parts. Organize which parts to keep and which parts will be affected by the cut.

The Extruded Cut feature uses the Cut-Extrude PropertyManager. The Cut-Extrude PropertyManager provides the following selections:

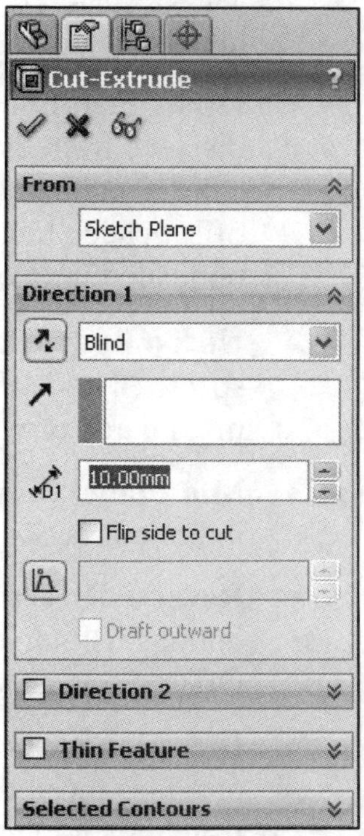


- ***From***. Displays the start location of the initial extrude feature. The From dialog box provides the following available Start conditions:
  - **Sketch Plane**. Selected by default. Initiates the extrude feature from the selected Sketch plane.
  - **Surface/Face/Plane**. Initiates the extrude feature from a valid selected entity. A valid entity is a surface, face or plane
  - **Vertex**. Initiates the extrude feature from the selected vertex.
  - **Offset**. Initiates the extrude feature on a plane that is offset from the current Sketch plane. Set the Offset distance in the Enter Offset Value box.
- ***Direction 1***. Provides the ability to select an End Condition Type in Direction 1. This option provides the ability to cut in a single direction from the Sketch plane. The available End Condition Types for Direction 1 are feature dependent:

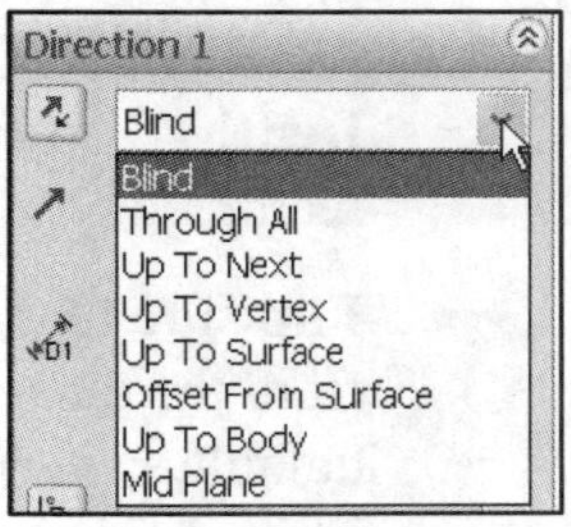


  - **Blind**. Selected by default. Cuts the feature for a specified depth.
  - **Through All**. Cuts the feature from the Sketch plane through all existing geometry.

- **Up To Next**. Cuts the feature from the Sketch plane to the next surface that intercepts the entire profile. The intercepting surface must be on the same part to use the Up To Next option.
- **Up To Vertex**. Cuts the feature from the Sketch plane to a plane which is parallel to the Sketch plane, and passing through the specified vertex. Sketch vertices are valid selections for Up To Vertex extrusions.
- **Up To Surface**. Cuts the feature from the Sketch plane to the selected surface. The extrusion is shaped by the selected surface. Only one surface selection is allowed.
- **Offset From Surface**. Cuts the feature from the Sketch plane to a specified distance from the selected surface. You are required to enter a value with this option selected. Select the Reverse offset check box to offset the specified distance in the opposite direction if required.
- **Up To Body**. Cuts the feature from the sketch plane to a specified body. Use the Up To Body type with assemblies, mold parts, or multi-body parts.
- **Mid Plane**. Cuts the feature from the Sketch plane equally in both directions.
- **Reverse Direction**. Only available for the following options: Blind, Through All, Up To Next, Up To Surface, Offset From Surface and Up To Body.

- **Direction of Extrusion**. The Direction of Extrusion box provides the ability to display the selected direction vector from the Graphics Window to extrude the sketch in a direction other than normal to the sketch profile
- **Depth**. Displays the selected depth of the extruded cut feature.
- **Flip side to cut**. Removes all material from the outside of the profile. By default, material is removed from the inside of the profile.

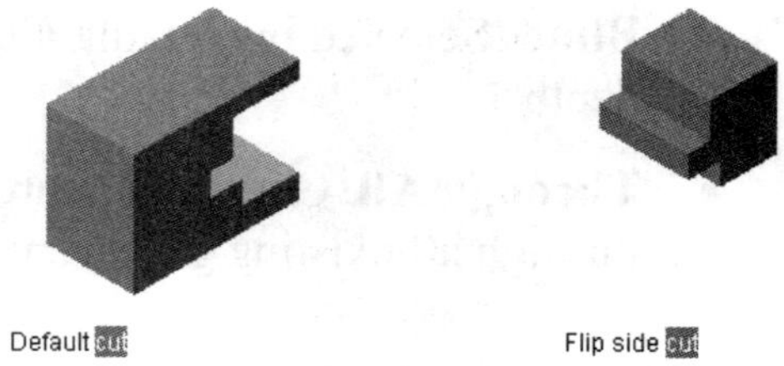


- **Draft On/Off**. Adds a draft to the extruded cut feature. The Draft On/Off option provides two selections:
  - **Required draft angle**. Input the required draft angle value.
  - **Draft outward**. Modifies the direction of the draft if required.

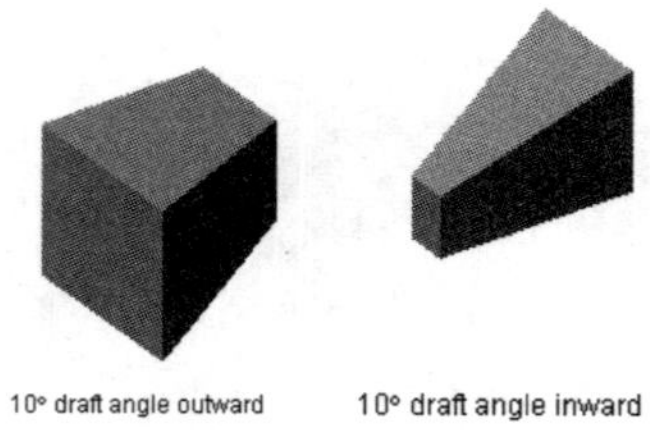

- **Vertex**. Only available for the Up To Vertex option. Displays the selected vertex for the extruded cut feature.
- **Face/Plane**. Only available for the Up To Surface and Offset From Surface option. Displays the selected face or plane and provides the ability to select either a face or plane from the Graphics window or FeatureManager.
- **Reverse offset**. Only available for the Offset From Surface option. Reverses the offset direction if required.

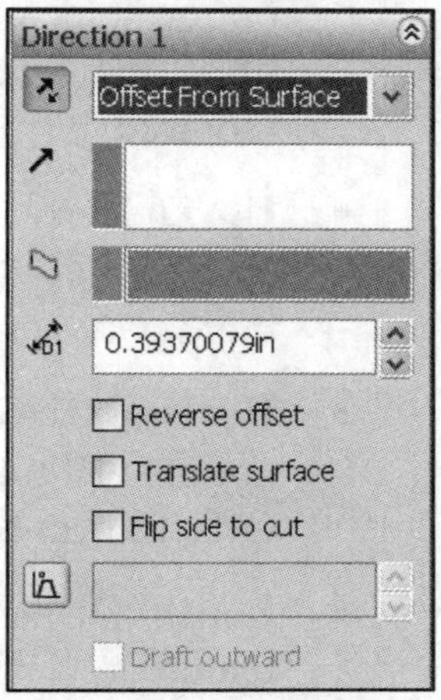


- **Translate surface**. Only available for the Offset From Surface option. Provides the ability to make the end of the extrusion a translation of the reference surface, rather than a true offset.
- **Solid/Surface Body**. Only available for the Up To Body option. Displays the selected solid or surface body and provides the ability to select either a solid or surface from the Graphics window or FeatureManager.
- **Normal cut**. Only available for Sheet metal cut extrudes. Provides the ability to ensure that the cut is created normal to the Sheet metal thickness for folded Sheet metal parts.

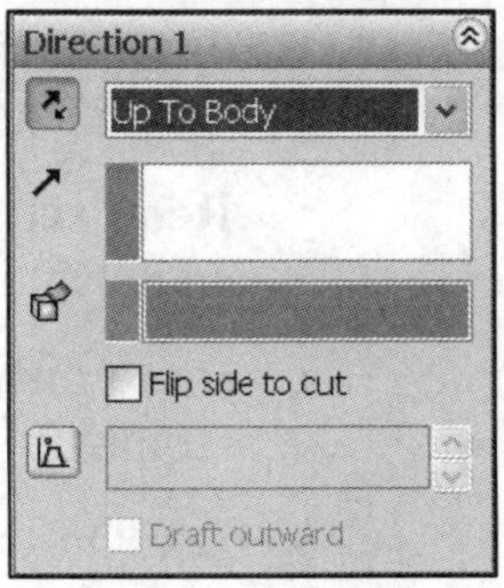


Set an End Condition Type for Direction 1 and Direction 2 to cut in two directions with different depths.

- ***Direction 2***. Provides the ability to select an End Condition Type in Direction 2. Extrudes in a second direction from the Sketch plane. The available End Condition Types for Direction 2 are feature dependent:
  - **Blind**. Selected by default. Extends the feature from the Sketch plane for a specified distance.
  - **Through All**. Cuts the feature from the Sketch plane through all existing geometry.
  - **Up To Next**. Cuts the feature from the Sketch plane to the next surface that intercepts the entire profile. The intercepting surface must be on the same part to use the Up To Next option.

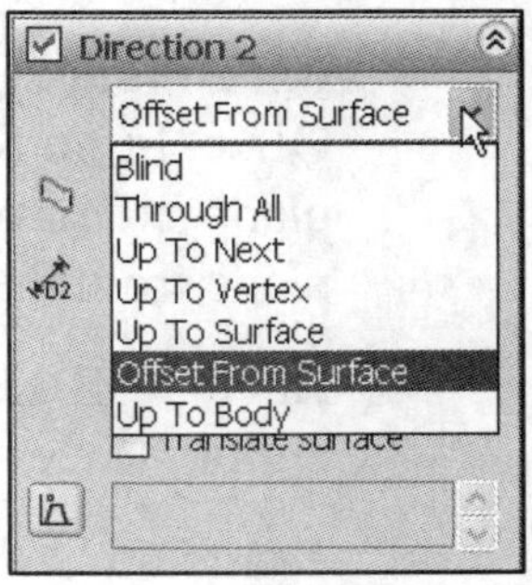

- **Up To Vertex**. Cuts the feature from the Sketch plane to a plane which is parallel to the Sketch plane, and passing through the specified vertex. Sketch vertices are valid selections for Up To Vertex extrusions.
- **Up To Surface**. Cuts the feature from the Sketch plane to the selected surface. The extrusion is shaped by the selected surface. Only one surface selection is allowed.
- **Offset From Surface**. Cuts the feature from the Sketch plane to a specified distance from the selected surface. You are required to enter a value with this option selected. Select the Reverse offset check box to offset the specified distance in the opposite direction if required.
- **Up To Body**. Cuts the feature from the sketch plane to a specified body. Use the Up To Body type with assemblies, mold parts, or multi-body parts.

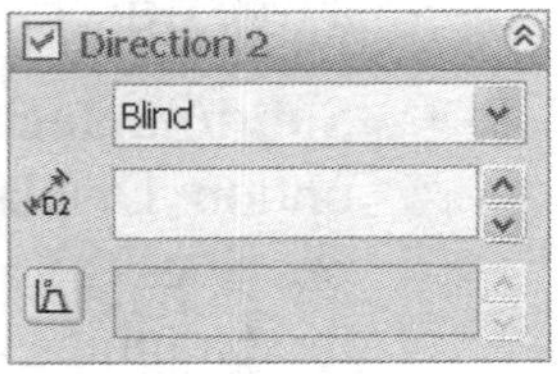


- **Reverse Direction**. Only available for the following options: Blind, Through All, Up To Next, Up To Surface, Offset From Surface and Up To Body.
- **Depth**. Displays the selected depth of the extruded feature.

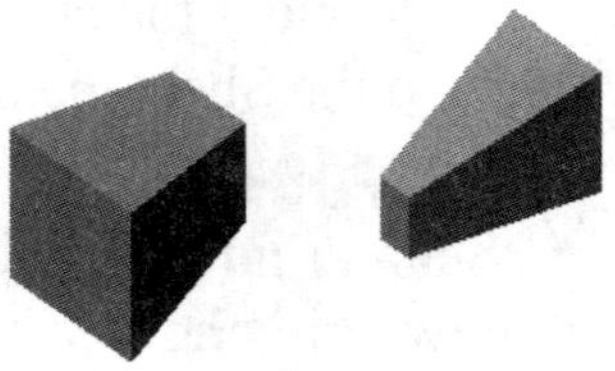
10° draft angle outward 10° draft angle inward

- **Draft On/Off**. Adds a draft to the extruded feature. The Draft On/Off option provides two selections:
  - **Required draft angle**. Input the required draft angle value.
  - **Draft outward**. Modifies the direction of the draft if required.

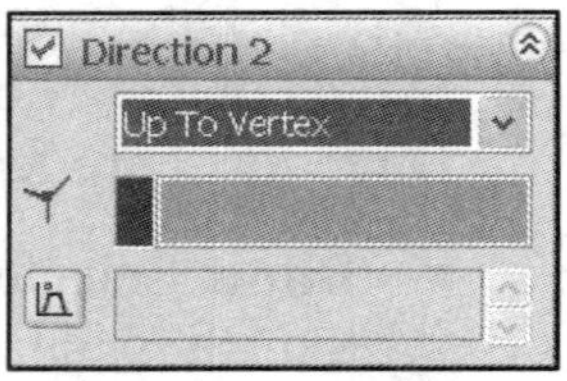


- **Vertex**. Only available for the Up To Vertex option. Displays the selected vertex for the extruded feature.
- **Face/Plane**. Only available for the Up To Surface and Offset From Surface option. Displays the selected face or plane and provides the ability to select either a face or plane from the Graphics window or FeatureManager.

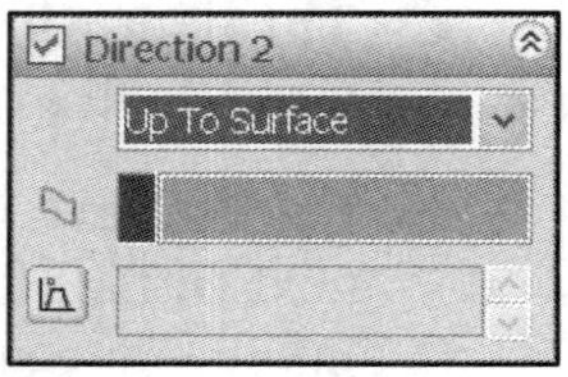


- **Reverse offset**. Only available for the Offset From Surface option. Reverses the offset direction if required.
- **Translate surface**. Only available for the Offset From Surface option. Provides the ability to make the end of the extrusion a translation of the reference surface, rather than a true offset.

- **Solid/Surface Body**. Only available for the Up To Body option. Displays the selected solid or surface body and provides the ability to select either a solid or surface from the Graphics window or FeatureManager.

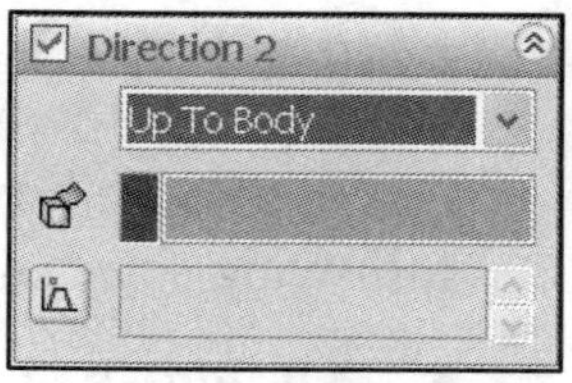


- ***Thin Feature***. Controls the extrude thickness of the profile. This is not the depth. Create a Thin feature by using an active sketch profile and applying a wall thickness. Apply thickness to a Thin feature either to the inside or outside of the sketch, evenly on both sides of the sketch, or unevenly on either side of the sketch. Thin feature creation is automatically invoked for active contours that are extruded or revolved. Create a Thin feature from a closed contour. The following options are available:
  - **Type**. Displays the selected type of thin feature cut. There are three conditions:

    - **One-Direction**. Displays the selected extrude thickness feature in one direction, outwards from the sketch. The Direction 1 Thickness option is available.
    - **Mid-Plane**. Displays the selected extrude thickness feature equally in both directions from the sketch. The Thickness option is available.

    - **Two-Direction**. Displays the selected extrude thickness in two directions, outward from the sketch. The Direction 1 and Direction 2 Thickness option is available.

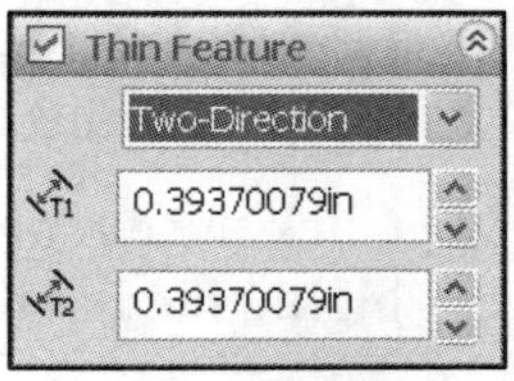


  - **Reverse Direction**. Reverses the direction of the Thin Feature if required.
  - **Direction 1 Thickness**. Displays the selected cut extrude thickness in one direction, outward from the sketch.

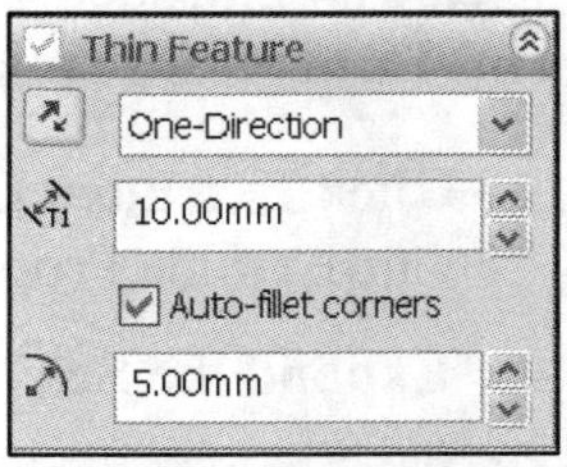


  - **Auto-fillet corners**. Only available for an open sketch. Rounds each edge where the lines meet at an angle.
  - **Fillet Radius**. Only available if the Auto-fillet corners option is selected. Sets the inside radius of the round.
- ***Selected Contours***. Displays the selected contours and to use a partial sketch to create extrude features. Select sketch contours and model edges from the Graphics window.

- ***Feature Scope***. Apply features to one or more multi-body parts. The Feature Scope box provides the following selections:

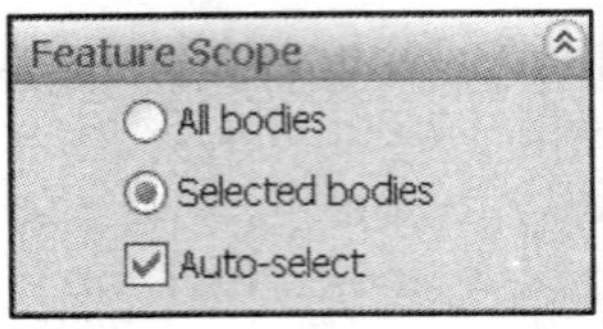


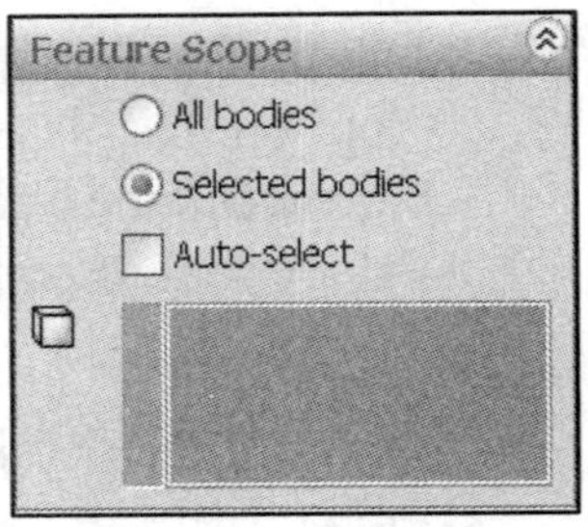


  - **All bodies**. Applies the feature to all bodies every time the feature regenerates. If you add new bodies to the model that are intersected by the feature, these new bodies are also regenerated to include the feature.
  - **Selected bodies**. Selected by default. Applies the feature to the selected bodies.
  - **Auto-select**. Only available if you select the Selected bodies option**.** When you first create a model with multi-body parts, the feature automatically processes all the relevant intersecting parts. Auto-select is faster than All bodies because it processes only the bodies on the initial list and does not regenerate the entire model.
  - **Solid Bodies to Affect**. Only available if Auto-select is not active. Displays the selected bodies to affect from the Graphics window.

### *Tutorial: Extruded Cut 6-1*

Create Extruded Cut features using various End Condition options.

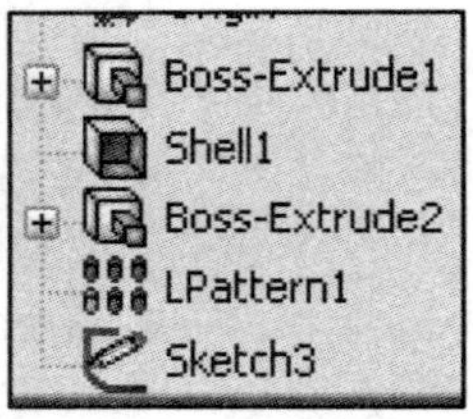


1. Open **Extruded Cut 6-1** from the SolidWorks 2010 folder. The Extruded Cut 6-1 FeatureManager displays two Extrude features, a Shell feature, and a Linear Pattern feature.
2. Click the circumference of the **front most circle**. Sketch3 is highlighted in the FeatureManager.

Create an Extruded Cut feature using the Selected Contours and Through All options.

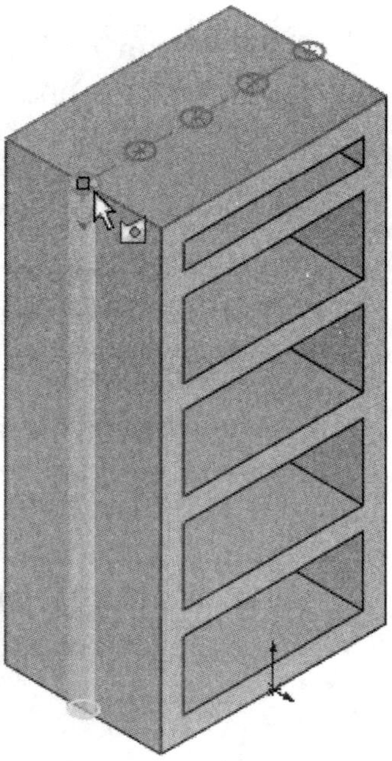

3. Click **Extruded Cut** from the Features toolbar. The Cut-Extrude PropertyManager is displayed.
4. **Expand** the Selected Contours box.
5. Click the circumference of the **front most circle**. Sketch3-Contour<1> is displayed in the Selected Contours box. The direction arrow points downward, if not click the Reverse Direction button.
6. Select **Through All** for the End Condition in Direction 1. Only the first circle of your sketch is extruded.
7. Click **OK** from the Cut-Extruded PropertyManager. Cut-Extrude1 is displayed in the FeatureManager.

Create an Extruded Cut feature using the Selected Contours and the Up To Next option.

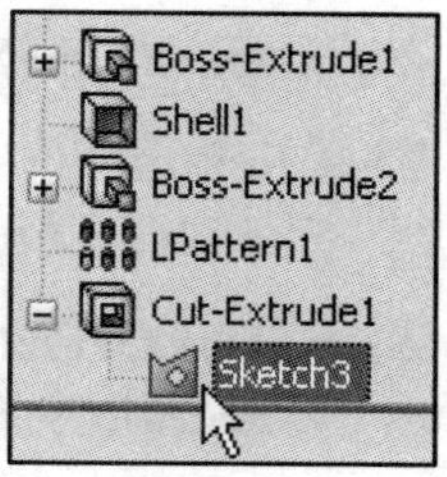


8. Click **Sketch3** from the FeatureManager.
9. Click **Extruded Cut** from the Features toolbar. The Cut-Extrude PropertyManager is displayed.
10. **Expand** the Selected Contours box.
11. Click the circumference of the **second circle** from the left. Sketch3-Contour<1> is displayed in the Selected Contours box.

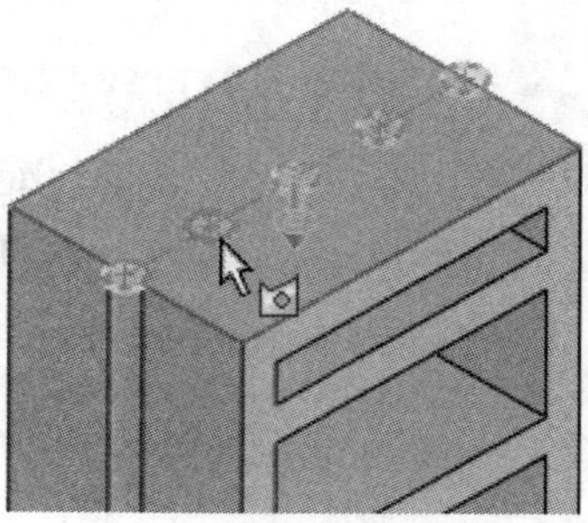

12. Select **Up To Next** for the End Condition in Direction 1. Only the second circle of your sketch is extruded.
13. Click **OK** from the Cut-Extrude PropertyManager. Cut-Extrude2 is displayed in the FeatureManager.
14. **Rotate** your model and view the created cut through the first plate.

Create an Extruded Cut feature using the Selected Contours and the Up To Vertex option.

15. Click **Sketch3** from the FeatureManager.
16. Click the **Extruded Cut** Features tool. The Cut-Extrude PropertyManager is displayed.
17. **Expand** the Selected Contours box.

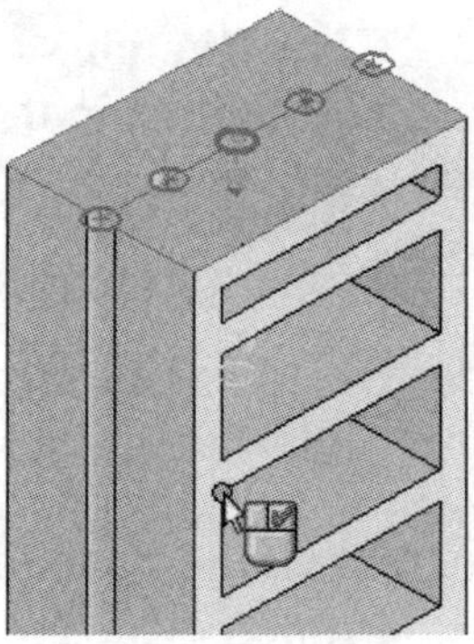

18. Click the circumference of the **third circle** from the left. Sketch3-Contour<1> is displayed in the Selected Contours box.
19. Select **Up To Vertex** for the End Condition in Direction 1. Only the third circle of your sketch is extruded.
20. Select a **vertex point** below the second shelf as illustrated. Vertex<1> is displayed in the Vertex box in Direction 1.
21. Click **OK** from the PropertyManager. Cut-Extrude3 is displayed in the FeatureManager. The third circle has an Extruded Cut feature through the top two shelves.

Create an Extruded Cut feature using the Selected Contours and the Offset From Surface option.

22. Click **Sketch3** from the FeatureManager.
23. Click the **Extruded Cut** Features tool.

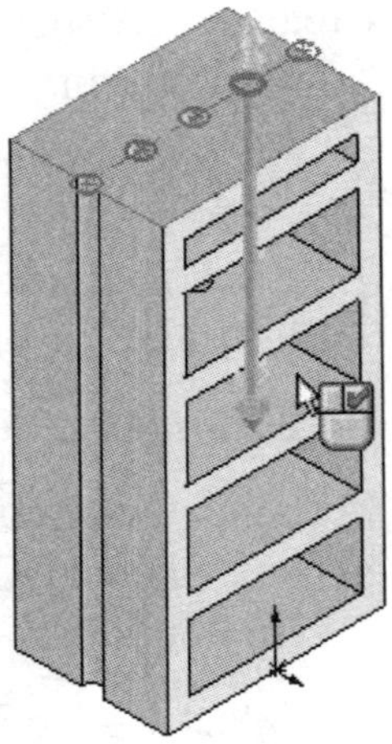

24. **Expand** the Selected Contours box.
25. Click the circumference of the **fourth circle** from the left. Sketch3-Contour<1> is displayed in the Selected Contours box.
26. Select **Offset From Surface** for the End Condition in Direction 1. Click the **face** of the third shelf. Face<1> is displayed in the Face/Plane box in Direction1.
27. Enter **60**mm for Offset Distance.
28. Click the **Reverse offset** box if required.
29. Click **OK** ✔ from the PropertyManager. Cut-Extrude4 is displayed in the FeatureManager.

30. Click **Isometric** view. View the created features.
31. **Close** the model.

### *Tutorial: Extruded Cut 6-2*

Create various Extruded Cut features using the Through All option.

1. Open **Extruded Cut 6-2** from the SolidWorks 2010 folder. View the Extruded Cut 6-2 FeatureManager.

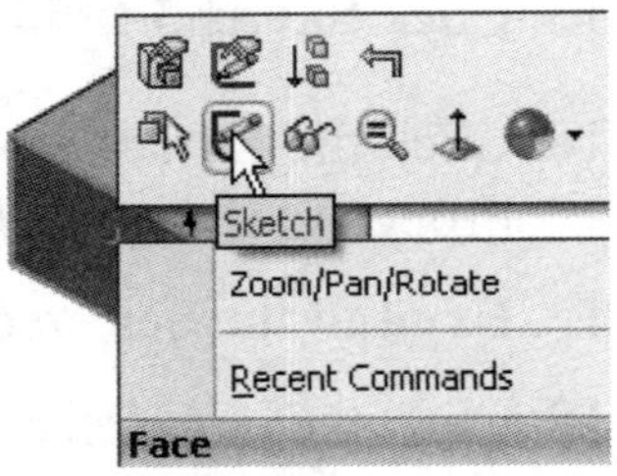


2. Right-click the **Front face**. This is your Sketch plane.
3. Click **Sketch** from the Context toolbar. Extrude1 is highlighted in the FeatureManager.
4. Click the **Line** Sketch tool. The Insert Line PropertyManager is displayed.
5. Sketch a **line** from the midpoint of the top edge to the midpoint of the right edge as illustrated.

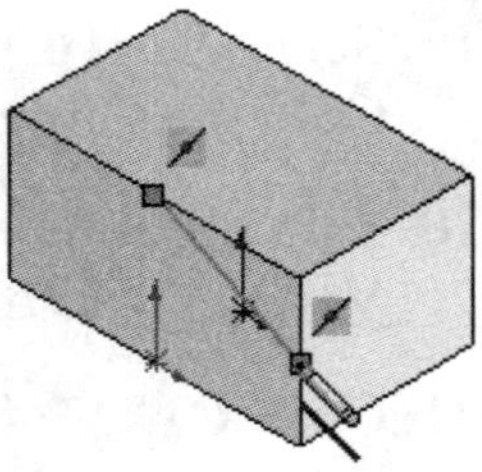

6. Click the **Extruded Cut** Features tool. The Cut-Extrude PropertyManager is displayed. Through All is the default option.
7. Click **OK** ✔ from the Cut-Extrude PropertyManager. Cut-Extrude1 is displayed in the FeatureManager.

Create a second Cut-Extrude feature using the Right Plane.

8. Right-click **Right Plane** from FeatureManager. This is your Sketch plane.

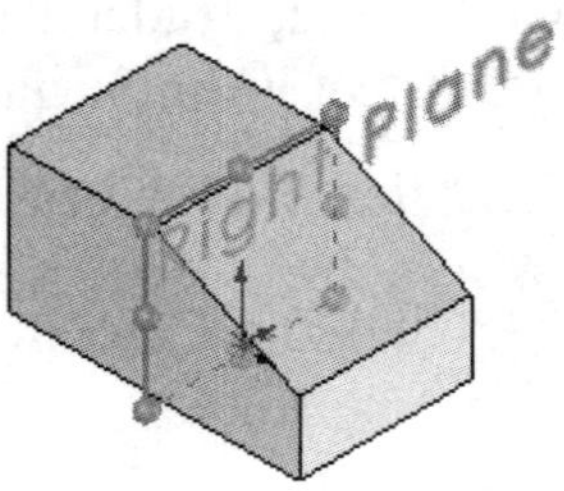


9. Click **Sketch** from the Context toolbar.

10. Click the **Line** Sketch tool.
11. Click **Right view**.
12. Sketch a **line** from the top midpoint of the model to the midpoint of the left edge as illustrated.

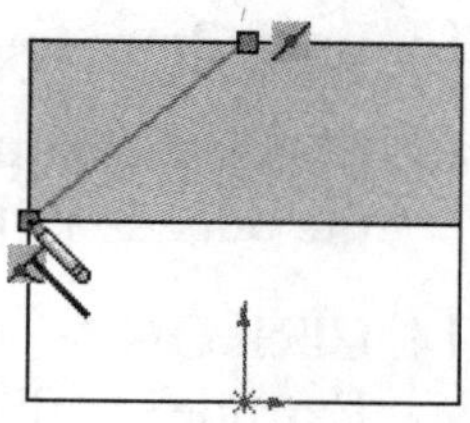

13. Click the **Extruded Cut** Features tool. The Cut-Extrude PropertyManager is displayed.
14. Check the **Flip side to cut** box in Direction 1. The cut is upwards and to the left.
15. Click **OK** from the Cut-Extrude PropertyManager. Cut-Extrude2 is displayed in the FeatureManager.
16. Display an **Isometric view**.
17. **Close** the model.

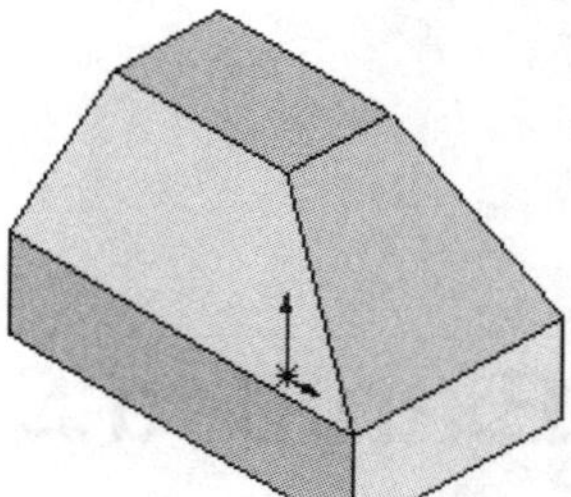

***Tutorial: Extruded Cut 6-3***

Create an Extruded Cut feature using the Offset Start Condition.

1. Open **Extruded Cut 6-3** from the SolidWorks 2010 folder.
2. Right-click the **Top face** of the small cylinder in the Graphics window. This is your Sketch plane.
3. Click **Sketch** from the Context toolbar. The Top face is your Sketch plane. Extrude2 is highlighted in the FeatureManager.

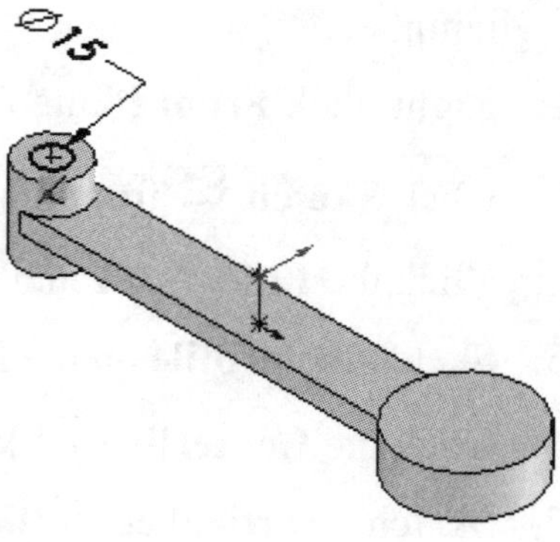


4. Click the **Circle** Sketch tool. The Circle PropertyManager is displayed.
5. Sketch a **circle** concentric with the circular edge of the small cylinder.
6. Click **Smart Dimension**. The Dimension PropertyManager is displayed.
7. Dimension the circle to **15**mm.
8. Click **Extruded Cut** from the Features toolbar. The Cut-Extrude PropertyManager is displayed.
9. Select **Offset** for Start Condition.
10. Enter **5**mm for Offset Value.
11. Click the **Reverse direction** box. The Offset direction is downwards.

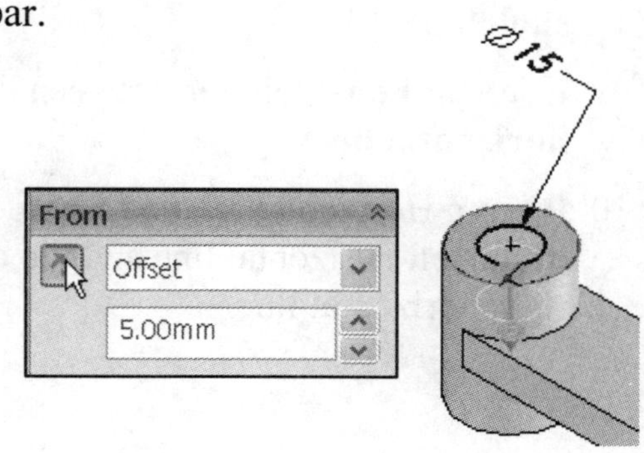

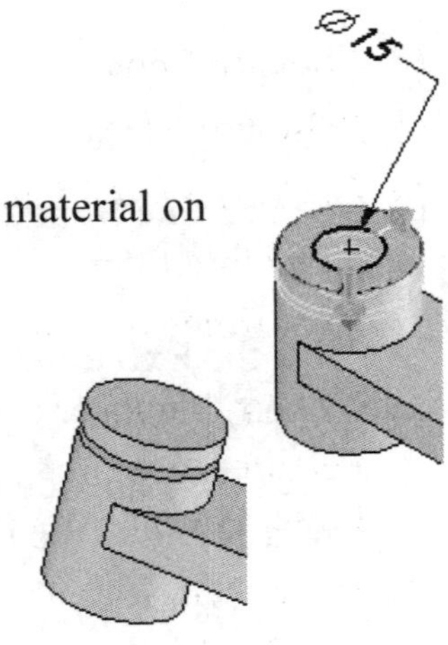


Blind is the default End Condition in Direction 1.

12. Enter **2**mm for Depth in Direction 1.
13. Check the **Flip Side to cut** option in the Direction 1 box. The material on the outside of the 15mm circle is removed.
14. Click **OK** from the Cut-Extrude PropertyManager. Cut-Extrude1 is displayed in the FeatureManager.
15. **Close** the model.

---

# Extruded Solid Thin Feature

An Extruded Solid Thin feature is a feature with an open profile and a specified thickness.

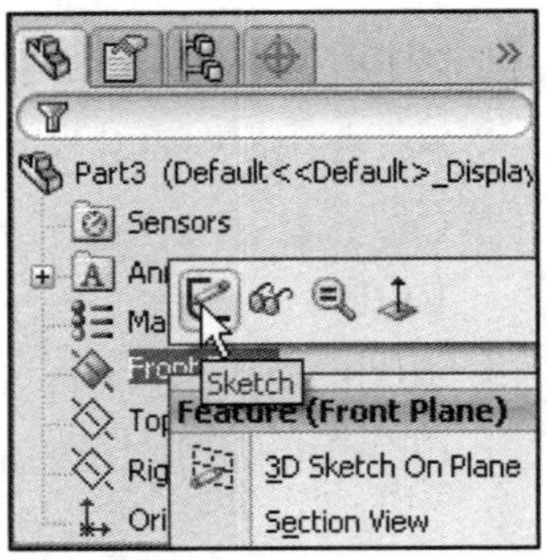


***Tutorial: Solid Thin 6-1***

Create an Extruded Solid Thin feature using the Mid Plane option.

1. Create a **New** part. Use the default ANSI, MMGS Part template.
2. Right-click **Front Plane** from the FeatureManager.
3. Click **Sketch** from the Context toolbar.
4. Click the **Line** Sketch tool.
5. Sketch the **profile** on the Front plane as illustrated.
6. Click the **Centerline** Sketch tool.
7. Sketch a **vertical centerline** through the origin and to the bottom of the profile.

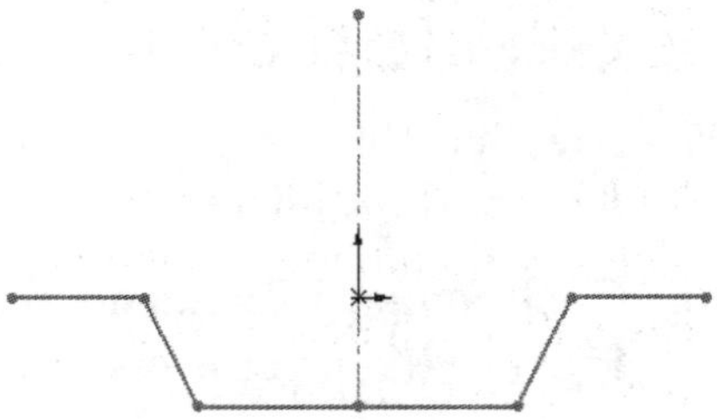

8. Insert a Midpoint relation between the **bottom endpoint of the centerline** and the **bottom of the sketch profile**.
9. Insert an Equal relation between the **two horizontal lines**.
10. Insert a Horizontal relation between the **endpoint** of the left horizontal line and the **endpoint** of the right horizontal line.

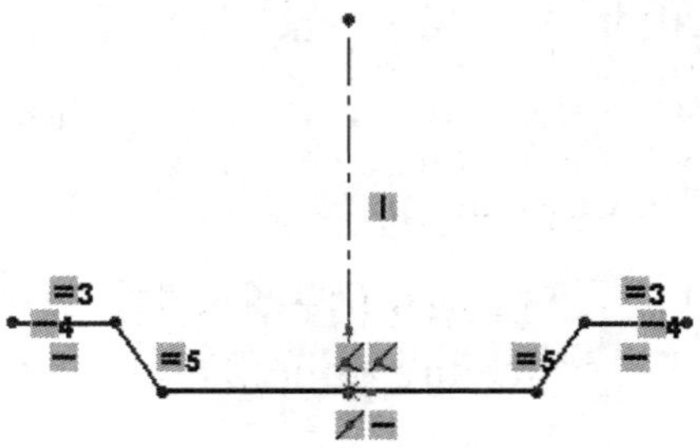

11. Insert an Equal relation between the **two diagonal lines**.
12. Click **Smart Dimensions**. The Smart Dimension PropertyManager is displayed.
13. Add **dimensions** as illustrated.

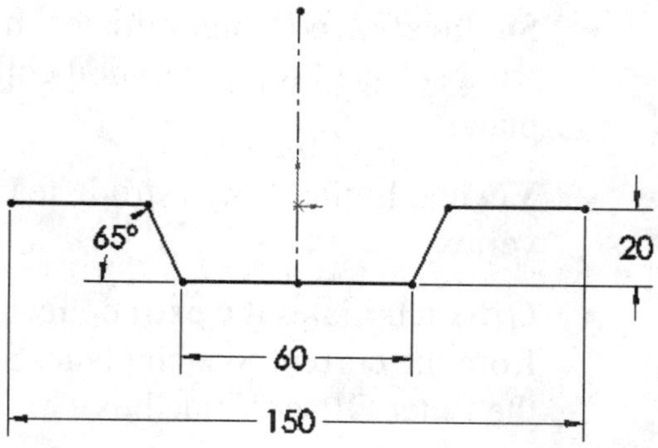


14. Click **Extruded Boss/Base** from the Features toolbar. The Boss-Extrude PropertyManager is displayed.
15. Select **Mid Plane** for End Condition in Direction 1.
16. Enter **25**mm for Depth.
17. **Expand** the Thin Feature box. One-Direction is the default.

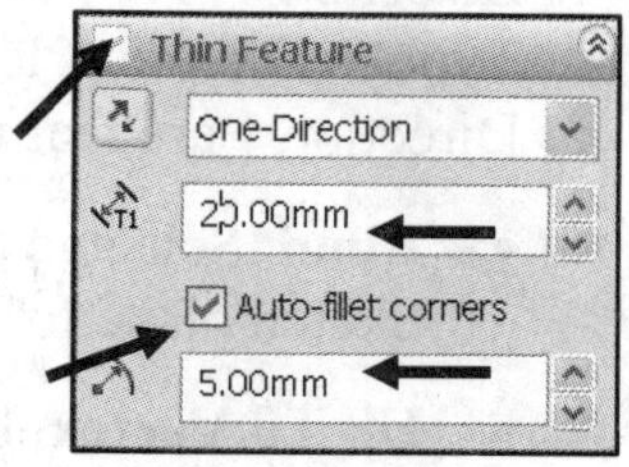


18. Enter **20**mm for Thickness.
19. Check the **Auto-fillet corners** box.
20. Enter **5**mm for Fillet Radius.
21. Click **OK** from the Boss-Extrude PropertyManager. The Extrude-Thin1 feature is created and is displayed in the FeatureManager.

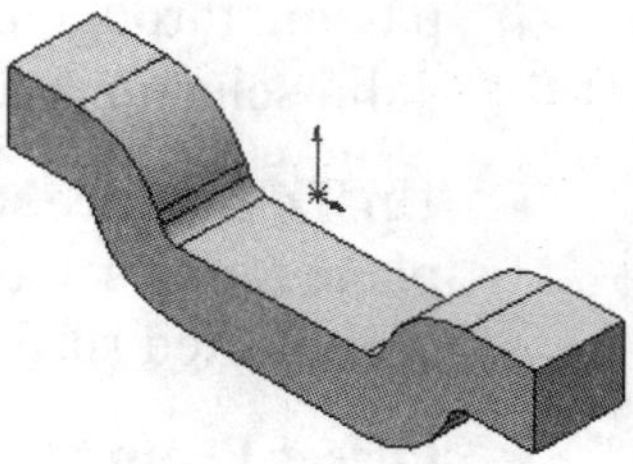

22. **Close** the model.

# Extruded Surface Feature

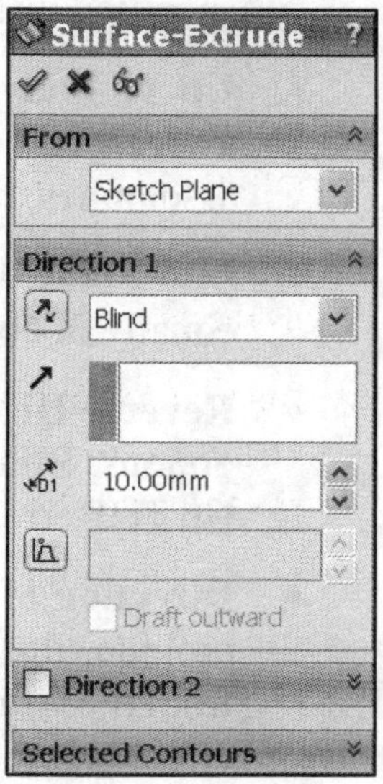


An Extruded Surface feature is created by projecting a 2D sketch perpendicular to the Sketch plane to create a 3D surface. The entity can be planar or non-planar. Planar entities do not have to be parallel to your sketch plane. Your sketch must be fully contained within the boundaries of the non-planar surface or face.

The Extruded Surface feature uses the Surface-Extrude PropertyManager. The Surface-Extrude PropertyManager provides the following selections:

- ***From***. Displays the location of the initial extruded feature. The available options are:
  - **Sketch Plane**. Selected by default. Initiates the extrude feature from the selected Sketch plane.

- **Surface/Face/Plane**. Initiates the extrude feature from a valid selected entity. A valid entity is a surface, face, or plane.
- **Vertex**. Initiates the extrude feature from the selected vertex.
- **Offset**. Initiates the extrude feature on a plane that is offset from the current Sketch plane. Set the Offset distance in the Enter Offset Value box.

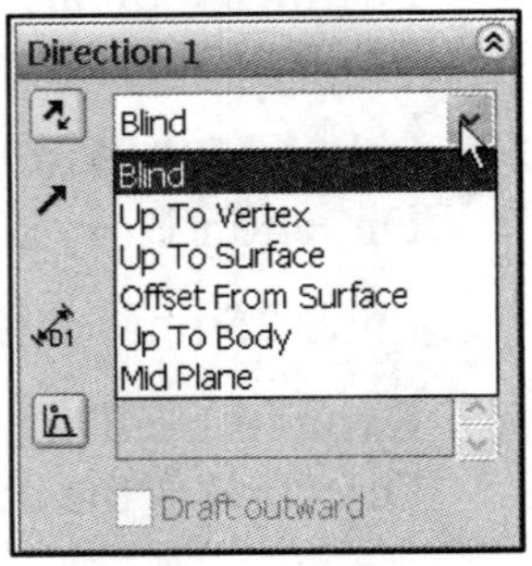


- ***Direction 1***. Provides the ability to select an End Condition Type in Direction 1. The available End Condition Types in Direction 1 are feature dependent:
  - **Blind**. Selected by default. Extrudes the feature from the Sketch plane for a specified distance.
  - **Up To Vertex**. Extrudes the feature from the Sketch plane to a plane which is parallel to the Sketch plane, and passing through the specified vertex. Sketch vertices are valid selections for Up To Vertex extrusions.
  - **Up To Surface**. Extrudes the feature from the Sketch plane to the selected surface. The extrusion is shaped by the selected surface. Only one surface selection is allowed.
  - **Offset From Surface**. Extrudes the feature from the Sketch plane to a specified distance from the selected surface. You are required to enter a value with this option selected. Select the Reverse offset check box to offset the specified distance in the opposite direction if required.
  - **Up To Body**. Extrudes the feature from the sketch plane to a specified body. Use the Up To Body type with assemblies, mold parts or multi-body parts.
  - **Mid Plane**. Extrudes the feature from the Sketch plane equally in both directions.

  - **Reverse Direction**. Only available for the following options: Blind, Up To Surface, Offset From Surface and Up To Body.
  - **Direction of Extrusion**. The Direction of Extrusion box provides the ability to display the selected direction vector from the Graphics Window to extrude the sketch in a direction other than normal to the sketch profile
  - **Depth**. Displays the selected depth of the extruded cut feature.

- **Draft On/Off**. Adds a draft to the extruded cut feature. The Draft On/Off option provides two selections:
  - **Required draft angle**. Input the required draft angle value.
  - **Draft outward**. Modifies the direction of the draft if required.
- **Vertex**. Only available for the Up To Vertex option. Displays the selected vertex for the extruded cut feature.

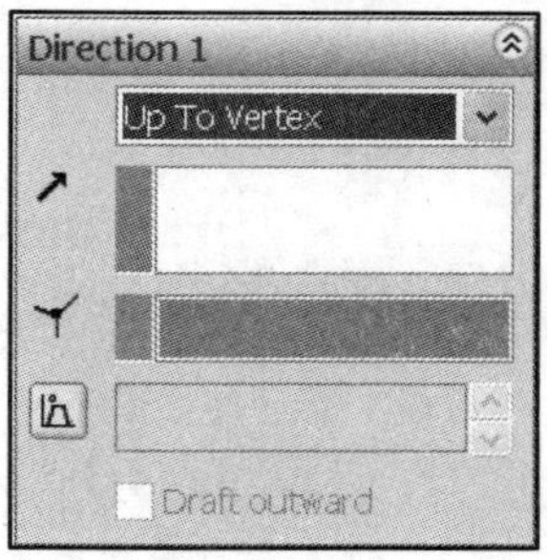


- **Face/Plane**. Only available for the Up To Surface and Offset From Surface option. Displays the selected face or plane and provides the ability to select either a face or plane from the Graphics window or FeatureManager.
- **Solid/Surface Body**. Only available for the Up To Body option. Displays the selected solid or surface body and provides the ability to select either a solid or surface from the Graphics window or FeatureManager.

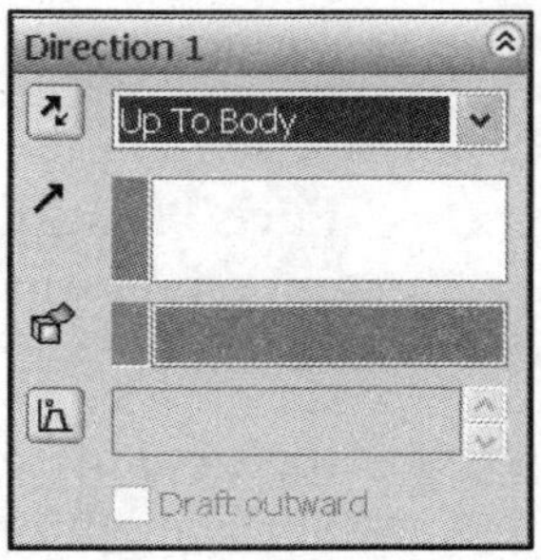


Set an End Condition Type for Direction 1 and Direction 2 to extrude in two directions with different depths.

- ***Direction 2***. Provides the ability to select an End Condition Type in Direction 2. Extrudes in a single direction from the Sketch plane. The available End Condition Types in Direction 2 are feature dependent:

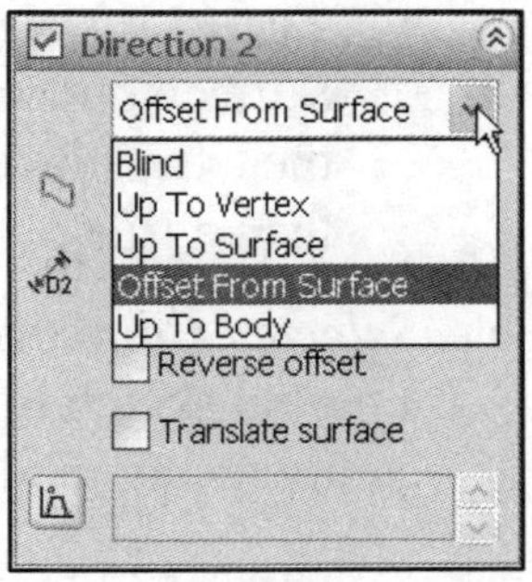


  - **Blind**. Selected by default. Extends the feature from the Sketch plane for a specified distance.
  - **Up To Vertex**. Extends the feature from the Sketch plane to a plane which is parallel to the Sketch plane, and passing through the specified vertex. Sketch vertices are valid selections for Up To Vertex extrusions.
  - **Up To Surface**. Extends the feature from the Sketch plane to the selected surface. The extrusion is shaped by the selected surface. Only one surface selection is allowed.
  - **Offset From Surface**. Extends the feature from the Sketch plane to a specified distance from the selected surface. You are required to enter a value with this option selected. Select the Reverse offset check box to offset the specified distance in the opposite direction if required.

- **Up To Body**. Extends the feature from the sketch plane to a specified body. Use the Up To Body type with assemblies, mold parts, or multi-body parts.

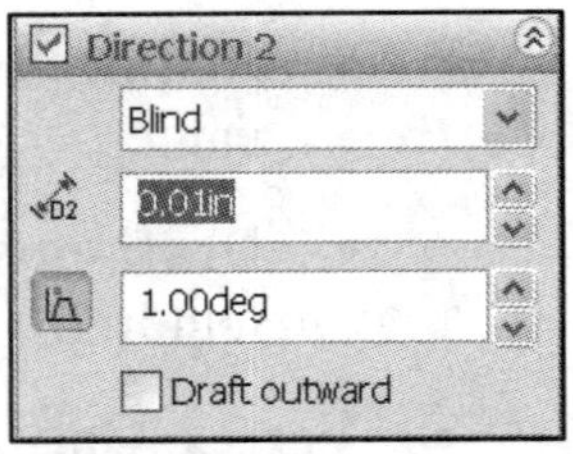


- **Depth**. Displays the selected depth of the extruded feature.
- **Draft On/Off**. Adds a draft to the extruded feature. The Draft On/Off option provides two selections:
  - **Required draft angle**. Input the required draft angle value.
  - **Draft outward**. Modifies the direction of the draft if required.

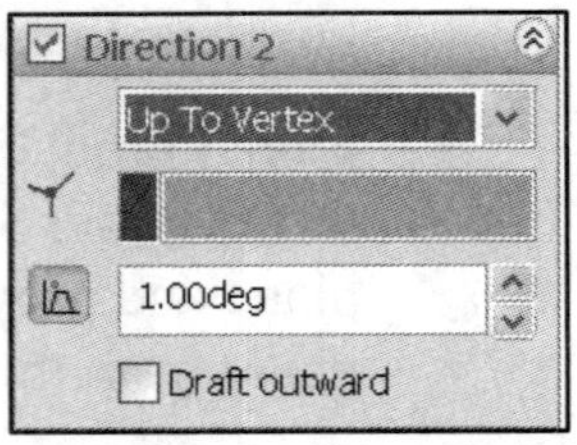


- **Vertex**. Only available for the Up To Vertex option. Displays the selected vertex for the extruded feature.

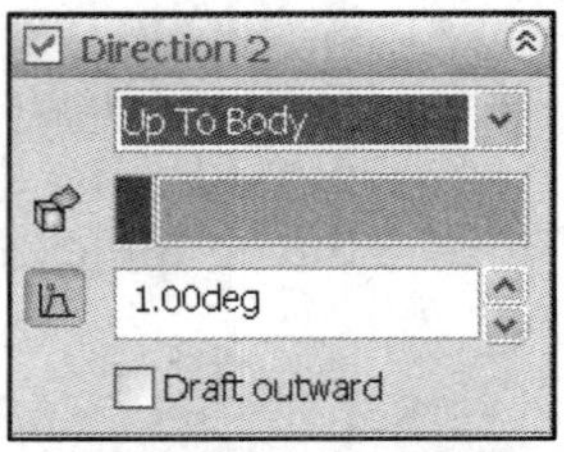


- **Solid/Surface Body**. Only available for the Up To Surface and Up To Body option. Displays the selected solid or surface body from the Graphics window or FeatureManager.

- **Face/Plane**. Only available for the Offset From Surface option. Displays the selected face or plane from the Graphics window or FeatureManager.
- **Reverse offset**. Only available for the Offset From Surface option. Reverses the offset direction if required.
- **Translate surface**. Only available for the Offset From Surface option. Provides the ability to make the end of the extrusion a translation of the reference surface, rather than a true offset.

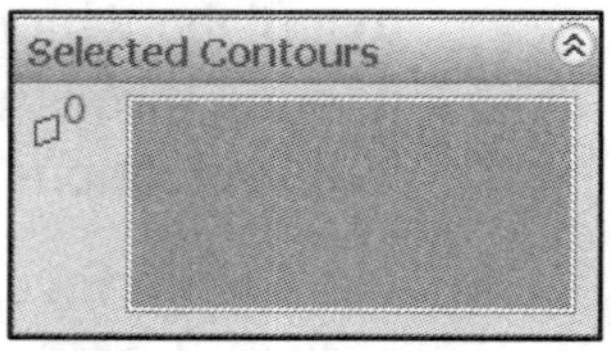


- ***Selected Contours***. Displays the selected contours and to use a partial sketch to create extrude features. Select sketch contours and model edges from the Graphics window.

### *Tutorial: Surface 6-1*

Create an Extruded Surface feature using the sketch Spline tool.

1. Create a **New** part. Use the default ANSI, MMGS Part template.
2. Right-click **Front Plane** from the FeatureManager. This is your Sketch plane.

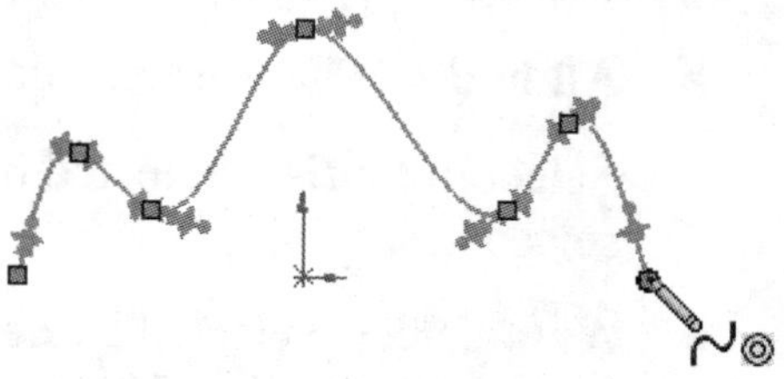

3. Click **Sketch** from the Context toolbar. The Sketch toolbar is displayed.
4. Click the **Spline** Sketch tool. The Spline icon is displayed on the mouse pointer.
5. Sketch a **Spline** as illustrated. The sketch remains under defined.
6. Right-click **End Spline**.

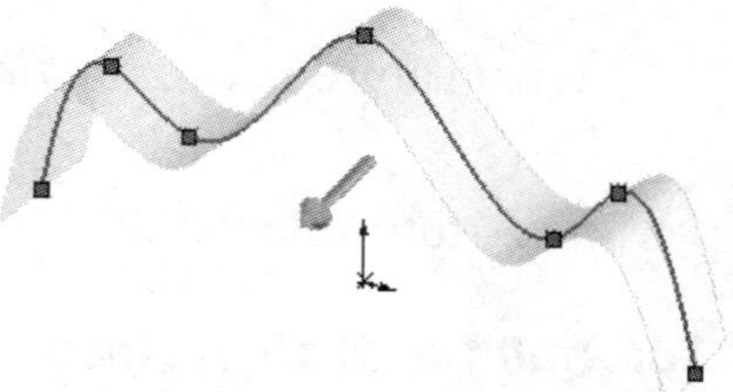

7. Click **Extruded Surface** from the Surfaces toolbar. The Surface-Extrude PropertyManager is displayed. Blind is the Default End Condition.
8. Select **Mid Plane** for End Condition in Direction 1.
9. Enter **30**mm for Depth in Direction 1.
10. Check the **Draft on/off** box in Direction 1.
11. Enter a **5**deg draft angle.

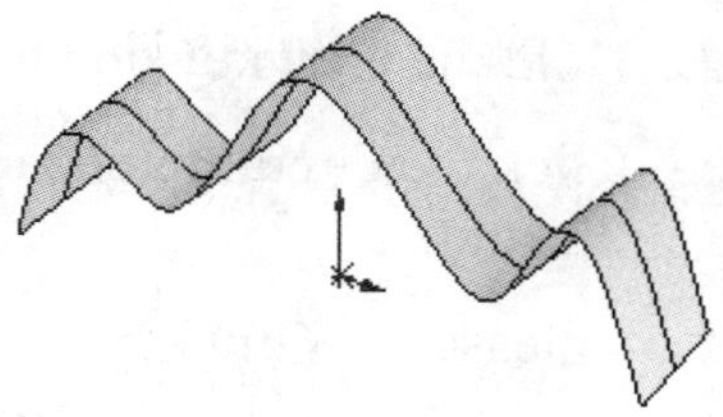

12. Click **OK** from the Surface-Extrude PropertyManager. Surface-Extrude1 is displayed in the FeatureManager.
13. **Close** the model.

## Cut With Surface Feature

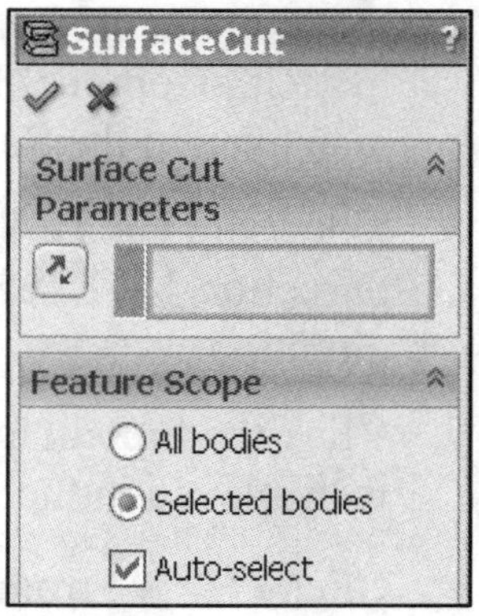


A Cut With Surface feature cuts a solid model by removing material with a plane or a surface. With multi-body parts, you can select which bodies to keep with the Feature Scope option.

The Cut With Surface feature uses the SurfaceCut PropertyManager. The SurfaceCut PropertyManager provides the following selections:

- ***Surface Cut Parameters***. The Surface Cut Parameters box provides the following options:
  - **Selected surface for cut**. Displays the selected surface or plane to be used to cut the solid bodies.
  - **Flip cut**. Reverses the direction of the cut if required.

- ***Feature Scope***. Provides the ability to select one of the following options:
  - **All bodies**. The surface cuts all bodies each time the feature is rebuilt.
  - **Selected bodies**. Selected by default. The surface cuts only the bodies which are selected.
  - **Auto-select**. Selected by default. The system automatically selects all relevant intersecting bodies. This option is faster than the All bodies option because the system only processes the bodies on the initial list. The system does not rebuild your entire model.

The Feature Scope option is only available with a multi-body part model.

The Auto-select option is only available with the Selected bodies option activated.

***Tutorial: Cut With Surface 6-1***

Create a Cut With Surface feature.

1. Open **Cut With Surface 6-1** from the SolidWorks 2010 folder.
2. Hold the **Ctrl** key down.
3. Click the circumference of the **left** and **right** circles as illustrated.
4. Release the **Ctrl** key.

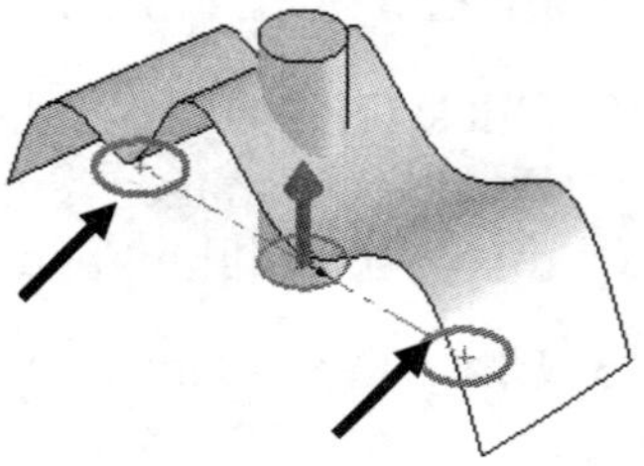

5. Click **Extruded Boss/Base** from the Features toolbar. The Boss-Extrude PropertyManager is displayed. Sketch2-Contour<1> and Sketch2-Contour<2> are displayed in the Selected Contours box.
6. Select the **Up To Surface** End Condition for Direction 1. The Extrude2 feature points in an upward direction.
7. Click the **top surface** as illustrated. Surface-Extrude1 is displayed in the Face/Plane box.

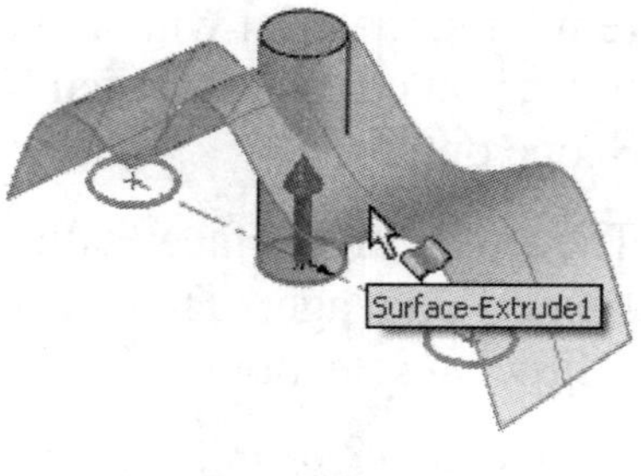


8. Click **OK** from the Boss-Extrude PropertyManager. Boss-Extrude3 is created.
9. Click the top face of the **center cylinder** from the Graphics window. Extrude2 is highlighted in the FeatureManager.
10. Click **Insert > Cut > With Surface** . The SurfaceCut PropertyManager is displayed.

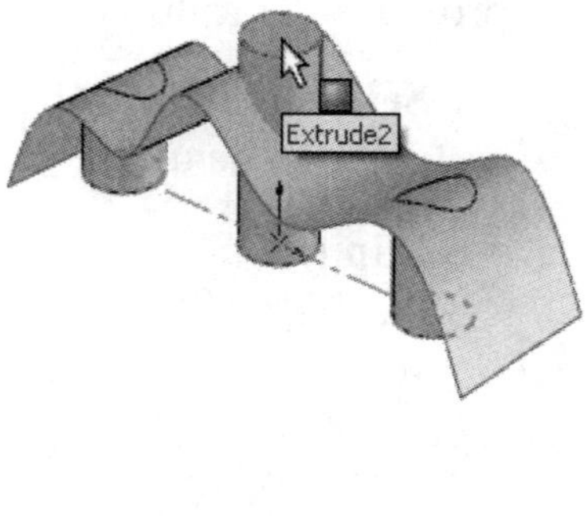

11. Click **Surface-Extrude1** from the Graphics window. Surface-Extrude1 is displayed in the Selected Surface for cut box. You are cutting the cylindrical surface with Surface-Extrude1.

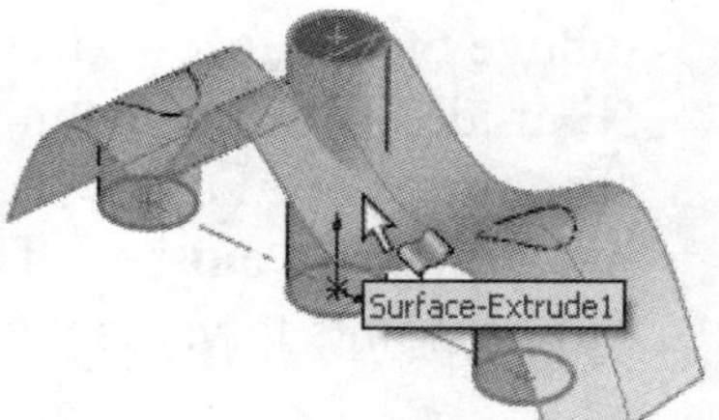


12. Un-check **Auto-Select** from the Feature Scope option box.

Select the side of the cylinder that you want to keep.

13. Click the **Top face (Extrude2)** of the cylinder.

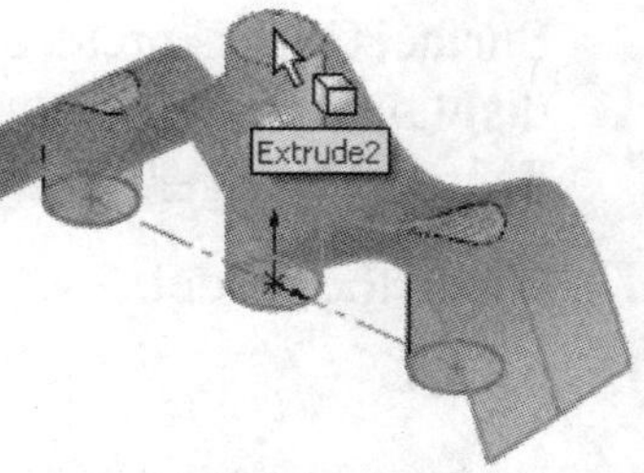


14. Click the **Flip Cut** option box. The direction arrow points to the front.
15. Click **OK** from the SurfaceCut PropertyManager. SurfaceCut1 is created and is displayed in the FeatureManager.
16. **Expand** the Surface Bodies folder from the FeatureManager.

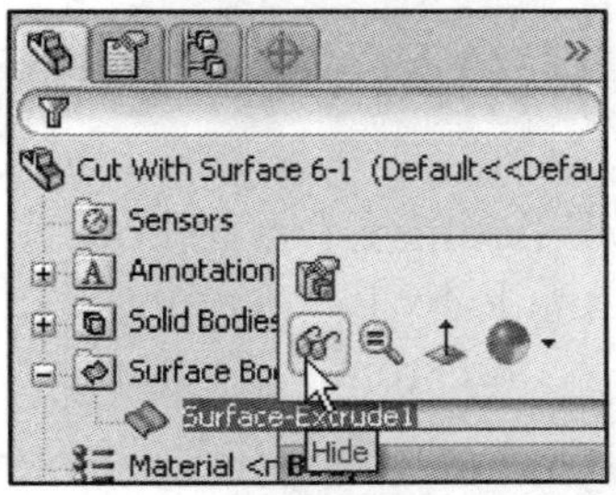


17. Right-click **Surface-Extrude1**.
18. Click **Hide**.
19. Right-click **Sketch2** from the FeatureManager.
20. Click **Hide**. View the results.
21. **Close** the model.

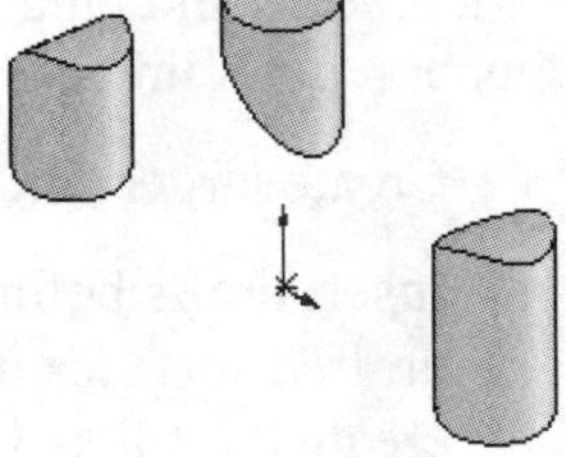

Press the **g** key to activate the Magnifying glass tool. Use the Magnifying glass tool to inspect a model and make selections without changing the overall view.

### *Tutorial: Cut With Surface 6-2*

Use the SurfaceCut PropertyManager. Cut the body using a plane.

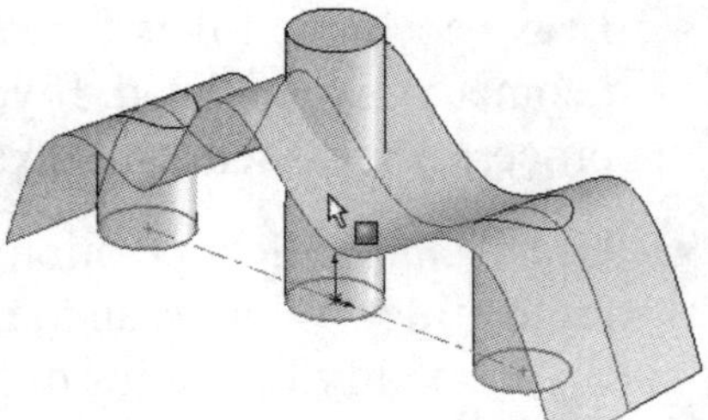

1. Open **Cut With Surface 6-2** from the SolidWorks 2010 folder.
2. Click **Insert ➢ Cut ➢ With Surface**. The SurfaceCut PropertyManager is displayed.

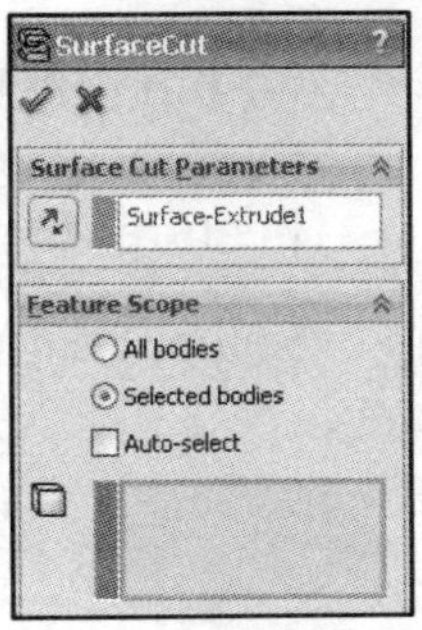


3. Click **Surface-Extrude1** from the fly-out FeatureManager or from the Graphics window as illustrated. Surface-Extrude1 is displayed in the Selected surface for cut box.
4. Uncheck the **Auto-select** box.

5. Click the **center cylinder** above the Surface-Extrude1. Extrude2 is displayed in the Feature Scope box. If required, click the **Flip cut** box. The arrow points towards the back.
6. Click **OK** ✔ from the SurfaceCut PropertyManager. SurfaceCut1 is created and is displayed in the FeatureManager.
7. **Close** the model.

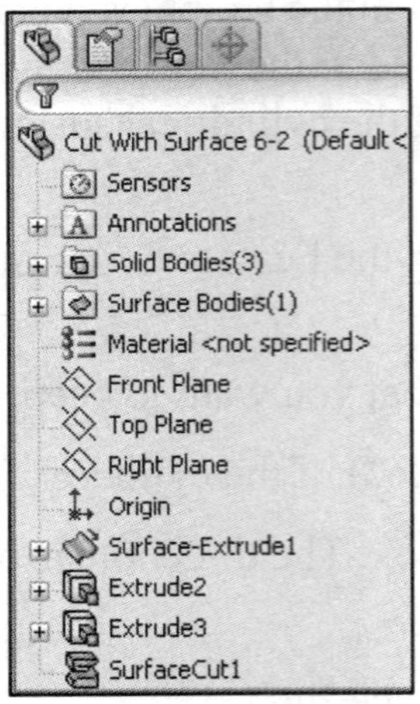


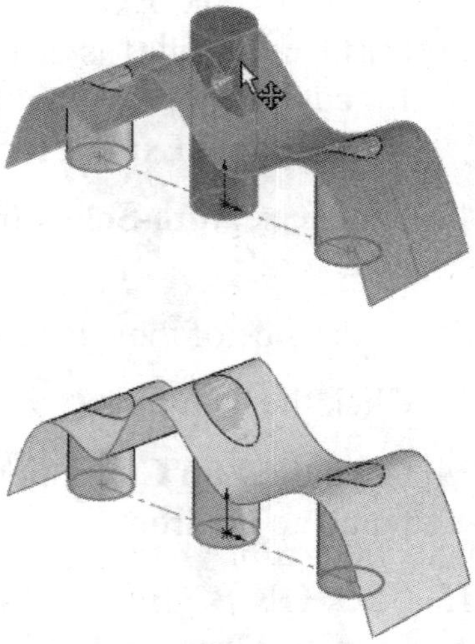

# Fillets in General

Filleting refers to both fillets and rounds. The distinction between fillets and rounds is made by the geometric conditions, and not by the command. Fillets add volume, and rounds remove volume.

Create fillets on a selected edge, selected edges, selected sets of faces, and edge loops. The selected edges can be selected in various ways. Options exist for constant or variable fillet radius and tangent edge propagation in the Fillet PropertyManager. There are a few general guidelines which you should know before creating fillets in a model. They are:

- Create larger fillets before you create smaller ones.
- Insert drafts before you create fillets. Example: There are numerous filleted edges and drafted surfaces in a cast part or a molded part. Insert the draft features before you create the fillets in your model.
- Leave cosmetic fillets for the end. Insert cosmetic fillets after most of your other geometry is completed. If you add the cosmetic fillets too early in your modeling process, the system will take longer to rebuild your model.
- Use a single fillet operation to address more than one edge which requires an equal radius fillet. Why? A single operation enables the model to rebuild quicker. However, if you modify the radius of that fillet, all other fillets created in the same operation will also be modified.
- Group Fillets together into a Fillet folder. Positioning Fillets into a file folder reduces the time spent for your mold designer or toolmaker to locate each fillet in the FeatureManager design tree. This saves time and cost.
- Select Features to fillet from the FeatureManager.

# Fillet Feature

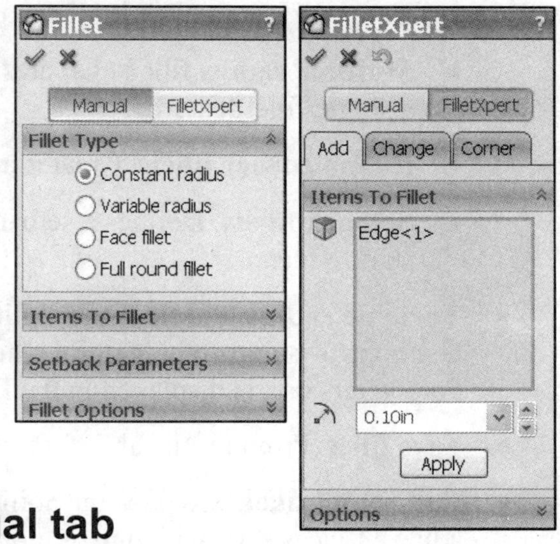


The Fillet tool uses the Fillet PropertyManager. The Fillet PropertyManager provides the ability to create various fillet types.

The Fillet PropertyManager provides the ability to select either the *Manual* or *FilletXpert* tab.

Each tab has different menus and options. The Fillet PropertyManager displays the appropriate selection based on the type of fillet you create.

## Fillet PropertyManager: Manual tab

Select the Manual tab to maintain control at the feature level. The following selections and options are available: *Constant radius*, *Variable radius*, *Face fillet* and *Full round fillet* each with a unique menu.

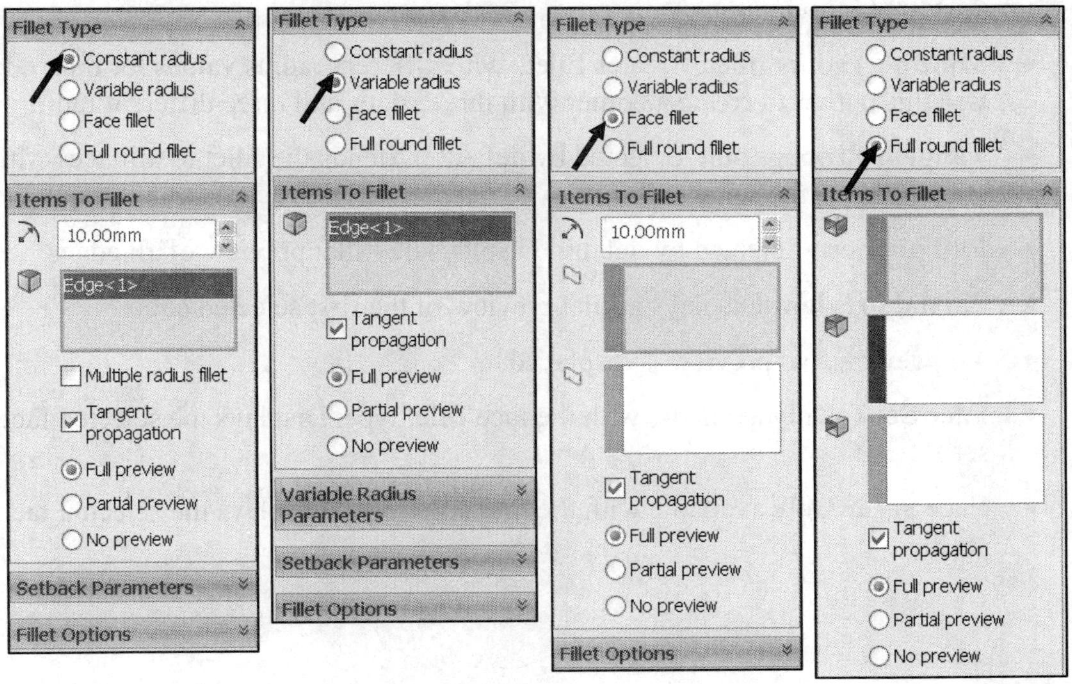

- ***Fillet Type***. Provides the ability to select four fillet types:
  - **Constant radius**. Selected by default. Provides the ability to create a fillet with a constant radius for the entire length of the fillet. After you select the Constant radius option, set the PropertyManager options to create the following:
    - **Multiple radius fillets**. Creates fillets that have different radius values within a single fillet feature.
    - **Round corner fillets**. Creates a smooth transition where fillet edges meet.
    - **Setback fillets**. Defines a setback distance from a vertex at which the fillets start to blend.
  - **Variable radius**. Provides the ability to create fillet with changeable radii values. Use control points to help define the fillet. When checked, the Variable Radius Parameters box is displayed in the PropertyManager.
  - **Face fillet**. Provides the ability to blends non-adjacent, non-continuous faces.
  - **Full round fillet**. Provides the ability to create fillets that are tangent to three adjacent faces sets, with one or more faces tangent.
- ***Items To Fillet***. Provides the ability to select the following options. The available options are dependent on the fillet type:
  - **Radius**. Sets the radius value of the fillet.
  - **Edges, Faces, Features, and Loops**. Displays the selected entities to fillet from the Graphics window.
  - **Multiple radius fillet**. Creates fillets with different radius values for their edges. Use this option to create a corner with three edges and three different radii.
  - **Tangent Propagation**. Selected by default. Extends the fillet to all faces which are tangent to the selected face.
  - **Full preview**. Selected by default. Displays the fillet preview of all edges.
  - **Partial preview**. Displays a fillet preview of the first selected edge.
  - **No preview**. No preview is displayed.
  - **Face Set 1**. Only available with the face fillet type. Displays the selected face for set 1.
  - **Face Set 2**. Only available with the face fillet type. Displays the selected face for set 2.

- **Side Face Set 1**. Only available with the Full round fillet type.
- **Center Face Set**. Only available with the Full round fillet type.
- **Side Face Set 2**. Only available with the Full round fillet type.

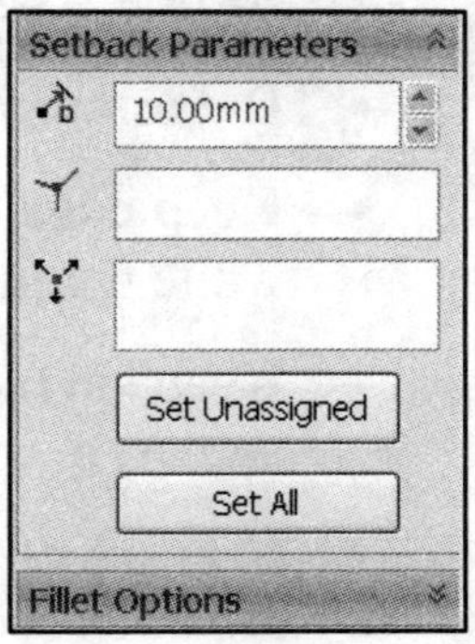


- ***Setback Parameters***. Creates an even transition connecting the blended surface, along the edge of the part, into the fillet corner. Select a vertex and a radius, then assign a different or the same setback distances for each edge. The setback distance is the distance along each edge at which the fillet starts to merge into the three faces which combine into the common vertex. The Setback Parameters box is only available for the Constant radius type and Variable radius type fillet. The available selections are:
  - **Distance**. Sets the fillet setback distance from the vertex.
  - **Setback Vertices**. Displays the selected vertices from the Graphics window. The setback fillet edges intersect at the selected vertices.
  - **Setback Distances**. Displays the edge numbers with the corresponding setback distance value.
  - **Set Unassigned**. Applies the current Distance option value to all edges that do not have an assigned distance under the Setback Distances option.
  - **Set All**. Applies the current Distance option value to all edges that are under the Setback Distances option.

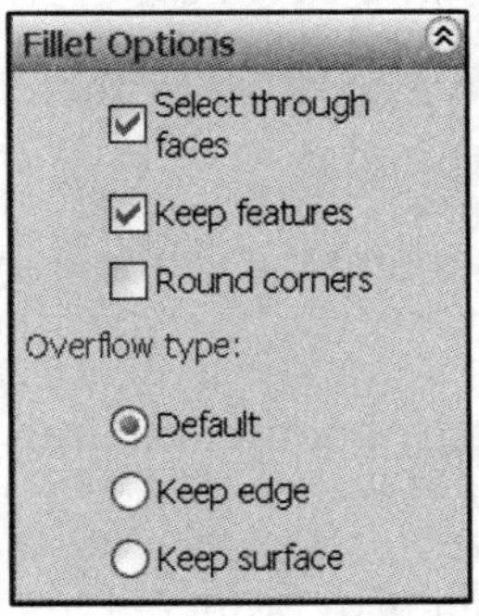


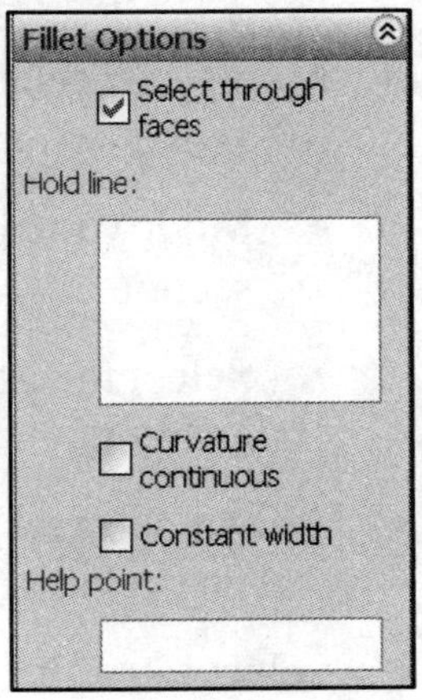


- ***Fillet Options***. The Fillet Options box is only available for the Constant radius type, Variable radius type, and face fillet type. The available options are dependent on the fillet type. The options are:
  - **Select through faces**. Selected by default.
  - **Keep Features**. Selected by default. Provides the ability to keep boss or cut features viewable from the Graphics window if you apply a large fillet radius to cover them.

Clear the Keep Features option to cover the Boss or Cut features with the fillet.

- **Round corners**. Creates constant radius fillets with rounded corners. You need to select at two or more adjacent edges to fillet.
- **Overflow type**. Controls the way fillets on single closed edges, splines, circles, ellipses, etc. behave when they meet edges. There are three options under this section. They are:
- **Default**. Provides the ability to select the Keep edge or Keep surface option.
- **Keep edge**. Provides the ability for the edge of the model to remain unchanged, while the fillet is adjusted.
- **Keep surface**. Provides the ability for the fillet edge to adjust to be uninterrupted and even, while the model edge alters to match the fillet edge.
- **Feature attachment**. Provides the ability to control attachment of edges between the intersection features.

Select a feature in the FeatureManager design tree to display the Feature attachment option in the PropertyManager. View SolidWorks Help for additional detail information.

## Control Points

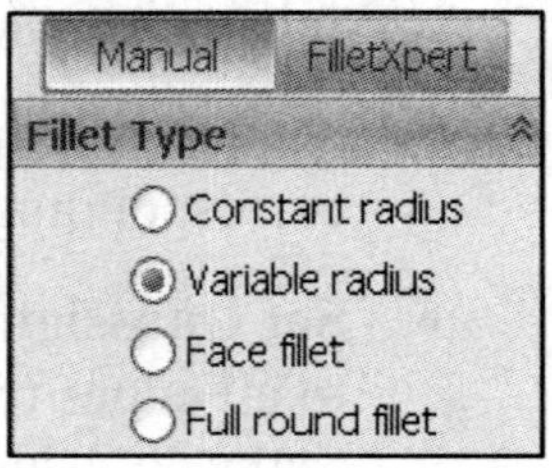


Use control points to define a Variable radius fillet type. Control and assign radius values to the control points between the vertices of the fillet. How do you use control point? Use the following as guidelines:

- Assign a radius value to each control point, or assign a value to one or both enclosing vertices.
- Modify the relative position of the control point by using the following two methods:
  - Modify the percentage of the control point in the callout section.
  - Select the control point and drag the control point to a new location.
- Add or subtract control points along the edge of the fillet which you selected. This can be performed at any time.
- Select more than one sketch entity to fillet. Complete each entity before selecting additional entities. Perform the following three step procedure to select sketch entities to fillet in the Items to Fillet section: 1.) *Apply a radius to each selected vertex*, 2.) *Apply a radius value to one or all control points, modify the position of a control point at any time, either before or after you apply a value for the radius.*

The system defaults to three control points located at equidistant increments of 25%, 50% and 75% along the edge between the two variable radii.

Adding or subtracting control points along the edge positions the control points in equidistant increments along that edge.

### *Tutorial: Fillet 6-1*

Create a fillet feature using the Tangent propagation option with the manual tab.

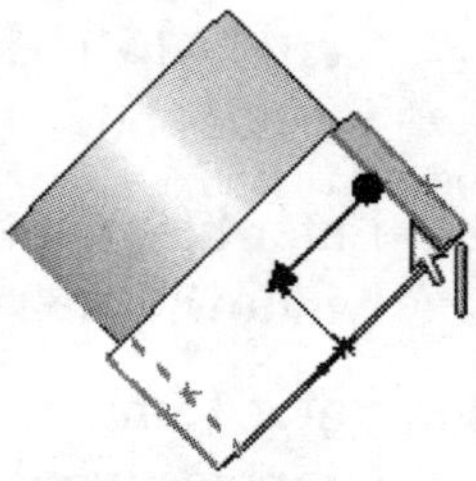

1. Open **Fillet 6-1** from the SolidWorks 2010 folder. The Fillet 6-1 FeatureManager is displayed.
2. Select the **four vertical edges** of Extrude1 using the Ctrl key. Note: You will need to release the Ctrl key to rotate the model.
3. Click **Fillet** from the Features toolbar. The Fillet PropertyManager is displayed.
4. Click the **Manual** tab. The four selected edges are displayed in the Edges, Faces, Features, and Loop box. Constant radius is the default Fillet type.

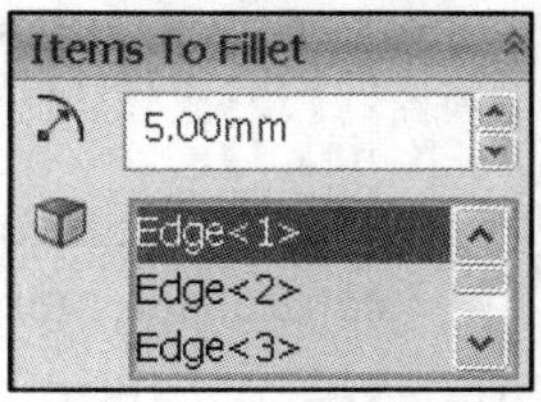


5. Enter **5**mm for Radius.
6. Click **OK** from the Fillet PropertyManager. Fillet1 is displayed in the FeatureManager.
7. Display an **Isometric view**. Click the **front face** of Extrude1.

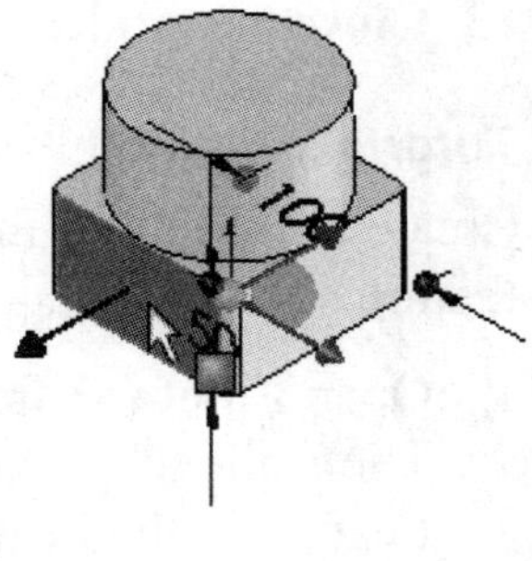

8. Click **Fillet** from the Features toolbar.
9. Check **Tangent propagation** and **Full preview**. This will pick all tangent faces and propagate around your model.

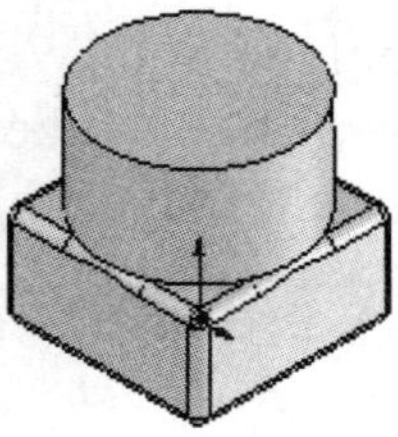

10. Click **OK** from the Fillet PropertyManager. The Fillet2 feature is displayed in the FeatureManager.
11. **Close** the model.

### *Tutorial: Fillet 6-2*

Create a fillet feature using the Setback Parameters option.

1. Open **Fillet 6-2** from the SolidWorks 2010 folder.
2. Click all **vertical** and **horizontal** edges of Extrude1. Note: You will need to release the Ctrl key to rotate the model.

3. Click **Fillet** from the Features toolbar. The selected entities, Edges<1> - Edges<12> are displayed in the Edges, Faces, Features, and Loop box.
4. Enter **5**mm for Radius.
5. Click the **Set Unassigned** button from the Setback Parameters box.
6. Click inside the **Setback Vertices** box.
7. Click the **Right top Vertex** of Extrude1. Vertex<1> is displayed in the Setback Vertices box.

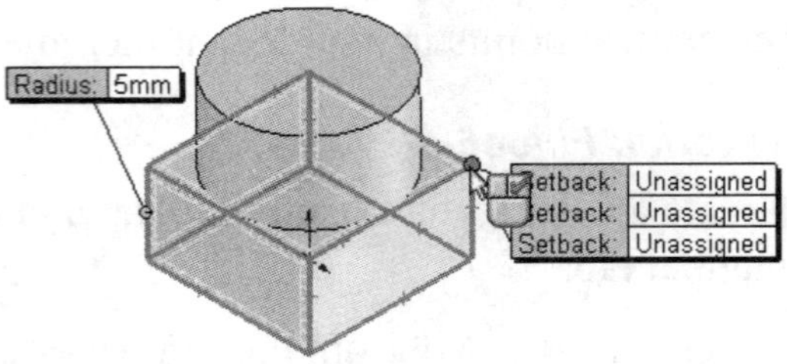


8. Enter **8**mm in the first Setback box in the Graphics window. The arrow direction points to the left.
9. Enter **15**mm in the second Setback box in the Graphics window. The arrow direction points downward.
10. Enter **8**mm in the third Setback box in the Graphics window. The arrow direction points to the back.

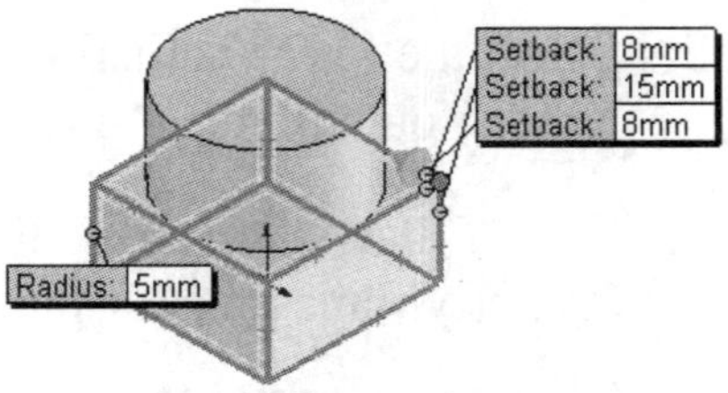


11. Click **OK** from the Fillet PropertyManager. Fillet1 is created and is displayed in the FeatureManager.
12. **View** the model in the Graphics window.
13. **Close** the model.

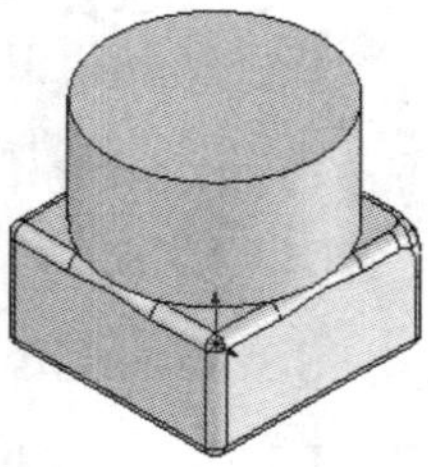

***Tutorial Fillet 6-3***

Create a full round fillet and a multiple radius fillet feature.

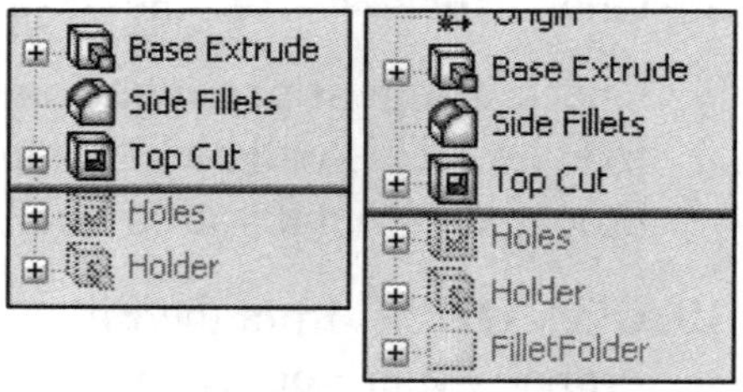


1. Open **Fillet 6-3** from the SolidWorks 2010 folder. The Rollback bar is positioned below the Top Cut Feature in the FeatureManager as illustrated.
2. Click **Hidden Lines Visible** from the Heads-up View toolbar.
3. Click **Fillet** from the Features toolbar. The Fillet PropertyManager is displayed.
4. Click the **Manual** tab.
5. Click **Full round fillet** for Fillet Type.
6. Click the **inside Top Cut face** for Side Face Set 1.
7. Click **inside** the Center Face Set box.

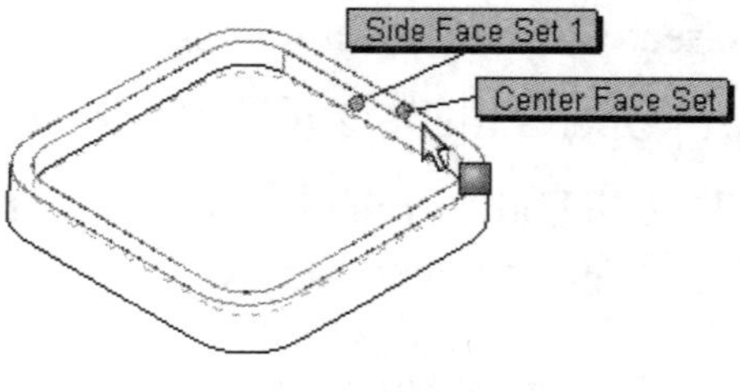

8. Click the **top face** of Base Extrude for Center Face Set.
9. Click **inside** the Side Face Set 2 box.
10. **Rotate** the part and click the **outside Base Extrude face** for Side Face Set 2 as illustrated.

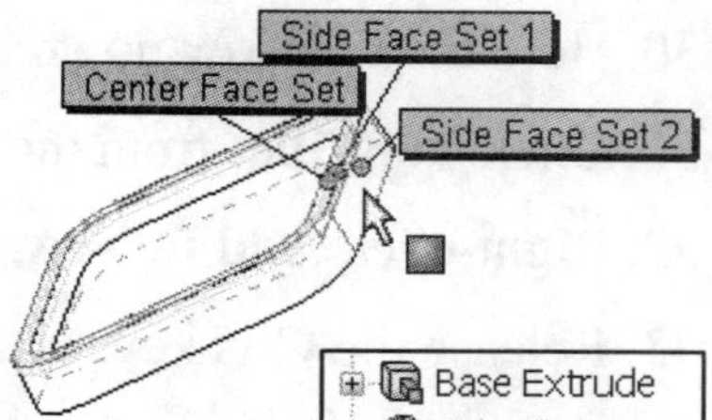


11. Click **OK** ✔ from the Fillet PropertyManager.
12. Rename **Fillet1** to **TopFillet**.
13. Drag the **Rollback** bar down to the bottom of the FeatureManager.

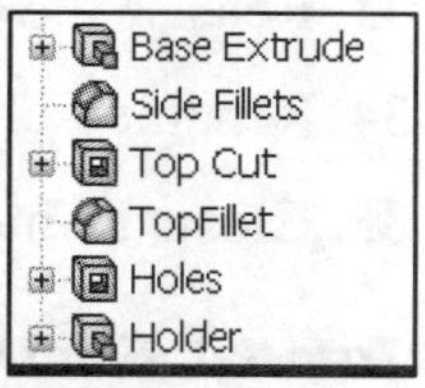


14. Display an **Isometric view**.
15. Display a **Shaded With Edges** view.
16. Click the **bottom outside circular edge** of the Holder as illustrated.

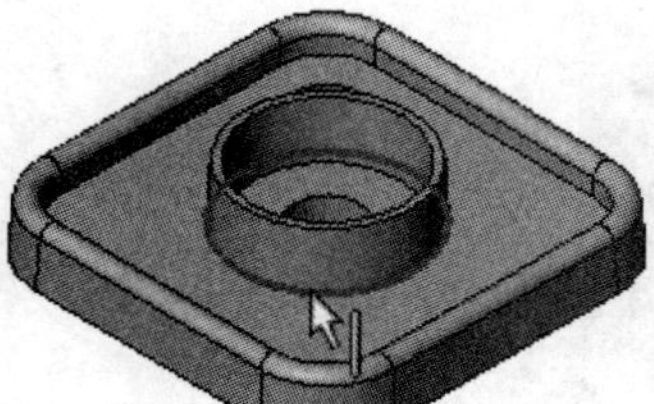

17. Click **Fillet** from the Features toolbar. The Fillet PropertyManager is displayed.
18. Enter **.050**in for Radius.

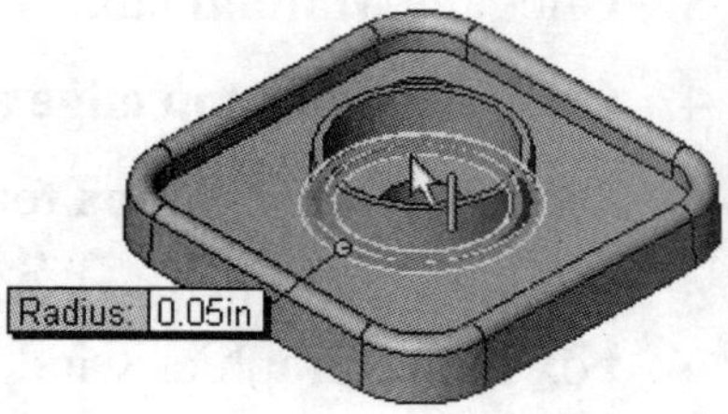


19. Click the **bottom inside circular edge**, “Top Cut” inside of the Holder as illustrated.
20. Click the **inside edge** of the right Top Cut as illustrated. Edge<1>, Edge<2>, and Edge<3> are displayed in the Items To Fillet box.
21. Check **Tangent Propagation**.
22. Check **Multiple radius fillet**. Modify the Fillet values.

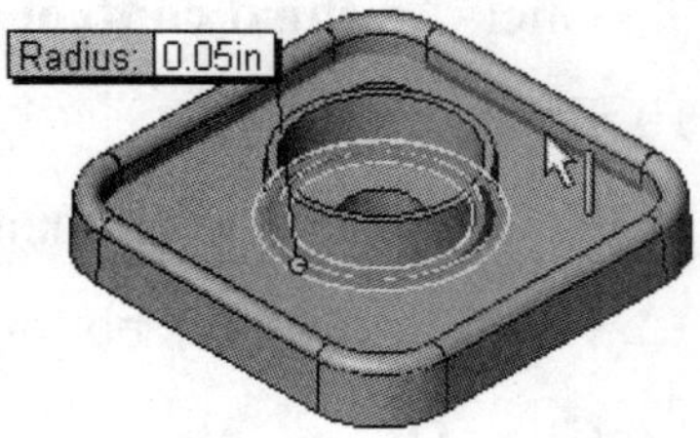


23. Click the **Radius** box for the Holder outside edge.
24. Enter **0.060**in.
25. Click the **Radius** box for the Top Cut inside edge.
26. Enter **0.040**in.
27. Click **OK** ✔ from the Fillet PropertyManager.
28. Rename **Fillet2** to **HolderFillet**.

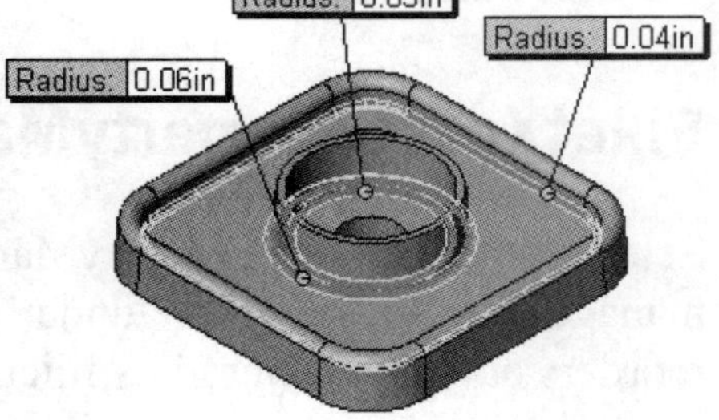


Group the Fillets into a Folder.

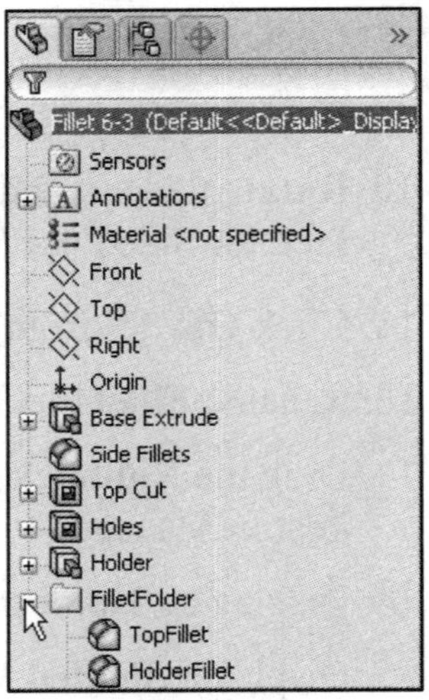


29. Click and drag **TopFillet** from the FeatureManager directly above HolderFillet in the FeatureManager.
30. Hold the **Ctrl** key down.
31. Click **TopFillet** from the FeatureManager.
32. Right-click **Add to New Folder**.
33. Release the **Ctrl** key.
34. Rename **Folder1** to **Fillet Folder**.
35. **Close** the model.

***Tutorial: Fillet 6-4***

Create a variable radius Fillet feature.

1. Open **Fillet 6-4** from the SolidWorks 2010 folder.

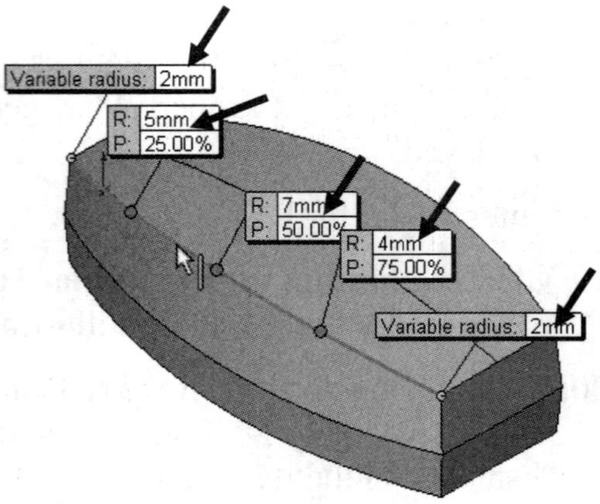


2. Click the **Fillet** Features tool. The Fillet PropertyManager is displayed.
3. Click the **Manual** tab.
4. Click the **front top edge** as illustrated.
5. Click **Variable radius** for Fillet Type.
6. Enter **2mm** in the top left Variable radius box in the Graphics window.
7. Click the **second control** point.
8. Enter **5mm** for R.
9. Click the **third control** point.
10. Enter **7mm** for R.
11. Enter **4mm** in the remaining control point.
12. Enter **2mm** in the bottom right Variable radius box as illustrated.
13. Click **OK** from the Fillet PropertyManager. The VarFillet1 feature is displayed. View the results.
14. **Close** the model.

## FilletXpert PropertyManager

Select the FilletXpert PropertyManager when you want the SolidWorks software to manage the structure of the underlying features. The FilletXpert manages, organizes, and reorders only constant radius fillets. The FilletXpert provides the ability to: 1. *Create multiple fillets,* 2. *Automatically invoke the FeatureXpert,* 3. *Automatically reorder fillets when required,* 4. *Manage the desired type of fillet corner.*

The FilletXpert PropertyManager remembers the last used state. The FilletXpert can ONLY create and edit *Constant radius* fillets.

## FilletXpert PropertyManager: Add tab

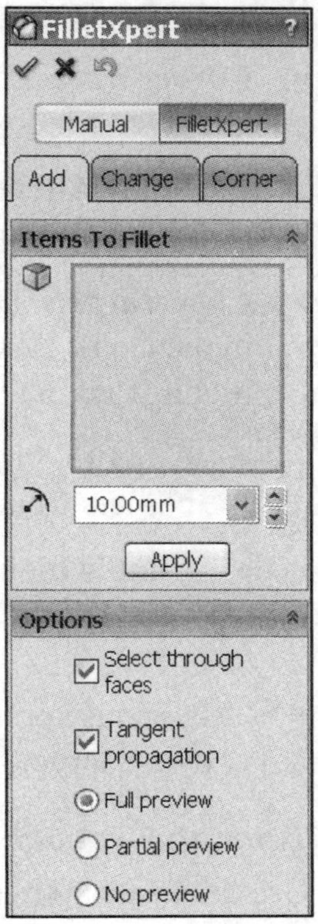


The FilletXpert PropertyManager provides the ability to create a new constant radius fillet. The FilletXpert PropertyManager provides the following selections:

- ***Items To Fillet***. The Items To Fillet box provides the following selections:
  - **Edges, Faces, Features and Loops**. Displays the selected items to fillet for Edges, Faces, Features and Loops.
  - **Radius**. Enter the radius value.
  - **Apply**. Calculates and creates the fillets. The FilletXpert uses the FeatureXpert to create the fillet.
- ***Options***. The Options box provides the following selections: **Select through faces, Tangent propagation**, **Full preview**, **Partial preview** and **No preview**.

## FilletXpert PropertyManager: Change tab

Provides the ability to remove or resize a constant radius fillet. The FilletXpert PropertyManager provides the following selections:

- ***Fillets to change***. The Fillets to change box provides the following selections:
  - **Filleted Faces**. Displays the selected fillets to resize or to remove.
  - **Radius**. Enter the radius value.
  - **Resize**. Modifies the selected fillets to the new radius value.
  - **Remove**. Removes the selected fillets from the model.
- ***Existing Fillets.*** Provides the following options:
  - **Sort by Size**. Filters all fillets by size. Select a fillet size from the list to select all fillets with that value in the model and display them under Filleted faces.

## FilletXpert PropertyManager: Corner tab

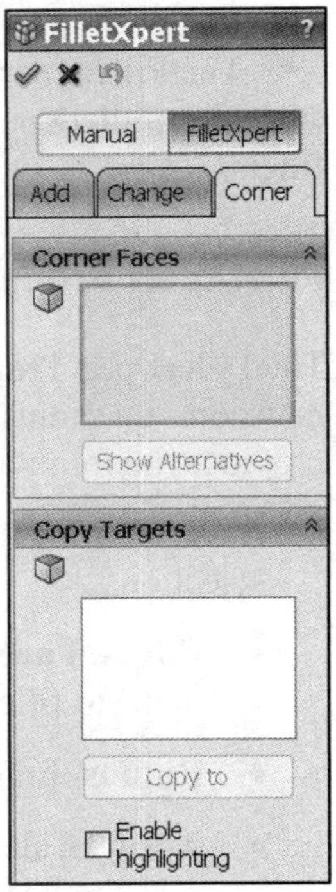


Provides the ability to create and manage the fillet corner feature where three filleted edges meet at a single vertex. The FilletXpert PropertyManager provides the following selections:

- ***Corner Faces***. Displays the selected fillet corners from the Graphics window.
  - **Show Alternatives**. Displays alternative fillet corner previews in a pop-up.
- ***Copy Targets***. Displays the selected target fillet corners. Click in the Copy Targets box, compatible target fillet corners are highlighted in the Graphics window.
  - **Copy to**. Provides the ability to copy selected target fillet corners from the Corner Faces box to a selected location.
  - **Enable highlighting**. Provides the ability to highlight compatible target fillet corners in the Graphics window.

The mouse pointer displays the fillet corner icon when you hover over a target fillet corner.

***Tutorial: Fillet 6-5***

Use the FeatureXpert tool to insert a Fillet feature.

1. Open **Fillet 6-5** from the SolidWorks 2010 folder.
2. Click the **top face** of Extrude1 as illustrated. Extrude1is highlighted in the FeatureManager.

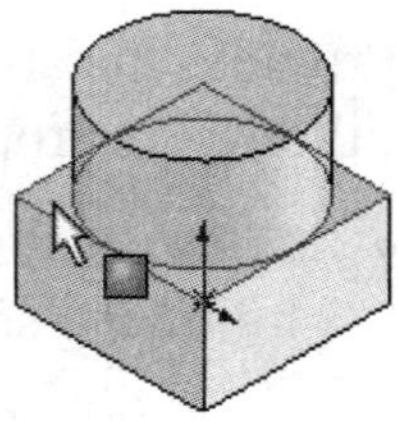

3. Click the **Fillet** Features tool. The Fillet PropertyManager is displayed. Enter **5**mm for Radius in the Item To Fillet box.
4. Click **OK** from the Fillet PropertyManager. The What's Wrong box is displayed. You failed to create a Fillet. Use the FeatureXpert.
5. Click the **FeatureXpert** button from the What's Wrong box. The FeatureXpert solved your fillet problem and created two fillet features: Fillet1 and Fillet2. The 5mm Radius fillet was not possible with the selected Extrude1 face. The FeatureXpert solved the problem with edges for a smoother transition.

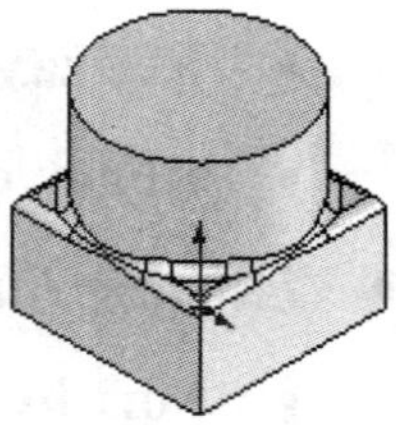

6. **Edit** both Fillet1 and Fillet2 from the FeatureManager to review the created fillets.
7. **Close** the model.

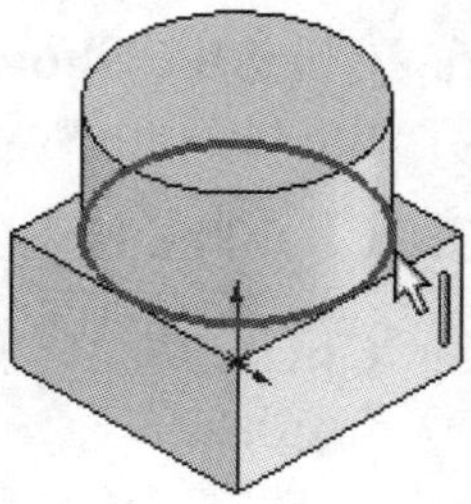

### *Tutorial: Fillet 6-6*

Use the FilletXpert tab option to create a Fillet feature.

1. Open **Fillet 6-6** from the SolidWorks 2010 folder.
2. Click the **bottom circular edge** of Extrude2.
3. Click the **Fillet** Features tool. The Fillet PropertyManager is displayed.

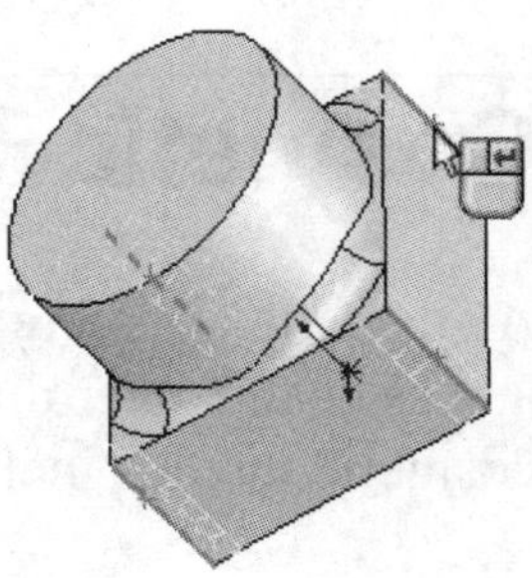

4. Click the **FilletXpert** tab. The FilletXpert PropertyManager is displayed. The selected edge is displayed in the Edges, Faces, Features and Loop box.
5. Enter **10**mm for Radius.
6. Click the **Apply** button.
7. Click the **4 vertical corners** of Extrude1.
8. Click the **Apply** button. The FilletXpert added two fillet features without leaving the FilletXpert PropertyManager. Modify the first fillet using the FilletXpert. Expand the FeatureManager to view Fillet1 and Fillet2.

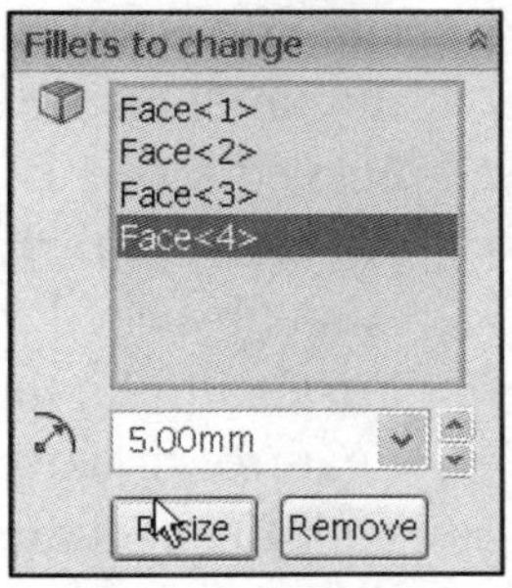


9. Click the **Change tab**.
10. Click **Fillet2** from the flyout FeatureManager.
11. Enter **5.00**mm for Radius.
12. Click the **Resize** button. The model is modified and the existing Fillets are sorted by size.
13. Click **OK** from the FilletXpert PropertyManager. View the results.
14. **Close** the model.

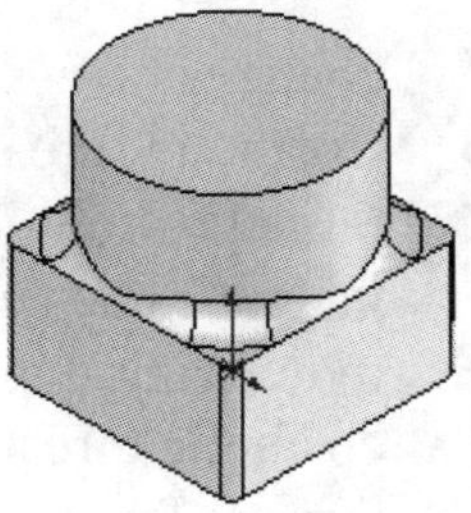

### *Tutorial: Fillet 6-7 fillet corner tab*

Apply the FilletXpert Corner Tab option. Remember, the Corner tab option requires three constant radius filleted edges of mixed convexity meeting at a single vertex.

1. Open **Fillet 6-7** from the SolidWorks 2010 folder.
2. Right-click **Fillet-Corner1** from the FeatureManager.
3. Click **Edit Feature** from the Context toolbar. The FilletXpert Property Manager is displayed.

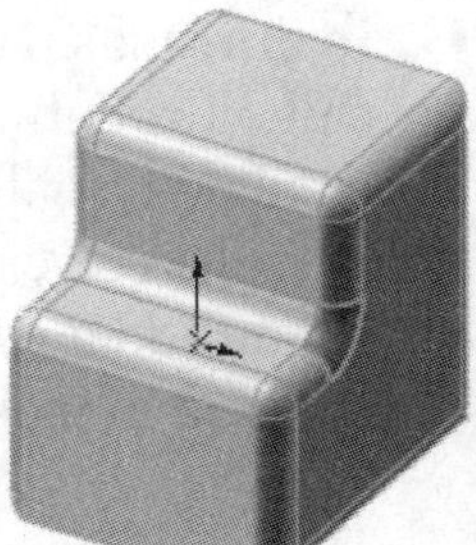

4. Click the **FilletXpert** tab.
5. Click the **Corner** tab.
6. Click the **Show Alternatives** button. Two options are displayed in the Graphics window.
7. Click the **right option**.
8. Click **OK** from the FilletXpert PropertyManager. View the results.
9. **Close** the model.

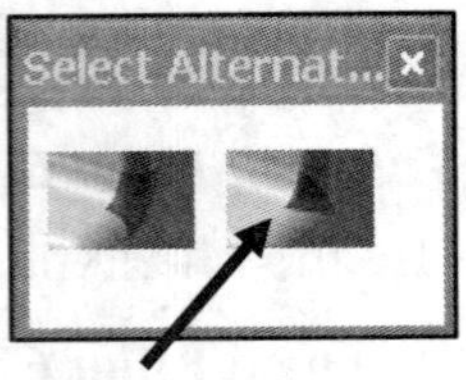


# Cosmetic Thread Feature

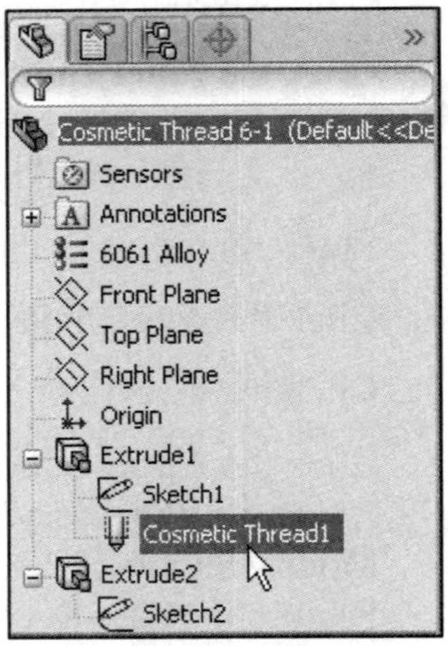


A cosmetic thread represents the inner diameter of a thread on a boss or the outer diameter of a thread. The properties of cosmetic threads include:

- You can represent threads on a part, assembly or drawing, and you can attach a thread callout note in drawings. You can add cosmetic threads to conical holes. If the conical thread does not end at a flat face, it is trimmed by the curved face.
- A cosmetic thread differs from other annotations in that it is an absorbed feature of the item to which it is attached. For example, the cosmetic thread on a hole is in the FeatureManager design tree under the **Hole** feature, along with the sketches used to create the hole.
- When the pointer is over a cosmetic thread, the pointer changes to .
- Cosmetic threads in part documents are inserted automatically into drawing views. A thread callout is also inserted if the drawing document is in the ANSI standard. (You insert thread callouts in the Cosmetic Thread PropertyManager, but they appear only in drawing documents.) Note: When creating a cosmetic thread, you can now define cosmetic threads using international standard sizes in 2010. To insert cosmetic threads from assembly documents into drawings, click **Insert**, **Model Items** and click **Cosmetic thread**.
- In drawings, **Insert Callout** appears in the Context toolbar. If a cosmetic thread callout is defined in the part or assembly but is not displayed in the drawing, you can display the callout by selecting this menu item. A leader attaches to the thread by default. The callout is a note. You can edit the callout as you would edit any note.
- If you add a cosmetic thread while working in a drawing view, the part or assembly is updated to include a Cosmetic Thread feature.

- You can dimension both the circular cosmetic thread and the linear dimension of the sides in drawings. You cannot dimension cosmetic threads in part or assembly documents
- The visibility of cosmetic threads follows the visibility of the parent feature. When you change display mode, add features to the **Show Hidden Edges** list, or hide a component, the visibility of cosmetic threads changes automatically.
- You can set High quality cosmetic threads to check all cosmetic threads to determine if they should be visible or hidden.
- You can reference patterned cosmetic threads.
- For tap and pipe tap holes, you can add cosmetic threads in the Hole Wizard. See the Hole Wizard section in the book for additional information.

The Cosmetic Thread feature uses the Cosmetic Thread PropertyManager. The Cosmetic PropertyManager provides the following default selections:

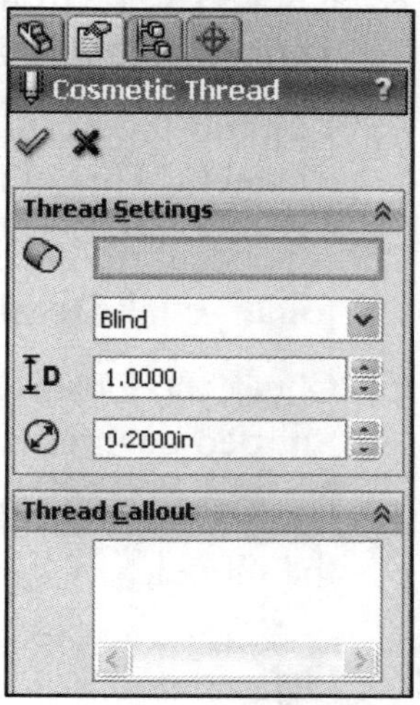


- ***Thread Settings***. Provides the following options:
  - **Circular Edge**. Select a circular edge of the model in the Graphics window.
  - **End Condition**. The cosmetic thread extends from the edge selected above to the end condition. The following End Conditions are available:
    - **Blind**. A specified depth. Specify the depth below.
    - **Through**. Completely through the existing geometry.
    - **Up To Next**. To the next entity that intercepts the thread.
  - **Depth**. Enter a value when the End Condition is Blind.
  - **Minor Diameter**, **Major Diameter** or **Conical Offset**. Sets the diameter for the dimension corresponding to the entity type with the cosmetic thread.

***Thread Callout***. Type text to appear in the thread callout. (The thread callout appears in drawing documents only.)

### *Tutorial: Cosmetic thread 6-1*

Apply a Cosmetic thread: 1/4-20x2 UNC.

1. Open **Cosmetic thread 6-1** from the SolidWorks 2010 folder.

Create a Cosmetic thread. Produce the geometry of the thread. A thread profile needs a Helix and a profile Sweep cut (to remove material) along the helix.

Start the Helix.

2. Click the **bottom edge** of the part as illustrated.
3. Click **Insert**, **Annotations**, **Cosmetic Thread** from the Menu bar menu. View the Cosmetic Thread PropertyManager. Edge<1> is displayed.

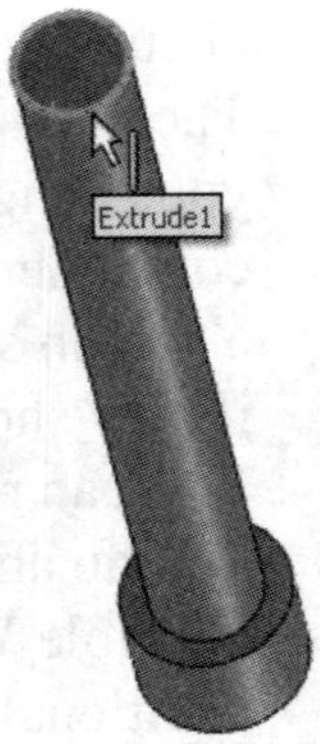


4. Select **Blind** for End Condition.
5. Enter **1.00** for depth.
6. Enter **.200** for min diameter.
7. Enter **¼-20-2 UNC 2A** in the Thread Callout box.
8. Click **OK** ✔ from the Cosmetic Thread FeatureManager.
9. **Expand** the FeatureManager. View the Cosmetic Thread feature.
10. If needed, right-click the **Annotations** folder, click **Details**.
11. Check the **Cosmetic threads**, and **Shaded cosmetic threads** box.
12. Click **OK**. View the cosmetic thread on the model.

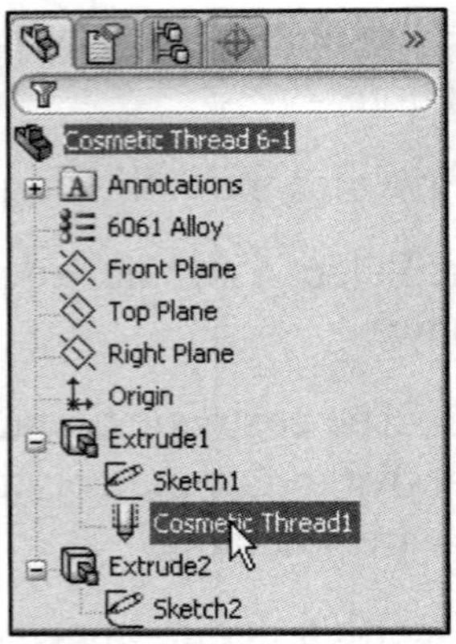


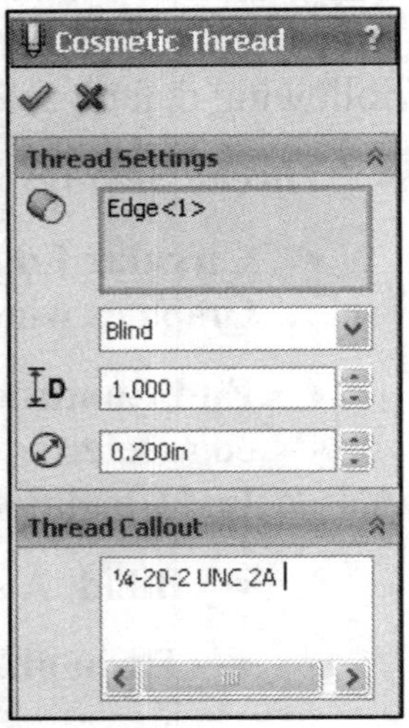


💡 The Thread Callout: ¼-20-2UNC 2A is automatically inserted into a drawing document, if the drawing document is in the ANSI drafting standard.

💡 ¼-20-2 UNC 2A – ¼ inch drill diameter – 20 threads / inch, Unified National Coarse thread series, Class 2, External threads

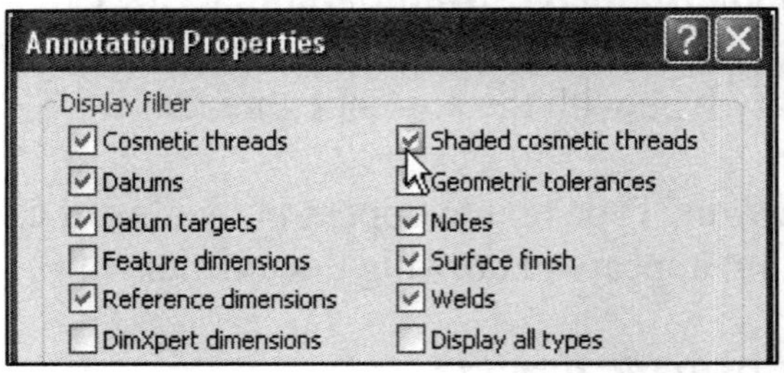

💡 When creating a cosmetic thread, you can now define cosmetic threads using international standard sizes in 2010.

# Summary

In this chapter, you learned about the Extruded Bose/Base, Extruded Cut, Fillet and the Cosmetic Thread features in SolidWorks. An extrusion is the Base feature which adds material and is the first feature created in a part.

An Extruded Boss feature adds material onto an existing feature. A cut feature removes material from the part. The Thin feature parameter option allows you to specific thickness of the extrusion. Extrude features can be solids or surfaces. Solids are utilized primary for machined parts and contain mass properties. Surfaces are utilized surfaces for organic shapes which contain no mass properties. You reviewed and applied the Extruded Boss/Base Feature, Extruded Cut Feature, Extruded Solid/Thin Feature, Extruded Surface Feature and the Cut With Surface Feature.

You also learned that Filleting refers to both fillets and rounds. The distinction between fillets and rounds is made by the geometric conditions, and not by the command. Fillets add volume, and rounds remove volume.

Create fillets on a selected edge, selected edges, selected sets of faces, and edge loops. The selected edges can be selected in various ways. Options exist for constant or variable fillet radius and tangent edge propagation in the Fillet PropertyManager.

You reviewed the Manual tab in the Fillet PropertyManager, using control points, surfaces, and the FilletXpert PropertyManager with the Add. Change and Corner tab.

You addressed adding a Cosmetic Thread to a simple part. View SolidWorks online help for additional information on Cosmetic threads and the Hole Wizard section in the next chapter.

In Chapter 7, explore and address the Revolved Boss/Base feature, Revolved Cut feature, Hole / Hole Wizard feature and the Dome feature.

**Notes:**

# CHAPTER 7: REVOLVED, HOLE AND DOME FEATURES

## Chapter Objective

Chapter 7 provides a comprehensive understanding of Revolved, Hole, and Dome features.

On the completion of this chapter, you will be able to:

- Comprehend and utilize the following Revolved features:
  - Revolved Boss/Base
  - Revolved Cut
  - Revolve Boss Thin
  - Revolved Surface
- Understand and utilize the following Hole features:
  - Simple Hole
  - Hole Wizard
- Know and utilize the Dome feature

## Revolved Boss/Base Feature

The Revolved Boss/Base feature adds material by revolving one or more profiles about a centerline. SolidWorks provides the ability to create Revolved Boss/Base, Revolved Cut, or Revolved Surface features.

The Revolved feature can be a solid, thin or surface. There are a few general guidelines that you should be aware of when creating a Revolved feature. They are:

- The sketch for a solid revolved feature can contain multiple intersecting profiles. Activate the Selected Contours box from the Revolve PropertyManager. The Selected Contours icon is displayed on the mouse pointer. Click one or more intersecting or non-intersecting sketches to create the Revolved feature.

- The sketch for a thin or surface revolved feature can contain multiple open or closed intersecting profiles.
- Profiles cannot cross the centerline. Select the centerline you wish to use as your axis of revolution if the sketch contains one or more centerlines.

The sketch cannot lie on the centerline for revolved surfaces and revolved thin features.

The Revolved Boss/Base feature uses the Revolve PropertyManager. The Revolve PropertyManager provides the following selections:

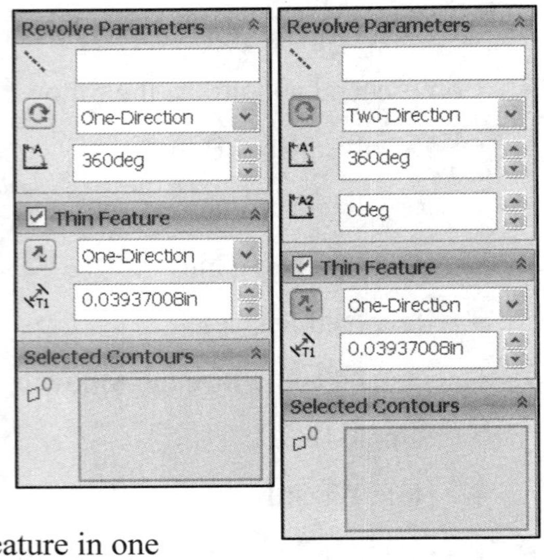


- ***Revolve Parameters***. The Revolve Parameters box provides the ability to select the following options:
  - **Axis of Revolution**. Displays the selected axis around which the feature revolves. The Axis of Revolution can be a line, centerline, or even an edge. Your selection is depended on the type of revolve feature you create.
  - **Revolve Type**. Defines the revolve direction type from your Sketch plane. There selections are:
    - **One-Direction**. Creates the revolve feature in one direction from your Sketch plane.
    - **Mid-Plane**. Creates the revolve feature in a clockwise and counter-clockwise direction from your Sketch plane. The Mid-Plane is in the middle of the revolve angle.
    - **Two-Direction**. Creates the revolve feature in a clockwise and counter-clockwise direction from your Sketch plane. Set the Direction 1 Angle and the Direction 2 Angle. The total of the two angles can't exceed 360degrees.
      - **Reverse Direction**. Reverses the revolve feature direction if required.
      - **Angle**. Defines the angle value covered by the revolve type feature. The default angle is 360 degrees. The angle is measured clockwise from the selected Sketch plane.
- ***Thin Feature***. The Thin Feature controls the revolve thickness of your profile. This is not the depth. Create Thin Features by using an active sketch profile and then applying a wall thickness. Apply the wall thickness to the inside or outside of your sketch, evenly on both sides of the sketch or unevenly on either side of your sketch. Thin Feature creation is automatically invoked for active contours which are revolved or extruded. You can also create a Thin Feature from a closed contour. The Thin Feature box provides the following selections:

- **Type**. Defines the direction of thickness. There are three selection:
- **One-Direction**. Adds the thin-walled volume in one direction from your Sketch plane.
- **Mid-Plane**. Adds the thin-walled volume using your sketch as the midpoint. This option applies the thin-walled volume equally on both sides of your sketch.
- **Two-Direction**. Adds the thin-walled volume to both sides of your sketch. The Direction 1 Thickness adds thin-walled volume outward from the sketch. Direction 2 Thickness adds thin-walled volume inward from your sketch.
  - **Reverse Direction**. Reverses the direction of the thin-walled volume if required. View the thin-walled volume from the Graphics window.
  - **Direction 1 Thickness**. Sets the thin-walled volume thickness for the One-Direction option and the Mid-Plane option for the Thin Feature option.

- ***Selected Contours***. The Selected Contours box provides the following option:
  - **Select Contours**. Displays the selected contours. Select the contours from the Graphics window.
  - ***Feature Scope***. Apply features to one or more multi-body parts. The Feature Scope box provides the following selections:

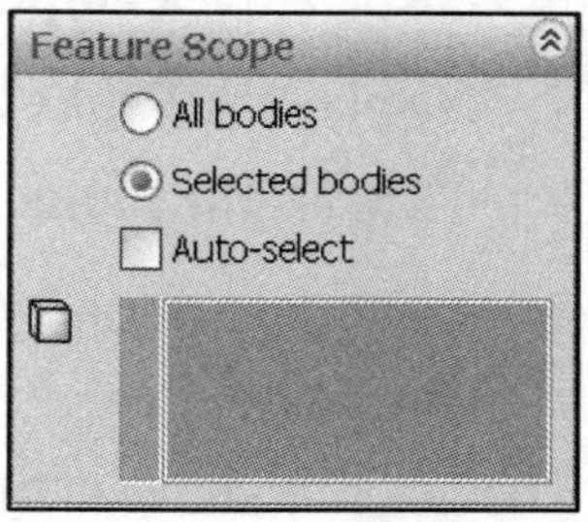


  - **All bodies**. Applies the feature to all bodies every time the feature regenerates. If you add new bodies to the model that are intersected by the feature, these new bodies are also regenerated to include the feature.
  - **Selected bodies**. Selected by default. Applies the feature to the selected bodies.
  - **Auto-select**. Only available if you select the Selected bodies option. When you first create a model with multi-body parts, the feature automatically processes all the relevant intersecting parts. Auto-select is faster than All bodies because it processes only the bodies on the initial list and does not regenerate the entire model.
  - **Solid Bodies to Affect**. Only available if Auto-select is not active. Displays the selected bodies to affect from the Graphics window.

Press the **g** key to activate the Magnifying glass tool. Use the Magnifying glass tool to inspect a model and make selections without changing the overall view.

### *Tutorial: Revolve Boss/Base 7-1*

Create a Revolve Base feature and a Revolve Boss feature for a light bulb.

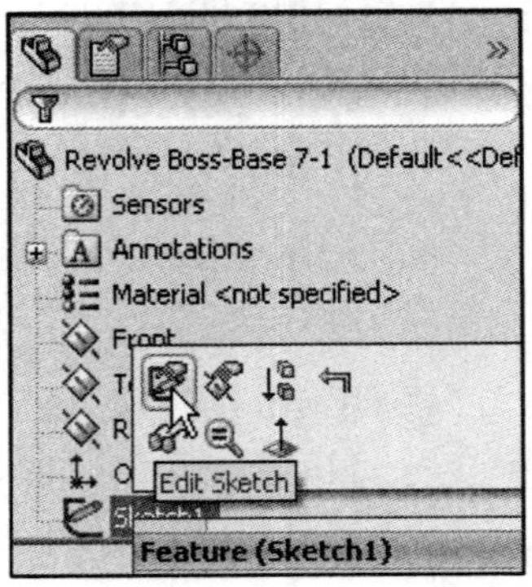


1. Open **Revolve Boss-Base 7-1** from the SolidWorks 2010 folder. The Revolve Boss-Base 7-1 FeatureManager is displayed.
2. **Edit** Sketch1. Display an **Isometric** view.
3. Click the **Revolved Boss/Base** Features tool. The Revolve PropertyManager is displayed.
4. Click the **centerline** from the Graphics window. Line1 is displayed in the Axis of Revolution box. Accept the defaults.

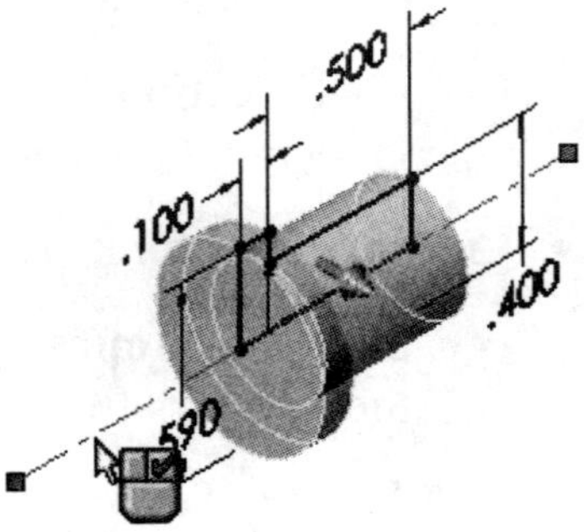


5. Click **OK** from the Revolve PropertyManager. Revolve1 is created and is displayed in the FeatureManager.
6. Display the **Temporary Axes**.
7. Display the **Right** view.
8. Click **Right Plane** from the FeatureManager.

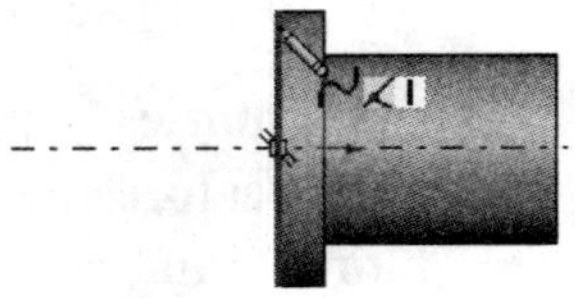

9. Click the **Spline** Sketch tool. The Spline icon is displayed on the mouse pointer.
10. Click the **left vertical edge** of the Base feature for the start point.
11. **Drag** the mouse pointer to the left.

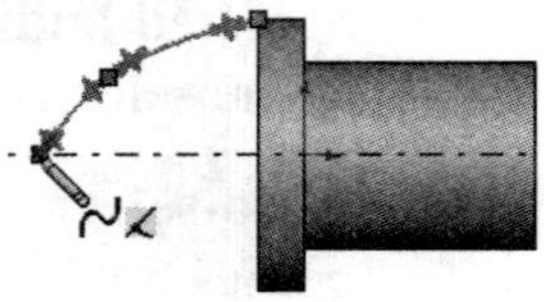

12. Click a **position** above the Temporary Axis. This is your control point.
13. Double-click the **Temporary Axis** to end the Spline. This is the end point.
14. Click **OK** from the Spline PropertyManager.
15. Click the **Line** Sketch tool.
16. Sketch a **horizontal line** from the Spline endpoint to the left edge of the Base Revolved feature.

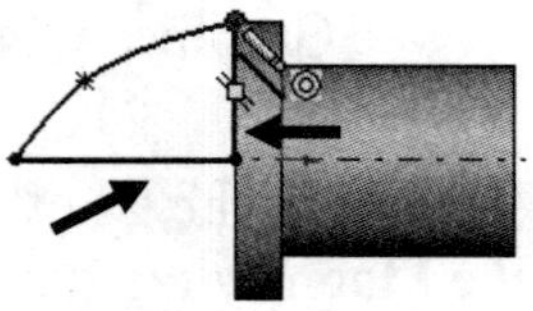

17. Sketch a **vertical line** to the start point of the Spline.
18. Deselect the Sketch tool. Right-click **Select**.
19. Click the **Temporary Axis** in the Graphics window.

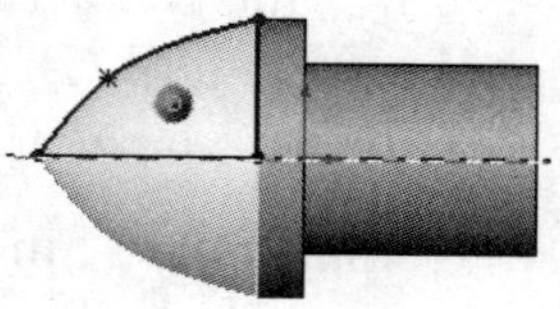

20. Click the **Revolved Boss/Base** Features tool. The Revolve PropertyManager is displayed. Axis1 is displayed in the Axis of Revolution box.
21. Click **OK** from the Revolve PropertyManager. Revolve2 is created and is displayed in the FeatureManager. The points of the Spline dictate the shape of the Spline. You can edit the control point in the sketch later to produce different results/shapes for the Revolved feature.
22. **Close** the model.

### *Tutorial: Revolved Boss/Base 7-2*

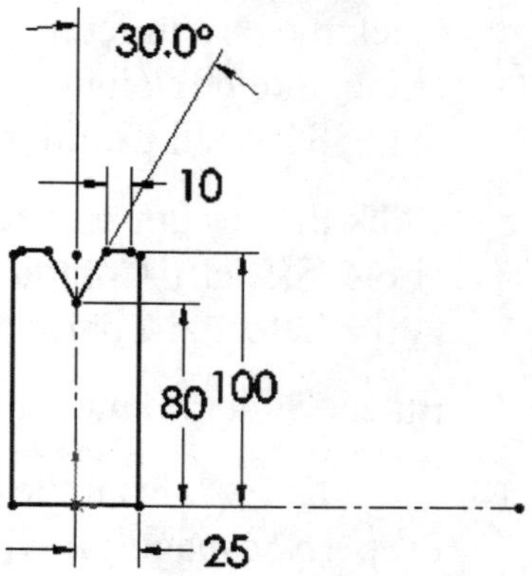


Create a pulley wheel using the Revolved Boss/Base Feature tool.

1. Open **Revolve Boss-Base 7-2** from the SolidWorks 2010 folder. The Revolve Boss-Base 7-2 FeatureManager is displayed.
2. **Edit** Sketch1.
3. Click the **Revolved Boss/Base** Feature tool. The Revolve PropertyManager is displayed.
4. Click the **horizontal centerline** from the Graphics window. Line13 is displayed in the Axis of Revolution box.
5. Enter **360**deg in the Angle box.
6. Click **OK** from the Revolve PropertyManager. Revolve1 is created and is displayed in the FeatureManager.
7. **Close** the model.

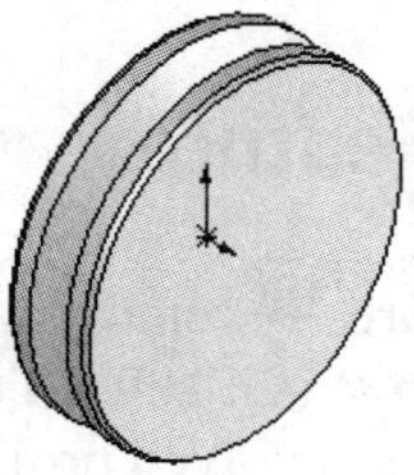

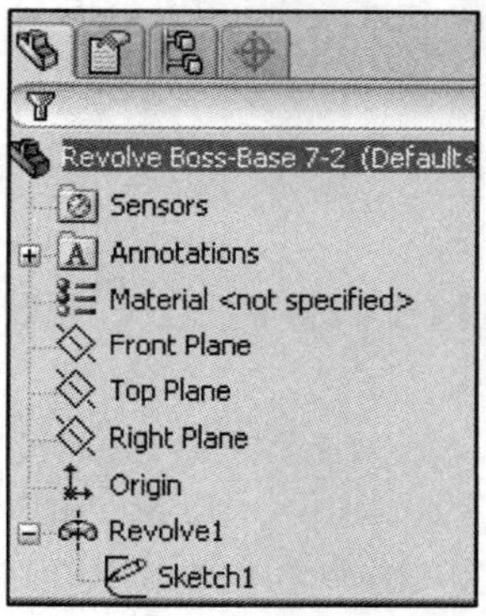


### *Tutorial: Revolved Boss/Base 7-3*

Create a Revolve Thin Feature using the Revolve Boss/Base Feature tool.

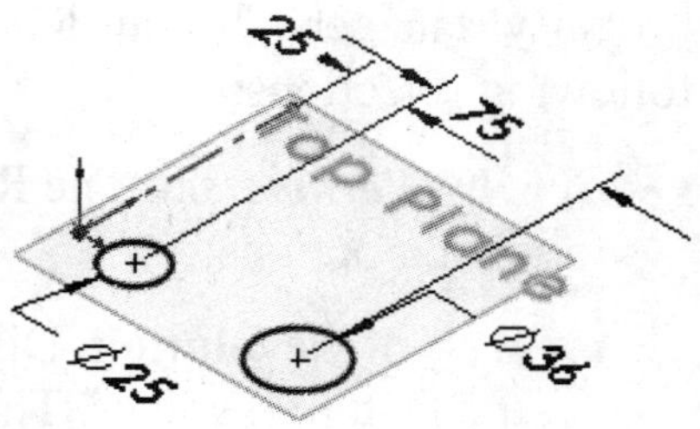


1. Open **Revolve Boss-Base 7-3** from the SolidWorks 2010 folder. The FeatureManager is displayed.
2. **Edit** Sketch1.

3. Click the **Revolved Boss/Base** Features tool. The Revolve PropertyManager is displayed.
4. **Expand** the Thin Feature box.
5. Check the **Thin Feature** box. The Thin Feature box displays Type and Direction thickness.
6. Enter **5**mm for Direction 1 Thickness. **Expand** the Selected Contours box.
7. Click the circumference of the **36**mm circle. Sketch1-Contour<1> is displayed in the Selected Contours box.
8. Click the circumference of the **25mm** circle. Sketch1-Contour<2> is displayed in the Selected Contours box.
9. Enter **180**deg in the Angle box.
10. Click **OK** from the Revolve PropertyManager. Revolve-Thin1 is created and is displayed in the FeatureManager.
11. **Close** the model.

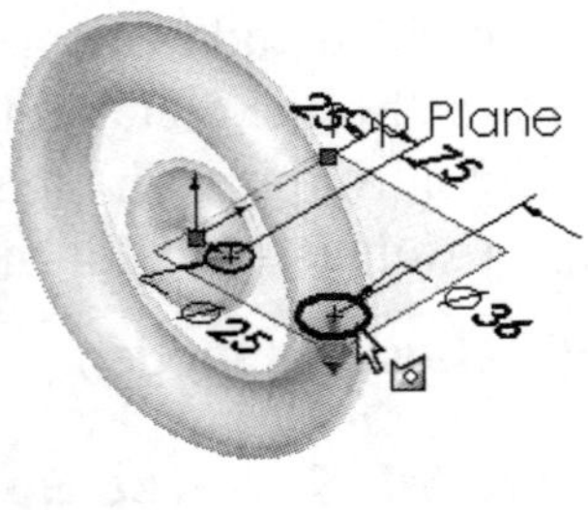


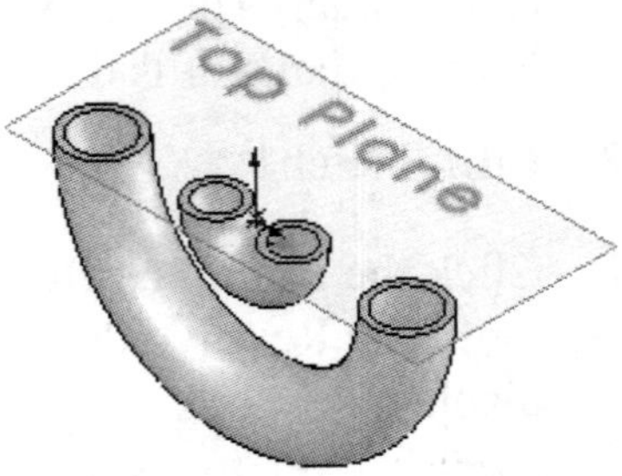


## Revolved Cut Feature

The Revolved Cut feature removes material by rotating an open sketch profile around an axis. Sketch a centerline to create a diameter dimension for a revolved profile. The Temporary axis does not produce a diameter dimension.

The Revolved Cut feature uses the Cut-Revolve PropertyManager. The Cut-Revolve PropertyManager provides the following selections:

- ***Revolve Parameters***. The Revolve Parameters box provides the following options:
  - **Axis of Revolution**. Displays the selected axis around which the feature revolves. The Axis of Revolution can be a line, centerline, or even an edge. Your selection is depended on the type of revolve feature you create.

- **Revolve Type**. Defines the revolve direction type from your Sketch plane. There are three selections:
  - **One-Direction**. Creates the revolve feature in one direction from your Sketch plane.
  - **Mid-Plane**. Creates the revolve feature in a clockwise and counter-clockwise direction from your Sketch plane. The Mid-Plane is in the middle of the revolve angle.
  - **Two-Direction**. Creates the revolve feature in a clockwise and counter-clockwise direction from your Sketch plane. Set the Direction 1 Angle and the Direction 2 Angle. The total of the two angles can't exceed 360 degrees.
    - **Reverse Direction**. Reverses the revolve feature direction if required.
    - **Angle**. Defines the angle value covered by the revolve type feature. The default angle is 360 degrees. The angle is measured clockwise from the selected Sketch plane.

- ***Thin Feature***. The Thin Feature controls the revolve thickness of your profile. This is not the depth. Create Thin Features by using an active sketch profile and then applying a wall thickness. Apply the wall thickness to the inside or outside of your sketch, evenly on both sides of the sketch or unevenly on either side of your sketch. Thin Feature creation is automatically invoked for active contours which are revolved or extruded. You can also create a Thin Feature from a closed contour. The Thin Feature box provides the following selections:
  - **Type**. Defines the direction of thickness. There are three selection:
    - **One-Direction**. Adds the thin-walled volume in one direction from your Sketch plane.
    - **Mid-Plane**. Adds the thin-walled volume using your sketch as the midpoint. This option applies the thin-walled volume equally on both sides of your sketch.
    - **Two-Direction**. Adds the thin-walled volume to both sides of your sketch. The Direction 1 Thickness adds thin-walled volume outward from the sketch. Direction 2 Thickness adds thin-walled volume inward from your sketch.
    - **Reverse Direction**. Reverses the direction of the thin-walled volume if required. View the thin-walled volume from the Graphics window.

  - **Direction 1 Thickness**. Sets the thin-walled volume thickness for the One-Direction option and the Mid-Plane option for the Thin Feature option.
  - **Direction 2 Thickness**. Sets the thin-walled volume thickness for the Two-Direction option.
- ***Selected Contours***. The Selected Contours box provides the following option:
  - **Select Contours**. Displays the selected contours. Select the contours from the Graphics window.

### *Tutorial: Revolved Cut 7-1*

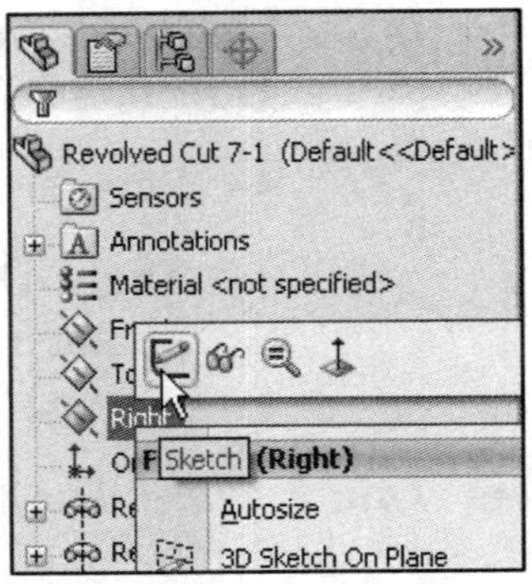


Insert a Revolved Cut Thin feature in a bulb part.

1. Open **Revolved Cut 7-1** from the SolidWorks 2010 folder.
2. Right-click **Right Plane** from the FeatureManager.
3. Click **Sketch** from the Context toolbar.
4. Click the **Line** Sketch tool. The Insert Line PropertyManager is displayed.
5. Click the **midpoint** of the top silhouette edge.
6. Sketch a **line** downward and to the right.
7. Sketch a horizontal **line** to the right vertical edge.

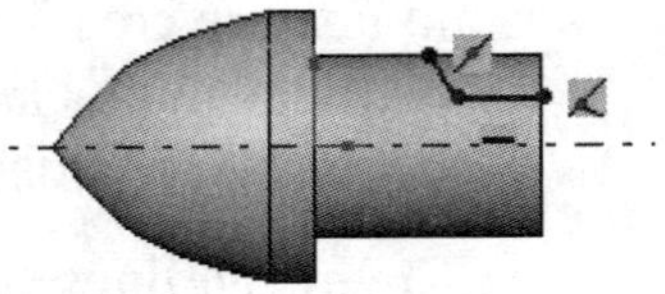

Deselect the Line Sketch tool.

8. Right-click **Select**.
9. Add a Coincident relation between the **end point of the line** and the **right vertical edge**.
10. Click **OK** from the Properties PropertyManager.

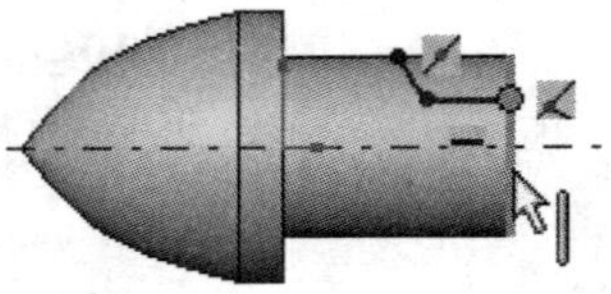

Deactivate the Temporary Axes.

11. Click **View**, ➤ uncheck **Temporary Axes** from the Menu bar.
12. Click the **Centerline** Sketch tool.
13. Sketch a **horizontal** centerline through the origin.

Insert dimensions.

14. Click the **Smart Dimension** Sketch tool.
15. **Dimension** the model as illustrated.
16. Click **OK** from the Dimension PropertyManager.
17. Click the **centerline** in the Graphics window.

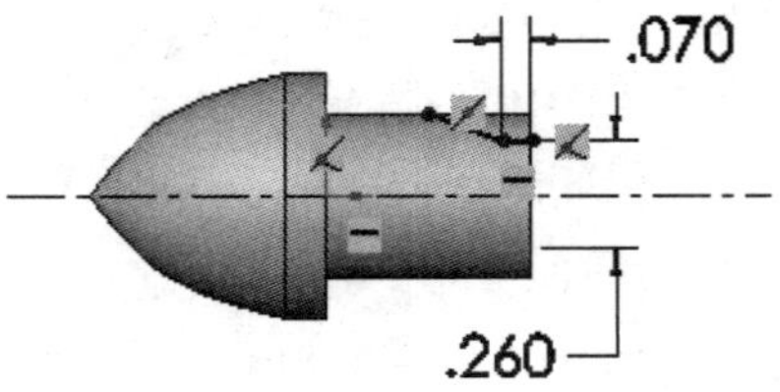

18. Click the **Revolved Cut** Features tool. The Cut-Revolve PropertyManager is displayed.
19. Click **No** to the Warning message in the Graphics window. The Cut-Revolve PropertyManager is displayed.
20. Click the **Thin Feature** check box.
21. Enter **.150**in for Direction 1 Thickness. Click **Reverse Direction** from the Thin Feature box.
22. Click **Reverse Direction** from the Revolve Parameters box.
23. Click **OK** from the Cut-Revolve PropertyManager. View the results. Cut-Revolve-Thin1 is displayed in the Graphics window.
24. **Close** the model.

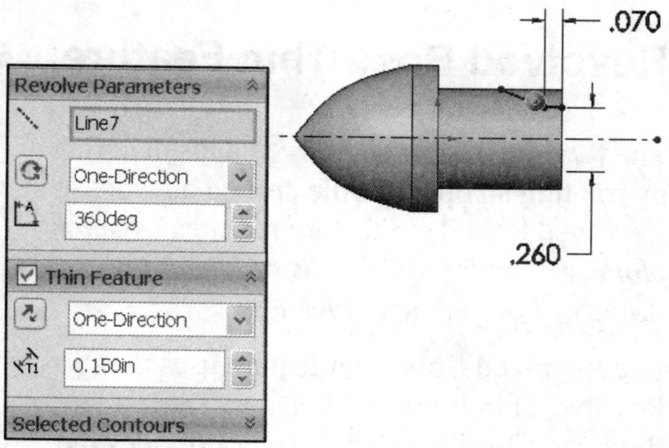


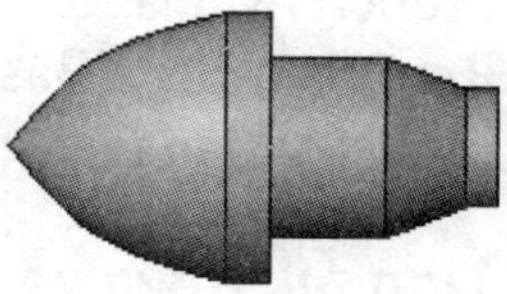

### *Tutorial: Revolved Cut 7-2*

Insert a Revolved Cut and Mirror feature.

1. Open **Revolved Cut 7-2** from the SolidWorks 2010 folder.
2. Click **Sketch2** from the FeatureManager.
3. Click the **Revolved Cut** Features tool. The Cut-Revolve PropertyManager is displayed. Accept the defaults.
4. Click **OK** from the Cut-Revolve PropertyManager. The Cut-Revolve1 feature is displayed in the FeatureManager.
5. Click **Right Plane** from the FeatureManager. Click the **Mirror** Features tool. The Mirror PropertyManager is displayed.
6. Click **Cut-Revolve1** from the flyout FeatureManager. Cut-Revolve1 is displayed in the Features to Mirror box.
7. Click **OK** from the Mirror PropertyManager. The Mirror1 feature is displayed.

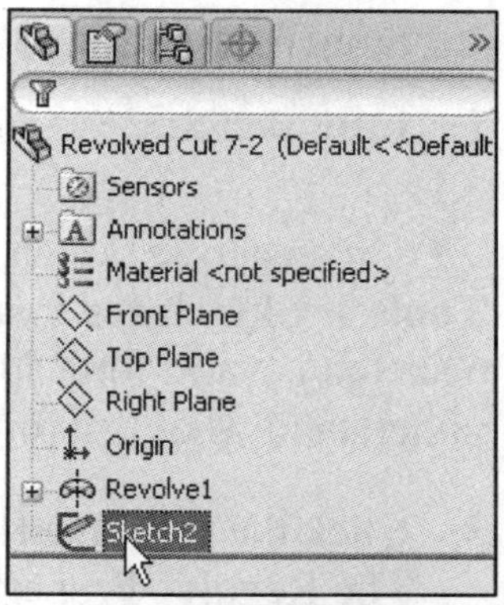


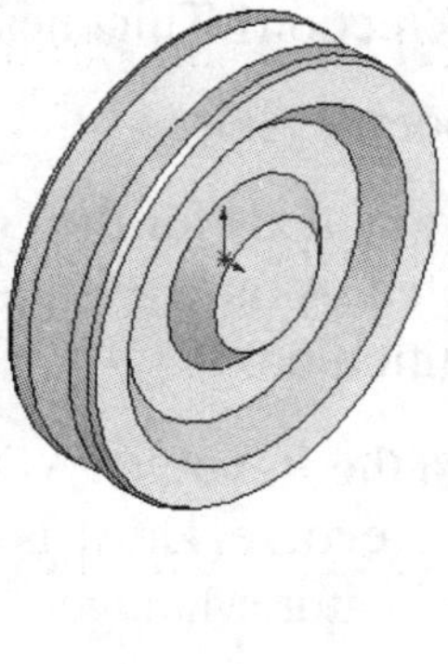

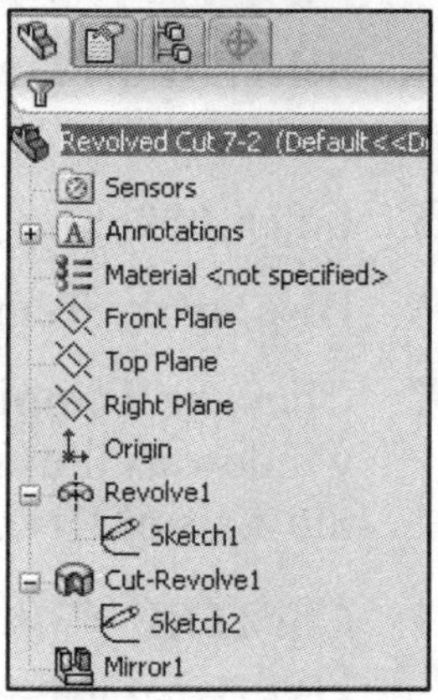

8. **Close** the model.

## Revolved Boss Thin Feature

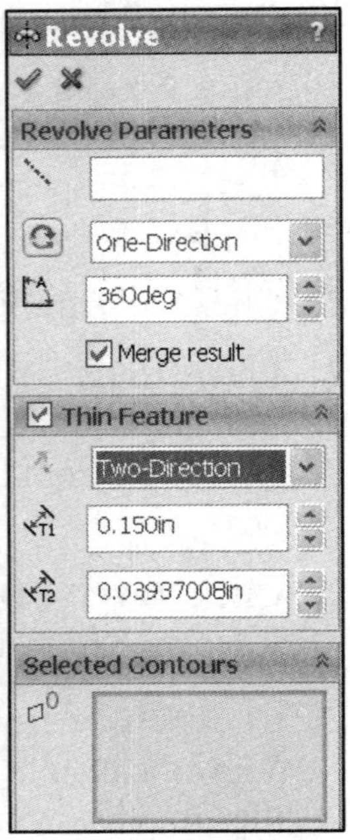


The Revolved Boss feature adds material by rotating an open profile around an axis. A Revolved Boss Thin feature requires a *Sketch plane*, a *Sketch profile*, *Axis of Revolution*, *Angle of Rotation* and *thickness*.

The Revolved Boss Thin feature uses the Revolve-Thin PropertyManager. The Revolve-Thin PropertyManager provides the same selections as the Revolve PropertyManager. View the section on Revolved Boss/Base for detail PropertyManager information.

### *Tutorial: Revolve Boss Thin 7-1*

Insert a Revolve Boss Thin feature.

1. Open **Revolve Boss Thin 7-1** from the SolidWorks 2010 folder.
2. **Edit** Sketch5.

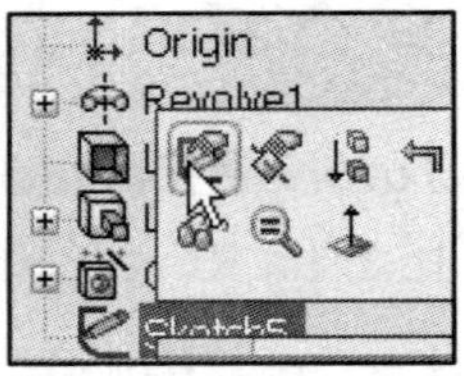


In an active sketch, click **Tools ➢ Sketch Tools ➢ Sketch for Feature Usage** to determine if a sketch is valid for a specific feature and to understand what is wrong with a sketch.

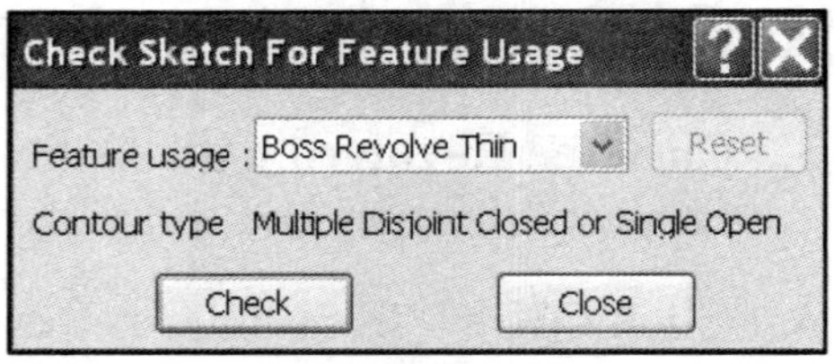


3. Click the **Revolved Boss/Base** Features tool. The Revolve PropertyManager is displayed.
4. Select **Mid-Plane** from the Thin Feature Type box.
5. Enter **.050**in for Direction1 Thickness.
6. **Display** the Temporary Axis.
7. Click the **Temporary Axis** for the Graphics window as illustrated. Axis<1> is displayed in the Axis of Revolution box.

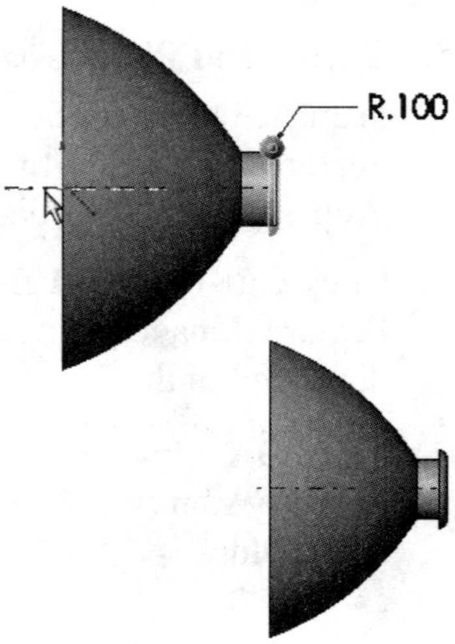


8. Click **OK** from the Revolve PropertyManager. Revolve-Thin1 is created and is displayed in the FeatureManager.
9. **Close** the model.

A Revolved sketch that remains open results in a Thin-Revolve feature 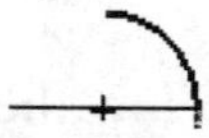. A Revolved sketch that is automatically closed, results in a line drawn from the start point to the end point of the sketch. The sketch is closed and results in a non-thin Revolve feature. 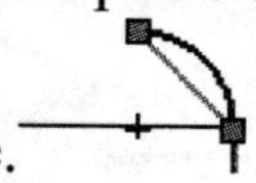.

## Revolved Surface Feature

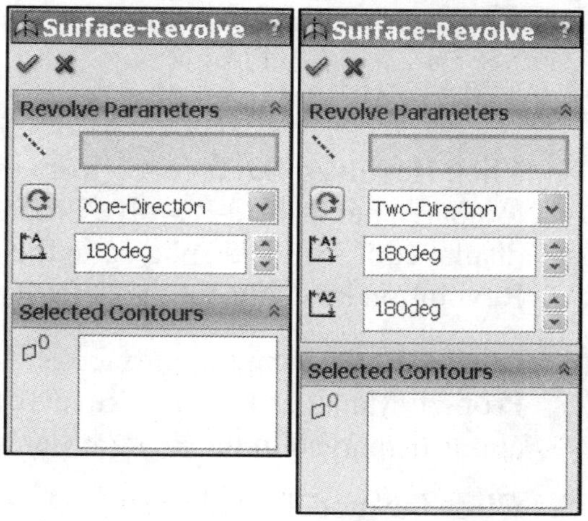


The Revolved Surface feature adds material by rotating a profile about an axis. The Revolved Surface feature uses the Surface-Revolve PropertyManager.

The Surface-Revolve PropertyManager provides the following selections:

- ***Revolve Parameters***. The Revolve Parameters box provides the following options:
  - **Axis of Revolution**. Displays the selected axis around which the feature revolves. The Axis of Revolution can be a line, centerline, or even an edge. Your selection is depended on the type of revolve feature you create.
  - **Revolve Type**. Defines the revolve direction type from your Sketch plane. There are three selections:
    - **One-Direction**. Creates the revolve feature in one direction from your Sketch plane.
    - **Mid-Plane**. Creates the revolve feature in a clockwise and counter-clockwise direction from your Sketch plane. The Mid-Plane is in the middle of the revolve angle.
    - **Two-Direction**. Creates the revolve feature in a clockwise and counter-clockwise direction from your Sketch plane. Set the Direction 1 Angle and the Direction 2 Angle. The total of the two angles can't exceed 360 degrees.
      - **Reverse Direction**. Reverses the revolve feature direction if required.
      - **Angle**. Defines the angle value covered by the revolve type feature. The default angle is 360 degrees.
- ***Selected Contours***. The Selected Contours box provides the following option:
  - **Select Contours**. Displays the selected contours. Select the contours from the Graphics window.

View the illustrated Surfaces toolbar.

***Tutorial: Revolved Surface 7-1***

Create a Revolved Surface feature.

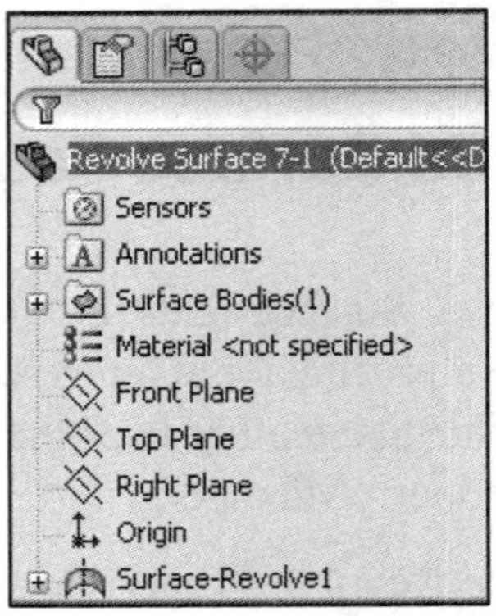


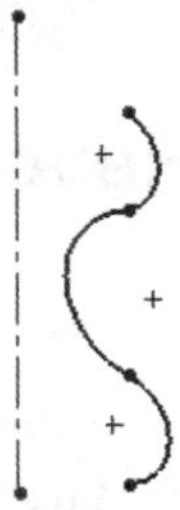

1. Open **Revolve Surface 7-1** from the SolidWorks 2010 folder.
2. **Edit** Sketch1.
3. Click **Revolved Surface** from the Surfaces toolbar. The Surface-Revolve PropertyManager is displayed. Line5 is displayed in the Axis of Revolution box. Accept the defaults.
4. Click **OK** from the Surface-Revolve PropertyManager. Surface-Revolve1 is created and is displayed in the FeatureManager.
5. **Close** the model.

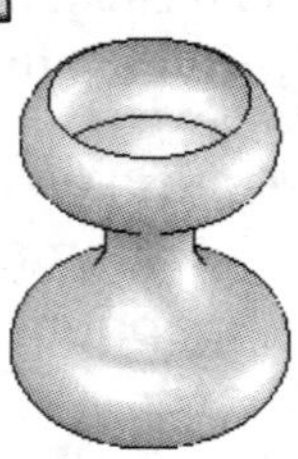

***Tutorial: Revolved Surface 7-2***

Create a Revolved Surface feature using the Selected Contour option.

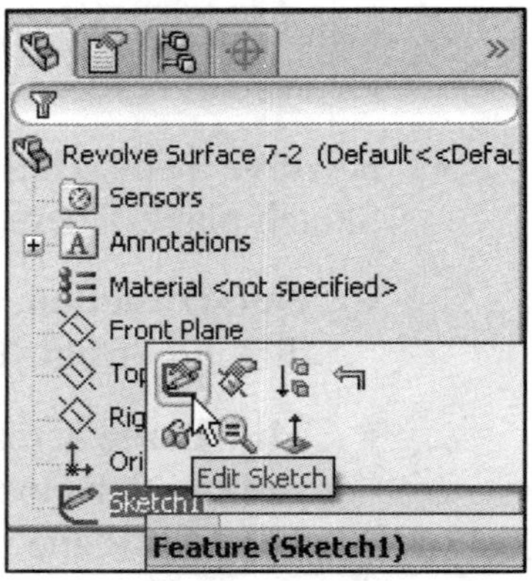


1. Open **Revolve Surface 7-2** from the SolidWorks 2010 folder.
2. Right-click **Sketch1**.
3. Click **Edit Sketch** from the Context toolbar.
4. Click **Insert ➢ Surface ➢ Revolve**. The Surface-Revolve PropertyManager is displayed.
5. **Expand** the Selected Contours box.
6. Click the **C-shape** contour in the Graphics window as illustrated. Sketch1-Region<1> is displayed in the Selected Contours box.
7. Click the **Reverse Direction** button. The arrow points upwards as illustrated.
8. Enter **360**deg for Angle.

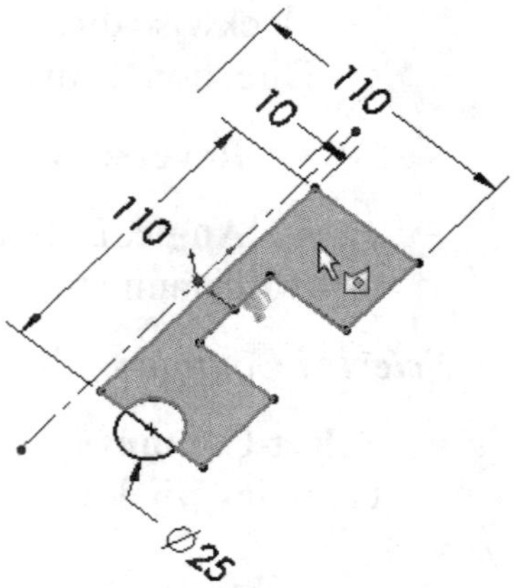

9. Click **inside** the Axis of Revolution box.
10. Select the **centerline** from the Graphics window. Line10 is displayed in the Axis of Revolution box.
11. Click **OK** from the Surface-Revolve PropertyManager. Surface-Revolve1 is created and is displayed in the FeatureManager.
12. **Close** the model.

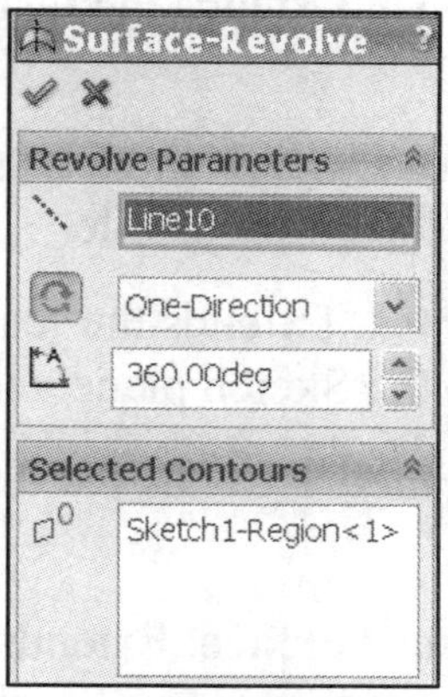


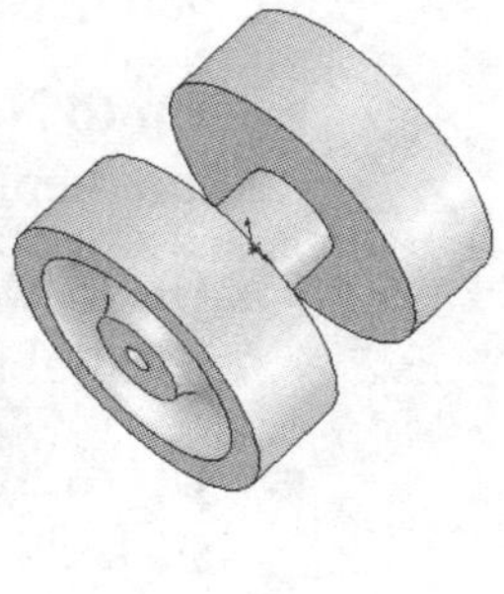

## Simple Hole Feature

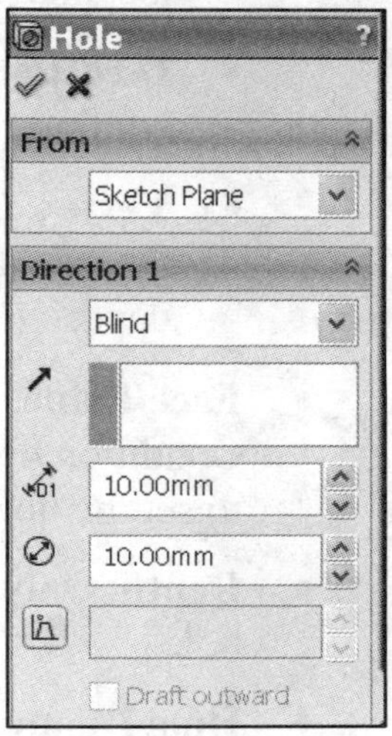


The Simple Hole feature provides the ability to create a hole in your model. In general, it is best to create holes at the end of your design process. This helps you to avoid inadvertently adding material inside an existing hole. The Simple Hole feature uses the Hole PropertyManager. The Hole PropertyManager provides the following selections:

- ***From***. The From box provides the following options:
  - **Start Condition**. Sets the starting condition for the simple hole feature. The following selections are available:
    - **Sketch Plane**. Starts the hole from the same plane on which the sketch is located.
    - **Surface/Face/Plane**. Starts the hole from the selected entity displayed in the Start A Surface/Face box
    - **Vertex**. Starts the hole from the selected vertex displayed in the Select A Vertex box.
    - **Offset**. Starts the hole on a plane that is offset from the displayed Enter Offset Value box from the current Sketch plane.

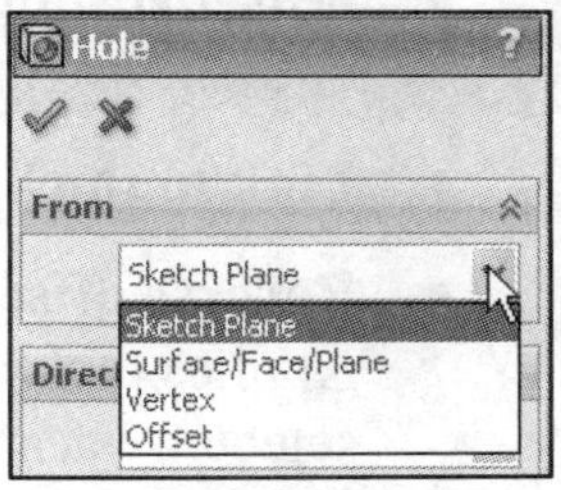


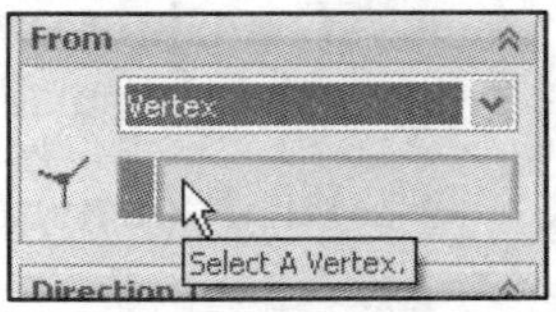


- ***Direction 1***: The Direction 1 box provides the following feature dependent options:
  - **End Condition**. Provides the ability to select one of the following feature dependent End Condition types:
    - **Blind**. Selected by default. Extends the feature from the Sketch plane from a specified distance.

- **Through All**. Extends the feature from the Sketch plane through all existing geometry.
- **Up to Next**. Extends the feature from the Sketch plane to the next surface that intercepts the entire profile.
- **Up to Vertex**. Extends the feature from the Sketch plane to a plane that is parallel to the Sketch plane and passes through the selected vertex.
- **Up to Surface**. Extends the feature from the Sketch plane to the selected surface.
- **Offset from Surface**. Extends the feature from the Sketch plane to a specified distance from the selected surface.
- **Direction of Extrusion**. Display the selected sketch entity from the Graphics window.
- **Vertex**. Only available for the Up To Vertex End Condition option. Displays the selected vertex or midpoint from the Graphics window to set the hole depth.

- **Face/Plane**. Only available for the Up To Surface, and Offset From Surface End Condition options. Displays the selected face or plane from the Graphics window to set the hole depth.
- **Depth**. Only available for the Blind End Condition option. Sets the depth of the hole.
- **Hole Diameter**. Sets the Hole diameter value.
- **Offset Distance**. Only available for the Offset from Surface End Condition option. Sets the Offset distance.
- **Link to thickness**. Applies the linked thickness.
- **Reverse offset**. Only available for the Offset From Surface End Condition option. Applies the specified Offset Distance value in the opposite direction from the selected Face/Plane.
- **Translate surface**. Applies the specified Offset Distance value relative to the selected surface or plane.
- **Draft outward**. Adds draft outwards to the hole. Set the Draft Angle value.

***Tutorial: Simple Hole 7-1***

Create a Simple Hole feature in a part.

1. Open **Simple Hole 7-1** from the SolidWorks 2010 folder.

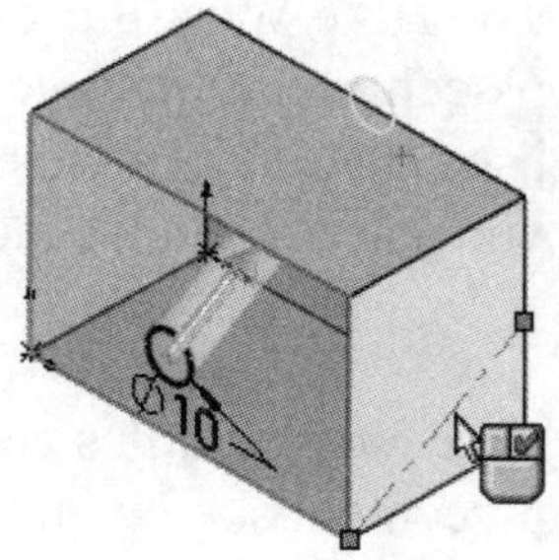


2. Click the **Front face** of Extrude1.
3. Click **Insert ➢ Features ➢ Hole ➢ Simple**. The Hole PropertyManager is displayed.
4. Click **Through All** for End Condition in Direction 1.
5. Click inside the **Direction of Extrusion** box.
6. Select the illustrated **sketched line** on the Right face of Extrude1 for the vector direction. Line1@Sketch2 is displayed.
7. Enter **10**mm for Hole Diameter.
8. Click **OK** from the Hole PropertyManager. Hole1 is created and is displayed in the FeatureManager and in the Graphics window.
9. **Edit** Sketch3.
10. Click the **Smart Dimension** Sketch tool.
11. Insert a **40mm** horizontal dimension and a **15mm** vertical dimension as illustrated from the center point of the circle.
12. **Rebuild** the model. View the results.
13. **Close** the model.

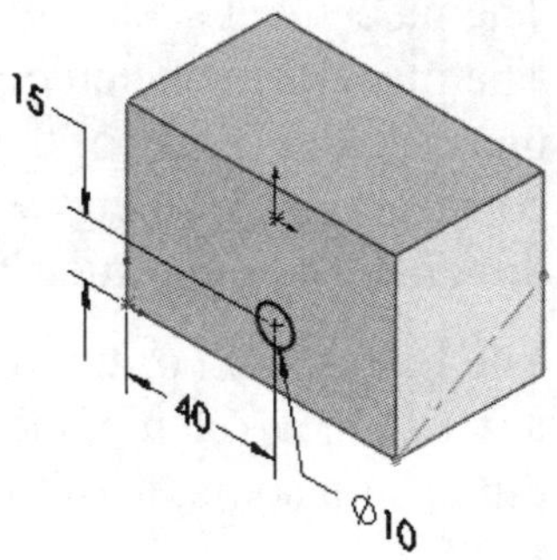


## Hole Wizard Feature

The Hole Wizard feature provides the ability to create cuts in the form of holes. This feature provides the ability to create holes on a plane as well as holes on planar and non-planar faces. Holes on a plane allow you to create holes at an angle to your feature. When you create a hole using the Hole Wizard, the type and size of the hole is displayed in the FeatureManager design tree.

The Hole Wizard information from the model propagates to the drawing when the Hole Callout button is selected.

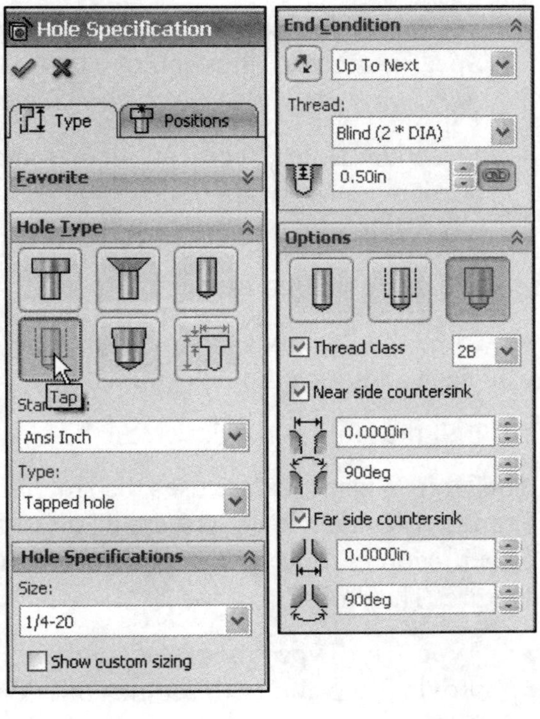

The Hole Wizard uses either a 2D or 3D sketch for the placement of the holes in the model. The 3D sketch type is used by default, with the 2D sketch type being used when you select a planar face prior to selecting the Hole Wizard  feature.

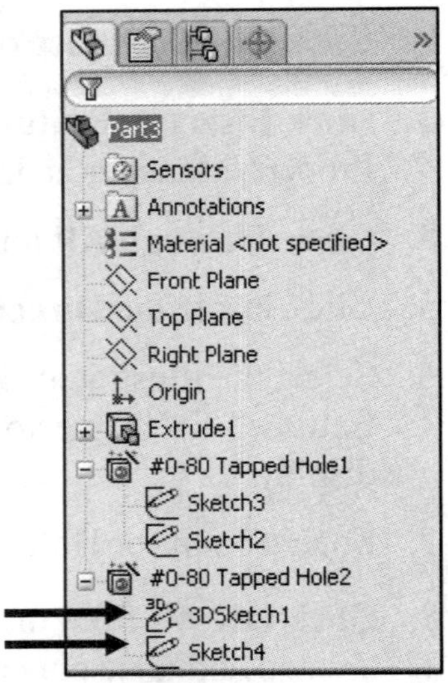


Hole Wizard holes consist of two sketches: a center placement sketch and a revolved cut profile as illustrated in the first Hole Wizard feature in the FeatureManager.

The placement sketch is listed first under the Hole feature. The placement sketch contains one or more sketch points marking the center of the hole. It may also contain construction geometry with geometry relations and dimensions to parametrically locate the hole centers.

The hole sketch or the revolved cut profile sketch is not in an identifiable sketch plane. You can modify the hole sketch dimensions outside of the hole wizard.

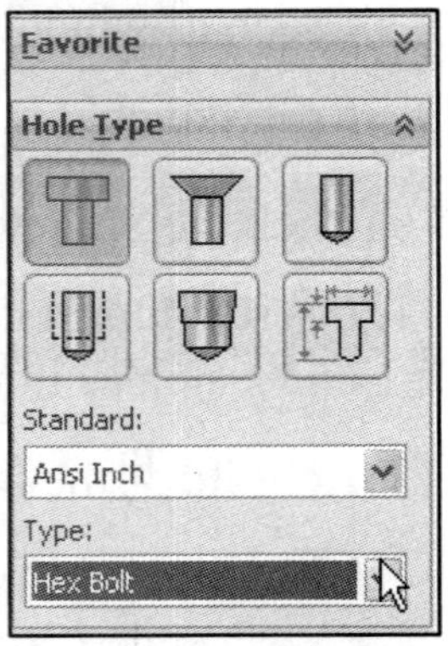


The Hole Wizard enables you to place holes, for many types of screws with normal, loose or close fit types. Below is a recommended process of applying the Hole Wizard tool:

- Select the face to position the hole. Note: This is not required.
- Select the fastener Type: *Counterbore*, *Countersunk*, *Drilled Hole*, *Tapped Hole*, *Pipe Tab or Legacy*.
- Set the Drafting standard and Unit System (Hole Specifications). This should match your document standard: *ANSI Inch*, *ANSI Metric*, *ISO*, *JIS*, etc.

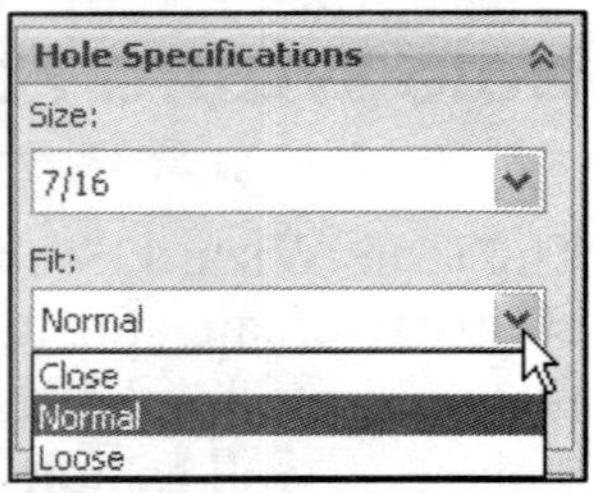


- Select the Hole Specification: *Size* and *Fit* or any other needed requirements.
- Select the End Condition: *Blind*, *Through All*, *Up To Next*, *etc.* and any other requirements.
- Click the Positions tab to either apply dimensions and or to place additional hole positions.
- Exit the Hole Wizard.

The Hole Wizard feature uses the Hole Specification PropertyManager. Two tabs are displayed in the Hole Specification PropertyManager when you active the Hole Wizard feature. They are:

- **Type**. The Type tab is the default tab. The Type option provides the ability to set the Hole Type parameters.

- **Positions**. The Positions tab options provides the ability to locate the hole on a planar or non-planar face and to apply dimensions. You can switch between these two tabs.
- ***Hole Type***. The Hole Type box provides ability to select from six set hole types. The different hole types determines the hole capabilities, available selections, and Graphic window previews. Select a hole type. Then determine the appropriate fastener from the Hole Specification box. The fastener dynamically updates the appropriate menu parameters. The selections are: **Counterbore**, **Countersink**, **Hole**, **Tap Hole**, **Pipe Tap** and **Legacy**.

Legacy holes are holes which were created prior to the SolidWorks 2000 release.

- **Standard**. The Standard drop-down menu provides twelve selections to choose from. Example: **Ansi Metric**, **Ansi Inch**, **ISO, JIS**, etc.
- **Type**. The Type drop-down menu provides the ability to select numerous fastener types. Example: **Hex Screw**, **Pan Slot Head**, etc.
- ***Hole Specifications***. The Hole Specification selections vary depending on the selected Hole Type. The available options are:

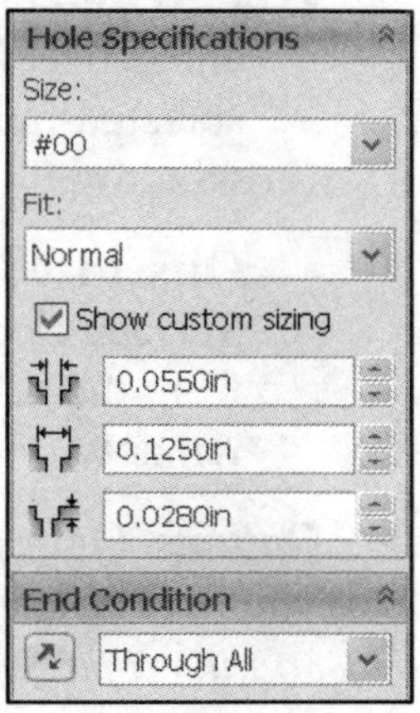


  - **Size**. The Size drop-down menu provides the ability to select the size for the selected fastener. The Size options are depended on Hole type.
  - **Fit**. Only available for the Counterbore and Countersink Hole type. The Fit drop down-menu provides the following options: **Close**, **Normal** and **Loose**.
  - **Show custom sizing**. Not selected by default. The Custom Sizing box selection varies depending on your selected hole type. Use the PropertyManager images and descriptive text to set options such as **diameter**, **depth** and **angle at bottom**.
- ***End Condition***. The End Condition box provides the following feature dependent options:
  - **End Condition**. The drop-down box provides six selections:
  - **Blind**. Extends the feature from your Sketch plane for a specified distance.
  - **Through All**. Extends the feature from your Sketch plane through all existing geometry.

- **Up To Next**. Extends the feature from your Sketch plane to the next surface that intercepts the entire profile. The intercepting surface must be on the same part.
- **Up To Vertex**. Extends the feature from your Sketch plane to a plane which is parallel to your Sketch plane and passes through a specified vertex.
- **Up To Surface**. Extends the feature from your Sketch plane to the selected surface.
- **Offset From Surface**. Extends the feature from your Sketch plane to a specified distance from the selected surface. Select a face to specify the surface. Specify an offset distance.
- **Reverse Direction**. Reverses the End Condition direction if required.
- **Blind Hole Depth**. Only available for the Blind End Condition. Sets the hole depth. For tap holes, set the thread depth and type. For pipe tap holes, set the thread depth.
- **Vertex**. On available for the Up to Vertex Condition. Select a vertex.

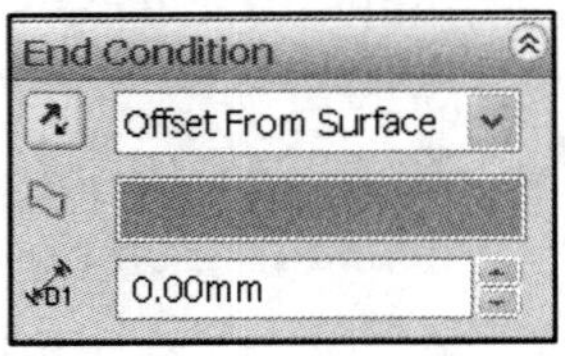


- **Face/Surface/Plane**. Only available for the Up to Surface and Offset From Surface End Condition. Displays the selected face, surface, or plane from the Graphics window.
- **Offset Distance**. Only available for the Offset From Surface End Condition. Displays the offset distance from the selected face, surface, or plane in the Graphics window.

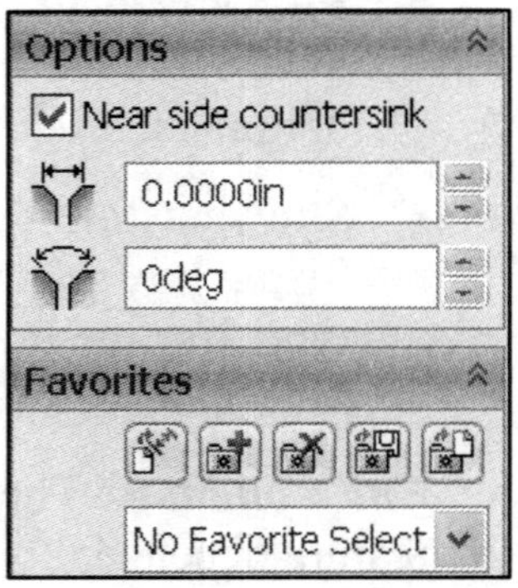


- ***Options***. Options vary depending on the selected Hole type. The option selections are: *Head clearance*, *Near side countersink*, *Under head countersink*, *Far side countersink*, *Cosmetic thread and Thread class*. If you select any of the choices from the Options section, the revolved sketch profile is altered to accommodate the modification.
- ***Favorites***. The Favorites box provides the ability to manage a list of favorite Hole Wizard holes which you can reuse in your models. The available selections are:
  - **Apply Defaults/No Favorites**. Resets to No Favorite selected and the system default settings.
  - **Add or Update Favorite**. Adds the selected Hole Wizard hole to your Favorites list.
  - **Delete Favorite**. Deletes the selected favorite for your Favorites list.

- **Save Favorite**. Saves the selected favorite to your Favorites list.
- **Load Favorite**. Loads the selected favorite.
- ***Feature Scope***. The Feature Scope applies Hole Wizard holes to one or more multi-body parts. Select which bodies should include the holes.

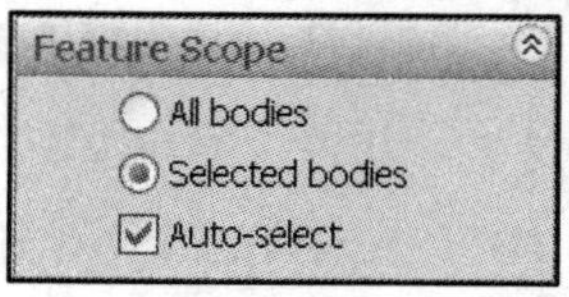


- **All bodies**. Applies the feature to all bodies each time the feature is regenerated. If you add a new body or bodies to your model that is intersected by a feature, the new body will regenerate to include the feature.
- **Selected bodies**. Displays the selected bodies. If you added new bodies to the model that are intersected by the feature, use the Edit Feature function to edit the extrude feature. Displays the selected bodies.

If you do not add your new bodies to the existing list of selected bodies, the new bodies will remain intact.

- **Auto-select**. Only available if you select the Selected bodies option. When you first create a model with multi-body parts, the feature automatically processes all the relevant intersecting parts.

The Auto-select option is faster than the All bodies option because the system only processes the bodies on the initial list and does not regenerate the entire model.

- **Solid Bodies to Affect**. Only available if you clear the Auto-select option. Displays the selected solid bodies to affect from the Graphics window.
- **Positions tab**. Locates the Hole Wizard hole on either a planar or non-planar face. Use the dimension and other sketch tools to position the center of the hole. To position Hole Wizard holes, click a face to place the center of the hole. Place multiple holes of the same type.

### *Tutorial: Hole Wizard 7-1*

Use the Hole Wizard tool to create a custom Counterbore Hole using the 2D sketch method.

1. Open **Hole Wizard 7-1** from the SolidWorks 2010 folder.
2. Click the small **inside circular** back face of the LensShell.

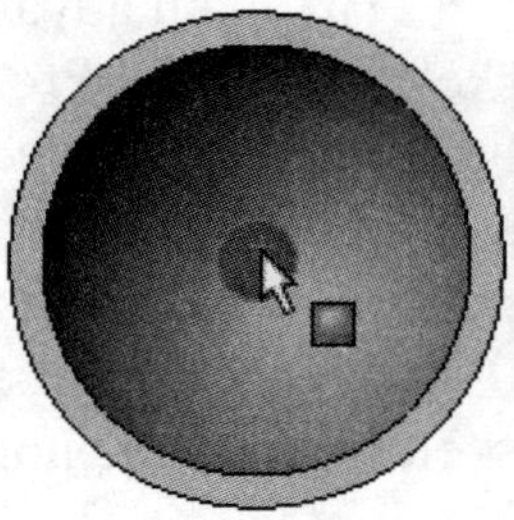

3. Click the **Hole Wizard** Features tool. The Hole Specification PropertyManager is displayed.
4. Select **Counterbore** for Hole Type.
5. Select **Ansi Inch** for Standard.

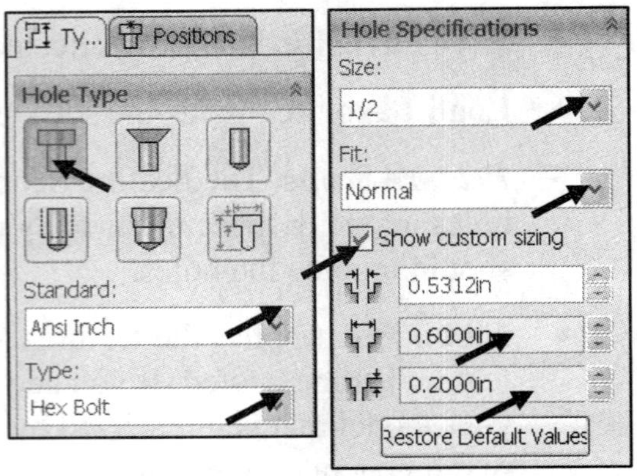


6. Select **Hex Bolt** for fastener Type.
7. Select **1/2** for Size.
8. Select **Normal** for Fit.
9. Select **Through All** for End Condition.
10. Check the **show custom sizing** box.
11. Enter **.600**in in the Counter bore Diameter box.
12. Enter .**200**in in the Counter bore Depth box.
13. Click the **Positions tab**. The Hole Position PropertyManager is displayed.
14. Deselect the point tool. Right-click **Select**.
15. Add a Coincident relation between the **center point** of the Counterbore hole and the **origin**.

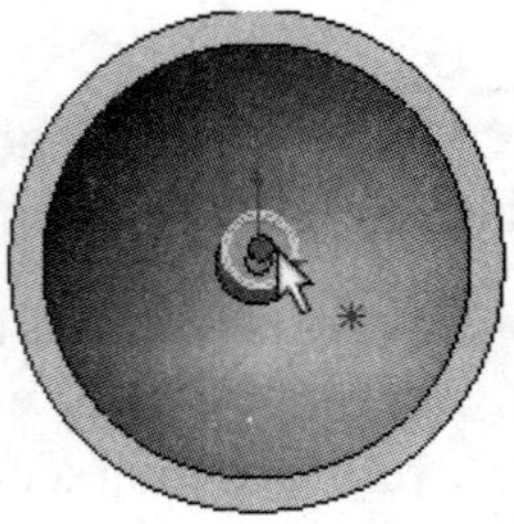

16. Click **OK** ✔ from the Properties PropertyManager.
17. Click the **Type** Tab.

Add a new hole type to your Favorites list.

18. Select the **Add or Update Favorite** button from the Favorites box.
19. Enter **CBORE for bulb.**
20. Click **OK.**
21. Click **OK** ✔ from the Hole Specification PropertyManager.
22. **Expand** CBORE for 1/2 Hex Head Bolt1 from the FeatureManager. Sketch3 and Sketch4 create the CBORE feature. View the results.
23. **Close** the model.

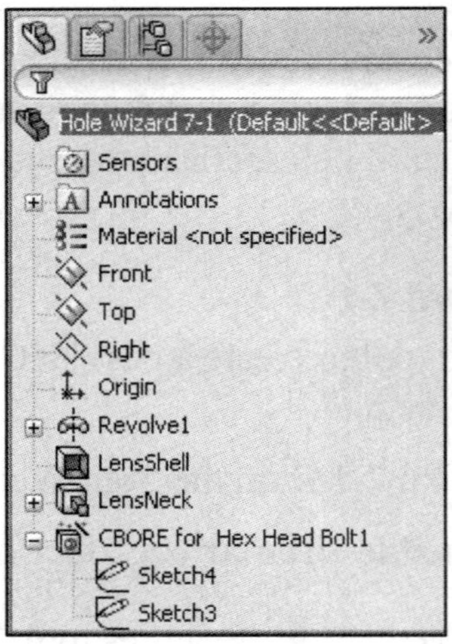


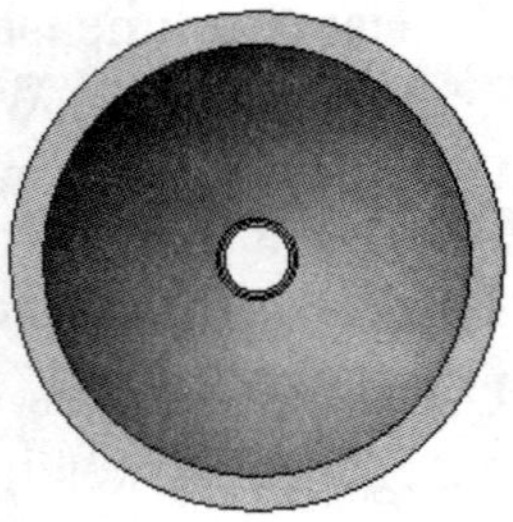

The main advantage of the 2D sketch method, (Pre-select a flat face) is the simplicity and completeness of the available tool. Most users know how to manage 2D sketches, sketch planes and dimensions. A limitation of the 2D sketch is that the holes that you create, are limited to a single planar face.

### *Tutorial: Hole Wizard 7-2*

Create a Countersunk hole located on a bolt circle using the 2D sketch method.

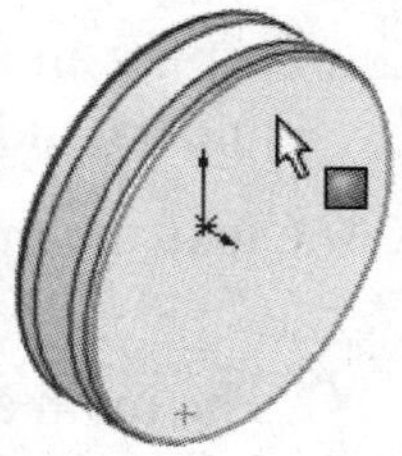

1. Open **Hole Wizard 7-2** from the SolidWorks 2010 folder.
2. Click a **position** on the upper right face of Revolve1 as illustrated.
3. Click the **Hole Wizard** Features tool. The Hole Specification PropertyManager is displayed.
4. Select the **Countersink** Hole Type.
5. Select **Ansi Metric** for Standard.
6. Select **Socket Countersunk Hex** for fastener Type.
7. Select **M8** for Size.
8. Select **Normal** for Fit.
9. Select **Through All** for End Condition.
10. Click the **Positions** Tab. The Hole Position PropertyManager is displayed.
11. Display a **Right view**. The Point sketch tool is activated.
12. Click the **Circle** Sketch tool.
13. Sketch a **circle** from the center point of the Revolve1 feature to the center point of the Countersink as illustrated.
14. Check the **For construction** box from the Circle PropertyManager.
15. Click the **Centerline** Sketch tool.
16. Sketch a **horizontal centerline** from the center point of the Revolve1 feature to the quadrant point of the construction circle as illustrated.
17. Click the **Smart Dimension** Sketch tool.
18. Click the **centerpoint** of the Countersink, the **origin** and the **right end point** of the centerline.
19. Click a **position** to position the angle dimension.
20. Enter **30**deg.

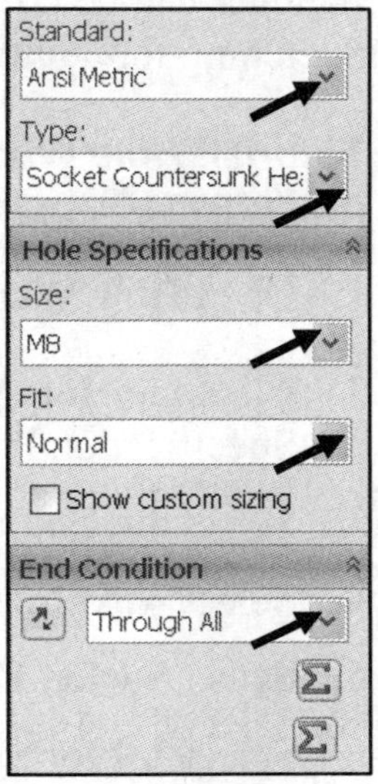


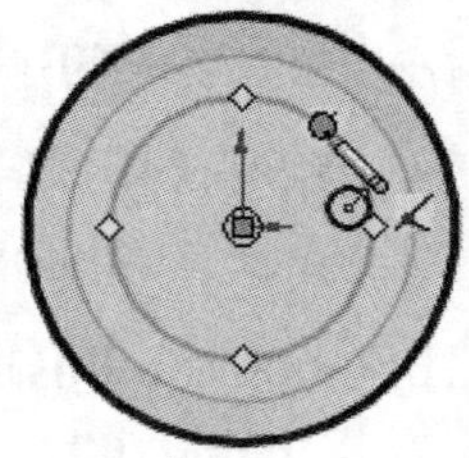

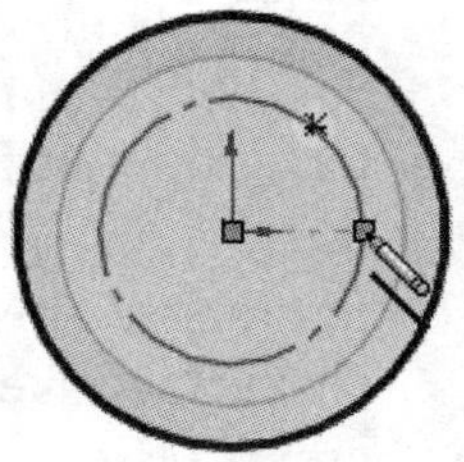

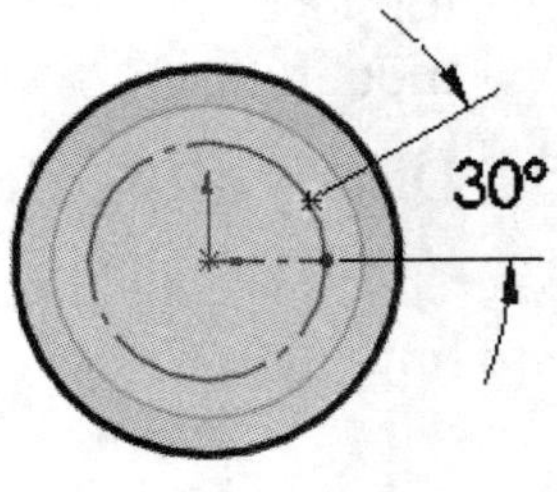

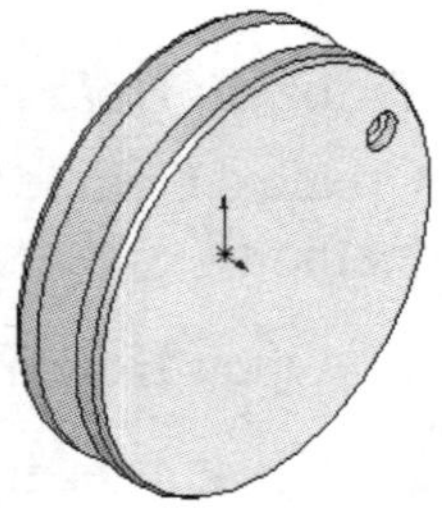

21. Click **OK** from the Hole Position Property Manager.
22. Display an **Isometric view**. View the results in the Graphics window and FeatureManager.
23. **Close** the model.

The main advantages of the 3D sketch placement method is that it can place a set of holes on any set of solid faces, regardless of whether they are at different levels, are non-parallel. A limitation, 3D sketches can be fairly cumbersome and difficult. See section on 3D Sketching for additional details.

### *Tutorial: Hole Wizard 7-3*

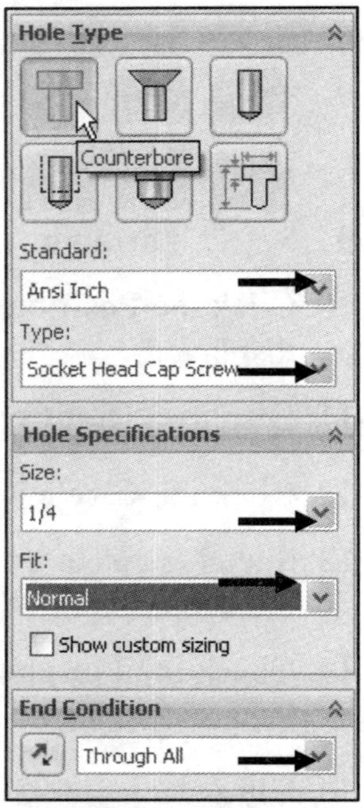


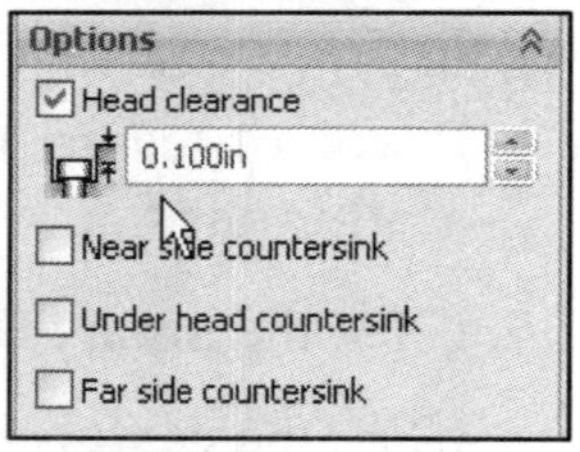


Create a Counterbore using the 3D sketch placement method.

1. Open **Hole Wizard 7-3** from the SolidWorks 2010 folder.
2. Click the **Hole Wizard** Features tool. The Hole Specification PropertyManager is displayed.
3. Select the **Counterbore** Hole Type.
4. Select **Ansi Inch** for Standard.
5. Select **Socket Head Cap Screw** for fastener Type.
6. Select **1/4** for Size.
7. Select **Normal** for Fit.
8. Select **Through All** for End Condition.
9. Enter **.100** for Head clearance in the Options box.
10. Click the **Positions** Tab. The Hole Position PropertyManager is displayed. SolidWorks displays a 3D interface with the Point tool active. Note: When the Point tool is active, wherever you click, you will create a point.
11. Click the **top face** of the model as illustrated. The selected face is displayed in orange. This indicates that an OnSurface sketch relations will be created between the sketch point and the top face. The hole is displayed in the model.
12. Display a **Top view**.

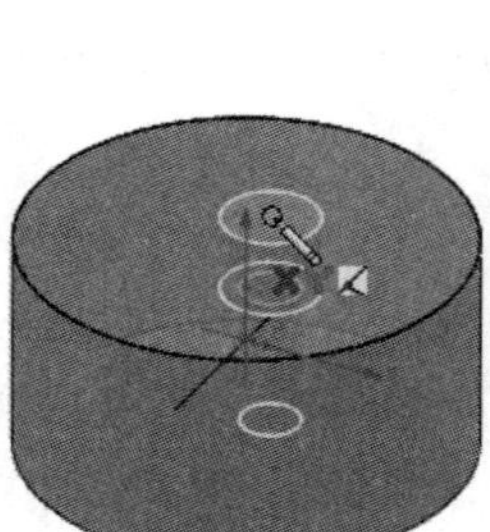

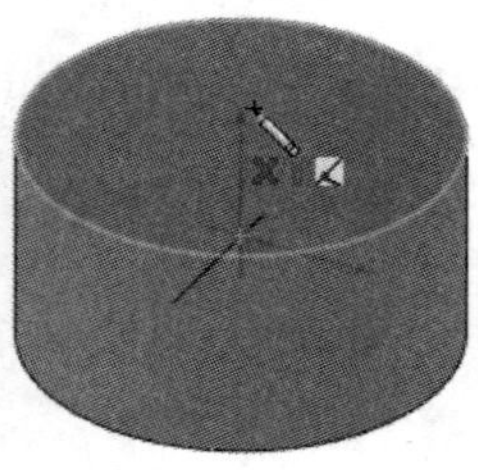

13. Add a Geometric Relation. Right-click **Select** to deselect the 3D Sketch tool.
14. Click the **centerpoint** of the hole.
15. Hold the **Ctrl** key down.
16. Click the **Origin**.
17. Release the **Ctrl** key.
18. Click **Along Y**.

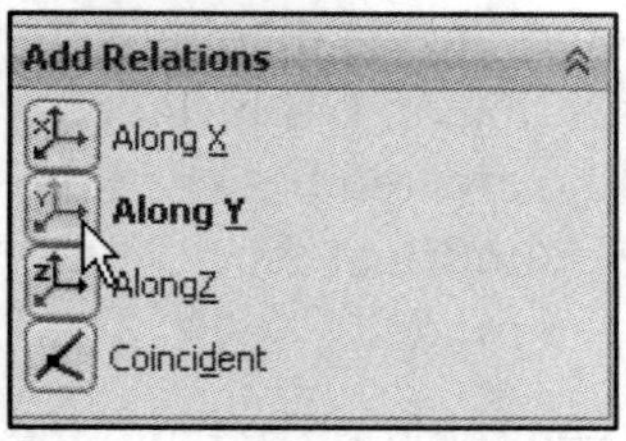


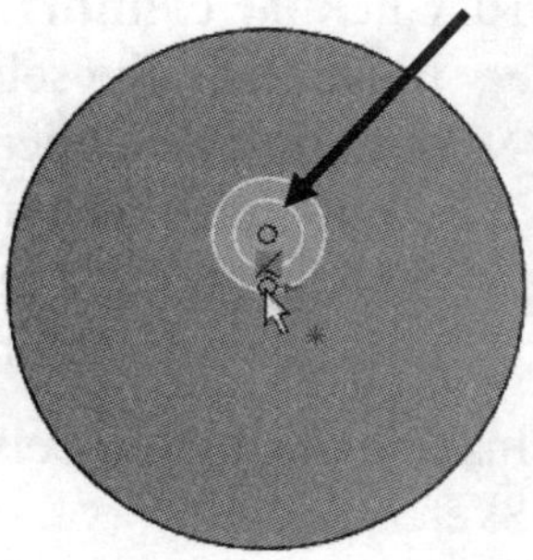

19. Click **OK** from the Properties PropertyManager.
20. Click **OK** from the Hole Position PropertyManager.
21. **Expand** the FeatureManager. View the created hole and 3D Sketch.
22. Display an **Isometric view**. View the results in the Graphics window and FeatureManager.
23. **Close** the model.

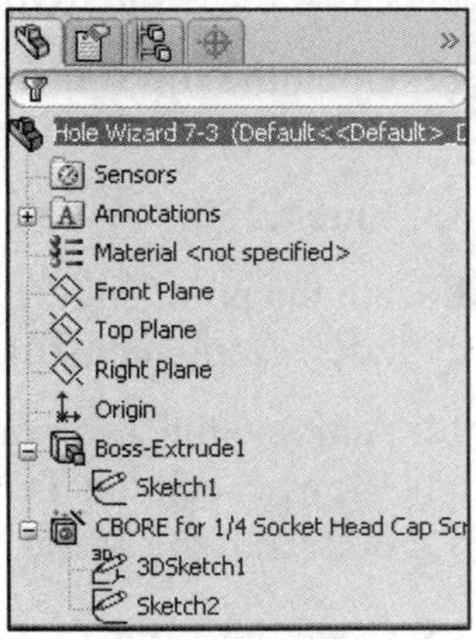


### *Tutorial: Hole Wizard 7-4*

Using the 3D sketch placement method, apply dimensions on a cylindrical face with the Hole Wizard feature.

1. Open **Hole Wizard 7-4** from the SolidWorks 2010 folder.
2. Click the **Hole Wizard** Features tool. The Hole Specification PropertyManager is displayed.
3. Select the **Counterbore** Hole Type.
4. Select **Ansi Inch** for Standard.
5. Select **Socket Head Cap Screw** for fastener Type.
6. Select **1/4** for Size. Select **Normal** for Fit.
7. Select **Through All** for End Condition.
8. Enter **.100** for Head clearance in the Options box.
9. Click the **Positions** Tab. The Hole Position PropertyManager is displayed. SolidWorks displays a 3D interface with the Point tool active.

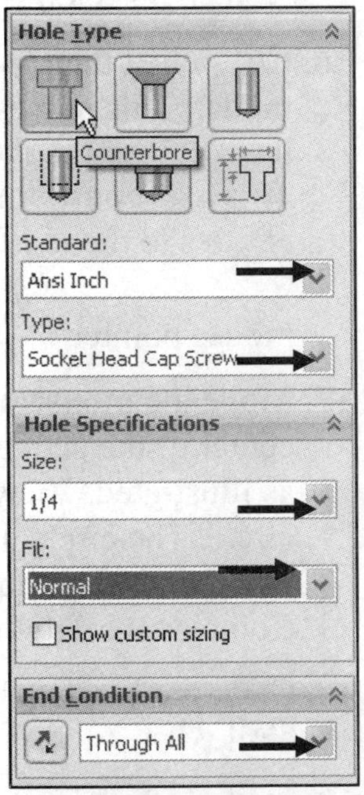


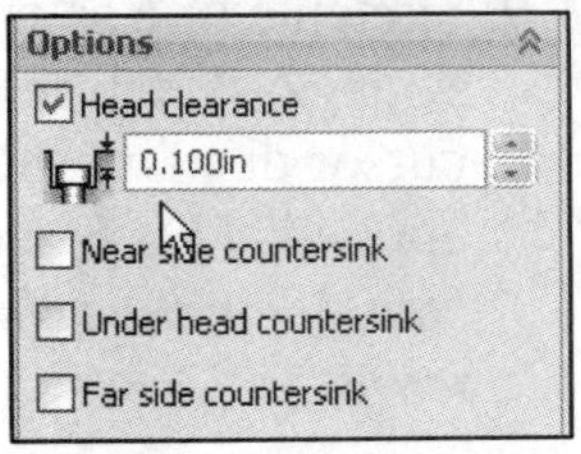


When the Point tool is active, wherever you click, you will create a point

10. Click the **cylindrical face** of the model as illustrated. The selected face is displayed in orange. This indicates that an OnSurface sketch relations will be created between the sketch point and the cylindrical face. The hole is displayed in the model.

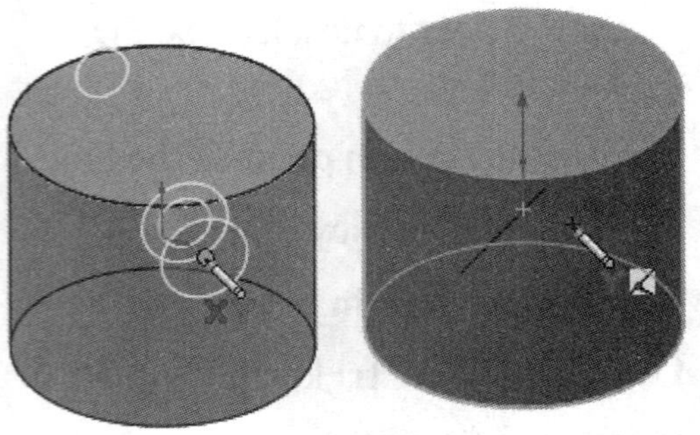

Insert a dimension between the top face and the Sketch point.

11. Click the **Smart Dimension** Sketch tool.
12. Click the **top flat face** of the model and the **sketch point**.
13. Enter **.25in**.

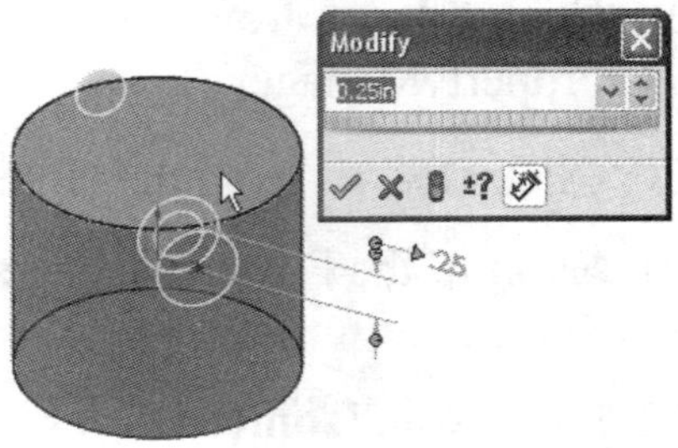


Locate the point angularly around the cylinder. Apply construction geometry.

14. Activate the Temporary Axes. Click **View**, check the **Temporary Axes** box from the Menu bar toolbar.
15. Click the **Line** Sketch tool. Note: 3D sketch is still activated.

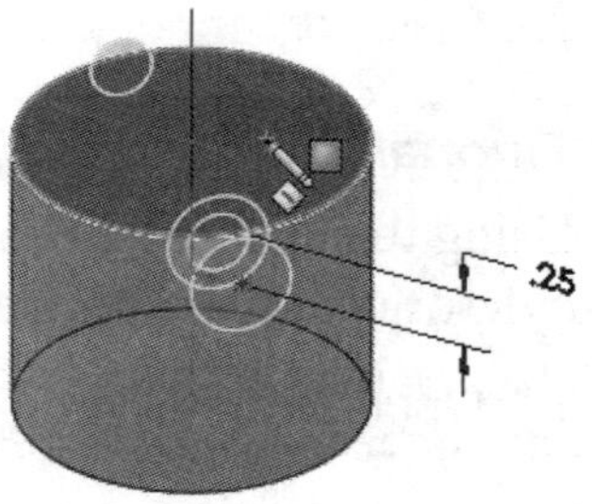


16. Ctrl - click the **top flat face** of the model. This moves the red space handle origin to the selected face. This also constrains any new sketch entities to the top flat face. Note the mouse pointer icon.

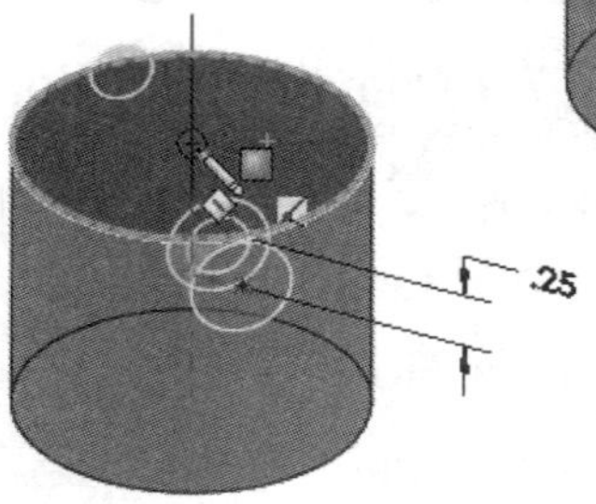


17. Move the **mouse pointer** near the center of the activated top flat face as illustrated. View the small black circle. The circle indicates that the end point of the line will pick up a Coincident relation.
18. Click the **centerpoint** of the circle.

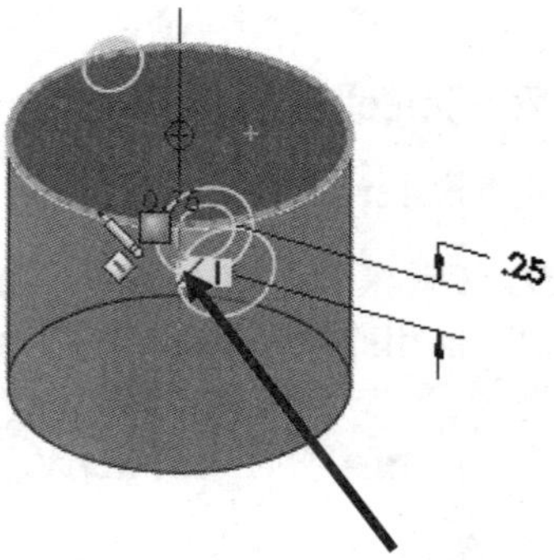


19. Sketch a **line** so it picks up the AlongZ sketch relation. The cursor displays the relation to be applied. ***This is a very important step! View the relation feedback icons.***

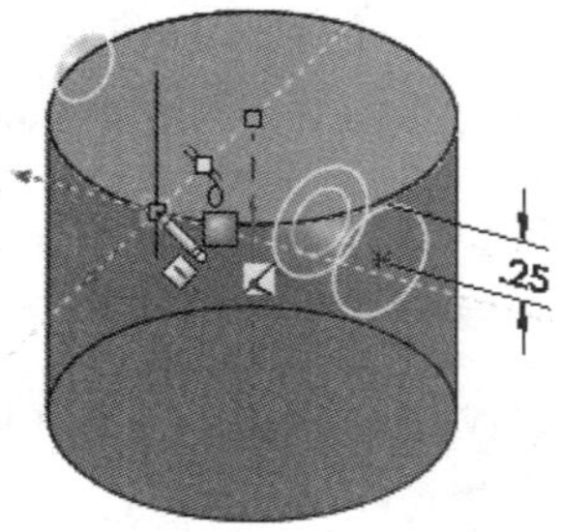

20. Create an **AlongY sketch relation** between the centerpoint of the hole on the cylindrical face and the endpoint of the sketched line as illustrated.

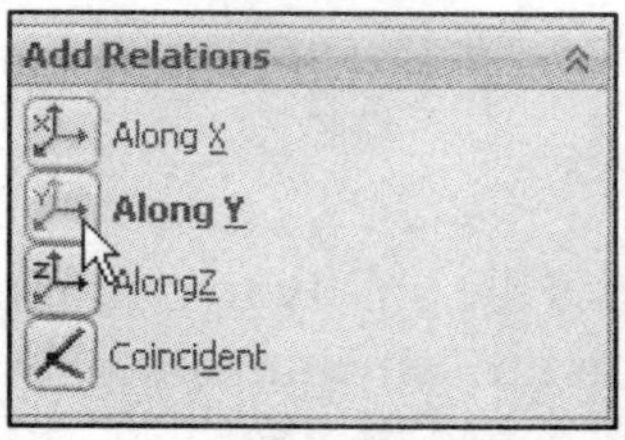


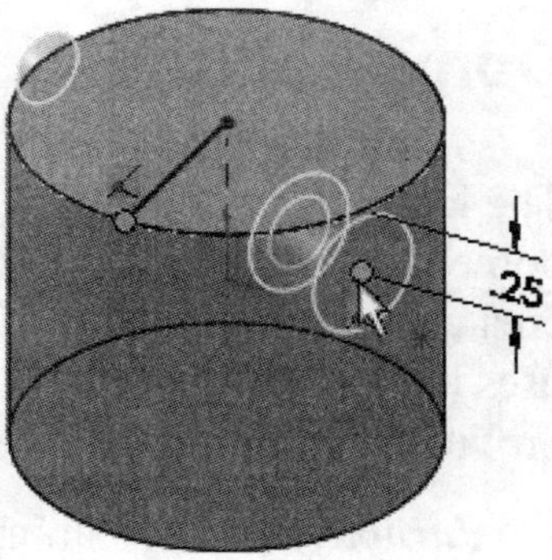


21. Click **OK** from the Properties PropertyManager.
22. Click **OK** from the Hole Position PropertyManager.

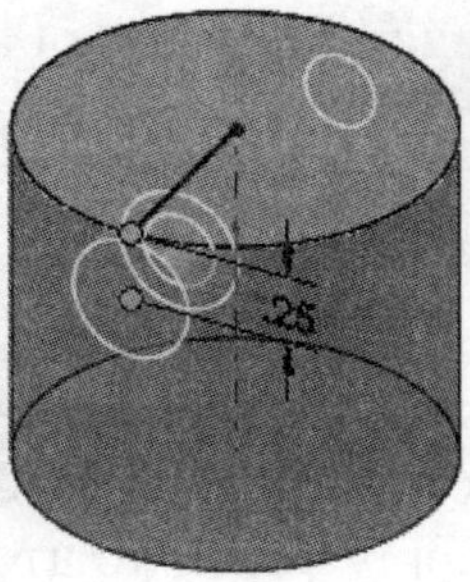


23. **Expand** the FeatureManager and view the results. The two sketches are fully defined.
24. **Close** the model.

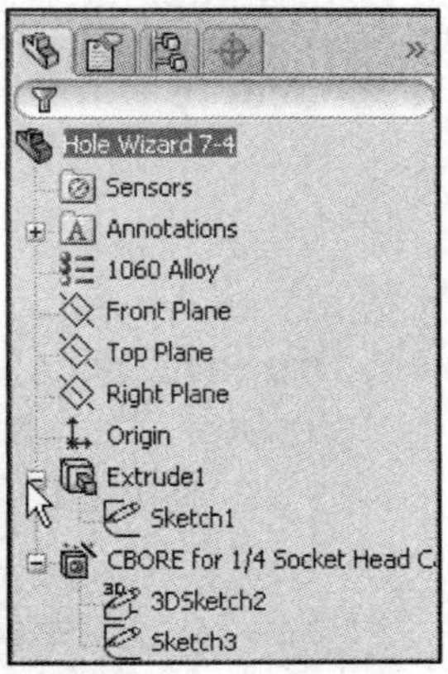


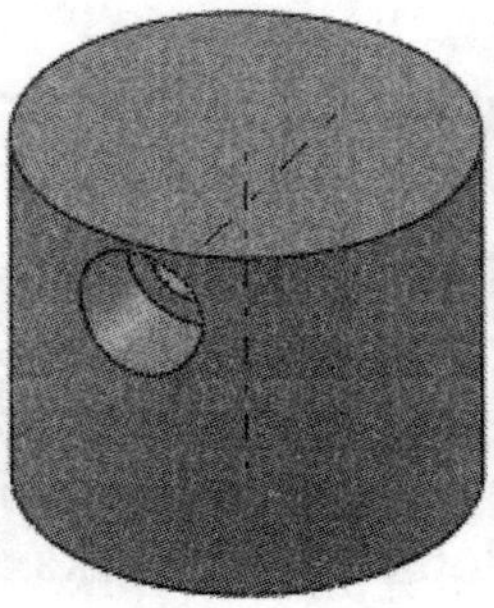

You can create a second sketched line and insert an angle dimension between the two lines. This process is used to control the position of the centerpoint of the hole on the cylindrical face as illustrated. Insert an AlongY sketch relation between the centerpoint of the hole on the cylindrical face and the end point of the second control line. Control the hole position with the angular dimension.

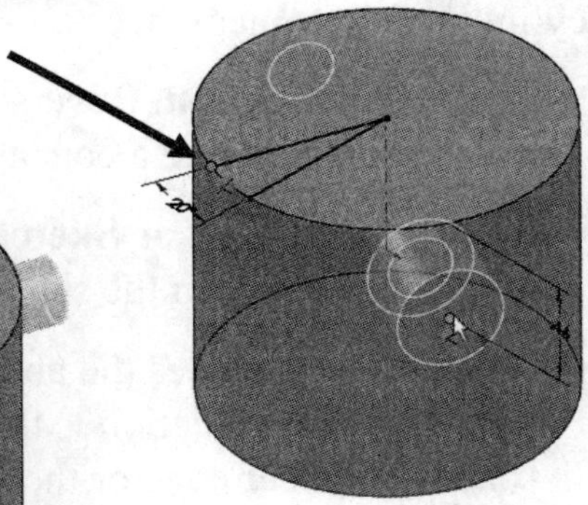

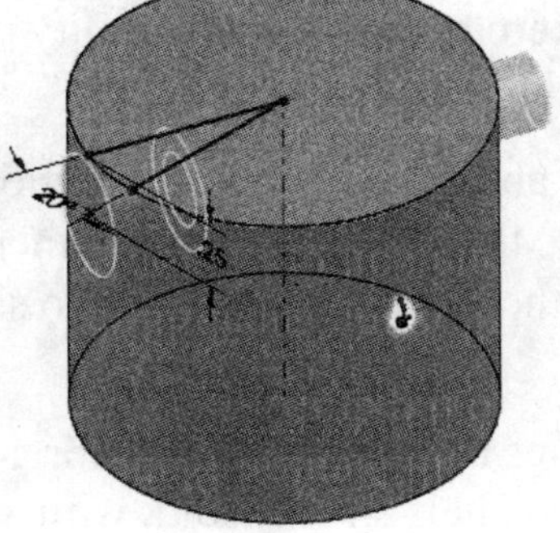


When creating a cosmetic thread, you can now define cosmetic threads using international standard sizes in 2010.

When creating a Hole Wizard hole, straight pipe tapped holes for all standards, not just DIN, are now provided.

In 2010, when creating a Hole Wizard hole, you no longer have to preselect a planar face to create a 2D sketch. For a 3D sketch, select a non-planar face or explicitly request a 3D sketch. At the time of SP0, this function still had a few issues.

## Dome Feature

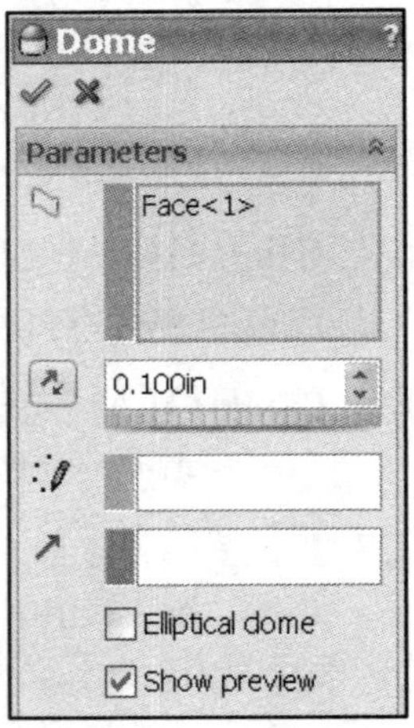


The Dome Feature provides the ability to create one or more dome features concurrently on the same model. A Dome feature creates spherical or elliptical shaped geometry. The Dome feature uses the Dome PropertyManager. The Dome PropertyManager provides the following selections:

- ***Parameters***. The Parameters box provides the ability to select the following options:
- **Faces to Dome**. Displays the selected planar or non-planar faces. Apply domes to faces whose centroid lies outside the face. This allows you to apply domes to irregularly shaped contours.
- **Distance**. Set a value for the distance in which the dome expands. The Distance option is disabled when you use a sketch as a constraint.

Set the Distance option to 0 on your cylindrical and conical models. SolidWorks calculates the distance using the radius of the arc as a basis for the dome. SolidWorks creates a dome which is tangent to the adjacent cylindrical or conical face.

- **Reverse Direction**. Reverses the direction of the Dome feature if required. Provides the ability to create a concave dome. The default is convex.
- **Constraint Point or Sketch**. Provides the ability to control the dome feature. Select a sketch to constrain the shape of the sketch.
- **Direction**. Provides the ability to choose a direction vector from the Graphics window. The direction is to extrude the dome other than normal to the face. You can choose a linear edge or the vector created by two sketch points as your direction vector.
- **Elliptical dome**. Specifies an elliptical dome for a cylindrical or conical model. An elliptical dome's shape is a half an ellipsoid, with a height that is equal to one of the ellipsoid radii.

The Elliptical dome option is not available when you use the Constraint Point or Sketch option or when you use the Direction option.

- **Continuous dome**. Specifies a continuous dome for a polygonal model. A continuous dome's shape slopes upwards, evenly on all sides. If you clear Continuous dome, the shape rises normal to the edges of the polygon.

The Continuous dome option is not available when you use a Constraint Point or Sketch or a Direction vector

- **Show preview**. Displays the total preview of the model.

### *Tutorial: Dome 7-1*

Create an Elliptical dome using the Dome feature.

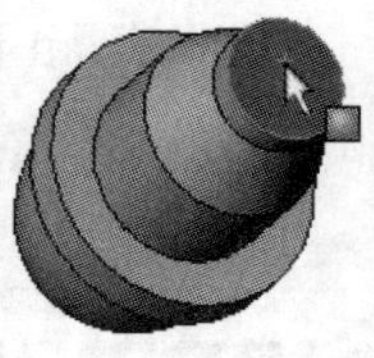

1. Open **Dome 7-1** from the SolidWorks 2010 folder.
2. Click the **back face** of Revolve1.
3. Click the **Dome** Features tool. The Dome PropertyManager is displayed. Face<1> is displayed in the Faces to Dome box. Click the **Elliptical dome** box.

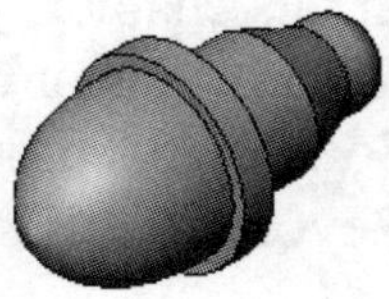

4. Enter **.100**in in the Distance box.
5. Click **OK** from the Dome PropertyManager. Dome1 is created and is displayed in the FeatureManager.
6. **Close** the model.

### *Tutorial: Dome 7-2*

Create a dome on a non-planar face using the Dome Feature to create irregular shaped contours.

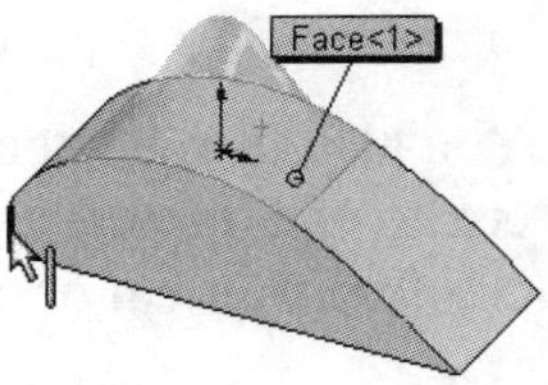


1. Open **Dome 7-2** from the SolidWorks 2010 folder. The Dome 7-2 FeatureManager is displayed.
2. Click the **top curved face** of Extrude1.
3. Click the **Dome** Features tool. The Dome PropertyManager is displayed. Face<1> is displayed in the Faces to Dome box.
4. Enter **50**mm for Distance.

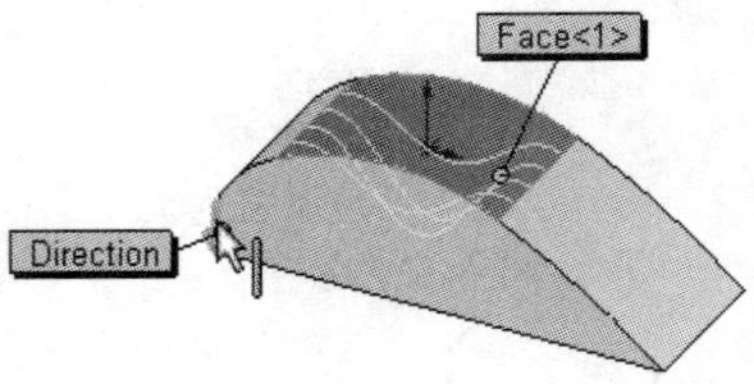


5. Click **inside** of the Direction box.
6. Select the **front left vertical edge**. Edge<1> is displayed. The Dome direction is downward.
7. Click **OK** from the Dome Feature Manager. Dome1 is created.
8. Click the **front face** of Extrude1.

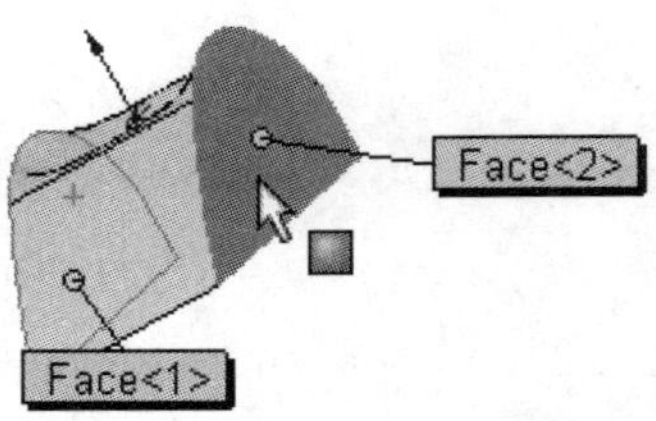


9. Click the **Dome** Features tool. The Dome PropertyManager is displayed.

10. Click the **back face**. Face<1> and Face<2> are displayed in the Faces to Dome box.
11. Enter **40**mm for Distance.
12. Click **OK** ✔ from the Dome Feature Manager. Dome2 is created and is displayed.

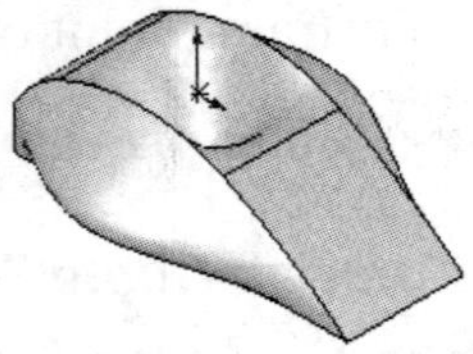

13. Display an **Isometric** view. View the results.
14. **Close** the model.

---

# Summary

In this chapter, you learned about the Revolved, Hole and Dome Features. A Revolved feature adds or removes material by revolving one or more profiles about a centerline. SolidWorks provides the ability to create Revolved Boss/Base, Revolved Cut, or Revolved Surface features. The Revolve feature can be a solid, thin, or a surface.

You learned about the Simple Hole and the Hole Wizard feature. The Simple Hole feature provides the ability to create a simple hole in your model. In general, it is best to create holes at the end of your design process. This helps you to avoid inadvertently adding material inside an existing hole.

The Hole Wizard feature provides the ability to create cuts in the form of standard holes. This feature provides the ability to create holes on a plane as well as holes on planar and non-planar faces. The Hole Wizard information from the model propagates to the drawing when the Hole Callout button is selected.

You also learned about the Dome Feature. The Dome Feature provides the ability to create one or more dome features concurrently on the same model. A Dome feature creates spherical or elliptical shaped geometry.

In Chapter 8, explore and address the Shell feature, Draft feature and the Rib feature.

# CHAPTER 8: SHELL, DRAFT AND RIB FEATURES

## Chapter Objective

Chapter 8 provides a comprehensive understanding of Shell, Draft and Rib features in SolidWorks. On the completion of this chapter, you will be able to:

- Understand and utilize the following Shell features:
  - Shell uniform thickness
  - Shell Error Diagnostics
  - Shell with Multi-thickness
- Understand and utilize the following Draft features:
  - Draft PropertyManager: Manual tab
  - DraftXpert PropertyManager:
    - Add tab
    - Change tab
    - Draft Analysis
- Understand and utilize the Rib feature

## Shell Feature

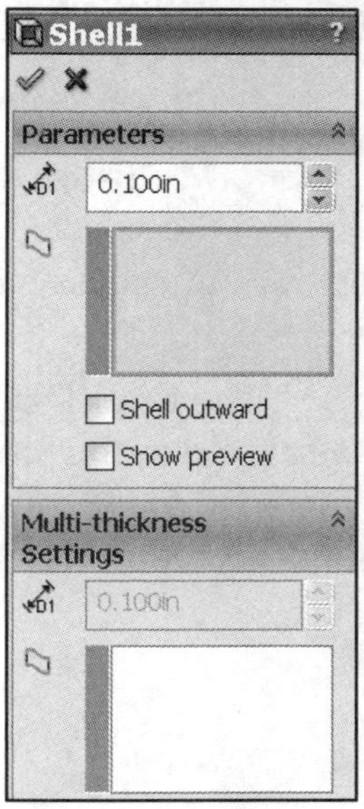


The Shell feature provides the ability to "hollow out" a solid part. Select a face or faces on the model. The Shell feature leaves the selected faces open and creates a thin-walled feature on the remaining faces.

If a face is not selected on the model, the Shell feature provides the ability to shell a solid part, creating a closed, hollow model.

You can also shell a model using the multiple thicknesses option for different faces. You can remove faces, set a default thickness for the remaining faces, and then set the different thicknesses for the faces that you selected from the remaining faces.

Most plastic parts have rounded corners. If you insert fillets to the edges prior to shelling, and the fillet radius is larger than the wall thickness, the inside corners of the part will automatically be rounded. The radius of the inside corners will be the same as the fillet radius minus the selected wall thickness. If the wall thickness is greater than the fillet radius, the inside corners will be sharp.

Insert fillets into your model, before you apply the Shell feature.

The Shell feature uses the Shell PropertyManager. The Shell PropertyManager provides the following selections:

- ***Parameters***. The Parameters box provides the ability to select the following options:
  - **Thickness**. Displays the selected thickness of the faces that you decide to keep.
  - **Faces to remove**. Displays the selected faces from the Graphics window to remove from the model.

To create a hollow part, do not select the Faces to remove option. Do not remove any faces from your model.

  - **Shell outward**. Increases the outside dimensions of the part.
  - **Show preview**. Displays a preview of the Shell feature. Clear the Show preview check box before selecting the faces. If you do not clear the Show preview check box, the preview will update with each face selection. This will slow your system operation down.
- ***Multi-thickness Settings***. The Multi-thickness Settings box provides the following selections:
  - **Multi-thickness(es)**. Displays the selected thickness for a multi-thickness model.
  - **Multi-thickness Faces**. Displays the selected faces of the multi-thickness model.

The Error Diagnostics section is displayed in the Shell PropertyManager if the Shell tool exhibits a modeling problem and a Rebuild error is displayed.

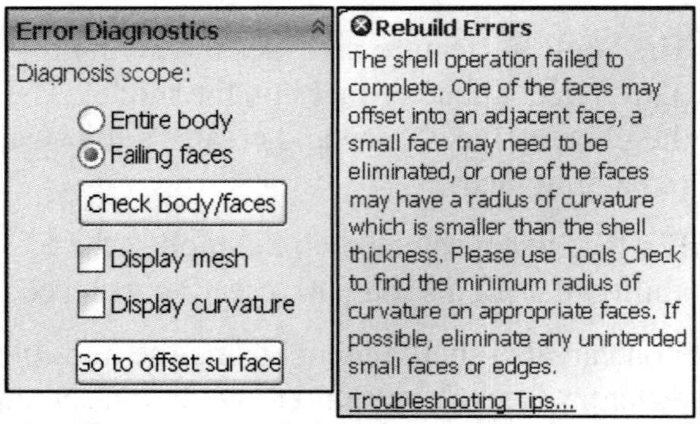

***Tutorial: Shell 8-1***

Create a Shell feature using the Check tool to remove the front face of the model.

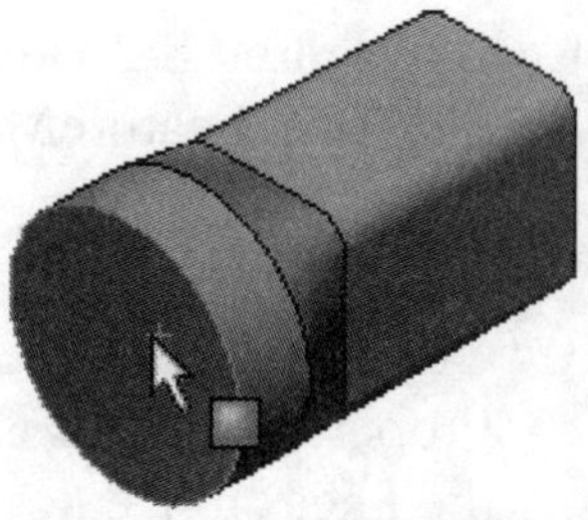

1. Open **Shell 8-1** from the SolidWorks 2010 folder. The Shell 8-1 FeatureManager is displayed.
2. Click the **Shell** Features tool. The Shell PropertyManager is displayed. Click the **front face** of Base-Extrude.
3. Enter **1.100**in for Thickness in the Parameters box.

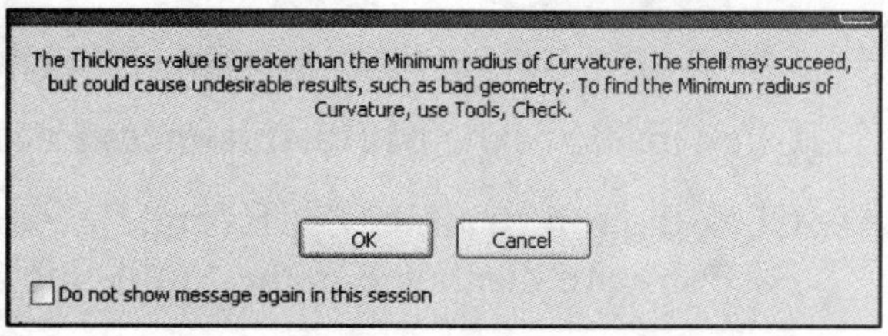


4. Click **OK** from the Shell1 PropertyManager. A warning message is displayed. The Thickness value is greater than the Minimum radius of Curvature. Find the Minimum radius of Curvature.

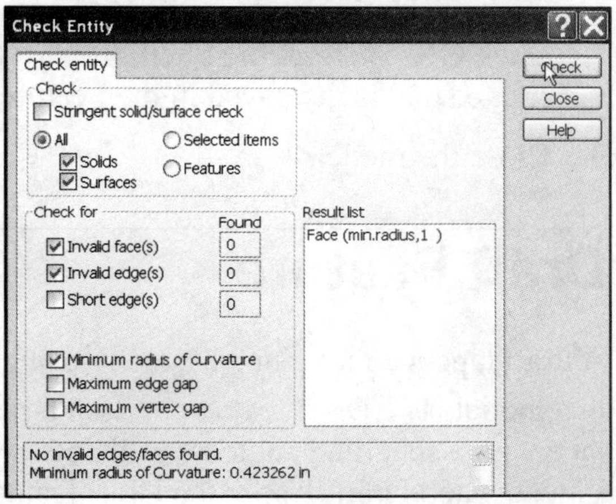


5. Click the **Cancel** button from the SolidWorks dialog box.
6. Click **Cancel** from the Shell PropertyManager.
7. Click **Check** from the Evaluate tab in the CommandManager. The Check Entity dialog box is displayed.
8. Check the **Minimum radius of curvature** box.
9. Click the **Check** button. The Minimum radius of Curvature that the system calculated is .423in.
10. Click the **Close** button from the Check Entity dialog box.
11. Click the **Shell** Features tool. The Shell PropertyManager is displayed.
12. Click the **front face** of Base-Extrude. Enter **.3**in for Thickness in the Parameters box.

13. Click **OK** from the Shell PropertyManager. Shell2 is created and is displayed in the FeatureManager.
14. **Close** the model.

***Tutorial: Shell 8-2***

Create a Shell feature using the Multi-thickness option.

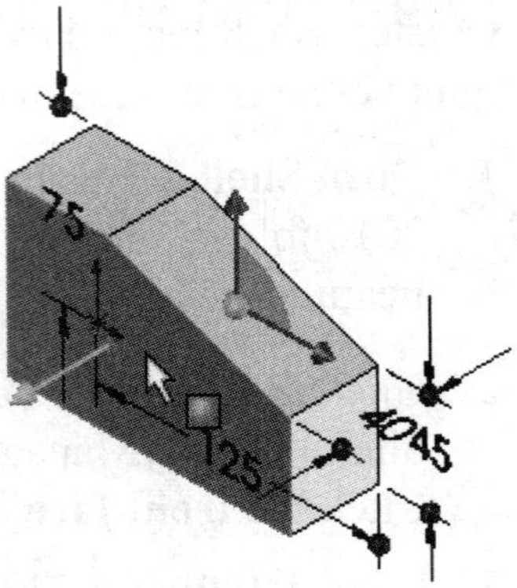


1. Open **Shell 8-2** from the SolidWorks 2010 folder. The Shell 8-2 FeatureManager is displayed.
2. Click the **front face** of Extrude1.
3. Click the **Shell** Features tool. The Shell PropertyManager is displayed. Face<1> is displayed in the Faces to Remove box.
4. Enter **2**mm for Thickness in the Parameters box.
5. Click inside of the **Multi-thickness Faces** box.
6. Click the **top two faces** of Extrude1. Face<2> and Face<3> are displayed in the Multi-thickness Faces box.
7. Enter **10**mm for Multi-thickness(es).
8. Click **OK** from the Shell PropertyManager. Shell1 is created and is displayed in the FeatureManager.
9. **Close** the model.

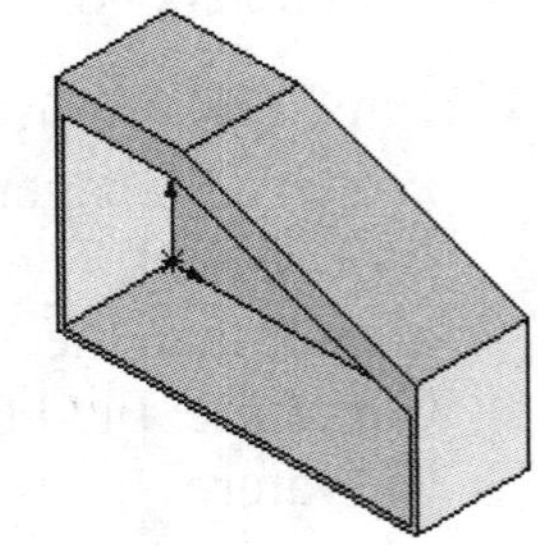

# Draft Feature

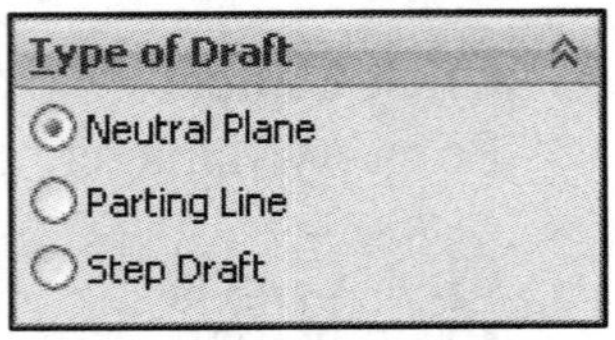


A draft tapers a face using a specified angle to the selected face in a model. The Draft feature tool tapers a selected model face with a specified angle by utilizing a Neutral Plane, Parting Line, or Step Draft. Apply the Draft feature to solid and surface models.

In order for a model to eject from a mold, all faces must draft away from the parting line which divides the core from the cavity. Cavity side faces display a positive draft and core side faces display a negative draft. Design specifications include a minimum draft angle, usually less than 5deg.

For the model to eject successfully, all faces must display a draft angle greater than the minimum specified by the Draft Angle. The Draft PropertyManager and DraftXpert PropertyManager utilizes the draft angle to determine what faces require additional draft base on the direction of pull.

You can apply a draft angle as a part of an Extruded Boss/Base or Cut feature.

## Draft PropertyManager

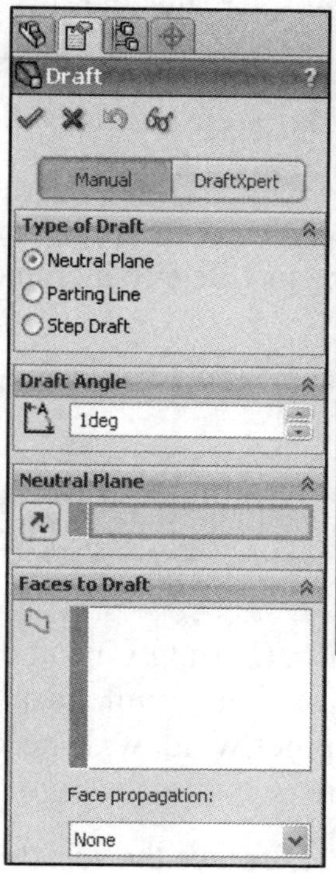

The Draft feature uses the Draft PropertyManager. The Draft PropertyManager provides the ability to create various draft types.

The Draft PropertyManager provides the ability to select either the *Manual* or *DraftXpert* tab. Each tab has a separate menu and option selection. The PropertyManager displays the appropriate options based on the type of draft you create.

The PropertyManager remembers its last used state.

### Draft PropertyManager: Manual tab

The Manual tab provides the ability to display and select various parameters for the Draft feature. Use this tab to maintain control at the feature level. The following selections and options are available under the Manual tab:

- ***Type of Draft***. The Type of Draft box provides the following type options:

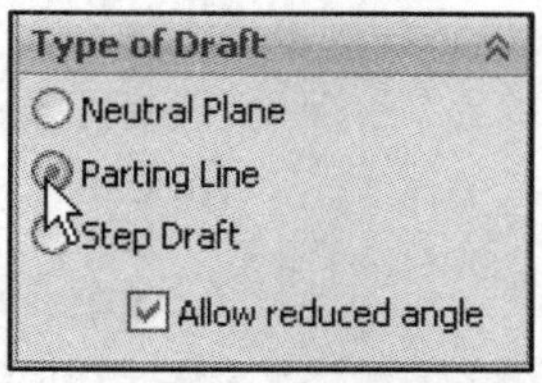


  - **Neutral Plane**. Selected by default. Creates a feature that tapers selected model faces by a specified angle, using a Neutral Plane (A Neutral Plane is the plane or face that you choose to determine the pull direction when creating a mold).
  - **Parting Line**. Drafts surfaces around a Parting line. The Parting line can be non-planar. Using a Parting line in a draft can also include a step draft.
  - **Allow reduced angle**. Allows you to create a draft when the sum of the angle produced by the maximum angle and the Draft Angle is 90° or greater.
  - **Step Draft**. The Step Draft option is a variation of a Parting Line draft. This option creates a single face rotated around the plane used as the direction of pull.

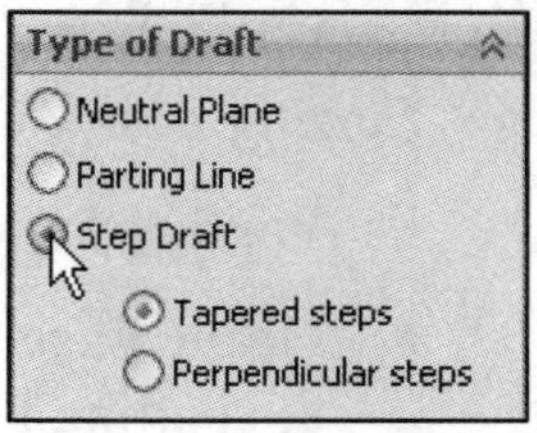

- **Tapered steps**. Creates the surfaces in the same manner as the tapered surfaces.
- **Perpendicular steps**. Creates the surfaces perpendicular to the original main face.

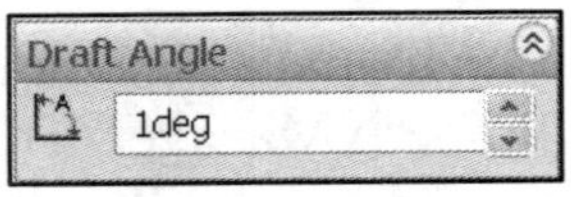


- ***Draft Angle***. Sets the draft angle, measured perpendicular to the neutral plane in 1 degree increments.

The draft angle is measured perpendicular to the Neutral plane.

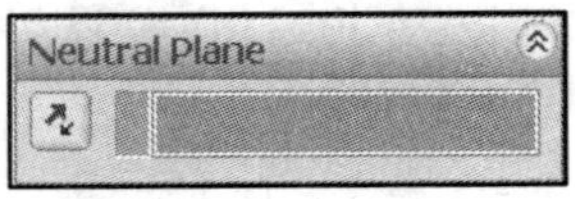


- ***Neutral Plane***. (Neutral Plane only). Select a planar face or a plane feature. If necessary, select Reverse direction to slant the draft in the opposite direction.

- ***Direction of Pull***. (Parting Line and Step Draft option only). Indicates the direction of pull. Displays the selected edge or face in the Graphics window. If necessary, select the Reverse direction option.

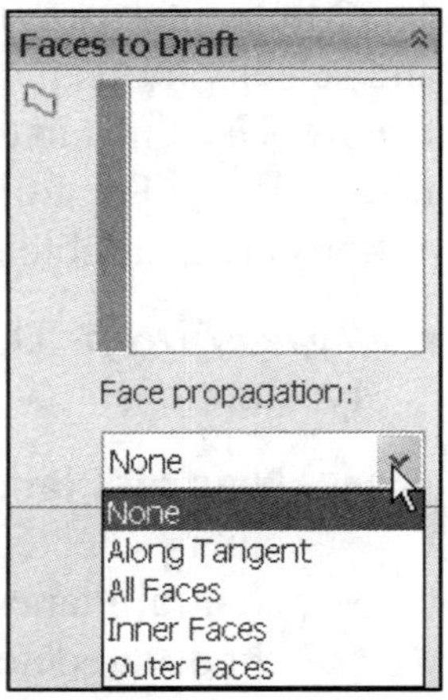


- ***Faces to Draft***. Displays the selected faces to draft from the Graphics window.
  - **Face Propagation**. Only available for the Neural Plane Draft option. The default option is None. If the Parting Line or Step Draft option is selected, only the None and Along Tangent selections are available. The available options are:
    - **None**. Selected by default. Drafts only the selected faces.
    - **Along Tangent**. Extends the draft to all faces which are tangent to the selected face.
    - **All Faces**. Drafts all faces extruded from the neutral plane.
    - **Inner Faces**. Drafts all inner faces extruded from the neutral plane.
    - **Outer Faces**. Drafts all outer faces next to the neutral plane.
- ***Parting Lines***. Only available for the Parting Line and Step Draft options.
  - **Parting Lines**. Displays the selected parting lines from the Graphics window.
  - **Other Face**. Allows you to specify a different draft direction for each segment of the parting line. Click the name of the edge in the **Parting Lines** box, and click **Other Face**.

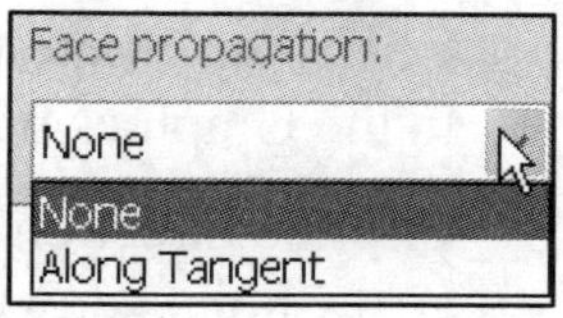


- **Face Propagation**. Propagates the draft across additional faces. Select an item:
  - **None**. Drafts only the selected face.
  - **Along Tangent**. Extends the draft to all faces that are tangent to the selected face.

### *Tutorial: Draft 8-1*

Create a Draft feature with a Neutral Plane.

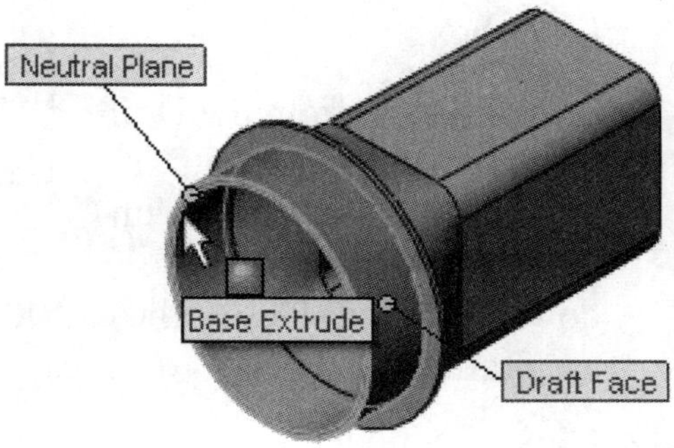


1. Open **Draft 8-1** from the SolidWorks 20010 folder. The Draft 8-1 FeatureManager is displayed.
2. Click the **Draft** Features tool.
3. Click the **Manual** tab. The Draft PropertyManager is displayed. Neutral Plane is displayed as the Type of Draft
4. **Zoom in** and click the **thin front circular face** of the Base Extrude feature. This is your Neutral Plane.
5. Click the **outside circular face** of the Base Extrude feature. Face<2> is displayed in the Faces to Draft box.
6. Enter **8.5**deg for Draft Angle.
7. Click **OK** from the Draft PropertyManager. Draft1 is created and is displayed.
8. Display the **Right** view.
9. Click **Hidden Lines Removed**. View the created Draft Angle. **Close** the model.

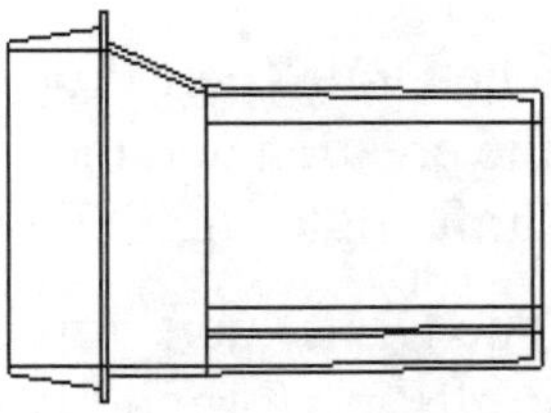

### *Tutorial: Draft 8-2*

Create a Draft feature with a Parting Line.

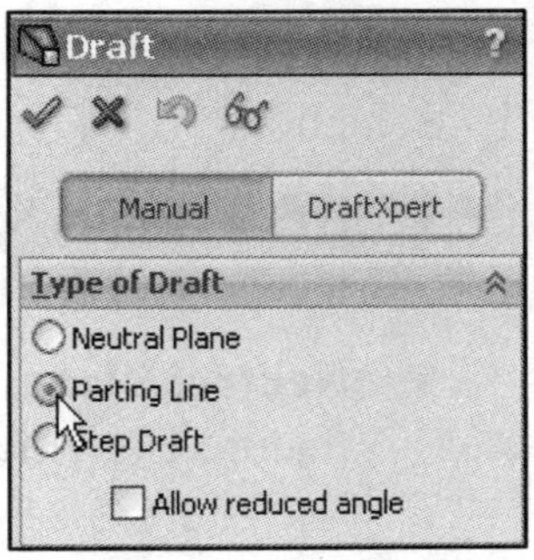


1. Open **Draft 8-2** from the SolidWorks 2010 folder. The Draft 8-2 FeatureManager is displayed.
2. Click the **Draft** Features tool.
3. Click the **Manual** tab. The Draft PropertyManager is displayed.
4. Select **Parting Line** for Type of Draft.
5. Enter **3**deg for Draft Angle.
6. Click inside the **Direction of Pull** box.

7. Click **Top Plane** from the flyout FeatureManager in the Graphics window.
8. **Flip** the direction so that the Direction of Pull arrow points downward.
9. **Rotate** the model and right-click the **bottom front edge** Sweep1.

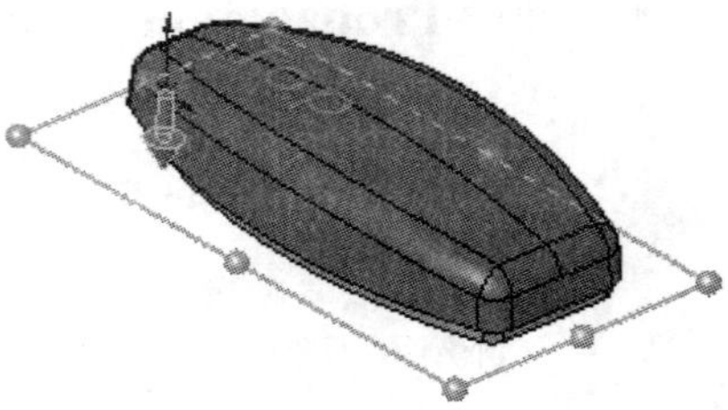

10. Click **Select Tangency** to display all bottom edges. Edge<1> - Edge<8> is displayed in the Parting Lines box.

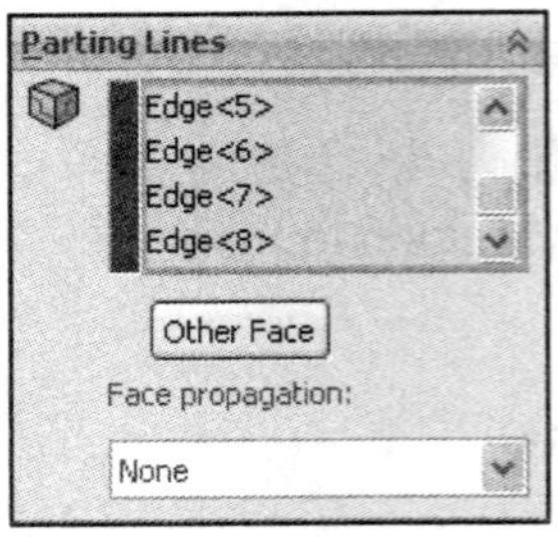


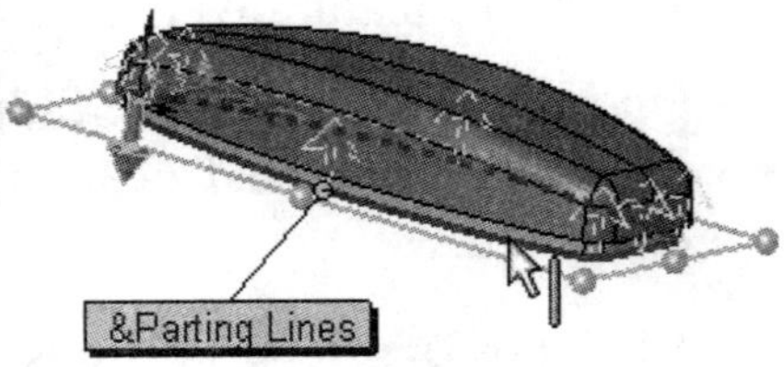


11. Click **OK** ✔ from the Draft PropertyManager. Draft2 is created and displayed. With the Direction of Pull downward, the sides of the extruded cut feature are drafted inward by 3 degrees.
12. **Close** the model.

## DraftXpert PropertyManager: Add/Change tabs

The DraftXpert PropertyManager provides the ability to manage the creation and modification of all Neutral Plane drafts. Select the draft angle and the references to the draft.

The DraftXpert provides the following capabilities: create multiple drafts, perform draft analysis, and edit drafts for (Neutral plane drafts only).

The DraftXpert PropertyManager provides the following selections:

### DraftXpert PropertyManager / Add tab

- ***Items to Draft***. The Items to Draft box provides the following selections:
  - **Draft Angle**. Sets the draft angle. The draft angle is measured perpendicular to the neutral plane.
  - **Neutral Plane**. Displays the selected planar face or plane feature from the flyout FeatureManager.

- **Reverse Direction**. Reverses the direction of the draft if required.
- **Items to Draft**. Displays the selected the faces to draft from the Graphics window.
- **Apply**. Calculates the draft.

- ***Draft Analysis***. The Draft Analysis box provides the following selections:
  - **Auto paint**. Enables the draft analysis of your model. Select a face for the Neutral plane.
  - **Color contour map**. Displays the range of draft in the model by color and numerical value, and the number of faces with Positive draft and Negative draft.
  - Click **Show** or **Hide** to toggle the display of faces that include or require draft.

## DraftXpert PropertyManager / Change tab

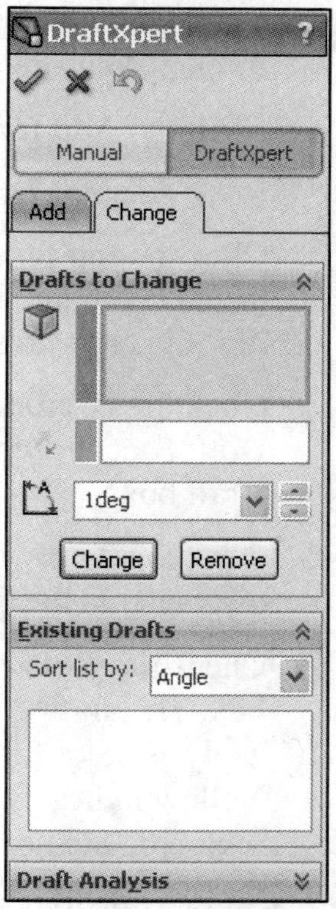


Use the Change tab to modify or remove Neutral Plane drafts. The DraftXpert PropertyManager remembers the last used state.

- ***Drafts to change***. The Drafts to change box provides the following selections:
  - **Draft Items**. Displays the selected faces with draft to change or remove from the Graphics window.
  - **Neutral Plane**. Displays the selected planar face or plane feature from the flyout FeatureManager. Not required if you select the Draft Angle option.
  - **Reverse Direction**. Reverses the direction of the draft if required.
  - **Draft Angle**. Sets the draft angle. The draft angle is measured perpendicular to the Neutral plane.
  - **Change**. Changes the draft.
  - **Remove**. Removes the draft.

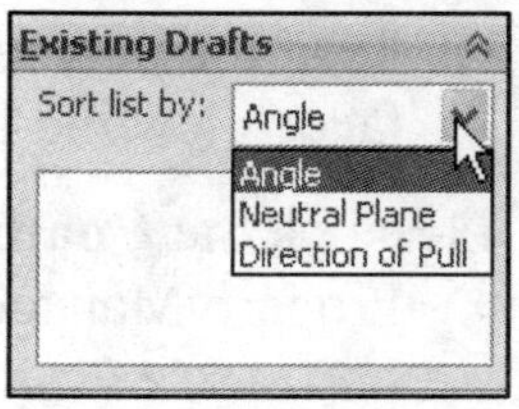


- ***Existing Drafts***. The Existing Drafts box provides the following selections:
  - **Sort list by**. Filters all drafts by the followings selections: **Angle**, **Neutral Plane** and **Direction of Pull**.

- *Draft Analysis*. The Draft Analysis box provides the following selections:
  - **Auto paint**. Enables the draft analysis of your model. Select a face for the Neutral plane.
  - **Color contour map**. Displays the range of draft in the model by color and numerical value, and the number of faces with Positive draft and Negative draft.
  - Click **Show** or **Hide** to toggle the display of faces that include or require draft.

### *Tutorial: DraftXpert 8-1*

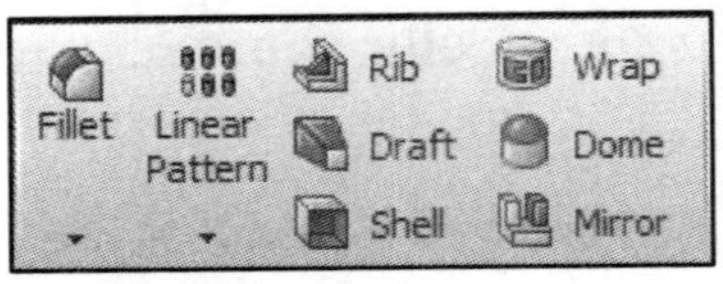


Apply DraftXpert to add and change a draft feature.

1. Open **DraftXpert 8-1** from the SolidWorks 2010 folder.
2. Click the **Draft** Features tool.
3. Click the **DraftXpert** tab. The DraftXpert PropertyManager is displayed.
4. Click the **Add** tab.
5. Enter **4**deg for Draft Angle.
6. Click the **top face** of Extrude1. Face<1> is displayed in the Neutral Plane box. The Direction of Pull is upwards.
7. Click the **circular face** of Extrude1. This is the Draft Face. Face<2> is displayed in the Items To Draft box.

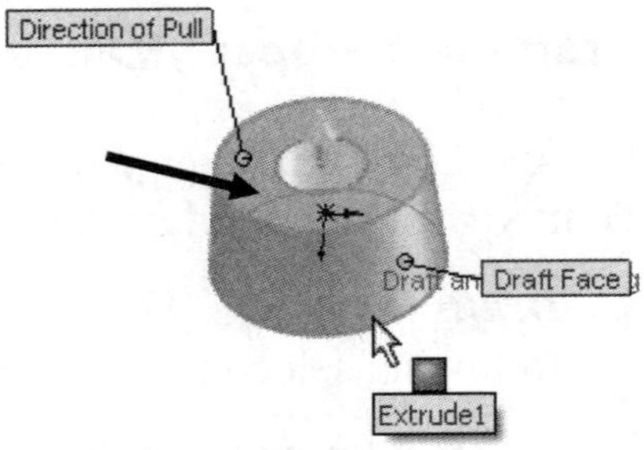


8. Click the **Apply** button. The draft is applied and is displayed in the Graphics window.
9. Check the **Auto paint** box in the Draft Analysis box. The drafted face displays the Draft analysis color for 4 degrees of draft. Note: Yellow indicates no draft. View positive, required, and negative draft surfaces with the Show/Hide toggle tool.

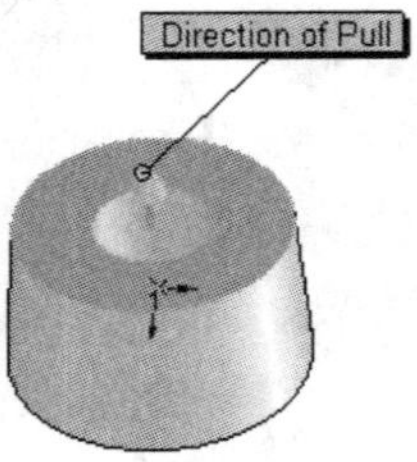


10. Drag the **mouse pointer** over the drafted face. View the feedback display.
11. Click the **Change** Tab from the DraftXpert PropertyManager.

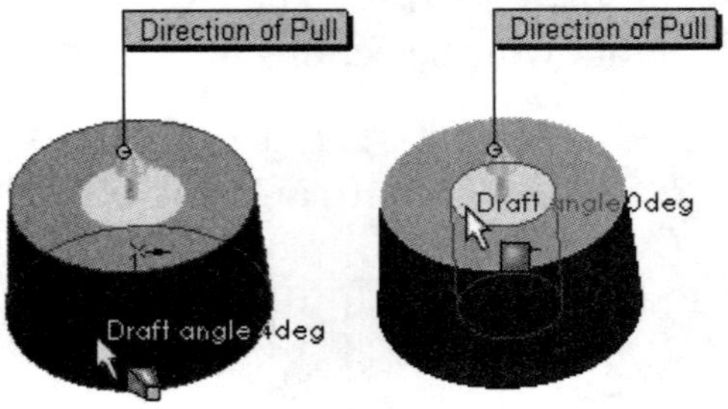

12. Click **4deg** inside the Existing Drafts box.
13. Enter **5deg** from the Draft Angle box.
14. Click the **Change** button in the Drafts to change box. View the changes in the draft in the Graphics window.
15. Click **OK** from the DraftXpert PropertyManager.
16. **Close** the model.

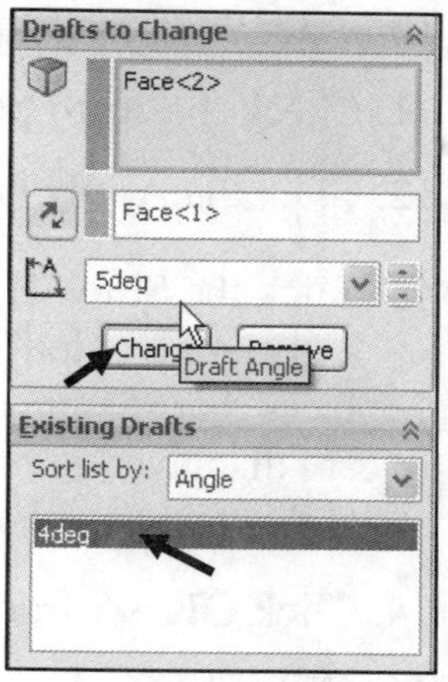


A Draft Analysis provides the designers of plastic parts and mold tooling manufacturers to check the correct application of draft to the faces of their part. With a draft analysis, you can verify draft angles, examine angle changes within a face, as well as locate parting lines, injection, and ejection surfaces in parts.

### *Tutorial: DraftXpert 8-2*

Apply DraftXpert to analyze a draft.

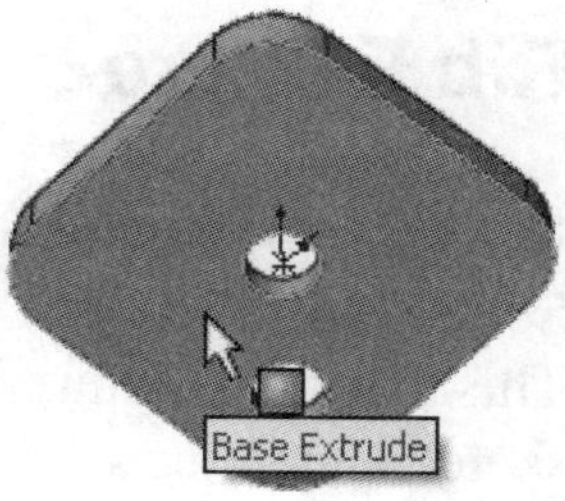


1. Open **DraftXpert 8-2** from the SolidWorks 2010 folder.
2. Click the **Draft** Features tool.
3. Click the **DraftXpert** tab. The DraftXpert PropertyManager is displayed.
4. Click the **Add** tab

Create the Direction of pull.

5. **Rotate** the model and click the **back face**. Face<1> is displayed in the Direction of Pull box.
6. Click the **Reverse direction** button. The direction arrow points upward.
7. Display an **Isometric** view.

Select a face to draft.

8. Zoom in and click the **inside hole face** of the large center hole. Face<2> is displayed in the Faces to Draft box.
9. Zoom in and click the **inside hole face** of the small hole. Face<3> is displayed.

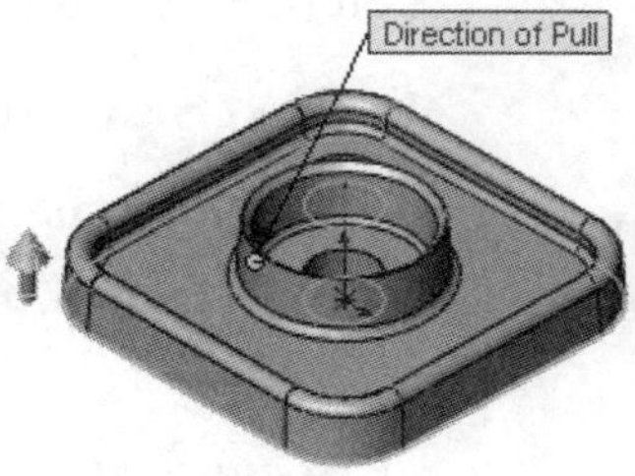

10. Enter **2**deg for Draft Angle.
11. Check the **Auto paint** button.
12. Click the **Apply** button.
13. Click the **Show/Hide** toggle tool to view positive, required, and negative draft surfaces tool. Rotate the part to display the faces that require a draft. By default, the faces that require draft are displayed in red. In the model, the Top Cut feature and the Holes feature requires a draft.
14. Click **OK** from the DraftXpert PropertyManager.
15. **Close** the model.

## Rib Feature

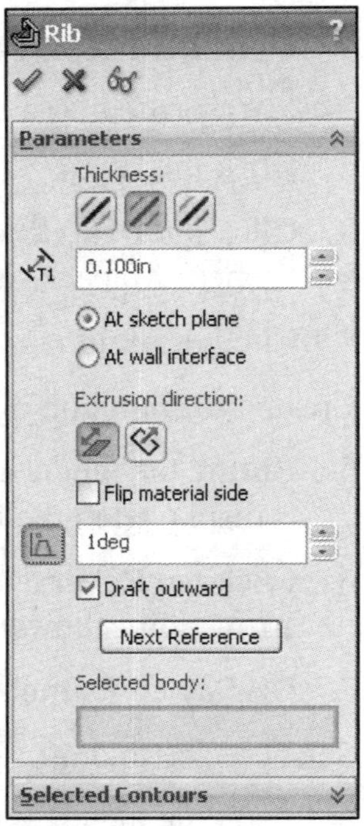


The Rib tool provides the ability to create Ribs in a SolidWorks model. A Rib is a unique type of extruded feature. This extruded feature is created from the opening or closing of sketched contours.

A Rib adds material of a specified thickness in a specified direction between the contour and an existing part. A Rib can be created using single or multiple sketches. You can also create a rib feature with draft, or select a reference contour to draft of sketches. A Rib requires: a sketch, thickness, and an extrusion direction.

Use Ribs to add structural integrity to a part.

The Rib feature uses the Rib PropertyManager. The Rib PropertyManager provides the following selections:

- ***Parameters***. Provides the ability to select the following options:
  - **Thickness**. Adds thickness to the selected side of the sketch. Select one of the following three options:
    - **First Side**. Adds material only to one side of the sketch.
    - **Both Sides**. Selected by default. Adds material equally to both sides of the sketch.
    - **Second Side**. Adds material only to the other side of the sketch.
  - **Rib Thickness**. Enter the rib thickness or select the thickness using the drop-down menu in .1inch increments using the ANSI, (IPS) unit standard.

Rule of thumb states that the Rib thickness should be ½ of the part wall thickness.

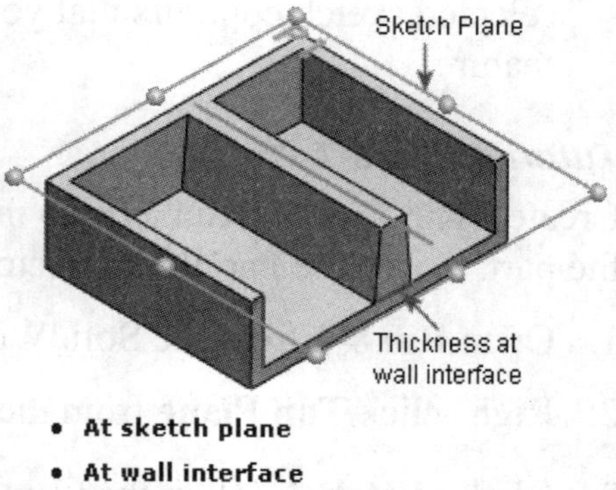


- **At sketch plane**. If you add draft, you can set the thickness at the sketch plane.
- **At wall interface**. If you add draft, you can set the thickness at the wall interface.
- **Extrusion Direction**. Selects the Extrude direction. There are two options:
  - **Parallel to Sketch**. Selected by default. Creates the rib extrusion parallel to your sketch.
  - **Normal to Sketch**. Creates the rib extrusion normal to your sketch.
- **Flip material side**. Changes the direction of the extrusion.
- **Draft On/Off**. Provides the ability to add draft to the rib.
- **Draft Angle**. Sets the value for the Draft Angle for the rib.
- **Draft outward**. Only available when the Draft On/Off option is active. Creates an outward draft angle. If you un-check this box, it will create an inward draft angle.

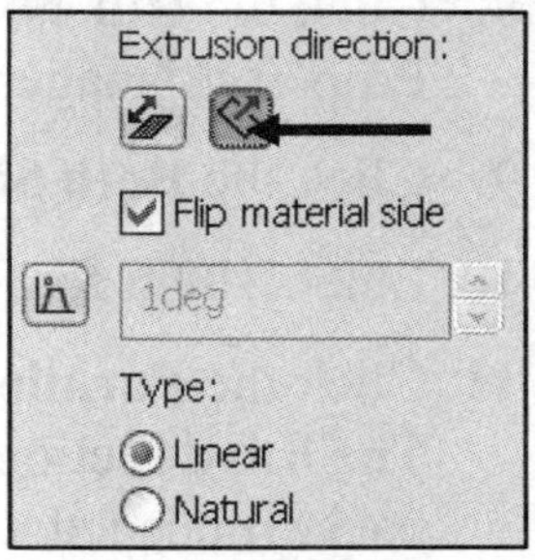


- **Type**. The Type option provides two selections for Rib type. The two Type options are:
  - **Linear**. Creates a rib which extends the sketch contours normal to the direction of your sketch, until they meet a boundary.
  - **Natural**. Creates a rib which extends the sketch contours, continuing with the same contour equation until your rib meets a boundary. Example: The sketch is an arc of a circle. The Natural option extends your rib using the circle equation, until it meets a boundary.
- **Next Reference**. Only available when you select the Parallel to Sketch option for the Extrusion Direction and the Draft On/Off is also selected. Provides the ability to toggle through the sketch contours, to select the contour to use as your reference contour for the draft.
- **Selected Body**. Available only for a multi-body part. After you create a sketch for the rib, select a body.

- ***Selected Contours***. The Selected Contours box displays the selected sketch contours that you are using to create the Rib feature.

### *Tutorial: Rib 8-1*

Create a Rib feature. Add a rib to increase structural integrity of the part. Apply the Parallel to Sketch option with a draft.

1. Open **Rib 8-1** from the SolidWorks 2010 folder.
2. Right-click **Top Plane** from the FeatureManager.
3. Click **Sketch** from the Context toolbar.
4. Click the **Line** Sketch tool.
5. Sketch a **horizontal line** as illustrated on the model. The endpoints are located on either side of the Handle as illustrated.

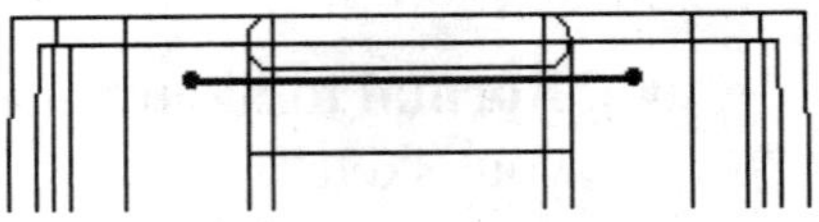

6. Click the **Smart Dimension** Sketch tool. The Dimension PropertyManager is displayed.
7. **Dimension** the model as illustrated.

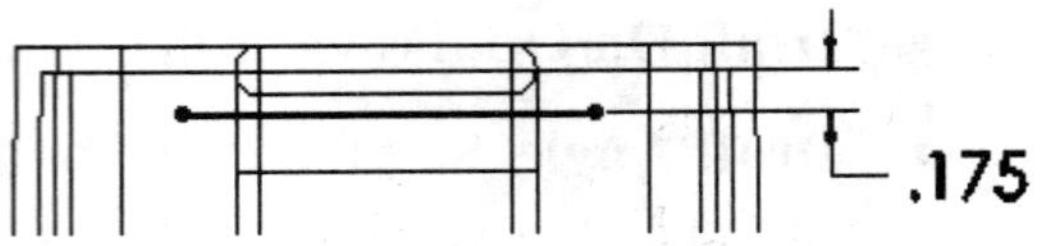


8. Click the **Rib** Features tool. The Rib PropertyManager is displayed.
9. Click the **Both Sides** button.
10. Enter **.100**in for Rib Thickness.

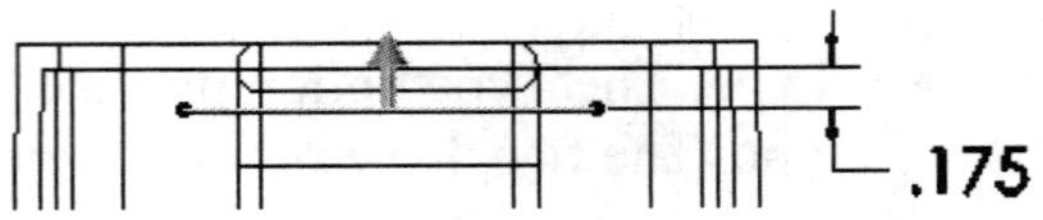


11. Click the **Parallel to Sketch** button. The Rib direction arrow points to the back. If needed, click the **Flip material side** check box.
12. Click the **Draft On/Off** button.
13. Enter **1**deg for Draft Angle.
14. Display a **Front view**.
15. Click the **back inside face** of the HOUSING for the Body. The selected entity is displayed.
16. Click **OK** from the Rib PropertyManager.

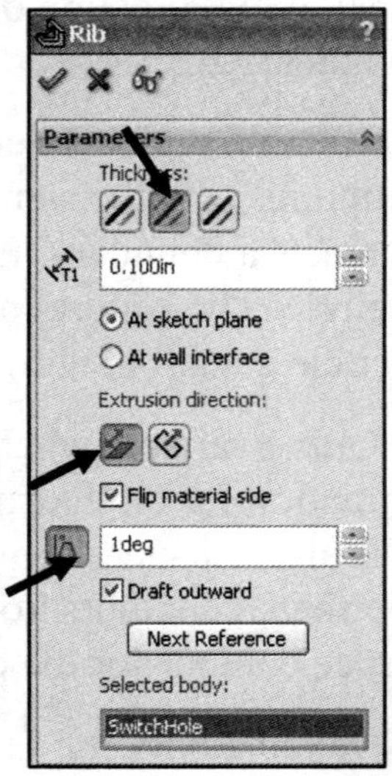


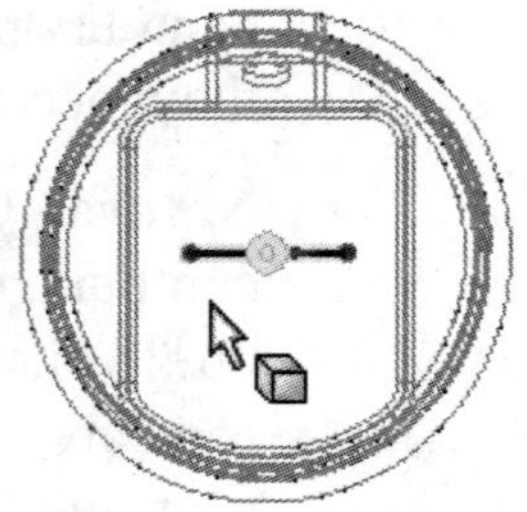

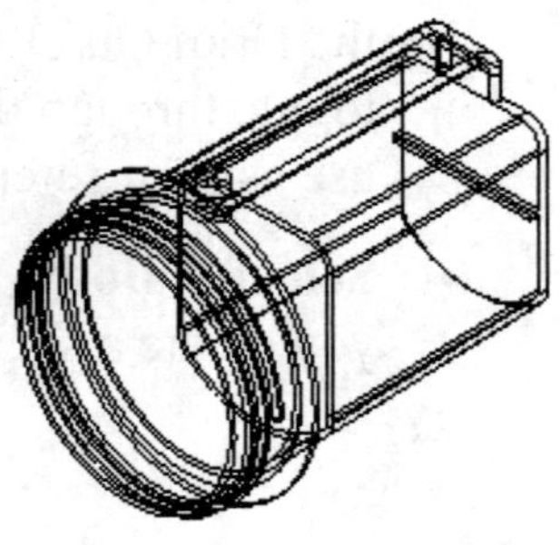

17. Display an **Isometric view**. Rib1 is created and is displayed in the FeatureManager. View the Rib in the Graphics window.
18. **Close** the model.

### *Tutorial: Rib 8-2*

Create a Rib feature. Apply the Parallel to Sketch option with a draft.

1. Open **Rib 8-2** from the SolidWorks 2010 folder.
2. **Edit** Sketch9 from the FeatureManager.
3. Click the **Rib** Features tool. The Rib PropertyManager is displayed.
4. Click the **Both Sides** button.
5. Enter **.100**in for Rib Thickness.
6. Click the **Parallel to Sketch** button. The Rib direction arrow points downwards.
7. Check the **Flip material side** box if required. The direction arrow points downwards.
8. Click the **Draft On/Off** button.
9. Enter **2**deg for Draft Angle.
10. Click **OK** from the Rib PropertyManager. Rib1 is displayed.
11. **Close** the model.

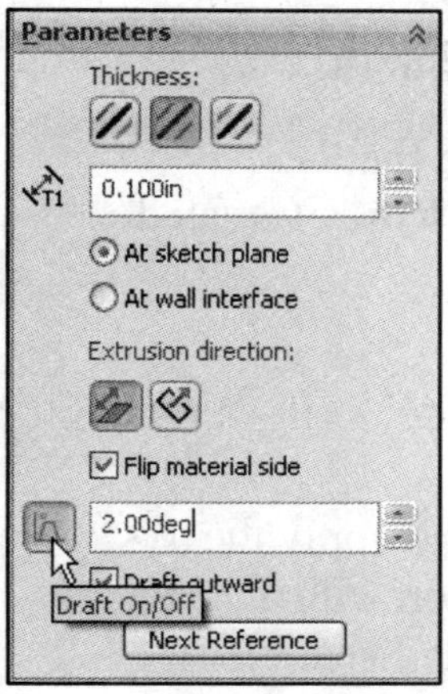


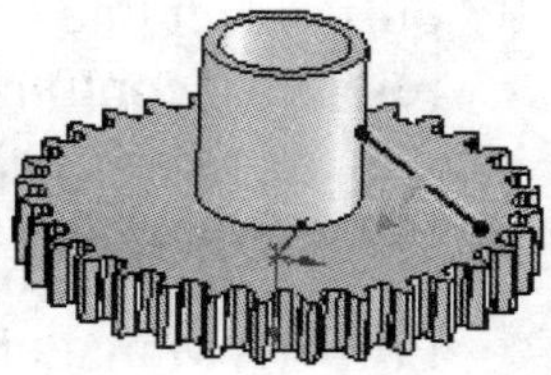

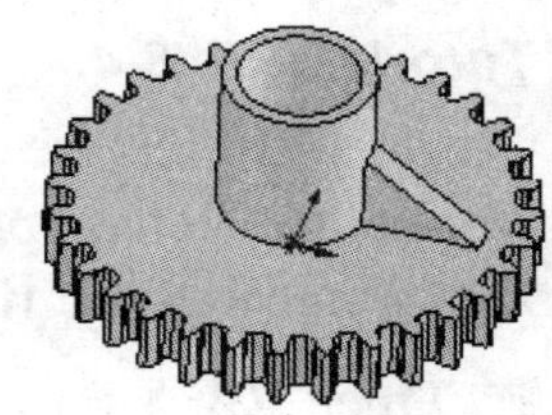

### *Tutorial: Rib 8-3*

Create a Rib feature with the Next Reference option.

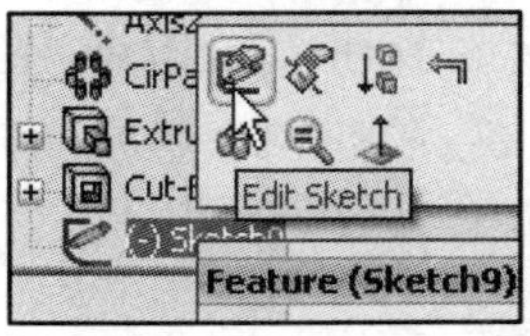


1. Open **Rib 8-3** from the SolidWorks 2010 folder.
2. **Edit** Sketch9 from the FeatureManager.
3. Click the **Rib** Features tool. The Rib PropertyManager is displayed.
4. Click the **Both Sides** button.
5. Enter **.150**in for Rib Thickness.

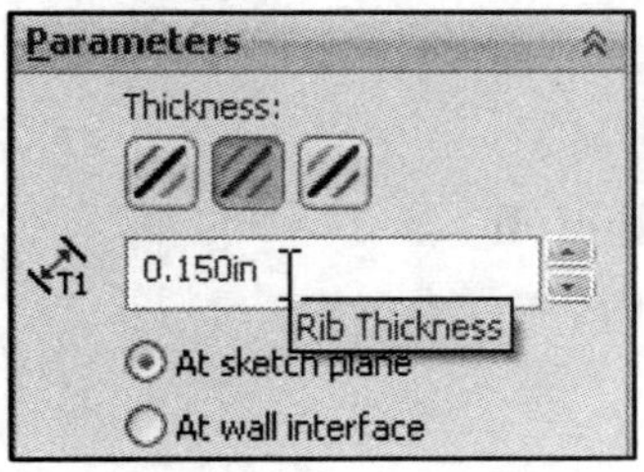


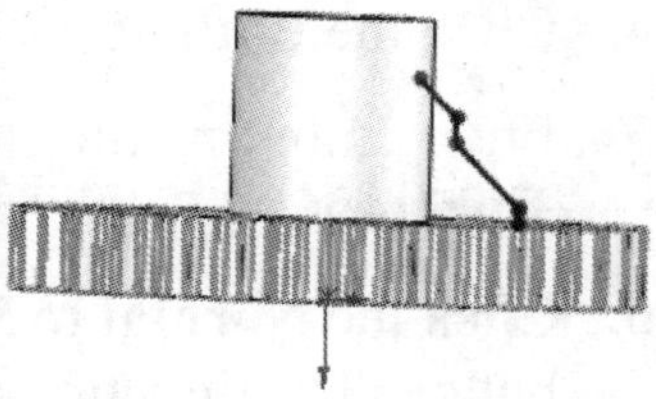

6. Click the **Parallel to Sketch** button. The Rib direction arrow points to the back.

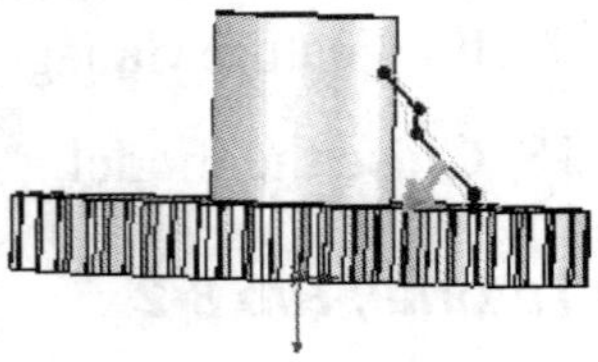

7. Click the **Flip material side** box. The direction arrow points downwards.
8. Click the **Draft On/Off** button.
9. Enter **3**deg for Draft Angle.

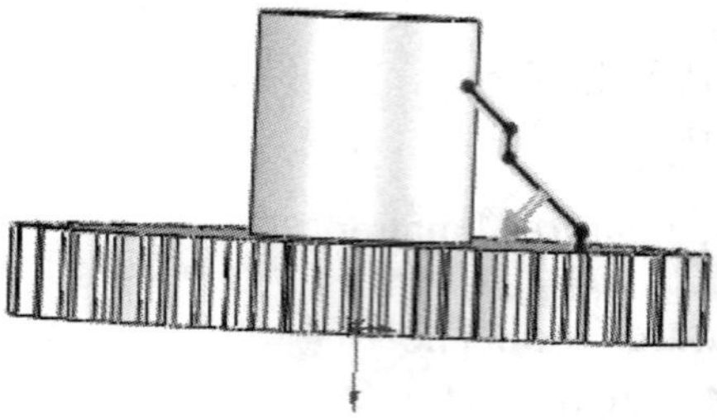

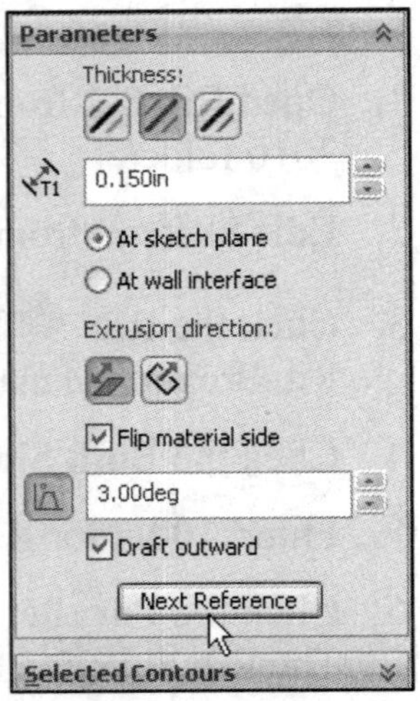


10. Click the **Next Reference** button until you select the contour as illustrated. You can only select one reference contour on which to base your draft.
11. Click **OK** from the Rib PropertyManager. Rib1 is created and is displayed.

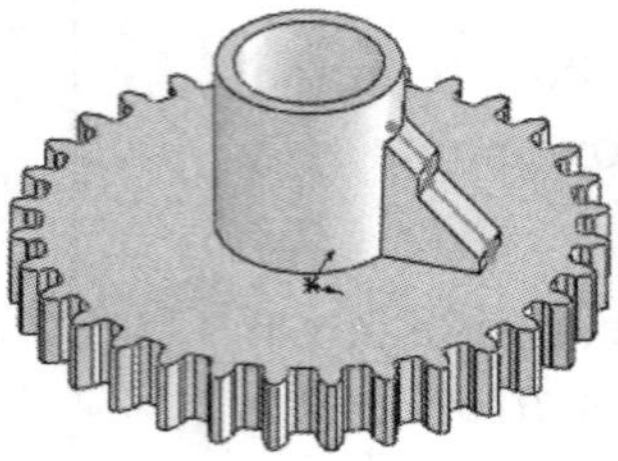

12. **Close** the model.

***Tutorial: Rib 8-4***

Create a Rib feature and apply the Normal to Sketch option with a Linear and Natural Rib Type.

1. Open **Rib 8-4** from the SolidWorks 2010 folder.
2. Click **SketchRib** from the FeatureManager.

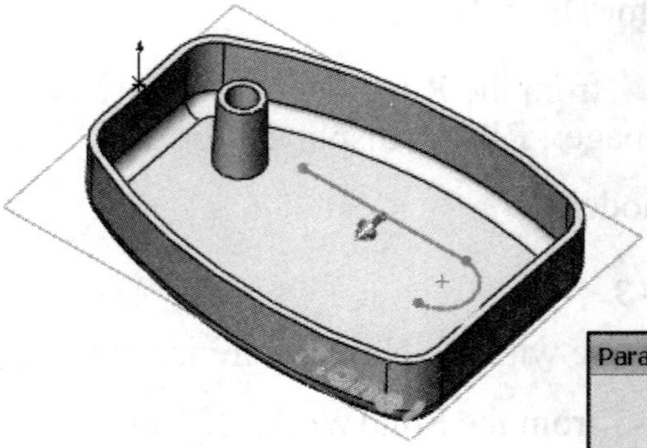

3. Click the **Rib** Features tool. The Rib PropertyManager is displayed. The direction arrow points toward the front as illustrated.
4. Click the **Both Sides** button.
5. Enter **2**mm for Rib Thickness.
6. Click the **Normal to Sketch** button. The direction arrow points downwards.

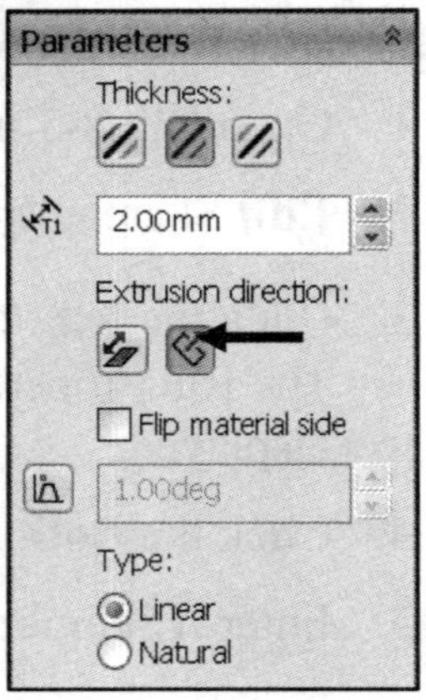

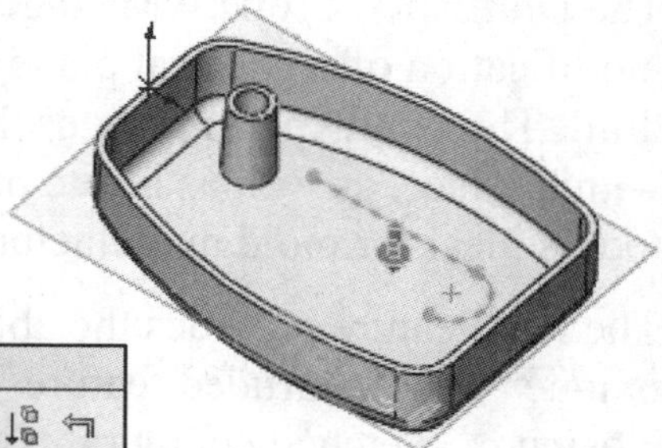

7. Check the **Linear** box for Type.
8. Click **OK** ✔ from the Rib PropertyManager.
9. Right-click **Rib1** from the FeatureManager.
10. Click **Edit Feature**.
11. Check the **Natural** box for Type.
12. Click **OK** ✔ from the Rib PropertyManager. View the results.
13. **Close** the model.

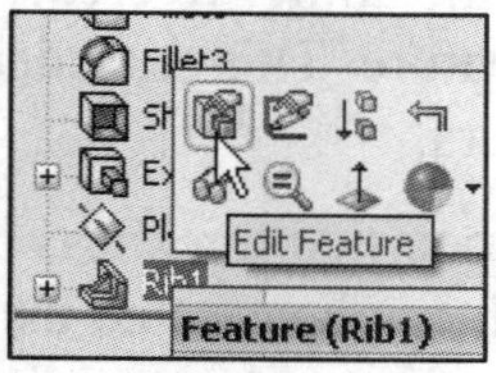


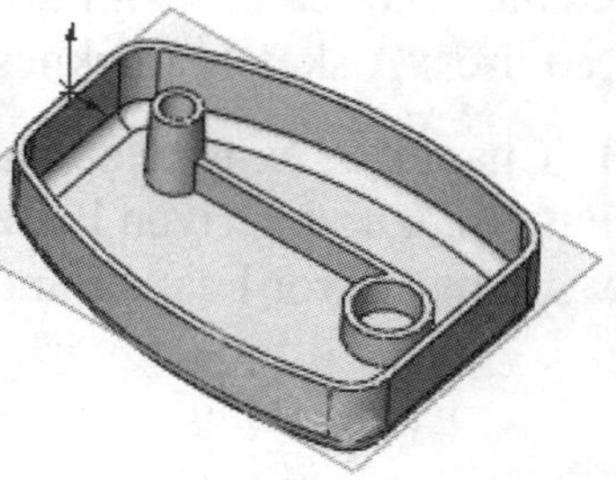

💡 The Fastening Feature toolbar provides access to additional features utilized in mold design. These tools combine Extrude, Draft, and Rib features. For example, the Mounting Boss feature contains parameters to define the Extruded Boss, hole size, draft and number of fins.

💡 Press the **g** key to activate the Magnifying glass tool. Use the Magnifying glass tool to inspect a model and make selections without changing the overall view.

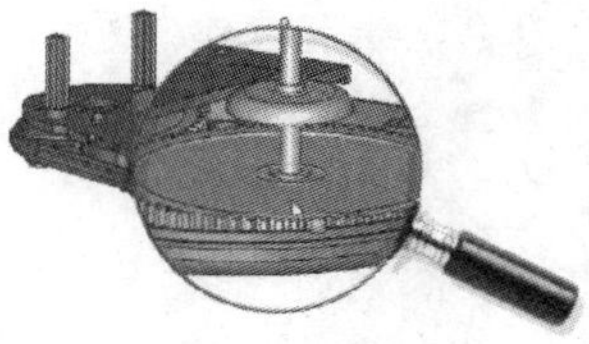

# Summary

In this chapter, you learned about the Shell, Draft and Rib Features in SolidWorks. The Shell feature provides the ability to "hollow out" a solid part. Select a face or faces on the model. The Shell feature leaves the selected faces open and creates a thin-walled feature on the remaining faces. If a face is not selected on the model, the Shell feature provides the ability to shell a solid part, creating a closed hollow model.

You can also shell a model using the multiple thicknesses option for different faces. You can remove faces, set a default thickness for the remaining faces, and then set the different thicknesses for the faces that you selected from the remaining faces.

Most plastic parts have rounded corners. If you insert fillets to the edges prior to shelling, and the fillet radius is larger than the wall thickness,

The Draft feature tapers a selected model face with a specified angle by utilizing a Neutral Plane, Parting Line, or Step Draft. Apply the Draft feature to solid and surface models.

In order for a model to eject from a mold, all faces must draft away from the parting line which divides the core from the cavity. Cavity side faces display a positive draft and core side faces display a negative draft. Design specifications include a minimum draft angle, usually less than 5 degrees.

The DraftXpert PropertyManager provided the ability to manage the creation and modification of all neutral plane drafts. Select the draft angle and the references to the draft. The DraftXpert manages the rest. It can verify draft angles, examine angle changes within a face, as well as locate parting lines, injection, and ejection surfaces in parts. This tool is ideal for mold manufacturing.

The Rib Feature provides the ability to create Ribs in a SolidWorks model. A Rib is a unique type of extruded feature. This extruded feature is created from the opening or closing of sketched contours.

A Rib adds material of a specified thickness in a specified direction between the contour and an existing part. A Rib can be created using single or multiple sketches. You can also create a rib feature with draft, or select a reference contour to draft of sketches. A Rib requires: A sketch, thickness and an extrusion direction.

In Chapter 9, explore and address various Pattern Features; Linear Pattern, Circular Pattern, Curve Driven Pattern, Sketch Pattern, Table Driven Pattern, Fill Pattern along with the Mirror Feature and Coordinate System PropertyManager.

# CHAPTER 9: PATTERN AND MIRROR FEATURES

## Chapter Objective

Chapter 9 provides a comprehensive understanding of Pattern and Mirror features in SolidWorks. On the completion of this chapter, you will be able to:

- Understand and utilize the following Pattern features:
  - Linear Pattern
  - Circular Pattern
  - Curve Driven Pattern
  - Sketch Driven Pattern
  - Table Driven Pattern
  - Fill Pattern
- Address the Coordinate System PropertyManager
- Recognize and utilize the Mirror feature

## Linear Pattern Feature

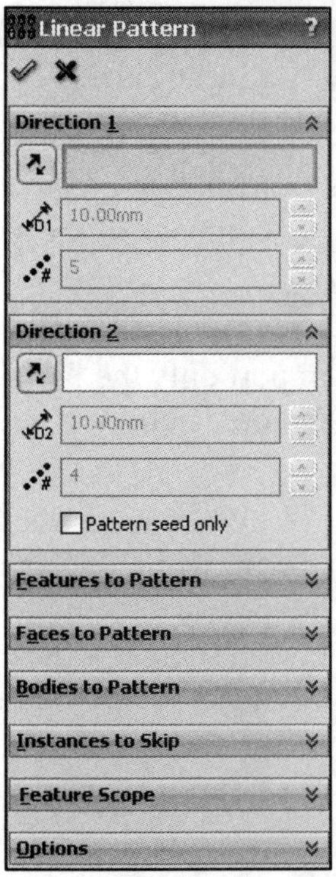


The Linear Pattern feature provides the ability to create copies, or instances, along one or two linear paths in one or two different directions. The instances are dependent on the selected originals. Changes to the originals are passed onto the instanced features.

Set an option in Direction 1 and Direction 2 to create a Linear Pattern feature in both directions from the Sketch plane.

The Linear Pattern feature uses the Linear PropertyManager. The Linear Pattern PropertyManager is feature dependent and provides the following selections:

- ***Direction 1***. Provides the following feature dependent options:

- **Pattern Direction**. Displays the selected linear edge, line, axis, or dimension from the Graphics window.
- **Reverse Direction**. Reverses the Direction 1 pattern if required.
- **Spacing**. Displays the set spacing value between the pattern instances for Direction 1.
- **Number of Instances**. Displays the set value of the number of pattern instances for Direction 1. The Number of Instances includes the original features or selections.

The options in Direction 1 are the same as the options in Direction 2 except for the Pattern seed only check box.

- ***Direction 2***. Provides the following feature dependent options:

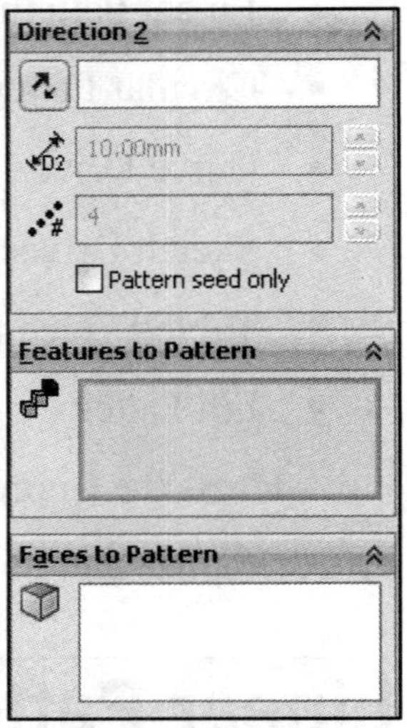


  - **Pattern Direction**. Displays the selected linear edge, line, axis, or dimension from the Graphics window.
  - **Reverse Direction**. Reverses the Direction 2 pattern if required.
  - **Spacing**. Displays the set spacing value between the pattern instances for Direction 2.
  - **Pattern seed only**. Creates a linear pattern in Direction 2, only using the Seed feature, without duplicating the Direction 1 pattern instances.
- ***Features to Pattern***. Displays the selected seed to create the Linear Pattern.
- ***Faces to Pattern***. Displays the selected faces of the seed feature to create the Linear Pattern utilizing the faces that compose of the seed feature.

The Faces to Pattern option is very useful with models that import only the faces that compose of the feature, and not the feature itself.

When using the Faces to Pattern option, your pattern must remain within the same boundary or face. The pattern cannot cross boundaries. Example: a cut across the complete face or different levels, such as a raised edge would create separate faces and a boundary, stopping the pattern from spreading.

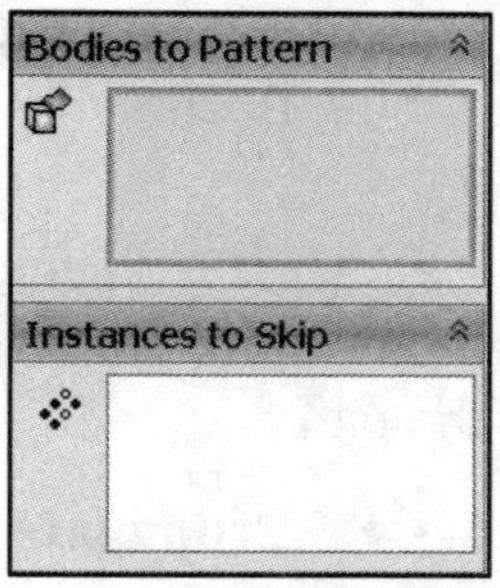


- ***Bodies to Pattern Direction***. Displays the selected Solid/Surface Bodies and to create the pattern using the bodies that is selected in the multi-body part.
- ***Instances to Skip***. Displays the selected coordinates of the instances from the Graphics window which you do not want to include in the pattern. The mouse pointer changes when you float over each pattern instance in the Graphics window. Click to select a pattern instance.

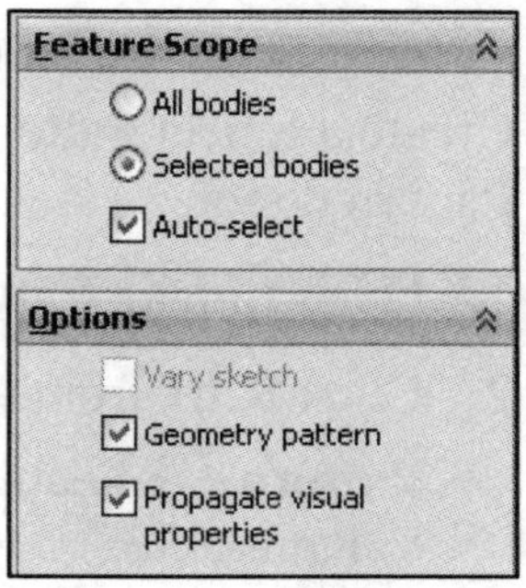


- ***Feature Scope***. Applies various features to one or more multi-body parts. Check the Geometry pattern option box from the Options section to apply features to a multi-bound part. The available selections are:
  - **All bodies**. Applies a feature to all bodies, each time the feature is regenerated. If a new body is added to your model that is intersected by the feature, the new body is also regenerated to include that feature.
  - **Selected bodies**. Selected by default. Applies a feature to the body that is selected. If a new body is added, to your model which is intersected by the feature, you are required to use the Edit Feature command to edit the pattern features. Select the bodies, and add them to the list of your selected bodies. If you do not add the new bodies to your selected list of selected bodies, they will remain intact.
  - **Auto-select**. Selected by default. Only available if you click the Selected bodies option. Provides the ability when you first create a model with multi-body parts, the features automatically process all the relevant intersecting parts.

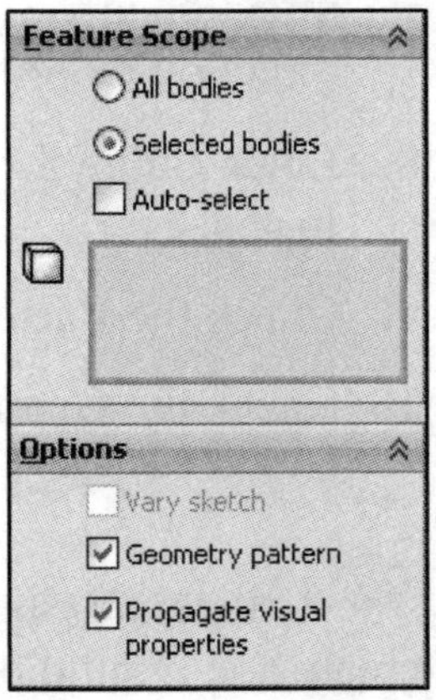


The Auto-select option is faster than the All bodies option because the Auto-select option processes only the bodies on the initial list, and does not regenerate your entire model.

  - **Bodies to Affect**. Only available if you un-check the Auto-select check box. Display the selected bodies from the Graphics window.
- ***Options***. The Options box provides the following selections:
  - **Vary sketch**. Allows the pattern to change as it repeats.

- **Geometry pattern**. Creates the pattern using only the geometry of faces and edges of the features, rather than patterning and resolving each instance of the features.

The Geometry Pattern option speeds up the creation and rebuilding of the pattern. You cannot create geometry patterns of features that have faces merged with the rest of the part.

- **Propagate Visual Properties**. Propagates SolidWorks textures, colors, and cosmetic thread data to all pattern instances.

### *Tutorial: Linear Pattern 9-1*

Create a Linear Pattern feature using the Pattern seed only option and the Geometry Pattern option.

1. Open **Linear Pattern 9-1** from the SolidWorks 2010 folder.
2. Click **Rib1** from the FeatureManager. Click the **Linear Pattern** Features tool. Rib1 is displayed in the Features to Pattern box.
3. Click inside the **Pattern Direction** box for Direction 1.
4. Click the **hidden upper back vertical edge** of Shell1. Edge<1> is displayed in the Pattern Direction box. The direction arrow points upward. Click the Reverse direction button if required.

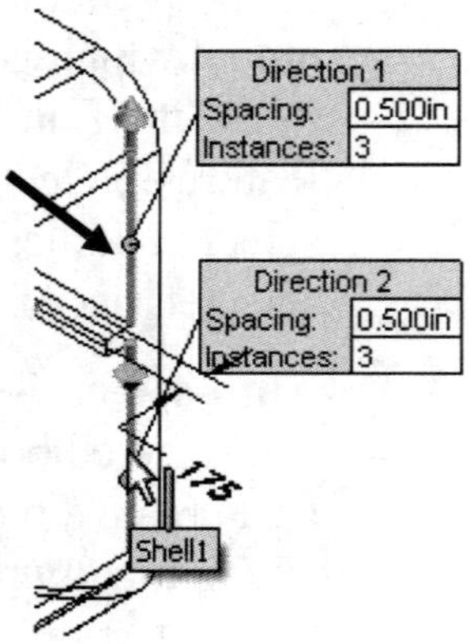


5. Enter **.500**in for Spacing.
6. Enter **3** for Number of Instances.
7. Click the **hidden lower back vertical edge** of Shell1. The direction arrow points downward. Click the Reverse direction button if required.
8. Enter **.500**in for Spacing. Enter **3** for Number of Instances.
9. Check the **Pattern seed only** box.
10. Check the **Geometry Pattern** box in the Options box.

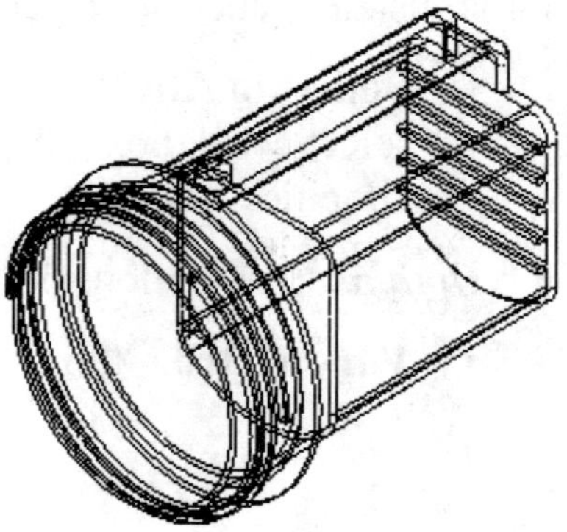

Utilize the Geometry Pattern option to efficiently create and rebuild patterns.

11. Click **OK** from the Linear Pattern PropertyManager. LPattern1 is created and is displayed in the FeatureManager.
12. **Close** the model.

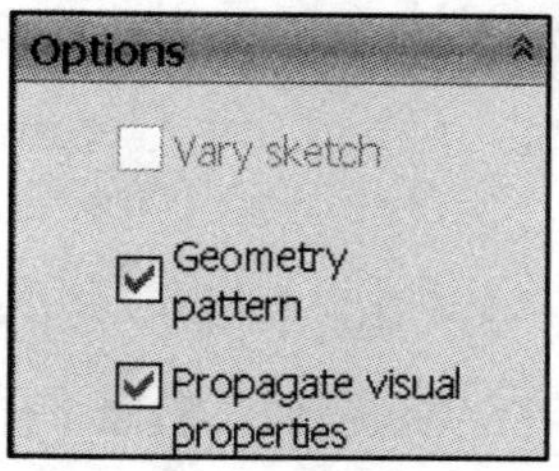


Know when to check the Geometry pattern box. Check the Geometry Pattern box when you require:

- An exact copy of the seed feature.
- Each instance is an exact copy of the faces and edges of the original feature.
- End conditions are not calculated.
- Saving rebuild time.
- Uncheck the Geometry Pattern box when you require:
  - The end condition to vary.
  - Each instance to have a different end condition.
  - Each instance is offset from the selected surface by the same amount.

***Tutorial: Linear Pattern 9-2***

Create a Linear Pattern feature using the Instances to skip option.

1. Open **Linear Pattern 9-2** from the SolidWorks 2010 folder.
2. Click **Cut-Extrude1** from the FeatureManager. Cut-Extrude1 is highlighted in the Graphics window.
3. Click the **Linear Pattern** Features tool. Cut-Extrude1 is displayed in the Features to Pattern box.
4. Click inside the **Pattern Direction** box for Direction 1.
5. Click the **top horizontal edge** of Extrude1. The direction arrow points to the right. Click the Reverse direction button if required.

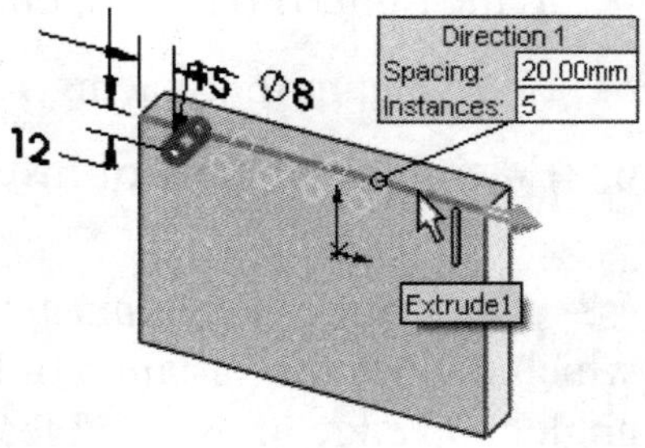


6. Enter **20**mm for Spacing.
7. Enter **5** for Number of Instances.
8. Click inside the **Pattern Direction** box for Direction 2.
9. Click the **left vertical edge** of Extrude1. Edge<2> is displayed in the Pattern Direction box. The direction arrow points downward. Click the Reverse direction button if required.

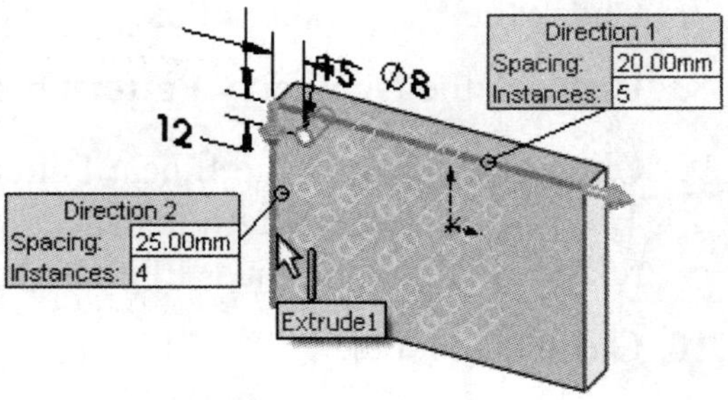


10. Enter **25**mm for Spacing.
11. Enter **4** for Number of Instances.

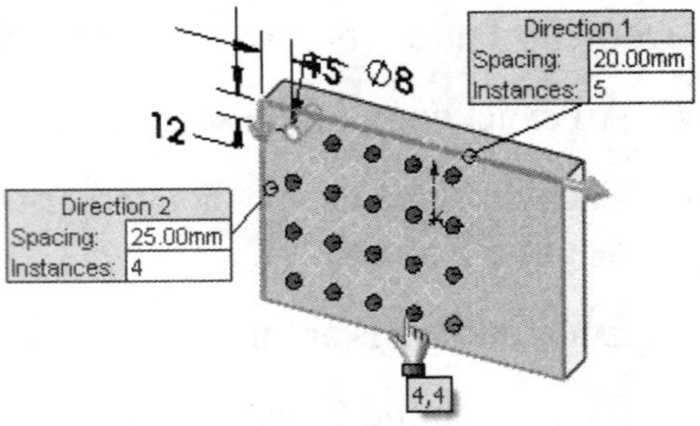


12. Un-check the **Pattern seed only** box.
13. Check the **Geometry pattern** box in the Options dialog box.
14. Click inside of the **Instances to skip** box.
15. Select **(5,4)** & **(4,4)** from the Graphics window. (5,4) & (4,4) is displayed in the Instances to Skip box.
16. Click **OK** from the Linear Pattern PropertyManager. LPattern1 is created and is displayed in the FeatureManager.

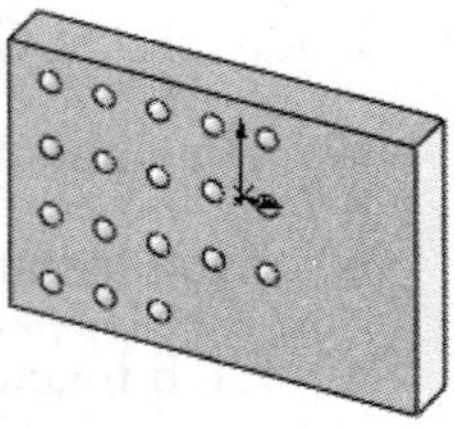

17. **Close** the model.

***Tutorial: Linear Pattern 9-3***

Create a Linear Pattern feature using the Vary sketch option. Use the seed feature to pattern three times to the left.

1. Open **Linear Pattern 9-3** from the SolidWorks 2010 folder.
2. Click **Cut-Extrude2** from the FeatureManager.
3. Click the **Linear Pattern** Features tool. The Linear Pattern PropertyManager is displayed.
4. Click the **9**mm driving dimension from the Graphics window. D4@Sketch2 is displayed in the Pattern Direction box. The pattern direction arrow is displayed to the right. If required, click the Reverse Direction box.

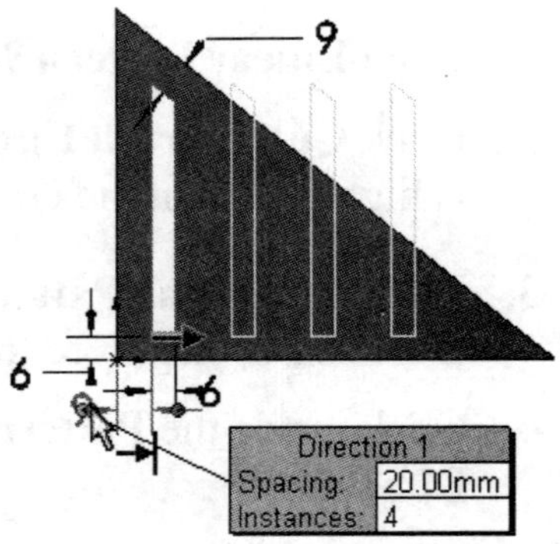


5. Enter **20**mm for Spacing.
6. Enter **4** for Number of Instances.

The feature sketch must be constrained to the boundary which defines the variation of the pattern instances. The angled top edge of the seed feature is parallel and is dimensioned to the angled edge on the base part. The feature sketch should be fully defined.

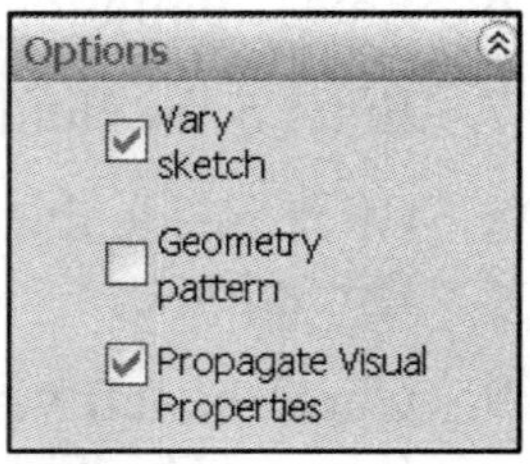


7. Check the **Vary sketch** box.
8. Uncheck the **Geometry Pattern** box.
9. Click **OK** from the Linear Pattern PropertyManager. The height of the pattern instances vary while other relations are maintained. LPattern1 is created.

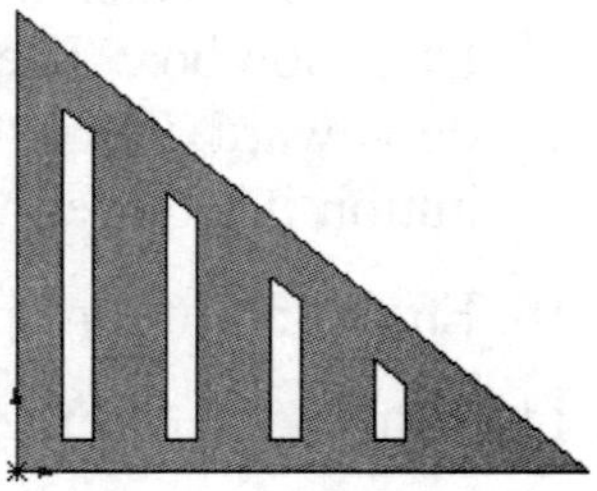

10. **Close** the model.

***Tutorial: Linear Pattern 9-4***

Create a Linear Pattern feature using the Feature Scope Selected bodies option.

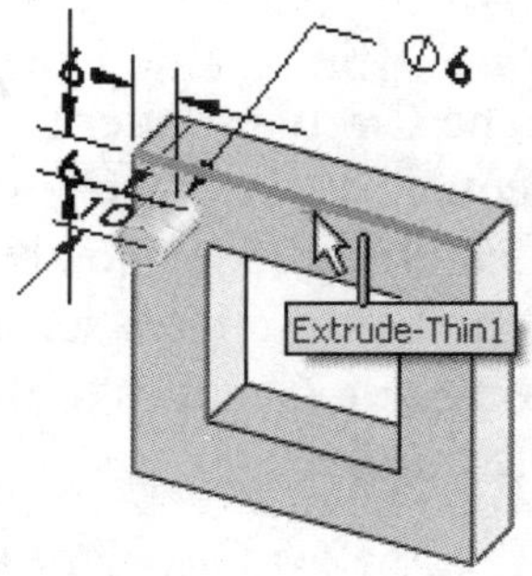


1. Open **Linear Pattern 9-4** from the SolidWorks 2010 folder.
2. Click **Extrude1** from the FeatureManager. Extrude1 is highlighted in the Graphics window.
3. Click the **Linear Pattern** Feature tool. The Linear Pattern PropertyManager is displayed. Extrude1 is displayed in the Features to Pattern box.
4. Click the **top edge** of Extrude-Thin1 as illustrated. Edge<1> is displayed in the Pattern Direction box for Direction 1. The direction arrow points to the right. Click the Reverse Direction button if required.

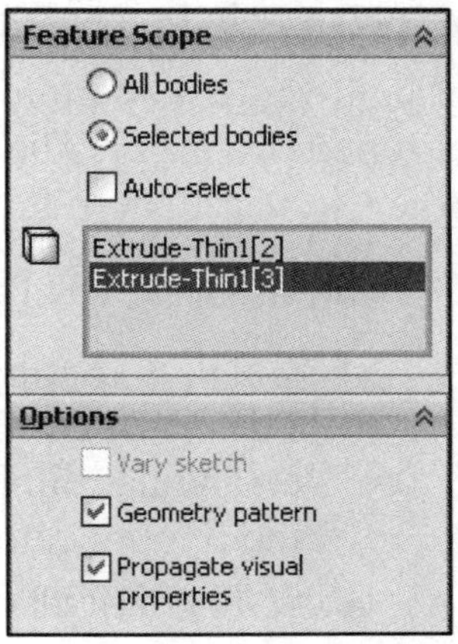


5. Enter **20**mm for Spacing.
6. Enter **9** for Number of Instances.
7. Uncheck **Auto-select** in the Feature Scope box.
8. Check **Selected bodies** in the Feature Scope box.
9. Click the **middle Extrude-Thin 1** feature in the Graphics window. Extrude-Thin1[2] is displayed in the Feature Scope box.
10. Click the **right Extrude-Thin1** feature in the Graphics window. Extrude-Thin1[3] is displayed in the Feature Scope box.

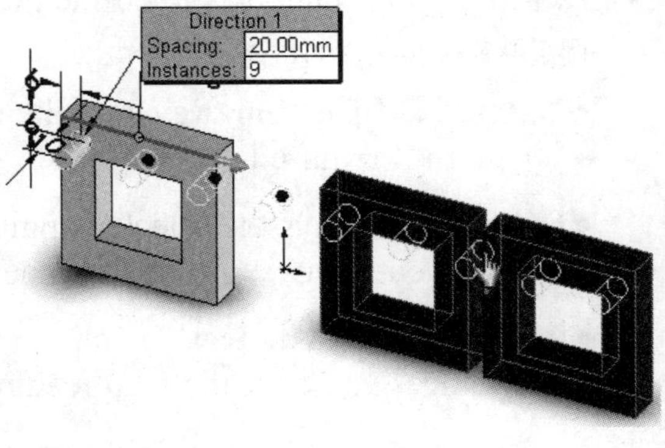


11. Check **Geometry pattern** in the Options box.
12. **Expand** the Instances to Skip box.
13. Select **(7,1)** from the Graphics window. (7,1) is displayed in the Instances to Skip box.
14. Click **OK** from the Linear Pattern PropertyManager. LPattern1 is displayed. View the results.
15. **Close** the model.

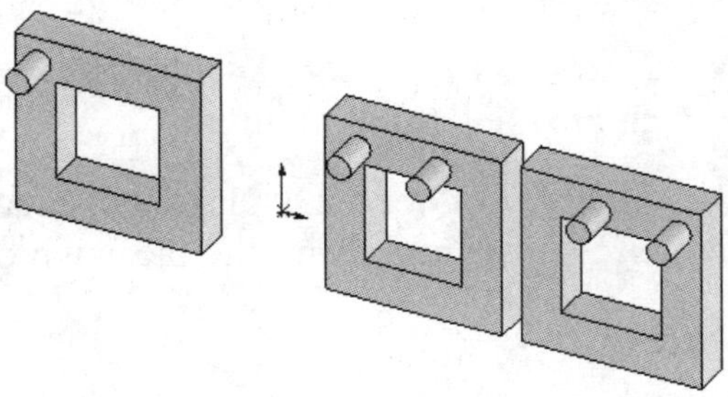

## Circular Pattern Feature

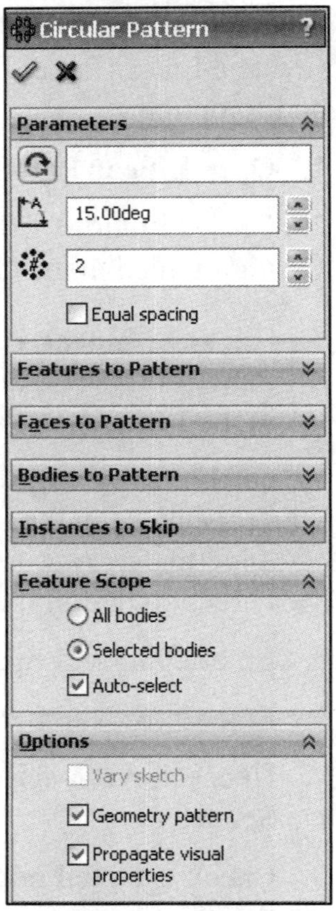


The Circular Pattern feature provides the ability to create copies, or instances in a circular pattern. The Circular Pattern feature is controlled by a center of rotation, an angle, and the number of copies selected. The instances are dependent on the original. Changes to the originals are passed to the instanced features.

To create a Circular Pattern, select the features and an axis or edge as the center of rotation. Specify the total number of instances and the angular spacing between instances or the total number of instances and the total angle in which to create the circular pattern.

The Circular Pattern feature uses the Circular Pattern PropertyManager. The following selections are available from the Circular Pattern PropertyManager:

- ***Parameters***. The Parameters box provides the following options:
  - **Pattern Axis**. Displays the selected axis, model edge, or an angular dimension from the Graphics window or from the flyout FeatureManager. The circular pattern is created around the selected axis.

Axes are types of Reference Geometry that can be used with various Pattern features to define their direction or rotational axes.

  - **Reverse Direction**. Reverses the direction of the circular pattern if required.
  - **Angle**. Displays the selected angle value, in 1deg increments between each instance.
  - **Number of Instances**. Displays the selected number of instances value for the seed feature.
  - **Equal spacing**. Sets spacing equal between each Circular Pattern instance.
- ***Features to Pattern***. Displays the selected seed feature from the Graphics window to create the Circular Pattern.
- ***Faces to Pattern***. Displays the selected faces from the Graphics window to create the circular pattern using the faces which composes the feature.

The Faces to Pattern option is very useful with models that import only the faces that compose the feature, and not the total feature itself.

When using the Faces to Pattern option, your pattern must remain within the same face or boundary. It cannot cross boundaries. Example: a cut across the complete face or different levels, such as a raised edge would create a boundary and separate faces, stopping the pattern from spreading.

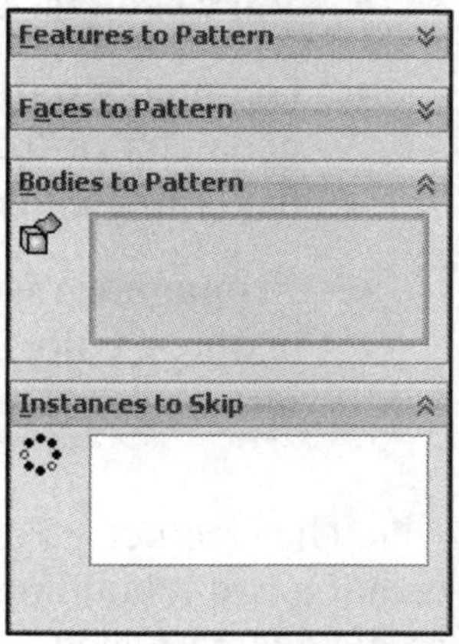


- ***Bodies to Pattern***. Displays the selected multi-body parts to create the pattern using bodies.
- ***Instances to Skip***. Display the selected instances coordinates from the Graphics window which you want to skip in the circular pattern. The mouse pointer changes when you float over each pattern instance. To restore a pattern instance, click the instance again.
- ***Feature Scope***. Applies features to one or more multi-body parts. Check the Geometry pattern box under the Options section of the Circular Pattern PropertyManager. Use this option to choose which bodies should include the feature. The following options are:

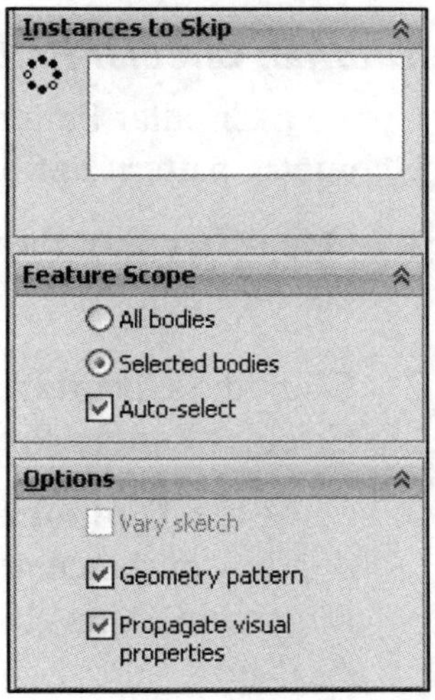


  - **All bodies**. Applies the feature to all bodies, each time the feature is regenerated. If a new body is added to your model that is intersected by a feature, the new body is also regenerated to include that feature.
  - **Selected bodies**. Selected by default. Applies a feature to the body that is selected. If a new body is added, to your model which is intersected by the feature, you are required to use the Edit Feature command to edit the pattern features. Select the bodies, and add them to the list of your selected bodies.
  - **Auto-select**. Only available if you click the Selected bodies option. With the Auto-select option activated, when you first create a model with multi-body parts, the features automatically process all the relevant intersecting parts.

The Auto-select option is faster than the All bodies option because the Auto-select option processes only the bodies on the initial list, and does not regenerate your entire model.

- **Bodies to Affect**. Only available if you un-check the Auto-select option. Affects only the selected bodies from the Graphics window.

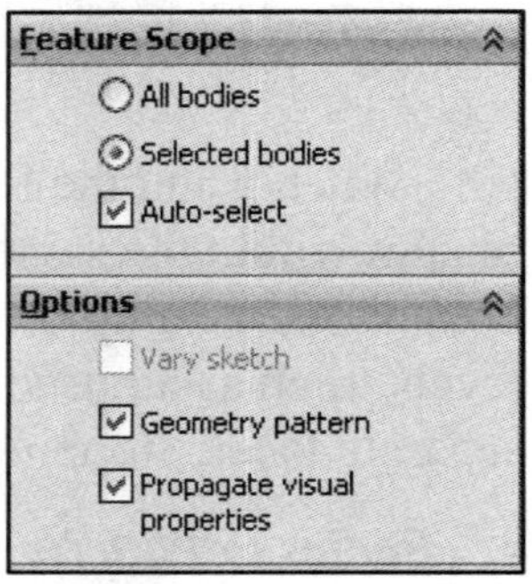


- ***Options***. The Options box provides two selections. They are:
  - **Vary sketch**. Allows the pattern to change as it repeats.
  - **Geometry pattern**. Creates the pattern using only the geometry of face and edge of the feature, rather than patterning and resolving each instance of the feature.
  - **Propagate Visual Properties**. Propagates SolidWorks textures, colors, and cosmetic thread data to all pattern instances.

The Geometry Pattern option speeds up the creation and rebuilding of the pattern. You cannot create geometry patterns of features that have faces merged with the rest of the part

***Tutorial: Circular Pattern 9-1***

Create a Circular Pattern feature not using the Geometry pattern option.

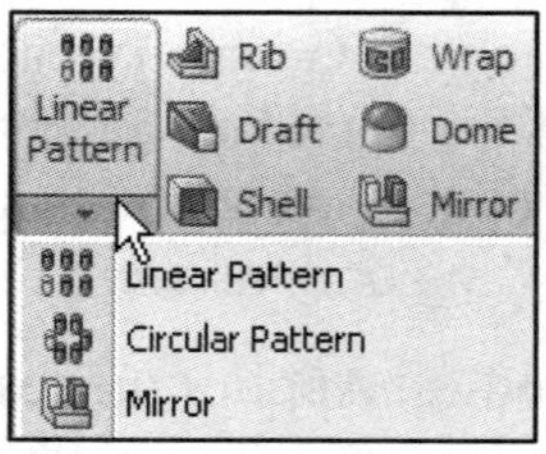

1. Open **Circular Pattern 9-1** from the SolidWorks 2010 folder.
2. Click the **Circular Pattern** Features tool. The Circular Pattern PropertyManager is displayed.
3. Click the **Temporary Axis** from the Graphics window at the center of the Hexagon as illustrated. Axis<1> is displayed in the Pattern Axis box.

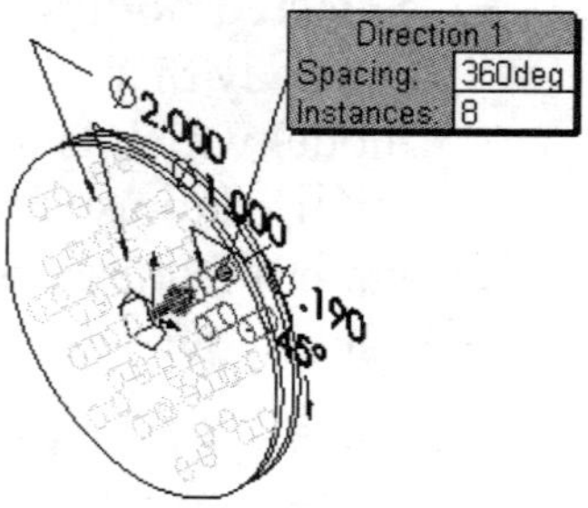


4. Check the **Equal spacing** box.
5. Enter **360**deg for Angle.
6. Enter **8** for Number of Instances.
7. Click inside the **Features to Pattern** box.
8. Click **Cut-Extrude1** and **Cut-Extrude2** for Features to Pattern from the flyout FeatureManager. Note: Cut-Extrude1 and Cut-Extrude2 are your seed features to pattern.
9. Un-check the **Geometry pattern** box.

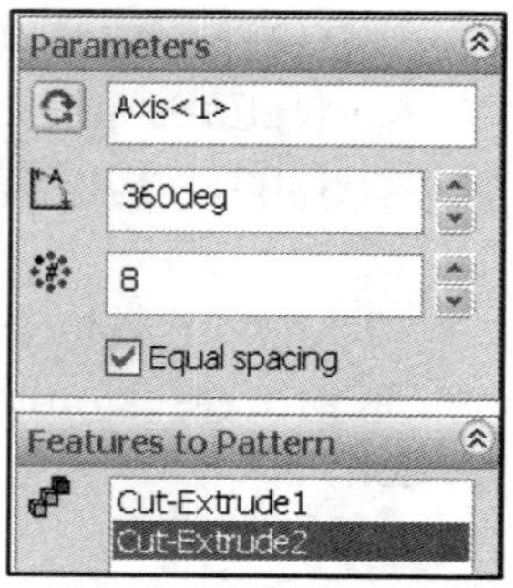

10. **Expand** the Instances to Skip box.

11. Select hole section (**5**) from the Graphics window. (5) is displayed in the Instances to Skip box.

12. Click **OK** ✓ from the Circular Pattern PropertyManager. CirPattern1 is created and is displayed in the FeatureManager.

13. **Close** the model.

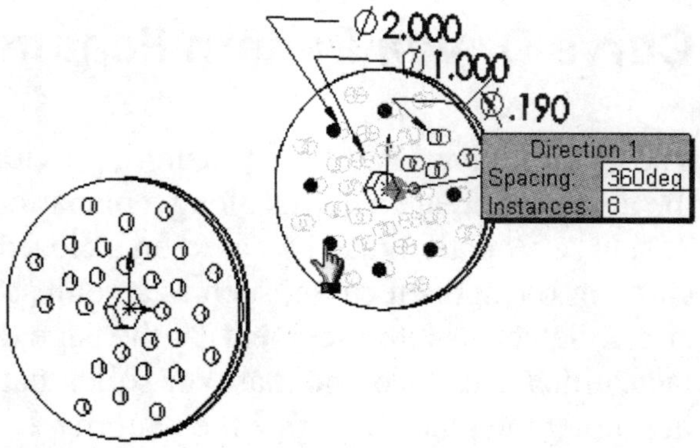


***Tutorial: Circular Pattern Gear 9-1***

Create a Circular Pattern feature using the Faces to Pattern option.

1. Open **Circular Pattern Gear 9-1** from the SolidWorks 2010 folder.

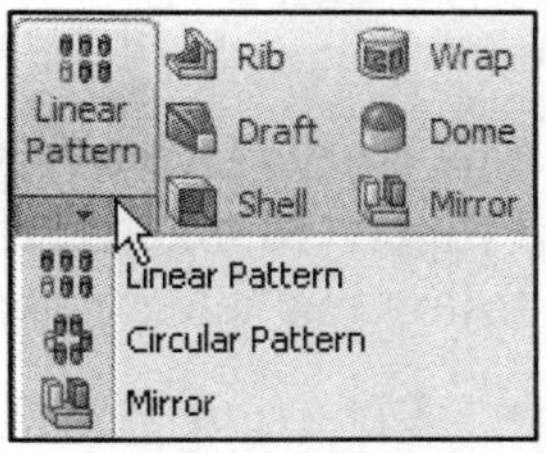


2. Click the **Circular Pattern** Features tool. The Circular Pattern PropertyManager is displayed.

3. Click **Axis2** from the flyout FeatureManager. Axis2 is displayed in the Pattern Axis box.

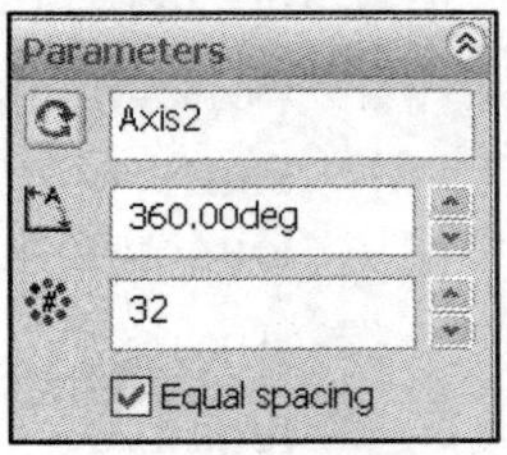


4. Enter **360**deg for Angle.

5. Enter **32** for Number of Instances.

6. Check **Equal spacing**.

7. Click inside the **Faces to Pattern** box.

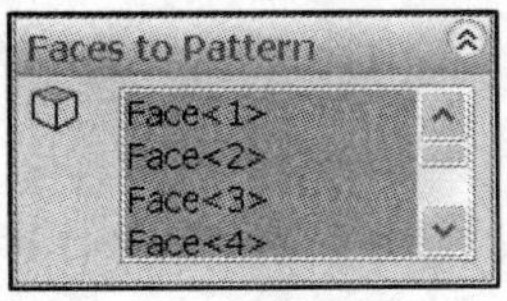


8. Click the **9 faces** of the Gear tooth in the Graphics window as illustrated. The selected faces are displayed in the Faces to Pattern box. The Geometry pattern and Propagate Visual Properties option is selected by default.

9. Click **OK** ✓ from the Circular Pattern PropertyManager. CirPattern1 is displayed. View the model in the Graphics window.

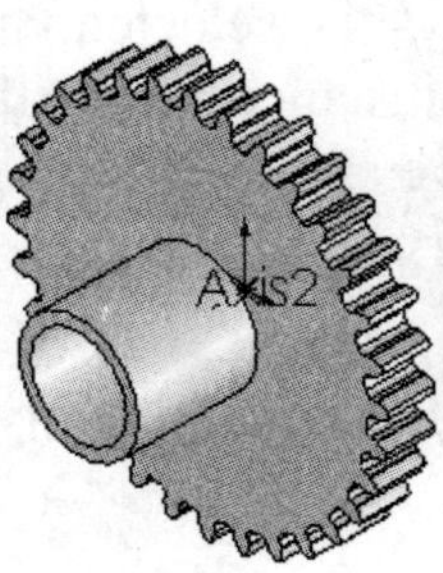


10. **Close** the model.

## Curve Driven Pattern Feature

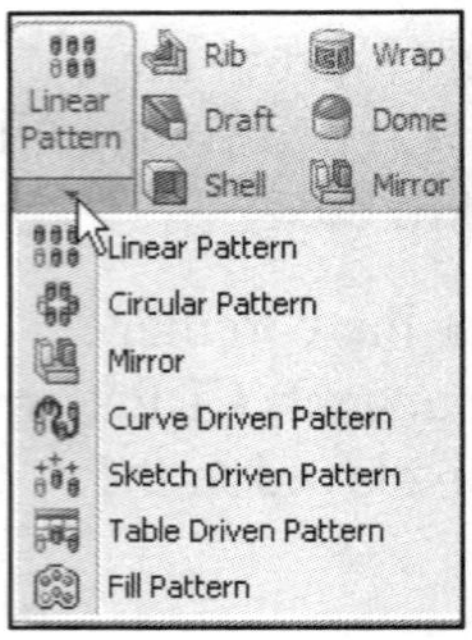


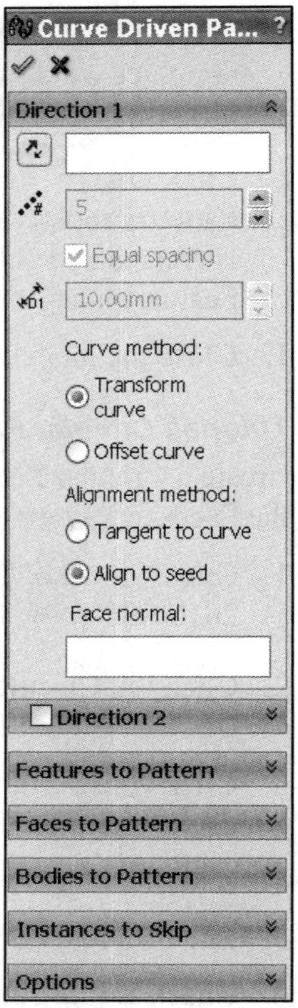


The Curve Driven Pattern feature provides the ability to create patterns along a planar or 3D curve. A pattern can be based on a closed curve or on an open curve, such as an ellipse or circle. Select a sketch segment, or the edge of a face, either a surface, (no mass) or solid, that lies along the plane to define the pattern.

To create a Curve Driven Pattern, select the features and a sketch segment or edge on which to pattern your feature. Then specify the curve type, curve method, and the alignment method.

The Curve Drive Pattern feature uses the Curve Driven Pattern PropertyManager. The Curve Drive PropertyManager provides the following selections:

- ***Direction 1***. The Direction 1 box provides the following feature dependent options:
  - **Pattern Direction**. Displays the selected edge, sketch entity, or curve to use as the path for your pattern in Direction 1.
  - **Reverse Direction**. Reverses the direction of the pattern if required.
  - **Number of Instances**. Displays the selected value for the number of instances of the seed feature in your pattern.
  - **Equal spacing**. Sets spacing equal between each Curve Driven Pattern instance. The separation between instances is depended on the curve that you select from the Pattern Direction box and on the Curve method option.
  - **Spacing**. Displays the selected value for the distance between pattern instances along the curve. The distance between the curve and the Features to Pattern is measured normal to the curve.

The Spacing option is available only if you do not select the Equal spacing option.

  - **Curve method**. Defines the direction of the pattern by transforming how you use the curve selected for the Pattern Direction option box. There are two methods. They are:

   - **Transform curve**. Selected by default. Uses the delta X and delta Y distances from the origin of the selected curve to the seed feature. These distances are maintained for each instance.
   - **Offset curve**. Normal distance from the origin of your selected curve to the seed feature. This distance is maintained for each instance.

- **Alignment method**. Defines the Alignment method for Direction 1. There are three methods:
   - **Tangent to curve**. Aligns each instance tangent to the curve selected for the Pattern Direction option box.
   - **Align to seed**. Selected by default. Aligns each instance to match the original alignment of the seed feature.
   - **Face normal**. Only available for 3D curves. Select the face on which the 3D curve lies to create the Curve Driven pattern.

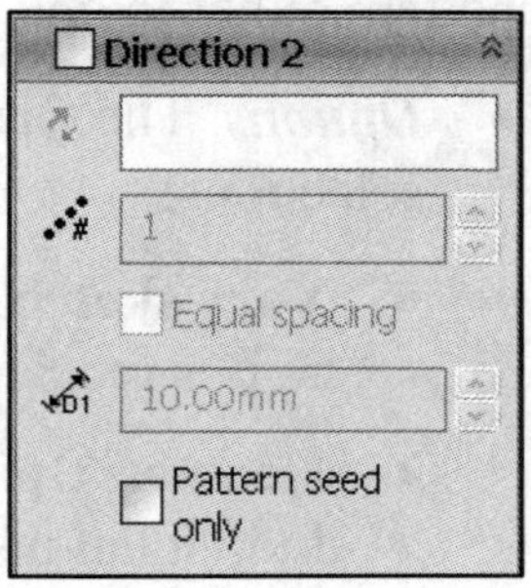


- ***Direction 2***. The Direction 2 box provides the following feature dependent options:

If you select the Direction 2 check box without selecting a sketch element or edge for the Pattern Direction option box from the Direction 2 section, an implicit pattern is created.

The created pattern is based on your selections from the Pattern Direction option under the Direction 1 section.

- **Pattern Direction**. Displays the selected edge, sketch entity, or curve to use as the path for your pattern in Direction 2.
- **Reverse Direction**. Reverses the direction of the pattern.
- **Number of Instances**. Displays the selected value for the number of instances of the seed feature in Direction 2.
- **Equal spacing**. Sets spacing equal between each pattern instance. The separation between instances is depended on the curve that you selected for the Pattern Direction box and on the Curve method option in Direction 2.
- **Spacing**. Displays the selected value for the distance between pattern instances along your curve. The distance between instances depends on the curve selected for the Pattern Direction and on the Curve method option selected under Direction 1.
- **Pattern seed only**. Replicates only the seed pattern. This option creates a curve pattern under Direction 2, without replicating the curve pattern created under the Direction 1 section.

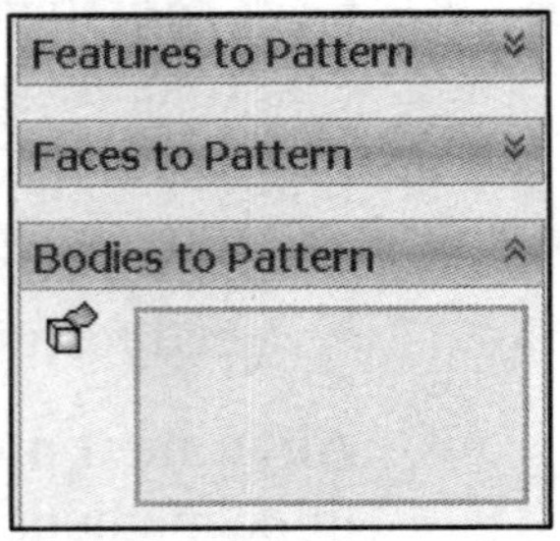


- ***Features to Pattern***. Displays the selected seed feature from the Graphics window.
- ***Faces to Pattern***. Displays the selected faces from the Graphics window. This is a useful option with models that only imports the faces that construct the feature, and not the feature itself.
- ***Bodies to Pattern***. Displays the selected bodies to pattern from the Graphics window for multi-body parts.
- ***Instances to Skip***. Displays the selected pattern instance to skip from the Graphics window. Selected instances are removed from your pattern.

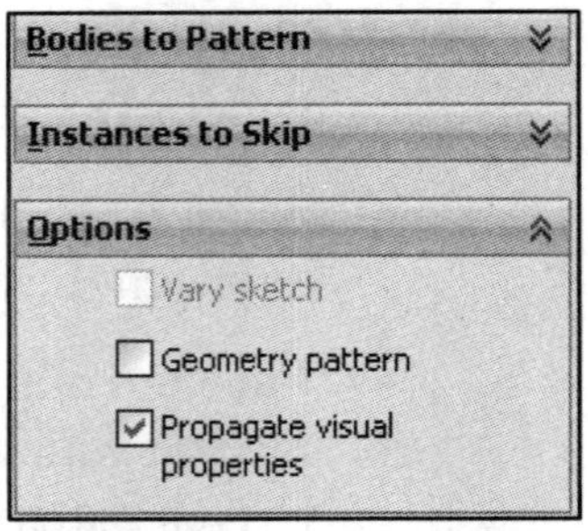


Like other pattern types, such as Linear Pattern or Circular Pattern, you can select and skip pattern instances, and pattern either in one or two directions.

- ***Options***. The Options box provides the following selections:
  - **Vary sketch**. Allows the pattern to change dimensions as it is repeated.
  - **Geometry pattern**. Creates a pattern using an exact copy of the seed feature. Individual instances of the seed feature are not solved. The End conditions and calculations are disregarded.
  - **Propagate Visual Properties**. Propagates SolidWorks colors, cosmetic thread data and textures to all pattern instances.

The Geometry Pattern option speeds up the creation and rebuilding time of a pattern.

### *Tutorial: Curve Driven 9-1*

Create a Curve driven pattern.

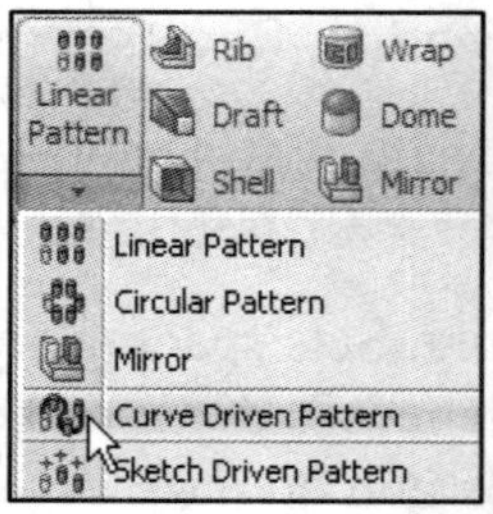


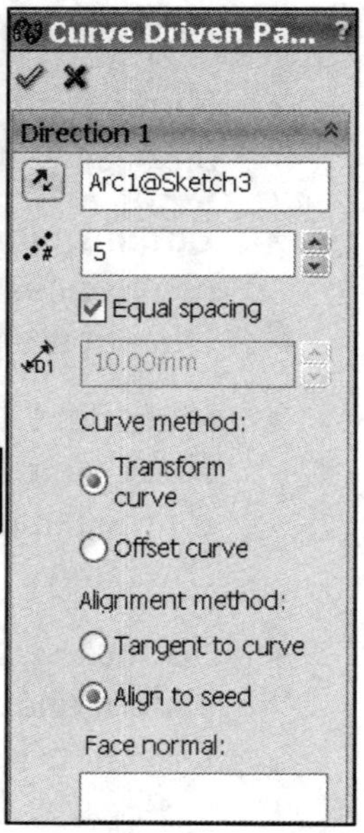


1. Open **Curve Driven 9-1** from the SolidWorks 2010 folder.
2. Click the **Curve Driven Pattern** Features tool.
3. Click the **sketched arc** on Extrude1. Arc1@Shketch3 is displayed in the Pattern Direction box.
4. Enter **5** for Number of Instances.

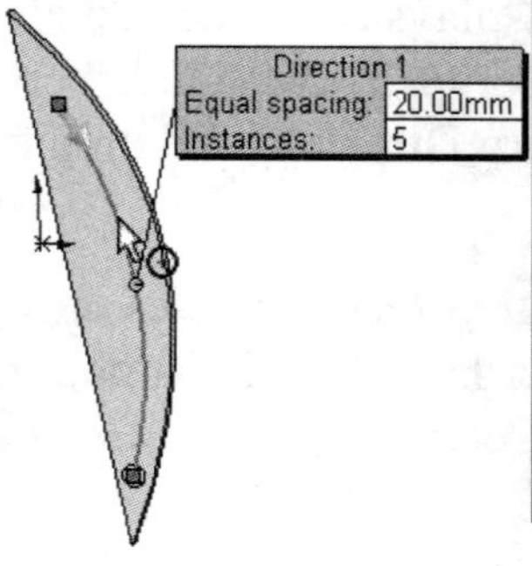

5. Check **Equal spacing**.
6. Click inside of the **Features to Pattern** box.
7. Click **Cut-Extrude1** for the flyout FeatureManager. The Direction arrow points upward. If required, click the Reverse Direction button in the Direction 1 box.
8. Click **OK** from the Curve Driven Pattern PropertyManager. CrvPattern2 is created and is displayed in the FeatureManager.
9. **Close** the model.

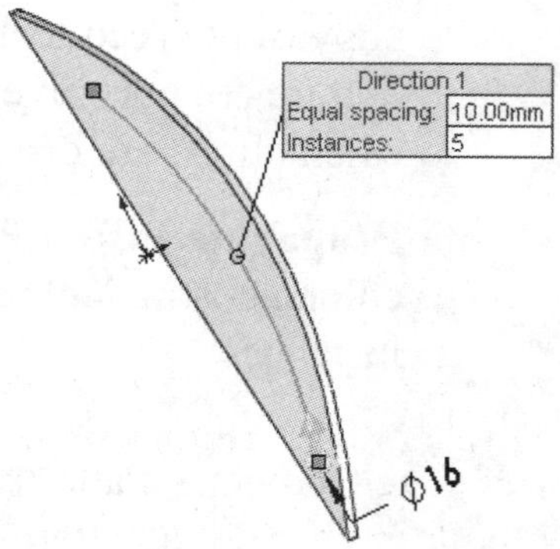


## Sketch Driven Pattern

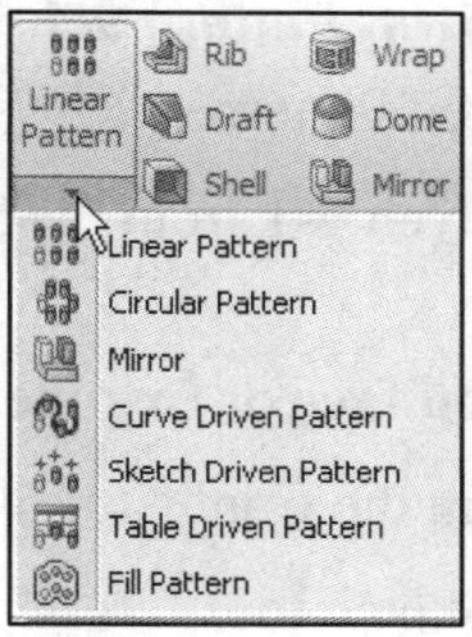


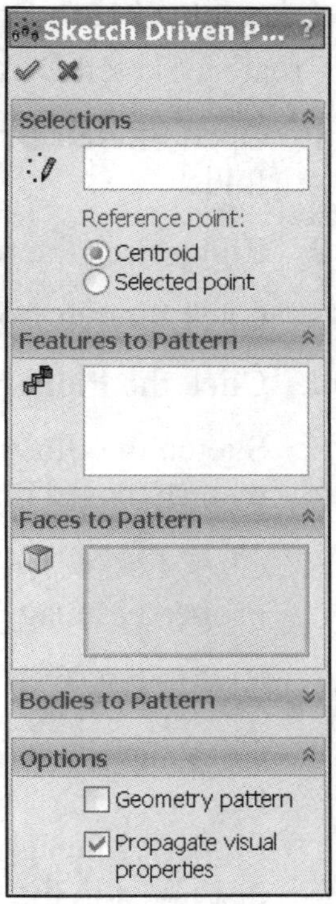


The Sketch Driven Pattern feature provides the ability to use sketch points within a sketch for a pattern. The sketch seed feature propagates throughout the pattern to each point in the sketch pattern. You can use sketch driven patterns for holes or other feature instances.

The Sketch Driven Pattern feature uses the Sketch Driven Pattern PropertyManager. The following selections are available:

- ***Selections***. The Selections box provides the following options:
  - **Reference Status**. Displays the selected sketch entity for the seed feature either from the Graphics window or from the fly-out FeatureManager.
  - **Centroid**. Provides the ability to use the centroid of the seed feature.
  - **Selected point**. Provides the ability to use another point as the reference point.
- ***Features to Pattern***. Displays the selected seed feature from the Graphics window to create the Sketch Driven Pattern.
- ***Bodies to Pattern***. Displays the selected bodies to pattern from the Graphics window for multi-body parts.
- ***Options***. The Options box provides the following selections:

- **Geometry pattern**. Creates a pattern using an exact copy of the seed feature. Individual instances of the seed feature are not solved. The End conditions and calculations are disregarded.
- **Propagate Visual Properties**. Propagates SolidWorks colors, cosmetic thread data and textures to all pattern instances.

The Geometry Pattern option speeds up the creation and rebuilding time of a pattern.

***Tutorial: Sketch Driven Pattern 9-1***

Create a Sketch Driven Pattern.

1. Open **Sketch Driven 9-1** from the SolidWorks 2010 folder.
2. Right-click the **top face** of Extrude1.
3. Click **Sketch** from the Context toolbar.
4. Click the **Point** Sketch tool.
5. Sketch the illustrated **points** to represent a pattern, based on the seed feature.

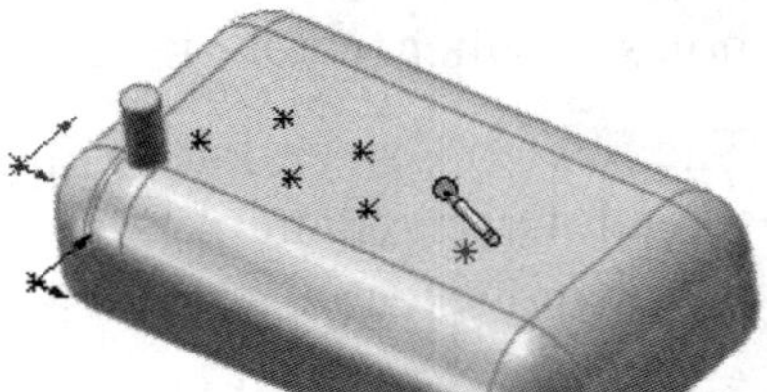

6. Click **OK** from the Point PropertyManager.
7. Right-click **Exit Sketch**.
8. Click the **Sketch Driven Pattern** Features tool. The Sketch Driven Pattern PropertyManager is displayed. Sketch3 is displayed in the Selections box.

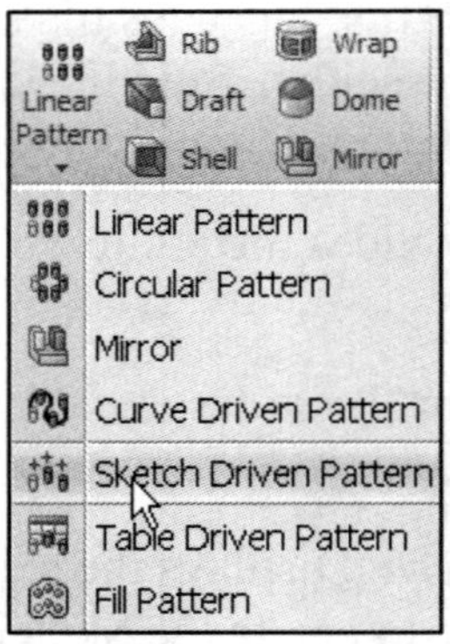


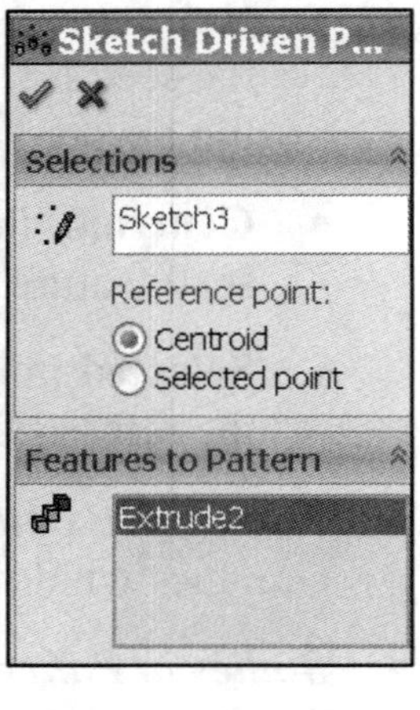


9. Click **inside** the Features to Pattern box.
10. Click **Extrude2** from the fly-out FeatureManager. Extrude2 is your seed feature to pattern!
11. Click **OK** from the Sketch Driven Pattern PropertyManager. Sketch-Pattern1 is displayed. View the results.
12. **Close** the model.

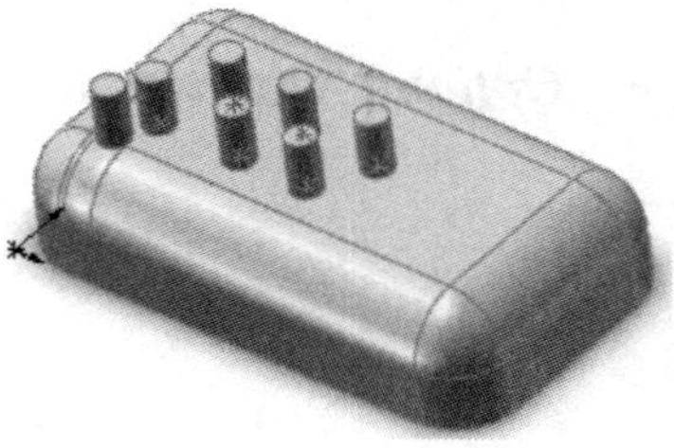

## Table Driven Pattern Feature

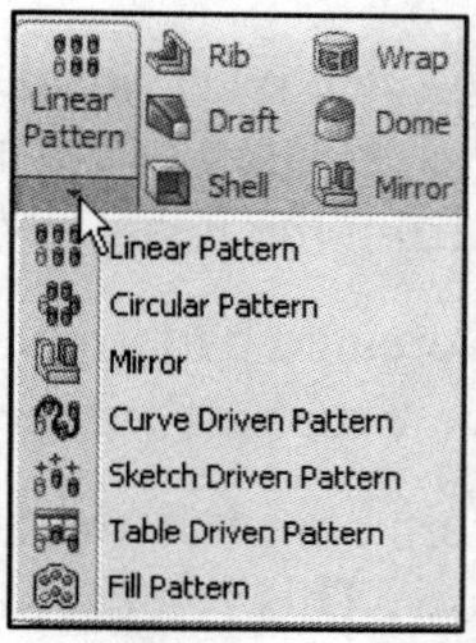


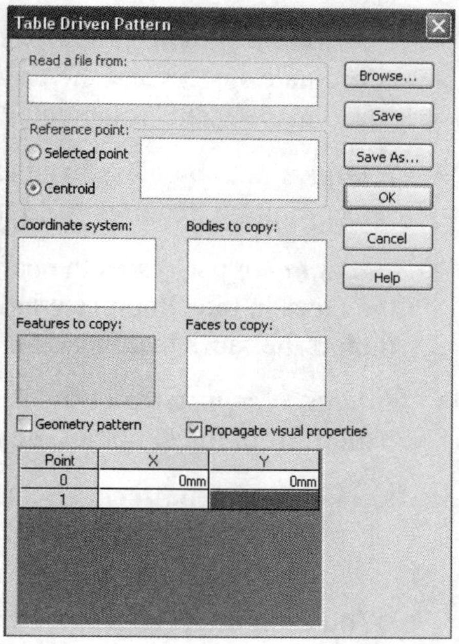


The Table Driven Pattern feature provides the ability to specify a feature pattern using the X-Y coordinates. For a Table Pattern, create a coordinate system or retrieve a previously created X-Y coordinates to populate a seed feature on the face of the model.

The origin of the created or retrieved coordinate system becomes the origin of the table pattern, and the X and Y axis define the plane in which the pattern occurs.

Hole patterns using X-Y coordinates are a frequent application for the Table pattern feature. You can also use other seed features, such as a boss, with your table driven patterns.

The Table Driven Pattern feature uses the Table Driven Pattern dialog box. The Table Driven Pattern dialog box provides the following selections:

Save and load the X-Y coordinates of a feature pattern, and then apply them to a new part later.

- ***Read a file From***: Displays the selected imported pattern table or text file with X-Y coordinates. Click the Browse button on the right side of the Table Driven Pattern dialog box. Select a pattern table (*.sldptab) file or a text (*.txt) file to import into an existing X-Y coordinates.

Text files can only have two columns. A single column for the X coordinate and a single column for the Y coordinate. The two columns must be separated by a delimiter.

- ***Reference point***. Specifies the point to which the X-Y coordinates are applied when placing pattern instances. The X-Y coordinates of the reference point are displayed as Point 0 in the pattern table. There are two available selections:
  - **Selected point**. Sets the reference point to the selected vertex or sketch point.

- **Centroid**. Sets the reference point to the centroid of the seed feature.

- ***Coordinate system***. Display the selected coordinate system, including the origin. The coordinate system and the origin are used to create the table pattern. Select the coordinate system you created from the FeatureManager design tree.
- ***Features to copy***. Displays the created pattern based on the selected features. You can select multiple features from the Graphics window.
- ***Faces to copy***. Creates the pattern based on the faces that make up the feature. Select the faces in the Graphics window. This is a useful option with models that only import the faces that make up the feature, and not the feature itself.
- ***Bodies to copy***. Creates the pattern based on multi-body parts. Select the bodies to pattern from the Graphics window.
  - **Geometry pattern**. Creates the pattern only using the geometry, edges and faces of the features. It does not use pattern and solve each instance of the feature.

You cannot create geometry patterns of features that have faces merged with the rest of the part. The Geometry Pattern option speeds up the creation and rebuilding time of a pattern.

- **Propagate Visual Properties**. Selected by default. Propagates SolidWorks colors, cosmetic thread data, and textures to all pattern instances.
- **X-Y coordinate table**. Creates the location points for the pattern instance using the X-Y coordinates. Double-click the area under Point 0 to enter the X-Y coordinates for each instance of the table pattern. The X-Y coordinates of the reference point are displayed for Point 0.

You can use positive or negative coordinates. To enter a negative coordinate, precede the value with a minus (-).

## Coordinate System PropertyManager

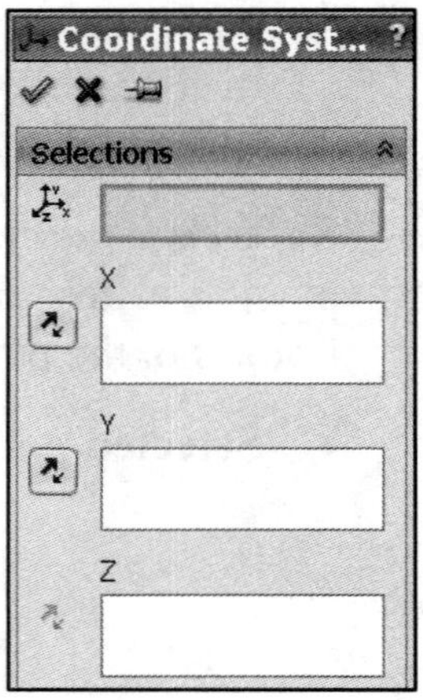


Before you create a Table Driven Pattern, review the Coordinate System PropertyManager. The Coordinate System PropertyManager is displayed when you add a new coordinate system to a part or assembly or when you edit an existing coordinate system. The Coordinate System PropertyManager provides the following selections:

- *Selections*. The Selections box provides the following options:
  - **Origin**. Displays the selected vertex, point, midpoint, or the default point of the origin on a part or assembly for the coordinate system origin.
  - **X axis**. Displays the selected X axis for the Axis Direction Reference. The available options are:
    - **Midpoint**, **vertex**, or **point**. Aligns the axis toward the selected point.
    - **Sketch line** or **linear edge**. Aligns the axis parallel to the selected edge or line.
    - **Sketch entity** or **Non-linear edge**. Aligns the axis toward the selected location on the selected entity.
    - **Planar face**. Aligns the axis in the normal direction of the selected face.
    - **Reverse Axis Direction**. Reverses the direction of an axis if required.
  - **Y axis**. Displays the selected Y axis for the Axis Direction Reference. The available options are:
    - **Midpoint**, **vertex**, or **point**. Aligns the axis toward the selected point.
    - **Sketch line** or **linear edge**. Aligns the axis parallel to the selected edge or line.
    - **Sketch entity** or **non-linear**. Aligns the axis toward the selected location on the selected entity.
    - **Planar face**. Aligns the axis in the normal direction of the selected face.
    - **Reverse Axis Direction**. Reverses the direction of an axis if required.
  - **Z axis**. Displays the selected Z axis for the Axis Direction Reference. The available options are:
    - **Midpoint**, **vertex**, or **point**. Aligns the axis toward the selected point.
    - **Sketch line** or **linear edge**. Aligns the axis parallel to the selected edge or line.
    - **Sketch entity** or **non-linear edge**. Aligns the axis toward the selected location on the selected entity.
    - **Planar face**. Aligns the axis in the normal direction of the selected face.
    - **Reverse Axis Direction**. Reverses the direction of an axis if required.

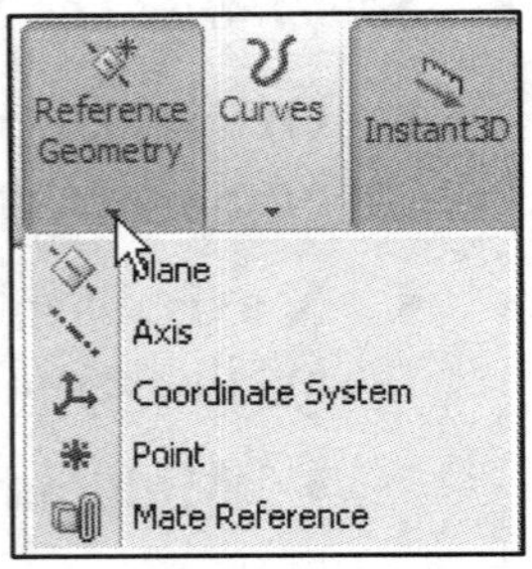


### *Tutorial: Table Driven 9-1*

Create a coordinate system. The origin of the coordinate system becomes the origin of the table pattern. The X and Y axes define the plane in which the pattern occurs. Create a Table Driven Pattern.

1. Open **Table Driven 9-1** from the SolidWorks 2010 folder.
2. Click **Coordinate System** from the Consolidated Reference Geometry Features toolbar. The Coordinate System PropertyManager is displayed.

Create the coordinate system.

3. Click the **bottom left vertex** as illustrated. Vertex<1> is displayed in the Origin box.
4. Click **OK** from the Coordinate System PropertyManager. Coordinate System1 is created and is displayed in the FeatureManager.

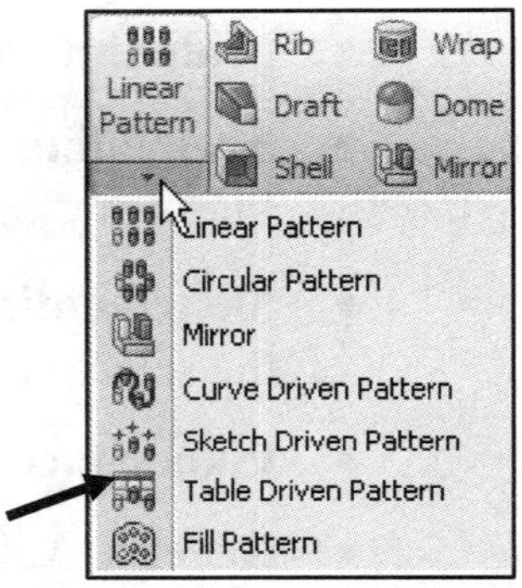


Create a Table Driven pattern.

5. Click the **Table Driven Pattern** Features tool. The Table Driven Pattern dialog box is displayed.
6. Click inside the **Coordinate system** box.
7. Click **Coordinate System1** from the FeatureManager.

Use coordinate systems with the Measure and Mass Properties tools, and for exporting SolidWorks documents to STL, IGES, STEP, ACIS, Parasolid, VRML and VDA.

8. Click inside the **Features to copy** box.
9. Click **Extrude2** from the FeatureManager.

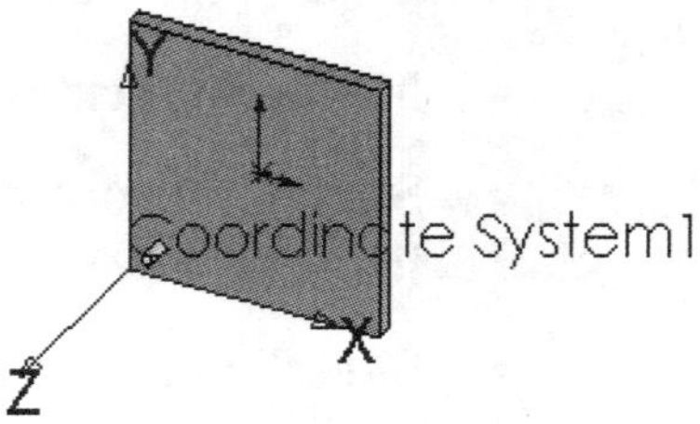

10. Double-click the **white text box** in the X column.
11. Enter **100mm**.
12. Double-click the **white text box** in the Y column.
13. Enter **50mm**.
14. Enter the remaining **X-Y** points as illustrated.
15. Click the **OK** from the Table Driven Pattern dialog box. TPattern1 is created and is displayed in the FeatureManager. View the results.
16. **Close** the model.

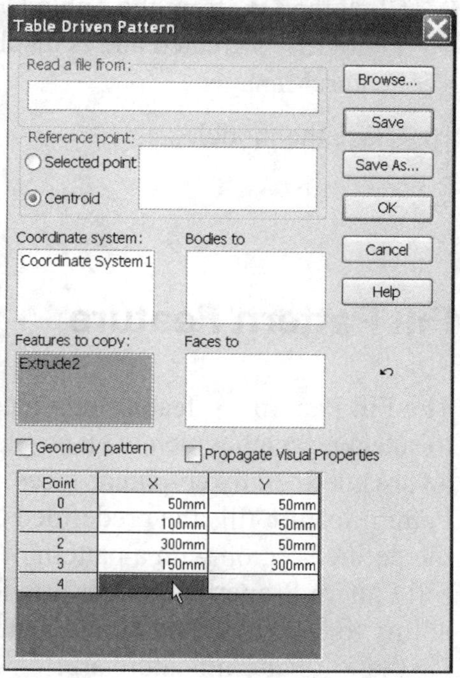


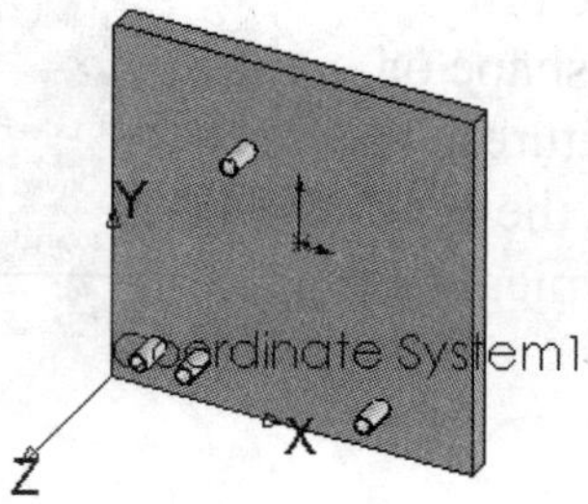


*Tutorial: Table Driven 9-2*

Utilize a SolidWorks Pattern Table data file to create a Table Driven Pattern.

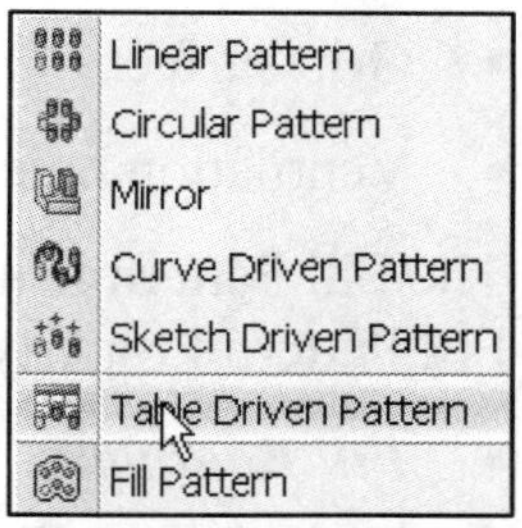


1. Open **Table Driven 9-2** from the SolidWorks 2010 folder.
2. Click the **Table Driven Pattern** Feature tool. The Table Driven Pattern dialog box.
3. Click the **Browse** button from the Table Driven Pattern dialog box.
4. Double-click **PT1.sldptab** from the SolidWorks 2010 folder. The Pattern Table data file contains X-Y coordinates and can be created in Notepad.
5. Click inside the **Coordinate system** box.
6. Click **Coordinate System1** from the FeatureManager.
7. Click inside the **Features to copy** box.
8. Click **Extrude2** from the FeatureManager.

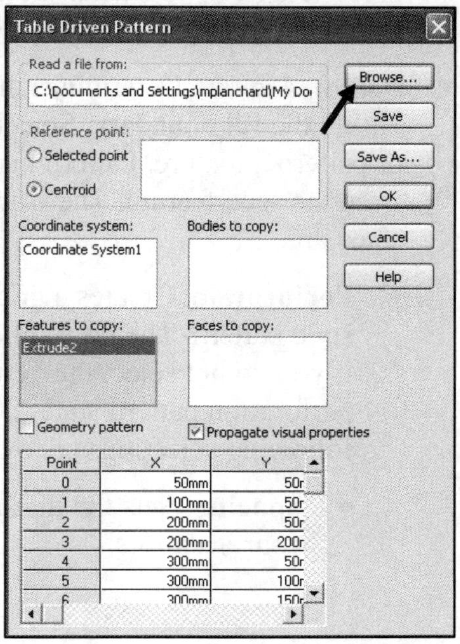

9. Click the **OK** from the Table Driven Pattern dialog box. TPattern1 is created and is displayed in the FeatureManager.
10. **Close** the model.

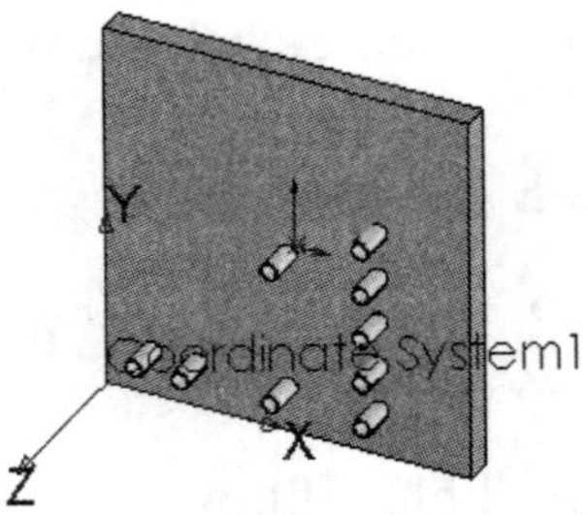


## Fill Pattern Feature

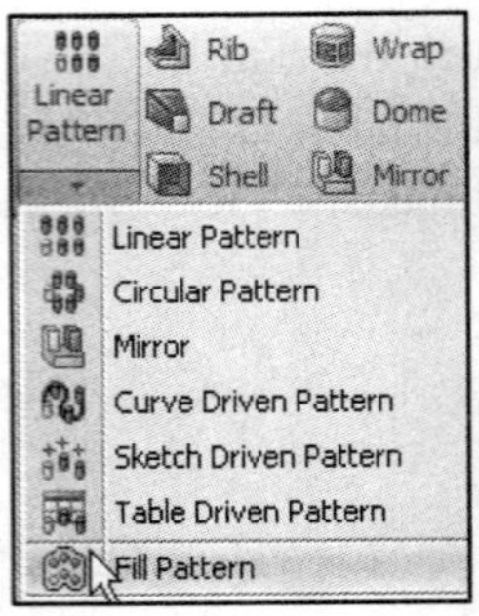


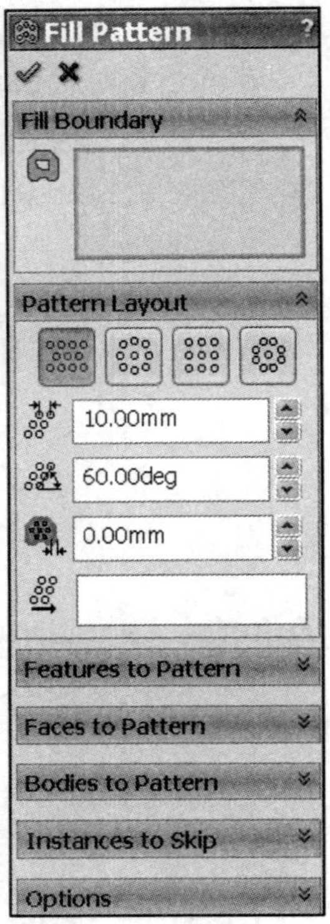


The Fill Pattern feature provides the ability to select a sketch which is on co-planar faces or an area defined by co-planar faces. The Fill Pattern feature fills the predefined cut shape or the defined region with a pattern of features. The Fill Pattern PropertyManager provides the ability to control the pattern layout. Typical uses for the Fill Pattern Feature are:

- Weight reduction
- Grip surfaces
- Ventilation holes

The Fill Pattern feature uses the Fill Pattern PropertyManager. The Fill Pattern PropertyManager provides the following selections:

- ***Fill Boundary***. Displays the selected sketches, planar curves on faces, a face, or co-planar faces. If you use a sketch for the boundary, you may need to select the pattern direction.
- ***Pattern Layout***. Determines the layout pattern of the instances within the fill boundary. Select a customizable shape to pattern, or pattern a feature. Pattern instances are laid out concentrically from the seed feature. There are four Pattern layout selections. They are:
  - **Perforation**. Creates a grid for a sheet metal perforation-style pattern. The perforation pattern is centered on the face if you do not select the vertex. If you select the vertex, the perforation pattern starts from the selected vertex. The following selections are available:
    - **Spacing**. Sets the distance value between the centers of your instances.

- **Stagger Angle**. Sets the stagger angle value between rows of instances, starting at the vector used for your pattern direction.
- **Margins**. Sets the margin value between the fill boundary and your outermost instance.

You can set a value of zero for margins.

- **Pattern Direction**. Displays the selected the direction reference. If you do not specify your reference, the system uses the most appropriate reference. Example: The longest linear edge of the selected region.

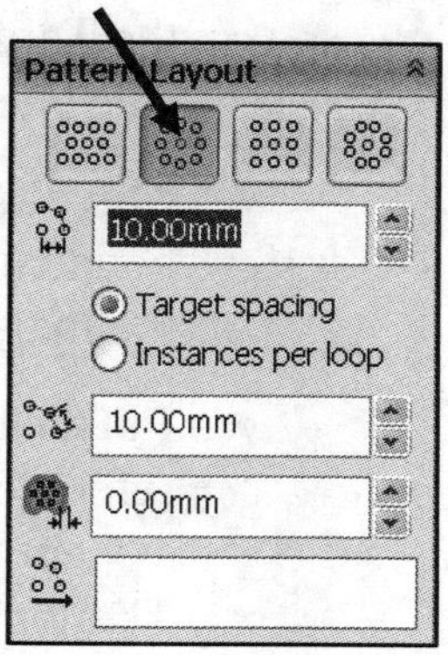


- **Circular**. Creates a circular-shaped pattern. The following selections are available:
  - **Spacing**. Sets the distance between loops of instances using their centers.
  - **Target spacing**. Fills the area using the Spacing option value to set the distance between instances within each loop using their centers. Spacing can vary for each loop.
  - **Instances per loop**. Fills the area using the Number of Instances option per loop.
  - **Instances Spacing**. Sets the distance value between centers of instances within each loop. Check the Target spacing check box. Uncheck the Instances per loop check box.
  - **Number of Instances**. Sets the number value of instances per loop. Check the Instances per loop check box. Uncheck the Target spacing check box.
  - **Margins**. Sets the margin value between the fill boundary and the outermost instance. A zero value for margins can be set.
  - **Pattern Direction**. Displays the selected direction reference. If you do not specify your reference, the system uses the most appropriate reference. Example: The longest linear edge of the selected region.

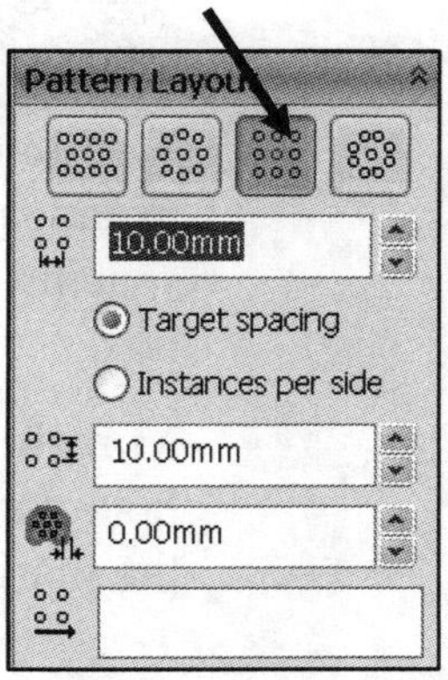


- **Square**. Creates a square-shaped pattern. The following selections are available:
  - **Spacing**. Sets the distance between loops of instances using their centers.

    - **Target spacing**. Fills the area using the Spacing option value to set the distance between instances within each loop using their centers. Spacing can vary for each loop.
    - **Instances per side**. Fills the area using the Number of Instances option per side of each square.
    - **Instances Spacing**. Sets the distance value between centers of instances within each loop. Check the Target spacing check box. Uncheck the Instances per side check box.
    - **Number of Instances**. Sets the number value of instances per loop. Uncheck the Target spacing check box. Check the Instances per side check box.
    - **Margins**. Sets the margin value between the fill boundary and the outermost instance. A value of zero for the margins can be set.
    - **Pattern Direction**. Displays the selected direction reference. If you do not specify your reference, the system uses the most appropriate reference. Example: The longest linear edge of the selected region.

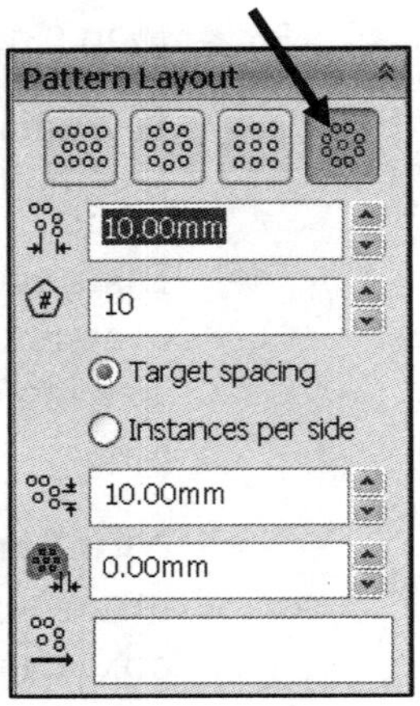


- **Polygon**. Creates a polygonal-shaped pattern. The following selections are available:
    - **Spacing**. Sets the distance between loops of instances using their centers.
    - **Sides**. Sets the number of sides in your pattern.
    - **Target spacing**. Fills the area using Spacing to set the distance between your instances within each loop using their centers. Actual spacing can vary for each loop.
    - **Instances per side**. Fills the area using the Number of Instances option, per side for each polygon.
    - **Instance Spacing**. Sets the distance value between centers of instances within each loop. Check the Target spacing check box. Uncheck the Instances per side check box.
    - **Number of Instances**. Sets the number value of instances per side of each polygon. Uncheck the Target spacing check box. Check the Instances per side check box.
    - **Margins**. Sets the selected margin value between the fill boundary and the outermost instance. A value of zero for the margins can be set.

- **Pattern Direction**. Displays the selected direction reference. If you do not specify your reference, the system uses the most appropriate reference. Example: The longest linear edge of the selected region.

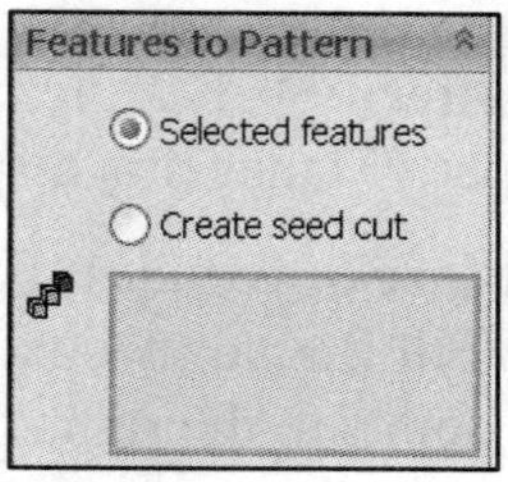


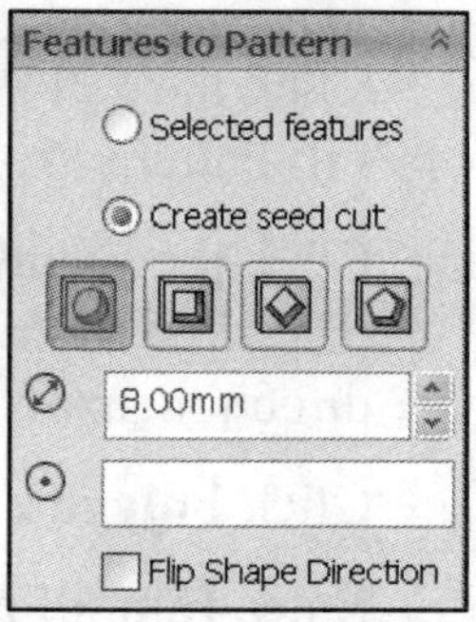


- ***Features to Pattern***. Provides the ability address selected features and predefined cut shapes. The following selections are available:
  - **Selected features**. Provides the ability to select a feature to pattern in the Features to Pattern box.
  - **Create seed cut**. Provides the ability to customize a cut shape for the seed feature to pattern. The predefined cut shapes are: **Circles**, **Squares**, **Diamonds**, **Polygons**.
  - **Flip Shape Direction**. Reverses the direction of the seed feature about the face selected in the Fill Boundary option if required.

If you select a vertex, the shape seed feature is located at the vertex. Otherwise, the seed feature is located at the center of the fill boundary.

- ***Faces to Pattern***. Displays the selected faces which you want to pattern. The selected faces must form a closed body which contacts the fill boundary face.
- ***Bodies to Pattern***. Displays the selected bodies which you want to pattern.
- ***Instances to Skip***. Displays the selected pattern instance to skip from the Graphics window. Selected instances are removed from your pattern.

- ***Options***. The Options box provides the following selections:
  - **Vary sketch**. Allows the pattern to change dimensions as it is repeated.
  - **Propagate Visual Properties**. Propagates SolidWorks colors, textures, and cosmetic thread data to all pattern instances.
  - **Show preview**. Displays a preview in the Graphics window.

***Tutorial: Fill Pattern 9-1***

Create a Fill Pattern feature.

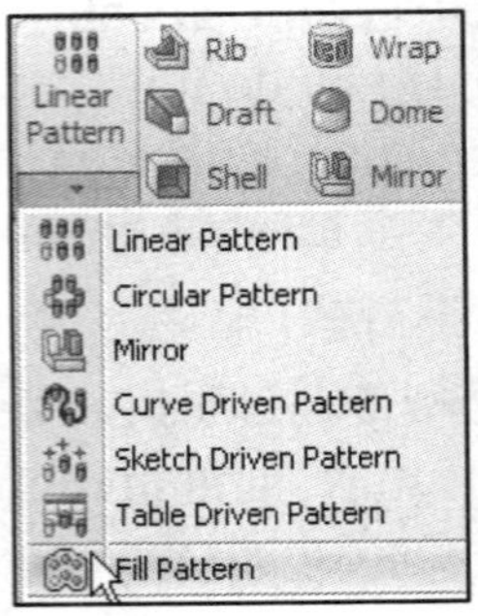


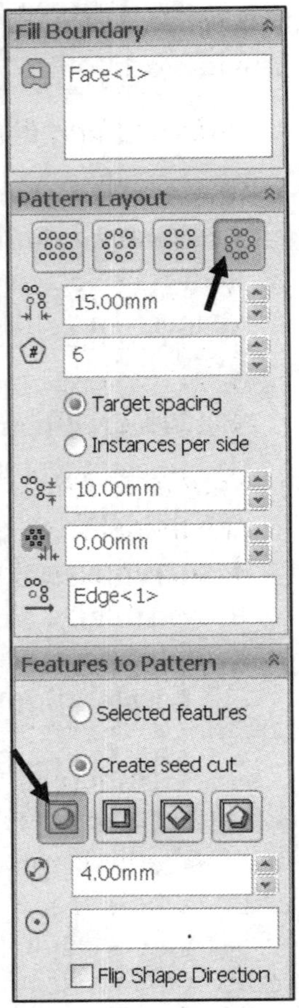


1. Open **Fill Pattern 9-1** from the SolidWorks 2010 folder.
2. Click the **Fill Pattern** Features tool. The Fill Pattern PropertyManager is displayed.
3. Click the **Front face** of Extude1. Face<1> is displayed in the Fill Boundary box. The direction arrow points to the right.
4. Click **Polygon** for Pattern Layout.
5. Enter **15**mm for Loop Spacing.
6. Enter **6** for Polygon sides.
7. Check the **Target spacing** box.
8. Enter **10**mm for Instances Spacing.
9. Click **Create seed cut**.
10. Click **Circle** for Features to Pattern.
11. Enter **4mm** for Diameter.
12. Click **OK** from the Fill Pattern PropertyManager. Fill Pattern1 is created and is displayed in the FeatureManager.
13. **Close** the model.

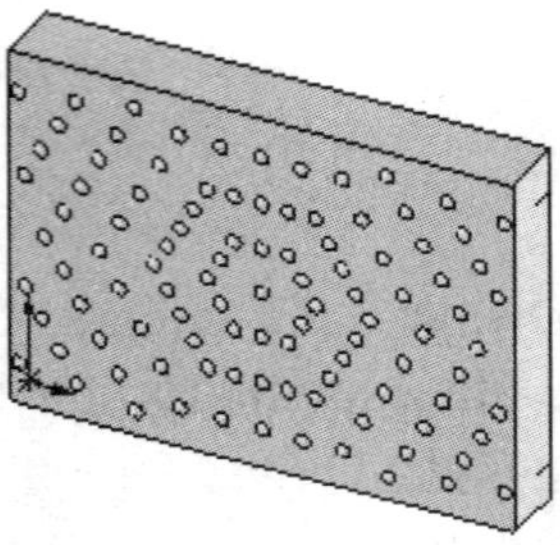

# Mirror Feature

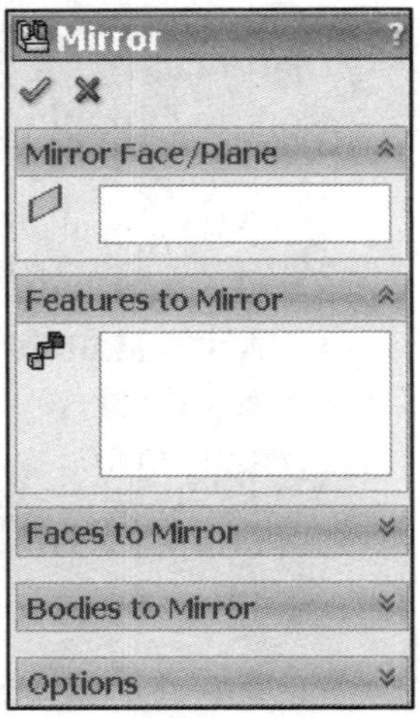


The Mirror feature provides the ability to create a copy of a feature, or multiple features, mirrored about a selected face or plane. The Mirror feature provides the option to either select the feature or select the faces that compose of the feature.

A mirror part creates a mirrored version of an existing part. This is a good way to generate a left-hand version and a right-hand version of a part. The mirrored version is derived from the original version. The two parts always match!

The Mirror feature uses the Mirror PropertyManager. The Mirror PropertyManager provides the following selections:

- ***Mirror Face/Plane***. Displays the selected face or plane from the Graphics window.
- ***Features to Mirror***. Displays the selected features, or a faces to mirror. The Geometry Pattern check box is available when using the Features to Mirror option.
- ***Faces to Mirror***. Displays the selected imported parts where the import process included the selected faces of the feature, but not the feature itself. In the Graphics window, click the faces that make-up the feature you want to mirror. The Geometry Pattern check box is available when using the Faces to Mirror option.
- ***Bodies to Mirror***. Displays the selected entire model. Select the model from the Graphics window or flyout FeatureManager. The mirrored model attaches to the face you selected.

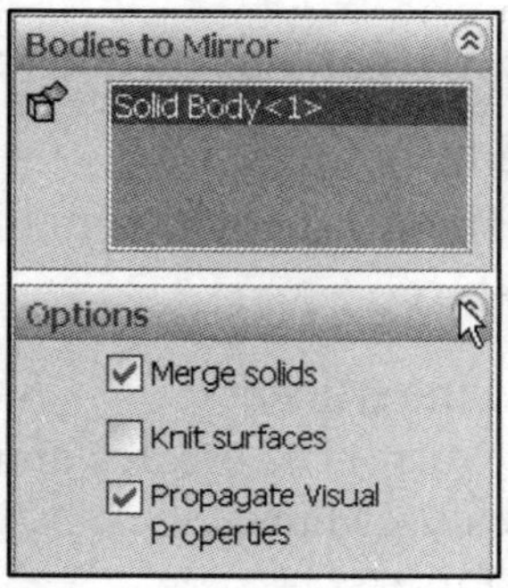


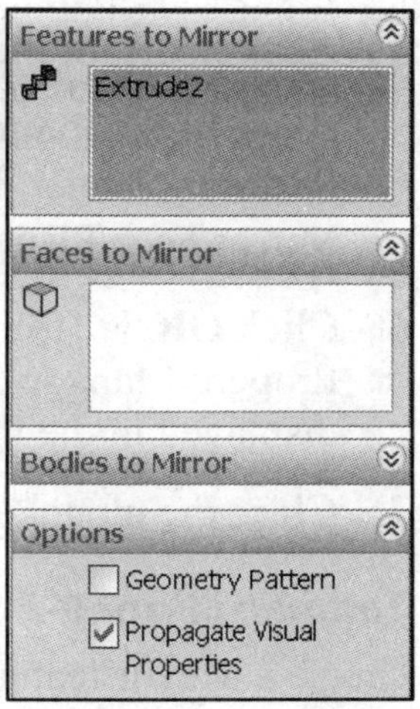


- ***Options***. The Options box provides the following selections:
  - **Geometry Pattern**. Mirrors only the geometry, faces and edges of the features, rather than solving the whole feature.
  - **Propagate Visual Properties**. Mirrors the visual properties of the mirrored entities. Example: Select the Propagate Visual Properties option to propagate SolidWorks colors, textures, and cosmetic thread data to all pattern instances and mirrored features.

If you select the Bodies to Mirror option, the following options are displayed in the Option section:

- **Merge solids**. Creates a mirrored box that is attached to the original body, but is a separate entity. You need to select a face on a solid part, and then clear the Merge solids option check box. If you select the Merge solid option check box, the original part and the mirrored part become a single entity.

- **Knit surfaces**. Provides the ability to knot two surfaces together. Select to mirror a surface by attaching the mirror face to the original face without intersections or gaps between the surfaces.

***Example: Mirror 9-1***

Create a Mirror feature. Mirror an existing rib to increase structural integrity.

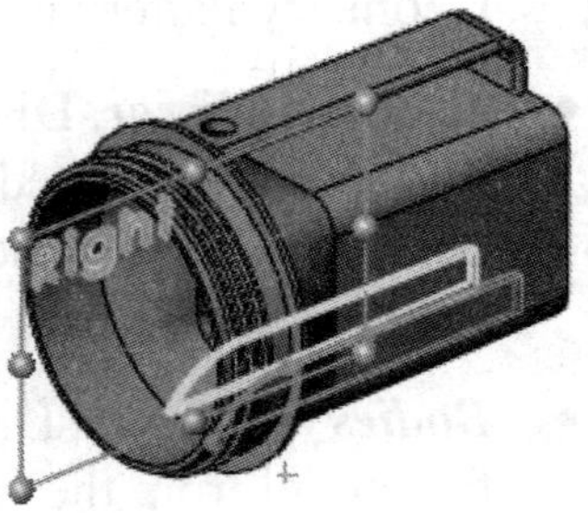


1. Open **Mirror 9-1** from the SolidWorks 2010 folder.
2. Click **Rib2** from the FeatureManager.
3. Click the **Mirror** Features tool. The Mirror PropertyManager is displayed. Rib2 is displayed in the Features to Mirror box.
4. Click inside of the **Mirror Face/Plane** box.
5. Click **Right Plane** from the flyout FeatureManager. Right is displayed in the Mirror Face/Plane box.
6. Click **OK** from the Mirror PropertyManager. Mirror1 is creates and is displayed in the FeatureManager.
7. **Close** the model.

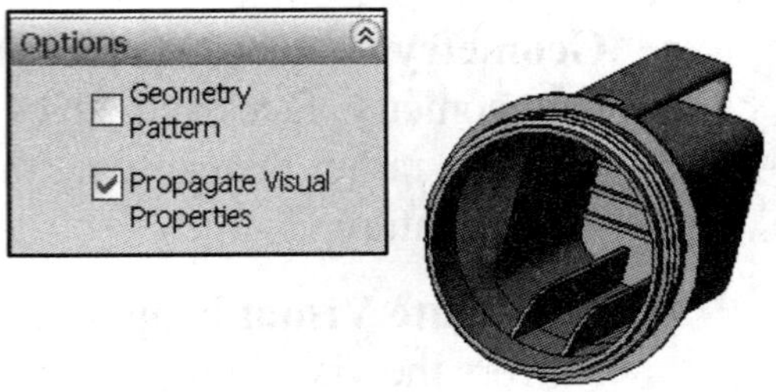


***Tutorial: Mirror 9-2***

Create a Mirror feature using the Geometric Pattern option.

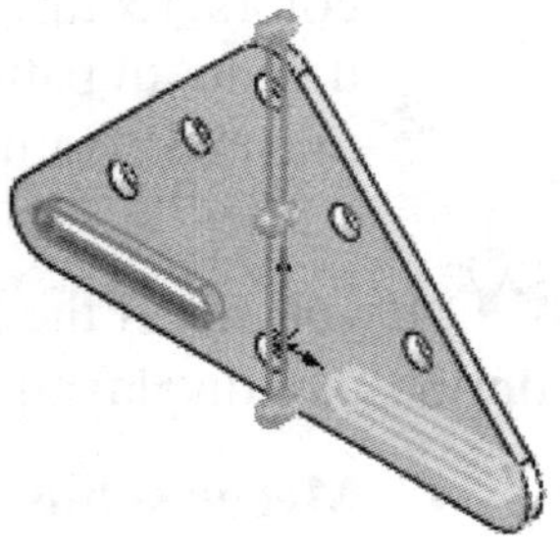

1. Open **Mirror 9-2** from the SolidWorks 2010 folder. Mirror an existing extruded cut feature.
2. Click **Cut-Extrude2** from the FeatureManager.
3. Click the **Mirror** Features tool. The Mirror PropertyManager is displayed. Cut-Extrude2 is displayed in the Features to Mirror box.
4. Click inside of the **Mirror/Face/Plane** box.
5. Click **Right Plane** from the FeatureManager.
6. Click the **Geometry Pattern** check box.
7. Click **OK** from the Mirror PropertyManager. Mirror1 is creates and is displayed in the FeatureManager.

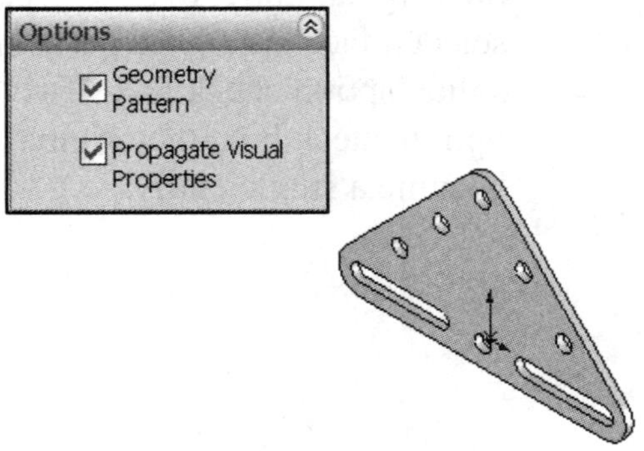

8. **Close** the model.

# Summary

In this chapter, you learned about the Pattern and Mirror Features in SolidWorks. The Linear Pattern feature provides the ability to create copies, or instances, along one or two linear paths in one or two different directions. The instances are dependent on the selected originals.

The Circular Pattern feature provides the ability to create copies, or instances in a circular pattern. The Circular Pattern feature is controlled by a center of rotation, an angle, and the number of copies selected. The instances are dependent on the original.

The Curve Driven Pattern feature provided the ability to create patterns along a planar or 3D curve. A pattern can be based on a closed curve or on an open curve, such as an ellipse or circle.

The Sketch Driven Pattern feature provided the ability to use sketch points within a sketch for a pattern. The sketch seed feature propagates throughout the pattern to each point in the sketch pattern. You can use sketch driven patterns for holes or other feature instances.

The Table Pattern feature provided the ability to specify a feature pattern using the X-Y coordinates. For a Table Pattern, create a coordinate system or retrieve a previously created X-Y coordinates to populate a seed feature on the face of the model. The origin of the created or retrieved coordinate system becomes the origin of the table pattern, and the X and Y axes define the plane in which the pattern occurs.

The Fill Pattern feature provided the ability to select a sketch which is on co-planar faces or an area defined by co-planar faces. The Fill Pattern feature fills the predefined cut shape or the defined region with a pattern of features.

The Mirror feature provided the ability to create a copy of a feature, or multiple features, mirrored about a selected face or plane. The Mirror feature provides the option to either select the feature or select the faces that compose of the feature.

A mirror part created a mirrored version of an existing part. This is a good way to generate a left-hand version and a right-hand version of a part. The mirrored version is derived from the original version. The two parts always match.

In Chapter 10, explore and address the Swept Boss/Base, Swept Cut, Lofted Boss/Base, Lofted Cut, Wrap and Flex Features in SolidWorks.

## Notes:

# Chapter 10: Swept, Loft, Wrap and Flex Features

## Chapter Objective

Chapter 10 provides a comprehensive understanding of the Swept, Loft, Wrap and Flex features with a general overview of the Flex PropertyManager in SolidWorks. On the completion of this chapter, you will be able to:

- Understand and utilize the following Swept features:
  - Swept Base with various options
  - Swept Boss with Helix/Spiral
  - Swept Thin with options
  - Swept Cut with options
- Understand and utilize the following Loft features:
  - Lofted Boss/Base with options
  - Lofted Cut with options
  - Adding a Loft Section
- Apply the Wrap feature
- Understand the Flex PropertyManager

## Swept Feature

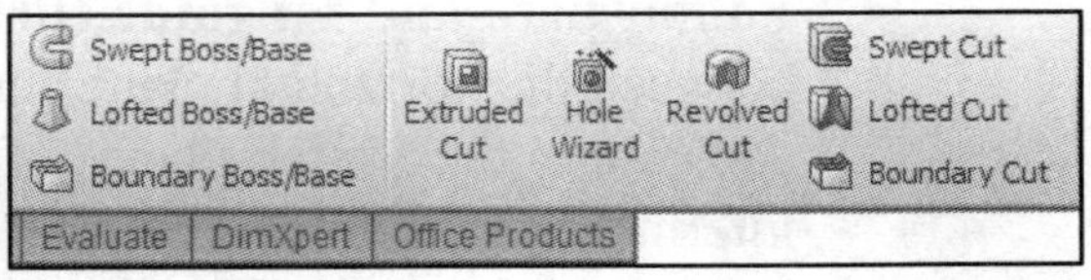


A Swept feature creates a base, boss, cut, or surface by moving a profile along a path. There are a few rules that you should know when creating a Swept feature: **1.)** *The path can be open or closed.* **2.)** *The start point of the path is required to be on the plane of the profile.* **3.)** *A closed profile is required for a Base or Boss Swept feature. The profile can be closed or open for a Surface Swept feature.* **4.)** *The path can be a set of sketched curves contained in a curve, a single sketch, or a set of edges.* **5.)** *The section, the path, nor the resulting solid can be self-intersecting.*

Example of a simple Swept Base feature. Note: The Path and Profile are on different planes.

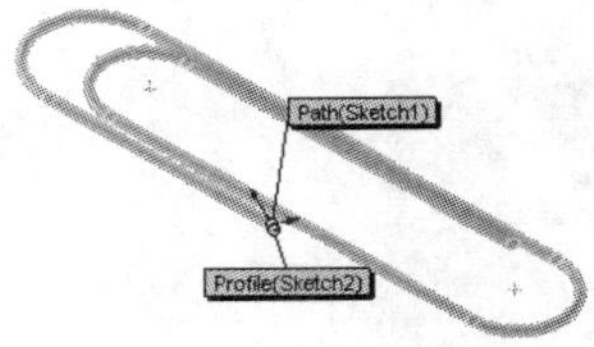

## Swept Boss/Base Feature

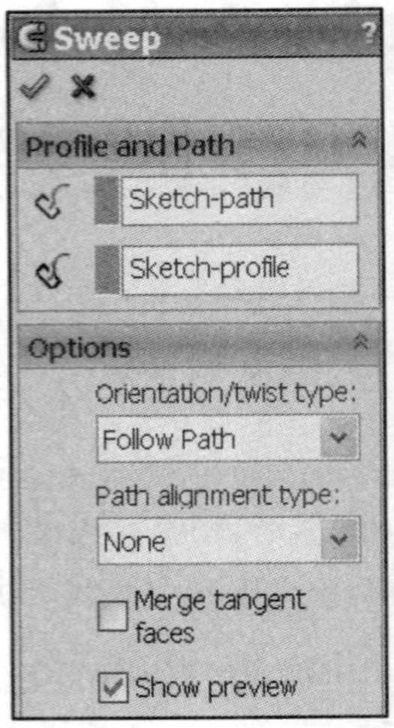


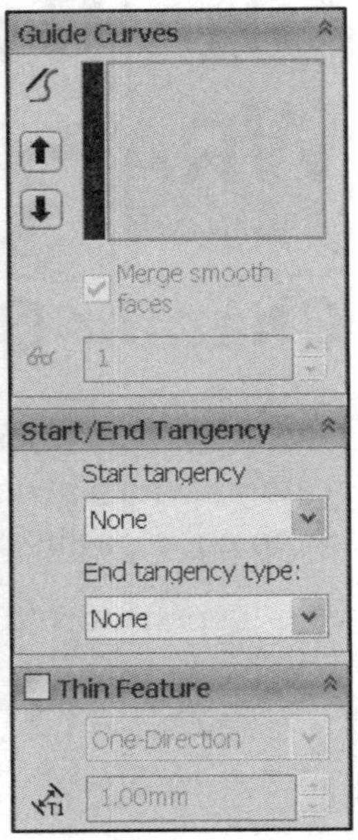


The Swept Boss/Base feature uses the Sweep PropertyManager. The Sweep PropertyManager provides the following selections:

- ***Profile and Path***. The Profile and Path box provides two selections. They are:
  - **Profile**. Displays the selected sketch profile or section from the Graphics window or FeatureManager.
  - **Path**. Displays the selected path along which the profile sweeps from the Graphics window or FeatureManager.
- ***Options***. The Options box provides the following feature dependent selections:

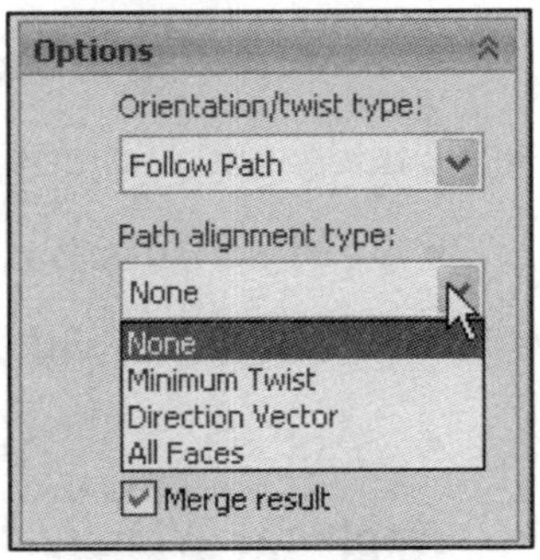


  - **Orientation/twist type**. Provides the ability to select one of six types to control the orientation of the Profile as it sweeps along the Path. The Type options are:
    - **Follow Path**. Selected by default. The section remains at the same angle with respect to the path at all times. Options for Path alignment type are: *None, Minimum, Twist, Direction Vector, and All Faces.*
    - **Keep normal constant**. The section remains parallel to the beginning section at all times. The available options are: *Merge tangent faces, show preview and Merge result.*

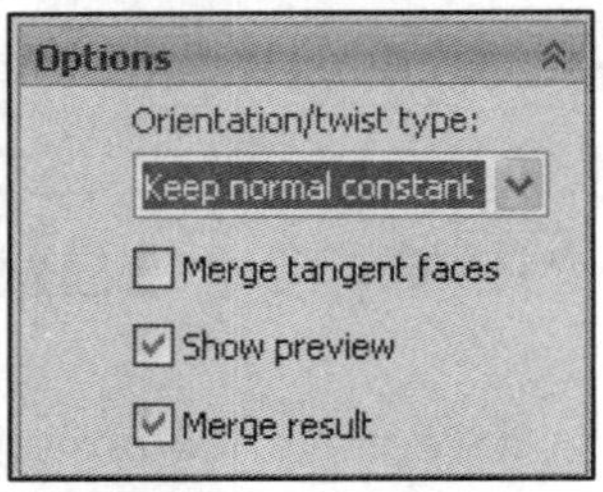


    - **Follow path and 1st guide curve**. The angle between the horizontal plane and the vector remains constant in the Sketch planes of all of the intermediate sections. The twist of the intermediate sections is determined by the vector from the path to the first guide curve.
    - **Follow 1st and 2nd guide curves**. The twist of the intermediate section is determined by the vector from the first to the second guide curve.

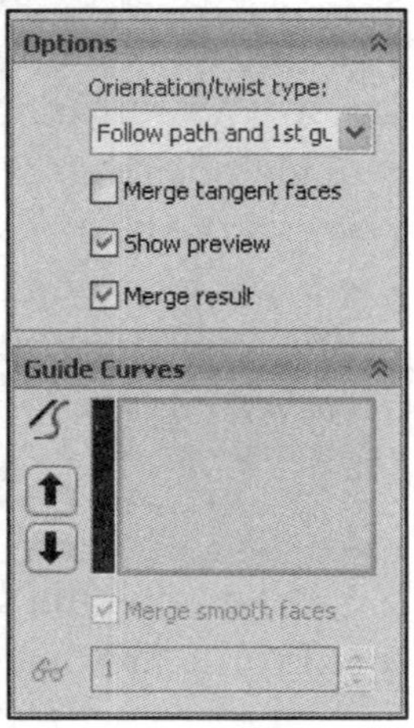

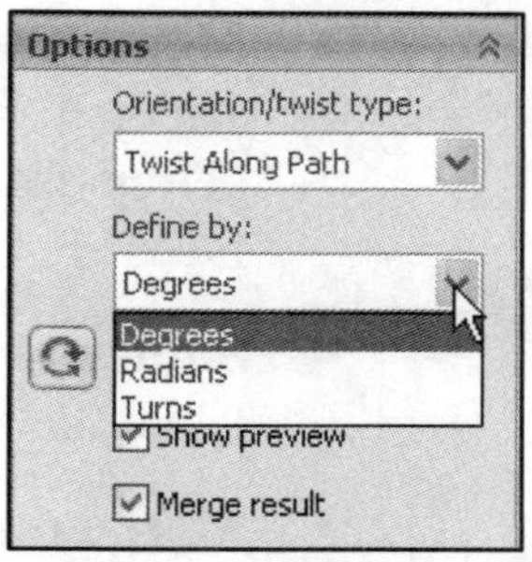


- **Twist Along Path**. Twists the section along the path. Defines the twist by *degrees, radians or turns* in the Define by section. Enter the required value.
- **Twist Along Path With Normal Constant**. Twists the section along the selected path. This option keeps the section parallel to the beginning section as it twists along the path. Defines the twist by *degrees, radians or turns* in the Define by section.

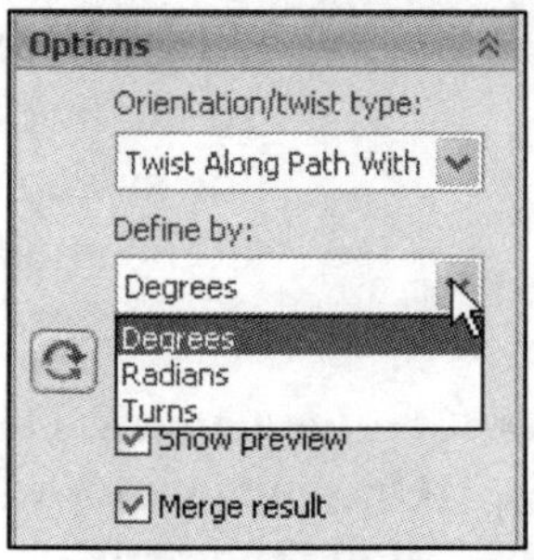


- **Define by**. Only available when either the Twist Along Path or Twist Along Path With Normal Constant type is selected. The Define by option provides two selections:
  - **Twist definition**. Defines the twist. Select *degrees, radians or turns*.
  - **Twist angle**. Sets the number of *degrees, radians or turns* in the twist.

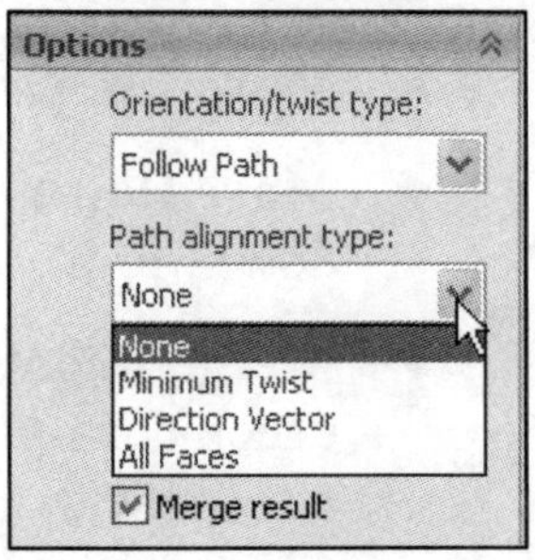


- **Path alignment type**. Only available when the Follow Path type is selected. Select one of the four options to stabilize the profile when small and uneven curvature fluctuations along the path occur. This issue can cause your profile to misalign. The Path alignment type options are:
  - **None**. Selected by default. Only available with the Follow Path option selected. Aligns the profile normal to the path. No correction is applied.
  - **Minimum Twist**. Only available with the Follow Path option selected and for 3D paths. Prevents the profile from becoming self-intersecting as it follows the path.
  - **Direction Vector**. Only available with the Follow Path option selected. Aligns the profile in the direction selected for Direction Vector. Select entities to set the direction vector.
  - **All Faces**. Only available with the Follow Path option selected. Creates the sweep profile tangent to the adjacent face where geometrically possible when the path includes adjacent faces.

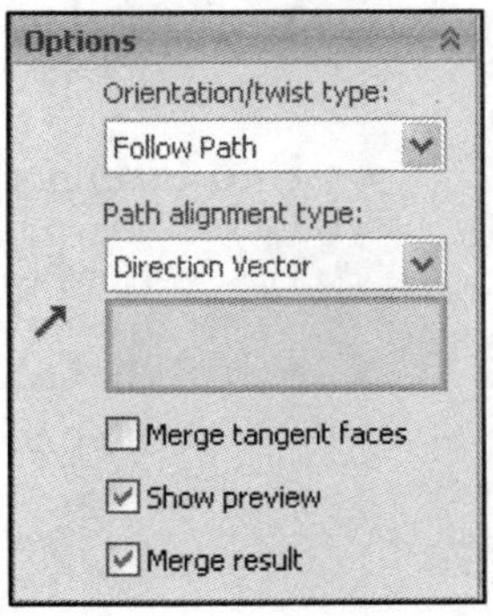


  - **Direction Vector**. The Direction Vector selection is available with the Direction Vector type selected and the Follow Path type selected. Sets the direction vector. Select a plane, planar face, line, edge, cylinder, axis or a pair of vertices on a feature.

- **Merge tangent faces**. Causes the corresponding surfaces in the resulting sweep to be tangent if the sweep profile has tangent segments. Faces that can be represented as a plane, cylinder, or cone are maintained. Other adjacent faces are merged, and the profiles are approximated.
- **Show preview**. Selected by default. Displays a shaded preview of the sweep. Clear the Show preview check box to only display the profile and path.
- **Merge result**. Merges the solids into a single body.
- **Align with end faces**. Continues the sweep profile up to the last face encountered by the path. The faces of the sweep are extended or truncated to match the faces at the ends of the sweep without requiring additional geometry. This option is commonly used with helices.

- ***Guide Curves***. Displays the selected guide curves from the Graphics window. This option guides the profile as it sweeps along the path.

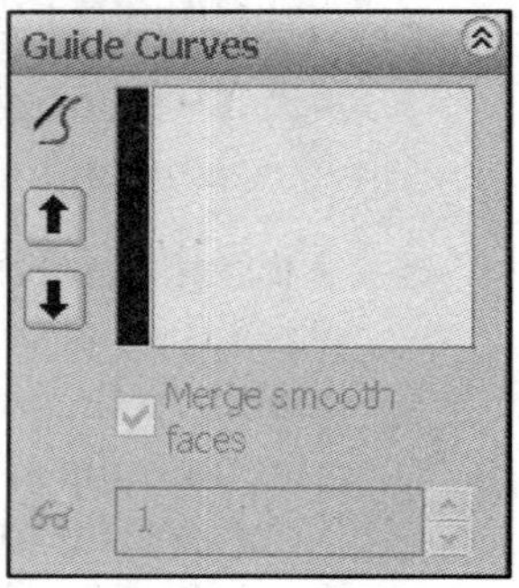


  - **Move Up Arrow**. Adjusts the profile order upwards.
  - **Move Down Arrow**. Adjusts the profile order downwards.
  - **Merge smooth faces**. Clear the Merge smooth faces check box option to improve your system performance of sweeps with guide curves and to segment the sweep at all points where the guide curve or path is not curvature continuous.
  - **Show Sections**. Displays the sections of the sweep. Select the arrows to view and troubleshoot the profile by the Section Number.

- ***Start/End Tangency***. The Start/End Tangency box provides the following selections:

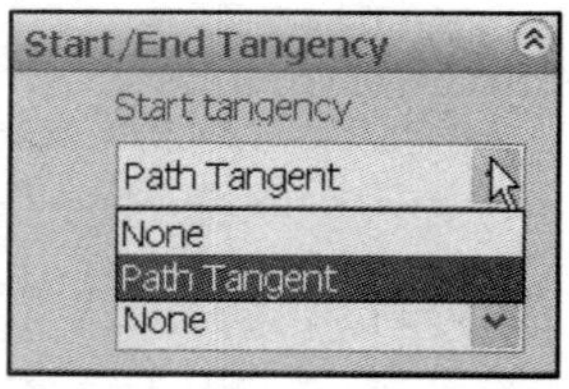


  - **Start tangency type**. The available options are:
    - **None**. No tangency is applied.
    - **Path Tangent**. Creates the sweep normal to the path at the start point.
  - **End tangency type**. The available options are:
    - **None**. No tangency is applied.
    - **Path Tangent**. Creates the sweep normal to the path at the end point.

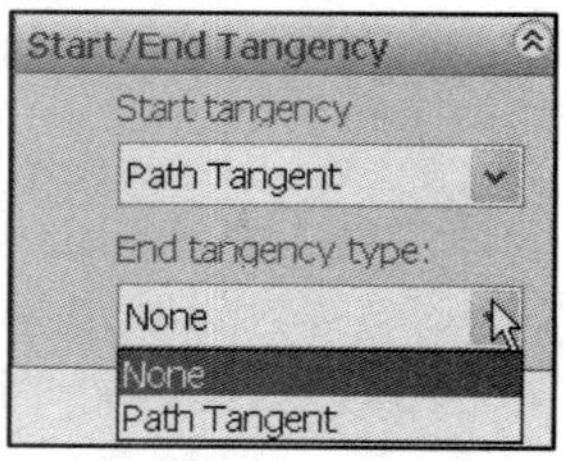

  - **All Faces**. Creates the sweep tangent to the adjacent faces of existing geometry at the start or end. This selection is only available when the sweep is attached to existing geometry.

- ***Thin Feature***. Provides the ability to set the type of thin feature sweep. The available options are:
  - **One-Direction**. Creates the thin feature in a single direction from the profiles using the Thickness value.
  - **Reverse Direction**. Reverses the profile direction if required.
  - **Mid-Plane**. Creates the thin feature in two directions from the profiles, applying the same thickness value in both directions.
  - **Two-Direction**. Creates the thin feature in both directions from the profiles. Set individual values for both thicknesses.

***Tutorial: Swept Base 10-1***

Create a Swept Base feature to create an o-ring part.

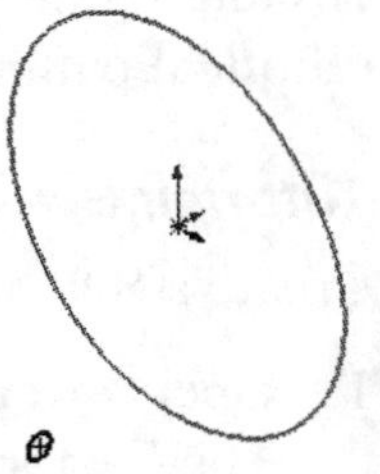

1. Open **Swept Base 10-1** from the SolidWorks 2010 folder. The FeatureManager is displayed.
2. Right-click **Right Plane** from the FeatureManager.
3. Click **Sketch** from the Context toolbar.
4. Click the **Circle** Sketch tool. The Circle PropertyManager is displayed.
5. Create a **small circle** left of the Sketch-path on the Right Plane as illustrated.

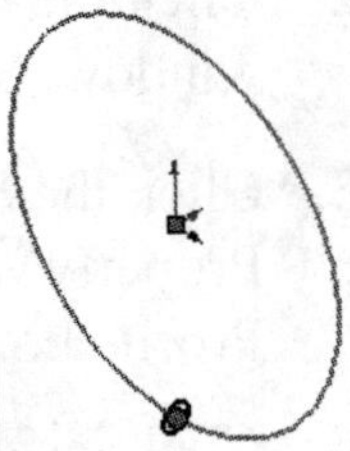

Deselect the Circle Sketch tool.

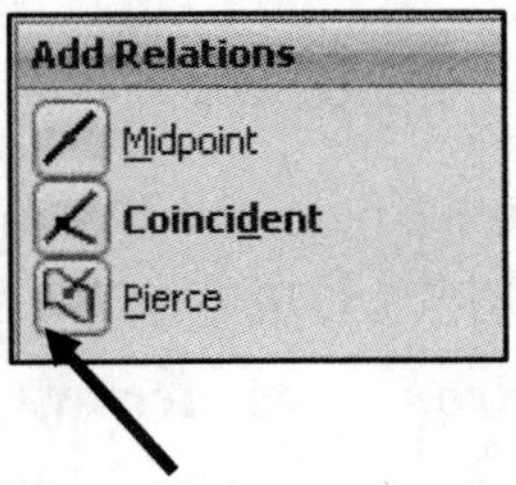


6. Right-click **Select**.
7. Insert a **Pierce** relation between the **center point** of the small circle and the **large circle** circumference.
8. Click **OK** from the Properties PropertyManager. Click the **Smart Dimension** Sketch tool. **Dimension** the circle as illustrated.
9. **Rebuild** the model. The Sketch is fully defined.

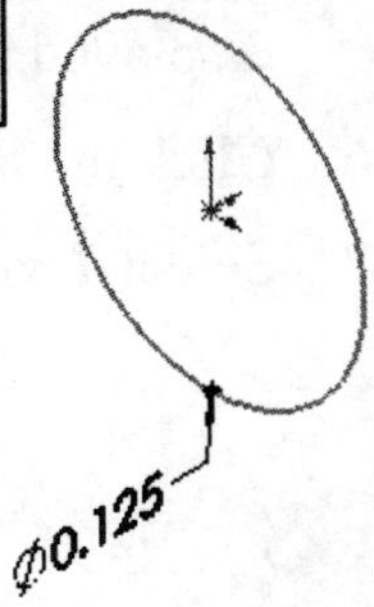

10. Rename **Sketch** to **Sketch-profile**. The FeatureManager displays two sketches: Sketch-path and Sketch-profile.
11. **Rebuild** the model.
12. Click the **Swept Boss/Base** Features tool. The Sweep PropertyManager is displayed. Sketch-profile is displayed in the Profile box.

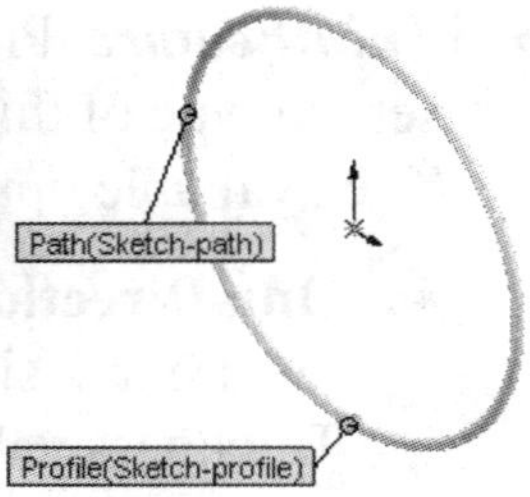


13. Click inside the **Path** box.
14. Click **Sketch-path** from the FeatureManager.
15. Click **OK** from the Sweep PropertyManager. Sweep1 is created and is displayed in the FeatureManager.
16. Rename **Sweep1** to **Base-Sweep**.
17. **Close** the model.

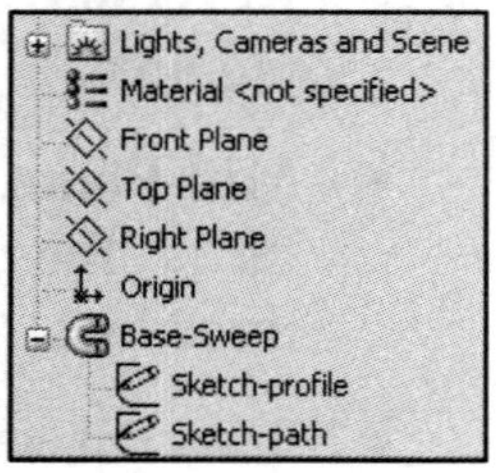


Can you have utilized a Revolved feature to create the o-ring part? Yes, if the circular profile is about the centerline. A Swept feature is required if the o-ring contains a non-circular path. A Revolved feature would not work with an elliptical path or a more complex curve as in a square clip.

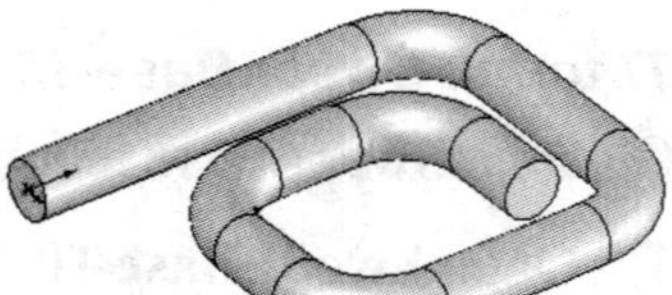

### *Tutorial: Swept Base 10-2*

Create a Swept Base feature. Create a simple spring.

1. Open **Swept Base 10-2** from the SolidWorks 2010 folder. The FeatureManager is displayed. View two simple sketches on the Front Plane.
2. Click the **circumference** of the circle in the Graphics window, Sketch2.

3. Click the **Swept Boss/Base** Features tool. The Sweep PropertyManager is displayed. Sketch2 is displayed in the Profile box.
4. Click inside the **Path** box.
5. Click **Sketch1** from the fly-out FeatureManager. Sketch1 is displayed in the Profile box.
6. Click the **drop-down arrow** to expand the Options box.
7. Select **Twist Along Path**.

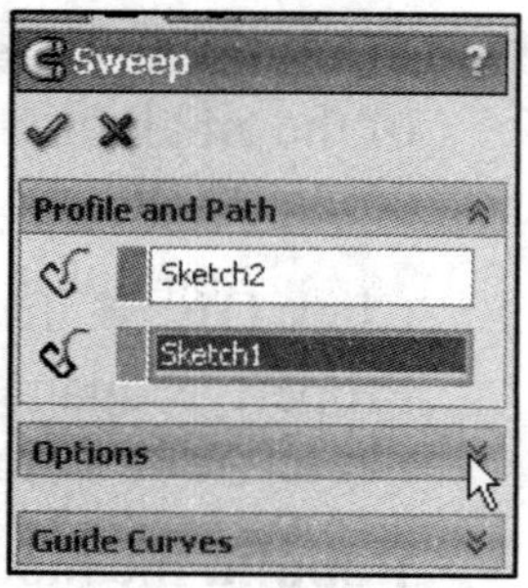

8. Select **Turns** from the Define by drop-down menu.
9. Enter **6** for the number of Turns as illustrated.
10. Click **OK** ✔ from the Sweep PropertyManager. Sweep1 is created and is displayed in the FeatureManager. View the results.
11. **Close** the model.

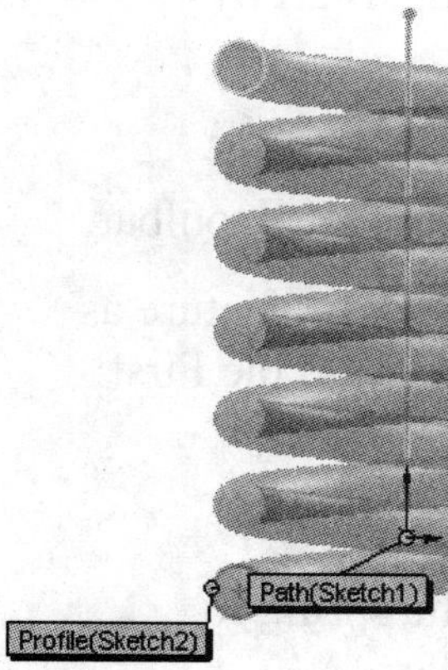


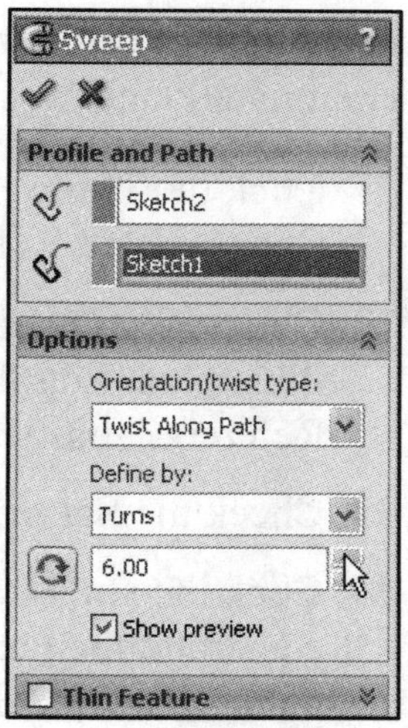


Example of a simple Swept Base feature. Note: The Path and Profile are on different planes using a Pierce geometric relation.

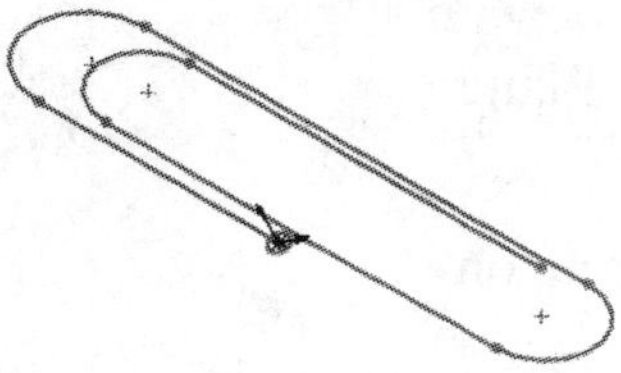

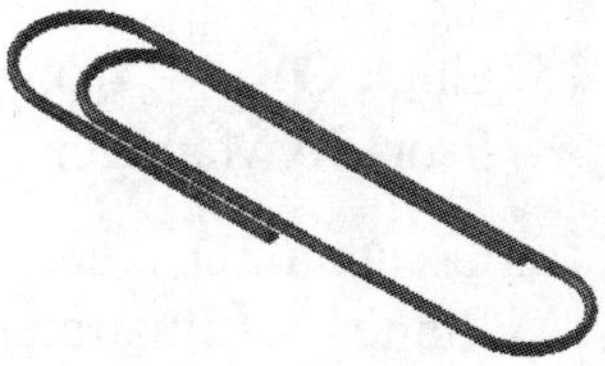

### *Tutorial: Swept Boss 10-1*

Create a Swept Boss feature using the Helix/Spiral PropertyManager. Create a variable pitch helix for a spring.

1. Open **Swept Boss 10-1** from the SolidWorks 2010 folder. The FeatureManager is displayed.
2. Edit **Sketch1**.
3. Click **Insert**, **Curve**, **Helix/Spiral** from the Menu bar menu. The Helix/Spiral PropertyManager is displayed. The default direction of rotation is clockwise. Pitch and Revolution Type is selected by default.
4. Check the **Variable Pitch** box.
5. Create a **Region Parameters table.** Create a spring with 7 coils. Enter the following information as illustrated. Coils 1,2,5, 6 & 7 are the closed ends of the spring. The spring has a diameter of .020in. The pitch needs to be slightly larger than the wire.
6. Enter **.021**in for the Pitch.
7. Enter **.080**in for the free state of the two active coils.
8. Enter Start angle of **0**deg.
9. Click **OK** ✔ from the Helix/Spiral PropertyManager.
10. Click **Isometric** view. View the results.

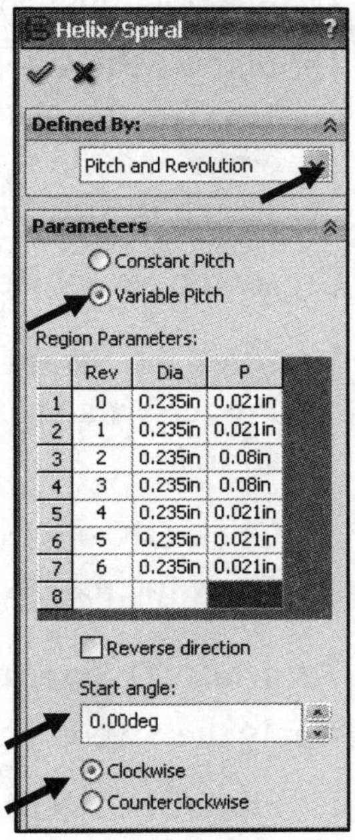


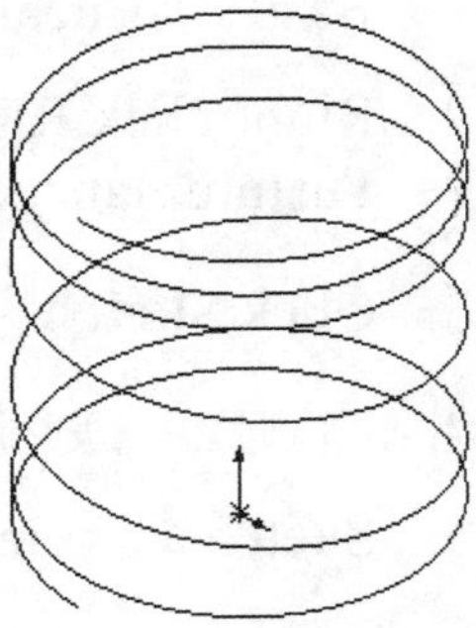

Create the Profile for the spring. Start by creating a Plane.

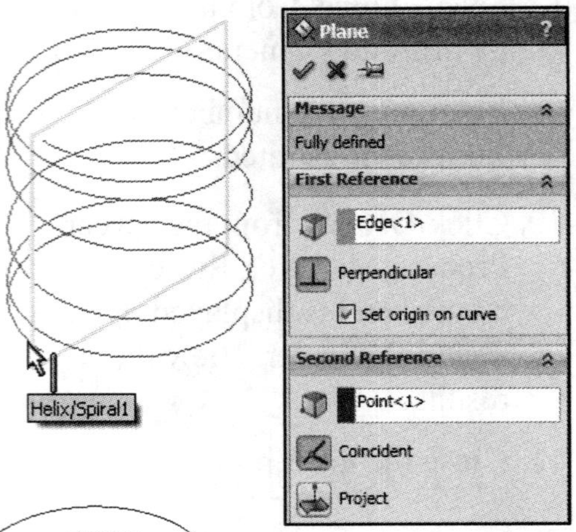


11. Click the **Plane** tool from the Consolidated Reference Geometry toolbar.
12. Click the **start edge** of the Helix feature as illustrated. Edge1 is displayed in the First Reference entities box.
13. Check the **Set origin on curve** box.
14. Click the **start point** on the spring to constraint the Perpendicular plane. The model is fully defined.
15. Click **OK** from the Plane PropertyManager.

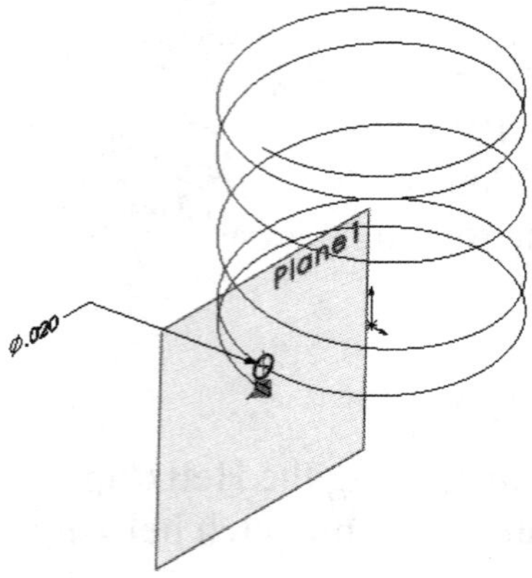


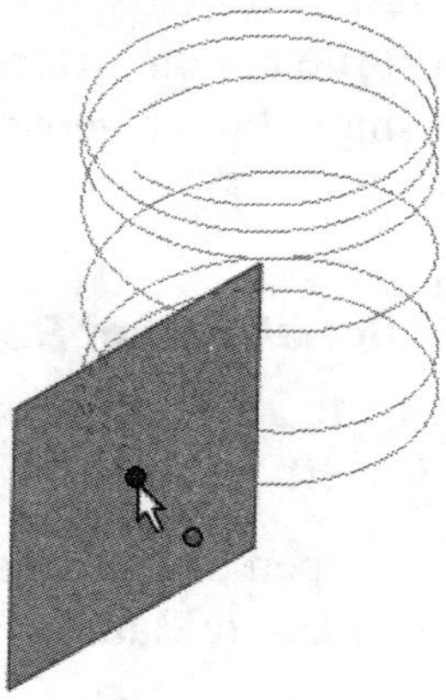

16. Create a 2D sketch, **circle** on Plane1 as illustrated.
17. Insert a dimension, **.020**in.
18. Insert a **Pierce** relation between the centerpoint of the circle and the starting edge of the spring as illustrated. The sketch is fully defined. **Exit** the Sketch.

Create the Swept Boss feature.

19. Click the **Swept Boss/Base** Features tool. The Sweep PropertyManager is displayed. Input the **Path** and **Profile** for the spring.
20. Click **OK** from the PropertyManager. View the results. **Close** the model.

***Tutorial: 3D Swept Base 10-1***

Apply the Swept feature in a 3D Sketch.

1. Open **3D Swept Base 10-1** from the SolidWorks 2010 folder. The 3D Swept Base 10-1 FeatureManager is displayed.
2. Right-click **Right Plane** from the FeatureManager.
3. Click **Sketch** from the Context toolbar.
4. Click the **Circle** Sketch tool.
5. Sketch a **circle** at the origin as illustrated.

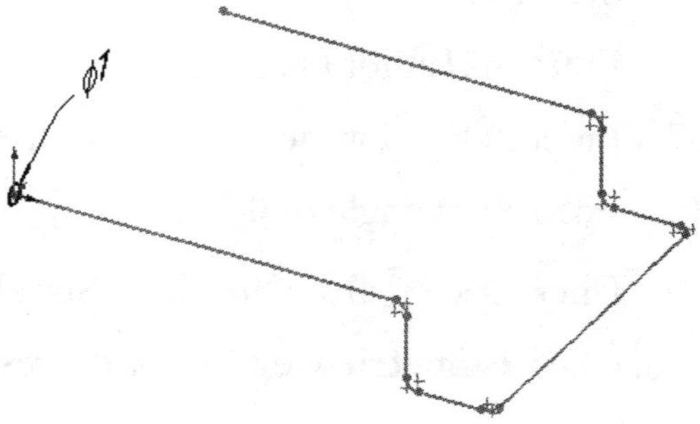

6. Click the **Smart Dimension** Sketch tool.
7. **Dimension** the circle with a 7mm diameter.
8. Click **OK** from the Dimension PropertyManager.
9. **Exit** the Sketch.
10. Click the **Swept Boss/Boss** Features tool. The Sweep PropertyManager is displayed. Sketch1 is displayed in the Profile box.
11. Click inside the **Path** box.
12. Click **3DSketch1** from the Fly-out FeatureManager. 3DSketch1 is displayed in the Path box.

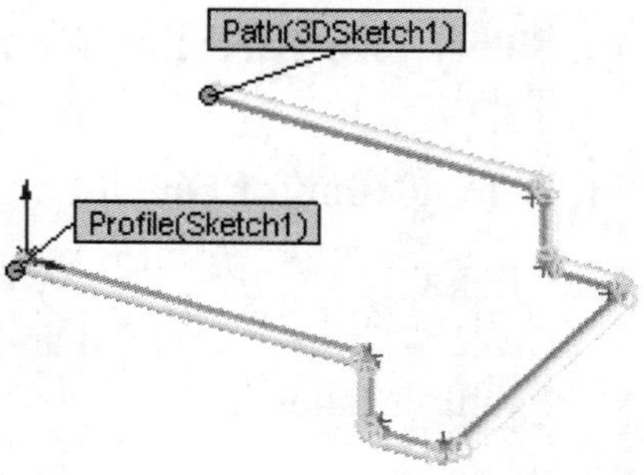


13. Click **OK** from the Sweep PropertyManager. Sweep1 is displayed in the FeatureManager. View the results.
14. **Close** the model.

## Sweep Thin Feature

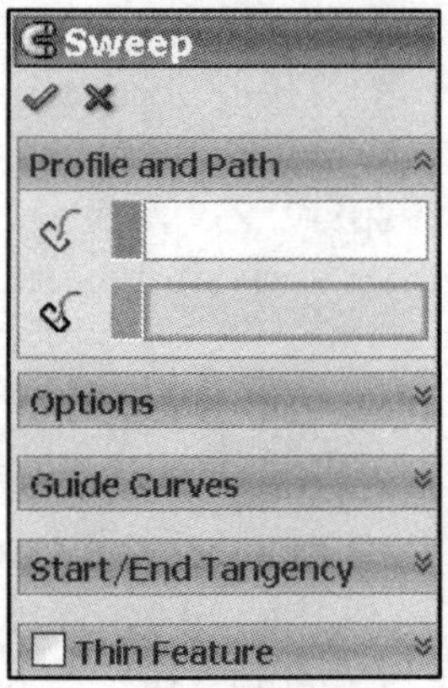


A Sweep Thin feature adds material by moving an open profile with a specified thickness along a path. A Sweep Thin feature requires a sketched profile, thickness, and path. The Sweep Thin feature uses the Sweep PropertyManager.

### *Tutorial: Sweep Thin 10-1*

Create a Sweep Thin profile. Remember, to create a sweep you need a sketch; a closed, non-intersecting profile on a face or a plane and you need to create the path for the profile.

1. Open **Sweep Thin 10-1** from the SolidWorks 2010 folder.
2. Check **View ➤ Display ➤ Zebra Stripes** from the Menu bar. The Zebra Stripes PropertyManager is displayed.
3. Click **Sketch-Profile** from the flyout FeatureManager.
4. Click the **Swept Boss/Base** Features tool. The Sweep PropertyManager is displayed. The Sketch-Profile is displayed in the Sweep-Profile text box.

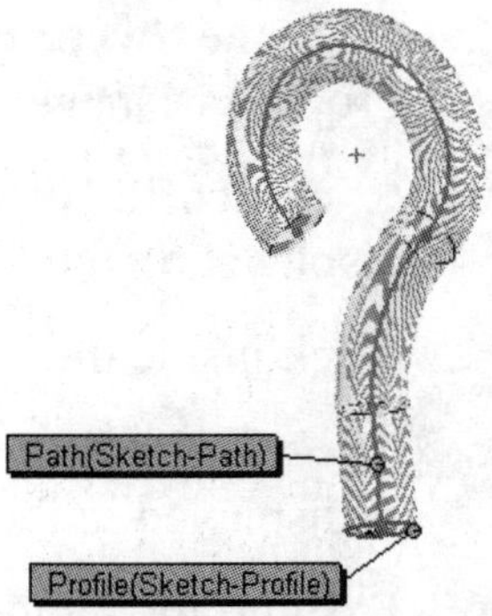


5. Click inside the **Sweep-Path** box.
6. Click **Sketch-Path** from the flyout FeatureManager. Sketch-Path is displayed in the Sweep-Path text box.

7. **Expand** the Options box.
8. Select **Twist Along Path** for Orientation/twist type.
9. Enter **0** for Angle. Review the surface, there is a single surface with smooth Zebra stripes.
10. Select **Two-Direction** for Thin Feature Type.
11. Enter **.010**in for Direction 1 and Direction 2 Thickness.

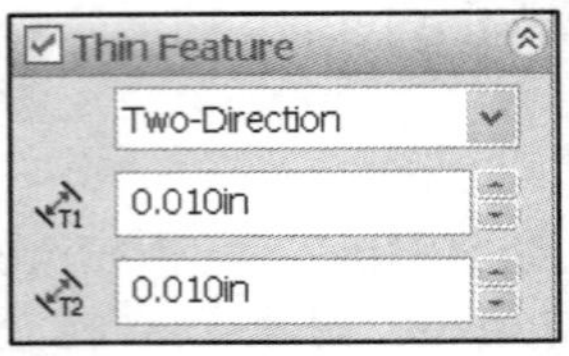

12. Click **OK** from the Sweep PropertyManager. Sweep-Thin1 is created and is displayed in the FeatureManager.
13. Right-click in the **Graphics window**.
14. Uncheck the **Zebra strips** box. The Zebra strips are removed from the model.
15. Display an **Isometric view**. View the results.
16. Close the model.

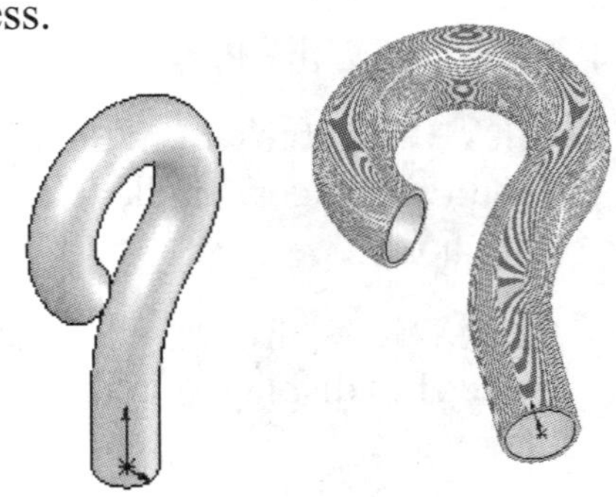

The Zebra stripes function provides the ability to display small changes in a surface which may be difficult to view with a standard display. Zebra stripes simulate the reflection of long strips of light on a very shiny surface.

### *Tutorial: Sweep Guide Curves 10-1*

Create a Swept feature utilizing the Guide Curves option.

1. Open **Sweep Guide Curves 10-1** from the SolidWorks 2010 folder. The Sweep Guide Curves 10-1 FeatureManager is displayed.
2. Click the **Swept Boss/Base** Features tool. The Sweep PropertyManager is displayed.
3. Click **Profile1** from the flyout FeatureManager. Profile1 is displayed in the Profile box.
4. Click inside the **Path** box.
5. Click **Path1** from the flyout FeatureManager. Path1 is displayed in the Path box.
6. **Expand** the Guide Curves box.
7. Click the **Guide Curve** spline sketch for the Graphics window as illustrated. Guide Curve1 is displayed.

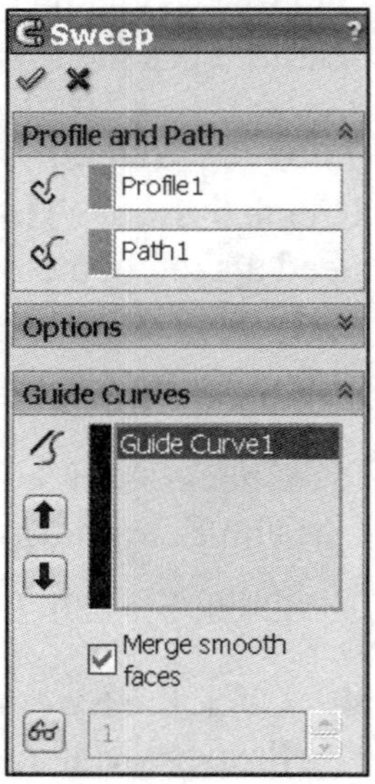


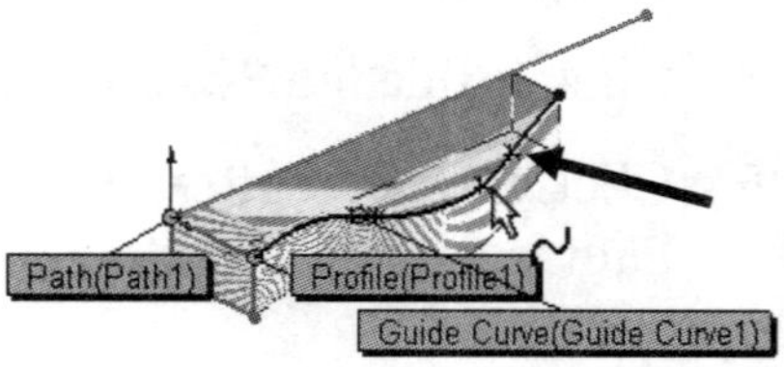

8. Click **OK** from the Sweep PropertyManager. Sweep1 is created and is displayed in the FeatureManager.
9. **Close** the model.

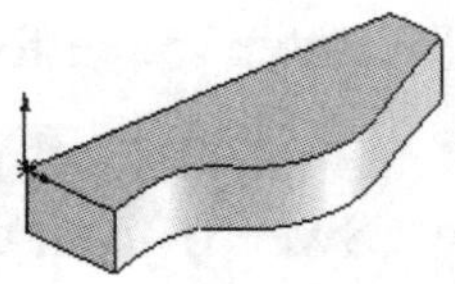

To insert an additional Guide Curve, insert a sketch before the Swept feature. Then edit the Swept feature to insert the new Guide Curve.

### *Tutorial: Sweep Guide Curves 10-2*

Create a Swept feature utilizing the Guide Curves option.

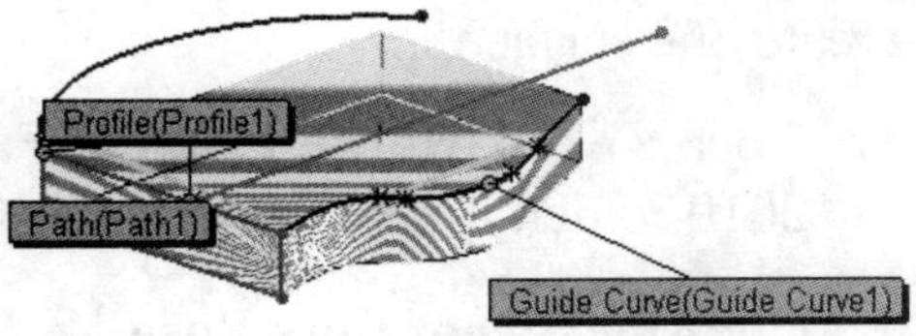


1. Open **Sweep Guide Curves 10-2** from the SolidWorks 2010 folder.
2. Click **Sweep1** from the FeatureManager.
3. Right-click **Edit Feature**. The Sweep1 PropertyManager is displayed.
4. Click inside the **Guide Curves** box.
5. Click **Guide Curve2** from the flyout FeatureManager. Guide Curve2 is displayed in the Guide Curves box.
6. Click **OK** from the Sweep PropertyManager. View the FeatureManager.
7. **Close** the model.

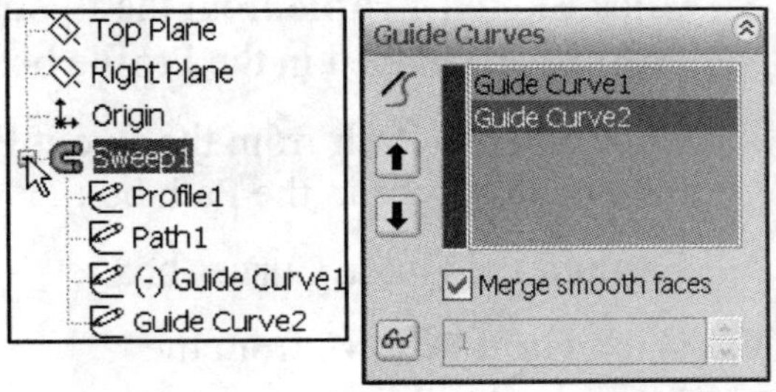


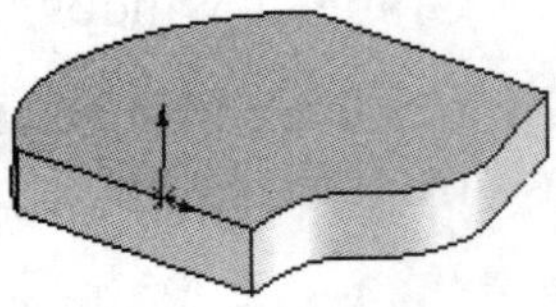

### *Tutorial: Sweep Twist 10-1*

Create a Swept profile. Utilize the Orientation/twist option to twist 75 degrees along the path.

1. Open **Sweep Twist 10-1** from the SolidWorks 2010 folder.
2. Click the **Swept Boss/Base** Features tool. The Sweep PropertyManager is displayed.
3. Click **Sketch2** from the flyout FeatureManager. Sketch2 is displayed in the Profile box.
4. Click **Sketch1** from the flyout FeatureManager. Sketch1 is displayed in the Path box.
5. **Expand** the Options box.

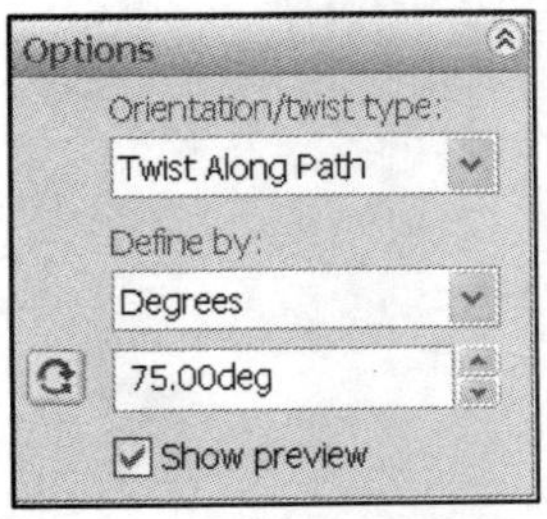

6. Select **Twist Along Path** for Orientation/twist type.
7. Enter **75**deg for Angle.
8. Click **OK** ✓ from the Sweep PropertyManager. View Sweep1 from the FeatureManager.
9. Display an **Isometric view**. View the results.
10. **Close** the model.

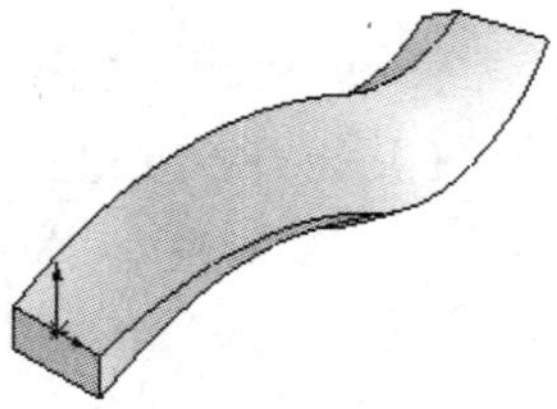

### *Tutorial: Sweep Merge Tangent Faces 10-1*

Create a Sweep profile with Guide Curves. Utilize the Orientation Merge tangent faces option and Merge smooth faces option to create one surface.

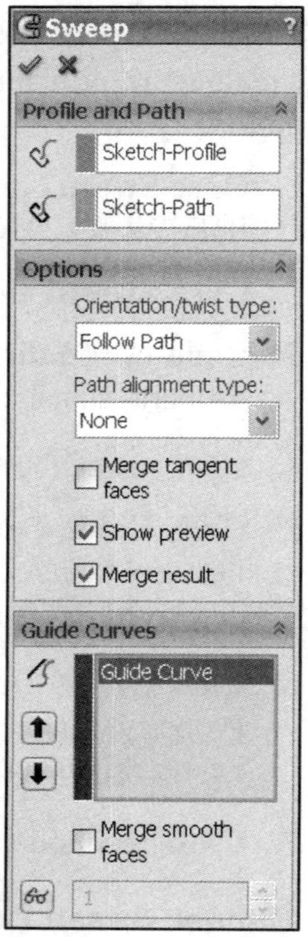


1. Open **Sweep Merge Tangent Faces 10-1** from the SolidWorks 2010 folder.
2. Click the **Swept Boss/Base** Features tool. The Sweep PropertyManager is displayed.
3. Click **Sketch-Profile** from the flyout FeatureManager. Sketch-Profile is displayed in the Profile box.
4. Click **Sketch-Path** from the flyout FeatureManager. Sketch-Path is displayed in the Path box.
5. **Expand** the Guide Curves box.
6. Click **Guide Curve** from the flyout FeatureManager. Guide Curve is displayed in the Graphics window.
7. Uncheck **Merge smooth faces** from the Guide Curves box.
8. Click **OK** ✓ from the Sweep PropertyManager. Sweep1 is created. There are four faces displayed in the Graphics window.

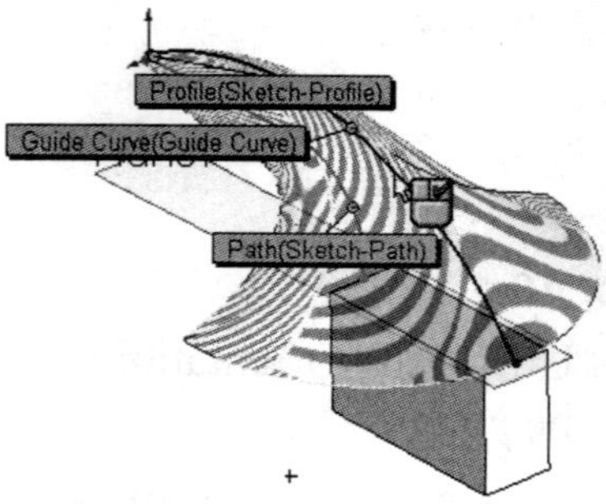


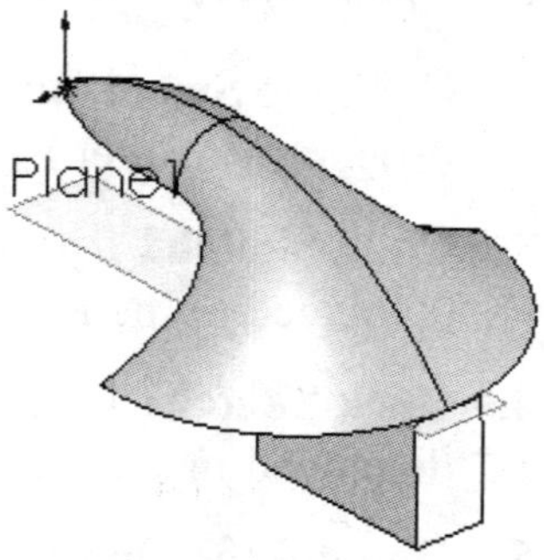

9. Right-click **Sweep1** from the FeatureManager.
10. Click **Edit Feature**. The Sweep1 PropertyManager is displayed.
11. Check **Merge tangent faces** in the Options box.
12. Check **Merge smooth faces** in the Guide Curves box.
13. Click **Yes** to the warning message.
14. Click **OK** ✔ from the Sweep PropertyManager. A single face is displayed in the Graphics window.
15. **Close** the model.

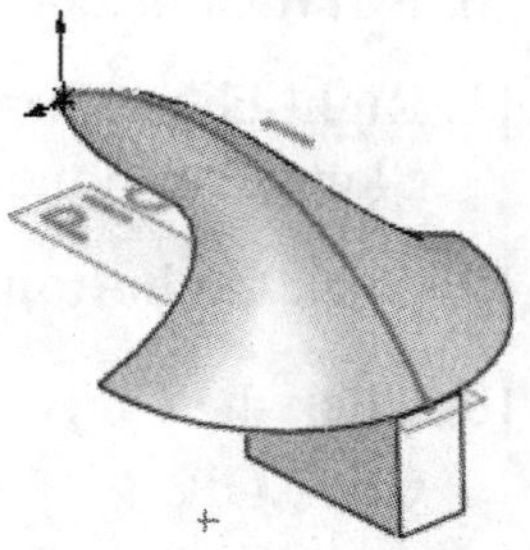

## Swept Cut Feature

A Swept Cut feature removes material from a part. A Swept Cut requires a sketched profile and path. Utilize the Swept Cut feature to create threads. The Swept Cut feature uses the Cut-Sweep PropertyManager.

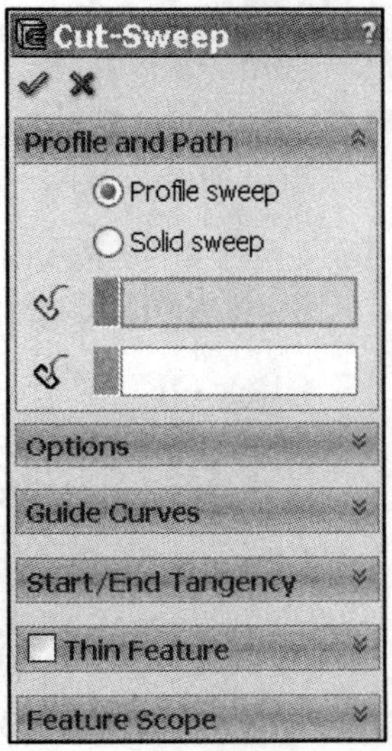


### *Tutorial: Sweep Cut Feature 10-1*

Create a Swept Cut feature.

1. Open **Sweep Cut 10-1** from the SolidWorks 2010 folder. Create an Offset Reference Plane.
2. Click the **bottom circular** face of Sweep1. Sweep1 is highlighted in the FeatureManager.

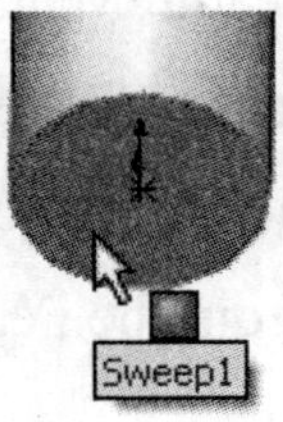


3. Click **Plane** from the Consolidated Reference Geometry Features toolbar. The Plane PropertyManager is displayed. Face<1> is displayed in the First Reference entity box.
4. Enter **.020**in for Distance.
5. Check the **Flip** box. Plane1 is above the Top Plane.

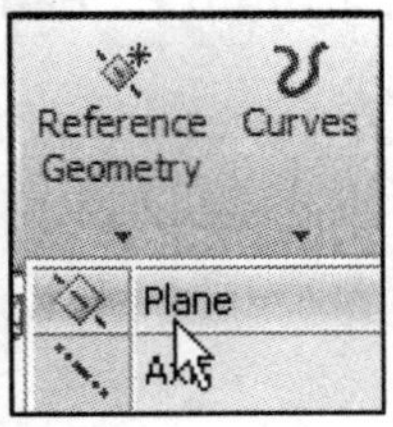


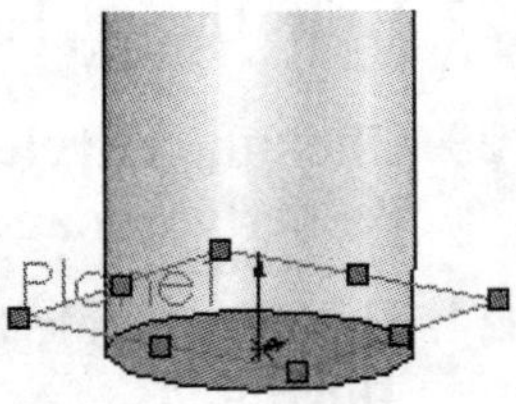


6. Click **OK** ✔ from the Plane PropertyManager. Plane1 is created and is displayed.
7. Rename **Plane1** to **Threadplane** in the FeatureManager.
8. Display an **Isometric** view.
9. Select **Hidden Lines Removed** from the Heads-up View toolbar.

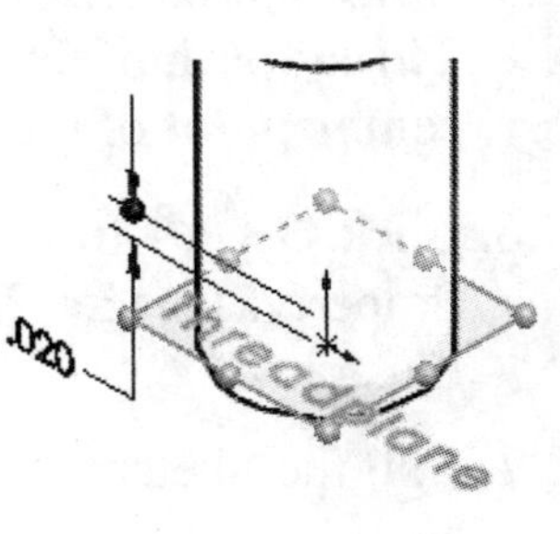

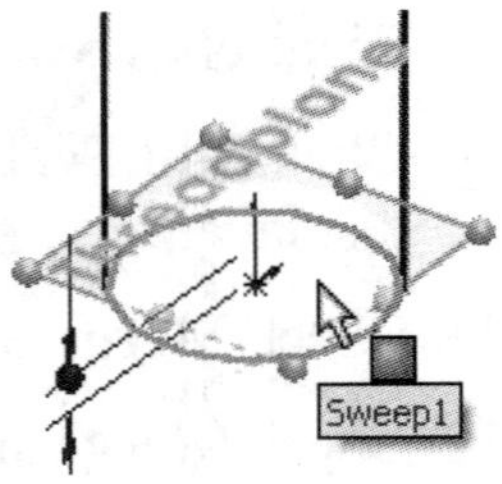


Create the Thread path.

10. **Rotate** and **Zoom to Area** on the bottom of Sweep1.
11. Right-click **Threadplane** from the FeatureManager. Click **Sketch** from the Context toolbar.
12. Click the **bottom** of Sweep1.
13. Click the **Convert Entities** Sketch tool. Click **OK**.

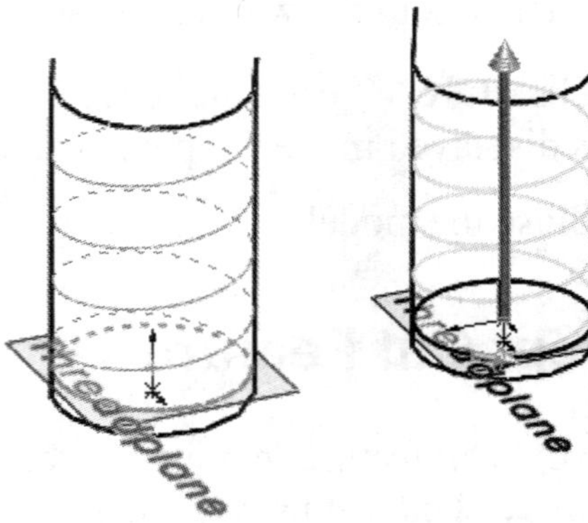


14. Click **Insert ➤ Curve ➤ Helix/Spiral** or click **Helix Spiral** from the Consolidated Curves toolbar. The Helix/Spiral PropertyManager is displayed.
15. Enter **.050**in for Pitch.
16. Check the **Reverse direction** box. The direction arrow points upward.
17. Enter **4** for Revolutions. Enter **0**deg for the Start angle. Check the **Clockwise** box.

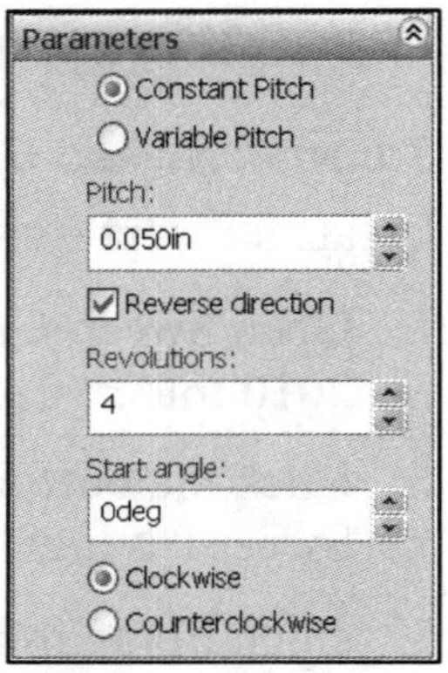


18. Click **OK** from the Helix/Spiral PropertyManager. Helix/Sprial1 is created and is displayed in the FeatureManager.
19. Rename **Helix/Sprial1** to **Threadpath**.

Create the Thread Profile, (cross section).

20. Click **Right Plane** from the FeatureManager.
21. Display a **Right** view.
22. **Hide** Threadplane from the FeatureManager.
23. Click the **Circle** Sketch tool. The Circle PropertyManager is displayed.
24. Sketch a **circle** to the right of the profile as illustrated.

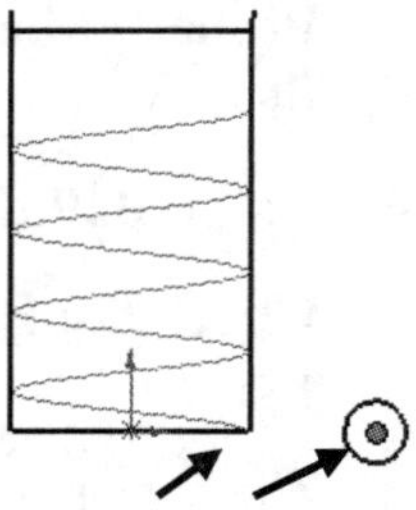

25. Add a Pierce relation between the **start of the Threadpath** of the helical curve and the **center point** of the circle.
26. Click **OK** from the Properties PropertyManager. **Dimension** the circle as illustrated.
27. **Exit** the Sketch.
28. Rename **Sketch2** to **Threadprofile**.

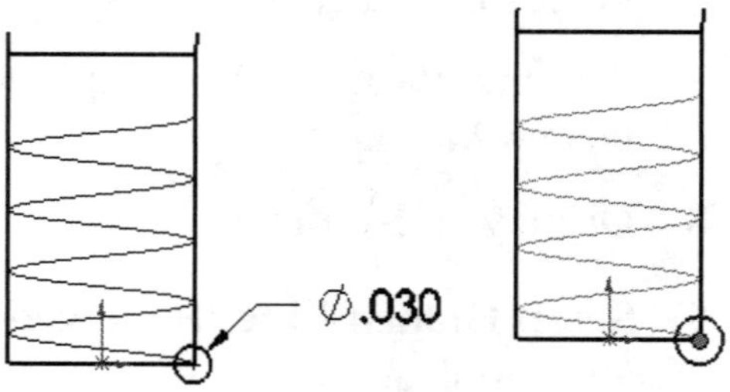

29. Click **Insert ➢ Cut ➢ Sweep**. The Cut-Sweep PropertyManager is displayed. The Threadprofile is displayed in the Sweep Profile text box.
30. Click the **Sweep Path** box.
31. Click **Threadpath** from the flyout FeatureManager. Threadpath is displayed in the Sweep Path box

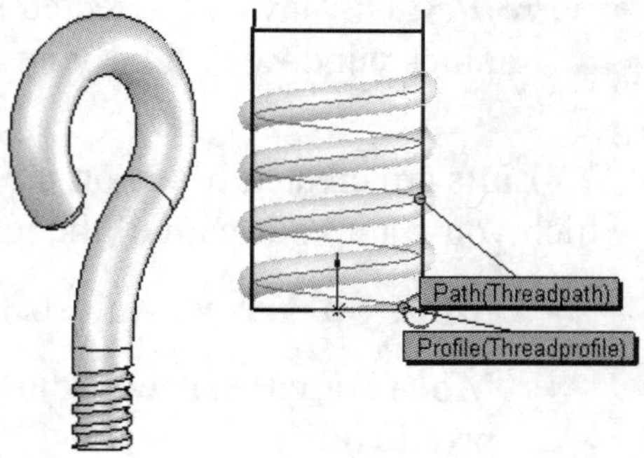


32. Click **OK** from the Cut-Sweep PropertyManager.
33. Rename **Cut-Sweep1** to **Thread**. View the model in the Graphics window. **Close** the model.

***Tutorial: Sweep Cut Feature 10-2***

Create a Simple Swept Cut. Create a Swept Cut along a handle.

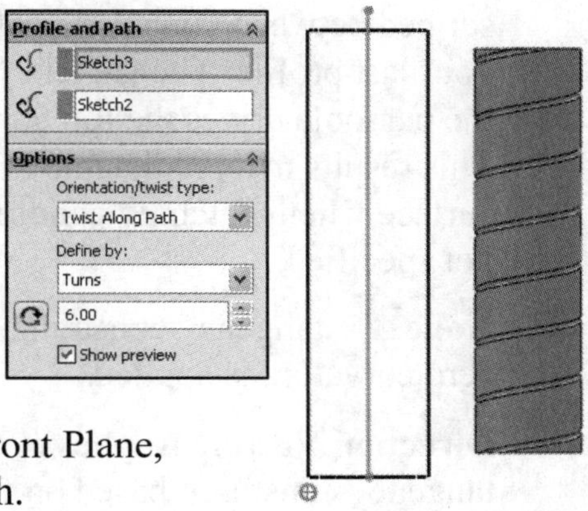


1. Open **Sweep Cut 10-2** from the SolidWorks 2010 folder.
2. Sketch a vertical **Line** from the Origin above the top of the model on the Front Plane. **Exit** the Sketch.
3. Sketch a **small circle** below the model on the Front Plane, near the left corner as illustrated. **Exit** the Sketch.
4. Click **Swept Cut** from the Features toolbar.
5. Select the **Profile** and the **Path** for the Swept Cut.
6. Select **Twist Along Path**, **Turns** and **6** in the Options box.
7. Click **OK** from the Cut-Sweept PropertyManager. View the results. **Close** the model.

## Loft Feature

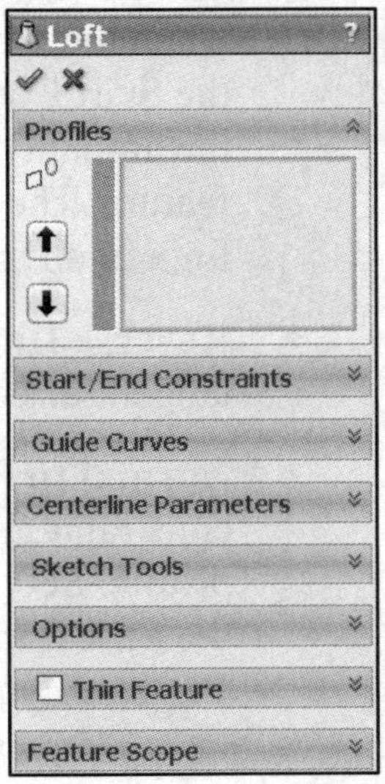


The Loft feature provides the ability to create a feature by creating transitions between profiles. A loft can be a Base, Boss, Cut, or Surface feature. Create a Loft feature by using two or more profiles. Only the first, last, or first and last profiles can be points. All sketch entities, including guide curves and profiles, can be enclosed in a single 3D sketch.

The Loft feature uses the Loft PropertyManager. The Loft PropertyManager provides the following selections:

- ***Profiles***. Displays the selected faces, sketch profiles, or edges selected from the Graphics window or the flyout FeatureManager.

Lofts are created based on the order of the profile selection. Select the point in which you want your path of the loft to travel for each profile.

  - **Move Up Arrow**. Adjusts the profile order upwards.
  - **Move Down Arrow**. Adjusts the profile order downwards.

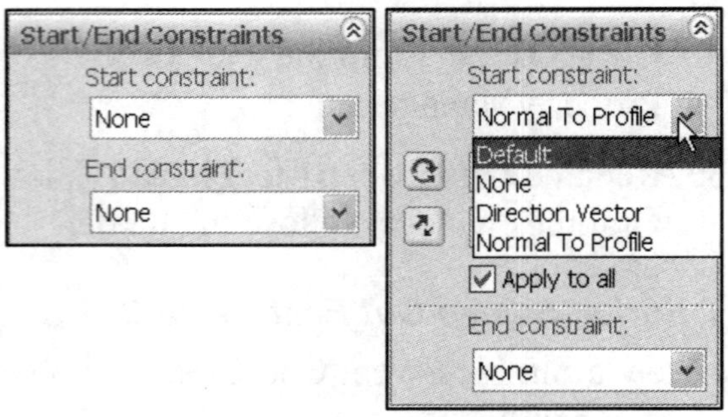


- ***Start/End Constraints***. Applies a constraint to control tangency for the start and end profiles. The selections for the Start constraints are:
  - **Default**. Approximates a parabola scribed between your first profile and your last profile. The tangency from the parabola drives the loft surface. This results in a predictable loft surface when matching conditions are not specified.
  - **None**. No tangency constraint. A zero curvature is applied.
  - **Direction Vector**. Applies a tangency constraint based on the selected entity which is used as a start direction vector. Select the Direction Vector option. Set the Draft angle option and the Start Tangent Length option.
  - **Start Tangent Length**. Not available when the None option is selected from the Start Constraint section. Controls the amount of influence on the loft feature. The effect of tangent length is limited up to the next section.
  - **Reverse Direction**. Reverses the tangent direction length if required.
  - **Normal to Profile**. Applies a tangency constraint normal to the selected start profile. Set the Draft angle option. Set the Start Tangent Length or End Tangent Length option.

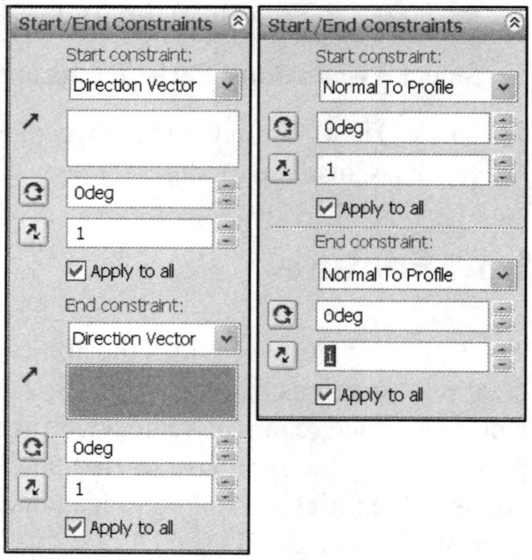

- **Tangency to Face**. Only available when attaching a loft to existing geometry. This option makes the adjacent faces tangent at your selected start profile.
- **Curvature to Face**. Only available when attaching a loft feature to existing geometry. Applies a smooth curvature continuous loft at your selected start profile.
- **Next Face**. Only available with the Tangency to Face option selected or when the Curvature to Face option is selected from the Start section. Ability to toggle the loft feature between available faces.
- **Direction Vector**. Only available with the Direction Vector option selected for Start or End constraint. Applies a tangency constraint based on the selected entity used as a direction vector. The loft is tangent to the selected linear edge or axis, or to the normal of a selected face or plane.
- **Draft angle**. Only available with the Direction Vector or Normal to Profile option selected for the Start or End constraint. Applies a draft angle to the start or end of your profile.
- **Start and End Tangent Length**. Not available with the None option selected from the Start or End constraint. Controls the amount of influence on the loft.
- **Apply to all**. Displays one handle that controls all the constraints for the entire profile. Clear this option to display multiple handles that permit individual segment control. Drag the handles to modify the tangent length.

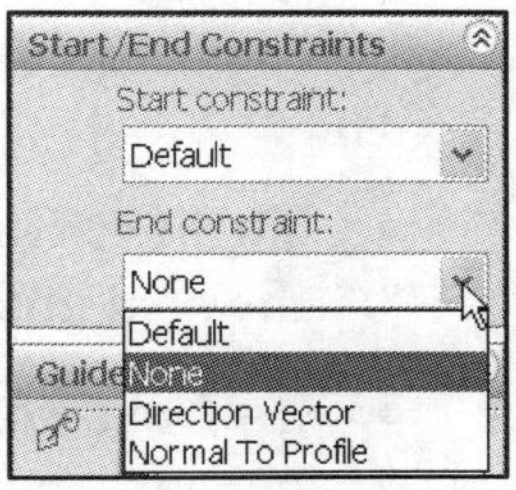


- *End Constraints*. Applies a constraint to control tangency of the end profile. The options for the End constraints are:
  - **Default**. Approximates a parabola scribed between the first profile and your last profile. The tangency from the parabola drives the loft surface. This results in a predictable loft surface when matching conditions are not specified.
  - **None**. Provides no tangency constraint. A zero curvature is applied.
  - **Direction Vector**. Only available with the Direction Vector option selected from the Start Constraint section. Applies a tangency constraint based on your selected entity used as a direction vector. The loft feature is tangent to your selected axis, linear edge or to the normal of a selected face or plane.

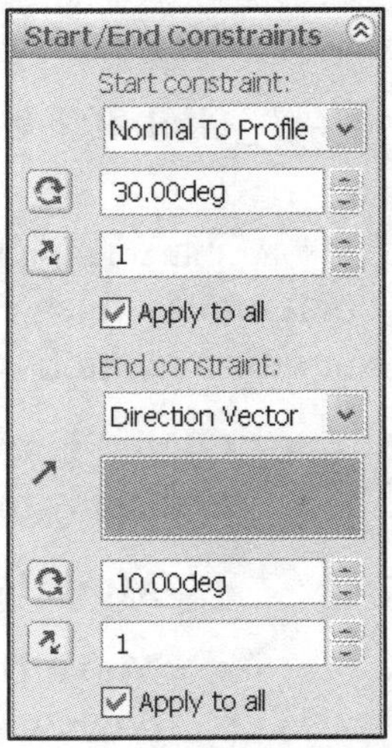

- **Draft angle**. Only available when the Direction Vector option or the Normal to Profile option is selected from the End Constraint section. Set a draft angle to end of your profile.

- **Reverse Direction**. Reverses the direction of the applied draft angle if required.

- **End Tangent Length**. Not available when the None option is selected from the Start or End Constraint section. Controls the amount of influence on the loft feature. The effect of tangent length is limited up to the next section.

  - **Reverse Direction**. Reverses the tangent direction length if required.

  - **Apply to all**. Display a handle which controls the constraints for the entire profile.

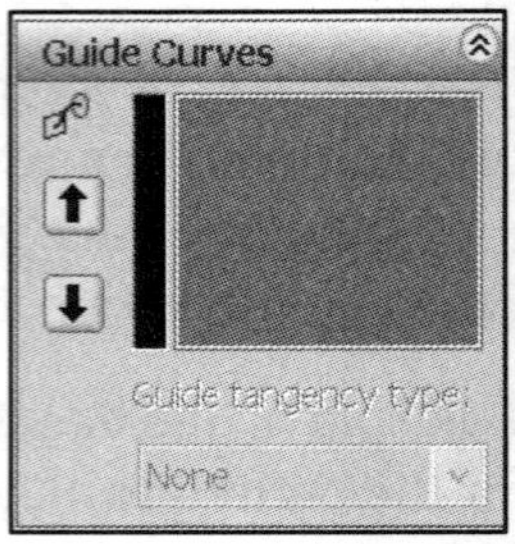


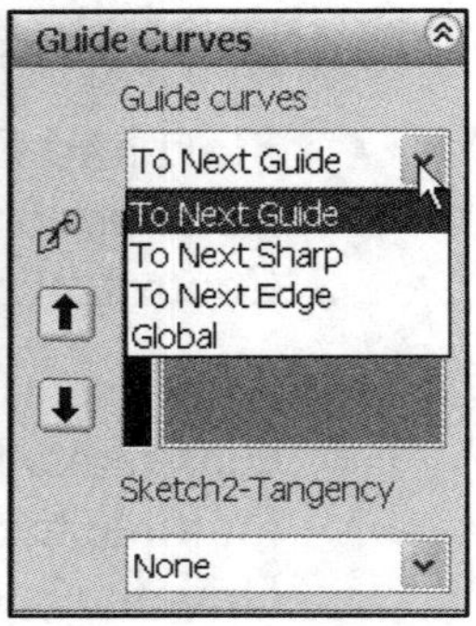


Clear the Apply to all check box option to display multiple handles. Clearing this option permits individual segment control. Drag the handles to modify the tangent length.

- *Guide Curves*. The Guide Curves influence box provides the ability to control the influence of the guide curves on the loft. The available options are:

  - **To Next Guide**. Extends your guide curve influence only to the next guide curve.

  - **To Next Sharp**. Extends your guide curve influence only to the next sharp.

  - **To Next Edge**. Extends your guide curve influence only to the next edge.

  - **Global**. Extends the guide curve influence to the entire loft.

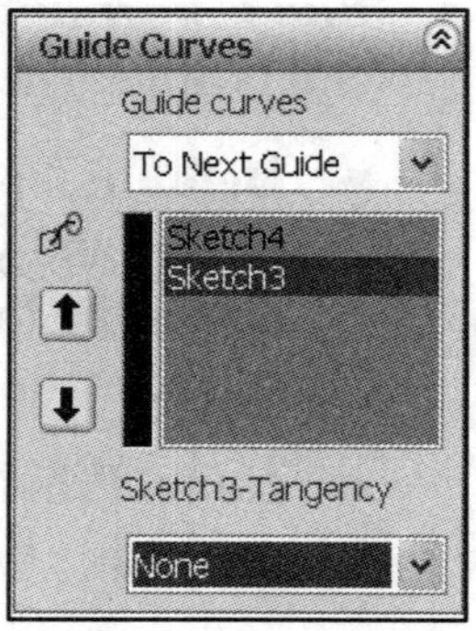


A sharp is a hard corner of a profile. Example: any two contiguous sketch entities that do not have a tangent or an equal curvature relation with each other.

- **Global Curves**. The Global Curves box provides the ability to display the select guide curves to control the loft feature.

  - **Move Up Arrow**. Adjusts the profile order upwards.

  - **Move Down Arrow**. Adjusts the profile order downwards.

- **Guide tangency type**. Provides the ability to control the tangency where your loft feature meets the guide curves. The available options are:
    - **None**. No tangency constraint.
    - **Normal To Profile**. Applies a tangency constraint normal to your plane of the guide curve. Set the Draft angle option.
    - **Direction Vector**. Applies a tangency constraint based on your selected entity used as the direction vector. Select the Direction Vector option. Set the Draft angle option.
    - **Tangency to Face**. Only available when a guide curve lies on the edge of existing geometry. Adds side tangency between adjacent faces that lie along the path of a guide curve, creating a smoother transition between adjacent faces.
    - **Direction Vector**. Only available when the Direction Vector option is selected from the Guide tangency type section. Applies a tangency constraint based on your selected entity used as the direction vector. The loft feature is tangent to your selected linear axis or edge, or to the normal of a selected plane or face.
    - **Draft angle**. Only available when the Direction Vector option or the Normal to Profile option is selected from the Start or End Constraint section. Applies a draft angle to the loft feature along the guide curve.
    - **Reverse Direction**. Reverses the direction of the draft if required.

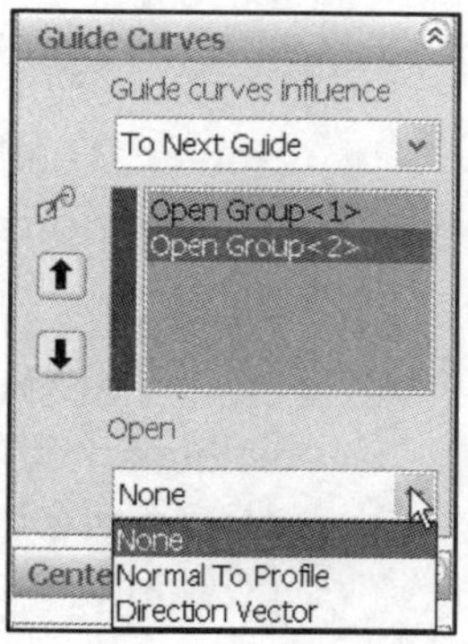


- ***Centerline Parameters***. The Centerline Parameters box provides three options. They are:
    - **Centerline**. Guides the loft feature shape using a centerline. Select a sketch from the Graphics window.
    - **Number of Sections**. Provides the ability to add sections between your profile and the centerline. Click and drag the slider to regulate the number of sections.
    - **Show Sections**. Displays the loft feature sections. Click the arrows in this option to display the required sections.

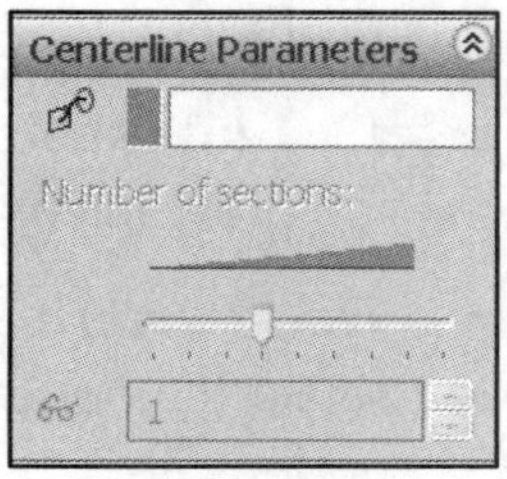


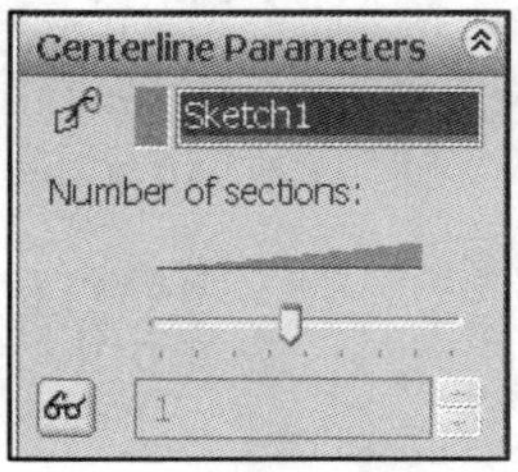


Enter your **section number**, click the **Show Sections** option and directly go to your desired section.

- ***Sketch Tools***. Provides the ability to define a loft section and a guide curve from contours within the same sketch. This is especially useful with a 3D sketch. The following options are available:
  - **Select**. The Select option only addresses sketch entities. This option cannot be selected for sketch contours.
  - **Chain Contour Select**. Provides the ability to select chains of sketch segments as contours. SolidWorks selects the best chain of sketch segments. Sketch chaining prefers planar contours over non-planar contours. Sketch chaining also prefers closed contours over open contours.

Select the plane or a sketch segment to select a contour on a 3D sketch plane. In a single loft feature, all 3D sketch contours must be in the same 3D sketch. Contours used in the same loft feature cannot share the same segment. Use a 3D sketch to produce contours in multiple loft features.

  - **Single Contour Select**. Provides the ability to select a single sketch segment at a time as a contour. Selections are displayed in the list as a separate single segment contours.
  - **Join**. Only for profiles guide curves. Forms a single contour from multiple intersecting contours. Select your contours from the Profiles list. Click the Join option.
  - **Drag Sketch**. Enables the drag mode. Use the drag mode to drag any 3D sketch segments, planes, or points from the 3D sketch from which contours have been defined for your loft feature in the Edit mode. The 3D sketch updates as you drag. You can also edit your 3D sketch to dimension the contours using dimensioning tools.
  - **Undo sketch drag**. Provides the ability to undo your previous drag and returns the view to its previous state.

- ***Thin Feature***. The Thin Feature box provides the ability to select the options required to create a thin loft feature. The options are:
  - **Thin feature type**. Sets the type of thin loft feature. The available options are:
    - **One-Direction**. Creates the thin feature in a single direction from the profiles using the Thickness value.
    - **Reverse Direction**. Reverses the direction of the profile if required.

- **Mid-Plane**. Creates the thin feature in two directions from the profiles. This option applies the same Thickness value in both directions.
- **Two-Direction**. Creates the thin feature in two directions from the profiles. There are two selections:

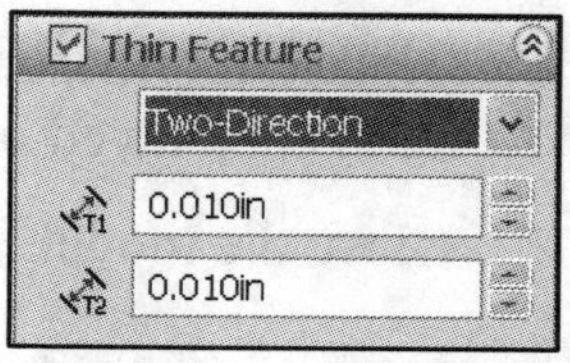


- **Thickness 1**. Thickness value in the first direction.
- **Thickness 2**. Thickness value in the second direction.

- ***Options***. The Options box provides the following selections:

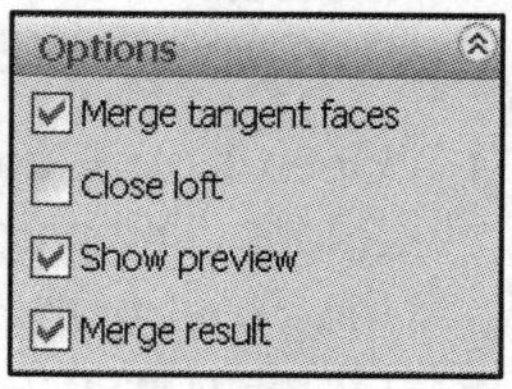


  - **Merge tangent faces**. Only if the corresponding segments are tangent. Causes the surfaces in the resulting loft feature to be tangent.
  - **Close loft**. Creates a closed body along the loft feature direction. The closed body connects your first and last sketch automatically.
  - **Show preview**. Displays the shaded preview of the loft feature. Uncheck the Show preview box to only view the path and the guide curves.
  - **Merge result**. Merges all of the loft elements. Uncheck the Merge result box, if you do not want to merge all of the loft feature elements.

***Tutorial: Loft 10-1***

Create a Loft feature using the Normal To Profile End constraint.

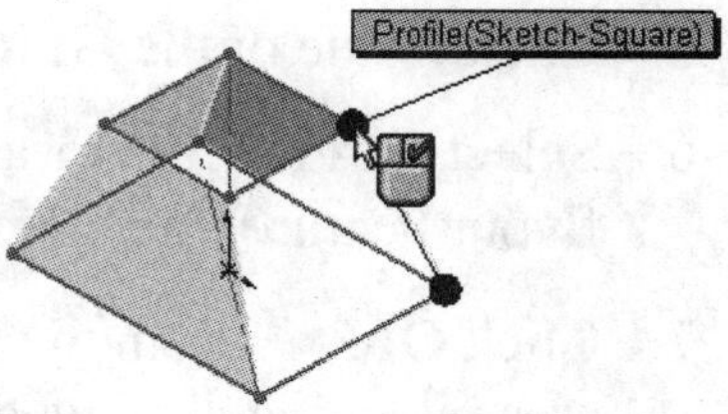


1. Open **Loft 10-1** from the SolidWorks 2010 folder.
2. Click **Lofted Boss/Base** from the Features toolbar. The Loft PropertyManager is displayed.
3. Click the **back right corner point** of Sketch-Rectangle.

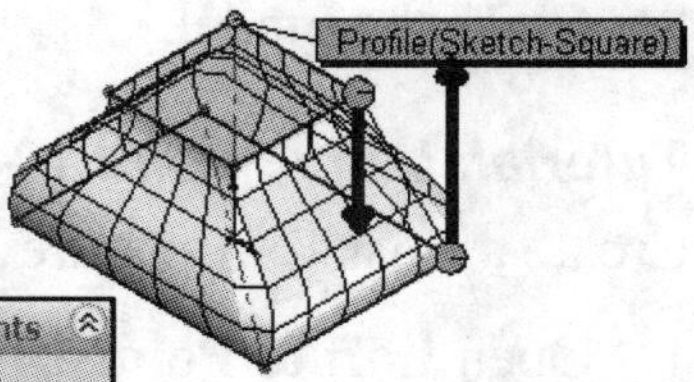


4. Click the **back right corner point** of Sketch-Square. Sketch-Rectangle and Sketch-Square are displayed in the Profile box.
5. Select **Normal To Profile** for the Start constraint.
6. Enter **30**deg for Draft angle.
7. Enter **1.5** for Start Tangent Length.
8. Select **Normal To Profile** for the End constraint.

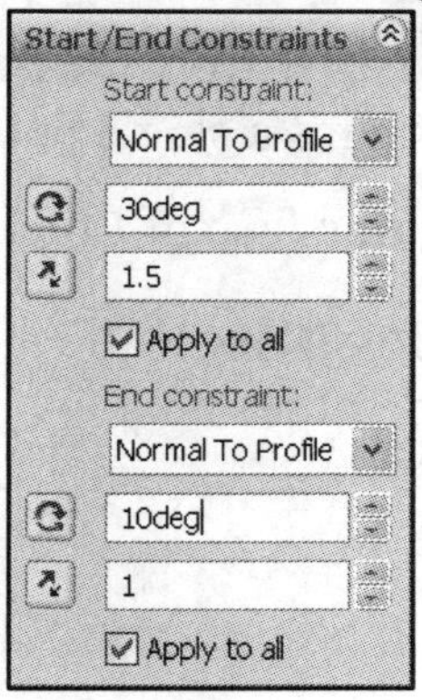


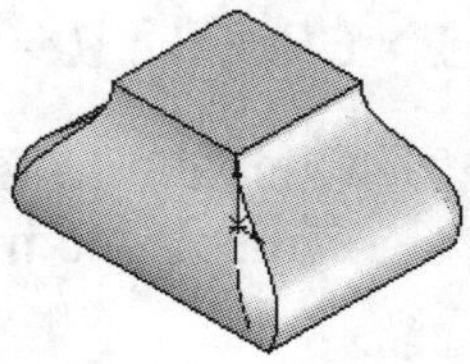

9. Enter **10**deg for Draft angle.
10. Enter **1** for End Tangent Length.
11. Click **OK** ✔ from the Loft PropertyManager. Loft1 is created and is displayed in the FeatureManager.
12. **Close** the model.

### *Tutorial: Loft Guide Curves 10-1*

Create a Loft base feature with profiles on different planes and two Guide Curves.

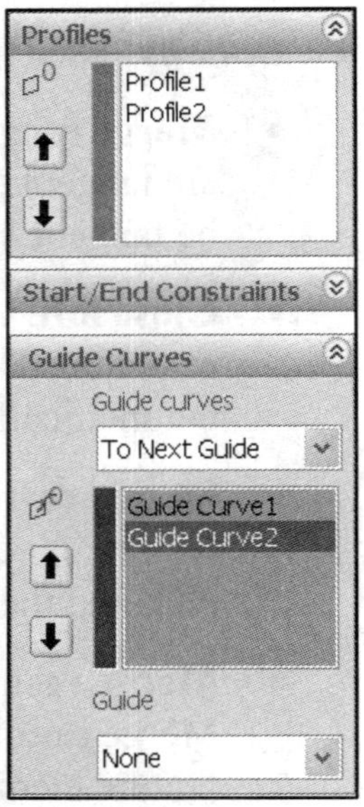


1. Open **Loft Guide Curves 10-1** from the SolidWorks 2010 folder. The part contains four sketches. Profile1 is sketched on the Front plane. Profile 2 is sketch on Plane1. Guide Curve1 and Guide Curve 2 are sketched on the Right plane.
2. Click the **Lofted Boss/Base** Features tool. The Loft PropertyManager is displayed.

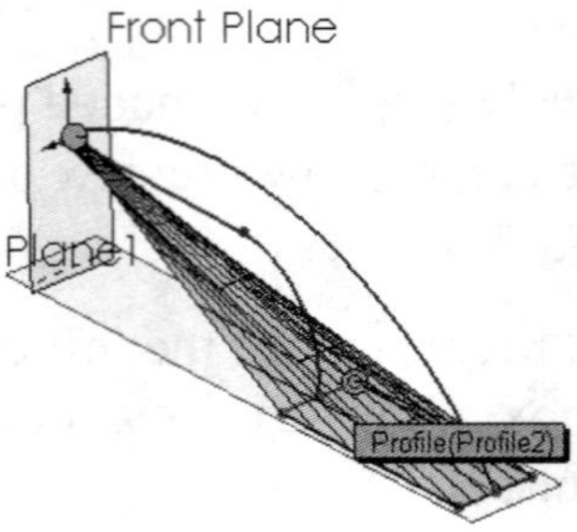


3. Click **Profile1** from the flyout FeatureManager.
4. Click **Profile2** from the flyout FeatureManager. Profile1 and Profile2 are displayed in the Profiles box.
5. Click inside of the **Guide Curves** box.

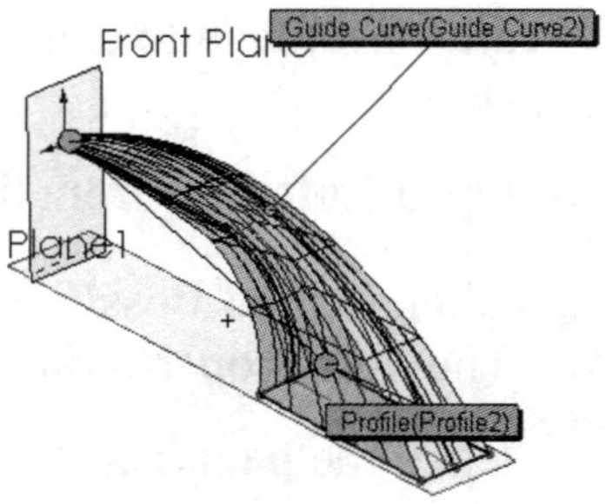


6. Select **Guide Curve1** and **Guide Curve2** from the flyout FeatureManager.
7. Click **OK** ✔ from the Loft PropertyManager. Loft1 is created and is displayed in the FeatureManager.
8. **Close** the model.

### *Tutorial: Loft to Point 10-1*

Create a Boss Loft feature utilizing a point for a profile.

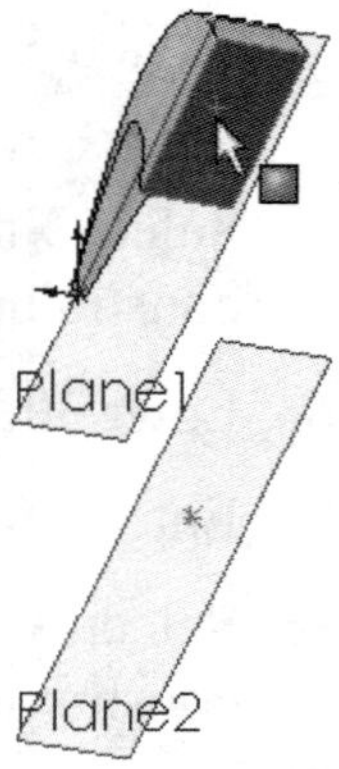


1. Open **Loft to Point 10-1** from the SolidWorks 2010 folder. Sketch1 contains a single point on Plane2.
2. Click the **Rectangular** face of Loft1 as illustrated.
3. Click the **Lofted Boss/Base** Features tool. Face<1> is displayed in the Profiles box.

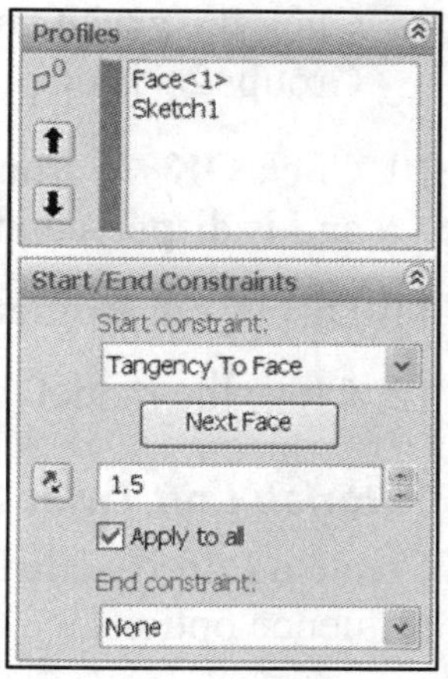


4. Click **Sketch1** from the flyout FeatureManager. Sketch1 is displayed in the Profiles box.

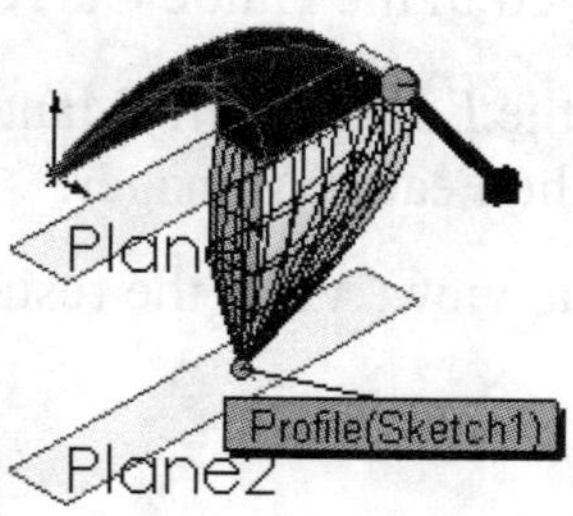


5. Select **Tangency To Face** for Start constraint.
6. Enter **1.5** Start Tangent Length.
7. Display an **Isometric** view. Accept the default conditions.
8. Click **OK** from the Loft PropertyManager. Loft2 is created and is displayed in the FeatureManager.
9. **Close** the model.

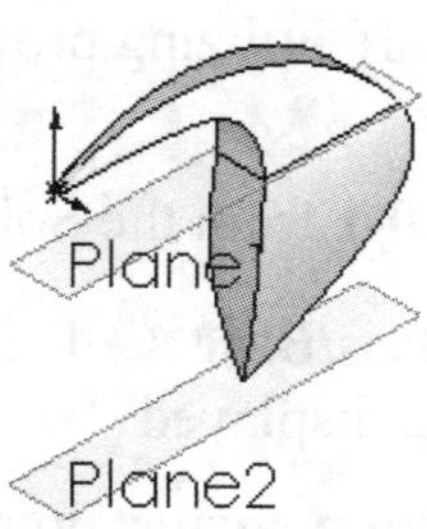


***Tutorial: Loft Multibody 10-1***

Create a Loft boss feature utilizing two individual bodies.

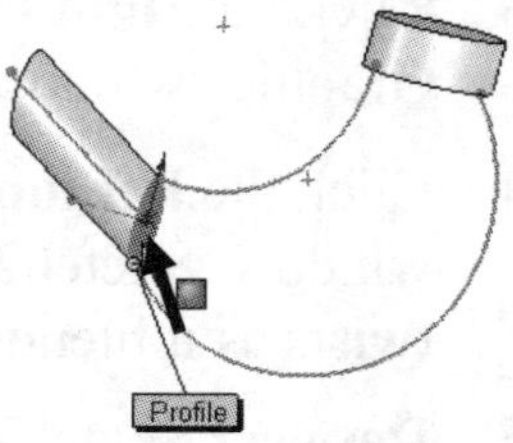


1. Open **Loft Multibody 10-1** from the SolidWorks 2010 folder. The Loft Multibody 10-1 FeatureManager is displayed.
2. Click the **Lofted Boss/Base** Features tool.
3. Click the **left circular face** of Extrude1 as illustrated. Face<1> is displayed in the Profiles box.

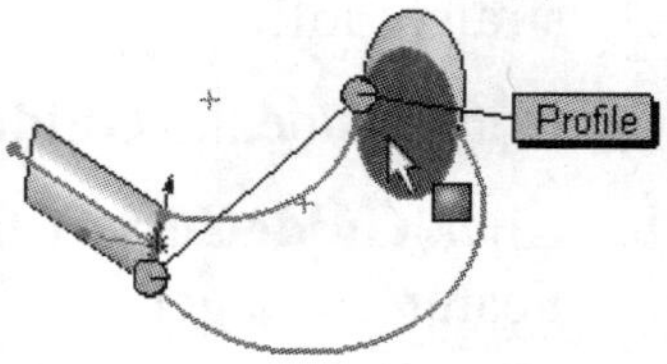


4. Click the **right bottom elliptical face** of Extrude2 as illustrated. Face<2> is displayed in the Profiles box.
5. Click inside the **Guide Curves** box.
6. Click the **bottom arc** for the first Guide Curve.

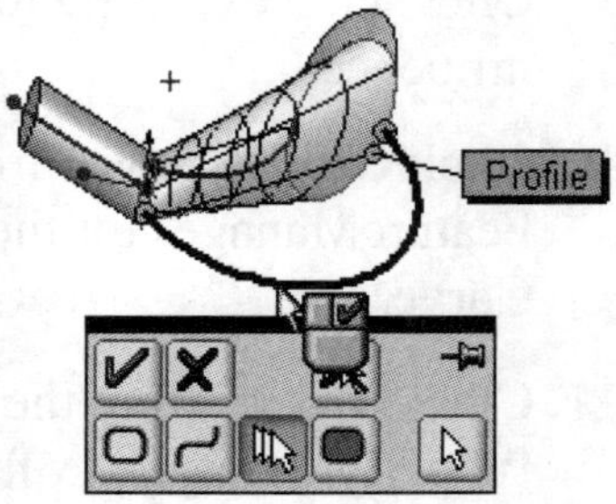


7. Click the **green check mark** to Select Open Loop. Open Group <1> is displayed in the Guide Curves box.

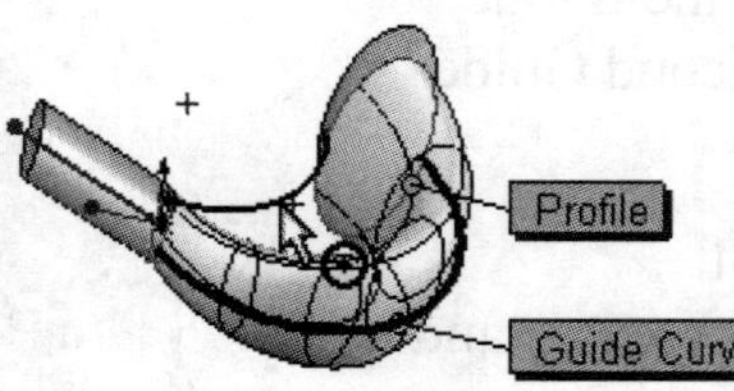


8. Click the **top arc** for the second Guide Curve.

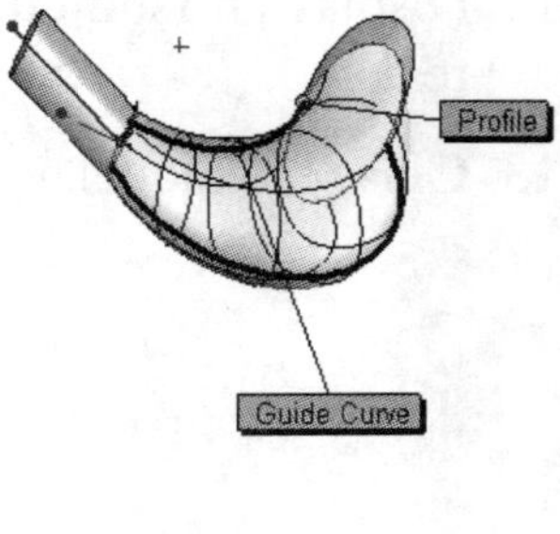

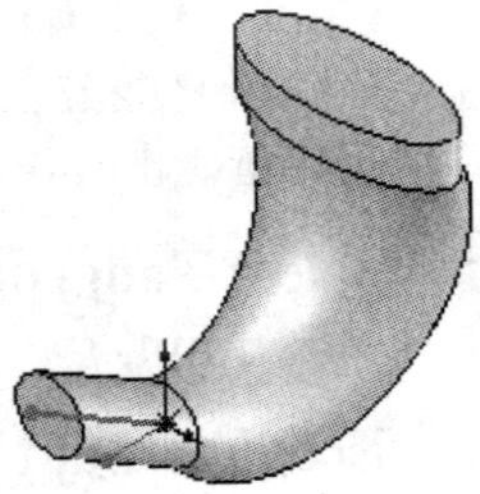

9. Click the **green check mark** to Select Open Loop. Open Group<2> is displayed in the Guide Curves box.
10. Click **OK** from the Loft PropertyManager. Loft1 is created and is displayed in the FeatureManager.
11. Display an **Isometric** view. View the results.
12. **Close** the model.

***Tutorial: Loft Twist 10-1***

Create a Loft base feature utilizing profiles and the Guide Curve influence options.

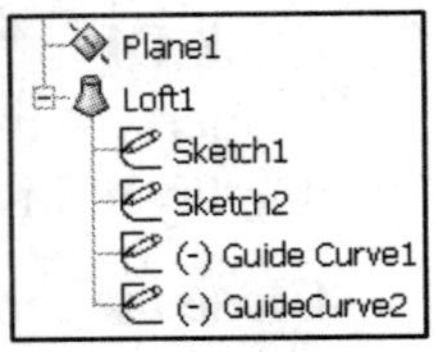


1. Open **Loft Twist 10-1** from the SolidWorks 2010 folder.
2. Click the **Lofted Boss/Base** Features tool. The Loft PropertyManager is displayed.
3. Click the **right bottom corner** point of Sketch1 in the Graphics window. Sketch1 is displayed in the Profiles box.

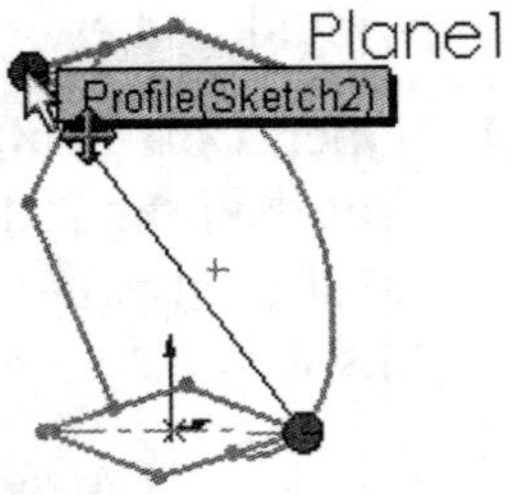


4. Click the **left top corner point** of Sketch2 in the Graphics window. Sketch2 is displayed in the Profiles box. The loft twists as it blends the two profiles.
5. **Deselect** Sketch2 in the Profiles box.
6. Click the **right top corner point** of Sketch1 to create a straight loft.

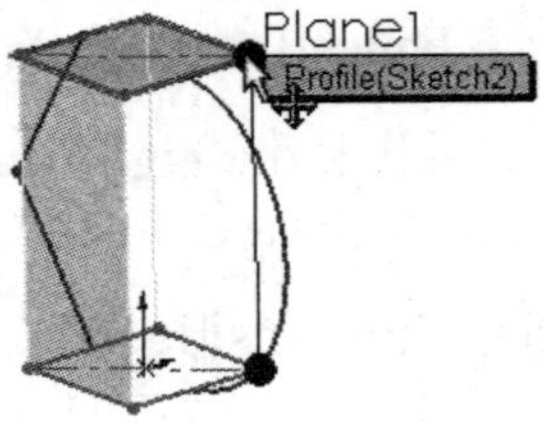


7. Click inside the **Guide Curves** box.
8. Click **GuideCurve1** from the flyout FeatureManager.
9. Click **To Next Edge** for Guide curves influence.
10. Click **GuideCurve2** from the flyout FeatureManager for the second Guide Curve.

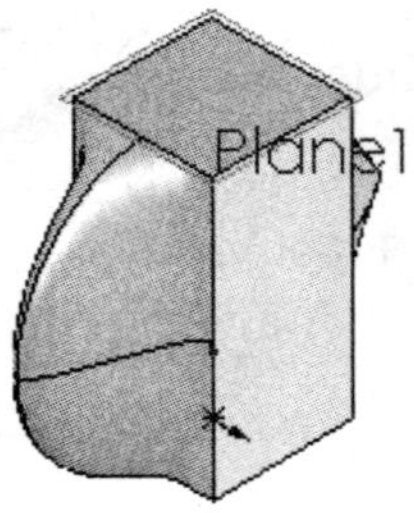


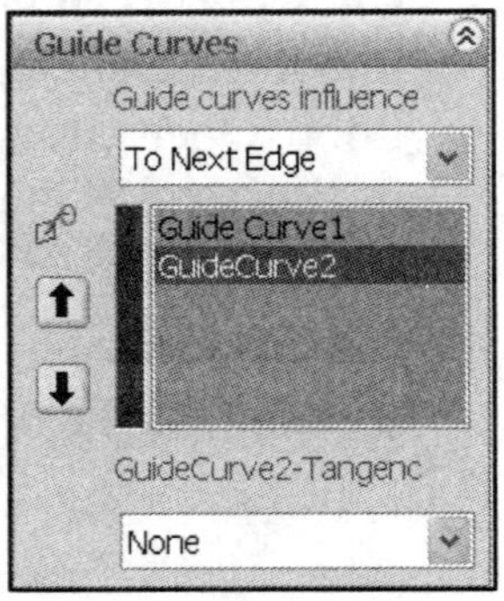


11. Click **OK** from the Loft PropertyManager. Loft1 is created and is displayed in the FeatureManager.
12. Display an **Isometric** view. View the results.
13. **Close** the model.

## Lofted Cut Feature

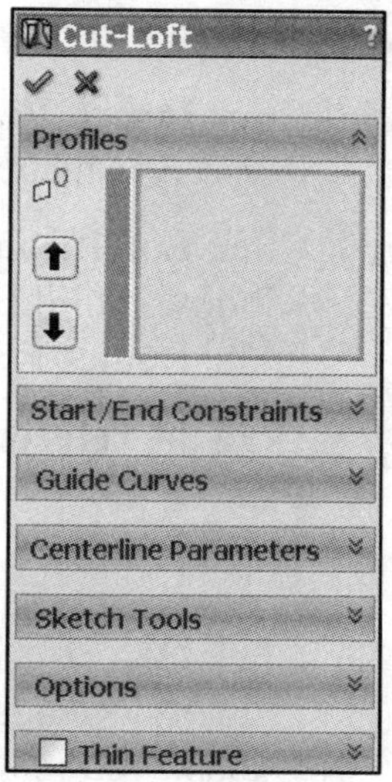


The Lofted Cut feature removes material by blending two or more sketches on different planes. A Lofted Cut feature requires a minimum of two sketched profiles. The Lofted Cut feature uses the Cut-Loft PropertyManager.

### *Tutorial: Loft Cut 10-1*

Create a Lofted Cut feature utilizing two profiles.

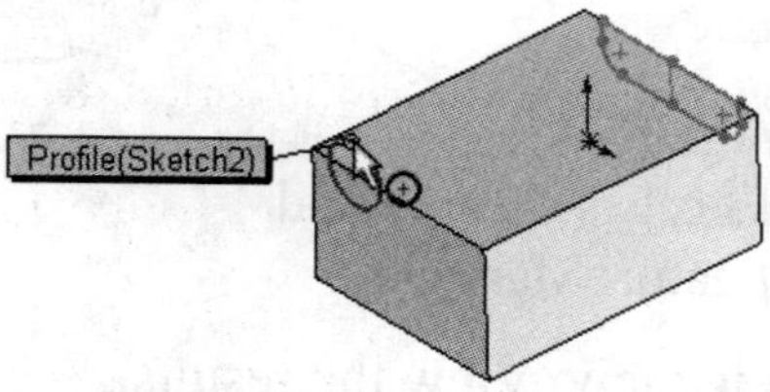


1. Open **Loft Cut 10-1** from the SolidWorks 2010 folder. The Cut Loft 10-1 FeatureManager is displayed.
2. Click the **Lofted Cut** Features tool. The Cut-Loft PropertyManager is displayed.
3. Click the **circumference** of the circle. Sketch2 is displayed in the Profiles box.
4. Click the top edge of **Sketch3** as illustrated. Sketch3 is displayed in the Profiles box.
5. Click **OK** from the Cut-Loft PropertyManager. Cut-Loft1 is displayed in the FeatureManager.
6. Display an **Isometric** view. View the results.
7. **Close** the model.

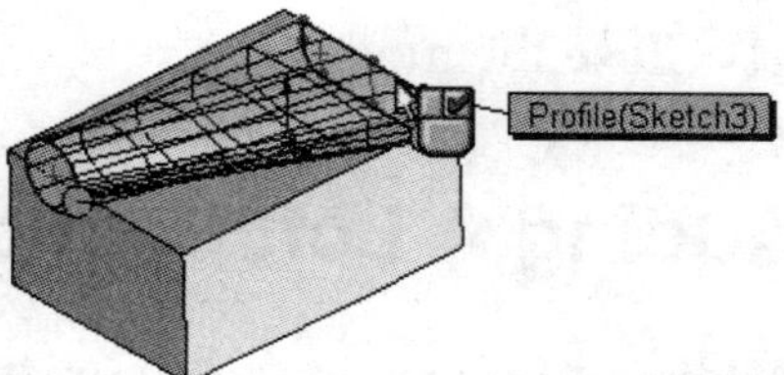


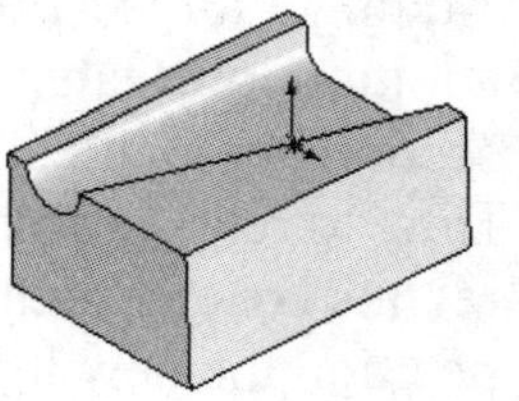

### *Tutorial: Loft Flex 10-1*

Create a Flex feature to modify a Loft feature.

1. Open **Loft Flex 10-1** from the SolidWorks 2010 folder. The Loft Flex 10-1 FeatureManager is displayed.
2. Click the **Lofted Boss/Base** Features tool. The Loft PropertyManager is displayed.
3. Click the **top right endpoint** for each profile in the Graphics window. Sketch1, Sketch2 and Sketch3 are displayed in the Profiles box.

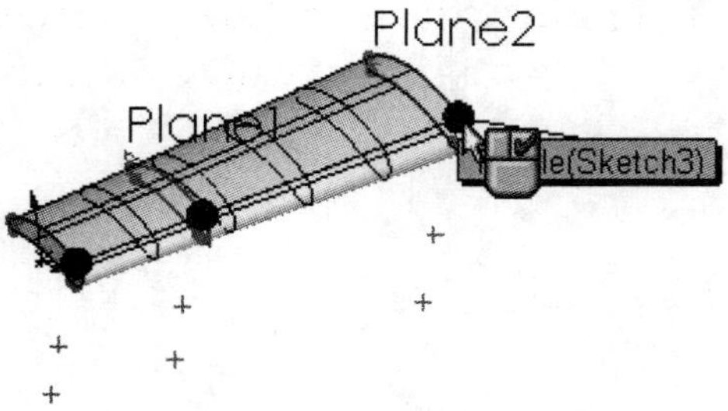

4. Click **OK** ✔ from the Loft PropertyManager. Loft1 is created and is displayed in the PropertyManager.
5. Click **Insert**, **Features**, **Flex**. The Flex PropertyManager is displayed.

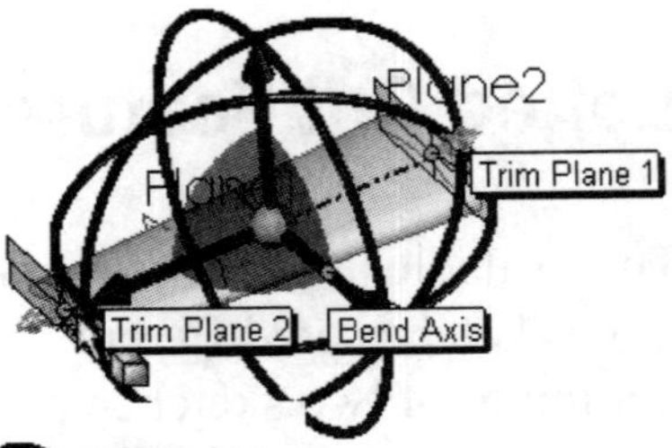


6. Click **Loft1** from the Graphics window. Solid Body<1> is displayed in the Bodies For Flex box.
7. Drag the **reference triad** towards Plane2.
8. Enter **15**deg for Angle.

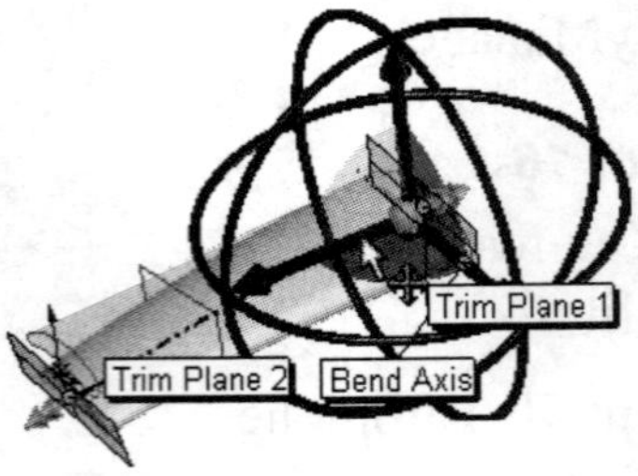


9. Click **OK** ✔ from the Flex PropertyManager. Flex1 is created and is displayed in the FeatureManager.
10. Display an **Isometric** view. View the results.
11. **Close** the model.

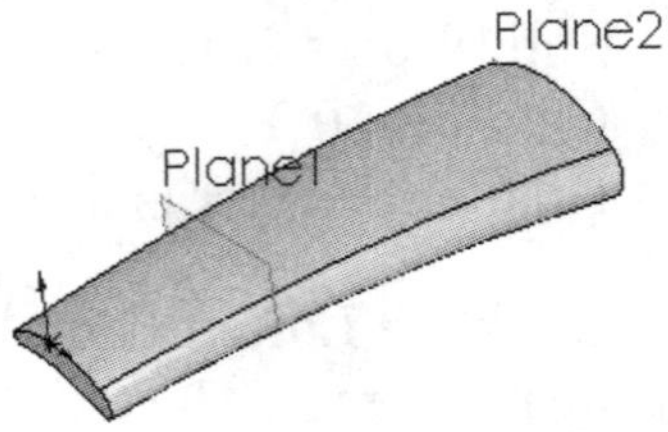


## Adding A Loft Section

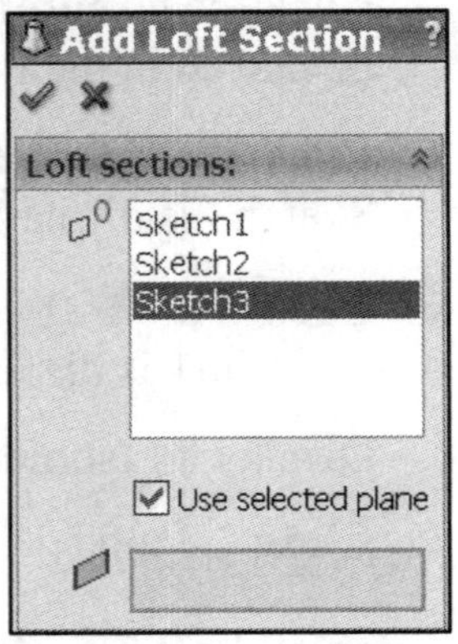


Adding a loft section to an existing Loft feature creates an addition loft feature and a temporary plane. The new loft section automatically creates pierce points at the end points. Drag to reposition the guide curve, the new loft section retains contact with the guide curve. Drag the plane to position the new loft section along the axis of the path. Use a pre-existing plane to position the new loft section.

Use the Context toolbar, (Right-click) to edit the new loft section. Edit the loft section in the same way that you would edit any other sketch element; add relations, dimension, modify shape, etc.

***Tutorial: Add Loft Section 10-1***

Create a Loft Section and modify the sketch.

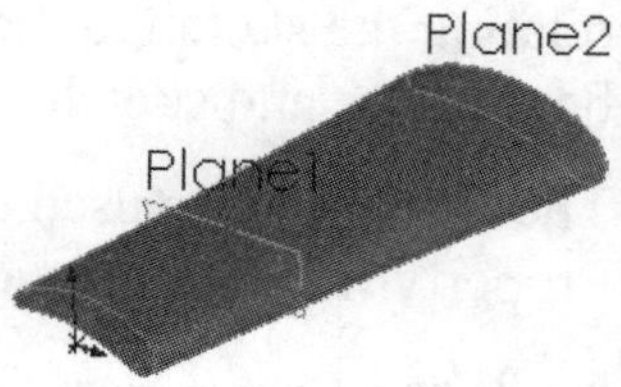


1. Open **Add Loft Section 10-1** from the SolidWorks 2010 folder. The Add Loft Section 10-1 FeatureManager is displayed.
2. Right-click **Loft1** from the FeatureManager.
3. Click **Add Loft Section**. The Add Loft Section PropertyManager is displayed.
4. Click and drag the **plane** from the Graphics window by the arrow behind Plane1 as illustrated.
5. Click **OK** ✓ from the Add Loft Section PropertyManager.

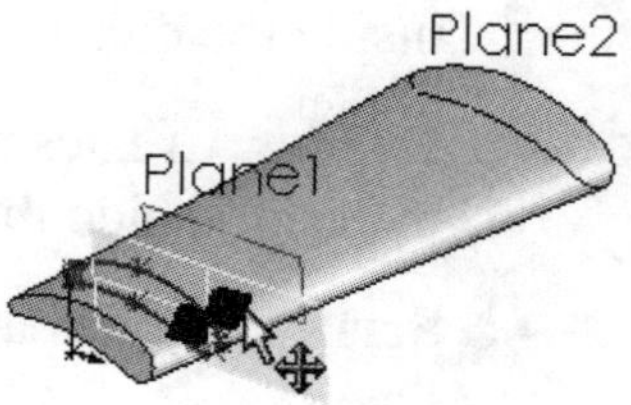


6. **Expand** Loft1 from the FeatureManager.
7. Click **Sketch4**.
8. Right-click **Edit Sketch**.
9. Drag the **top arc point** upward.

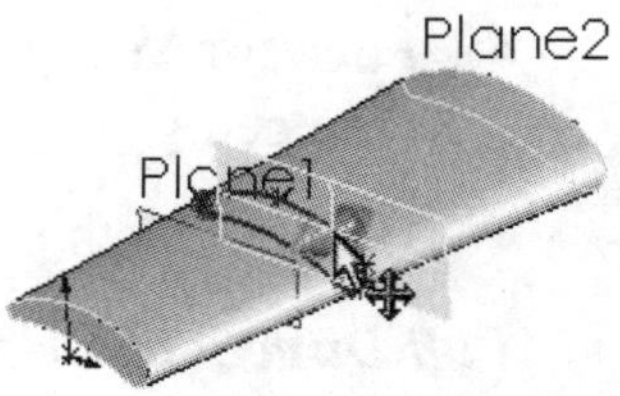


10. Click **OK** ✓ from the Point PropertyManager.
11. Click **Exit Sketch** from the Sketch toolbar to display the modified Loft1 feature.
12. Display an **Isometric** view. View the results.
13. **Close** the model.

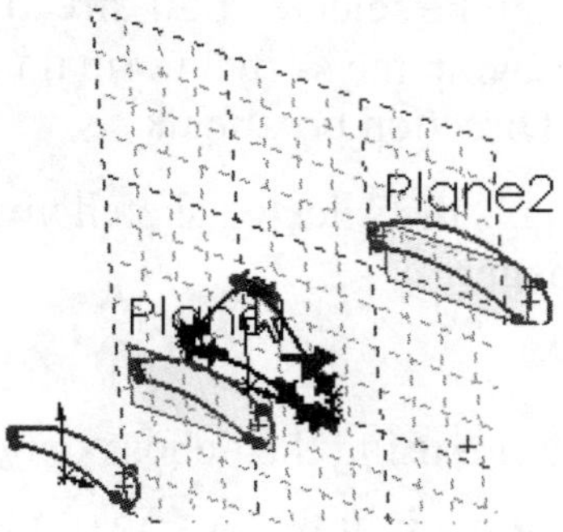


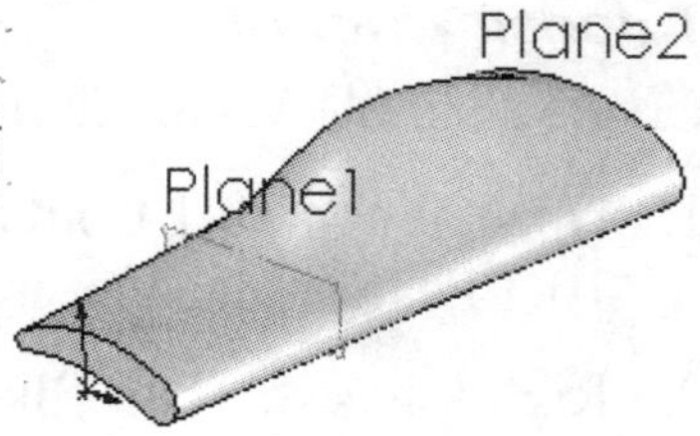


If you want to use a previously created plane instead of the temporary plane, select **Use selected plane** and select the **created plane**.

## Wrap Feature

The Wrap feature wraps a 2D sketch onto a planar or non-planar face. You can create a planar face from cylindrical, conical, or extruded models. You can also select a planar profile to add multiple, closed spline sketches.

The Wrap feature supports contour selection and sketch reuse.

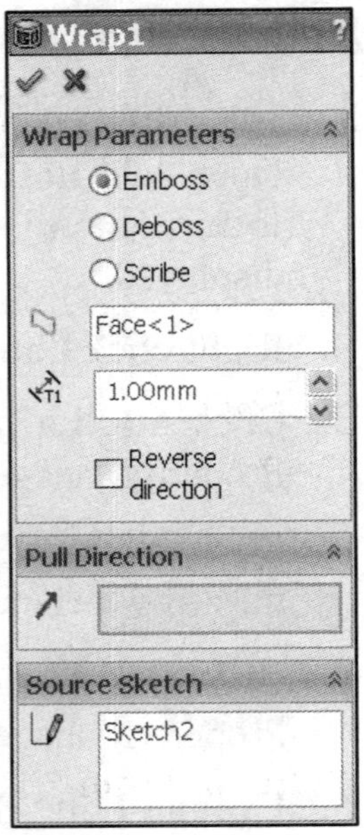


The Wrap feature provides the ability to flatten the selected face, relating the sketch to the flat pattern, and them mapping the face boundaries and sketch back onto the 3D face.

The Wrap feature used the Wrap PropertyManager. The Wrap PropertyManager provides the following selections:

- ***Wrap Parameters***. The Wrap Parameters box provides the following selections:
  - **Emboss**. Creates a raised feature on the face, adds material inside the closed loop.
  - **Deboss**. Creates an indented feature on the face, removes material inside the closed loop.
  - **Scribe**. Creates an imprint of the sketch contours on the face.
  - **Face for Wrap Sketch**. Displays the selected face to be wrapped.
  - **Depth**. Depth of the selected feature.
- ***Pull Direction***. Display the selected pull direction from the Graphics window. To wrap the sketch normal to the sketch plane, leave the Pull Direction box blank.
- ***Source Sketch***. Displays the selected sketch you want to wrap from the FeatureManager.

***Tutorial: Wrap 10-1***

Create a simple Wrap feature using the deboss option.

1. Open **Wrap 10-1** from the SolidWorks 2010 folder. The Wrap 10-1 FeatureManager is displayed.
2. Right-click the **Top Plane** from the FeatureManager. Click **Sketch** from the Context toolbar. Click the **Circle** Sketch tool. Sketch a **circle** as illustrated. Note the location of the origin.

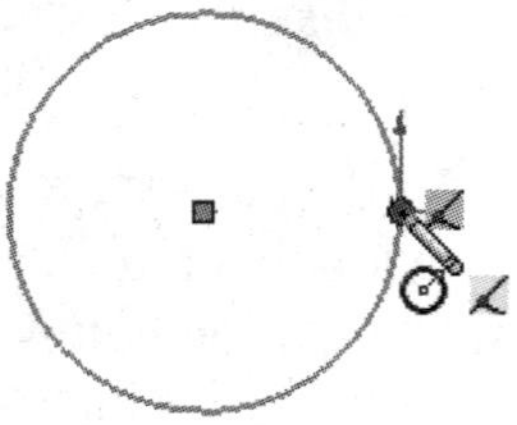

3. Click the **Extruded Boss/Base** Features tool. Blind is the default End Condition in Direction 1.
4. Enter **70**mm for Depth.

Create the sketch to Wrap.

5. Right-click the **Right Plane** from the FeatureManager. Click **Sketch** from the Context toolbar.

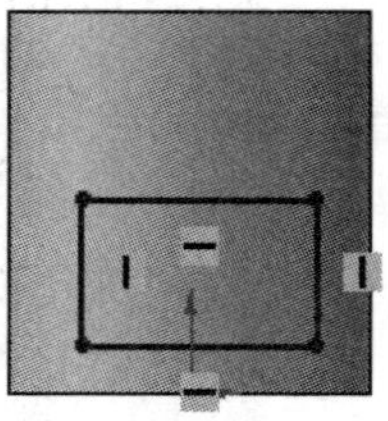

6. Click the **Corner Rectangle** Sketch tool.
7. Display a **Right** view. Sketch a **rectangle** as illustrated.

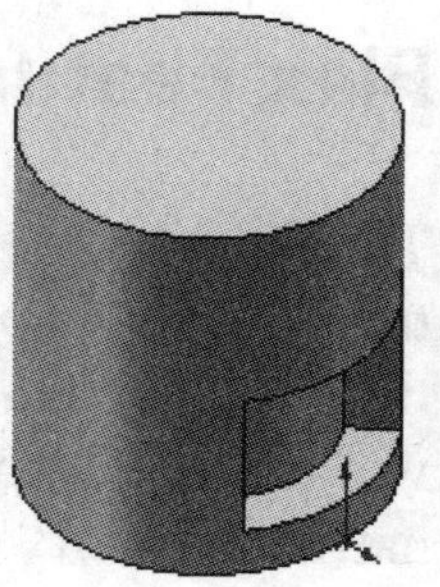

8. **Rebuild** the model. Click **Sketch2** from the FeatureManager.
9. Click the **Wrap** Features tool. The Wrap PropertyManager is display. Sketch2 is displayed in the Source Sketch box. Check the **Deboss** option.
10. Click the **right cylindrical face** of Extrude1. Face<1> is displayed in the Face for Wrap Sketch box. Enter **10**mm for Depth.
11. Click **OK** from the Wrap PropertyManager. View the results. Remember, The Sketch plane must be tangent to the face, allowing the face normal and the sketch normal to be parallel at the closest point and you cannot create a wrap feature from a sketch that contains any open contours.

***Tutorial: Wrap 10-2***

Create a simple Wrap feature using the deboss option and the Sketch Text PropertyManager.

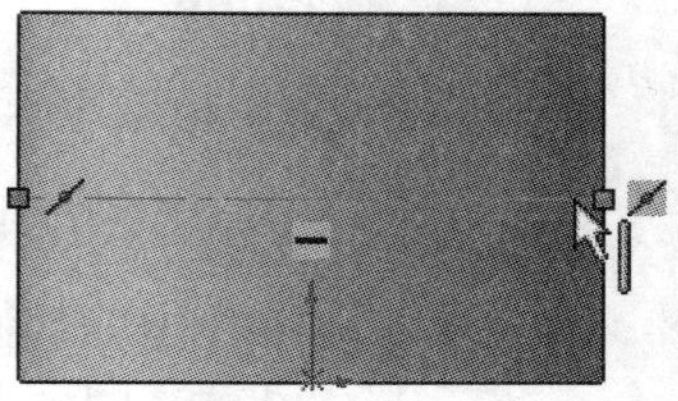

1. Open **Wrap 10-2** from the SolidWorks 2010 folder. The Wrap 10-2 FeatureManager is displayed.
2. Right-click the **Right Plane** from the FeatureManager.
3. Click **Sketch.**
4. Display a **Right** view. Sketch a horizontal **construction line** midpoint on Extrude1.

Create a text sketch.

5. Click the **Text** Sketch tool. The Sketch Text PropertyManager is displayed.
6. Click the **construction line** from the Graphics window.
7. Click **inside** the Text box.
8. Enter **Made in USA** in the Text box.
9. Click the **Center Align** button. Uncheck the **Use document font** box. Enter **150%** in the Width Factor box. Enter **120%** in the Spacing box.
10. Click **OK** from the Sketch Text PropertyManager. **Rebuild** the model.
11. Click **Sketch2** from the FeatureManager. Click the **Wrap** Features tool. The Wrap PropertyManager is display. Sketch2 is displayed in the Source Sketch box. Select the **Deboss** option.
12. Click the **right cylindrical face** of Extrude1. Face<1> is displayed in the Face for Wrap Sketch box. Enter **10**mm for Depth.
13. Click **OK** from the Wrap PropertyManager. View the results.
14. **Close** the model.

# Flex Feature

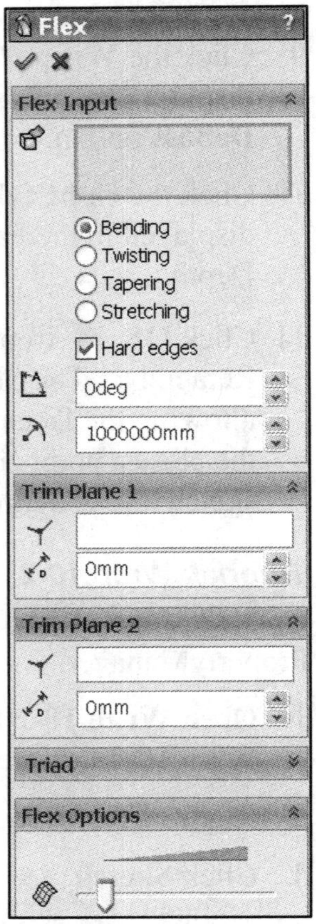


The Flex feature takes existing SolidWorks geometry and modifies its shape. The Flex feature provides the ability to modify the entire model, or just a portion of the model. The Flex feature works on both solid and surface bodies as well as imported and native geometry.

The Flex feature uses the Flex PropertyManager. The Flex PropertyManager provides the following selections:

- ***Flex Input***. The available selections are:
  - **Bodies for Flex** box. Displays the selected bodies to flex.
  - **Flex types**: The available selections are:
    - **Bending**. Bends one or more bodies about the triad's red X-axis (the bend axis). Position the triad and trim planes to control the degree, location, and extent of bending.
      - **Angle**. Displays the bend angle.
      - **Radius**. Displays the bend radius.
    - **Twisting**. Twists solid and surface bodies. Position the triad and trim planes to control the degree, location, and extent of twisting. Twisting occurs about the triad's blue Z-axis.
      - **Angle**. Displays the angle of twist.
    - **Tapering**. Tapers solid and surface bodies. Position the triad and trim planes to control the degree, location, and extent of tapering. Tapering follows the direction of the triad's blue Z-axis.
      - **Taper factor**. Sets the amount of taper. Note: The trim planes do not move when you adjust the Taper factor.
    - **Stretching**. Stretches solid and surface bodies. Specify a distance or drag the edge of a trim plane with the left mouse button. Stretching follows the direction of the triad's blue Z-axis.
      - **Stretch distance**. Displays the amount of stretch.
- ***Trim Planes***. The Trim Plane section provides two options. They are:
  - **Select a reference entity for Trim Plane**. Locates the origin of the trim plane to a selected point on the model.

- **Trimming distance**. Moves the trim plane from the outer extents of the bodies along the trim plane axis (blue Z-axis) of the triad. Set a value.
- ***Triad***. The Triad box provides the following selections:
  - **Select a coordinate system feature**. Locks the position and orientation of the triad to a coordinate system. Note: You must add a coordinate system feature to the model to use this option.
  - **Rotation Origin**. Moves the triad along the specified axis, relative to the triad's default location.
  - **Rotation Angle**. Rotates the triad around the specified axis, relative to the triad itself. Set values. The angle represents rotations about the component coordinate system and are applied in this order: Z, Y, X.
- ***Flex Options***. Provides the following selection:
  - **Flex accuracy**. Controls surface quality. Increasing the quality also increases the success rate of the flex feature. For example, if you get an error message, move the slider towards the right. Move the slider only as needed; increasing surface accuracy decreases performance.

# Summary

In this chapter, you learned about the Swept Boss/Base feature, Swept Cut feature, Swept Thin feature, Loft Boss/Base feature, Wrap feature and a general overview of the Flex feature in SolidWorks. A Swept feature creates a base, boss, cut, or surface by moving a profile along a path. You addressed the Swept Boss/Base feature, Sweep Thin feature, Sweep Guide feature and the Swept Cut feature.

The Loft feature provides the ability to create a feature by creating transitions between profiles. A loft can be a Base, Boss, Cut, or Surface feature. You created a Loft feature by using two or more profiles. Remember, only the first, last, or first and last profiles can be points. You addressed the Lofted Boss/Base feature, Lofted Cut feature and added a Loft Section.

The Wrap feature provides the ability to wrap a 2D sketch onto a planar or non-planar face. You can create a planar face from either a cylindrical, conical, or extruded model. The wrap feature supports contour selection and sketch reuse. The Wrap feature provides the ability to flatten the selected face, relating the sketch to the flat pattern, and them mapping the face boundaries and sketch back onto the 3D face.

The Flex feature takes existing SolidWorks geometry and modifies its shape. The Flex feature provides the ability to modify the entire model, or just a portion of the model. The Flex feature works on both solid and surface bodies as well as imported and native geometry.

In Chapter 11, explore and address Assembly modeling using the Bottom-up assembly modeling technique and the ability to insert Standard Mates, Advance Mates, Mechanical Mates, SmartMates, InPlace Mates and Mate References. You will also explore the Large Assembly mode, resolving Mating problems with the MateXpert tool and applying Instant3D in an Assembly.

# CHAPTER 11: BOTTOM-UP ASSEMBLY MODELING

## Chapter Objective

Chapter 11 provides a comprehensive understanding of Bottom-up assembly modeling techniques, the ability to address Standard Mates, Advance Mates, Mechanical Mates, InPlace Mates, SmartMates, Mate References, Large Assembly mode and Instant3D in an assembly. On the completion of this chapter, you will be able to:

- Apply Bottom-up assembly modeling techniques
- Understand various Assembly configuration methods:
  - Manual(Add Configuration command)
  - Configure component /Configure dimension tool
  - Design Tables
- Create an Assembly Task List – Before you begin
- Comprehend an Assembly Template
- Identify sections of the Assembly FeatureManager and various Component States
- Recognize the various Mate types:
  - Standard
  - Advanced
  - Mechanical
  - SmartMates
  - InPlace
- Apply the Mate PropertyManager:
  - Mates tab and Analysis tab
- Know and apply SmartMates
- Understand and apply Mate References
- Resolve Mating problems with the MateXpert tool
- Employ the Large Assembly mode
- Utilize the AssemblyXpert tool
- Apply Instant3D in an Assembly

# Bottom-up Assembly Modeling Technique

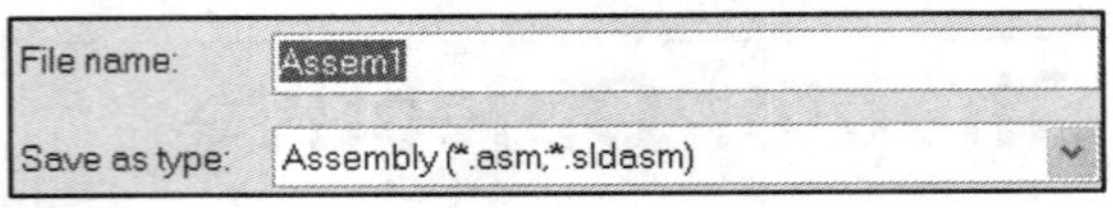


An assembly combines two or more parts. A part inserted into an assembly is called a component. A sub-assembly is a component contained within an assembly.

When you create your first assembly, Assem1.sldasm is the default document name. The Assembly document end with the extension .sldasm.

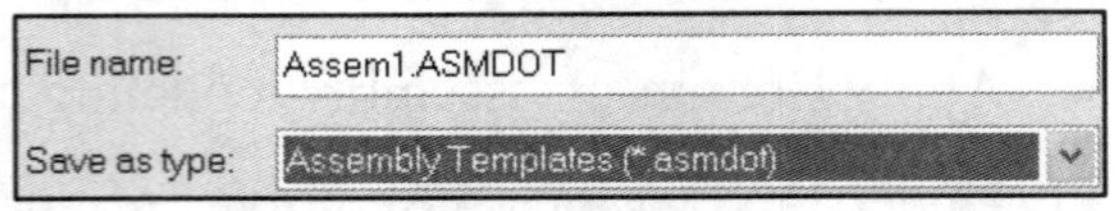


The foundation for a SolidWorks assembly is the Assembly Template. Define drawing standards, units and other properties in the Assembly Template. The Assembly Template document ends with the .asmdot extension. See Chapter 2 for additional information on templates and file locations.

## Terminology Review

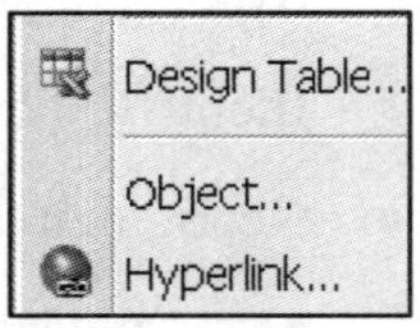


*Design Table*: Design tables are used to control dimensions values for distance and angle mates, assembly features, the suppression state or visibility of components and the configurations of components within the assembly.

*Hide components*: The Hide component tool provides the ability to remove a component's graphics without removing the component or its dependents. Mates associated with hidden components are still evaluated.

*Lightweight components*: When an operation requires model data that is not loaded for a lightweight component, the software fully resolves the part for you, to gain access to the additional data. This happens automatically when you do any of the following things: Right-click a part or feature, and select **Edit Part**, **Edit Sketch** or **Edit Feature**. The part becomes fully resolved, and you are in **Editing Part** mode.

*Suppress*: The Suppress tool provides the ability to temporarily remove a component. When a component is suppressed, the system treats the component as if it does not exist.

This means other components and mates that are dependent, will be suppressed. In addition, suppressed components are removed from memory, freeing up system resources. Suppressed components can be resolved (un-suppressed) at any time.

## Assembly Configurations Methods

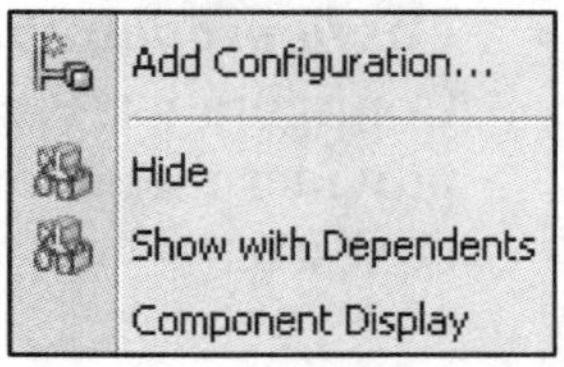


You can create assemblies using the Bottom-Up design approach, the Top-Down design approach, or a combination of both methods. This chapter focuses on the Bottom-up design approach technique. The Bottom-up design approach is the traditional method that combines individual components. Based on design criteria, the components are developed independently. There are several ways to create assembly configurations. Three ways are explored in this book. Note: See Chapter 12 for additional information and short tutorials on these methods.

- *Manual(Add Configuration)*
- *Design Tables*
- *Configure component tool / Configure dimension tool*

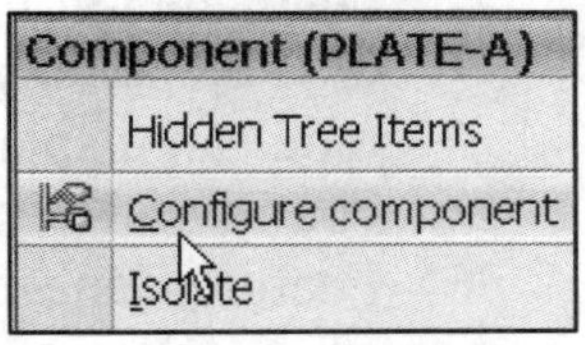


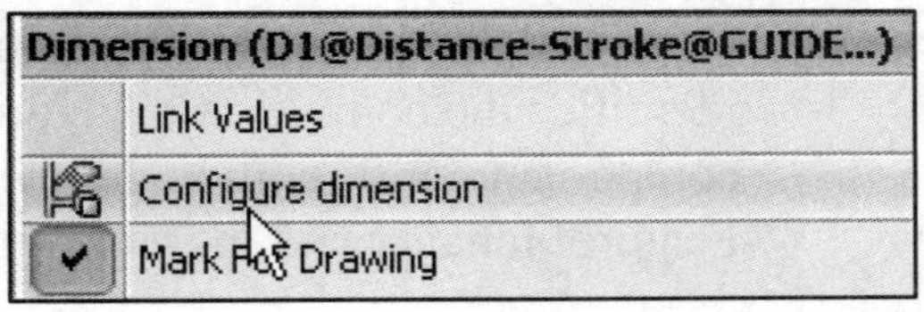


The three major steps in a Bottom-up design approach are:

1. Create each component independent of any other component in the assembly.
2. Insert the components into the assembly.
3. Mate the components in the assembly as they relate to the physical constraints of your design.

The Bottom-up design approach is the preferred technique for previously constructed, off-the-shelf parts, or standard components. Example: hardware, pulleys, motors, etc. These parts do not change their size and shape based on the design unless you choose a different component.

## Manual (Add Configuration)

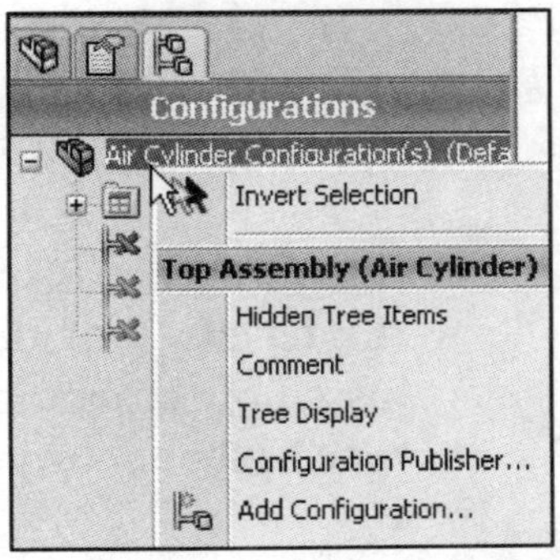


The Manual (Add Configuration) method uses the Add Configuration PropertyManager. Right-click the assembly name in the ConfigurationManager and click the Add Configuration command. The Add Configuration PropertyManager is displayed.

The Add Configuration PropertyManager is document dependent. The Add Configuration PropertyManager provides the following options:

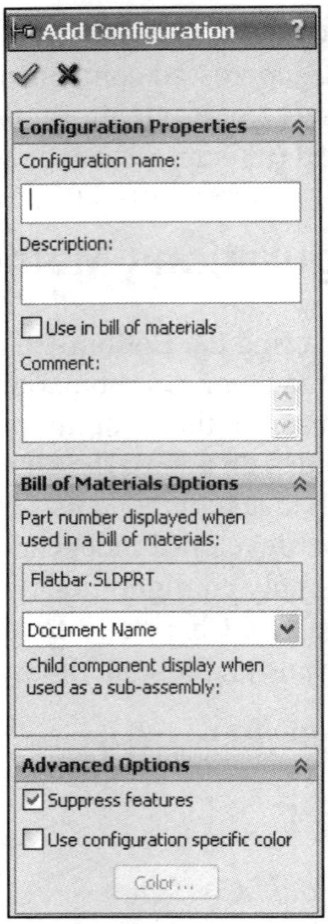


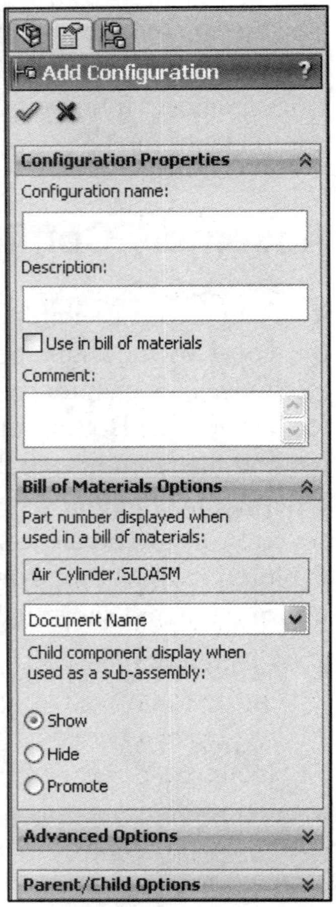


- ***Configuration Properties***. The Configuration Properties box provides the following dialog boxes:

  - **Configuration name**. Type a name for the configuration. The name must not include the forward slash (/) or "at" sign (@). A warning message is displayed when you close the dialog box if the name field contains either of these characters, if the field is blank, or if the name already exists. You can display component configuration names in the FeatureManager design tree.

  - **Description** (optional). Type a description that identifies the configuration. You can display component configuration descriptions in the FeatureManager and the ConfigurationManager.

  - **Use in bill of materials**. Specify how the assembly or part is listed in a Bill of Materials.

  - **Comment** (Optional). Type additional descriptive information about the configuration.

  - **Custom Properties** (available only when editing properties of an existing configuration). Click to access Configuration Specific properties in the Summary Information dialog box.

- ***Bill of Materials Options***. The Bill of Materials Options box provides the following dialog boxes:

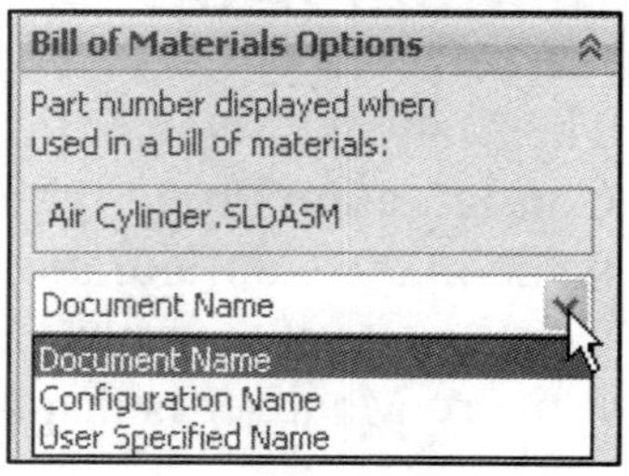


  - **Part number displayed when used in a bill of materials**. Provides the ability to specify how the assembly or part is listed in a Bill of Materials. Select one of the following: **Document Name**. The part number is the same as the document name, **Configuration Name**. The part number is the same as the configuration name, **Link to Parent Configuration**. (For derived configurations only.) The part number is the same as the parent configuration name, and **User Specified Name**. The part number is a name that you type.

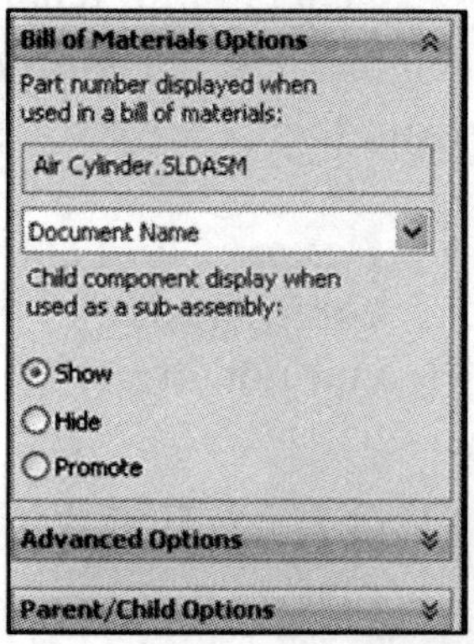


- **Show**. Selected by default. Show child components in BOM when used as sub-assembly (assemblies only).

- **Hide.** When selected, the sub-assembly is always shown as a single item in the Bill of Materials.

- ***Advanced Options***. The Advanced Options box provides the following dialog boxes: Note: The following properties control what happens when you add new items to another configuration, and then activate this configuration again. Options are document dependent.

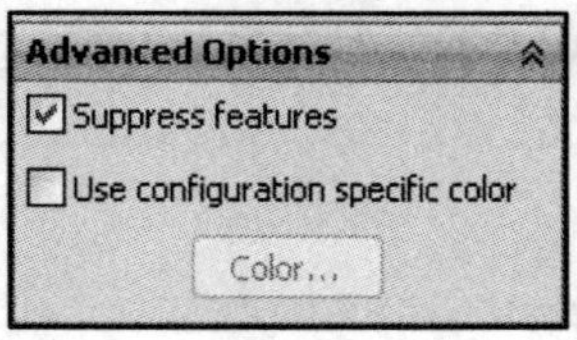


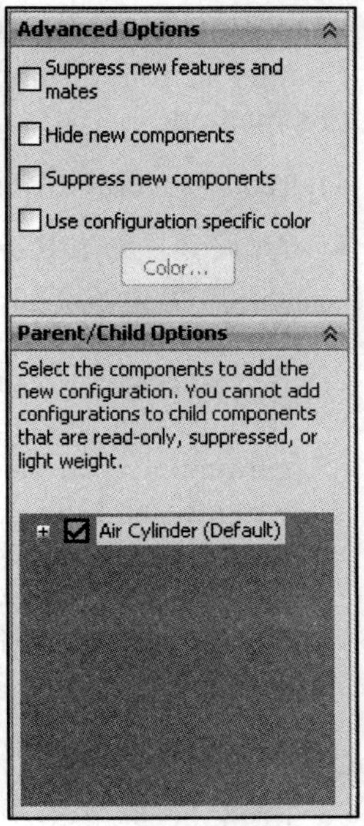


- **Suppress new features and mates** (assembly only). When selected, new features added to other configurations are suppressed in this configuration. Otherwise, new features are included (not suppressed) in this configuration.

- **Hide new components** (assemblies only). When selected, new components added to other configurations are hidden in this configuration. Otherwise, new components are displayed in this configuration.

- **Suppress new components** (assemblies only). When selected, new components added to other configurations are suppressed in this configuration. Otherwise, new components are resolved (not suppressed) in this configuration.

- **Use configuration specific color**. Provides the ability to specify a color for the configuration. Select the check box. Click **Color** to choose a color from the color palette.

By default, when you create a sub-assembly, it is in the rigid mode. Right-click the **component** in the assembly. Click **Component Properties** from the Context toolbar. Set the desired mode.

- ***Parent/Child Options*** (assemblies only). Available when adding a new configuration to the assembly or one of its components. Select the components to which you want to add the new configuration.

## Design Tables

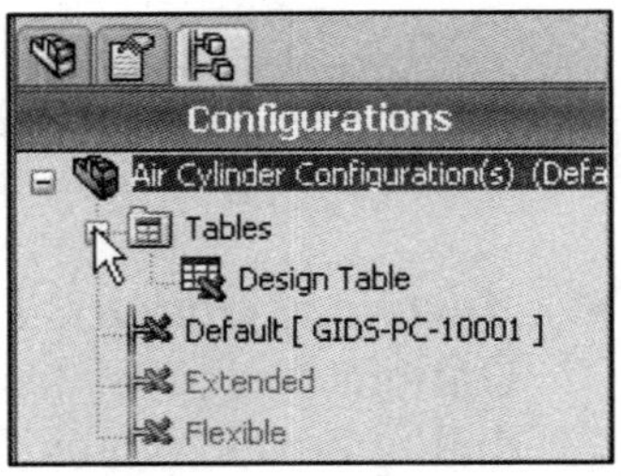


A design table provides the ability to build multiple configurations of parts or assemblies by specifying parameters in an embedded Microsoft Excel worksheet. Note: See Chapter 12 for additional information and short tutorials on this method.

There are several different ways to insert a design table. You can:

- ***Have the SolidWorks Software automatically insert one for you***. In a part or assembly document, click **Design Table** from the Tools toolbar, or click **Insert**, **Design Table** from the Menu bar menu. In the PropertyManager, under Source, select **Auto-create**. Set any needed settings or Options. Click **OK**. Depending on the settings you selected, a dialog box may appear that asks which dimensions or parameters you want to add. An embedded worksheet is displayed in the Graphics window, and the SolidWorks toolbars are replaced with Excel toolbars. Cell A1 identifies the worksheet as Design Table for: *<model_name>*. Click anywhere **outside** of the worksheet, in the Graphics area to close the design table. A message lists the configurations that were created. The Design Table is displayed in the ConfigurationManager.

- ***Insert a blank design table***. In a part or assembly document, click **Design Table** from the Tools toolbar, or click **Insert**, **Design Table** from the Menu bar menu. The Design Table PropertyManager is displayed. In the PropertyManager, under Source, click **Blank**. Set any needed settings or Options. Click **OK**. Depending on the settings you selected, a dialog box may appear that asks which dimensions or parameters you want to add. An embedded worksheet is displayed in the Graphics window, and the SolidWorks toolbars are replaced with Excel toolbars. Cell A1 identifies the worksheet as Design Table for: *<model_name>*. Cell A3 contains the default name for the first new configuration, First Instance.

In row **2**, type the parameters that you want to control. Leave cell **A2** blank. Notice that cell B2 is active. In column **A** (cells **A3**, **A4**, etc), type the names of the configurations that you want to create. The names can include numeric but must not include the forward slash (/) or at (@) characters. Type the parameter values in the worksheet cells. When you finish adding information to the worksheet, click **outside** the table to close it.

You can also enter parameters by double-clicking the feature or dimension in the graphics area or in the FeatureManager design tree. When you double-click a feature or dimension, its associated value is displayed in the **Default** row.

- ***Insert an external MS Excel table as a design table***. In a part or assembly document, click **Design Table** from the Tools toolbar, or click **Insert**, **Design Table** from the Menu bar menu. The Design Table PropertyManager is displayed. In the PropertyManager, under Source, click **From file**, click **Browse** to locate the Excel file. To link the design table to the model, select the **Link to file** check box. A linked design table reads all of its information from an external Excel file. Note: If you update a linked design table in Microsoft Excel, then open the SolidWorks model, you can choose to update either. Click **OK**. An embedded worksheet is displayed in the window, and the SolidWorks toolbars are replaced with Excel toolbars. Click anywhere **outside** of the worksheet (but in the graphics window) to close the design table.

An External reference is created when one document is dependent on another document for its solution. If the referenced document changes, the dependent document also changes.

Check **Options**, **External References**, **Do not create references external to the model**. New features or parts created in the assembly will not be created with External References.

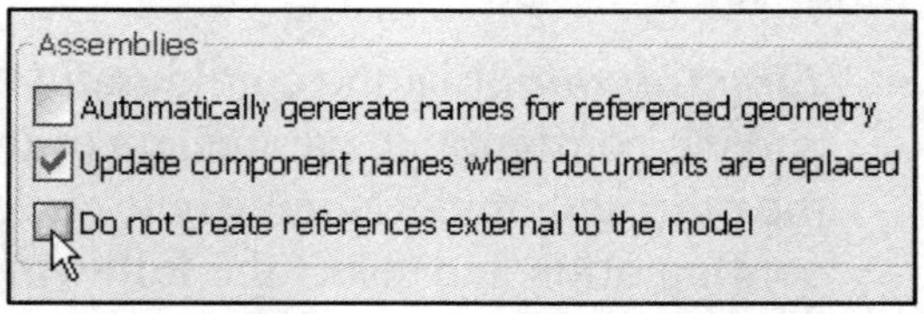


Know the default SW colors. A selected feature in the Graphics window is displayed in blue. The corresponding feature entry in the FeatureManager is displayed in blue. Fully defined sketched dimensions are displayed in black. Extruded depth dimensions are displayed in blue. Modify default colors in **Options**, **System Options**, **Colors**, **Color scheme setting**.

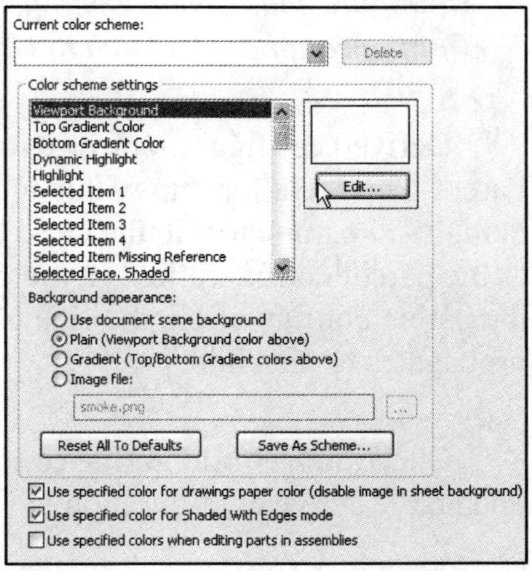


Assemblies support Instant3D. Use Instant3D to edit components within the assembly or to edit assembly level sketches, assembly features and mate dimensions. See the Instant3D assembly section at the end of this chapter.

## Configure component tool / Configure dimension tool

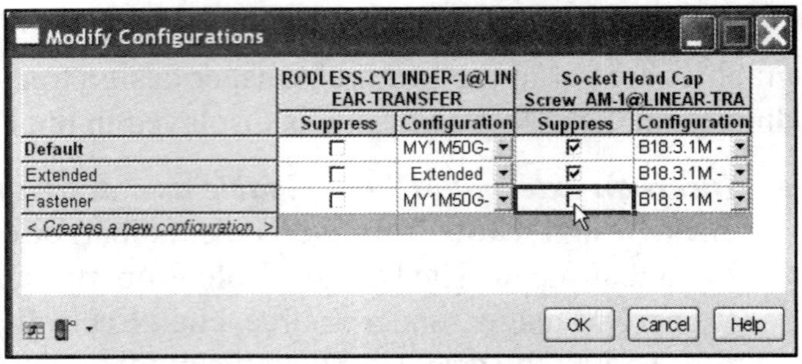


The Configure component tool / Configure dimension tool provides access to the Modify Configurations dialog box. The Modify Configurations dialog box facilitates creating and modifying configurations for commonly configured parameters in parts and assemblies. You can add, delete, and rename configurations and modify which configuration is active. Note: See Chapter 12 for additional information and a short tutorial on this method.

For features and sketches in parts, you can configure the following: Dimensions, and Suppression states.

In assemblies, you can configure the following: Which configurations of components to use, Suppression states of components, Assembly features, and mates, and Dimensions of assembly features and mates.

The Modify Configurations dialog box provides the following options:

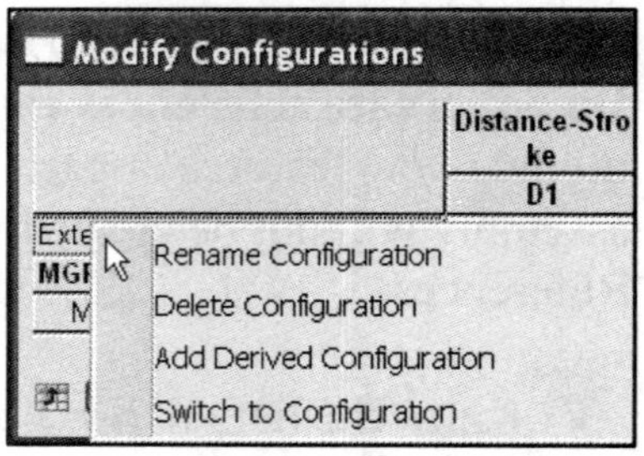


- ***First Column***. List the configurations of the model and the configurable parameters of the selected item in the other columns. Note: Right-click any configuration and select the following: *Rename Configuration, Delete Configuration, Add Derived Configuration and Switch to Configuration.*

Derived configurations provide the ability to create a Parent-Child relationship within a configuration. By default, all parameters in the child configuration are linked to the parent configuration. If you change a parameter in the parent configuration, the change automatically propagates to the child.

Click the **Rebuild active configuration** icon to update the active configuration.

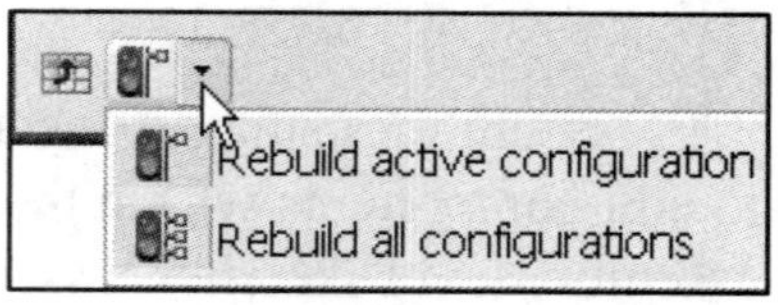


- ***Parameter Columns***. Provides the ability to click in a cell and; Type to change the numeric values, Select from a list of component configurations, or to Change the suppression state of features, sketches, components and mates.

# Assembly Task List – Before you begin

You are required to perform numerous tasks before you create a SolidWorks assembly. Review the following tasks.

- Review the Assembly Layout Diagram. Group components into sub-assemblies.
- Comprehend the geometric and functional requirements of purchased components. Understand the interaction between components in the assembly. Examine the fit and function of each component. Obtain model files and data specifications from your vendors.
- Place yourself in the position of the machinist, manufacturing technician, field service engineer, or customer. This will aid in the process to identify potential obstacles or design concerns before you start the assembly.
- Prepare and create the Part, Assembly, Drawing Templates ahead of time. Identify your units, dimensioning standards, and other document properties.
- Organize your documents into file folders. Place the created templates, vendor components, library components, parts, assemblies, and drawings in a specific location with a descriptive name.
- Acquire unique part numbers for your components. A unique part number will avoid duplication problems in the assembly later in the process.

# Assembly Templates

Templates are the foundation for assemblies, parts, and drawings. Document Properties address: dimensioning standards, units, text style, center marks, witness lines, arrow styles, tolerance, precision, and other important parameters. Document Properties apply only to the current document.

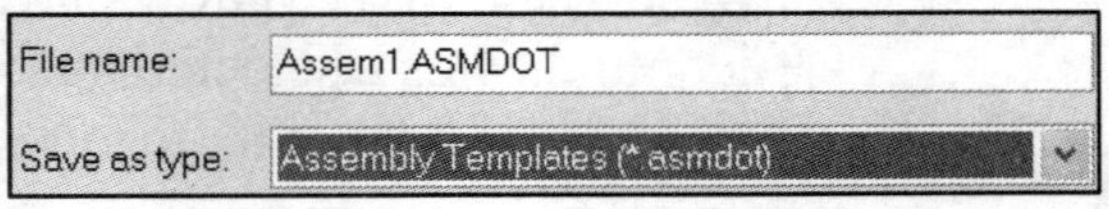


The foundation of a SolidWorks assembly is the Assembly Template. The custom Assembly Template begins with the default Assembly Template. You created a custom Assembly Template in Chapter 2 in the SolidWorks 2010\MY-TEMPLATE folder.

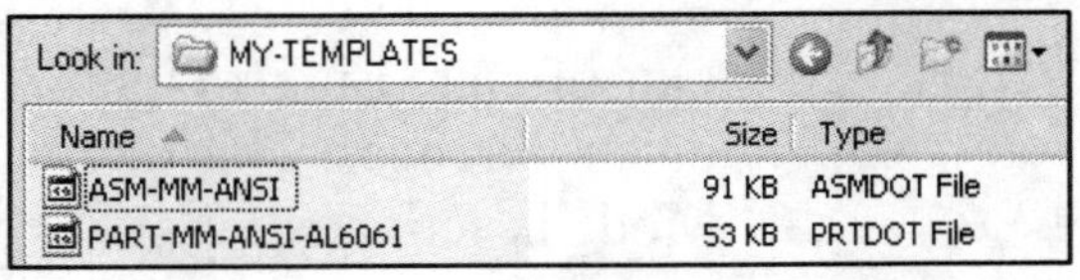


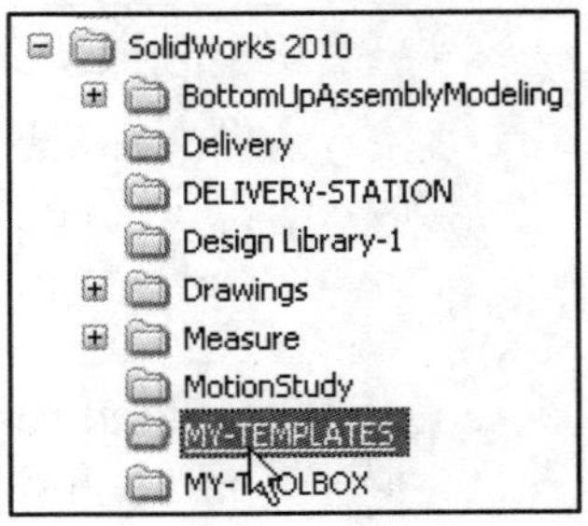


All templates are included on the CD in the book.

Conserve modeling time. Store Document Properties in the Assembly Template. Set the parameters for the Drafting standard and Units.

# Assembly FeatureManager and Component States

How do you distinguish the difference between an assembly and a part in the FeatureManager? Answer: The assembly icon contains a green square block and an upside down yellow “T” extrusion. The part icon contains an upside down yellow “T” extrusion. Entries in the FeatureManager design tree have specific definitions. Understanding syntax and states saves time when creating and modifying assemblies. Review the columns of the MGPTube part syntax in the FeatureManager.

Column 1: A resolved component (not in lightweight state) displays a plus icon. The plus icon indicates that additional feature information is available. A minus icon displays the fully expanded feature list.

Column 2: Identifies a component’s (part or assembly) relationship with other components in the assembly.

| Component States: | |
|---|---|
| **Symbol:** | **State:** |
|  | Resolved part. A yellow part icon indicates a resolved state. A blue part icon indicates a selected, resolved part. The component is fully loaded into memory and all of its features and mates are editable. |
| 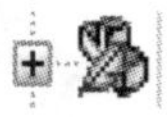 | Lightweight part. A blue feather on the part icon indicates a lightweight state. When a component is lightweight, only a subset of its model data is loaded in memory. |
|  | Out-of-Date Lightweight. A red feather on the part icon indicates out-of-date references. This option is not available when the Large Assembly Mode is activated. |
|  | Suppressed. A gray icon indicates the part is not resolved in the active configuration. |
|  | Hidden. A clear icon indicates the part is resolved but invisible. |
|  | Hidden Lightweight. A clear feather over a clear part icon indicates the part is hidden and lightweight. |

| | |
|---|---|
|  | Hidden, Out-of-Date, Lightweight. A red feather over a clear part icon indicates the part is hidden, out-of-date, and lightweight. |
|  | Hidden Smart Component. A transparent star over a transparent icon indicates that the component is a Smart Component and hidden. |
|  | Smart Component. A star overlay is displayed on the icon of a Smart Component. |
| 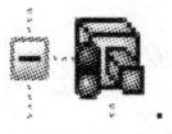 | Rebuild. A rebuild is required for the assembly or component. |
|  | Resolved assembly. Resolved (or unsuppressed) is the normal state for assembly components. A resolved assembly is fully loaded in memory, fully functional, and fully accessible. |

Column 3: The MGPTube part is fixed (f). You can fix the position of a component so that it cannot move with respect to the assembly origin. By default, the first part in an assembly is fixed; however, you can float it at any time.

It is recommended that at least one assembly component is either fixed, or mated to the assembly planes or origin. This provides a frame of reference for all other mates, and helps prevent unexpected movement of components when mates are added. The Component Properties are:

| **Component Properties in an Assembly** | |
|---|---|
| **Symbol:** | **Relationship:** |
| (-) | A floating, under defined component has a minus sign (-) before its name in the FeatureManager and requires additional information. |
| (+) | An over-defined component has a plus sign (+) before its name in the FeatureManager. |
| (f) | A fixed component has a (f) before its name in the FeatureManager. The component does not move. |
| None | The Base component is mated to three assembly reference planes. |
| (?) | A question mark (?) indicates that additional information is required on the component. |

Column 4: MGPTube - Name of the part.

Column 5: The symbol <#> indicates the particular inserted instance of a component. The symbol <1> indicates the first inserted instance of a component, "MGPTube" in the assembly. If you delete a component and reinsert the same component again, the <#> symbol increments by one.

Column 6: The Resolved state displays the MGPTube icon with an external reference symbol, "->". The state of external references is displayed as follows:

- If a part or feature has an external reference, its name is followed by ->. The name of any feature with external references is also followed by ->.
- If an external reference is currently out of context, the feature name and the part name are followed by ->?
- The suffix ->* means that the reference is locked.
- The suffix ->x means that the reference is broken.

There are modeling situations in which unresolved components create rebuild errors. In these situations, issue the forced rebuild command, Ctrl+Q. The Ctrl+Q command rebuilds the model and all its features. If the mates still contain rebuild errors, resolve all the components below the entry in the FeatureManager that contains the first error.

# General Mate Principles

Mates create geometric relationships between assembly components. As you add mates, you define the allowable directions of linear or rotational motion of the components. You can move a component within its degrees of freedom, visualizing the assembly's behavior. When creating mates, there are a few basic procedures to remember:

- Click and drag components in the Graphics window to assess their degrees of freedom.
- Remove display complexity. Hide components when visibility is not required.
- Utilize Section views to select internal geometry. Utilize Transparency to see through components required for mating.
- Apply the Move Component and Rotate Component tool from the Assembly toolbar before mating. Position the component in the correct orientation.
- Use a Coincident mate when the distance value between two entities is zero. Utilize a Distance mate when the distance value between two entities in not zero.
- Apply various colors to features and components to improve visibility for the mating process.
- Rename mates, key features, and reference geometry with descriptive names.
- Resolve a mate error as soon as it occurs. Adding additional mates will not resolve the earlier mate problem.
- Avoid redundant mates. Although SolidWorks allows some redundant mates (all except distance and angle), these mates take longer to solve and make the mating scheme harder to understand and diagnose if problems occur.

If a component is causing problems, it is often easier to delete all its mates and re-create them instead of diagnosing each one. This is especially true with aligned/anti-aligned and dimension direction conflicts (you can flip the direction that a dimension is measuring).

- Use the View Mates tool, (Right-click a **component** and select **View Mates**) or expand the component in the FeatureManager design tree using **Tree Display**, **View Mates** and **Dependencies** to view the mates for each component.

Use limit mates sparingly because they take longer to solve and whenever possible, mate all components to one or two fixed components or references. Long chains of components take longer to solve and are more prone to mate errors.

# Mate PropertyManager

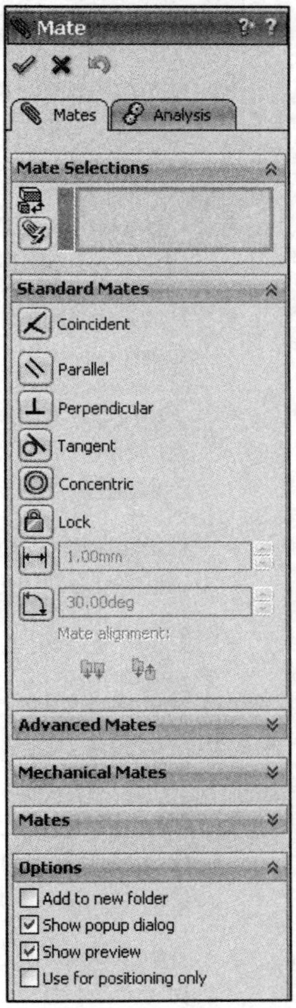


Mates provide the ability to create geometric relationships between assembly components. Mates define the allowable directions of *rotational* (3 degrees of freedom) and *linear motion* (3 degrees of freedom) of the components in the assembly.

Move a component within its degrees of freedom in the Graphics window, to view the behavior of an assembly.

Mates are solved together as a system. The order in which you add mates does not matter. All mates are solved at the same time. You can suppress mates just as you can suppress features.

The Mate PropertyManager provides the ability to select either the *Mates* or *Analysis* tab. Each tab has a separate menu. The Mate PropertyManager displays the appropriate selections based on the type of geometry you select.

## Mate PropertyManager: Mates tab

The Mates tab is the default tab. The Mates tab provides the ability to insert a *Standard, Advanced or Mechanical* mate.

- ***Mate Selections***. The Mate Selections box provide the following selections:
  - **Entities to Mate**. Displays the selected faces, edges, planes, etc. that you want to mate.
  - **Multiple mate mode**. Mates multiple components to a common reference in a single operation. When activated, the following selections are available:

- **Common references**. Displays the selected entity to which you want to mate several other components.
- **Component references**. Displays the selected entities on two or more other components to mate to the common reference. A mate is added for each component.
- **Create multi-mate folder**. Groups the resulting mates in a Multi-Mates folder.
- **Link dimensions**. Only available for Distance and Angle mates in a multi-mate folder. Provides the ability to link dimensions. The variable name in the Shared Values dialog box is the same as the multi-mate folder name.

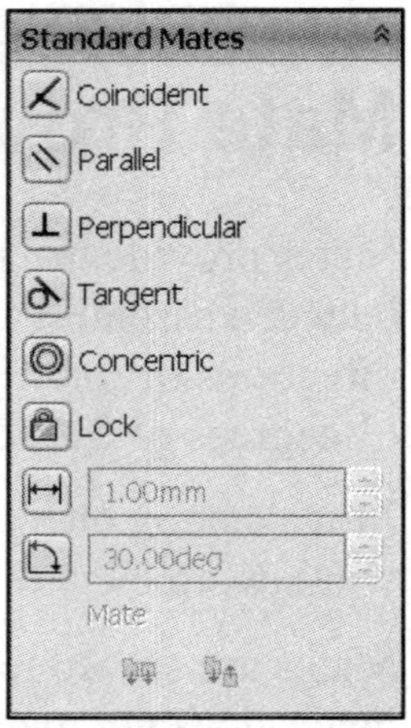


- ***Standard Mates***. The Standard Mates box provide the following selection:
  - **Coincident mate**. Locates the selected faces, edges or planes so they use the same infinite line. A Coincident mate positions two vertices for contact.
  - **Parallel mate**. Locates the selected items to lie in the same direction and to remain a constant distance apart.
  - **Perpendicular mate**. Locates the selected items at a 90 degree angle to each other.
  - **Tangent mate**. Locates the selected items in a tangent mate. At least one selected item must be either a conical, cylindrical, spherical face.
  - **Concentric mate**. Locates the selected items so they can share the same center point.
  - **Lock mate**. Enables two components to be fully constrained to each other without needing to create a rigid sub-assembly. Maintains the position and orientation between two components.

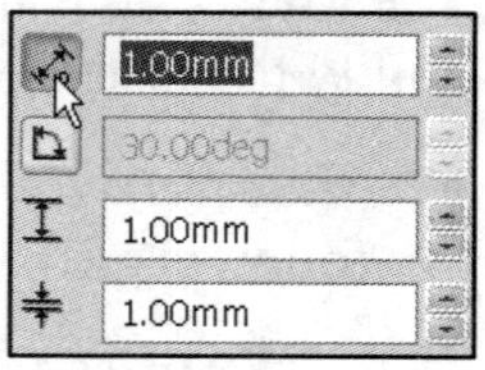


  - **Distance mate**. Locates the selected items with a specified distance between them. Use the drop-down arrow box or enter the distance value directly.
  - **Angle mate**. Locates the selected items at the specified angle to each other. Use the drop-down arrow box or enter the angle value directly.
  - **Mate alignment**. Provides the ability to toggle the mate alignment as necessary. There are two options:
    - **Aligned**. Locates the components so the normal or axis vectors for the selected faces point in the same direction.

- **Anti-Aligned**. Locates the components so the normal or axis vectors for the selected faces point in the opposite direction.

- ***Advance Mates***. The Advance Mates box provide the following selections:

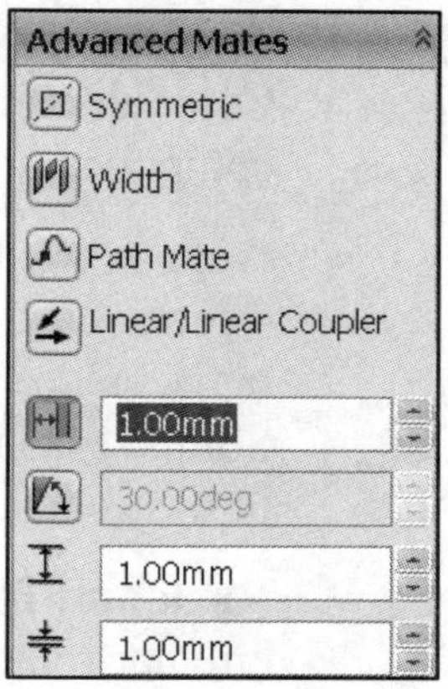


- **Symmetric mate**. Forces two similar entities to be symmetric about a planar face or plane.
- **Width mate**. Centers a tab within the width of a groove. The Width mate is used to replace the Symmetric mate where components have tolerance and a gap rather than a tight fit.
- **Path mate**. Enables any point on a component to be set to follow a defined path.
- **Linear/Linear Coupler mate**. Establishes a relationship between the translation of one component and the translation of another component.
- **Limit mate**. Provides the ability to allow components to move within a range of values for distance and angle. Select the angle and distance from the provided boxes. Specify a starting distance or angle as well as a maximum and minimum value.
  - **Distance**. Locates the selected items with a specified distance between them. Use the drop-down arrow box or enter the distance value directly (Limit mate).

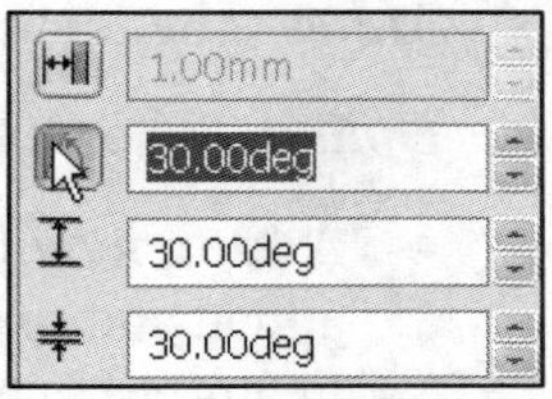


  - **Angle**. Locates the selected items at the specified angle to each other. Use the drop-down arrow box or enter the angle value directly.
- **Mate alignment**. Provides the ability to toggle the mate alignment as necessary. There are two options:
  - **Aligned**. Locates the components so the normal or axis vectors for the selected faces point in the same direction.
  - **Anti-Aligned**: Locates the components so the normal or axis vectors for the selected faces point in the opposite direction.

- ***Mechanical Mates***. The Mechanical Mates box provide the following selections:

- **Cam mate**. Forces a plane, cylinder, or point to be tangent or coincident to a series of tangent extruded faces. Four conditions can exist with the Cam mate: *Coincident, Tangent, CamMateCoincident and CamMateTangent.*

Create the profile of the cam from lines, arcs, and splines as long as they are tangent and form a closed loop. View SolidWorks help for additional information.

- **Hinge mate**. Limits the movement between two components to one rotational degree of freedom. It has the same effect as adding a Concentric mate plus a Coincident mate. You can also limit the angular movement between the two components.
- **Gear mate**. Forces two components to rotate relative to one another around selected axes. The Gear mate provides the ability to establish gear type relations between components without making the components physically mesh. Note: SolidWorks provides the ability to modify the gear ratio without changing the size of the gears. Align the components before adding the Mechanical gear mate.
- **Rack and Pinion mate**. Linear translation of one component (the rack) causes circular rotation in another component (the pinion), and vice versa. You can mate any two components to have this type of movement relative to each other. The components do not need to have gear teeth.
- **Screw mate**. Constrains two components to be concentric, and adds a pitch relationship between the rotation of one component and the translation of the other. Translation of one component along the axis causes rotation of the other component according to the pitch relationship. Likewise, rotation of one component causes translation of the other component. Align the components before adding the Mechanical screw mate.
- **Universal Joint mate**. The rotation of one component (the output shaft) about its axis is driven by the rotation of another component (the input shaft) about its axis.

- ***Mates***. The Mates box displays the activated selected mates.
- ***Options***. The Options box provide the following selections:
  - **Add to new folder**. Provides the ability for new mates to be added and to be displayed in the Mates folder in the FeatureManager design tree.
  - **Show popup dialog**. Selected by default. Displays a standard mate, when added in the Mate pop-up toolbar.
  - **Show preview**. Selected by default. Displays a preview of a mate when enough selections for a valid mate occur.
  - **Use for positioning only**. When selected, components move to the position defined by the mate. A mate is not added to the FeatureManager design tree.

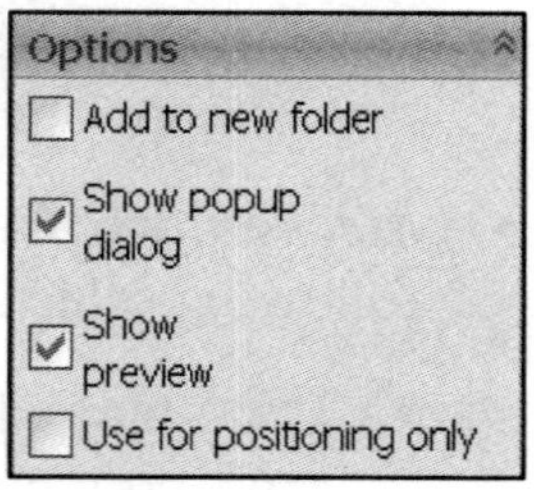


The *Use for positioning only* check box option is an alternative to adding numerous mates, then afterward deleting those mates in the FeatureManager design tree.

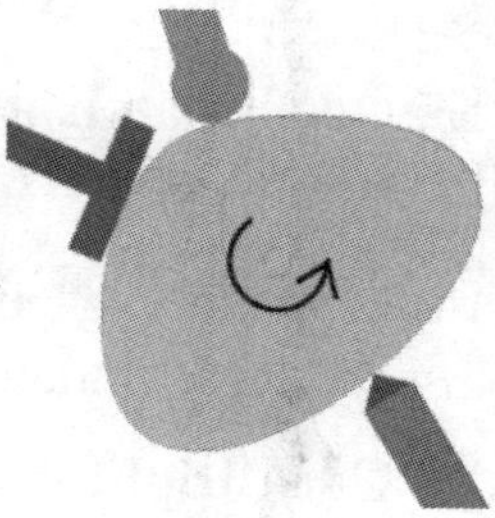

A Cam-follower mate is a type of Tangent or Coincident mate. It allows you to mate a *cylinder*, *plane* or *point* to a series of tangent extruded faces; such as you would find on a cam. Create the cam profile from lines, arcs and splines as long as they are tangent and form a **closed** loop.

When starting a Gear or Screw mate, SolidWorks creates the mate based on the current position of the models. *Align the components before adding* the Mechanical mate. To align the two components, move them manually or add a mate to get them where they need to be and then suppress the mate. The advantage in using this technique is if you need to make changes, you can suppress / unsuppress the mate to jog your component back to the starting location.

### *Tutorial: Standard Mate 11-1*

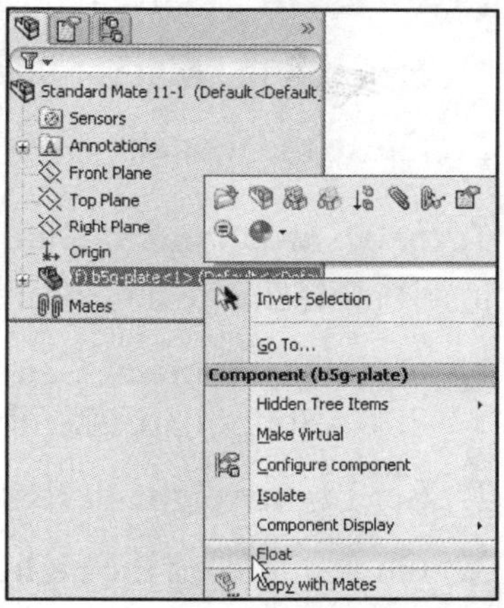


Modify the component state from fixed to float. Insert two Coincident mates, a Distance mate and apply the Align Standard mate option.

1. Open **Standard Mate 11-1** from the SolidWorks 2010\ BottomUpAssemblyModeling folder.
2. Set **Lightweight to Resolved** if needed for the model.
3. Right-click **bg5-plate** from the FeatureManager.
4. Click **Float**. The bg5-plate part is no longer fixed to the origin.

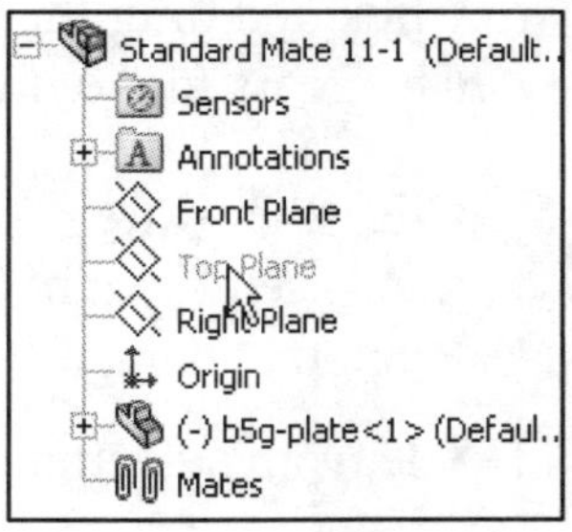


5. Click the **Mate** tool from the Assembly tab. The Mate PropertyManager is displayed. The Mates tab is selected by default.
6. Click **Top Plane** of Standard Mate 11-1 from the flyout FeatureManager.
7. Click the **back face** of bg5-plate. Top Plane and Face<1>@b5g-plate-1 are displayed in the Mate Selections box. Coincident is selected by default.

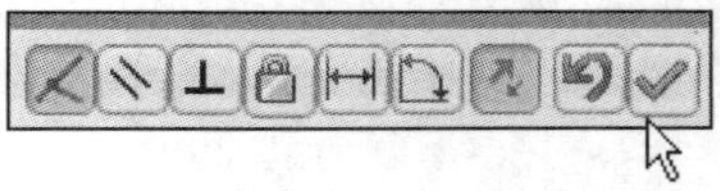

8. Click the **green check mark** from the Mate dialog box.
9. Click **Front Plane** of the Standard Mate 11-1 from the flyout FeatureManager.
10. Click **Top Plane** of bg5-plate from the flyout FeatureManager.
11. Click **Aligned** from the Standard Mate box.

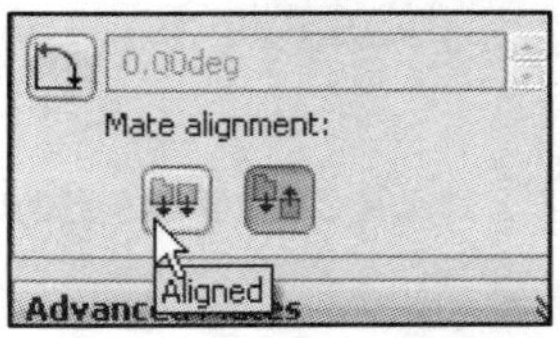

12. Click **Anti-Aligned** to review the position.
13. Display an **Isometric** view. The narrow cut faces front.

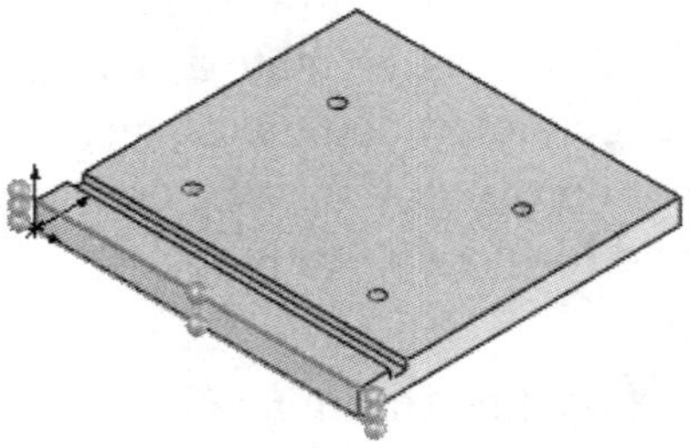

14. Click **OK** ✔ from the Coincident PropertyManager.
15. Click **Right Plane** of Standard Mate 11-1 from the flyout FeatureManager.
16. Click the **Right Plane** of bg5-plate from the flyout FeatureManager.

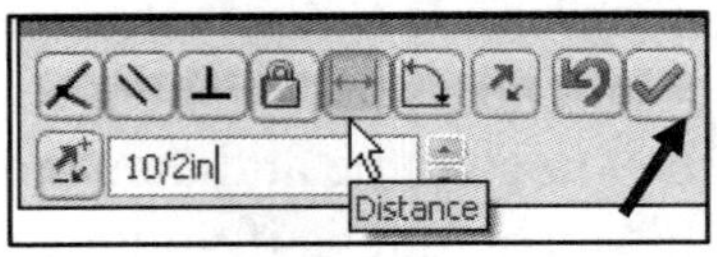


17. Select **Distance**.
18. Enter **10/2in**. The part is in inches and the assembly is in millimeter units.
19. Click the **green check mark**.
20. Click **OK** ✔ from the Mate Property Manager.
21. **Expand** the Mates folder. View the created mates.
22. **Close** the model.

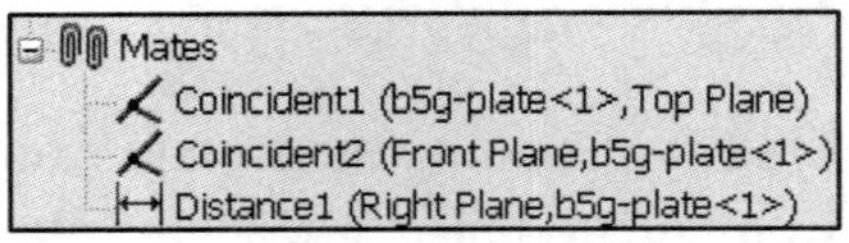


### *Tutorial: Mechanical Gear Mate 11-1*

Insert a Mechanical Gear mate between two gears.

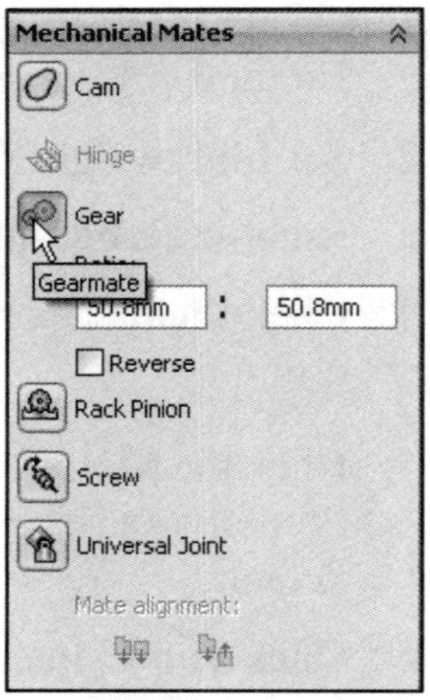


1. Open **Mechanical Gear Mate 11-1** from the SolidWorks 2010\BottomUpAssemblyModeling folder.
2. Set **Lightweight to Resolved** if needed for the model.
3. Click and drag the **right gear**.
4. Click and drag the **left gear**. The gears move independently.
5. Click the **Mate** tool from the Assembly tab. The Mate PropertyManager is displayed.

6. **Clear** all selections.
7. **Align the components** before adding the Mechanical mate. To align the two components, select a Front view and move them manually or add a mate to get them where they need to be and then suppress the mate.
8. Select the **inside cylindrical face** of the left hole.

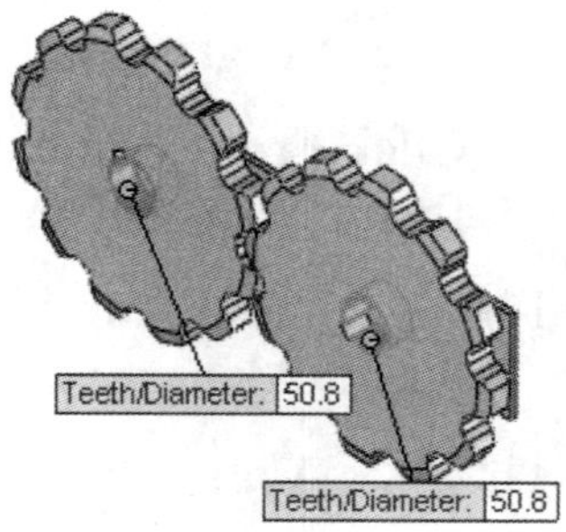

9. Select the **inside cylindrical face** of the right hole.
10. **Expand** the Mechanical Mates box from the Mate PropertyManager.
11. Click **Gear** mate from the Mechanical Mates box. The GearMate1 PropertyManager is displayed. Accept the default settings.
12. Click **OK** from the GearMate1 PropertyManager.

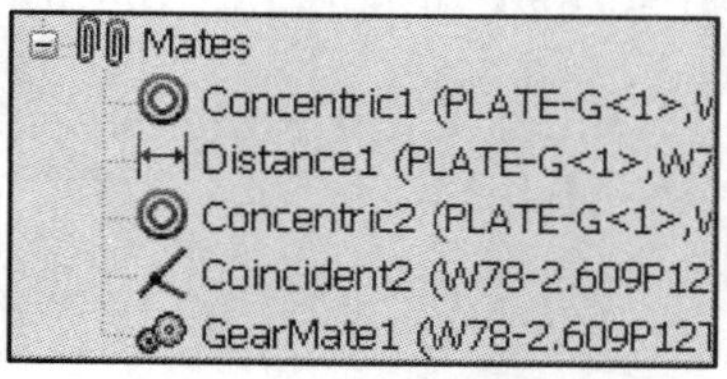


13. Click **OK** from the Mate PropertyManager.
14. **Expand** the Mates folder. View the created GearMate1.
15. **Rotate** the Gears in the Graphics window. View the results.
16. **Close** the model.

***Tutorial: Mechanical Cam Mate 11-1***

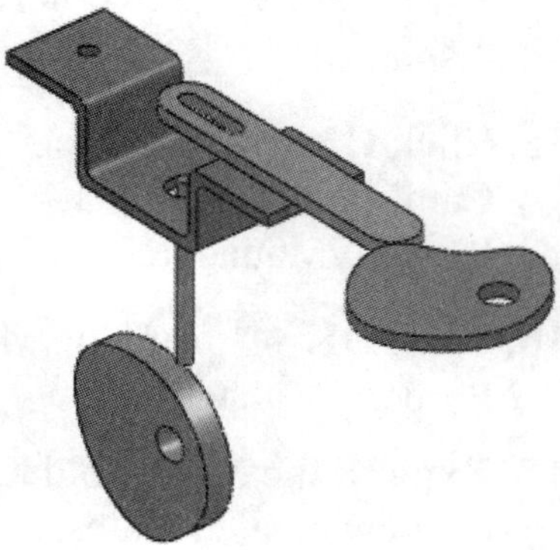

Create a tangent Cam follower mate and a Coincident Cam follower mate. A cam-follower mate is a type of Tangent or Coincident mate. It allows you to mate a cylinder, plane or point to a series of tangent extruded faces; such as you would find on a cam.

Create the profile of the cam from lines, arcs and splines as long as they *are tangent and form a closed loop.*

1. Open **Cam Mate 11-1** from the SolidWorks 2010\BottomUpAssemblyModeling folder. View the model. The model contains two cams.
2. Set **Lightweight to Resolved** if needed for the model.
3. **Expand** the Mates folder to view the existing mates.

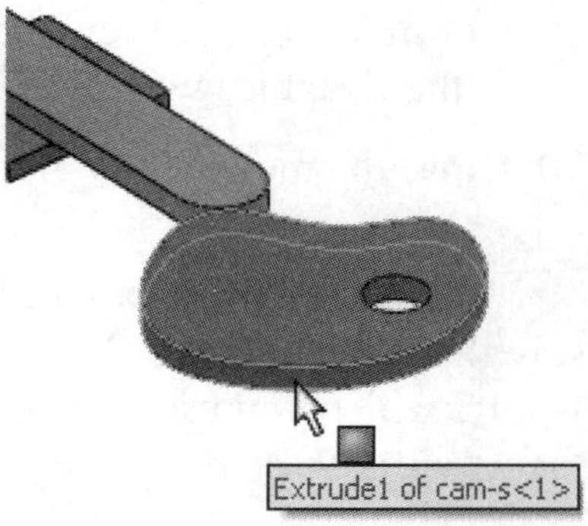


Insert a tangent Cam follower mate.

4. Click the **Mate** tool from the Assembly tab.
5. **Expand** the Mechanical Mates box from the Mate PropertyManager
6. Click **Cam Follower** mate from the Mechanical Mates box.
7. Click the **outside face** of cam-s<1> as illustrated.
8. Click **inside** the Cam follower box.

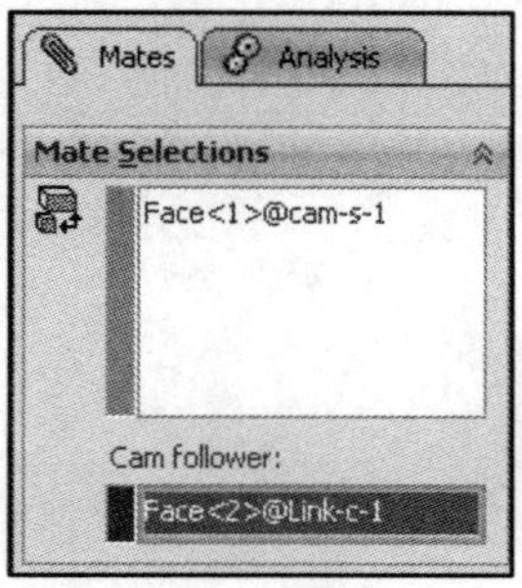


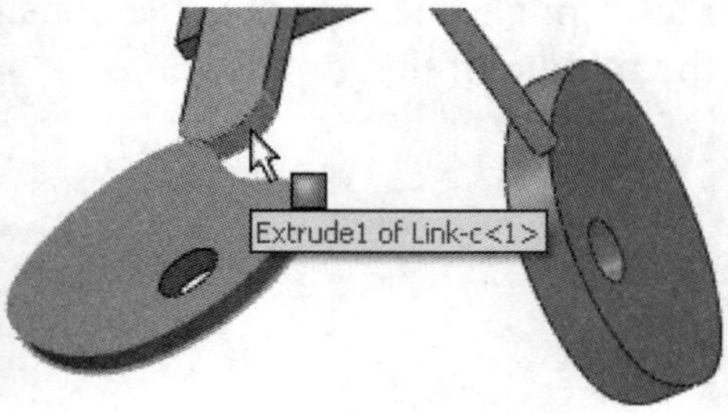

9. Click the **face of Link-c<1>** as illustrated. Face<2>@Link-c-1 is displayed.

10. Click **OK** ✔ from the CamMateTangent1 PropertyManager.

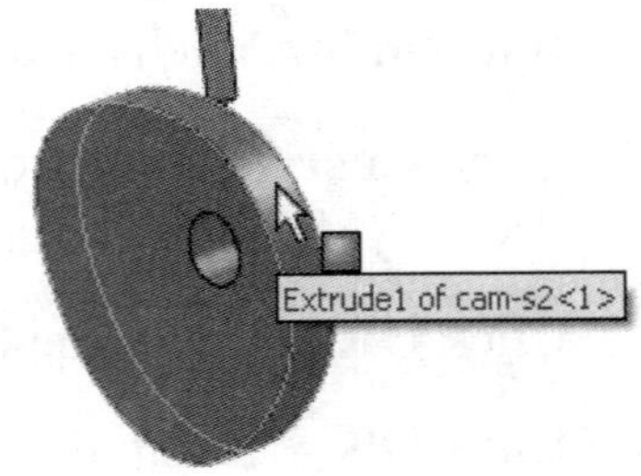


Insert a Coincident Cam follower mate.

11. Click **Cam Follower** mate from the Mechanical Mates box.

12. Click the **outside face** of cam-s2<1>.

13. Click **inside** the Cam follower box.

14. Click the vertex of **riser<1>** as illustrated. Vertex<1>@riser-1 is displayed.

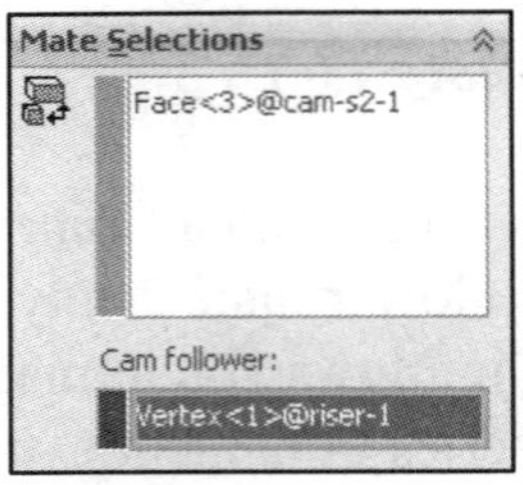


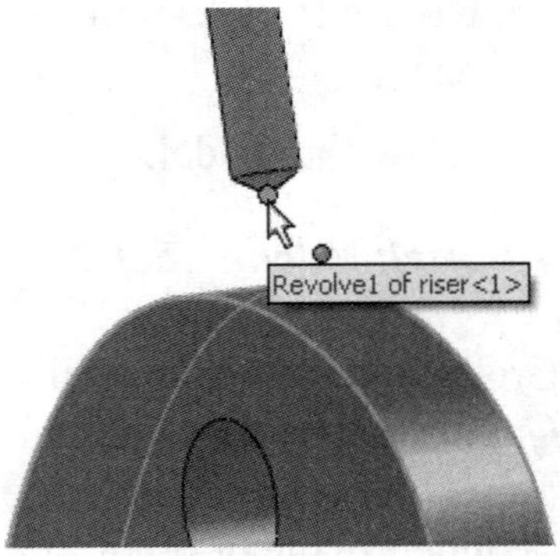


15. Click **OK** ✔ from the CamMateCoincident1 PropertyManager.

16. Click **OK** ✔ from the Mate PropertyManager.

17. **Expand** the Mates folder. View the new created mates.

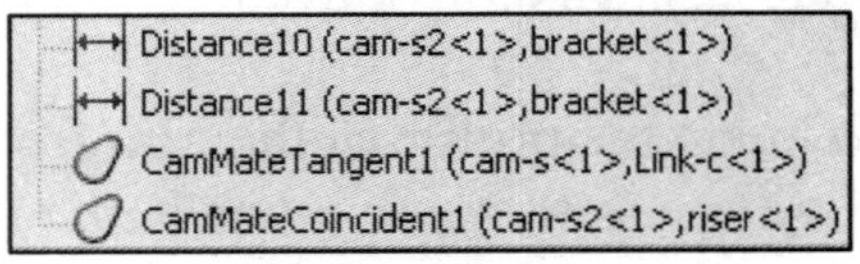


18. Display an **Isometric** view.

19. **Rotate** the cams. View the results in the Graphics window.

20. **Close** the model.

When creating a cam follower mate, make sure that your Spline or Extruded Boss/Base feature which you use to form the cam contact face *does nothing but forms the face*.

In the next tutorial of the spur gear and rack, the gear's pitch circle <u>*must be tangent*</u> to the rack's pitch line, which is the construction line in the middle of the tooth cut.

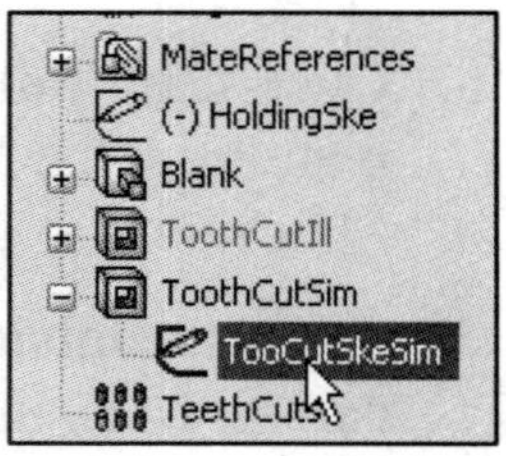

### *Tutorial: Mechanical Rack Pinion Mate 11-1*

The Spur gear and rack components for this tutorial were obtained from the SolidWorks Toolbox folder marked Power Transmission. Apply the Rack Pinion mate.

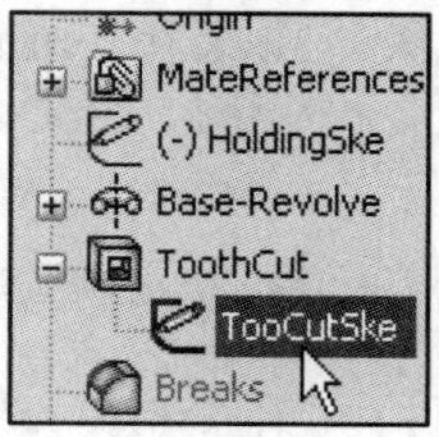


1. Open **Rack Pinion Mate 11-1** from the SolidWorks 2010\BottomUpAssemblyModeling folder. The sketches containing the tooth cut dimensions are displayed.
2. Set **Lightweight to Resolved** if needed for the model. View the displayed sketches: (TooCutSkeSim and TooCutSke).

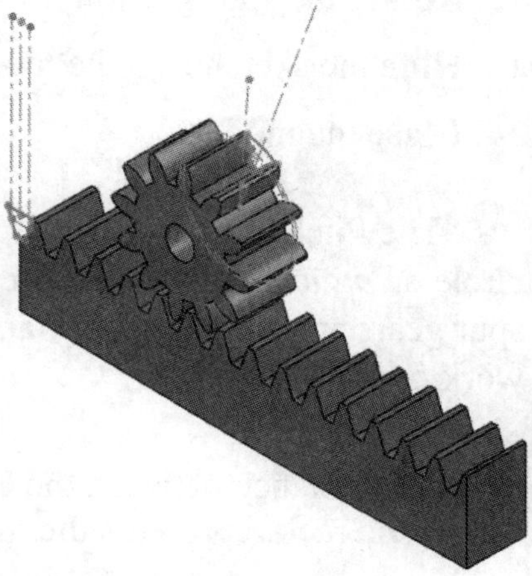

The Diametral Pitch, Pressure Angle and Face Width values should be the same for the spur gear as the rack.

Tangency is required between the spur gear and rack.

3. **Expand** the Mates folder to view the existing mates. Four Coincident mates and a Distance mate were created in the assembly.

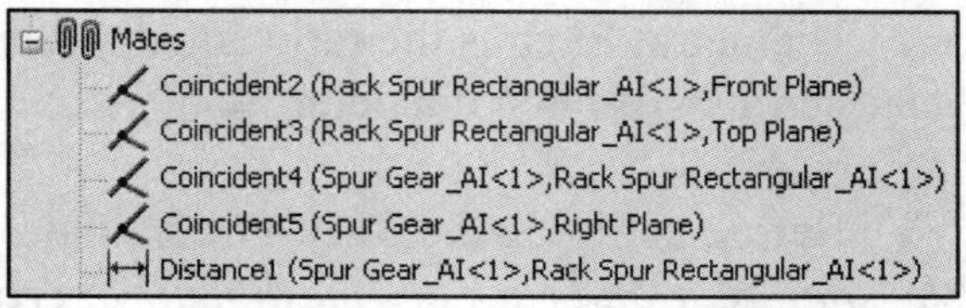


Insert a Rack Pinion mate.

4. Click the **Mate** tool from the Assembly tab.
5. **Expand** the Mechanical Mates box from the Mate PropertyManager.
6. Click **Rack Pinion** mate from the Mechanical Mates box.
7. Mate the rack. Make sure the teeth of the spur gear and rack are **meshing properly**; they are not interfering with each other. It is important to create a starting point were the gear and rack has no interference.

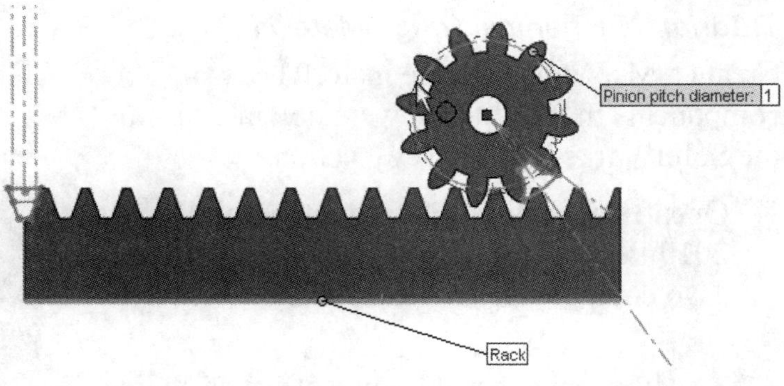

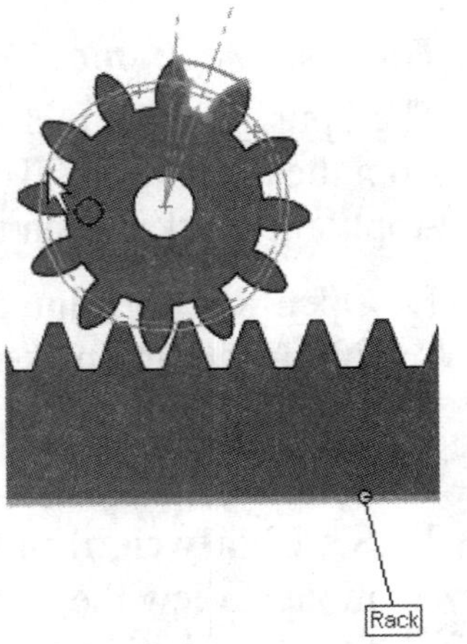


8. Click the **bottom linear edge of the rack** in the direction of travel. Any linear edge that runs in the direction of travel is acceptable.
9. Click the **spur gears's pitch circle** as illustrated. The Pinion pitch diameter, 1in is taken from the sketch geometry. Accept the default settings.
10. Click **OK** from the RackPinionMate1 PropertyManager.
11. Click **OK** from Mate PropertyManager.
12. **Rotate** the spur gear on the rack. View the results.
13. **Hide** the sketches in the model.
14. **Close** the model.

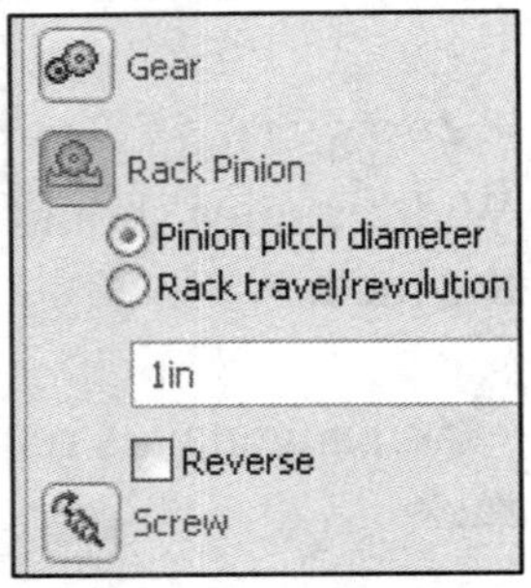


The Pitch Diameter is the diameter of an imaginary pitch circle on which a gear tooth is designed. Pitch circles of the two spur gears are required to be tangent for the gears to move and work properly.

The distance between the centerpoint of the gear and the pitch line of the rack represents the theoretical distance required.

Diametral Pitch is the ratio equal to the number of teeth on a gear per inch of pitch diameter.

Before applying the Rack Pinion mate, make sure the *teeth of the spur gear and rack are meshing properly*.

Pressure Angle is the angle of direction of pressure between contacting teeth. Pressure angle determines the size of the base circle and the shape of the involute teeth. It is common for the pressure angle to be 20 or 14 1/2 degrees.

### *Tutorial: Mechanical Hinge Mate 11-1*

Create a Mechanical Hinge mate. The two components in this tutorial were obtained from the SolidWorks What's New section.

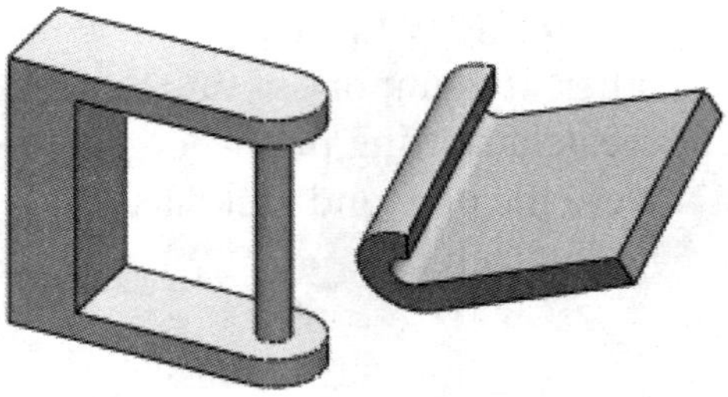

1. Open **Hinge Mate 11-1** from the SolidWorks 2010\BottomUpAssemblyModeling folder. Two components are displayed.

A Hinge mate has the same effect as adding a Concentric mate plus a Coincident mate. You can also limit the angular movement between the two components.

2. Set **Lightweight to Resolved** if needed for the model.

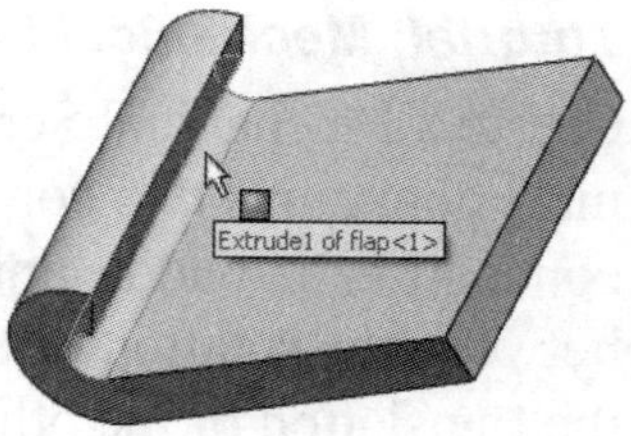


3. Click the **Mate** tool from the Assembly tab.
4. **Expand** the Mechanical Mates box from the Mate PropertyManager.
5. Click **Hinge** mate from the Mechanical Mates box.

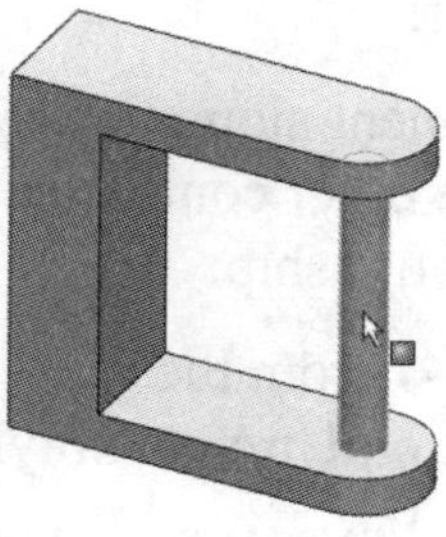

Set the two Concentric faces.

6. Click the **inside cylindrical face** of the first component as illustrated.
7. Click the **outside cylindrical face** of the second component as illustrated. The two selected faces are displayed.

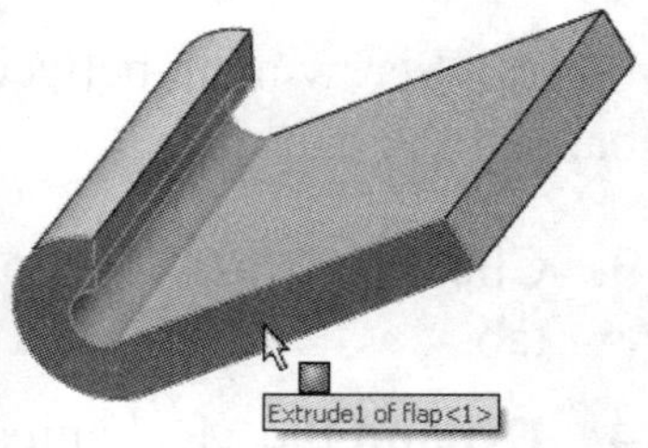


Set the two Coincident faces.

8. Click the **front flat face** of the first component as illustrated.
9. Click the **bottom flat face** of the second component as illustrated. View the results in the Graphics window.

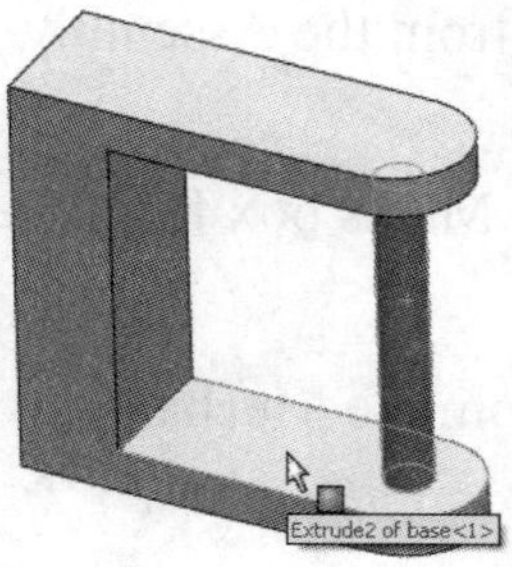


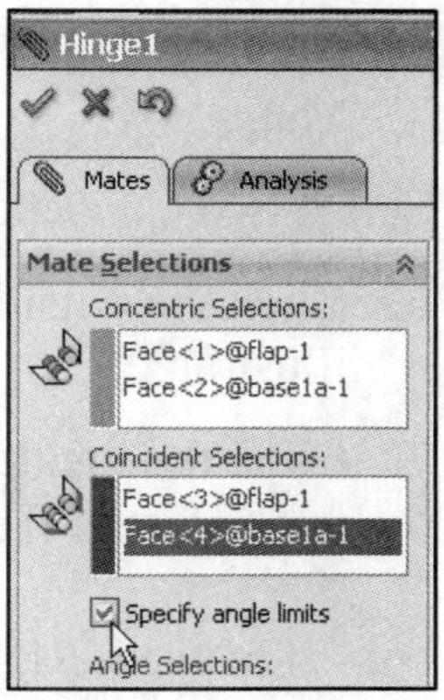


You can specify a limit angle for rotation by checking the **Specify angle limits** box and selecting the required faces.

10. Click **OK** from the Hinge1 PropertyManager.
11. Click **OK** from the Mate PropertyManager.
12. **Rotate** the flap component about the pin.
13. **Close** the model.

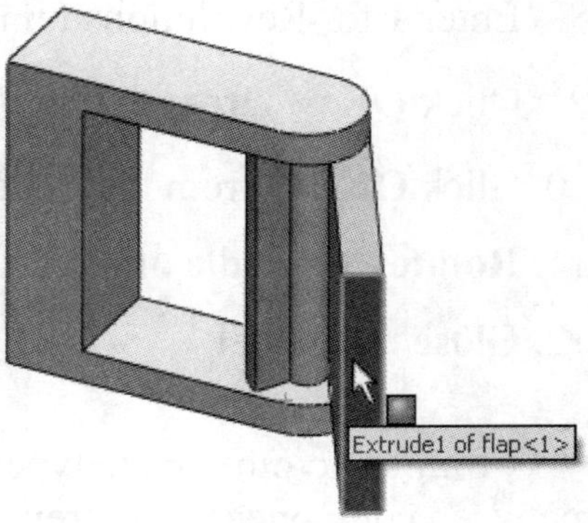


A Hinge mate limits the movement between two components to one rotational degree of freedom.

Similar to other mate types, Hinge mates do not prevent interference or collisions between components. To prevent interference, use Collision Detection or Interference Detection.

### *Tutorial: Mechanical Screw Mate 11-1*

Create a Mechanical Screw mate. A Screw mate constrains two components to be concentric, and adds a pitch relationship between the rotation of one component and the translation of the other.

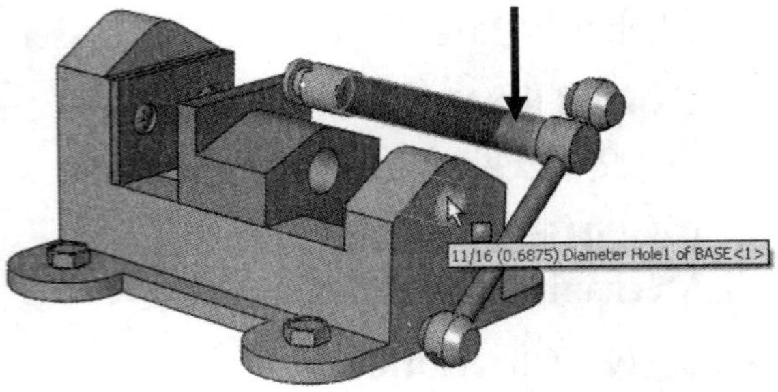


Translation of one component along the axis causes rotation of the other component according to the pitch relationship.

1. Open **Screw Mate 11-1** from the SolidWorks 2010\BottomUpAssemblyModeling folder.
2. Set **Lightweight to Resolved** if needed for the model.

Insert a Screw mate between the screw bar and the base of the clamp.

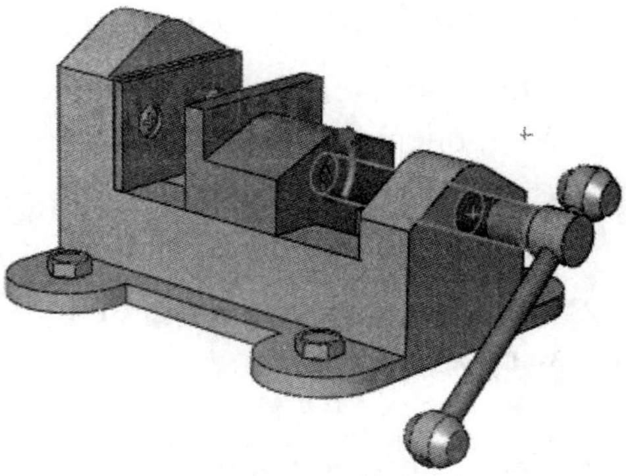

3. Click the **Mate** tool from the Assembly tab.
4. **Expand** the Mechanical Mates box from the Mate PropertyManager.
5. Click **Screw** mate from the Mechanical Mates box.

Select two Concentric faces.

6. Click the outside **cylindrical face** of the vice_screw bar as illustrated.
7. Click the **inside face of Diameter Hole1** as illustrated. The two selected faces are displayed.

If needed, Right-click and use the Select Other command to select the inside cylindrical face of the Hole.

8. Enter **1** for Revolutions/mm
9. Click **OK** from the Screw1 PropertyManager.
10. Click **OK** from the Mate PropertyManager.
11. **Rotate** the handle of the screw-bar. View the results.
12. **Close** the model.

Similar to other mate types, Screw mates do not prevent interference or collisions between components. To prevent interference, use Collision Detection or Interference Detection.

### *Tutorial: Advanced Path Mate 11-1*

Create an Advanced Path mate. The Path mate constrains a selected point on a component to a path. In this example, the Path mate is the selected sketch point of the ball to the spiral trough.

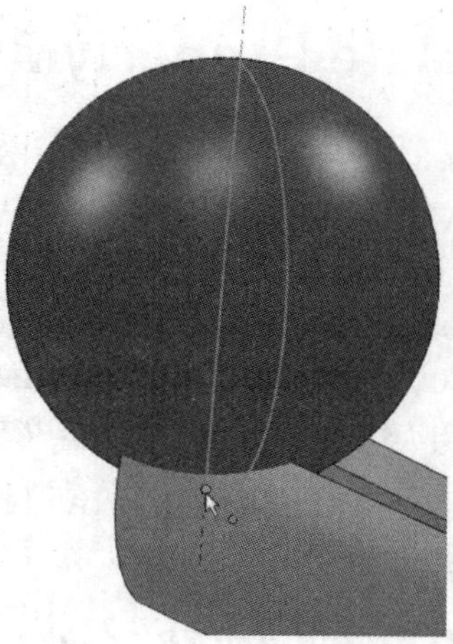

1. Open **Path Mate 11-1** from the SolidWorks 2010\BottomUpAssemblyModeling folder.
2. Set **Lightweight to Resolved** if needed for the model.
3. Click the **Mate** tool from the Assembly tab.
4. **Expand** the Advanced Mates box from the Mate PropertyManager.
5. Click **Path Mate** from the Advanced Mates box.

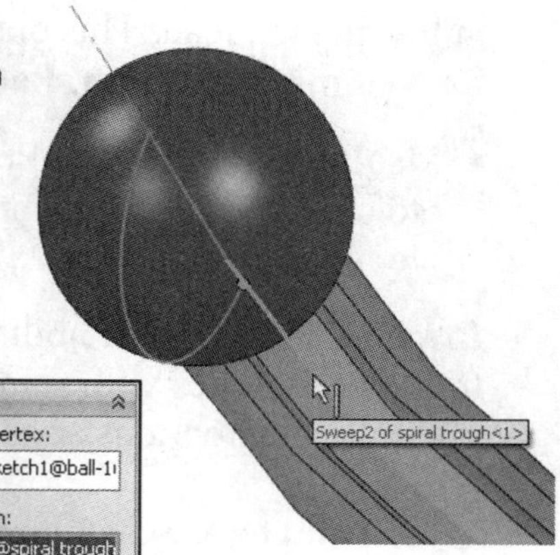


Select the component vertex of the ball (Bottom point of the Revolved Base sketch).

6. Zoom in and click the **Revolved Base sketch vertex** as illustrated.

Select the path for the Path Mate.

7. Zoom in and click the **bottom inside edge of the spiral trough**. Accept the default settings.

13. Click **OK** from the PathMate1 PropertyManager.
14. Click **OK** from the Mate PropertyManager.
15. Click **Isometric** view.
16. **Zoom in** on the ball. Click and drag the **ball** and view the PathMate along the spiral trough.
17. **Close** the model.

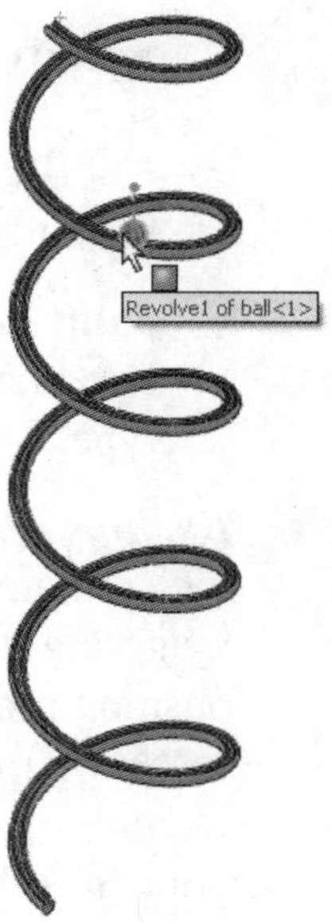


You can define pitch, yaw, and roll of the component as it travels along the path. You can also add Motion!

## Mate PropertyManager: Analysis tab

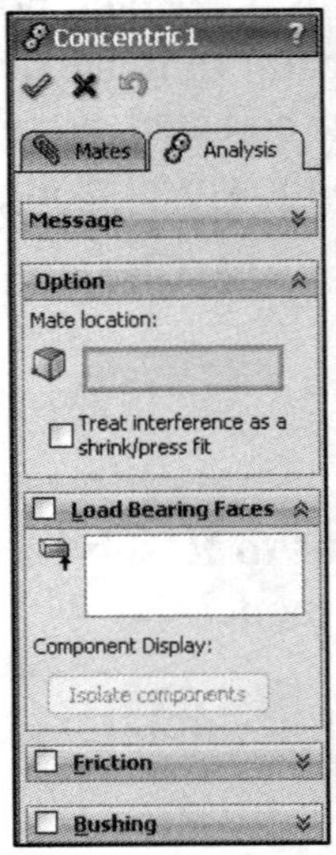


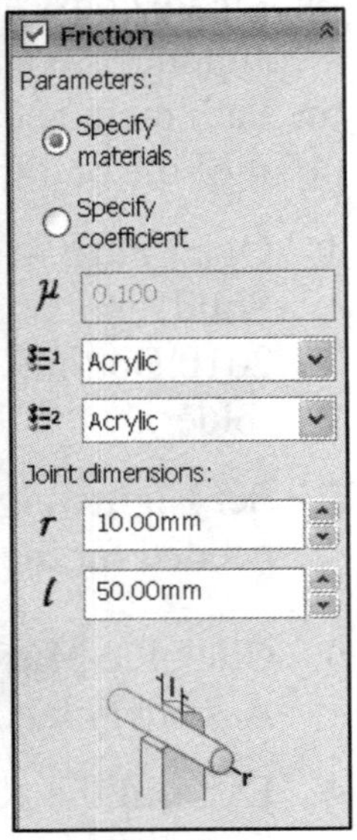


Assign mate properties for use in a SolidWorks Motion analysis or SolidWorks Simulation. Motion studies use mate location points to determine how parts move in relation to each other. Modify the mate location used for Motion studies. The Analysis tab option is *Mate dependent.*

The Analysis tab provides the following options for a selected mate:

- ***Load Bearing Faces***. Associates additional faces with the selected mate to define which faces share in bearing the load. This option is not available for **Symmetric**, **Width**, **Path** or **Cam** mates.
  - **Isolate components**. Provides the ability to only display the components referenced by the mate.

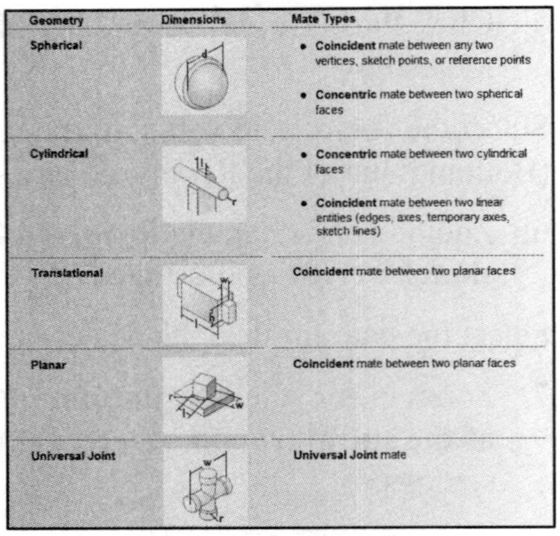

| Geometry | Dimensions | Mate Types |
|---|---|---|
| Spherical | | • **Coincident** mate between any two vertices, sketch points, or reference points<br>• **Concentric** mate between two spherical faces |
| Cylindrical | | • **Concentric** mate between two cylindrical faces<br>• **Coincident** mate between two linear entities (edges, axes, temporary axes, sketch lines) |
| Translational | | **Coincident** mate between two planar faces |
| Planar | | **Coincident** mate between two planar faces |
| Universal Joint | | **Universal Joint** mate |

- ***Friction***. Provides the ability to associate friction properties with some types of mates. The following options are available:
  - **Parameters**. Select how to define the friction properties of the mate.
  - **Specify materials**. Select the materials of the components from the first and second lists.
  - **Specify coefficient**. Provides the ability to specify the following: **Dynamic Friction Coefficient** by typing a number or moving the slider between **Slippery** and **Sticky.**
  - **Joint dimensions**. Available dimensions vary depending on geometry and mate type. They are:

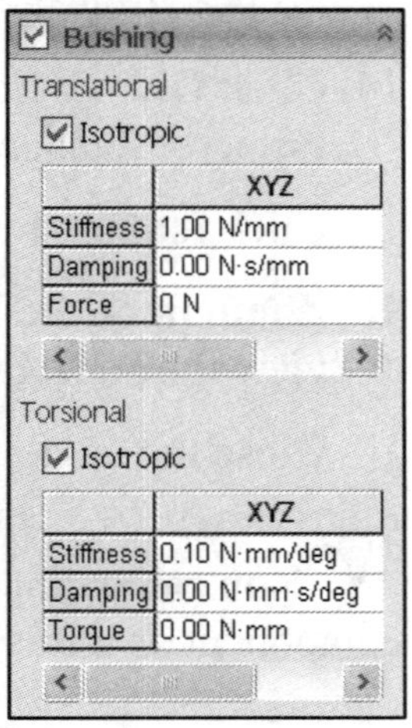


- ***Bushing***. Provides the ability to associate bushing properties with a mate. Bushing properties make a mate somewhat flexible by giving it spring and damper characteristics. Mates with bushing properties can produce a more realistic distribution of forces.

See SolidWorks help for additional information on this topic.

## *Tutorial: Assign mate properties with the Analysis Tab 11-1*

Apply the Analysis tab. Assign mate properties for use in a SolidWorks Motion analysis.

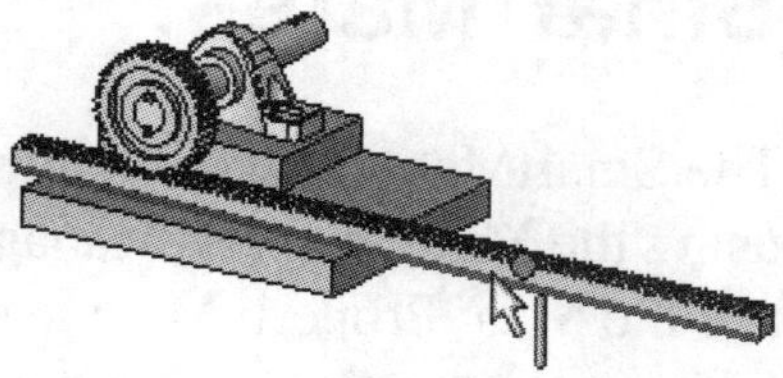

1. Open **Analysis 11-1** from the SolidWorks 2010\BottomUpAssemblyModeling folder.
2. Set **Lightweight to Resolved** if needed for the model.
3. Click and drag the **Rack** in the Graphics window. The Rack moves linear.
4. Click and drag the **Gear**. The Rack and Gear moves independently of each other. Edit the Coincident1 Mate under the gearrackpbaseplate component.
5. Right-click **Coincident1** as illustrated.
6. Click **Edit Feature**. The Coincident1 PropertyManager is displayed.

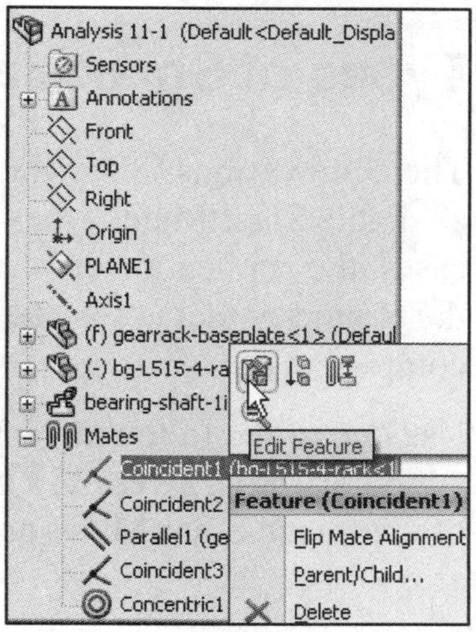


7. Click the **Analysis** tab.
8. Check the **Load Bearing Faces** dialog box as illustrated.

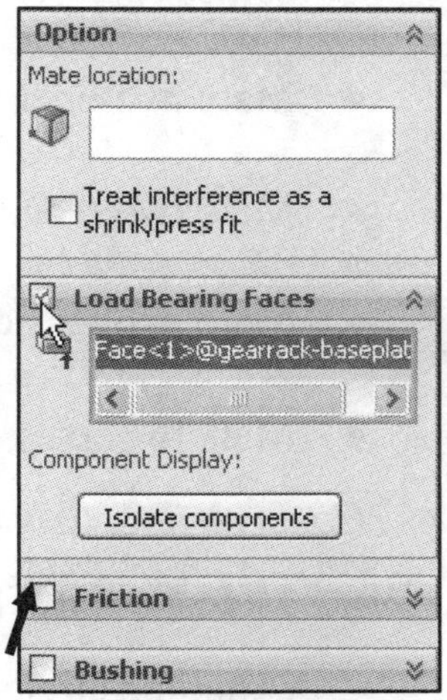


9. Click the **top face** of the gearrack-baseplate as illustrated. The selected face is displayed in the Load Bearing Faces dialog box.

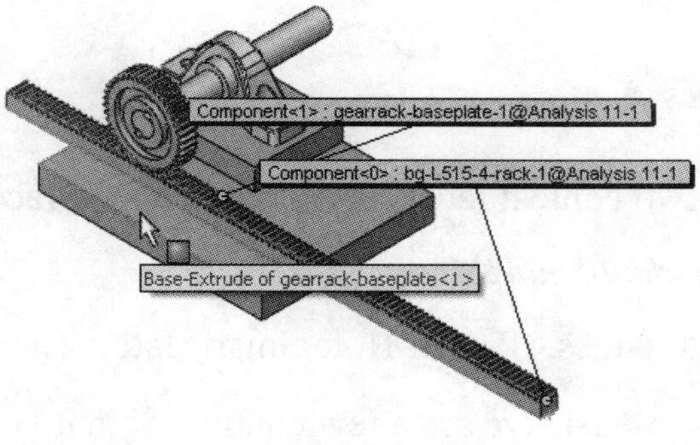


10. Check the **Friction** box. Specify material properties.
11. Select **Aluminum(Greasy)** for both material properties to define friction. Accept the default Busing options.
12. Click **OK** ✔ from the Coincident1 PropertyManager.
13. Click **OK** ✔ from the Mate PropertyManager. You assigned mate properties for use in a Motion analysis.
14. **Close** the model. Do not save.

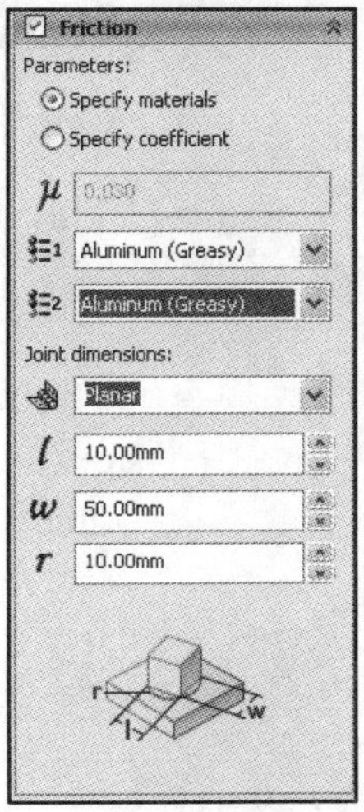

# SmartMates:

The SmartMates tool saves time by allowing you to create commonly used mates without using the Mate PropertyManager. Standard Mates, Advance Mates and Mechanical Mates use the Mate PropertyManager.

## Types of SmartMates

There are various SmartMates types that are available to you in SolidWorks. The available SmartMates types are depended on the application and your situation. In most cases, the application creates a single mate. The type of SmartMate created depends on the geometry that is selected, "to drag" and the type of geometry which you drop the component.

Use one of the following entities to drag the component: a linear or circular edge, a temporary axis, a vertex, a planar face, or a cylindrical/conical face. The following types of automatic SmartMates are supported and are displayed on your mouse pointer. They are:

- *Coincident SmartMate:*
  - Mate two linear edges
  - Mate two planar faces
  - Mate two vertices
  - Mate two axes, two conical faces, or a single conical face and a single axis
- *Concentric & Coincident SmartMate:*
  - Mate two circular edges, (Peg-in-Hole SmartMate). The edges do not have to be complete circles. There are a few conditions that you need to know to apply the Peg-in-Hole SmartMate. They are:
    - One feature must be a Base or Boss.
    - The other feature must be a Hole or a Cut.
    - The features must be Extruded or Revolved.
    - The faces that are selected in the mate must both be of the same type, either a cylinder or a cone or a cylinder. Both need to be the same. You can not have one of each type.

- A planar face must be adjacent to the conical/cylindrical face of both features.
- Mates two circular patterns on flanges, (Flange SmartMate).

For parts that you typically mate the same way every time, you can set up Mate References to define the mates used and the part geometry being mated. Mate references specify one or more entities of a component to use for automatic mating.

***Tutorial: SmartMate 11-1***

Insert two Concentric SmartMates and a Coincident SmartMate into an Assembly.

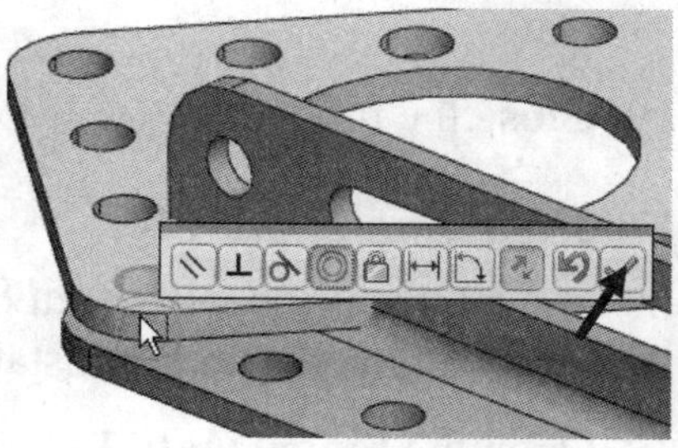

1. Open the **SmartMate 11-1** assembly from the SolidWorks 2010\BottomUpAssemblyModeling folder.
2. Set **Lightweight to Resolved** if needed for the model.
3. Click the **left back cylindrical hole** face of the IM15-MOUNT part.
4. Hold the **Alt** key down.
5. Drag the mouse pointer to the **left cylindrical hole** face of the Angle Bracket part. The Concentric SmartMate icon is displayed.
6. Release the **Alt** key. Release the **mouse button**. Concentric is selected by default.
7. Click the **green check mark**.

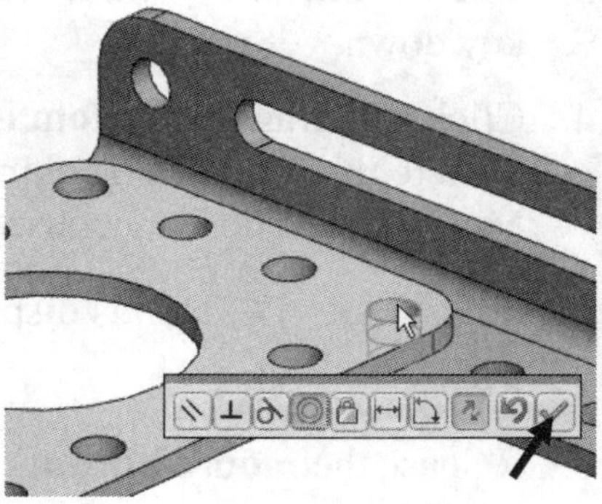

Insert a second Concentric SmartMate.

8. Click the **right back cylinder hole** face of the IM15-MOUNT part.
9. Hold the **Alt** key down.
10. Drag the mouse pointer to the **right cylindrical hole** face of the Angle Bracket part. The Concentric SmartMate icon is displayed.
11. Release the **Alt** key.
12. Release the **mouse button**. Concentric is selected by default.
13. Click the **green check mark**.

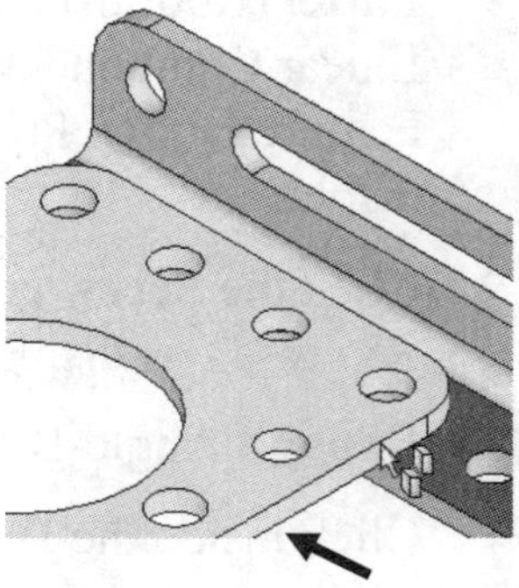

Insert a Coincident SmartMate.

14. Click the **right bottom edge** of the IM15-Mount part.
15. Hold the **Alt** key down. Drag the mouse pointer to the **top front edge** of the Angle Bracket part. The Coincident SmartMate icon is displayed.
16. Release the **Alt** key. Release the **mouse button**. Coincident is selected by default.

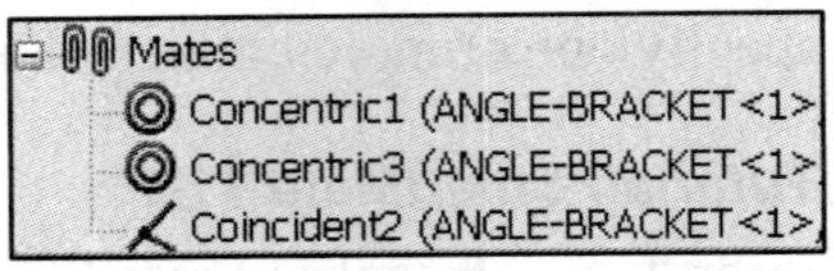


17. Click the **green check mark**.
18. **Expand** the Mates folder. View the three inserted mates.
19. **Close** the model.

***Tutorial: SmartMate 11-2***

Insert a Concentric/Coincident SmartMate. Utilize the Feature Driven PropertyManager with the Instances to Skip option.

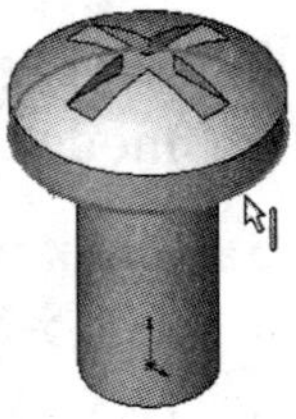

1. Open the **SmartMate 11-2** assembly from the SolidWorks 2010\BottomUpAssemblyModeling folder. Set **Lightweight to Resolved** if needed for the model.
2. Open the **SCREW** part from the SolidWorks 2010\BottomUpAssemblyModeling folder.
3. Click **Window ➢ Tile Horizontally**. Hold the **Alt** key down.
4. Click and drag the **bottom edge** of the Screw head to the **top left circular edge** of the IM15-Mount part. The Concentric/Coincident SmartMate icon is displayed.

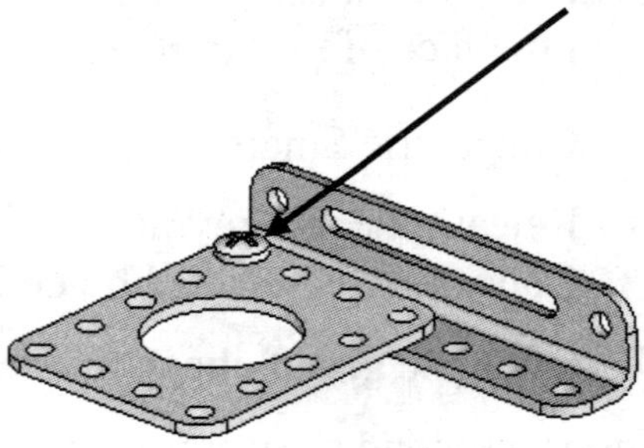

5. Release the **Alt** key.
6. Release the **mouse button**.
7. **Close** the Screw part.
8. Click the **Feature Driven Component Pattern** tool from the Consolidated Linear Component toolbar. The Feature Driven PropertyManager is displayed.

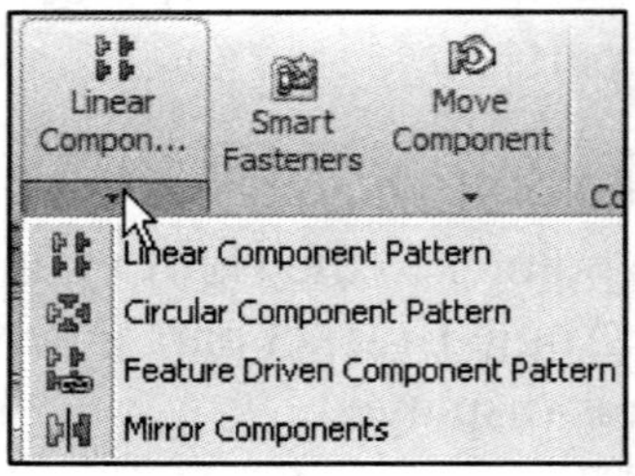


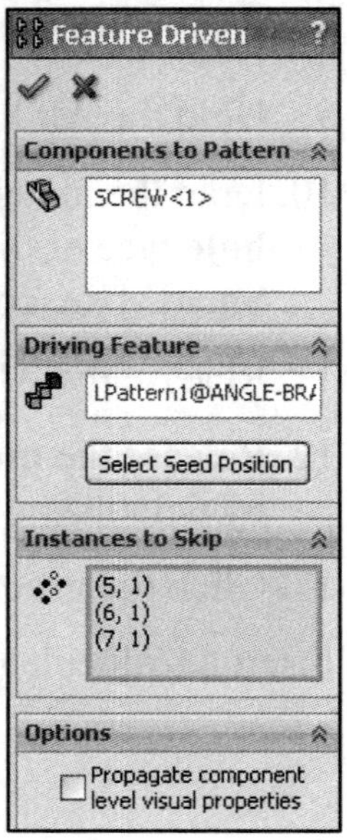


9. Click the **Screw** component from the Graphics window. Screw<1> is displayed in the Components to Pattern box.
10. **Expand** Angle-Bracket from the flyout FeatureManager.
11. Click inside the **Driving Feature** box.

12. Click **LPattern1** from the flyout FeatureManager. LPattern1 is displayed in the Driving Feature box.
13. Click inside the **Instances to Skip** box.
14. Select **(5, 1)**, **(6, 1)**, and **(7, 1)**, from the Graphics window to skip. Note: Select the bottom control point.

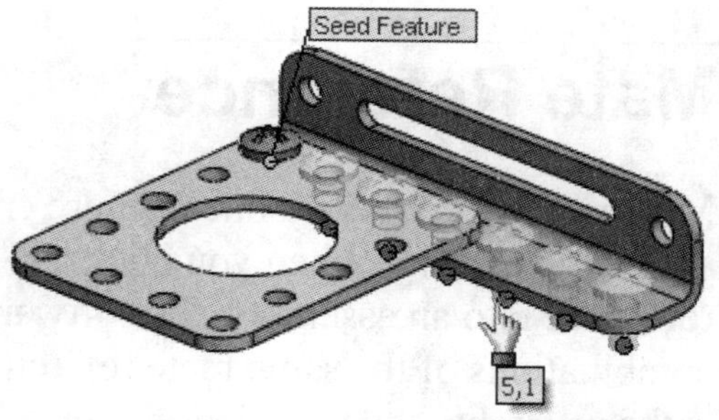


15. Click **OK** ✔ from the Feature Driven PropertyManager. The DrivedLPattern feature is created and is displayed.
16. **Close** all models.

---

# InPlace Mates

InPlace Mates are created automatically for In-context components. InPlace Mates are created to prevent movement of the component.

The In-context component is attached to geometry of components in the assembly through External references, references that cross between component at the assembly level.

An InPlace Mate is a Coincident Mate created between the Front Plane of a new component and the selected planar geometry of the assembly. The component is fully defined; no additional Mates are required to position the component. By default, SolidWorks uses the default templates for new parts and assemblies developed In-context of an existing assembly.

To select a custom Template, define the System Options, Document Templates option before you insert a new component into the assembly. See Chapter 12 for additional information.

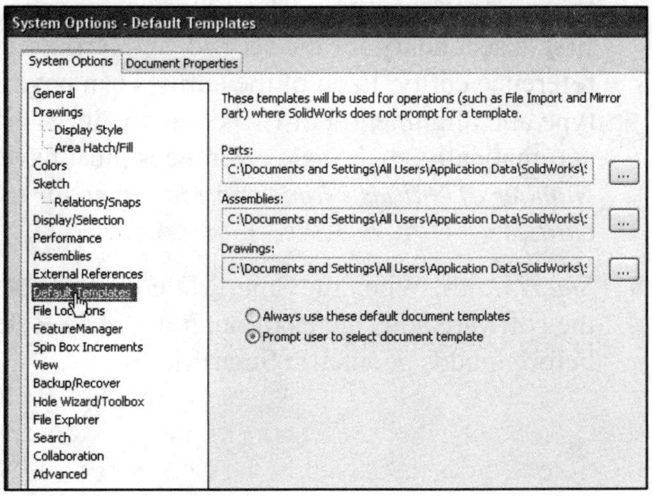

# Mate Reference

Mate references specify one or more entities of a component to use for automatic mating. When you click and drag a component with a mate reference into an assembly, the software tries to locate other combinations of the same mate reference name and type. If the name is the same, but the type does not match, the software does not add the mate.

The Mate Reference tool is located in the Reference Geometry toolbar and under the Assembly tab in the CommandManager. Below are a few items to be aware of when using the Mate Reference tool:

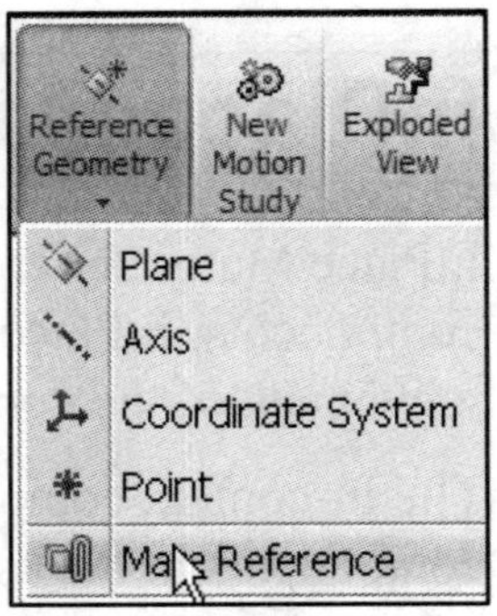


- *Components*. You can add mate references to parts and assemblies. Select assembly geometry, example: a plane in the assembly or component geometry, example: the face of a component.
- *Multiple mate references*. More than a single mate reference can be contained in a component. All mate references are located in the Mate References folder in the FeatureManager design tree. Example: You have a component in an assembly with two mate references: nut and bolt. When you click and drag a fastener with a mate reference named nut into your assembly, mates are inserted between the entities with the same mate reference name.
- *Multiple mated entities*. Each mate reference may contain one to three mated entities. The mated entities are: a primary for the first, a secondary for the second, and tertiary for the three reference entity. Each of the entities can have an assigned mate type and alignment. For two components to mate automatically, their mate references must have the same: *Number of entities*, *Name* and *Mate type for corresponding entities*.
- *SmartMates*. When the SmartMate PropertyManager is active, the software adds mates through the Mate References tool before it adds geometric SmartMates.

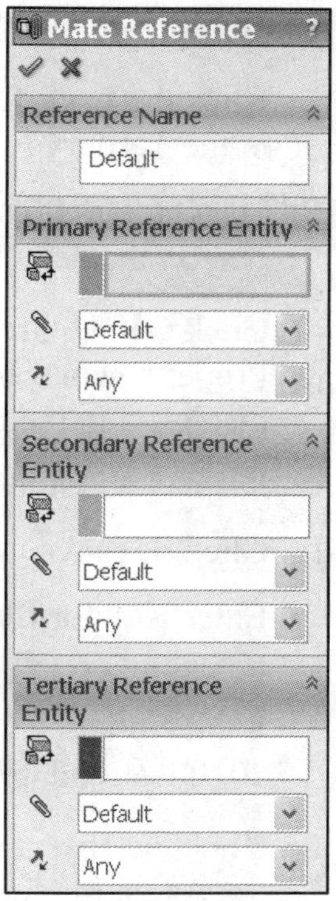


The Mate Reference tool uses the Mate Reference PropertyManager. The Mate Reference PropertyManager provides the following selections:

- ***Reference Name***. Displays the name for the mate reference. Default is the default name reference. Accept Default or type a name in the mate reference box.
- ***Primary Reference Entity***. Displays the selected face, edge, vertex, or plane for the Primary reference entity. The selected entity is used for potential mates when dragging a component into an assembly.
  - **Mate Reference Type**. Provides the ability to select the following mate types: **Default**, **Tangent**, **Coincident**, **Concentric** and **Parallel**.
  - **Mate Reference Alignment**. Provides the ability to define the default mate for the reference entity. The following Alignment options are available: **Any**, **Aligned**, **Anti-Aligned** and **Closest**.

Secondary and tertiary entities options are the same as the Primary Reference Entity box.

***Tutorial: Mate Reference 11-1***

Utilize the Reference Mate tool. Insert a Concentric and a Coincident Mate Reference Type.

1. Open the **Mate Reference 11-1** part from the SolidWorks 2010\BottomUpAssemblyModeling folder.
2. Set **Lightweight to Resolved** if needed for the model.
3. Click the **Mate Reference** tool from the Reference Geometry toolbar. The Mate Reference PropertyManager is displayed. The Reference Name is Default.

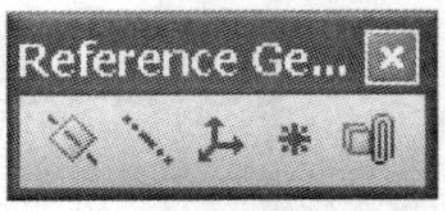


4. Display an **Isometric** view.

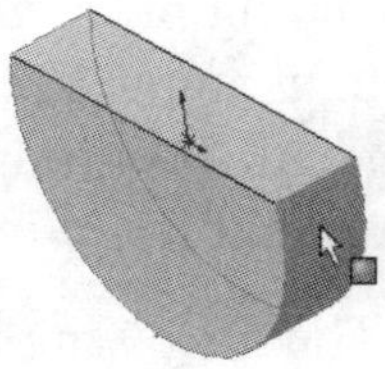

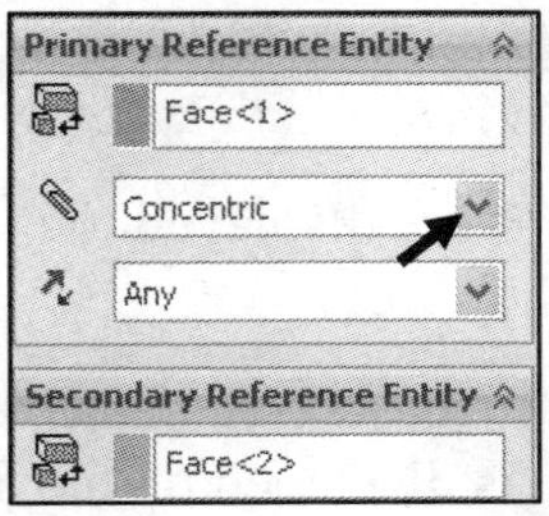


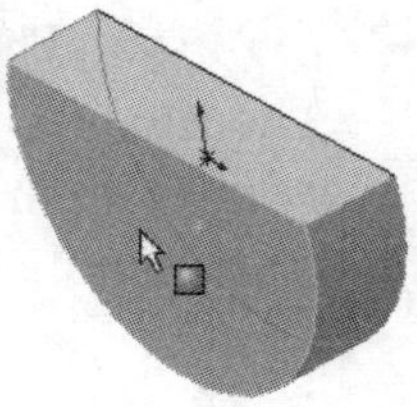

5. Click the **cylindrical right face** in the Graphics window as illustrated. Face<1> is displayed in the Primary Reference Entity box.
6. Select **Concentric** for Mate Reference Type. Accept Any as the default option
7. Click the **front face** in the Graphics window. Face<2> is displayed in the Secondary Reference Entity box.

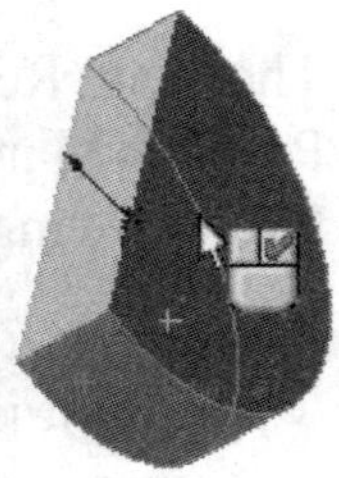

8. Select **Coincident** for Mate Reference Type. Accept Any as the default option.
9. Click the **back face** from the Graphics window. Face<3> is displayed in the Tertiary Reference Entity box.
10. Select **Coincident** for Mate Reference Type. Accept Any as the default option.

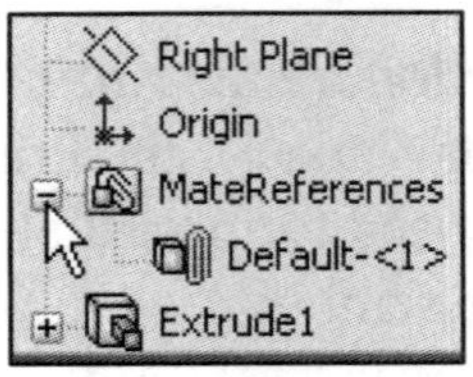


11. Click **OK** from the Mate Reference PropertyManager. The Mate References folder is displayed in the FeatureManager.
12. Display an **Isometric** view.
13. Click **Save As** from the Menu bar.
14. Enter **Key** for file name.
15. Open the **Mate Reference Shaft 11-1** assembly from the SolidWorks 2010\BottomUpAssemblyModeling folder.

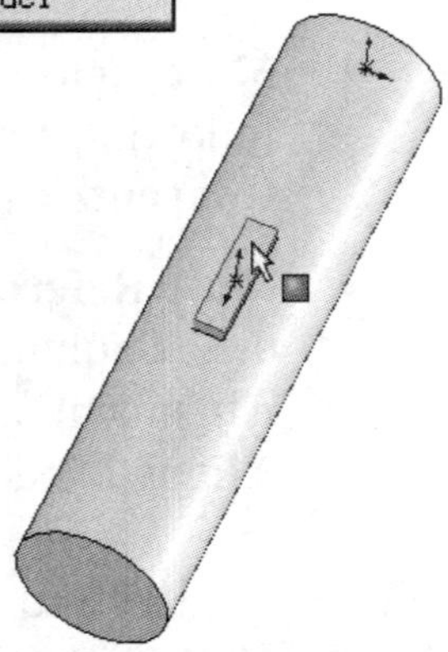

16. Click the **Insert Components** tool from the Assembly toolbar.
17. Click **Key** from the Part/Assembly to insert box.

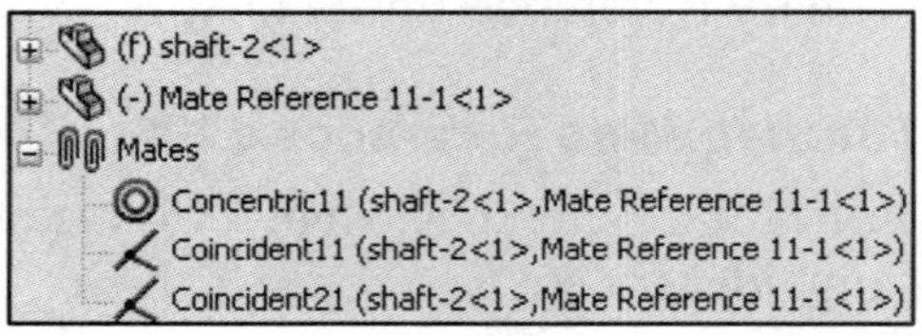


18. Click the **cylindrical face** of Shaft-2 inside cut as illustrated. View the results. Three mates are created.
19. **Close** the model.

---

# Mate Diagnostics/MateXpert

The Mate Diagnostics tool provides the ability to recognize mating problems in an assembly. The tool provides information to examine the details of mates which are not satisfied and identifies groups of mates which are over define in your assembly.

The following icons are displayed to indicate errors or warnings in an assembly. They are:

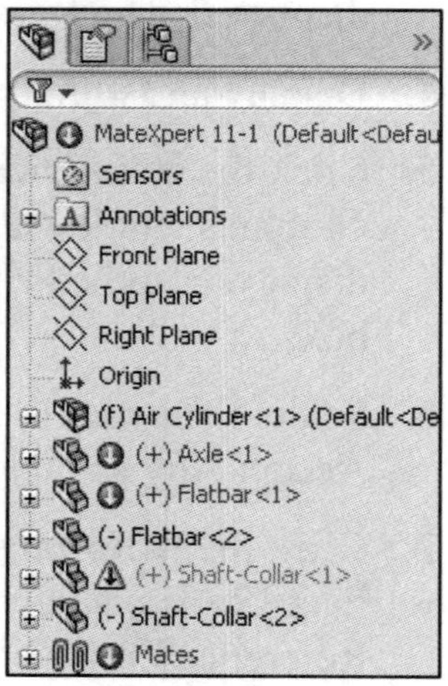


- *Error*. The Error icon indicates an error in your model. The Error icon is displayed on the document name at the top of the FeatureManager design tree and on the component that contains the error.

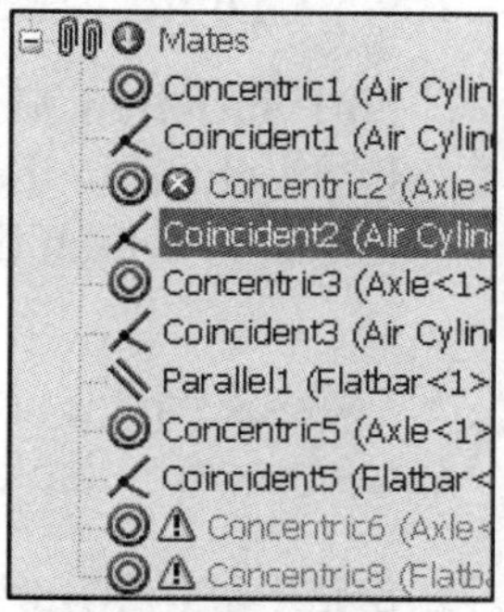


- *Warning*. The Warning icon indicates a warning in your model. The Warning icon is displayed on the component that contains the feature that issued the warning. When it is displayed on the Mates folder, it indicates that all the mates are satisfied, but one or more mates are over defined.

View the What's Wrong dialog box for additional information on identifying errors and warnings in your parts or assemblies. The following icons indicate the status of the mates:

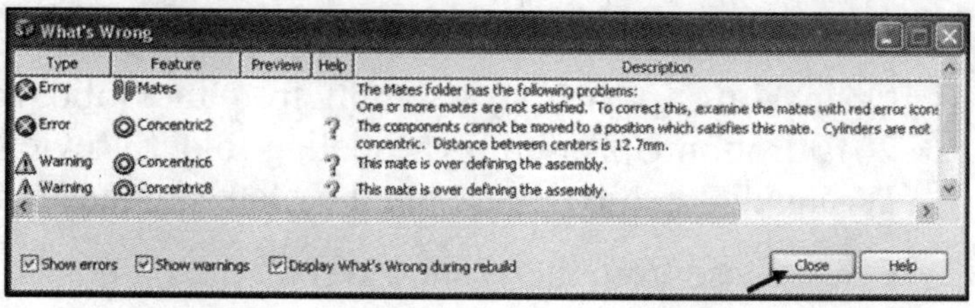


- *Not Satisfied*. The Not Satisfied icon indicates that all mates are not satisfied in you assembly. Use the Mate Diagnostics tool to address.
- *Satisfied but over defined*. The Satisfied icon indicates that the mates are satisfied, but they are over defined the assembly. Use the Mate Diagnostic tool to address.

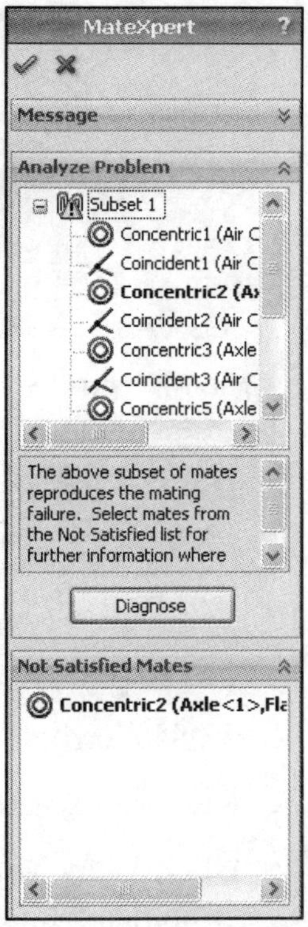


The MateXpert tool uses the MateXpert PropertyManager. To active the MateXpert PropertyManager, click **Tools** ➤ **MateXpert**, or right-click the **Mates** folder or any mate in the **Mates** folder, and click **MateXpert**.

The MateXpert PropertyManager provides the following selections:

- ***Analyze Problem***. The Analyze Problem box provides the following options:
  - **Analyze**. Displays one or more subsets of mates with problems. The components that are not related to the current subset are displayed transparent in the Graphics window. A message is displayed with information on the mating problem.

- **Diagnose**. Performs the diagnoses of the displayed mates in the Analyze box.
- **Not Satisfied Mates.** Displays the unsolved mates. The selected unsolved mate is highlighted in the Graphics window. A message informs you that the distance or angle by which the mated entities are currently misaligned.

Mates which are displayed in both the **Analyze** box and the and **Not Satisfied Mates** box are displayed in bold.

### *Tutorial: MateXpert 11-1*

View Mate errors. Utilize the Mate Diagnostics tool. Resolve a Mate conflict.

1. Open **MateXpert 11-1** assembly from the SolidWorks 2010\BottomUpAssemblyModeling folder. Review the Mate errors on the What's Wrong dialog box. These are the Mates in questions.
2. Click **Close** from the What's Wrong dialog box.

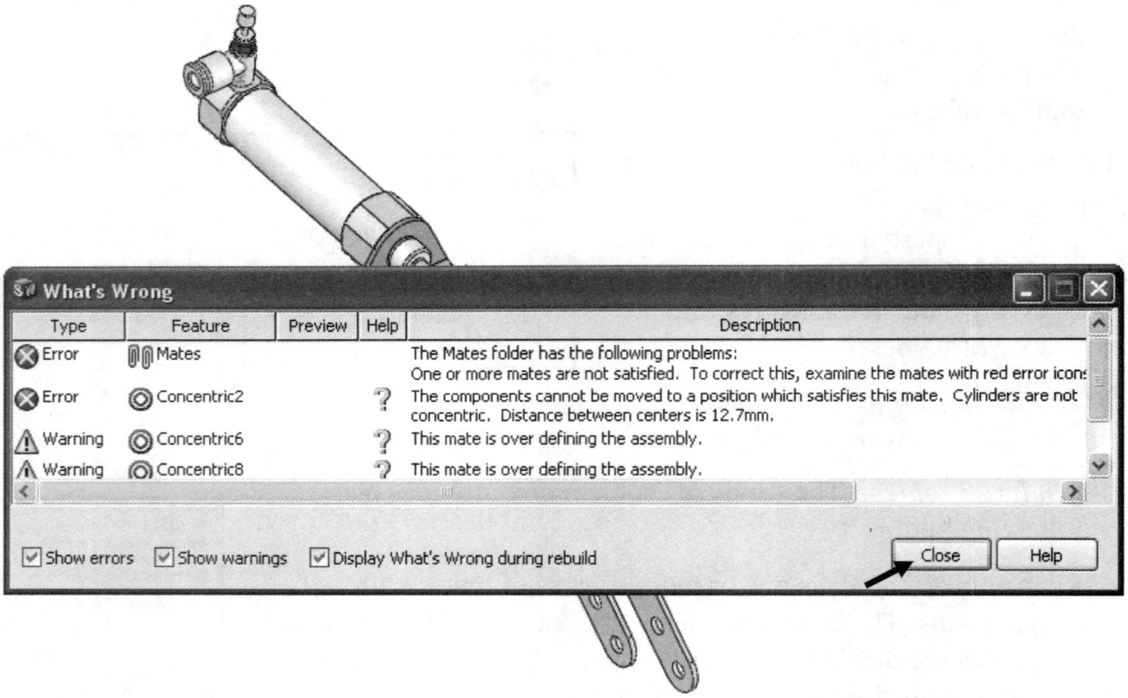


View Mate errors.

3. Right-click **Axle<1>** from the FeatureManager.
4. Click **View Mate Errors**. View the display in the Graphics window. Additional mates are displayed.

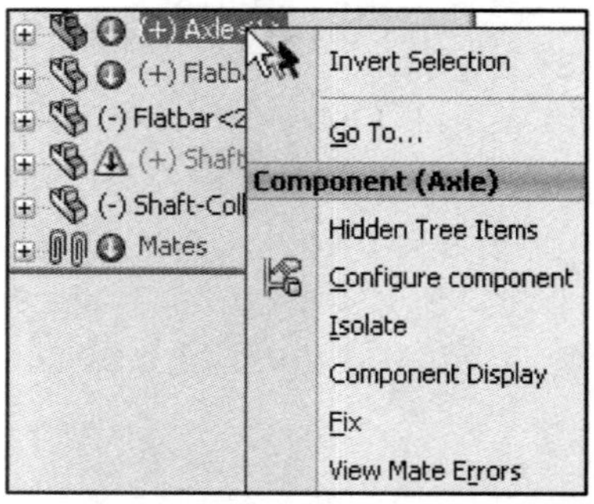

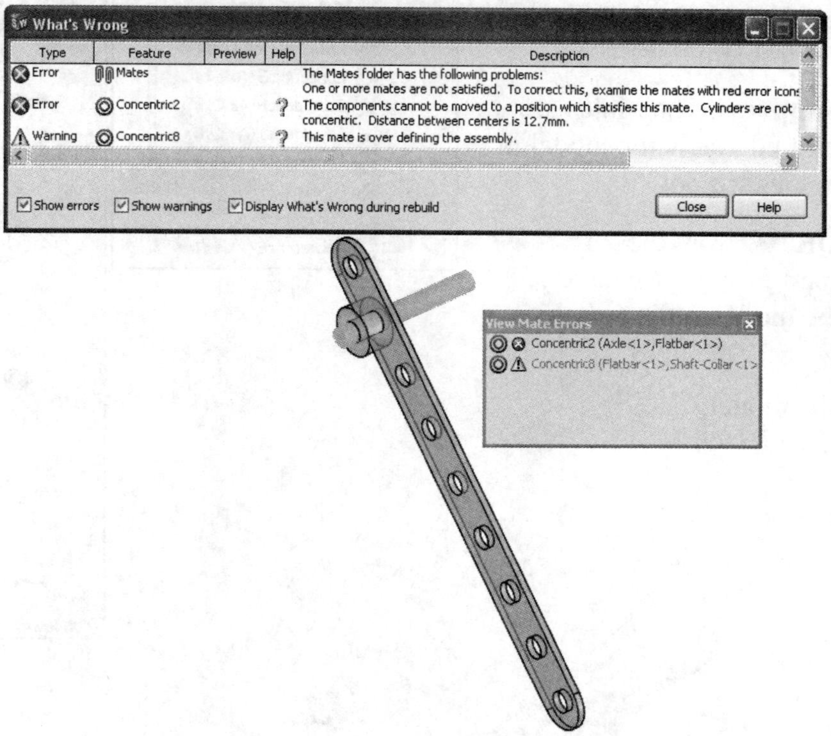


View the Mate PropertyManager.

5. Click **Close** from the What's Wrong dialog box.
6. **Close** the View Mate Errors dialog box to return to the standard FeatureManager and display in the Graphics window.

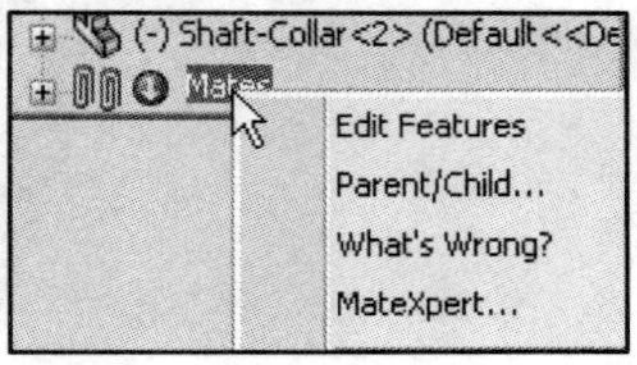


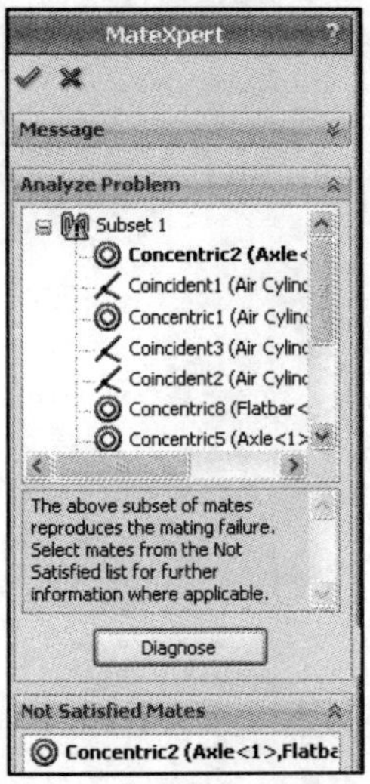


7. Right-click the **Mates** folder from the FeatureManager.
8. Click **MateXpert**. The MateXpert PropertyManager is displayed.
9. Click **Diagnose** from the Analyze Problem box.
10. **Expand** Subset1 and review the mates. A message is displayed with information on the mating problem, "The above subset of mates reproduces the mating failure. Select mates from the Not Satisfied list for further information where applicable."
11. Click **Concentric2(Axle<1>, Flatbar<1>)** from the Not Satisfied Mates box. View the Axle in the Graphcis window. Concentric6 mates the Axle to the Shaft-Collar. Concentric8 mates the Flatbar second hole to the Shaft-Collar. Concentric2 mates the Axle to the first hole of the Flatbar. The Shaft-Collar cannot be physically located concentrically at both the first hole and the second hole of the Flatbar.

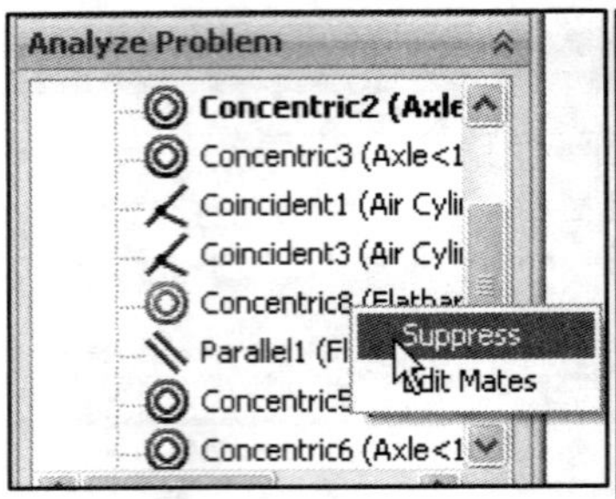


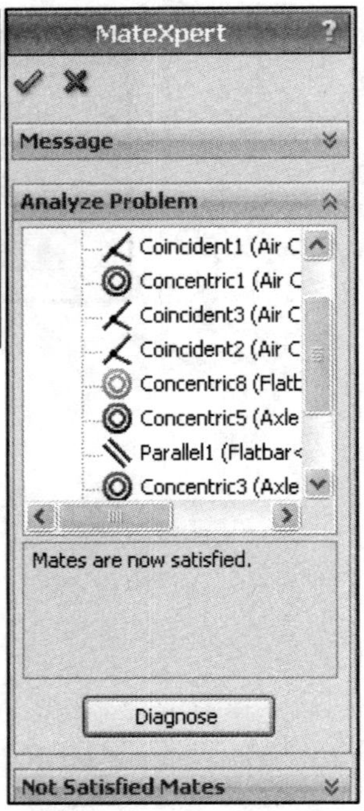


12. Right-click **Concentric8** from the Analyze Problem box.
13. Click **Suppress**. The Mates are now satisfied. View the model in the Graphics window.
14. Click **OK** ✔ from the MateXpert PropertyManager. View the model in the Graphics window.
15. **Close** the model.

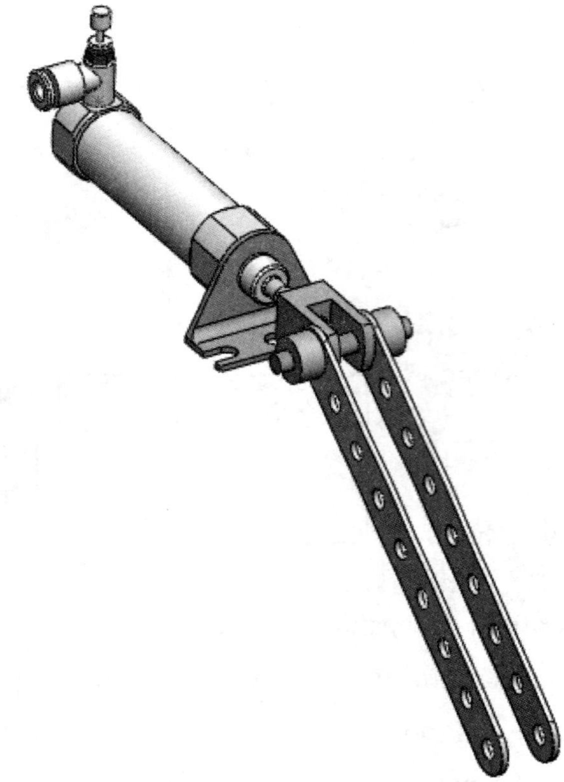

Click the **Over Defined** tab in the lower right corner of the Graphics window to view Mate Errors in the Graphics window and to obtain the View Mate Errors PropertyManager. Select **each** mate in the View Mate Errors PropertyManager to highlight in the Graphics window.

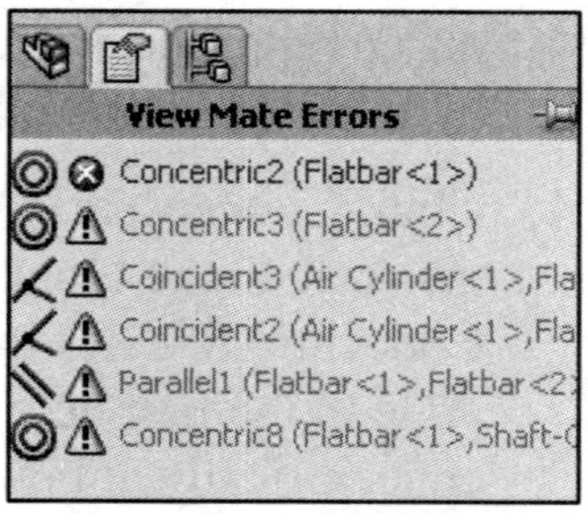

# AssemblyXpert

AssemblyXpert analyzes performance of assemblies and suggests possible actions you can take to improve performance. This is useful when you work with large and complex assemblies. In some cases, you can select to have the software make changes to your assembly to improve performance.

Although the conditions identified by the AssemblyXpert can degrade assembly performance, they are not errors. It is important that you understand and think about the recommendations before you modify the model. In some cases, implementing the system recommendations could improve your assembly performance, but could also compromise the design intent of your model.

***Tutorial: AssemblyXpert 11-1***

Utilize the AssemblyXpert tool.

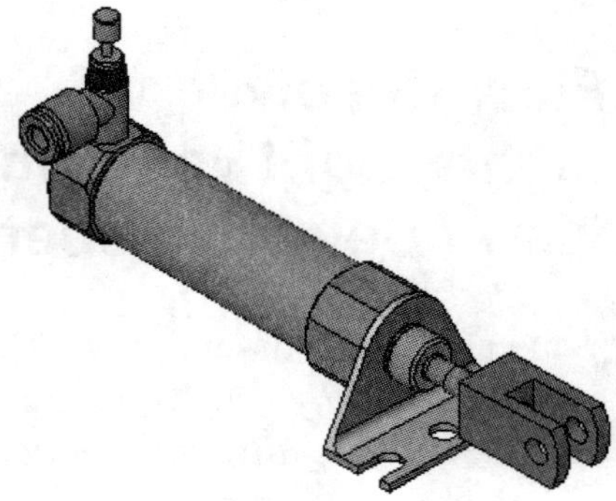

1. Open **AssemblyXpert 11-1** assembly from the SolidWorks 2010\BottomUpAssemblyModeling folder.
2. Set **Lightweight to Resolved** if needed for the model.
3. Click the **AssemblyXpert** tool from the Evaluate tab in the CommandManager. View the AssemblyXpert dialog box.
4. **Close** the model.

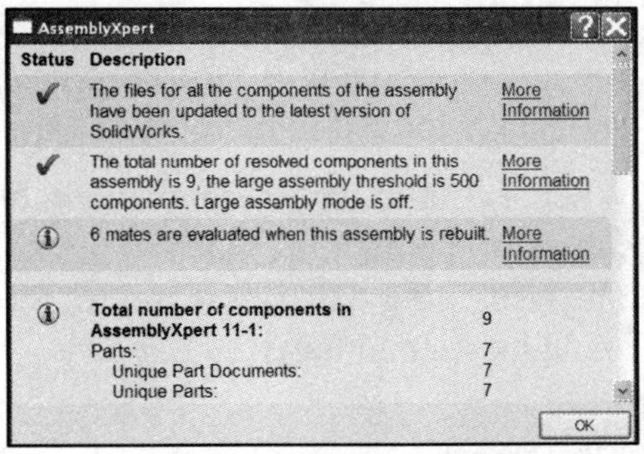


New in SolidWorks 2010 is the Assembly Visualization tool from the Evaluate tab in the CommandManager. This tool provides the ability to display and sort an assembly's components in a list and in the Graphics window.

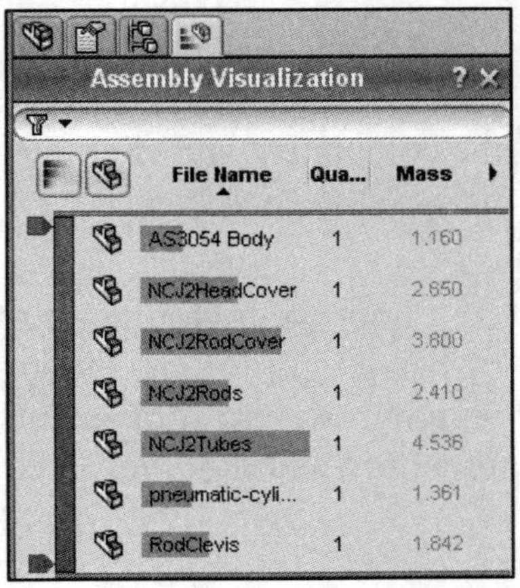

# Large Assembly mode

Large Assembly mode is a collection of system settings that improves the performance for large assemblies. See Chapter 2 on System Options for additional details.

Set a threshold for the number of components, and have Large Assembly mode active automatically when that threshold is reached. The default setting is 500 components as illustrated.

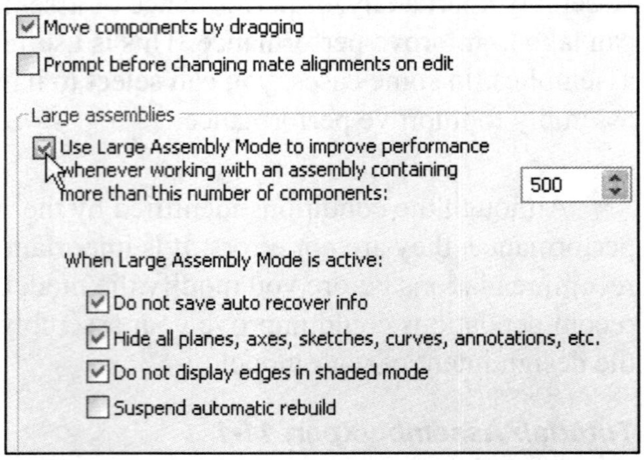


## Fully Resolved vs. Lightweight vs. Quick view / Selective open

You can load an assembly with its active components *fully resolved* or in a *lightweight or Quick view mode*. Both parts and assemblies can be opened with either mode.

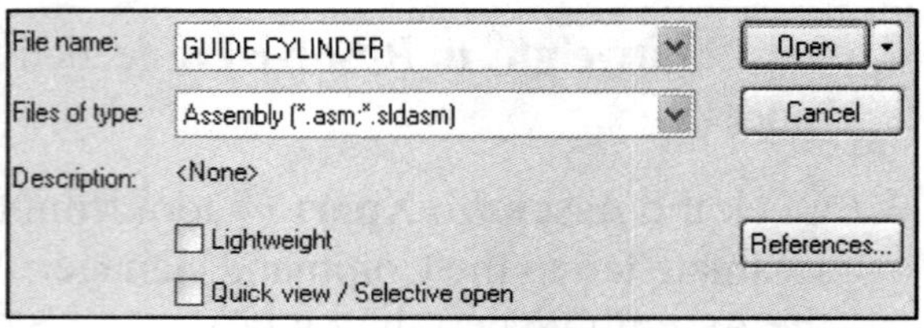


When a component is *fully resolved*, all of the data is loaded in memory.

When a component is *lightweight*, only a subset of the data is loaded in memory. The remaining data of the model is loaded on an as-needed basis.

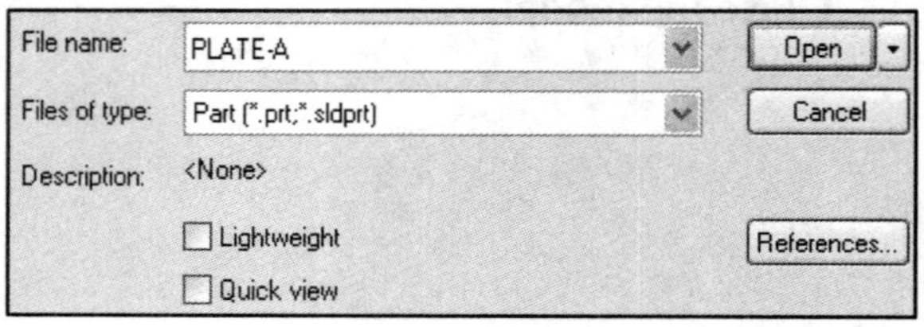


A feather is displayed in the FeatureManager for a Lightweight component in an assembly. Right-click on the component and click Set to Resolved to resolve the component.

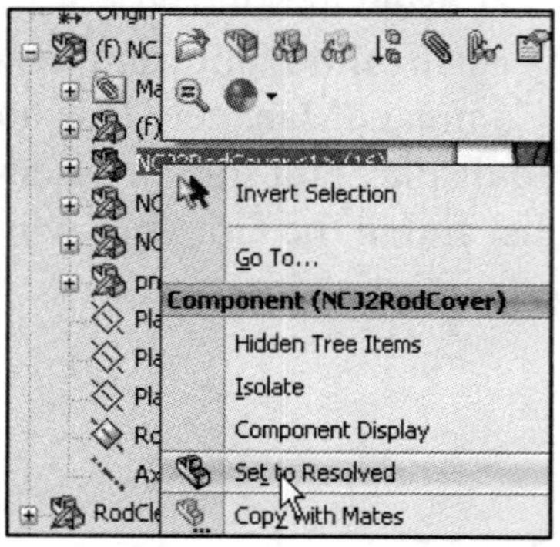


Improve performance of large assemblies significantly by using lightweight components. Loading an assembly with lightweight components is faster than loading the same assembly with fully resolved components.

Assemblies with lightweight components rebuild faster because less data is evaluated. Only components that are affected by changes that you make in the current editing session become fully resolved.

You can perform the following assembly operations on lightweight components without resolving them: *Add/remove mates*, *Interference detection*, *Collision detection*, *Edge/ Face/Component selection*, *Annotations*, *Measure*, *Dimensions*, *Section Properties*, *Assembly Reference Geometry*, *Mass Properties*, *Section View*, *Exploded View* and *Basic Motion*.

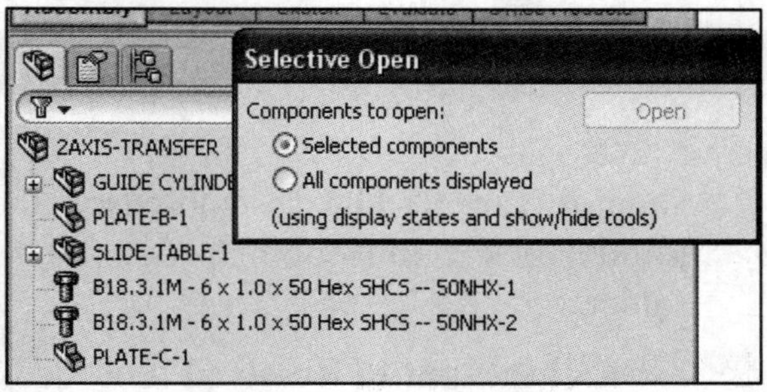


Large assemblies can consist of hundreds, even thousands of components. Reasons to simplify a large assembly include:

- Improve performance and reduce rebuild times.
- Improve display speed during dynamic view operations (zoom, pan, rotate, etc).
- Focus your work on a subset of components.

The Quick View / Selective Open option opens a simplified representation of the assembly. You specify which components to load; other components are not loaded and not visible, but the effects of their mates are / should be retained.

The Quick View / Selective Open option is not used in this book.

The Level of detail option affects performance. Drag the slider to the right for a faster display and a reduced level of detail in the Performance section of System Options.

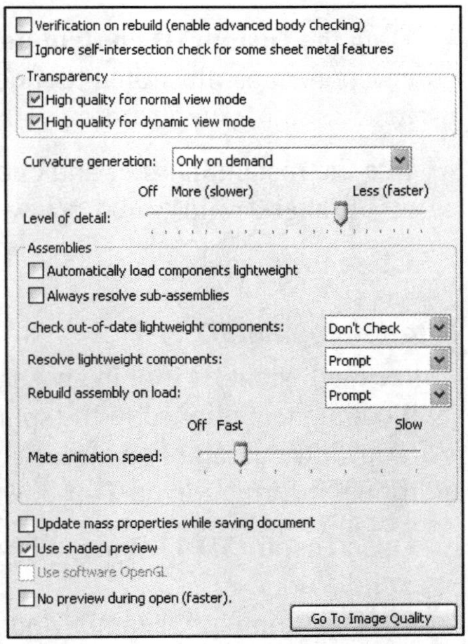


The Large Assembly Mode by default hides all planes, axes, sketches, curves, and annotations. Uncheck the Hide all planes, axes, sketches, curves, annotations, etc. option when working with Layout Sketches.

# Instant3D in an Assembly

Instant3D supports assemblies. You can apply the Instant3D tool to edit components within the assembly or to edit assembly level sketches, assembly features and mate dimensions.

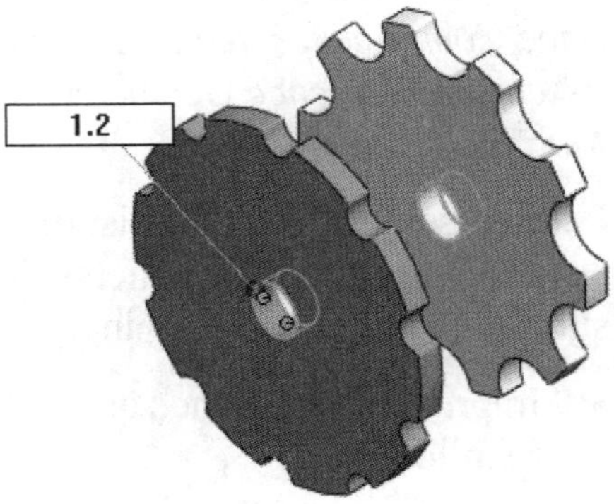


***Tutorial: Instant3D 11-1***

Utilize the Instant3D tool in an Assembly to modify a Distance Mate.

1. Open **Instant3D 11-1** assembly from the SolidWorks 2010\BottomUpAssemblyModeling folder.
2. Set **Lightweight to Resolved** if needed for the model.
3. Click the **Hole1** feature in the FeatureManager. Zoom-in and view the dimension in the Graphics window.
4. Modify the **0.6** dimension to **1.2**.
5. **Expand** the Mates folder.
6. Click **Distance1** from the Mates folder.
7. Drag the **Instant3D control point** on the component as illustrated to modify the Distance mate.
8. Use the Instant3D ruler and click a control point at **3 inches** as illustrated. View the results.
9. **Close** the model.

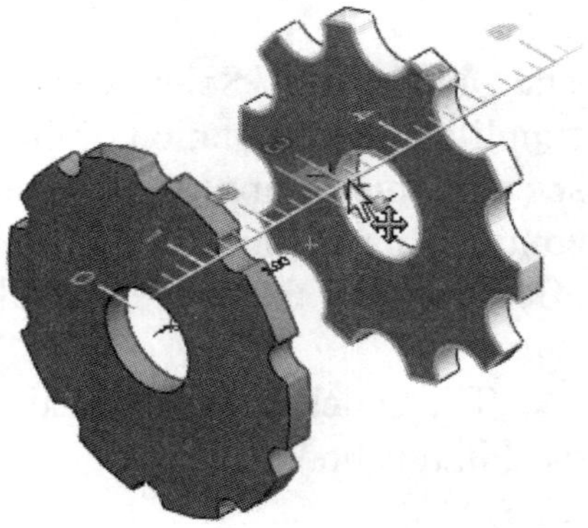

***Tutorial: Instant3D 11-2***

Utilize the Instant3D tool in an Assembly to add a shaft component aligned to the spur gear. Note: This is a Top-down assembly approach. See Chapter 12 for additional information on Top-down assembly.

1. Open **Instant3D 11-2** assembly from the SolidWorks 2010\BottomUpAssemblyModeling folder.
2. Insert a new part into the Assembly. Click **Insert**, **Component**, **New Part** from the Menu bar toolbar. The mouse pointer

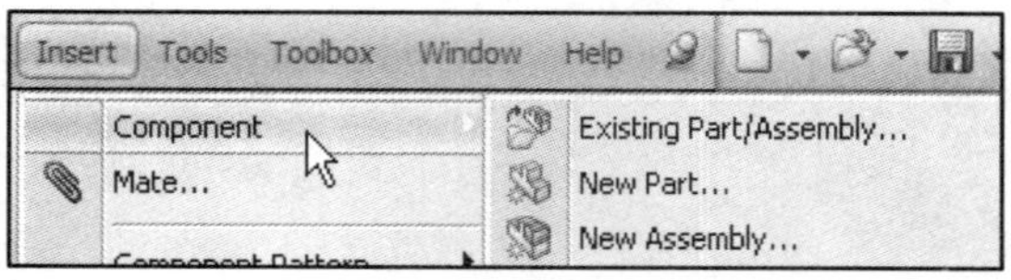

displays the  icon. The new part is displayed in the FeatureManager with a name in the form **[Part*n^assembly_name*]**. The square brackets indicate that the part is a virtual component.

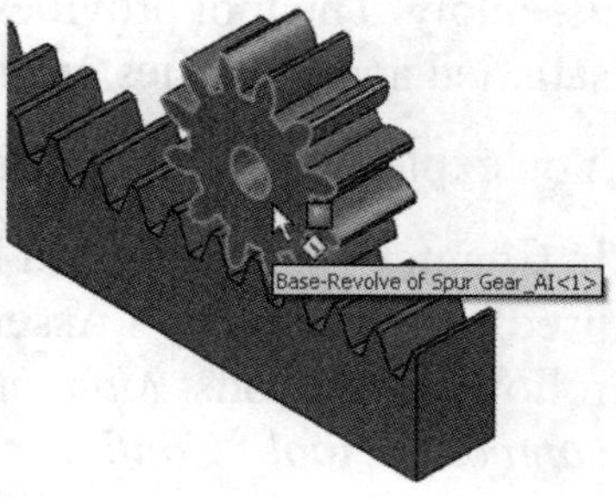


3. Click the **front face** of the Spur Gear component as illustrated.
4. Click the **circular face** of the hole in the spur gear. This is your Sketch plane.
5. Click the **Convert Entities** Sketch tool.
6. Click the **Exit Sketch** tool.

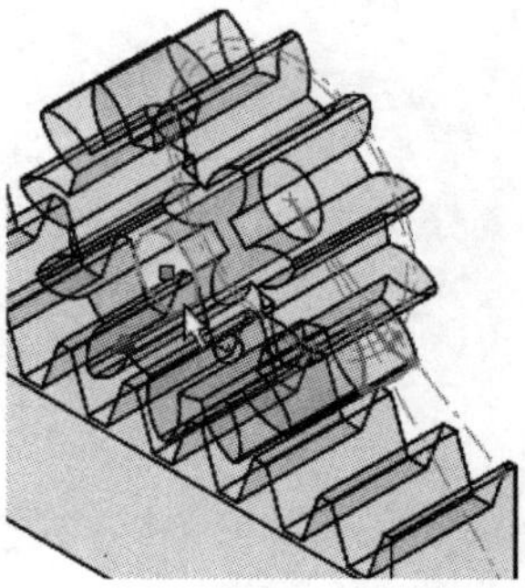

7. Click the **circumference of the circle** as illustrated. View the direction arrow.
8. Click and drag the **green arrow backwards** to create a shaft with an InPlane mate.
9. Click a position **at -50** on the Instant3D ruler as illustrated. You created a shaft with an InPlace mate using the Instant3D tool. View the results.
10. Click **Edit Component** from the CommandManager.
11. **Close** the model.

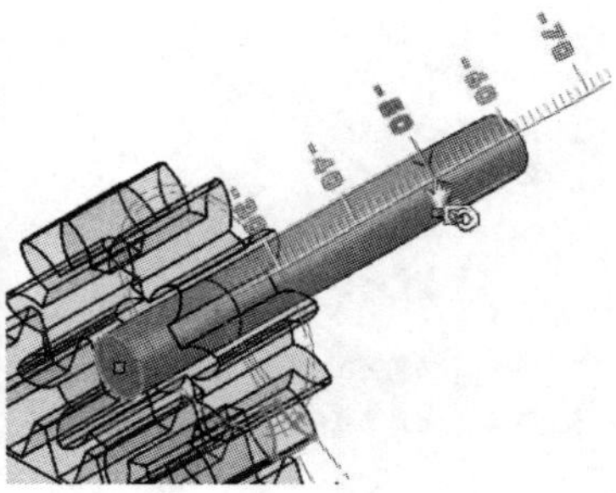

# Summary

In this chapter, you learned about Assembly modeling and the Bottom-up Assembly Modeling techniques. An assembly combines two or more parts. A part inserted into an assembly is called a component. A sub-assembly is a component contained within an assembly. When you create your first assembly, Assem1 is the default document name. The Assembly document end with the extension .sldasm.

You reviewed the various Assembly configuration methods: *Manual (Add Configuration command), Configure component /Configure dimension tool,* and *Design Tables* and addressed the before you begin an assembly task list. See Chapter 12 for additional tutorials on assembly configuration methods.

You reviewed the Assembly FeatureManager and the various Component States of an assembly. You also reviewed an applied the Mate PropertyManager, (Mates and Analysis tabs), reviewed Standard Mates, Mechanical Mates, Advanced Mates, SmartMates, InPlane Mates and Mate References.

The Mate Diagnostics tool provided the ability to recognize mating problems in an assembly. The tool provides information to examine the details of mates which are not satisfied and identifies groups of mates which are over define in your assembly.

You explored the Large Assembly mode.

In Chapter 12, explore and learn how to create and apply Assembly modeling methods used in the Top-down Assembly modeling approach along with configurations using the following methods; *Manual(Add Configuration command), Design Tables* and *Configure component tool / Configure dimension tool.*

# CHAPTER 12: TOP-DOWN ASSEMBLY MODELING AND MORE

## Chapter Objective

Chapter 12 provides a comprehensive understanding of the modeling methods used in the Top-down assembly approach, Motion Studies and Assembly configurations. On the completion of this chapter, you will be able to:

- Know and apply the three different Top-down assembly methods:
  - Individual features, Complete parts and Entire assembly
- Recognize and utilize the following tools from the Assembly toolbar:
  - Insert Components, New Part, New Assembly, Copy with Mate, Mate, Linear Component Pattern, Smart Fasteners, Move Component, Rotate Component, Show Hidden Component, Assembly Features, Reference Geometry, Bill of Materials, Exploded View, Exploded View Sketch, Interference Detection, Clearance Verification and AssemblyXpert
- Create and address Motions Studies:
  - MotionManager, Animation, Basic Motion
- Understand and implement design Assembly configurations methods:
  - Manual (Add Configuration command)
  - Configure component /Configure dimension tool
  - Design Tables
- Comprehend the difference between In-Context and Out-of-Context
- Create and apply equations

# Top-Down Assembly Modeling

In the Top-down assembly modeling design approach, one or more features of the part are defined by something in the assembly. Example: A layout sketch or the geometry of another part. The design intent of the model, examples: the size of the features, location of the components in the assembly, etc. take place from the top level of the assembly and translates downward from the assembly to the component.

A few advantages of the Top-down modeling approach are that design details of all components are not required and much less rework is required when a design change is needed. The model requires individual relationships between components. The parts know how to update themselves based on the way you created them.

Designers usually use the Top-down assembly modeling approach to lay their assemblies out and to capture key design aspects of custom parts specific in the assemblies. There are three key methods to use for the Top-down assembly modeling approach. They are:

# Assembly Methods

- *Individual features method.* The Individual features method provides the ability to reference the various components and sub-components in an existing assembly. Example: Creating a structural brace in a box by using the Extruded Boss/Base feature tool. You might use the Up to Surface option for the End Condition and select the bottom of the box, which is a different part. The Individual features method maintains the correct support brace length, even if you modify the box in the future. The length of the structural brace is defined in the assembly. The length is not defined by a static dimension in the part. The Individual features method is useful for parts that are typically static but have various features which interface with other assembly components in the model.
- *Entire assembly method.* The Entire assembly method provides the ability to create an assembly from a layout sketch. The layout sketch defines the component locations, key dimensions, etc. A major advantage of designing an assembly using a layout sketch is that if you modify the layout sketch, the assembly and its related parts are automatically updated. The entire assembly method is useful when you create changes quickly, and in a single location.

You can create an assembly and its components from a layout of sketch blocks.

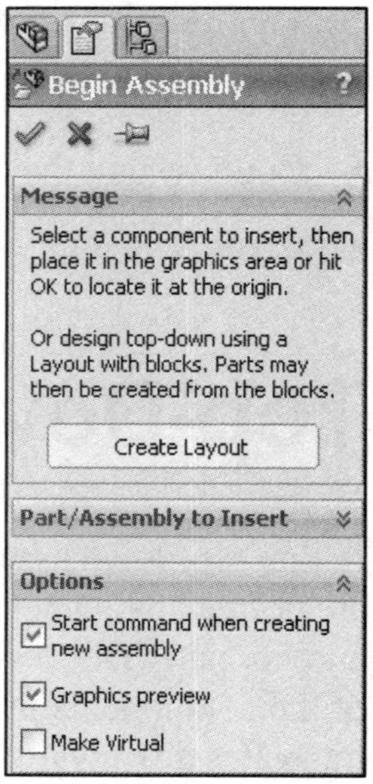


- *Complete parts method.* The Complete parts method provides the ability to build your model by creating new components In-Context of the assembly. The component you build is actually mated to another existing component in the assembly. The geometry for the component you build is based upon the existing component.

This method is useful for parts like brackets and fixtures, which are mostly or completely dependent on other parts to define their shape and size.

Whenever you create a part or feature using the Top-Down approach, external references are created to the geometry you referenced.

The Top-down assembly approach is also referred to as "In-Context".

## In-Context

You can create a new part In-Context of an assembly. That way you can use the geometry of other assembly components while designing the part. The new part is saved as a virtual component. Virtual components are saved internally in the assembly file in which they are created, instead of in a separate part file. When you create components in the context of an assembly, the software saves them inside the assembly file as virtual components. Later, you can save the components to external files or delete them.

During the conceptual design process, when you frequently experiment with and make changes to the assembly structure and components, using virtual components has several advantages over the Bottom-up assembly method:

- You can rename these virtual components in the FeatureManager design tree, avoiding the need to open, save as a copy, and use the Replace Components command.

- You can make one instance of a virtual component independent of other instances in a single step.

- The folder where you store your assembly is not cluttered with unused part and assembly files resulting from iterations of component designs.

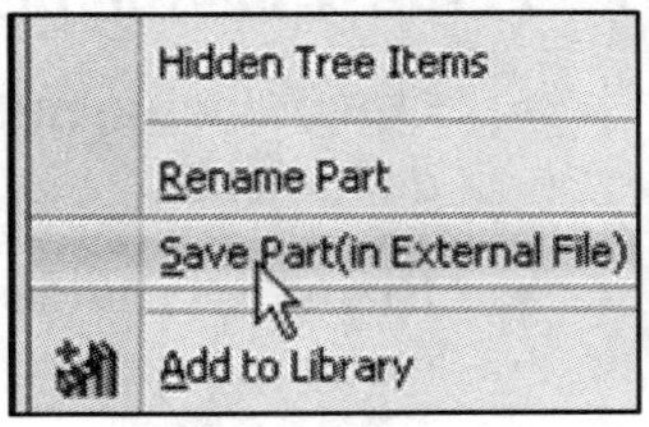


To save a virtual component to its own external file, right-click the component and select **Save Part (in External File)** or **Save Assembly (in External file)**.

To rename the virtual component in the assembly, right-click the **virtual component** and click **Rename Part**.

## Out of Context

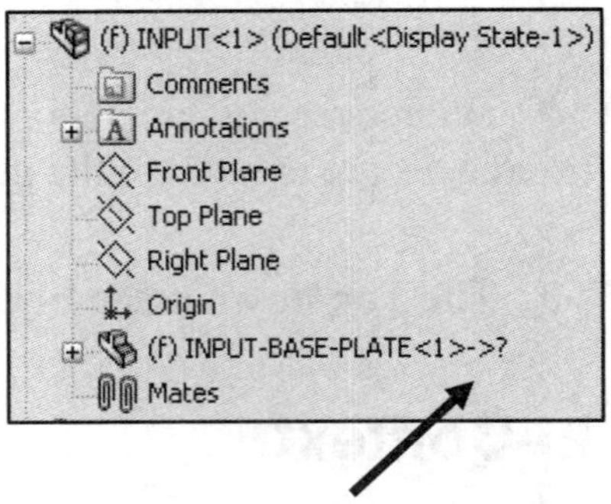


Look at the External reference symbols. If you see the notation "->?" appended to a component, the ? indicates that the External reference is out of context.

To put an out of context component back into context, open the externally referenced document. The Edit In Context automatically opens the document that is referenced by an External reference. This is quite a time saver because you do not have to query the feature to identify the references file, browse to the locate it, and then open it manually.

# Assembly Toolbar

The Assembly toolbar controls the management, movement, and mating of components. The Assembly options are dependent on the views displayed in your Graphics window. The tools and menu options that are displayed in gray are called gray-out. The gray icon or text cannot be selected. Additional information is required for these options. View SolidWorks Help for additional information on the Assembly toolbar and its options.

## Insert Components tool

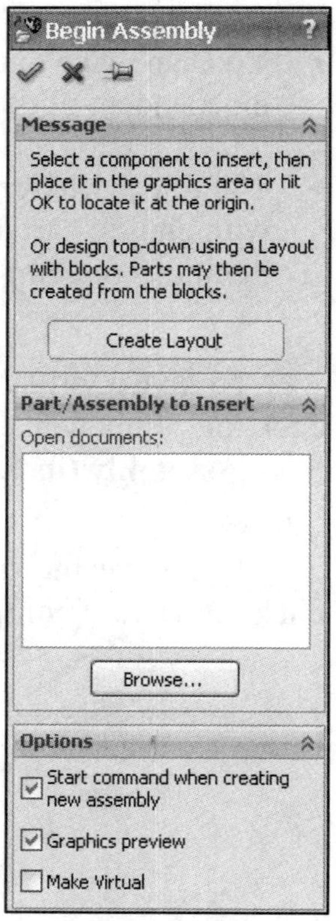


The Insert Components tool provides the ability to add a part or sub-assembly to the assembly. The Insert Components tool uses the Insert Component PropertyManager. The Insert Component PropertyManager provides the following selections:

- ***Part/Assembly to Insert***. Provides the following selections:
  - **Open documents**: Displays the active parts and assembly documents.
  - **Browse**. Provides the ability to select a part or assembly to insert into your model. Click a location in the Graphics window to place the selected component in your model.

Active documents are displayed in the Part/Assembly to Insert box.

- ***Options***. The Options box provides the following selections:
  - **Start command when creating new assembly**. Default setting. Opens the Insert Component PropertyManager when you create a new assembly.

- **Graphics preview**. Provides a preview of the selected document in the Graphics window under your mouse pointer.
- **Make Virtual**. Makes the component you are inserting virtual. Making a component virtual breaks the link to the external component file and stores the component definition inside the assembly file.

## New Part

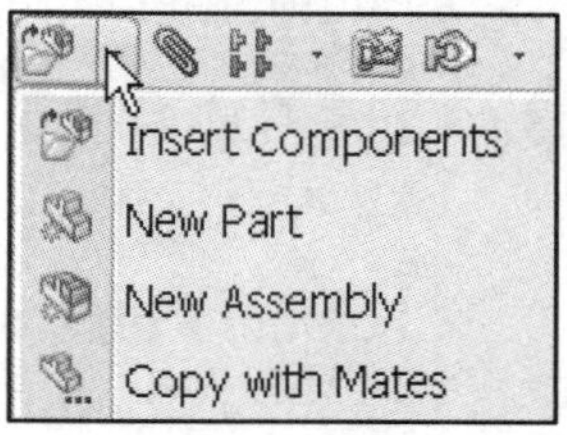


The New Part tool provides the ability to create a new part In-Context of an assembly. The New Part tool provides the ability to apply the geometry of other assembly components while designing the part. The new part is saved internally in the assembly file as a virtual component. Later, you can save the part to its own part file.

You can also create a new sub-assembly In-Context of the top-level assembly.

## New Assembly

The New Assembly tool provides the ability to insert a new, empty sub-assembly at any level of the assembly hierarchy.

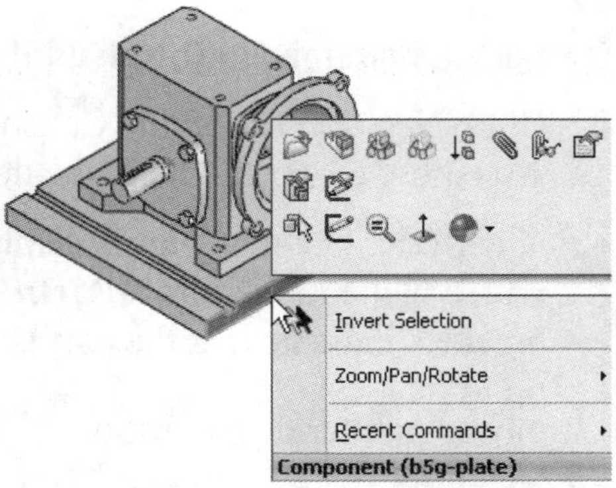


### *Tutorial: Insert a feature In-Context of an assembly 12-1*

Insert a feature In-Context of an assembly. Utilize the Individual features Top-Down assembly method.

1. Open **Individual Features 12-1** from the SolidWorks 2010\TopDownAssemblyModeling folder. Set **Lightweight to Resolved** if needed for the model.
2. Right-click the right face of the **b5g-plate** from the Graphics window as illustrated.

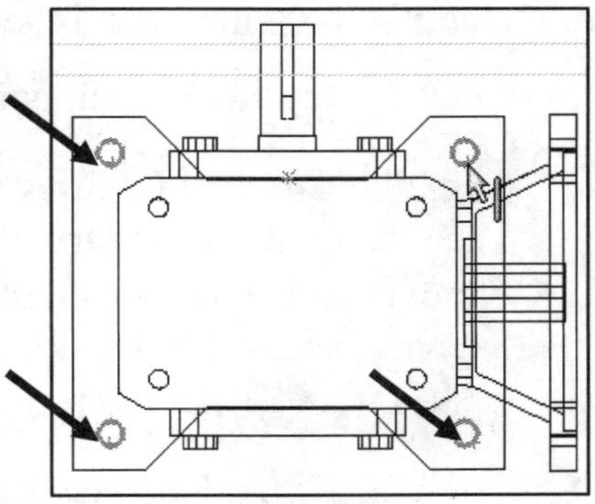

3. Click **Edit Part** from the Context toolbar. The b5g-plate part is displayed in blue in the FeatureManager. Right-click the **bottom face** of b5g-plate for the Sketch plane.
4. Click **Sketch** from the Context toolbar.
5. Display a **Bottom** view. Display **Wireframe**.

6. Ctrl-select the **4 circular edges** of the f718b-30-b5-g mounting holes. Click the **Convert Entities** Sketch tool. The 4 circles are projected on the Sketch plane of the b5g-plate part. Click **OK** from the PropertyManager.

7. Click the **Extruded Cut** Features tool. The PropertyManager is displayed. Select **Through All** for End Condition in Direction 1.

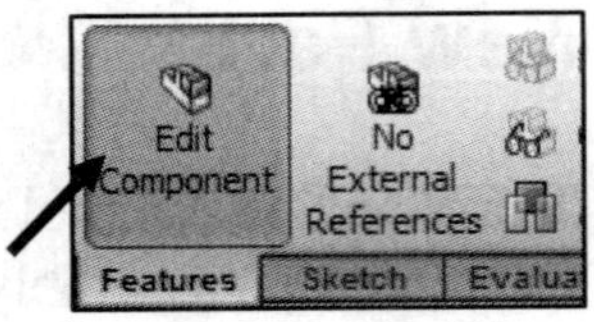


8. Click **OK** from the Cut-Extrude PropertyManager. Cut-Extrude3 -> is displayed.

9. Click the **Edit Component** tool to return to the assembly. **Rebuild** the assembly. The b5g-plate part is updated. Display a **Shaded With Edges** view. Display an **Isometric** view. View the Through all mounting holes in the assembly. **Close** the model.

### *Tutorial: New Part In-Context of the assembly 12-1*

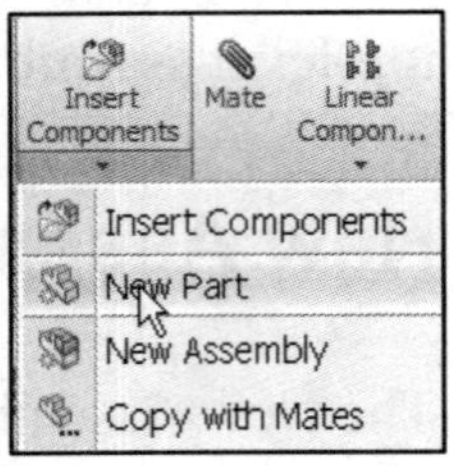


Create a New Part In-Context of the assembly. Utilize the Complete Part Top-Down assembly method.

1. Open **Complete Parts 12-1** from the SolidWorks 2010\TopDownAssemblyModeling folder.
2. Set **Lightweight to Resolved** if needed for the model.
3. Click **New Part** from the Consolidated Insert Components Assembly toolbar. Accept the default Part Template.

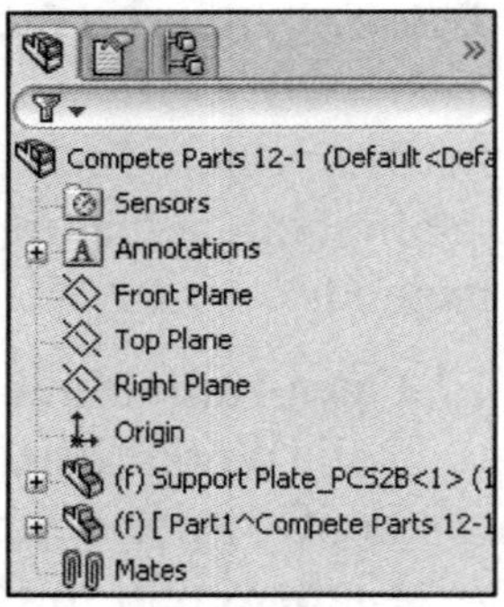


4. Click **OK**. The new part is displayed in the FeatureManager with a name in the form **[Part*n*^*assembly_name*]**. The square brackets indicate that the part is a virtual component. The mouse pointer displays the icon.
5. Click the **top face** of Support Plate_PCS2B for your Sketch plane. Edit Component is selected. A new sketch opens.
6. Click the **top face** of Support Plate_PCS2B.
7. Click the **Convert Entities** Sketch tool. The rectangular boundary of the Support Plate_PCS2B is projected onto the current Sketch plane of the Top Plate_PCS2B part. Click **OK** from the PropertyManager.

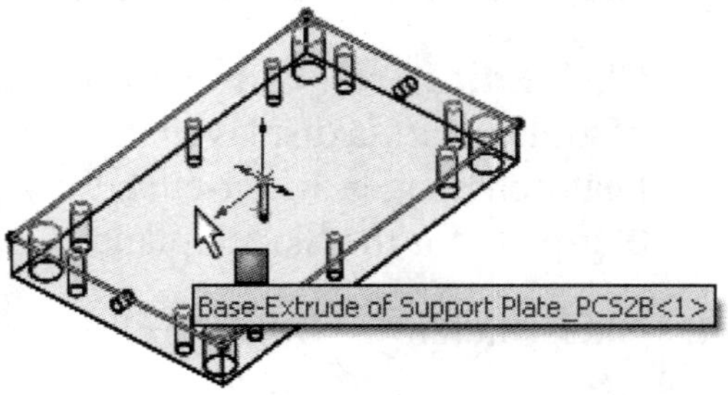


8. Click the **Extruded Boss/Base** Features tool. The Boss-Extrude PropertyManager is displayed. The extrude direction is upward.

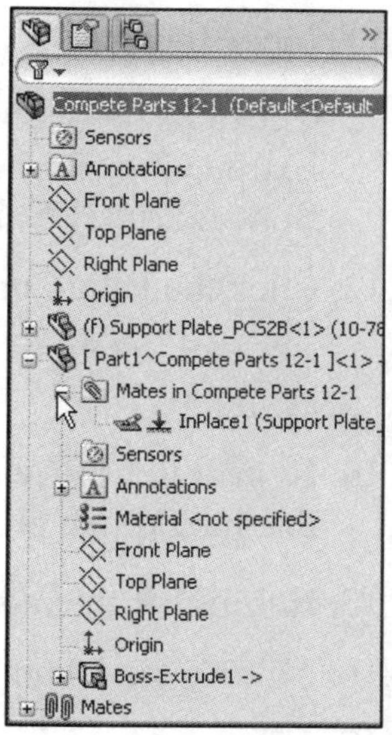


9. Enter **50**mm for Depth in Direction 1. Blind is the default End Condition.

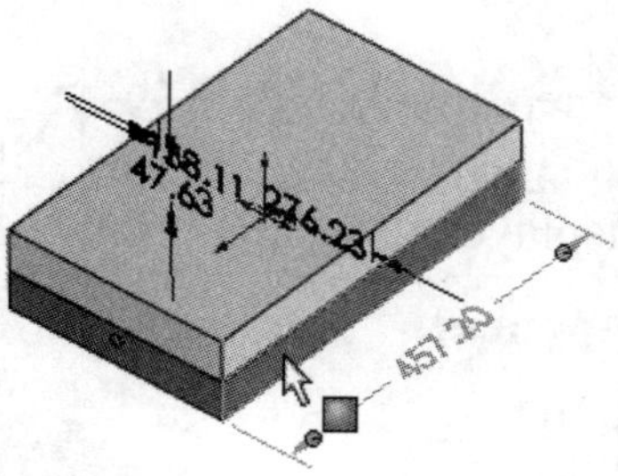


10. Click **OK** from the Boss-Extrude PropertyManager.
11. Click the **Edit Component** tool to return to the assembly.
12. Double-click the **right face** of Support Plate_PCS-2B as illustrated. Double-click **457.20**.
13. Enter **500**. **Rebuild** the model to modify the Support Plate_PCS2B and the Top Plate. View the results. Note: To name the new virtual component, right-click the component, click Open part. Click Save. Enter the desired name.
14. View the created InPlace Mate. **Close** the model.

***Tutorial: Layout Sketch Assembly 12-1***

Create components from a Layout sketch utilizing blocks.

1. Open **Layout Sketch Assembly 12-1** from the SolidWorks 2010\TopDownAssemblyModeling folder. Three blocks are displayed.

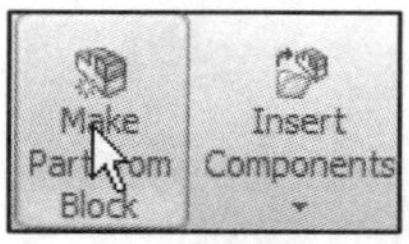


Activate the Make part from block tool.

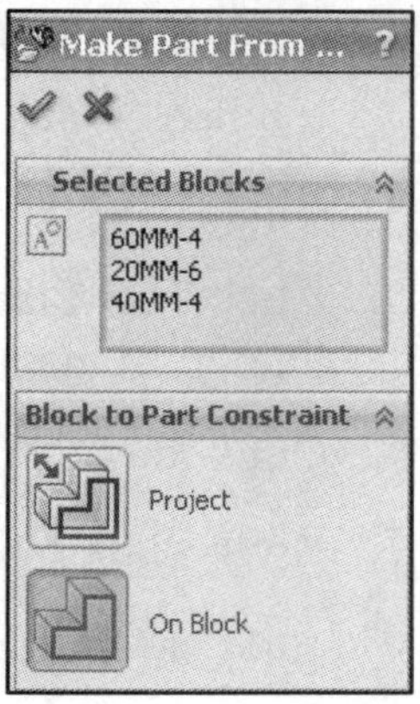


2. Click the **Make Part from Block** tool from the Layout tab. The Make Part from Block PropertyManager is displayed.
3. Ctrl-Select the **three blocks** from the Graphics window. The selected entities are displayed in the Selected Blocks box.
4. Click the **On Block** option.
5. Click **OK** from the Make Part From Block PropertyManager. Accept the default Part Template.
6. Click **OK**. The three blocks are displayed in the FeatureManager and the Layout icon is displayed in the assembly FeatureManager. Rebuild if needed.

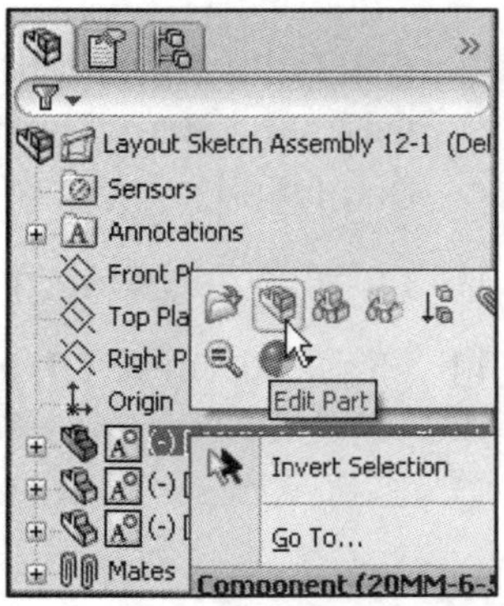


7. Right-click the **20MM** part in the FeatureManager.
8. Click **Edit Part** from the Context toolbar. The 20MM-1 part is displayed in blue.
9. **Expand** the 20MM part from the FeatureManager.
10. Click **Sketch1**. Click the **Extruded Boss/Base** Features tool. Blind is the default End Condition in Direction 1.

11. Enter **10**mm.
12. Click **OK** ✓ from the Boss-Extrude PropertyManager. Boss-Extrude1 is displayed.
13. Click the **Edit Component** tool to return to the assembly.
14. **Repeat** the above steps for the **40MM** and **60MM** parts.
15. **Rebuild** the model. View the model.
16. **Modify** the 80mm dimension to 70mms.
17. **Close** the model.

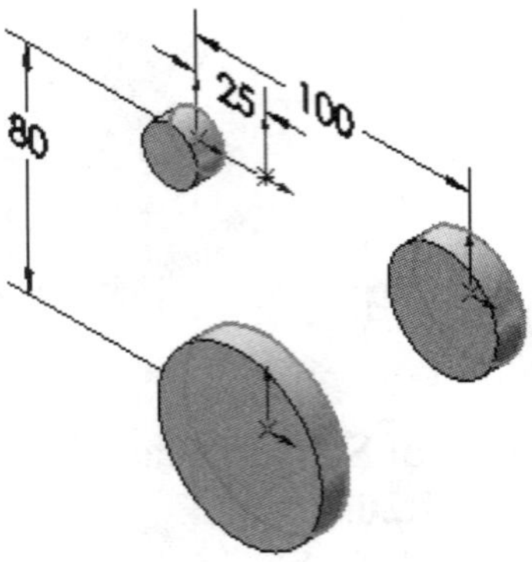


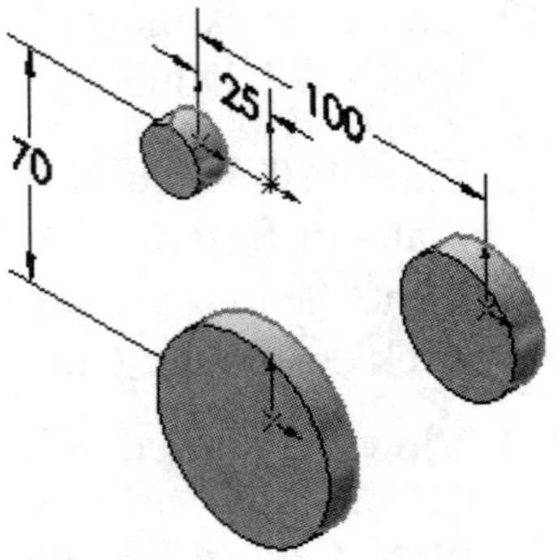


***Tutorial: Entire Assembly 12-2***

Create an assembly from a Layout sketch. Utilize the Entire assembly method.

1. Open **Entire Assembly 12-2** from the SolidWorks 2010\TopDownAssemblyModeling folder. Layout is the first Sketch.
2. Double-click the **Layout** sketch from the FeatureManager to display the sketched dimensions.
3. Click **New Part** from the Consolidated Insert Components toolbar. Accept the default Part Template.

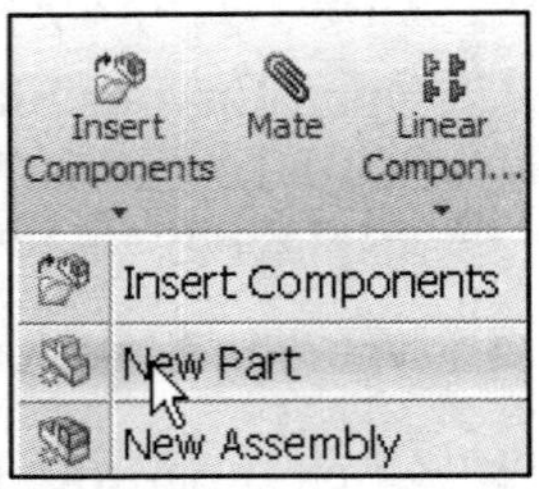


4. Click **OK**.
5. Click **Top Plane** from the Entire Assembly 12-2 FeatureManager.
6. Click the **bottom horizontal line** from the Graphics window.
7. Right-click **Select Chain**. The outside lines are selected.

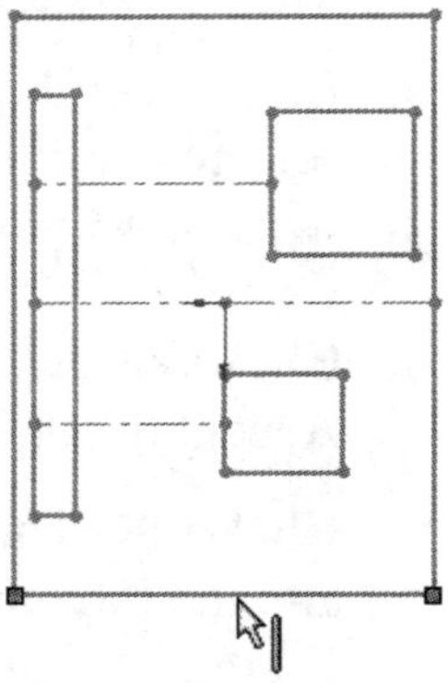

8. Click the **Convert Entities** Sketch tool. Click **OK** ✓ from the PropertyManager.
9. Click the **Extruded Boss/Base** Features tool. The Boss-Extrude PropertyManager is displayed.
10. Display an **Isometric** view.
11. Click **Reverse Direction**. The direction arrow point downward into the screen.

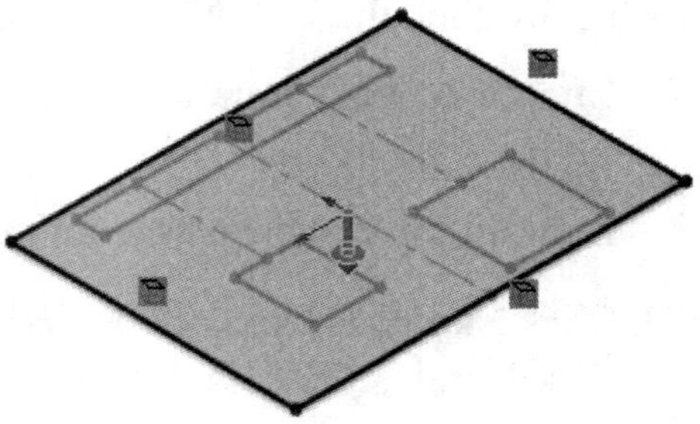

12. Enter **20**mm for Depth in Direction 1. Blind is the default End Condition.
13. Click **OK** from the Boss-Extrude PropertyManager.
14. Click the **Edit Component** tool to return to the assembly.

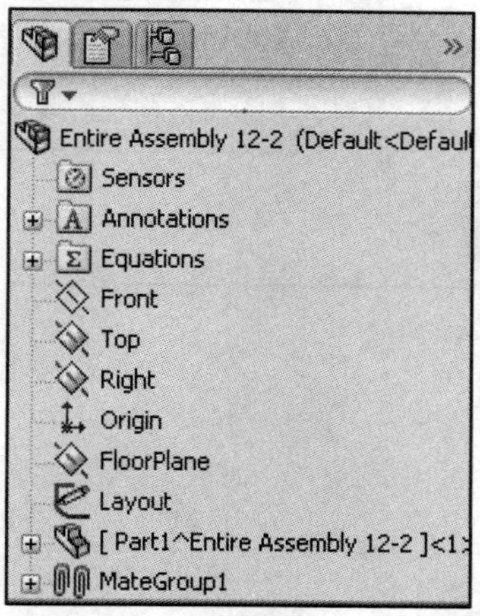

15. **Rebuild** the model. View the results.
16. Click **Save**. Enter the desired **part name**.

Note: To name the new virtual component, right-click the component, click Open part. Click Save. Enter the desired name.

17. **Close** the model.

***Tutorial: Layout Tool with Block Assembly 12-3***

Apply the Layout tool with blocks to address motion.

1. Open **Layout 12-3** from the SolidWorks 2010\TopDownAssemblyModeling folder.
2. Set **Lightweight to Resolved** if needed for the model. Block B translates vertically and represents the motion of the Linear Transfer assembly.
3. Click the **Layout** tool from the Layout tool bar in the CommandManager. Remember block B translates vertically and represents the motion of the Linear Transfer assembly.
4. Drag **Block B** vertically. Note: Block C translates horizontally and represents the motion of a 2AXIS-TRANSFER assembly.
5. Drag **Block C** horizontally a few mm's.
6. **Return** Block B and Block C to their original positions.

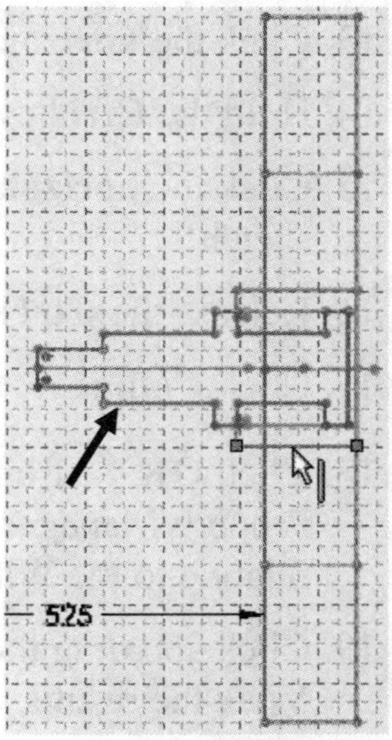


7. Click the **Insert Block** tool from the Layout toolbar. The Insert Block PropertyManager is displayed.
8. Click the **Browse** button.
9. **Browse** to the SolidWorks 2010\TopDownAssemblyModeling folder.

10. Double-click **Rack**. Rack is displayed in the Blocks to Insert box.
11. Click a **position** at the midpoint of the end of the Slider block as illustrated.

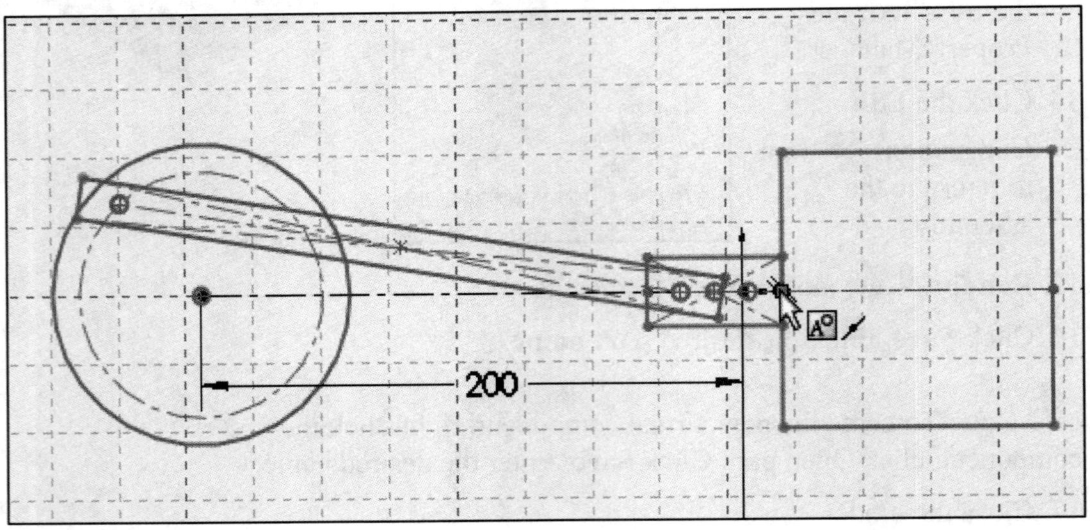


12. Click **OK** from the Insert Block PropertyManager.

Insert a Collinear Geometric relation.

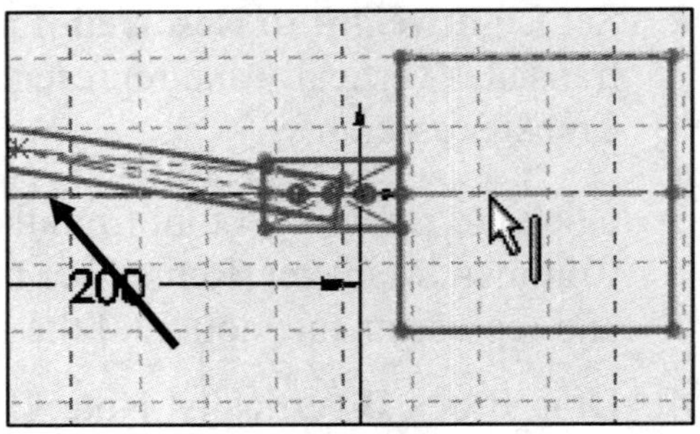


13. Click the **horizontal centerline** of the Rack.
14. Hold the **Ctrl** key down.
15. Click the **horizontal centerline** in the Layout sketch.
16. Release the **Ctrl** key.
17. Click **Collinear**.
18. Click **OK** from the Properties PropertyManager. Verify the Rack motion relative to the Wheel.
19. Click and drag the **wheel** counterclockwise. View the results.

Exit the Layout Sketch.

20. Click the **Layout** tool from the Layout toolbar in the CommandManager.
21. **Close** all models. Do not save.

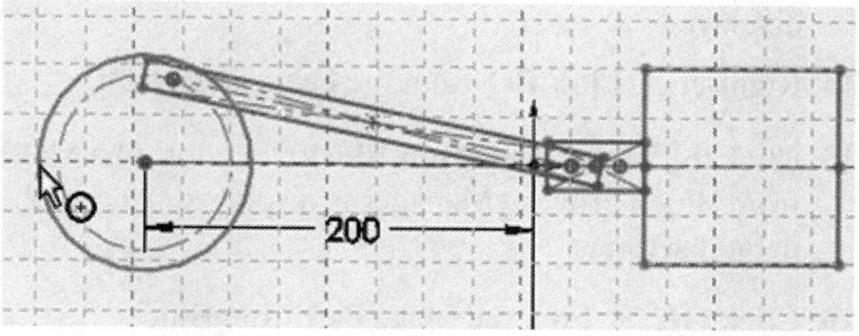


### *Tutorial: Layout Tool with Block Assembly 12-4*

Apply the Layout tool with blocks to address motion. You can make a block from any single or combination of multiple sketch entities. Saving each block individually, provides extensive design flexibility.

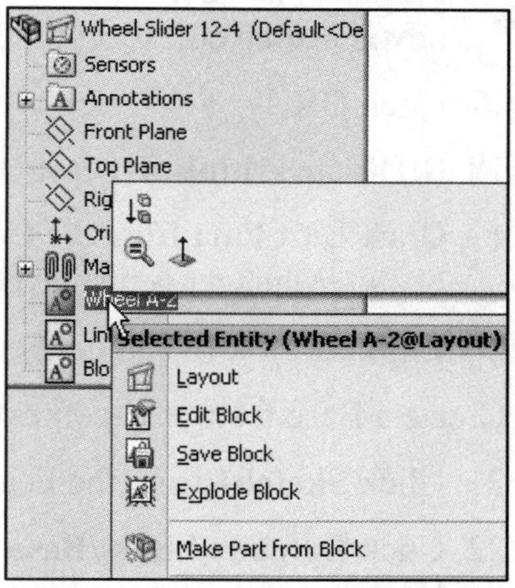


1. Open the **Wheel-Slider 12-4** assembly from the SolidWorks 2010\TopDownAssemblyModeling folder. View the FeatureManager.

Create a Base feature for Wheel A-2.

2. Right-click the **Wheel A-2** block from the FeatureManager.
3. Click the **Make Part From Block** tool. The Make Part from Block PropertyManager is displayed. On Block is selected. Accept the default settings.

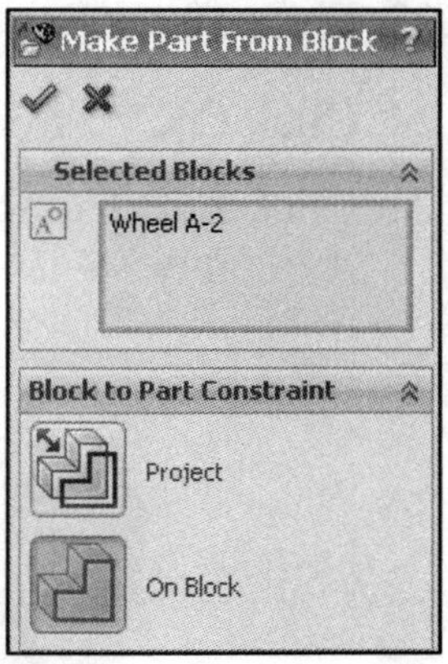


4. Click **OK** from the Make Part from Block PropertyManager. The New SolidWorks Document dialog box is displayed. Accept the default Part Template.
5. Click **OK**.
6. Right click **Wheel A** from the FeatureManager.
7. Click **Open Part** from the Context toolbar. The Part FeatureManager is displayed.
8. Click **Sketch1** from the FeatureManager.
9. Click **Extruded Boss/Base** from the Features toolbar. The Boss-Extrude PropertyManager is displayed.

10. Click the **Reverse Direction** arrow. The arrow points towards the back of the model.
11. Enter **10** for Depth. Blind is the default End Condition in Direction 1.
12. Click **OK** from the Boss-Extrude PropertyManager. **Close** the part.

13. Click **Yes** to rebuild. The Wheel-Slider assembly is displayed.

14. Right-click **Link B-1** from the FeatureManager.

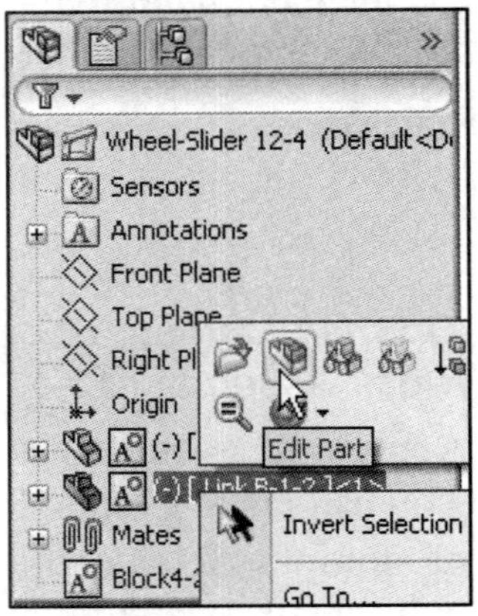


15. Click the **Make Part from Block** tool. The Make Part from Block PropertyManager is displayed. Accept the default settings.

16. Click **OK** from the Make Part from Block PropertyManager. The New SolidWorks Document dialog box is displayed. Accept the default Part Template.

17. Click **OK**.

18. Right-click **Link B-1** from the FeatureManager.

19. Click **Edit Part** from the Context toolbar. The Link B-1 FeatureManager is displayed in blue.

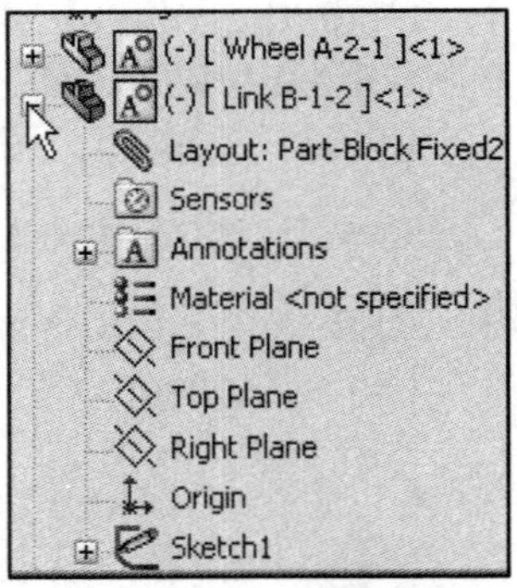


20. **Expand** Link B-1 in the FeatureManager.

Create a Base feature in-context.

21. Click **Sketch1** from the FeatureManager.

22. Click **Extruded Boss/Base** from the Features toolbar. The Boss-Extrude PropertyManager is displayed. Blind is the default End Condition in Direction 1.

23. Enter **10** for Depth.

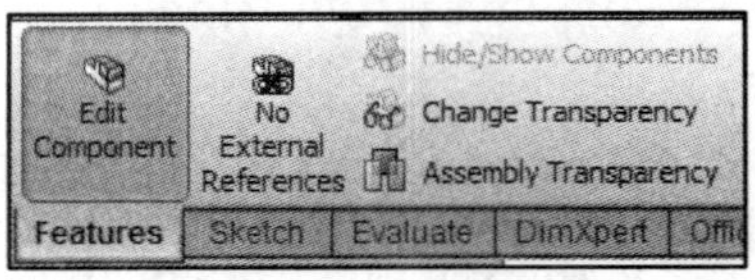


24. Click **OK** from the Boss-Extrude PropertyManager.

25. Click **Edit Component** to return to the Wheel Slider Assembly.

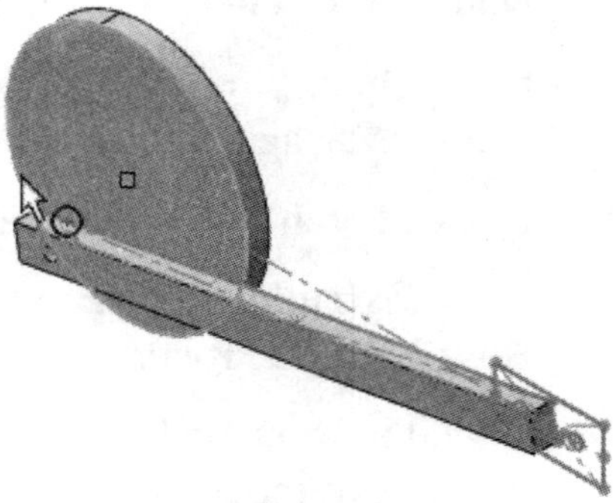

26. Click **Isometric** view. View the results.

27. Drag **Wheel A** counterclockwise. View the results.

Insert a new part into the assembly. Extrude with a different Start Condition.

28. Right-click **Block 4-2** from the FeatureManager.

29. Click the **Make Part from Block** tool. The Make Part from Block PropertyManager is displayed. Accept the default settings.

30. Click **OK** from the Make Part from Block PropertyManager. The New SolidWorks Document dialog box is displayed. Accept the default Part Template.

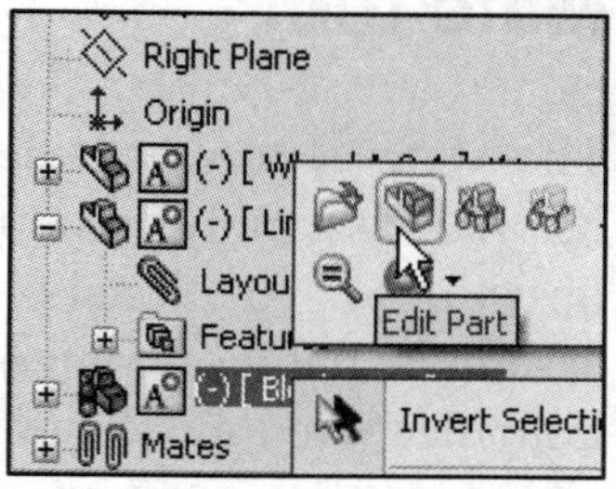


31. Click **OK**.

32. Right-click **Block 4-2** from the FeatureManager.

33. Click **Edit Part**. The Block 4-2 FeatureManager is displayed in blue.

34. **Expand** Block4-2 in the FeatureManager.

35. Click **Sketch1**.

Create a Base feature in-context.

36. Click **Extruded Boss/Base** from the Features toolbar. The Boss-Extrude PropertyManager is displayed. Blind is the default End Condition in Direction 1.

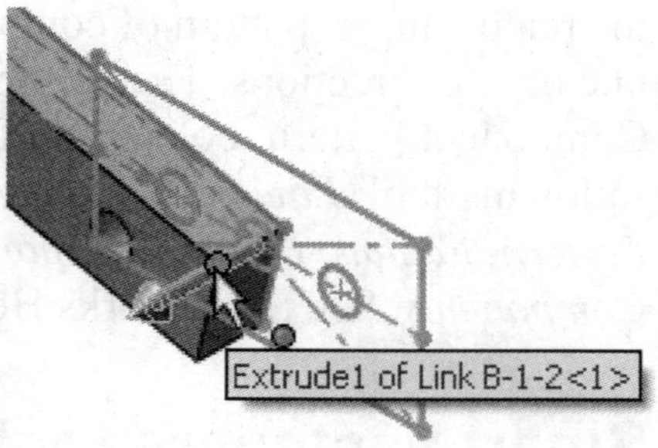


37. Select **Vertex** for Start Condition.

38. Enter **10** for Depth. Click the **Vertex** location as illustrated.

39. Click **OK** from the Boss-Extrude PropertyManager. View the results.

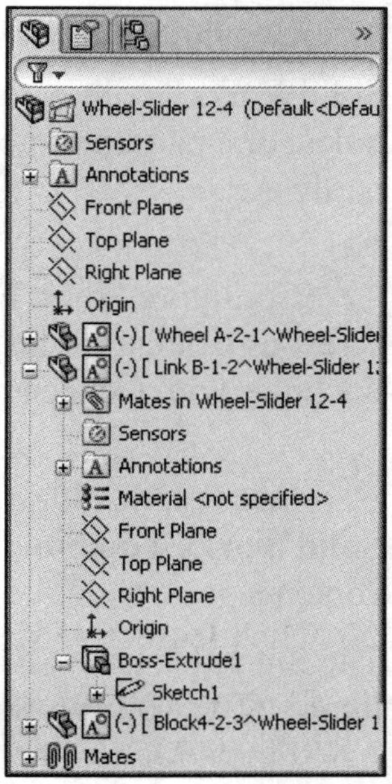


40. Click **Edit Component** to return to the Wheel Slider Assembly.

Deactivate displayed sketches.

41. Click **View**, uncheck **Sketches** from the Menu bar menu.

42. Click **Isometric** view. View the results.

43. **Close** the model. Do not save.

## Copy with Mates tool

The Copy with Mates tool provides the ability to copy components and their associated mates. The Copy with Mates tool uses the Copy With Mates PropertyManager.

## Mate tool

The Mate tool provides the ability to create Geometric relations between assembly components. Mates define the allowable directions of rotational or linear motion of the components in the assembly. Move a component within its degrees of freedom in the Graphics window, to view the behavior of an assembly. View Chapter 11 for additional information.

## Linear Component Pattern tool

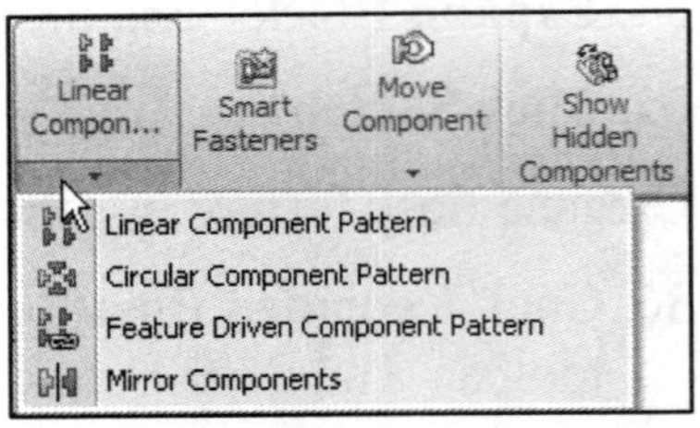


The Linear Component Pattern tool provides the ability to create a linear pattern of components in an assembly in one or two directions. The Consolidated Linear Component Pattern toolbar provides access to the following tool: *Linear Component Pattern*, *Circular Component Pattern*, *Feature Driven Component Pattern* and *Mirror Components*. See SolidWorks Help for additional information.

## Smart Fasteners tool

The Smart Fasteners tool automatically adds fasteners from the SolidWorks Toolbox to your assembly if there is a hole, a series of holes, or a pattern of holes, which is sized to accept standard hardware.

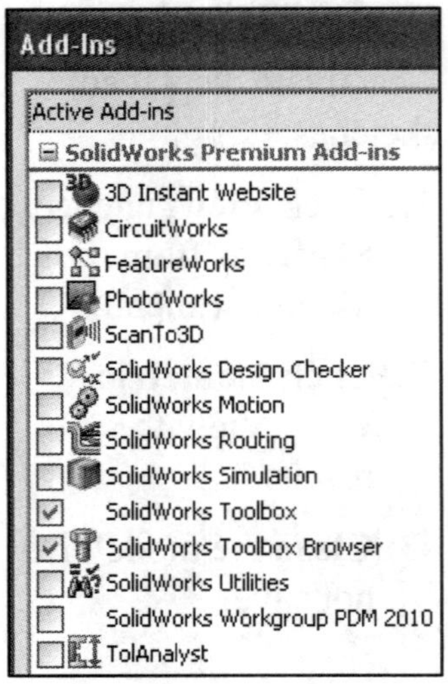


Configure Smart Fasteners to add any type of bolt or screw as a default. The fasteners are automatically mated to the holes with Concentric and Coincident mates.

Install and Add-in the **SolidWorks Toolbox** and **SolidWorks Toolbox Browser** to access SolidWorks Toolbox contents.

The Smart Fasteners feature uses the SolidWorks Toolbox library. The SolidWorks Toolbox provides a large variety of ANSI inch, Metric and other standard hardware.

The Smart Fasteners tool uses the Smart Fasteners PropertyManager. The Smart Fasteners PropertyManager has been updated to include direct controls for adding top and bottom stack components as well as accessing all fastener properties. The Smart Fasteners PropertyManager provides the following selections:

- ***Selection***. The Selection box provides the following options:
  - **Selection**. Displays the selected hole, face or component to add a fastener.
  - **Add**. Adds fasteners to selected holes. You can select holes, faces, or components. If you select a face, the Smart Fasteners tool locates all available holes which pass through the surface. If you select a component, the Smart Fasteners tool locates all available holes in that component.
  - **Populate All**. Adds fasteners to all holes in the assembly.

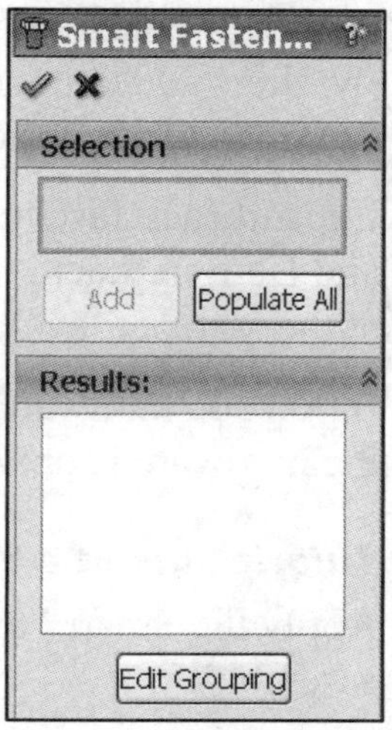


When you click the Add or Populate All option, new fasteners are added to the assembly. The length of a new fastener is the next smallest national standard length for a blind hole, and the next longest national standard length for a through hole. When holes are deeper than the longest fastener length, the longest one is used.

- ***Results***. The Results box displays groups of fasteners you are adding or editing. Select a group to make changes to its fastener type and properties under the **Series Components** and **Properties** option box.
- ***Series Components***. Displays the fastener type for the item that you select in the Results list.
  - **Fastener**. Right-click to change fastener type or to revert to the default fastener type.
  - **Top Stack / Bottom Stack**. Select items from **Add to Top Stack** and **Add to Bottom Stack** to add hardware to the top and bottom stacks.

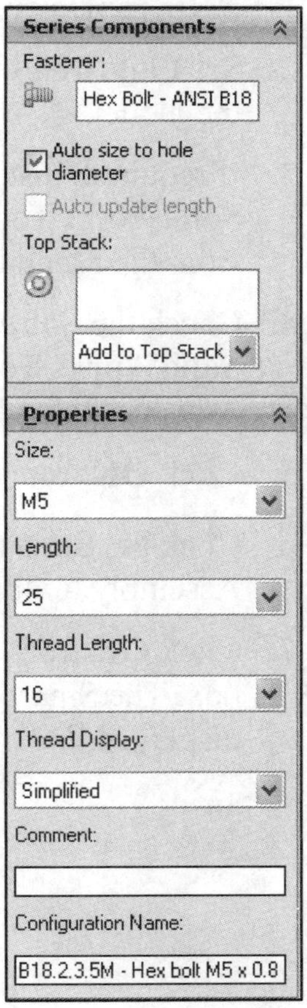


Top Stack, washers under the head of the fastener.

Bottom Stack, (Available for through holes only.) Washers and nuts at the end of the fastener.

  - **Auto size to hole diameter**. Selected by default. Automatically updates the hardware size whenever the hole diameter changes. In the FeatureManager design tree, fasteners and their associated mates are identified with a star if they have this option applied in System options.

- ***Properties***. Displays the properties of the hardware selected under Series Components. Available properties vary depending on the hardware type. You can edit properties such as size, length, and display.
- ***Edit Grouping***. Provides the ability to display and edit the fastener tree.

The Smart Fasteners tool does not automatically insert the needed washers or nuts. You must add theses item by editing the fastener or the series.

Add standard nuts and washers to Smart Fasteners from the Smart Fasteners PropertyManager. Each Series of fasteners has an associated Top Stack (washers added under the head of the fastener) and Bottom Stack (washers and nuts added to the end of the fastener).

Expand each fastener series from the Fasteners box to view its Top Stack and Bottom Stack. If you add hardware to the Top Stack or Bottom Stack at the fastener level, that hardware is displayed in each Series.

If you add hardware to the Top Stack or Bottom Stack at the Series level, the hardware is only displayed in that Series.

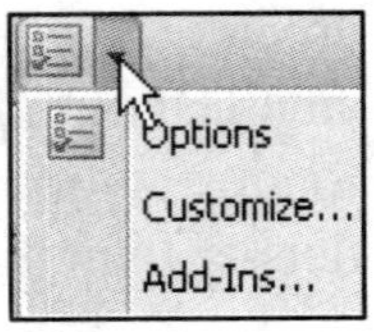


### *Tutorial: Insert a Smart Fastener 12-1*

Apply the Smart Fastener tool. Insert Smart Fasteners into an assembly.

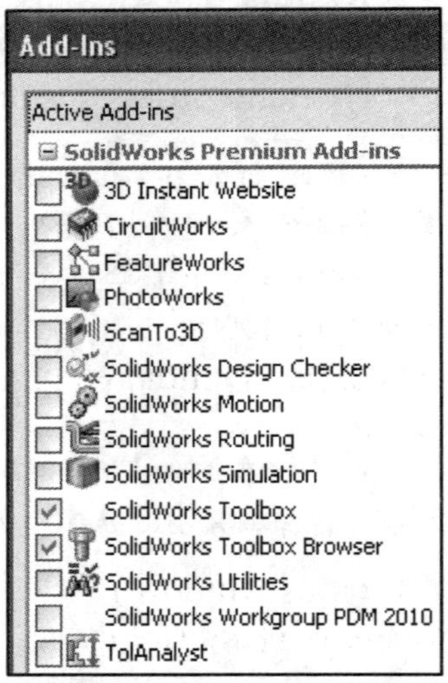


1. Open **SmartFastener 12-1** from the SolidWorks 2010\TopDownAssemblyModeling folder.
2. Set **Lightweight to Resolved** if needed for the model.
3. If required, install SolidWorks Toolbox and SolidWorks Toolbox Browser. Click **Add-Ins** from the Menu bar toolbar.
4. Check the **SolidWorks Toolbox** and **SolidWorks Toolbox Browser** box from the Add-Ins dialog box.
5. Click **OK** from the Add-Ins dialog box.
6. Click the **Smart Fasteners** tool from the Assembly toolbar.
7. Click **OK** from the SolidWorks 2010 dialog box. The Smart Fasteners PropertyManager is displayed.

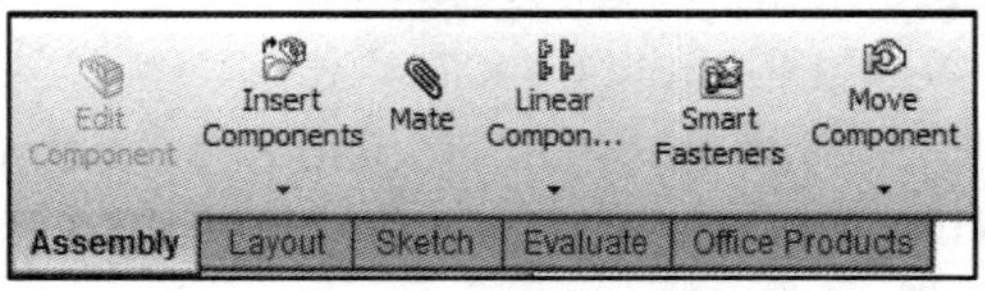

8. Click **CBORE for M5 Hex Head Bolt1** of SF_plate1 from the flyout FeatureManager. CBORE is the seed feature for the DerivedLPattern1.

9. Click the **Add** button from the Smart Fasteners PropertyManager. View the results.

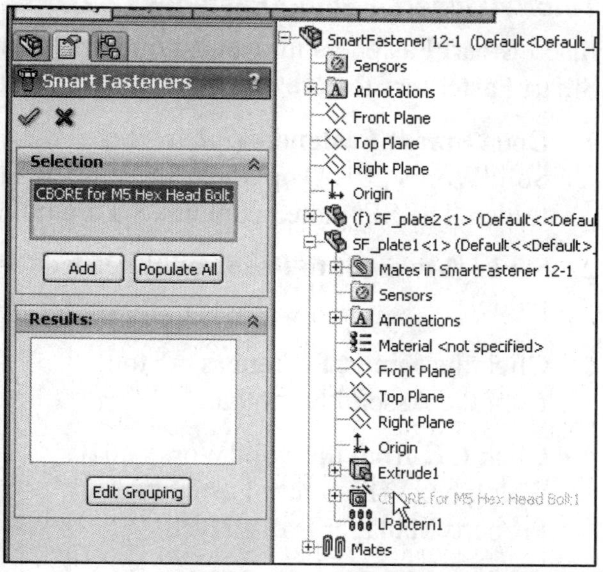


Right-click in the Fastener box to change fastener type or to revert to the default fastener type.

10. Click **OK** ✔ from the Smart Fasteners PropertyManager. View the model with the inserted Smart Fasteners and the FeatureManager.

11. **Expand** the Smart Fastener1 folder in the FeatureManager. View the created DerivedLPattern feature.

12. **Close** the model.

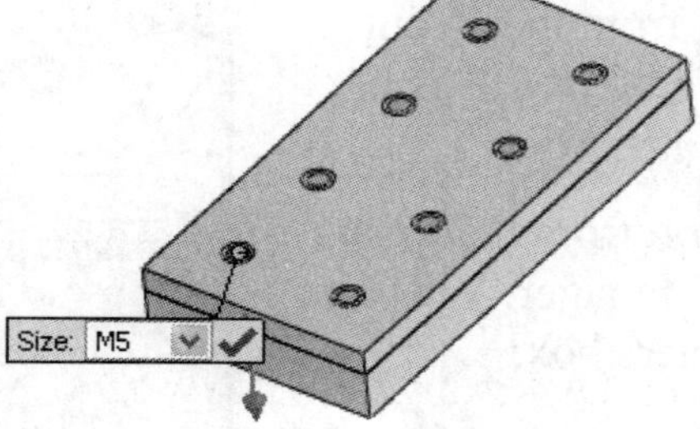


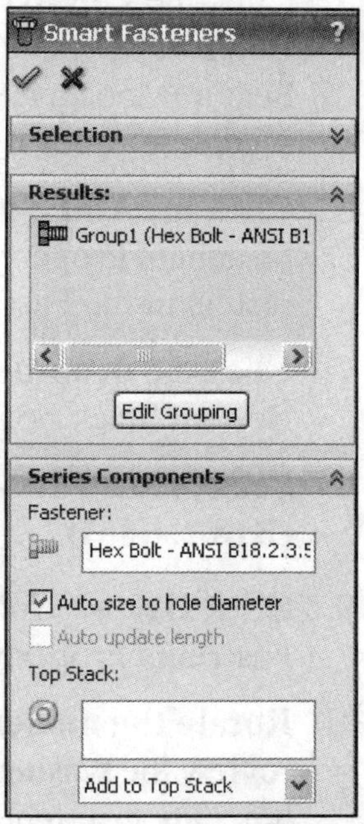


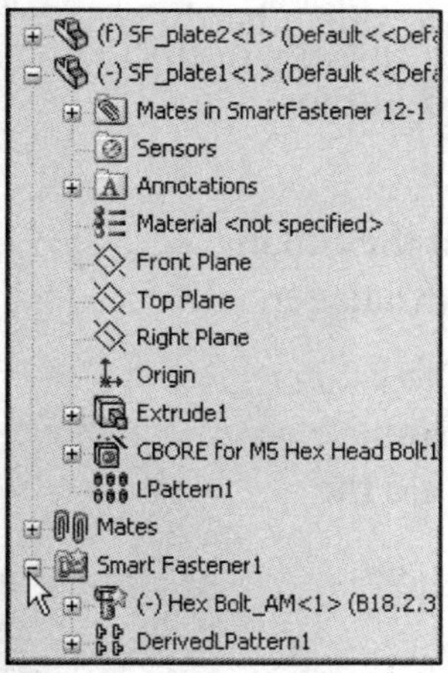


Press the **g** key to activate the Magnifying glass tool. Use the Magnifying glass tool to inspect a model and make selections without changing the overall view.

Right-click and drag in the Graphics window to view the display wheel (mouse gestures). Use the display wheel to reduce mouse travel.

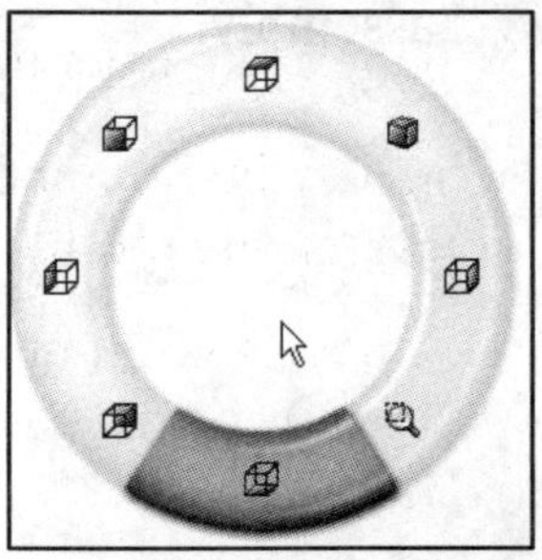

### *Tutorial: Insert a Smart Fastener 12-2*

Insert Smart Fasteners into an assembly. Use the Smart Fasterners feature and insert a bottom Stack.

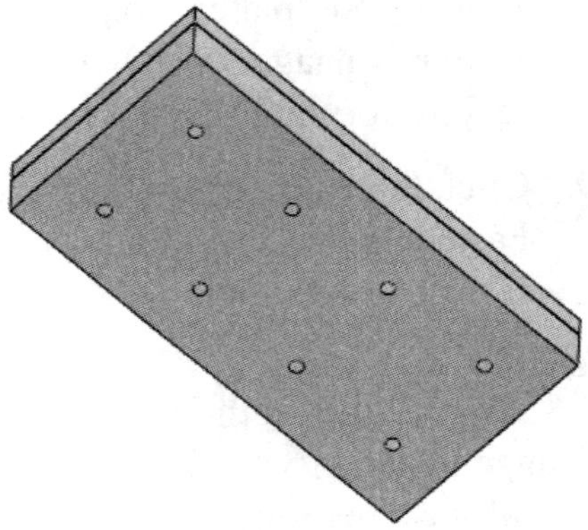

1. Open **Smart Fastener 12-2** from the SolidWorks 2010\TopDownAssemblyModeling folder. The SF_plate3 contains 8 Thru holes.
2. Set **Lightweight to Resolved** if needed for the model.
3. Click the **Smart Fasteners** tool from the Assembly toolbar.
4. Click **OK** from the SolidWorks 2010 dialog box. The Smart Fasteners PropertyManager is displayed.

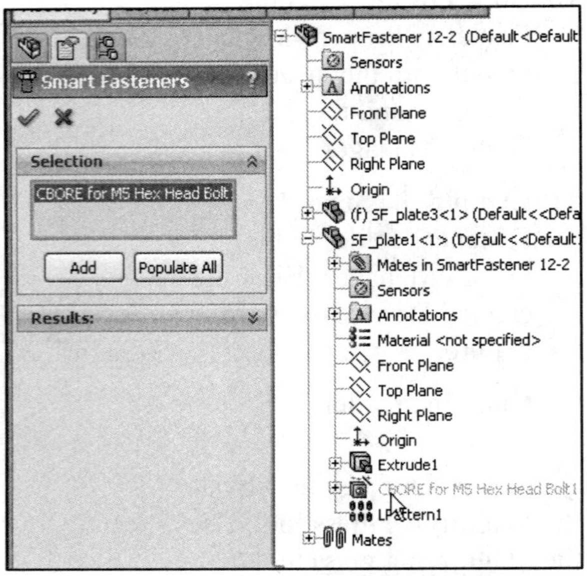


5. Click the **CBORE for M5 Hex Head Bolt1** of SF_plate1 from the flyout FeatureManager. The CBORE is the seed feature for LPattern1.
6. Click the **Add** button from the Smart Fasteners PropertyManager. View the results in the Fasteners box.
7. Click the **drop-down arrow** from the Bottom Stack box to select hardware.
8. Select **Hex Nuts - Flange (B18.2.4.4M)**.
9. Click **OK** from the Smart Fasteners PropertyManager.
10. **Rotate the model** to review the washers and hex nuts inserted into the assembly.

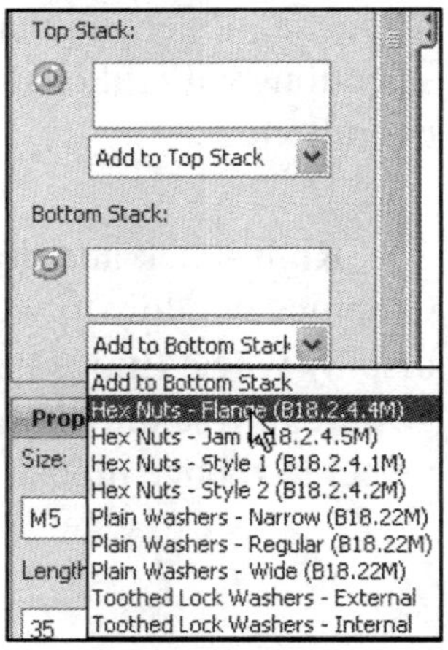


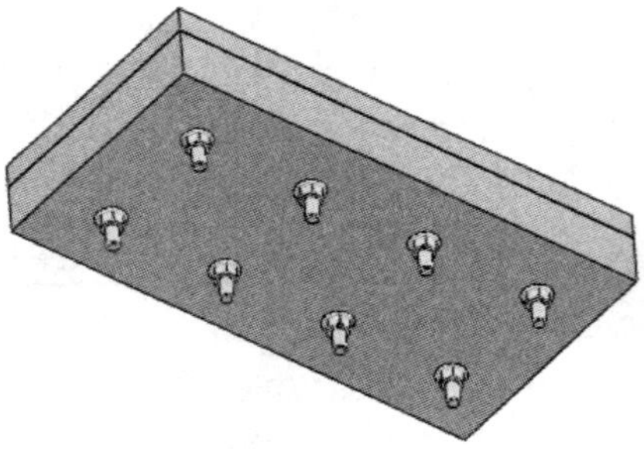

11. **Expand** SmartFastener1 from the FeatureManager. View the results.

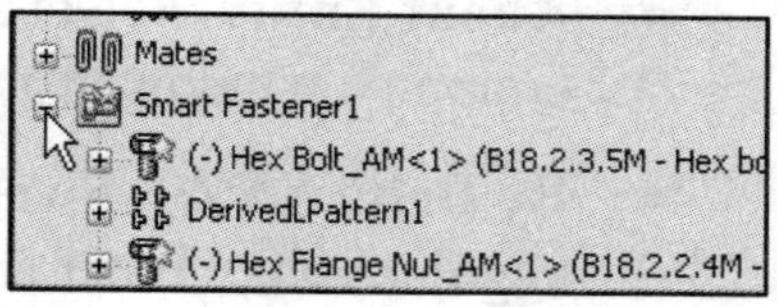


12. **Close** the model.

## Move Component tool

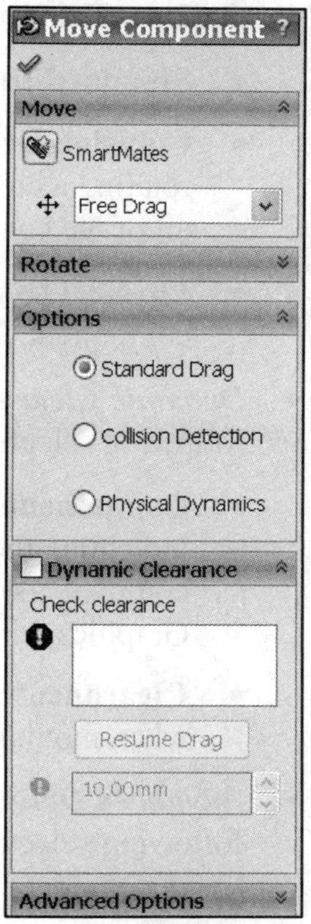


The Move Component tool provides the ability to drag and move a component in the Graphics window. The component moves within its degrees of freedom.

The Move Component tool uses the Move Component PropertyManager. The Move Component PropertyManager provides the following capabilities: *Move a component, Add SmartMates while moving a component, Rotate a component, Detect collision with other components, Activate Physical Dynamics and Dynamically detect the clearance between selected components*.

The available selections are dependent on the selected options. The Move Component PropertyManager provides the following selections:

- ***Move***. The Move box provides the ability to move the selected component with the following options:
  - **SmartMates**. Creates a SmartMate while moving a component. The SmartMates PropertyManager is displayed.
  - **Move**. The Move box provides the following options: *Free Drag, Along Assembly XYZ, Along Entity, By Delta XYZ and To XYZ Position.*
- ***Rotate***. Provides the ability to rotate a component in the Graphics window. The Rotate box provides the following selections:

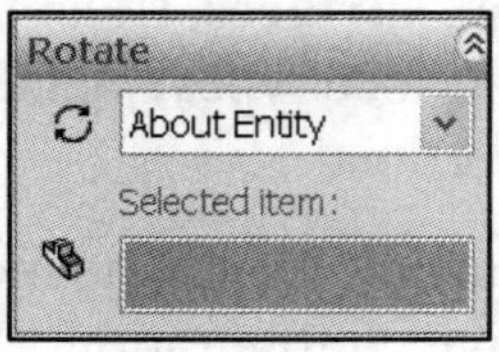


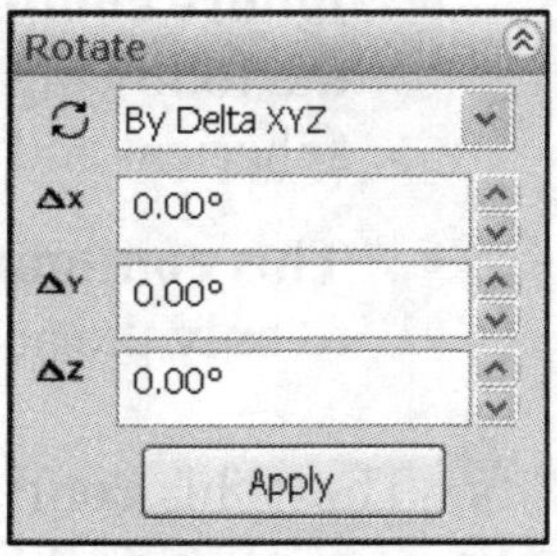


  - **Free Drag**. Provides the ability to drag a selected component in any direction.

- **About Entity**. Select a line, an edge, or an axis. Drag a component from the Graphics window around the selected entity.
- **By Delta XYZ**. Moves a component around an assembly axes by a specified angular value. Enter an X, Y, or Z value in the Move Component PropertyManager. Click Apply.

- ***Options***. The Options box provides the followings selections:
  - **Standard Drag**. Provides a standard drag to the mouse pointer.
  - **Collision Detection**. Detects collisions with other components when moving or rotating a component. Locate collisions for either the selected components or for all of the components that move as a result of mates to the selected components.
  - **Physical Dynamics**. View the motion of the assembly components. Drag a component. The component applies a force to components that it touches.
- ***Dynamic Clearance***. The Dynamic Clearance box provides the following selections:
  - **Components for Collision Check**. Displays the dimension indicating the minimum distance between the selected components when moving or rotation a component in the Graphics window.
  - **Clearance.** Specify a distance between two components when moving or rotating.
- ***Advanced Option***. The Advance Option box provides the following selections:

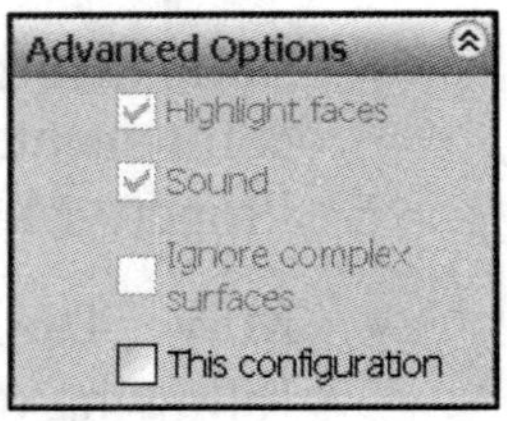


  - **Highlight faces**. Selected by default. Faces in the Graphics window are highlighted.
  - **Sound**. Selected by default. The computer beeps when the minimum distance in the Clearance box is reached.
  - **Ignore complex surfaces**. Clearances are only detected on the following surface types: planar, cylindrical, conical, spherical and torodial.
  - **This configuration**. Apply the movement of the components to only the active configuration.

The "This configuration" check box does not apply to Collision Detection, Physical Dynamics, or Dynamic Clearance. It applies only to Move Component or Rotate Component.

## Rotate Component tool

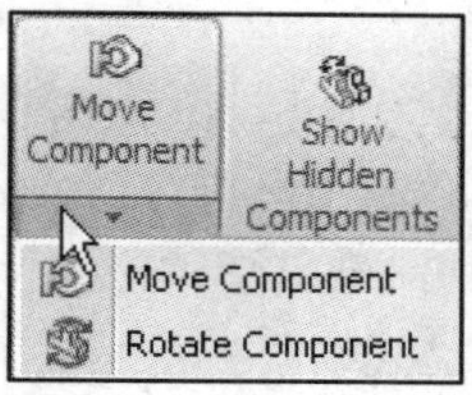


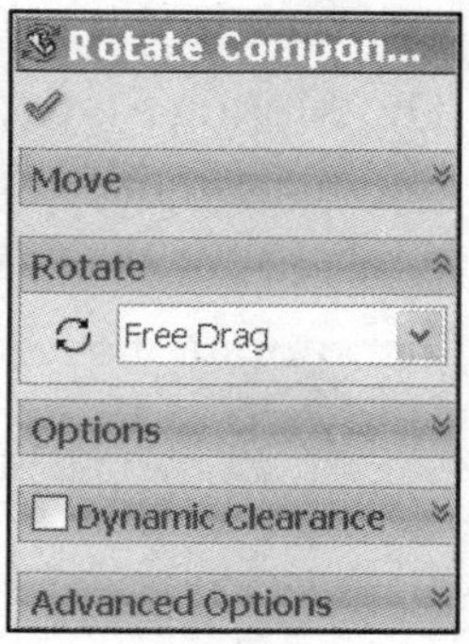


The Consolidated Rotate tool provides the ability to rotate a component within the degrees of freedom defined by its mates. The Rotate Component tool uses the Rotate Component PropertyManager. The Rotate Component PropertyManager provides the same selections as the Move PropertyManager. View the Move Component tool section for detail PropertyManager information.

## Show Hidden Components tool

The Show Hidden Components tool provides the ability to toggle the display of hidden and shown components in an assembly. The tool provides the ability to select which hidden component to be displayed in the Graphics window.

## Consolidated Assembly Features toolbar

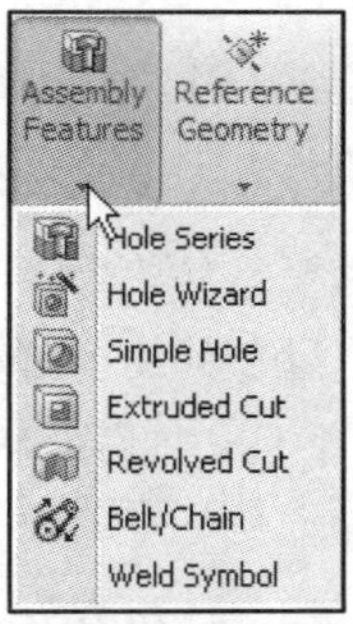


The Consolidated Assembly Features toolbar provides the ability to access the following tools for an assembly: *Hole Series, Hole Wizard, Simple Hole, Extruded Cut, Revolved Cut, Belt/Chain and Weld Symbol*.

## Consolidated Reference Geometry toolbar

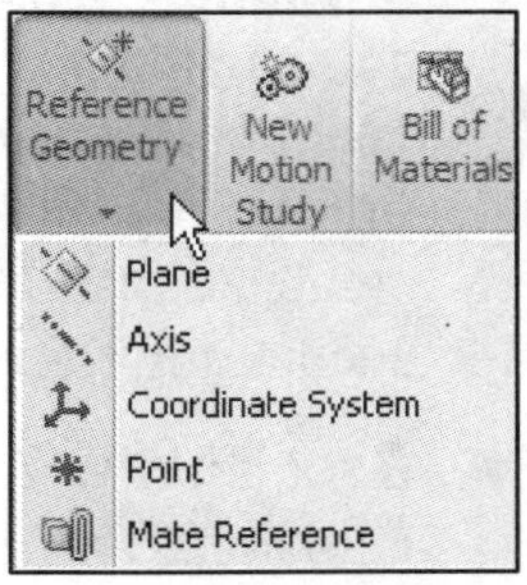


The Consolidated Reference Geometry toolbar provides access to the following options: *Plane, Axis, Coordinate System, Point and Mate Reference.*

## Bill of Materials tool

The Bill of Materials tool provides the ability to create a Bill of Materials directly in an Assembly. The created BOM is displayed in the Tables folder in the FeatureManager design tree. The name of the configuration to which the BOM applies is displayed beside the BOM feature.

## Motion Study tool

The Motion Study tool provides the ability to create graphical simulations of motion for an assembly. Access the MotionManager from the Motion Study tab. The Motion Study tab is located in the bottom left corner of the Graphics window.

Incorporate visual properties such as lighting and camera perspective. Click the Motion Study tab to view the MotionManager. Click the Model tab to return to the FeatureManager design tree.

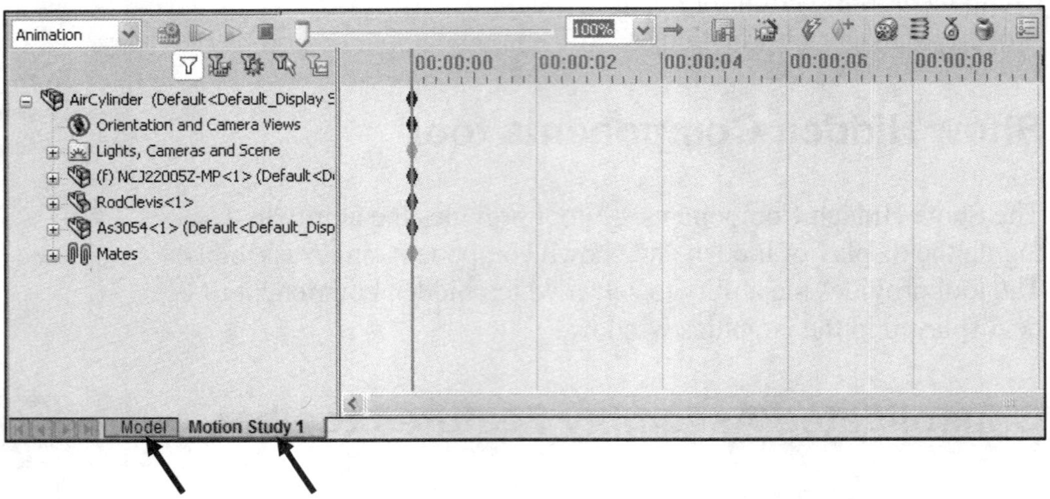


The MotionManager display a timeline-based interface and provide the following selections from the drop-down menu as illustrated:

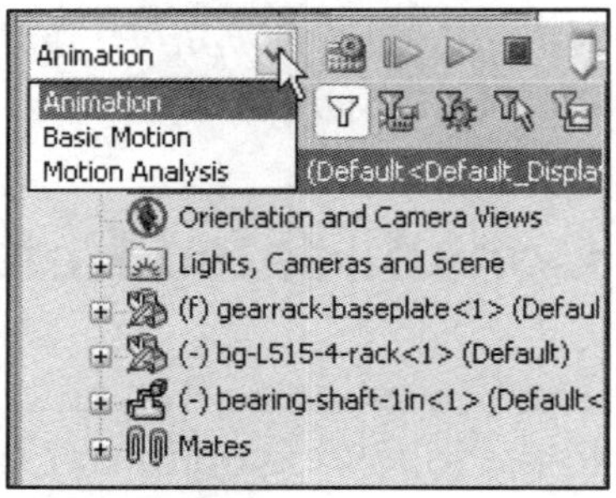


- *Animation:* Default setting. Apply Animation to animate the motion of an assembly. Add a motor and insert positions of assembly components at various times using set key points. Use the Animation option to create animations for motion that does **not** require accounting for mass or gravity.
- *Basic Motion.* Apply Basic Motion for approximating the effects of motors, springs, collisions, and gravity on assemblies. Basic Motion takes mass into account in calculating motion. Basic Motion computation is relatively fast, so you can use this for creating presentation animations using physics-based simulations. Use the Basic Motion option to create simulations of motion that account for mass, collisions or gravity.
- *Motion Analysis.* Only available with SolidWorks Motion as an Add-In. See SolidWorks Help for additional information.

If the Motion Study tab is not displayed in the Graphics window, click **View ➤ MotionManager** from the Menu bar.

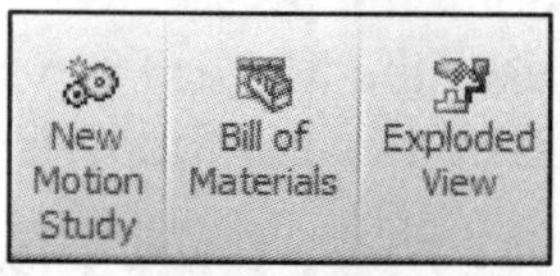


Create a new Motion Study, click **Insert ➤ New Motion Study** from the Menu bar or click the **New Motion Study** tool from the Assembly tab in the CommandManager.

## Animation Wizard

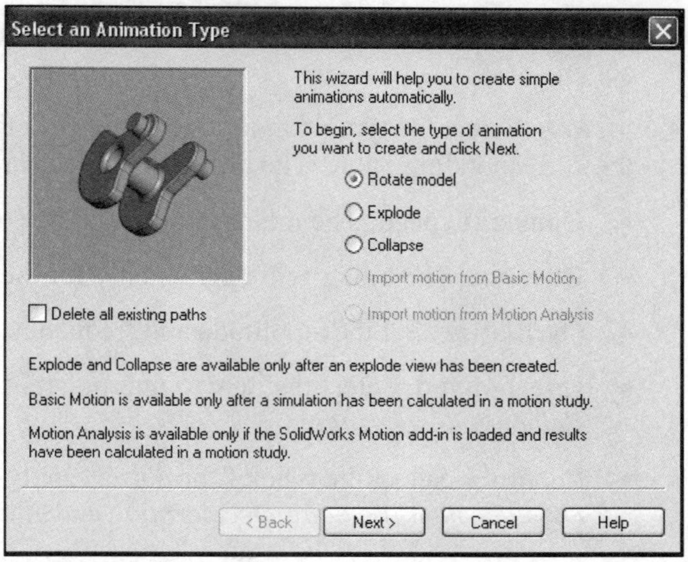


The Animation Wizard tool provides the ability to rotate parts or assemblies or explode or collapse assemblies using a simple wizard format. The following selections are available:

- ***Select an axis of rotation:*** Provides the ability to select the *X-axis*, *Y-axis* or *Z-axis*.
- ***Number of rotations***: Provides the ability to enter the desired number of rotations either Clockwise or Counterclockwise.
- ***Set the duration of the animation***. Provides the ability to set the duration of the animation in seconds.
- ***Set the start time***. Provides the ability to delay the movement of objects at the beginning of the animation.

To apply the Animation Wizard in the Explode and Collapse option, you must first create an Exploded view of your assembly.

# Basic Motion

Basic Motion provides the ability to simulate the effects of motors, springs and gravity on your assemblies. When you record a simulation, the affected components move to a new location in the assembly. Physical Simulation uses the following options. *Linear Motor* , *Rotary Motor* , *Springs* , *Contacts* *and Gravity* .

## Linear / Rotary Motor tool

The Linear / Rotary Motor tool simulates elements that move components around an assembly. The Linear / Rotary Motor tool uses the Motor PropertyManager. The Motor PropertyManager provides the following selections:

- ***Motor Type***. Select Rotary or Linear.
- ***Component / Direction***. Select the component the motor will act on.
- ***Motion***. Select the type of motion to apply with the motor, and the corresponding value. The available options are:
  - **Constant speed**. The motor's value will be constant.
  - **Distance**. The motor will operate only for the set distance.
  - **Oscillating**. Set the amplitude and frequency.
  - **Interpolated**. Select the item to interpolate, *Displacement*, *Velocity*, *Acceleration*.
  - **Formula**. Select the type of formula to apply, *Displacement*, *Velocity*, *Acceleration* and enter the formula.
- ***More Options***. Provides the ability to set motion relative to another part, and to select components for Load-bearing Faces/Edges to transfer them to a Simulation analysis.

Motors move components in a selected direction, but they are not forces. Motor strength does not vary based on component size or mass. For example, a small cube moves at the same speed as a large cube if you set the velocity of the motor to a given value in both cases.

## Spring

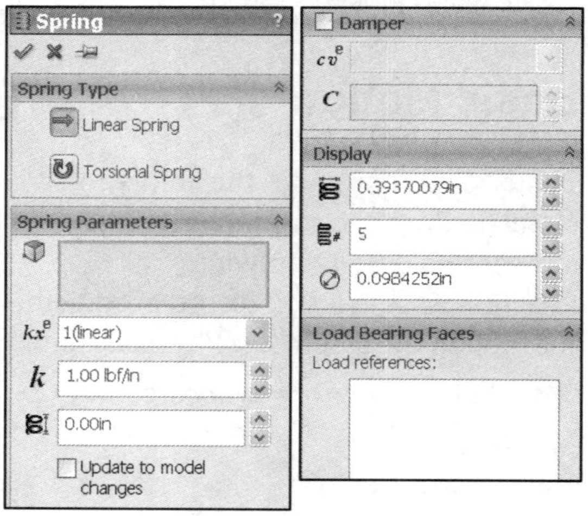


The Spring tool simulates elements that move components around an assembly using Physical Simulation. Physical Simulation combines simulation elements with other tools such as Mates and Physical Dynamics to move components within the components degrees of freedom. The Spring PropertyManager provides the following selections:

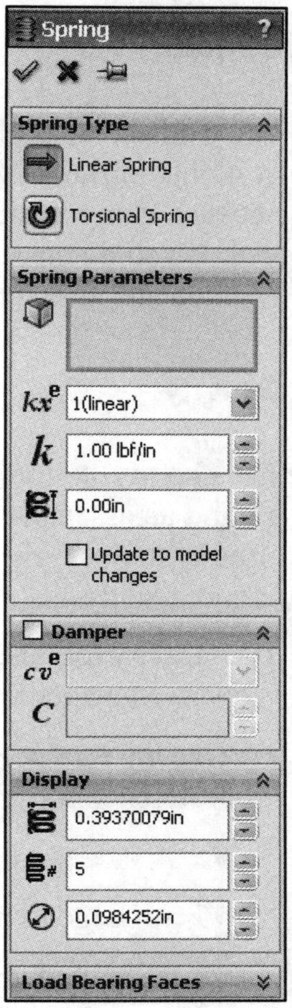


- ***Spring Type***. Select Linear Spring or Torsional Spring.
  - **Linear Spring**. Only available in Basic Motion and SolidWorks Motion Analysis. Represents forces acting between two components over a distance and along a particular direction.
  - **Torsional Spring**. Only available in SolidWorks Motion Analysis. Represents torsional forces acting between two components.
- ***Spring Parameters***. Select the following options:
  - **Spring Endpoints**. Select two features for Spring Endpoints.
  - **Exponent of Spring Force Expression**. Based on the Functional Expressions for Springs.
  - **Spring Constant**. Based on the Functional Expressions for Springs.
  - **Free Length**. The initial distance is the distance between the parts as currently displayed in the Graphics window.
  - **Update to model changes**. Provides the ability to have the free length dynamically update to model changes while the PropertyManager is open.
- ***Damper***. Only available in SolidWorks Motion Analysis. Provides two options:
  - **Exponent of Damper Force Expression**
  - **Damping Constant**
- ***Display***. View the display values only when the **Spring** PropertyManager is open, or when you calculate the study. Provides three options:
  - **Coil Diameter**
  - **Number of Coils**
  - **Wire Diameter**
- ***Load Bearing Faces***. Select components for Load-bearing Faces/Edges to transfer them to a SolidWorks Motion Analysis.

## Contact

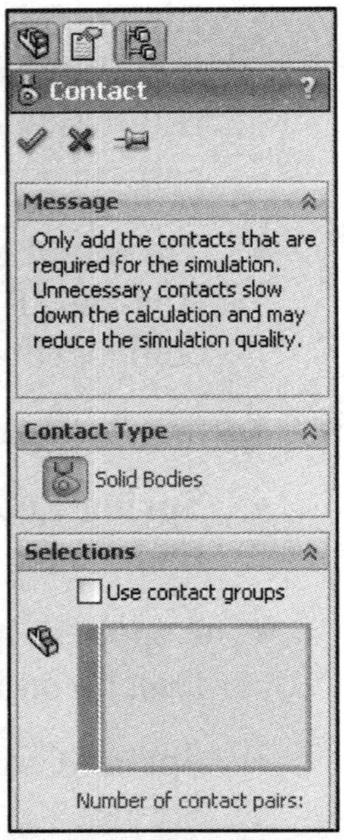


The Contact tool uses the Contact PropertyManager. Only available in Basic Motion and SolidWorks Motion Analysis. Contact between components is ignored unless you apply the 3D Contact tool. If you do not use the Contact tool to specify contact, components pass through each other.

## Gravity

The Gravity tool is a simulation element that moves components around an assembly by inserting a simulated gravitational force. The Gravity tool is only available in Basic Motion and SolidWorks Motion Analysis.

The Gravity tool uses the Gravity PropertyManager. The Gravity PropertyManager provides the following options:

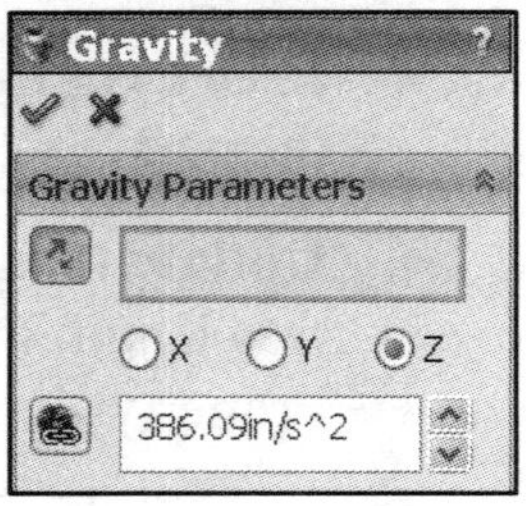


- ***Gravity Parameters***. Provides the ability to set a Direction Reference for gravity.
  - A face to orient gravity parallel to the normal.
  - An edge to orient gravity parallel to the edge.
  - X, Y, or Z to orient gravity in the chosen direction in the assembly reference frame.
  - **Numeric gravity value**. Set the Numeric gravity value. Default is standard gravity.

### *Tutorial: Motion Study 12-1*

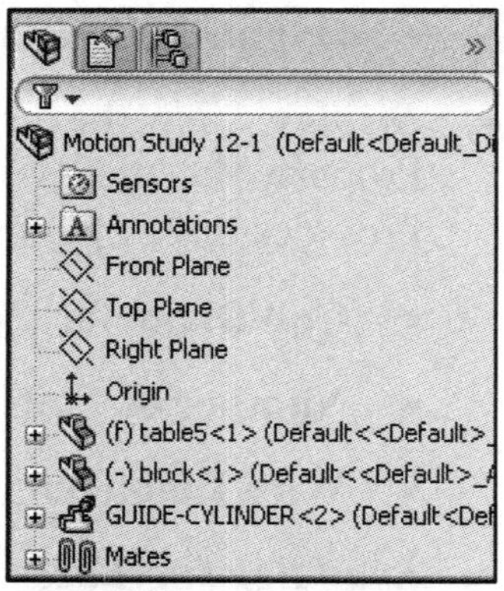


Perform a Motion Study with an assembly using the linear motor and gravity options.

1. Open **Motion Study 12-1** from the SolidWorks 2010\TopDownAssemblyModeling folder.
2. Set **Lightweight to Resolved** if needed for the model.
3. Click the **Motion Study1** tab in the lower left corner of the Graphics window.

4. Select **Basic Motion** for Study type from the drop-down menu.

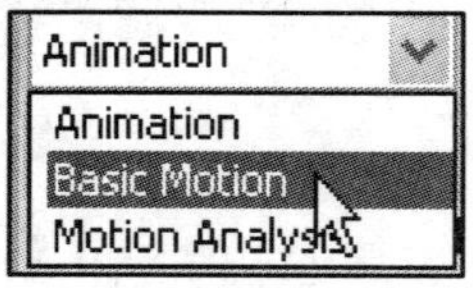

5. Click the **linear right front edge** of Plate of MGPRod<1> as illustrated.

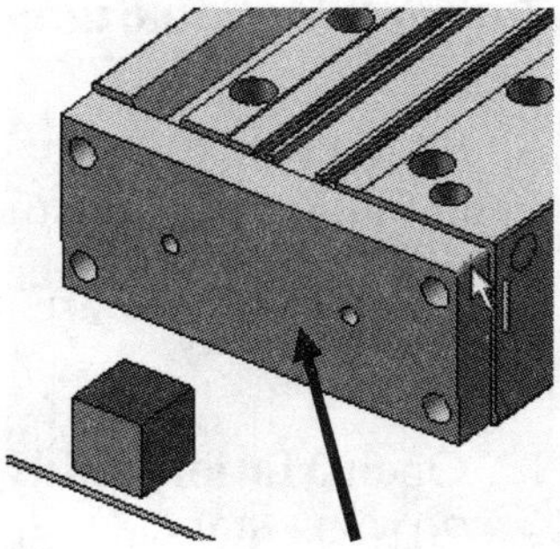

6. Click the **Motor** tool from the Basic Motion toolbar. The Motor PropertyManager is displayed. Edge<1>@GUIDE-CYLINDER is displayed in the Motor direction box.
7. Click the **Linear Motor** button.

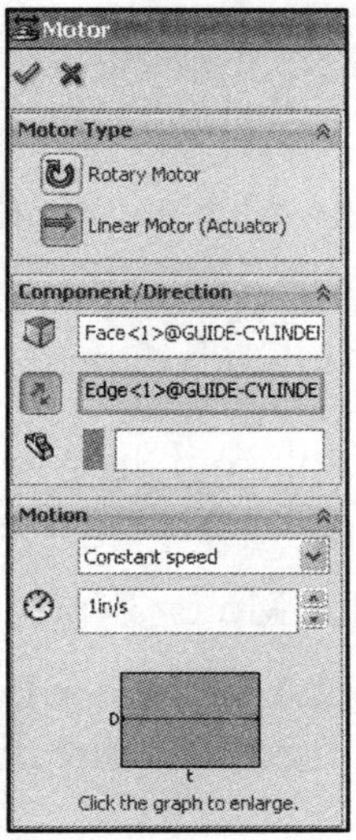


8. Click the **Reverse Direction** button. The direction arrow points to the front.
9. Click the **front face** of the plate. Accept the defaults.
10. Click **OK** from the Motor PropertyManager.
11. Click the **top face** of the plate part as illustrated.

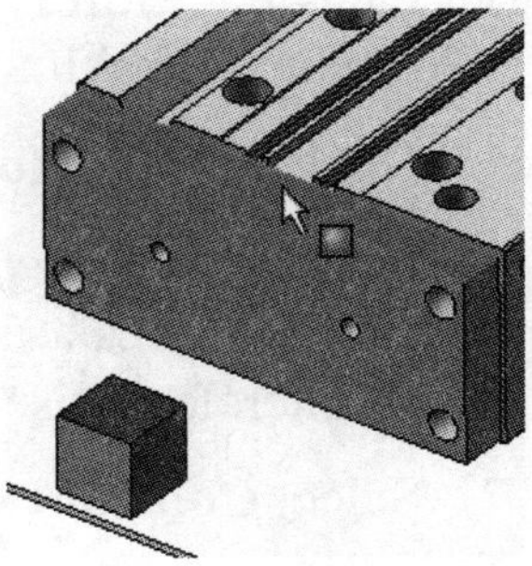

12. Click the **Gravity** tool from the Basic Motion toolbar. The Gravity PropertyManager is displayed. The direction arrow points downward. If required, click the **Reverse Direction** button.
13. Click **OK** from the Gravity PropertyManager.
14. Click **Calculate** from the MotionManager. The piston moves and pushes the block of the table.

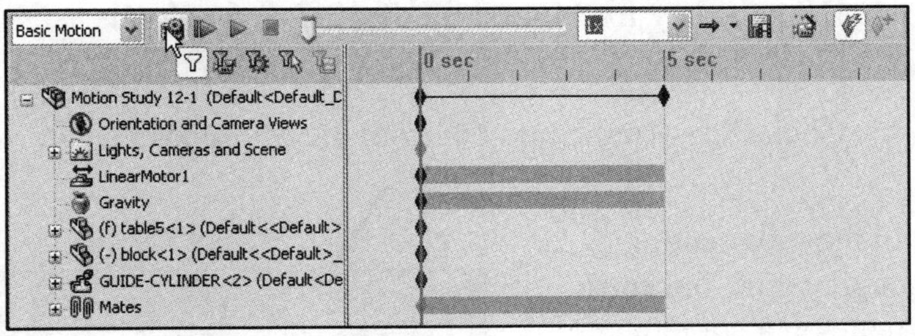


Return to the FeatureManager.

15. Click the **Model** tab to return to SolidWorks.
16. **Close** the model.

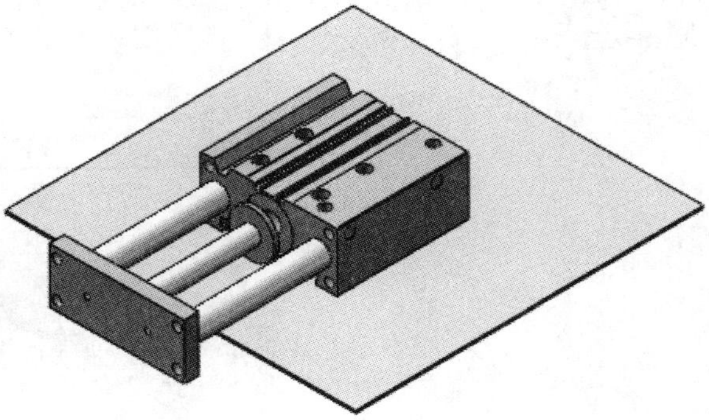

### *Tutorial: Motion Study 12-2*

Apply a motor to move components in an assembly. Set up an animation motion study. Use the motion study time line and the MotionManager design tree to suppress mates in the motion study.

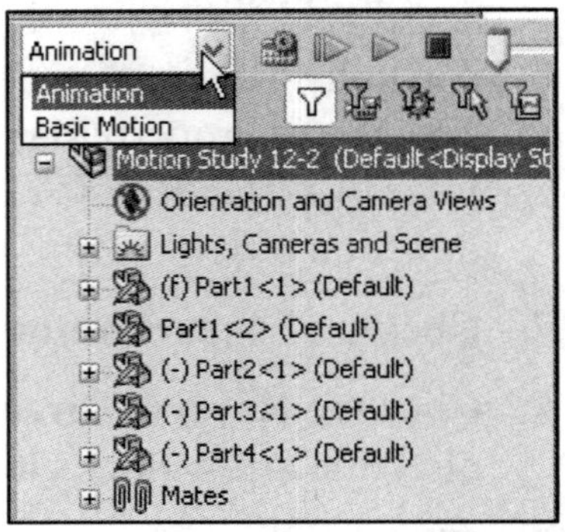


1. Open **Motion Study 12-2** from the SolidWorks 2010\TopDownAssemblyModeling folder.
2. Click the **Motion Study 1** tab at the bottom of the Graphics window.
3. Select **Basic Motion** for Study type.
4. Click the **Motor** tool from the MotionManager toolbar. The Motor PropertyManager is displayed.
5. Click **Rotary Motor** for Motor Type.
6. Select **Face<1>@Part2-1** for Motor Direction, in the Graphics area as illustrated. The direction arrow point counterclockwise.

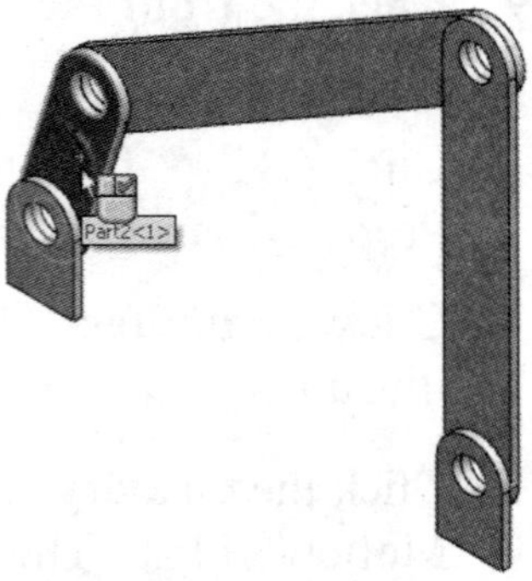


7. Select **Constant speed** for Motor Type.
8. Enter **30** for Constant Speed Motor.
9. Click **OK** from the Motor PropertyManager.

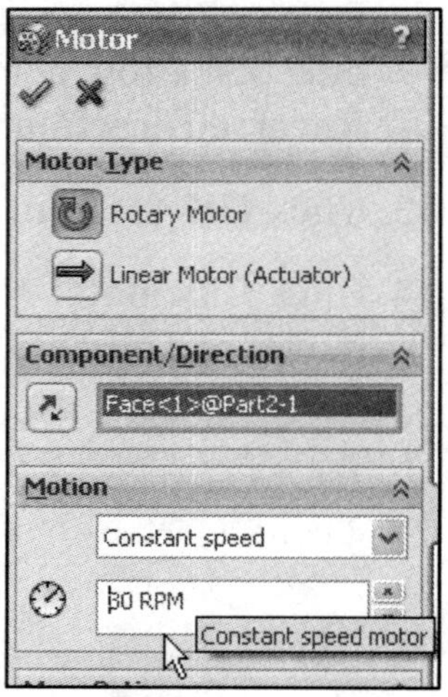


Set the duration and run your animation on the 4bar-Linkage.

10. Drag the key for Motion Study 12-2 to **6** seconds as illustrated.
11. Click **Play from Start** from the MotionManager. View the results.

In the next section, suppress a Concentric mate on a component. View the results in the Motion Study.

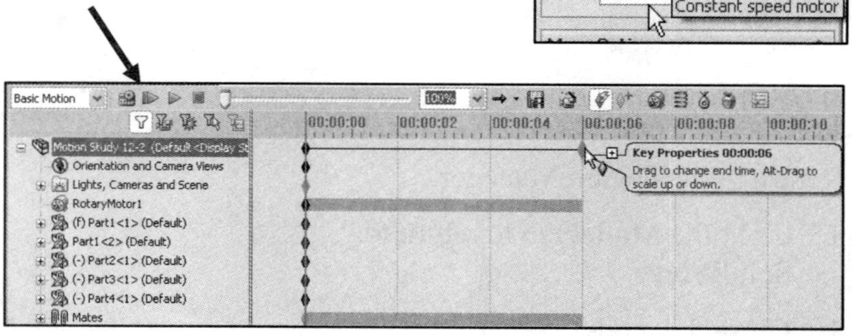


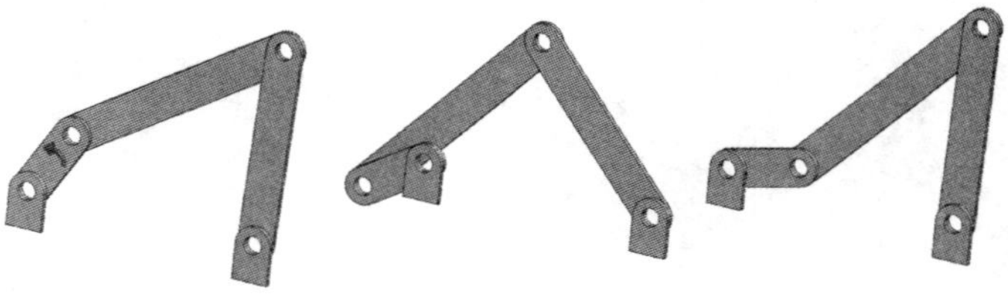

12. **Expand** the Mate folder in the MoitionManager Design tree.
13. Right-click at 2 seconds and select **Place Key** for the Concentric2 mate.
14. Right-click at 4 seconds and select **Place Key** for the Concentric2 mate.

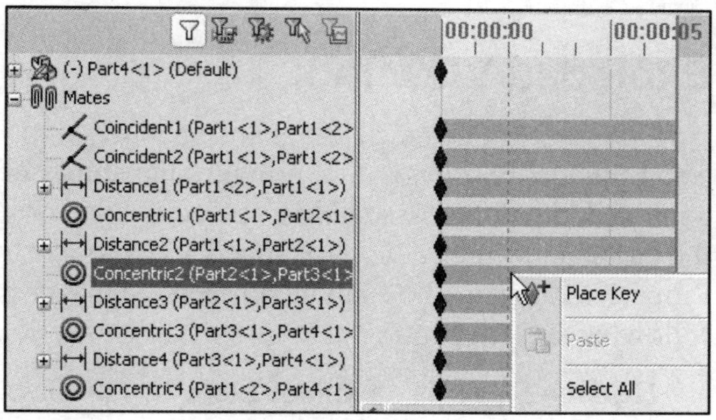


15. Set the time bar to **2 seconds**.
16. Right-click **Concentric2** in the MotionManager design tree.
17. Click **Suppress**. The mate is suppressed between the 2 and 4 second marks.

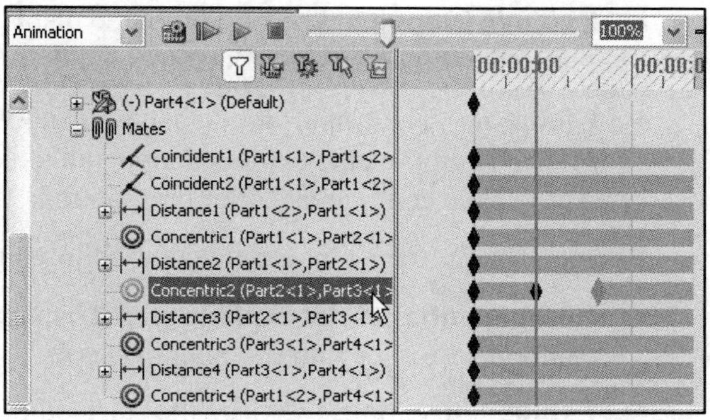


18. Click the **Calculate** tool. After calculating a motion study, you can view it again.
19. Click **Play from Start** from the MotionManager toolbar. View the results. Explore your options and the available tools. View SolidWorks Help for additional information on a Motion Study.

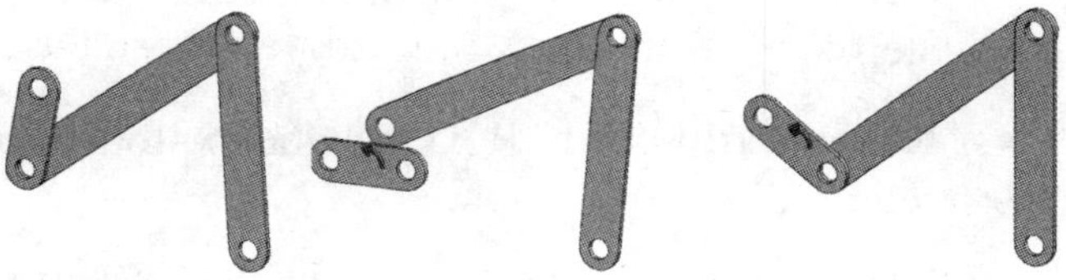

Return to the FeatureManager.

20. Click the **Model** tab to return to SolidWorks.
21. **Close** the model.

## Exploded View tool

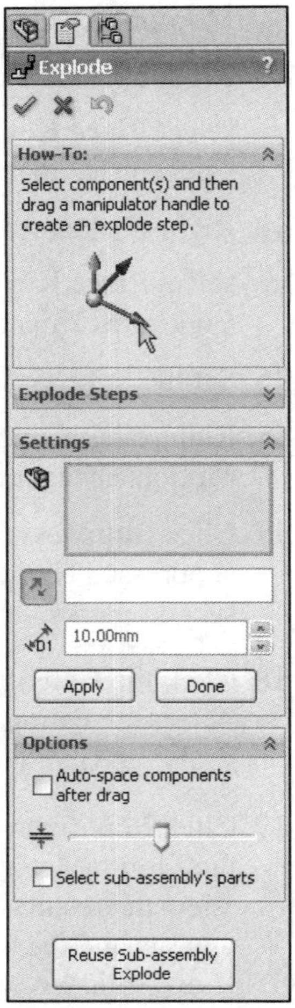


The Exploded View tool provides the ability to create an exploded view of an assembly by selecting and dragging parts in the Graphics window. The Exploded View tool uses the Explode PropertyManager. The Explode PropertyManager provides the following selections:

- ***Explode Steps***. The Explode Steps box displays the selected components exploded in the Graphics window. The Explode Steps box displays the following items:
  - **Explode Step<n>**. The Explode Step displays one or more selected components exploded to a single position.
  - **Chain<*n*>**. The Chain<n> displays a stack of two or more selected components exploded along an axis using the Auto-space components after drag option.
- ***Setting***. The Settings box provides the following selections:
  - **Component(s) of the explode step**. Displays the selected component for the current explode step.
  - **Explode direction**. Displays the selected direction, (X, Y or Z) and component name for the current explode step.
  - **Reverse direction**. Reverses the explode direction if required.
  - **Explode distance**. Displays the selected distance to move the component for the current explode step.
  - **Apply**. Previews the changes to the explode steps.
  - **Done**. Completes the new or changed explode steps.
- ***Option***. The Option box provides the following selections:
  - **Auto-space components after drag**. Spaces a group of components equally along an axis.
  - **Adjust the spacing between chain components**. Adjusts the distance between components placed by the Auto-space components after drag option.
  - **Select sub-assembly's parts**. Enables you to select individual components of a sub-assembly. When cleared, you can select an entire sub-assembly.

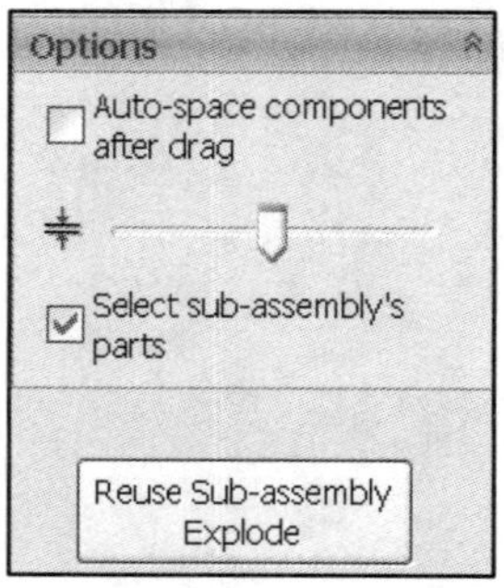

- **Re-use Sub-assembly Explode**. Uses the explode steps that you defined previously in a selected sub-assembly.

***Tutorial: Exploded View 12-1***

Use the Exploded View tool. Insert an Exploded View into an assembly.

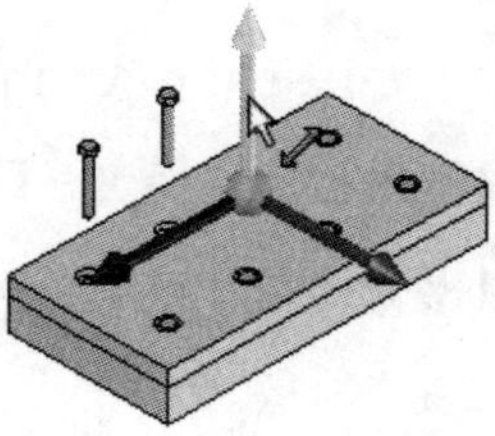

1. Activate **SolidWorks Toolbox** and **SolidWorks Toolbox browser**.
2. Open **ExplodedView 12-1** from the SolidWorks 2010\TopDownAssemblyModeling folder.
3. Set **Lightweight to Resolved** if needed for the model.
4. Click the **Exploded View** tool. The Explode PropertyManager is displayed.
5. Click each of the **8 Hex bolts** in the Graphics window and drag upward using the triad. Explode Step1 - 8 are created in the Explode Steps box.
6. Click the **SF_plate1** in the Graphics window and drag the plate backwards using the triad as illustrated. Explode Step9 is created.
7. Click each of the **8 Hex Flange Nuts** and drag them downward using the triad from the Graphics window as illustrated.
8. Click **OK** from the Explode PropertyManager.
9. Click the **ConfigurationManager** tab.
10. **Expand** the Default configuration.
11. Right-click **ExplView1**.
12. Click **Animate collapse**. View the Animation.
13. Click **Loop** from the Animation Controller. The model will continue to play until you stop it.
14. Click **Play** from the Animation Controller.
15. Click **Stop** from the Animation Controller.

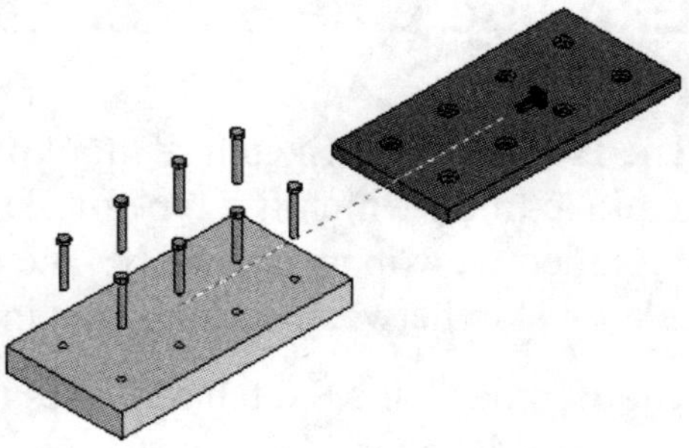

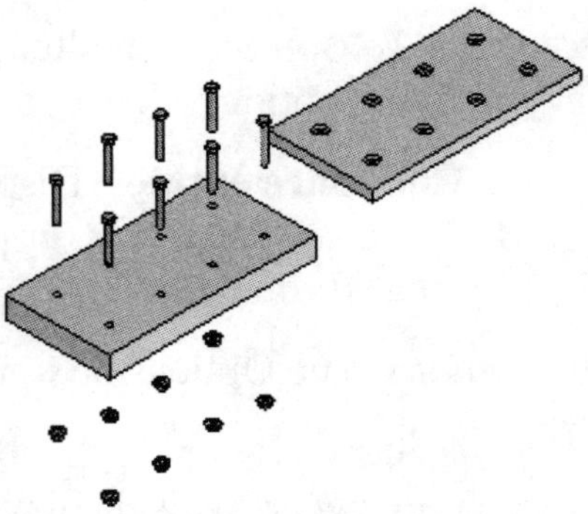

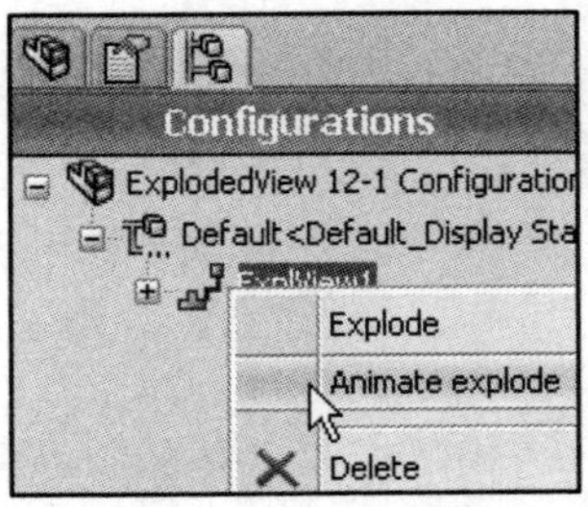

Click End from the Animation Controller. The End option brings the model to the end point in the animation.

16. **Close** the Animation Controller.

17. **Return** to the FeatureManager.

18. **Close** the model.

For collapse and explode animation that resemble manufacturing procedures, create the exploded steps in the order of disassembling a physical assembly.

## Explode Line Sketch tool

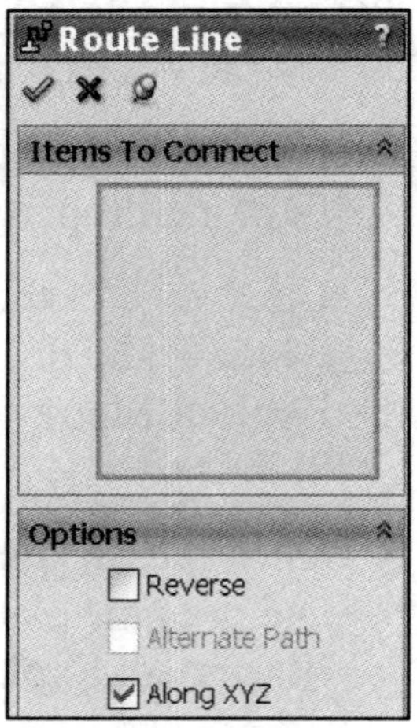


The Explode Line Sketch tool provides the ability to add explode lines, which is a type of 3D sketch that you add to an exploded view in an assembly. The explode lines indicate the relationship between components in the assembly.

The Explode Line Sketch tool uses the Route Line PropertyManager. The Route Line PropertyManager provides the following selections:

- ***Items To Connect***. The Items To Connect box provides the following option:
  - **Reference entities**. Displays the selected circular edges, faces, straight edges, or planar faces to connect with your created route line.
- ***Options***. The Options box provides the following selections:
  - **Reverse**. Reverses the direction of your route line. A preview arrow is displayed in the direction of the route line.
  - **Alternate Path**. Displays an alternate possible path for the route line.
  - **Along XYZ**. Selected by default. Creates a path parallel to the X, Y, and Z axis directions.

### *Tutorial: Explode Line Sketch 12-1*

Use the Explode Line Sketch tool. Insert an Explode Line feature.

1. Open **ExplodeLine Sketch 12-1** from the SolidWorks 2010\TopDownAssemblyModeling folder.
2. Set **Lightweight to Resolved** if needed for the model.

You require an Exploded view to create an Explode Line Sketch.

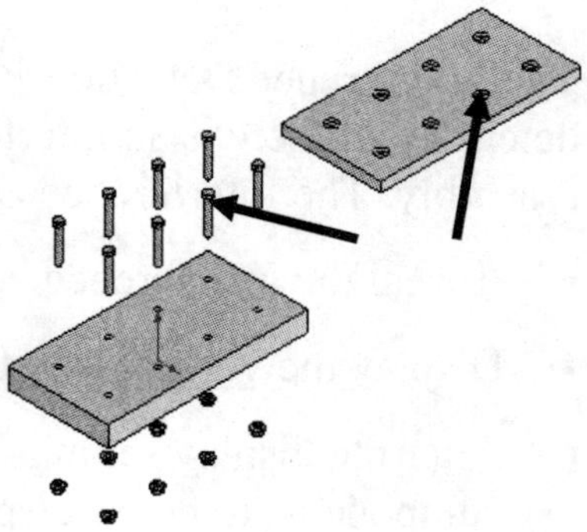

3. Click the **Explode Line Sketch** tool. The Route Line PropertyManager is displayed.
4. Click the cylindrical face of the **third hex bolt** in the front row. The direction arrow points upward.
5. Click the inside face of the **third front hole** of SF_plate1. The direction arrow points downward.
6. Click the inside face of the **third front hole** of SF_plate3. The direction arrow points downward.
7. Click the inside face of the **third hex flange nut** in the front row. The direction arrow points downward.

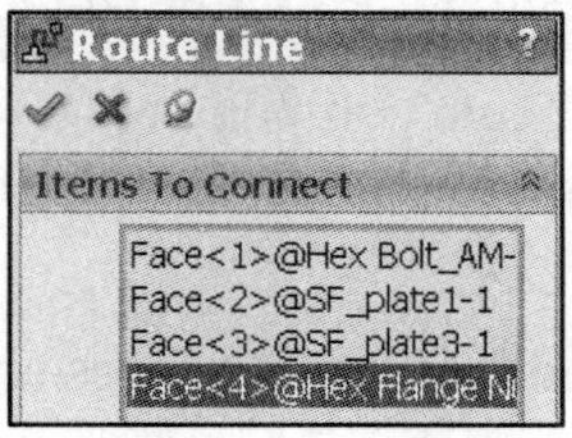


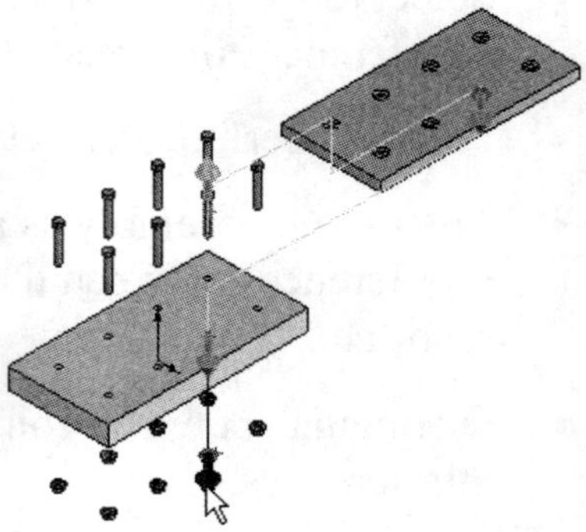

8. Click **OK** from the Route Line PropertyManager.
9. Repeat the above Explode Line Sketch procedure for the **fourth hex bolt** in the front row.
10. Click **OK** from the Route Line PropertyManager.
11. Click **OK** from the Route Line PropertyManager.

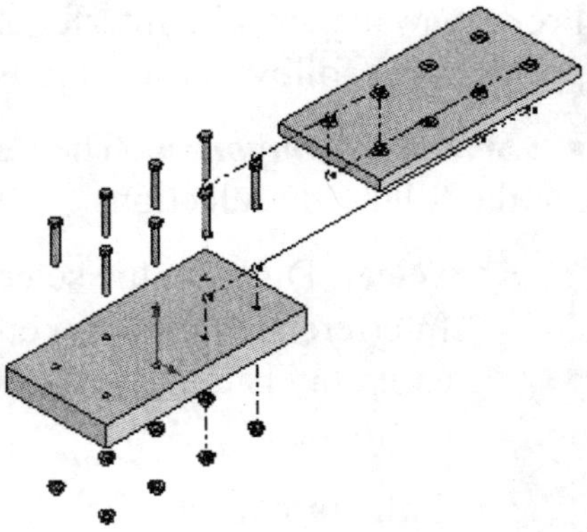

12. Click and drag the two **Explode Line Sketch** segments upward to create spacing between the line.
13. Click **OK** from the Line Properties PropertyManager. View the results.
14. **Close** the model.

The Explode Line Sketch, 3DExplode<n> is located in the ConfigurationManager under ExplView<n>. To edit the Explode Line, right-click **3DExplode<n>**. Click **Edit Sketch**.

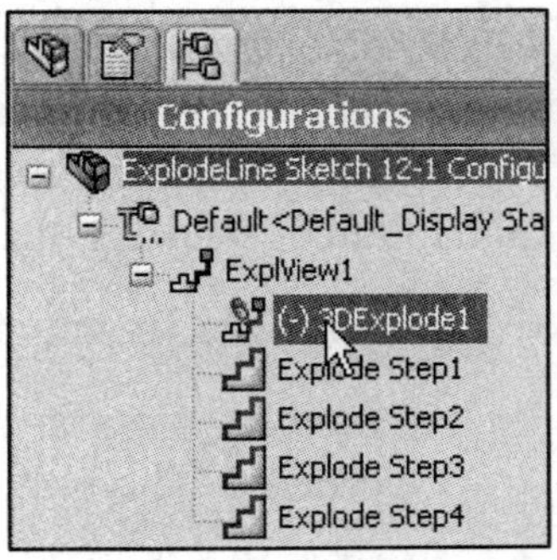

# Interference Detection tool

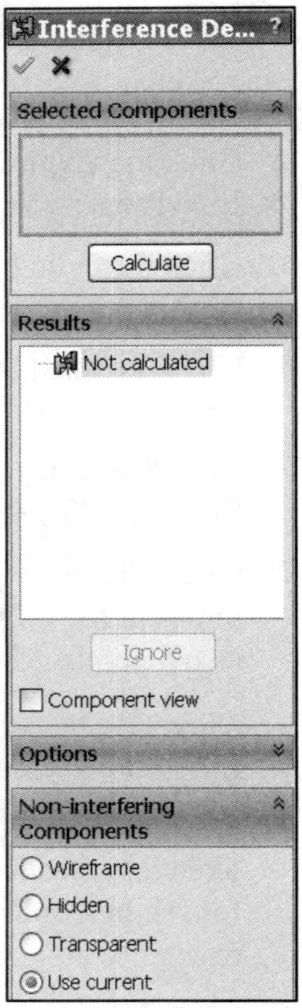


The Interference Detection tool provides the ability to visually determine if there is an interference between components in an assembly. The Interference Detection tool can:

- Reveal the interference between components.
- Display the volume of interference as a shaded volume.
- Alter the display settings of the interfering and non-interfering components to better display the interference.
- Select to ignore interferences that you want to exclude, such as, interferences of threaded fasteners, press fits, etc.
- Include interferences between bodies within a multi-body part.
- Treat a sub-assembly as a single component, so that interferences between the sub-assembly's components are not reported.
- Distinguish between coincidence interferences and standard interferences.

The Interference Detection tool uses the Interference Detection PropertyManager. The Interference Detection PropertyManager provides the following selections:

- ***Selected Component***. The Selected Component box provides the following selections:
  - **Select**. Displays the selected components to perform the Interference Detection on. By default, the top-level assembly is displayed unless you pre-select other component.
  - **Calculate**. Performs the Interference detection process.

When you check an assembly for interference, all of its components are checked by default. If you select a single component, only the interferences that involve that component are reported. If you select two or more components, only the interferences between the selected components are reported.

- ***Results***. The Results box provides the following selections:
  - **Results**. Displays the results of the Interference detection process. The volume of each interference is displayed to the right of each listing.

- **Ignore**. Switches between the ignored and un-ignored mode for the selected interference in the Results box. If an interference is set to the Ignore mode, the interference remains ignored during subsequent interference calculations.
- **Component view**. Displays the interferences by component name instead of interference number.

- *Options*. The Options box provides the following selections:

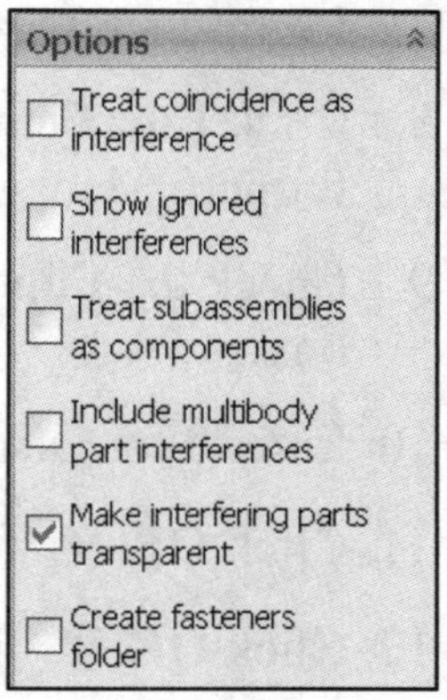


  - **Treat coincidence as interference**. Reports coincident entities as interferences.
  - **Show ignored interferences**. Displays ignored interferences in the Results list, with a gray icon. When this option is cleared, ignored interferences are not listed.
  - **Treat subassemblies as components**. Treats sub-assemblies as single components. Interferences between a sub-assembly's components are not reported.
  - **Include multibody part interferences**. Reports interference between bodies within multi-body parts.
  - **Make interfering parts transparent**. Selected by default. Displays the components of the selected interference in transparent mode.
  - **Create fasteners folder**. Segregates interferences between fasteners into a separate folder under Results.

- *Non-interfering Components*. The Non-interfering Components box provides the ability to display non-interfering components in a selected display mode. Use current is selected by default. The available display modes are: **Wireframe**, **Hidden**, **Transparent**, and **Use current**.

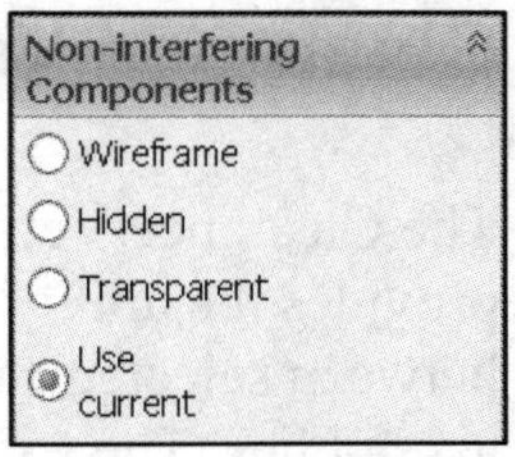


### *Tutorial: Interference Detection 12-1*

Use the Interference Detection tool. Calculate the interference in the assembly.

1. Open **Interference Detection 12-1** from the SolidWorks 2010\TopDownAssemblyModeling folder.
2. Set **Lightweight to Resolved** if needed for the model.
3. Click the **Interference Detection** tool from the Evaluate tab in the CommandManager.

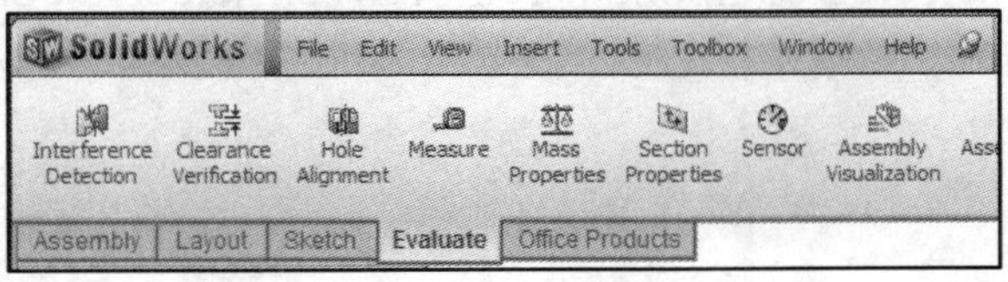

4. Click the **Calculate** button from the Selected Components box. The volume of Interference is displayed in red. The components that interfere are transparent.

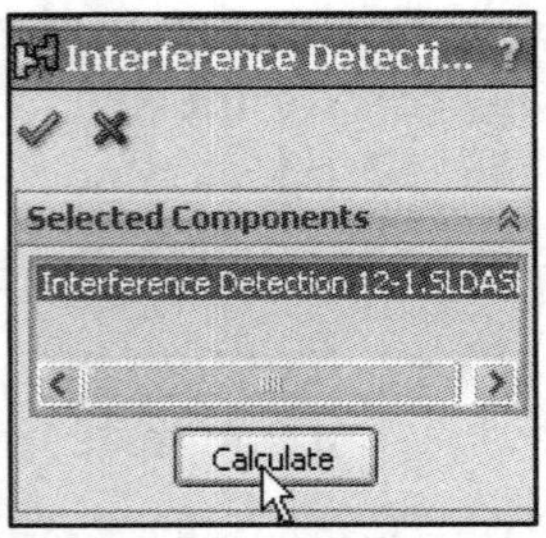


5. Click **OK** from the Interference Detection PropertyManager.
6. **Expand** the Mates folder from the FeatureManager.

7. Right-click **Distance1**.
8. Click **Edit Feature**. The Distance1 Mate PropertyManager is displayed.
9. Check the **Flip direction** box from the Standard Mates box.

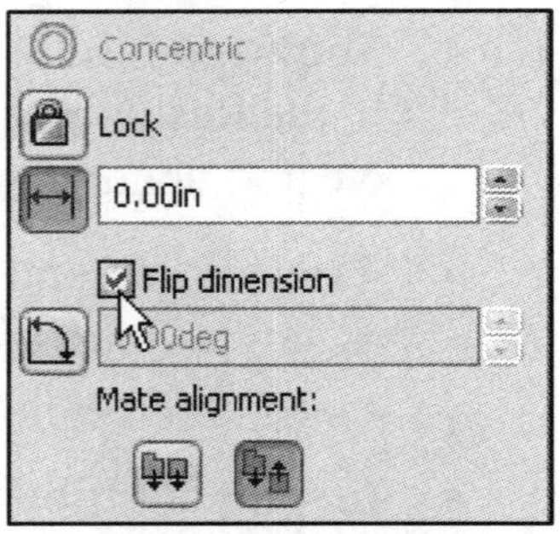


10. Enter **0** for Distance.
11. Click **OK** from the Distance1 PropertyManager.
12. Click **OK** from the Mate PropertyManager.
13. Click the **Interference Detection** tool.
14. Click the **Calculate** button. There are no interferences.
15. Click **OK** from the Interference Detection PropertyManager.
16. **Close** the model.

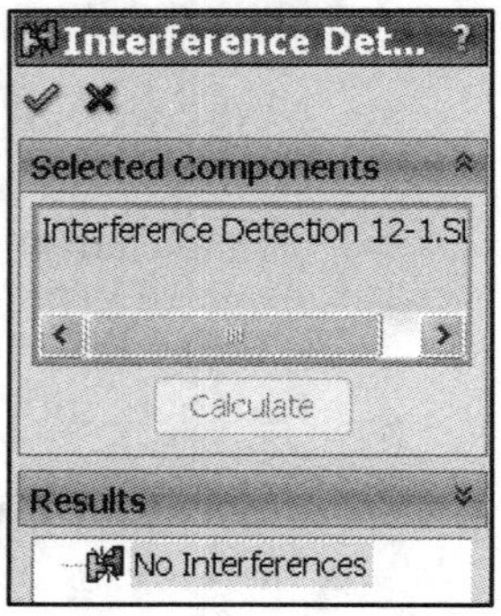


## Clearance Verification

The Clearance Verification tool provides the ability to check the clearance between selected components in assemblies. The software checks the minimum distance between the components and reports clearances that fail to meet the minimum acceptable clearance you specify.

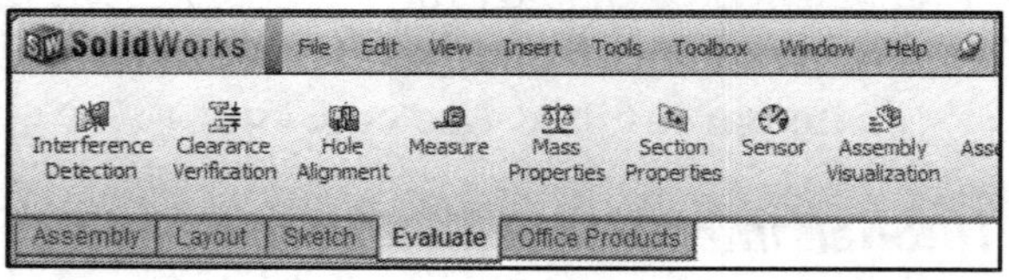


You can select entire components or particular faces of components. You can check between just the selected components, or between selected components and the rest of the assembly.

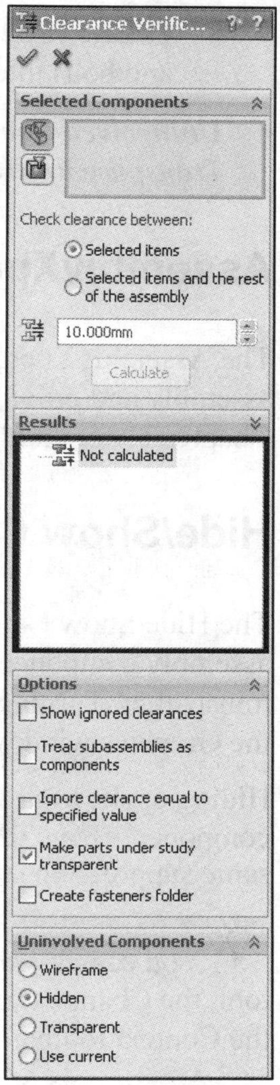


The Clearance Verification tool uses the Clearance Verification PropertyManager. The Clearance Verification PropertyManager provides the following selections:

- ***Selected Component***. The Selected Component box provides the following selections:
  - **Select**. Lists entities selected for the clearance check.
  - **Select Components**. Selected by default. To filter the type of entity you want to select.
  - **Select Faces**. To filter the type of entity you want to select.
  - **Selected items**. Selected by default. Specifies whether to check only between the entities you select, or between the entities you select and the rest of the assembly.
  - **Selected items and the rest of the assembly**. Specifies whether to check only between the entities you select, or between the entities you select and the rest of the assembly.
  - **Minimum Acceptable Clearance**. Clearances less than or equal to this value are reported in Results.
  - **Calculate**. Click to run the clearance check.
- ***Results***. Lists clearances that fail to meet the minimum acceptable clearance. The value of each failed clearance appears in its listing. When you select a clearance under Results, it highlights in the graphics area.
- ***Options***. Provides the following options:
  - **Show ignored clearances**. Select to show ignored clearances in the Results list, with a gray icon. When this option is cleared, ignored clearances are not listed.
  - **Treat subassemblies as components**. Treats sub-assemblies as single components, so clearances between a sub-assembly's components are not checked.
  - **Ignore clearance equal to specified value**. Reports only clearances less than the specified value.
  - **Make parts under study transparent**. Selected by default. Displays in transparent mode the components whose clearances are being verified.

    - **Create fasteners folder**. Segregates clearances between fasteners (such as a nut and bolt) into a separate folder under Results.

- ***Uninvolved Components***. Provides the following options: *Wireframe, Hidden, Transparent, Use current display.*

## AssemblyXpert

The AssemblyXpert tool provides the ability to analyze the performance of an assembly and provides possible actions you can take to improve performance. View Chapter 11 for additional information.

## Hide/Show Components tool from the Display Pane

The Hide/Show Components tool provides the ability to hide or display the selected assembly component. You can hide the component completely from view or make it 75% transparent. Turning off the display of a component temporarily removes it from view in the Graphics window. This provides the ability to work with the underlying components.

Hiding or showing a component only affects the visibility of the component. Hidden components have the same accessibility and behaviors as displayed components in the same suppression state.

You can also right-click on a component in an assembly and apply the Hide / Show tool, the Change transparent tool, and obtain access to the color and texture options from the Context toolbar.

### *Tutorial: Component States 12-1*

Utilize the Hide/Show Components tool. Use Show Display Pane for the Transparency, Color and Hide features.

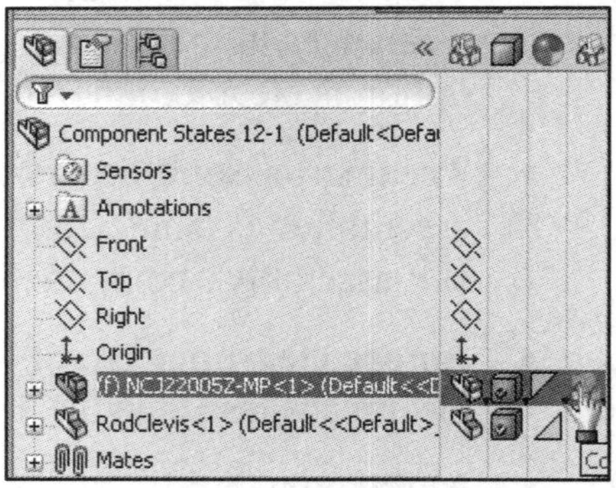


1. Open **Component States 12-1** from the SolidWorks 2010\TopDownAssemblyModeling folder.
2. Set **Lightweight to Resolved** if needed for the model.
3. Click the **Show Display Pane** icon at the top of the Component States 12-1 FeatureManager.
4. Right-click the **Transparency** column to the right of the NCJ22005Z-MP assembly.
5. Click **Change Transparency**. The component is transparent in the model.
6. Right-click inside the **Appearances** column to the right of RodClevis<1>.
7. Click **Appearance**. The Color PropertyManager is displayed.

8. Select **blue** for a Color Swatch. The color set in the assembly overrides the part color.
9. Click **OK** from the Color PropertyManager.
10. **Expand** the NCJ22005Z-MP assembly.
11. Right-click the **Transparency** column next to NCJ2TUBES<1>.
12. Click **Hide**. View the assembly in the Graphics window.
13. **Close** the model.

## Edit Component tool

The Edit Component tool provides the ability to move between editing a part or sub-assembly and the main assembly.

In the Top-Down assembly method, relationships are created while editing a part within an assembly. This method is referred to as In-Context editing. You create or edit your feature In-Context of the assembly, instead of in isolation, as you traditionally create parts.

In-Context editing provides the ability to view your part in its location in the assembly as you create new features in the assembly. Use geometry of the surrounding parts to define the size or shape of the new feature.

Relations that are defined In-Context are listed as External references. External references are created when one document is dependent on another document for its solution. If the referenced document is modified, the dependent document is also modified. In-Context relations and External references are powerful tools in the design phase.

In the FeatureManager, an item with an External reference has a suffix which displays the reference status. They are:

- -> The reference is In-Context. It is solved and up-to-date.
- ->? The reference is out-of-context. The feature is not solved or not up-to-date. To solve and update the feature, open the assembly that contains the update path.
- ->* The reference is locked.
- ->**x** The reference is broken.

Mastering assembly modeling techniques with In-Context relations requires practice and time. Planning and selecting the correct reference and understanding how to incorporate changes are important.

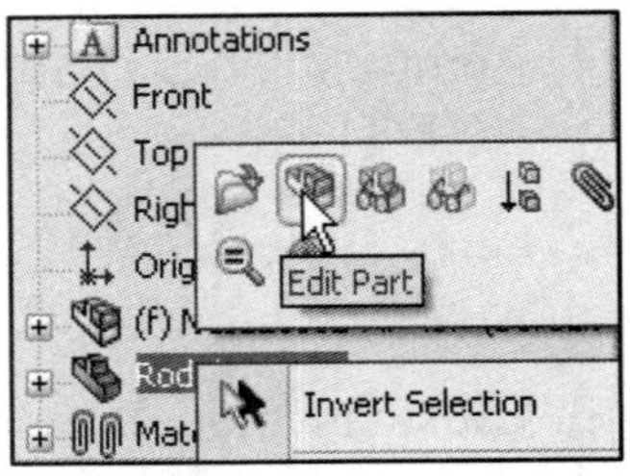


Right-click a component and the click Edit Part tool to obtain the ability to move between editing a part or sub-assembly and the main assembly.

***Tutorial: Edit Component 12-1***

Edit a Component In-Context to an assembly.

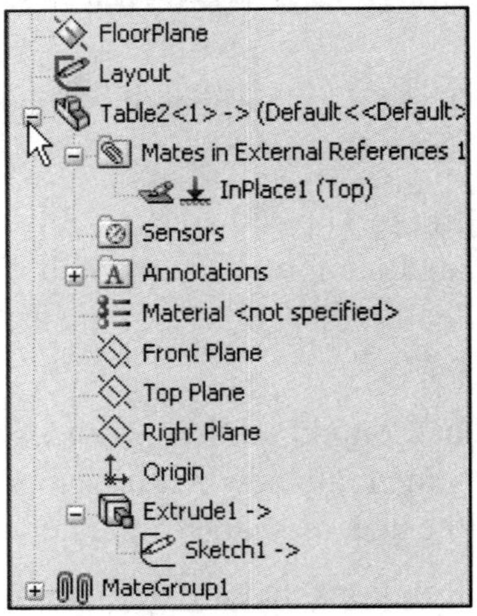


1. Open **External References 12-1** from the SolidWorks 2010\TopDownAssemblyModeling folder.
2. Set **Lightweight to Resolved** if needed for the model.
3. **Expand** Table2<1> -> from the FeatureManager. The -> symbol indicates External references, In-Context. View the InPlace1(Top) mate from the Table2 component. The Table2 component references the Top Plane in the assembly. The InPlace1 mate is also displayed in the MateGroup1 folder.
4. **Expand** Extrude1 -> from the FeatureManager. Extrude1 -> and Sketch1 -> in the FeatureManager contains External references. The references were created from four converted lines in an assembly Layout sketch.

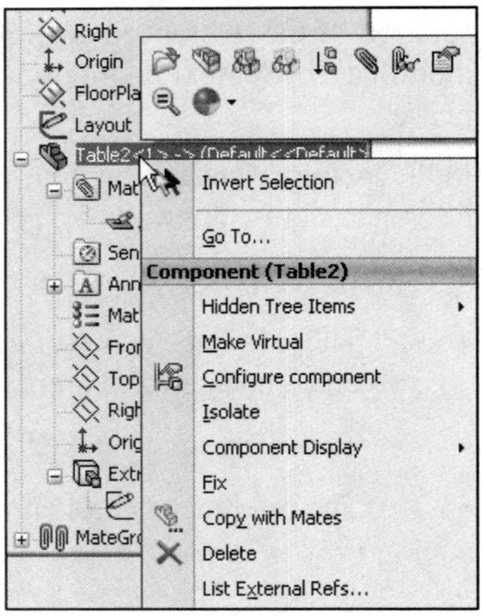


5. Right-click **Table2<1> ->** from the FeatureManager.
6. Click **List External Refs**. The External References For: Table2 dialog box lists the sketched lines of the Layout sketch. View your options. Click the HELP button to learn additional information.
7. Click **OK** from the External References For: Table2 dialog box.
8. Click the **InPlace1(Top)** mate from the FeatureManager.
9. Right-click **Delete**.
10. Click **Yes** to delete.
11. Click **Yes** to delete references. The Table2 component is free to move in the assembly.

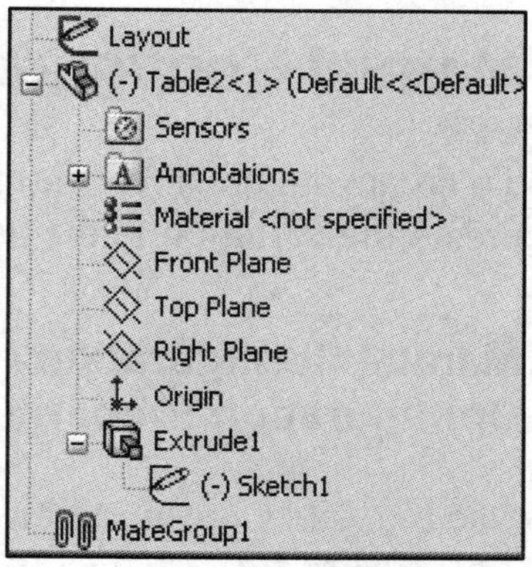


12. **Rebuild** the model.
13. **Expand** Extrude1 from the FeatureManager. Sketch1 is under defined and requires dimensions and relations. The External References are removed.
14. **Close** the model.

To list External references on a part or feature: Right-click the **component** or the **feature** with the External reference, ➤ **List External Refs**. The referenced components, features, and entities are listed.

## Assembly ConfigurationManager

SolidWorks provides the ability to create multiple variations of a part or assembly model within a single document. The ConfigurationManager provides the tools to develop and manage families of models with various dimensions, components, or other key design parameters.

The ConfigurationManager is located on the left side of the SolidWorks window. You can split the ConfigurationManager to either display two ConfigurationManager instances, or combine the ConfigurationManager with the FeatureManager, PropertyManager, or a third party application that uses the panel. Use Configurations for part, assembly, and drawing documents.

In a part document, the part ConfigurationManager provides the ability to create a family of parts with unique dimensions, features, and properties, including custom properties.

In an assembly document, the assembly ConfigurationManager provides the ability to create simplified versions of the design by suppressing components and families of assemblies with unique configurations of the components, with various parameters for assembly features, dimensions, or custom properties.

In a drawing document, the drawing ConfigurationManager provides the ability to display views of the various configurations that were created in the part and assembly documents.

The icons in the ConfigurationManager indicate how the configuration was created: *Manual*, *With a design table*, *Manually, with an explode state or a derived configuration*, *and with a design table, and an explode state or a derived configuration*.

# Manual Configurations

To create a manual configuration, first specify the properties. Then modify the model to create the variation in the new configuration. You can add or edit manual configurations.

## Manual Configuration / Add Configuration Property Manager

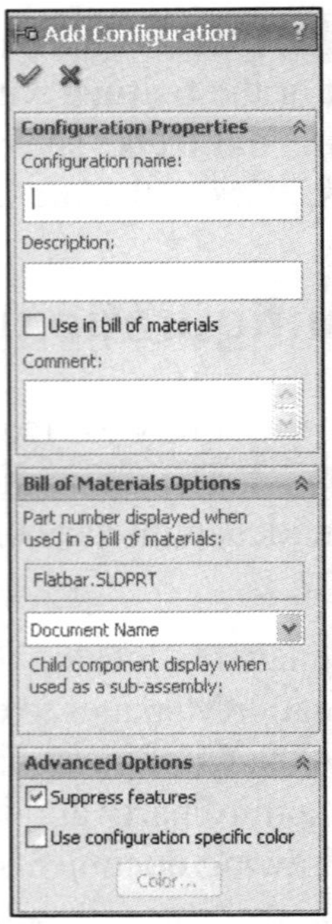


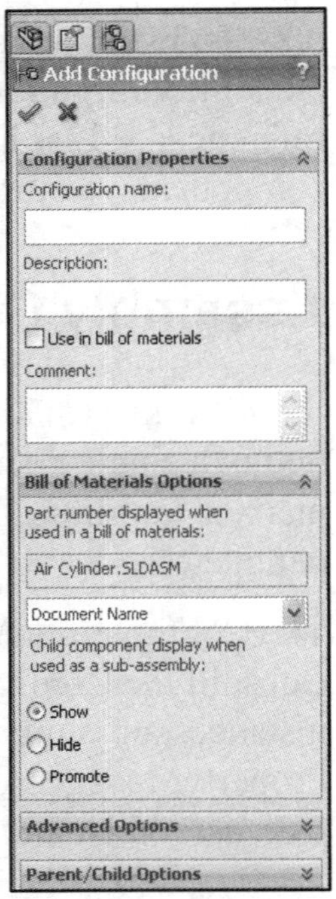


Use the Add Configuration PropertyManager to add a new configuration. To display the Add Configuration PropertyManager, click the **ConfigurationManager** tab, then right-click **Add Configuration**. The Add Configuration PropertyManager is document dependent and provides the following selections:

- ***Configuration Properties***. The Configuration Properties box provides the following selections:
    - **Configuration name**. Displays the entered name for the configuration. The name can not include the following: forward slash (/) or "at" sign (@). A warning message is displayed when you close the dialog box if the name field contains either of these characters, or if the field is blank.
    - **Description**. (Optional). Displays the entered description of the configuration.
    - **Use in bill of materials**. Specify how the assembly or part is listed in a Bill of Materials.
    - **Comment**. (Optional). Displays the entered additional descriptive information on the configuration.
    - **Custom Properties** Only available only when editing properties of an existing configuration.
- ***Bill of Materials Options***. Specifies how the part or assembly is listed in the Bill of Materials. The box provides the following selections:
    - **Document Name**. Displays the part number. The Part number is the same as the document name.

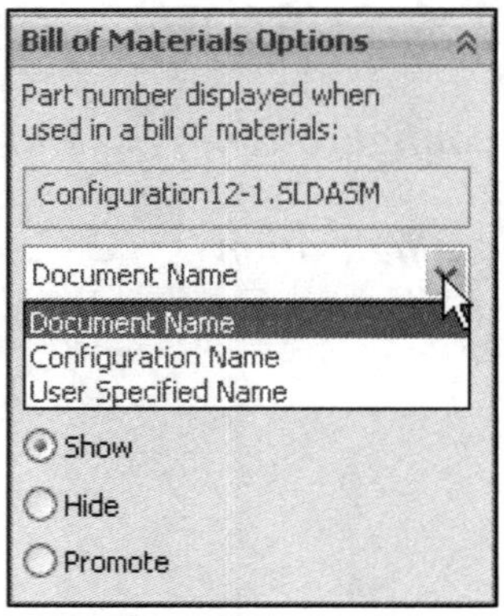

- **Configuration Name**. Displays the part number. The Part number is the same as the configuration name.
- **User Specified Name**. The part number is a name that you type.
- **Show**. Selected by default. Show child components in BOM when used as sub-assembly (assemblies only).
- **Hide**. When selected, the sub-assembly is always shown as a single item in the Bill of Materials (assemblies only).
- **Promote**.

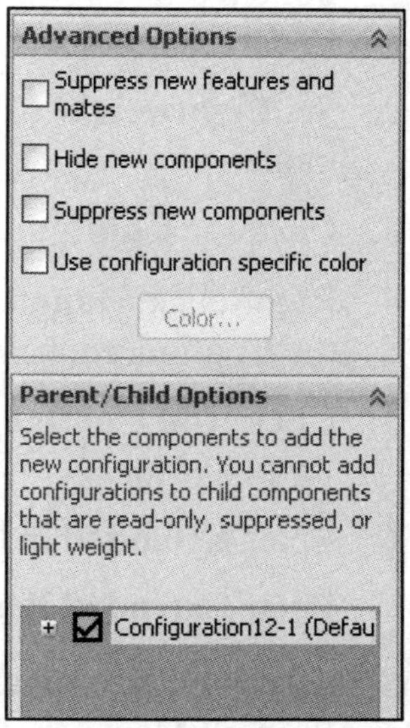


- *Advanced Options*. The following selections control what happens when you add new items to another configuration, and then activate this configuration again. The selection are:
  - **Suppress new features and mates**. Only for assemblies. When selected, new mates and features added to other configurations are suppressed in this configuration. Otherwise, new mates and features are contained, not suppressed in this configuration.
  - **Hide new components**. Only for assemblies. When selected, new components added to other configurations are hidden in this configuration. Otherwise, new components are displayed in this configuration.
  - **Suppress new components**. Only for assemblies. When selected, new components added to other configurations are suppressed in this configuration. Otherwise, new components are resolved, not suppressed in this configuration.
  - **Suppress features**. Only for parts. When selected, new features added to other configurations are suppressed in this configuration. Otherwise, new features are contained, not suppressed in this configuration.

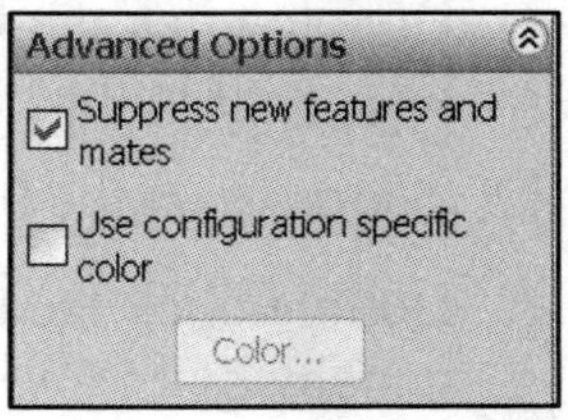


  - **Use configuration specific color**. Specifies a color for the configuration.
  - **Color**. Choose a color from the color palette. If the color for wireframe and HLR modes is the same as the color for shaded mode, the configuration-specific color applies to all three modes. If the color is not the same for the three modes, the configuration specific color is applied only to the shaded mode.

- ***Parent/Child Options***. Only available for assemblies and when adding a new configuration to the assembly or one of its components. Select the components to which you want to add the new configuration.

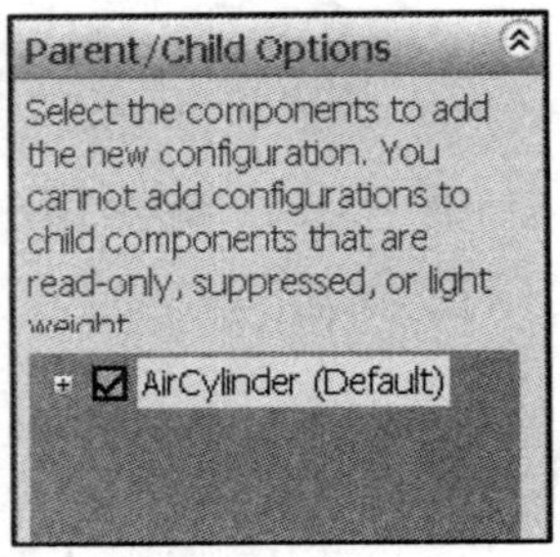


### *Tutorial: Manual Configuration 12-1*

Create a manual assembly configuration with the Add Configuration PropertyManager.

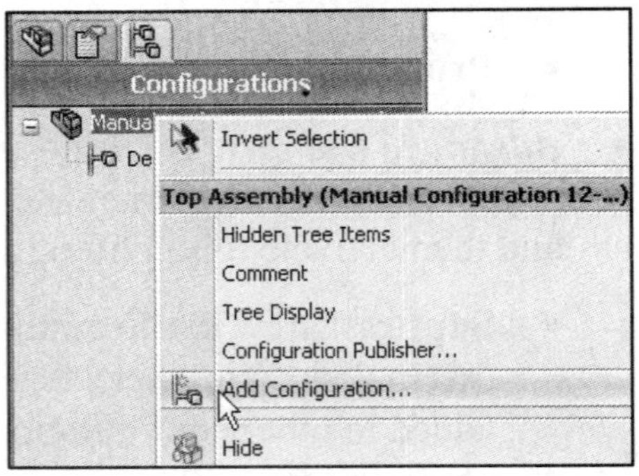


1. Open **Manual Configuration 12-1** from the SolidWorks 2010\TopDownAssemblyModeling folder.
2. Set **Lightweight to Resolved** if needed for the model.
3. Click the **ConfigurationManager** tab.
4. Right-click **Manual Configuration 12-1** from the ConfigurationManager.
5. Click **Add Configuration**. The Add Configuration PropertyManager is displayed.
6. Enter **Extended** in the Configuration name box.
7. Enter **Extended Position 10mm** for Description.
8. Click **OK** ✔ from the Add Configuration PropertyManager. The Extended Configuration is currently selected.
9. **Return** to the FeatureManager.
10. **Expand** the Mates folder in the FeatureManager.
11. Double-click the **Distance1** Mate. The 0 dimension is displayed in the Graphics window.
12. **Zoom-in** on the 0 dimension in the Graphics window.
13. Double-click the **0** dimension from the Graphics window.

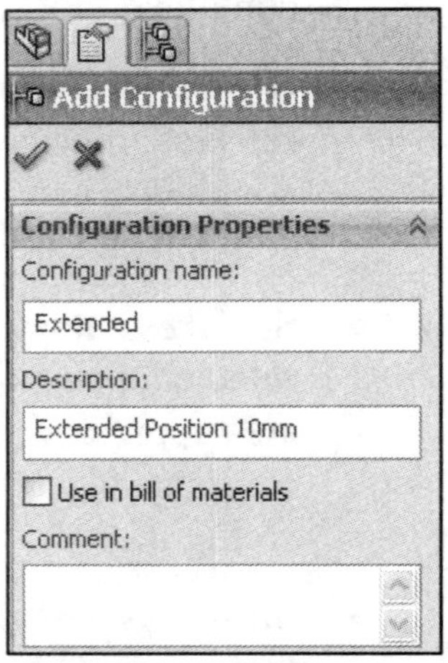


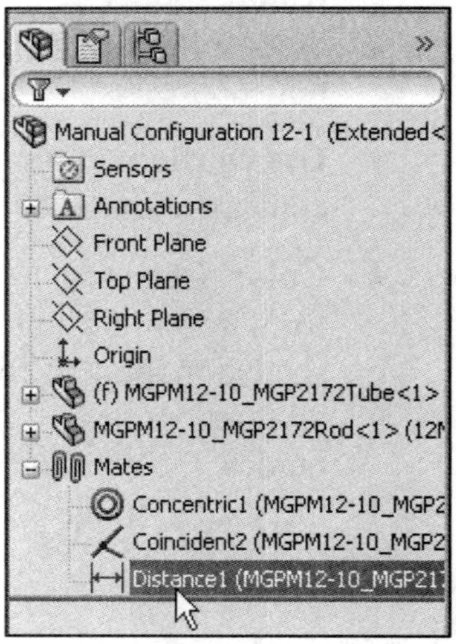


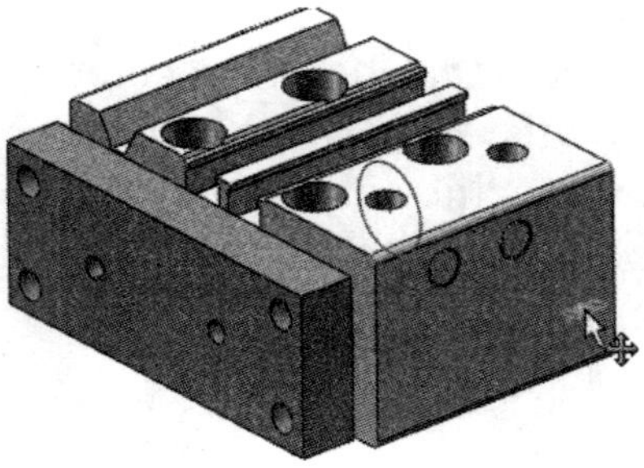

14. Enter **10mm**.
15. Select **This Configuration** as illustrated in the Modify dialog box.
16. **Rebuild** the model from the Modify dialog box. The piston is extended 10mm in the Graphics window.
17. Click the **green check mark** in the Modify dialog box.
18. Click **OK** ✔ from the Dimension PropertyManager.
19. **Return** to the ConfigurationManager.
20. Double-click the **Default** Configuration in the ConfigurationManager. View the results in the Graphics window.
21. **Return** to the FeatureManager.
22. **Close** the model.

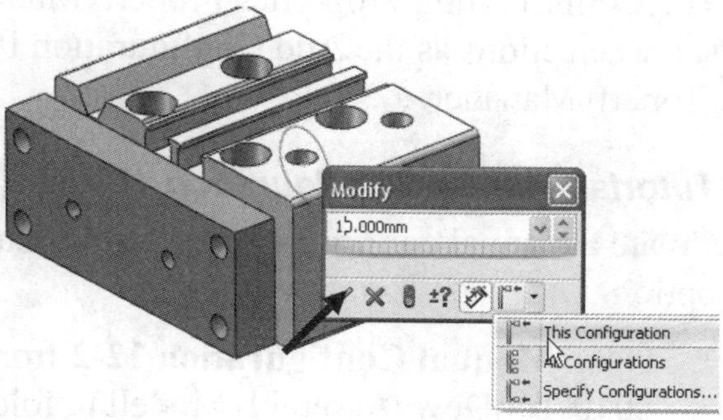


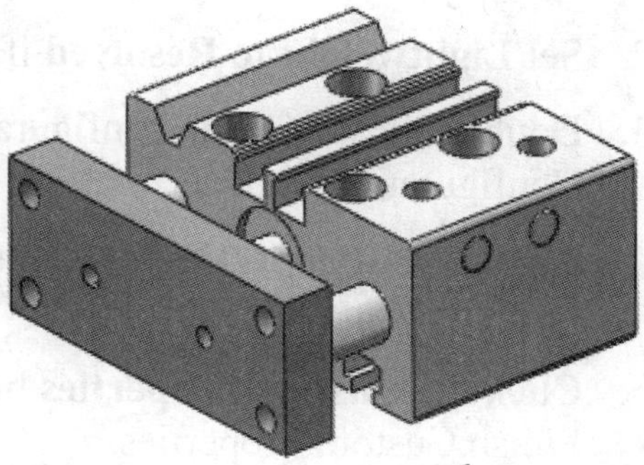

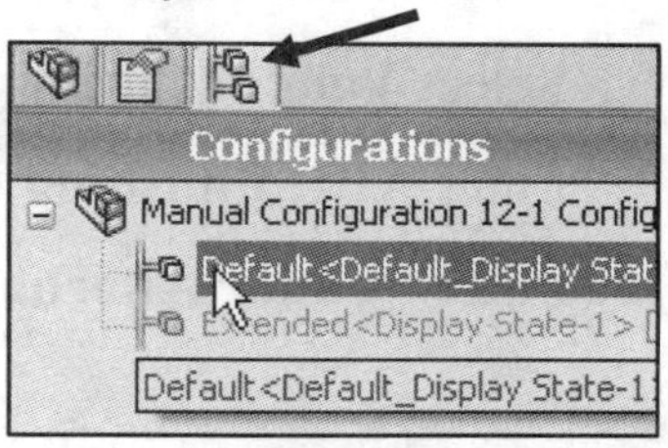


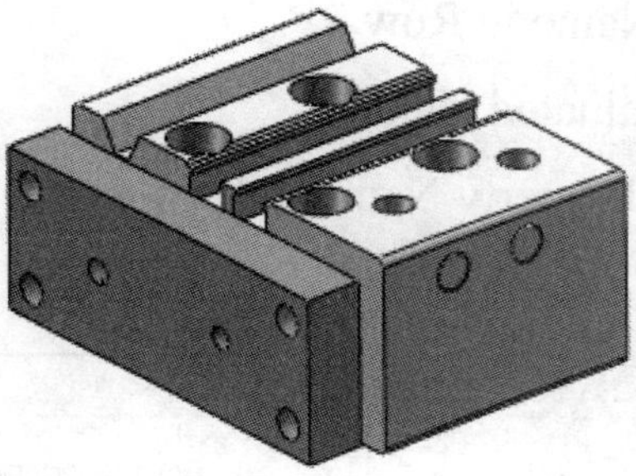

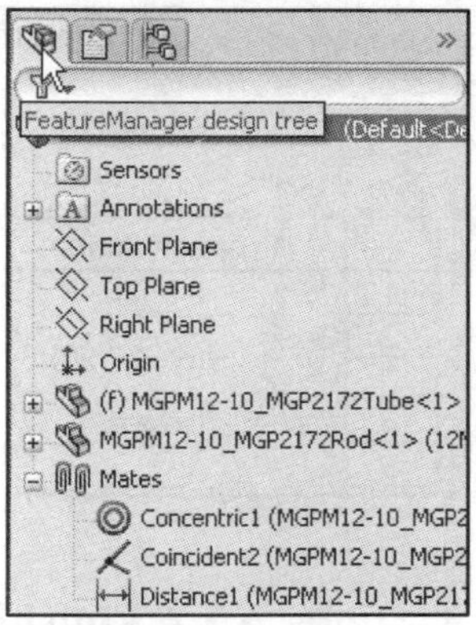


## Manual Configuration / Edit Configuration

Use the Configuration Properties PropertyManager to edit an existing configuration. To display the Configuration Properties PropertyManager, click the **ConfigurationManager** tab ➤ right-click **Properties** on a configuration.

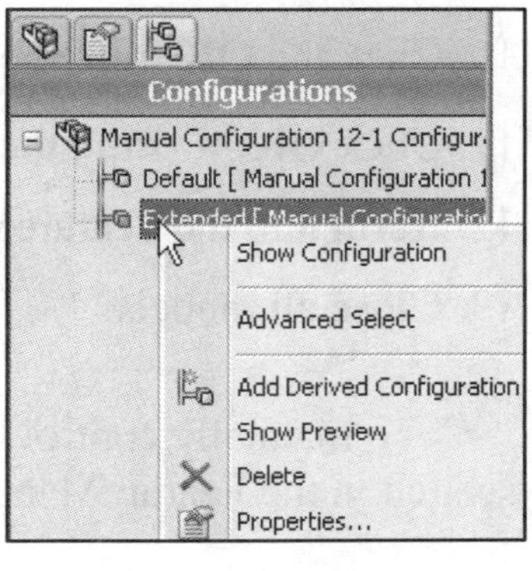

The Configuration Properties PropertyManager provides the same selections as the Add Configuration Properties PropertyManager.

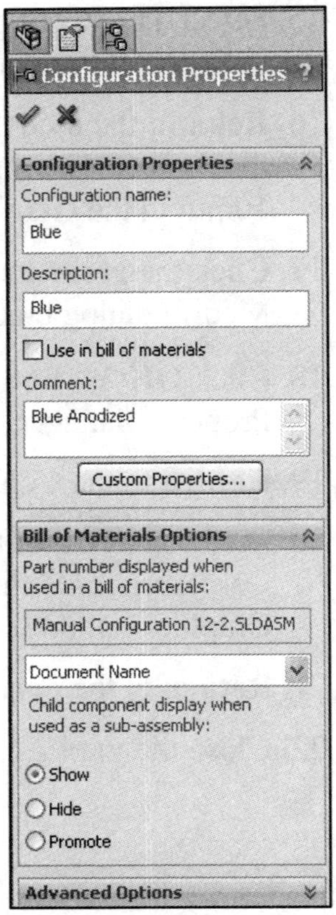


### *Tutorial: Manual Configuration 12-2*

Create a manual configuration using the Custom Properties option.

1. Open **Manual Configuration 12-2** from the SolidWorks 2010\TopDownAssemblyModeling folder.
2. Set **Lightweight to Resolved** if needed for the model.
3. Double-click the **Blue** configuration from the ConfigurationManager.
4. Right-click **Properties**. The Configuration Properties PropertyManager is displayed.
5. Click the **Custom Properties** button. Review the Cost and Finish Custom Properties.
6. Select **Vendor** for Property Name in Row 3.
7. Enter **ABC Finishing** for Evaluated Value.
8. Enter **Vendor Alternate** for Property Name in Row 4.

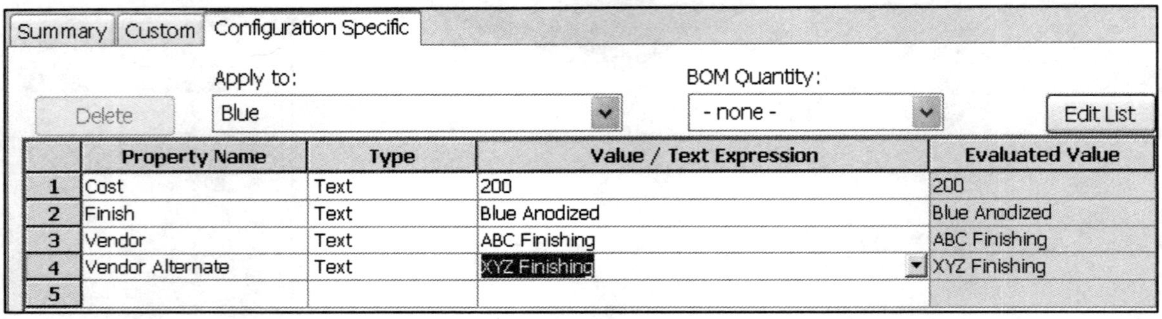


9. Enter **XYZ Finishing** for Evaluated Value.
10. Click the **OK** from the Summary Information dialog box.
11. Click **OK** ✔ from the Configuration Properties PropertyManager.
12. **Return** to the FeatureManager. The Blue configuration is active.
13. **Close** all models.

To manually control individual color states for parts in an assembly, select the color swatch in the FeatureManager. Select the configuration.

## Automatic Configuration: Design Tables

To create a design table, define the names of the configurations, specify the parameters to control, and assign the value for each parameter.

There are several ways to create a design table:

- Insert a new, empty design table in the model. Enter the design table information directly in the worksheet. When you finish entering the design table information, the new configurations are automatically created in the model.
- Have SolidWorks automatically create the design table. SolidWorks loads all configured parameters and their associated values from a part or assembly.
- Create a design table worksheet as a separate operation in Microsoft Excel. Save the worksheet. Insert the worksheet in the model document to create the configurations.
- Insert a partially completed worksheet. Edit the partially completed worksheet later to add additional configurations, to control additional parameters, or to update values.

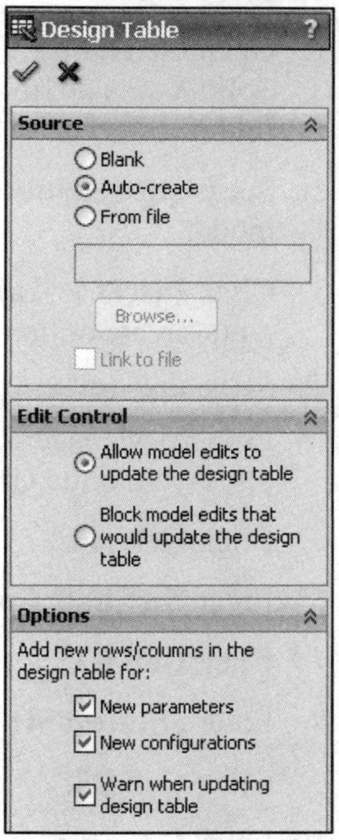


The Design Table PropertyManager provides the ability to create an excel file which automatically creates a design table. To Display the Design Table PropertyManager click **Insert ➢ Design Table**. The Design Table PropertyManager provides the following selections:

- ***Source***. The Source box provides the following selections:
  - **Blank**. Inserts a blank design table where you fill in the parameters.
  - **Auto-create**. Selected by default. Automatically creates a new design table, and loads all configured parameters and their associated values from a part or assembly.
  - **From file**. References a Microsoft Excel table.
  - **Browse**. Browse to a file location to select a Microsoft Excel table.
  - **Link to file**. Links the Excel table to the model. When a design table is linked, any changes you make to the table outside of SolidWorks are reflected in the table within the SolidWorks model.

- ***Edit Control***. The Edit Control box provides the following selections:
  - **Allow model edits to update the design table**. If you modify the model, the changes are updated in the design table.
  - **Block model edits that would update the design table**. You are not allowed to modify the model, if the change updates the design table.
- ***Options***. The Options box provides the following selections:
  - **New parameters**. Selected by default. Adds a new column to the design table if you add a new parameter to the model.
  - **New configurations**. Selected by default. Adds a new row to the design table if you add a new configuration to the model.
  - **Warn when updating design table**. Selected by default. Warns you that the design table will change based on the parameters you updated in the model.

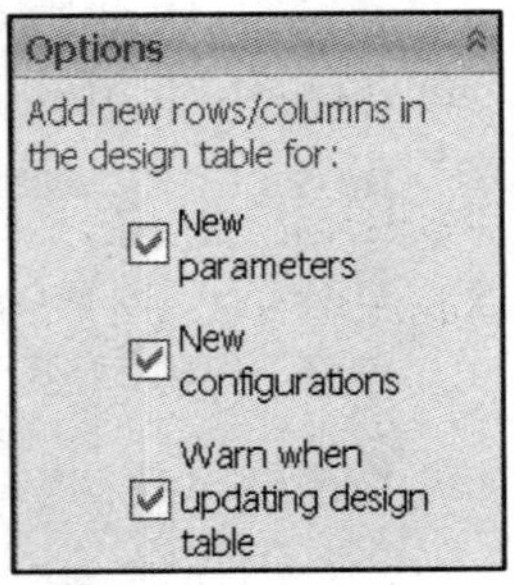


### *Tutorial: Design Table 12-1*

Insert a design table.

1. Open the **Design Table 12-1** assembly from the SolidWorks 2010\TopDownAssemblyModeling folder.
2. Set **Lightweight to Resolved** if needed for the model.
3. Click **Insert ➢ Tables ➢ Design Table**. The Auto-create option is selected.
4. Click **OK** ✔ from the Design Table PropertyManager. A blank design table is displayed in the Graphics window.
5. Click **Cell A4**.
6. Enter **No Shaft Collar**.
7. Click **Cell B2**.
8. Enter **$State@SHAFT-COLLAR<2>**.
9. Click **Cell B3**.
10. Enter **R** for Resolved.
11. Click **Cell B4**. Enter **S** for Suppressed.
12. Click a **position** outside the Design Table.
13. Click **OK** to display the No Shaft Collar configuration.

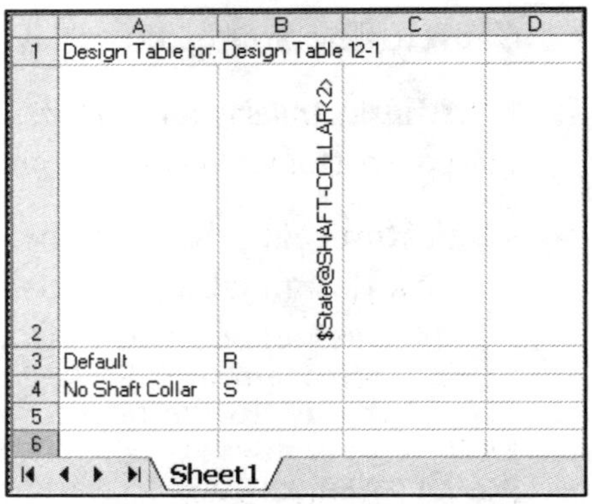


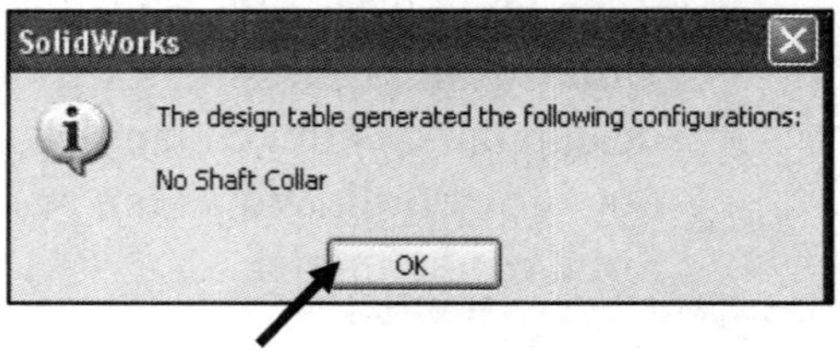

14. Double-click the **No Shaft Collar** configuration from the ConfigurationManager. View the model.

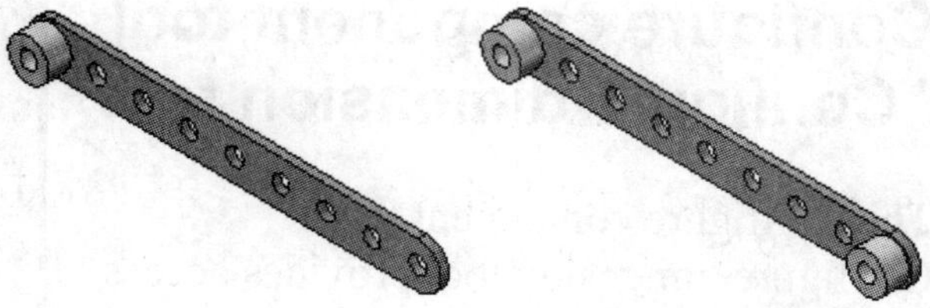

15. Double-click **Default** from the ConfigurationManager. View the model. Display an **Isometric** view.
16. **Close** all models.

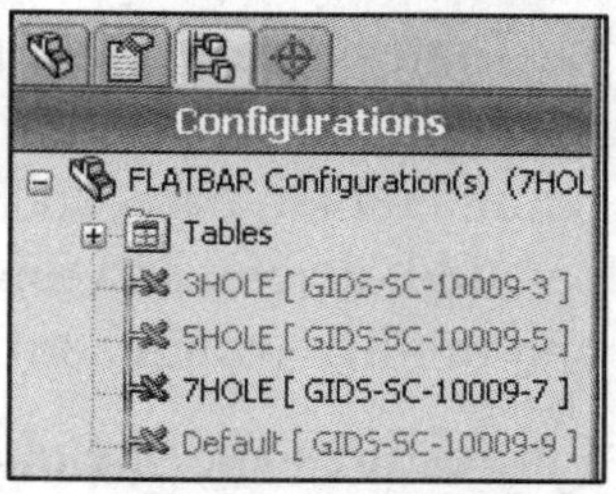


***Tutorial: Design Table 12-2***

Modify a design table. Apply the Custom properties option.

1. Open the **FLATBAR** part from the SolidWorks 2010\TopDownAssemblyModeling folder.
2. Set **Lightweight to Resolved** if needed for the model.
3. Double-click the **3HOLE**, **5HOLE** and **7HOLE** configuration from the ConfigurationManager. View the part configurations in the Graphics window. The three configurations were created with a design table.

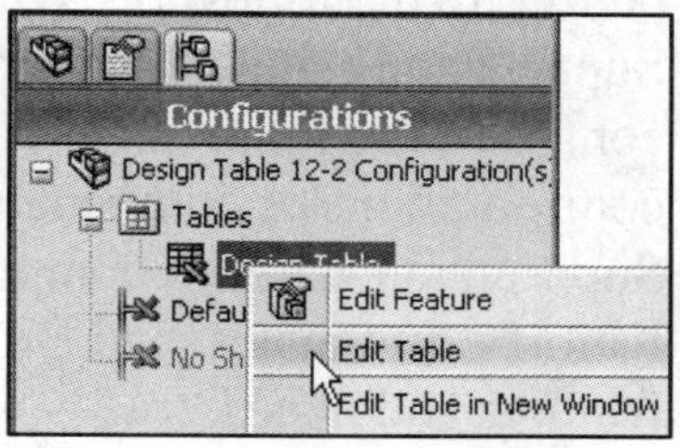


4. Open **Design Table 12-2** from the SolidWorks 2010\ TopDownAssemblyModeling folder.
5. Right-click **Design Table** from the ConfigurationManager.
6. Click **Edit Table**.
7. Click **Cancel** to the message. The design table is displayed in the Graphics window.

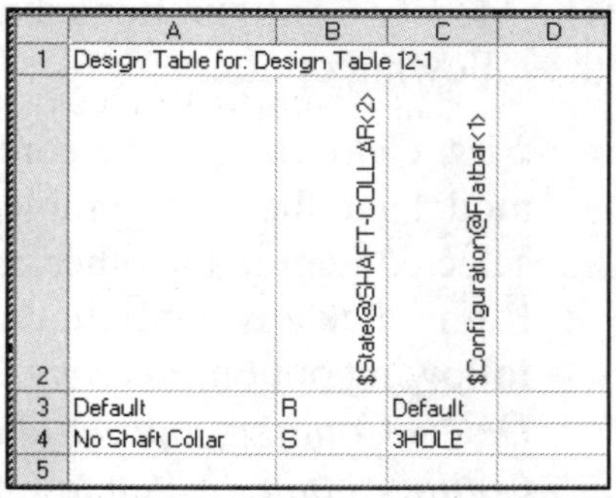

| | A | B | C | D |
|---|---|---|---|---|
| 1 | Design Table for: Design Table 12-1 | | | |
| 2 | | $State@SHAFT-COLLAR<2> | $Configuration@Flatbar<1> | |
| 3 | Default | R | Default | |
| 4 | No Shaft Collar | S | 3HOLE | |
| 5 | | | | |

8. Click **Cell C4**.
9. Enter **3HOLE**.
10. Click a **position** outside the Design Table.
11. Double-click the **No Shaft Collar** configuration from the ConfigurationManager. The 3HOLE configuration is displayed in the Graphics window.

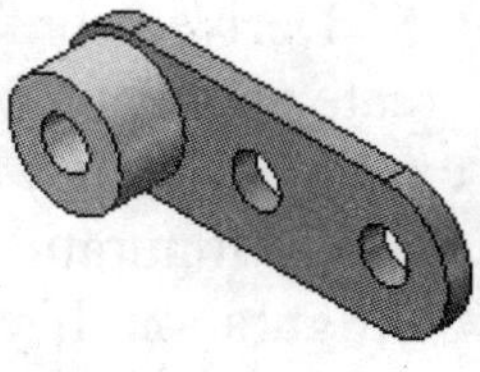

12. Double-click the **Default** configuration from the ConfigurationManager. The default configuration is displayed in the Graphics window.
13. Display an **Isometric** view.
14. **Return** to the FeatureManager.
15. **Close** all models.

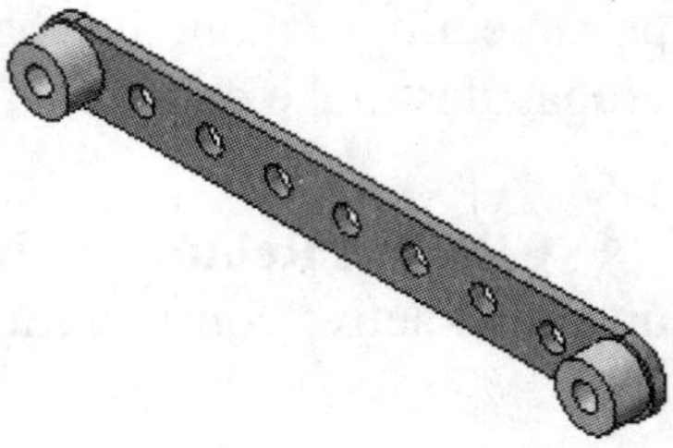

## Configure component tool / Configure dimension tool

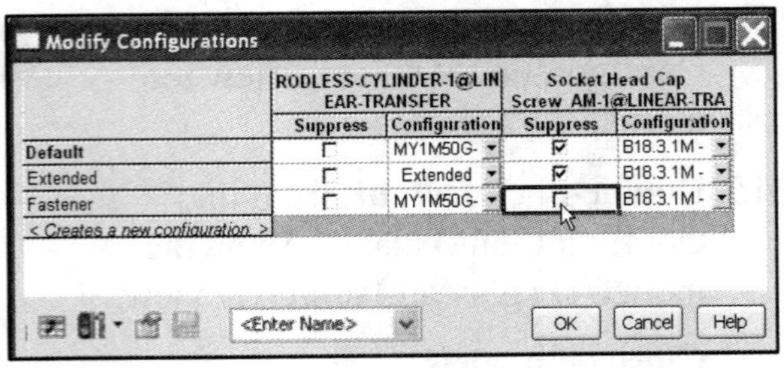


The Configure component tool / Configure dimension tool provides access to the Modify Configurations dialog box. The Modify Configurations dialog box facilitates creating and modifying configurations for commonly configured parameters in parts and assemblies. You can add, delete, and rename configurations and modify which configuration is active.

For features and sketches in parts, you can configure the following: Dimensions, and Suppression states. In assemblies, you can configure the following: Which configurations of components to use, Suppression states of components, Assembly features, and mates, and Dimensions of assembly features and mates.

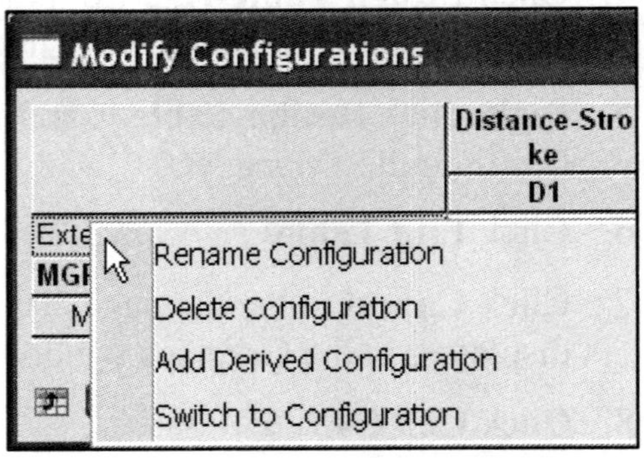


The Modify Configurations dialog box provides the following options:

- ***First Column***. List the configurations of the model and the configurable parameters of the selected item in the other columns. Note: Right-click any configuration and select the following option: *Rename Configuration, Delete Configuration, Add Derived Configuration, Switch to Configuration.*

Derived configurations provide the ability to create a Parent-Child relationship within a configuration. By default, all parameters in the child configuration are linked to the parent configuration. If you change a parameter in the parent configuration, the change automatically propagates to the child.

Click the **Rebuild active configuration** icon to update to active configuration.

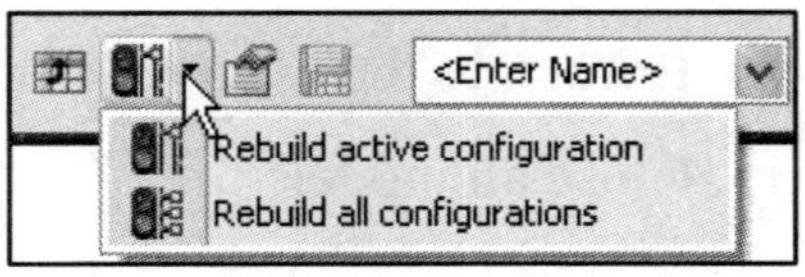

- ***Parameter Columns***. Provides the ability to select one of the following: *Type to change the numeric values, Select from a list of component configurations or to Change the suppression state of features, sketches, components and mates.*

***Tutorial: Configure component / Dimension tool 12-1***

Add a new configuration. Utilize the Configure dimension tool.

1. Open the **GUIDE-CYLINDER 12-1** assembly from the SolidWorks 2010\TopDownAssemblyModeling folder.
2. Set **Lightweight to Resolved** if needed for the model.
3. Click the **ConfigurationManager** icon. View the configurations.

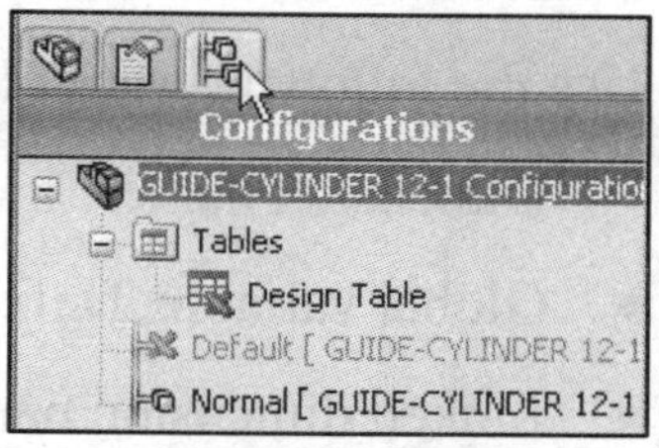


Create a new configuration.

4. **Return** to the FeatureManager.
5. Double-click the **Distance-Stroke** mate from the MateGroup1 folder. View the illustrated dimension in the Graphics window.

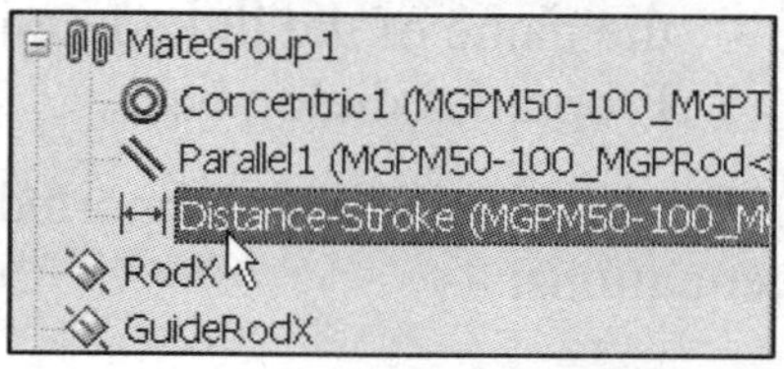


6. Right-click NEAR the **0** dimension text.
7. Click **Configure dimension** from the Context toolbar. The Modify Configurations dialog box is displayed.

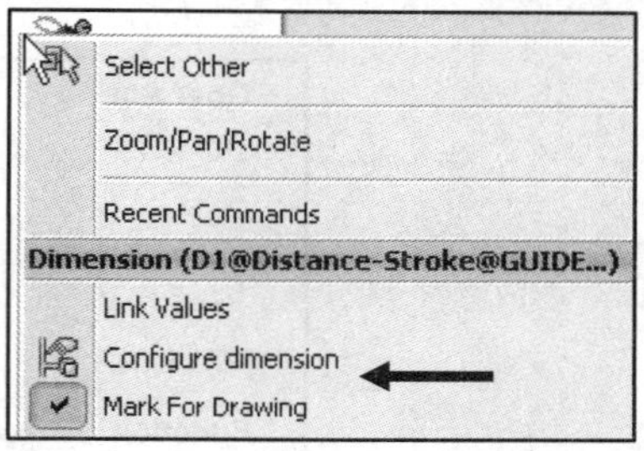


8. Click inside the **Creates a new configuration** box.
9. Enter **Extended**.
10. Enter **100**mm as illustrated.
11. Click **OK** from the Modify Configuration dialog box. View the results in the Graphics window.

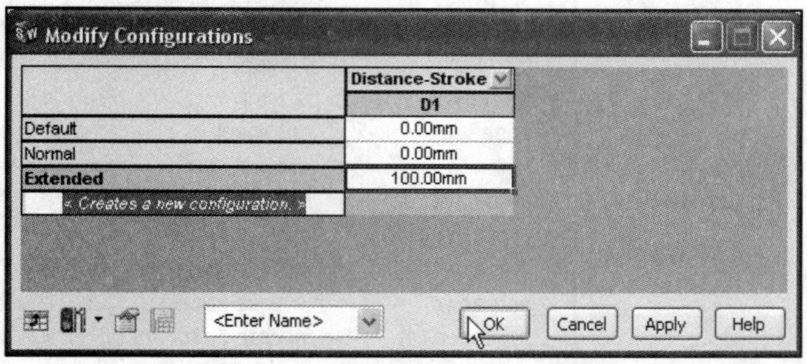


12. Click the **ConfigurationManager** tab. View the new configuration.
13. Double-click the **Extended** configuration.
14. **Return** to the Normal configuration.
15. **Return** to the FeatureManager.
16. **Close** the model.

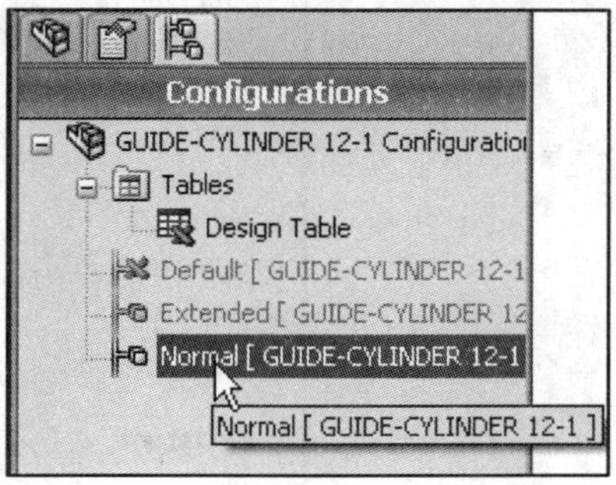

# Equations

Use equations Σ to create mathematical relations between the dimensions of your model. Use dimension names as variables. Set equations in an assembly between multiple parts, a part and a sub-assembly, with mating dimensions, etc.

Use the following variables to create an equation:

- Dimension name.
- Global variable. Define global variables in the Add Equation dialog box.
- Linked dimension names. Specify a variable name. The Specified variable becomes the name of the linked dimension and is displayed in the Name box of the Dimension Properties dialog box.

Use the SolidWorks supported operations, constants and functions listed below in your equations:

| **Operator** | **Name** | **Notes** |
|---|---|---|
| + | plus sign | addition |
| - | minus sign | subtraction |
| * | asterisk | multiplication |
| / | forward slash | division |
| ^ | caret | exponentiation |
| | | |
| **Function** | | |
| sin (*a*) | sine | *a* is the angle; returns the sine ratio |
| cos (*a*) | cosine | *a* is the angle; returns the cosine ratio |
| tan (*a*) | tangent | *a* is the angle; returns the tangent ratio |
| sec (*a*) | secant | *a* is the angle; returns the secant ratio |
| cosec (*a*) | cosecant | *a* is the angle; returns the cosecant ratio |
| cotan (*a*) | cotangent | *a* is the angle; returns the cotangent ratio |
| arcsin (*a*) | inverse sine | *a* is the sine ratio; returns the angle |
| arccos (*a*) | inverse cosine | *a* is the cosine ratio; returns the angle |
| atn (*a*) | inverse tangent | *a* is the tangent ratio; returns the angle |
| arcsec (*a*) | inverse secant | *a* is the secant ratio; returns the angle |
| arccosec (*a*) | inverse cosecant | *a* is the cosecant ratio; returns the angle |
| arccotan (*a*) | inverse cotangent | *a* is the cotangent ratio; returns the angle |
| abs (*a*) | absolute value | returns the absolute value of *a* |
| exp (*n*) | exponential | returns e raised to the power of *n* |
| log (*a*) | logarithmic | returns the natural log of *a* to the base e |
| sqr (*a*) | square root | returns the square root of *a* |
| int (*a*) | integer | returns *a* as an integer |
| sgn (*a*) | sign | returns the sign of *a* as -1 or 1<br><br>For example: sgn(-21) returns -1 |
| | | |
| **Constant** | | |
| pi | pi | ratio of the circumference to the diameter of a circle (3.14...) |

***Tutorial: Equations 12-1***

Display the Equations dialog box.

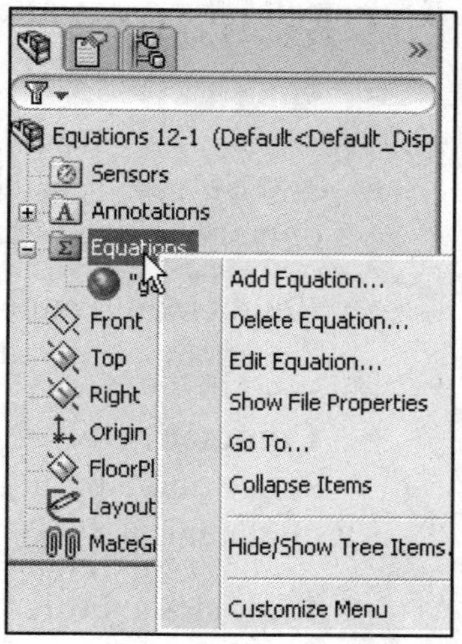


1. Open **Equations 12-1** from the SolidWorks 2010\TopDownAssemblyModeling folder.
2. Click **Tools** ➤ **Equation**. View the Equations dialog box.
3. Click **Close** from the Equations dialog box.
4. Right-click the **Equations folder** from the FeatureManager. View your options.
5. **Close** the model.

Existing equations are listed in the dialog box.

## Equations tool

The Equations tool uses the Equations dialog box. The Equations box provides the following selections:

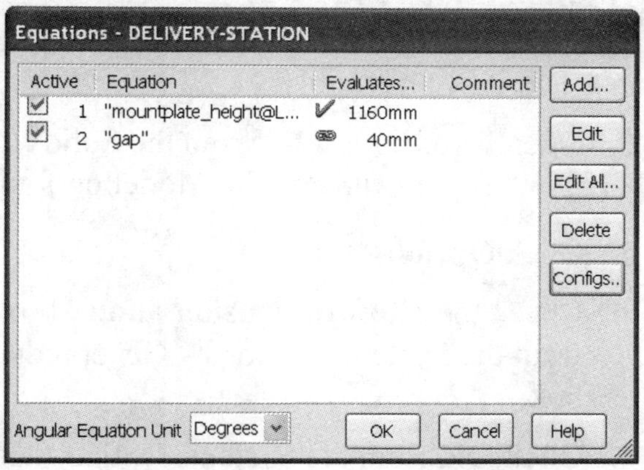


- ***Add***. Creates a new equation.
- ***Edit***. Edits the selected equation.
- ***Edit All***. Edits all of the equations in the dialog box.
- ***Delete***. Deletes the selected equation.
- ***Configs***. Specifies the configurations to apply to the selected equation.
- ***Angular Equations Units***. The Angular Equations Units drop down box provides two selections: **Degrees**, and **Radians**.
- ***Active***. The Active column provides the ability to display the following items:
  - The active equation with a check mark.
  - A non active equation, no check mark.
- ***Equation***. The Equation column displays the equations in the model. Equations are solved from left to right.

- ***Evaluates***. The Evaluates column displays the solutions of your equations. An icon indicates the status of each equation:
  - **Solved** - ✔. The equation is solved without errors.
  - **Not Solved** - !. The Not Solve icon is displayed when you delete a feature or dimension that is used in the equation.
  - **Read Only** - . The Read Only icon is displayed when you rename an assembly that includes an equation between assembly components.
  - **Comment Only** - **A**. The Comment Only icon is displayed when you add a single quote (') at the beginning of an equation, making the entire equation a comment.
  - **Linked Variable** - . The Linked Variable icon is displayed when the equation is a linked dimension name.
- ***Comments***. The Comments column displays inserted comments on the equation.

Linked dimension names cannot be edited from the equations dialog.

***Tutorial: Equations 12-2***

Create an Equation to define the Layout sketch in a Top-down assembly.

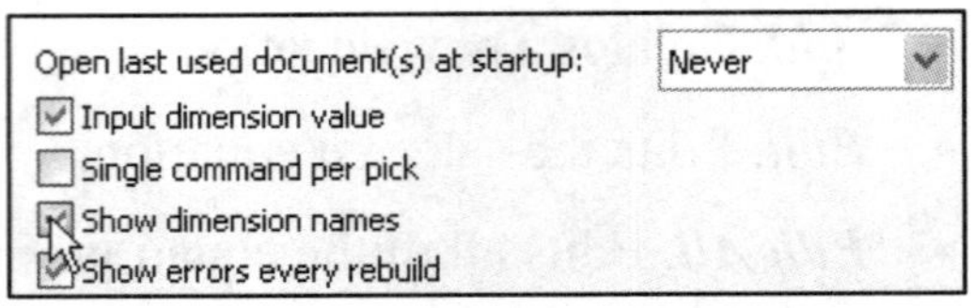


1. Open **Equations 12-2** from the SolidWorks 2010\TopDownAssemblyModeling folder.
2. Click **Options** .
3. Check the **Show dimension names** box from the Systems Options – General dialog box.

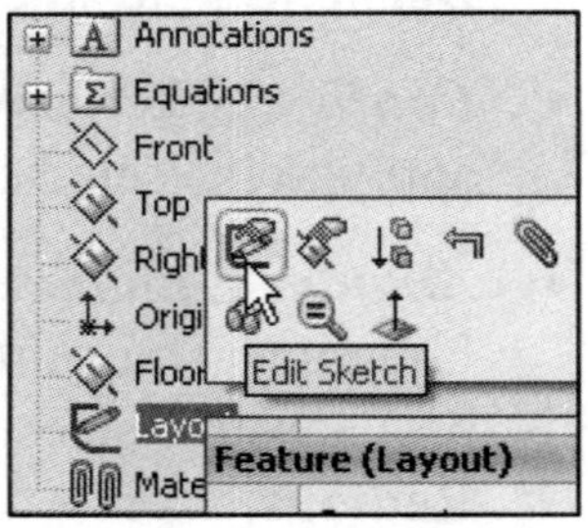


4. Click **OK** from the Systems Option - General dialog box.
5. Right-click **Layout** from the FeatureManager.
6. Click **Edit Sketch** from the Context toolbar.
7. Right-click the **Equations** folder from the FeatureManager.
8. Click **Add Equation**. The Add Equation dialog box is displayed.

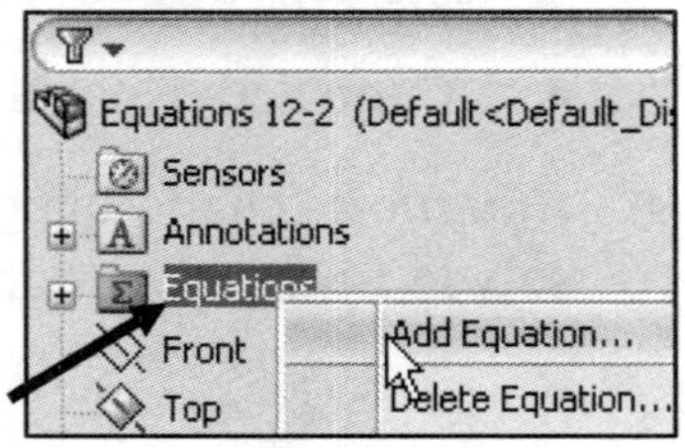


9. Click the mountplate_height dimension, **1160** from the Graphics window. The variable "mountplate_height@Layout" is added to the equation text box.

10. Press **Equals** [=] from the Add Equation keypad.

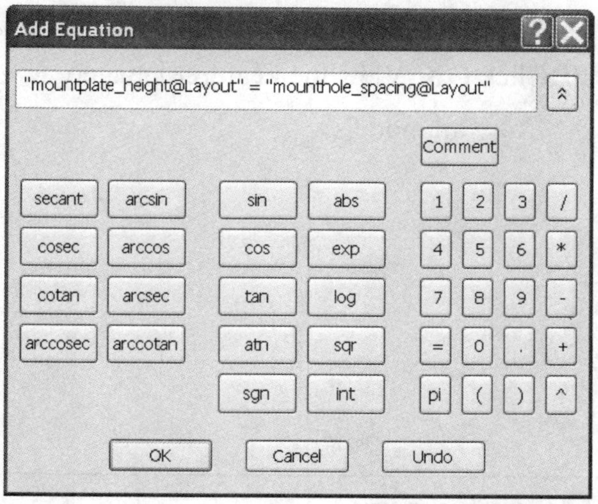


11. Click mounthole_spacing dimension, **880**. The variable “mounthole_spacing@Layout” is added to the equation text box.

12. Press [+] [2] [*] [(] from the Add Equation keypad.

13. Click gap, **40** from the Graphics window. The variable “gap@Layout” is added to the equation text box.

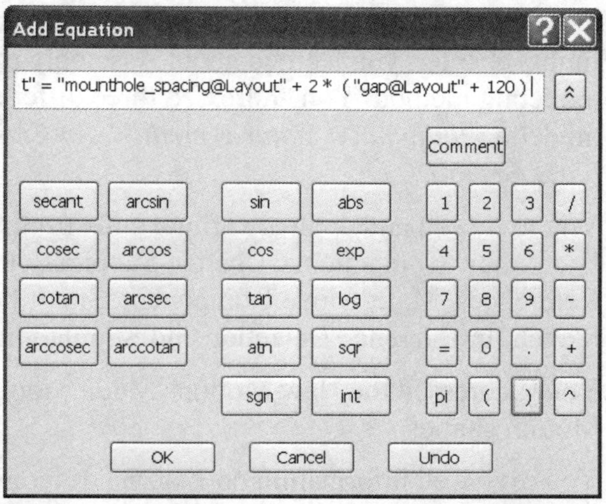


14. Press [+] [1] [2] [0] [)] from the Add Equation keypad.

15. Click **OK** from the Add Equation dialog box. The new equation is added to the Equations dialog box.

16. Click **OK** from the Equations dialog box. The variable, mountplate_height equals 1200 and is displayed in the Graphics window.

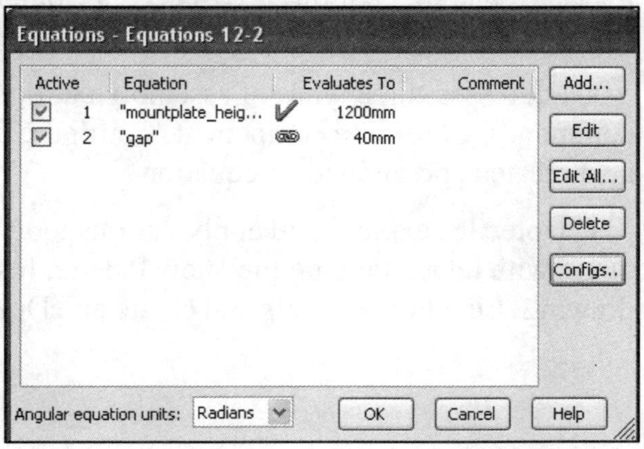


17. Click **Exit Sketch**.

18. Click **Options**.

19. Uncheck the **Show dimension names** box from the Systems Options – General dialog box.
20. Click **OK**. View the FeatureManager.
21. **Close** all models.

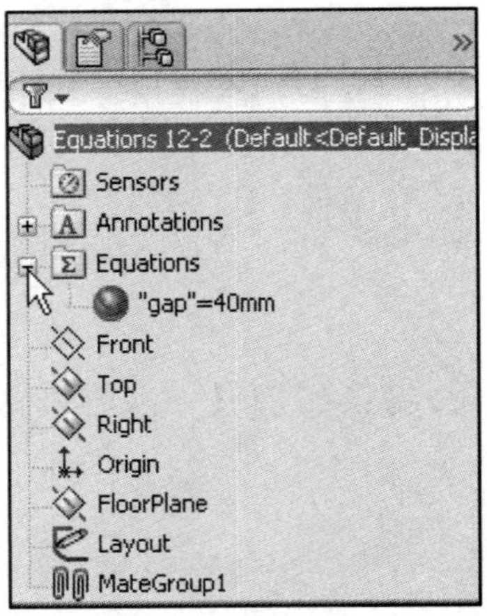


# Summary

In this chapter, you learned about Assembly modeling with the Top-down assembly modeling method. You addressed three different Assembly methods for Top-down modeling: *Individual features method, An Entire assembly method and the Complete parts method.*

You reviewed and applied various tools from the Assembly toolbar: Insert Components, Hide/Show Components, Change Suppression State, Edit Component, No External References, Mate, Move Component, Smart Fasteners, Explode View, Explode Line Sketch, Interference Detection and Simulation.

Your addressed the New Motions Studies tool, the MotionManager and created Basic Motion studies.

You reviewed information on External references, In-Content components, and InPlace mates. Remember, an InPlace Mate is a Coincident Mate created between the Front Plane of a new component and the selected planar geometry of the assembly.

You addressed three types of assembly configurations: Manual (Add Configuration command), Configure component /Configure dimension tool, and Design Tables. You also created and applied an equation.

In Chapter 13, explore and apply various tools from the Drawing and Annotations toolbar along with understanding the View Palette, Inserting DimXpert Annotations into a drawing, Line Format tools and create an eDrawing.

# CHAPTER 13: DRAWINGS AND EDRAWINGS

## Chapter Objective

Chapter 13 provides a comprehensive understanding of document properties, setting and the ability to create dimensioned multi view drawings from a part or assembly and more. On the completion of this chapter, you will be able to:

- Address Sheet format, size and Document Properties
- Understand and apply the SolidWorks View Palette
- Address and utilize the following tools from the View Layout toolbar:
  - Model View, Projected View, Auxiliary View, Section View, Aligned Section View, Detail View, Standard 3 View, Broken-out Section, Break, Crop View and Alternate Position View
- Know and utilize the following tools from the Annotation toolbar:
  - Smart Dimension, Model Items, Note, Spell Checker, Format Painter, Balloon, AutoBalloon, Surface Finish, Weld Symbol, Geometric Tolerance, Datum Feature, Datum Target, Hole Callout, Revision Symbol, Area Hatch/Fill, Block, Center Mark, Centerline and Tables
- Insert DimXpert Annotation using the SolidWorks View Palette
- Understand and utilize tools from the SolidWorks eDrawings toolbar
- Recognize and utilize the following tools from the Line Format toolbar:
  - Layer Properties, Line Color, Line Thickness, Line Style, Hide edge, Show Edge and Color Display Mode

# Drawings

Create 2D drawings of a 3D part or assembly. Parts, assemblies and drawings are linked documents. This means that any changes that you incorporate into the part or assembly will modify the associate drawing document.

Drawings consist of one or more views produced from a part or assembly. The part or assembly connected with the drawing must be saved before you can create the drawing. Drawing files have the .slddrw extension.

A new drawing takes the name of the first model inserted. The name is displayed in the title bar. When you save the drawing, the name of the model is displayed in the Save As dialog box as the default file name.

Create a drawing within a part or assembly document.

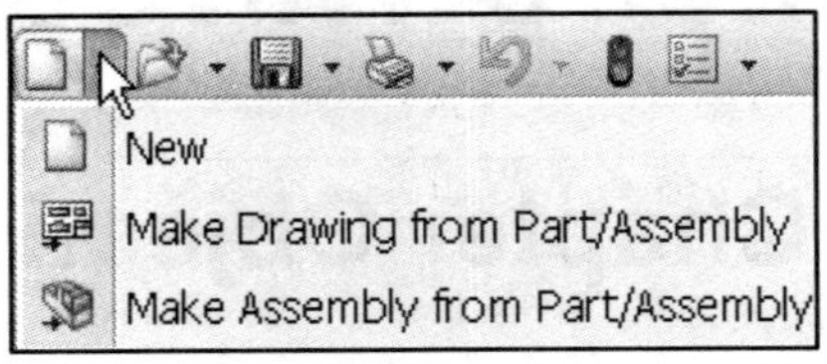


The foundation of a SolidWorks drawing is the Drawing Template. Drawing sheet size, drawing standards, company information, manufacturing and or assembly requirements; units, layers, line styles and other properties are defined in the Drawing Template.

The Sheet Format is incorporated into the Drawing Template. The Sheet Format contains the following; sheet border, title block and revision block information, company name, and or logo information, Custom Properties and SolidWorks Properties.

SolidWorks starts with a default Drawing Template, Drawing.drwdot. The default Drawing Template is located in the \SolidWorks\data\templates folder. SolidWorks is the name of the installation folder.

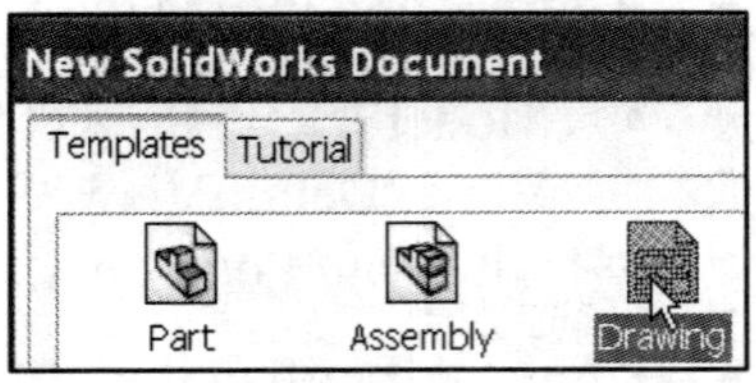


# Sheet Format, Size and Properties

The Sheet Format/Size dialog box defines the Sheet Format and the paper size. The U.S. default Standard Sheet Format is A (ANSI)-Landscape.slddrt. The Display sheet format option toggles the sheet format display on/off. The Standard Sheet Formats are located in the \SolidWorks\data folder.

## ASME Y14.1 Drawing Sheet Size and Format

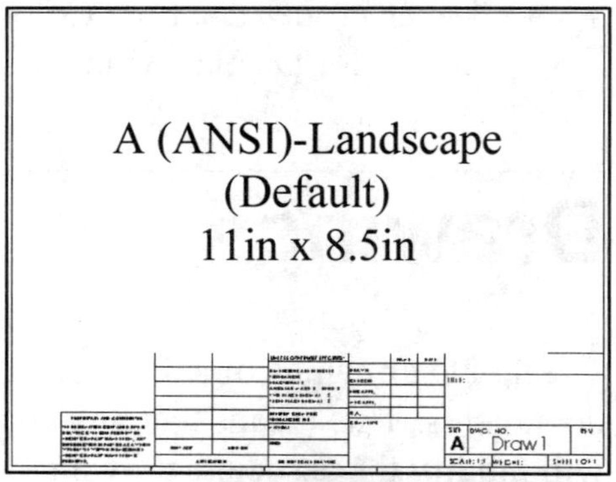


There are two ASME standards that define sheet size and format. They are:

1. ASME Y14.1-1995 Decimal Inch Drawing Sheet Size and Format.
2. ASME Y14.1M-1995 Metric Drawing Sheet Size.

The Hole Wizard information from the model propagates to the drawing when the Hole Callout button is selected.

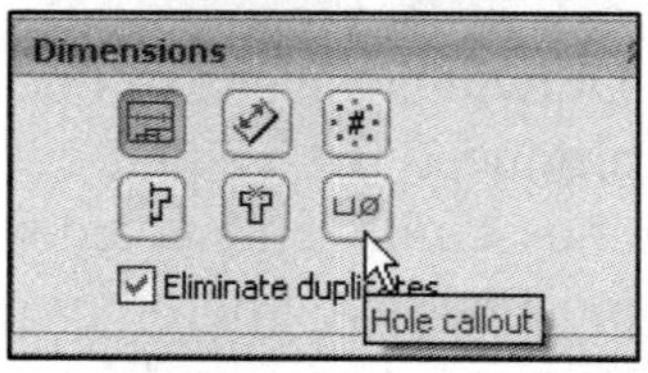

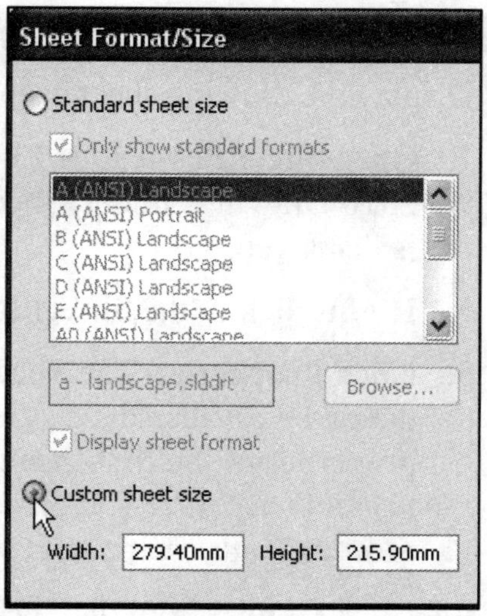


Drawing size refers to the physical paper size used to create the drawing. The most common paper size in the U.S. is the A size: (8.5in. x 11in.). The most common paper size internationally is the A4 size: (210mm x 297mm). The ASME Y14.1-1995 and ASME Y14.1M-1995 standards contain both a horizontal and vertical format for A and A4 size respectively. The corresponding SolidWorks format is Landscape for horizontal and Portrait for vertical.

SolidWorks predefines U.S. drawing sizes A through E. Drawing sizes F, G, H, J & K utilize the Custom sheet size option. Enter values for Width and Height. SolidWorks predefines metric drawing sizes A4 through A0. Metric roll paper sizes utilize the Custom sheet size option.

The ASME Y14.1-1995 Decimal Inch Drawing and ASME Y14.1M-1995 Metric Sheet Size standard are as follows:

| **Drawing Size:**<br>**"Physical Paper"** | **Size in inches:**<br>**Vertical**<br>**Horizontal** | |
|---|---|---|
| A horizontal (landscape) | 8.5 | 11.0 |
| A vertical (portrait) | 11.0 | 8.5 |
| B | 11.0 | 17.0 |
| C | 17.0 | 22.0 |
| D | 22.0 | 34.0 |
| E | 34.0 | 44.0 |
| F | 28.0 | 40.0 |
| G, H, J and K apply to roll sizes, User Defined | | |

| **Drawing Size:**<br>**"Physical Paper"**<br>**Metric** | **Size in Millimeters:**<br>**Vertical**<br>**Horizontal** | |
|---|---|---|
| A0 | 841 | 1189 |
| A1 | 594 | 841 |
| A2 | 420 | 594 |
| A3 | 297 | 420 |
| A4 horizontal (landscape) | 210 | 297 |
| A4 vertical (portrait) | 297 | 210 |

Use caution when sending electronic drawings between U.S. and International colleagues. Drawing paper sizes will vary. Example: An A-size (11in. x 8.5in.) drawing (280mm x 216mm) does not fit a A4 metric drawing (297mm x 210mm). Use a larger paper size or scale the drawing using the printer setup options.

Sheet Properties display properties of the selected sheet. Sheet Properties define the following: Name of the Sheet, Sheet Scale, Type of Projection (First angle or Third angle), Sheet Format, Sheet Size, View label and Datum label.

The Sheet Format and Sheet size are set in the default Drawing Template. The Sheet Format file extension is .drt. The Sheet Format option is grayed out. The C Paper size, width and height dimensions are listed under the Custom sheet size option.

### *Tutorial: Sheet Properties 13-1*

Display the drawing sheet properties.

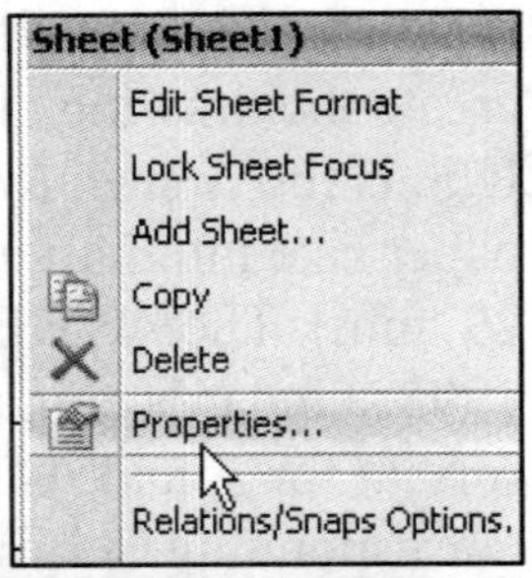


1. Open **Sheet Properties 13-1*slddrw** from the SolidWorks 2010\Drawings folder. Sheet1 of the COVERPLATE drawing is displayed.
2. **Right-click** in the Sheet1 boundary.
3. Click **Properties**. The Sheet Properties dialog box is displayed. View the properties of the first sheet: *Third angle projection*, *Scale: 1:1*, *Display sheet format*, *Sheet1* name, etc.
4. Click **Cancel** from the Sheet Properties dialog box.
5. **Close** the drawing.

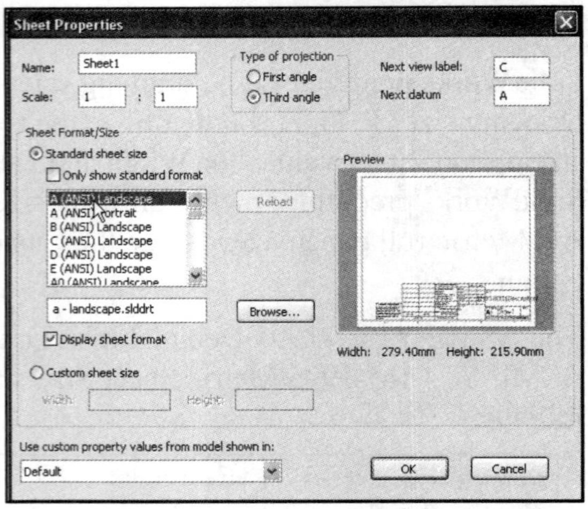


Note: ANSI, Third Angle projection is illustrated and used in this book.

# View Palette

The View Palette is located in the Task Pane. Apply the View Palette tool to insert images of *Standard views*, *Annotation views*, *Section views*, and *flat patterns* (sheet metal parts) of an active part or assembly, or click the Browse button to locate your desired model.

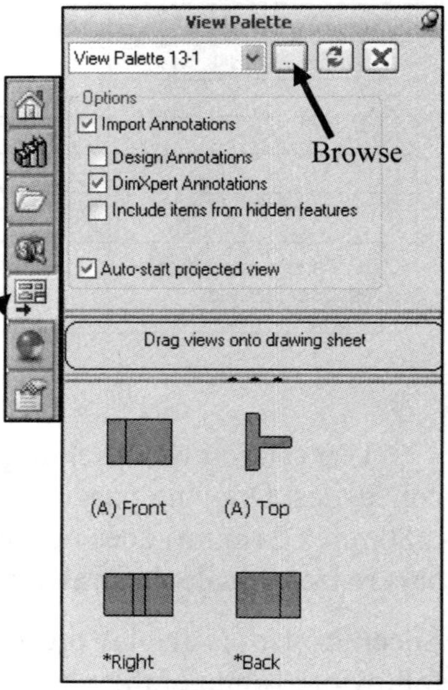


Click and drag the selected model view from the View Palette onto an active drawing sheet to create the drawing view.

The View Palette provides the following options: *Import Annotations, Design Annotations, DimXpert Annotations, Include items from hidden features and Auto-start projected view*.

The selected model is View Palette 13-1 in the illustration. The **(A) Front** and **(A) Top** drawing views are displayed with DimXpert Annotations which was applied at the part level.

***Tutorial: View Palette / Import Annotations 13-1***

Create a three (3) standard view drawing using the View Palette with DimXpert dimensions.

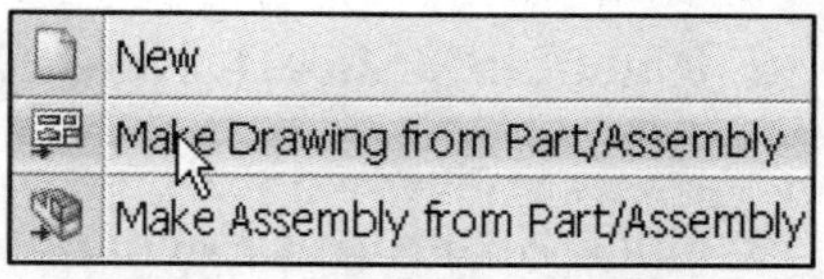


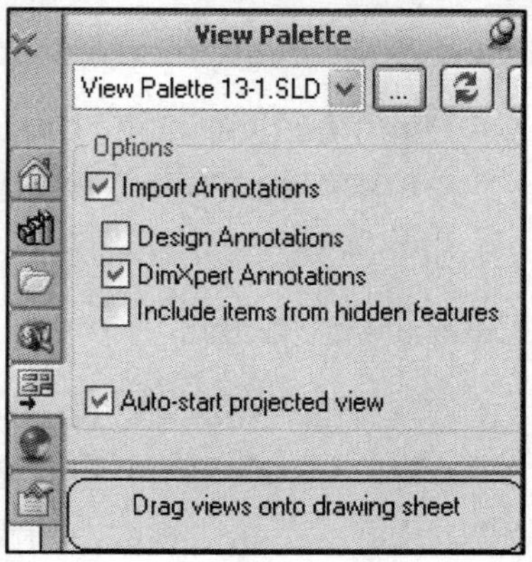


1. Open **View Palette 13-1.sldprt** from the SolidWorks 2010\Drawings folder. View the model with the created DimXpert dimensions.
2. Click **Make Drawing from Part/Assembly** from the Menu bar. The New SolidWorks Document dialog box is displayed. Drawing is selected by default.
3. Click **OK**. Accept the Standard Sheet size and format.
4. Click **OK** from the Sheet Format/Size dialog box.
5. Click the **View Palette** tab from the Task Pane. View Palette 13-1 is displayed with the available views.
6. Check the **Import Annotations** box.
7. Check the **DimXpert Annotations** box.
8. Click and drag the **(A) Front** drawing view into Sheet1.
9. Click a **position** directly above the Front view. The Top view is created.
10. Click a **position** directly to the right of the Front view. The Right view is created.
11. Click **OK** from the Projected View PropertyManager. You created a drawing with the default drawing template, using the View Palette and imported Annotations from DimXpert. Note: There are numerous ways to create a drawing. At this time, (SP0) SolidWorks does not let the user move DimXpert dimensions from one view to the other.

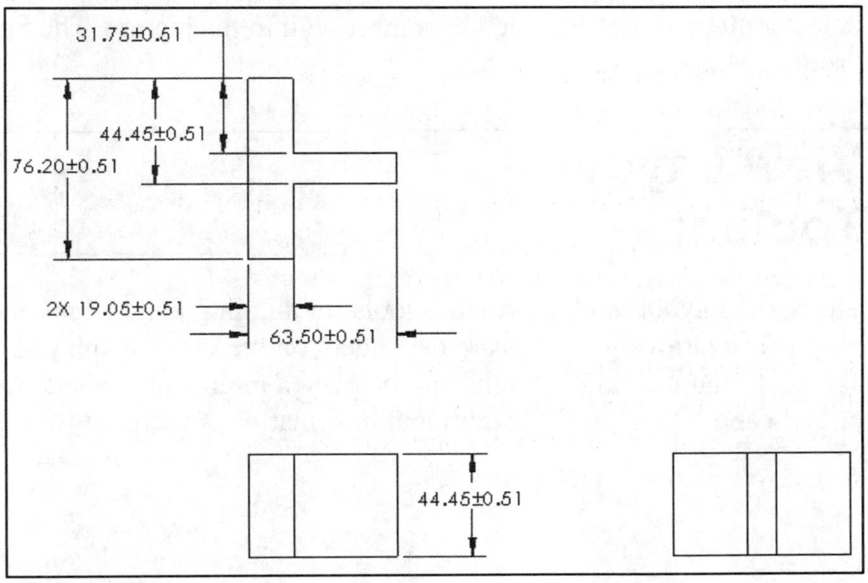

Modify the Title block.

12. Right-click **Sheet1**. Note: Do not click inside a drawing view.

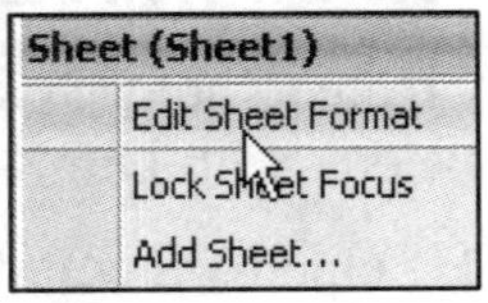


13. Click **Edit Sheet Format**.

Modify the Drawing No. text.

14. **Double-click** inside the DWG. NO. box. The Formatting toolbar is displayed.

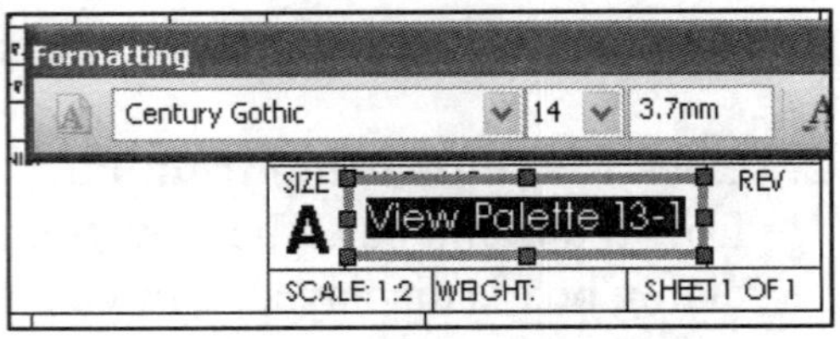


15. Select **14** for text size.

Enter a Title name.

16. Click the **Note** A tool from the Annotation tab. The Note PropertyManager is displayed.

17. Click a position inside the **Title box** below the TITLE: text.

18. Enter **TUTORIAL**.

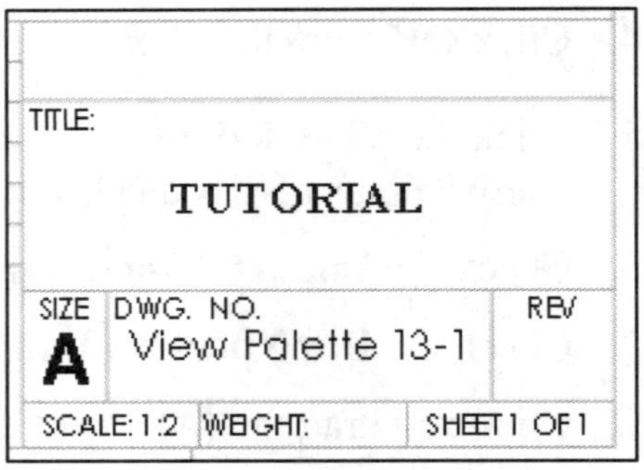


19. Click **OK** from the Note PropertyManager.

20. Right-click **Sheet1**.

21. Click **Edit Sheet**. View the finished drawing.

22. **Close** all models.

If you delete a view from a drawing, you can re-insert the view from the View Palette by clicking the **Refresh** button at the top of the palette.

To insert a picture into a drawing, click **Insert ➢ Picture** from the Menu bar menu. Select a **picture file**. The picture is inserted into the picture. The Sketch Picture PropertyManager is displayed.

## View Layout Toolbar

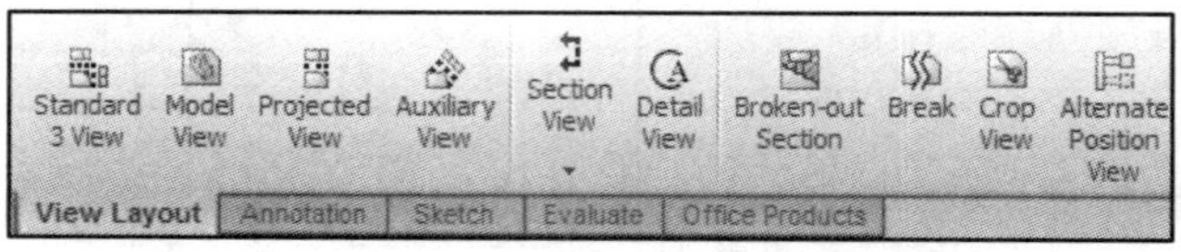


The View Layout toolbar provides tools for aligning dimensions and creating drawing views. The Drawing options are dependent on the views displayed in the drawing sheet. The tools and menu options that are displayed in gray are called gray-out. The gray icon or text cannot be selected. Additional information is required for these options.

## Standard 3 Views tool

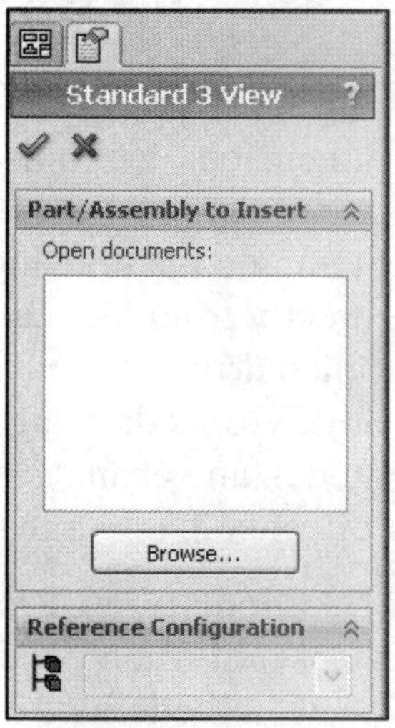


The Standard 3 Views tool provides the ability to add three standard, orthogonal views. The type and orientation of the views can be 1st or 3rd Angle. The alignment of the top and side views is fixed in relation to the front view. The Standard 3 Views tool uses the Standard 3 View PropertyManager. The PropertyManager provides the following selections:

- ***Part/Assembly to Insert***. The Part/Assembly to Insert box provides the ability to select a document from the following selections. They are:
  - **Open documents**. Displays the active part or assembly file. Select the part or assembly file.
  - **Browse**. Browse for the needed part or assembly file.
- ***Reference Configuration***. Provides the ability to select the model configuration.

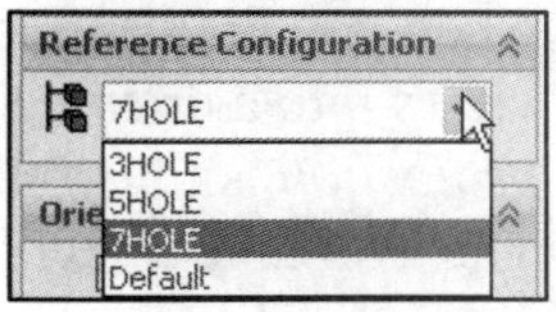


### *Tutorial: Standard 3 Views 13-1*

Apply the Standard 3 View drawing tool.

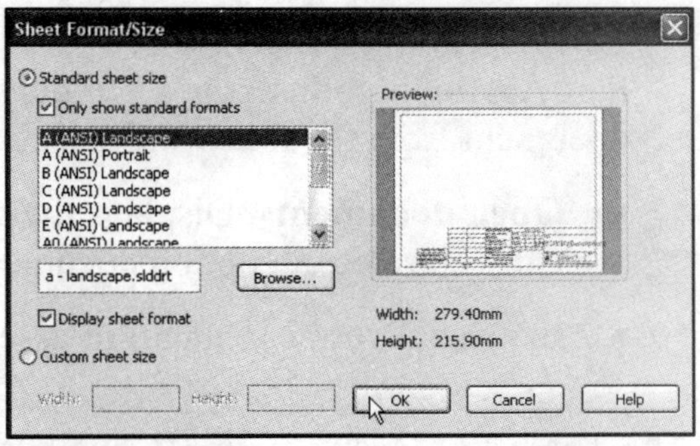


1. Create a **New** drawing. Use the ANSI Drafting standard, Third Angle projection, A (ANSI) Landscape template.
2. Click the **Standard 3 View** drawing tool from the View Layout toolbar.
3. Click the **Browse** button from the Part/Assembly to Insert box.
4. Double-click the **Shaft-Collar** part from the SolidWorks 2010\Drawings folder. Three standard views are inserted on Sheet1. Note: *First Angle projection* vs. *Third angle projection* is displayed in this example.
5. If needed, **modify** the Sheet scale to fit Sheet1. View the results.
6. **Close** the drawing.

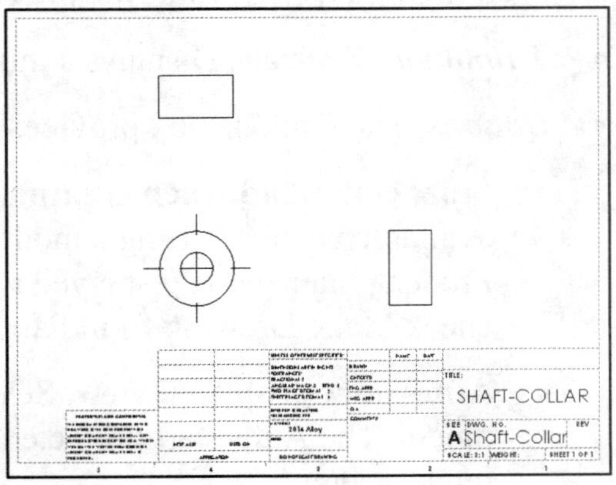


To modify the drawing view scale, click inside the desired view. Click the Use custom size box. Enter the needed scale.

## Model View tool

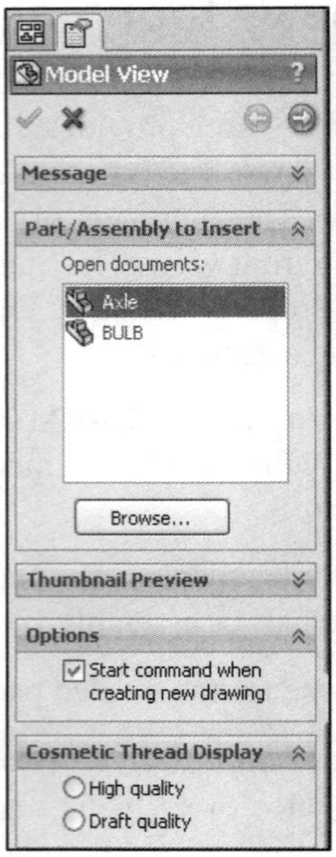


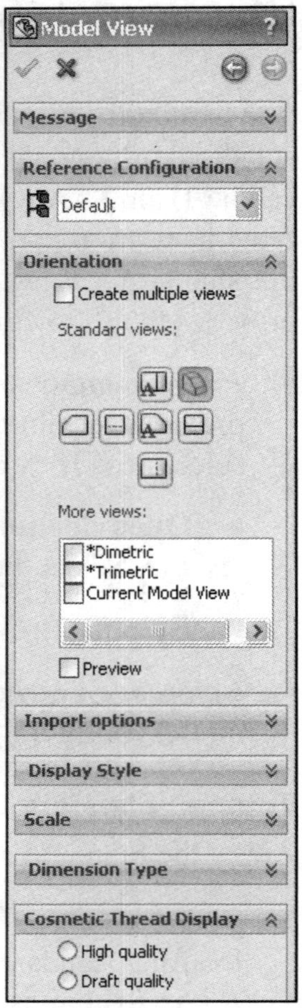


The Model View tool imports various dimensions, symbols and annotations that where used to create the model, and puts them into the drawing. Dimenions that come directly from the features or sketches are called driven dimensions. Dimensions in a SolidWorks drawing are associated with the model, and changes in the model are reflected in the drawing.

The Model View PropertyManager is displayed when you insert or select a Model View, a Predefined View, an Empty View or when you drag a model with annotation views into a drawing. Note: *Third Angle projection* is illustrated and used in this book. The available selections in the Model View are *dependent* on the type of view selected.

The options are:

- ***Part/Assembly to Insert***. The Part/Assembly to Insert box provides the ability to select a document from the following selections:
  - **Open documents**. Displays the open part or assembly files. Click to select an option document.
  - **Browse**. Browse to a part or assembly file.

The list of Open documents includes saved models, both parts and assemblies that are open in SolidWorks windows, plus models that are displayed in drawing views.

- ***Thumbnail Preview***. Displays a thumbnail view of the selected part or assembly.
- ***Options***. The Options box provides the following selections:
  - **Start command when creating new drawing**. Selected by default. Only available when inserting a model into a new drawing. The Model View PropertyManager is displayed whenever you create a new drawing except if you check Make Drawing from Part/Assembly.
  - **Auto-start projected view**. Selected by default. Inserts projected views of the model. The Auto-start projected view option is displayed after you insert the model view.

- ***Cosmetic Thread Display***. Sets either the High quality or Draft quality settings from the Model View PropertyManager for Assembly drawings only. The setting in the Cosmetic Thread Display, if different will override the Cosmetic thread display option that is set in the Document Properties, Detailing section.

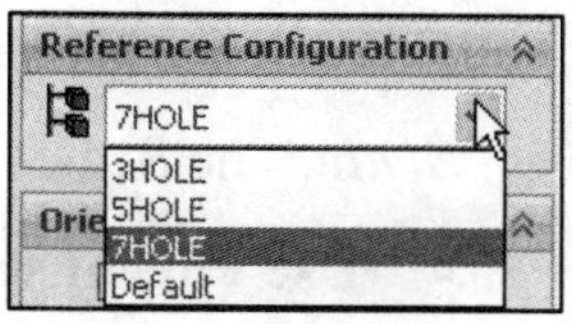


- ***Reference Configuration***. Provides the ability to change drawing view configurations.
- ***Select Bodies***. Provides the ability to select the bodies of a multi-body part for inclusion in the drawing view. For flat patterns of multi-body sheet metal parts, you can use one body per view.
- ***Orientation***. The Orientation box provides the following selections:

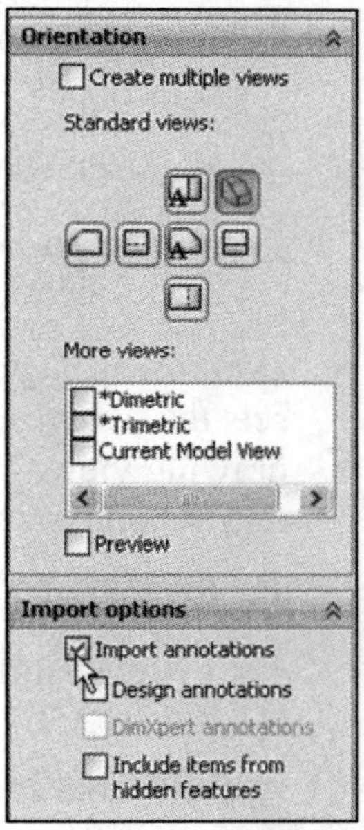


  - **Create multiple views**. Ability to display multiple drawing views.
  - **Standard views**. Provides the following views: ***Front**, ***Back**, ***Top**, ***Bottom**, ***Right**, ***Left** and ***Isometric**.
  - **Annotation view**. Displays annotation views if created. The selections are: ***Front**, ***Back**, ***Top**, ***Bottom**, ***Right**, ***Left** and ***Isometric**.
  - **More views**. This option is application dependent. Displays additional views such as **Current Model View**, ***Trimetric**, ***Dimetric**, **Annotation View 1** & **Annotation View 2**.
  - **Preview**. Only available with a singe drawing view. Displays a preview of the model while inserting a view.
- ***Import Options***. The available options are: **Import annotations**, **Design annotations**, **DimXpert annotations**, and **Include Items for hidden feature**.

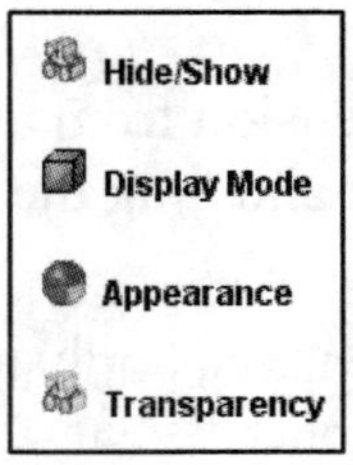


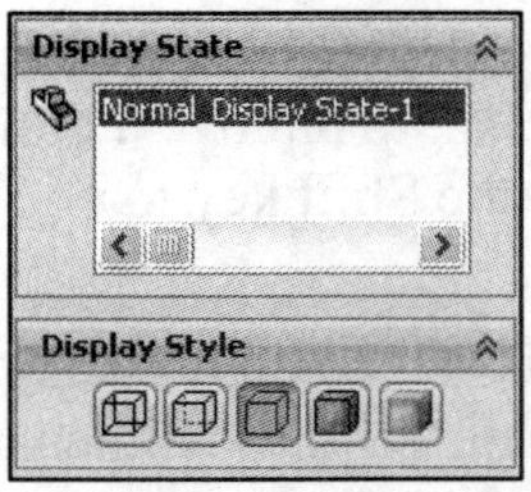


- ***Display State***. Only available for assemblies. Defines different combinations of settings for each component in an assembly. Saves the settings in Display States. The available settings are: **Hide/Show state**, **Display Mode**, **Appearance** and **Transparency**.

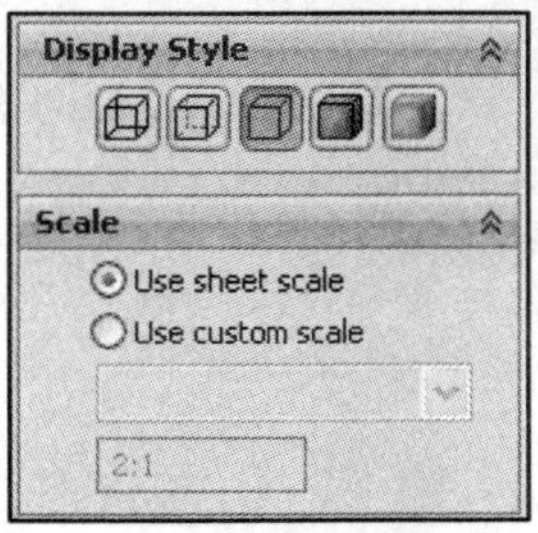


- ***Display Style***. Provides the following view display styles: **Wireframe**, **Hidden Lines Visible**, **Hidden Lines Removed**, **Shaded With Edges** and **Shaded**.

The Use parent style check box option provides the ability to apply the same display style used from the parent.

In the Hidden Lines Visible or Hidden Lines Removed mode, you can select a style for Tangent Edge Display.

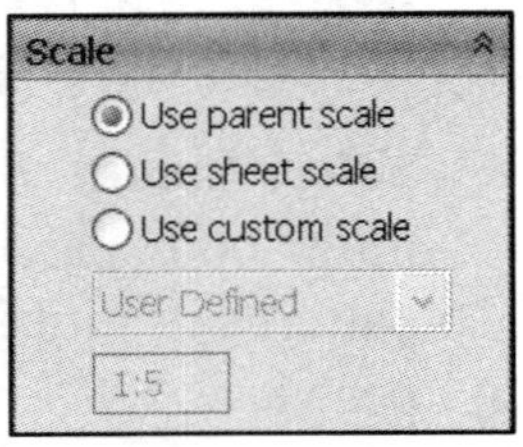


- ***Scale***. The Scale box provides the following sections:
  - **Use Parent scale**. Applies the same scale used for the parent view. If you modify the scale of a parent view, the scale of all child views that use the parent scale is updated.
  - **Use sheet scale**. Applies the same scale used for the drawing sheet.

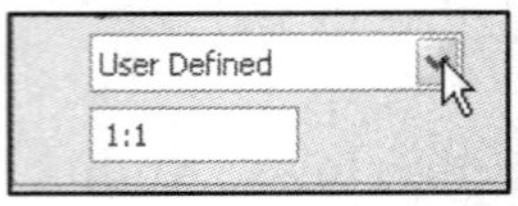


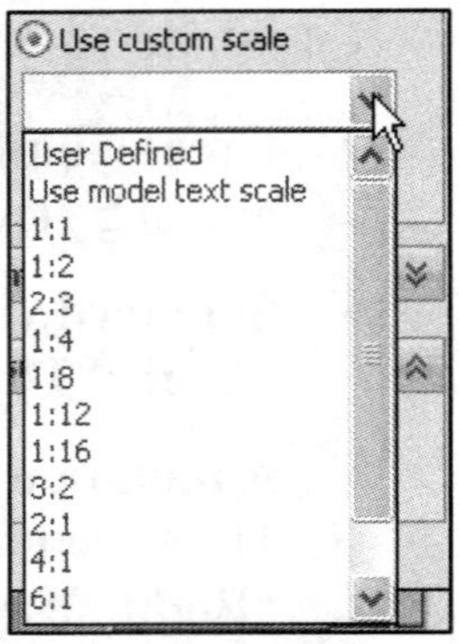


  - **Use custom scale**. Creates a custom scale for your drawing. There are two selections:
    - **User Defined**. Enter a scale value.
    - **Use model text scale**. Uses the scale of the model.
- ***Dimension Type***. The Dimension Type box sets the dimension type when you insert a drawing view. The Dimension Type box provides two dimension type selections:
  - **Projected**. Displays 2D dimensions.
  - **True**. Displays accurate model values.

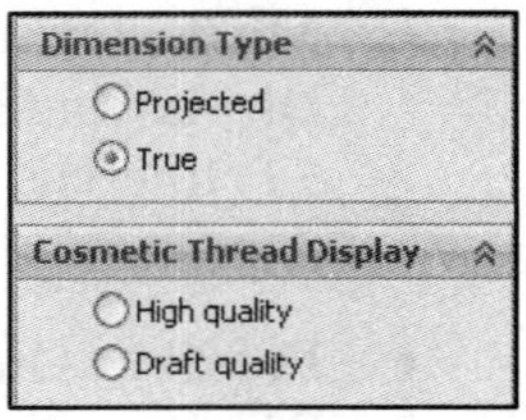


SolidWorks specifies Projected type dimensions for standard and custom orthogonal views and True type for Isometric, Dimetric and Trimetric views.

To move a dimension from one view to another view, apply the Shift key to click and drag the required dimension.

To copy a dimension, apply the Ctrl key, and click and drag the required dimension.

To open a part from an active drawing view, right-click inside the drawing view, click Open Part from the Context toolbar.

- ***Cosmetic Thread Display***. Sets either the High quality or Draft quality settings from the Model View PropertyManager. The setting in the Cosmetic Thread Display, if different will override the Cosmetic thread display option that is set in the Document Properties, Detailing section. The selections are:

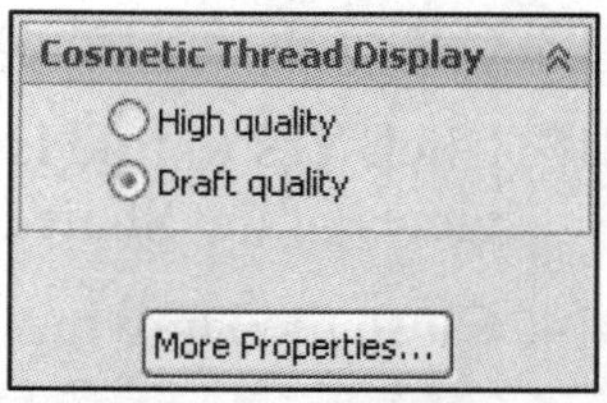


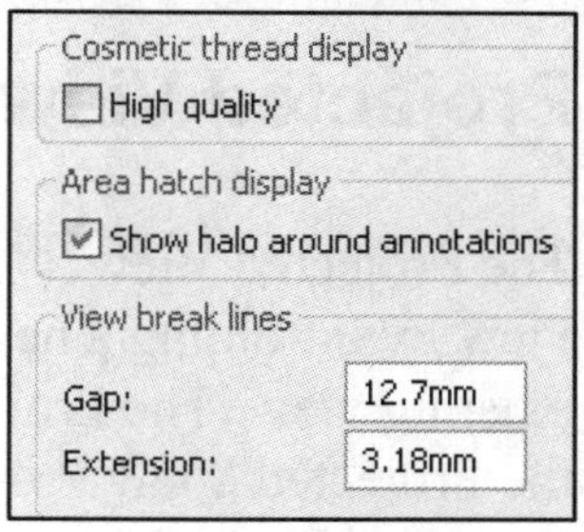


  - **High quality**. Displays precise line fonts and trimming in cosmetic threads. If a cosmetic thread is only partially visible, the High quality option will display only the visible portion.
  - **Draft quality**. Displays cosmetic threads with less detail. If a cosmetic thread is only partially visible, the Draft quality option will display the entire feature.
  - **More Properties**. The More Properties button provides the ability to modify the bill or materials information, show hidden edges, etc. after a view is created or by selecting an existing view from the drawing sheet or FeatureManager.

***Tutorial: Model View 13-1***

Create a new drawing using the Model View tool.

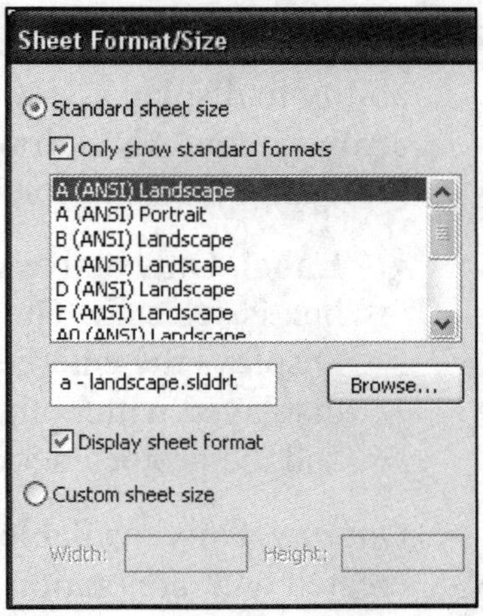


1. Create a **New** drawing. Use the ANSI Drafting standard, Third Angle projection, A (ANSI) Landscape default drawing template.
2. Click **OK** from the Sheet Format/Size dialog box.
3. If required, click the **Model View** tool from the View Layout tab. The Model View PropertyManager is displayed.
4. Click the **Browse** button.
5. Click **Shaft Collar** from the SolidWorks 2010\Drawings folder.
6. Check **Multiple views** from the Number of Views box.
7. Click ***Isometric**, ***Top** and ***Right** view. Front view is selected by default. Note: Third angle projection is used in this book.

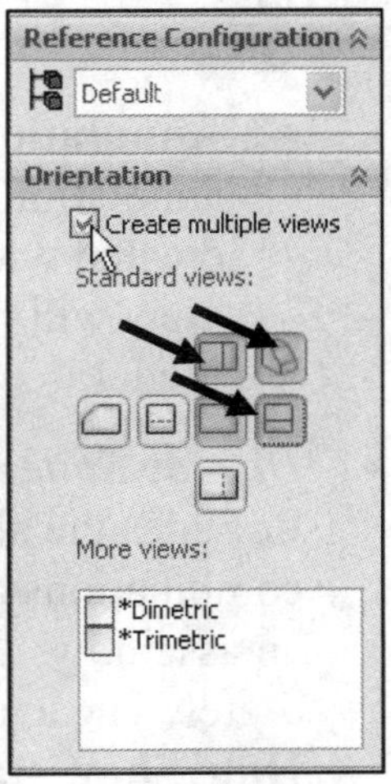


8. Click **Shaded With Edges** from the Display Style box.
9. Check **Use custom scale.**
10. Select **User Defined**.
11. Enter **3:1**.

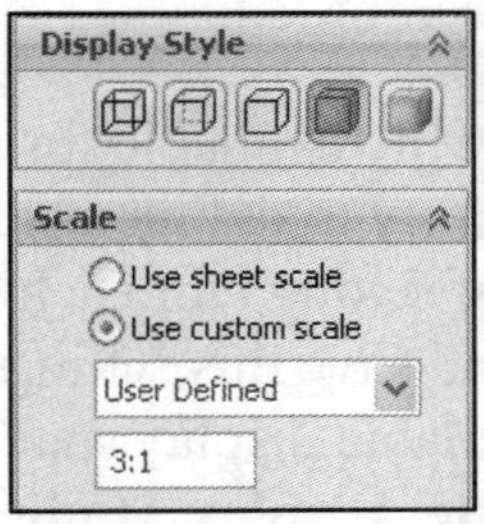

12. Click **OK** from the Model View PropertyManager.
13. Click **Yes** to true Isometric dimensions. You created four views of the Shaft Collar on Sheet1.
14. **Close** the Drawing.

## Projected View tool

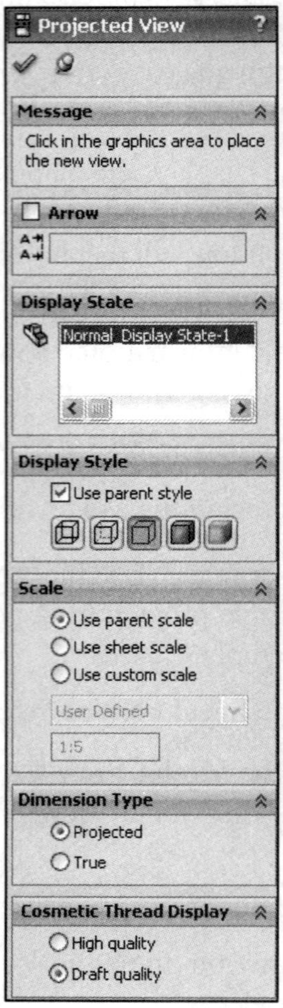


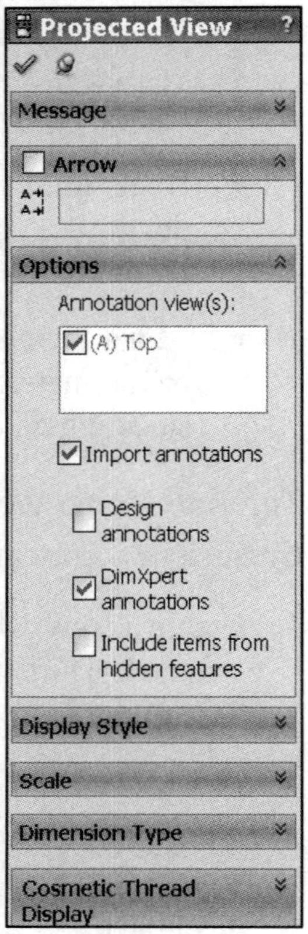


The Projected View tool adds a projected view by unfolding a new view from an existing view. The Projected View tool uses the Projected View PropertyManager. The Projected View PropertyManager is displayed when you create a Projected View in a drawing, or when you select an existing Projected View. The Projected View PropertyManager provides the following selections:

- ***Arrow***. The Arrow box provides the ability to display a view arrow, or a set of arrows in the ANSI drafting standard indicating the direction of the projection.
  - **Label**. Only active when the Arrow box is selected. The first Label is A. Displays the entered text to be displayed with both the parent view and the projected view.
- ***Options***. Only available if the model was created with annotation views. The Options box provides the following selections.
  - **Annotation view(s)**. Select an annotation view, if the model was created with annotation views. The view will include annotations from the model.
- ***Display State***. Only available for assemblies. Provides the ability to define different combinations of settings for each component in an assembly, and save this settings in Display States. The available display state settings are: **Hide/Show state**, **Display Mode**, **Appearance** and **Transparency**.

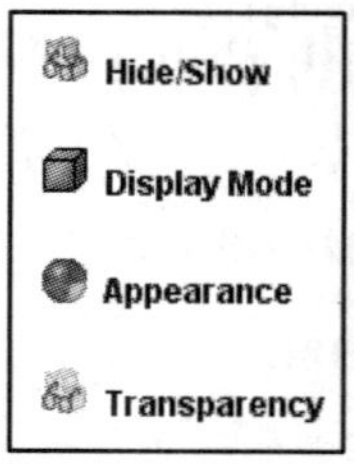

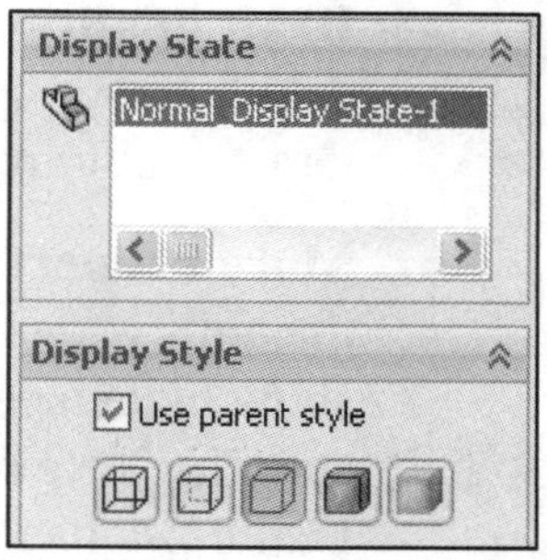


- ***Display Style***. Displays drawing views in the following modes. They are: **Wireframe**, **Hidden Lines Visible**, **Hidden Lines Removed**, **Shaded With Edges** and **Shaded**.

The Use parent style check box option provides the ability to apply the same display style used from the parent.

When in the Hidden Lines Visible or Hidden Lines Removed mode, you can select a style for Tangent Edge Display.

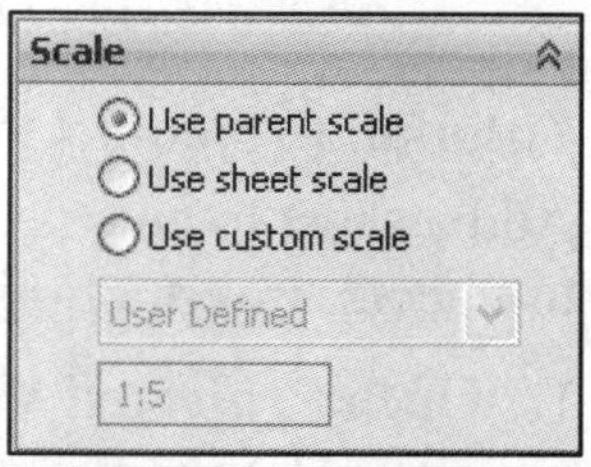


- ***Scale***. The Scale box provides the following sections. They are:
  - **Use Parent scale**. Applies the same scale used for the parent view. If you modify the scale of a parent view, the scale of all child views that use the parent scale is updated.
  - **Use sheet scale**. Applies the same scale used for the drawing sheet.
  - **Use custom scale**. Create a custom scale for your drawing. There are two selections:
    - **User Defined**. Enter a scale value.
    - **Use model text scale**. Uses model scale.

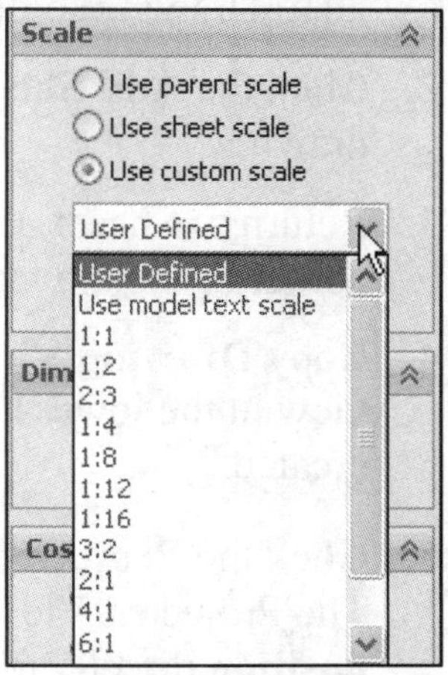


- ***Dimension Type***. Sets the dimension type when you insert a drawing view. The Dimension Type box provides two dimension type selections. They are:
  - **Projected**. Displays 2D dimensions.
  - **True**. Displays accurate model values.

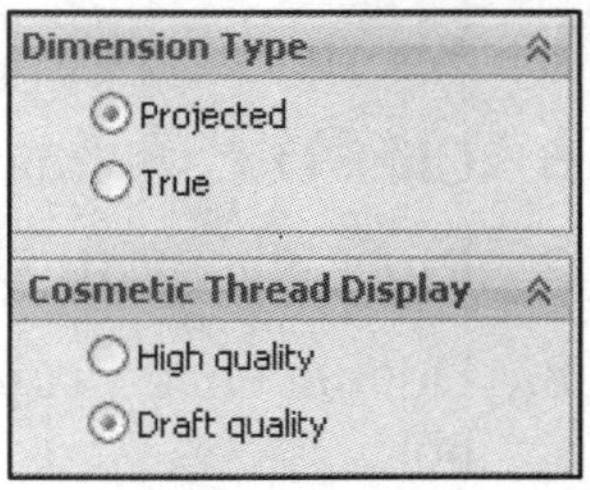


SolidWorks specifies Projected type dimensions for standard and custom orthogonal views and True type for Isometric, Dimetric and Trimetric views.

- ***Cosmetic Thread Display***. Set either the High quality or Draft quality settings from the Model View PropertyManager. The setting in the Cosmetic Thread Display, if different will override the Cosmetic thread display option that is set in the Document Properties, Detailing section. The selections are:
  - **High quality**. Displays precise line fonts and trimming in cosmetic threads. If a cosmetic thread is only partially visible, the High quality option will display only the visible portion.

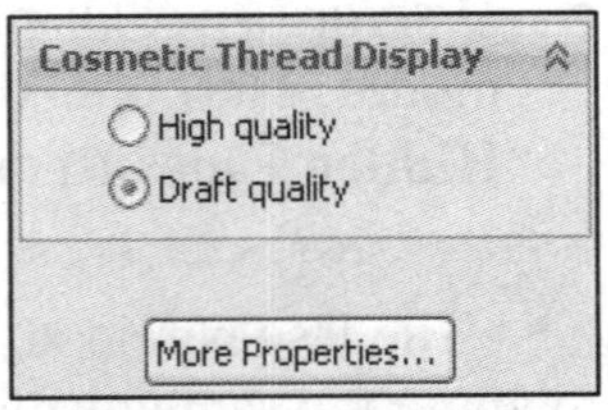


- **Draft quality**. Displays cosmetic threads with less detail. If a cosmetic thread is only partially visible, the Draft quality option will display the entire feature.
- **More Properties**. The More Properties button provides the ability to modify the bill or materials information, show hidden edges, etc. after a view is created or by selecting an existing view from the drawing sheet or FeatureManager. The More Properties option activates the Drawing View Properties dialog box.

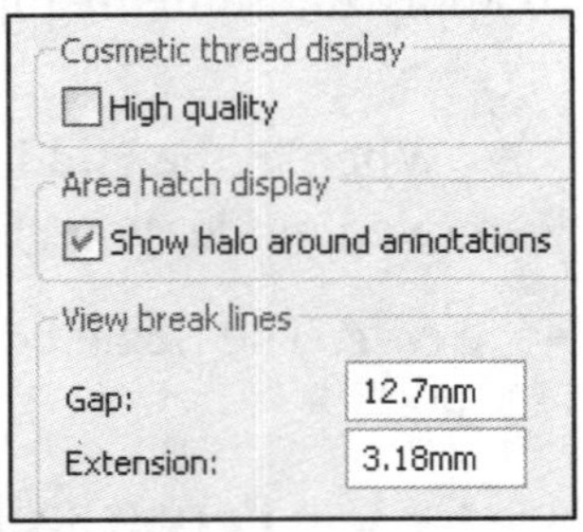


***Tutorial: Projected View 13-1***

Add a sheet to an existing drawing. Copy a drawing from Sheet1 to Sheet2. Insert a Projected View. Modify the Title box.

1. Open **Projected View 13-1** from the SolidWorks 2010\Drawing folder. Add a Sheet to the drawing.

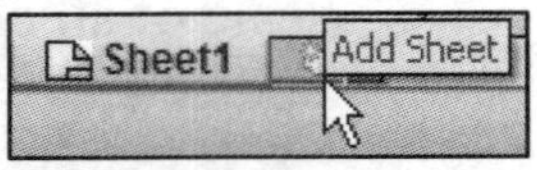


2. Click the **Add Sheet** icon in the bottom left corner of the drawing.

3. Return to Sheet1. Click the **Sheet1** tab in the bottom left corner of the drawing.
4. Copy **Drawing View1** from Sheet1 to Sheet2. **Position** the view in the lower left corner of Sheet2. Drawing View5 is created.

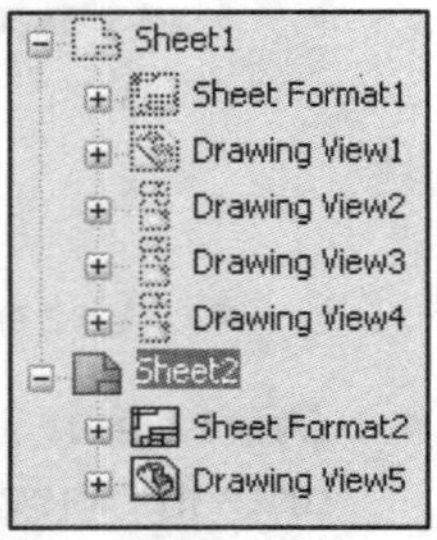


5. Click the **Projected View** tool from the View Layout tab. The Projected View PropertyManager is displayed. Click a **position** directly to the right of Drawing View5. Drawing View6 is displayed.
6. Click **OK** from the Projected View PropertyManager.

7. Right-click **Edit Sheet Format** in the Graphics window.
8. Double-click **Projected View 13-1** in the DWG NO. box.

9. Select **12** font from the Formatting dialog box.
10. Click **OK** from the Note PropertyManager.
11. Right-click in the **Graphics window**.
12. Click **Edit Sheet**. **Return** to Sheet1.
13. **Close** the drawing.

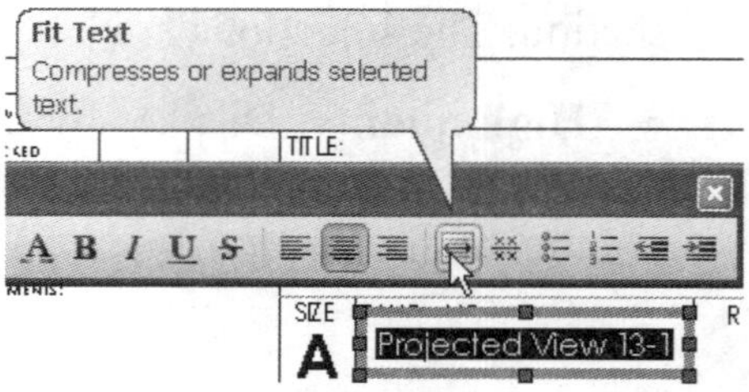


Select the **Fit text** option from the Formatting dialog box to compress or expand selected text using control points.

## Auxiliary View tool

The Auxilary View tool adds a view by unfolding a new view from a linear entity. Example: Edge, sketch entity, etc. An Auxiliary View is similar to a Projected View, but it is unfolded normal to a reference edge in an existing view. The Auxiliary View tool uses the Auxiliary View PropertyManager. The Auxiliary View PropertyManager provides the following selections:

- ***Arrow***. The Arrow box provides the ability to display a view arrow, or a set of arrows in the ANSI drafting standard indicating the direction of the projection.
  - **Label**. Only active when the Arrow box is selected. The first Label is A. Displays the entered text to be displayed with both the parent view and the auxiliary view.
- ***Options***. Only available if the model was created with annotation views. The Options box provides the following selections.
  - **Annotation view(s)**. Select an annotation view, if the model was created with annotation views. The view will include annotations from the model.
- ***Display State***. Only available for assemblies. Defines different combinations of settings for each component in an assembly, and save this settings in the Display State. The available settings are: **Hide/Show state**, **Display Mode**, **Appearance** and **Transparency**.

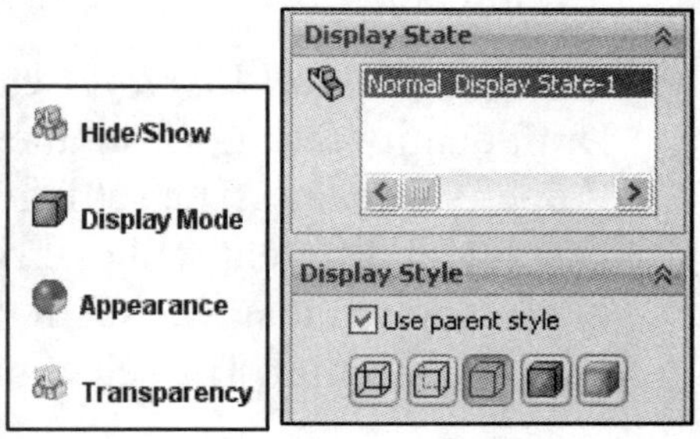


- ***Display Style***. Displays drawing views in the following modes. They are: **Wireframe**, **Hidden Lines Visible**, **Hidden Lines Removed**, **Shaded With Edges** and **Shaded**.

The Use parent style check box option provides the ability to apply the same display style used from the parent.

Reference dimensions show measurements of the model, but they do not drive the model and you cannot change their values. However, when you change the model, the reference dimensions update accordingly. Reference dimensions are enclosed in parentheses by default.

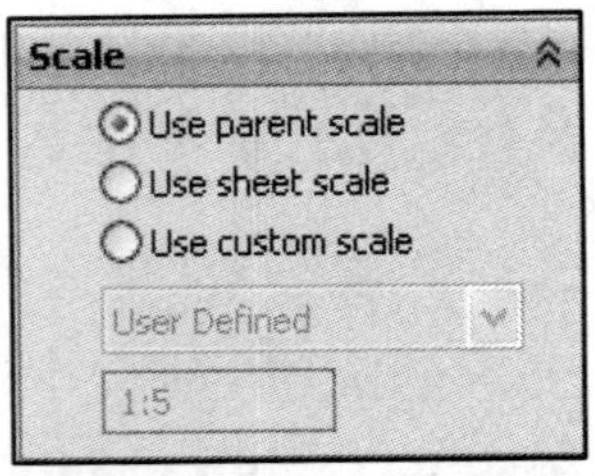


- ***Scale***. The Scale box provides the following sections. They are:
  - **Use Parent scale**. Applies the same scale used for the parent view. If you modify the scale of a parent view, the scale of all child views that use the parent scale is updated.
  - **Use sheet scale**. Applies the same scale used for the drawing sheet.
  - **Use custom scale**. Create a custom scale for your drawing. There are two selections:
    - **User Defined**. Enter a scale value.
    - **Use model text scale**. Uses the model scale.

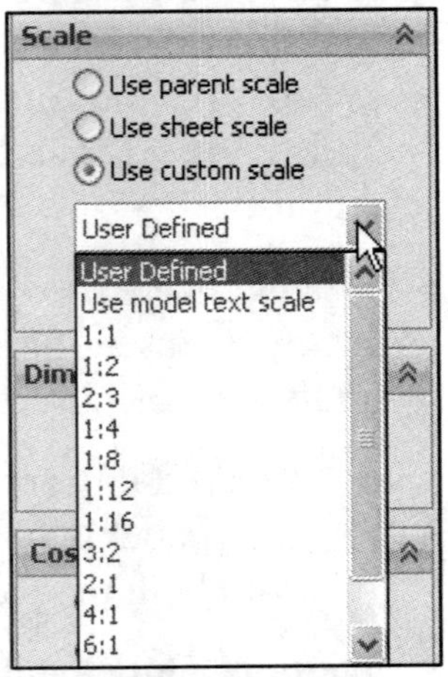


  - **Dimension Type**. Sets the dimension type when you insert a drawing view. The Dimension Type box provides two dimension type selections:
    - **Projected**. Displays 2D dimensions.
    - **True**. Displays accurate model values.

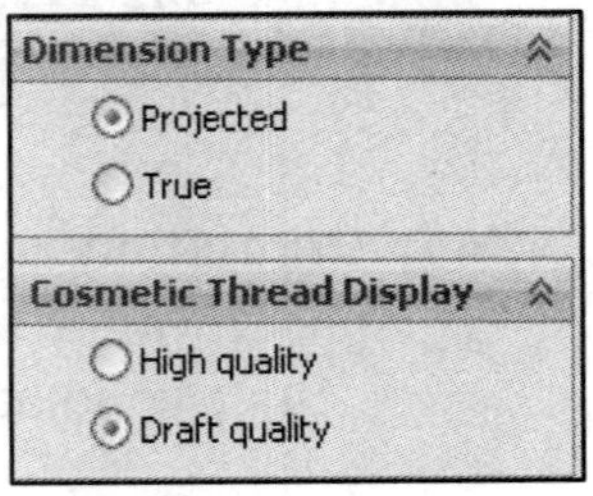


SolidWorks specifies Projected type dimensions for standard and custom orthogonal views and True type for Isometric, Dimetric and Trimetric views.

- ***Cosmetic Thread Display***. Sets either the High quality or Draft quality settings from the Model View PropertyManager. The setting in the Cosmetic Thread Display, if different will override the Cosmetic thread display option that was set in the Document Properties, Detailing section. The selections are:
  - **High quality**. Displays precise line fonts and trimming in cosmetic threads. If a cosmetic thread is only partially visible, the High quality option will display only the visible portion.
  - **Draft quality**. Displays cosmetic threads with less detail. If a cosmetic thread is only partially visible, the Draft quality option will display the entire feature.
  - **More Properties**. The More Properties button provides the ability to modify the bill or materials information, show hidden edges, etc. after a view is created or by selecting an existing view from the drawing sheet or FeatureManager.

### *Tutorial: Auxiliary View 13-1*

Create an Auxilary view from an existing Front view. Reposition the view.

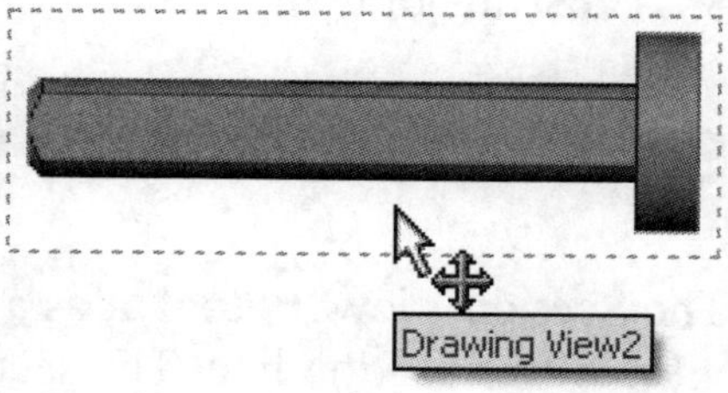


1. Open **Auxiliary View 13-1** from the SolidWorks 2010\Drawing folder.
2. Click inside the **Front view** boundary of Drawing View2.
3. Click the **Auxiliary View** drawing tool. The Auxiliary View PropertyManager is displayed.

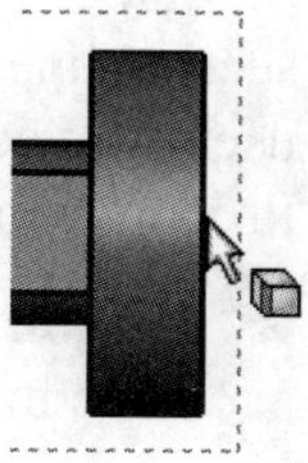

4. Click the **right vertical edge** of Drawing View2 as illustrated.
5. Hold the **Ctrl** key down.
6. Click a **position** above Drawing View2.
7. Release the **Ctrl** key. Flip the arrows if required.

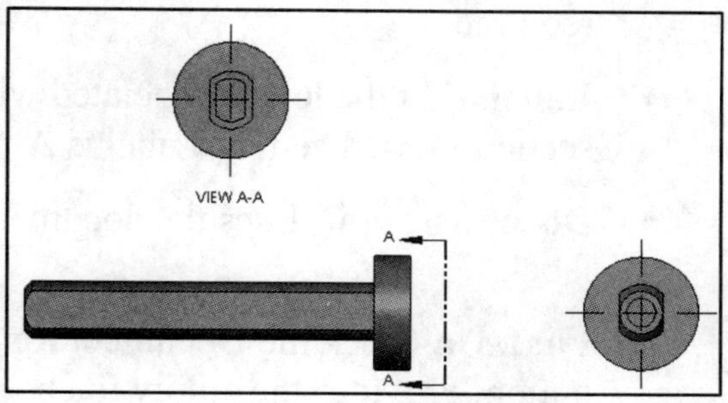


8. Drag the **View A-A** text below the Drawing View3 view boundary.
9. Drag the **A-A arrow** as illustrated.
10. Click **OK** from the Auxiliary View PropertyManager.
11. **Rebuild** the drawing.
12. **Close** the drawing.

### *Tutorial: Auxiliary View 13-2*

Create an Auxilary view from an existing Front view.

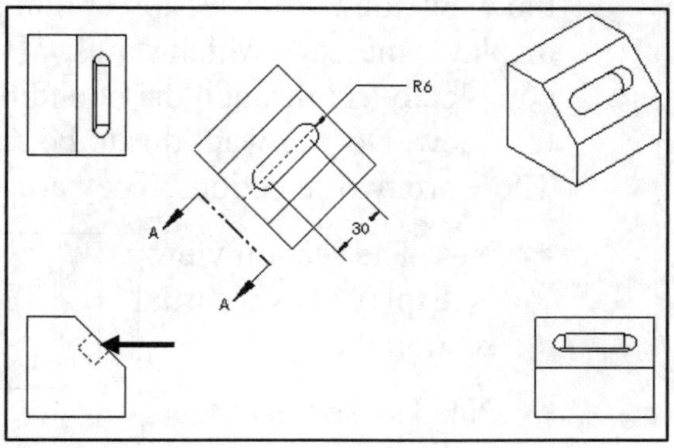


1. Open **Auxiliary View 13-2** from the SolidWorks 2010\Drawing folder.
2. Click the **angled edge** in Drawing View1 as illustrated.
3. Click the **Auxiliary View** drawing tool.
4. Click a **position** up and to the right.
5. Drag the **A-A arrow** as illustrated.
6. Drag the **text** off the view.

7. Click **OK** from the Auxiliary View PropertyManager.
8. **Close** the drawing.

## Section View tool

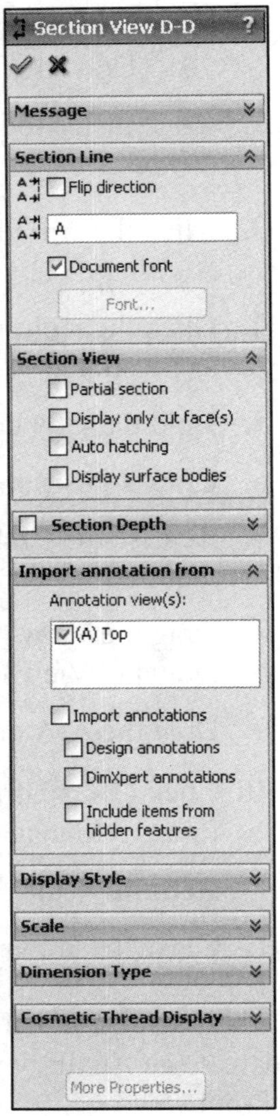


The Section View tool adds a section view by cutting the parent view with a section line. The section view can be a straight cut section or an offset section defined by a stepped section line. The section line can also include concentric arcs. The Section View tool uses the Section View PropertyManager. The Section View PropertyManager provides the following selections:

- ***Section Line***. The Section Line box provides the following selections:
  - **Flip direction**. Flips the direction of the section cut if required.
  - **Label**. Edit the letter associated with the section line and section view. The first Label is A by default.
  - **Document font**. Uses the document font for the section line label.
  - **Font**. Un-check the Document font box to use the Font button. Provides the ability to choose a font for the section line label other than the document's font.
- ***Section View***. The Section View box provides the following selections:
  - **Partial section**. If the section line does not completely cross the view, the Partial section option provides the ability to display a message which states, "The section line does not completely cut through the bounding box of the model in this view. Do you want this to be a partial section cut?" There are two selections. They are:
    - **Yes**. The section view is displayed as a partial section view.
    - **No**. The section view is displayed with not cut.

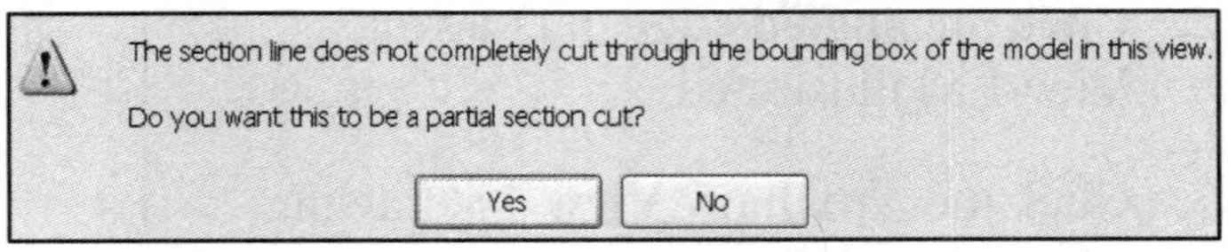


  - **Display only cut faces(s)**. Only displays the faces cut by the section line.

- **Auto hatching**. Provides the ability to crosshatch patterns alternate between components in assemblies, or between bodies in multi-body parts and weldments.
- **Displays surface bodies**. Surface body is a general term that describes connected zero-thickness geometries such as single surfaces, knit surfaces, trimmed and filleted surfaces, and so on.

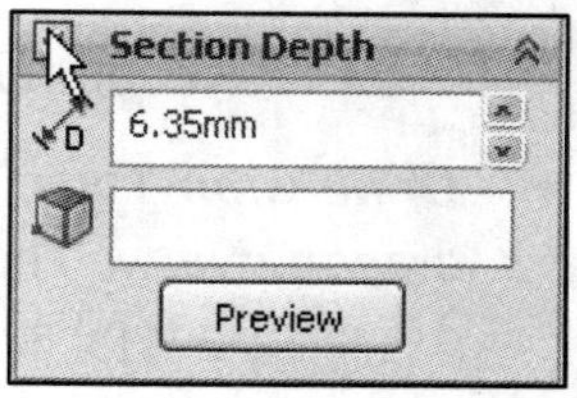


- ***Section Depth***. The Section Depth box provides the following options:
  - **Depth**. Enter Section depth.
  - **Depth Reference**. Select geometry, such as an edge or an axis, in the parent view for the Depth Reference. Drag the pink section plane in the Graphics window to set the depth of the cut.
  - **Preview**. Provides the ability to view how the section view will look with the section depth settings before you close the Section View PropertyManager.

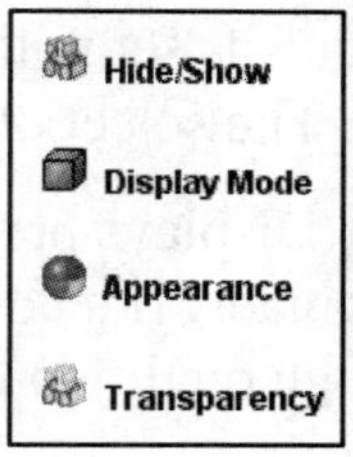


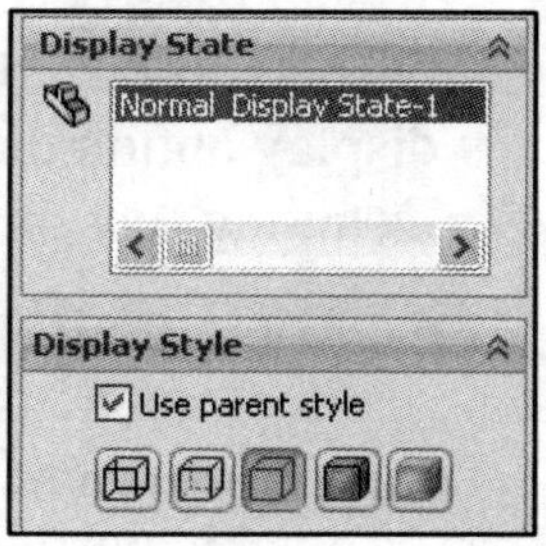


- ***Display State***. Only available for assemblies. Defines different combinations of settings for each component in an assembly, and save this settings in Display States. The available settings are: **Hide/Show state**, **Display Mode**, **Appearance** and **Transparency**.
- ***Display Style***. Displays drawing views in the following style modes. They are: **Wireframe**, **Hidden Lines Visible**, **Hidden Lines Removed**, **Shaded With Edges** and **Shaded**.

The Use parent style check box option provides the ability to apply the same display style used from the parent.

When in the Hidden Lines Visible or Hidden Lines Removed mode, you can select a style for Tangent Edge Display.

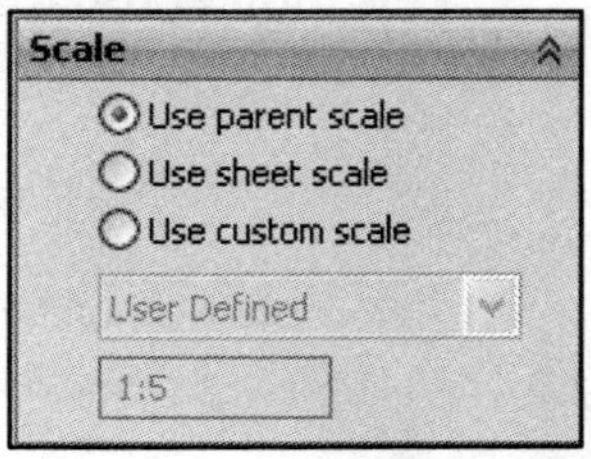


- ***Scale***. The Scale box provides the following sections. They are:
  - **Use Parent scale**. Applies the same scale used for the parent view. If you modify the scale of a parent view, the scale of all child views that use the parent scale is updated.

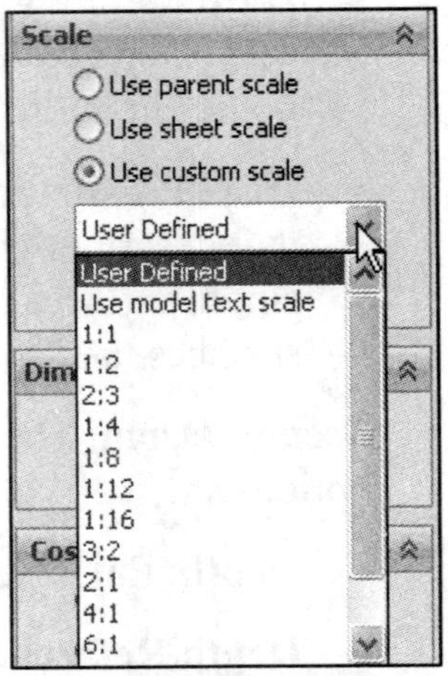


- **Use sheet scale**. Applies the same scale used for the drawing sheet.
- **Use custom scale**. Creates a custom scale for your drawing. There are two selections:
  - **User Defined**. Enter a scale value.
  - **Use model text scale**. Uses the model scale.
- ***Dimension Type***. Set the dimension type when you insert a drawing view. The Dimension Type box provides two dimension type selections. They are:
  - **Projected**. Displays 2D dimensions.
  - **True**. Displays accurate model values.

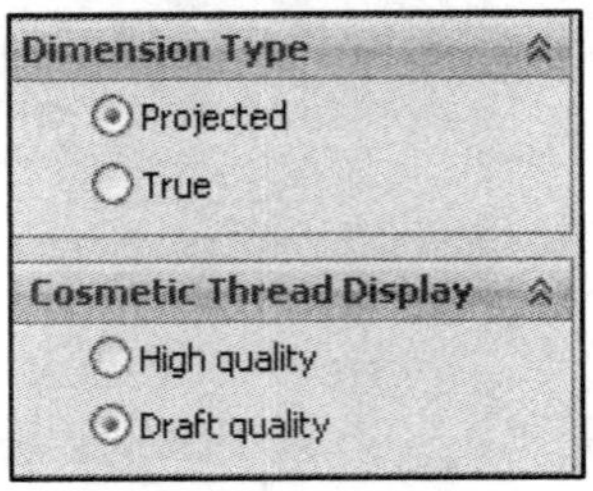


SolidWorks specifies Projected type dimensions for standard and custom orthogonal views and True type for Isometric, Dimetric and Trimetric views.

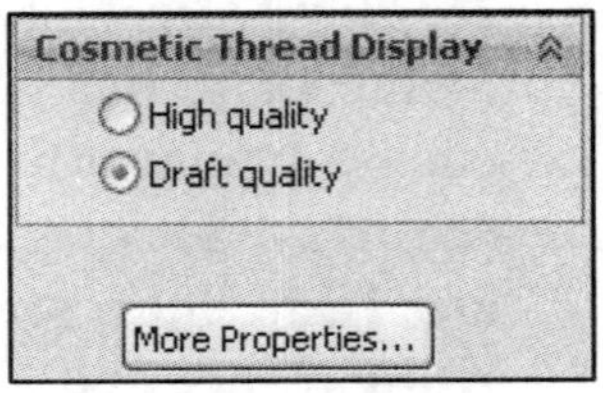


- ***Cosmetic Thread Display***. Provides the ability to set either the High quality or Draft quality settings from the Model View PropertyManager. The setting in the Cosmetic Thread Display, if different will override the Cosmetic thread display option that was set in the Document Properties, Detailing section. The selections are:
  - **High quality**. Displays precise line fonts and trimming in cosmetic threads. If a cosmetic thread is only partially visible, the High quality option will display only the visible portion.
  - **Draft quality**. Displays cosmetic threads with less detail. If a cosmetic thread is only partially visible, the Draft quality option will display the entire feature.
  - **More Properties**. Provides the ability to modify the bill or materials information, show hidden edges, etc. after a view is created or by selecting an existing view from the drawing sheet or FeatureManager. The More Properties option activates the Drawing View Properties dialog box.

***Tutorial: Section View 13-1***

Create a Section view and modify the drawing view scale.

1. Open **Section View 13-1** from the SolidWorks 2010\Drawing folder.
2. Click inside the **Drawing View1** view boundary. The Drawing View1 PropertyManager is displayed.

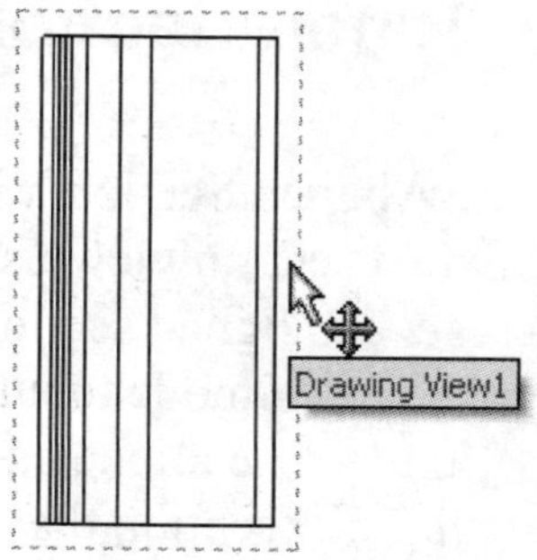


Display the origins on Sheet1.

3. Click **View ➤ Origins** from the Menu bar.
4. Click the **Section View** drawing tool. The Section View PropertyManager is displayed.
5. Sketch a **vertical section line** coincident with the Right plane through the origin as illustrated.
6. Click **Yes** to continue.
7. Click a **position** to the right of Drawing View1. The section arrows point to the right. If required, click Flip direction.
8. Check **Auto hatching** from the Section View box.
9. Check the **Shaded With Edges** option from the Display Style box.

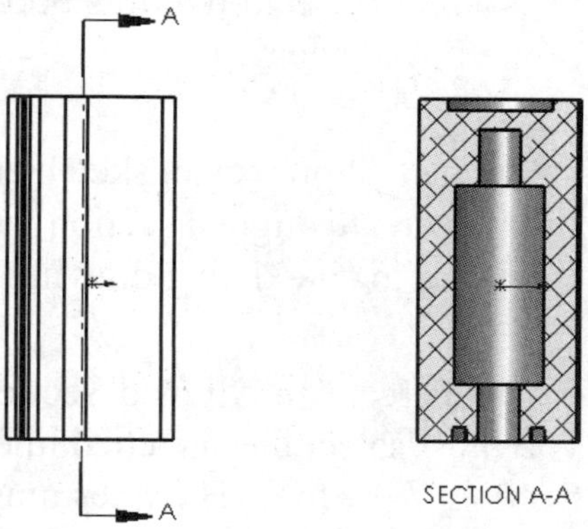


10. Click **OK** from the Section View A-A PropertyManager. Section View A-A is created and is displayed in the Drawing FeatureManager.
11. Click inside the **Drawing View1** view boundary. The Drawing View1 PropertyManager is displayed.

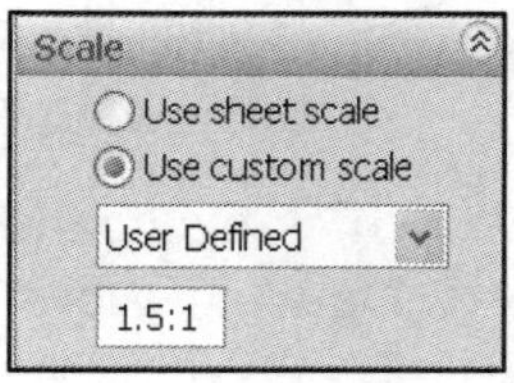


12. Modify the Scale to **1.5:1**.
13. Click **OK** from the Drawing View1 PropertyManager. Both drawing views are modified.
14. **Close** the drawing.

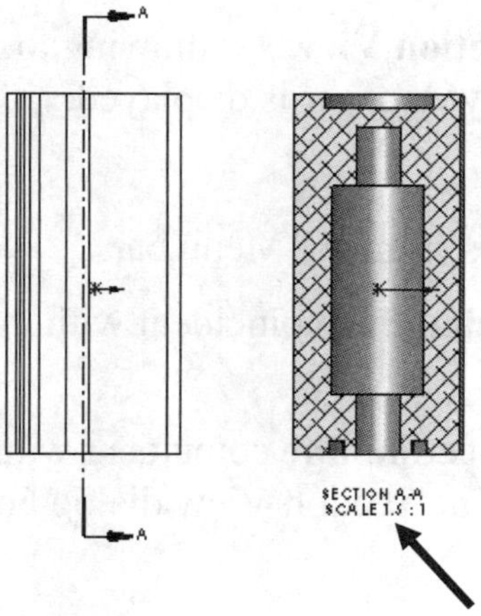


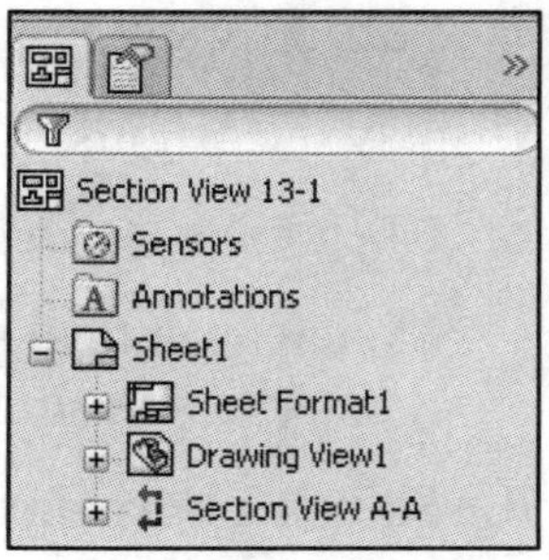

# Aligned Section View tool

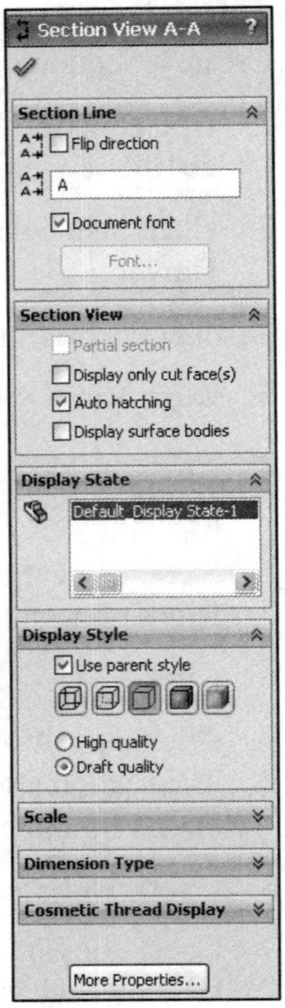


The Aligned Section View tool provides the ability to add an aligned section view using two lines connected at an angle. You can create an aligned section view in a drawing through a model, or portion of a model, that is aligned with a selected section line segment. The aligned section view is very similar to a section view, with the exception that the section line for an aligned section comprises of two or more lines connected at an angle. The Aligned Section View tool uses the Section View PropertyManager. View the Section View section in this book for detail information on the PropertyManager.

You can pre-select sketch entities that belong to the drawing sheet to create aligned section views. The sketch entities do not have to belong to an existing drawing view.

To create an Aligned Section view with more than two lines, you must select the sketched lines before clicking the Aligned Section View tool. The lines must be connected at an angle and cannot form multiple contours.

### *Tutorial: Aligned Section View 13-1*

Create an Aligned Section view.

1. Open **Aligned Section View 13-1** from the SolidWorks 2010\Drawing folder.
2. Click inside the **Drawing View1** view boundary. The Drawing View1 PropertyManager is displayed.

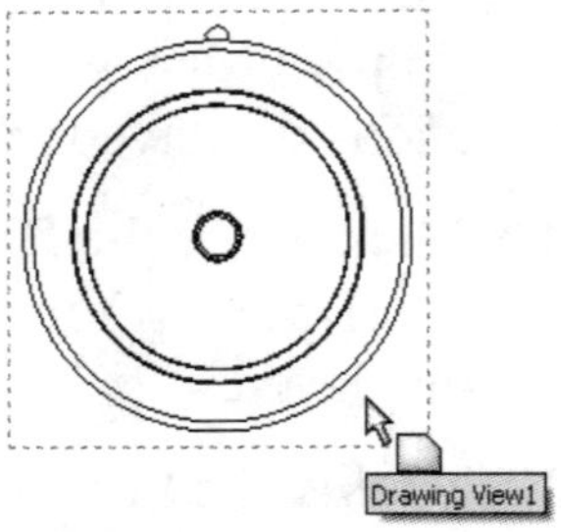


3. Click the **Aligned Section View** drawing tool. The Section View PropertyManager is displayed.

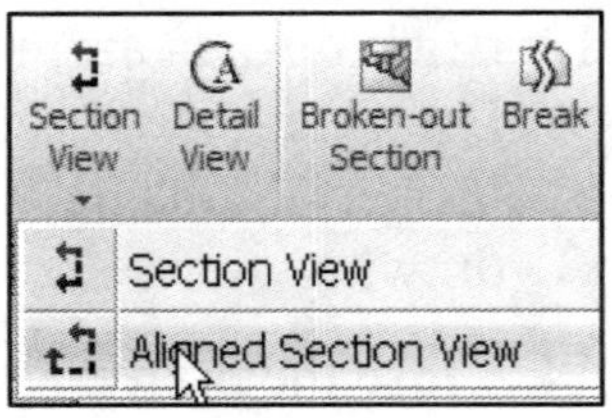


Display the origins.

4. Click **View ➢ Origins** from the Menu bar.
5. Sketch a **vertical section line** coincident with the origin (center) as illustrated.
6. Sketch a **horizontal section line** coincident with the origin as illustrated. The Section View dialog box is displayed.

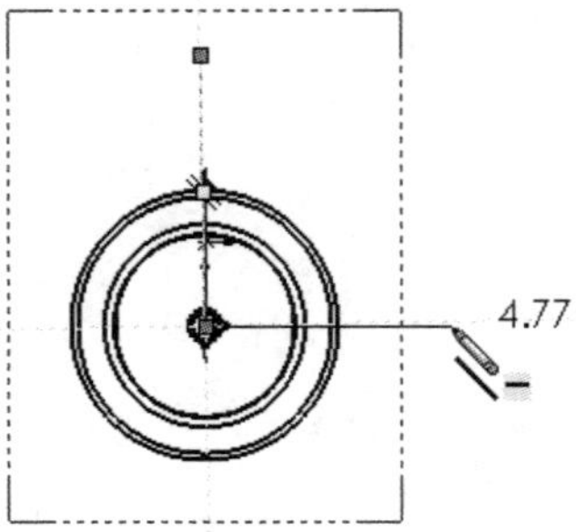

7. Click the **LENSCAP** in the Graphics window as illustrated. The LENSCAP component is displayed in the Excluded components box.
8. Check the **Auto hatching** box.
9. Click **OK** from the Section View dialog box.
10. Click a **position** above Drawing View1.
11. Click **OK** from the Section View A-A PropertyManager.
12. Modify the **scale to 1:4**.

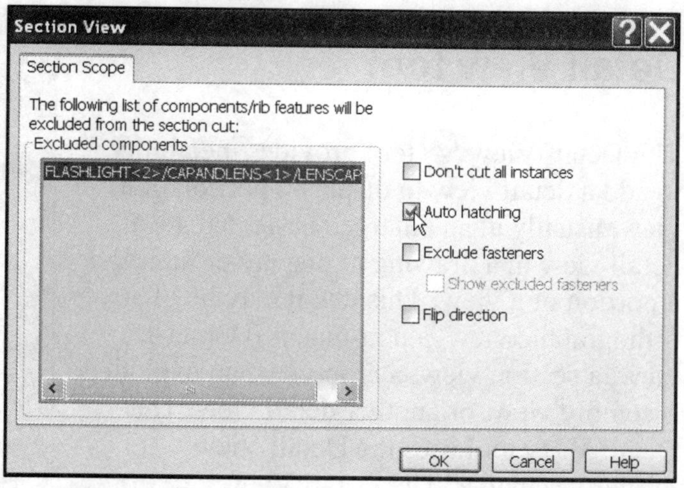


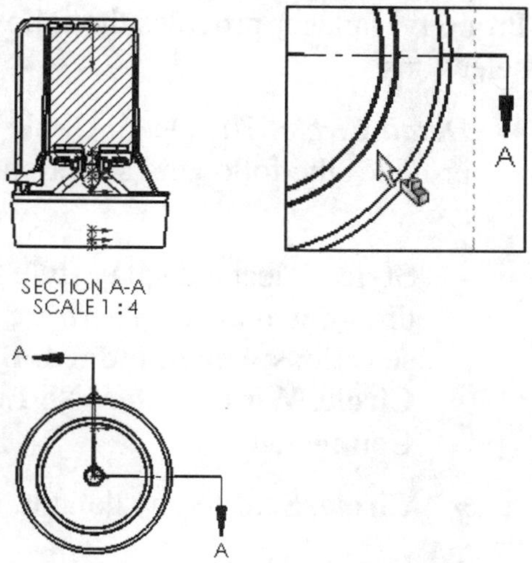


Deactivate the origin display.

13. Click **View** ➢ uncheck **Origins** from the Menu bar.
14. **Rebuild** the drawing.
15. **Move** the Drawing Views to fit the Sheet. View the drawing FeatureManager.
16. **Close** the drawing.

You can copy sheets within the same document or between documents.

***Tutorial: Copy / Paste 13-1***

1. Open **Copy-Paste 13-1** from the SolidWorks 2010\Drawing folder.
2. Right-click the **Sheet1** tab at the bottom of the Graphics window.
3. Click **Copy**.
4. Right-click the **Sheet1 tab** at the bottom of the Graphics window.
5. Click **Paste**. The Insert Paste dialog box is displayed.
6. Check the **After selected sheet** box.
7. Click **OK**. View the results. You copied the drawing view from Sheet1 to Sheet2.
8. **Close** the model.

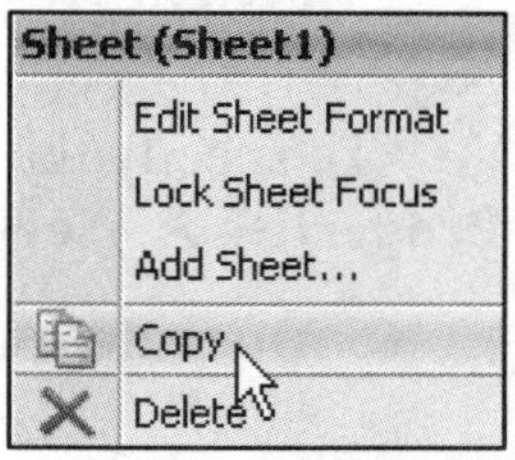


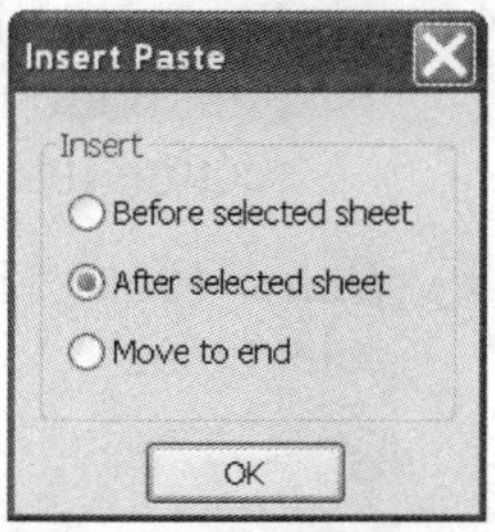

## Detail View tool

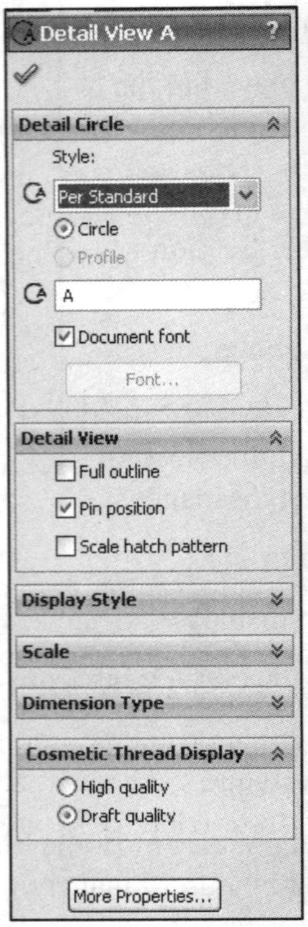


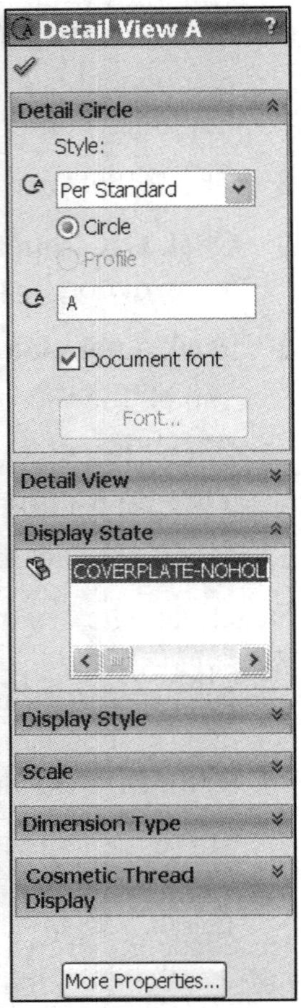


The Detail View tool provides the ability to add a detail view to display a portion of a view, usually at an enlarged scale. Create a detail view in a drawing to display or highlight a portion of a view. This detail may be of an orthographic view, a non-planar (isometric) view, a section view, a crop view, an exploded assembly view, or another detail view. The Detail View tool uses the Detail View PropertyManager. The Detail View PropertyManager provides the following selections:

- ***Detail Circle***. The Detail Circle box provides the following selections. They are:
  - **Style**. Select a display style from the drop-down menu. There are five selections: **Per Standard**, **Broken Circle**, **With Leader**, **No Leader** and **Connected**.
  - **Circle**. Selected by default. Displays a circle.
  - **Profile**. Displays a profile.
  - **Label**. Provides a letter associated with the section line and section view. The first Label is A by default.

To specify the label format, click **Options** ➢ **Document Properties** ➢ **View Labels** from the Menu bar.

  - **Document font**. Uses the document font for the section line label.
  - **Font**. Un-check the Document font check box to use the Font button. Provides the ability to choose a font for the section line label other than the document's font.

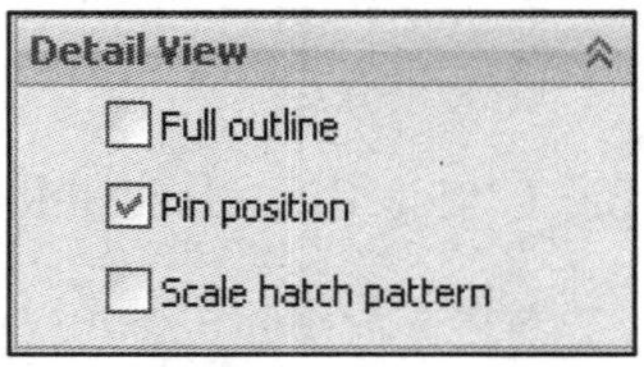


- ***Detail View***. The Detail View box provides the following selections:

- **Full outline**. Displays the profile outline in the detail view.
- **Pin position**. Selected by default. Keeps the detail view in the same relative position on the drawing sheet if you modify the scale of the view.
- **Scale hatch pattern**. Displays the hatch pattern based on the scale of the detail view rather than the scale of the section view. This option applies to detail views created from section views.

- ***Options***. Only available if the model was created with annotation views. The Options box provides the following selections.
  - **Annotation view(s)**. Select an annotation view, if the model was created with annotation views. The view will include annotations from the model.
- ***Display State***. Only available for assemblies. Defines the different combinations of settings for each component in an assembly, and save this settings in Display States. The available settings are: **Hide/Show state, Display Mode, Appearance** and **Transparency**.

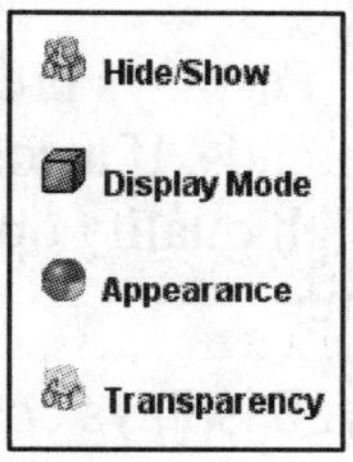


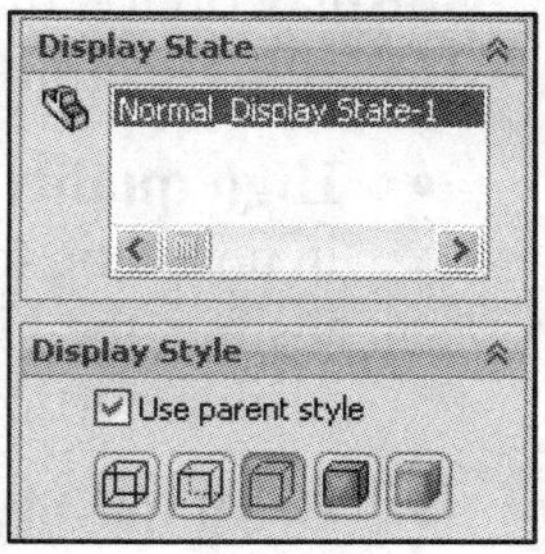


- ***Display Style***. Displays drawing views in the following style modes. They are: **Wireframe, Hidden Lines Visible, Hidden Lines Removed, Shaded With Edges** and **Shaded**.

The Use parent style check box option provides the ability to apply the same display style used from the parent.

When in the Hidden Lines Visible or Hidden Lines Removed mode, you can select a style for Tangent Edge Display.

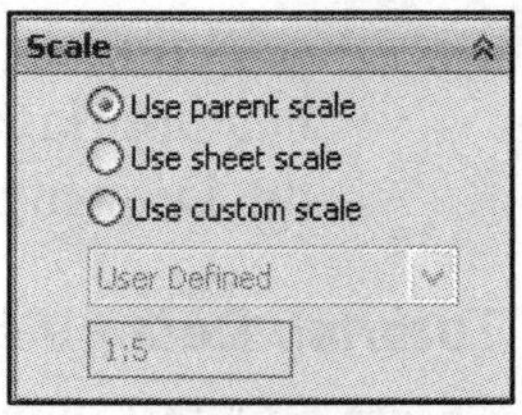


- ***Scale***. The Scale box provides the following sections. They are:
  - **Use Parent scale**. Applies the same scale used for the parent view. If you modify the scale of a parent view, the scale of all child views that use the parent scale is updated.
  - **Use sheet scale**. Applies the same scale used for the drawing sheet.
  - **Use custom scale**. Creates a custom scale for your drawing. There are two selections:
    - **User Defined**. Enter a scale value.

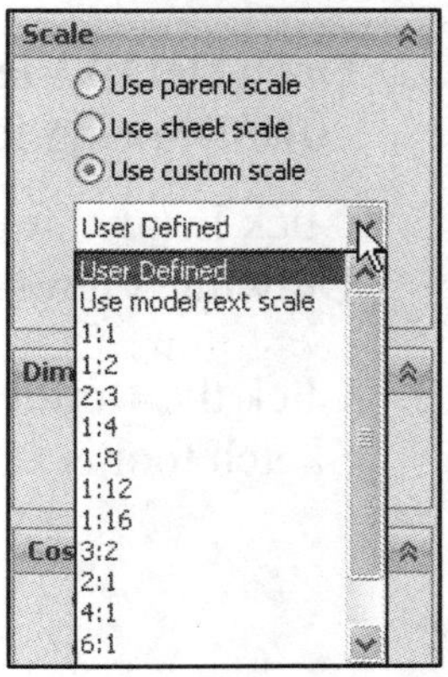

- **Use model text scale**. Uses model scale.

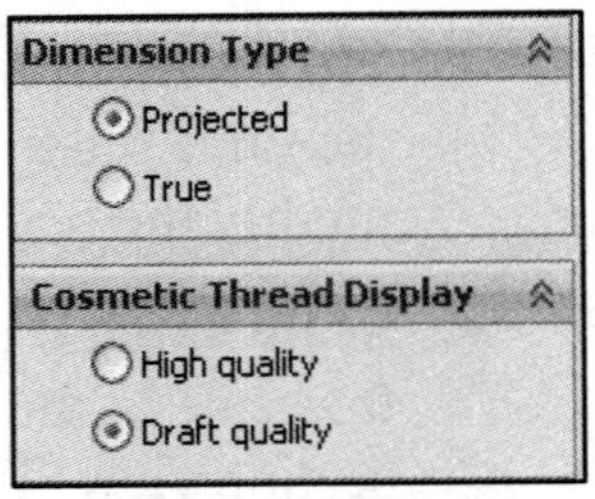


- ***Dimension Type***. Sets the dimension type when you insert a drawing view. The Dimension Type box provides two dimension type selections. They are:
  - **Projected**. Displays 2D dimensions.
  - **True**. Displays accurate model values.

SolidWorks specifies Projected type dimensions for standard and custom orthogonal views and True type for Isometric, Dimetric and Trimetric views.

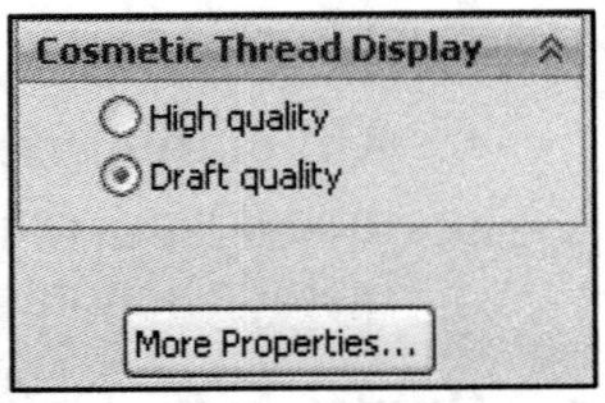


- ***Cosmetic Thread Display***. Sets either the High quality or Draft quality settings from the Model View PropertyManager. The setting in the Cosmetic Thread Display, if different will override the Cosmetic thread display option that was set in the Document Properties, Detailing section. The selections are:
  - **High quality**. Displays precise line fonts and trimming in cosmetic threads. If a cosmetic thread is only partially visible, the High quality option will display only the visible portion.
  - **Draft quality**. Displays cosmetic threads with less detail. If a cosmetic thread is only partially visible, the Draft quality option will display the entire feature.
  - **More Properties**. The More Properties button provides the ability to modify the bill or materials information, show hidden edges, etc. after a view is created or by selecting an existing view from the drawing sheet or FeatureManager. The More Properties option activates the Drawing View Properties dialog box.

### *Tutorial: Detail View 13-1*

Create a Detail view from an existing view.

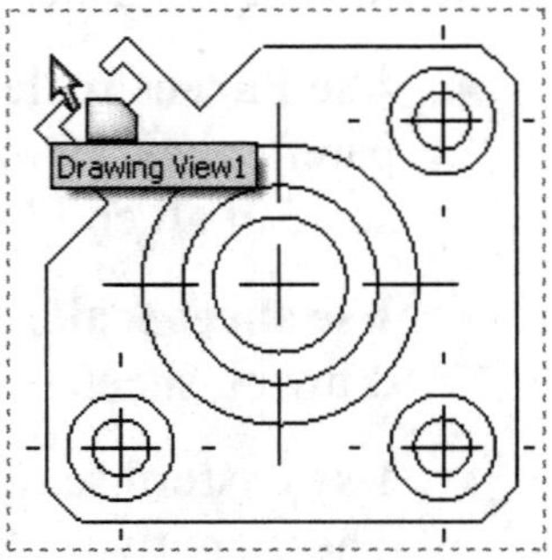


1. Open **Detail View 13-1** from the SolidWorks 2010\Drawing folder.
2. Click inside the **Drawing View1** view boundary. The Drawing View1 PropertyManager is displayed.
3. Click the **Detail View** drawing tool. The Circle Sketch tool is activated.

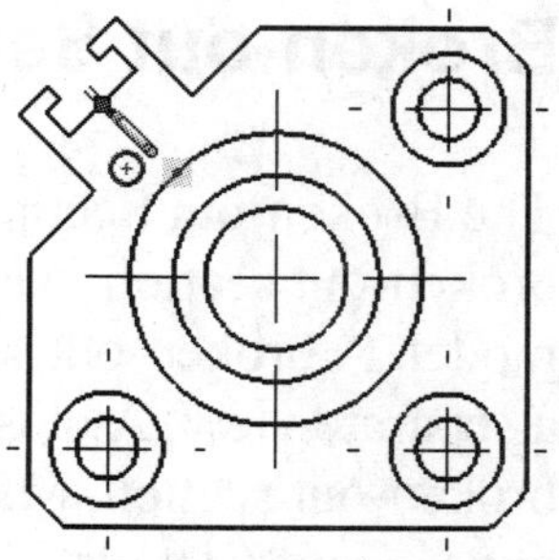

4. Click the **middle** of the Switch Grove in the Front view as illustrated.
5. Drag the **mouse pointer** outward.
6. Click a **position** just below the large circle to create the sketched circle. The Detail View A PropertyManager is displayed.
7. Click a **position** to the left of DrawingView1.
8. Check the **Use custom scale** box.
9. Select **User Defined**.
10. Enter **3:1** in the Custom Scale text box.
11. Click **Hidden Lines Visible** from the Display Style box.
12. Click **OK** from the Detail View A PropertyManager.

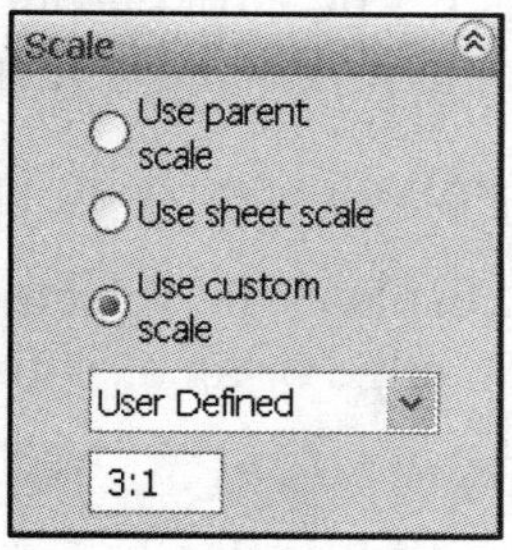


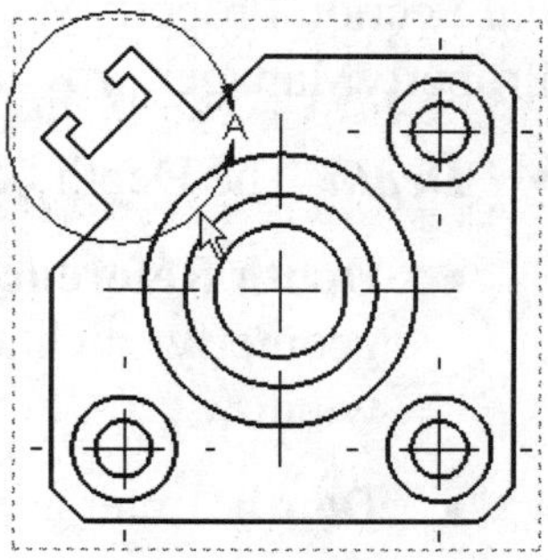


13. Drag the **text** off the profile lines.
14. **Rebuild** the drawing.
15. **Close** the drawing.

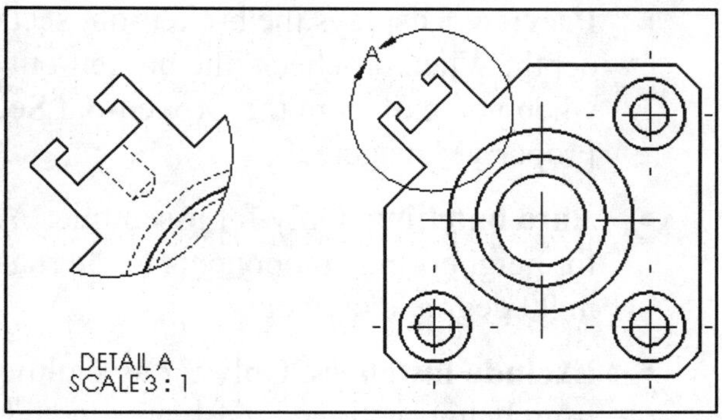


The Hole Wizard information from a model propagates to the drawing when the Hole Callout button is selected.

Use the Smart Dimension tool to input drawing dimensions. Typically, you create dimensions as you create each part feature, then insert those dimensions into the various drawing views. Changing a dimension in the model updates the drawing and changing an inserted dimension in a drawing changes the model.

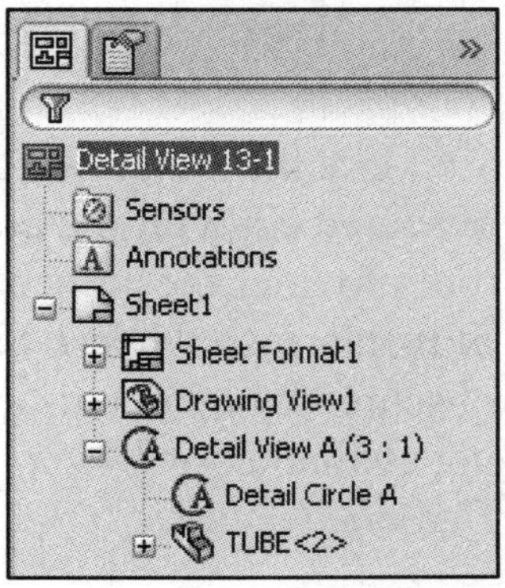


Reference dimensions show measurements of the model, but they do not drive the model and you cannot change their values. However, when you change the model, the reference dimensions update accordingly. Reference dimensions are enclosed in parentheses by default.

## Broken-out Section tool

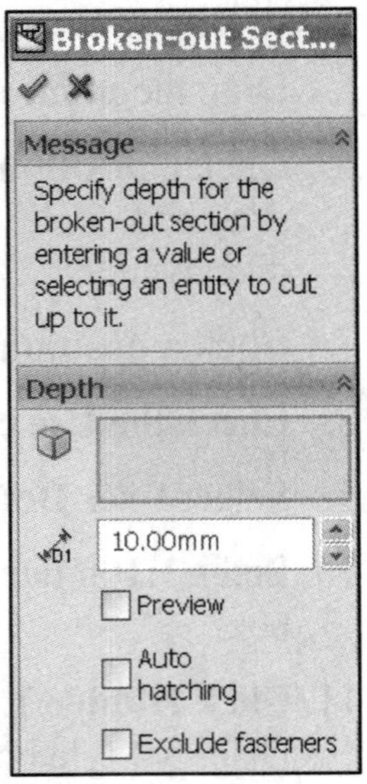


The Broken-out Section tool provides the ability to add a broken-out section to an existing view exposing inner details of a model. A broken-out section is part of an existing drawing view, not a separate view. A closed profile, usually a spline, defines the broken-out section. Material is removed to a specified depth to expose inner details. The Broken-out Section tool uses the Broken-out Section PropertyManager. The Broken-out Section PropertyManager provides the following selections:

- ***Depth***. The Depth box provides the following options:
  - **Depth Reference**. Displays the selected depth reference geometry, such as an edge or an axis from the Graphic window.
  - **Depth**. Enter a value for the depth.
  - **Preview**. Displays the broken-out section as you change the depth. When un-check, the broken-out section is applied when you exit from the Broken-out Section PropertyManager.
  - **Auto hatching**. Only for assemblies. Automatically adjust for neighboring components to alternate crosshatch patterns in 90 degree increments.
  - **Exclude fasteners**. Only for assemblies. Excludes fasteners from being sectioned. Fasteners include any item inserted from SolidWorks Toolbox (nuts, bolts, washers, etc).

Use the 3D drawing view tool to select an obscured edge for the depth. The 3D drawing view tool provides the ability to rotate a drawing view out of its plane so you can view components or edges obscured by other entities. 3D drawing view mode is not available for *Detail, Broken, Crop and Empty or Detached views*.

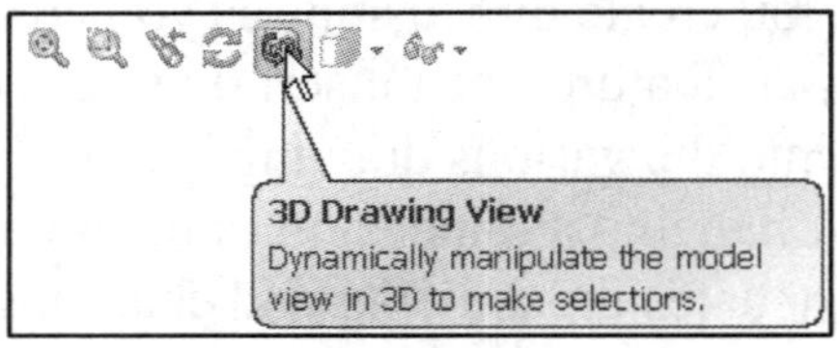


#### *Tutorial: Broken-out Section View - 3D drawing View 13-1*

Create a Broken-out Section view using the Spline Sketch tool and the 3D drawing view tool.

1. Open **Broken-out Section View 13-1** from the SolidWorks 2010\Drawing folder.
2. Click inside the **Drawing View1** view boundary. The Drawing View1 PropertyManager is displayed. Apply the 3D drawing view tool.

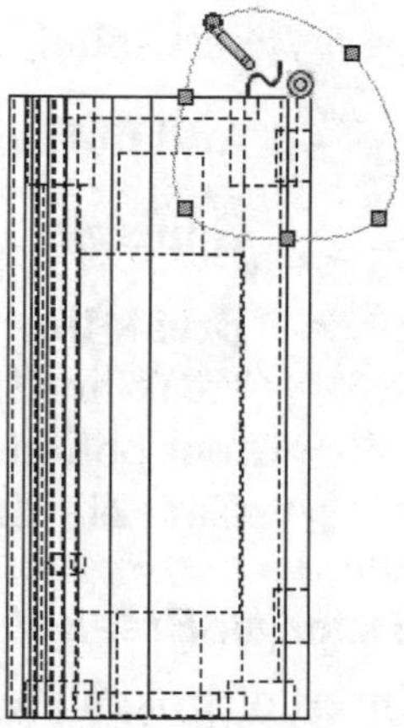

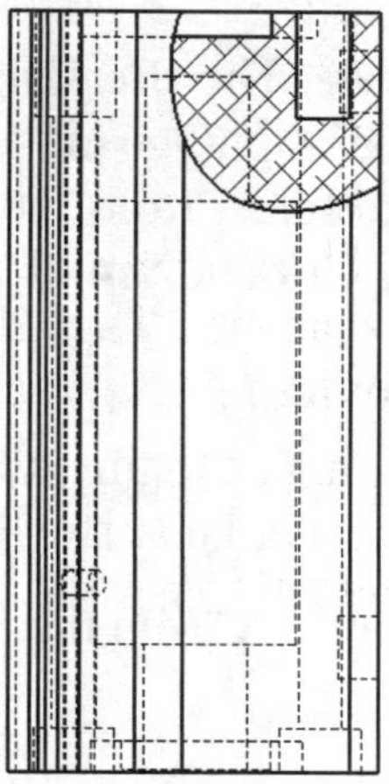

3. Click the **3D drawing view** tool from the View toolbar. The Rotate icon is displayed.
4. **Rotate** the view.
5. Click the **green check mark** to exit the 3D drawing view mode and to return to the normal view.
6. Click the **Spline** Sketch tool. The Spline PropertyManager is displayed.
7. Sketch a **closed Spline** in the top right corner as illustrated.
8. Right-click **End Spline**.
9. Click the **Broken-out Section** drawing tool. The Broken-out Section PropertyManager is displayed.
10. Enter **.3**in for Depth.
11. Check **Preview**. View the Broken-out Section preview in the Graphics window.
12. Click **OK** from the Broken-out Section PropertyManager. View the Drawing FeatureManager.
13. **Close** the drawing.

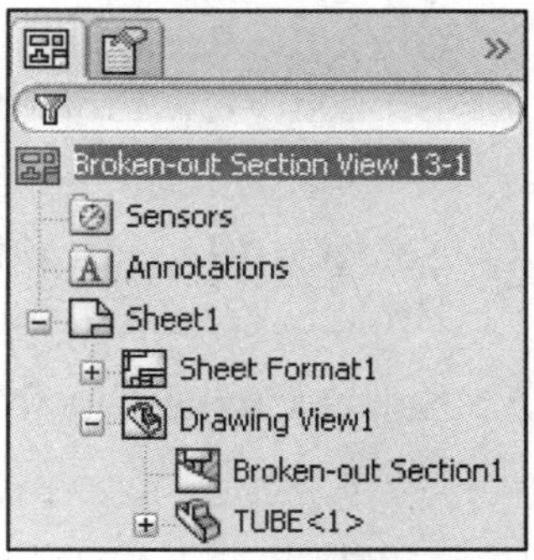


You cannot create a broken-out section on a detail, section, or alternate position view. If you create a broken-out section on an exploded view, the view is no longer exploded.

## Break tool

The Break tool provides the ability to add a break line to a selected view. Create a broken (or interrupted) view in a drawing. Use the Broken view to display the drawing view in a larger scale on a smaller size drawing sheet. Reference dimensions and model dimensions associated with the broken area reflect the actual model values. The Break tool uses the Broken View PropertyManager. The Broken View PropertyManager provides the following selections:

- ***Broken View Settings***. The Broken View Settings box provides the following options:

- **Add vertical break line**. Selected by default. Adds a vertical break line.
- **Add horizontal break line**. Adds a horizontal break line.
- **Gap size**. Sets the value of the space between the gap.
- **Break line style**. The Break line style option defines the break line type. Zig Zag Cut selected by default. There are four options to select from. They are: **Straight Cut**, **Curve Cut**, **Zig Zag Cut** and **Small Zig Zag Cut**.

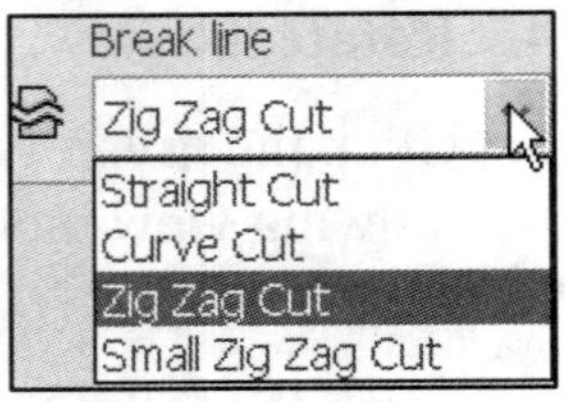


***Tutorial: Break View 13-1***

Insert a Broken view in an existing drawing view. Use the Break drawing tool. Note the available Break line options.

1. Open **Break View 13-1** from the SolidWorks 2010\Drawing folder.
2. Click **inside** the Drawing View1 view boundary. The Drawing View1 PropertyManager is displayed.
3. Click the **Break** drawing tool. The Broken View PropertyManager is displayed.

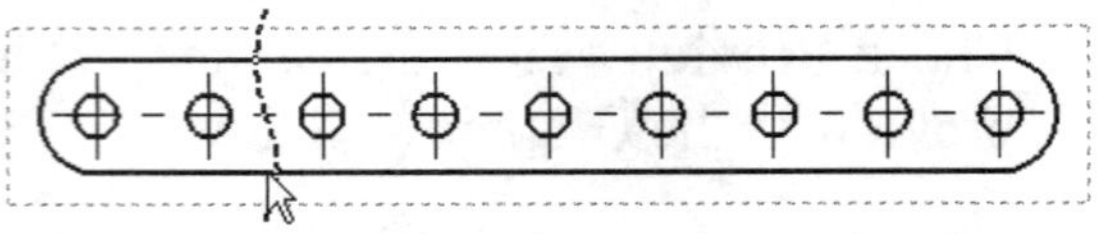

4. Select **Add vertical break line** from the Broken View Settings box.
5. Select **Curve Cut** from the Break line box.

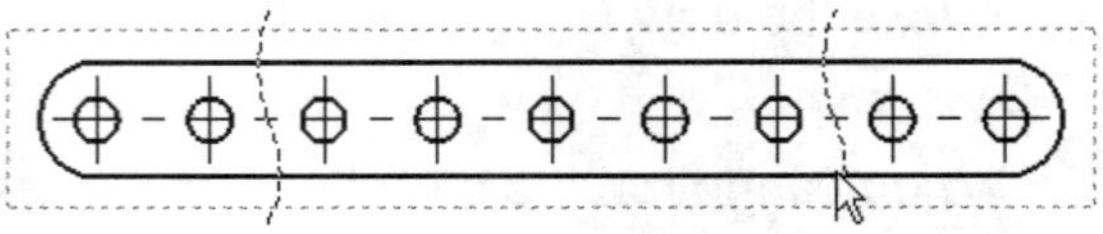

6. Enter .**4**in for Gap.
7. Click the **two locations** as illustrated in the Graphics window.

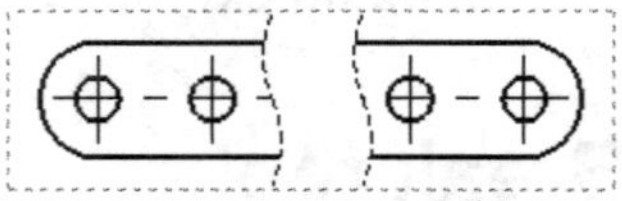

8. Click **OK** from the Broken View PropertyManager. View the Drawing FeatureManager.
9. **Close** the drawing.

# Crop tool

The Crop tool provides the ability to crop an existing drawing view. You can not use the Crop tool on a Detail View, a view from which a Detail View has been created, or an exploded view. Use the Crop tool to save steps. Example: instead of creating a Section View and then a Detail View, then hiding the unnecessary Section View, use the Crop tool to crop the Section View directly. The Crop tool does not use a PropertyManager.

***Tutorial: Crop view 13-1***

Crop an existing drawing view. Apply the Crop View drawing tool with the Spline Sketch tool.

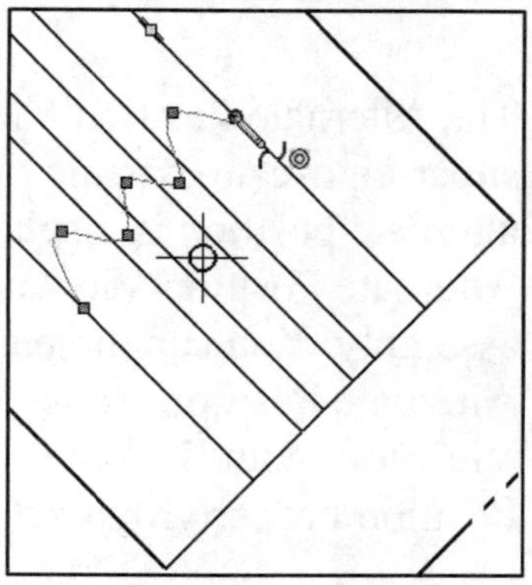

1. Open **Crop View 13-1** from the SolidWorks 2010\Drawing folder.
2. Click inside the **Drawing View2** view boundary. The Drawing View2 PropertyManager is displayed.
3. Click the **Spline** Sketch tool. The Spline PropertyManager is displayed.
4. Sketch **7 control points** as illustrated.
5. Right-click **End Spline**.

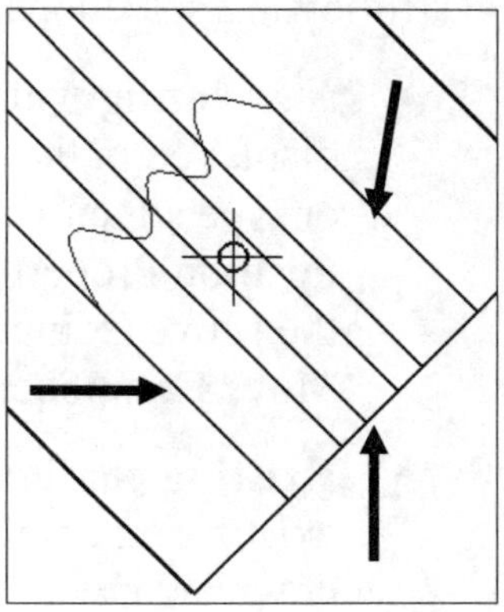

6. Click the **Line** Sketch tool. The Insert Line PropertyManager is displayed.
7. Sketch **three lines** as illustrated. The first line, the first point must display Endpoint interference with the first point of the spline. The second line is collinear with the bottom edge of the view. The third line, the last point must display Endpoint interference with the last point of the spline.
8. Right-click **Select** in the Graphics window.
9. Window-Select the **three lines** and the **Spline**. The selected sketch entities are displayed in the Properties PropertyManager.

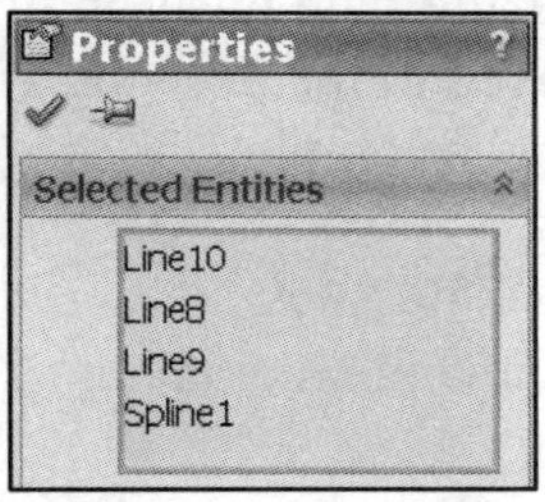


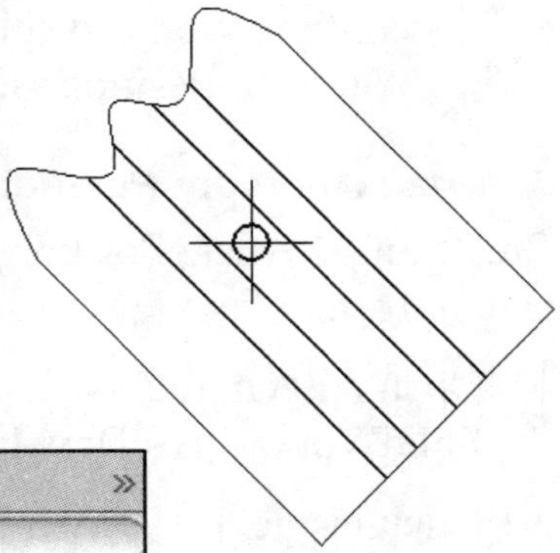

10. Click the **Crop View** drawing tool. The selected view is cropped.
11. Click **OK** from the Properties PropertyManager. View the Drawing FeatureManager.
12. **Close** the drawing.

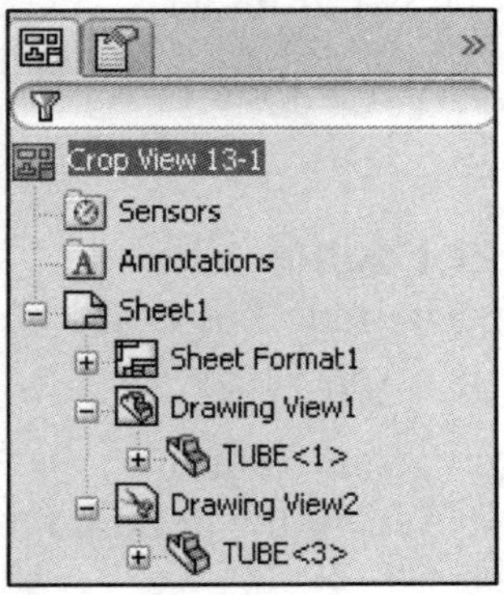

## Alternate Position View tool

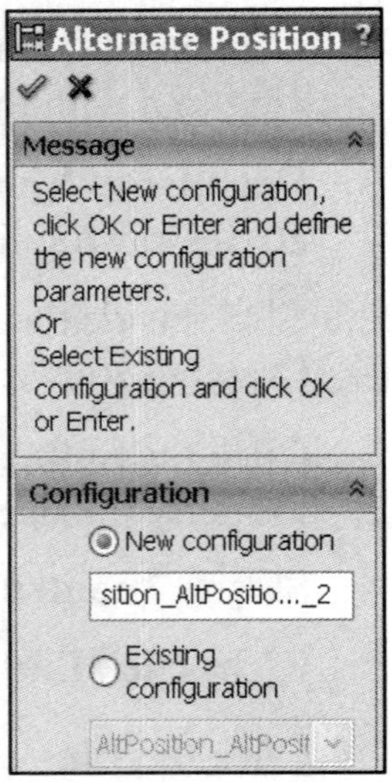


The Alternate Position View tool provides the ability to superimpose an existing drawing view precisely on another. The alternate position is displayed with phantom lines. Use the Alternate Position View is display the range of motion of an assembly. You can dimension between the primary view and the Alternate Position View. You can not use the Alternate Position View tool with Broken, Section, or Detail views. The Alternate Position PropertyManager provides the following selections:

- ***Configuration box***. The Configuration box provides the following selections:
  - **New configuration**. Selected by default. A default name is displayed in the configuration box. Accept the default name or type a name of your choice. Click OK from the Alternate Position PropertyManager. The assembly is displayed with the Move Component PropertyManager. See section on the Move Component PropertyManager for additional details.
  - **Existing configuration**. Provides the ability to select an existing assembly configuration that is displayed in the drop down arrow box. Click OK from the Alternate Position PropertyManager. The alternate position of the selected configuration is displayed in the drawing view. The Alternate Position view is complete.

### *Tutorial: Alternate Position View 13-1*

Create an Alternate Position view in an existing assembly drawing view.

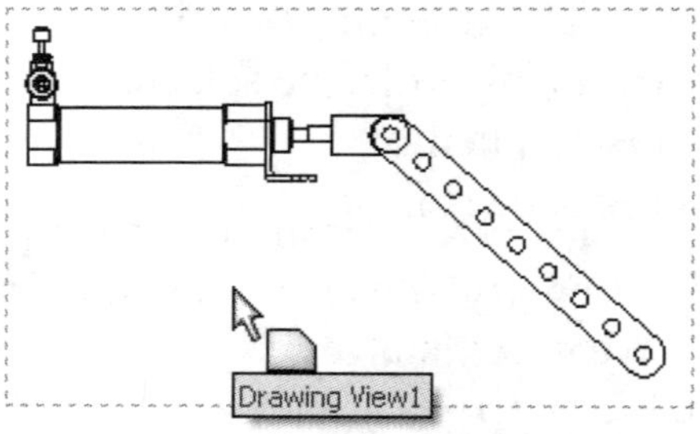


1. Open **Alternate Position View 13-1** from the SolidWorks 2010\Drawing folder.
2. Click inside the **Drawing View1** view boundary.
3. Click the **Alternate Position View** drawing tool. The Alternate Position PropertyManager is displayed.
4. Click **New configuration** from the Configuration box. Accept the default name.

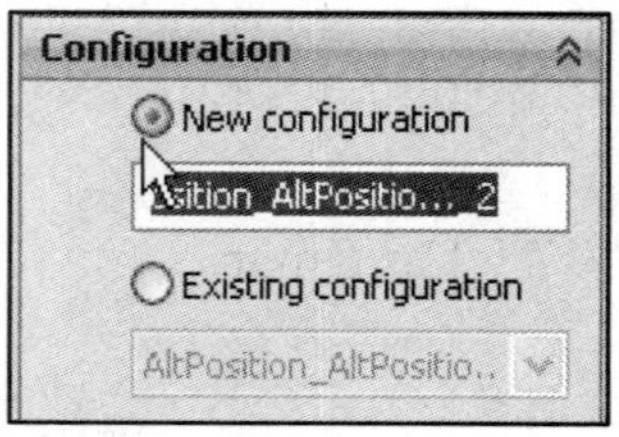

5. Click **OK** ✓ from the Alternate Position PropertyManager. If the assembly document is not already open, it opens automatically. The assembly is displayed with the Move Component PropertyManager. Free drag is selected by default in the Move box.

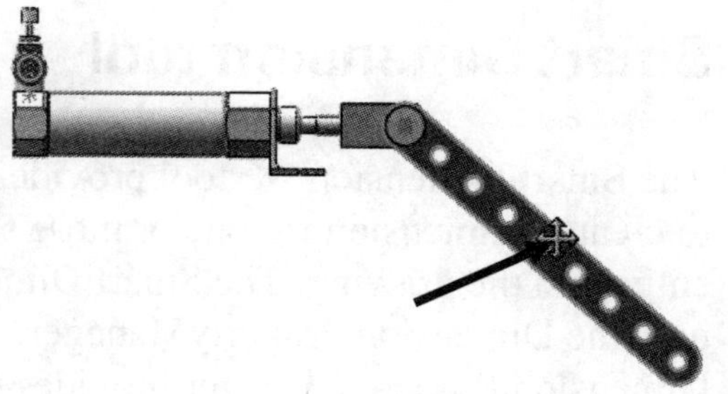

6. Click the **flatbar** in the Graphics window as illustrated.

7. Drag the **flatbar** upward to create the Alternate position.

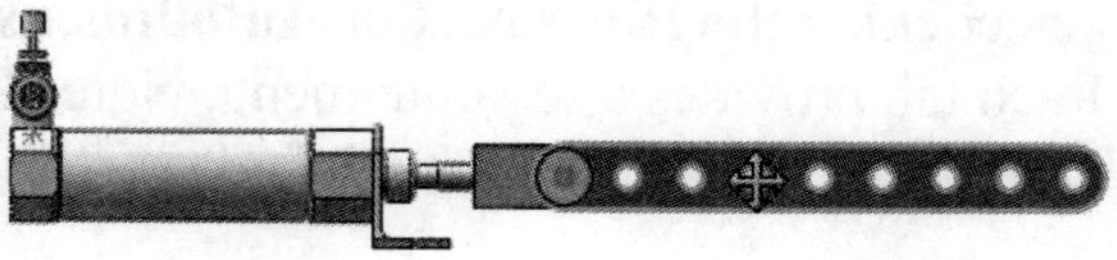

8. Click **OK** ✓ from the Move Component PropertyManager. The Alternate Position view is displayed in the Graphics window.

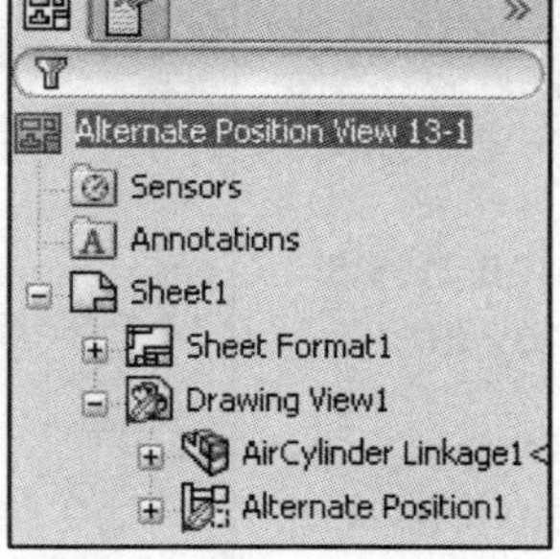


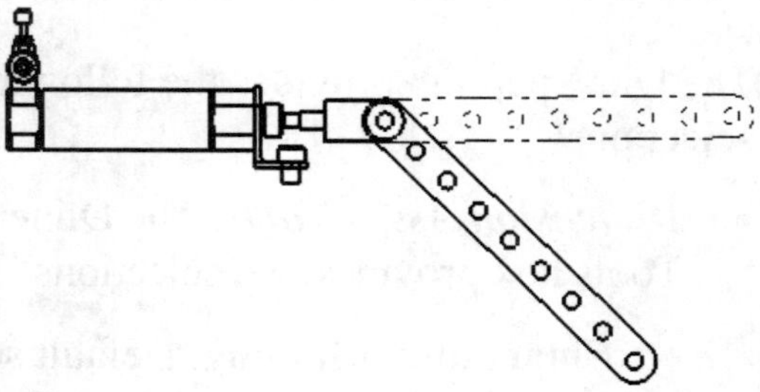

9. **Close** the drawing.

# Annotation Toolbar

Add annotations to a drawing document using the Annotation toolbar from the CommandManager.

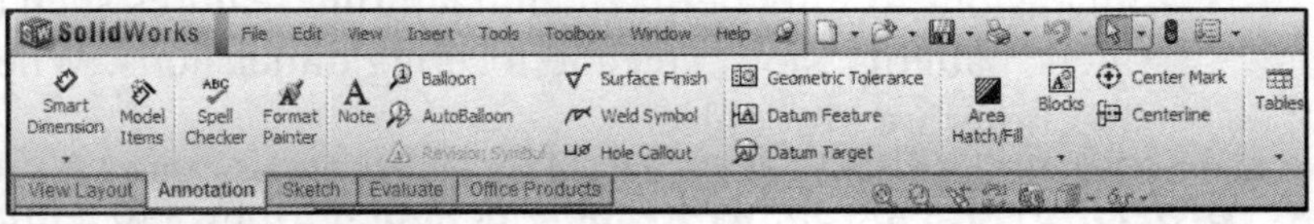


You can add most annotation types in a part or assembly document, then insert them into a drawing document. However there are some types, such as Center Marks and Area Hatch that you can only add in a drawing document.

Annotations behave like dimensions in a SolidWorks document. You can add dimensions in a part or assembly document, then insert the dimensions into the drawing, or create dimensions directly in the drawing.

The Smart Dimension drop-down menu provides access to the following options: *Horizontal Dimension, Vertical Dimension, Baseline Dimension, Ordinate Dimension, Horizontal Ordinate Dimension, Vertical Ordinate Dimension and Chamfer Dimension.*

## Smart Dimension tool

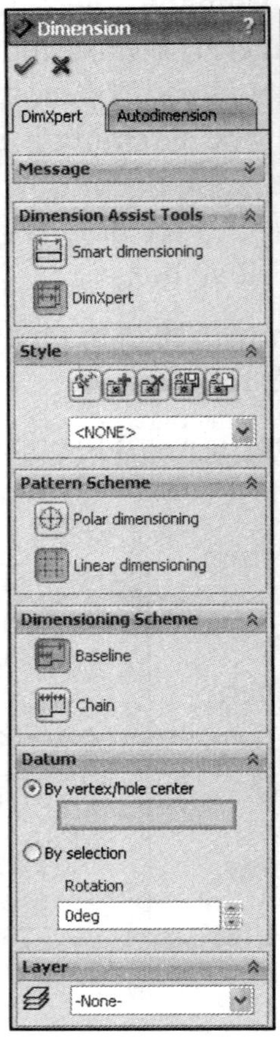


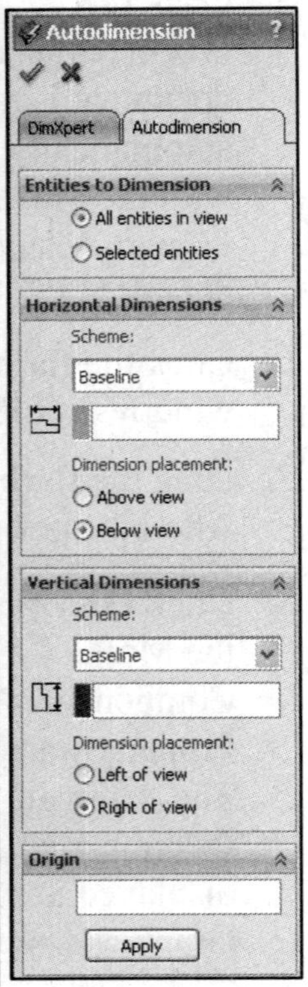


The Smart Dimension tool provides the ability to create a dimension for one or more selected entities in the drawing. The Smart Dimension tool uses the Dimension PropertyManager. The Dimension PropertyManager provides the ability to select either the **DimXpert** or **Autodimension** tab. Each tab provides a separate menu. Note: The DimXpert tab is selected by default.

### Smart Dimension tool: DimXpert tab

The DimXpert tab provides the following selections:

- ***Dimension Assist Tools***. The Dimension Assist Tools box provides two selections. They are:
  - **Smart dimensioning**. Default setting. Provides the ability to create dimensions with the Smart Dimension tool. View Chapter 5 on Smart dimensions for detail command and PropertyManager information.
  - **DimXpert**. The DimXpert provides the ability to apply dimensions to fully define manufacturing features such as: fillets, patterns, slots, etc. and locating dimensions. When selected, the following selections are available:
- ***Style***. Provides the ability to apply default attributes to a dimension, add, delete, save or load a style.
- ***Pattern Scheme***. The Pattern Scheme box provides the ability to apply a select a dimensioning scheme. The two pattern schemes are:
  - **Polar dimensioning**. Creates a scheme consisting of a callout and sometimes an angular locating dimension.
  - **Linear dimensioning**. Selected by default. Creates linear dimensions for a pattern.
- ***Dimensioning Scheme***. Baseline selected by default. The Dimensioning Scheme box provides the ability to select a dimensioning scheme. The two dimensioning schemes are: **Baseline** and **Chain**.

- ***Datum***. The Datum box provides the following selections. They are:

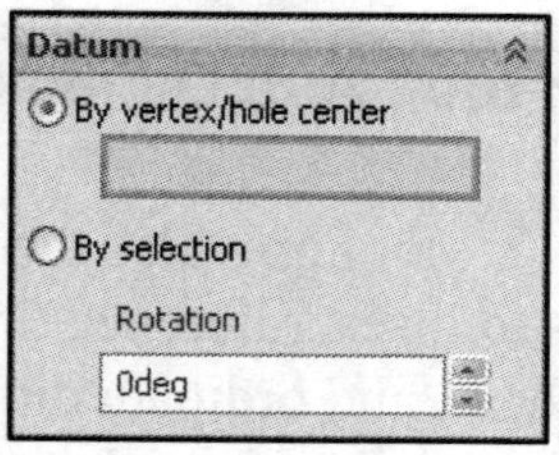


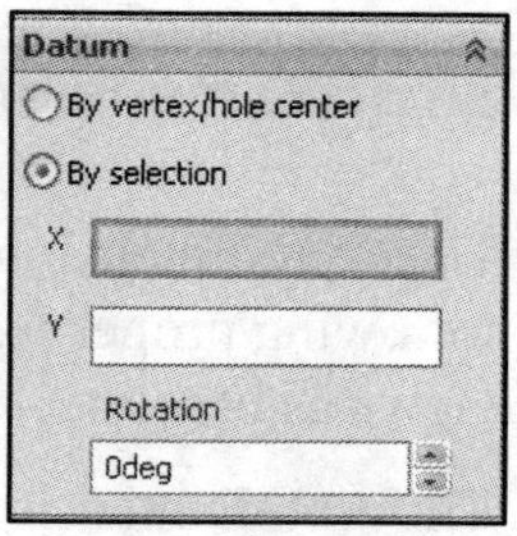


  - **By Vertex/hole center**. Measures the manufacturing features and the locating dimensions from the selected vertex in the Graphics window.
  - **By selection**. Measures the manufacturing features and the locating dimensions. Set the following selections:
  - **X**. Select the X edge to create a virtual point.
  - **Y**. Select the Y edge to create a virtual point.
  - **Rotation**. Set the angle or drag the origin to rotate if required.

If the X and Y edges intersect, you must use the By vertex/hole center option.

***Tutorial: Smart Dimension 13-1***

Dimension a part drawing view using the Smart Dimension tool with the DimXpert option.

1. Open **Smart Dimension 13-1** from the SolidWorks 2010\Drawing folder.
2. Click the **Smart Dimension** tool. The Smart Dimension PropertyManager is displayed.
3. Click the **DimXpert** tab from the Dimension Assist Tools box. The Dimension PropertyManager is displayed.
4. Click **Linear dimensioning** for Pattern Scheme.

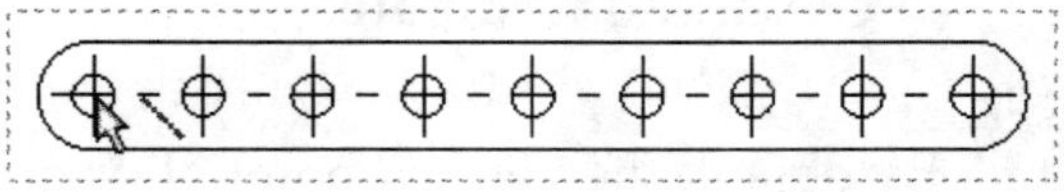

5. Click **Baseline** for Dimensioning Scheme. Check the **By vertex/hole center** box.

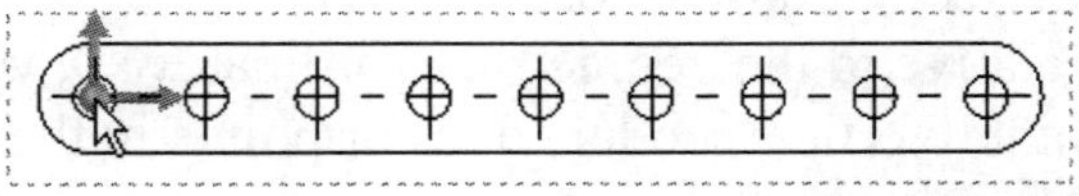

6. Click the **Axis** of the left most hole. Axis<1> is displayed in the Datum box.

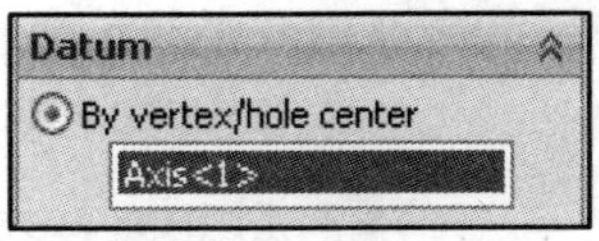


7. Click the **circular edge** of the left most hole.
8. Click **OK** to the Warning message. The hole dimension is displayed.
9. Click **OK** from the Dimension PropertyManager. The dimensions are displayed on Drawing View1.
10. **Close** the drawing.

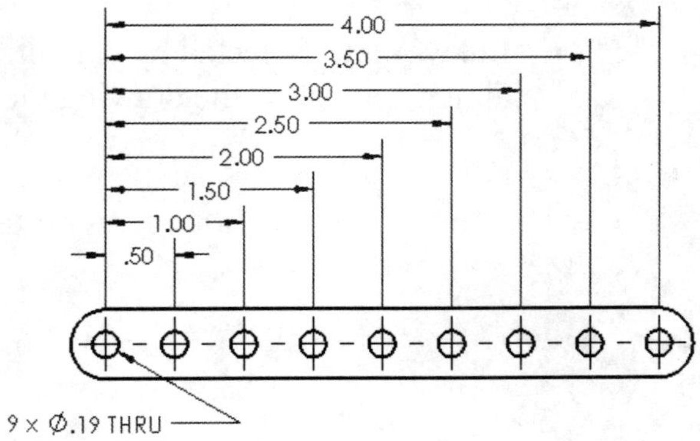

## Smart Dimension tool: AutoDimension tab

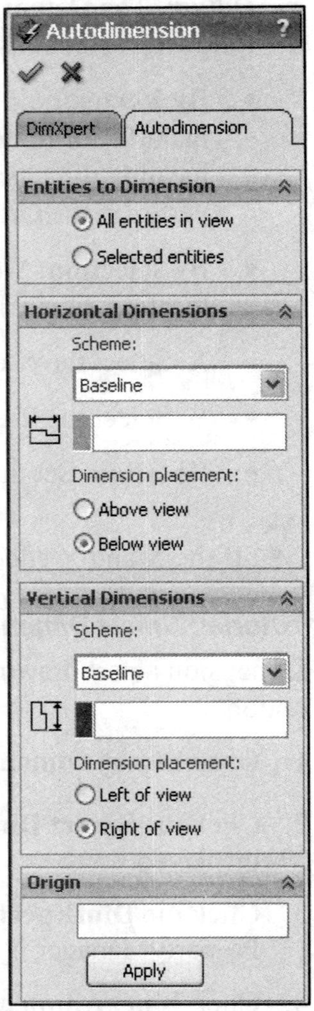


The Autodimension tool provides the ability to specify the following properties to insert reference dimensions into drawing views as baseline, chain, and ordinate dimensions.

The AutoDimension tool uses the Autodimension PropertyManager. The Autodimension PropertyManager provides the following selections:

- ***Entities to Dimension***. The Entities to Dimension box provides two selections. They are:
  - **All entities in view**. Selected by default. Dimensions all entities in the drawing view.
  - **Selected entities**. Displays the selected entities to dimension.
- ***Horizontal Dimensions***. The Horizontal Dimensions box provides the following selections:
  - **Scheme**. Baseline selected by default. Sets the Horizontal Dimensioning Scheme and the entity used as the vertical point of origination (Datum - Vertical Model Edge, Model Vertex, Vertical Line or Point) for the dimensions. The Horizontal Dimensions Scheme provides three types of dimensions. They are: **Baseline**, **Chain** and **Ordinate**.

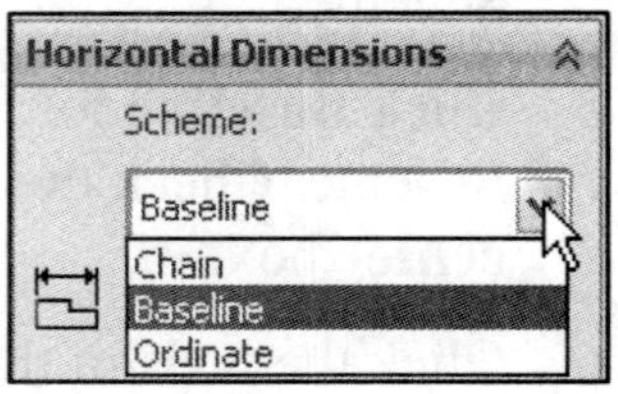


By default the vertical point of origination for the horizontal dimensions is based on the first vertical entity relative to the geometric coordinates x0, y0. You can select other vertical model edges or points in the drawing view.

- **Dimension placement**. The Dimension placement section provides two options. They are:
  - **Above view**. Locates the dimension above the drawing view.
  - **Below view**. Selected by default. Locates the dimension below the drawing view.

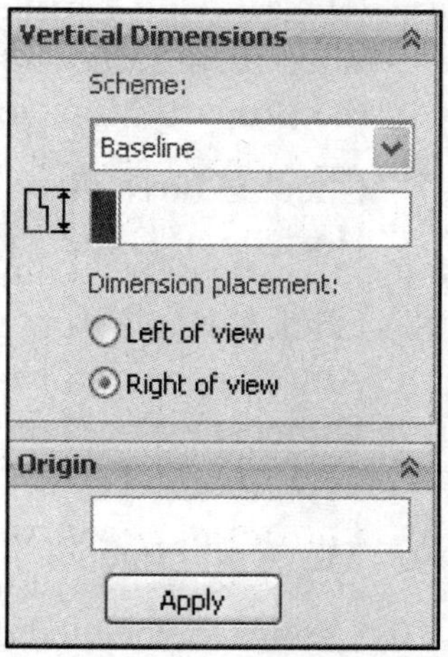


- ***Vertical Dimensions***. The Vertical Dimensions box provides the following selections:
  - **Scheme**. Baseline selected by default. Sets the Horizontal Dimensioning Scheme and the entity used as the vertical point of origination (Datum - Vertical Model Edge, Model Vertex, Vertical Line or Point) for the dimensions. The Horizontal Dimensions Scheme provides three types of dimensions: **Baseline, Chain** and **Ordinate**.

By default, the horizontal point of origination for the vertical dimensions (Datum - Horizontal Model Edge, Model Vertex, Horizontal Line or Point) is based on the first horizontal entity relative to the geometric coordinates x0,y0. You can select other horizontal model edges or points in the drawing view.

  - **Dimension placement**. Right of view selected by default. The Dimension placement section provides two selections. They are:
    - **Left of view**. Locates the dimension to the left of the drawing view.
    - **Right of view**. Select by default. Locates the dimension to the right of the drawing view.
- ***Origin***. Sets the origin for the dimensions. Select a horizontal edge to set as the zero starting point for all dimensions.
  - **Apply**. Modifies the selected edge. Select a different edge. Click the Apply button.

### *Tutorial: Autodimension 13-1*

Insert Autodimensions into an existing drawing view. Note your options.

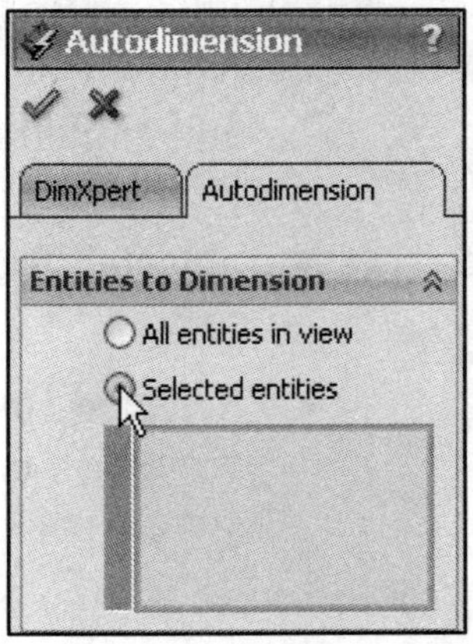


1. Open **Autodimension 13-1** from the SolidWorks 2010\Drawing folder.
2. Click the **Smart Dimension** tool.
3. Click the **Autodimension** tab. The Autodimension PropertyManager is displayed.
4. Check the **Selected entities** box.
5. Click inside the **Drawing View1** view boundary.

6. Click the **left radius** of the flatbar as illustrated. Edge<3> is displayed in the PropertyManager.

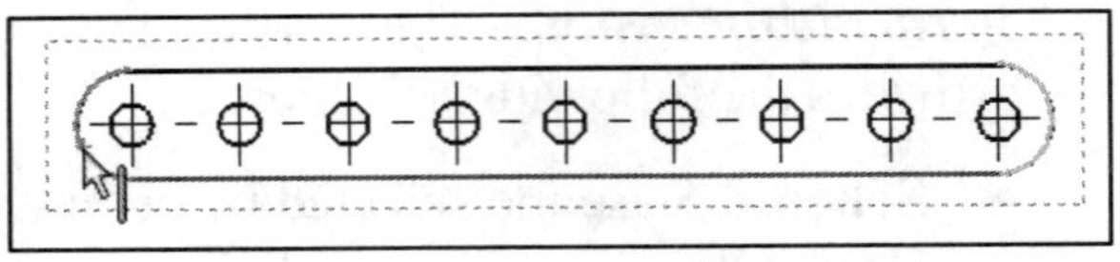

7. Check **Above view** from the Horizontal Dimensions box.
8. Click **OK** from the Autodimension PropertyManager. Dimensions are applied to the front view.

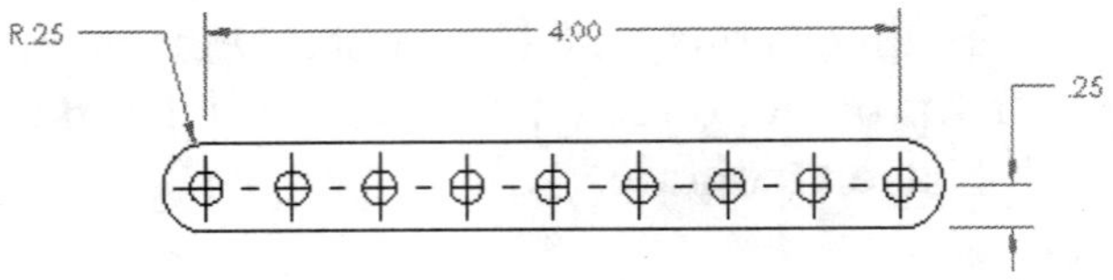


9. **Move** all dimensions off the view.
10. **Create** the needed dimension gaps as illustrated.
11. **Close** the drawing.

## Model Items tool

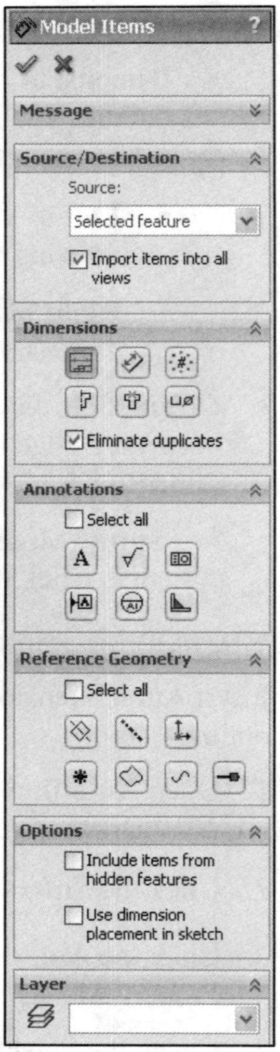


The Model Items tool provides the ability to import dimensions, annotations, and reference geometry from the referenced model into the selected view of the drawing. You can insert items into a selected feature, an assembly component, an assembly feature, a drawing view or all views. When inserting items into all drawing views, dimensions and annotations are displayed in the most appropriate view. Edit the inserted locations if required.

The Model Items tool uses the Model Items PropertyManager. The Model Items PropertyManager provides the following selections:

- ***Source/Destination***. The Source/Destination box provides the following options:

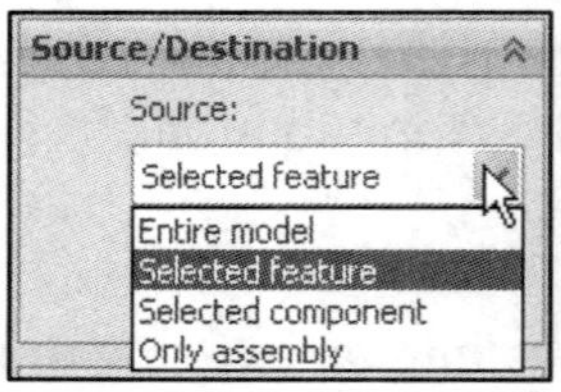


  - **Source**. Selects the source of the model to inset the dimensions. There are four options. They are:
    - **Entire model**. Inserts model items for the total model.
    - **Selected feature**. Inserts model items for the selected feature.
    - **Selected component**. Only available for assembly drawings. Inserts model items for the selected component.

- **Only assembly**. Assembly drawing only. Inserts model items only for assembly features.
- **Import items into all views**. Inserts model items into all drawing views on the selected sheet.
- **Destination view(s)**. Lists the drawing views where the model items will be inserted.

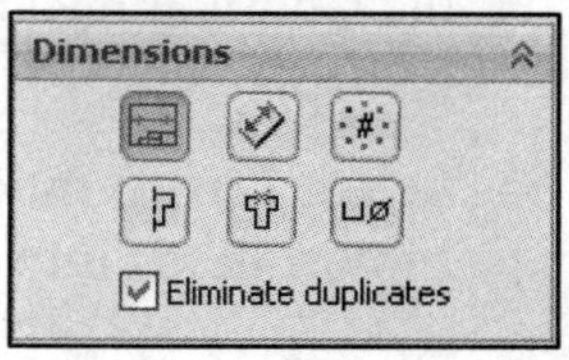


- ***Dimensions***. The Dimensions box provides various selections to insert the following model items if they exist. The available selections are: **Marked for drawing, Not marked for drawing, Instance/Revolution counts, Hole Wizard Profiles, Hole Wizard Locations** and **Hole callout**.

Hole Wizard information from the model propagates to the drawing when the Hole Wizard Profiles, Hole Wizard Locations and Hole callout buttons are selected.

- **Eliminate duplicates**. Selected by default. Inserts only unique model items. Duplicates are not inserted.

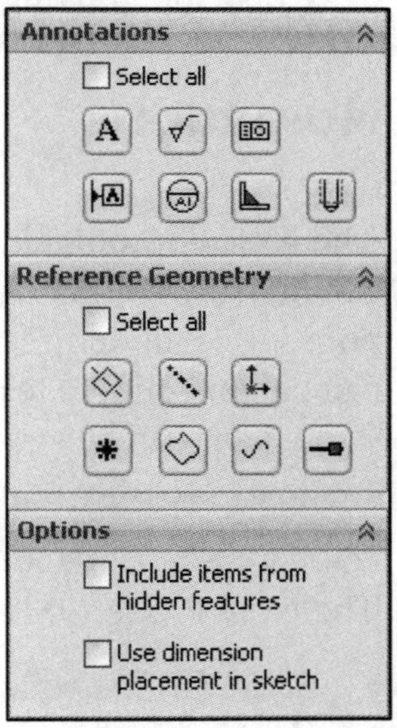


- ***Annotations***. The Annotations box provides selections to insert the following model items if they exist. If not, select the Select all option. The available selections are: **Select all**, **Notes, Surface finish, Geometric tolerances, Datums, Datum targets, Welds** and **Cosmetic thread**.
- ***Reference Geometry***. The Reference Geometry box provides eight selections to insert the following model items if they exist. If not, select the Select all option. The available selections are: **Select all, Planes, Axis, Origins, Points, Surfaces, Curves** and **Routing points**.
- ***Options***. The Options box provides the following selections:
  - **Include items from hidden features**. Clear this option to prevent the insertion of annotations that belong to hidden model items. Performance is slower while hidden model items are filtered.
  - **Use Dimension placement in sketch**. Uses the dimension location of the sketch.

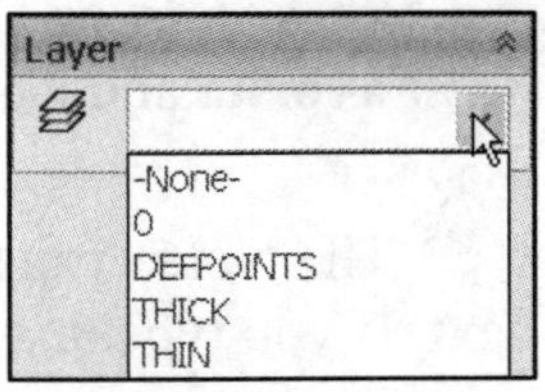


- ***Layer***. The Layer box provides the ability to insert the model items to a specified drawing layer using the drop-down menu.

***Tutorial: Model Items view 13-1***

Insert Annotations into a single drawing using the Model Items tool.

1. Open **Model Items 13-1** from the SolidWorks 2010\Drawing folder.
2. Click the **Model Items** tool from the Annotations tab in the CommandManager. The Model Items PropertyManager is displayed.
3. Select **Entire model** from the Source/Destination box. Import items into all views is checked by default.
4. Click **OK** from the Model Items PropertyManager. Dimensions are inserted into Drawing View1.
5. Click and drag each **dimension** off the model. View the results. Note: You can manually insert dimensions (Smart Dimension tool) and move dimensions from one drawing view to the other.
6. **Close** the drawing.

## Note tool

The Note **A** tool adds a note to the selected drawing sheet. A note can be free floating or fixed. A note can be placed with a leader pointing to an item, face, edge, or vertex in your document. A note can contain simple text, symbols, parametric text, and hyperlinks. The leader can be straight, bent or multi-jog. Use the Note tool to create a note or to edit an existing note, balloon note or a revision symbol. The Note tool uses the Note PropertyManager.

The Note PropertyManager provides the following selections:

- ***Style***. Define styles for dimensions and various annotations, (Notes, Geometric Tolerance Symbols, Surface Finish Symbols, Weld Symbols, etc.). The favorite box provides the following six selections. They are: **Apply the default attributes to selected Notes**, **Add or Update a Favorite**, **Delete a Favorite**, **Save a Favorite** and **Load Favorites**.

The Note PropertyManager has two types of Styles: 1.) With text. If you type text in a note and save it as a style, the text is saved with the note properties. 2.) Without text. If you create a note without text and save it as a style, only the note properties are saved.

The extensions for styles are: Dimensions: .sldfvt, Notes: .sldnotefvt, Geometric Tolerance Symbols: .sldgtolfvt and Weld Symbols: .sldweldfvt

- ***Text Format***. The Text Format box provides the following format selections. They are:
  - **Left Align**. Aligns the text to the left.
  - **Center Align**. Aligns the text in the center.
  - **Right Align**. Aligns the text to the right.
  - **Angle**. Enter the angle value. A positive angle rotates the note counterclockwise.
  - **Insert Hyperlink**. Includes a Hyperlink in the note.
  - **Link to Property**. Links a note to a document property.
  - **Add Symbol**. Adds a symbol from the Symbols dialog box.
  - **Lock/Unlock note**. Only available for a drawings. Fixes the note to a selected location.
  - **Insert Geometric Tolerance**. Inserts a geometric tolerance symbol into the note. Use the Geometric Tolerance PropertyManager and the Properties dialog box.
  - **Insert Surface Finish Symbol**. Inserts a surface finish symbol into the selected note. Use the Surface Finish PropertyManager.
  - **Insert Datum Feature**. Inserts a datum feature symbol into the selected note. Use the Datum Feature PropertyManager.
  - **Manual view label**. Only for projected, detail, section, aligned section, and auxiliary views. Overrides the options in **Tools**, **Options**, **Document Properties**, View labels. When selected, you can edit the label text.
  - **Use document font**. Use the document font which is specified in the Tools, Options, Document Properties, Notes section of the Menu bar menu.
  - **Font**. Select a new font style, size, etc. from the Choose Font dialog box.
  - **Block Attribute**. Only available when you are editing a note in a block.
    - **Attribute name**. Displays the text for notes with attributes imported from AutoCAD. There are three options: **Read only**, **Invisible** and **Both**.

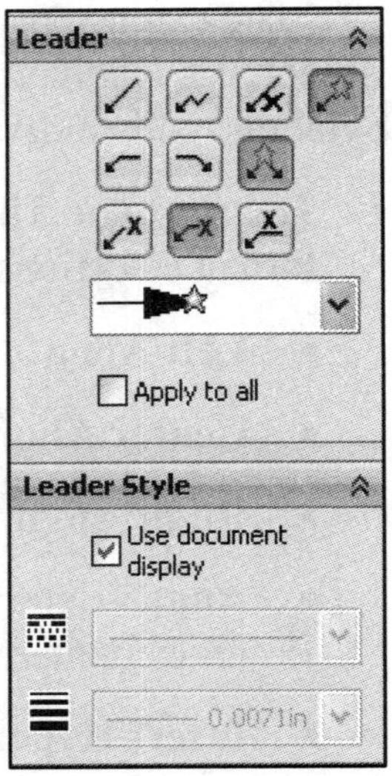


The Attribute name and its properties are displayed in the Attributes editor from the Block PropertyManager.

- *Leader*. Provides the ability to select the required Leader type. Document dependent. The available types are:
  - **Leader**. Create a simple leader from the note to the drawing.
  - **Multi-jog leader**. Create a leader from the note to the drawing with one or more bends.
  - **No Leader**.
  - **Auto Leader**. Selects leader or multi-jog depending on the location of the note.
  - **Left Leader**. Originates from the left of the note.
  - **Right Leader**. Originates from the right of the note.
  - **Nearest Leader**. Originates from the closest point.
    - Choose whether the leader is: **Straight, Bent** or **Underlined**.
- *Leader Style*. Provides the ability to customize Leader style at the document level for line thickness and style.
  - **Use document display**. Selected by default.
  - **Leader Style**. Select a Leader Style from the drop-down menu.
  - **Leader Thickness**. Select a Leader thickness from the drop-down menu.

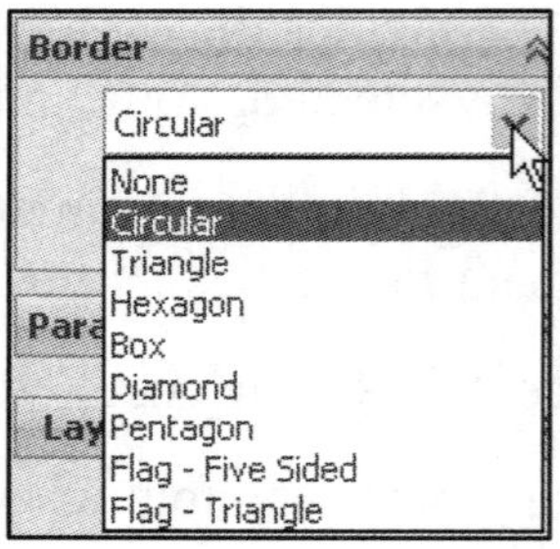


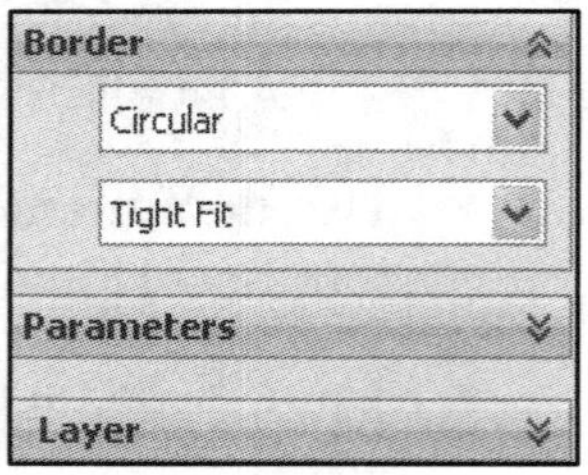


- *Border*. Provides the following style and size selections. They are:
  - **Style**. Circular is selected by default. The Style option provides nine selections. Specify the style of the border from the drop-down arrow box. The Style selections are: **None**, **Circular**, **Triangle**, **Hexagon**, **Box**, **Diamond**, **Pentagon**, **Flag - Five Sided** and **Flag - Triangle**.

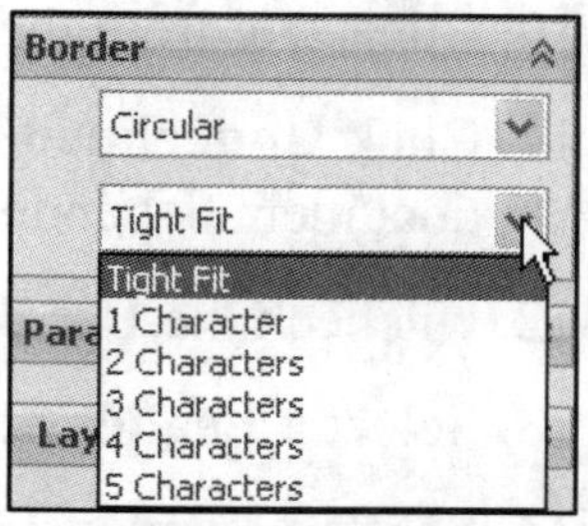


- **Size**. Tight Fit is selected by default. The Size option provides six selections. Specify the required size of the border from the drop-down arrow box. The Size selections are: **Tight Fit, 1 Character**, **2 Characters, 3 Characters**, **4 Characters** and **5 Characters**.

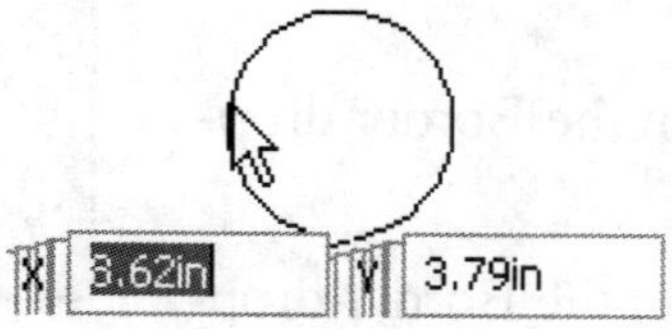


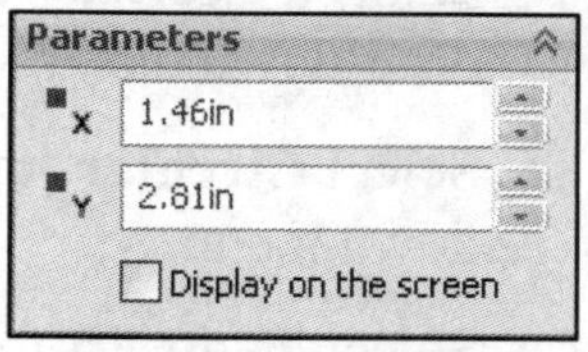


- ***Parameters***. Provides the ability to input or view the X and Y coordinate of the Note on the drawing.
  - **X**. X coordinates
  - **Y**. Y coordinates
  - **Display on the screen**.

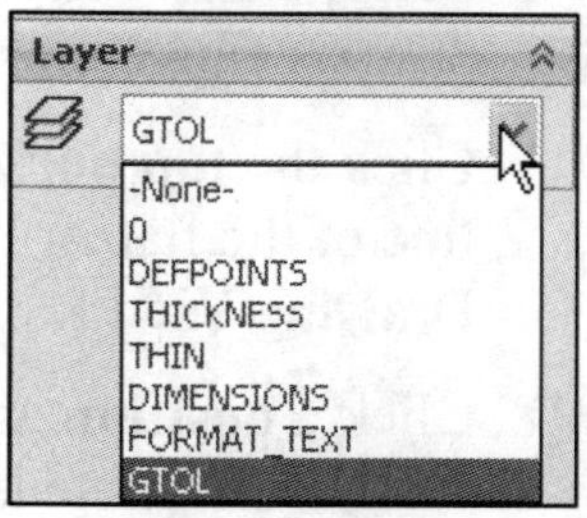


- ***Layer***. The Layer box provides the ability to select a created Layer for the drawing view.

***Tutorial: Note 13-1***

Create a linked note in a drawing.

1. Open **Note 13-1** from the SolidWorks 2010\Drawing folder.
2. Click the **Note** **A** tool from the Annotation tab. The Note PropertyManager is displayed.
3. Click **Left Align** from the Text Format box.

4. Click **Link to Property** from the Text Format box. The Link to Property dialog box is displayed.
5. Click the **Files Properties** button. The Summary Information dialog box is displayed.
6. Enter **Link** for Keywords.
7. Click **OK** from the Summary Information dialog box.
8. Check the **Current document** box.
9. Select **SW-Keywords** from the drop-down menu.

10. Click **OK** from the Link to Property dialog box.
11. Click **Underlined Leader** from the Leader box. Remember, document dependent.
12. Uncheck the **Use document display** box as illustrated.
13. Select a **Leader Style** from the drop-down menu.
14. Select a **Leader Thickness** from the drop-down menu.
15. Select **Circular** from the Border drop-down menu.
16. Select **Tight Fit** from the Border drop-down menu.

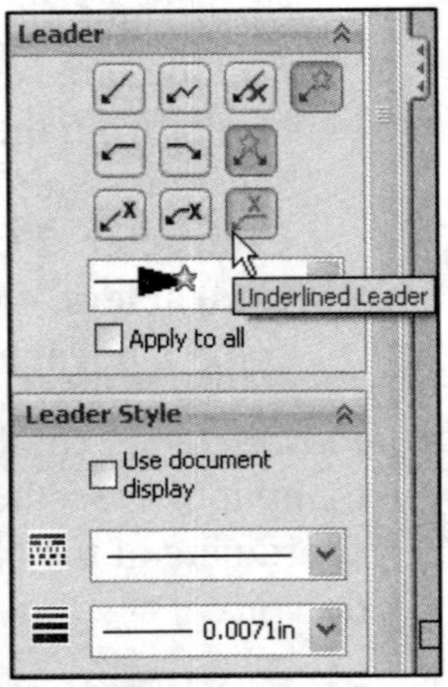


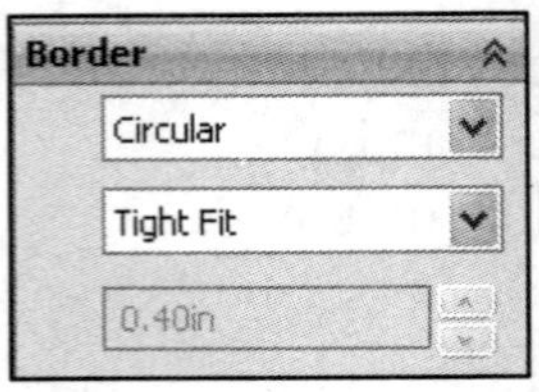


17. Click the **top horizontal** line of the flatbar in Drawing View1.
18. Click a **position** above the view as illustrated.

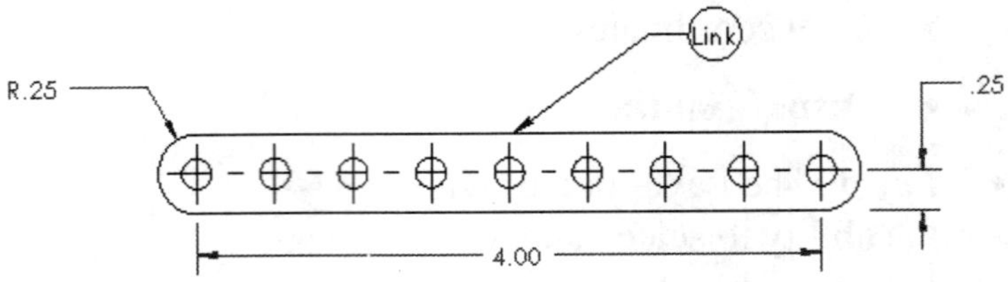


19. Click **OK** from the Note PropertyManager. View the results.
20. **Close** the drawing.

## Spell Checker tool

The Spell Checker tool checks for miss spelled words in documents. This tool checks: notes, dimensions with text, and drawing title blocks, when you are in the Edit Sheet Format mode. The Spell Checker tool will not check words in a table and is only available in English using Microsoft Word 2000 or later.

The Spell Checker tool uses the Spelling Check PropertyManager. The Spelling Check PropertyManager provides the following selections:

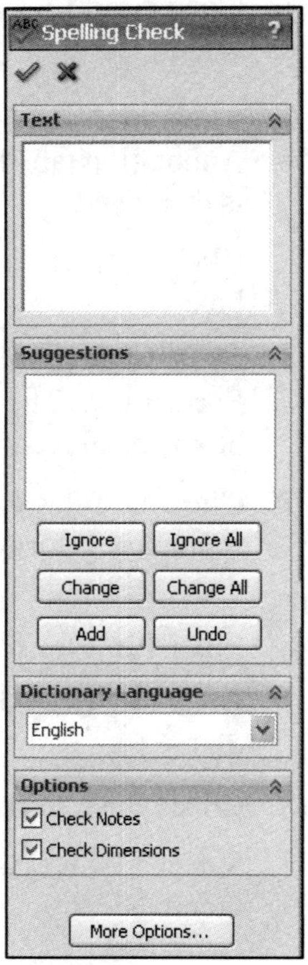


- ***Text***. The Text box displays the misspelled word. Edit the word if required or use the supplied words in the Suggestions box.
- ***Suggestions***. The Suggestions box displays a list of possible replacements words associated with the misspelled word.
  - **Ignore**. Skips the instance of the misspelled word.
  - **Ignore All**. Skips all instances of the misspelled word.

- **Change**. Changes the misspelled word to the highlighted word in the Suggestions box.
- **Change All**. Changes all instances of the misspelled word to the highlighted word in the Suggestions box.
- **Add**. Adds the currently selected word to the dictionary.
- **Undo**. Undoes the last action.

- ***Dictionary Language***. List the language used for the Microsoft dictionary. English is the default option.
- ***Options***. The Options box provides the following selections:
    - **Check Notes**. Selected by default. Checks the spelling of notes.
    - **Check Dimensions**. Selected by default. Checks the spelling of dimensions.
    - **More Options**. Provides the ability to customize your spell checking options.

## Format Painter tool

The Format Painter tool moved from SolidWorks Utilities into core SolidWorks. The Format Painter tool provides the ability to paint the properties or styles used in one annotation to another.

The Format tool uses the Format PropertyManager. The Format Painter supports the following:

- Annotations properties such as; font, leader line style, line thickness and layer (except for centerlines and center marks).
- Component line fonts in drawings.
- Crosshatch.

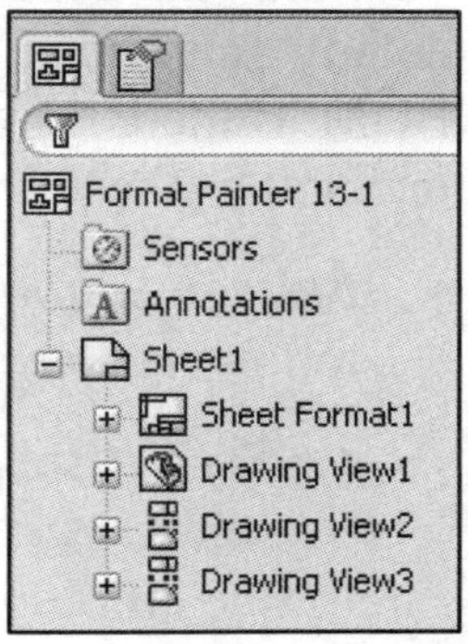


### *Tutorial: Format Painter 13-1*

Apply the Format Painter tool to a Front drawing view.

1. Open the **Format Painter 13-1** drawing from the SolidWorks 2010\Drawing folder.
2. Click the **Format Painter** tool from the Annotation tab. The Format Painter PropertyManager is displayed.

Select the source dimension for the format.

3. Click the **1.932** dimension as illustrated.

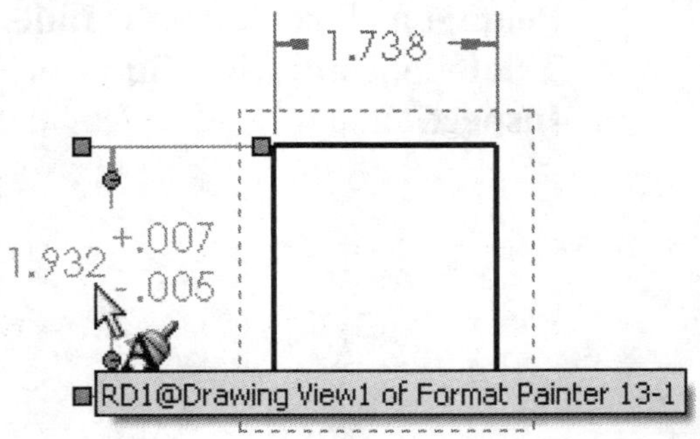

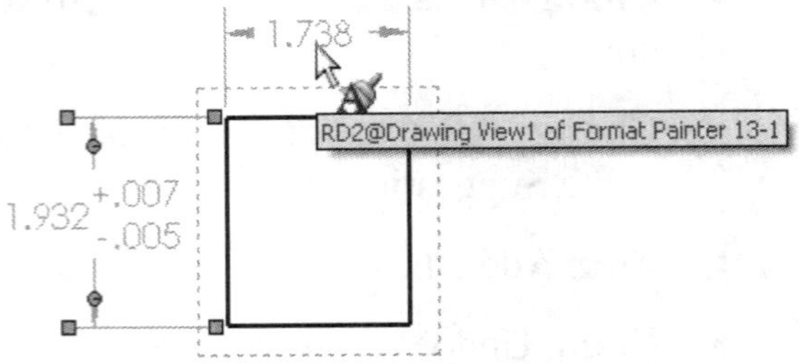


Select the destination dimension to paint with the source dimension format.

4. Click the **1.738** dimension in the view as illustrated. The destination dimension changes to the bilateral format and applies the same tolerance values.

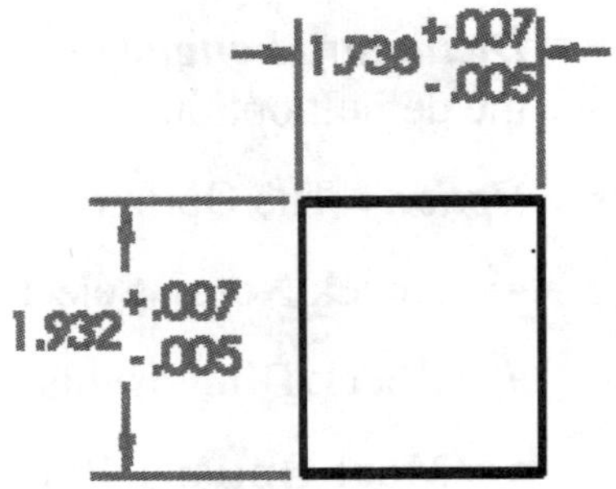


If the destination dimension has a tolerance, the Format Painter tool applies the bilateral format by will not override the tolerance values.

5. Click **OK** from the Format Painter PropertyManager.
6. **Close** the drawing.

## Balloon tool

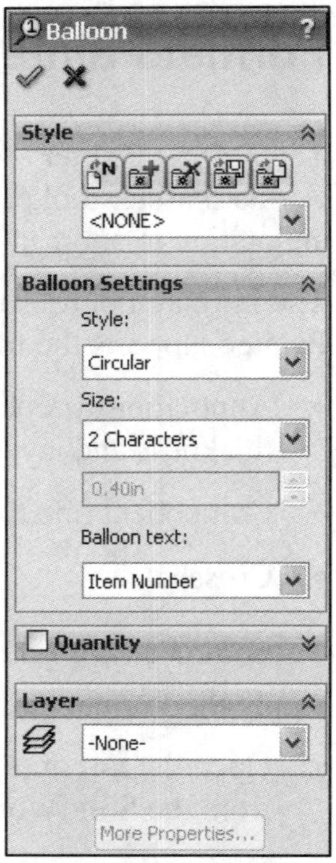


The Balloon tool provides the ability to create a single balloon or multi balloons in an assembly or drawing document. The balloons label the parts in the assembly and relate them to item numbers on the bill of materials (BOM). The Balloon tool uses the Balloon PropertyManager. The Balloon PropertyManager provides the following selections:

You do not have to insert a BOM in order to add balloons. If your drawing does not have a BOM, the item numbers are the default values that SolidWorks would use if you did have a BOM. If there is no BOM on the active sheet, but there is a BOM on another sheet, the numbers from that BOM are used.

- ***Balloon Settings***. The Balloon Settings box provides the following selections. They are:
  - **Style**. Circular selected by default. Provides the ability to select a style for the shape and border of the balloon from the drop-down list. The available styles are: **None**, **Circular**, **Triangle**, **Hexagon**, **Box**, **Diamond**, **Pentagon**, **Circular Split Line**, **Flag - Five Sided**, **Flag - Triangle**, **Underline**, **Square**, **Square Circle and Inspection**.

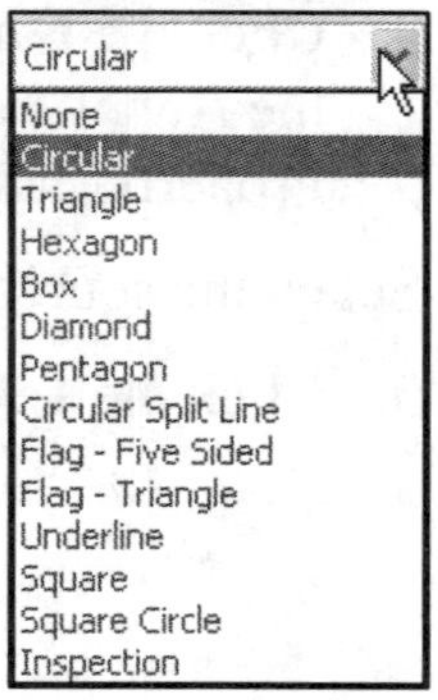

- **Size**. 2 Characters is selected by default. Provides the ability to select a size of the balloon from the drop-down list. The available sizes are: **Tight Fit**, **1 Character**, **2 Characters**, **3 Characters**, **4 Characters** and **5 Characters** and **User Defined**.

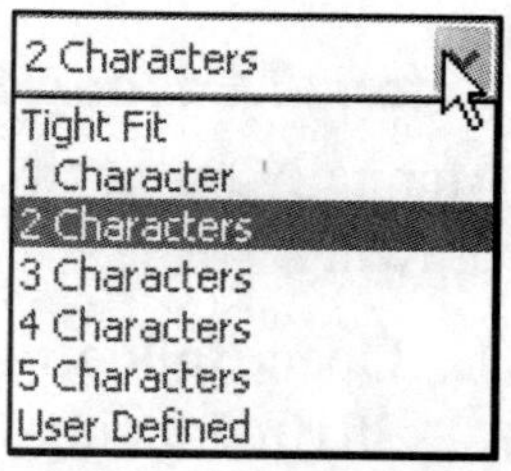


- **Balloon text**. Item Number is selected by default. Provides the ability to select the type of text for the balloon, or for the upper section of a split balloon from the drop-down list. The available options are:
  - **Text**. Type custom text in the balloon.
  - **Item Number**. Displays the item number from the Bill of Materials.
  - **Quantity**. Displays the quantity of this item in the assembly.
  - **Custom Properties**. Provides the ability to select a custom property.
  - **Component Reference.** Shows the text specified for **Component Reference** in the **Component Properties dialog box**.

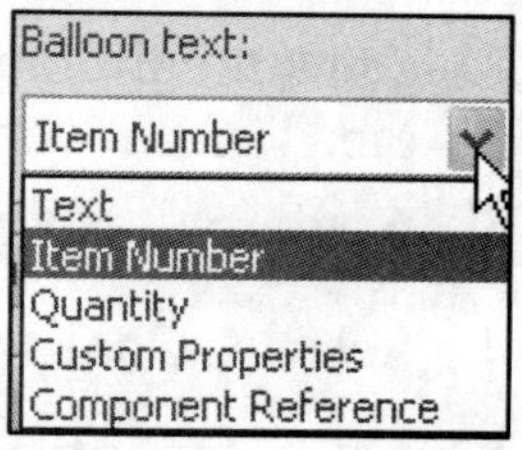


- *Quantity*. Provides the following selections:
  - **Placement**. Displays the quantity to the **Left, Right, Top or Bottom of the balloons.**
  - **Denotation**. Lets you set a label for the quantity. **User Defined** lets you type a custom label.
  - **Quantity value**. Displays the quantity to appear in the balloon (read-only).
  - **Override value**. Lets you override a balloon's quantity. For example, you might insert a balloon in a drawing view that shows only two components, but the total number of assembly components is five. In one view a balloon can display a "2" and in the other view it can display a "3."

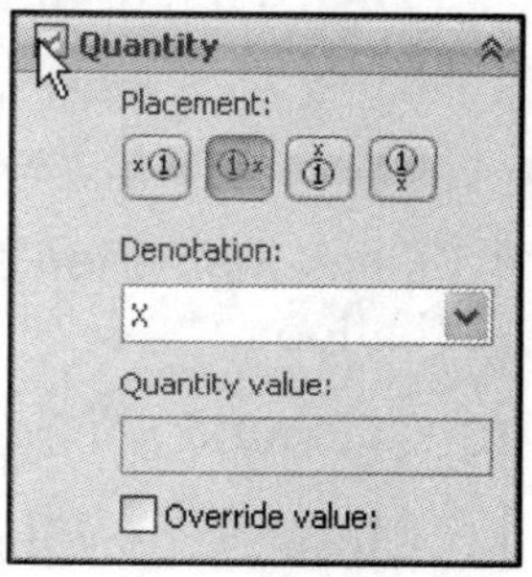


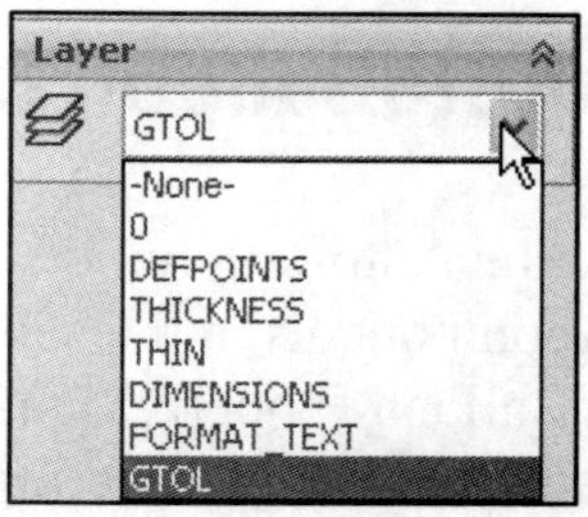


- *Layer*. The Layer box provides the ability to apply the balloon to a specified drawing layer that you created.
  - **More Properties**. Provides the ability to customize your setting by using the Note PropertyManager.

***Tutorial: Balloon 13-1***

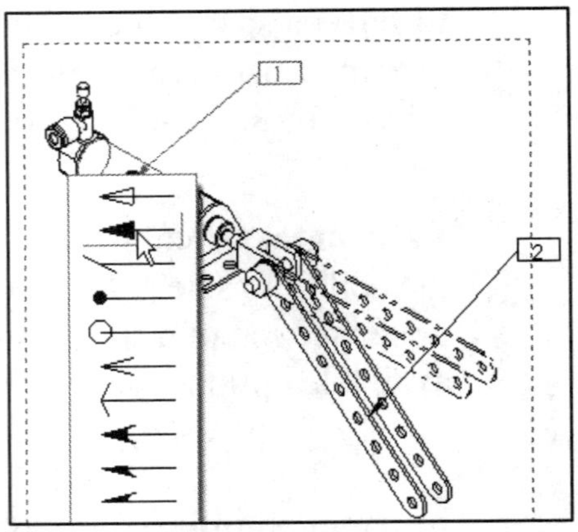


Manually insert two balloons in an assembly drawing.

1. Open **Balloon 13-1** from the SolidWorks 2010\Drawing folder.
2. Click the **Balloon** tool from the Annotation tab. The Balloon PropertyManager is displayed.
3. Select **Box** for Style.
4. Select **2 Characters** for Size.
5. Select **Quantity** for Balloon text.
6. Click **Base-Extrude of NCJ2 Tubes<1>** as illustrated in the Graphics window.
7. Click a **position** above the tube for the first balloon.
8. Click **Extrude1 of Flatbar<1>** as illustrated in the Graphics window.
9. Click a **position** above the flatbar for the second balloon.
10. Click **OK** from the Balloon PropertyManager.
11. **Close** the drawing.

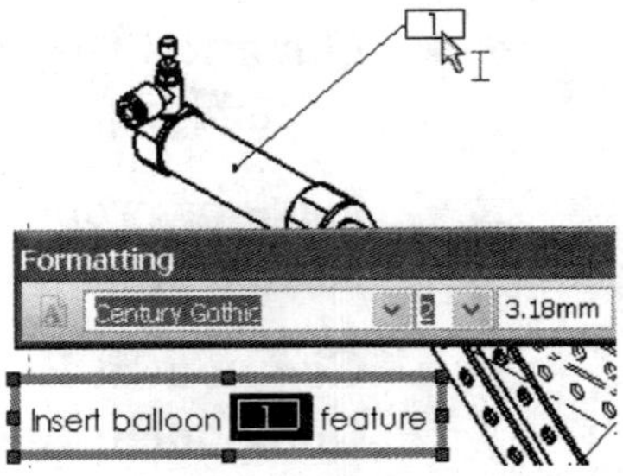


You can insert a balloon directly into a Note text simply be selecting the desired balloon from the active drawing sheet.

## AutoBalloon tool

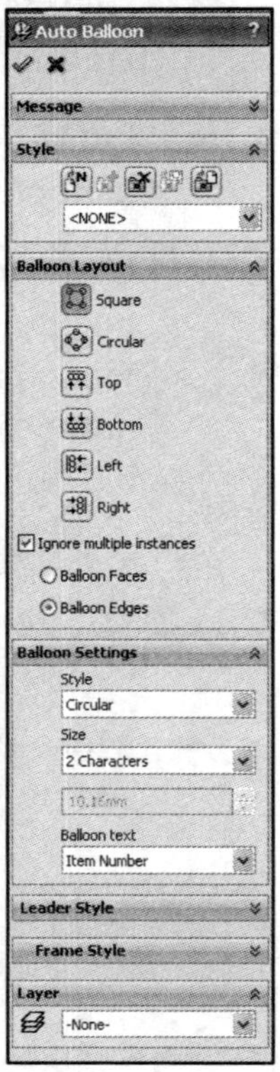


The AutoBalloon tool provides the ability to add balloons for all components in the selected views. The AutoBalloon tool uses the Auto Balloon PropertyManager. The Auto Balloon PropertyManager provides the following selections:

- ***Style***. None selected by default. Provides the ability to select a style for the shape and border of the balloon.
- ***Balloon Layout***. Square selected by default. Provides the following balloon selections: **Square**, **Circular**, **Top**, **Bottom**, **Left** and **Right**.
  - **Ignore multiple instances**. Selected by default. Applies a balloon to only one instance for components with multiple instances.

   - **Balloon Faces**. Applies the leader to the face of the reference item.
   - **Balloon Edges**. Selected by default. Applies the leader to the edge of the reference item.

- ***Balloon Settings***. The Balloon Settings box provides the following selections:

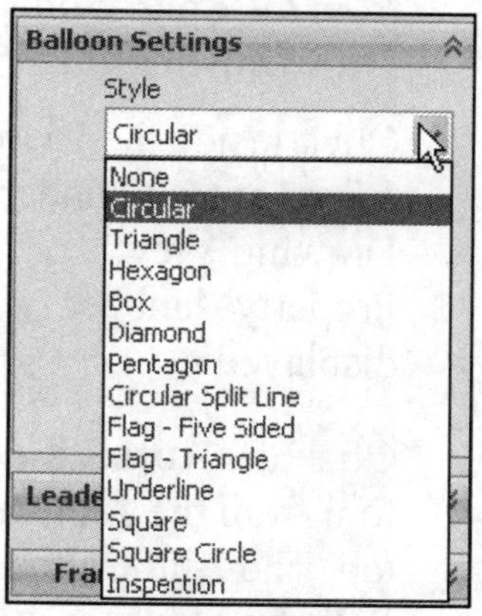


   - **Style**. Circular selected by default. Provides the following style option: **None, Circular, Triangle, Hexagon, Box, Diamond, Pentagon, Circular Split Line, Flag - Five Sided, Flag - Triangle, Underline, Square, Square Circle** and **Inspection**.
   - **Size**. 2 Characters selected by default. The Size box provides the following options from the drop-down list. They are: **Tight Fit, 1 Character, 2 Characters, 3 Characters, 4 Characters, 5 Characters** and **User Defined.**

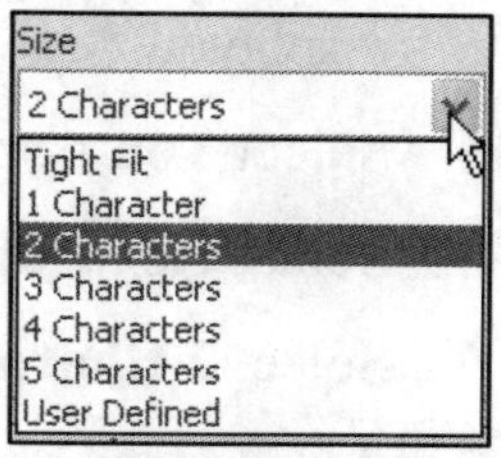


- ***Leader Style.*** Use document display selected by default. Provides the ability to apply the default document leader style set in the Document Properties section or to select a custom leader style for the drop-down menus.

- ***Frame Style.*** Use document display selected by default. Provides the ability to apply the default document Frame style set in the Document Properties section or to select a custom frame style from the drop-down menus.
- ***Layer***. The Layer box provides the ability to apply the balloon to a specified drawing layer that you created.

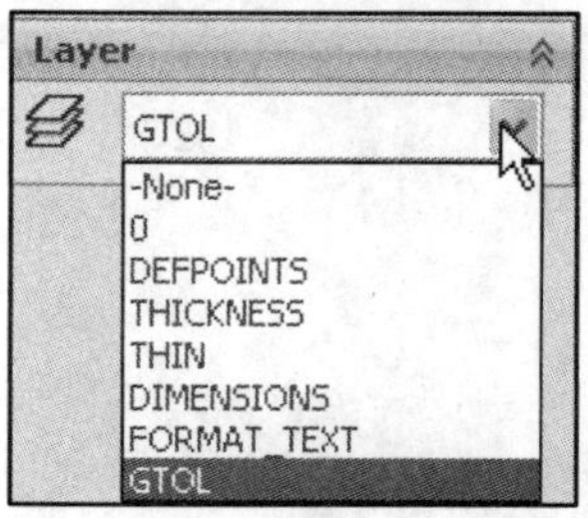

### *Tutorial: AutoBalloon 13-1*

Apply the AutoBalloon tool.

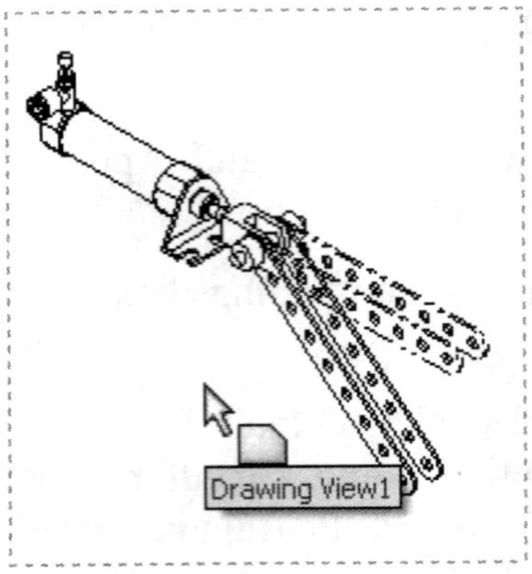


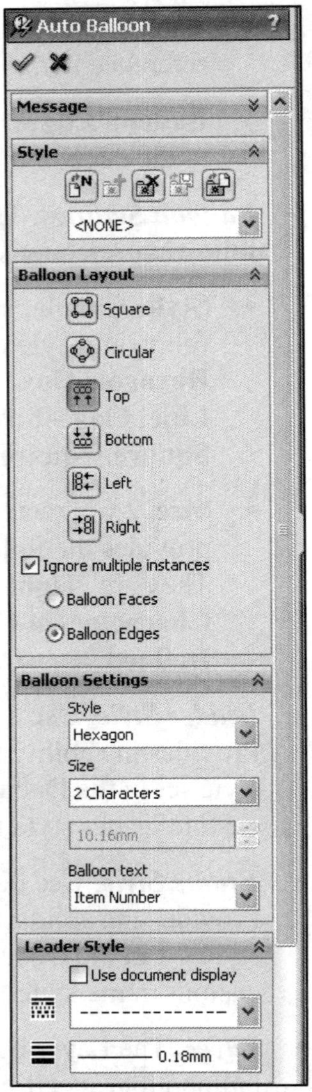


1. Open **AutoBalloon 13-1** from the SolidWorks 2010\Drawing folder.
2. Click inside the **Drawing View1** view boundary. The Drawing View1 PropertyManager is displayed.
3. Click the **AutoBalloon** tool from the Annotation tab. The AutoBalloon PropertyManager is displayed.
4. Select **Top** from the Balloon Layout box.
5. Select **Hexagon** from the Balloon Settings box.
6. Select **2 Characters** for Size.
7. Select **Item Number** for Balloon text.
8. **Uncheck** the Use document display box in the Leader Style.
9. Select **dotted** from the Leader Style box as illustrated.
10. Click **OK** from the AutoBalloon PropertyManager. View the created balloons in the drawing.
11. Click and drag the **balloons** to arrange in the drawing view.
12. **Close** the drawing.

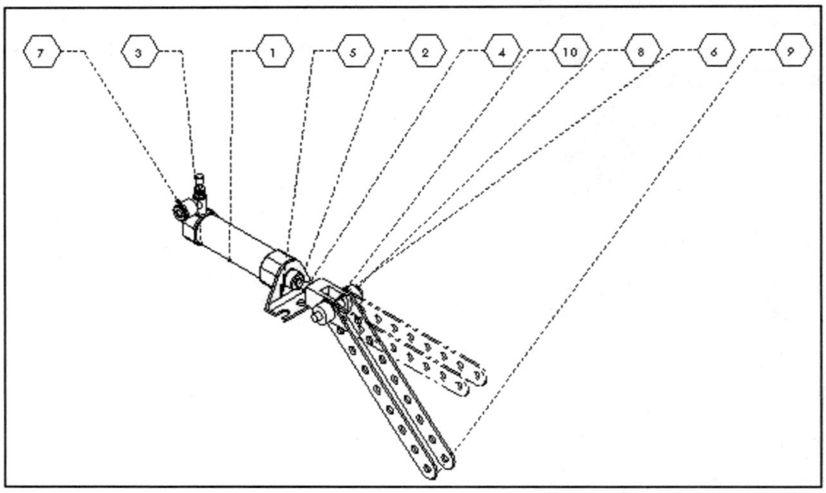

## Surface Finish tool

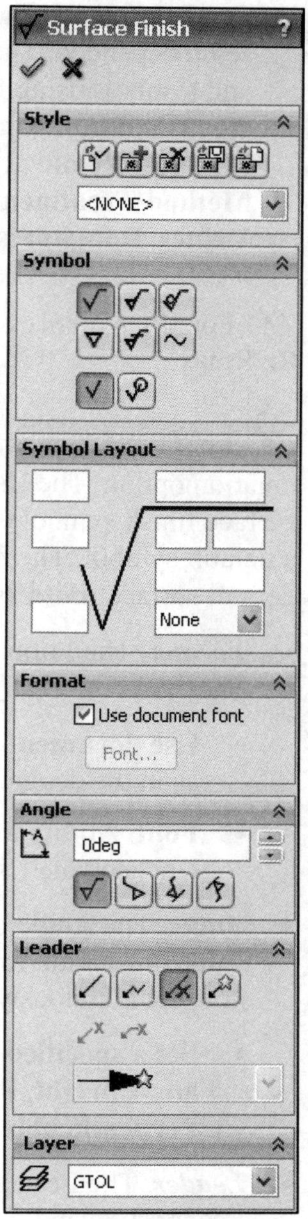


The Surface Finish tool provides the ability to add a surface finish symbol to the selected drawing view. The Surface Finish tool uses the Surface Finish PropertyManager. The Surface Finish PropertyManager provides the following selections:

- ***Style***. The Style box provides the ability to define styles for dimensions and various annotations (Notes, Geometric Tolerance Symbols, Surface Finish Symbols, Weld Symbols, etc). The style box provides the following selections. They are: **Apply the default attributes to selected Surface Finish Symbols**, **Add or Update a Style**, **Delete a Style**, **Save a Style** and **Load Style**.

The extensions for styles are:

| | |
|---|---|
| Dimensions: | .sldfvt |
| Notes: | .sldnotefvt |
| Geometric Tolerance Symbols: | .sldgtolfvt |
| Surface Finish Symbols: | .sldsffvt |
| Weld Symbols: | .sldweldfvt |

- ***Symbol***. Basic and Local are selected by default. The Symbol box provides the following selections for Surface Finish symbols. They are: **Basic**, **Machining Required**, **Machining Prohibited**, **JIS Basic**, **JIS Machining Required**, **JIS Machining Prohibite Local** and **All Around**.

If you select JIS Basic or JIS Machining Required, several surface textures are available.

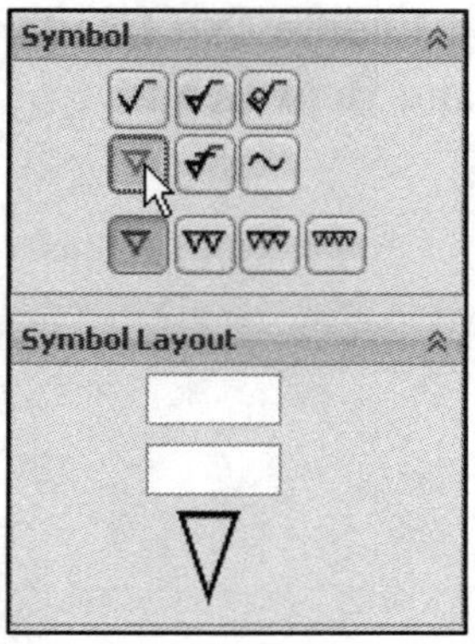


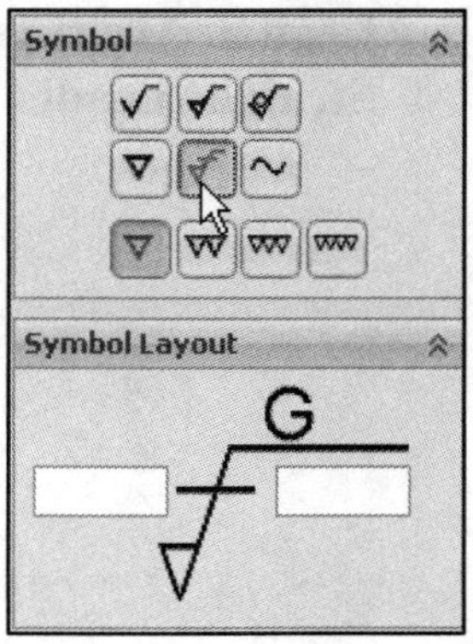

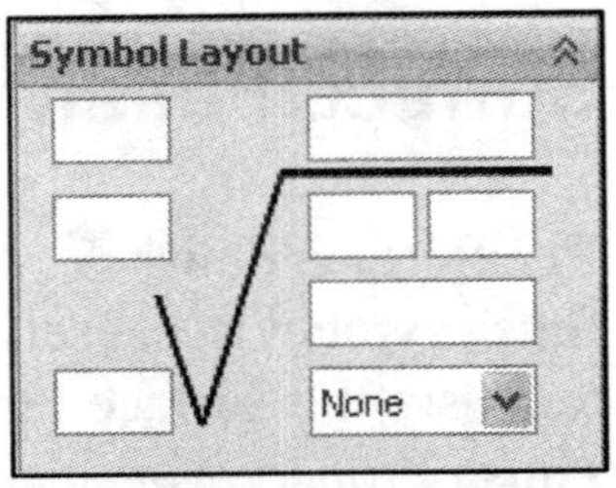


- ***Symbol Layout***. The Symbol Layout box selections are setup depended. The available selections for ANSI symbols and symbols using ISO and related standards prior to 2002 are: **Maximum Roughness**, **Minimum Roughness**, **Material Removal Allowance**, **Production Method/Treatment**, **Sampling Length**, **Other Roughness Values**, **Roughness Spacing** and **Lay Direction**.

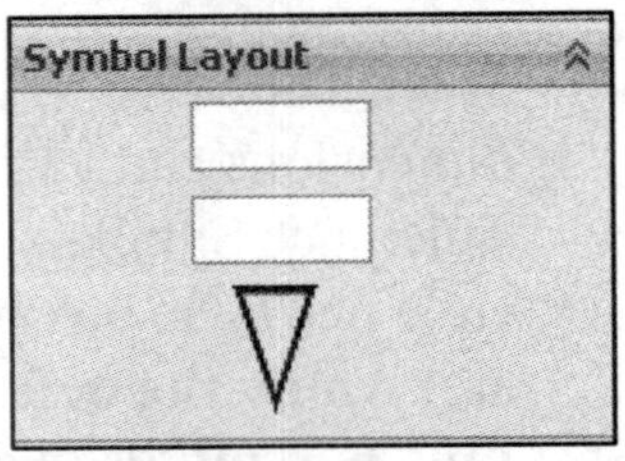


For JIS symbols, specify: Roughness Ra, and Roughness Rz/Rmax.

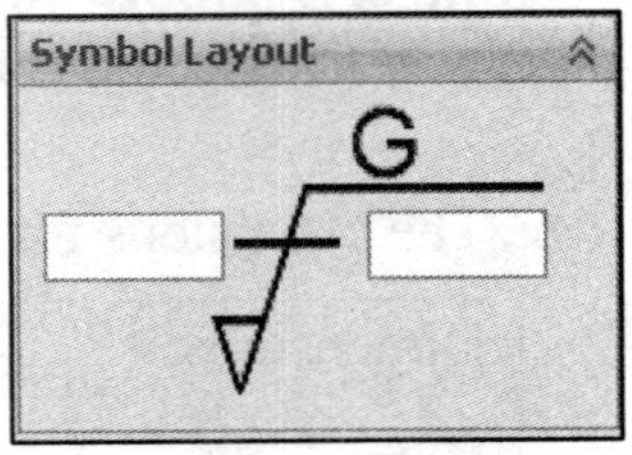


For GOST symbols, you can also select the Use for notation option. The Use for notation option displays the surface finish symbol 0.5 times larger than the default size. Add a default symbol. The Add default symbol selection displays the default surface finish symbol in parenthesis.

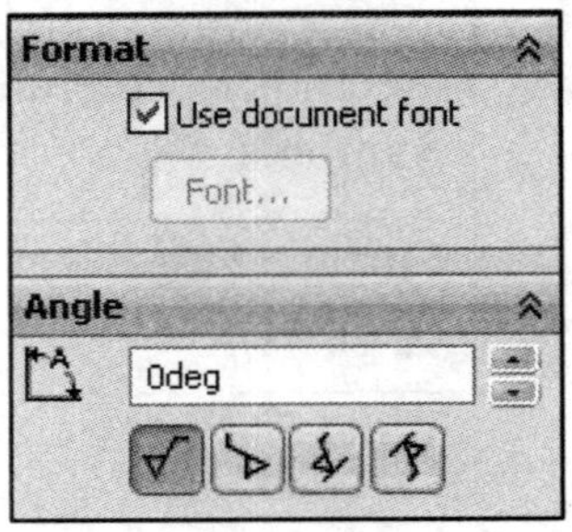


- ***Format***. The Format box provides the following selections. They are:
  - **Use document font**. Uses the same font style and type as in the document.
  - **Font**. Ability to customize the font for the document. Uncheck the Use document font check box.
- ***Angle***. The Angle box provides the ability to set the angle value of rotation for the symbol. A positive angle rotates the note counterclockwise.
  - **Set a specified rotation**: There are four selections. They are: **Upright**, **Rotated 90deg**, **Perpendicular** and **Perpendicular (Reverse)**.

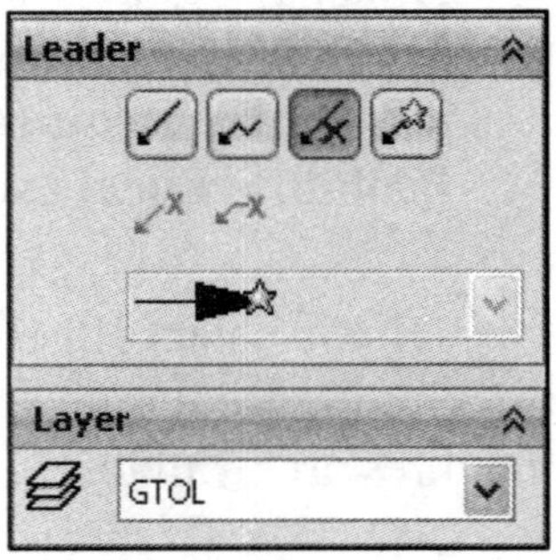


- ***Leader***. The Leader box provides the ability to select the Leader style and Arrow style. The available selections are: **Leader**, **Multi-jog Leader**, **No Leader**, **Auto Leader**, **Straight Leader** and **Bent Leader**.

- **Select an Arrow Style**. Provides the ability to select an Arrow Style from the drop down box.

- ***Layer***. The Layer box provides the ability to apply the Surface finish to a specified drawing layer.

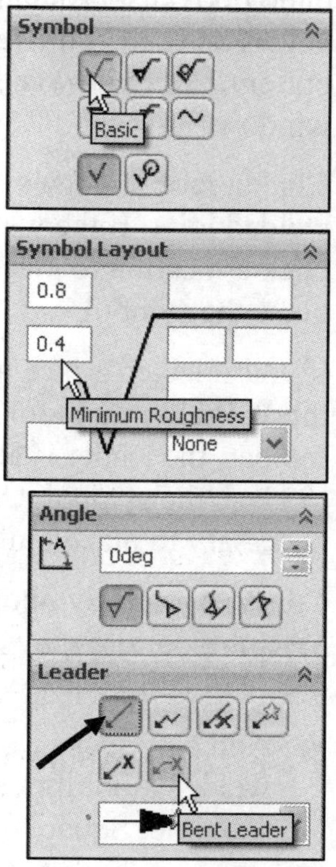


***Tutorial: Surface Finish 13-1***

Manually apply a Surface Finish to a drawing view.

1. Open **Surface Finish 13-1** from the SolidWorks 2010\Drawing folder. **Zoom in** on the Top view.
2. Click the **Surface Finish** tool from the Annotation tab. The Surface Finish PropertyManager is displayed.
3. Click **Basic** for Symbol.
4. Enter **0.8** micrometers for Maximum Roughness.
5. Enter **0.4** micrometers for Minimum Roughness.
6. Click **Leader** from the Leader box.
7. Click **Bent Leader** from the Leader box.
8. Click the **top horizontal edge** of the Top view for the arrowhead attachment.
9. Click a **position** for the Surface Finish symbol.
10. Click **OK** from the Surface Finish PropertyManager.

Create Multiple Leaders to the Surface finish symbol.

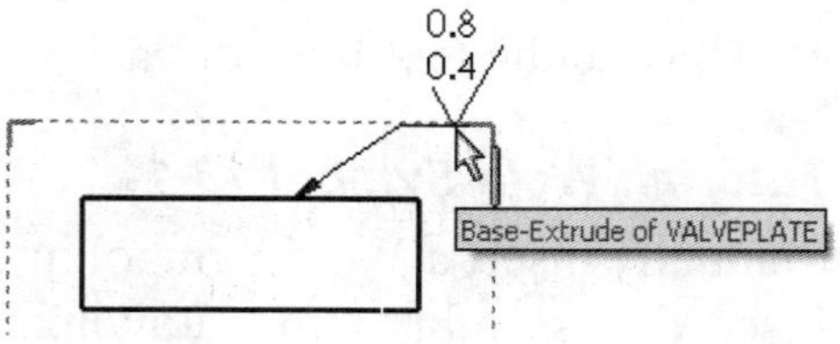


11. Click the **tip** of the arrowhead.
12. Hold the **Ctrl** key down.
13. Drag the **arrowhead** to the bottom edge of the Top view as illustrated.
14. Release the **Ctrl** key.
15. Release the **mouse button**. View the results.
16. **Close** the drawing.

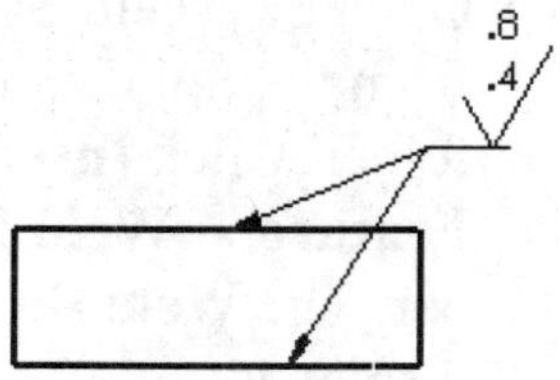


## Weld Symbol tool

The Weld Symbol tool provides the ability to add a weld symbol on a selected entity, edged, face, etc. Create and apply the weld symbol by using the Properties dialog box under the ANSI Weld Symbol tab.

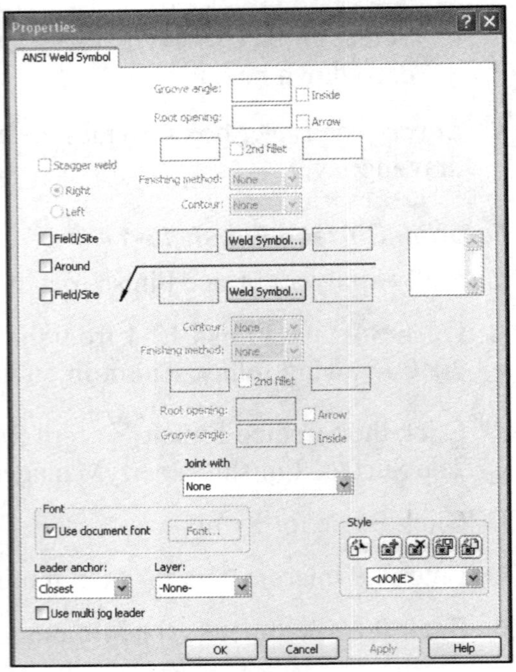


The dialog box is displayed for ISO, BSI, DIN, JIS and GB standards. Different dialog boxes are displayed for ANSI and GOST standards. The book addresses the ANSI dialog box. The dialog box displays numerous selections. Enter values and select the required symbols and options. A preview is displayed in the Graphics window.

Click a face or edge where you want to locate a welded joint. If the weld symbol has a leader, click a location to place the leader first. Click to place the symbol.

If you selected a face or edge before you click the Weld Symbol tool from the Annotation toolbar, the leader is already placed; click once to place the symbol. Click as many times as necessary to place multiple weld symbols.

Construct weld symbols independently in a part, assembly, or drawing document. When you create or edit your weld symbol, you can:

- Add secondary weld fillet information to the weld symbol for certain types of weld, example; Square or Bevel.
- Choose a Leader anchor of None.
- Choose the text font for each weld symbol.

### *Tutorial: Weld Symbol 13-1*

Manually insert a Weld Symbol into an assembly. Insert the assembly into a drawing.

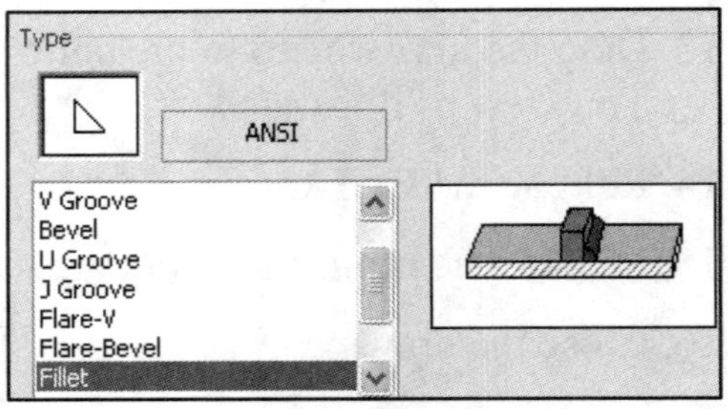


1. Open the **Weld Symbol 13-1** assembly from the SolidWorks 2010\Drawing folder. Click **Insert ➢ Assembly Feature ➢ Weld Bead** from the Menu bar. The Weld Bead Type dialog box is displayed.
2. Click **Fillet** for Weld Type.
3. Click **Next>**.
4. Click **Concave** for Surface Shape.
5. Enter **1.00**mm for the Top Surface Delta.
6. Enter **6.00**mm for Radius.

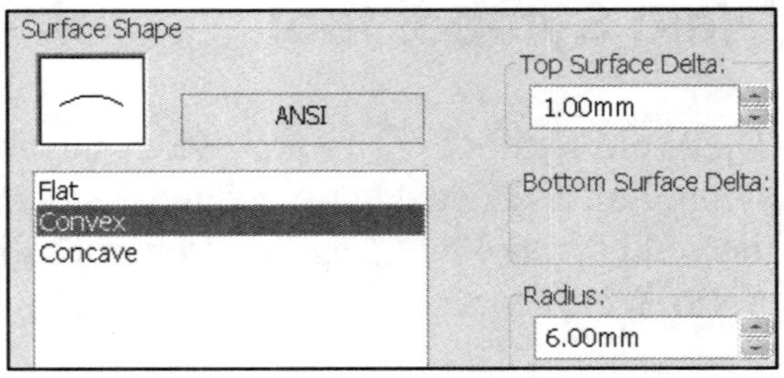

7. Enter **Next>**.
8. Click the **outside cylindrical face** of TUBE<1>. Face<1>@TUBE1-W-1 is displayed in the Contact Faces box.
9. Click the **top face** of PLATE<1>. Face<2>@PLATE1-W-1 is displayed in the Contact Faces box.

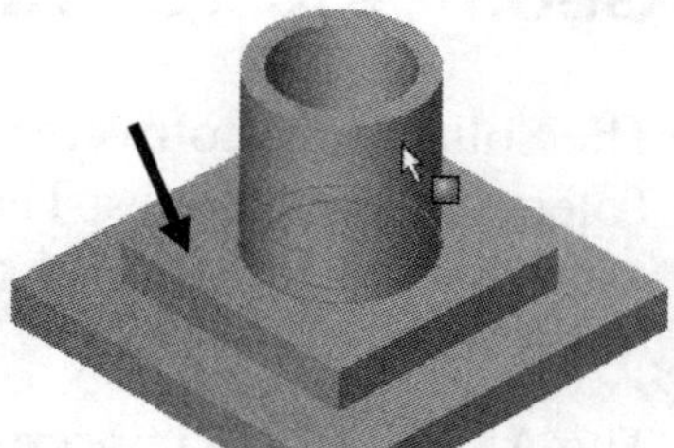

10. Click **Next>**. Bead#.sldprt is located in the SolidWorks 2010\Drawing folder.
11. Click **Finish** from the Weld Bead Part dialog box.
12. Right-click the **Annotations** folder from the FeatureManager.
13. Click **Display Annotations**.
14. Drag the **Weld Symbol** off the profile.

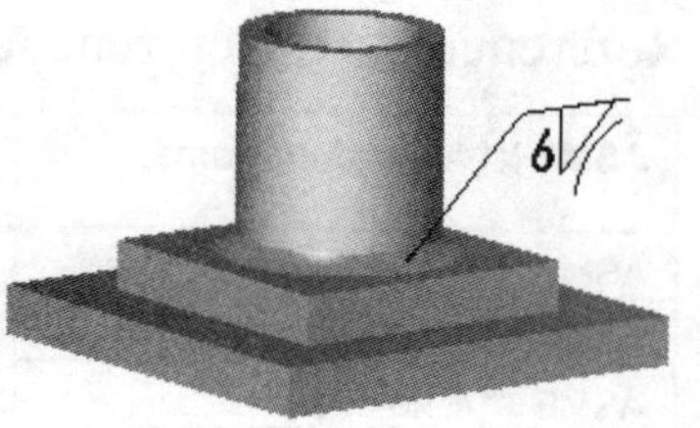


15. Click **Make Drawing from Part/Assembly** from the Menu bar.

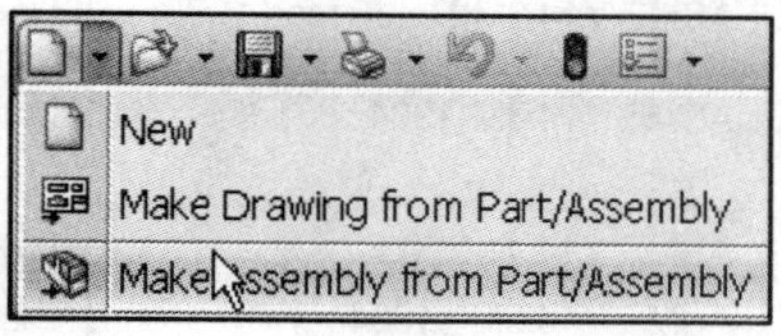


16. Click **No**.
17. Click **OK**.
18. Click **OK**.
19. Click and drag the **Front view** from the View Palette into the active drawing sheet.

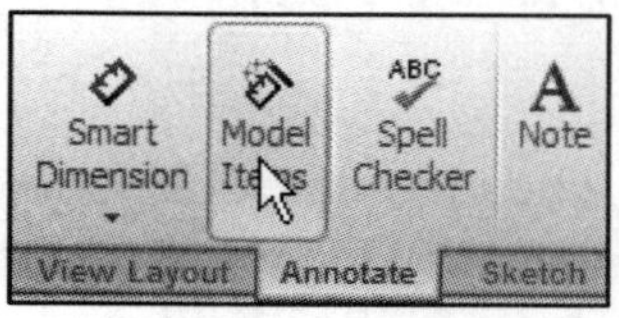


20. Click **OK** from the Projected View PropertyManager. The Front View is displayed on Sheet1.
21. Create a **1:1** scale.

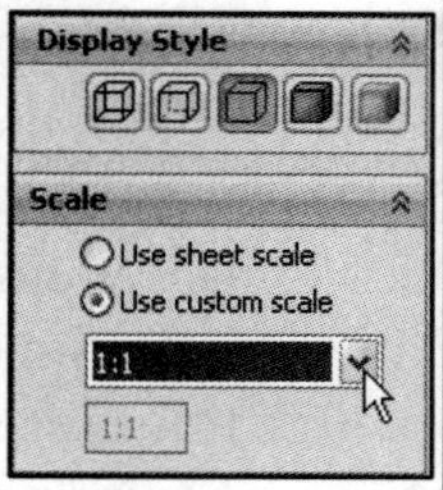


22. Click **Model Items** from the Annotation tab. The Model Items PropertyManager is displayed.
23. Select **Entire model** for Source.
24. Deselect **Marked for Drawing**.
25. Click **Welds** from the Annotations box.
26. Click **OK** from the Model Items PropertyManager. The Weld Symbol from the assembly is displayed in the drawing.
27. **Close** the drawing.

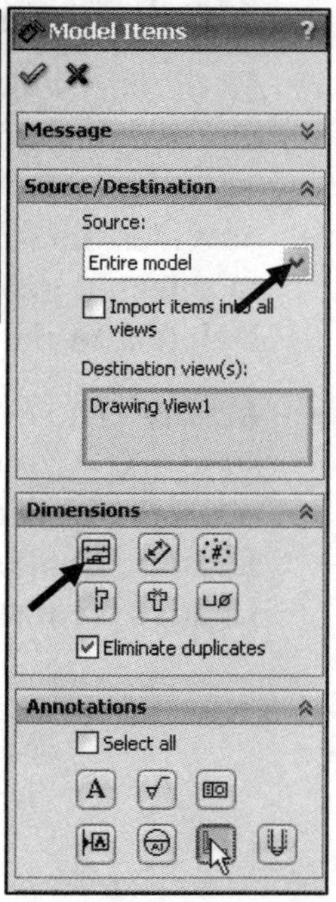

# Geometric Tolerance tool

The SolidWorks software supports the ANSI Y14.5 Geometric and True Position Tolerancing guidelines. These standards represent the drawing practices used by U.S. industry. The ASME Y14 practices supersede the American National Standards Institute ANSI standards.

The ASME Y14 Engineering Drawing and Related Documentation Practices are published by The American Society of Mechanical Engineers, New York, NY. References to the current ASME Y14 standards are used with permission.

| ASME Y14 Standard Name: | American National Standard Engineering Drawing and Related Documentation: | Revision of the Standard: |
|---|---|---|
| ASME Y14.100M-1998 | Engineering Drawing Practices | DOD-STD-100 |
| ASME Y14.1-1995 | Decimal Inch Drawing Sheet Size and Format | ANSI Y14.1 |
| ASME Y14.1M-1995 | Metric Drawing Sheet Size and Format | ANSI Y14.1M |
| ASME Y14.24M | Types and Applications of Engineering Drawings | ANSI Y14.24M |
| ASME Y14.2M(Reaffirmed 1998) | Line Conventions and Lettering | ANSI Y14.2M |
| ASME Y14.3M-1994 | Multi-view and Sectional View Drawings | ANSI Y14.3 |
| ASME Y14.41-2003 | Digital Product Definition Data Practices | N/A |
| ASME Y14.5M –1994 (Reaffirmed 1999) | Dimensioning and Tolerancing | ANSI Y14.5-1982 (R1988) |

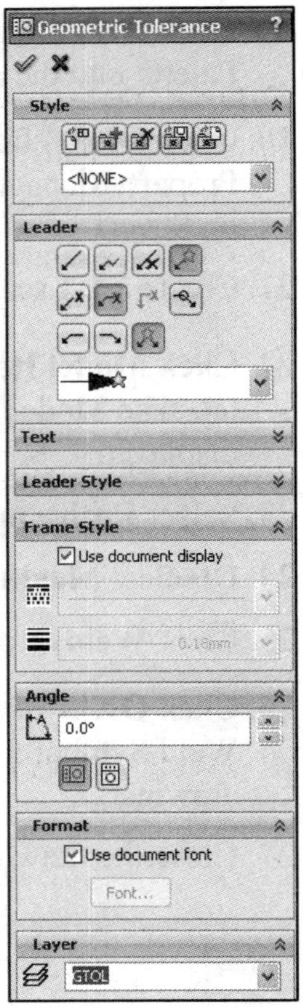


The Geometric Tolerance tool uses the Properties dialog box and the Geometric Tolerance PropertyManager. As items are added, a preview is displayed. The Geometric Tolerance PropertyManager provides the following selections:

- ***Style***. The Style box provides the ability to define styles, for dimensions and various annotations (Notes, Geometric Tolerance, Surface Finish, Weld Symbols, etc.). The style box provides the following selections: **Apply the default attributes to selected geometric tolerance**, **Add or Update a Style**, **Delete a Style**, **Save a Style** and **Load Style**.
- ***Leader***. The Leader box provides the ability to select the Leader style and Arrow style. The available selections are: **Leader**, **Straight Leader**, **Leader Left**, **Multi-jog Leader**, **Bend Leader**, **Leader Right**, **No Leader**, **Perpendicular Leader**, **Leader Nearest**, **Auto Leader** and **All Around Leader**.

- ***Text***. Default text <Gtol>.
- ***Frame Style***. Use document display selected by default. Provides the ability to apply the default document frame style set in the Document properties section or to select a custom frame style for the drop-down menus.
- ***Angle***. The Angle box provides the ability to set the angle value of rotation for the symbol. A positive angle rotates the note counterclockwise.
- ***Format***. The Format box provides the following selections. They are:
  - **Use document font**. Uses the same font style and type as in the document.
  - **Font**. Provides the ability to customize the font for the document. Uncheck the Use document font box.
- ***Layer***. The Layer option provides the ability to apply the Geometric Tolerance to a specified drawing layer.

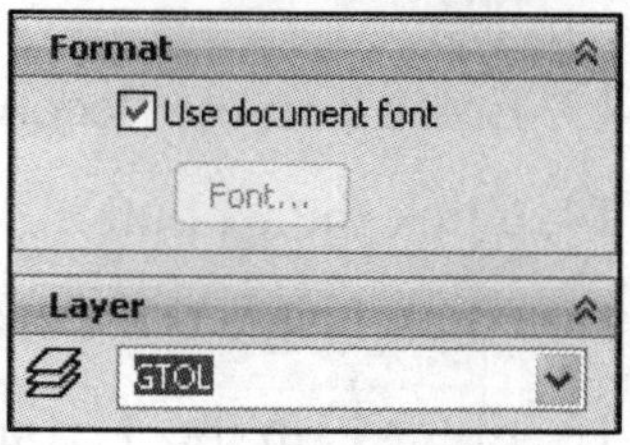


When you use the Auto Leader option, you must float over the entity to highlight the entity and to attach the leader. The leader is not displayed until you float over the entity with the mouse pointer.

***Tutorial: Geometric Tolerance 13-1***

Insert a Geometric tolerance. Add a Feature Control frame for the Ø22 hole dimension in the Front view.

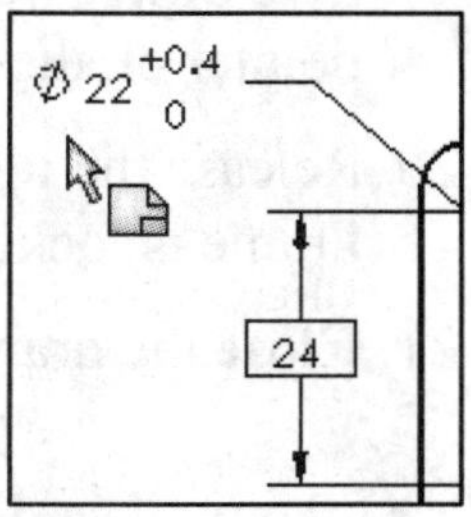


1. Open **Geometric Tolerance 13-1** from the SolidWorks 2010\ Drawing folder.
2. Click a position below the **Ø22 hole dimension** text in the Front view.
3. Click the **Geometric Tolerance** tool from the Annotation tab. The Geometric Tolerance Properties dialog box is displayed.
4. Click the **Symbol Library** Geometric Tolerance drop-down arrow.
5. Click the **Position** icon as illustrated. The Feature Control Frame displays the Position symbol in the Preview box.

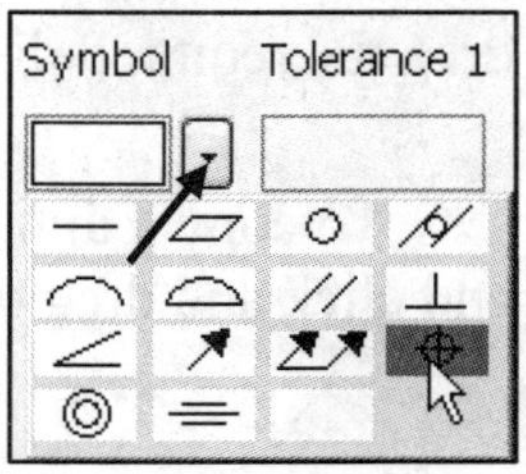

6. Click inside the **Tolerance 1** box.
7. Click the **Diameter** Ø button.
8. Enter **0.25** in the Tolerance 1 box.
9. Click the **M** button. The Maximum Material Condition Modifying Symbol is displayed.

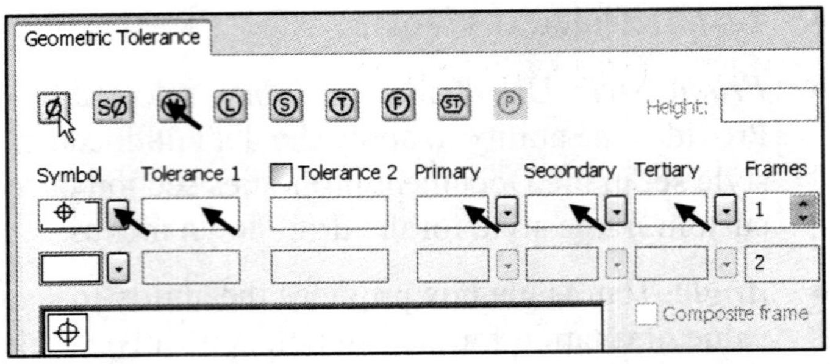


10. Click inside the **Primary** box.
11. Enter **A** in the Primary box.
12. Click inside the **Secondary** box.
13. Enter **B** in the Secondary box.
14. Click the **M** button.
15. Click inside the **Tertiary** box.
16. Enter **C** in the Tertiary box.
17. Click the **M** button.
18. Click **OK** from the Properties dialog box.

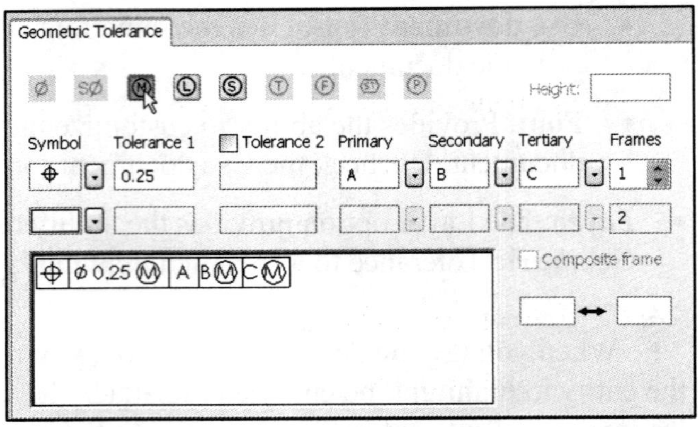


Attach the Feature Control Frame.

19. Drag the Feature Control Frame to the **Ø22 hole dimension** text and position the mouse pointer on the Ø22.
20. Release the **mouse**. The Feature Control Frame is locked to the dimension text.
21. **Close** the drawing.

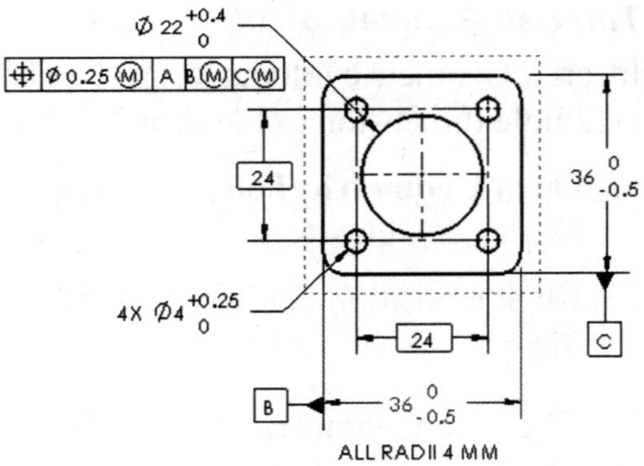


To move a dimension from one view to another view, apply the Shift key to click and drag the required dimension.

To copy a dimension, apply the Ctrl key, and click and drag the required dimension.

# Datum Feature tool

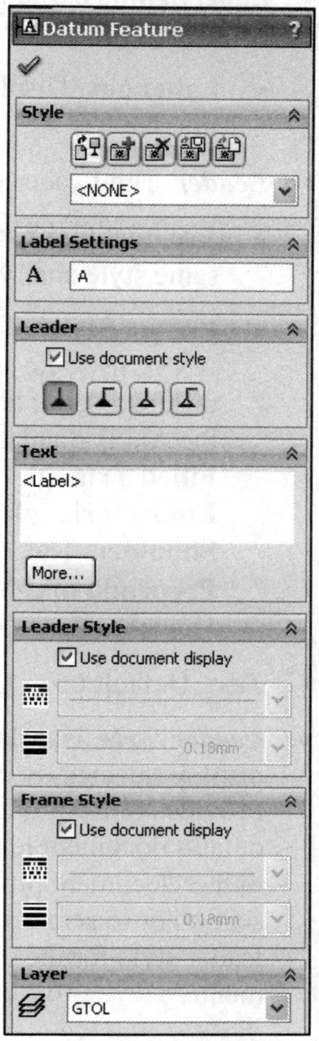


The Datum Feature tool adds a Datum Feature symbol. Attach a datum feature symbol to the following items:

- In an assembly or part, on a reference plane, or on a planar model surface.
- In a drawing view, on a surface that is displayed as an edge, not a silhouette or on a section view surface.
- A geometric tolerance symbol frame.
- In a note.
- On a dimension, with the following exceptions:
  - Chamfer dimensions.
  - Angular dimensions, unless the symbols are displayed per the 1982 standard.
  - Ordinate dimensions.
  - Arc dimensions.

The Datum Feature symbol name automatically increments every time you select the symbol. The Datum Feature tool uses the Datum Feature PropertyManager. The Datum Feature PropertyManager provides the following selections:

- ***Style***. None selected by default. The Style box provides the ability to define styles, for dimensions and various annotations. The style box provides the following selections: **Apply the default attributes to selected datum feature, Add or Update a Style, Delete a Style, Save a Style** and **Load Style**.

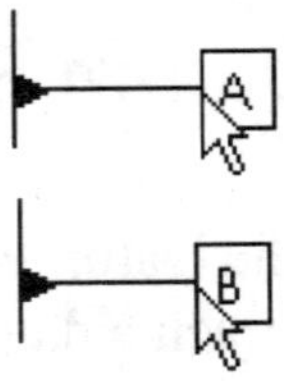


- ***Label Settings***. The Label Settings box provides the following option:
  - **Label box**. Displays a Label to the leader line. The first label is A.
- ***Leader***. The Leader box provides the following options:
  - **Use document style**. Selected by default. Uses the same style and type as in the document.
  - **Pre-set Styles**. The available pre-set styles follow the ANSI, ISO, etc standards. Each style of box has a different set of attachment styles. The book addresses the ANSI standard. The available styles for Square are: **Filled Triangle, Filled Triangle With Shoulder, Empty Triangle** and **Empty Triangle With Shoulder**. The styles for Round (GB) are: **Perpendicular Vertical** and **Horizontal**.

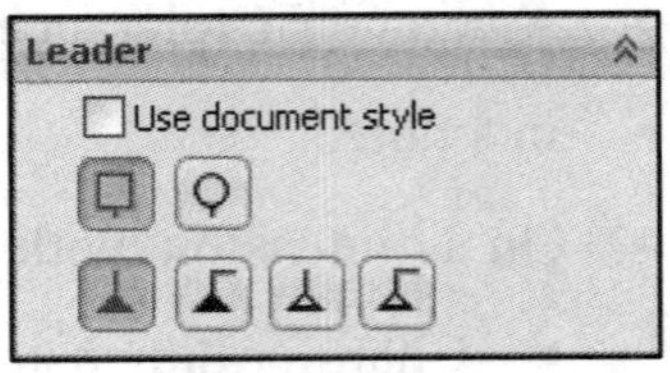


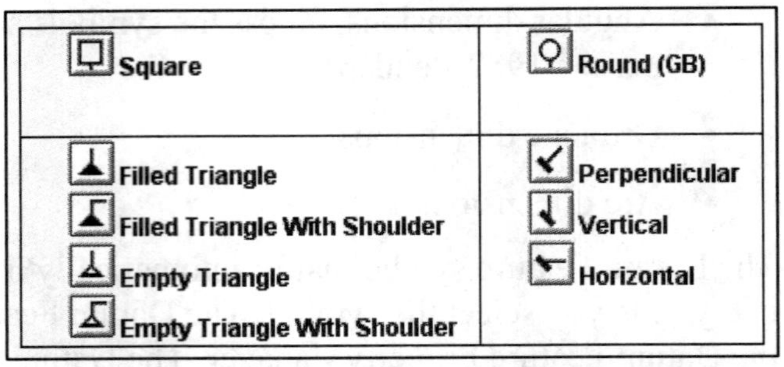


- ***Text***. Default text <Gtol>.
- ***Leader Style***. Use document display selected by default. Provides the ability to apply the default document leader style set in the Document properties section or to select a custom leader style for the drop-down menu.
- ***Frame Style.*** Use document display selected by default. Provides the ability to apply the default document frame style set in the Document properties section or to select a custom frame style for the drop-down menu.
- ***Layer***. The Layer option provides the ability to apply the Datum Feature to a specified drawing layer.

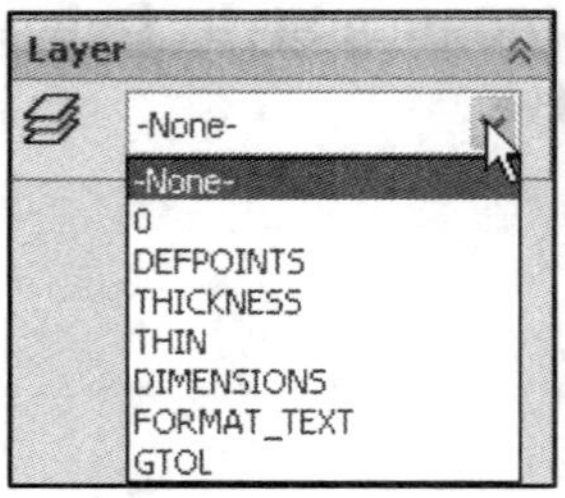

### *Tutorial: Datum Feature 13-1*

Create two datum features. The method to insert a datum feature and a geometric tolerance symbols is the same for a part or drawing. There is one exception. When a geometric tolerance frame is created in the drawing, anchor the frame to the corresponding dimension. In the part, position the geometric tolerance near the dimension. The frame is free to move.

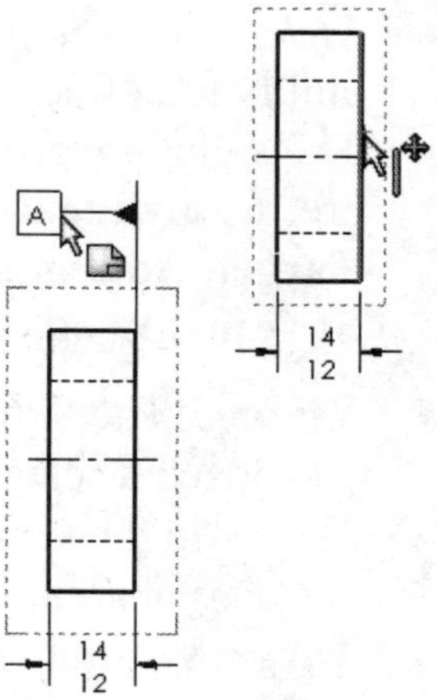


1. Open **Datum Feature 13-1** from the SolidWorks 2010\ Drawing folder.
2. Click the **right vertical edge** of Drawing View2 as illustrated. The Drawing View2 PropertyManager is displayed.
3. Click the **Datum Feature** tool from the Annotation tab. The Datum Feature PropertyManager is displayed. The Label Settings box displays an A. If not, enter A.
4. Drag the **Datum Feature Symbol A** above the top profile line in the Right view.
5. Click a **position** to the left of the vertical edge as illustrated.
6. Drag the **Datum Feature Symbol B** to the left vertical edge in the Front view.
7. Click the **left vertical edge** in the Front view as illustrated.
8. Click a **position** below the bottom profile line in the Front view.
9. Click **OK** from the Datum Feature PropertyManager. View the two created datum features. Note: The default Leader and Frame style is applied.
10. **Close** the drawing.

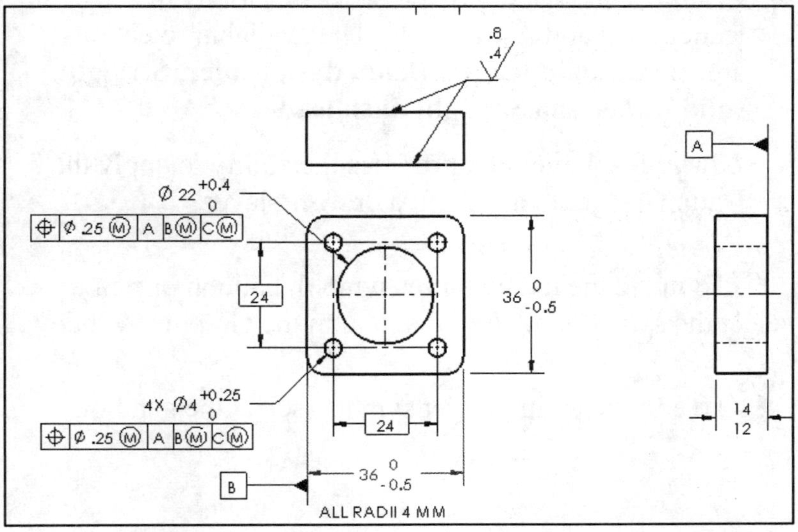

# Datum Target tool

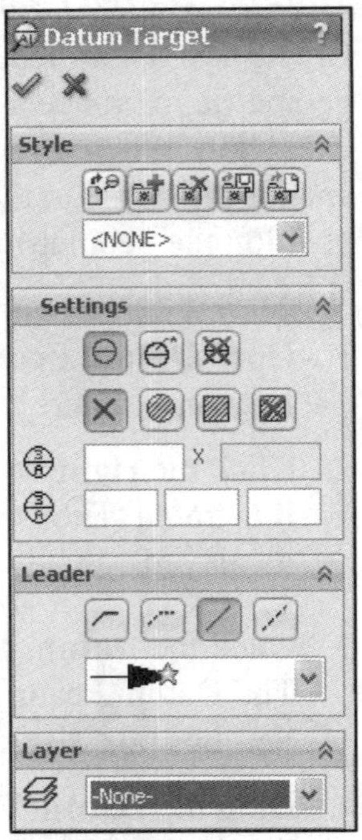


The Datum Target tool provides the ability to attach a datum target and symbol to a model face or edge in a document. The Datum Target tool uses the Datum Target PropertyManager. The Datum Target PropertyManager provides the following selections:

- ***Style***. None selected by default. The Style box provides the ability to define styles for dimensions and various annotations. The style box provides the following selections. They are: **Apply the default attributes to selected Datum Target**, **Add or Update a Style**, **Delete a Style**, **Save a Style** and **Load Style**.
- ***Settings***. The Settings box provides the ability to select and attach a selected symbol to a model face or edge. The Setting box provides selections for Target symbols and Target area. The available Target symbols are: **Target symbol**, **Target symbol with area size outside**, and **No target symbol**.

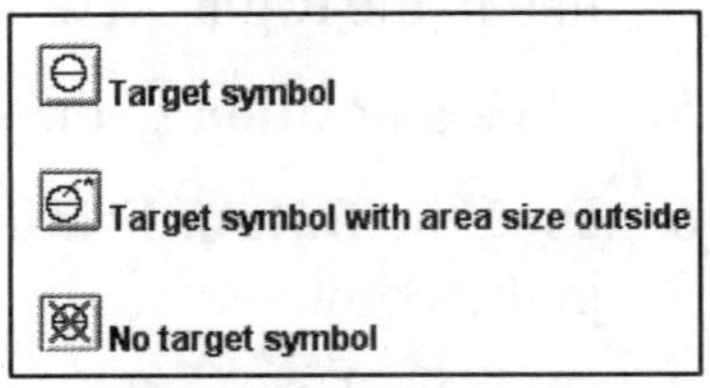


  - The available Target areas are: **X target area**, **Circular target area**, **Rectangular target area** and **Do not display target area**.

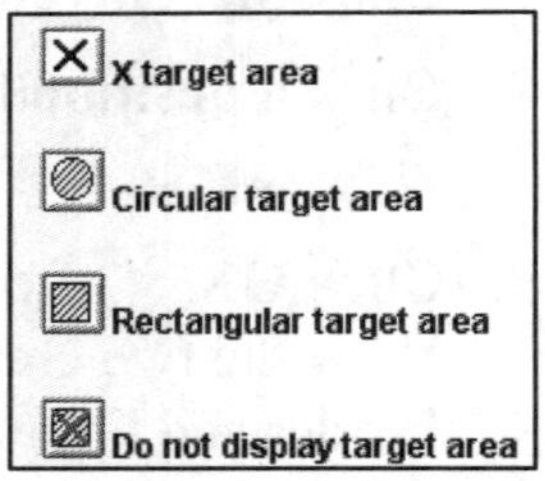


  - **Target areas size box**. Provides the ability to specify the width and height for rectangles or the diameter for circles.
  - **Datum references**. Provides the ability to specify up to three references.
- ***Leader***. The Leader box provides the ability to select the leader style and Arrow style. The available selections are: **Bend, solid leader**, **Bend, dash leader**, **Straight, solid leader** and **Straight dash leader**.

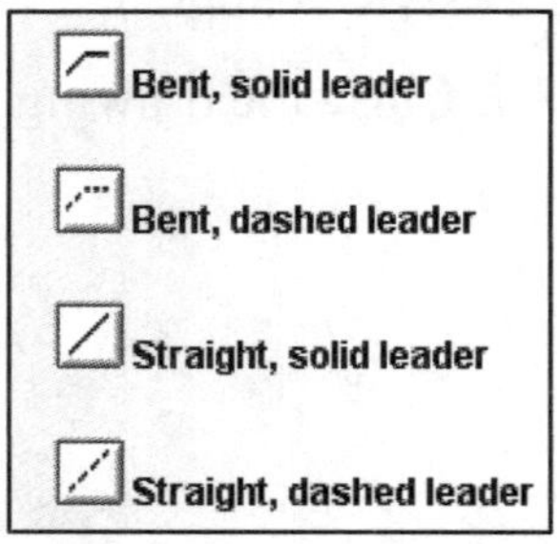


- ***Layer***. The Layer box provides the ability to apply the Datum Target to a specified drawing layer.

To move the datum target symbol, balloon or point, select the symbol and drag the item in the Graphics window.

To edit the datum target symbol, select the symbol.

## Hole Callout tool

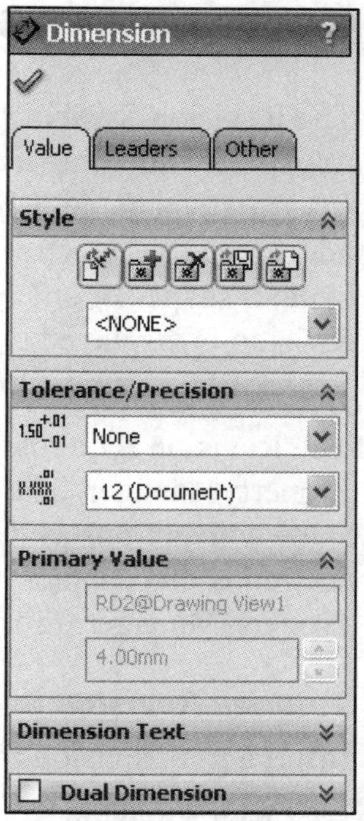


The Hole Callout ⌴⌀ tool adds a Hole Callout to the selected view in your drawing. The Hole callout contains a diameter symbol and the dimension of the hole diameter. If the depth of the hole is known, the Hole Callout will also contain a depth symbol and the dimension of the depth.

The number of instances is included in the hole callout if a hole in a Linear or Circular pattern was created in the Hole Wizard tool.

The Hole Callout tool uses the information from the Hole Wizard, if the hole was created by the Hole Wizard. The Dimension PropertyManager is displayed when using the Hole Callout tool. See Chapter 5 for additional information on the Dimension PropertyManager.

### *Tutorial: Hole Callout 13-1*

Insert a Hole Callout feature into a drawing view.

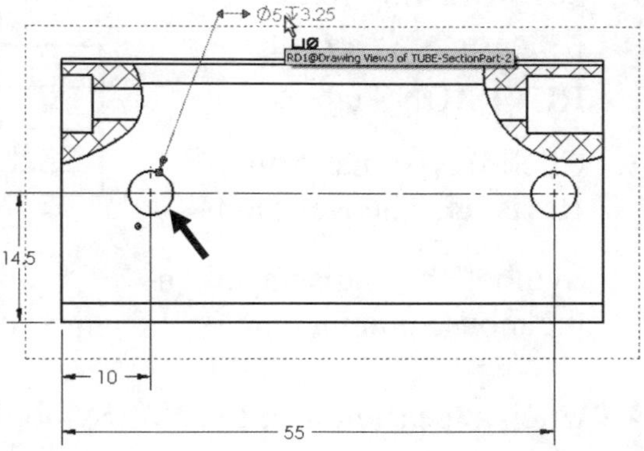


1. Open **Hole Callout 13-1** from the SolidWorks 2010\Drawing folder.
2. **Zoom in** on Drawing View3.
3. Click the **Hole CallOut** ⌴⌀ tool from the Annotation tab.
4. Click the **circumference of the left port** on Drawing View3.
5. Click a **position** above the profile. The Dimension PropertyManager is displayed.
6. Enter **2X** before the <DIM> text in the Dimension Text box as illustrated. Note: delete **R**.
7. Click **Yes** to the Break Link with Model dialog box.
8. Press the **space** key.
9. Click **OK** from the Dimension PropertyManager.
10. **Close** the drawing.

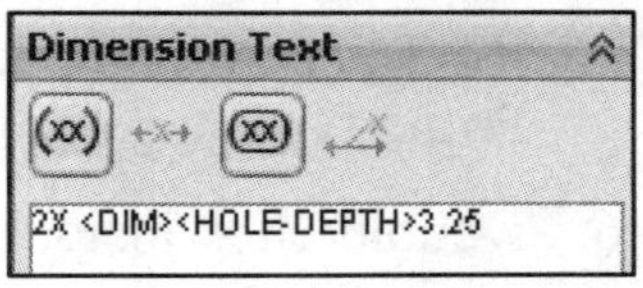


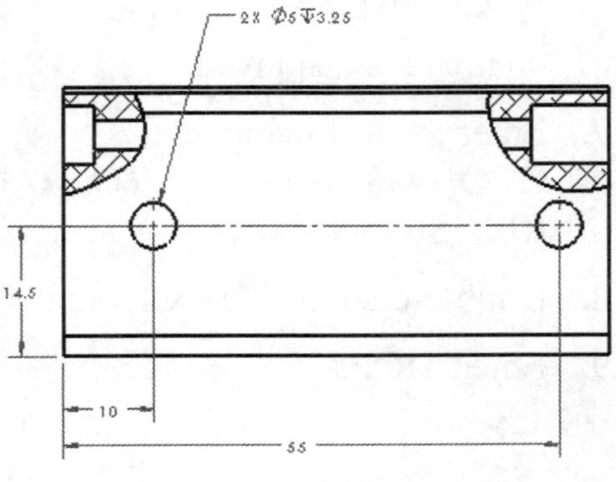

## Revision Symbol tool

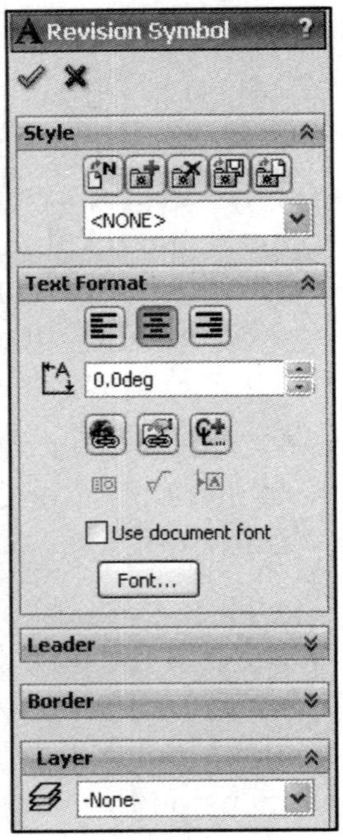


The Revision Symbol tool provides the ability to insert a revision symbol into a drawing with a revision already in the table. Insert a revision table into a drawing to track document revisions. In addition to the functionality for all tables, you can select: Revision symbol shapes or an alphabetic or numeric sequence. The latest revision is displayed under REV in the lower-right corner of a sheet format.

The Revision Symbol tool uses the Revision Symbol PropertyManager. The Revision Symbol PropertyManager uses the same conventions as the Note PropertyManager. View the Note tool section is this chapter, Annotation toolbar for detail PropertyManager information.

***Tutorial: Revision Symbol 13-1***

Insert a new revision into a drawing.

1. Open **Revision Symbol 13-1** from the SolidWorks 2010\Drawing folder.
2. Right-click inside the **REVISIONS** table.

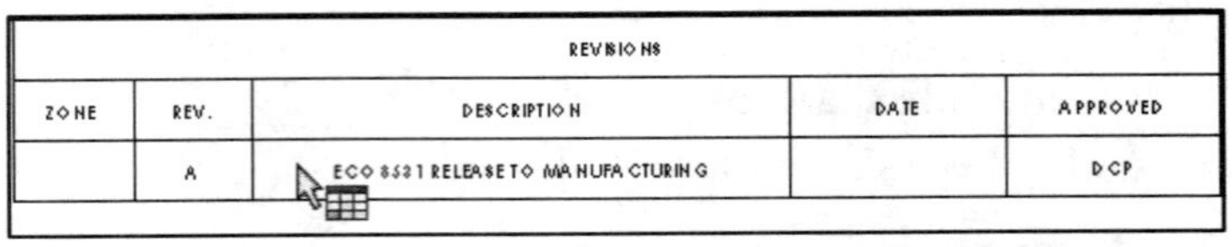


3. Click **Revisions, Add Revision**. The Revision Symbol is displayed on the mouse pointer.
4. Click a **location** near the Symbol in the drawing sheet.
5. Click **OK** from the Revision Symbol PropertyManager.

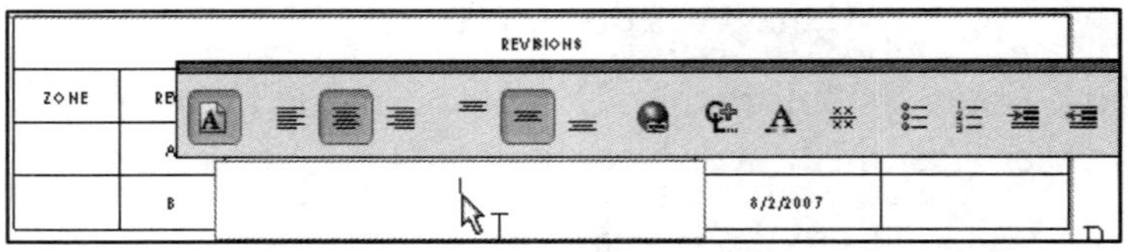


6. Double-click inside the empty **Cell** under DESCRIPTION. The Pop-up menu is displayed.
7. Enter the following text: **ECO 9443 RELEASE TO MANUFACTURING.** The Date is displayed in the REVISIONS table.
8. Double-click inside **Cell 4** under APPROVED.
9. Enter: **DCP**.

10. Click **outside** the REVISION table.

11. **Close** the drawing.

| REVISIONS | | | | |
|---|---|---|---|---|
| ZONE | REV. | DESCRIPTION | DATE | APPROVED |
| | A | ECO 8531 RELEASE TO MANUFACTURING | 9/10/2008 | DCP |
| | B | ECO 9443 RELEASE TO MANUFACTURING | 7/24/2009 | DCP |

## Area Hatch/Fill tool

The Area Hatch/Fill tool provides the ability to add an area hatch or fill pattern in a drawing. Apply a solid fill or a crosshatch pattern to a closed sketch profile, model face, or to a region bounded by a combination of model edges and sketch entities. You can only apply an Area Hatch in drawings. Some characteristics of Area Hatch include the following:

- If the Area Hatch is a solid fill, the default color of the fill is black.
- You can move an Area Hatch into a layer.
- You can select an Area Hatch in a Broken View only in its unbroken state.
- You cannot select an Area Hatch that crosses a break.
- Dimensions or annotations that belong to the drawing view are surrounded by a halo of space when they are on top of an area hatch or fill.

The Area Hatch / Fill tool uses the Area Hatch/Fill PropertyManager. The Area Hatch/Fill PropertyManager provides the following selections:

- ***Properties***. The Properties box provides the following selections and displays the Area Hatch and Fill. The selections are:
  - **Hatch**. Selected by default. Applies a hatch pattern to the region. Illustrated in the Properties box. ANSI31 is selected by default.
  - **Solid**. Applies a black fill to the region.
  - **None**. Removes the area hatch or fill from the region.
  - **Pattern Scale**. Only available for the Hatch option.
  - **Hatch Pattern Angle**. Only available for the Hatch option

- ***Area to Hatch***. The Area to Hatch box provides the following selections. They are:
  - **Region**. Applies the Area Hatch or Fill to a closed region bounded by model edges or sketch entities.
  - **Boundary**. Applies the Area Hatch or Fill to a combination of model edges and sketch entities that you select for Selected boundary or face.

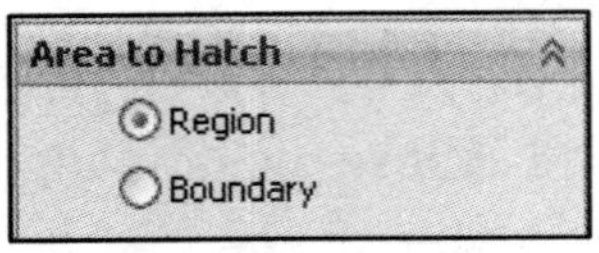


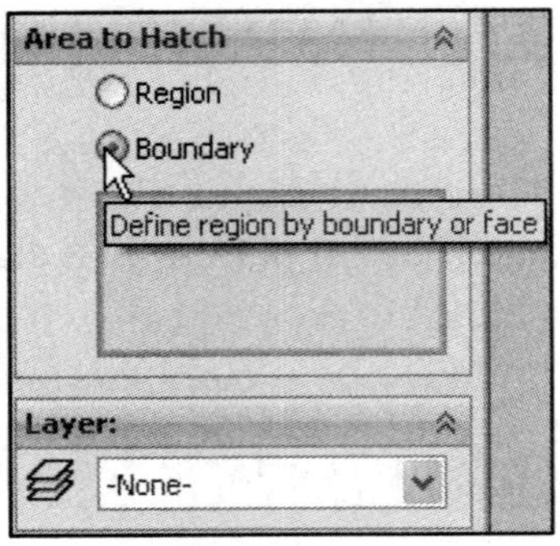


- ***Layer***. The Layer box provides the ability to apply the Area Hatch/Fill to a specified drawing layer.

### *Tutorial: Area Hatch/Fill 13-1*

Insert Area Hatch to a region of a drawing view.

1. Open **Area Hatch 13-1** from the SolidWorks 2010\ Drawing folder.
2. Click inside the **Drawing View9** view boundary as illustrated.

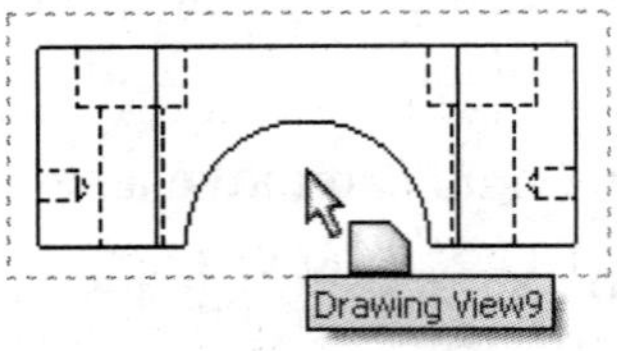


3. Click the **Area Hatch/Fill**  tool from the Annotation tab. The Area Hatch/Fill PropertyManager is displayed.
4. Check **Hatch** from the Properties box.
5. Select **Steel** for Hatch Pattern from the drop-down menu.
6. Select **4** for Hatch Pattern Scale. Accept the default angle. Region is checked by default.
7. Click on the **Drawing View** as illustrated. An area hatch is applied to the clamp in the selected region.

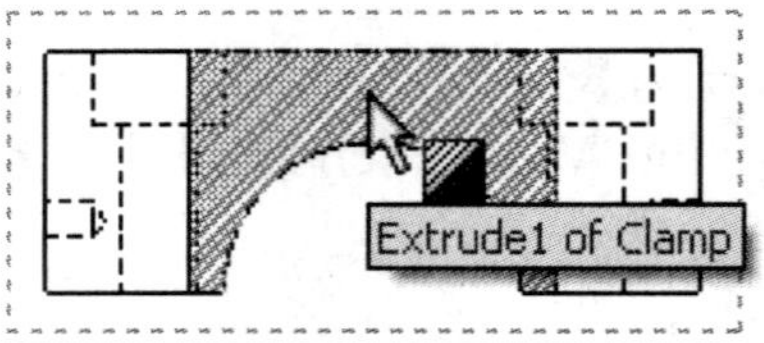


8. Click **OK** from the Area Hatch/Fill PropertyManager.
9. **Close** the drawing.

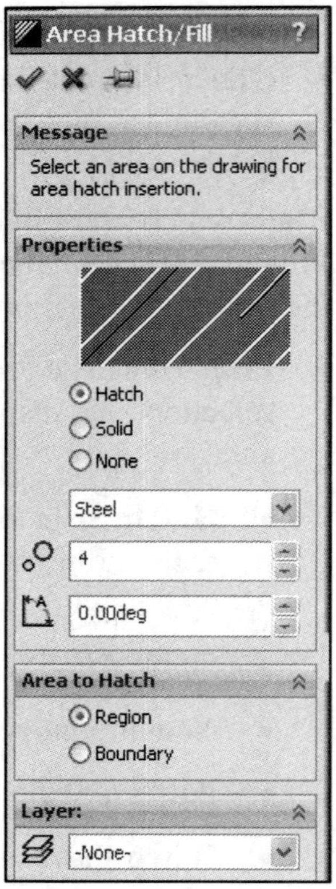

## Block tool

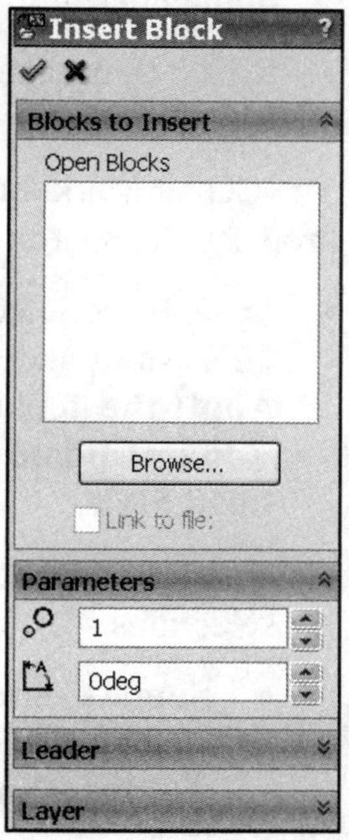


The Block tool from the Annotation toolbar provides the ability to either select the Make Block tool or the Insert Block tool. The Make Block tool uses the Make Block PropertyManager. The Insert Block tool uses the Insert Block PropertyManager.

You can make, save, edit, and insert blocks for drawing items that you use often, such as standard notes, title blocks, label positions, etc.

Blocks can include text, any type of sketch entity, balloons, imported entities and text, and area hatch. You can attach blocks to geometry or to drawing views, and you can insert them into sheet formats. You can also copy blocks between drawings and sketches, or insert blocks from the Design Library. View the Block section in Chapter 4 for additional information.

## Center Mark tool

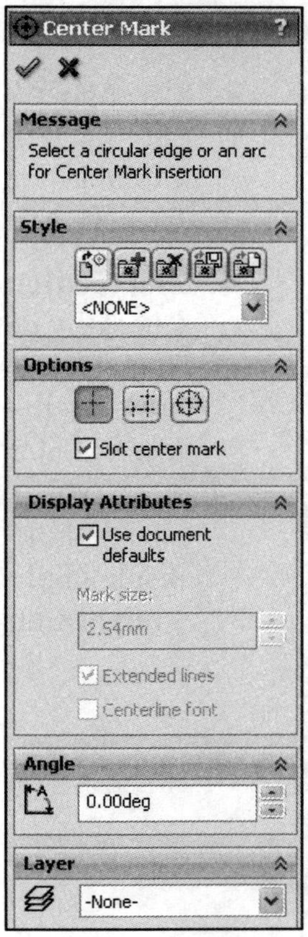


The Center Mark tool provides the ability to locate center marks on circles or arcs in a drawing. Use the center mark lines as references for dimensioning. A few items to note about center marks are:

- Center marks are available as single marks, in Circular, Linear patterns or in a Slot center mark.
- The axis of the circle or arc must be normal to the drawing sheet.
- Center marks can be inserted automatically into new drawing views for holes or fillets if required using the option selection.
- Center marks propagate or insert automatically into patterns if the pattern is created from a feature and not a body or face.

- Center marks in Auxiliary Views are oriented to the viewing direction such that one of the lines of the center mark is parallel to the view arrow direction.
- Rotate center marks individually by specifying the rotation in degrees. Using the Rotate Drawing View dialog box.

The Center Mark tool uses the Center Mark PropertyManager. The Center Mark PropertyManager provides the following selections:

- ***Style***. None selected by default. The Style box provides the ability to define styles for dimensions and various annotations. The style box provides the following selections: **Apply the default attributes to selected Center Mark**, **Add or Update a Style**, **Delete a Style**, **Save a Style** and **Load Style**.
- ***Options***. The Options box provides the following selections:
  - **Single Center Mark**. Inserts a center mark into a single arc or circle. You can modify the Display Attributes and rotation Angle of the center mark.
  - **Linear Center Mark**. Inserts center marks into a Linear pattern of arcs and circles. You can select Connection lines and Display Attributes for Linear patterns.
  - **Circular Center Mark**. Inserts center marks into a Circular pattern of arcs and circles. You can select Circular lines, Radial lines, Base center mark, and Display Attributes for Circular patterns.
  - **Slot Center mark**. Check by default. The Slot center mark option provides the ability to insert center marks in slots, which included slots in hole tables and display hole callouts for straight slots.

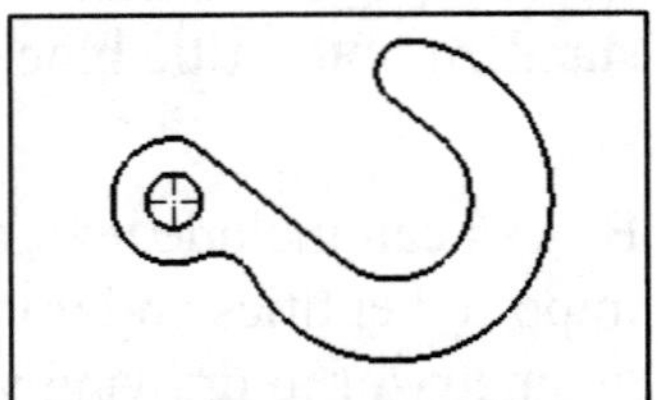

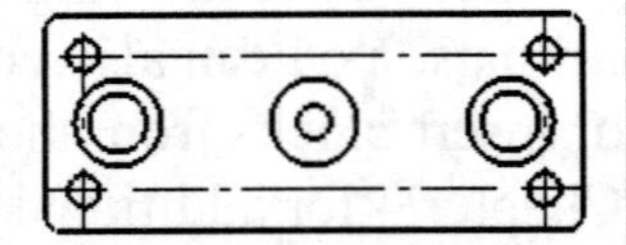

Linear center marks with connection lines

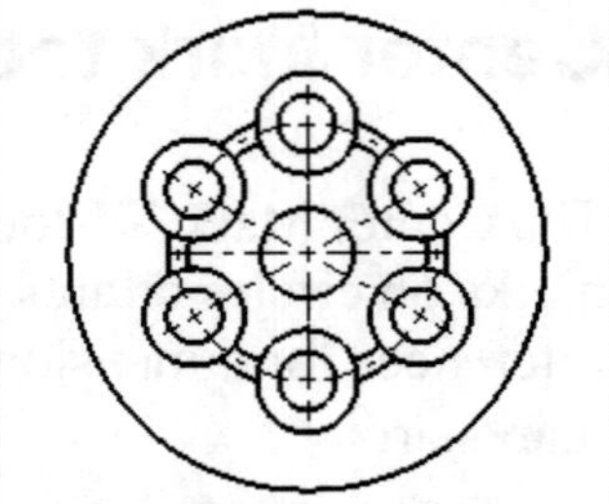

Circular center marks with circular lines, radial lines, and base center mark

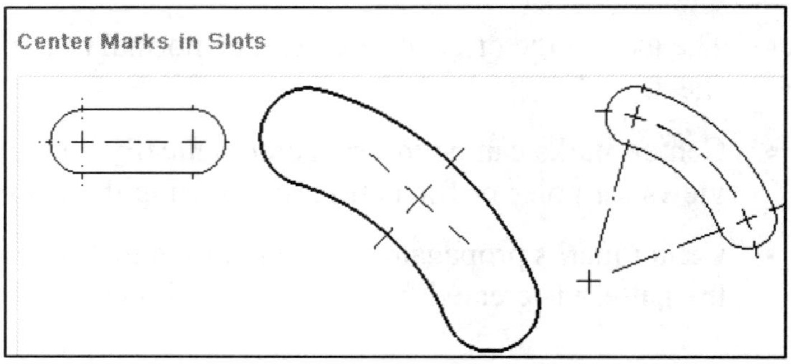

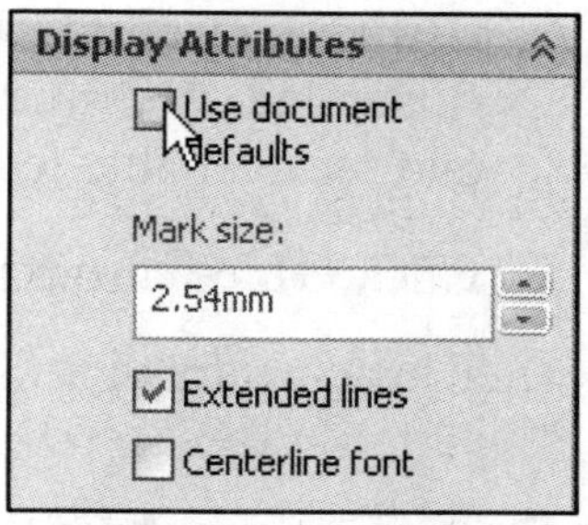


- ***Display Attributes***. The Display Attributes box provides the following selections. They are:
  - **Use document defaults**. Selected by default. Uses the default attributes set in the Documents Properties section.
  - **Mark size**. Sets a document value. Uncheck the Use document defaults option.
  - **Extended lines**. Displays the extended axis lines with a gap between the center mark and the extended lines. Uncheck the Use the document defaults option.

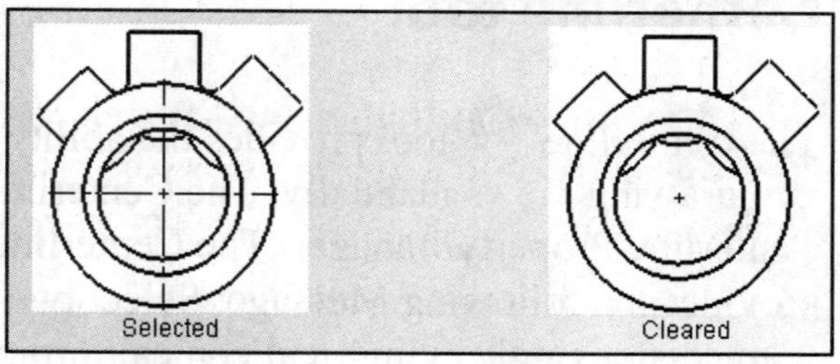


  - **Centerline font**. Displays the center mark lines in the centerline font. Uncheck the Use the document defaults option.

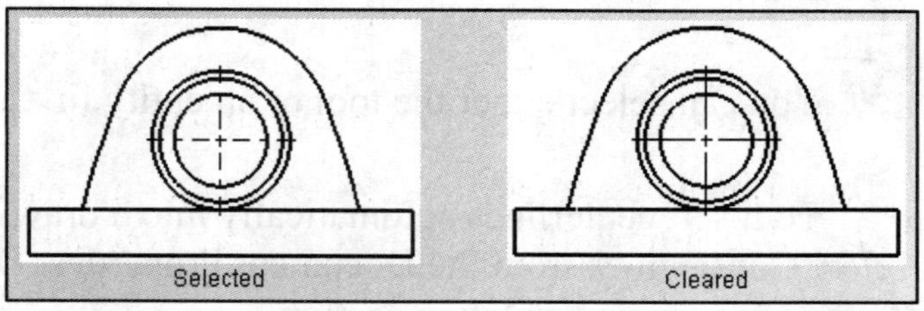


- ***Angle***. The Angle section provides the following option:
  - **Angle box**. Not available for Linear or Circular pattern center marks. Sets the angle of the center mark. If you rotate the selected center mark, the rotation angle is displayed in the Angle box.

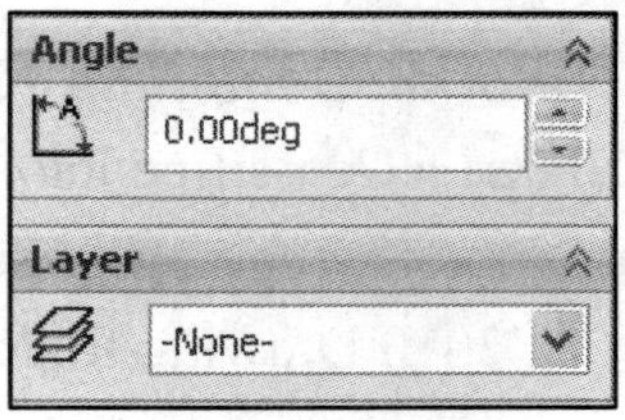


- ***Layer***. The Layer box provides the ability to apply the center mark to a specified drawing layer.

### *Tutorial: Center Mark 13-1*

Manually insert a Center Mark into a drawing view.

1. Open the **Center Mark 13-1** drawing from the SolidWorks 2010\Drawing folder. Drawing View1 has two center marks.

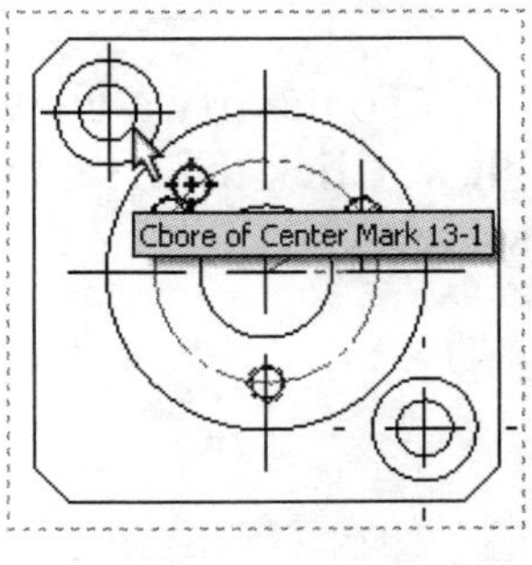


2. Click inside the **Drawing View1** view boundary. The Drawing View1 PropertyManager is displayed.
3. Click the **Center Mark** tool from the Annotation tab. The Center Mark PropertyManager is displayed.

4. Click the **circumference** of the small top left circle as illustrated. A Center Mark is displayed. View your options and the available features.
5. Click **OK** from the Center Mark PropertyManager.
6. **Close** the drawing.

## Centerline tool

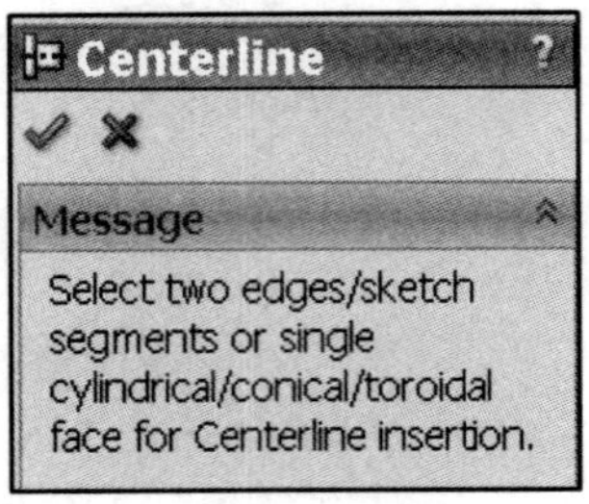


The Centerline tool provides the ability to insert centerlines into drawing views manually. The Centerline tool uses the Centerline PropertyManager. The Centerline PropertyManager provides the following Message: Select two edges/sketch segments or single cylindrical/conical/toroidal face for Centerline insertion.

You can select either the tool or an entity first.

To insert centerlines automatically into a drawing view, select **Centerlines** from the Document Properties, Detailing, Auto insert on view creation section.

***Tutorial: Centerline 13-1***

Insert a Centerline into a drawing view.

1. Open **Centerline 13-1** from the SolidWorks 2010\Drawing folder.
2. Click inside the **Drawing View9** view boundary as illustrated.

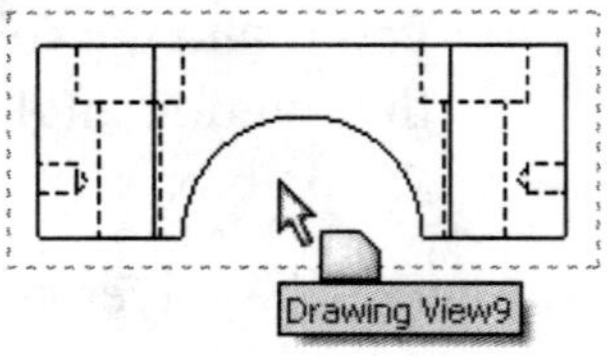


3. Click the **Centerline** tool from the Annotation tab. The Centerline PropertyManager is displayed. Centerlines are displayed in the selected view.
4. Click **OK** from the Centerline PropertyManager.
5. **Close** the drawing.

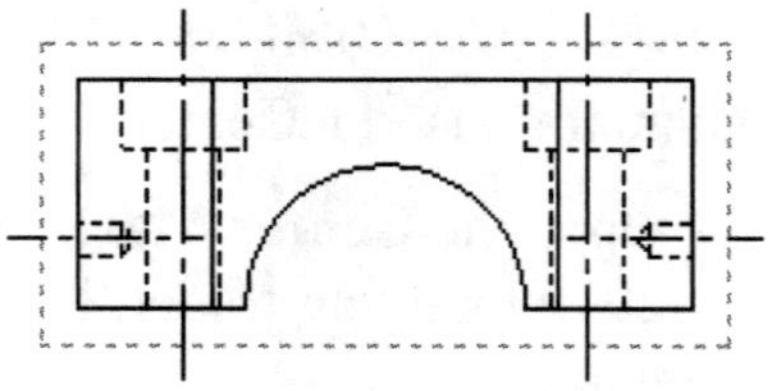

To modify a view scale, click inside the desired view. Click the Use custom size box. Enter the needed scale.

## Consolidated Table Toolbar

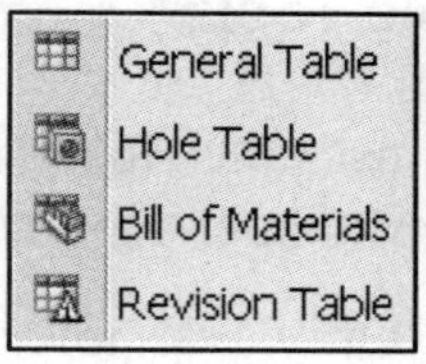


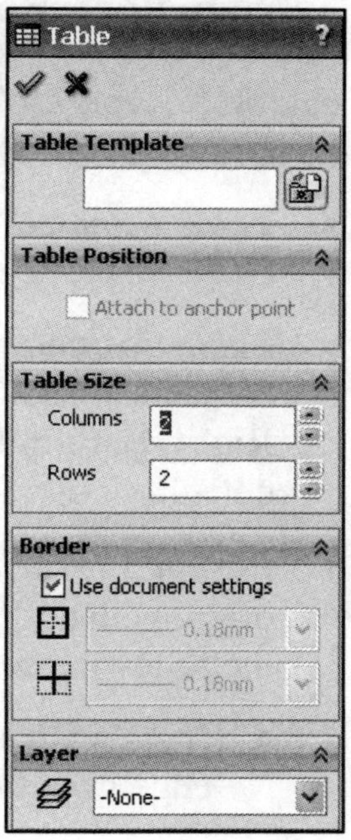


The Consolidated Table toolbar provides the ability to add a table in a drawing. The toolbar provides five selections: **General Table**, **Hole Table**, **Bill of Materials** and **Revision Table**.

### Table toolbar: General Table

The General Table option uses the Table PropertyManager. The Table PropertyManager provides the following selections:

- ***Table Template***. Only available during table insertion. Display the selected standard or custom template.
- ***Table Position***. Provides the ability to set the anchor corner to the table anchor. The available selections are: **Top Left**, **Top Right**, **Bottom Left** and **Bottom Right**. Note: Top Left is the default.
- ***Table Size***. The Table Size box provides the following selections:
  - **Columns**. Sets the number of columns in the table.
  - **Rows**. Sets the number of rows in the table.
- ***Border***. The Border box provides the ability to address the Border and Grip of the table. The selections are:
  - **Use document settings**. Selected by default. Apply the default document settings in the Document Properties section.
  - **Border**. Thin is selected by default. Border provides the following selections: **Thin, Normal, Thick, Thick (2), Thick (3), Thick (4), Thick (5)** and **Thick (6).**
  - **Grid**. Thin is selected by default. Grid provides the following selections: **Thin, Normal, Thick, Thick (2), Thick (3), Thick (4), Thick (5)** and **Thick (6).**
- ***Layer***: Select a layer type from the drop-down menu.

## Table toolbar: Hole Table

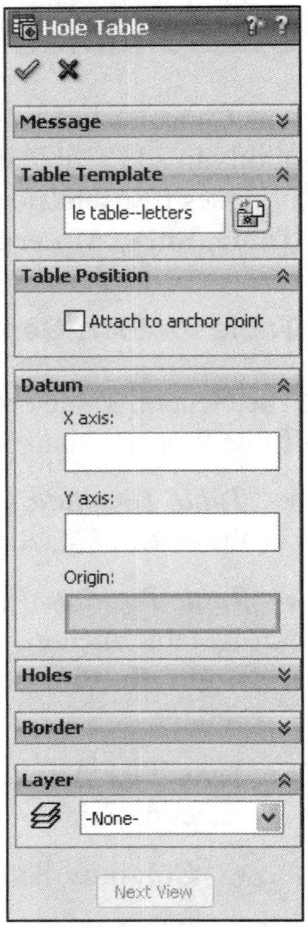


The Hole Table tool uses the Hole Table PropertyManager. The Hole Table PropertyManager provides the following selections:

- ***Table Template***. Only available during table insertion. Displays the selected standard or custom template.
- ***Table Position***. Provides the ability to set the anchor corner to the table anchor. The available selections are: **Top Left**, **Top Right**, **Bottom Left** and **Bottom Right**. Note: Top Left is the default.
- ***Datum***. Provides the ability to select a vertex to define the origin with an X axis and a Y axis. The Datum box provides the following selections:
  - **X Axis Direction Reference**. Select a horizontal model edge from the Graphics window.
  - **Y Axis Direction Reference**. Select a vertical model edge from the Graphics window.
  - **Origin**. Select an Origin.
- ***Holes***. The Holes box provides the ability to select individual hole edges, or select a model face to include all the holes in the face.

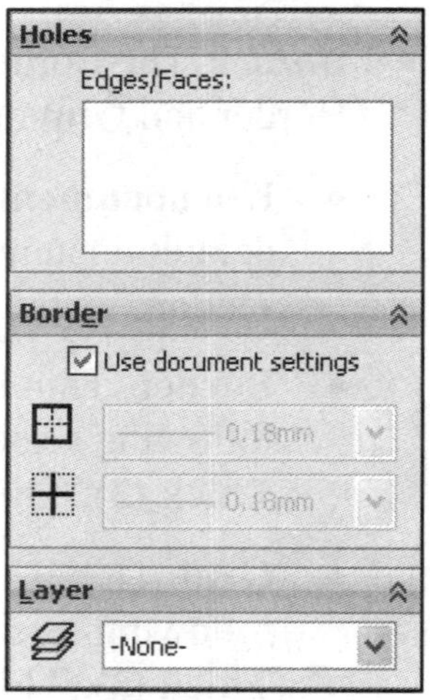


- ***Border***. Use document settings selected by default. Provides the ability to select a custom Box or Grid border.
- ***Layer***. None selected by default. The Layer box provides the ability to apply the hole table to a specified drawing layer.
  - **Next View**. Only available during table insertion. Provides the ability to set the Datum and Holes for another drawing view.

A One hole table can include several drawing views.

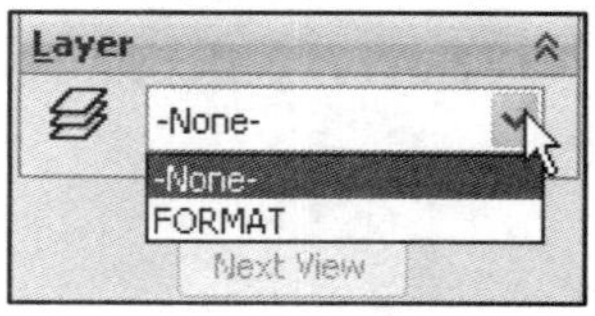

## Table toolbar: Bill of Materials

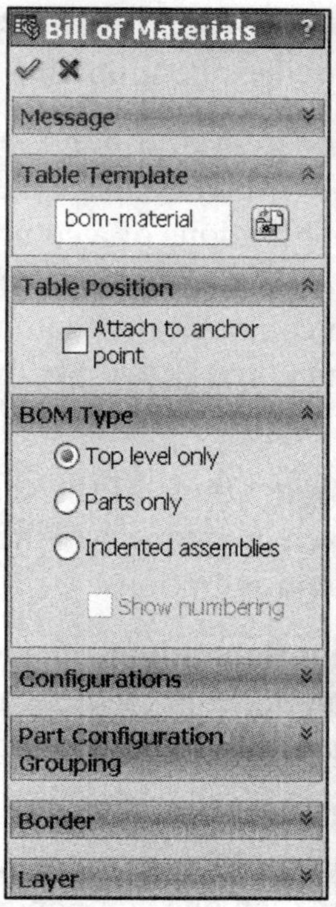


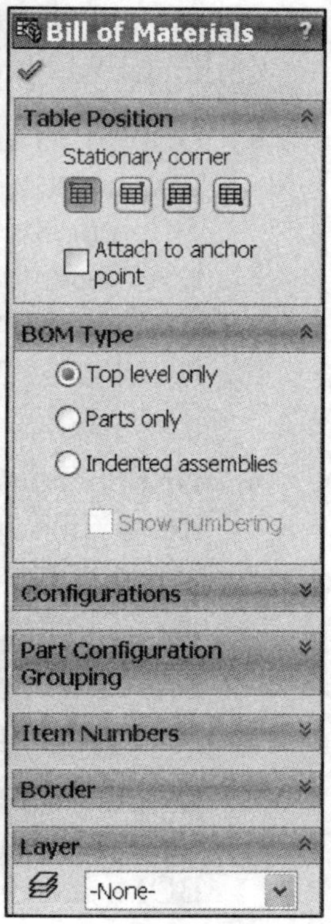


The Bill of Materials option uses the Bill of Materials PropertyManager. The Bill of Materials PropertyManager provides the following selections:

- ***Table Template***. Only available during table insertion. Displays the selected standard or custom template.
- ***Table Position***. Provides the ability to set the anchor corner to the table anchor. The available selections are: **Top Left**, **Top Right**, **Bottom Left** and **Bottom Right**. Note: Top Left is the default.
- ***BOM Type***. The BOM Type box provides the following selections. They are:
  - **Top level only**. Creates a parts and sub-assemblies BOM. This option does not create a sub-assembly components BOM.
  - **Parts only**. Creates a sub-assembly components, "as individual items" BOM.
  - **Indented assemblies**. Lists the sub-assemblies. List the indents sub-assembly components below their sub-assemblies.
  - **Show numbering**. Displays item numbers for the sub-assembly components.
- ***Configurations***. The Configurations box displays the list quantities in the Bill of Materials for all selected configurations. Select configurations manually, or use one of the following: **Select all configurations** and **Unselect all configurations**.

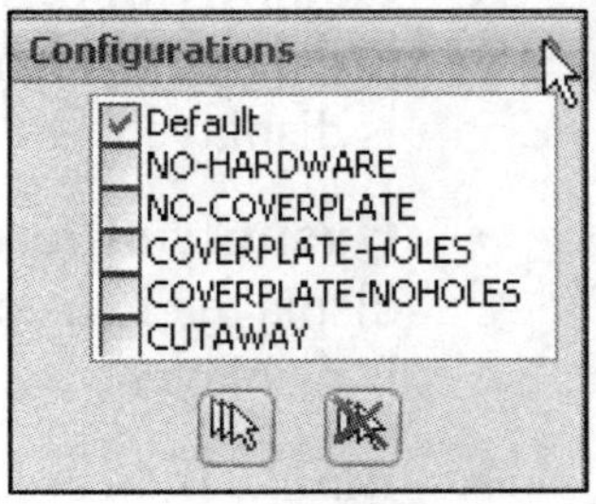

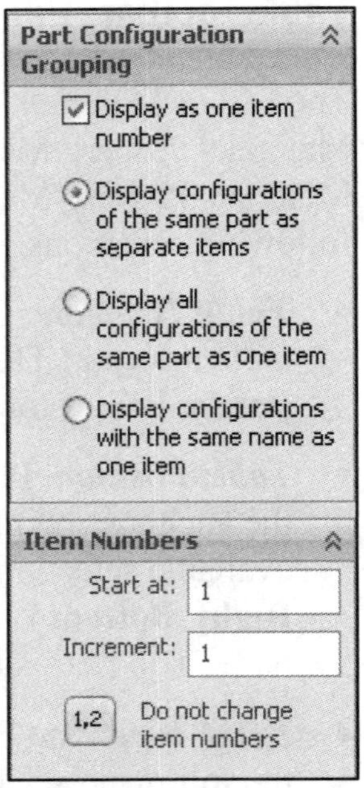


- ***Part Configuration Grouping***. The Part Configuration Grouping box provides the following selections:
  - **Display as one item number**. Only available when you first create a BOM. Uses the same item number for different configurations of a component in different top-level assembly configurations. Each unique component configuration can be present in only one of the assembly configurations in the BOM. Set the BOM Type to Top level only.
  - **Display configurations of the same part as separate items**. List each component in the BOM if a component has multiple configurations.
  - **Display all configurations of the same part as one item**. List each component in only one row in the BOM, if a component has multiple configurations.
  - **Display configurations with the same name as one item**. List one configuration name in one row of the BOM, if more than one component has the same configuration name.

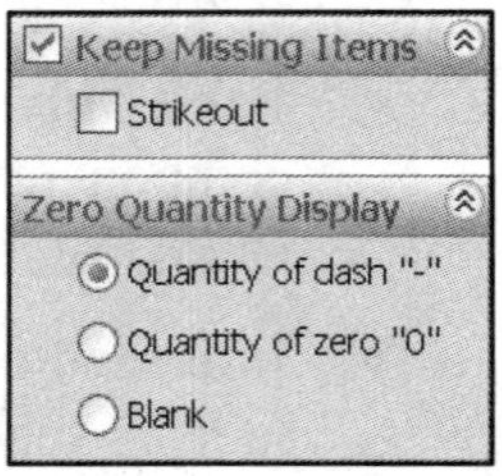


- ***Keep Missing Items***. Keep components listed in the table if components have been deleted from the assembly since the Bill of Materials was created.
  - **Strikeout**. If missing components are still listed, the text for the items is displayed with the Strikeout option.
- ***Zero Quantity Display***. The Zero Quantity Display box provides the following selections. They are:
  - **Quantity of dash "-"**. If an assembly component is not displayed in a configuration, the zero quantity with a dash (-) is displayed.
  - **Quantity of zero "0"**. If an assembly component is not displayed in a configuration, the zero quantity with a zero (**0**) is displayed.
  - **Blank**. If an assembly component is not displayed in a configuration, the zero quantity with a blank cell is displayed.

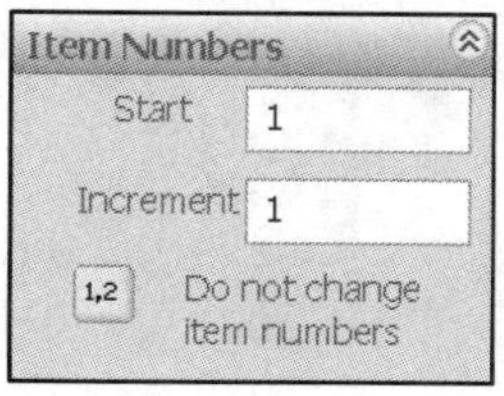


- ***Item Numbers box***. The Item Numbers box provides the following selections. They are:
  - **Start**. The Start option provides a value for the beginning of the item number sequence. The sequence increases by a single digit.
  - **Increment**. The Increment option provides the ability to set the increment value for item numbers in the BOM.
- ***Border***. The Border box provides the ability to address the Box and Grid of the table. The selections are:
  - **Border**. Thin is selected by default. Border provides the following selections: **Thin**, **Normal**, **Thick**, **Thick (2)**, **Thick (3)**, **Thick (4)**, **Thick (5)** and **Thick (6)**.
  - **Grid**. Thin is selected by default. Grid provides the following selections: **Thin**, **Normal**, **Thick**, **Thick (2)**, **Thick (3)**, **Thick (4)**, **Thick (5)** and **Thick (6)**.

### *Tutorial: Bill of Materials 13.1*

Insert a Bill of Materials in a drawing

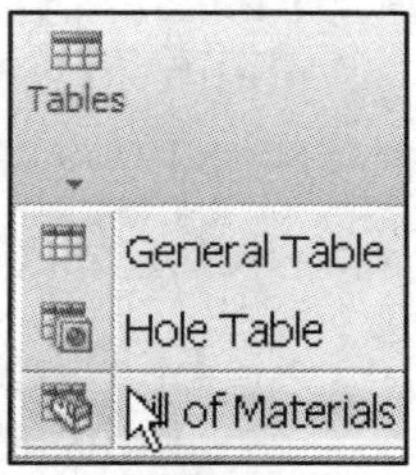


1. Open **Bill of Materials 13-1** from the SolidWorks 2010\Drawing folder.
2. Click **Bill of Materials** from the Annotation tab in the CommandManager.
3. Click inside the **Isometric view** boundary.
4. Select **bom-standard** from the Table Template.
5. Click **Top level only** from the BOM Type box.
6. Click **OK** from the Bill of Materials PropertyManager.
7. Click a **position** in the top left corner of Sheet1 to locate the Bill of Materials. The Bill of Materials PropertyManager is displayed.
8. **Close** the drawing.

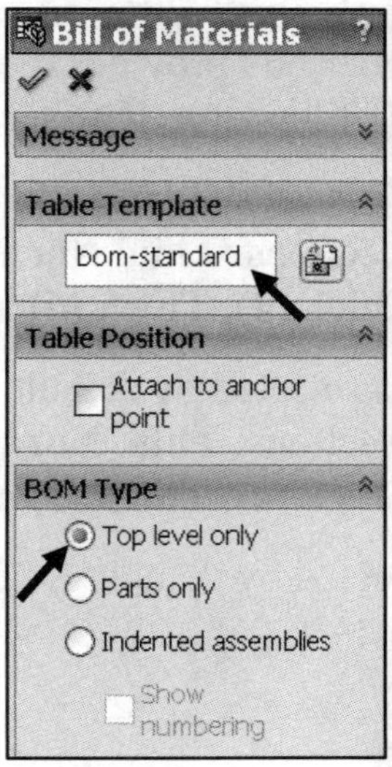


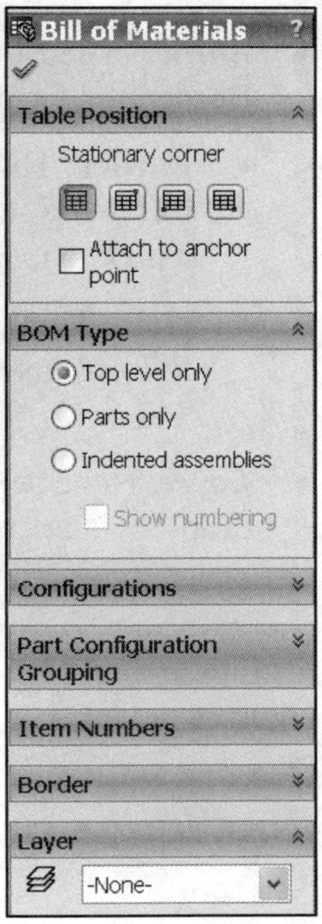

| ITEM NO. | PART NUMBER | DESCRIPTION | Default/QTY. |
|---|---|---|---|
| 1 | 99-1007-1 | TUBE4_ROD4 | 1 |
| 2 | 10-0411 | COLLAR | 1 |
| 3 | MP043BM1-17 | RING | 1 |
| 4 | 10-0410 | COVERPLATE | 1 |
| 5 | MP04-M3-05-16 | CAP SCREW | 2 |

## Table toolbar: Revision Table

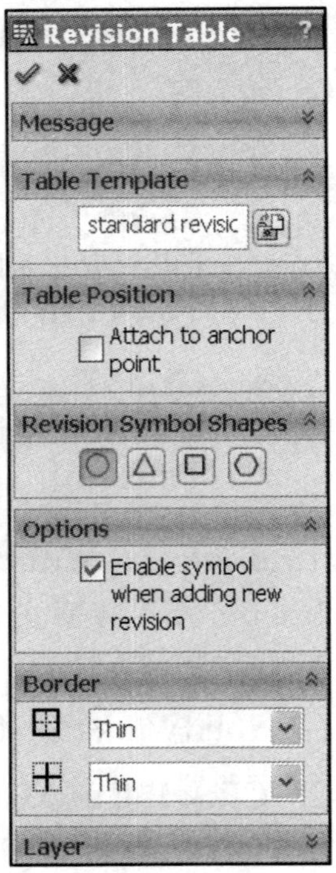


The Revision Table tool uses the Revision Table PropertyManager. The Revision Table PropertyManager provides the following selections:

- ***Table Template***. Only available during table insertion. Displays the selected standard or custom template.
- ***Table Anchor***. Provides the ability to set the anchor corner to the table anchor. The available selections are: **Top Left**, **Top Right**, **Bottom Left** and **Bottom Right**.
- ***Revision Symbol***. The Revision Symbol box provides the ability to select a border shape for revision symbols. The selections are: **Circle**, **Triangle**, **Square** and **Hexagon**.
- ***Options***. The Options box provides the following selection:
  - **Enable symbol when adding new revision**. Provides the ability to place revision symbols when you add a revision to the table.
- ***Border***. The Border box provides the ability to address the Border and Grip of the table. The selections are:
  - **Border**. Thin is selected by default. Border provides the following selections: **Thin**, **Normal**, **Thick**, **Thick (2)**, **Thick (3)**, **Thick (4)**, **Thick (5)** and **Thick (6)**.
  - **Grid**. Thin is selected by default. Grid provides the following selections: **Thin**, **Normal**, **Thick**, **Thick (2)**, **Thick (3)**, **Thick (4)**, **Thick (5)** and **Thick (6)**.
- ***Layer***: None selected by default. Select a layer type from the drop-down arrow.

# DimXpert Dimensions and Drawings

You can import dimensions and tolerances which you created using DimXpert for parts into drawings. If the DimXpert dimensions are not displayed in the drawing after import, follow the below procedure:

- In the FeatureManager design tree, right-click the **Annotations** folder.
- Select **Display Annotations** and **Show DimXpert Annotations.**

You can't use the Model Items PropertyManager to import DimXpert dimensions into a drawing.

***Tutorial: DimXpert 13-1***

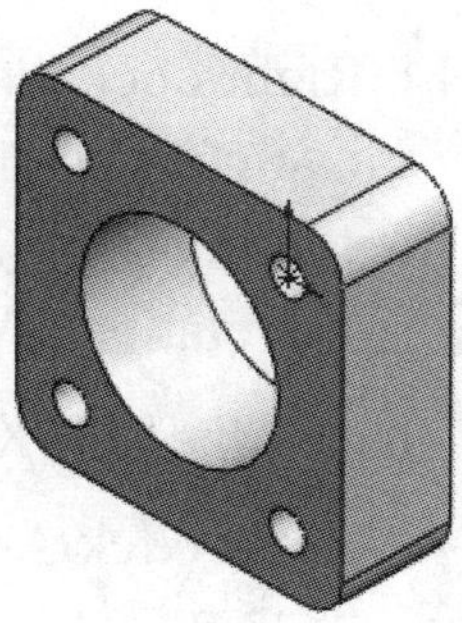

Apply DimXpert: Plus and Minus option. Insert three drawing views using the View Palette with DimXpert Annotations.

1. Open the **DimXpert 13-1** part from the SolidWorks 2010\Drawing folder. View the three Extrude features, Linear Pattern feature, and the Fillet feature.
2. Click the **DimXpertManager** tab.
3. Click the **Auto Dimension Scheme** tool from the DimXpertManager. The Auto Dimension PropertyManager is displayed. Prismatic and Plus and Minus is selected by default.

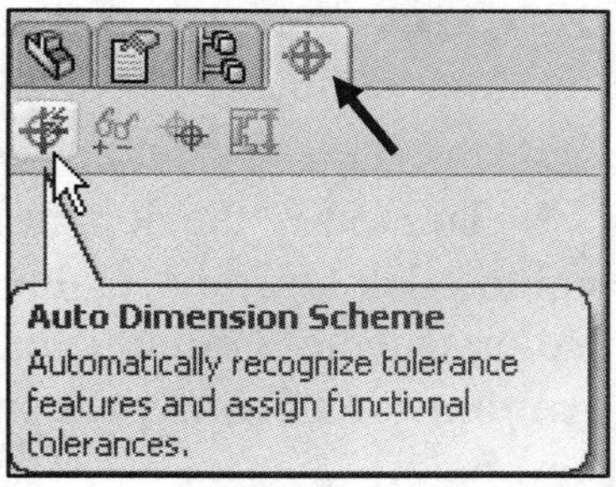


A key difference between the *Plus and Minus* option versus the *Geometric* option is how DimXpert controls the four-hole pattern, and how it applies tolerances to interrelate the datum features when in *Geometric* mode.

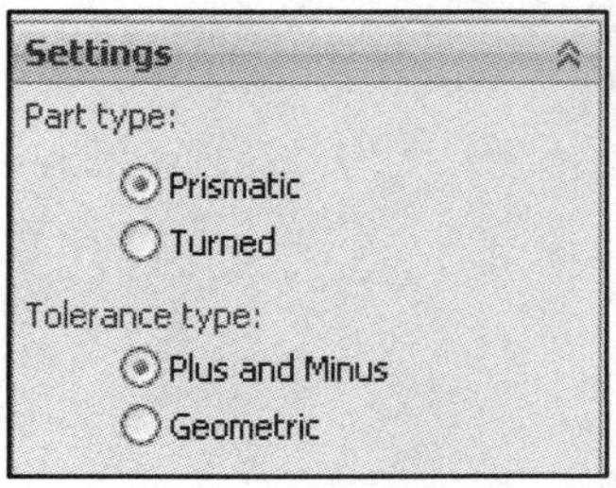


4. Check the **Prismatic** box.
5. Check the **Plus and Minus** box.
6. Click the **back face** of the model. Plane1 is displayed in the Primary Datum box.
7. Click **inside** the Secondary Datum box.

8. Click the **left face** of the model. Plane2 is displayed in the Secondary Datum box.
9. Click **inside** the Tertiary Datum box.
10. Click the **top face** of the model. The selected plane is displayed in the Tertiary Datum box.

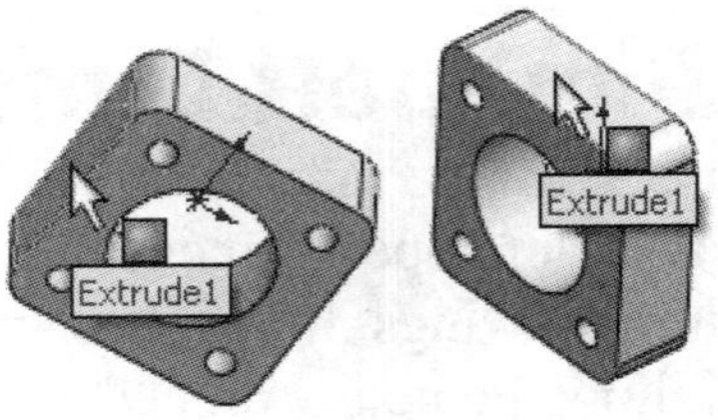


11. Click **OK** from the Auto Dimension PropertyManager.
12. Click **Isometric view**. View the dimensions. All features are displayed in green.
13. **Return** to the FeatureManager.
14. Right-click **Annotations** from the FeatureManager.
15. **Uncheck** Show DimXpert Annotations. View the results.

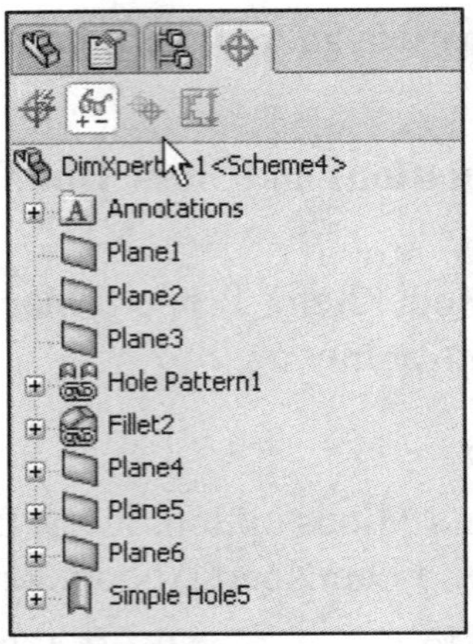


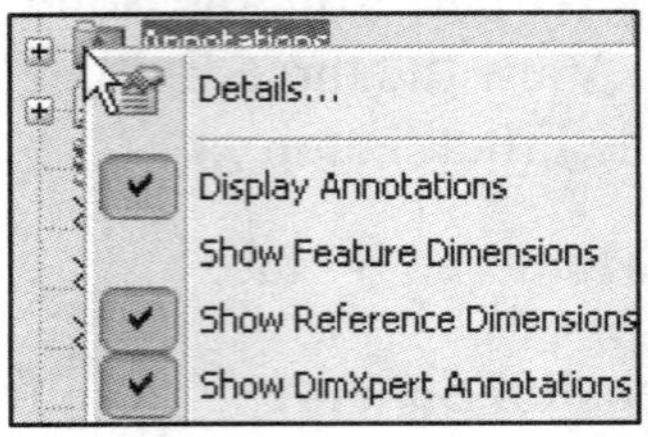


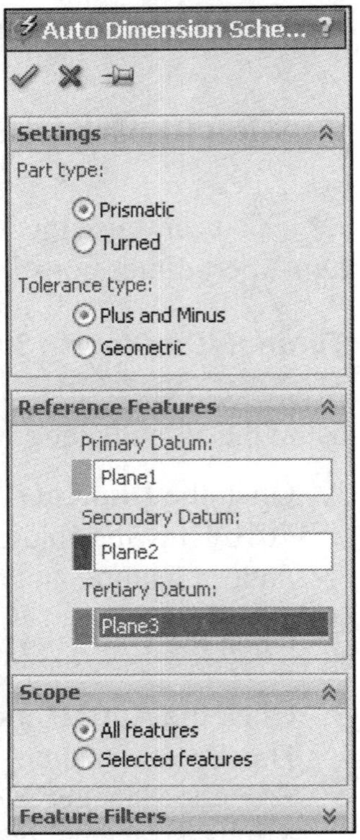


Display the DimXpert Annotations.

16. Right-click **Annotations** from the FeatureManager.
17. **Check** Show DimXpert Annotations.

To modify the default DimXpert color, click **Options**, **Colors**. Under Color scheme settings, select **Annotations**, **DimXpert** and pick the new color.

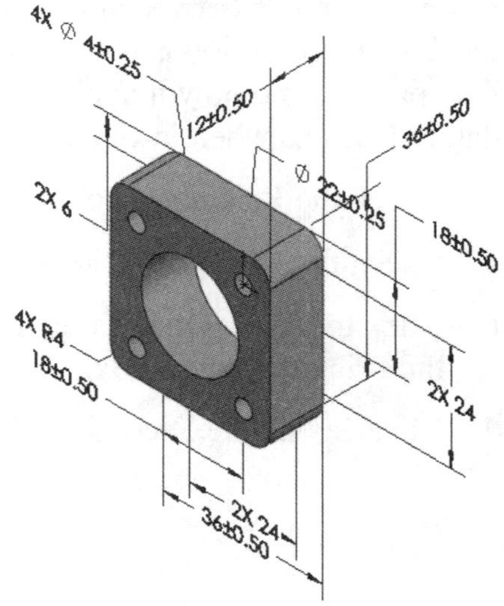

Create a new drawing.

18. Click the **Make Drawing from Part/Assembly** in the Menu bar toolbar.

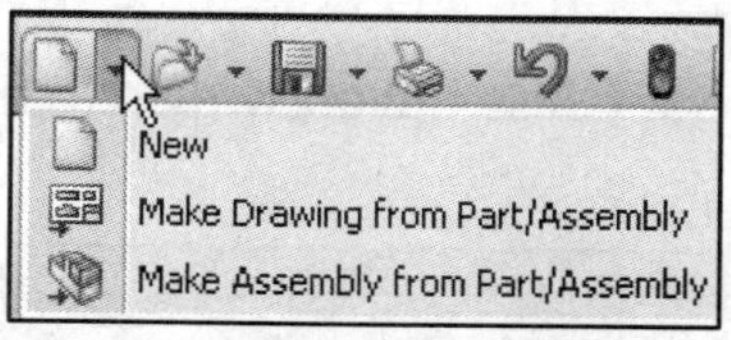


Accept the default Drawing Template.

19. Double-click the **Drawing** icon from the New SolidWorks Document dialog box.

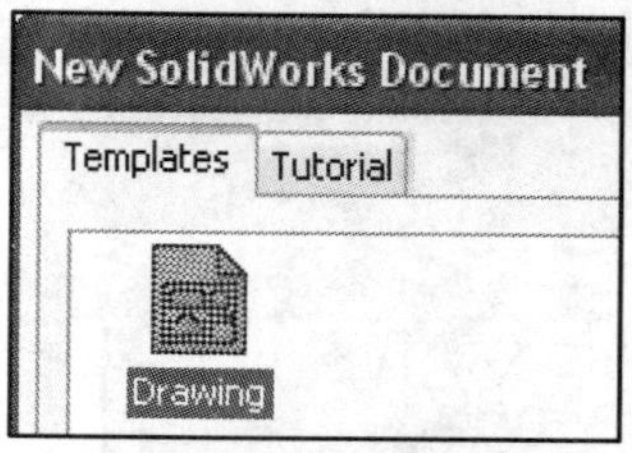


Accept the default settings. Note: *Third Angle, A-Landscape* is selected in this tutorial.

20. If required, click **OK** from the Sheet Format/Size dialog box.

Insert three drawing views using the View Palette.

21. Click the **View Palette** tab in the Task Pane. DimXpert13 is displayed in the drop-down menu.
22. Check the **Import Annotations** box.
23. Check the **DimXpertAnnotations** box.
24. Check the **Include items from hidden features** box. Note: The (A) next to the drawing view informs the user that DimXpert Annotations are present.

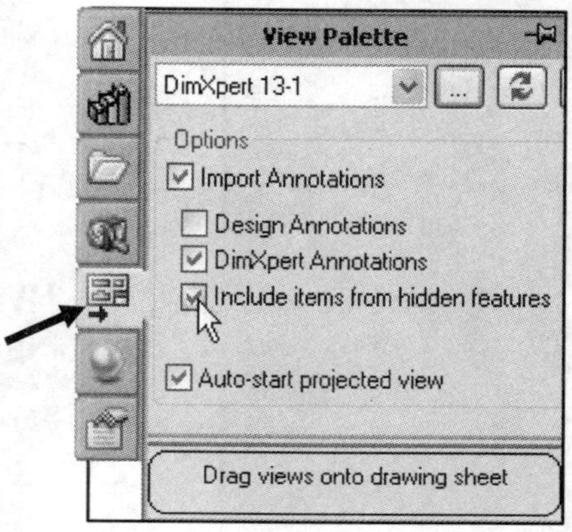


25. Click and drag the **(A) Front** view into Sheet1 in the lower left corner.
26. Click a **position** directly above the Front view.
27. Click a **position** directly to the right of the Front view. Three views are displayed.

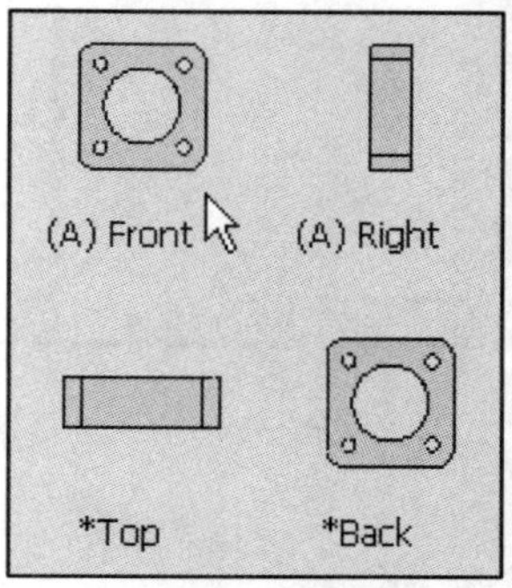


28. Click **OK** from the Projected View PropertyManager. View the results.

Set Sheet Properties to fit the views and dimensions to the drawing sheet.

29. Right-click **Properties** in Sheet1. Note: Do not select inside a drawing view. The Sheet Properties dialog box is displayed.

30. Set the **Sheet Scale** to fit the drawing.
31. Click **OK** from the Sheet Properties dialog box.

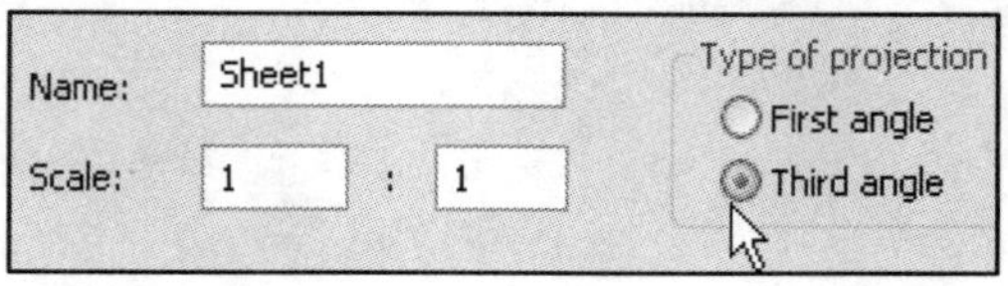

32. Click and drag the **dimensions** off the model as illustrated.

33. **Close** the drawing. Do not save the drawing.

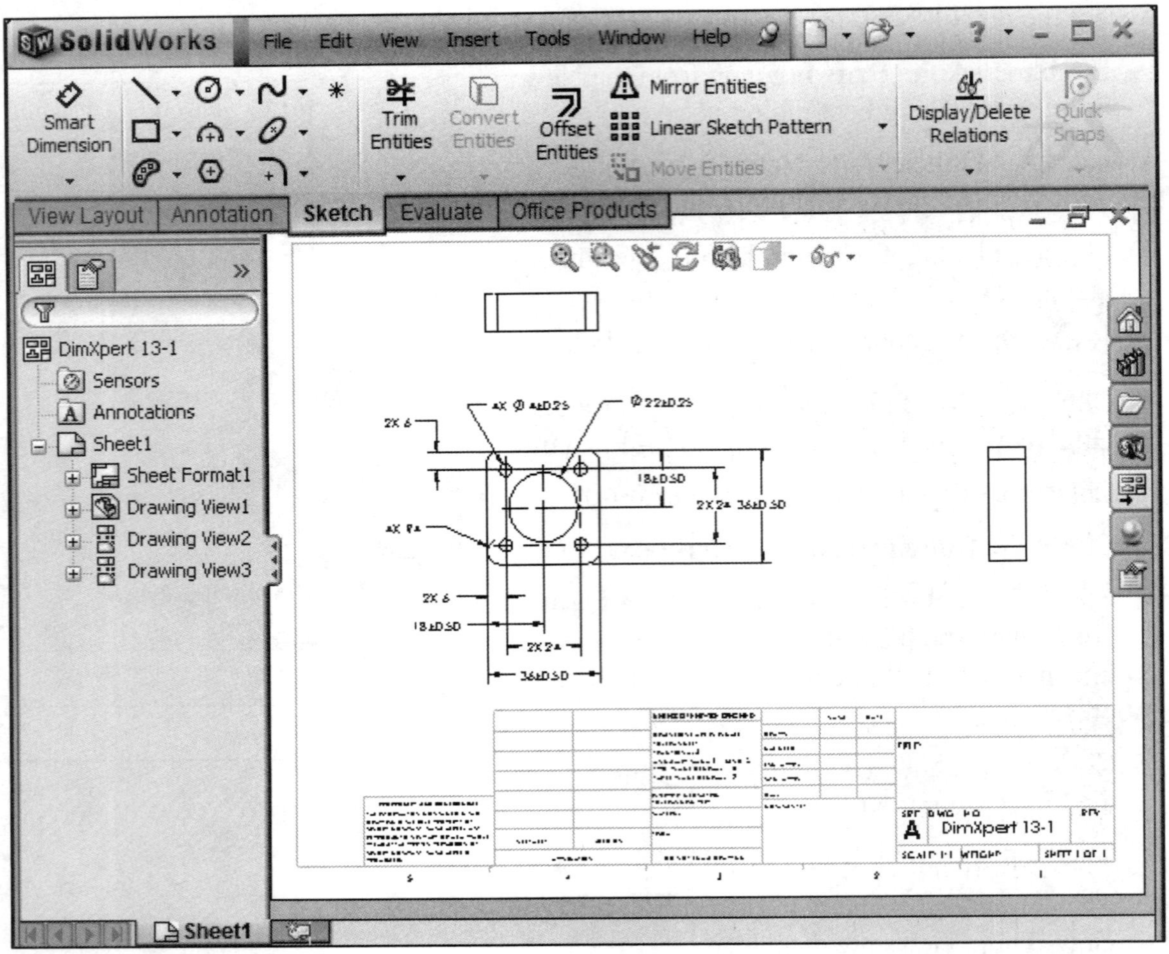

***Tutorial: DimXpert 13-2***

Apply DimXpert: Geometric option. Insert three drawing views using the View Palette with DimXpert Annotations.

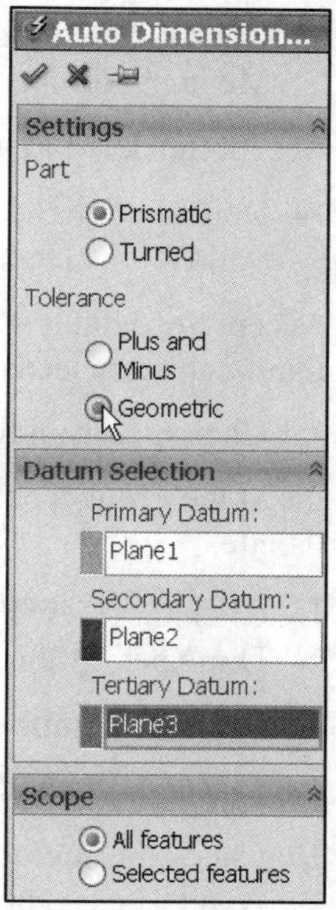


1. Open the **DimXpert 13-2** part from the SolidWorks 2010\ Drawing folder. The Part FeatureManager is displayed.

Apply DimXpert to the part.

2. Click the **DimXpertManager** tab.
3. Click the **Auto Dimension Scheme** tool from the DimXpertManager. The Auto Dimension PropertyManager is displayed. Prismatic and Plus and Minus is selected by default. In this section, select the Geometric option.

DimXpert: Geometric option provides the ability to locate axial features with position and circular runout tolerances. Pockets and surfaces are located with surface profiles.

4. Check the **Geometric** box as illustrated. Note: The Prismatic box is selected.
5. Click the **back face** of the model. Plane1 is displayed in the Primary Datum box.
6. Click **inside** the Secondary Datum box.
7. Click the **left face** of the model. Plane2 is displayed in the Secondary Datum box.
8. Click **inside** the Tertiary Datum box.
9. Click the **top face** of the model. Plane3 is displayed in the Tertiary Datum box.
10. Click **OK** from the Auto Dimension PropertyManager.
11. Click **Isometric view**. View the Datum's, Feature Control Frames and Geometric tolerances.
12. **Return** to the FeatureManager.

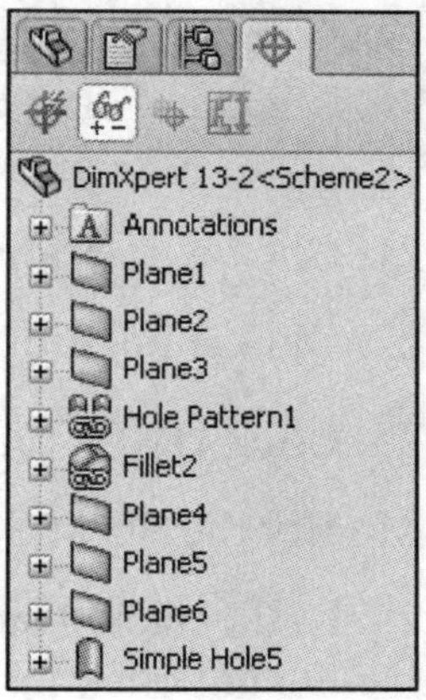


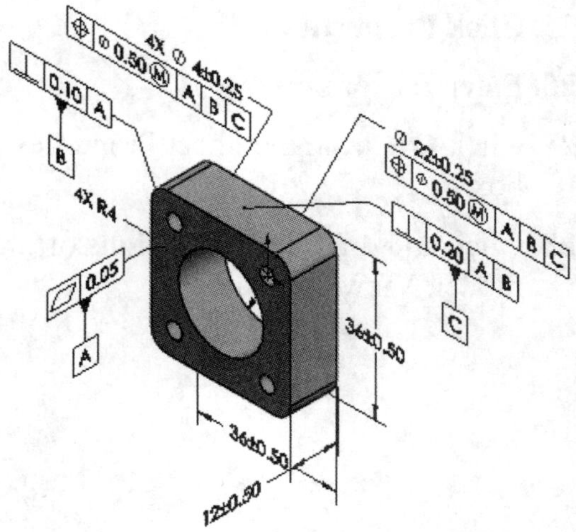

Create the drawing.

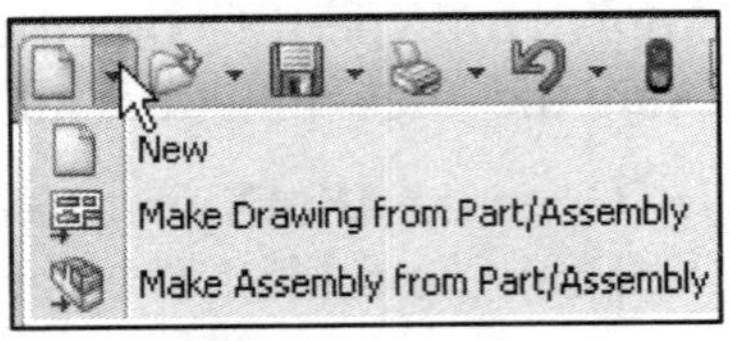


13. Click the **Make Drawing from Part/Assembly** in the Menu bar toolbar.

Accept the default Drawing Template.

14. Double-click the **Drawing** icon from the New SolidWorks Document dialog box.

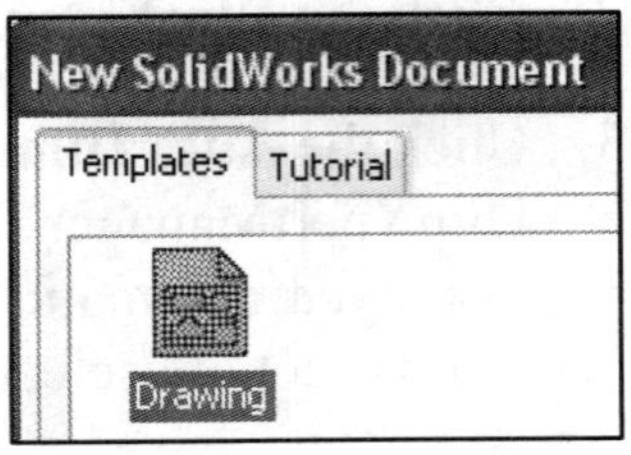


Accept the default settings. Note: Third Angle, A-Landscape is selected in this tutorial.

15. Click **OK** from the Sheet Format/Size dialog box.

Insert the Front, Top, and Right view from the View Palette.

16. Click the **View Palette** tab in the Task Pane. DimXpert13-2 is displayed in the drop-down menu.

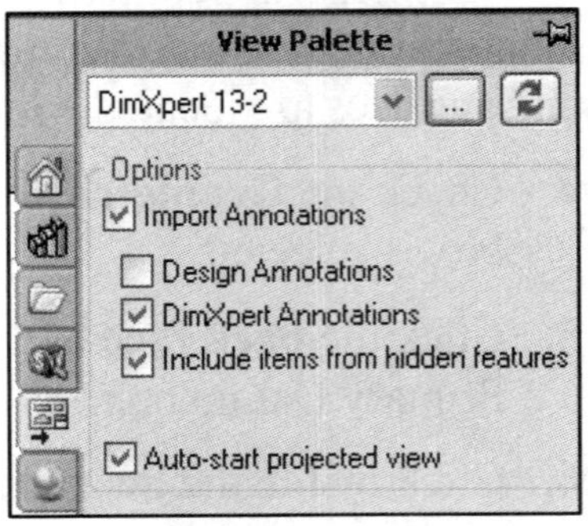


17. Check the **Import Annotations** box.
18. Check the **DimXpertAnnotations** box.
19. Check the **Include items from hidden features** box. Note: The (A) next to the drawing view informs the user that DimXpert Annotations are present.
20. Click and drag the **(A) Front view** into Sheet1 in the lower left corner.

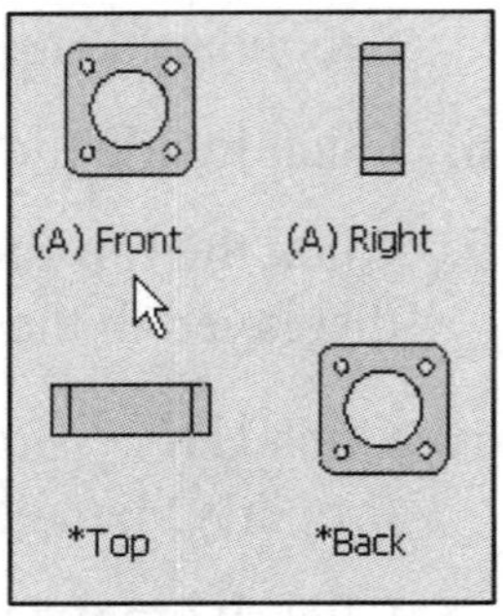


21. Click a **position** directly above the Front view.
22. Click a **position** directly to the right of the Front view.
23. Click **OK** from the Projected View PropertyManager.

Modify the Sheet Scale.

24. Right-click inside the **sheet boundary**. Note: Do not click inside a view.
25. Click **Properties**.
26. Enter **1:1** for Scale.

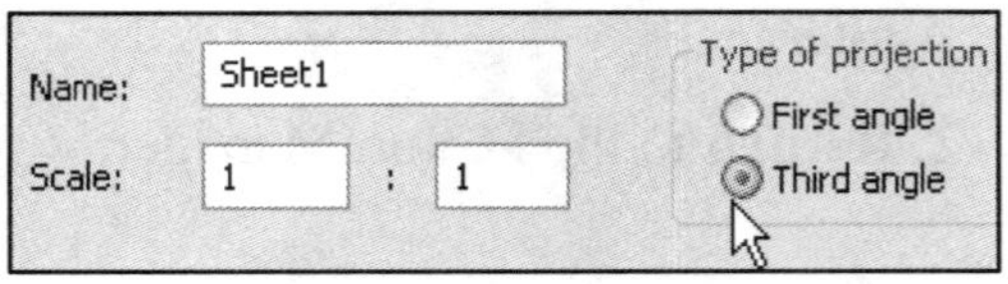


27. Click **OK** from the Sheet Properties dialog box.
28. Click and drag the **dimensions** off the model. View the drawing

Close the drawing.

29. Click **File**, **Close**. Do not save the drawing.

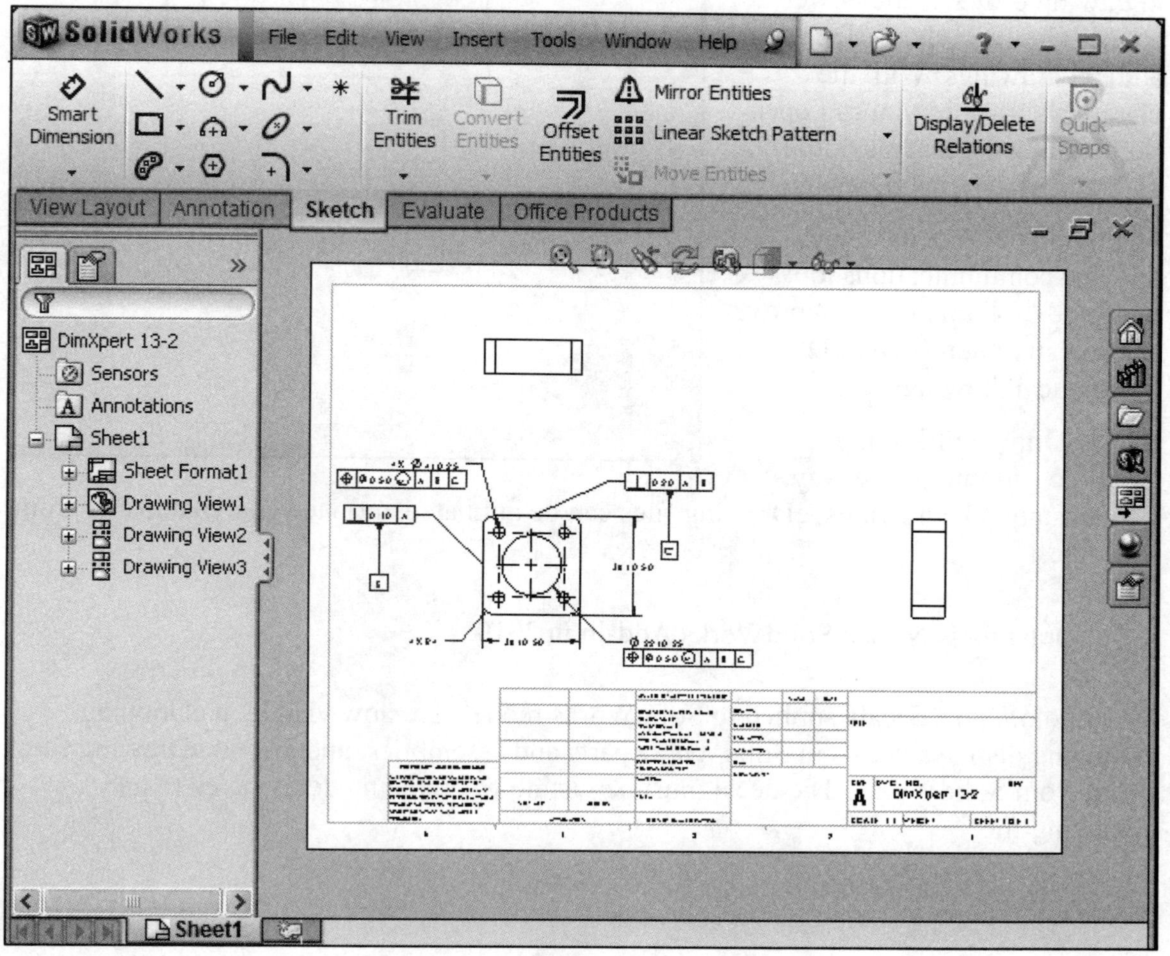

# eDrawing

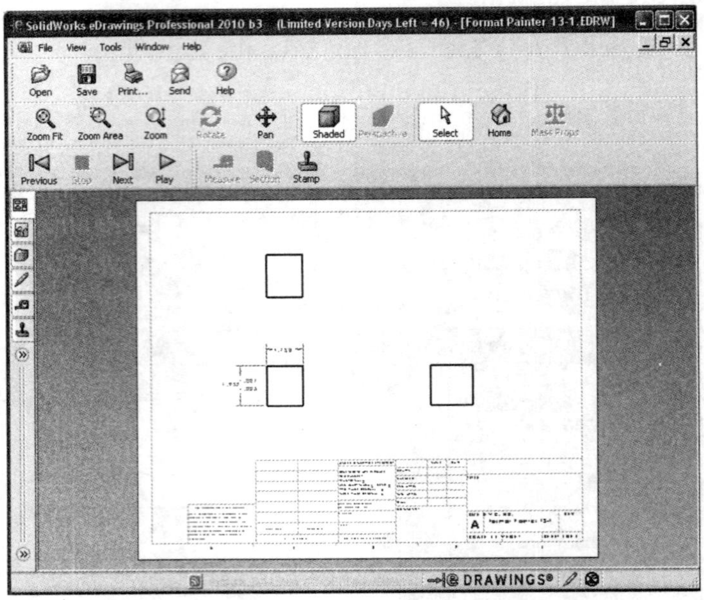


eDrawing provides the power to create, view and share 3D models and 2D drawings. With the eDrawing Viewer, you can open SolidWorks documents, modify, and then save as an eDrawing.

eDrawing files are an email-enabled communications tool designed to dramatically improve sharing and interpreting 2D mechanical drawings.

View eDrawing files in a dynamic and interactive way. Unlike static 2D drawings, eDrawing files can be animated and viewed dynamically from all angles.

eDrawing is NOT a SolidWorks Add-In in 2010.

PhotoWorks decals applied to SolidWorks models are now visible in eDrawing. eDrawing displays decals in SolidWorks parts and assemblies, and also in eDrawing files saved from SolidWorks. The decal must be visible when the model is saved to an eDrawing file.

# eDrawing Tools

## Publish eDrawings File tool

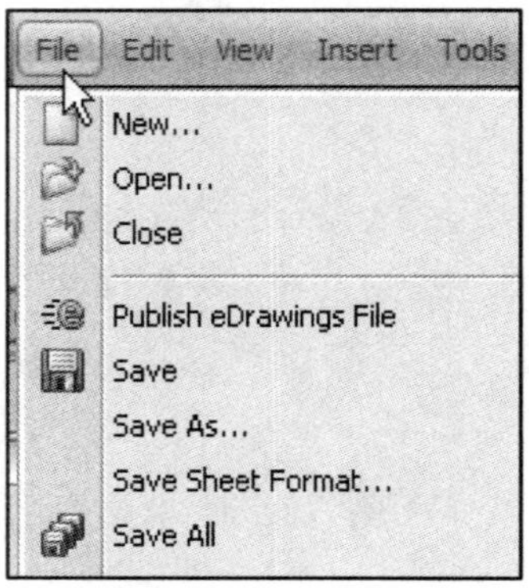


The Publish eDrawing File tool opens the eDrawings Viewer. The eDrawings Viewer provides the tools for viewing, shading, animating, hyperlinking and arranging drawing views.

With eDrawing's Print Preview, you can view your drawing or model exactly as it will be printed, eliminating wasted paper and time. You can also preview multiple sheets without having to exit Print Preview. Within the Print dialog box, you select a portion of the drawing to print.

With the Current screen image option selected, you can pan and zoom to fine-tune your selection before printing.

***Tutorial: eDrawing 13-1***

Create an eDrawing from a SW drawing.

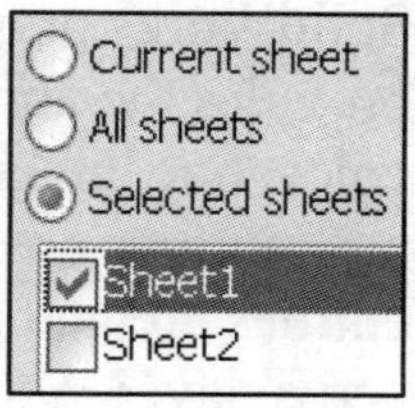


1. Open the **eDrawing 13-1** drawing from the SolidWorks 2010\Drawing folder.
2. Click **File**, **Publish eDrawing File** from the Main menu bar.
3. **Selected sheets** from the Pop-up dialog box.
4. Click **Sheet1**.

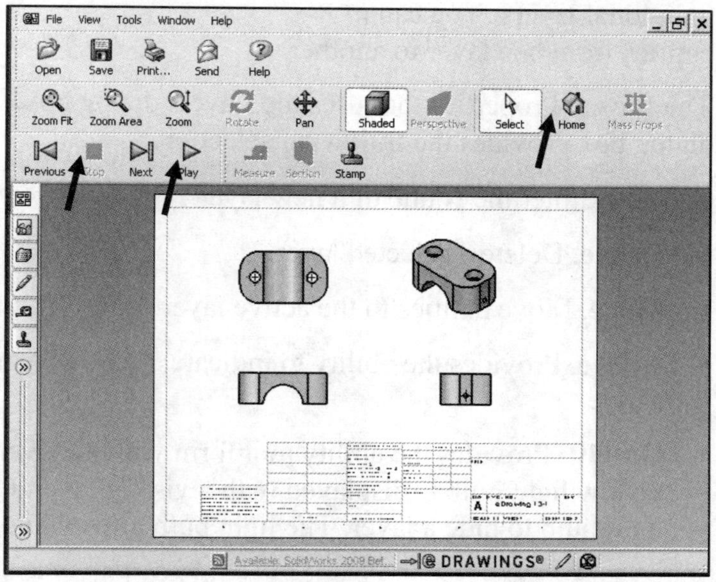


5. Click **OK** from the Save Sheets to eDrawings file dialog box. Review the Clamp eDrawing file.
6. Animate the eDrawing. Click **Play**. The eDrawings file is displayed showing you each view. This display continues until you stop it.
7. Click **Stop**.
8. Click **Home** to return the eDrawing file view to its starting point.
9. **Close** the eDrawing.

You can specify configurations and drawing sheets when you publish an eDrawings file.

# Line Formats Toolbar

The Line Formats toolbar provides the tools to change the appearance of individual lines, edges, and Sketch entities in a drawing. The Line Formats toolbar provides the following tools: **Layer Properties**, **Line Color**, **Line Thickness**, **Line Style** and **Color Display Mode**. Additional available tools: **Hide Edge** and **Show Edge**.

## Layer Properties tool

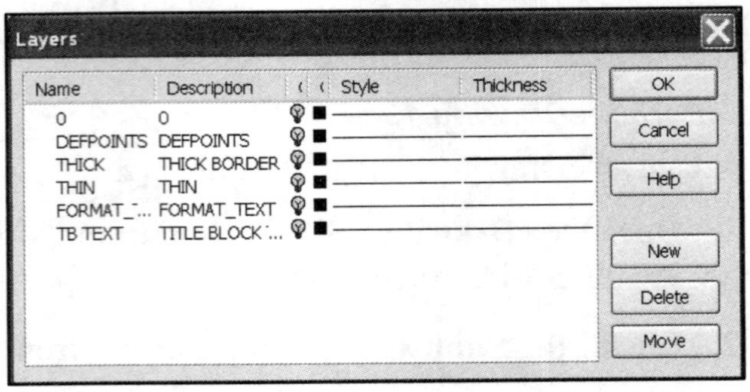


The Layer Properties tool provides the ability to create layers in a SolidWorks drawing. This option provides the ability to assign a line color, line thickness, and line style for new entities created on each layer. New entities are automatically added to the active layer. You can hide or show individual layers. You can move entities from one layer to another.

The Layers Properties tool uses the Layers dialog box. The Layers dialog box provides the following selections:

- **New**. Enter the Name of a new layer.
- **Delete**. Delete a selected layer.
- **Move**. Move entities to the active layer.
- **Active**. Provides the ability to indicate, “Arrow” which layer is active.
- **On/Off**. Provides the ability to inform you if a layer is hidden. A yellow light bulb is displayed with a visible layer. Click the yellow light bulb to hide a layer. The light bulb turns white.

## Line Color tool

The Line Color tool provides the ability to select a color from the color palette, or to select the Default option. The Line Color tool uses the Set Next Line Color dialog box.

## Line Thickness tool

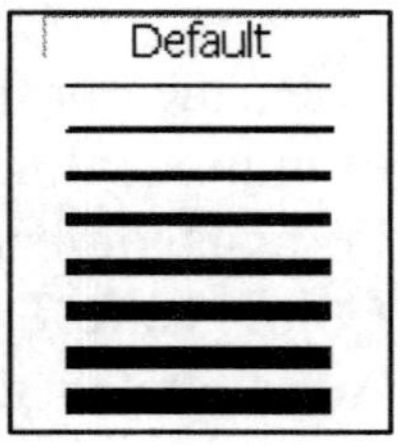


The Line Thickness tool provides the ability to set the thickness of the line. Select a thickness or the Default from the menu. Move the mouse pointer over the menu, the thickness name, Thin, Normal, Thick, etc is displayed in the Status Bar.

## Line Style tool

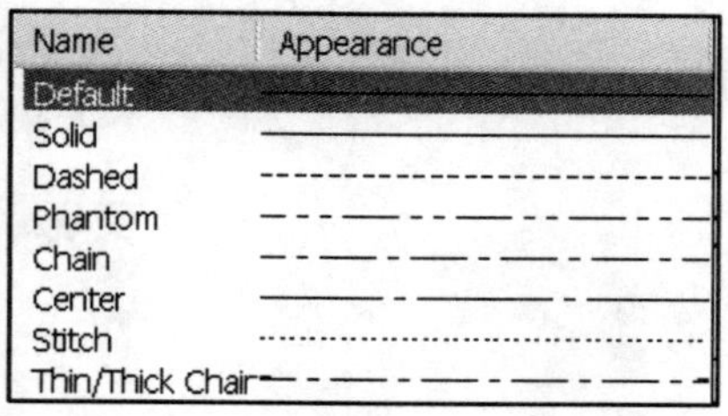


The Line Style tool provides the ability to select the style of the line in a drawing. Select a style or Default from the menu. You can also create a custom line style.

## Color Display Mode tool

The Color Display Mode tool provides the ability to toggle between aesthetic colors, colors chosen in layers or with the Line Color tool and the default system status colors for fully defined, under defined, etc. Sketch endpoints and dangling dimensions are always in the system status color.

# Summary

In this chapter, you learned about Drawings and eDrawings. You addressed Sheet Format, Size and Document Properties. You used the View Palette feature to insert drawing views into a drawing.

You reviewed and addressed each tool in the Drawing Toolbar: *Model View, Projected View, Auxiliary View, Section View, Aligned Section View, Detail View, Standard 3 View, Broken-out Section, Break, Crop View and Alternate Position View.*

You reviewed and addressed each tool in the Annotations Toolbar: *Smart Dimension, Model Items, Autodimension, Note, Spell Checker, Balloon, AutoBalloon, Surface Finish, Weld Symbol, Geometric Tolerance, Datum Feature, Datum Target, Hole Callout, Revision Symbol, Area Hatch/Fill, Block, Center Mark, Centerline and Tables.*

You Inserted DimXpert on a part, then applied the View Palette and inserted the DimXpert Annotation into drawing views.

You created an eDrawing and reviewed the Line Format Toolbar.

In Chapter 14, explore Sheet Meal features and their associated tools.

**Notes:**

# CHAPTER 14: SHEET METAL

## Chapter Objective

Chapter 14 provides a comprehensive understanding of the Sheet Metal features and their associated tools. On the completion of this chapter, you will be able to:

- Review and utilize the tools from the Sheet Metal toolbar:
  - Base-Flange/Tab, Convert to Sheet Metal, Lofted-Bend, Edge Flange, Miter Flange, Hem, Jog, Sketched Bend, Cross-Break, Closed Corners, Break-Corner/Corner-Trim, Extruded Cut, Simple Hole, Vent, Unfold, Fold, Flatten, No Bends, Insert Bends and Rip
- Examine and utilize the Sheet Metal Library feature

# Sheet Metal

Sheet metal parts are generally used as enclosures for components or to provide support to other components. There are two methods to create a sheet metal part:

1. Build a part. Then convert the built part to a sheet metal part. There are a few instances where this method is to your advantage. They are:

- **Imported Solid Bodies**. If you import a sheet metal file with bends from another CAD system, the bends are already in the model. Using the Insert Bends tool from the Sheet Metal toolbar is your best option for converting the imported file to a SolidWorks sheet metal part.
- **Conical Bends**. Conical bends are not supported by specific sheet metal features, such as Base Flange, Edge Flange, etc. You must build the part using extrusions, revolves, etc., and then convert it to add bends to a conical sheet metal part.

2. Create the part as a sheet metal part using specific sheet metal features from the Sheet Metal toolbar. This method eliminates extra steps because you create a part as sheet metal from the initial design stage.

The new DXF/DWG PropertyManager in SolidWorks 2010 exports sheet metal to .dxf or .dwg files. A preview shows what you are exporting and lets you remove unwanted entities, such as holes, cutouts and bend lines. The scale is 1:1 by default. Also automatically cleans up overlapping entities so a cleaner file is delivered to manufacturing.

# Sheet Metal toolbar

The Sheet Metal toolbar provides the tools to create sheet metal parts. The available Sheet Metal tool options are dependent on the selected mode and selected part or assembly. The tools and menu options that are displayed in gray are called gray-out. The gray icon or text cannot be selected. Additional information is required for these options.

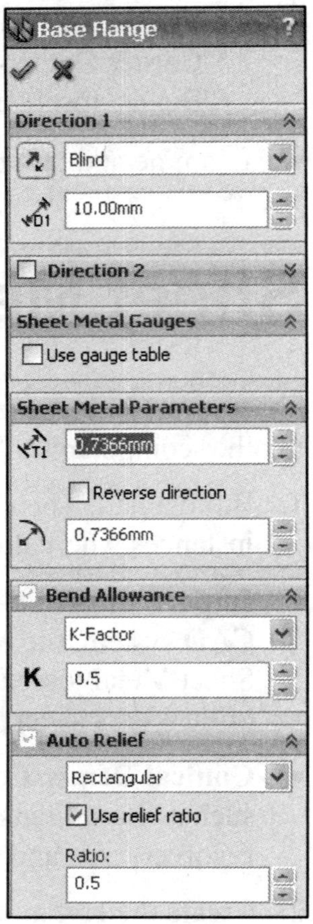


## Base-Flange/Tab tool

The Base-Flange/Tab tool provides the ability to add a base flange feature to a SolidWorks sheet metal part. A Base-Flange/Tab feature is the first feature in a new sheet metal part.

The Base-Flange/Tab feature is created from a sketch. The sketch can be a single closed, a single open, or multiple enclosed profiles. The part is marked as a sheet metal part in the FeatureManager.

The thickness and bend radius of the Base-Flange feature are the default values for the other sheet metal features.

The Base-Flange/Tab tool uses the Base Flange PropertyManager. The options on the Base Flange PropertyManager update according to the active sketch. Example, the Direction 1 and Direction 2 boxes are not displayed for a sketch with a single closed profile.

The Base Flange PropertyManager provides the following selections:

- ***Direction1***. Blind is the default End Condition. Provides the ability to set the End Condition and depth if needed. View Chapter 6 on End Condition details.
- ***Direction2***. Blind is the default End Condition. Provides the ability to set the End Condition and depth if needed.

- ***Sheet Metal Gauges***. The Sheet Metal Gauges box provides the following selections:

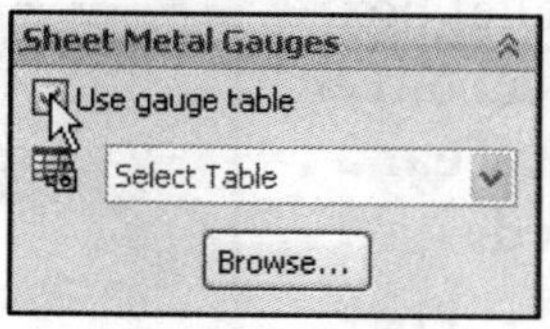

  - **Use gauge table**. Selected by default. Use the default gauge table.
  - **Select Table**. Select a Sheet Metal Gauge Table from the drop-down menu.
  - **Browse**. Browse to locate a Sheet Metal Gauge Table from the SW default folder.

- ***Sheet Metal Parameters***. The Sheet Metal Parameters box provides the following selections:

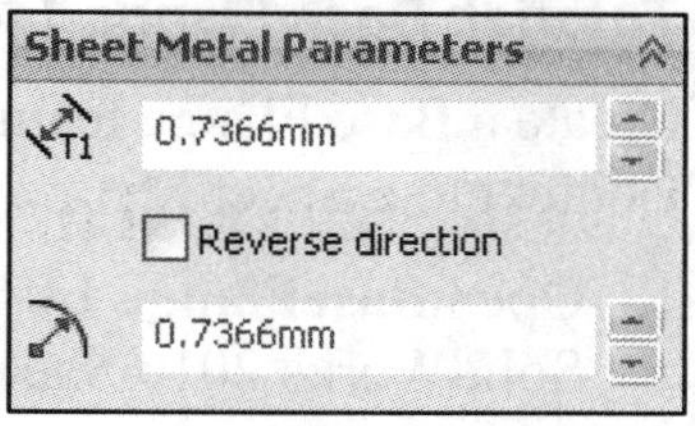


  - **Thickness**. Displays the selected value for the sheet metal thickness.
  - **Reverse direction**. Reverses the thicken sketch in the opposite direction if required.
  - **Bend Radius**. Displays the selected value for the bend radius.

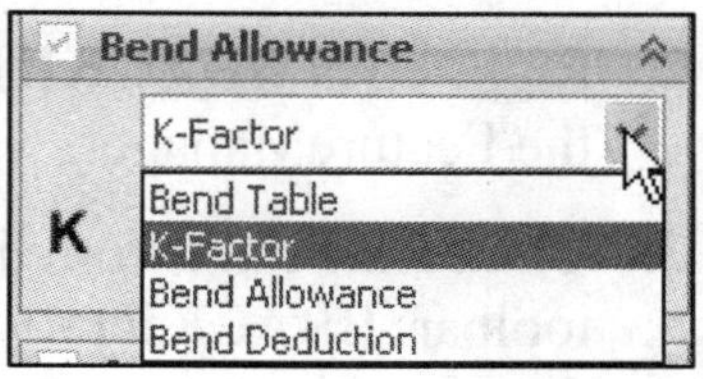


- ***Bend Allowance***. The Bend Allowance box provides the ability to select the following four types of bends:

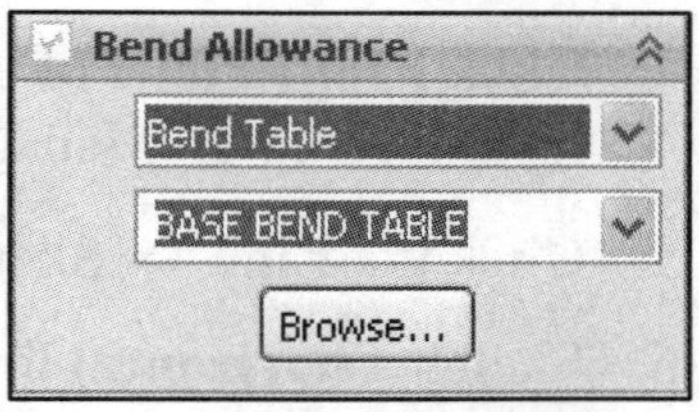


  - **Bend Table**. Select a bend table from the drop-down menu.
  - **Browse**. Browse to locate a bend table file.

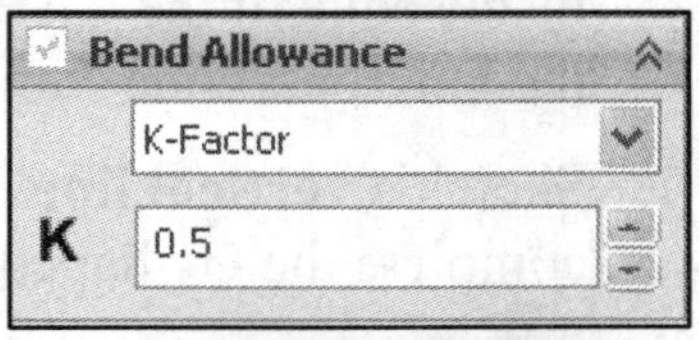


  - **K-Factor**. Selected by default. Enter a K-Factor value. A K-Factor is a ratio that represents the location of the neutral sheet with respect to the thickness of the sheet metal part.

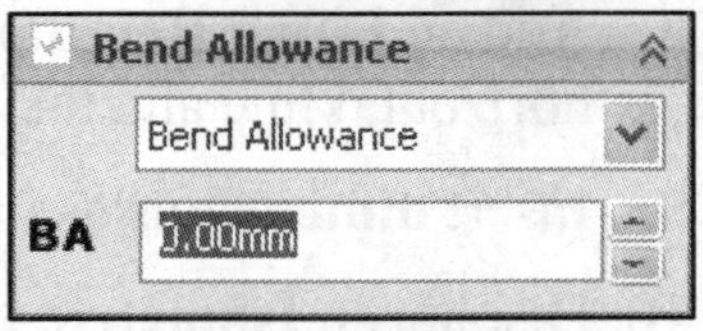


  - **Bend Allowance**. Enter a Bend Allowance value. A bend allowance is the arc length of the bend as measured along the neutral axis of the material.

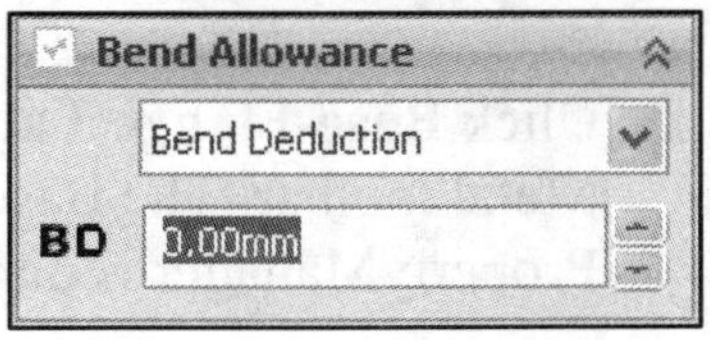


  - **Bend Deduction**. Enter a Bend Deduction value. A bend deduction is the difference between the bend allowance and twice the outside setback.

- ***Auto Relief***. The Auto Relief box provides the ability to select three relief types: **Rectangular**, **Tear** and **Obround** as illustrated.
  - **Use relief ratio**. Selected by default for the Rectangular and Obround option. Uncheck the Use relief ration to enter Width and Depth.

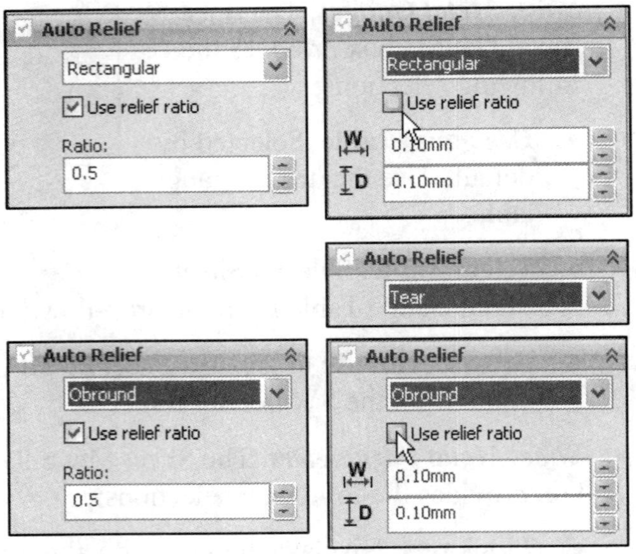


***Tutorial: Base/Flange 14-1***

Create a Base Flange feature In-Context to a Sheet Metal assembly.

1. Open **BaseFlange 14-1** from the SolidWorks 2010\SheetMetal folder.
2. Right-click **BRACKET1<1>** from the FeatureManager.
3. Click **Edit Part** from the Context toolbar. BRACKET<1> is displayed in blue.

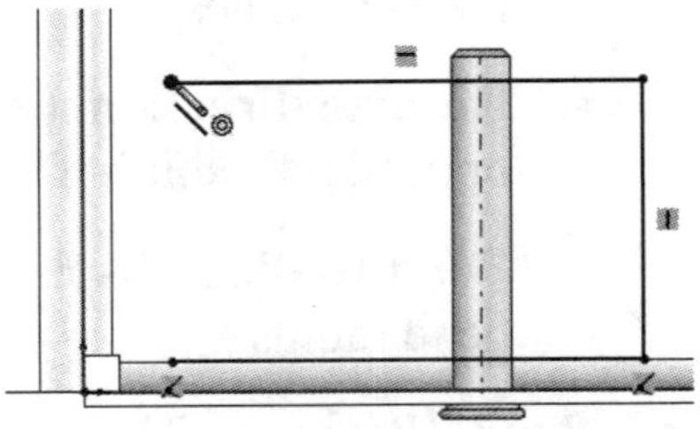

4. Click **Front Plane** of CABINET from the FeatureManager.
5. Click the **Line** Sketch tool.
6. Sketch a **horizontal line** collinear with the inside edge of the CABINET. Note: Sketch the horizontal line from left to right.
7. Sketch a **vertical line** and a **horizontal line** to complete the U-shaped profile as illustrated.

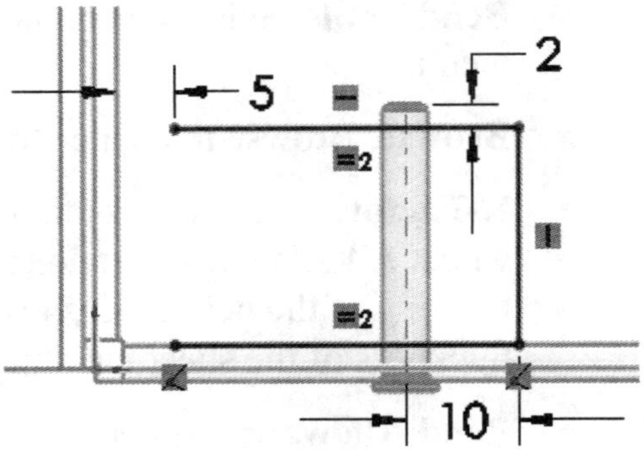


8. Add an **Equal Relation** between the top horizontal line and the bottom horizontal line.
9. Insert **dimensions** as illustrated.
10. Display an **Isometric** view.
11. Click **Base-Flange/Tab** from the Sheet Metal toolbar. The Base Flange PropertyManager is displayed.
12. Select **Up to Vertex** for End Condition in Direction 1.

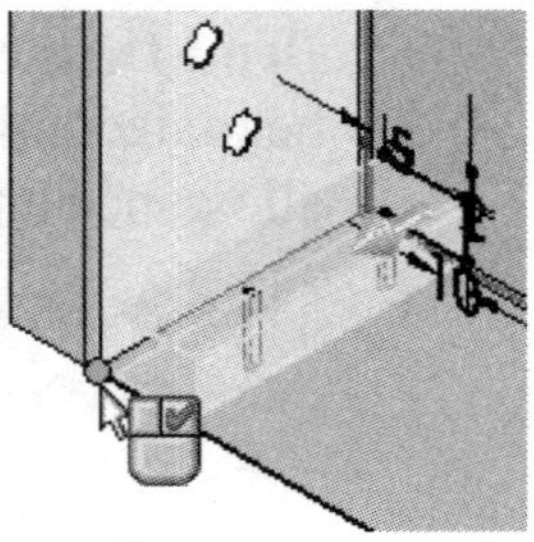

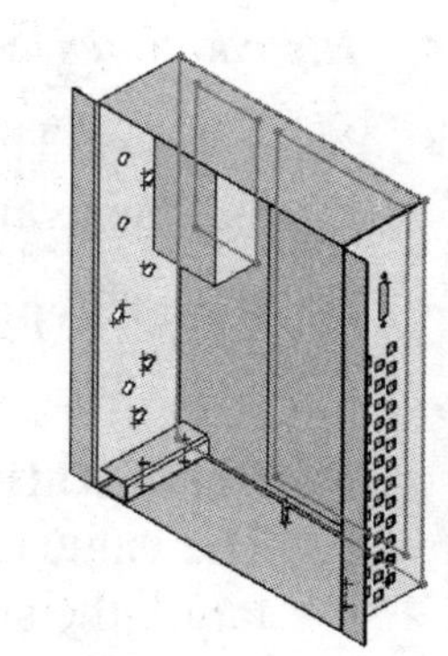

13. Click the CABINET **Extruded1 front left vertex** as illustrated. Vertex<1>@CABINET-1 is displayed in the Vertex box.
14. Enter **1.00**mm for Thickness in the Sheet Metal Parameters box.
15. Enter **2.00**mm for Bend Radius.
16. Enter **.45** for K factor.
17. Click **OK** from the Base Flange PropertyManager.

Return to the assembly.

18. Click the **Exit Component** tool. **Rebuild** the model. View the results.
19. **Close** the model.

## Convert to Sheet Metal tool

The Convert to Sheet Metal tool provides the ability to convert a solid or surface body to a sheet metal part. The solid body can be an imported sheet metal part.

The Convert to Sheet Metal tool uses the Convert To Sheet Metal PropertyManager. The PropertyManager provides the following selections:

- ***Sheet Metal Parameters***. The Sheet Metal Parameters box provides the following options:
  - **Select a fixed entity**. Select the face that remains in place when the part is flattened. You can select only one face.
  - **Sheet thickness**. Thick of the sheet.
  - **Default radius for bends**. Bend radius.
  - **Reverse Thickness**. Changes the direction in which the sheet thickness is applied.
- ***Bend Edges***. The Bend Edges box provides the following options:
  - **Select edges/faces that represent bends**. In the graphics window, click an edge to add it to the list of bend edges.
  - **Collect All Bends**. When there are pre-existing bends, such as in an imported part, finds all of the appropriate bends in the part.
- ***Rip Edges found (Read-only)***. When you select bend edges, the corresponding rip edges are selected automatically.

- ***Rip Sketches***. Select a 2D or 3D sketch to define a required rip.
- ***Auto Relief***. The software automatically adds relief cuts where needed when inserting bends. The available options are:
  - **Relief Type**. Select the type of relief cut to be added: **Rectangular**, **Obround** and **Tear**.
  - **Relief Ratio**. If you select Rectangular or Obround, you must set a relief ratio. The value of the relief ratio must be between .1 and 2. The higher the value, the larger the size of the relief cut added during the insertion of bends.

Use the Convert to Sheet Metal command with: Solid or surface bodies that have: No shells or fillets, either a shell or fillets, both a shell and fillets, or imported parts that are already in the form of a sheet metal part.

***Tutorial: Convert to Sheet Metal 14-1***

Apply the Convert to Sheet Metal tool.

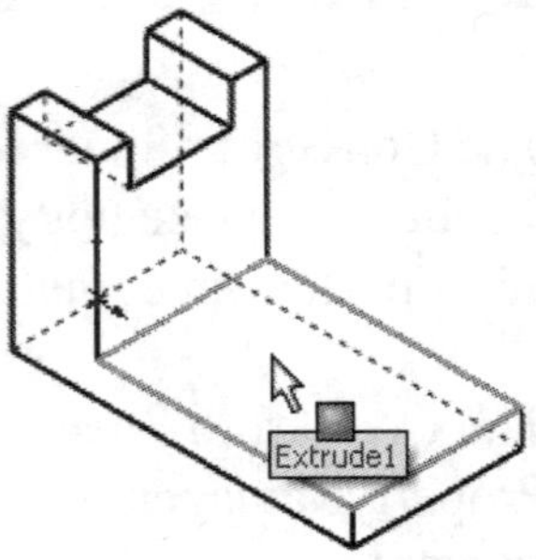


1. Open **Convert to Sheet Metal 14.1** from the SolidWorks 2010\SheetMetal folder.
2. Click **Convert to Sheet Metal** from the Sheet Metal toolbar. The Convert to Sheet Metal PropertyManager is displayed.

Select a face as the fixed face for the sheet metal part and set the sheet thickness and default bend radius. Under Bend Edges, select the model edges that will form bends.

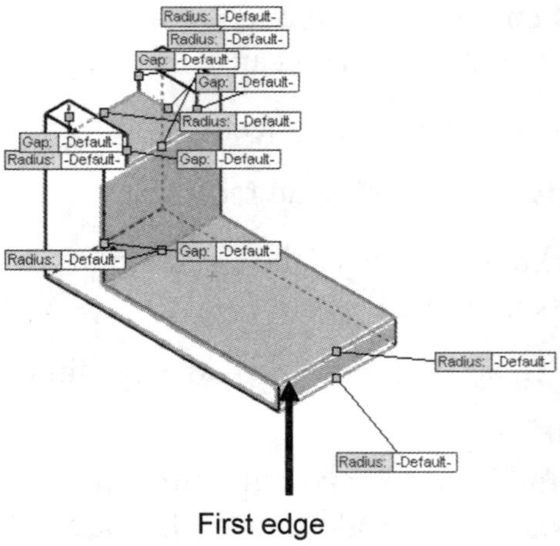


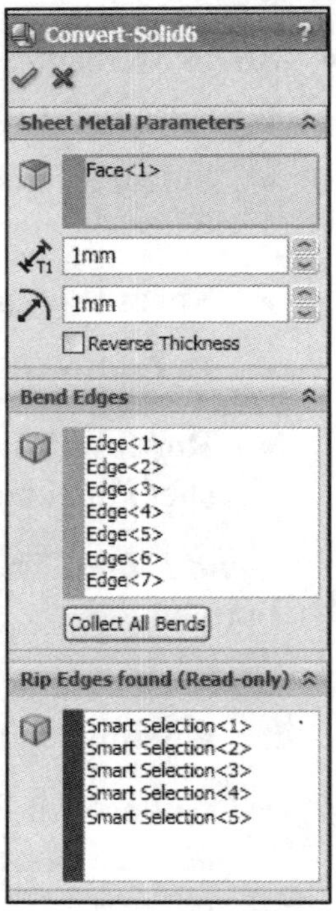


3. Click the **top face** of Extrude1 as illustrated.
4. Enter **1mm** for Sheet Thickness.
5. Enter **1mm** for Default Radius for bend.
6. Select the **top 7 edges** of the model as illustrated. The selected edges are displayed in the Bend Edges dialog box.

To provide access to needed edges, display your model in the Hidden Lines Visible mode.

7. Accept the default settings. Click **OK** from the Convert to Sheet Metal PropertyManager. View the results.

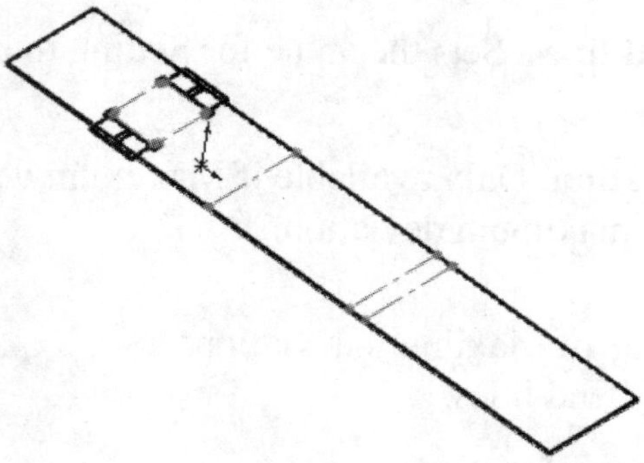

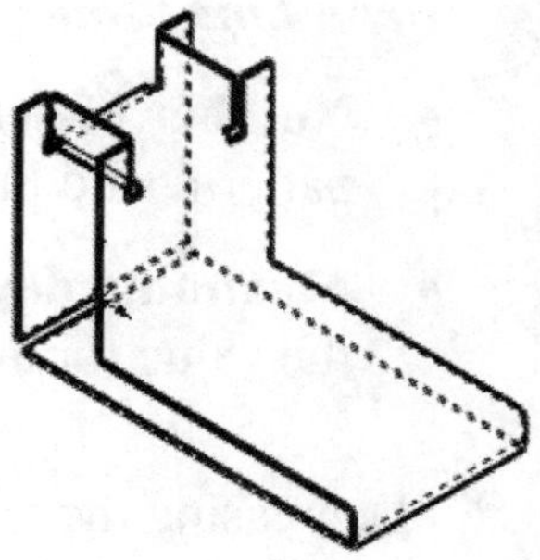

Display the model in a Flatten state.

8. Right-click **Flat-Pattern1** from the FeatureManager.

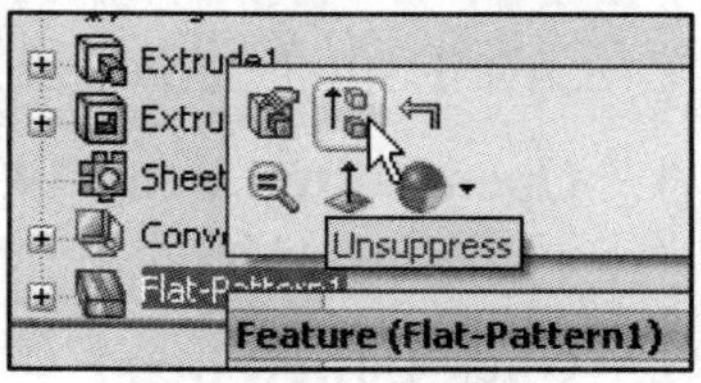


9. Click **Unsuppress**. View the results.
10. **Close** the model.

View SolidWorks Help for additional information on the Convert to Sheet Metal feature.

## Lofted Bend tool

The Lofted Bend tool provides the ability to create a sheet metal part between two sketches using a loft feature. Lofted bends in sheet metal parts use two open-profile sketches that are connected by a loft.

The Base-Flange feature is not used with the Lofted Bend feature.

They are some additional items to note about the Lofted Bend feature. They are:

1. You can not mirror a Lofted Bend feature.
2. Two sketches are required with the following restrictions:
   - An open profile is required without sharp edges.
   - An aligned profile is required to ensure flat pattern accuracy.

The Lofted Bend tool uses the Lofted Bend PropertyManager. The Lofted Bend PropertyManager provides the following selections:

- ***Profiles***. The Profiles box provides the following selections:
  - **Profile**. Displays the selected sketches. For each profile, select the point from which you want the path of the loft to travel.
  - **Move Up**. Adjusts the order of the profiles up.
  - **Move Down**. Adjusts the order of the profiles down.
- ***Thickness***. The Thickness box provides the ability to set the value for Thickness.
  - **Reverse Direction**. Reverses the direction of the lofted bend if required.

- ***Bend Line Control***. The Bend Line Control box provides the following selections:
  - **Number of bend lines**. Sets the value for Setting to control coarseness of the flat pattern bend lines.
  - **Maximum deviation**. Only available if Maximum deviation is not selected. Sets the value for the maximum deviation.

Decreasing the value of Maximum deviation increases the number of bend lines.

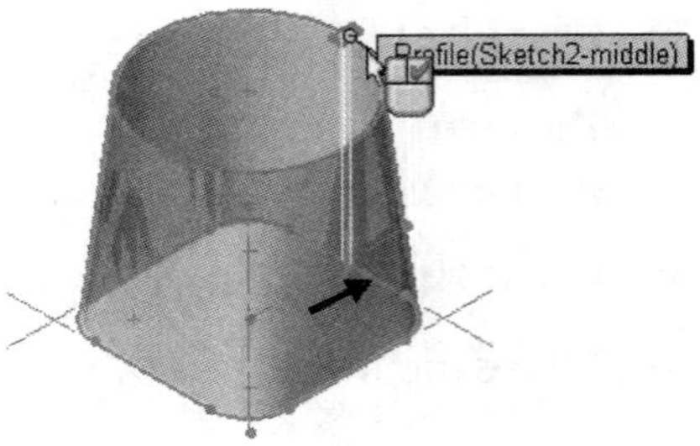


### *Tutorial: Lofted Bend 14-1*

Create a Lofted Bend feature in a Sheet Metal part.

1. Open **Lofted Bend 14-1** from the SolidWorks 2010\SheetMetal folder.
2. Click **Lofted Bend** from the Sheet Metal toolbar. The Lofted Bend PropertyManager is displayed.
3. Click **both sketches** in the Graphics window as illustrated. The selected profiles are the traveled loft path. Enter **.01**in for Thickness. The direction arrow points inward. Click the **Reverse Direction** button if required.
4. Click **OK** from the Lofted Bend PropertyManager. The Lofted Bend1 feature is displayed in the FeatureManager. View the results.
5. **Close** the model.

## Edge Flange tool

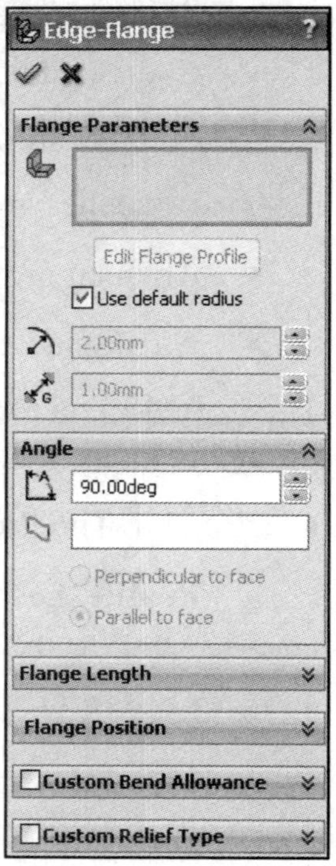


The Edge Flange tool provides the ability to add a wall to an edge of a sheet metal part. General edge flange characteristics include:

1. The thickness of the edge flange is linked to the thickness of the sheet metal part.
2. The sketch line of the profile must lie on the selected edge.

The Edge Flange tool uses the Edge-Flange PropertyManager. The Edge-Flange PropertyManager provides the following selections:

- ***Flange Parameters***. The Flange Parameters box provides the following options:
  - **Select edges**. Displays the selected edges from the Graphics window.
  - **Edit Flange Profile**. Edits the sketch of the profile. The Profile Sketch dialog box is used.

- **Use default radius**. Uses the default radius. Un-check to enter bend radius.
- **Bend Radius**. Only available when the Use default radius option is un-checked. Enter a bend radius value.
- **Gap distance**. Sets the value of the gap distance.

- *Angle*. The Angle box provides the following selections:
  - **Flange Angle**. Sets the value of the Flange Angle.
  - **Select face**. Provides the ability to select a face from the Graphics window.
  - **Perpendicular to face**. Flange angle perpendicular to selected face.
  - **Parallel to face**. Flange angel parallel to selected face.

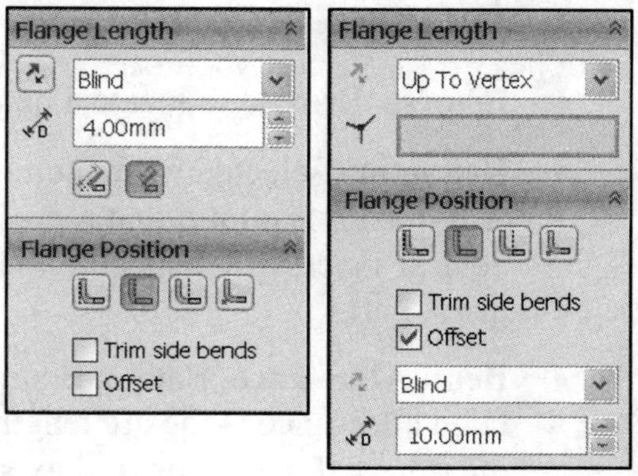


- *Flange Length*. The Flange Length box provides the following selections:
  - **Length End Condition**. Provides two selections:
    - **Blind**. Selected by default.
    - **Up To Vertex**. Select a Vertex from the Graphics window.
  - **Reverse Direction**. Reverses the direction of the edge flange if required.
  - **Length**. Only available if the Blind option is selected. Enter a **Length** value. Select the **origin** for the measurement. The selections are: **Outer Virtual Sharp** and **Inner Virtual Sharp**.

- *Flange Position*. The Flange Position box provides the following selections:
  - **Bend Position**. Select one of the following positions:
    - **Material Inside**. The top of the shaded preview of the flange coincides with the top of the fixed sheet metal entity.
    - **Material Outside**. The bottom of the shaded preview of the flange coincides with the top of the fixed sheet metal entity.
    - **Bend Outside**. The bottom of the shaded preview of the flange is offset by the bend radius.
    - **Bend from Virtual Sharp**. This preserves the dimension to the original edge and will vary the bend material condition to automatically match with the flange's end condition.

- **Trim side bends**. Not selected by default. Removes extra material.
- **Offset**. Not selected by default. Offsets the flange.
- **Offset End Condition**. Only available if the Offset option is checked. There are four End Conditions. They are: **Blind**, **Up To Vertex**, **Up To Surface** and **Offset From Surface**.
- **Offset Distance**. Only available if the Offset option is checked. Enter the Offset distance value.

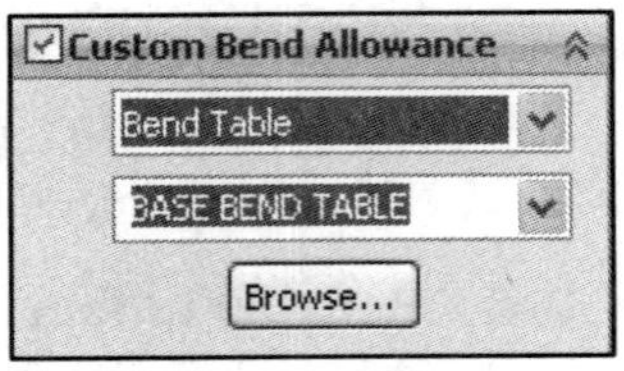


- ***Custom Bend Allowance***. Provides the following four selections:
  - **Bend Table**. Selects a bend table from the drop down menu
  - **Browse**. Browse to locate a bend table file.

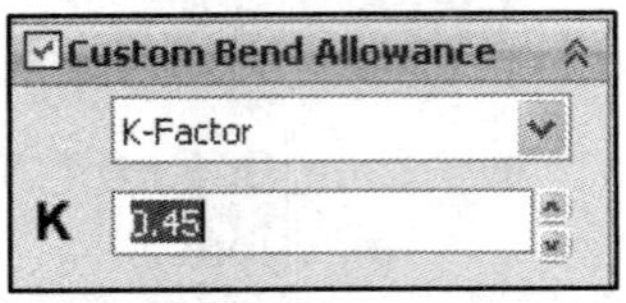


  - **K-Factor**. Selected by default. Enter a K-Factor value. A K-Factor is a ratio that represents the location of the neutral sheet with respect to the thickness of the sheet metal part.

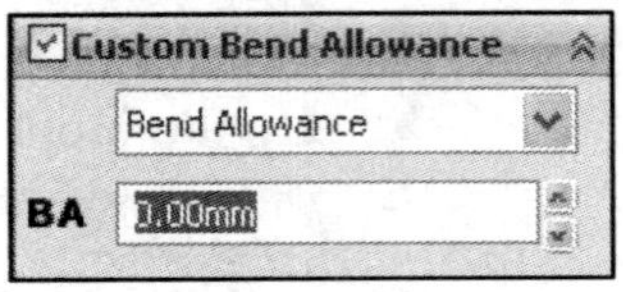


  - **Bend Allowance**. Enter a Bend Allowance value. A bend allowance is the arc length of the bend as measured along the neutral axis of the material.

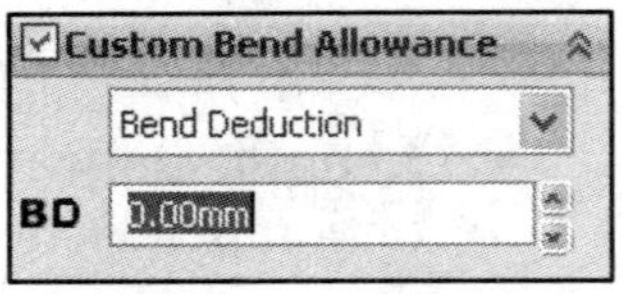


  - **Bend Deduction**. Enter a Bend Deduction value. A bend deduction is the difference between the bend allowance and twice the outside setback Bend Allowance Type.

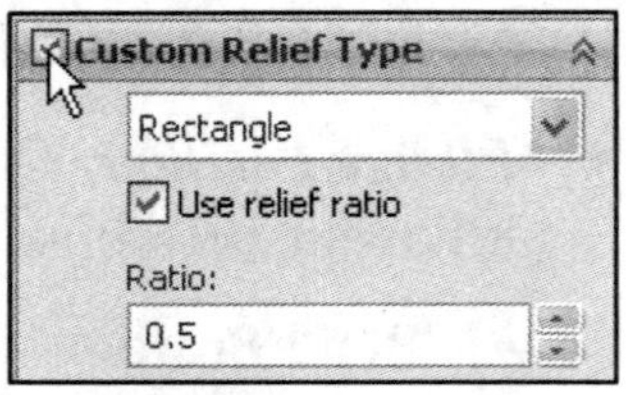


- ***Custom Relief Type***. Provides the ability to select three relief types. They are: **Rectanglar**, **Tear** and **Obround**. The Rectangle custom relief type is selected by default. Note: If you want to add a Rectangle or Obround relief, you must specify the Relief ratio. The value of the Relief ratio must be between 0.05 and 2.0. The higher the value, the larger the size of the relief cut added during insertion of bends. See SolidWorks help for additional information on Relief ratio.

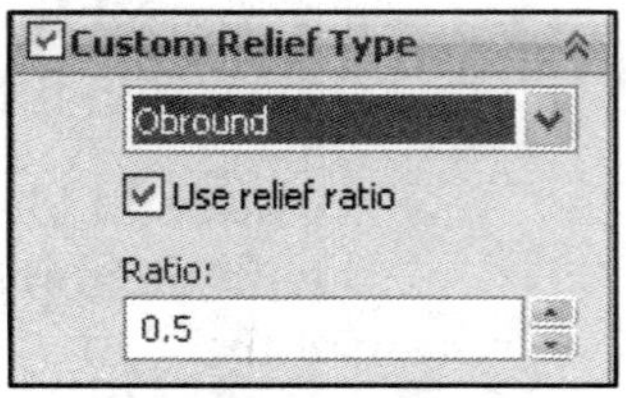


  - **Use relief ratio**. Uncheck the Use relief ratio box. Enter **Width** and **Depth**.

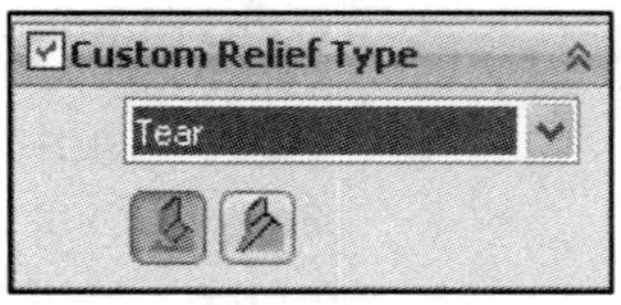


  - **Tear**. Reliefs are the minimum size required to insert the bend and flatten the part. Two options are provided: **Rip** and **Extended**. Rip is selected by default.

### *Tutorial: Edge Flange 14-1*

Create an Edge Flange feature on a Sheet metal part. Insert a front right flange.

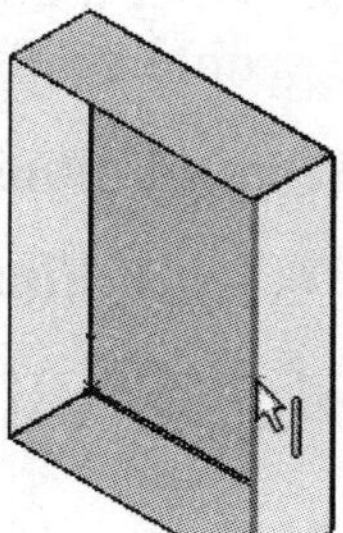

1. Open **Edge Flange 14-1** from the SolidWorks 2010\SheetMetal folder.
2. Click the **front right vertical** edge as illustrated.
3. Click **Edge Flange** from the Sheet Metal toolbar. The Edge-Flange PropertyManager is displayed. Edge<1> is displayed in the Select edges box.
4. Select **Blind** for Length End Condition.
5. Enter **30**mm for Length. The direction arrow points to the right. If required, click the **Reverse Direction** button. Inner Virtual Sharp is selected by default.
6. Select **Material Outside** for Flange Position. Accept all other defaults.

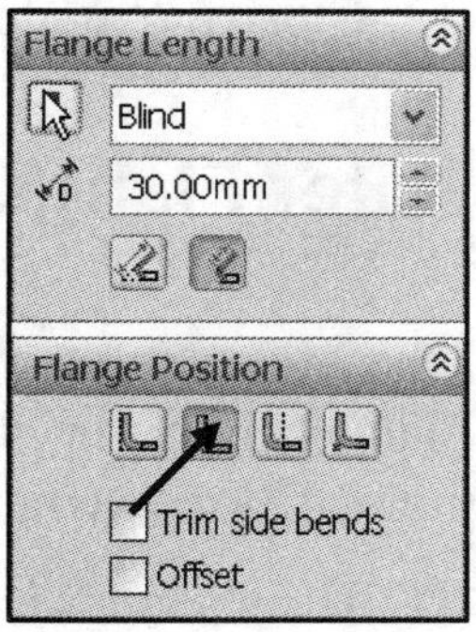


7. Click **OK** from the Edge-Flange PropertyManager. Edge-Flange1 is displayed in the FeatureManager.
8. **Close** the model.

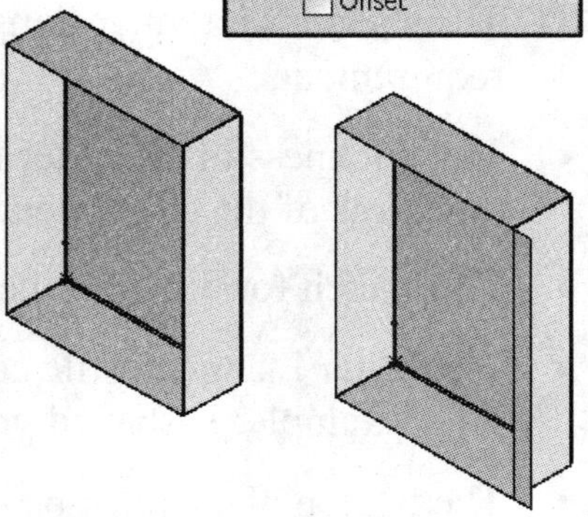

### *Tutorial: Edge Flange 14-2*

Create an Edge Flange feature on a Sheet metal part using the Edit Flange Profile option.

1. Open **Edge Flange 14-2** from the SolidWorks 2010\SheetMetal folder.
2. Click the **top left edge** of the BRACKET.

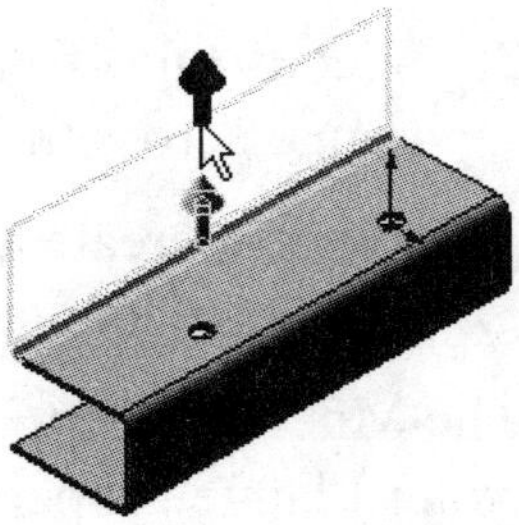

3. Click **Edge Flange** from the Sheet Metal toolbar. The PropertyManager is displayed. Edge<1> is displayed in the Select edges box.
4. Click a **position** above the BRACKET for direction. The direction arrow points upwards.
5. Enter **20**mm for Flange Length in the spin box.
6. Click the **Edit Flange Profile** button. Do not click the Finish button at this time.
7. Drag the **front left edge** of the edge flange towards the front hole as illustrated.

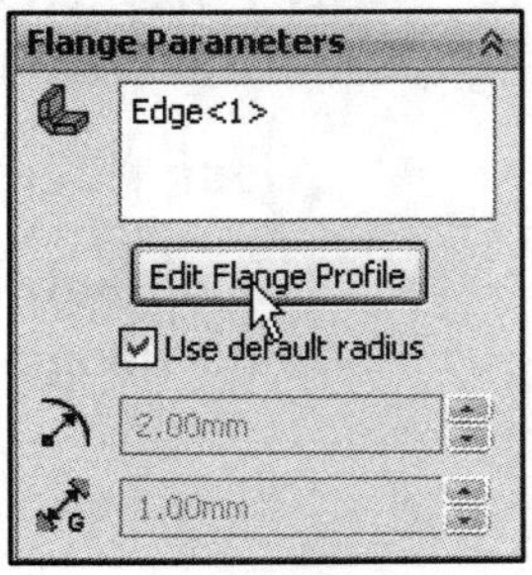

8. Drag the **back left edge** towards the front hole as illustrated.
9. Add **dimensions** as illustrated.
10. Click **Finish** from the Profile Sketch box.
11. Click **OK** from the PropertyManager. Edge-Flange1 is displayed in the FeatureManager.
12. **Close** the model.

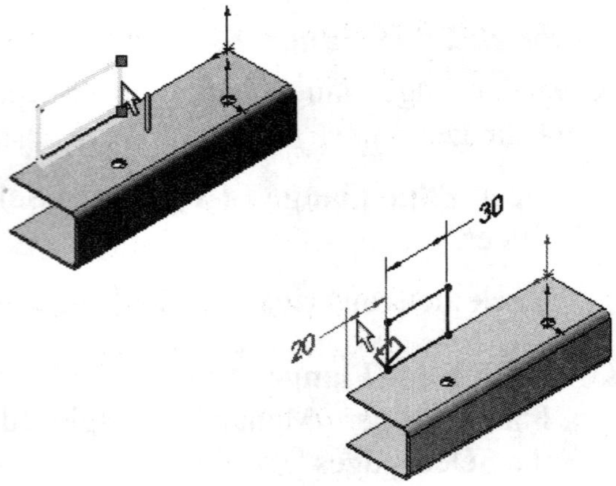


## Miter Flange tool

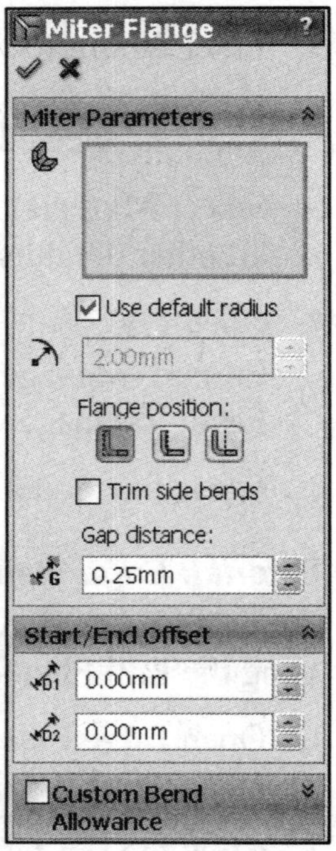


The Miter Flange tool provides the ability to add a series of flanges to one or more edges of a sheet metal part. There are a few items to know when using the miter flange feature. They are:

1. The sketch for a miter flange must adhere to the following requirements:

- The thickness of the miter flange is automatically linked to the thickness of the sheet metal part.
- The sketch for the miter flange can contain lines or arcs.
- The Miter Flange profile can contain more than one continuous line. Example: L-shaped profile
- The Sketch plane must be normal to the first created edge of the Miter Flange.

2. Specify an offset of the miter flange instead of creating a miter flange across the entire edge of a sheet metal part.
3. You can create a miter flange feature on a series of tangent or non-tangent edges.

The Miter Flange tool uses the Miter Flange PropertyManager. The Miter Flange PropertyManager provides the following selections:

- ***Miter Parameters***. The Miter Parameters box provides the following selections:
  - **Along Edges**. Displays the selected edge.
  - **Use default radius**. Uses the default bend radius for the miter flange.

- **Bend radius**. Only available when the Use default radius is un-checked. Set the bend radius value.
- **Flange position**. The Flange position section provides the following selections:
  - **Material Inside**. The top of the shaded preview of the flange coincides with the top of the fixed sheet metal entity.
  - **Material Outside**. The bottom of the shaded preview of the flange coincides with the top of the fixed sheet metal entity.
  - **Bend Outside**. The bottom of the shaded preview of the flange is offset by the bend radius.
- **Trim side bends**. Removes extra material.
- **Gap distance**. Sets the distance of the gap.

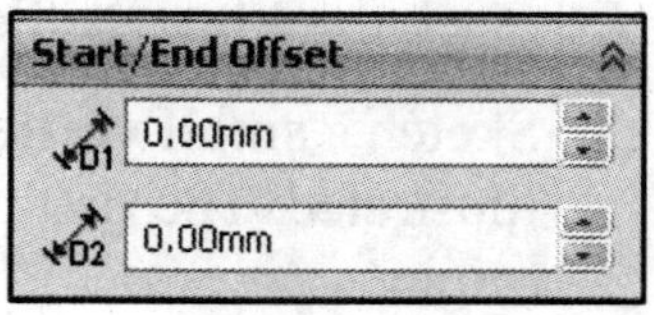


- ***Start/End Offset***. The Start/End Offset box provides the following selections:
  - **Start Offset Distance**. Enter the value for Start Offset Distance.
  - **End Offset Distance**. Enter the value for the Start Offset Distance.

If you want the miter flange to span the entire edge of the model, set the Start Offset and End Offset Distance values to zero.

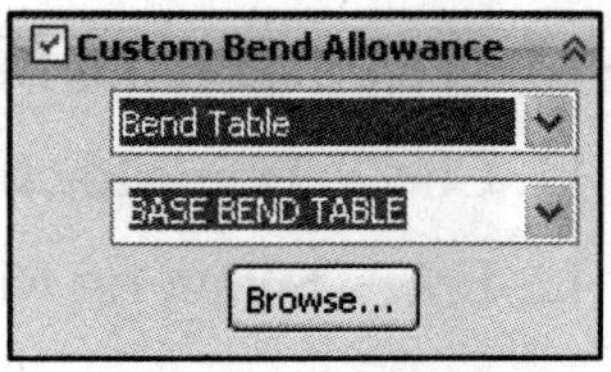


- ***Custom Bend Allowance***. The Custom Bend Allowance box provides the following four selections:
  - **Bend Table**. Select a bend table from the drop-down menu.
    - **Browse**. Browse to locate a bend table file.

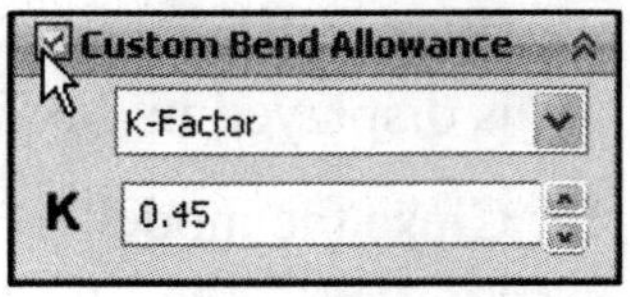


  - **K-Factor**. Selected by default. Enter a K-Factor value. A K-Factor is a ratio that represents the location of the neutral sheet with respect to the thickness of the sheet metal part.

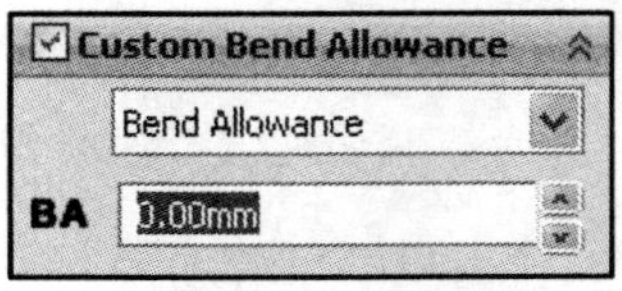


  - **Bend Allowance**. Enter a Bend Allowance value. A bend allowance is the arc length of the bend as measured along the neutral axis of the material.

- **Bend Deduction**. Enter a Bend Deduction value. A bend deduction is the difference between the bend allowance and twice the outside setback Bend Allowance Type.

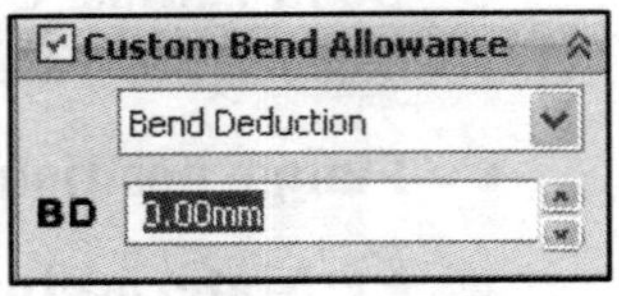


### *Tutorial: Miter Flange 14-1*

Create a Miter Flange feature in a Sheet metal part.

1. Open **Miter Flange 14-1** from the SolidWorks 2010\SheetMetal folder.

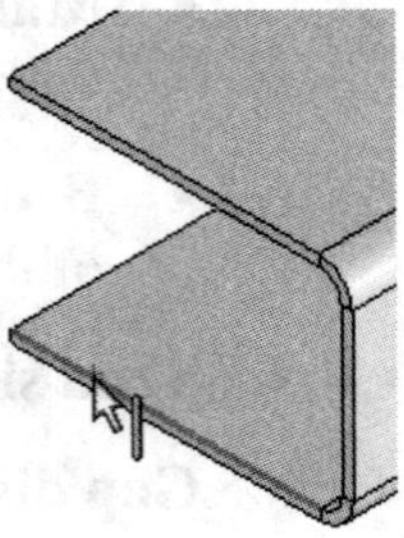

2. Click **Miter Flange** from the Sheet Metal toolbar. The PropertyManager is displayed.
3. Click the **front inside edge** of the BRACKET as illustrated.
4. Click the **Line** Sketch tool.
5. Sketch a **small vertical line** on the front inside left corner as illustrated. The first point is coincident with the new sketch origin.

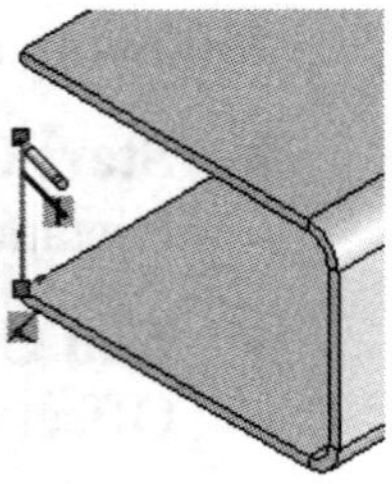

6. Add **dimensions** as illustrated. The line is 2mms.
7. **Exit** the Sketch. The Miter Flange PropertyManager is displayed.
8. Click the **Propagate** icon in the Graphics window to select inside tangent edges. The selected entities are displayed.

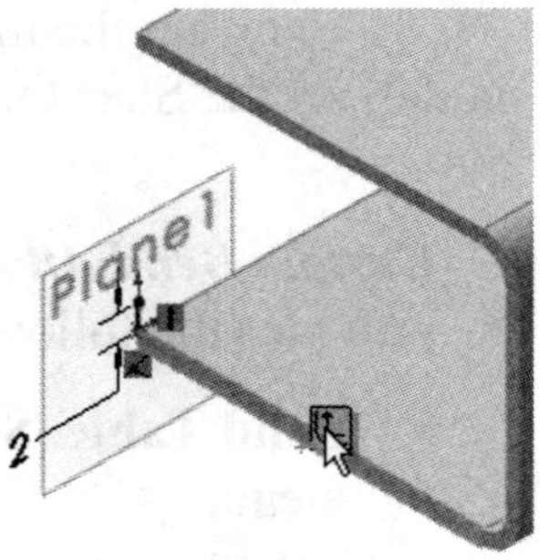


9. Uncheck **Use default radius.**
10. Enter **.50**mm for Bend Radius.
11. Check **Trim side bends.**
12. Enter **.50**mm for Rip Gap distance.
13. Click **OK** from the Miter Flange PropertyManager. The Miter Flange1 feature is displayed in the FeatureManager.
14. **Close** the model.

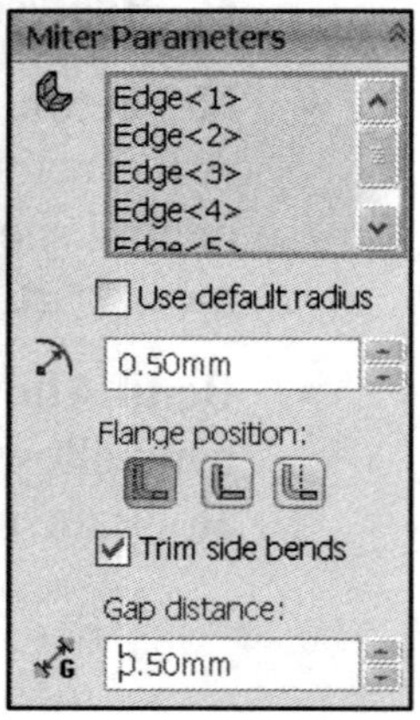

## Hem tool

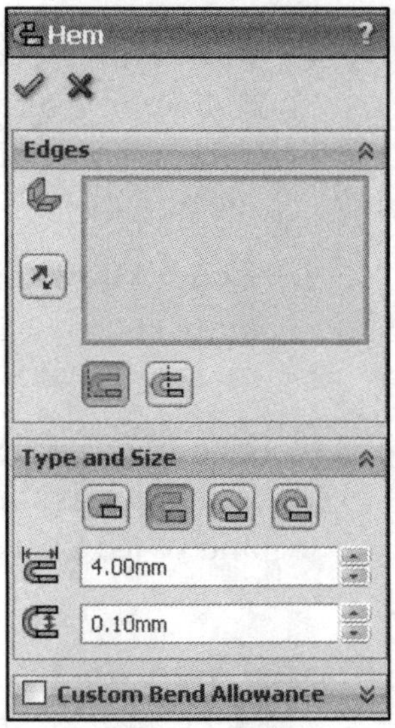


The Hem  tool provides the ability to curl or hem the edge of a sheet metal part. There are a few items to know when using the Hem feature. They are:

1. The selected edge to hem must be linear.
2. Mitered corners are automatically added to intersecting hems.
3. The edges must lie on the same face if you select multiple edges to hem.

The Hem tool uses the Hem PropertyManager. The Hem PropertyManager provides the following options:

- ***Edges***. The Edges box provides the following selections:
  - **Edges**. Displays the selected edges to hem from the Graphics window.
  - **Reverse Direction**. Reverse the direction of the hem if required.
  - **Material Inside**. Selected by default. The top of the shaded preview of the flange coincides with the top of the fixed sheet metal entity.
  - **Bend Outside**. The bottom of the shaded preview of the flange is offset by the bend radius.

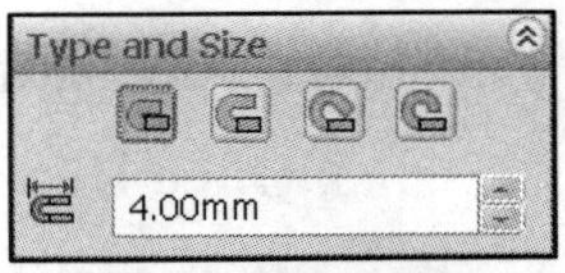


- ***Type and Size***. The Type and Size box provides the following selections:
  - **Closed**, **Open**, **Tear Drop** and **Rolled**.
  - **Length**. Sets the Length value.

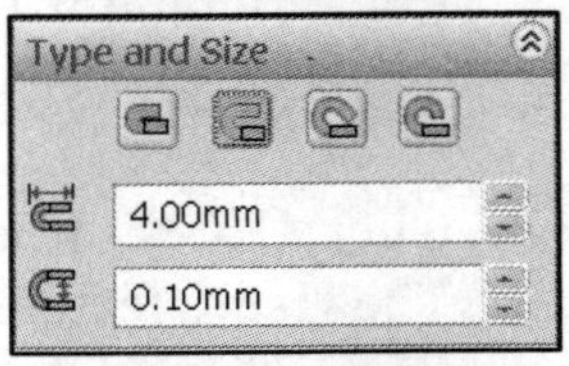


  - **Gap Distance**. Only available for the Open option. Sets the Gap distance value.
  - **Angle**. Only available for the Drop and Rolled options. Sets the Angle value.

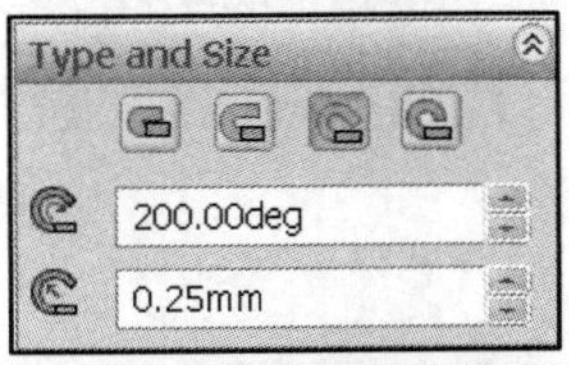


  - **Radius**. Only available for the Drop and Rolled options. Sets the Radius value.

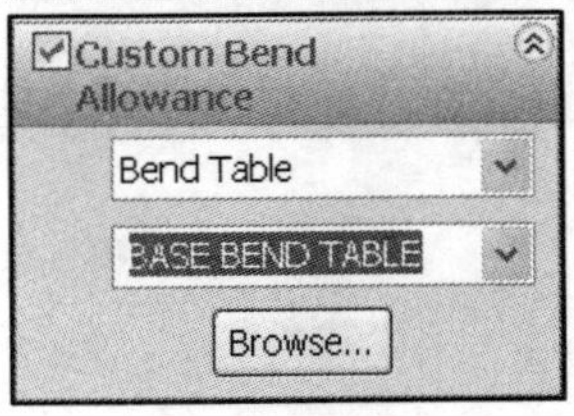


- ***Custom Bend Allowance***. The Custom Bend Allowance box provides the following selections:
  - **Bend Table**. Select a bend table from the drop-down menu.

- **Browse**. Browse to locate a bend table file.
- **K-Factor**. Selected by default. Enter a K-Factor value. A K-Factor is a ratio that represents the location of the neutral sheet with respect to the thickness of the sheet metal part.

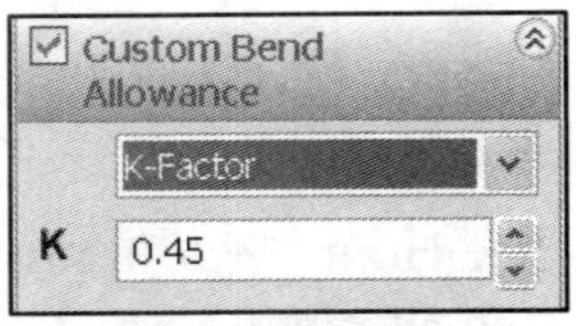


- **Bend Allowance**. Enter a Bend Allowance value. A bend allowance is the arc length of the bend as measured along the neutral axis of the material.

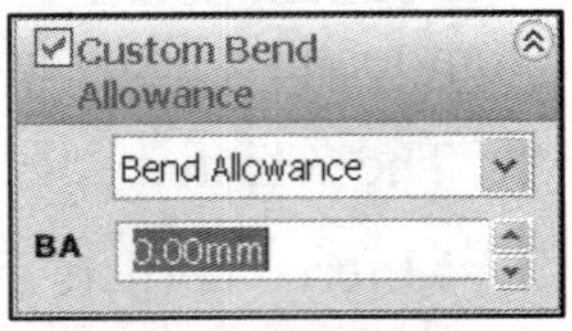


- **Bend Deduction**. Enter a Bend Deduction value. A bend deduction is the difference between the bend allowance and twice the outside setback Bend Allowance Type.

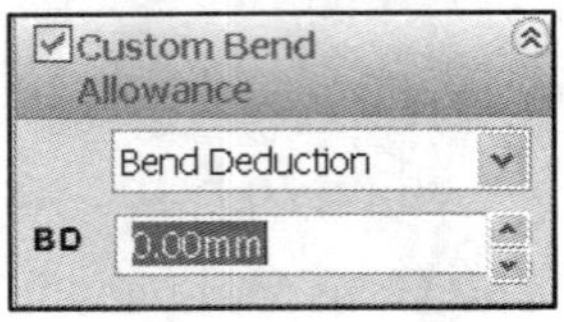


***Tutorial: Hem 14-1***

Create an Open type Hem feature on a Sheet metal part.

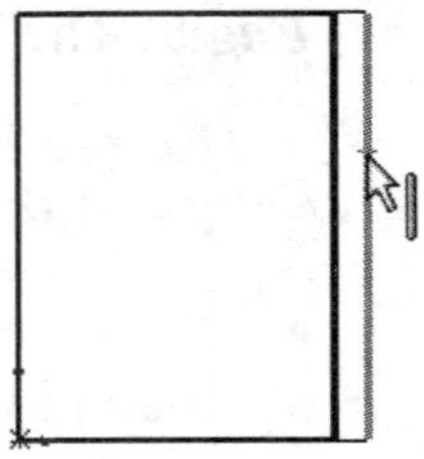

1. Open **Hem 14-1** from the SolidWorks 2010\ SheetMetal folder.
2. Display a **Front** view.
3. Click the **right vertical edge** of the right flange.
4. Click **Hem** from the Sheet Metal toolbar. The Hem PropertyManager is displayed. Edge<1> is displayed in the Edges box.
5. Display an **Isometric** view.
6. Click the **Reverse Direction** button.
7. Click **Open Hem** type.
8. Enter **10**mm for Hem Length.
9. Enter **.10**mm for Gap Distance.
10. Click **OK** from the Hem PropertyManager. The Hem1 feature is displayed in the FeatureManager.
11. **Close** the model.

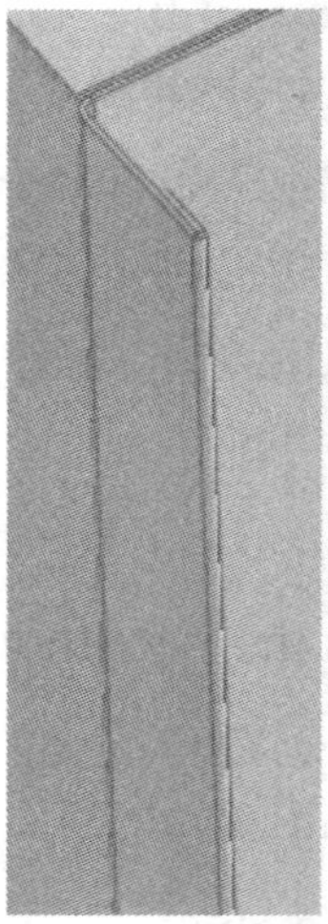

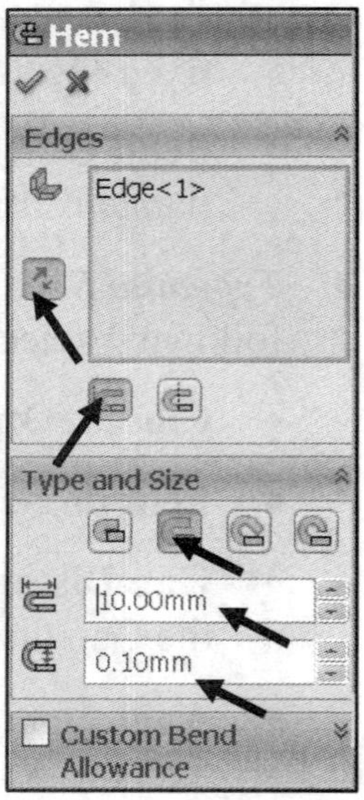

## Sketch Bend tool

The Sketch Bend tool provides the ability to add a bend from a selected sketch in a sheet metal part. You can add a bend line to the sheet metal part while the part is in the folded state with a sketched bend feature. There are a few items to know when using the Sketch Bend feature. They are:

1. Only lines are allowed in the sketch.
2. You can have more than one line per sketch.
3. The bend line does not have to be the same length of the faces you are bending.

The Sketch Bend tool uses the Sketched Bend PropertyManager. The Sketched Bend PropertyManager provides the following selections:

- ***Bend Parameters***. The Bend Parameters box provides the following selections:
  - **Fixed Faces**. Displays the selected face from the Graphics window. The Fixed face does not move as a result of the bend.
  - **Bend position**. Select one of the four bend positions:
    - **Bend Centerline**. Selected by default. The bend line is located such that it equally splits the bend region in the flattened part.
    - **Material Inside**. The top of the shaded preview of the flange coincides with the top of the fixed sheet metal entity.
    - **Material Outside**. The bottom of the shaded preview of the flange coincides with the top of the fixed sheet metal entity.
    - **Bend Outside**. The bottom of the shaded preview of the flange is offset by the bend radius
  - **Reverse Direction**. Reverses the direction of the bend position if required.
  - **Bend Angle**. 90deg selected by default. Sets the value of the bend angle.
  - **Use default radius**. Selected by default. Uses the default bend radius.
  - **Bend Radius**. Only available if the Use default radius is un-checked. Sets the radius of the bend.

- ***Custom Blend Allowance***. The Custom Blend Allowance box provides the following selections:

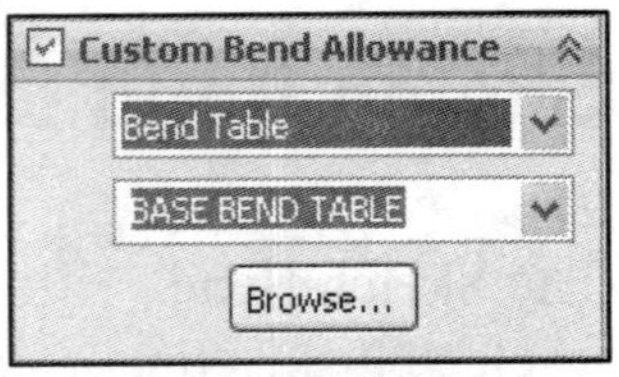


  - **Bend Table**. Select a bend table from the drop down menu.
    - **Browse**. Browse to locate a bend table file.

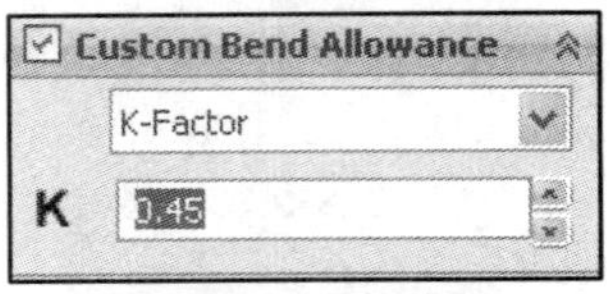


  - **K-Factor**. Enter a K-Factor value. A K-Factor is a ratio that represents the location of the neutral sheet with respect to the thickness of the sheet metal part.

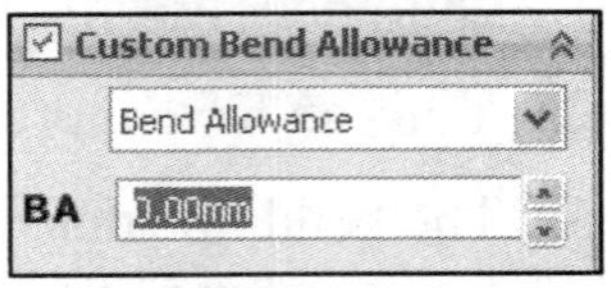


  - **Bend Allowance**. Enter a Bend Allowance value. A bend allowance is the arc length of the bend as measured along the neutral axis of the material.

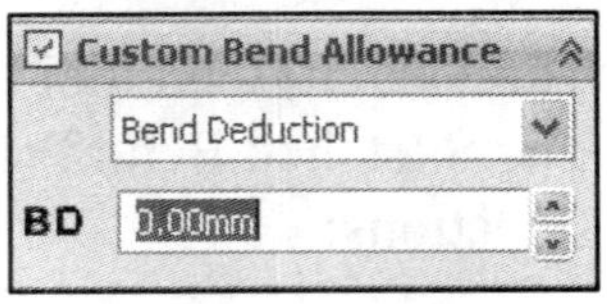


  - **Bend Deduction**. Enter a Bend Deduction value. A bend deduction is the difference between the bend allowance and twice the outside setback Bend Allowance Type.

### *Tutorial: Sketch Bend 14-1*

Create a Sketch Bend feature in a Sheet Metal part.

1. Open **Sketch Bend 14-1** from the SolidWorks 2010\SheetMetal folder.
2. Click the right **face** of Edge-Flange1.
3. Sketch a **line** on the planar face of the sheet metal part as illustrated.

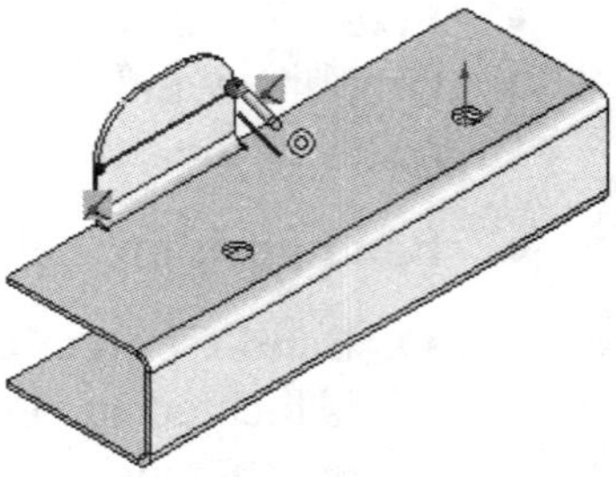

4. Click **Sketch Bend** from the Sheet Metal toolbar. The Sketched Bend PropertyManager is displayed.
5. Click the **face** below the sketch line as illustrated in the Graphics window. The selected section does not move as the result of the bend.
6. Click the **Reverse Direction** button. The direction arrow points towards the left.

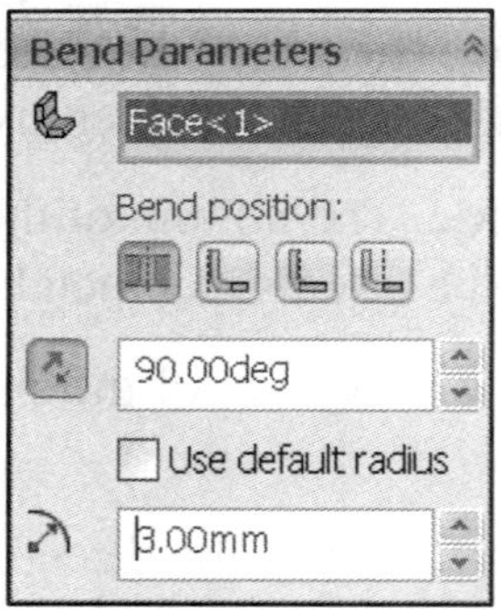


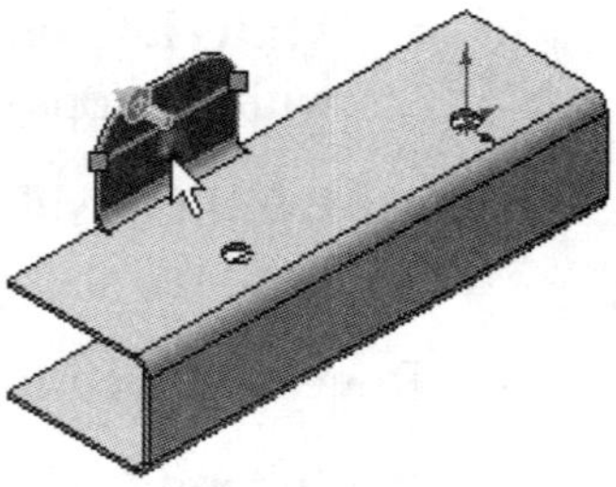

7. Enter **90**deg for Angle.
8. Uncheck **Use default radius**.
9. Enter **3.0**mm for Radius.

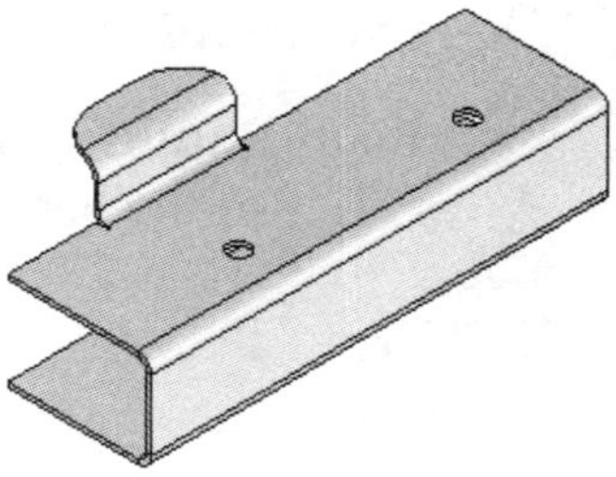

**10.** Click **OK** from the Sketched Bend PropertyManager. The Sketched Bend1 feature is displayed in the FeatureManager.

11. **Close** the model.

## Jog tool

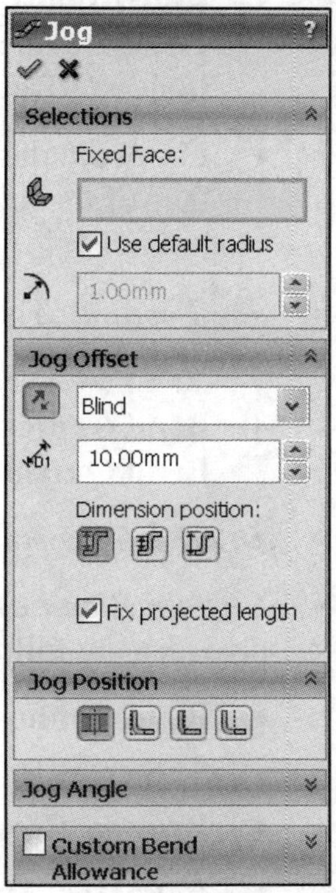


The Jog tool provides the ability to add two bends from a sketched line in a sheet metal part. There are a few items to know when using the Jog tool. They are some additional items to note about the Jog tool:

1. The line does not need to be vertical or horizontal.
2. Your sketch must contain a least one line.
3. The bend line does not have to be the same length of the faces that you are bending.

The Jog tool uses the Jog PropertyManager. The Jog PropertyManager provides the following selections:

- ***Selections***. The Selections box provides the following options:
  - **Fixed Face**. Displays the selected fixed face for the Jog.
  - **Use default radius**. Selected by default. Uses the default Jog radius.
  - **Bend Radius**. Only available if the Use default radius is un-checked. Sets the radius of the Jog.
- ***Jog Offset***. The Jog Offset box provides the following selections:
  - **End Condition**. Provides four End Condition selections:
    - **Blind**. Selected by default. Extends the feature from the Sketch plane from a specified distance.
    - **Up To Vertex**. Extends the feature from the Sketch plane to a plane that is parallel to the Sketch plane and passes through the selected vertex.
    - **Up To Surface**. Extends the feature from the Sketch plane to the selected surface.
    - **Offset From Surface**. Extends the feature from the Sketch plane to a specified distance from the selected surface.

- **Reverse Direction**. Reverses the direction of the Jog if required.
- **Offset Distance**. Displays the selected offset distance of the Jog.
- **Dimension Position**: Outside Offset selected by default. There are three position types. They are: **Outside Offset**, **Inside Offset** and **Overall Dimension**.
- **Fix projected length**. Provides the ability for the selected face of the jog to stay the same length. The overall length of the tab is preserved.

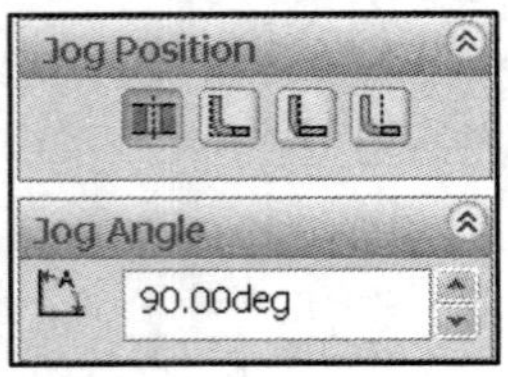


- ***Jog Position***. The Job Position box provides the following selections:
  - **Bend Centerline**, **Material Inside**, **Material Outside** and **Bend Outside**.
- ***Jog Angle***. Displays the selected Jog Angle value.

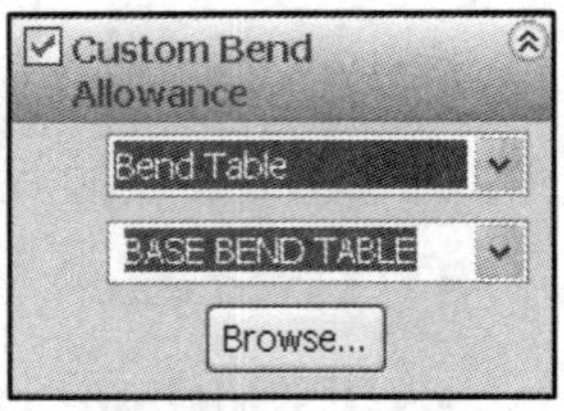


- ***Custom Blend Allowance***. The Custom Blend Allowance box provides the following selections:
  - **Bend Table**. Select a bend table from the drop down menu.
  - **Browse**. Browse to locate a bend table file.
  - **K-Factor**. Enter a K-Factor value. K-Factor is a ratio that represents the location of the neutral sheet with respect to the thickness of the sheet metal part.

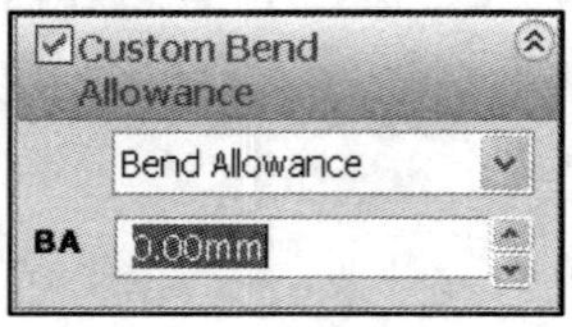


  - **Bend Allowance**. Enter a Bend Allowance value. A bend allowance is the arc length of the bend as measured along the neutral axis of the material.

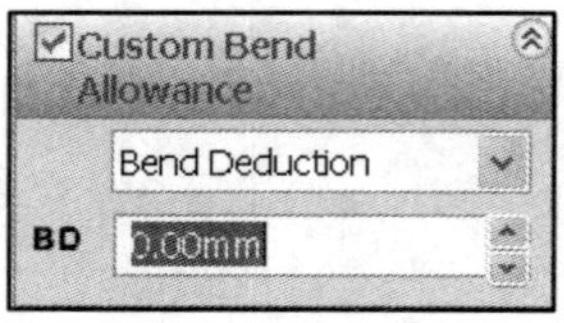


  - **Bend Deduction**. Enter a Bend Deduction value. A bend deduction is the difference between the bend allowance and twice the outside setback Bend Allowance Type.

### *Tutorial: Jog 14-1*

Insert a Jog feature in a Sheet Metal part.

1. Open **Jog 14-1** from the SolidWorks 2010\SheetMetal folder.
2. **Rotate** the model to view the back face of the tab.
3. Right-click the **back face** of the tab. Edge-Flange1 is highlighted in the FeatureManager.

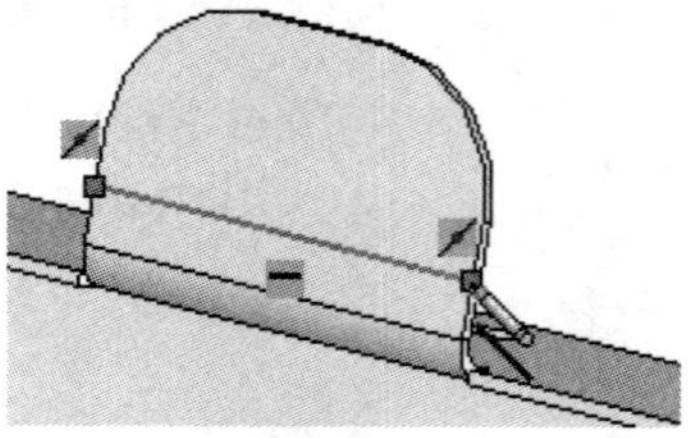

4. Click the **Line** Sketch tool.
5. Sketch a **horizontal line** across the midpoints of the tab as illustrated.

6. Click **Jog** from the Sheet Metal toolbar. The Jog PropertyManager is displayed.
7. Click the **back face** of the tab below the horizontal line.
8. Enter **5**mm for Jog Offset Distance.

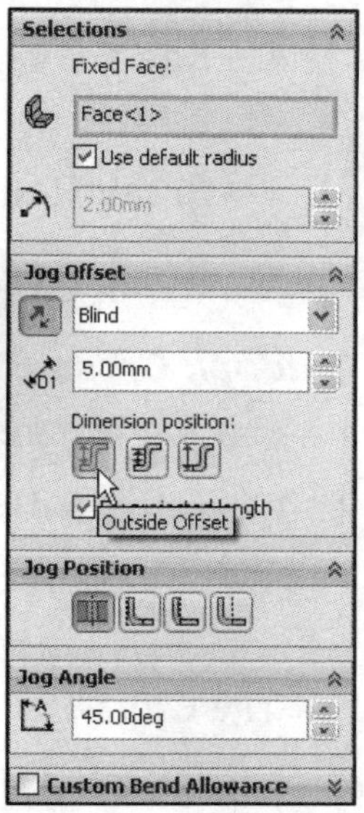


9. Display an **Isometric** view. The Jog direction arrow points to the left. If required, click the **Reverse Direction** button.
10. Click the **Outside Offset** button.
11. Enter **45**deg for Jog Angle.
12. Click **OK** from the Jog PropertyManager. The Jog1 feature is displayed in the FeatureManager.
13. **Close** the model.

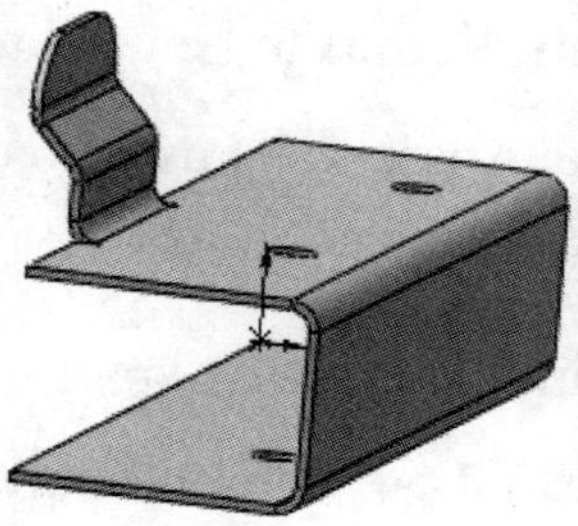

## Cross-Break tool

In HVAC or duct work design, cross-breaks are used to stiffen sheet metal. The Cross-Break tool provides the ability to insert a graphical representation of a cross break. There are a few items to know when using the Cross-Break feature. They are:

- You can flatten a sheet metal part with a cross break.
- You can add edge or miter flanges to the edge of a face that contains a cross break.
- The dimensions of a part with a cross break are not changed.
- You can edit the cross break sketch to move corners and change relationships.
- When you create a part with a cross break, the flattened view is labeled with the bend direction, bend radius, and bend angle.

The corners of the cross break must be at the ends of the edge.

The Cross-Break tool uses the Cross Break PropertyManager. Use the Cross Break PropertyManager to add a graphical representation of a cross break to a sheet metal part. The Cross-Break PropertyManager provides the following selections:

- ***Cross Break Parameters***. The Cross Break Parameters box provides the following selections:
  - **Faces**. Face on which the cross break is inserted.
  - **Reverse Direction**. Reverses the direction of the cross break in relation to the selected face.
  - **Edit Cross Profile**. Click to edit the profile sketch of the cross break to move corners and change relationships.
  - **Break Radius**. Radius to be used to create the cross break.
  - **Break Angle**. Angle to be used to create the cross break.

***Tutorial: Cross-Break 14-1***

Insert a Jog feature in a Sheet Metal part.

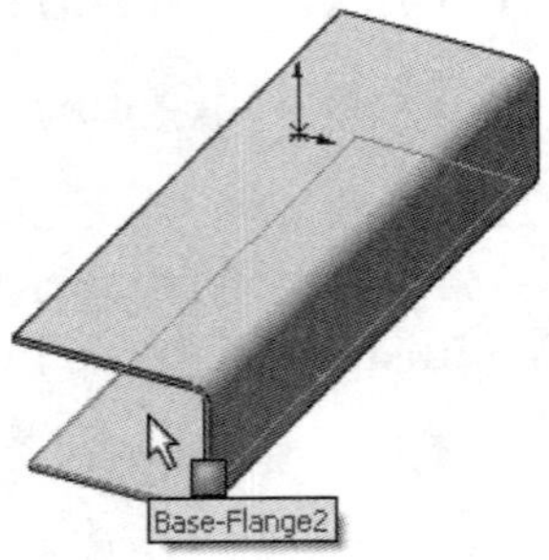


1. Open **Cross-Break 14-1** from the SolidWorks 2010\SheetMetal folder.
2. Click **Cross-Break** from the Sheet Metal toolbar. The Cross-Break PropertyManager is displayed.
3. Click the **bottom face** of Base-Flange2 as illustrated. The direction arrow points upwards.
4. Accept the default settings. Click **OK** from the Cross-Break PropertyManager. The Cross Break1 feature is displayed in the FeatureManager.
5. View the results in the Graphics window.
6. **Close** the model.

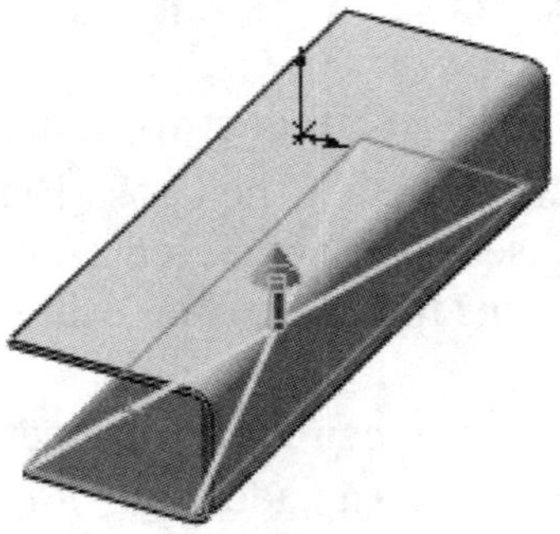

## Consolidated Corner toolbar

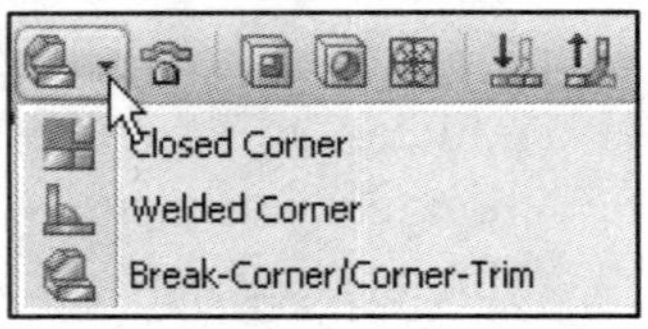


The Consolidated Corner toolbar provides access to the following sheet metals tools: **Closed Corner, Welded Corner** and **Break-Corner/Corner-Trim**.

External corners cut material. Internal corners add material.

You can use the Closed Corner tool to add material between sheet metal features: when there is a cut across flanges; with large radius bends; when the part is created using Insert Bends or Convert to Sheet Metal; with faces that are part of a larger corner.

# Closed Corner tool

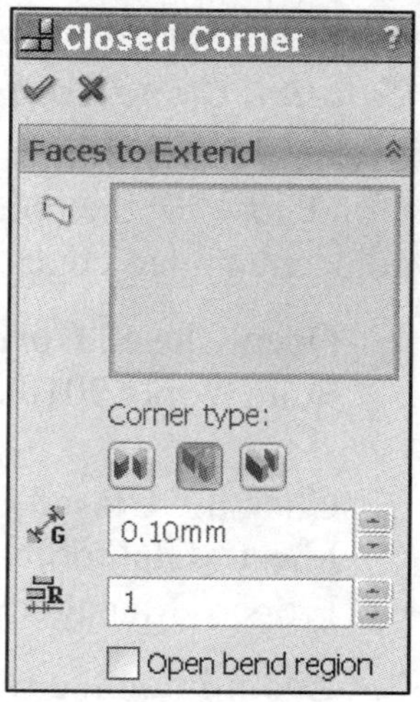


The Closed Corner tool provides the ability to extend, (add material) the face of a sheet metal part. Add closed corners between sheet metal flanges. The Closed Corner feature provides the following capabilities:

1. Close non-perpendicular corners.
2. Close or open the bend region.
3. Close multiple corners simultaneously by selecting the faces for all of the corners that you want to close.
4. Adjust the Gap distance. The distance between the two sections of material that area added by the Closed Corner feature.
5. Adjust the Overlap/underlap ratio. The ratio between the material that overlaps and the material that underlaps. A value of 1 indicates that the overlap and the underlap are equal.

The Closed Corner feature uses the Closed Corner PropertyManager. The Closed Corner PropertyManager provides the following selections:

- ***Faces to Extend***. The Faces to Extend box provides the following selections:
  - **Faces to Extend**. Displays the selected planar faces from the Graphics window.
  - **Corner type**. Overlap selected by default. Corner type provides three options. They are:
    - **Butt**
    - **Overlap**
    - **Underlap**

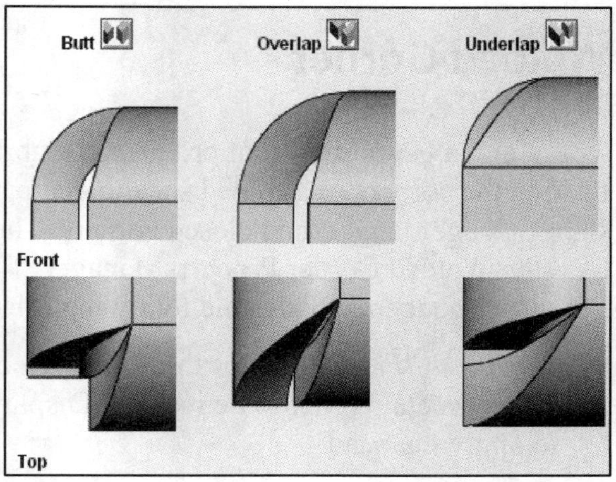


  - **Gap distance**. Set a value for Gap distance. Distance between the two sections of material that area added by the Closed Corner feature.
  - **Overlap/underlap ratio**. Only available with the Overlap or Underlap Corner type option. Sets the value. The value is the ratio between the material that overlaps and the material that underlaps.

- **Open bend region**. Opens the bend region.

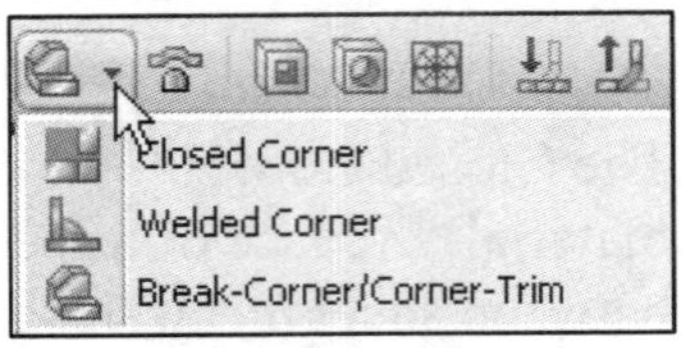


***Tutorial: Close Corner 14-1***

Create a Close Corner feature in a Sheet Metal part. Close off the open space between the adjacent angled edges.

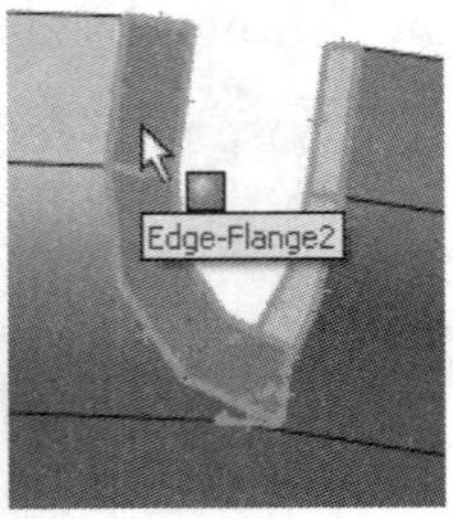


1. Open **Closed Corner 14-1** from the SolidWorks 2010\SheetMetal folder.
2. Click the **Closed Corner** tool from the Sheet Metal toolbar. The Closed Corner PropertyManager is displayed.
3. **Zoom in** on the right front corner as illustrated.
4. Click the **Edge-Flange2 planar face** as illustrated in the Graphics window. Face<1> is displayed in the Faces to Extend box.
5. Click **Overlap** for Corner type.
6. Enter **.10**mm for Gap distance.
7. Click **OK** from the Closed Corner PropertyManager. The Closed Corner1 feature is displayed in the FeatureManager.
8. **Close** the model.

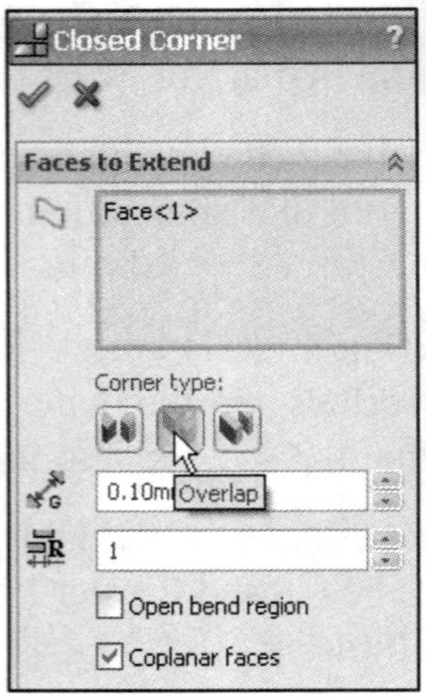


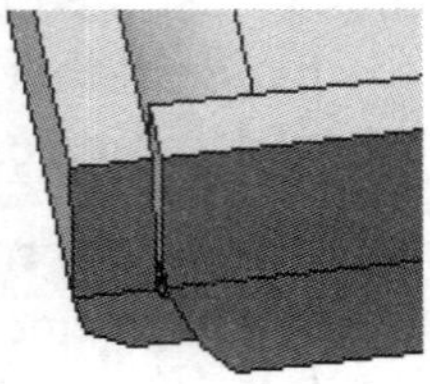

## Welded Corner

The Welded Corner tool provides the ability add a weld bead to the corners of a folded sheet metal part, including miter flanges, edge flanges, and closed corners. The Welded Corner uses the Welded Corner PropertyManager. The Welded Corner PropertyManager provides the following selections:

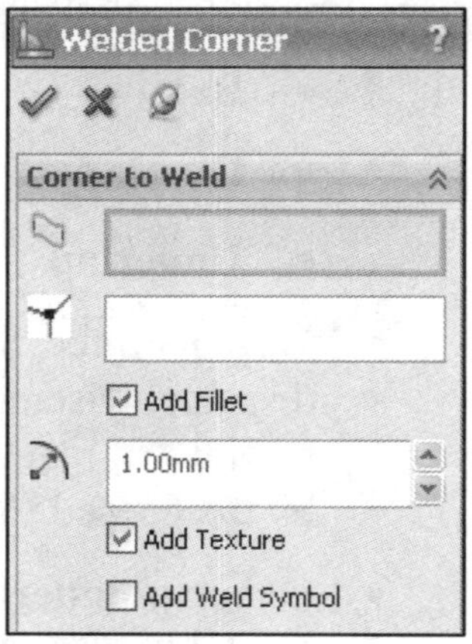


- ***Corner to Weld***. Provides the ability to select a side face of a sheet metal corner to be welded. Display the selected face to apply the bead.
  - **Add Fillet**. Selected by default. Inserts a Fillet.
  - **Fillet Radius**. The fillet radius must be less than a tangent arc connecting the outer edges.

- **Add Texture**. Selected by default. Adds a texture to the bead for display purposes.
- **Add Weld Symbol**. Adds a weld symbol for the created weld.

***Tutorial: Welded Corner 14-1***

Create a Welded Corner feature in a Sheet Metal part.

1. Open **Welded Corner 14-1** from the SolidWorks 2010\SheetMetal folder.
2. Click the **Welded Corner** tool from the Sheet Metal toolbar. The Welded Corner PropertyManager is displayed.
3. **Zoom in** on the right front side.
4. Click the flat face of **Edge-Flange1** as illustrated in the Graphics window. Face<1> is displayed.
5. Check the **Add Fillet** box.
6. Enter **2.00**mm for fillet radius. The fillet radius must be less than a tangent arc connecting the outer edges.
7. Click **OK** from the PropertyManager.
8. Click **OK** from the PropertyManager. Read the rebuild message. Click OK if required. View the FeatureManager. Welded Corner1 is displayed.

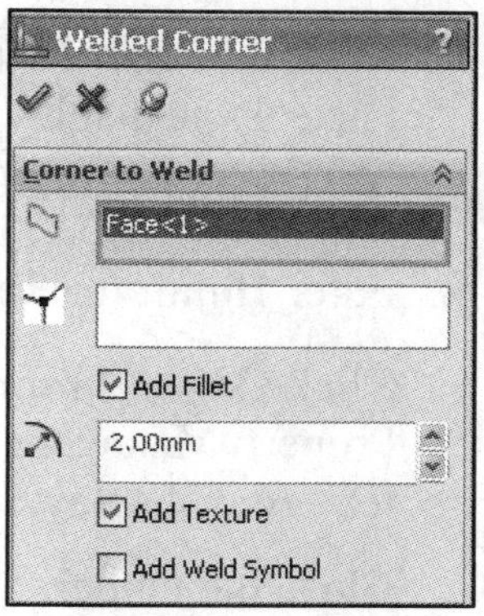


## Break Corner tool

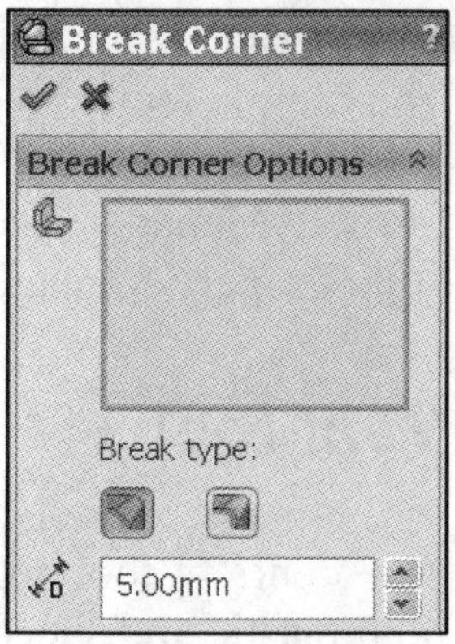


The Break-Corner/Corner Trim tool uses the Break Corner PropertyManager. The Break Corner PropertyManager provides the following selections:

- ***Break Corner Options***. The Break Corner Options box provides the following selections:
  - **Corner Edges and/or Flange Face**. Displays the selected corner edges and or Flange Face from the Graphics window.
  - **Break type**. Provides the following two break type selections:
    - **Chamfer** and **Fillet**.

- **Distance**. Only available for the Chamfer selection. Sets the value for the chamfer distance.
- **Radius**. Only available for the Fillet option. Sets the value for the fillet radius.

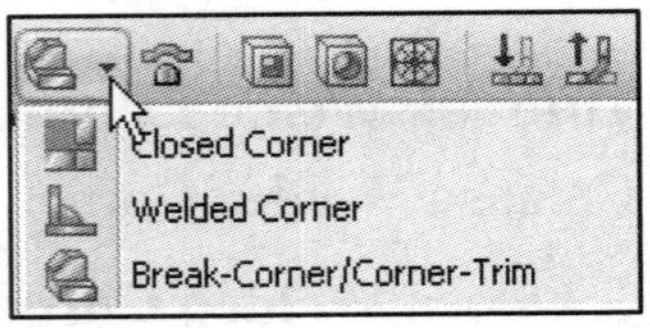


### *Tutorial: Break-Corner/Corner Trim 14-1*

Create a Break-Corner feature in a Sheet Metal part.

1. Open **Break-Corner 14-1** from the SolidWorks 2010\SheetMetal folder
2. Click **Break-Corner/Corner Trim** from the Sheet Metal toolbar. The Break Corner PropertyManager is displayed.
3. Click the **right face** of the tab as illustrated. Face<1> is displayed.
4. Click **Fillet** for Break type.
5. Enter **10**mm for Radius.
6. Click **OK** from the Break Corner PropertyManager. The Break-Corner1 feature is displayed in the FeatureManager.
7. **Close** the model.

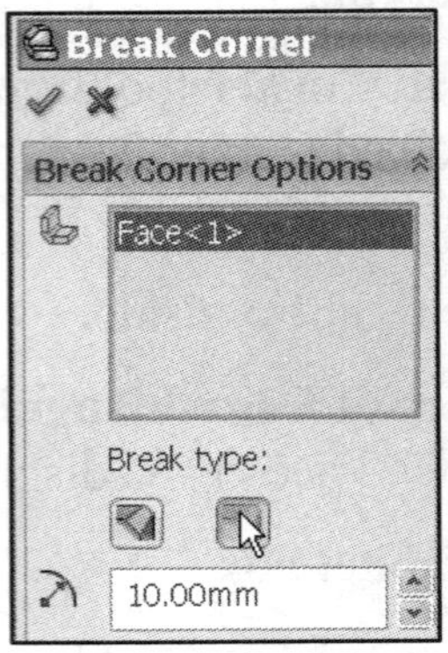


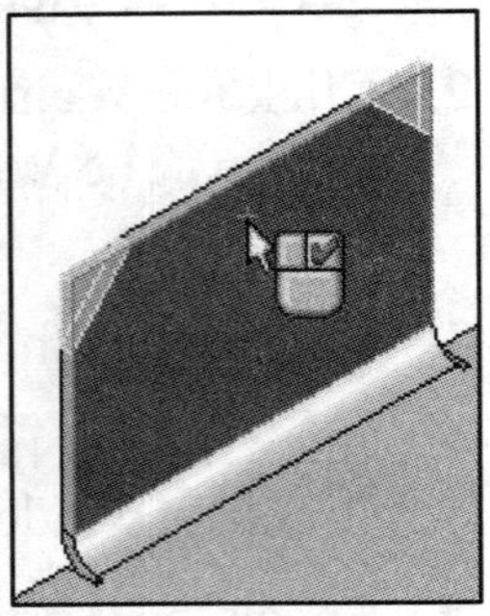

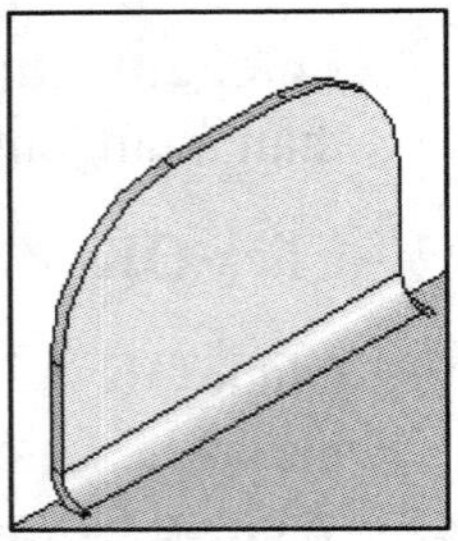

## Simple Hole tool

The Simple Hole tool provides the ability to create a simple hole in a sheet metal part. The Simple Hole tool uses the Hole PropertyManager. See Simple Hole Feature in Chapter 7 for detail Hole PropertyManager information.

## Vent tool

The Vent tool provides the ability to create various sketch elements for air flow in both plastic and sheet metal design. The Vent tool uses the Vent PropertyManager. The Vent PropertyManager provides the following selections:

- ***Boundary***. The Boundary box provides the following option:
  - **Select 2D sketch segments**. Displays the selected sketch segment from the Graphics window to form a closed profile as the outer vent boundary.

- ***Geometry Properties***. The Geometry Properties box provides the following selections:

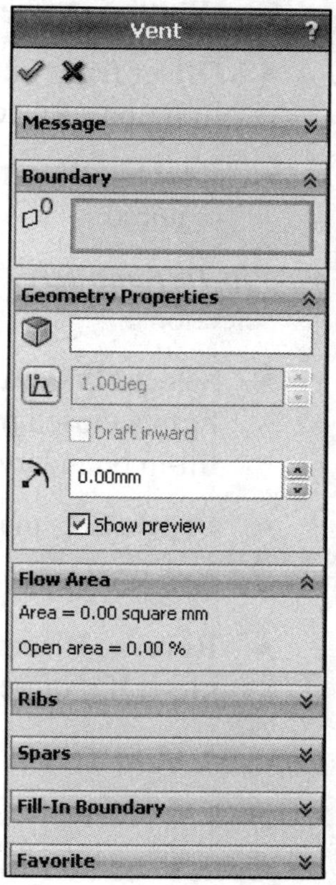


  - **Select a face**. Displays the selected planar or non-planar face from the Graphics window for the vent. The entire vent sketch must fit on the selected face.
  - **Draft Angle**. Click Draft On/Off to apply draft to the boundary, fill-in boundary, plus all ribs and spars.

For vents on planar faces, draft is applied from the Sketch plane.

  - **Radius for the fillets**. Sets the fillet radius, which is applied to all intersections between the boundary, spars, ribs, and the fill-in boundary.
  - **Show preview**. Display a preview of the feature.

- ***Flow Area***. The Flow Area box provide the following selections:
  - **Area**. Displays the total available area inside the boundary. This value remains fixed. The value is provided in square units.
  - **Open area**. Displays the open area inside boundary for air flow. This value updates as you add vent entities. Draft, fillets, ribs, spars, and the fill-in boundary reduce the open area value. The value is provided in percent.

- ***Ribs***. The Ribs box provides the following selections:

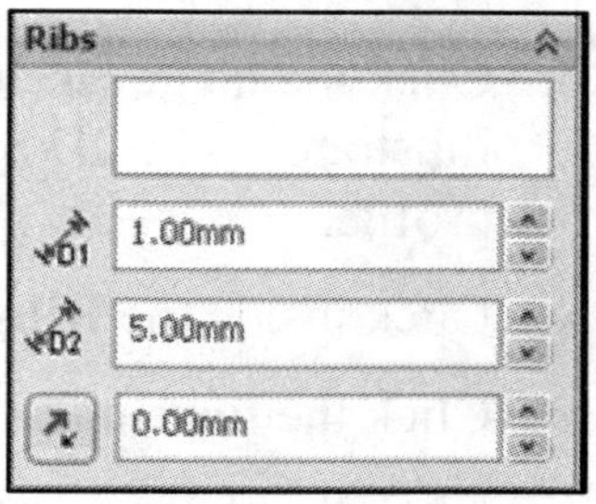


  - **Select 2D sketch segments**. Displays the selected sketch segments for ribs from the Graphics window.
  - **Depth**. Sets the depth value of the ribs.
  - **Width**. Sets the width value of the ribs.
  - **Offset from Surface**. Sets the offsets value for all ribs from the surface.
  - **Reverse Direction**. Reverses the direction of the offset if required.

You must create at least one rib before you can create spars.

- ***Spars***. The Spars box provides the following selections:

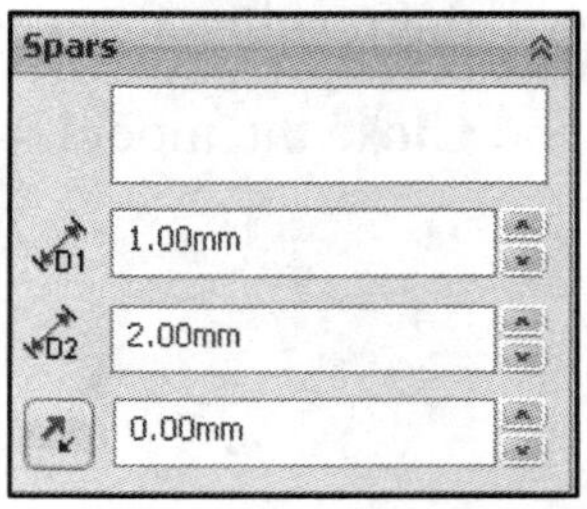


  - **Select 2D sketch segments**. Displays the selected sketch segments for spars from the Graphics window.
  - **Depth**. Sets the depth value of the spars.

- **Width**. Sets the width value of the spars.
- **Offset from Surface**. Sets the offset value for all spars from the surface.
- **Reverse Direction**. Reverses the direction of the offset if required.

- ***Fill-In Boundary***. The Fill-In Boundary box provides the selections:

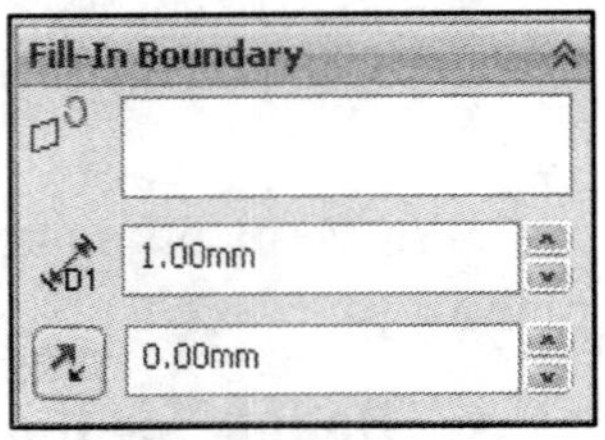


  - **Select 2D sketch segments**. Select sketch entities that form a closed profile. At least one rib must intersect the fill-in boundary.
  - **Depth**. Sets the depth value of the support area.
  - **Offset**. Offsets the fill-in boundary from the surface.
  - **Reverse Direction**. Reverses the direction of the offset if required.

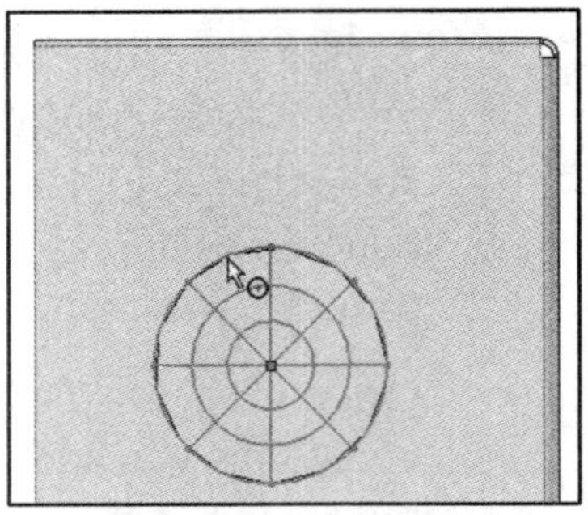

***Tutorial: Vent 14-1***

Create a Vent feature for a Sheet metal part.

1. Open **Vent 14-1** from the SolidWorks 2010\SheetMetal folder.
2. Click **Vent** from the Sheet Metal toolbar. The Vent PropertyManager is displayed.
3. Click the **large circle circumference** as illustrated. The 2D Sketch is a closed profile.
4. Click inside the **Ribs** box.
5. Click the **horizontal** sketch line.
6. Click the **three remaining lines** as illustrated. The selected entities are displayed in the Ribs box.

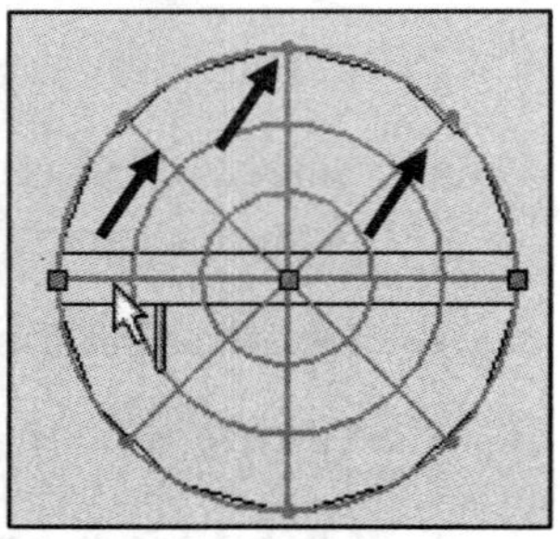

7. Click **OK** from the Vent PropertyManager. Vent1 is created and is displayed in the FeatureManager. View the results.
8. **Close** the model.

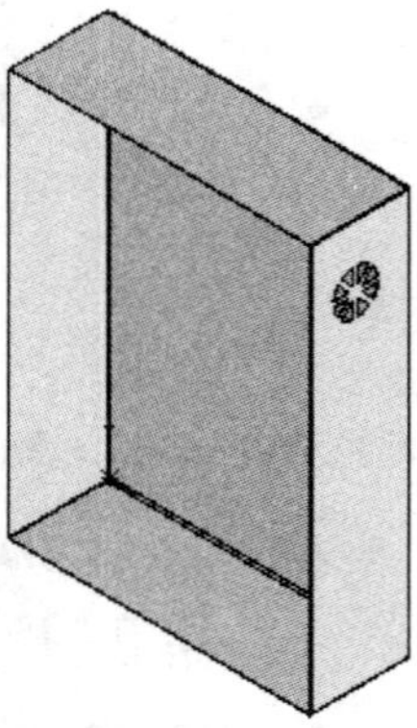

# Unfold tool

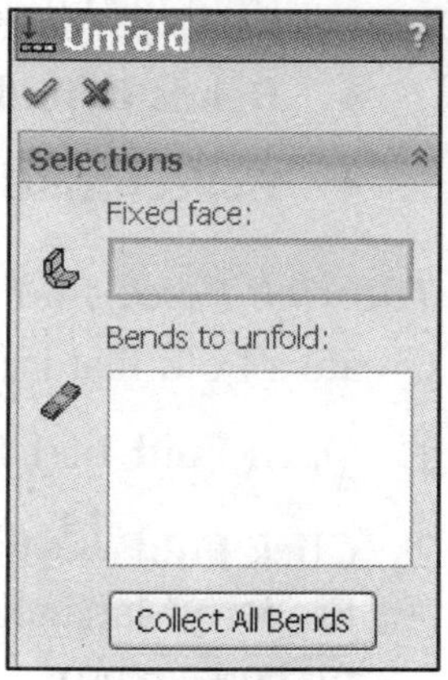


The Unfold tool provides the ability to flatten one or more bends in a sheet metal part. The Unfold tool uses the Unfold PropertyManager. The Unfold PropertyManager provides the following selections:

- ***Selections***. The Selections box provides the following options:
  - **Fixed face**. Displays the selected face that does not move as a result of the feature from the Graphics window.
  - **Bends to unfold**. Displays the selected bends from the Graphics window.
  - **Collect All Bends**. Selects all bends in the active part.

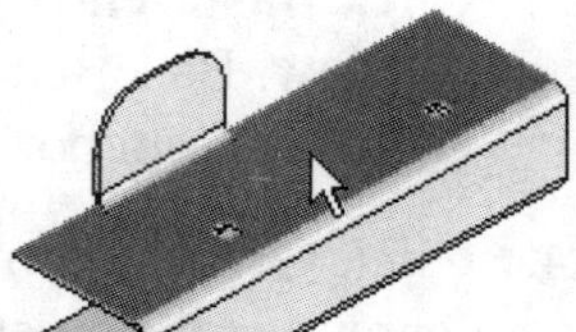

### *Tutorial: Unfold 14-1*

Create an Unfold feature in a Sheet Metal part.

1. Open **Unfold 14-1** from the SolidWorks 2010\SheetMetal folder.
2. Click **Unfold** from the Sheet Metal toolbar. The Unfold PropertyManager is displayed.
3. Click the **top face** of the bracket. Face<1> is displayed in the Fixed face box.
4. Click **BaseBend1** and **BaseBend2** from the Graphics window. BaseBend1 and BaseBend2 are displayed in the Bends to Unfold box.
5. Click **OK** from the Unfold PropertyManager. The Unfold1 feature is displayed in the FeatureManager.
6. Display an **Isometric** view. View the results.
7. **Close** the model.

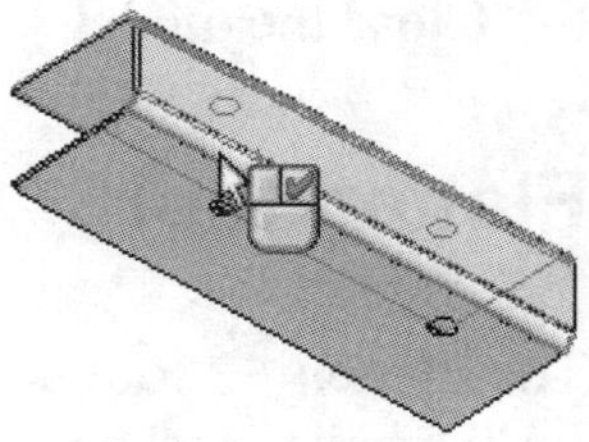

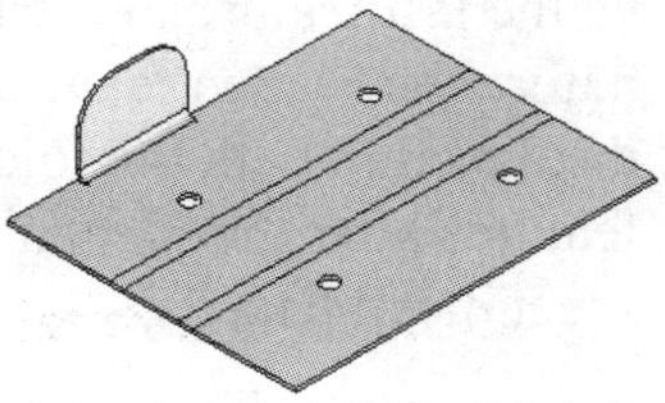

# Fold tool

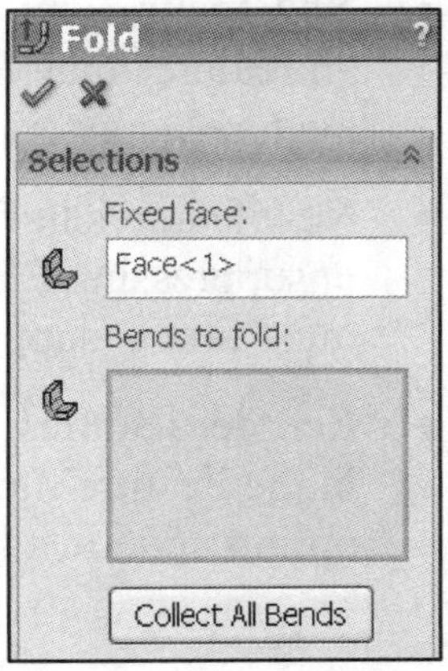


The Fold tool provides the ability to bend one or more sections in a sheet metal part. The Fold tool uses the Fold PropertyManager.

The Fold PropertyManager provides the following selections:

- ***Selections***. The Selections box provides the following options:

- **Fixed face**. Displays the selected face that does not move as a result of the feature from the Graphics window.
- **Bends to fold**. Displays the selected bends from the Graphics window.
- **Collect All Bends**. Selects all bends in the active part.

***Tutorial: Fold: 14-1***

Create a Fold feature in a Sheet Metal part.

1. Open **Fold 14-1** from the SolidWorks 2010\SheetMetal folder.
2. Click **Fold** from the Sheet Metal toolbar. The Fold PropertyManager is displayed. Face<1> is displayed in the Fixed face box.
3. Click **BaseBend1** and **BaseBend2** from the Graphics window. BaseBend1 and BaseBend2 are displayed in the Bends to Fold box.

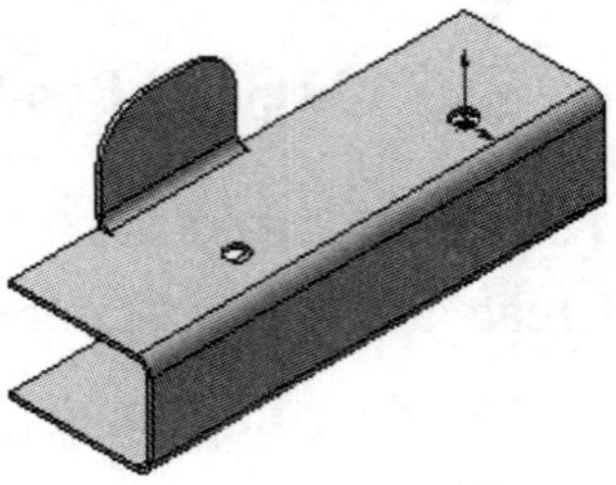

4. Click **OK** from the Fold PropertyManager. The Fold1 feature is displayed in the FeatureManager.
5. Display an **Isometric** view. View the results.
6. **Close** the model.

## Flatten tool

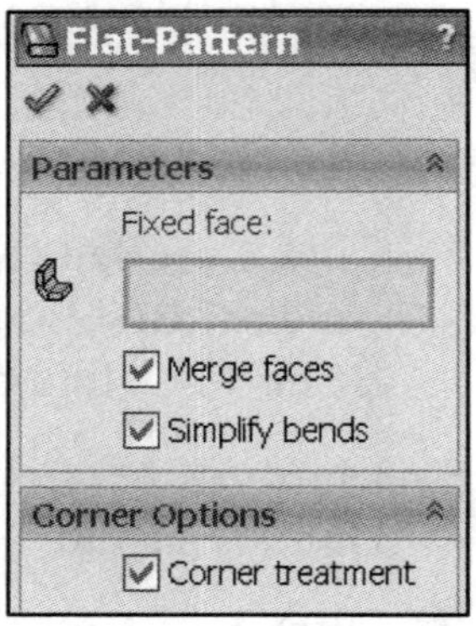


The Flatten tool provides the ability to display the Flat pattern for the existing sheet metal part. The Flatten feature is intended to be the last feature in the folded sheet metal part. All features before the Flatten feature in the FeatureManager design tree is displayed in both the folded and flattened sheet metal part. All features after the Flatten feature is displayed only in the flattened sheet metal part.

Items to note about the Flat-pattern feature.

- New features in folded part. When Flat-Pattern1 is suppressed, all features that you add to the part automatically appear before this feature in the FeatureManager design tree.
- New features in flattened part. You flatten the entire sheet metal part by unsuppressing Flat-Pattern1. To add features to the flattened sheet metal part, you must first unsuppress Flat-Pattern1.
- Reorder features. You cannot reorder sheet metal features to go below Flat-Pattern1 in the FeatureManager design tree. So, you cannot order a cut with the Normal cut option underneath Flat-Pattern1.

- Modify parameters. You can modify the parameters of Flat-Pattern1 to control how the part bends, to enable or disable corner options, and to control the visibility of the bend region in the flattened sheet metal part.
- Sketches. You can transform sketches and their locating dimensions from a folded state to a flattened state and back again. The sketch and locating dimensions are retained.

The Flatten tool uses the Flat-Pattern PropertyManager. The Flat-Pattern PropertyManager provides the following selections:

- ***Parameters***. The Parameters box provides the following options:
  - **Fixed face**. Displays the selected fixed face from the Graphics window.
  - **Merge faces**. Merges faces that are planar and coincident in the flat pattern.
  - **Simplify bends**. Straighten curved edges in the selected flat pattern.
- ***Corner Options***. The Corner Options box provides the following selection:
  - **Corner treatment**. Applies a smooth edge in the flat pattern.
  - **Add Corner trim**. Applies relief cuts in the flat pattern. When selected, you can choose from:
    - **Break Corner**. Cuts away material from an edge or a face. Click **Chamfer** or **Fillet** as the **Break type** and set the **Distance** or **Radius.**
    - **Relief type**. Sets the relief type for any relief cuts needed.
    - **Radius** or **Side length**. Set the **Radius** or **Side length** for the **Relief type**.
    - **Ratio to thickness**. Sets the relief type radius to a specified ratio of the sheet metal thickness. When selected, set the **Ratio of radius/distance to sheet metal thickness**.

### *Tutorial: Flatten 14-1*

Display a flatten state for a Sheet Metal part.

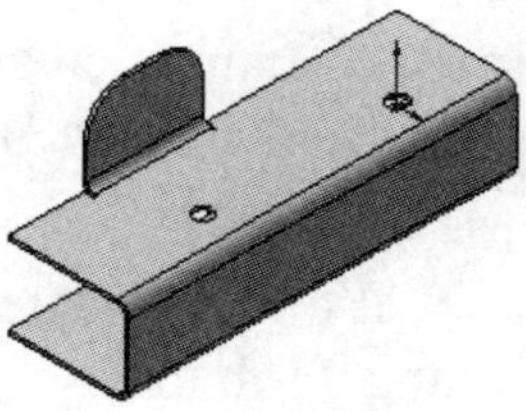

1. Open **Flatten 14-1** from the SolidWorks 2010\ SheetMetal folder.
2. Click **Flatten** from the Sheet Metal toolbar. The Sheet Metal part is flattened.

Display the part in its fully formed state.

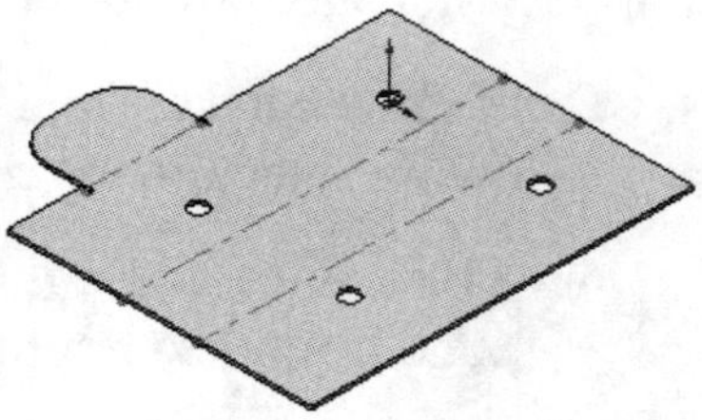

3. Click **Flatten** from the Sheet Metal toolbar. The part is returned to its fully formed state. View the Flat-Patten PropertyManager.

4. Right-click **Flat-Pattern1** from the FeatureManager.
5. Click **Edit Feature**. View the Flat Pattern PropertyManager.
6. Click **OK** from the Flat-Pattern PropertyManager. View the results.
7. **Close** the model.

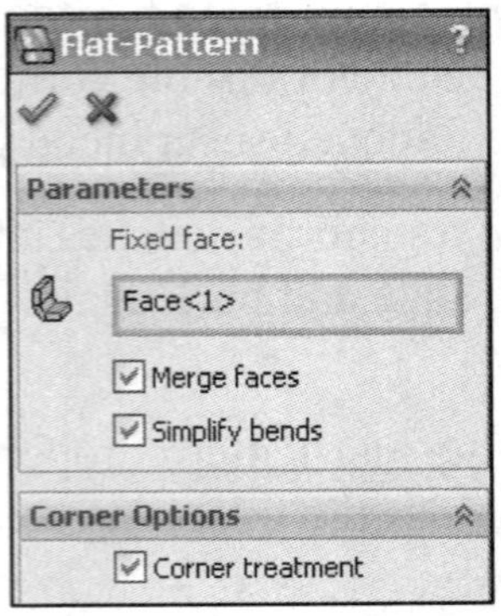


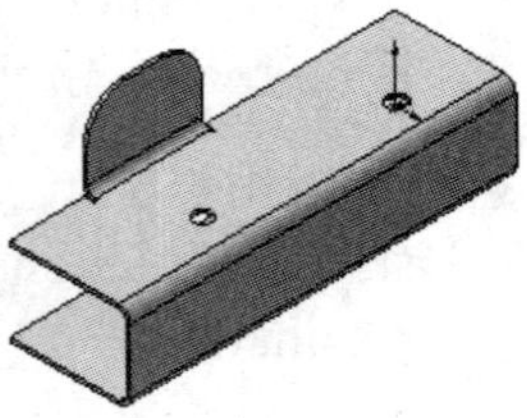

## No Bends tool

The No Bends tool provides the ability to roll back all bends from a sheet metal part in which bends have been inserted. This provides the ability to create additions, such as adding a wall. This tool is only available only in sheet metal parts with Flatten-Bends1 and Process-Bends1 features. The No Bends tool does not use a PropertyManager.

***Tutorial: No Bends 14-1***

1. Open **No Bends 14-1** from the SolidWorks 2010\SheetMetal folder.
2. Click **No Bends** from the Sheet Metal toolbar. The FeatureManager rolls back all bends from the sheet metal part.
3. View the FeatureManager. **Close** the model.

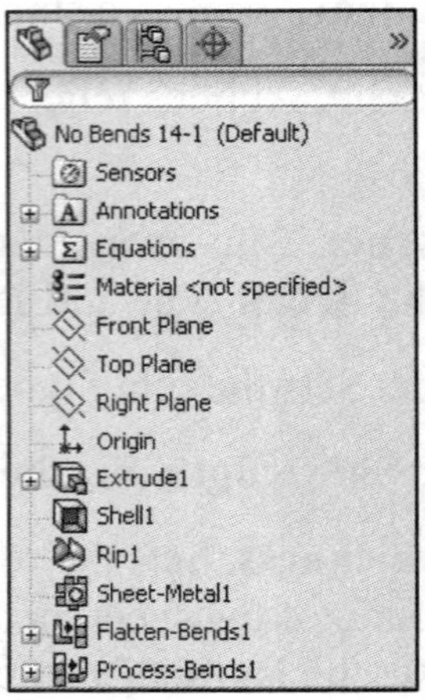


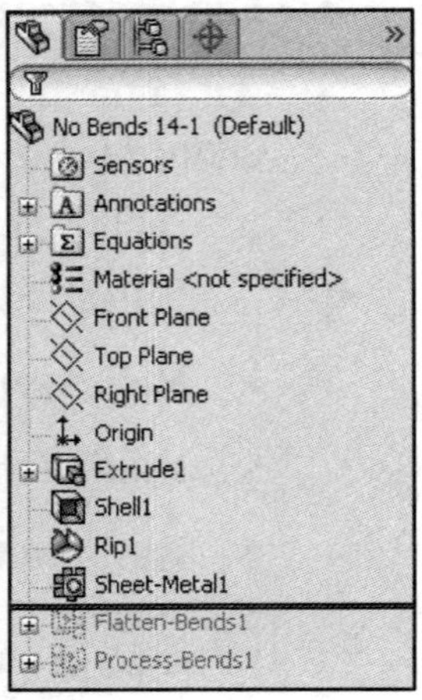


## Insert Bends tool

The Inset Bends tool creates a sheet metal part from an existing part. You must create a solid body with uniform thickness when you use the Insert Bends tool.

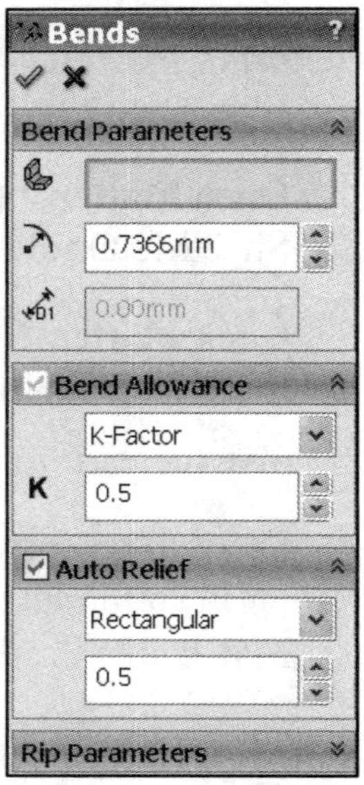


You can create a part directly out of sheet metal with the Base-Flange/Tab tool.

The Insert Bends tool uses the Bends PropertyManager. The Bends PropertyManager provides the following selections:

- ***Bend Parameters***. The Bend Parameters box provides the following selections:
  - **Fixed Face or Edge**. Displays the selected fixed face or edge from the Graphics window.
  - **Bend Radius**. Sets the required bend radius value.

- **Thickness**. Sets the required thickness value.

- ***Bend Allowance***. The Bend Allowance box provides the following selections:

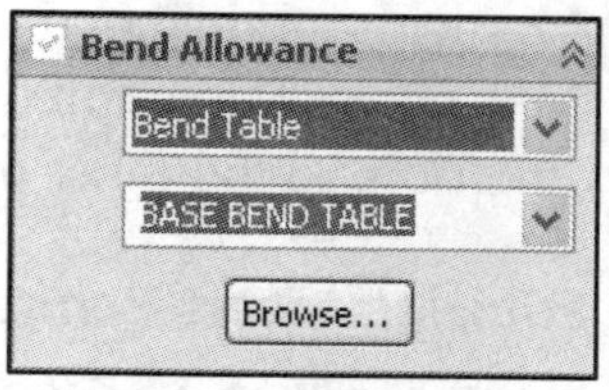


  - **Bend Table**. Select a bend table from the drop-down menu.
  - **Browse**. Browse to a bend table file.

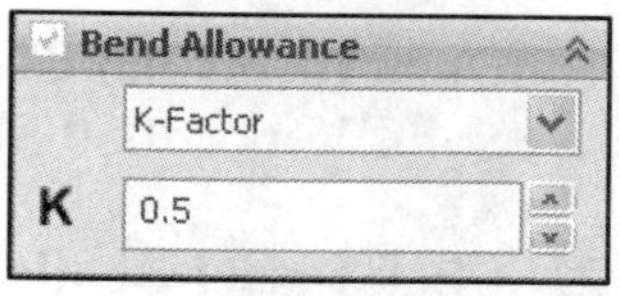


  - **K-Factor**. Enter a K-Factor value. K-Factor is a ratio that represents the location of the neutral sheet with respect to the thickness of the sheet metal part.

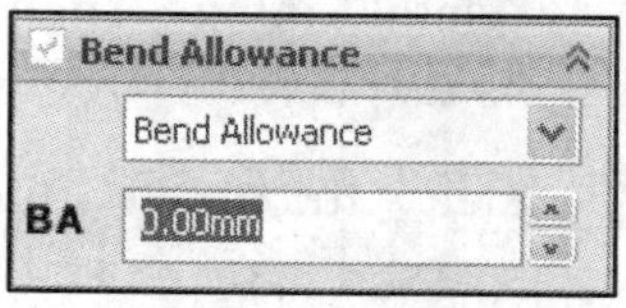


  - **Bend Allowance**. Enter a Bend Allowance value. A bend allowance is the arc length of the bend as measured along the neutral axis of the material.

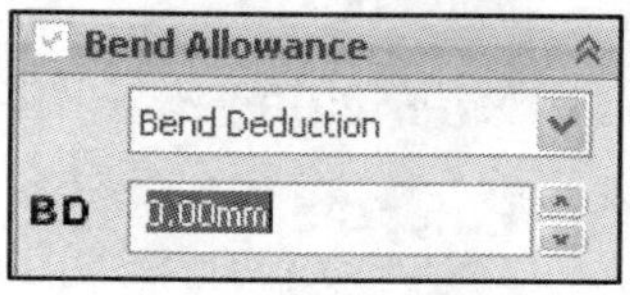


  - **Bend Deduction**. Enter a Bend Deduction value. A bend deduction is the difference between the bend allowance and twice the outside setback Bend Allowance Type.

- ***Auto Relief***. Provides the ability to select three Relief types. The Rectangle relief type is selected by default. Note: If you want to add a Rectangle or Obround relief, you must specify the Relief ratio. See SolidWorks help for additional information on Relief ratio.

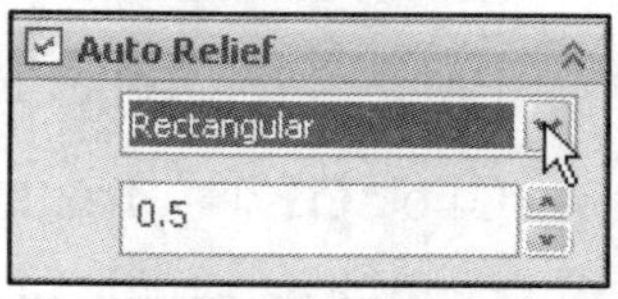


  - **Rectanglar**

  - **Tear**

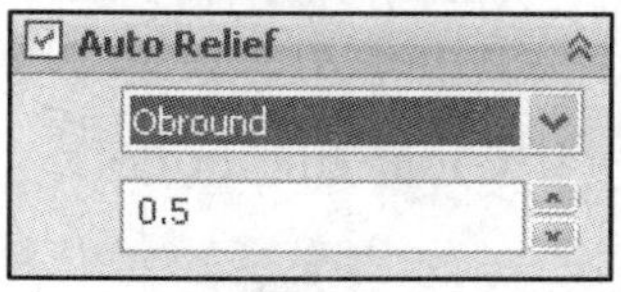


  - **Obround**
  - **Relief ratio**. Enter the Relief ratio.

- ***Rip Parameters***. The Rip Parameters box provides the following selections:

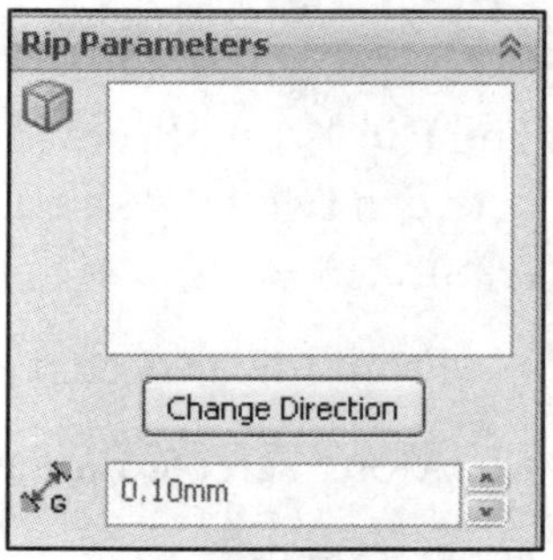


  - **Edges to Rip**. Displays the selected edge to rip from the Graphics window.
  - **Change Direction**. Reverses the direction of the rip if required.
  - **Rip Gap**. Sets a rip gap distance value.

Rips are inserted in both directions by default. Each time you select the Change Direction option, the rip direction sequences from one direction, to the other direction, and then back to both directions.

### *Tutorial: Insert Bends 14-1*

Insert bends in a Sheet Metal part.

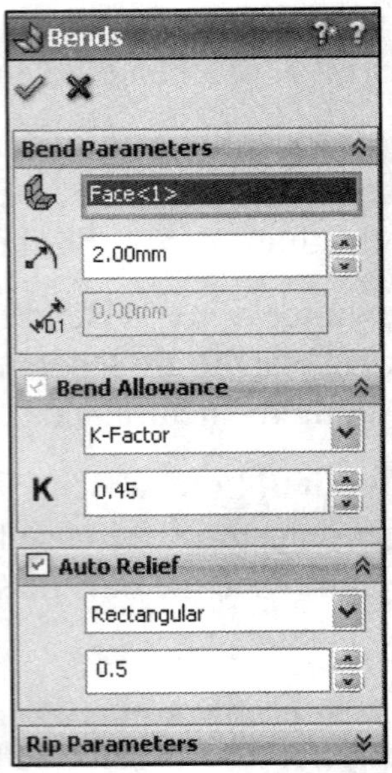


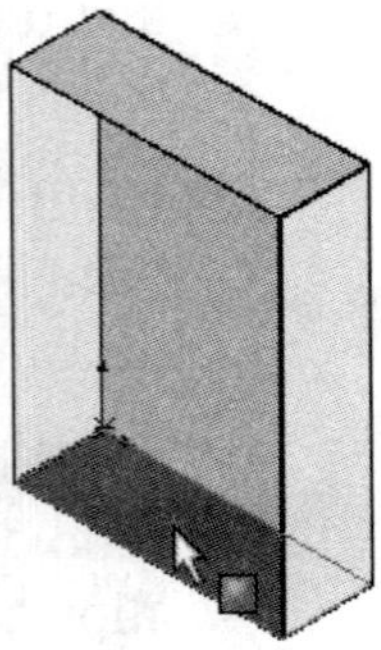

1. Open **Insert bends 14-1** from the SolidWorks 2010\SheetMetal folder.
2. Click **Insert Bends** from the Sheet Metal toolbar. The Bends PropertyManager is displayed.
3. Click the **inside bottom face** to remain fixed. Face<1> is displayed in the Fixed Face box.
4. Enter **2.00**mm for Bend Radius.
5. Enter **.45** for K-Factor.
6. Select **Rectangular** for Auto Relief Type.
7. Enter **.5** for Relief Ratio.
8. Click **OK** from the Bends PropertyManager.
9. Click **OK** to the message, "Auto relief cuts were made for one or more bends".
10. Display an **Isometric** view. View the created feature in the FeatureManager and in the Graphics window.
11. **Close** the model.

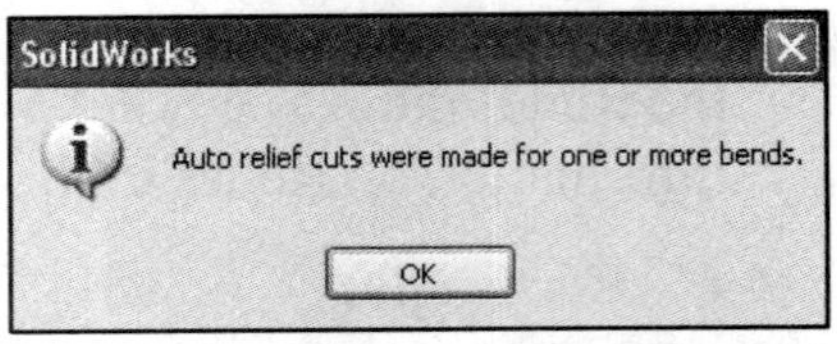

## Rip tool

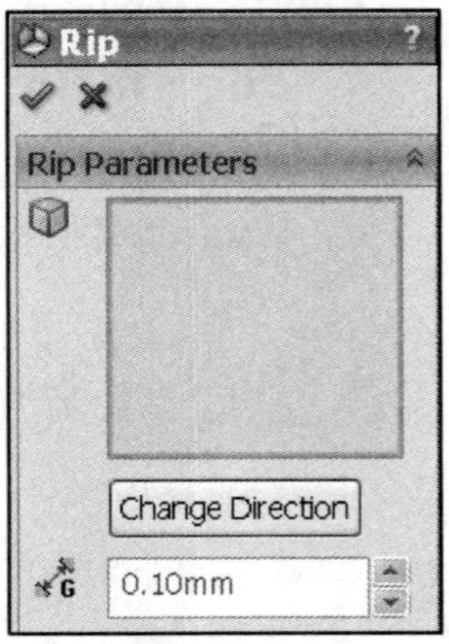


The Rip tool provides the ability to create a gap between two edges in a sheet metal part. Create a rip feature:

- From linear sketch entities.
- Along selected internal or external model edges.
- By combining single linear sketch entities and model edges.

A rip feature is commonly used to create sheet metal parts, but you can also add a rip feature to any part.

The Rip tool uses the Rip PropertyManager. The Rip PropertyManager provides the following selections. They are:

- ***Rip Parameters***. The Rip Parameters box provides the following selections:
  - **Edges to Rip**. Displays the selected edges to rip from the Graphics window.
  - **Change Direction**. Reverses the direction of the rip if required.
  - **Rip Gap**. Sets a rip gap distance.

Rips are inserted in both directions by default. Each time you select the Change Direction option, the rip direction sequences from one direction, to the other direction, and then back to both directions.

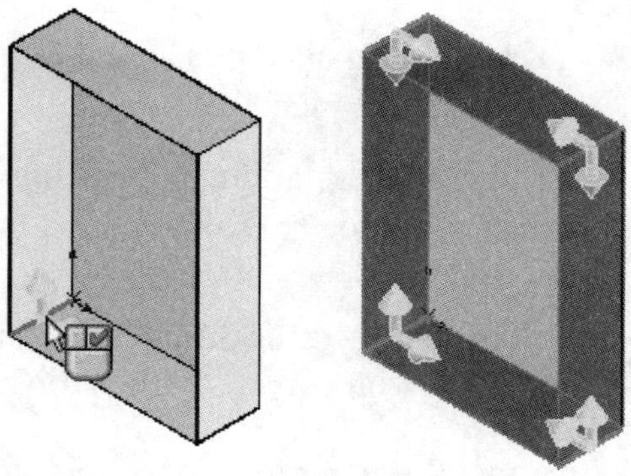

### *Tutorial: Rip 14-1*

Create a Rip feature in a Sheet metal part.

1. Open **Rip 14-1** from the SolidWorks 2010\SheetMetal folder.
2. Click **Rip** from the Sheet Metal toolbar. The Rip PropertyManager is displayed.
3. **Rotate** the part to view the inside edges.
4. Click the **inside lower left edge**.
5. Click the other **three inside edges**. The four selected edges are displayed in the Rip Parameters box.
6. Enter **.10mm** for Rip Gap.
7. Click **OK** from the Rip PropertyManager. Rip1 is created and is displayed in the FeatureManager.
8. **Close** the model.

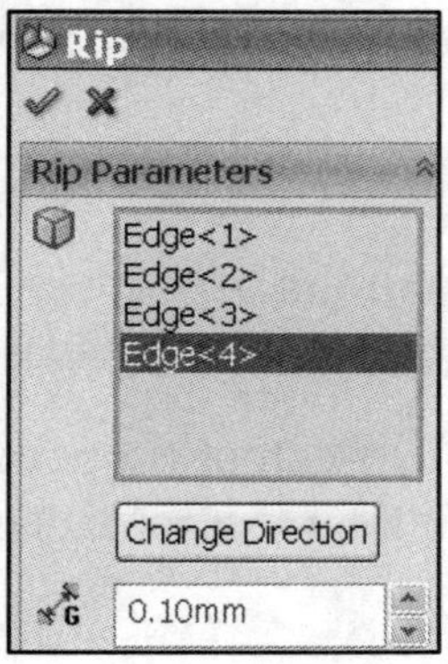


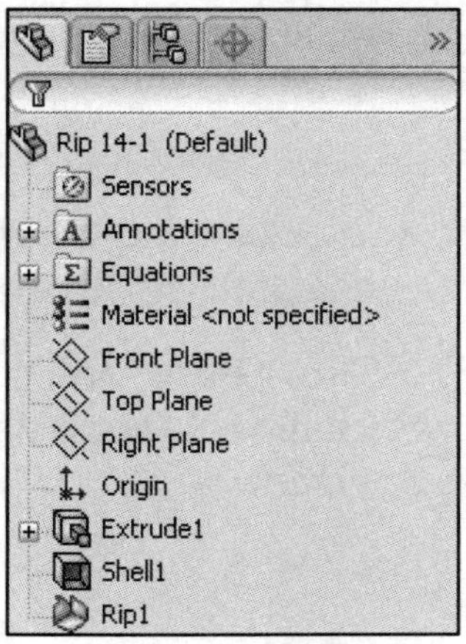

# Sheet Metal Library Feature

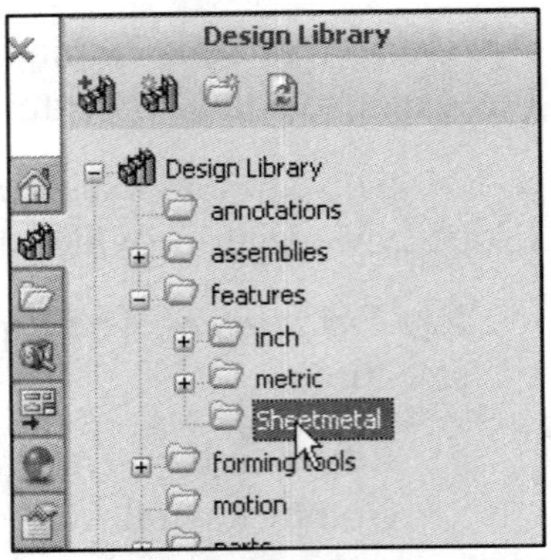


Sheet metal manufacturers utilize dies and forms to create specialty cuts and shapes. The Design Library contains information on dies and forms. The SW Design Library features folder contains examples of predefined sheet metal shapes.

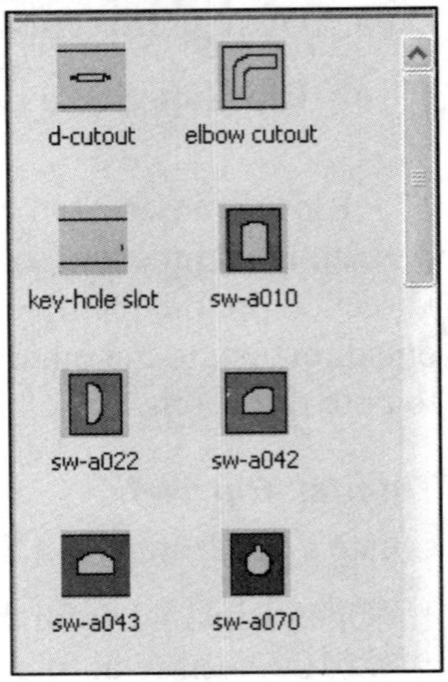


Forming tools act as dies that bend, stretch, or otherwise form sheet metal to create form features such as louvers, lances, flanges, and ribs. The SolidWorks software includes some sample forming tools. You can create forming tools and add them to sheet metal parts. When you create a forming tool:

- The locating sketch is added to position the forming tool on the sheet metal part
- The colors are applied to distinguish the Stopping Face from the Faces to Remove.

You can insert forming tools only from the Design Library and you can apply them only to sheet metal parts.

***Tutorial: Sheetmetal Library Feature 14-1***

Insert a Sheetmetal library feature.

1. Open **Sheetmetal library feature 14.1** from the SolidWorks 2010\SheetMetal folder.
2. Click **Design Library** from the Task Pane as illustrated.
3. **Expand** Design Library.
4. **Expand** features.
5. Click **Sheetmetal** from the features folder.
6. Click and drag the **d-cutout** Sheetmetal library feature to the right side of the Shell1 feature as illustrated. Accept the defaults.

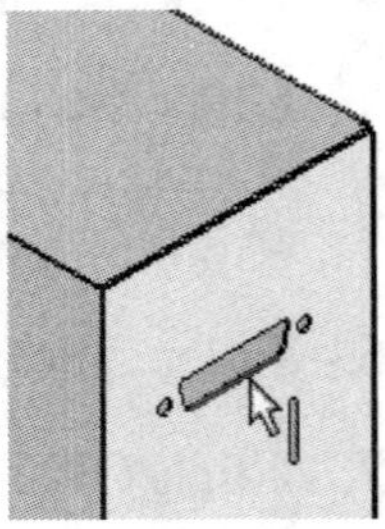

7. Click **OK** from the d-cutout PropertyManager. The d-cutout feature is displayed in the FeatureManager and in the Graphics window.
8. **Close** the model.

# Summary

In this chapter, you learned about Sheet Metal Features and the associated tools. You reviewed and addressed each tool in the Sheet Metal toolbar: *Base-Flange/Tab, Convert to Sheet Metal, Lofted-Bend, Edge Flange, Miter Flange, Hem, Jog, Sketched Bend, Cross-Break, Closed Corners, Break-Corner/Corner-Trim, Extruded Cut, Simple Hole, Vent, Unfold, Fold, Flatten, No Bends, Insert Bends and Rip.*

In Chapter 15, explore PhotoView 360.

SolidWorks 2010 will be the last release to include PhotoWorks. In subsequent releases, PhotoWorks will not be available and PhotoView 360 will be its functional replacement and the sole photorealistic solution for SolidWorks software.

## Notes:

# CHAPTER 15: SOLIDWORKS PHOTOVIEW 360

## Chapter Objective

Chapter 15 provides a general overview of SolidWorks PhotoView 360. On the completion of this chapter, you will be able to:

- Activate PhotoView 360 and address a part or assembly with the following tools:
  - *Open a File*
  - *Appearances*
  - *Environments*
  - *Settings*
  - *Final Render*
  - *Shared picture gallery*

SolidWorks 2010 will be the last release to include PhotoWorks. In subsequent releases, PhotoWorks will not be available and SolidWorks PhotoView 360 will be its functional replacement and the sole photorealistic solution for SolidWorks software.

## SolidWorks PhotoView 360

### Introduction

PhotoView 360 is a new visualization and rendering solution from Solidworks. It's a highly interactive environment for viewing your designs as well as for creating photorealistic renderings that you can use to showcase your designs.

PhotoView 360, based on SolidWorks Intelligent Feature Technology (SWIFT), helps beginning CAD users achieve expert results. Its simple-to-use progressive rendering tools lets users photorealistically render a scene while allowing the user to continue working on the same scene, unlike software that forces users to wait until scenes are complete.

PhotoView 360 provides the ability to import decals and additional appearances to your models.

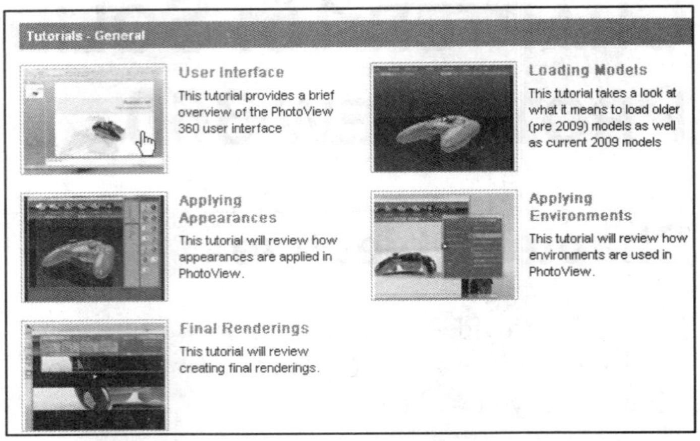


View the following website to obtain short tutorials on PhotoView 360: http://www.solidworksgallery.com/index.php?p=tutorials_general or visit http://www.dmeducation.net

PhotoView 360 is an integral part of SolidWorks 2010 Professional and SolidWorks 2010 Premium. Legacy users of PhotoWorks (such as SolidWorks Office and standalone PhotoWorks owners) also have access to PhotoView 360.

If you do not have the latest version of SolidWorks 2009 or 2010 or need to upgrade your version to the levels that include PhotoView 360, contact your SolidWorks Sales representative or Reseller.

## The PhotoView 360 User Interface

The PhotoView 360 User Interface for a Part provides the ability at the top level to address: Open File, Appearances, Environments, System Settings, Final Render, and access a shared Gallery along with a standard Window menu toolbar: *File*, *Edit*, *View*, *Render*, and *Help*.

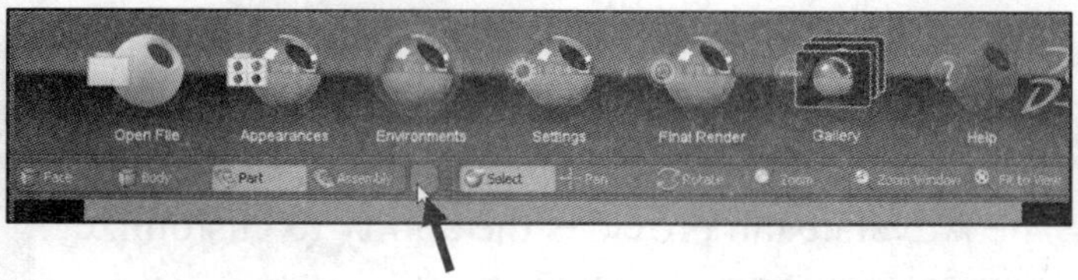


Below the large toolbar are two additional toolbars: one on the left side (Reference section filter toolbar) and one on the right side. There is an interface split by a small splitter bar between the two toolbars.

If you shrink your window, the top large icon toolbar will scale.

Click the double carrot icon to expand the lower toolbars if needed.

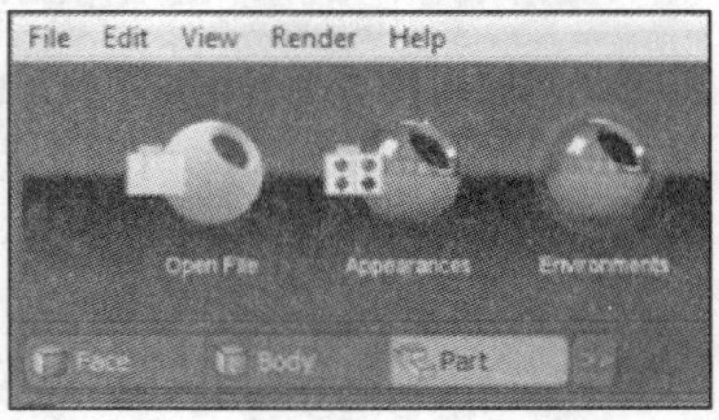


PhotoView 360 is not a SolidWorks Add-in application.

## Open File

Click the Open File icon from the large icon toolbar to browse to the needed file location.

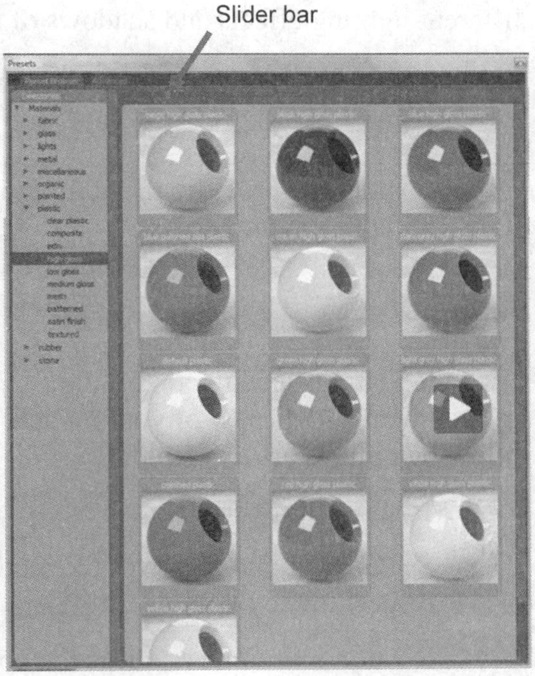


## Appearances

Click the Appearances icon to view the available default appearances. Drag and drop an appearance on to your model. To control what is being affected by the Appearance tool; use the Reference section filter toolbar: Part, Multi-body and Assembly. As illustrated, Part is selected.

The Presets dialog box is displayed. The Preset dialog box window is a split window: Tree on the left and thumbnail icons on the right. The Preset Brower tab is the default tab.

The slider bar at the top of the dialog box provides the ability to resize the display of the available thumbnail icons.

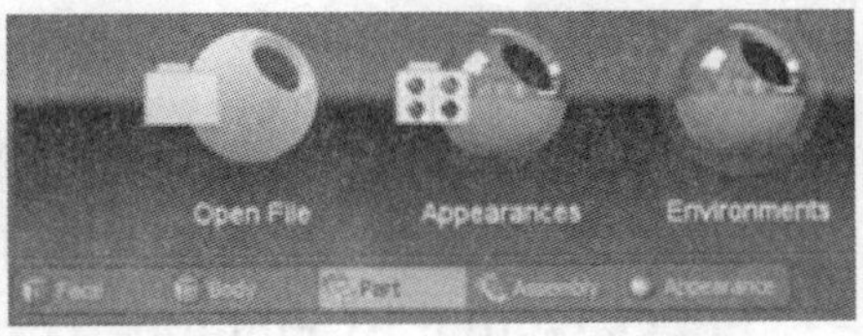


The Appearance filter relates to the Appearances set in SolidWorks.

PhotoView 360 provides the ability to apply material to a body, face, part or an assembly.

The Advance tab provides the ability to customize your selected appearance display.

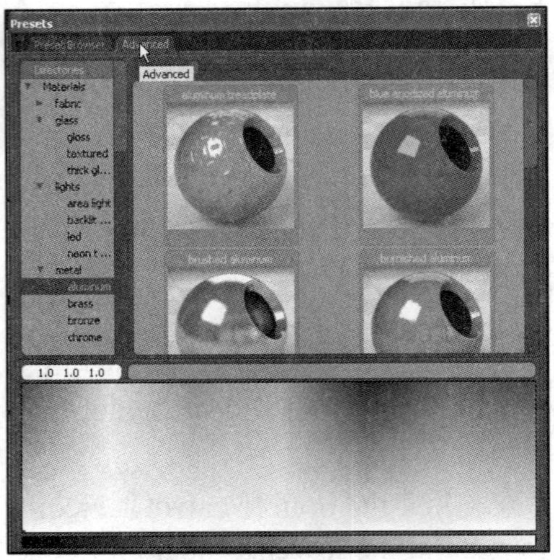


## Environments

Click the Environments icon to view the available default environments for your model. The Environments dialog box is very similar to the Appearance dialog box. Drag and drop an environment into your model.

As you rotate your model in the Environment setting, you will view the model and environment from a camera perspective.

All lighting in PhotoView 360 comes from the various environments. Different Environments will provide different lighting effects and shadows of the model.

To close the Environment dialog box, click the Close box or click the Environments icon again.

The slider bar provides the ability to resize the display of the available environments.

## Settings

Click the Settings icon to control the Environment and display of your model. The following options are available:

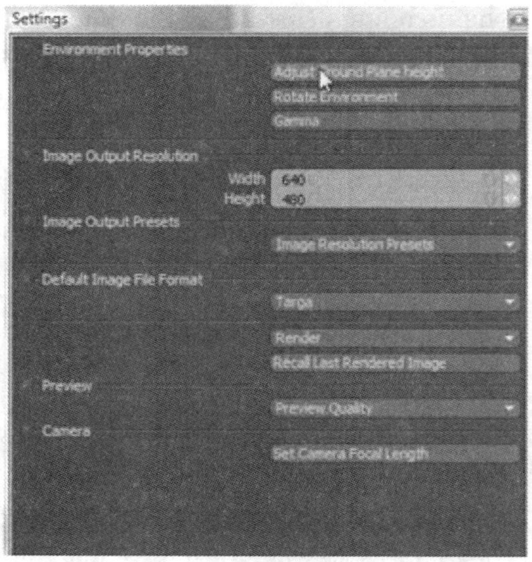


- Environment Properties:
  - Set Ground plane (moves the model with respect to the floor)
  - Rotate Environment (keeps the position of the model as you rotate the Environment)
  - Gamma (adjust how your screen displays colors or brightest of the render)
- Image Output Resolution
- Image Output Presents

- Default Image File Format
  - Targa is selected by default. View the available formats.
  - Render
  - Recall Last Rendered Image: History base.
- Preview
- Camera

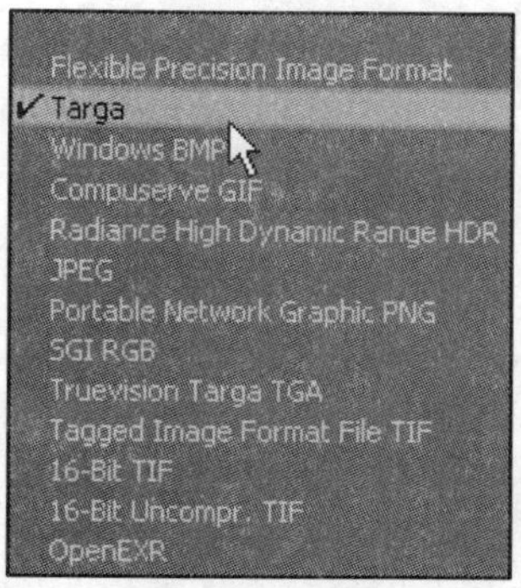


## Final Render

Click the Final Render icon to display the final render of your.

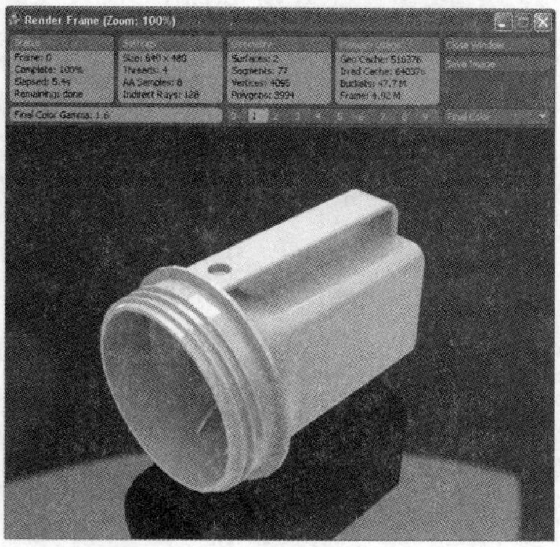


The Render Frame dialog box remembers the last nine renders of the model.

## Gallery

Click the Gallery icon to post or to share your models with other users on the internet.

### *Tutorial: PhotoView 15-1*

Apply PhotoView 360 to a SolidWorks part.

1. Click the **PhotoView 360** icon in the MS Windows area, or click **Start**, **All Programs**, **SolidWorks 2010**, **PhotoView 360**. The SolidWorks PhotoView 360 dialog box is displayed.

You do not need to run PhotoView 360 inside SolidWorks

View the various tools located in the PhotoView 360 dialog box.

Open a part.

2. Click the **Open File** icon from the large toolbar.
3. **Browse** to the SolidWorks 2010\PhotoView 360 folder.

4. Double-click **PhotoView 15-1**. The model is displayed in the SolidWorks PhotoView 360 dialog box.

Click and drag the splitter bar near the Select button to display the Face, Body, Part, Assembly and Appearance buttons.

Apply an Appearance to the outside face of the part model.

The selected material is applied to all of the common texture surfaces of the model.

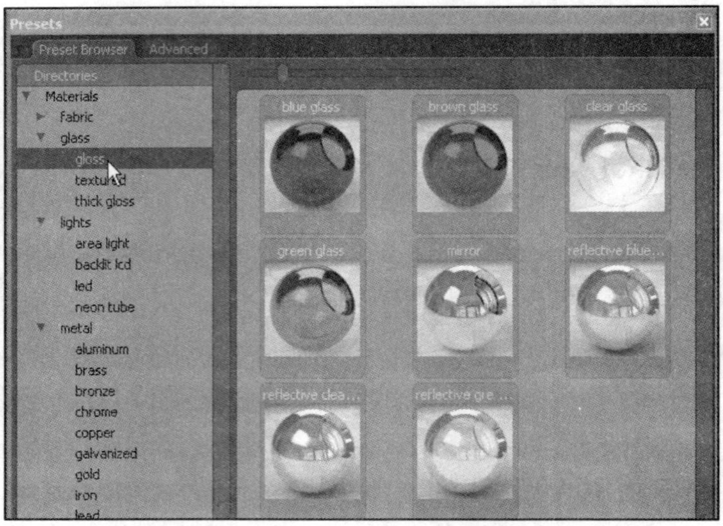


5. Click the **Part** icon in the Reference section filter toolbar.
6. Click the **Appearances** icon. View the Presets dialog box. Size the dialog box if needed.
7. Click the **Preset Browser** tab.
8. Click the drop-down arrow next to **Materials** in the Directories column.
9. Click the drop-down arrow next to **glass**.
10. Click **gloss** as illustrated. View your options.
11. Drag and drop **green glass** onto the model in the PhotoView 360 graphics area. All of the common texture surfaces of the part are displayed in green glass.
12. **Rotate** the model in the graphics area to view the results.

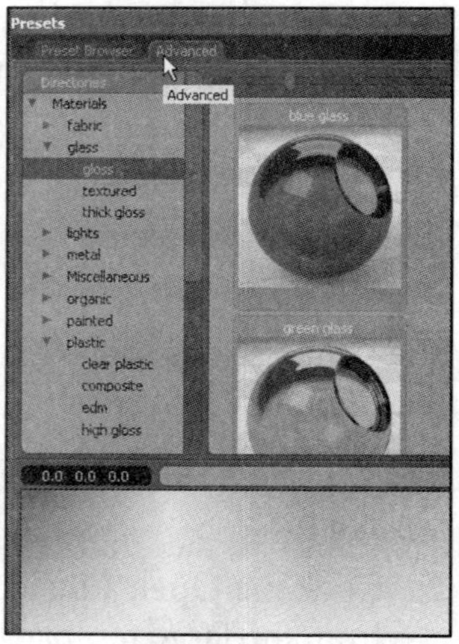


The slider bar provides the ability to resize the display of the available environments.

The Advance tab provides the ability to customize your selected appearance display.

13. **Close** the Presets dialog box.

Set an Environment for your model.

14. Click the **Environments** icon. View the Environments dialog box.
15. Drag and drop **abstract studio shadow** into the graphics area.

16. **Close** the Environment dialog box. View the results.

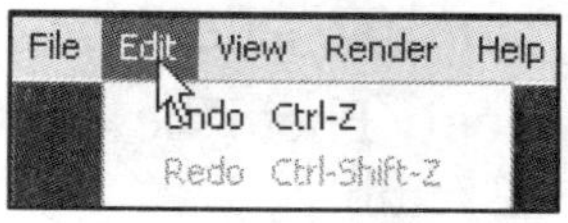


Click **Edit, Undo** to undo your last command.

View your Render Setting options.

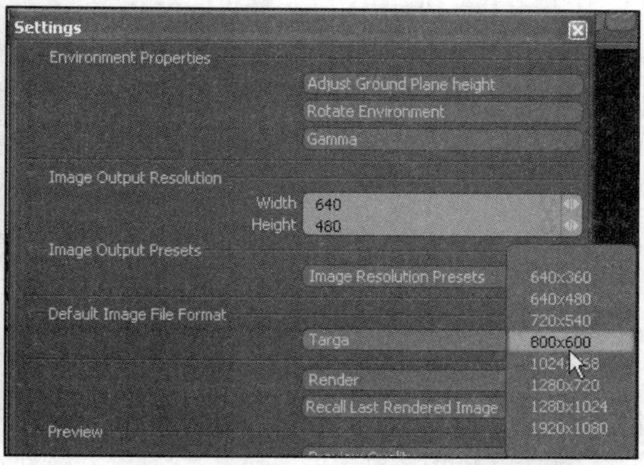


17. Click the **Settings** icon from the large toolbar. The Settings dialog box is displayed.
18. Click the drop-down arrow for **Image Resolution Presets**.
19. Select **800 x 600**.
20. Click **Better Quality** for Render Quality. The Render Quality options effects the shadows and transparencies of the display. View the results.

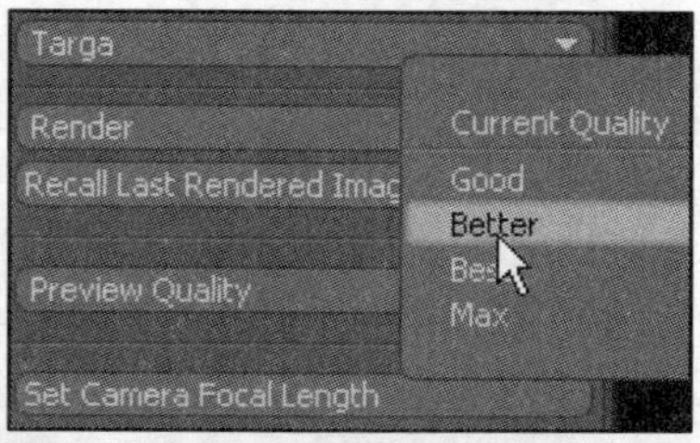


21. Click the **Close Window** button from the Render Frame dialog box. Return to the Render Settings dialog box.
22. **Close** the Settings dialog box.

Close the model. Save the changes and leave PhotoView 360 open.

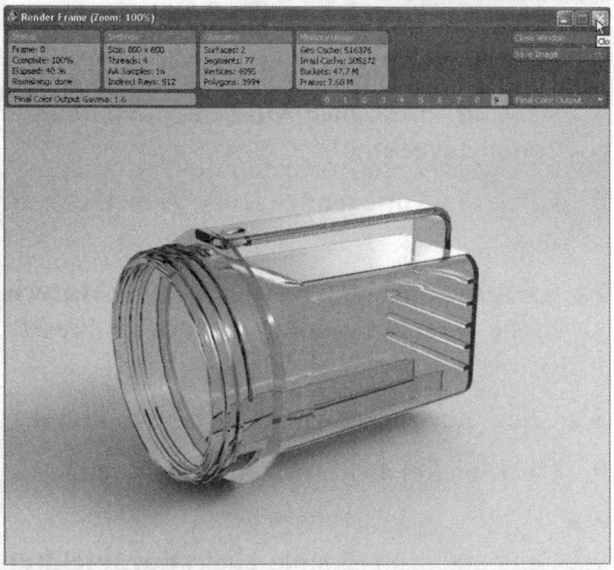

23. Click **File, Close Scene** from the Main menu.
24. Click **Save**. The SolidWorks PhotoView 360 dialog box is open. No models are displayed.

In PhotoView 360, you can now view PhotoWorks decals that were applied in SolidWorks and that were visible when the part or assembly was saved. First, save the part in SolidWorks 2010. Then open PhotoView 360 to view the decals.

### *Tutorial: PhotoView 15-2*

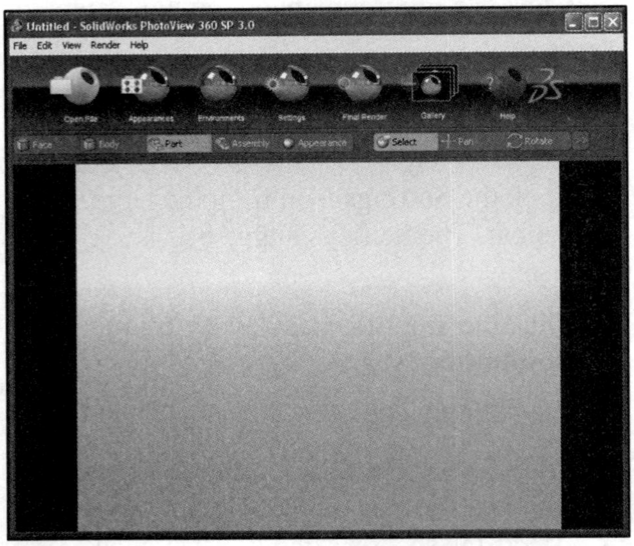


Apply PhotoView 360 to a SolidWorks Assembly.

1. Click the **PhotoView 360** icon in the MS Windows area, or click **Start**, **All Programs**, **SolidWorks 2010**, **PhotoView 360**. The PhotoView 360 dialog box is displayed.

View the various tools located in the dialog box.

Open the assembly.

2. Click the **Open File** icon from the Main menu.
3. **Browse** to the SolidWorks 2010\PhotoView 360 folder.
4. Double-click **PhotoView - 15-2**. The assembly model is displayed in the dialog box.

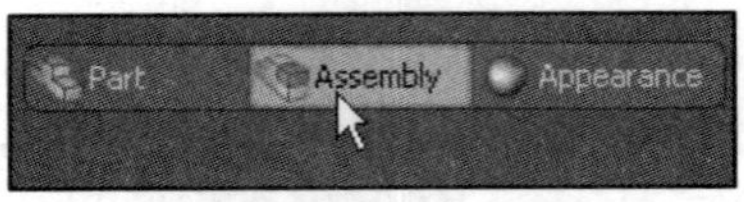


Apply Appearance to the assembly.

5. Click the **Assembly** icon as illustrated. The selected appearance will be applied to the complete assembly.
6. Click the **Appearance** icon. View the dialog box.
7. Click the drop-down arrow next to **Materials** in the Directories column under the Preset Browser tab.
8. Click the drop-down arrow next to **metal**.
9. Click **nickel** as illustrated. View your options.

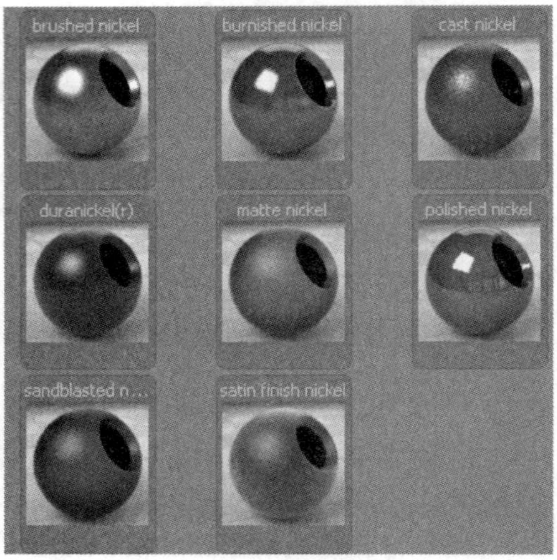


10. Drag and drop (double-click) **duranickl(r)** onto the model. View the results on the assembly.
11. **Close** the dialog box.

Set an Environment.

12. Click the **Environments** icon. View the Environments dialog box.

13. Drag and drop **daytime** into the graphics area.
14. **Close** the Environment dialog box. View the results.

View your Render Settings options.

15. Click the **Settings** icon from the large toolbar.
16. Click the drop-down arrow for **Image Resolution Presets**.
17. Select **800 x 600**.
18. Click **Better Quality** for Render Quality. The Render Quality options effects the shadows and transparencies of the display. View the results.
19. Click the **Close Window** button from the Render Frame dialog box. Return to the Render Settings dialog box.
20. **Close** the Render Settings dialog box.

Close the model. Save the changes and leave SolidWorks PhotoView open.

25. Click **File, Close Scene** from the Main menu.
21. Click **Save**. The SolidWorks PhotoView 360 dialog box is open. No models are displayed.

PhotoView 360 camera now supports additional effects; namely: you can switch between perspective and orthogonal views, create renderings where part of the image is in focus and other parts are not in focus through the Depth-of-field controls, and add a bloom effect to the final render to create a glow for emissive appearances or areas of very bright environment reflections.

***Tutorial: PhotoView 15-3***

Apply PhotoView 360 to a SolidWorks Assembly.

1. Click the **PhotoView 360** icon in the MS Windows area, or click **Start**, **All Programs**, **SolidWorks 2010**, **PhotoView 360**. The SolidWorks PhotoView 360 dialog box is displayed.

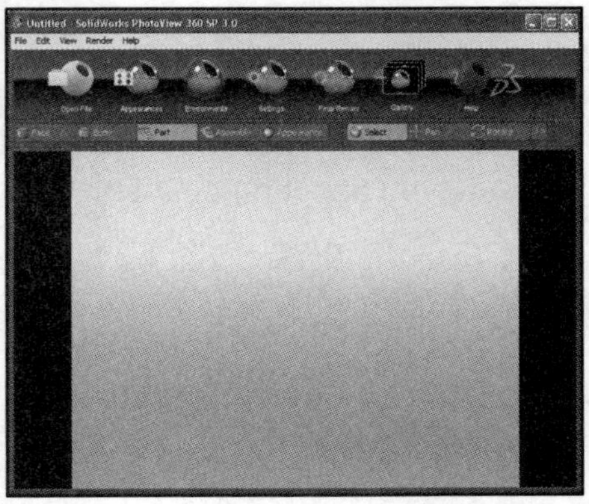

View the various tools located in the dialog box.

Open a SolidWorks Assembly.

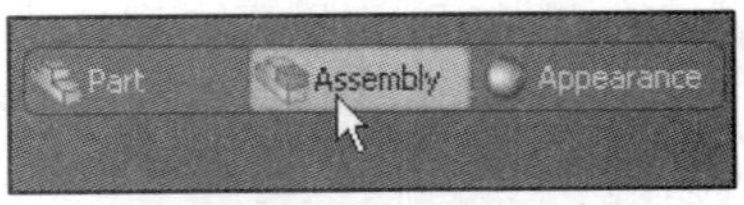


2. Click the **Open File** icon from the Main menu.
3. **Browse** to the SolidWorks 2010\PhotoView 360 folder.
4. Double-click **PhotoView 15-3**. The assembly model is displayed.
5. Click the **Assembly** icon as illustrated. The selected appearance will be applied to the complete assembly.

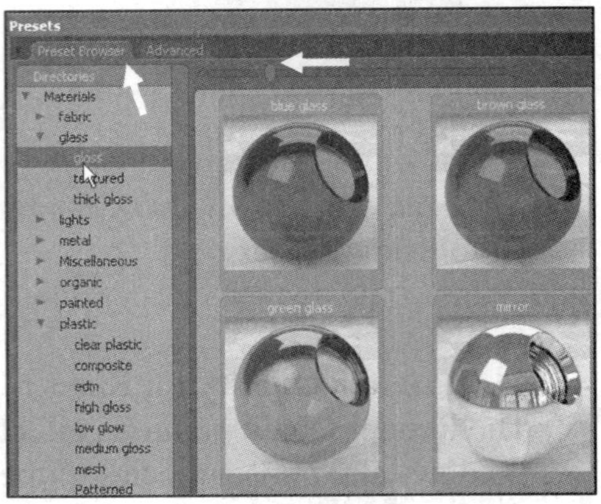


6. Click the **Appearances** icon. View the dialog box.
7. Click the drop-down arrow next to **Materials** in the Directories column under the Preset Browser tab.
8. Click the drop-down arrow next to **glass**.
9. Click **gloss** as illustrated. View your options.

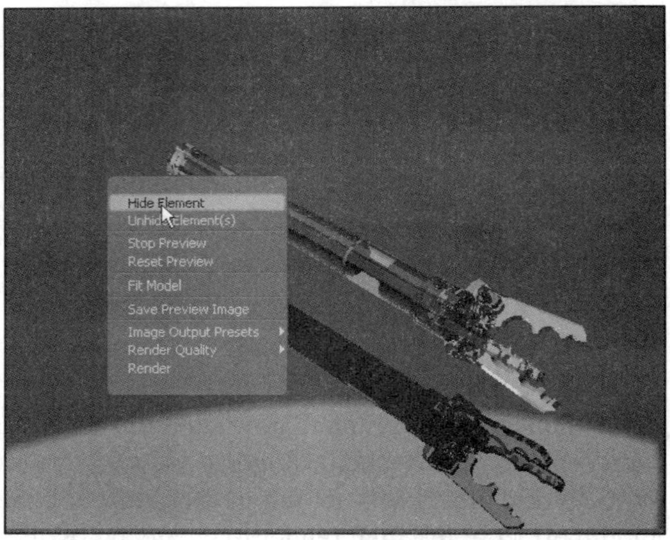


10. Drag and drop **green glass** onto the handle of the model in the SolidWorks PhotoView dialog box. View the results. All of the common surfaces of the assembly are displayed in green glass.
11. **Rotate** the model in the Graphics area to view the results.
12. **Right-click** in the Graphics area. View your options. PhotoView 360 provides the ability to hide top elements of an assembly to view inside your model.
13. Click inside the **graphics area**.
14. Click the **Advance** tab in the Presets dialog box. The Advance tab provides the ability to customize your selected appearance display.
15. **Close** the Presets dialog box.

Set an Environment.

16. Click the **Environments** icon. View the Environments dialog box.

17. Double-click the **abstract studio shadow** icon. View the results.

18. **Close** the Environments dialog box. View the results.

View your Render Settings options.

19. Click the **Settings** icon from the large icon toolbar.

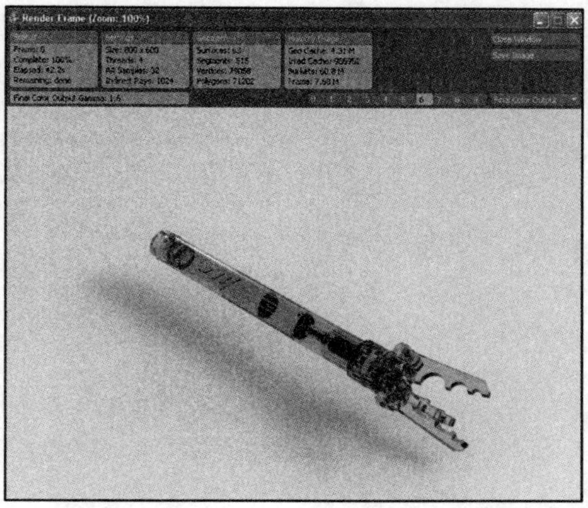

20. Click the drop-down arrow for **Image Resolution Presets**.

21. Select **800 x 600**.

22. Click **Better Quality** for Render Quality. The Render Quality options effects the shadows and transparencies of the display. View the results.

23. Click the **Close Window** button from the Render Frame dialog box. Return to the Render Settings dialog box.

24. **Close** the Render Settings dialog box.

Close the model. Save the changes and leave SolidWorks PhotoView open.

25. Click **File, Close Scene** from the Main menu.

26. Click **Save**. The SolidWorks PhotoView 360 dialog box is open. No models are displayed.

# Summary

In this chapter, you were exposed to a general overview of the PhotoView 360. PhotoView 360 is a new visualization and rendering solution from Solidworks. It's a highly interactive environment for viewing your designs as well as for creating photorealistic renderings that you can use to showcase your designs. PhotoView 360 is available in SolidWorks Professional and Premium.

In Chapter 16, explore SolidWorks Design Library, SolidWorks Explorer, Toolbox and the Measure tool.

SolidWorks 2010 will be the last release to include PhotoWorks. In subsequent releases, PhotoWorks will not be available and PhotoView 360 will be its functional replacement and the sole photorealistic solution for SolidWorks software.

# Notes:

# CHAPTER 16: DESIGN LIBRARY, EXPLORER, TOOLBOX AND MEASURE TOOL

## Chapter Objective

Chapter 16 provides a comprehensive understanding of the SolidWorks Design Library, SolidWorks Explorer, Toolbox and the Measure tool. On the completion of this chapter, you will be able to:

- Apply and use the SolidWorks Design Library
  - Add a folder
  - Use the Design Library tools
- Insert and configure the SolidWorks Toolbox
  - Use the SolidWorks Toolbox recourses
- Utilize SolidWorks Explorer:
  - Rename and Save components
- Know and apply the Measure tool

## Measure tool

The Measure tool measures distance, angle, radius and size of and between lines, points, surfaces and planes in sketches, 3D models, assemblies or drawings.

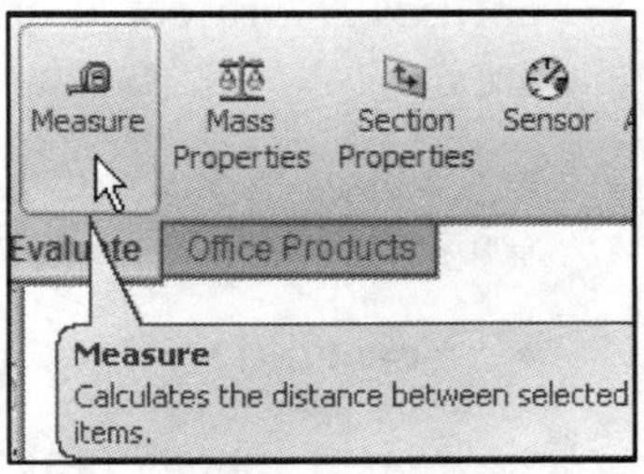


When you measure the distance between two entities, the delta x, y and z distances can also be displayed. When you select a vertex or sketch point, the x, y and z coordinates are displayed.

You have the ability to configure the Measure tool to display the results in dual dimensions. Click the **Measure** tool. Click **Units/Precision**. Select **Use custom settings**. Select the **first** length unit. Click **Use Dual Units**. Select the **second** length unit. Click **OK**.

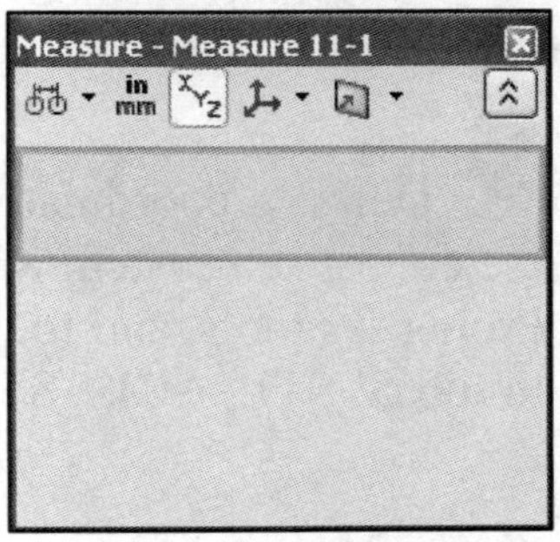

Use the Measure tool to measures distance, size, angle and radius in your model. Confirm geometric requirements between points, lines, surfaces, and planes in sketches, 3D models, assemblies, or drawings. The Measure tool uses the Measure dialog box. The Measure dialog box provides the following selections:

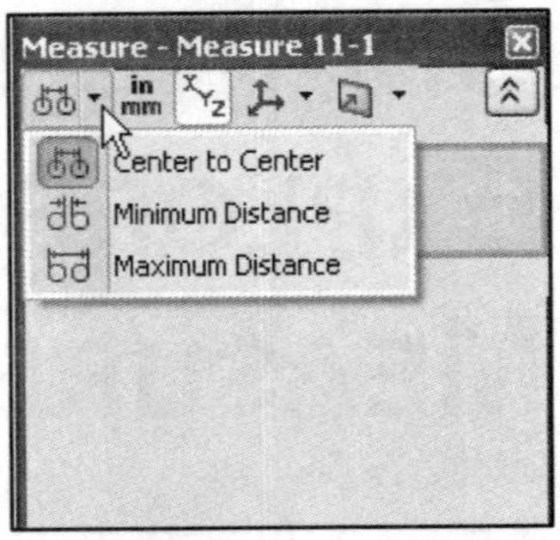


- ***Arc/Circle Measurements***. Specify the distance to display when arcs or circles are selected. The three options are:
  - **Center to Center**
  - **Minimum Distance**
  - **Maximum Distance**
- ***Units/Precision***. Provides access to the Measure Units/Precision dialog box. Enter the required units and values. Note: Location to add dual dimensions for the measure result.

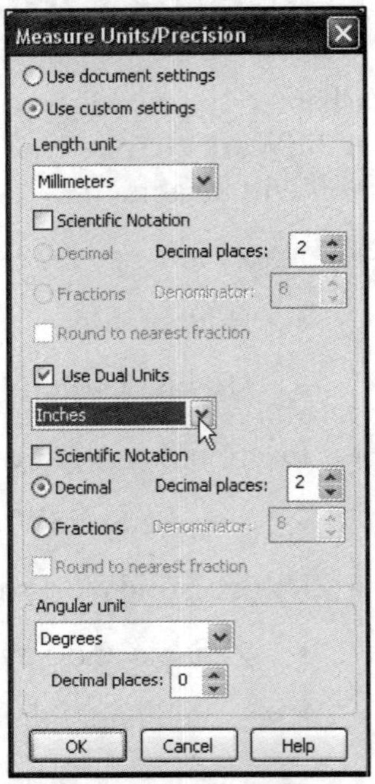


- ***Show XYZ Measurements***. Displays the dX, dY and dZ measurements between the selected entities in the Graphics window.
- ***XYZ Relative To***. Selects a coordinate system. The options are:
  - **Part Origin**. Default coordinate system of the part or assembly.
  - **Coordinate System**. Provides the ability to be user-defined.

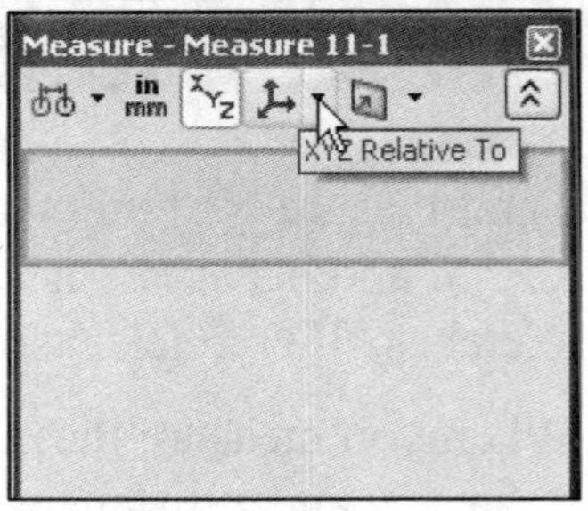


- ***Projected On***. Displays the distance between your selected entities as projected on one of the following. The options are:
  - **None**. Projection and Normal are not calculated. This is the default.
  - **Screen**. Displays in the Graphics window.
  - **Select Face/Plane**. Select a face or plane in the Graphics window or the FeatureManager design tree.

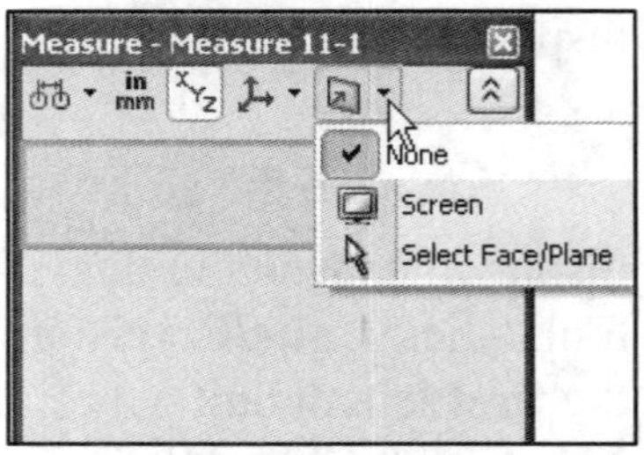


Define a coordinate system for a part or assembly. Use the coordinate system with the Measure and Mass Properties tools, and for exporting SolidWorks documents to IGES, STL, ACIS, STEP, Parasolid, VRML and VDA.

***Tutorial: Measure 16-1***

Apply the Measure tool to verify the design.

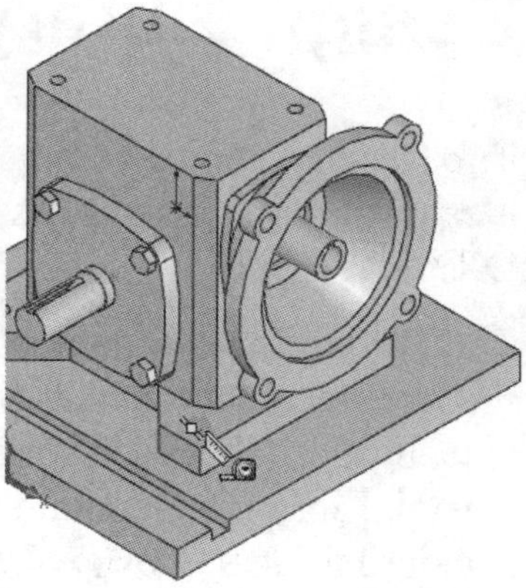

1. Open **Measure 16-1** from the SolidWorks 2010\Measure folder.
2. Click the **Measure** tool from the Evaluate tab. The Measure dialog box is displayed.
3. Click the circumference of the **right front hole** of the f718b-30-b5-g-1 assembly.
4. Click the circumference of the **right back hole** of the f718b-30-b5-g-1 assembly. The distance 114.3mm is displayed.

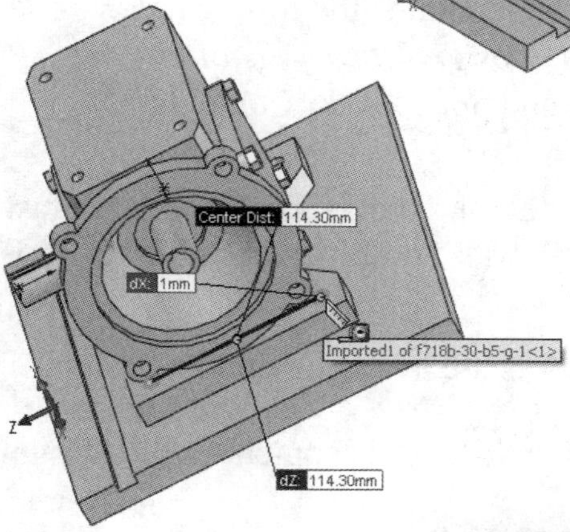


5. Right-click **Clear Selections** in the display box.
6. Click the **front shaft** as illustrated. View the results.

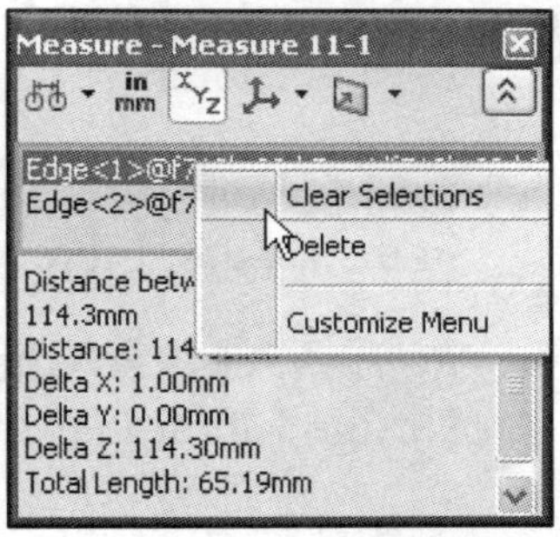


Apply Custom settings and dual dimensions.

7. Click **Units/Precision** from the Measure dialog box.
8. Check the **Use custom settings** box. Accept the default first length units (Millimeters).
9. Select **3** Decimal places.
10. Check the **Use Dual Units** box.

Select the second length unit.

11. Select **inches**. Click **OK**. View the updated results. **Close** the Measure dialog box.
12. **Close** the model.

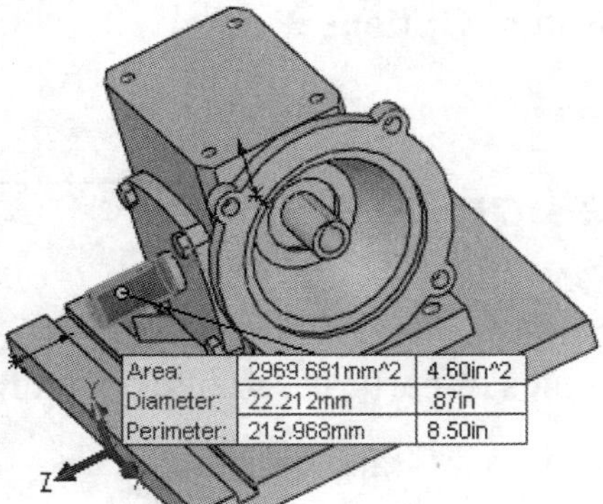


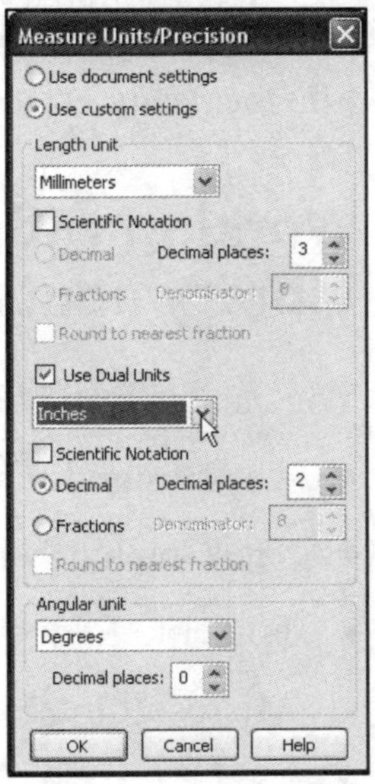

# Design Library

The Design Library tab in the Task Pane provides a central location for reusable elements: parts, assemblies, sketches, annotation favorites, blocks, library features and DXF/DWG files.

The Design Library does not recognize non-reusable elements such as SolidWorks drawings, text files, or other non-SolidWorks files. The Design Library tab contains the following standard folders: *Design Library*, *Toolbox*, *3D ContentCentral* and *SolidWorks Content*.

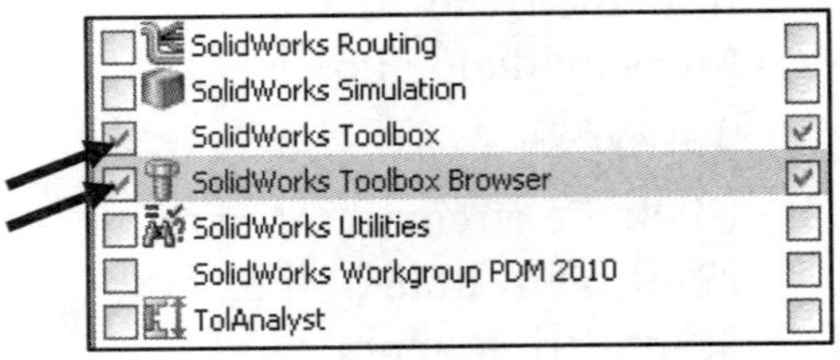


To access the SolidWorks Toolbox, you must install and add in the SolidWorks Toolbox and SolidWorks Toolbox Browser.

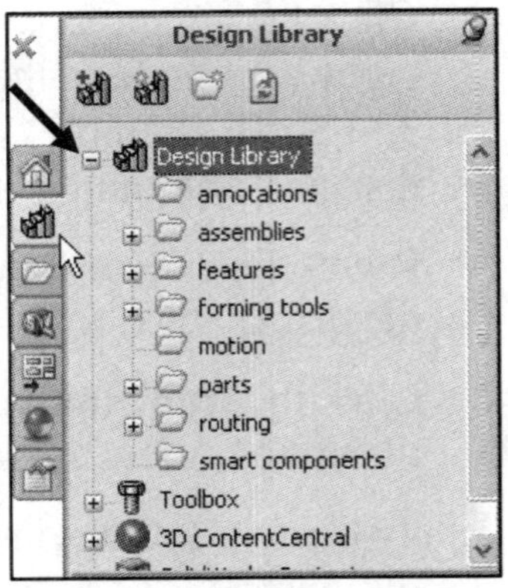


The following tools are available on the Design Library tab:

- *Add to Library*: Adds content to the Design Library.
- *Add File Location*: Adds an existing folder to the Design Library.
- *Create New Folder*: Creates a new folder on disk and in the Design Library.
- *Refresh*: Refreshes the view of the Design Library tab.

Specify folders for the Design Library by clicking **Options ➢ System Options ➢ File locations**.

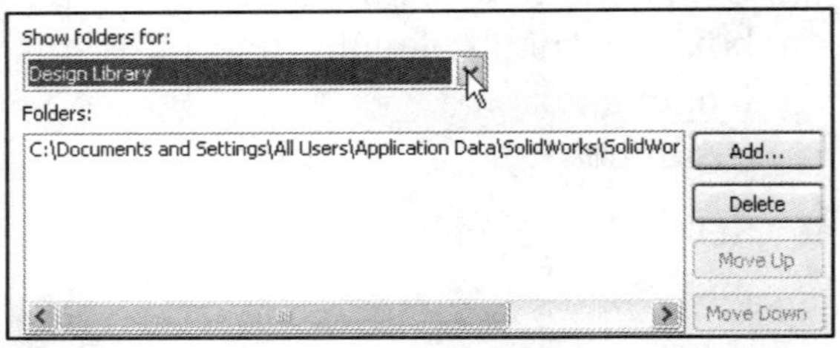


## Working with Design Library contents

You can click and drag copies of parts, assemblies, features, annotations, etc. from:

- The Design Library into your Graphics window.
- The Graphics window into the lower pane of the Design Library.
- Folder to folder in the Design Library.
- Microsoft Internet Explorer and Windows Explorer into the Design Library.

When you click and drag items into the Design Library, the Add to Library PropertyManager is displayed with a default file name, the default file type, and the selected folder for the Design Library folder.

***Tutorial: Assembly Design Library 16-1***

Create a new file location in the Design Library. Apply the *Add File Location* option.

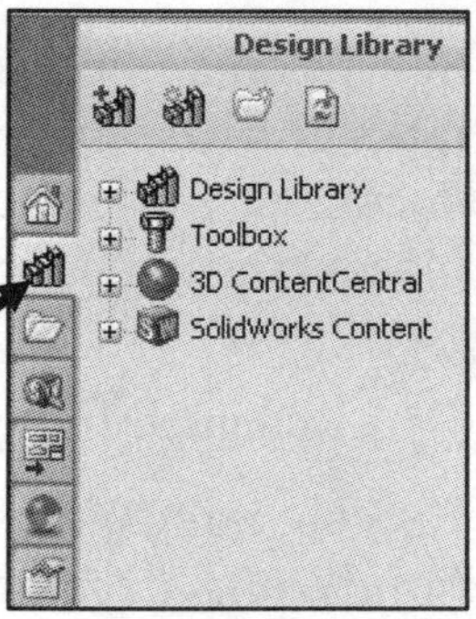


1. Open **Assembly Design Library 16-1** from the SolidWorks 2010\Design Library-1 folder.
2. Click the **Design Library** tab from the Task Pane.
3. Click the **Add File Location** icon.
4. Browse to the **SolidWorks 2010** Design Library-1 folder.
5. Click **OK** from the Choose Folder dialog box. The Design Library-1 folder is added to the Design Library.
6. Click the **Design Library-1** folder from the Design Library.
7. Click and drag the **f718b-30-b5-g-1** assembly into the Graphics window above the plate.
8. Click **Cancel** from the Insert Component PropertyManager. View the Assembly Design Library FeatureManager. The part is added to the assembly.
9. Display an **Isometric** view.
10. **Close** all models.

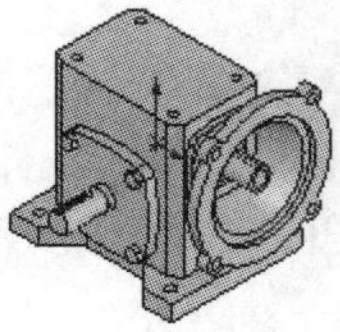

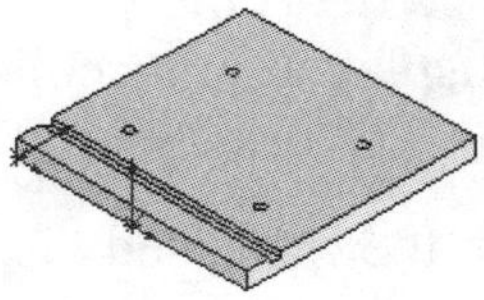

# Add a Design Library tab

Work directly from the Design Library. Add a Design Library tab to reference a folder. Note: In the illustration, the 2008 and 2009 Design Library folders are displayed.

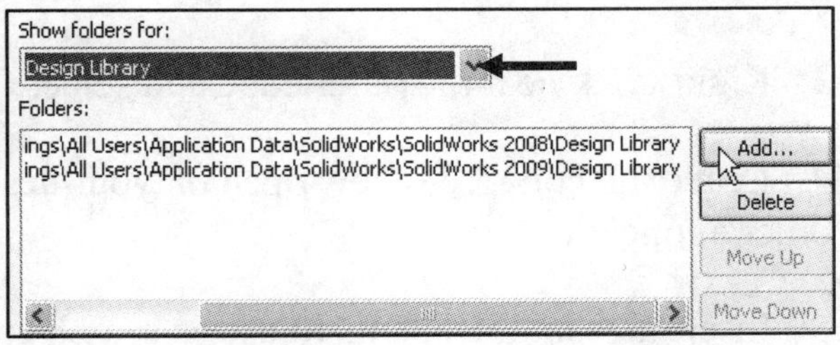


***Tutorial: Assembly Design Library 16-2***

Create a new file location for the Design Library.

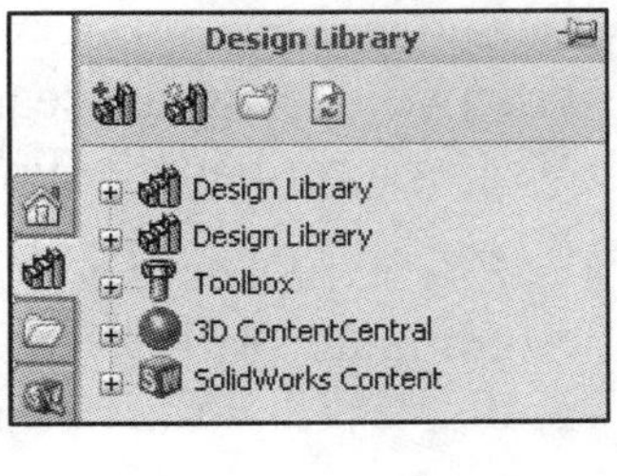


1. Click **Options**, **File Locations** from the Menu bar toolbar.
2. Select **Design Library** as illustrated.
3. Click the **Add** button. **Browse** to the folder that you want to add to the Design Library.

4. Click **OK** from the Browse dialog box. Note: In this case, the tab for the 2008 Design Library was added. Click **OK**. View the new tab in the Design Library.

# SolidWorks Explorer

SolidWorks Explorer is a file management tool designed to help you perform such tasks as *renaming*, *replacing* and *copying* SolidWorks files. You can display a document's references, search for documents using a variety of criteria, and list all the places where a document is used.

Renamed files are still available to those documents that reference them.

Execute SolidWorks Explorer within SolidWorks or directly from the desktop. The SolidWorks documents remain closed while manipulating names in SolidWorks Explorer.

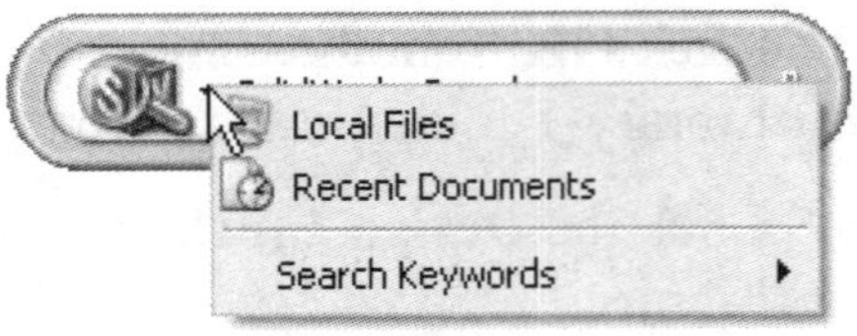


Apply SolidWorks Explorer with or without the SolidWorks application and with or without PDMWorks Workgroup added in.

The first time you open SolidWorks Explorer, it is displayed in its collapsed view, with only the SolidWorks Search box visible.

In the collapsed view, you can:

1.) Search for text strings and tags in all indexed documents, including SolidWorks and Microsoft Office documents.

2.) Click the **Expand** icon to display the File Explorer pane.

3.) Right-click near the outer edge and select **Close** or **Minimize**.

4.) Leave the collapsed view open on your desktop. It becomes transparent while you use other applications.

5.) Insert tags in documents to use as search criteria. Remember, tags provide the ability to associate keywords with documents to make it easier to search for them.

When you perform a search or click the **Expand** icon, the view expands to display the File Explorer pane, which has two tabs:

- *File Explorer.* The File Explorer tab displays the folders and documents on your computer. If PDM Works Workgroup Contributor is added in, the vault view is displayed at the bottom of the pane.

- *Results*. Displays results of the searches.

Activate SolidWorks Explorer from the SolidWorks Tools menu or from the Windows Start menu. The application is located on the SolidWorks installation CD's or on the SolidWorks website.

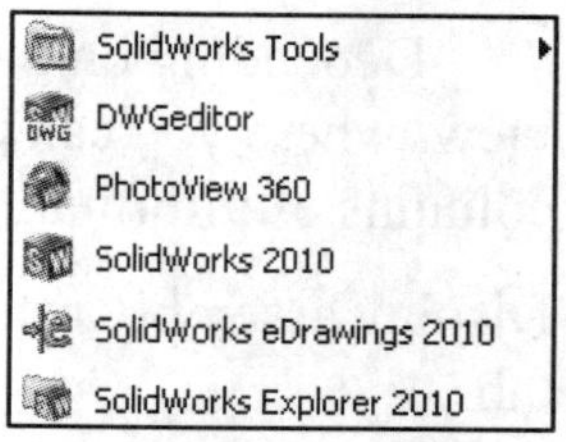


***Tutorial: SolidWorks Explorer 16-1***

Activate SolidWorks Explorer. Rename an assembly.

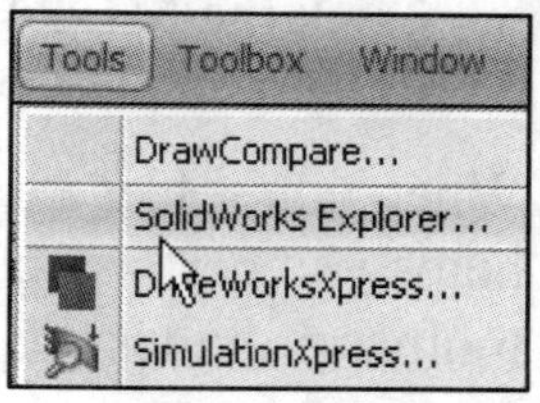


1. Click **Tools, SolidWorks Explorer** from the Menu bar menu. SolidWorks Explorer is displayed. Click **Accept** if needed.
2. Click **Cancel** from the SolidWorks Workgroup Login dialog box. The SolidWorks Search icon is displayed.
3. Click **Expand** as illustrated if this is your first time using SolidWorks Explorer.

Display the MGPM12-1010-11-1 assembly.

4. Click the **MGPM12-1010-11-1** assembly from the SolidWorks 2010\SolidWorks Explorer folder. The MGPM12-1010 assembly is displayed in the main window. Note: If you double-click MGPM12-1010-11-1, the assembly opens in the SolidWorks Graphics window. Do not open the assembly at this time.
5. Click the **Info** tab. View the results.

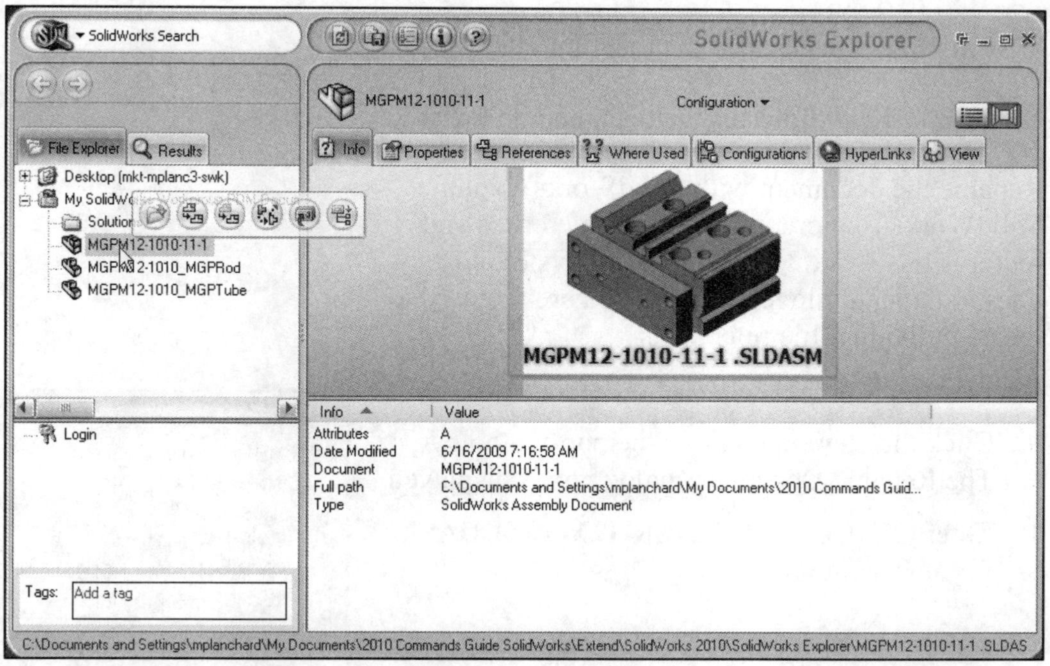


6. Click the **Properties** tab. View the results.

7. Click the **References** tab. View the results. Explore the other tabs.

Depending on the type of items selected, different tabs are displayed in the expanded view, where you can perform data management tasks. Each tab can contain several columns of information.

Display assembly references with the References tab.

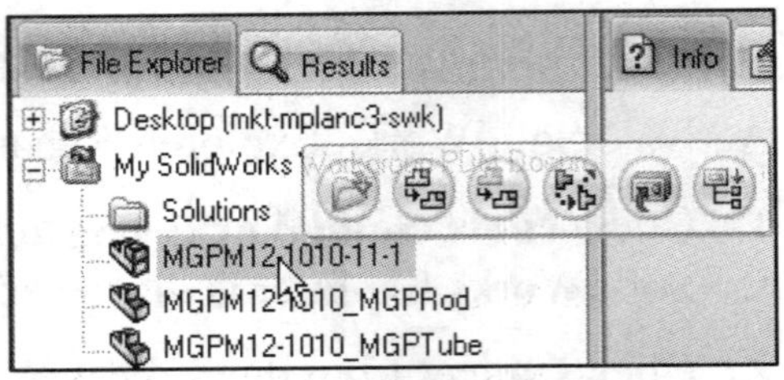


8. Click the **MGPM12-1010-11-1** assembly as illustrated. The pop-up toolbar is displayed.

When you select a document, a pop-up toolbar helps you perform additional tasks. The pop-up toolbar provides the following tools:

- *Open a document.* Opens the selected document.
- *SolidWorks Pack and Go.* Gathers all related files for a model design (parts, assemblies, drawings, references, design tables, Design Binder content, PhotoWorks content and Simulation / COSMOS results) into a folder or zip file. See SolidWorks Help for additional information. This is a very useful tool to take an entire assembly and save it, keeping al of it relations into another file structure.
- *Rename.* Renames one or more selected documents and updates all the references.
- *Replace.* Replaces a selected part or assembly document and updates its references.
- *Check In.* Checks the document into the vault.
- *Find in Vault.* Locates the document in the vault.

Rename the document with SolidWorks Explorer. SolidWorks Explorer updates file references and requires less work. Microsoft Windows Explorer does not update file references. You are required to locate individual file references.

Rename the MGPM12-1010-11-1 assembly.

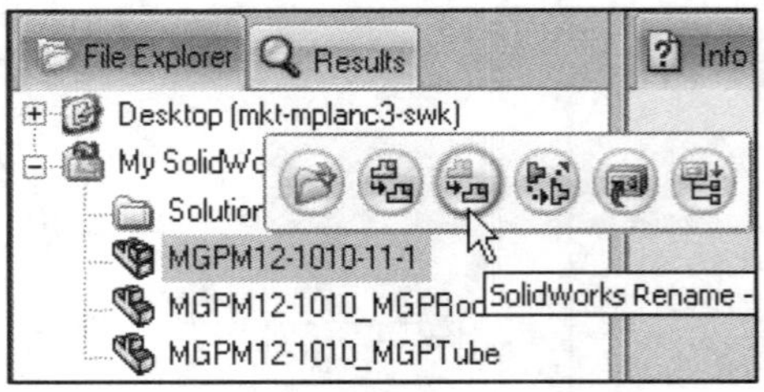


9. Click the **Rename** icon in the pop-up toolbar. The Rename Document dialog box is displayed.
10. Enter **GUIDE-CYLINDER-12MM.SLDASM** for new name.

11. Click **OK** from the Rename Document dialog box. View the results.
12. **Close** SolidWorks Explorer and return to SolidWorks.

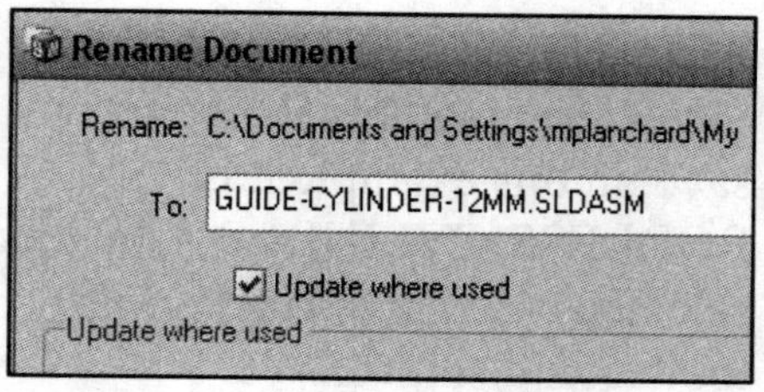


How do you save an assembly with multi components and references? You can either apply SolidWorks Explorer or the Save As command from the Menu bar menu.

First, apply the Save As command. Click Save As from the Menu bar menu. The Save As dialog box is displayed.

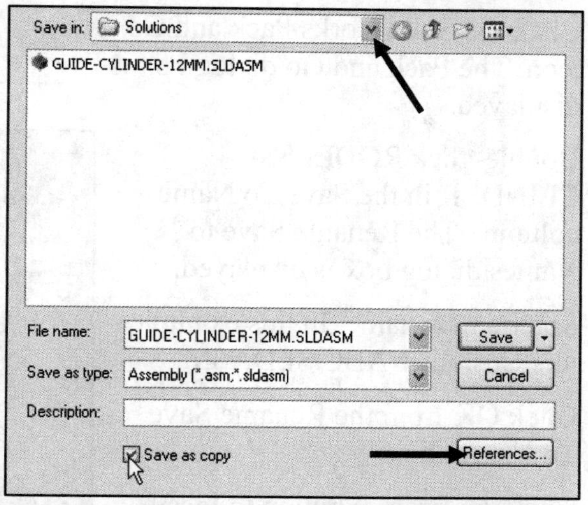


Check the Save as copy box. Select the assembly folder location (Save in).

Click the References button. The Save As with Reference dialog box is displayed.

Click the Browse button to locate the Destination folder (same as the Save in location).

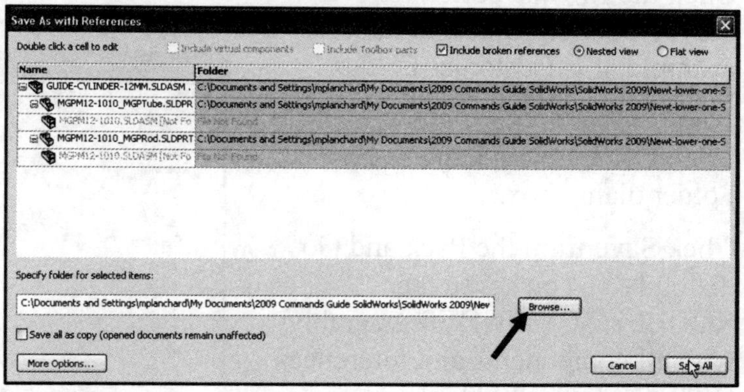


Click OK from the Browse For Folder dialog box.

Click the Save All button from the Save As with References dialog box.

You saved the GUIDE CYLINDER assembly with all of the reference components.

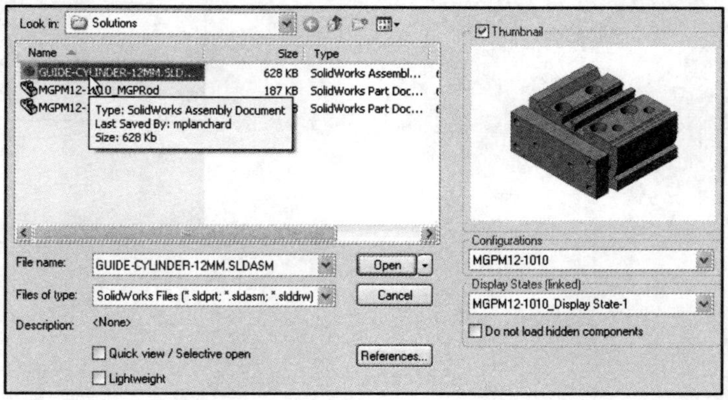

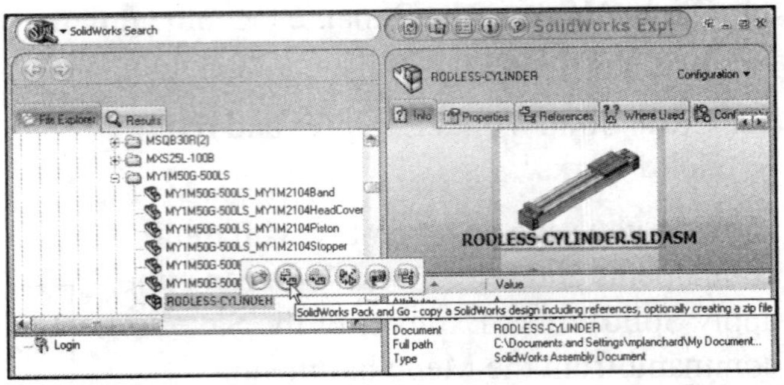


Second, apply SolidWorks Explorer. Select the assembly that you want to save, in this example it is RODLESS-CYLINDER. Click the selected assembly. The Pop-up toolbar is displayed.

Click the SolidWorks Pack and Go icon. The Pack and Go dialog box is displayed.

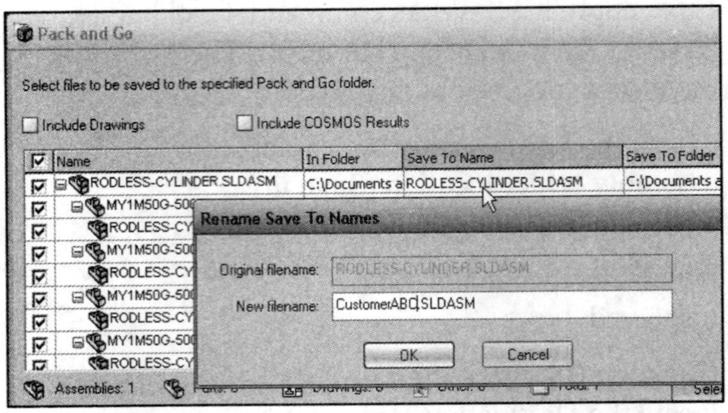


Double-click RODLESS-CLINDER in the Save To Name column. The Rename Save to Names dialog box is displayed.

Enter a new name. In this example it is Customer ABC.SLDASM.

Click OK from the Rename Save To Names box.

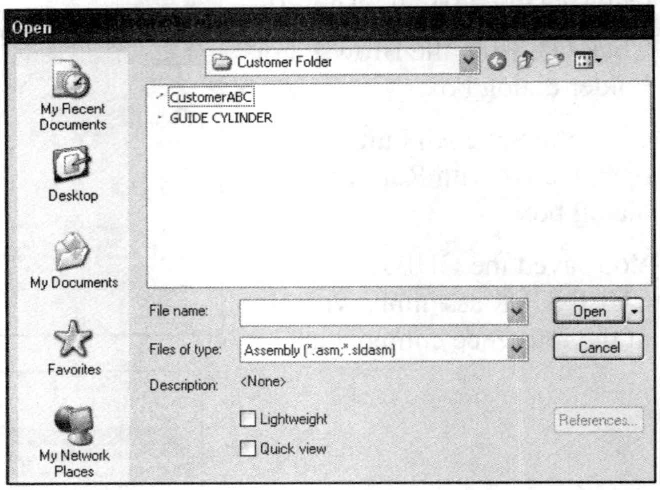


Click the Browse button to locate the Destination folder. In this example, it is Customer Folder. Locate your folder.

Click OK from the Browse For Folder dialog box.

Click Save from the Pack and Go dialog box. You saved the RODLESS-CYLINDER assembly with all components and references to the Customer Folder location.

# Summary

In this chapter, you applied the Measure tool to measure distance, size, angle and radius in your model. Use this tool to confirm geometric requirements between points, lines, surfaces, and planes in sketches, 3D models, assemblies, or drawings.

You explored and applied SolidWorks Explorer. SolidWorks Explorer is a file management tool designed to perform such tasks as renaming, replacing and copying SolidWorks files.

In Chapter 17, explore SolidWorks SimulationXpress and SustainabilityXpress. Every license of SolidWorks 2010, obtains a copy of SolidWorks SustainabilityXpress. SustainabilityXpress calculates environmental impact on a model in four key areas: *Carbon Footprint*, *Energy Consumption*, *Air Acidification* and *Water Eutrophication.*

Material and Manufacturing process region and Transportation Usage regions are used as input variables.

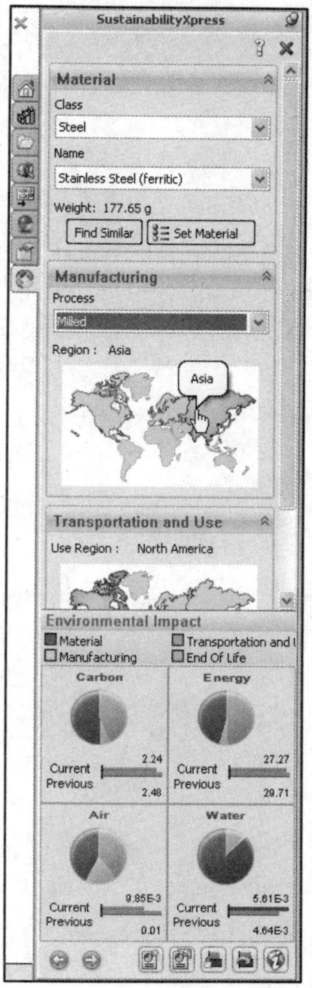

## Notes:

# CHAPTER 17: SIMULATIONXPRESS AND SUSTAINABILITYXPRESS

## Chapter Objective

Chapter 17 provides a general overview of SolidWorks SimulationXpress along with an understanding of SolidWorks SustainabilityXpress. On the completion of this chapter, you will be able to:

- Recognize the power of SolidWorks SimulationXpress:
- Apply the SolidWorks SimulationXpress Wizard:
  - Fixtures, Loads, Material, Run, Results and Optimization
- Comprehend and apply the strength of SolidWorks SustainabilityXpress:
  - Environmental Impact Factors: Carbon Footprint, Energy Consumption, Air Acidification and Water Eutrophication
  - Material and Manufacturing process region and Transportation Usage region
  - Material database
  - Customer report

## SolidWorks SimulationXpress

SolidWorks SimulationXpress offers an easy-to-use first pass stress analysis tool for SolidWorks users. This tool displays the effects of a force applied to a part, and simulates the design cycle and provides stress results. It also displays critical areas and safety levels at various regions in the selected part.

Based on these results, you can strengthen unsafe regions and remove material from over designed areas.

In this section, apply the SimulationXpress tool to analyze a Bent bar part. Perform a first-pass analysis on the Bent bar. View the Factor of Safety and the applied stresses for a given load. Apply the Optimization tool.

SimulationXpress calculates displacements, strains and stresses, but it only displays stresses and displacements.

The accuracy of the results of the analysis depends on selected material properties, restraints, and loads. For results to be valid, the specified material properties must accurately represent the part material, and the restraints and loads must accurately represent the part working conditions.

## SolidWorks SimulationXpress User Interface

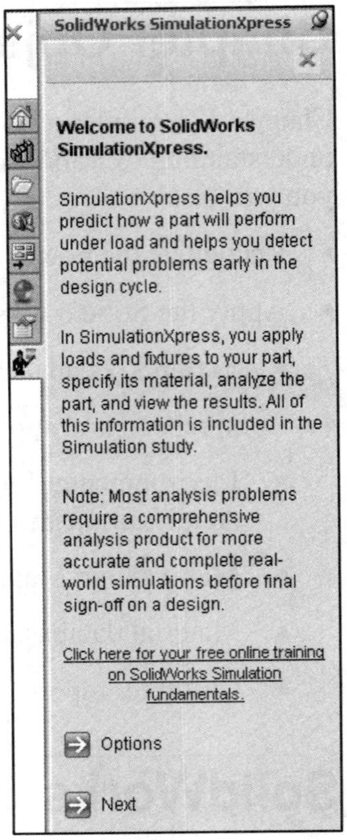


SimulationXpress guides you through various default steps to define fixtures, loads, material properties, analyze the model, view the results and the optional Optimization process.

The SimulationXpress interface consists of the following options:

- **Welcome Menu**. Allows you to set the default units, specify a folder for saving the analysis results, and to Start a new analysis.
- **Fixture Menu**. Applies Fixtures / restraints to faces of the part.
- **Loads Menu**. Applies forces and pressures to faces of the part.
- **Material Menu**. Applies material properties to the part. The material can be assigned from the material library or you can input the material properties.
- **Run Menu**. Provides the ability to either display the analysis with the default settings or to change the settings.
- **Results Menu**. Displays the analysis results in the following ways:
  - Show critical areas where the factor of safety is less than a specified value.
  - Display the stress distribution in the model with or without annotation for the maximum and minimum stress values.
  - Display resultant displacement distribution in the model with or without annotation for the maximum and minimum displacement values.
  - Show deformed shape of the model.
  - Generate an HTML report.
  - Generate eDrawing files for the analysis results.

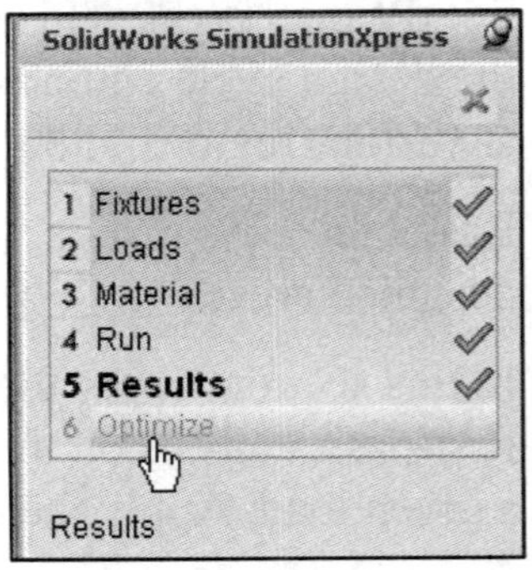

- **Optimize Menu**. Optimizes a model dimension based on a specified criterion.
- **Start Over button**. Deletes existing analysis data and results and starts a new analysis session.

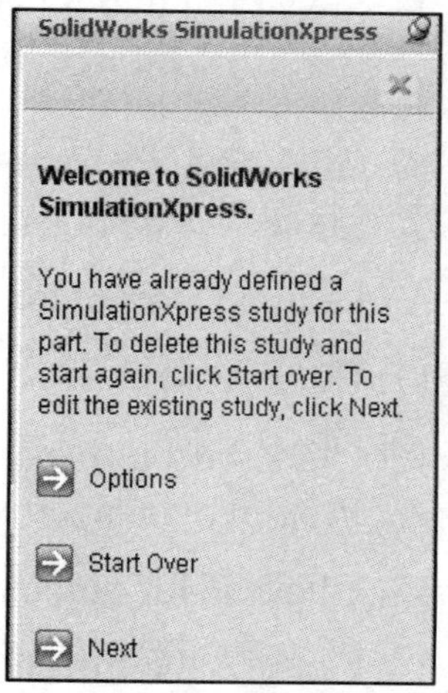


SimulationXpress automatically saves the analysis information and closes the current analysis session.

***Tutorial: SimulationXpress 17-1***

Close all parts, assemblies and drawings. Run SimulationXpress. Perform an analysis.

1. Open the **Bent Bar 17-1** part from the SolidWorks 2010/ SimulationXpress folder.
2. Click **SimulationXpress Analysis Wizard** from the Evaluate tab. The Welcome box is displayed.
3. Click the **Options** button to select the system units and to specify a save in folder.
4. Select **SI (MMGS)** for unit system.
5. Select the **Results location**; your file folder.
6. Click **OK** from the SimulationXpress Options dialog box.

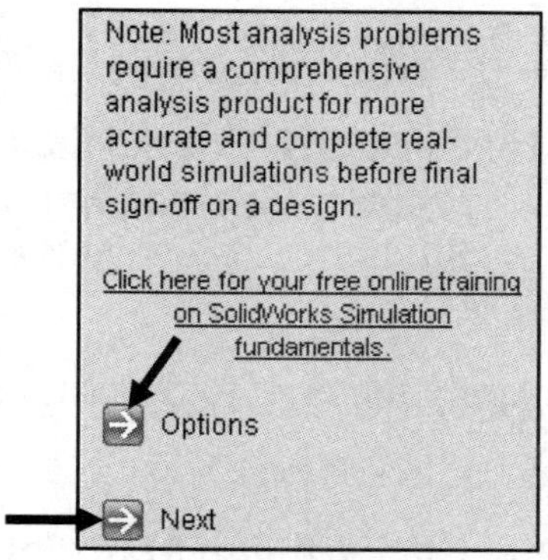


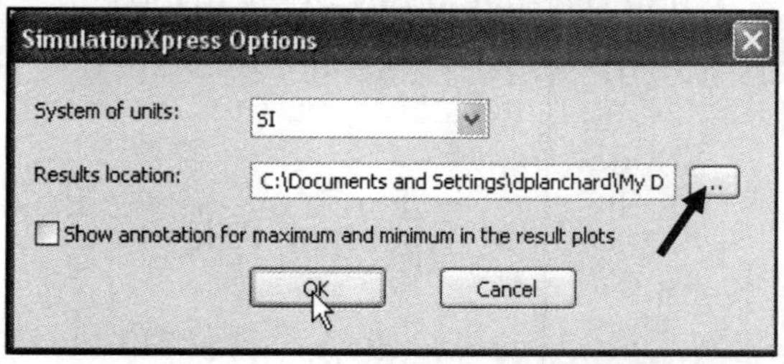


Add a Fixture. Fix the part to apply a load.

7. Click **Next**. Apply fixtures to keep the part from moving. View the warnings in the dialog box.
8. Click **Add a fixture**. The Fixture PropertyManager is displayed. This is new for SolidWorks 2010.

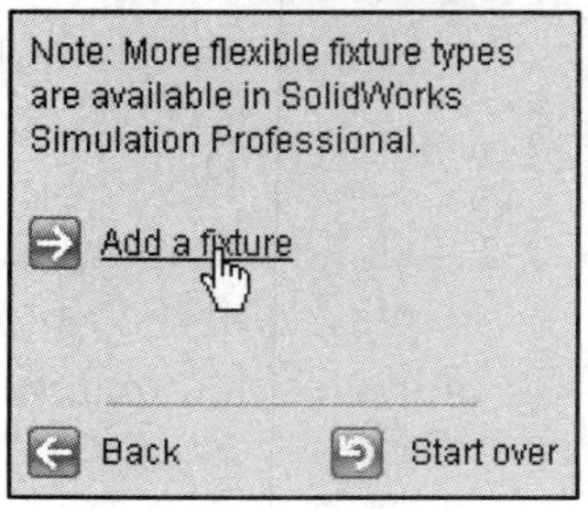


You can specify multiple sets of fixtures (restraints) for a part. Each set of fixtures can have multiple faces.

9. **Select** the two illustrated end faces of the Bent Bar as illustrated. Face1 and Face2 are displayed.

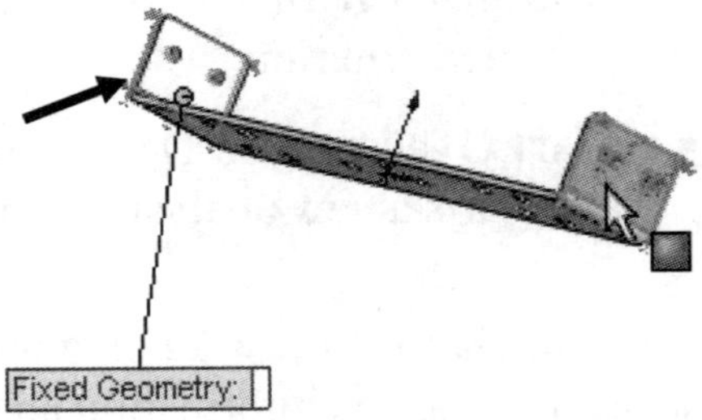


10. Click **OK** ✔ from the Fixture PropertyManager. Fixed-1 is displayed in the Study tree.

Add a Load (force) to the part.

11. Click **Next**.

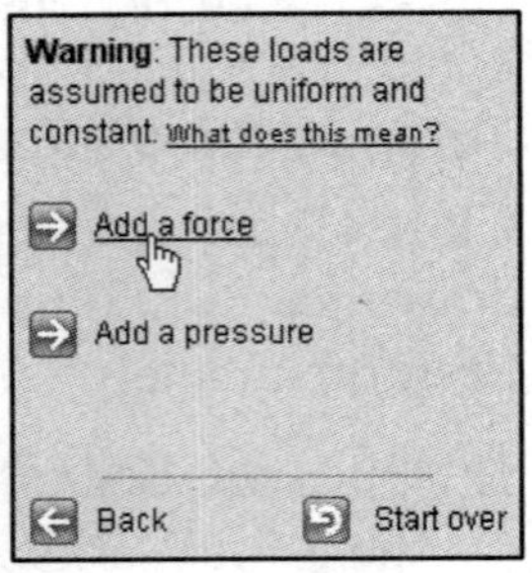


12. Click **Add a force**. The Force PropertyManager is displayed.

13. Click **SI** for units.

14. Click to the **top flat face** of the Bent Bar as illustrated. Note: The edges of the Bent Bar are fixed.

15. The direction of the applied force is displayed. The direction is downward and is normal to the selected face. Enter **5N** for Force Value.

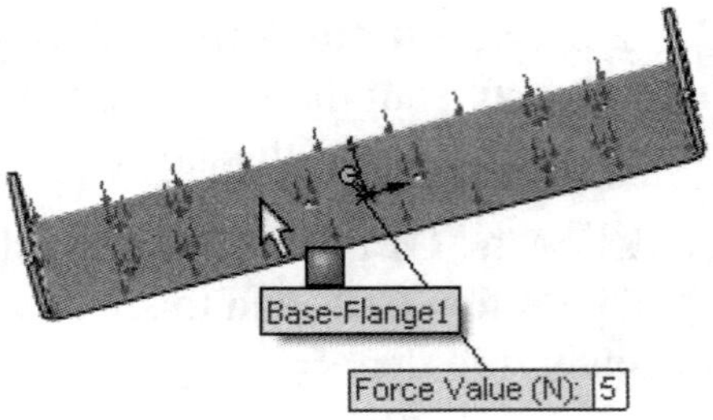


16. Click **OK** ✔ from the Force PropertyManager. Force-1 is displayed in the Study tree. View your options to edit, go back, etc.

Apply material to the part.

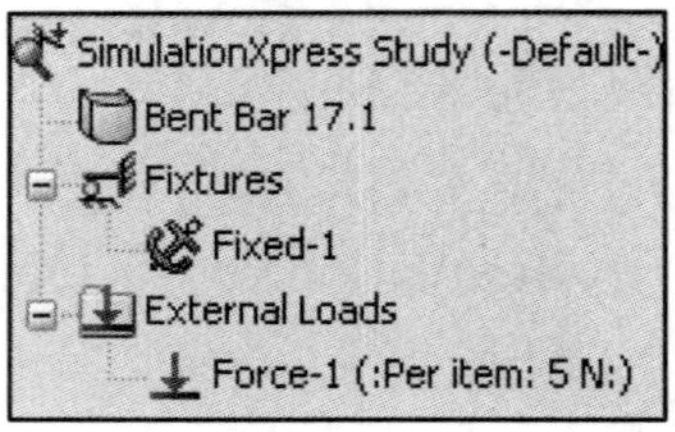


17. Click **Next**.

18. Click **Choose Material**. View the Material dialog box. This is the same information available when adding material to a part in SolidWorks.

19. **Expand** the Aluminum Alloys folder.

20. Select **6061 Alloy**. View the available material information.

21. Click **Apply**.

22. Click **Close**. A green check mark is displayed in the Study tree. This indicates that material is applied.

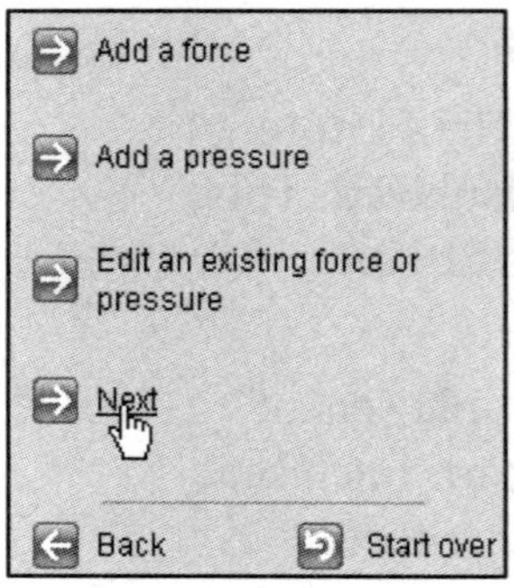


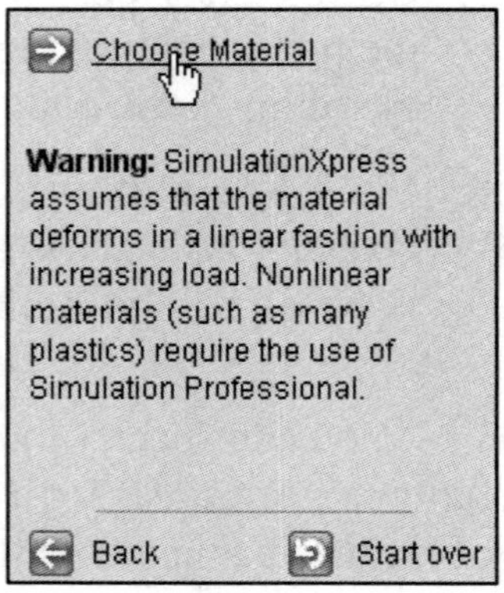

Brittle materials do not have a specific yield point and hence it is not recommended to use the yield strength to define the limit stress for the criterion.

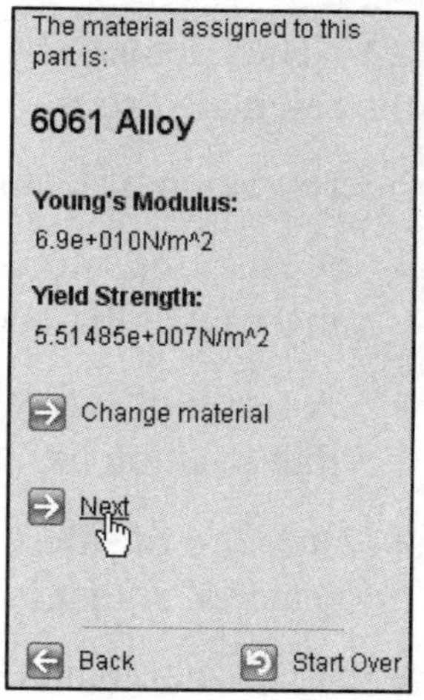


You can apply multiple pressures to a single face or to multiple faces. SimulationXpress applies pressure loads normal to each face.

Run the analysis.

23. Click **Next**. View your options.

24. Click **Change settings**. This option provides the ability to modify the element size and element tolerance during the mesh period to analyze the part. The larger the element size and element tolerance, the longer it will take to calculate. Accept the default conditions.

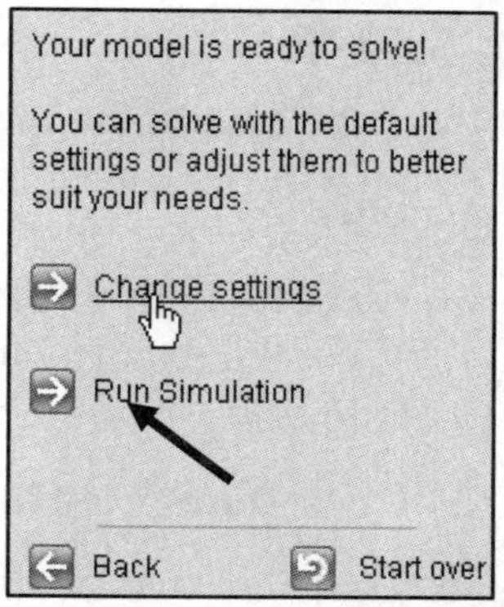


Specifying a smaller mesh element size provides a more accurate result.

25. Click **Back**. Click **Run Simulation**. View the animation in the Graphics window and the SimulationXpress Study tree. The Results folder displays: *Stress*, *Displacement*, *Deformation* and *Factor of Safety*.

26. Click **Stop animation**.

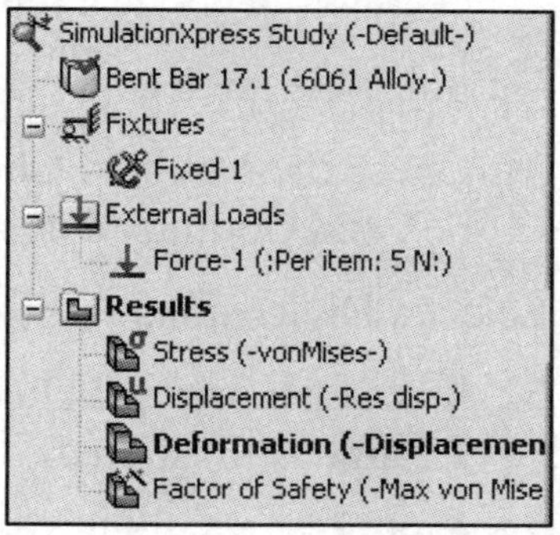


27. Double-click each results folder **(Stress, Displacement**, **Deformation**, and **Factor of Safety**) in the Results section of the Study tree to view the study plot. Explore your options. End viewing the Factor of Safety graph.

28. Click the **Yes, continue** button. The result is displayed. The Factor of Safety for the specified parameters is approximately 20. What does this mean? This indicated that the current design is safe or may be overdesigned.

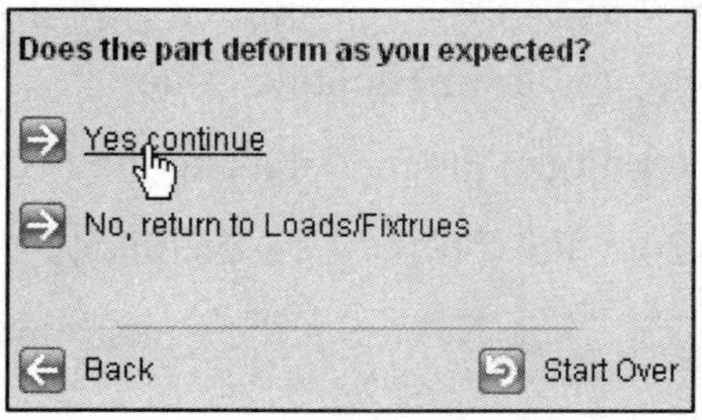


The FOS plot displays in red, where the FOS is less than 1. The plot displays in blue, where the FOS is greater than one.

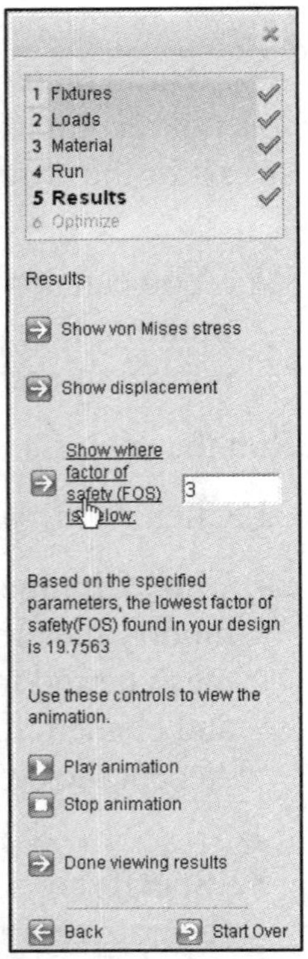


The Factor of Safety is a ratio between the material strength and the calculated stress.

Interpretation of factor of safety values:

- A factor of safety less than 1.0 at a location indicates that the material at that location has yielded and that the design is not safe.
- A factor of safety of 1.0 at a location indicates that the material at that location has just started to yield.
- A factor of safety greater than 1.0 at a location indicates that the material at that location has not yielded.
- The material at a location will start to yield if you apply new loads equal to the current loads multiplied by the resulting factor of safety.

View the area of the model with a FOS of 3 or below.

27. Enter **3**.
28. Click the **Show where factor of safety (FOS) is below**. View the results. Note: The color red indicates areas below 3.
29. Click **Done Viewing results**.
30. There are two kinds of reports that you can generate. As an exercise, generate a report. Click **Next**.

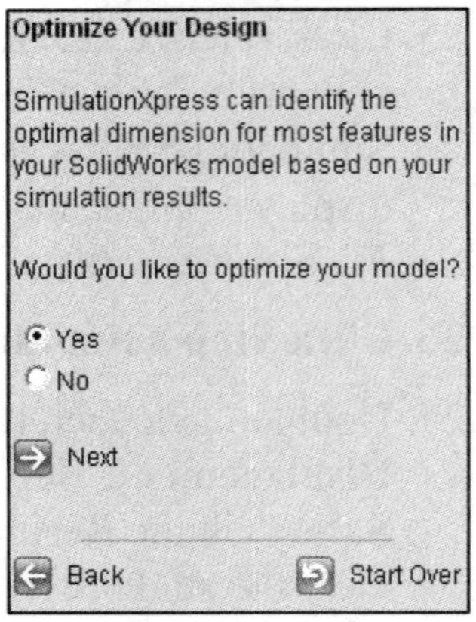


Optimize the model.

31. Check the **Yes** box. Click **Next**. The Add Parameters dialog box and Optimization table is displayed.

Select a Dimension.

32. Rotate the part and click the Sheet metal part thickness of **2.5mm** as illustrated.

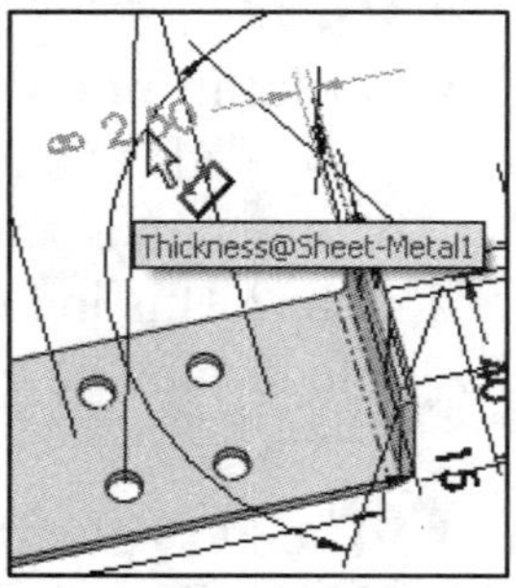


33. Click **OK** from the Add Parameters dialog. View the updated Optimization table. Accept the Min (1.25mm) and Max (3.75mm) default values.

Optimize the model using the Factor of Safety.

34. Click **Next**. View the dialog box.
35. Click **Next**. Set the Constraint in the next step.

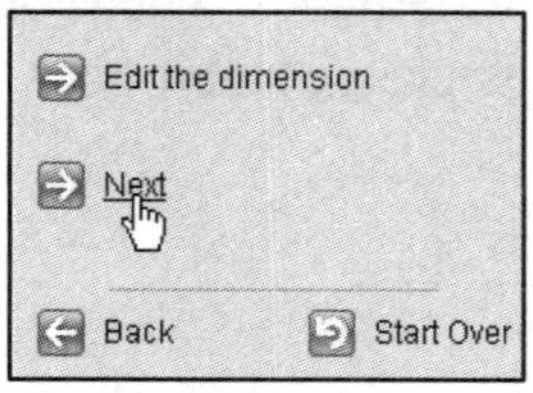

36. Click **Specify the constraint**.

37. Select **Factor of Safety** from the Constraints drop-down menu as illustrated.
38. Accept the default: Is greater than. Enter **6** in the for Min of Factor of Safety box.

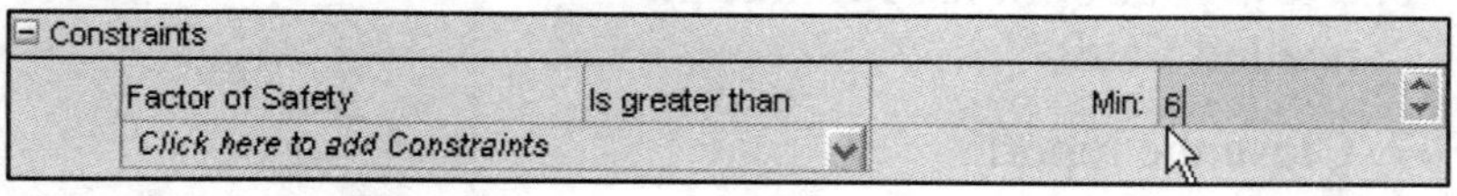


39. Click **Next**.
40. Click **Run the optimization**. Note: This may take 2- 3 minutes. View the results. To optimal value of 1.25mm, the Factor of Safety would be approximately 6. You have the option to select the Initial Value, or to select the Optimal Value.

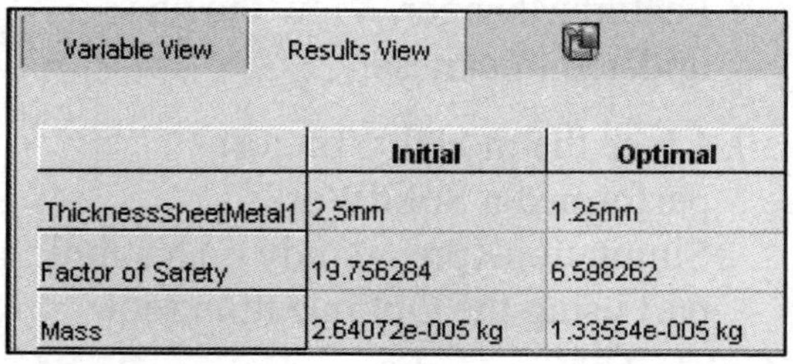


41. Check the **Optimal Value** box.
42. Click **Next**. The results are now out of date because the study parameters have changed. You must rerun the study to update the plot results (**Stress**, **Displacement**, **Deformation** and **Factor of Safety**).
43. Click **Run** in the Wizard window.
44. Re-run the Simulation. Click **Run Simulation**.

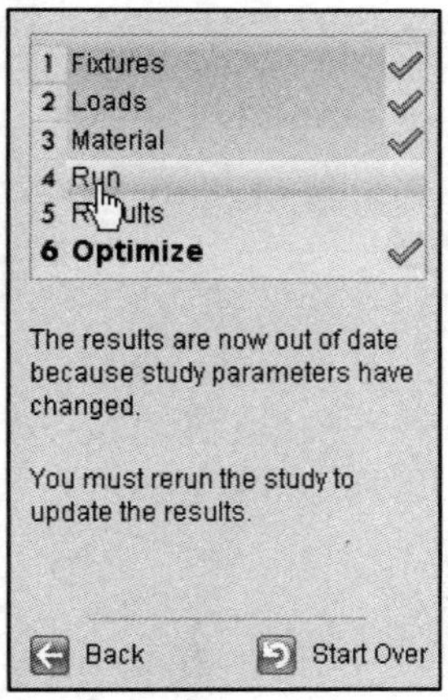


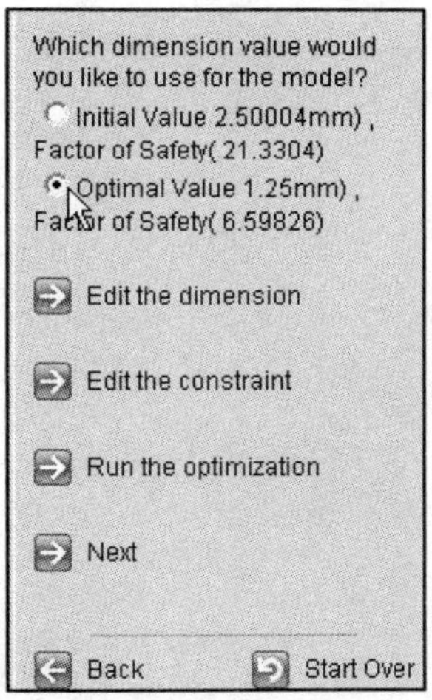


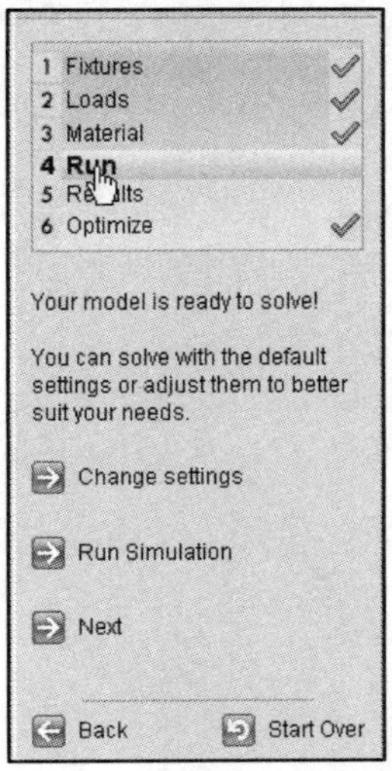

The SolidWorks SimulationXpress Wizard window is updated. Generate a HTML report.

45. Click **Generate HTML report**.

46. View your options. **Fill out** the needed fields.

47. **Close** the report.

48. **Save** the part.

49. Click **Sheet-Metal1** in the FeatureManager. View the new updated thickness.

50. **Close** the model. You just performed a SolidWorks SimulationXpress study on a simple part using the Optimization tool.

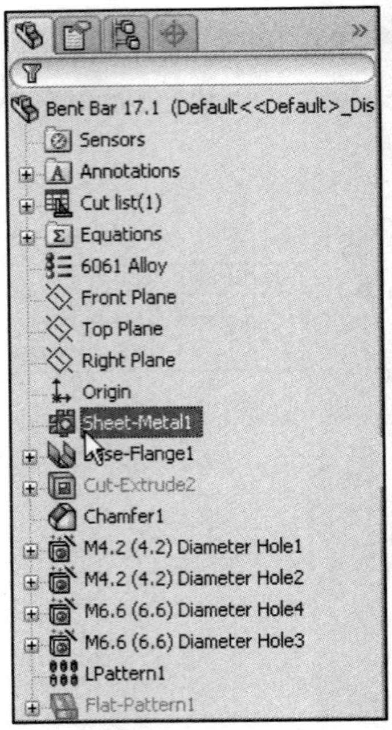


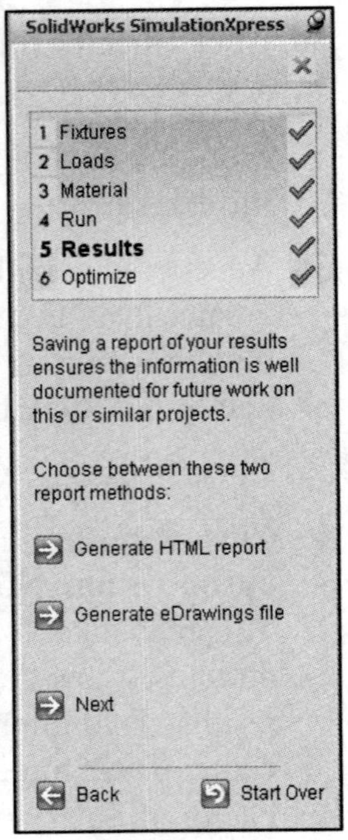


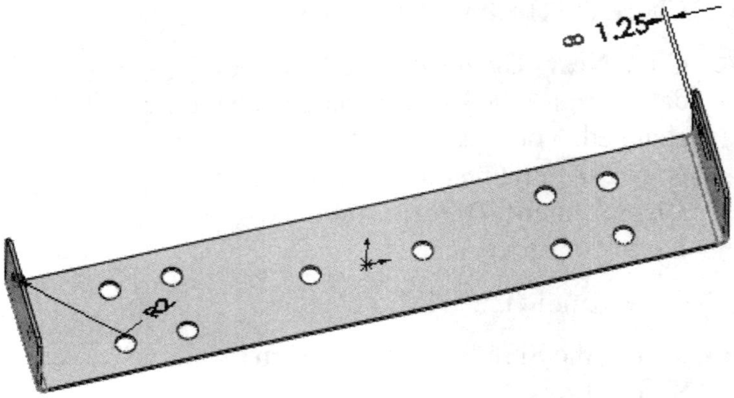

# SolidWorks Sustainability

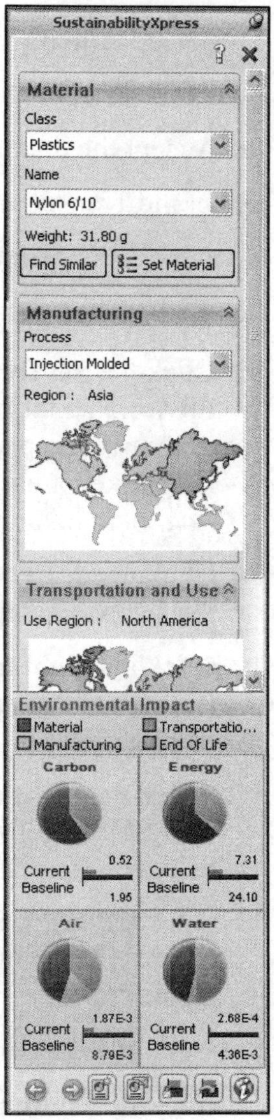


Every license of SolidWorks 2010, obtains a copy of SolidWorks SustainabilityXpress. SustainabilityXpress calculates environmental impact on a model in four key areas: *Carbon Footprint*, *Energy Consumption*, *Air Acidification* and *Water Eutrophication*.

Material and Manufacturing process region and Transportation Usage region are used as input variables. Two SolidWorks Sustainability products are available:

- **SolidWorks SustainabilityXpress**. Handles part documents and is included in the core software.

- **SolidWorks Sustainability**. Handles parts and assemblies, available as a separate product. Other functionality includes configuration support, expanded reporting and expanded environmental impact options.

SolidWorks Sustainability provides real-time feedback on key impact factors in the Environmental Impact Dashboard, which updates dynamically with any changes by the user. You can generate customize reports to share the results.

Run SustainabilityXpress and analyzes a part. Display the four environmental impact factors, view suitable alternative materials, compare their environmental impact factors and generate a customer report.

### *Tutorial: SustainabilityXpress 17-1*

Close all parts, assemblies and drawings. Run SustainabilityXpress. Perform an analysis.

1. Open the **SustainabilityXpress 17-1** part from the SolidWorks 2010/SustainabilityXpress folder.

Activate SustainabilityXpress.

2. Click **Tools, SustainabilityXpress** from the Main menu. SustainabilityXpress is displayed in the Task Pane area.

Select Material Class.

3. Select **Steel** from the drop-down menu.

Select Material Name.

4. Select **Stainless Steel (ferritic)** from the drop-down menu.

Select Manufacturing Process.

5. Select **Milled** from the drop-down menu.

Select the Manufacturing Region.

6. Accept the default setting: **Asia**.

Select the Transportation and Usage region.

7. Accept the default setting: **North America**.

Set the Baseline for your design.

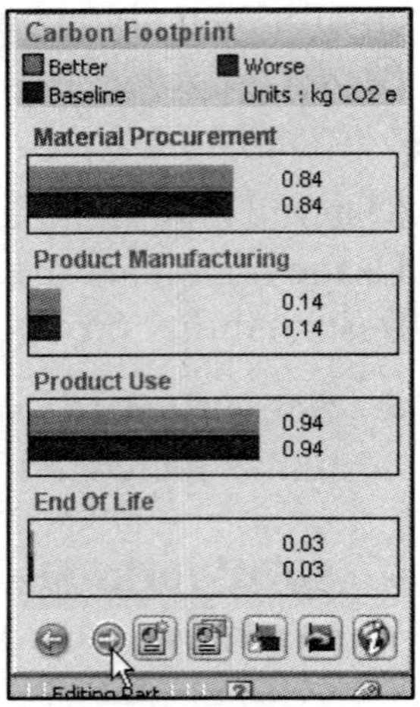


8. Click the **Set Baseline** tool from the bottom of the Environmental Impact screen. The Environmental Impact of this part is displayed. The Environmental Impact is calculated in four key areas: *Carbon Footprint*, *Energy Consumption*, *Air Acidification* and *Water Eutrophication*.

9. Click inside the **Carbon** box to display a Baseline bar chart of the Carbon Footprint.

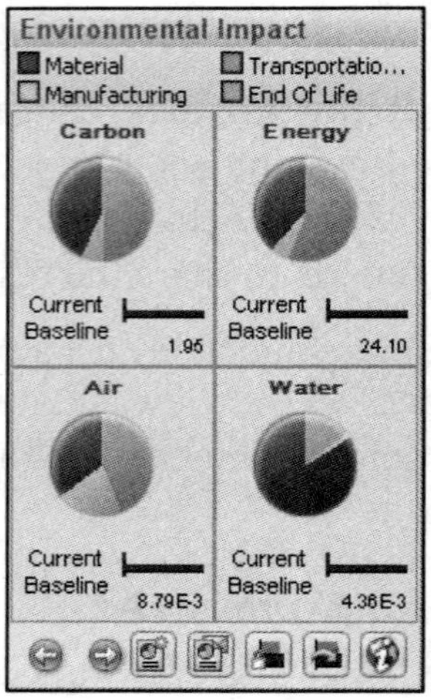


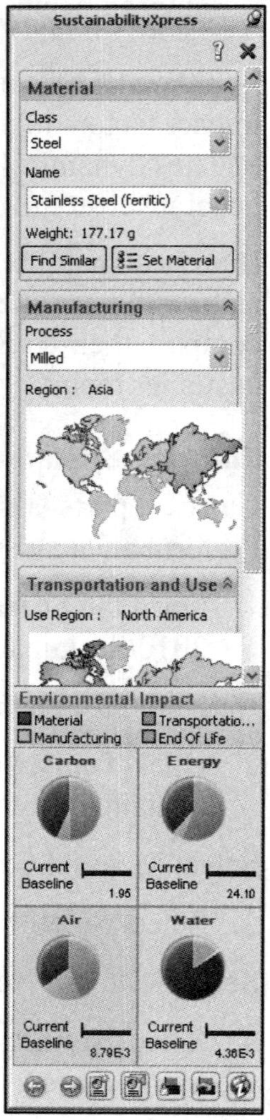


10. Click the **right arrow** to move to the next (Energy Consumption) impact screen to display a Baseline bar chart.

11. Click the **right arrow** to move to the next (Air Acidification) impact screen to display a Baseline bar chart.

12. Click the **right arrow** to move to the next (Water Eutrophication) impact screen to display a Baseline bar chart.

Return to the Baseline screen.

13. Click the **right arrow** to move to back to the original impact screen.

In the next section, compare the baseline design to a different design so you can determine if you can make a meaningful design change. Let's compare the present material Stainless Steel (ferritic) to Nylon 6/10.

Select a new Material Class.

14. Select **Plastic** from the drop-down menu.

Select a new Material Name.

15. Select **Nylon 6/10** from the drop-down menu.

Select new Manufacturing Process.

16. Select **Injection Molded.**

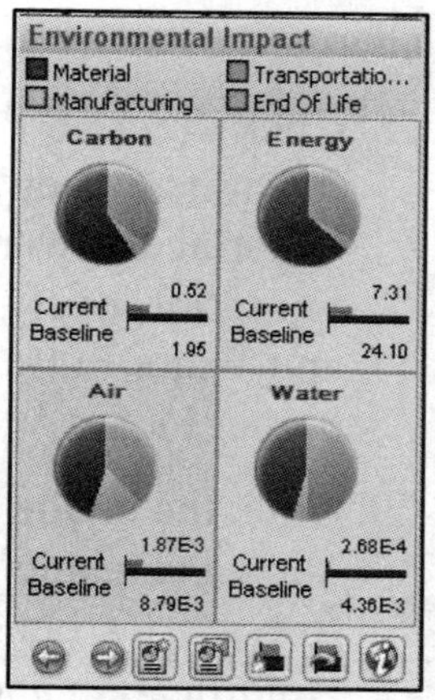


Select the Manufacturing Region.

17. Accept the default setting: **Asia.**

Select the Transportation and Usage region.

18. Accept the default setting: **United States.**

View the results. Changing the material from Stainless Steel to Nylon 6/10 and the manufacturing process from milled to injection molded had a positive environmental impact in all four categories, but a further material change may provide a better results!

19. Click **inside each** of the environmental categories to view the results. Return to the default Baseline Impact screen.

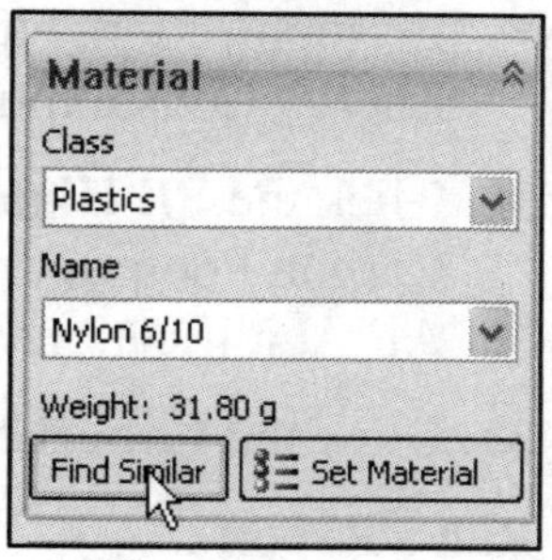


Fine a similar material and compare the Environmental Impact to Nylon 6/10.

20. Click the **Find Similar Material** button as illustrated. The Find Similar Material dialog box is displayed.

21. Click the **Value (-any-)** drop-down arrow.

22. Select **Plastic.** At this time, you can perform a general search or customize your search on physical properties of the material.

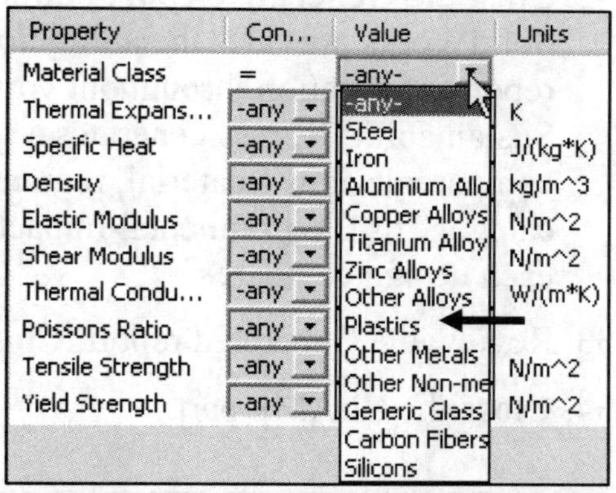


23. Click the **Find Similar** button as illustrated. SolidWorks provides a full list of comparable materials that you can further refine.

Select a Similar Material from the provided list.

24. Check the **ABS PC** box.

25. Check the **Nylon 101** box.

26. Check the **PE High Density** box.

27. Click **inside the top left box (Show Selected Only)** as illustrated. The selected materials are displayed.

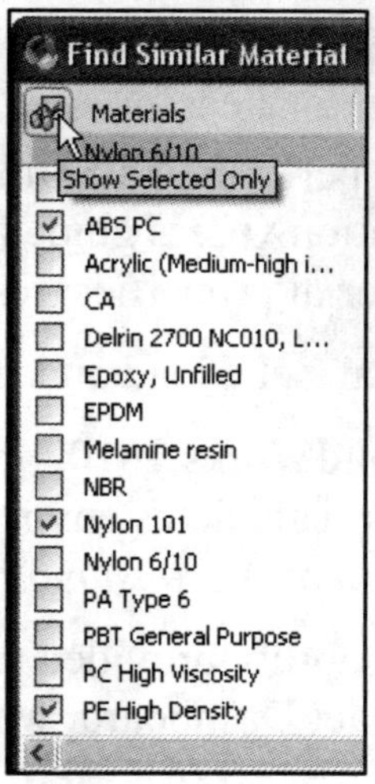


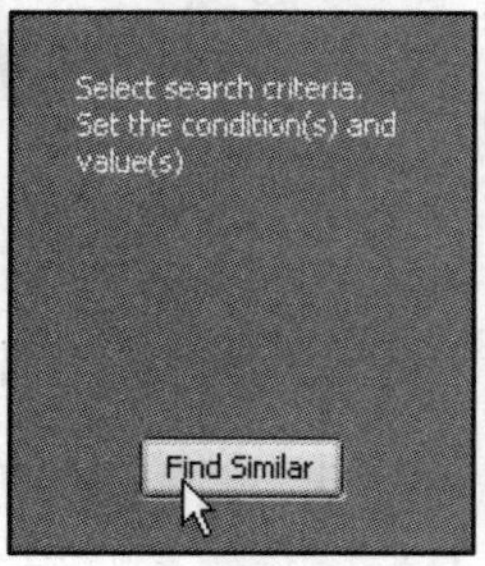

View the Environment Impact for the alternative materials.

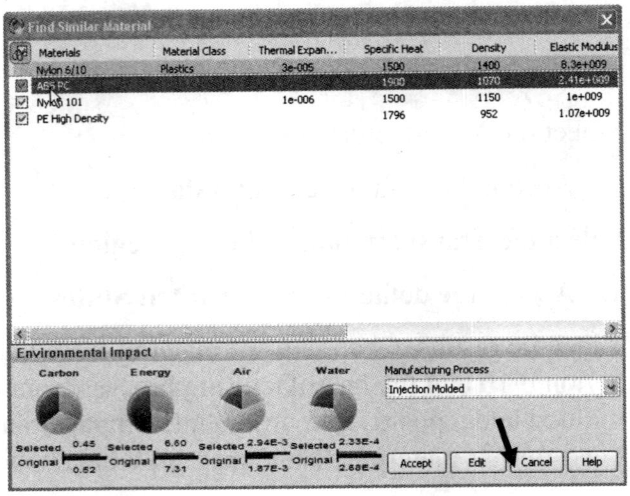


28. Click the **ABS PC** material row as illustrated. View the results. The material is lower in Carbon Footprint, Energy Consumption, and Water Eutrophication, but higher in Air Acidification.

29. Click the **Nylon 101** material row. View the results. The material is lower in Carbon Footprint, Air Acidification and Water Eutrophication, but higher in Energy Consumption.

30. Click the **PE High Density** material row. View the results. The material is lower in Carbon Footprint, Energy Consumption, and Water Eutrophication, but is higher in Air Acidification. You decide to stay with Nylon 6/10.

31. Click the **Cancel** button from the Find Similar Material dialog box.

Run a Report.

32. Click the **Generate Report** button as illustrated. SolidWorks provides the ability to communicate this report information throughout your organization. SustainabilityXpress generates a report that will compare designs (material, regions) and explain each category of Environmental Impact and show how each design compares.

33. Review the Generated report. **Close** the report.

34. **Close** the CLAMP part.

# Summary

In this chapter, you performed a SolidWorks SimulationXpress analysis on a part. SolidWorks SimulationXpress guided you through various default steps to define fixtures, loads, material properties, results and the optional Optimization process.

You applied material, set a load and fixtures and ran the optimization procedure.

Every license of SolidWorks 2010, obtains a copy of SolidWorks SustainabilityXpress. SustainabilityXpress calculates environmental impact on a model in four key areas: *Carbon Footprint*, *Energy Consumption*, *Air Acidification* and *Water Eutrophication.*

SolidWorks Sustainability provided real-time feedback on key impact factors in the Environmental Impact Dashboard, which updated dynamically with changes by the user.

You applied material, manufacturing process and selected the manufacturing process region and the part transportation and usage region. You then viewed the environmental impact of your design.

You viewed suitable alternative materials, re-ran the environmental impact study and compared their environmental impact factors in all four categories. A customer report was generated.

# Notes:

# Types of Decimal Dimensions ASME Y14.5M

| TYPES of DECIMAL DIMENSIONS (ASME Y14.5M) | | | |
|---|---|---|---|
| **Description:** | **UNITS: MM** | **Description:** | **UNITS: INCH** |
| Dimension is less than 1mm.<br>Zero precedes the decimal point. | 0.9<br>0.95 | Dimension is less than 1 inch.<br>Zero is not used before the decimal point. | .5<br>.56 |
| Dimension is a whole number.<br>Display no decimal point.<br>Display no zero after decimal point. | 19 | Express dimension to the same number of decimal places as its tolerance.<br>Add zeros to the right of the decimal point.<br>If the tolerance is expressed to 3 places, then the dimension contains 3 places to the right of the decimal point. | 1.750 |
| Dimension exceeds a whole number by a decimal fraction of a millimeter.<br>Display no zero to the right of the decimal. | 11.5<br>11.51 | | |

| TABLE 1<br>TOLERANCE DISPLAY FOR INCH AND METRIC DIMENSIONS (ASME Y14.5M) | | |
|---|---|---|
| **DISPLAY:** | **UNITS: INCH:** | **UNITS: METRIC:** |
| Dimensions less than 1 | .5 | 0.5 |
| Unilateral Tolerance | $1.417^{+.005}_{-.000}$ | $36^{0}_{-0.5}$ |
| Bilateral Tolerance | $1.417^{+.010}_{-.020}$ | $36^{+0.25}_{-0.50}$ |
| Limit Tolerance | .571<br>.463 | 14.50<br>11.50 |

## SolidWorks Keyboard Shortcuts

Listed below are some of the pre-defined keyboard shortcuts in SolidWorks:

| Action: | Key Combination: |
|---|---|
| **Model Views** | |
| Rotate the model horizontally or vertically: | **Arrow** keys |
| Rotate the model horizontally or vertically 90 degrees. | **Shift** + **Arrow** keys |
| Rotate the model clockwise or counterclockwise | **Alt** + left of right **Arrow** keys |
| Pan the model | **Ctrl** + **Arrow** keys |
| Magnifying glass | **g** |
| Zoom in | **Shift + z** |
| Zoom out | **z** |
| Zoom to fit | **f** |
| Previous view | **Ctrl + Shift + z** |
| **View Orientation** | |
| View Orientation menu | **Spacebar** |
| Front view | **Ctrl + 1** |
| Back view | **Ctrl + 2** |
| Left view | **Ctrl + 3** |
| Right view | **Ctrl + 4** |
| Top view | **Ctrl + 5** |
| Bottom view | **Ctrl + 6** |
| Isometric view | **Ctrl + 7** |
| NormalTo view | **Ctrl + 8** |
| **Selection Filters** | |
| Filter edges | **e** |
| Filter vertices | **v** |
| Filter faces | **x** |
| Toggle Selection Filter toolbar | **F5** |
| Toggle selection filters on/off | **F6** |
| **File menu items** | |
| New SolidWorks document | **Ctrl + n** |
| Open document | **Ctrl + o** |
| Open From Web Folder | **Ctrl + w** |
| Make Drawing from Part | **Ctrl + d** |
| Make Assembly from Part | **Ctrl + a** |
| Save | **Ctrl +s** |
| Print | **Ctrl + p** |
| **Additional shortcuts** | |
| Access online help inside of PropertyManager or dialog box | **F1** |
| Rename an item in the FeatureManager design tree | **F2** |
| Rebuild the model | **Ctrl + b** |
| Force rebuild – Rebuild the model and all its features | **Ctrl + q** |
| Redraw the screen | **Ctrl + r** |

| | |
|---|---|
| Cycle between open SolidWorks document | **Ctrl + Tab** |
| Line to arc/arc to line in the Sketch | **a** |
| Undo | **Ctrl + z** |
| Redo | **Ctrl + y** |
| Cut | **Ctrl + x** |
| Copy | **Ctrl + c** |
| **Additional shortcuts** | |
| Paste | **Ctrl + v** |
| Delete | **Delete** |
| Next window | **Ctrl + F6** |
| Close window | **Ctrl + F4** |
| View previous tools | **s** |
| Selects all text inside an Annotations text box | **Ctrl + a** |

In a sketch, the **Esc** key un-selects geometry items currently selected in the Properties box and Add Relations box. In the model, the **Esc** key closes the PropertyManager and cancels the selections.

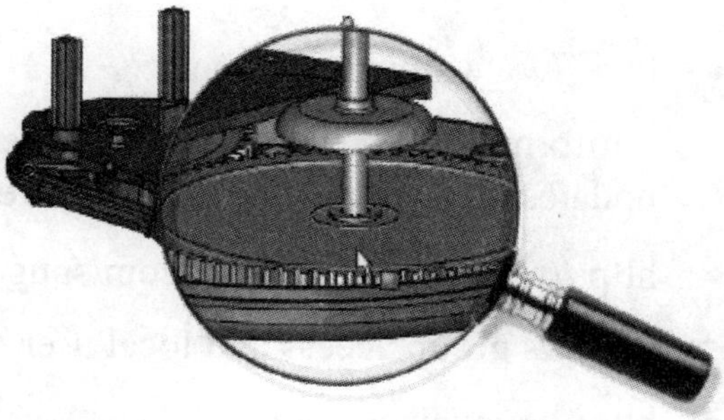

Use the **g** key to activate the Magnifying glass tool. Use the Magnifying glass tool to inspect a model and make selections without changing the overall view.

Use the **s** key to view/access previous command tools in the Graphics window.

## Windows Shortcuts

Listed below are some of the pre-defined keyboard shortcuts in Microsoft Windows:

| Action: | Keyboard Combination: |
|---|---|
| Open the Start menu | Windows Logo key |
| Open Windows Explorer | Windows Logo key + E |
| Minimize all open windows | Windows Logo key + M |
| Open a Search window | Windows Logo key + F |
| Open Windows Help | Windows Logo key + F1 |
| Select multiple geometry items in a SolidWorks document | Ctrl key (Hold the Ctrl key down. Select items.) Release the Ctrl key. |

# Helpful On-Line Information

The SolidWorks URL: http://www.solidworks.com contains information on Local Resellers, Solution Partners, Certifications, SolidWorks users groups and more.

Access 3D ContentCentral using the Task Pane to obtain engineering electronic catalog model and part information.

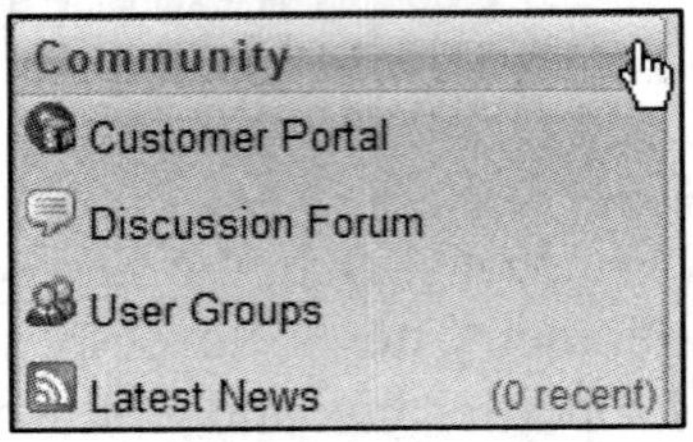


Use the SolidWorks Resources tab in the Task Pane to obtain access to Customer Portals, Discussion Forums, User Groups, Manufacturers, Solution Partners, Labs and more. Helpful on-line SolidWorks information is available from the following URLs:

- http://www.dmeducation.net

  Information on the CSWA Certification, software updates, design tips and new book releases.

- http://www.mechengineer.com/snug/

  News group access and local user group information.

- http://www.nhcad.com

  Configuration information and other tips and tricks.

- http://www.solidworktips.com

  Helpful tips, tricks on SolidWorks and API.

- http://www.topica.com/lists/SW

  Independent News Group for SolidWorks discussions, questions and answers.

Certified SolidWorks Professionals (CSWP) URLs provide additional helpful on-line information.

- http://www.scottjbaugh.com — Scott J. Baugh
- http://www.3-ddesignsolutions.com — Devon Sowell
- http://www.zxys.com — Paul Salvador
- http://www.mikejwilson.com — Mike J. Wilson
- http://www.dimontegroup.com — Gene Dimonte & Ed Eaton

*On-line tutorials are for educational purposes only. Tutorials are copyrighted by their respective owners.

# SolidWorks Document Types

SolidWorks has three main document file types: Part, Assembly and Drawing, but there are many additional supporting types that your may want to know. Below is a brief list of these supporting file types:

| **Design Documents** | **Description** |
|---|---|
| .sldprt | SolidWorks Part document |
| .slddrw | SolidWorks Drawing document |
| .sldasm | SolidWorks Assembly document |
| **Templates and Formats** | **Description** |
| .asmdot | Assembly Template |
| .asmprp | Assembly Template Custom Properties tab |
| .drwdot | Drawing Template |
| .drwprp | Drawing Template Custom Properties tab |
| .prtdot | Part Template |
| .prtprp | Part Template Custom Properties tab |
| .sldbt | General Table Template |
| .slddrt | Drawing Sheet Template |
| .sldbombt | Bill of Materials Template (Table-based) |
| .sldholtbt | Hole Table Template |
| .xls | Bill of Materials Template (Excel) |
| **Library Files** | **Description** |
| .sldlfp | Library Part file |
| .sldblk | Blocks |
| **Other** | **Description** |
| .sldstd | Drafting standard |
| .sldmat | Material Database |
| .sldclr | Color Palette File |

**Notes:**

# Index

# Index

## Index

## Index

## Index

# Official Certified SolidWorks Associate (CSWA) Examination Guide

**SolidWorks 2008, 2009, and 2010**

**Authors:** Planchard and Planchard
**Pages:** 312
**ISBN:** 978-1-58503-533-5

## Description

Specifying a Certified SolidWorks Associate (CSWA) certification on your resume is a great way to increase your chances of landing a new job, getting a promotion, or looking more qualified. This book covers the key topics contained on the exam with the aim of helping readers to master each topic as well as the exam itself.

This book is more than a collection of practice exam questions because it also devotes attention to the concepts and implementation details that underlie the CSWA process, providing readers with a thorough and comprehensive foundation in SolidWorks.

Each chapter in this book is geared toward helping you discover the topics that are on the CSWA exam, pinpoint where you have a knowledge deficiency, and determine what you need to know to master these topics. Ideal for anyone with a basic knowledge of SolidWorks and engineering fundamentals, this book will help you get the certification you need to land the best jobs, get promoted, and become a successful professional.

## Table of Contents Summary



This book is available for individual purchase at amazon.com
College bookstores can call SDC Publications to place course adoption orders.

# Assembly Modeling with SolidWorks 2010

**Authors:** Planchard and Planchard
**Pages:** 500
**ISBN:** 978-1-58503-564-9

## Description

Assembly Modeling with SolidWorks 2010 is written to assist the beginning SolidWorks user with a few months of design experience to the intermediate SolidWorks user who desires to enhance their skill sets in assembly modeling. The book provides a solid foundation in assembly modeling using competency-based projects.

The book is a self-paced tutorial in a realistic design setting. Complex models expose you to large assembly modeling techniques. You focus on the design process while learning the commands relative to assemblies.

The authors developed the industry scenarios by combining their own industry experience with the knowledge of engineers, department managers, vendors and manufacturers. These professionals are directly involved with SolidWorks everyday. They create assemblies with thousands of components and drawings with hundreds of sheets.

## Table of Contents Summary

1. SolidWorks 2010 User Interface
2. File Management, System Options, Templates, SolidWorks Explorer, and more
3. Assembly Modeling - Bottom-up design approach
4. Bottom-Up design assembly approach - Two Levels of Configurations
5. Top-down design assembly approach - Two Components with Configurations
6. Part and Assembly Configurations, Custom Properties, Design Tables, and References
7. Assembly Drawings with Revision Table and Bill of Materials - Multiple Sheets, Views, and Custom Properties
8. Top-down design, Layout Sketches, Block, Motion, and More

   Index

This book is available for individual purchase at amazon.com

**Notes:**

## Notes:

**Notes:**

## Notes:

**Notes:**

**Notes:**

**Notes:**

## Notes:

**Notes:**

## Notes:

**Notes:**

## Notes: